INTERNATIONAL LAW
NORMS, ACTORS, PROCESS

INTERNATIONAL LAW
NORMS, ACTORS, PROCESS

A Problem-Oriented Approach

Second Edition

Jeffrey L. Dunoff
Charles Klein Professor of Law and Government
Temple University Beasley School of Law

Steven R. Ratner
Professor of Law
University of Michigan Law School

David Wippman
Vice Provost for International Relations and Professor of Law
Cornell Law School

ΛSPEN

PUBLISHERS

76 Ninth Avenue, New York, NY 10011
http://lawschool.aspenpublishers.com

© 2006 Aspen Publishers, Inc.
a Wolters Kluwer business
http://lawschool.aspenpublishers.com

Printed in the United States of America.

3 4 5 6 7 8 9 0

ISBN 0-7355-5734-9

Library of Congress Cataloging-in-Publication Data

Dunoff, Jeffrey L., 1960-
    International law : norms, actors, process : a problem-oriented approach / Jeffrey L.
    Dunoff, Steven R. Ratner, David Wippman. — 2nd ed.
      p. cm.
    ISBN 0-7355-5734-9 (hardcover)
1. International law. I. Ratner, Steven R. II. Wippman, David, 1954- III. Title.

KZ3410.D86 2006
341–dc22

2006018503

About Aspen Publishers

Aspen Publishers, headquartered in New York City, is a leading information provider for attorneys, business professionals, and law students. Written by preeminent authorities, our products consist of analytical and practical information covering both U.S. and international topics. We publish in the full range of formats, including updated manuals, books, periodicals, CDs, and online products.

Our proprietary content is complemented by 2,500 legal databases, containing over 11 million documents, available through our Loislaw division. Aspen Publishers also offers a wide range of topical legal and business databases linked to Loislaw's primary material. Our mission is to provide accurate, timely, and authoritative content in easily accessible formats, supported by unmatched customer care.

To order any Aspen Publishers title, go to *http://lawshool.aspenpublishers.com* or call 1-800-638-8437.

To reinstate your manual update service, call 1-800-638-8437.

For more information on Loislaw products, go to *www.loislaw.com* or call 1-800-364-2512.

For Customer Care issues, e-mail *CustomerCare@aspenpublishers.com*; call 1-800-234-1660; or fax 1-800-901-9075.

Aspen Publishers
a Wolters Kluwer business

To
Theresa, Elizabeth, and Joel
Nancy, Benjamin, and Isabel
and
Meredith, Brianna, and Lauren

Summary of Contents

Contents

PART II
Participants in the International Legal Process   107

Chapter 3
The Traditional Actors: States and International
Organizations   111

Chapter 4
The Challenge of Non-State Actors

PART III
International Law and Domestic Law   263

Chapter 5
International Law in the Domestic Arena   267

I. The Monist-Dualist Debate   267

Chapter 6
The Reach of Domestic Law in the International Arena:
Jurisdiction and Its Limits

PART IV
The Protection of Human Dignity   437

Chapter 7
The Claims of Individuals on States: International
Human Rights   441

Chapter 8
Mitigating the Harms of War: International Humanitarian Law

Chapter 9
Individual Accountability for Violations of Human Dignity: International Criminal Law and Beyond

PART V
Interdependence and Integration: The Challenge of Collective Action Problems

695

Chapter 10
Responding to the First Global Commons Issue: The Law of the Sea

701

Chapter 11
Protecting the International Environment   761

Chapter 12
Managing the World Economy   827

PART VI
Challenges to International Law   873

Chapter 13
The Use of Force   875

Preface

Our book is designed to provide a general introduction to the range and reach—and the possibilities and limits—of contemporary international law. To do so, the book is built around a series of current problems that illustrate international law in action. These materials are intended to convey an understanding of the profound transformations that mark international law in the current era, and of recent theories and developments that challenge some of the discipline's most basic assumptions. Today's students and tomorrow's international lawyers will benefit from a casebook prepared with these fundamental shifts in the nature of the subject in mind.

The book is also designed to convey to students a keen sense of the process for the making, interpretation, and application of international legal norms, rather than focusing on law as a set of detailed rules or doctrines. It is our experience as teachers that the best way to get students interested in these processes and to show their relevance to modern society is to rely as much as possible on real situations where the law has made—or not made—a difference. Using real-world problems permits students to consider the formation and application of international law in the specific contexts in which such problems arise, and to appreciate the complexity and interrelated character of international legal issues as they appear to lawyers in practice. Moreover, we believe that only through an examination of international law's principal actors, methods of law making, and key subjects can a student fully understand what it means to have law in a context that lacks a single legislature, executive, or judiciary.

The problems are chosen, in part, for their importance or intrinsic interest and, in part, to highlight many of the profound transformations that characterize international law in the post-Cold War era. Thus, throughout the text we focus on creative new forms of law making, including "soft" law, as well as treaty regimes; the increased importance of non-state actors, such as corporations, sub-state units, and non-governmental organizations; new compliance strategies; the growth of critical subject areas, notably international criminal law and international economic law; and the erosion of traditional divisions among these subjects. Given our focus on current international legal controversies, we omit a number of classic doctrinal areas that receive extended treatment in other texts but that do not raise critical process-related issues as dramatically as those we have chosen.

We recognize that no limited number of problems can present the entire spectrum of international law. Indeed, we have consciously avoided the temptation to create a treatise, or to present encyclopedic treatments of the limited range of issues covered. Instead, our overriding goal has been to create a book that serves as an effective teaching tool. To this end, each chapter begins with a short introduction to the particular field of international law at issue, and each problem begins with an overview and a series of questions designed to orient the student to the materials that follow. Problems are followed by relevant primary and secondary source materials. These materials are both interdisciplinary and multi-perspectival and are intended to enrich the student's understanding of relevant issues. Notes and questions are kept to a minimum.

This book is organized into six parts, each consisting of two or more chapters for a total of fourteen chapters. Part I introduces students to international law and law making. Chapter 1 uses two problems to illustrate both basic concepts and the changing nature of contemporary international law. Chapter 2 uses a series of problems to serve as vehicles for a discussion of treaties, customary international law, and soft law. Part II focuses on the principal participants (other than individuals) in the international legal system. Chapter 3 reviews the processes of state formation and dissolution, self-determination, state succession, and related issues, as well as the legal status and powers of international organizations. In recognition of the prominence that non-state actors have assumed in contemporary international law, Chapter 4 includes four problems that explore the variety and roles that these entities play.

Part III explores the interactions between international and domestic law. Chapter 5 focuses on the impact of international law in domestic systems, while Chapter 6 explores the ways that states assert their authority abroad. Part IV focuses on the use of international law to protect human dignity. Chapter 7 covers human rights, including both civil and political rights, and economic, social, and cultural rights. We also include two chapters on rapidly evolving areas: Chapter 8 examines the legal regulation of the conduct of war, and Chapter 9 covers issues of individual accountability for human rights abuses. Part V focuses on issues generated by the interdependence of states and the need for collective action to protect international common resources and to facilitate international economic activity. Chapter 10 covers the law of the sea; Chapter 11 examines international environmental law; and Chapter 12 explores international economic law.

We take seriously the challenges of those who question the relevance, legitimacy, and justice of international law. Most casebooks bury these issues near the end of an introductory chapter, after which the issues disappear. As a conceptual matter, we think that starting a book with these issues often appears to be unduly defensive; as a practical matter, we think that discussing these issues before students have studied international law is unlikely to be productive. We also think the issues are too important to be treated in this way. Thus, we raise questions about the relevance and efficacy of international law throughout the text. We devote Part VI, the final part of the book, to an examination of the most important challenges to international law. Chapter 13 examines the use of force in international affairs. In Chapter 14, the book's final chapter, we focus more explicitly on the legitimacy, relevance, and justice of international law, through an examination of several contemporary issues, including the legal issues raised by the September 11, 2001, attacks on the United States and their aftermath.

The book is designed to stimulate interest in, and thinking about, international law. It is an invitation to share our commitment to exploration of the uses and limits of international law—where it succeeds, where it fails, and how it can be improved. We welcome your comments and suggestions.

Jeffrey L. Dunoff
Steven R. Ratner
David Wippman

July 2006

Acknowledgments

This volume is the product of countless interchanges with students, colleagues, and others who have contributed to the ideas in it. We begin by thanking all our students, whose reactions to this book as it progressed were our surest signal of where we needed to do more work.

At Temple Law School, we acknowledge with appreciation the outstanding work by Professor Dunoff's research assistants, including Kim Bartman, Brooke Birnbaum, Jon Cagan, Laurie Dow, Ben Franks, Sean Handler, Nhan Nguyen, Lori Odessa, Veronica Rice, Daniel Simons, Maggie Soboleski, and Keith Verrier. We also thank John Necci, Ethel Fiderer, Steve Pavlo, and others at the Temple Law School Library, and Joel Houkom, Freddie Sanford, and the secretarial staff at the Law School. Special thanks to Professor Dunoff's Temple colleagues for their support throughout this project. We wish to acknowledge Dean Robert Reinstein and Temple University Beasley School of Law for generous financial assistance in support of this project.

At the University of Texas School of Law, we thank research assistants Molly Leder and Elizabeth Herre for their superlative work. Professor Ratner also thanks his former Columbia Law School student, Amin Kassam, for excellent research assistance. At the Tarlton Law Library, we appreciate the assistance of Jonathan Pratter in locating some of our more unusual sources. Professor Ratner's tremendous faculty assistants, Melonie Alspaugh and Katrin Flechsig, made the many details of the publication process for the first edition flow smoothly. His colleagues at Texas were a constant source of pedagogical ideas for the book, and he particularly appreciates the insights of Douglas Laycock. Dean William Powers provided generous financial assistance with all aspects of this project.

At the University of Michigan Law School, we thank Scott Risner for his research assistance, Kimberly Latta for her superlative work on various production aspects of the book, and Dean Evan Caminker for his financial assistance in the form of the Wolfson and Cook Scholarship Funds.

At Cornell Law School, we would like to thank Ilana Buschkin, Jean Carmalt, Alayne Fleischmann, Maureen McKee, Benjamin Meier, and Victoria Orlowski for excellent research, cite-checking, and editing. Anne Cahanin and Pamela Finnigan provided outstanding and unflagging secretarial and administrative support. We also thank the Cornell Law School Library staff for their invaluable assistance in tracking down elusive documents. Professor Wippman acknowledges with great appreciation the faculty at Cornell Law School, particularly Professors John Barcelo and Muna Ndulo, for their advice, encouragement, and support. Dean Stewart Schwab and the Cornell Law School offered generous financial assistance in support of this project.

We have benefitted greatly from the perceptive comments of our colleagues at other schools who taught from the first edition, as well as earlier drafts of this text, including Daniel Bodansky, David Caron, Kal Raustiala, and Peter Spiro. We are also grateful to Alan Boyle, Philippe Gautier, Frederick Kirgis, John Knox, Sean Murphy, Michael Ratner, and Amy Sinden for various comments, suggestions, and assistance on aspects of the book. Bernard Oxman and J. Ashley Roach offered critically helpful commentary on all of Chapter 10. Aspen Publishers' anonymous reviewers offered many useful suggestions for which we are most grateful.

The photographs that appear in the book were located and obtained through the hard work of our professional picture researcher, Corinne Szabo, whose unfailing assistance we gratefully appreciate.

We also thank our colleagues at Aspen Publishing, in particular Susan Boulanger, Melody Davies, Carol McGeehan, Iris Greidinger, Christie Rears, and Kathy Yoon.

Finally, we thank our families, to whom this book is dedicated, for graciously tolerating the long hours required to complete this task—and for their creative efforts to devise enjoyable distractions from it.

The authors are grateful for permission to reprint material from the following sources:

Abbott, Kenneth. "International Relations Theory, International Law, and the Regime Governing Atrocities in Internal Conflicts." Reproduced with permission from 93 Am. J. Int'l L. 361 (1999). Copyright © The American Society of International Law.

Abi-Saab, Georges. "Whither the International Community?," 9 Eur. J. Int'l L. 248 (1998). Copyright © Oxford University Press. Reprinted by permission of Oxford University Press.

Allott, Philip. "Power Sharing in the Law of the Sea." Reproduced with permission from 77 Am. J. Int'l L. 1 (1983). Copyright © The American Society of International Law.

Alvarez, Jose E. "Judging the Security Council." Reproduced with permission from 90 Am. J. Int'l L. 1 (1996). Copyright © The American Society of International Law.

Amnesty International. "Rwanda: Gacaca: A Question of Justice," AI Index AFR 47/007/2002 (December 2002). Copyright © Amnesty International. Reprinted by permission.

Anand, R.P. "The Influence of History on the Literature of International Law," in The Structure and Process of International Law (R. St. J. Mac Donald and D. M. Johnston eds. 1983). Copyright © Martinus Nijhoff. Reprinted by permission.

Anghie, Anthony. "Finding the Peripheries: Sovereignty and Colonialism in Nineteenth-Century International Law," 40 Harv. Int'l L.J. 1 (1999). Copyright © 1999 by the President and Fellows of Harvard College and the Harvard International Law Journal.

An-Na'im, Abdullah Ahmed. "Human Rights in the Muslim World: Socio-Political Conditions and Scriptural Imperatives," 3 Harv. Hum. Rts. J. 13 (1990).

Associated Press. Photos of Lockerbie bombing and plane flying into World Trade Center. Reproduced with permission. AP Wide World Photos.

Baumol, William J., and Oates, Wallace E. Economics, Environmental Policy and the Quality of Life (1979). Reprinted by permission of William J. Baumol and Wallace E. Oates.

Benedick, Richard Elliot. Ozone Diplomacy: New Directions in Safeguarding the Planet. Copyright © 1991, 1998 by the President and Fellows of Harvard College. Reprinted by permission of the publisher.

Black, David. "The Long and Winding Road: International Norms and Domestic Political Change in South Africa," in The Power of Human Rights, edited by Thomas Risse, Stephen C. Ropp, and Kathryn Sikkink (1999).

Copyright © 1999 by Cambridge University Press. Reprinted with the permission of Cambridge University Press.

Bodansky, Daniel. "Bonn Voyage: Kyoto's Uncertain Revival," 65 The National Interest 45 (Fall 2001). Reprinted by permission of The National Interest.

Bodansky, Daniel. "The Legitimacy of International Governance: A Coming Challenge for International Environmental Law?" Reproduced with permission from 93 Am. J. Int'l L. 596 (1999). Copyright © The American Society of International Law.

Bodansky, Daniel. "*Non Liquet* and the Incompleteness of International Law," in International Law, the International Court of Justice and Nuclear Weapons, edited by Laurence Boisson de Chazournes and Philippe Sands (2000). Copyright © 2000 Cambridge University Press. Reprinted with the permission of Cambridge University Press.

Boraine, Alex. "Truth and Reconciliation in South Africa: The Third Way," in Truth v. Justice: The Morality of Truth Commissions, edited by Robert I. Rotberg and Dennis Thompson (2000). Copyright © 2000 by Princeton University Press. Reprinted by permission of Princeton University Press.

Brilmayer, Lea. "International Justice and International Law," 98 West Virginia Law Review 611 (1996). Republished with permission of the West Virginia Law Review.

Bronner, Ethan. "Population talks: the flip side; Unofficial groups get chance to tell world their views," The Boston Globe, Sept. 8, 1994. Republished with permission of The Boston Globe. Permission conveyed through Copyright Clearance Center, Inc.

Charlesworth, Hilary. "Alienating Oscar? Feminist Analysis of International Law," in Reconceiving Reality: Women and International Law, edited by Dorinda G. Dallmeyer (1993). Copyright © The American Society of International Law. Reproduced with permission.

Chart of CFC Production in Chapter 11 reproduced with permission of the United Nations Environment Programme.

Chart of Ozone Depletion in Chapter 11 reproduced with permission of the United Nations Environment Programme.

Chayes, Abram. "The Use of Force in the Persian Gulf," in Law and Force in the New World Order, edited by Lori Fisler Damrosch and David Scheffer (1991). Copyright © 1991 by The American Society of International Law. Reprinted by permission of Westview Press, a member of Perseus Books, L.L.C.

Chinkin, Christine. "Kosovo: A 'Good' or 'Bad' War?" Reproduced with permission from 93 Am. J. Int'l L. 841 (1999). Copyright © The American Society of International Law.

Chinkin, Christine. "Normative Development in the International Legal System," in Commitment and Compliance: The Role of Non-Binding Norms in the International Legal System, edited by Dinah Shelton (2000). Copyright © American Society of International Law 2000. Reprinted by permission of Oxford University Press.

Clagett, Brice M. "Ownership of Seabed and Subsoil Resources in the Caspian Sea Under the Rules of International Law," 1 Caspian Crossroads (Fall 1995). Copyright © 1995 United States-Azerbaijan Council. Reprinted by permission.

Clagett, Brice M. "Title III of the Helms-Burton Act is Consistent with International Law." Reproduced with permission from 90 Am. J. Int'l L. 435 (1996). Copyright © The American Society of International Law.

Cleaver, Martin. Photo of nose section of Pan Am 103. Reproduced with permission from AP/Wide World Photos.

Colburn, Jamison E. "Turbot Wars: Straddling Stocks, Regime Theory, and a New U.N. Agreement," 6 J. Transnat'l L. & Pol'y 323 (1997). Copyright © 1997 Journal of Transnational Law and Policy. Reprinted by permission.

Couvreur, Philippe (Registrar, International Court of Justice, The Hague). Case Concerning the Gabcikovo-Nagymoros Project, Opinion of the Court, p. 26, Sketch Map No. 3. Permission granted by the Registrar of the Court.

Donnelly, Jack. "Cultural Relativism and Universal Human Rights," 6 Hum. Rts. Q. 410 (1984). Copyright © The Johns Hopkins University Press. Reprinted with permission of The Johns Hopkins University Press.

Engle, Karen. "Female Subjects of Public International Law: Human Rights and the Exotic Other Female," 26 New England L. Rev. 1509 (1992). Reprinted by permission.

Falk, Richard. "Kosovo, World Order and the Future of International Law." Reproduced with permission from 93 Am. J. Int'l L. 848 (1999). Copyright © The American Society of International Law.

Farer, Tom. "A Paradigm of Legitimate Intervention," in Enforcing Restraint: Collective Intervention in Internal Conflicts, edited by Lori Fisler Damrosch (1993). Council on Foreign Relations Press.

Federal News Service, Transcript of Statement of Saddam Hussein, © Federal News Service, Washington, D.C.

Finnemore, Martha, and Sikkink, Kathryn. "International Norm Dynamics and Political Change," 52 Int'l Org. 887 (1998). Copyright © 1998 The IO Foundation and the Massachusetts Institute of Technology.

Fischer, Horst, "Proportionality, Principle of," in Crimes of War, edited by Roy Guttman and David Rieff (1999).

Fox, Gregory, Addendum to ASIL Insight on Terrorist Attacks, September 2001, http://www.asil.org/insights/insigh77.htm#addendum. Copyright © The American Society of International Law.

Franck, Thomas M. "The 'Powers of Appreciation': Who Is the Ultimate Guardian of UN Legality?" Reproduced with permission from 86 Am. J. Int'l L. 519 (1992). Copyright © The American Society of International Law.

Franck, Thomas M., and Patel, Faiza. "The Gulf Crisis in International and Foreign Relations Law: UN Police Action in Lieu of War: 'The Old Order Changeth.'" Reproduced with permission from 85 Am. J. Int'l L. 63 (1991). Copyright © The American Society of International Law.

French, Howard W. "The Ritual: Disfiguring, Hurtful, Wildly Festive," The New York Times, Jan. 31, 1997. Copyright © 2001 by the New York Times Co. Reprinted by permission.

Gerretsen, Chas, "Messe de la Junta, General Augusto Pinochet, Santiago de Chile, September 19, 1973." © Chas Gerretsen/The Netherlands Photo Archive.

Glennon, Michael. "Legal Authority for the Possible Use of Force Against Iraq." Reproduced with permission from 92 Am. Soc'y Int'l L. Proc. 136 (1998). Copyright © The American Society of International Law.

Gourevitch, Philip. We Wish to Inform You That Tomorrow We Will Be Killed With Our Families: Stories from Rwanda (1998). Copyright © 1998 by Philip Gourevitch. Reprinted by permission of Farrar, Straus and Giroux LLC.

Greenpeace. July 10th, 1985: The Greenpeace Flagship Rainbow Warrior in Auckland Harbour after bombing by French secret service agents—crew member Fernando Pereira was killed in the blast. © Greenpeace.

Grotitus, Hugo. De Jure Belli ac Pacis Libri Tres (Francis Kelsey trans. 1925) (1625). Reprinted by permission of the Carnegie Institution of Washington.

Gutman, Roy, and Kuttab, Daoud. "Indiscriminate Attack," in Crimes of War, edited by Roy Gutman and David Rieff (1999).

Gya, Giji, and Global Policy Forum, Table in Chapter 14 reproduced with permission of Global Policy Forum.

Hannum, Hurst, and Hawk, David. "The Case Against the Standing Committee of the Communist Party of Kampuchea, Draft Memorial for the International Court of Justice" (1986). Reprinted by permission of Hurst Hannum.

Hardin, Garrett. "Tragedy of the Commons," 162 Science 1243 (1968). Excerpted with permission. Copyright © 1968 American Association for the Advancement of Science.

Hart, H. L. A. The Concept of Law. Copyright © Oxford University Press 1961. Reprinted by permission of Oxford University Press.

Henkin, Louis. How Nations Behave (2d ed. 1979). Reprinted with permission of Columbia University Press.

Henkin, Louis. International Law: Politics and Values 8, 175 (1995). Reprinted with kind permission of Kluwer Academic Publishers.

Hersh, Seymour. "King's Ransom: How Vulnerable Are the Saudi Royals?" The New Yorker, Oct. 22, 2001, at 35.

Higgins, Rosalyn. Problems and Process: International Law and How We Use It (1994). Reprinted by permission of Oxford University Press.

Hudec, Robert E. "The New WTO Dispute Settlement Procedure: An Overview of the First Three Years," 8 Minnesota Journal of Global Trade 1 (1999). Reprinted with the permission of the publisher, University of Minnesota and Minnesota Journal of Global Trade.

Human Rights Watch. Getting Away with Torture: Command Responsibility for the U.S. Abuse of Detainees (2005). Copyright © Human Rights Watch. Reprinted by permission.

Human Rights Watch. "The Legal Prohibition Against Torture," www.hrw.org/press/2001/11/torture Q and A.htm. Reprinted by permission.

Hurrell, Andrew. "International Law and the Changing Constitution of International Society," in The Role of Law in International Politics: Essays in International Relations and International Law, edited by Michael Byers (2000). Reprinted by permission of Oxford University Press.

International Humanitarian Law: Answers to Your Questions (ICRC, 1998).

International Legal Materials. Permission to reprint the following: Award on the Merits in Dispute Between Texaco Overseas Petroleum Company/California Asiatic Oil Company and the Government of Libyan Arab Republic, 17 I.L.M. 1 (1977); Guidelines on the Treatment of Foreign Direct Investment, 31 I.L.M. 1363 (1992); Conference on Yugoslavia: Arbitration Commission Opinion Nos. 1, 2, 3, 4, and 6, 31 I.L.M. 1494, 1497, 1499, 1501, 1507 (1992); Declaration on the Guidelines on the Recognition of New States in Eastern Europe and in the Soviet

Union, 31 I.L.M. 1486 (1992); Declaration on Yugoslavia, 31 I.L.M. 1485 (1992); Joint Declaration of the Government of the United Kingdom of Great Britain and Northern Ireland and the Government of the People's Republic of China on the Question of Hong Kong, September 26, 1984, 23 I.L.M. 1366; Joint Communique and Declaration on the Establishment of the Arctic Council, 35 I.L.M. 1382 (1996); Memorandum of Understanding concerning the U.S. Helms-Burton Act and the U.S. Iran and Libya Sanctions Act, 36 I.L.M. 529 (1997); Public Committee Against Torture in Israel, Judgment Concerning the Legality of the General Security Service's Interrogation Methods, 38 I.L.M. 1471 (1999); Document of the Copenhagen Meeting of the Conference on the Human Dimension of the CSCE, 29 I.L.M. 1305 (1990); Framework Convention for the Protection of National Minorities, 34 I.L.M. 351 (1995); Ruling on the Rainbow Warrior Affair Between France and New Zealand, 26 I.L.M. 1346 (1987); Opinion of the Inter-American Juridical Committee on Resolution AG/DOC.3375/96 "Freedom of Trade and Investment in the Americas", 35 I.L.M. 1322 (1996); Inter-American Commission on Human Rights, Detainees in Guantanamo Bay, 41 I.L.M. 532 (2002). Copyright © The American Society of International Law.

International Telecommunication Union, "Explanation of Membership Policies," http://www.itu.int/members/sectmem/participation.html. © International Telecommunication Union. Reprinted with permission.

Jacobson, Harold K. Networks of Interdependence: International Organizations and the Global Political System. Reprinted by permission of Merelyn Jacobson.

Kahn, Paul. "Nuclear Weapons and the Rule of Law," 31 N.Y.U. J. Int'l L. & Pol. 349, 373-374 (1999). Reproduced with the permission of the New York University Journal of Law and Politics.

Kausikan, Bilihari. "Asia's Different Standard," 92 Foreign Policy 24 (1993).

Kearney, Richard, and Dalton, Robert. "The Treaty on Treaties." Reproduced with permission from 64 Am. J. Int'l L. 495 (1970). Copyright © The American Society of International Law.

Kennedy, David. "When Renewal Repeats: Thinking Against the Box," 22 N.Y.U. J. Int'l. L. & Pol. 33 (2000). Reproduced with permission of the New York University Journal of International Law and Politics.

Keohane, Robert O. "International Relations and International Law: Two Optics," 38 Harv. Int'l L.J. 487 (1997). Copyright © 1997 by the President and Fellows of Harvard College and the Harvard International Law Journal. Reprinted by permission.

Kingsbury, Benedict. "Sovereignty and Inequality," 9 Eur. J. Int'l L. 599 (1998). Copyright © Oxford University Press. Reprinted by permission of Oxford University Press.

Kirgis, Frederic L. "Cruise Missile Strikes in Afghanistan and Sudan," reproduced with permission from ASIL Insights, August 1998. Copyright © The American Society of International Law.

Kissinger, Henry A. "The Pitfalls of Universal Jurisdiction," Foreign Affairs, July/Aug. 2001. From Does America Need A Foreign Policy? by Henry Kissinger. Copyright © 2001 by Henry A. Kissinger. Abridged by permission of Simon & Schuster Adult Publishing Group.

Koskenniemi, Martti. "The Politics of International Law," 1 Eur. J. Int'l L. 7 (1990). Copyright © Oxford University Press. Reprinted by permission of Oxford University Press.

Krasner, Stephen. Sovereignty: Organized Hypocrisy (1999). Copyright © 1999 by Princeton University Press. Reprinted by permission of Princeton University Press.

Krauthammer, Charles. "The Curse of Legalism: International Law? It's Purely Advisory," The New Republic, Nov. 6, 1989, at 44. Copyright © 1989 The New Republic, LLC. Reprinted by permission of The New Republic.

Levi, Werner. Contemporary International Law (2 ed. 1991). Reprinted by permission of the author.

Lietzau, William K. "The United States and the International Criminal Court: International Criminal Law After Rome: Concerns from a U.S. Military Perspective," 64 Law & Contemp. Prob. 119. Copyright © Duke University School of Law. Reprinted by permission.

Lipson, Charles. "Why Are Some International Agreements Informal?," 45 Int'l Org. 495 (1991). © 1991 by the World Peace Foundation and the Massachusetts Institute of Technology.

Lissitzyn, Oliver J. "Efforts to Codify or Restate the Law of Treaties," 62 Colum. L. Rev. 1166 (1962). Reprinted by permission.

MacLaren, Malcolm, and Schenendimann, Felix. "An Exercise in the Development of International Law: The New ICRC Study on Customary International Humanitarian Law," 6 German L.J. (2005). Copyright © 2005 German Law Journal.

Malanczuk, Peter. Akehurst's Modern Introduction to International Law (7th ed. 1997). Reproduced with permission from Thomson Publishing Services.

Map of the Nile Basin in Chapter 11 was created for this text by Dana Costello.

Matheson, Michael J. "The Opinions of the International Court of Justice on the Threat or Use of Nuclear Weapons." Reproduced with permission from 91 Am. J. Int'l L. 434 (1997). Copyright © The American Society of International Law.

Mathews, Jessica, "Power Shift," Foreign Affairs, Jan/Feb. 1997, at 50. Copyright © Council on Foreign Relations.

Mayer, Ann. "Universal Versus Islamic Human Rights: A Clash of Cultures or a Clash with a Construct?" 15 Mich. J. Int'l L. 307 (1994).

McIntosh, C. Alison, and Finkle, Jason L. "The Cairo Conference on Population and Development: A New Paradigm?" 21 Population & Dev. Rev. 223 (1995). Copyright © 1995 Population Council. Reprinted with the permission of the Population Council.

Murphy, Sean D., ed. "Contemporary Practice of the United States Relating to International Law." Reproduced with permission from 93 Am. J. Int'l L. 628 (1999). Copyright © The American Society of International Law.

Mutua, Makau. "What is TWAIL?" Reproduced with permission from 94 ASIL Proc. 31, 34-35 (2000). Copyright © The American Society of International Law.

Naim, Moises. "Lori's War," Foreign Policy (Spring 2000). Copyright © 2000 by the Carnegie Endowment for International Peace. Reprinted by permission.

Nike Code of Conduct, www.nike.com. Courtesy of www.nikebiz.com.

O'Brien, Conor Cruise. United Nations: Sacred Drama. Copyright © Conor Cruise O'Brien, 1968. Reproduced by permission of Greene & Heaton Ltd.

Oppenheim, Lassa. International Law, Vol. 1, Peace (1905). Copyright ©
Longmans, Green and Co. Reprinted by permission.

Oxman, Bernard H. "Caspian Sea or Lake: What Difference Does It Make?" 1
Caspian Crossroads Magazine (Winter 1996). Copyright © 1996 United States-
Azerbaijan Council. Reprinted by permission.

Oxman, Bernard H., and Bantz, Vincent P. "International Decisions: The
'Camouco.'" Reproduced with permission from 94 Am. J. Int'l L. 713 (2000).
Copyright © The American Society of International Law.

Pictet, Jean, ed. Commentary, I Geneva Convention for the Amelioration of
the Condition of the Wounded and Sick in Armed Forces in the Field (1952).

Ratner, Steven R. "Corporations and Human Rights: A Theory of Legal
Responsibility," 111 Yale L.J. 443 (2001). Reprinted by permission of The Yale
Law Journal Company and William S. Hein Company.

Ratner, Steven R. "New Democracies, Old Atrocities: An Inquiry in
International Law," 87 Geo. L.J. 707 (1999). Reprinted with permission of the
publisher, Georgetown Law Journal © 1999.

Ratner, Steven R. "Terrorism and the Laws of War—September 11 and its
Aftermath: Expert Analysis." Crimes of War Project Web site, *www.crimesofwar.org*
(2001).

Ratner, Steven R. The New UN Peacekeeping: Building Peace in Lands of
Conflict after the Cold War (1995). Copyright © Steven R. Ratner. Reprinted with
permission of Palgrave.

Ratner, Steven R. "The Schizophrenias of International Criminal Law," 33
Tex. Int'l L.J. 237 (1998). Copyright © Texas International Law Journal,
University of Texas School of Law.

Ratner, Steven R., and Abrams, Jason S. Accountability for Human Rights
Atrocities in International Law: Beyond the Nuremberg Legacy (2d ed. 2001).
Copyright © 2001 Oxford University Press. Reprinted by permission of Oxford
University Press.

Reisman, W. Michael. "The Constitutional Crisis in the United Nations."
Reproduced with permission from 87 Am. J. Int'l L. 83 (1993). Copyright © The
American Society of International Law.

Reisman, W. Michael. "Law From the Policy Perspective," in International
Law Essays, edited by Myres S. McDougal and W. Michael Reisman. Copyright ©
1981 Foundation Press. Reprinted by permission, Foundation Press.

Reisman, W. Michael. "The Lessons of Qana," 22 Yale J. Int'l L. 381 (1997).

Reisman, W. Michael. "The Political Consequences of the General Assembly
Advisory Opinion," in The International Court of Justice and Nuclear Weapons,
edited by Laurence Boisson de Chazournes and Philippe Sands (1991). Reprinted
with the permission of Cambridge University Press.

Rostow, Eugene V. "The Gulf Crisis in International and Foreign Relations
Law, Continued: Until What? Enforcement Action or Collective Self-Defense?"
Reproduced with permission from 85 Am. J. Int'l L. 506 (1991). Copyright © The
American Society of International Law.

Rudolph, Christopher. "Constructing an Atrocities Regime: The Politics of
War Crimes Tribunals," 55 Int'l Org. 655 (2001). Copyright © 2001 by the IO
Foundation and the Massachusetts Institute of Technology. Reprinted by
permission.

Schachter, Oscar. "In Defense of International Rules on the Use of Force," 53
U. Chi. L. Rev. 113 (1986).

Scharf, Michael P. "A Preview of the Lockerbie Case," reproduced with permission from ASIL Insights, May 2000. Copyright © The American Society of International Law.

Schmitt, Michael N. "U.S. Security Strategies: A Legal Assessment," 27 Harv. J.L. & Pub. Pol'y 737 (2004). Copyright © 2004. Harvard Journal of Law & Public Policy.

Shanker, Thom, and Seelye, Katherine A. "Behind-the-Scenes Clash Led Bush to Reverse Himself on Applying Geneva Conventions," The New York Times, Feb. 22, 2002. Copyright © 2001 by the New York Times Co. Reprinted by permission.

Shelton, Dinah. "Law, Non-Law and the Problem of 'Soft Law,'" in Commitment and Compliance: The Role of Non-binding Norms in the International Legal System, edited by Dinah Shelton (2000). Reprinted by permission of Oxford University Press.

Shihata, Ibrahim. The Legal Treatment of Foreign Direct Investment. (Kluwer Academic Publishers, 1993). Reprinted with kind permission of Kluwer Law International and Mrs. Ibrahim Shihata.

Spiro, Peter J. "New Global Potentates: Nongovernmental Organizations and the 'Unregulated' Marketplace," 18 Cardozo L. Rev. 957 (1996). Copyright © 1996 Cardozo Law Review. Reprinted by permission of Cardozo Law Review.

Stromseth, Jane E. "Rethinking Humanitarian Intervention: The Case for Incremental Change," in Humanitarian Intervention: Ethical, Legal, and Political Dimensions, edited by J. L. Holzgrefe and Robert Keohane (2003). Reprinted by permission of the author.

Szasz, Paul. "Legal Authority for the Possible Use of Force Against Iraq." Reproduced with permission from 92 Am. Soc'y Int'l L. Proc. 136 (1998). Copyright © The American Society of International Law.

Taylor, Carmen, "A jet airliner is lined up on one of the World Trade Center towers in New York Tuesday, Sept. 11, 2001." Associated Press, KHBS KHOG. Reprinted with permission of AP/Wide World Photos.

Varley, Pamela; Voorhes, Meg; De Simone, Peter; Bateman Brenda; and Breen, Kerry. The Sweatshop Quandary: Corporate Responsibility on the Global Frontier (1998). Copyright © 1998 Investor Responsibility Research Center. Reprinted with permission of the Investor Responsibility Research Center.

Watts, Sir Arthur. "The Importance of International Law," in The Role of Law in International Politics: Essays in International Relations and International Law, edited by Michael Byers (2000). Reprinted by permission of Oxford University Press.

Wedgwood, Ruth. "NATO's Campaign in Yugoslavia." Reproduced with permission from 93 Am. J. Int'l L. 828 (1999). Copyright © The American Society of International Law.

Weiler, J. H. H. "The Transformation of Europe," 100 Yale L.J. 2403 (1991). Reprinted by permission of The Yale Law Journal Company and William S. Hein Company from the Yale Law Journal, Vol. 100, pages 2403-2483.

Welsh, Stephanie. "A circumciser holds a standard double-edged razor blade August 1995." Reprinted by permission of Getty Images.

Welsh, Stephanie. "Villagers gather to celebrate the circumcision of several adolescent girls and boys August 1995." Reprinted by permission of Getty Images.

Wiener, Jonathan Baert. "Global Environmental Regulation: Instrument Choice in Legal Context, " 108 Yale L.J. 677 (1999). Reprinted by permission of

The Yale Law Journal Company and William S. Hein Company from the Yale Law Journal, Vol. 108, page 677.

Williams, Paul R. "The Treaty Obligations of the Successor States of the Former Soviet Union, Yugoslavia, and Czechoslovakia: Do They Continue in Force?" 23 Den. J. Int'l L. & Pol'y 1 (1994). Reprinted with permission of the Denver Journal of International Law & Policy, University of Denver College of Law.

Williamson, Edwin D., and Osborn, John E. "A U.S. Perspective on Treaty Succession and Related Issues in the Wake of the Breakup of the USSR and Yugoslavia," 33 Va. J. Int'l L. 1. Copyright © Virginia Journal of International Law. Reprinted by permission.

Wippman, David. International Law and Ethnic Conflict in Cyprus, 31 Texas Int'l L.J. 141 (1996). Copyright © Texas International Law Journal, University of Texas School of Law.

Wright, Shelley. "Women and the Global Economic Order: A Feminist Perspective," 10 Am. U. Int'l L. Rev. 861 (1995). Reprinted with the permission of the publisher, Washington College of Law of The American University and American University International Law Review.

Authors' Note

In order to provide a sense of the appearance of original international legal documents, we have attempted as much as possible to retain the formatting of documents as they appear in the original, authoritative source. In some cases, this results in different typefaces in the text. For convenience, additions to excerpted material are indicated by brackets. Deletions are indicated by ellipses, unless the deletions occur at the beginning of court or tribunal decisions or dissents. Citations and footnotes are generally omitted from excerpted materials without using an ellipsis. Footnotes that appear in excerpted materials retain the numbering of the originals; footnotes denoted by an asterisk are the authors'.

Political Map of the World 2006

SOURCE: CIA World Factbook

INTERNATIONAL LAW
NORMS, ACTORS, PROCESS

PART I

Introduction to International Law and Law Making

International law, in one form or another, dates back thousands of years, and reflects the felt need of most independent political communities for agreed norms and processes to regulate their interactions. Part I of this casebook is designed to introduce you to the issues, processes, actors, and norms that constitute modern international law, and to the ways in which international legal norms are generated, interpreted, and applied. The problems in Part I illustrate in microcosm the kinds of issues that confront international decision makers and the ways in which international legal norms and processes may be used to analyze and resolve such issues.

Chapter 1 provides an overview of the evolution and historical development of international law and institutions in the context of two quite different problems that together illustrate the richness and complexity of contemporary international law and its role in international decision making. The first problem, the clash between Chad and Libya over control of the Aouzou Strip during the 1980s, represents a classic international law dispute. The actors are states, the issue in dispute is control over territory, the governing legal instruments are treaties, and the forum for decision is an international court. Similar issues have arisen countless times over the last several hundred years, and the legal principles relied upon by the International Court of Justice in reaching its decision would be instantly recognizable to lawyers from a much earlier era. The Chad-Libya problem highlights the continuing importance of states and territory in the international legal and political order and raises questions concerning the effect of international law and institutions on interstate relations and state behavior.

The second problem in Chapter 1, the *Rainbow Warrior* affair, illustrates some of the dramatic changes that have reshaped international law in the post-World War II era, including the rising prominence of non-state actors and issue areas such as human rights and the environment. The problem centers on the French government's decision to destroy a vessel used by a non-governmental organization to protest the effects of French nuclear testing on the environment. The actors include states, non-governmental organizations, individuals, and a variety of international organizations. The issues involve a complex mix of international security, trade, and environmental concerns, and illustrate the sometimes complicated relationship between international and

1

domestic legal systems. Like the Chad-Libya problem, the *Rainbow Warrior* affair also raises difficult questions concerning the manner and extent to which international law influences the behavior of international actors, though in a very different context.

Chapter 1 concludes by sketching some of the conceptual challenges that characterize the field, noting both the increasing legalization of international relations and the gaps, inadequacies, and problems that remain. Finally, Chapter 1 outlines some of the many different conceptual approaches that could be applied to understand international law, from natural law to positivism to more recent interdisciplinary methodologies.

Chapter 2 provides the basic analytical framework for understanding the generation, interpretation, and application of international legal norms. The chapter relies on several concrete problems to illustrate how states come to agree on international legal norms, why states and other actors might prefer one form of international law to another in a given context, and the processes by which international legal norms change over time. Together, Chapters 1 and 2 provide an overview of the field of international law as well as some of the analytical and substantive tools needed for analyzing the subject-specific problems that appear in the chapters that follow.

1

Tracing the Evolution of International Law Through Two Problems

I. THE CHAD-LIBYA WAR OVER THE AOUZOU STRIP

In the middle of the Sahara desert lies a narrow area of barren land known as the Aouzou Strip. Sparsely inhabited by a few thousand members of the nomadic Toubou people, the Strip sits on the border between Libya and Chad. The Strip's dimensions are defined not by nature but by humans: the Strip represents the core area of disagreement between the claims of Libya as to the location of its southern border and the claims of Chad as to the location of its northern border. The Strip has virtually no economic potential to either Chad or Libya, either on its surface or below; nor has either state seen the Strip as having any military or strategic value, given its isolation from population centers and its inhospitable climate. Yet since the independence of Libya from Italian colonial rule in 1951 and of Chad from French colonial rule in 1960, the two states have fiercely contested—including through recourse to armed force—the location of their common border and thus of title to the Strip.

The essence of Chad's claim to the territory is that the border was fixed by a treaty—but not a treaty between Libya and Chad. Rather, Chad has asserted that the 1955 Treaty of Friendship and Good Neighbourliness between Libya and France included a formal acceptance by Libya of France's claims to the borders of its colonial possessions in Africa. These borders had themselves been the subject of earlier agreements not between France and Libya, but between France and the previous colonial powers in the area—namely, Italy and Britain. Chad claimed that the 1955 Treaty that recognized the validity of these previous colonial agreements still bound Libya. Libya, for its part, asserted title not only to the Strip but to significant amounts of territory south of it, based on a variety of assertions, including the invalidity of the 1955 Treaty that France allegedly coerced Libya's king into signing; the lack of any recognition in that treaty of the Chad-Libya border in particular; the allegiance to Libya of various inhabitants of the region; and the prior title to the territory held by the Ottoman Empire and Italy, the predecessor colonial powers to Libya.

3

Libya asserted its claims in a variety of ways. In the early 1970s, Libya supported a rebellion by inhabitants of northern Chad against the central government; after the central government lost control of the Strip, the local leaders allowed Libyan military personnel into the area, following which Libya set up a de facto administration of the region. Diplomatic negotiations throughout the 1970s, mediated by the Organization of African Unity (OAU), failed to reach a solution. In 1980, as Chad's civil war intensified, Libya invaded large areas of Chad outside the Strip, captured the capital, N'Djamena, and ousted the official (although very weak) government in favor of its pro-Libyan rival; Libya and the new government even discussed the merger of the two states. The invasion was strongly condemned by the OAU and France. In 1982, after the OAU threatened to cancel its summit scheduled to take place in Tripoli, Libya agreed to pull its troops out of much of the country.

In 1983, with Libya still occupying much of northern Chad (including the Strip) and arming rebels, the Chad government appealed to the UN Security Council to demand Libya's withdrawal. The Soviet Union vetoed a UN resolution calling for the withdrawal. Chad succeeded in ousting the Libyan military from northern Chad—except for the Strip—in a lightning action in August 1987. After two more years of OAU-sponsored mediation and negotiation, the two states agreed in August 1989 to settle the border dispute by political means within one year or, if they failed to do so, to submit it for determination to the International Court of Justice (ICJ), the judicial organ of the United Nations, in The Hague. In late August and early September 1990, after the failure of negotiations, the two states asked the Court to determine their mutual border in accordance with principles of international law.

A. The Law of Nations in Its Traditional Incarnation

The dispute between Chad and Libya concerns international law, and not only political interactions, in two key senses. First, the parties themselves invoked legal arguments to assert their title to the disputed territory; and, second, they agreed, after much discussion and fighting, that they would allow a judicial body to resolve their dispute solely by recourse to legal rules. Throughout the pages that follow, the reader will see numerous problems in which the various actors—not always states—use legal arguments to make claims, justify their own actions, and acknowledge obligations. A decision by those parties to entrust the final resolution of their dispute to an international court is, however, relatively rare in the field of international law. Such regularized resort to tribunals for the settlement of international disputes represents an aspiration of many of the founders and modern practitioners of international law, but it is by no means the only way in which the law can prove decisive or influential to an outcome. We offer this case merely to demonstrate the role of law in the resolution of disputes without suggesting that the mechanism of a court decision is the only possible, or even the most common, arena for decision making.

The Aouzou Strip problem also provides an example of an international legal disagreement in its most traditional sense: the principal actors are states; the resource under dispute is territory; the legal instruments on which the two sides rely are quite formal—namely, treaties; the doctrinal arguments of the parties about the formal requisites of title to territory reflect (although they do not exclusively rely upon) concepts dating back to the conquest of much of the world by

European states 500 years ago. This sort of dispute could easily have arisen 100 or 200 years ago (with colonial powers replacing the states of today as parties).

To gain a sense of how international law developed to address these interstate disputes, one must have some grasp of its history. Legal historians differ significantly, however, in arriving at an appropriate starting point for such history. From their earliest days, organized political communities have entered into agreements to regulate interactions they might have. For instance, in the thirteenth century B.C., the Egyptian pharaoh Rameses II entered into a Treaty of Peace, Alliance, and Extradition with a neighboring king; Asian kingdoms routinely engaged in similar practices. Ancient entities settled some disputes through accords, though recourse to war was the more common enterprise. Most historians of international law nonetheless focus on Europe as the birthplace of international law as we know it today; as indicated in the following excerpt, they regard the law's key formative years as the time of the decline of the Holy Roman Empire and the birth of new states in Europe.

Werner Levi, *Contemporary International Law*

6-13 (2d ed. 1991)

Mainly as a result of new economic forces, the Holy Roman Empire broke down, which brought about the collapse of the at least nominally centralized order of Europe and foreshadowed the need for a different legal system. . . .

As new centers of independent power arose, laws regulating their coexistence and relations were needed, although until the age of absolutism had passed, these laws had to refer to the person of the rulers more than to political entities. Gradually, the relationships of subordination and superordination under the universalist reign of one emperor and pope were replaced by a system of coordination among sovereign rulers. The feudalistic entities with their relatively uncertain borders gave way to states based upon sharply defined territory. . . . The preeminent role of territory in international law began. . . .

Once the multitude of specific limited jurisdictions . . . was replaced by the principle of territoriality with one sovereign ruler as the basis of the state, a number of legal consequences followed. One was the absolute power and exclusive jurisdiction of one ruler in his or her territory. The second was the prohibition of interference by other monarchs in a state's internal affairs. The third was the rise of immunity. The fourth was the gradual elaboration of equality among states in diplomatic practice and of the principles regulating this practice. . . .

Many of the principles and norms developed during this time, especially those fortifying sovereignty, are still accepted today, with states replacing rulers as subjects of the law. But initially, the law was not applicable to peoples and territories outside Western society (except the United States when it became independent). . . . Rules legitimizing imperialism and its means . . . endured well into the twentieth century, until most colonies became independent.

EARLY WRITERS ON INTERNATIONAL LAW

During these first centuries in the development of international law, legal and political writers . . . collected existing norms and suggested new ones. And they provided the theoretical and philosophical foundations, justifications, and guidelines for the international legal system, always keeping in mind the interests of their countries.

. . . The Spaniard Francisco Vitoria (1480-1546) argued that Spain was obliged to treat the conquered Indians in the Americas humanely, and he even granted these Indians a limited right to conduct "just wars" against their cruel conquerors. But he defended Spain's right in principle to create overseas dependencies and to exploit them. Another Spaniard, Francisco Suárez (1548-1617), dealt with the by then obvious interactions of states and how to regulate them. Like all writers of the era he was particularly concerned with the nature of just war and rules for its conduct. The Italian Alberico Gentili (1552-1608)—in contrast to his Spanish colleagues, who were both professors of theology—emphasized the secular nature of international law. He therefore deduced the rules of the law not from some metaphysical source but from the practice of states and the writings of historians. He was thus the first representative of the "positivists," who argue that law is created by humans for definite conditions and purposes rather than by some supreme being for all eternity. . . .

Outstanding [among early treatises] was Hugo de Groot's (Grotius, 1583-1645) *De iure belli ac pacis* (On the Law of War and Peace), which brought him the sobriquet "father of international law." He became equally influential in writing on the laws of treaties, extraterritoriality, and the sea while focusing on the law of war and on the theoretical foundation of international law. Grotius believed that there was a law of nature (not necessarily divine) that could be implemented, not counteracted, by people using right reason. The combination of these two sources was, to Grotius, the foundation of international law. By this argument he avoided commitment to a particular religion and deliberately so, for he felt that to be effective, international law had to be acceptable to all, conceivably even "infidels." . . . Three doctrines [that are still relevant today] are the applicability of laws of war to all parties regardless of the justness of the war, freedom of the seas (argued in his book *Mare liberum* and a particularly important concept for a Dutchman to undo the claims of England and other states to dominion over the seas), and extraterritoriality of ambassadors. Philosophically, Grotius was the first representative of the eclectic school, which believes that the foundation of international law is a combination of natural and positive law.

In spite of Grotius's influence, writers continued to argue in their treatment of international law either the naturalist or the positivist view, although they did so with varying degrees. The Germans Samuel Pufendorf (1632-1694) and Christian Wolff (1676-1756) and the Swiss Emmerich de Vattel (1714-1767) could generally be classified as naturalists. The Englishman Richard Zouche (1590-1660) represented the positivist school. But few of these writers were extremists, and most took account of state practice. The contributions of these writers to the development of a body of international law continue to have some effect upon contemporary international law. Their works are still cited in the decisions of national and international courts and tribunals.

THE NINETEENTH CENTURY

. . . When the French Revolution and others ended the age of absolutism, the state became identified with its people rather than with the person of its monarch. This change required adjustments in the law. A state's territory or people could no longer be treated as appendixes of the ruler. The state itself became the subject of international law. The state's form or government personnel no longer affected the state's rights or obligations. The separation of the ruler's person from the objective legal existence of the state fulfilled the political need of including non-Christian states (Turkey, Japan, China) into the international community of states.

In increasing measure, treaties, especially multilateral treaties, implemented and eventually surpassed in volume custom as a source of international norms. The growing importance and numbers of treaties also meant a simplification of their conclusion, the routinization of what used to be prestige matters, and, most important to the new and Communist states today, a greater effectiveness of the rule that states cannot be bound against their will or that they should participate in the making of rules binding them.

The material covered by treaties was greatly augmented, reflecting both the growing volume of interaction among states and the multiplication of state interests. Agreements were reached on rules of state conduct. Communications, trade and commerce, financial matters, scientific and health subjects, and humanitarian concerns surpassed politics in volume, not importance, as topics of international conferences, thereby inaugurating a trend that continues in the contemporary era. Treaties establishing international organizations, mainly in the "noncontroversial" field of communications, made their appearance.

Grotius's natural law approach can be seen in the following passages from his treatise on war and peace.

Hugo Grotius, *De Jure Belli ac Pacis Libri Tres, book 1*

9, 12-13, 15 (Francis Kelsey trans. 1925) (1625)

1. . . . That body of law . . . which is concerned with the mutual relations among states or rulers of states, whether derived from nature, or established by divine ordinances, or having its origin in custom and tacit agreement, few have touched upon. Up to the present time no one has treated it in a comprehensive and systematic manner; yet the welfare of mankind demands that this task be accomplished. . . .

3. Such a work is all the more necessary because in our day, as in former times, there is no lack of men who view this branch of law with contempt as having no reality outside of an empty name. On the lips of men quite generally is the saying of Euphemus, which Thucydides quotes, that in the case of a king or imperial city nothing is unjust which is expedient. Of like implication is the statement that for those whom fortune favours might makes right, and that the administration of a state cannot be carried on without injustice.

Furthermore, the controversies which arise between peoples or kings generally have Mars as their arbiter. That war is irreconcilable with all law is a view held not alone by the ignorant populace; expressions are often let slip by well-informed and thoughtful men which lend countenance to such a view. Nothing is more common than the assertion of antagonism between law and arms. . . .

8. [M]aintenance of the social order . . . which is consonant with human intelligence, is the source of law properly so called. To this sphere of law belong the abstaining from that which is another's, the restoration to another of anything of his which we may have, together with any gain which we may have received from it,

the obligation to fulfil promises, the making good of a loss incurred through our fault, and the inflicting of penalties upon men according to their deserts.

9. From this signification of the word law there has flowed another and more extended meaning. . . . [I]t is meet for the nature of man, within the limitations of human intelligence, to follow the direction of a well-tempered judgement, being neither led astray by fear or the allurement of immediate pleasure, nor carried away by rash impulse. Whatever is clearly at variance with such judgement is understood to be contrary also to the law of nature, that is, to the nature of man. . . .

17. [J]ust as the laws of each state have in view the advantage of that state, so by mutual consent it has become possible that certain laws should originate as between all states, or a great many states; and it is apparent that the laws thus originating had in view the advantage, not of particular states, but of the great society of states. And this is what is called the law of nations. . . .

The geographical ambit of international law and its approach to the diversity of actors in the international system during its formative centuries remains a subject of great importance. Levi's more Eurocentric vision is echoed in the first edition of the leading English-language treatise on international law.

Lassa Oppenheim, *International Law, vol. 1, Peace*

30-31, 34, 218-19, 266-67 (1905)

§26. . . . There is no doubt that the Law of Nations is a product of Christian civilisation. It originally arose between the States of Christendom only, and for hundreds of years was confined to these States. Between Christian and Moham-medan nations a condition of perpetual enmity prevailed in former centuries. And no constant intercourse existed in former times between Christian and Buddhistic States. But from about the beginning of the nineteenth century matters gradually changed. A condition of perpetual enmity between whole groups of nations exists no longer either in theory or in practice. And although there is still a broad and deep gulf between Christian civilisation and others, many inter-ests, which knit Christian States together, knit likewise some non-Christian and Christian States.

§27. Thus the membership of the Family of Nations has of late necessarily been increased and the range of dominion of the Law of Nations has extended beyond its original limits. . . . [T]here are three conditions for the admission of new members into the circle of the Family of Nations. A State to be admitted must, first, be a civilised State which is in constant intercourse with members of the Family of Nations. Such State must, secondly, expressly or tacitly consent to be bound for its future international conduct by the rules of International Law. And, thirdly, those States which have hitherto formed the Family of Nations must expressly or tacitly consent to the reception of the new member. . . .

§29. The Law of Nations as a law between States based on the common consent of the members of the Family of Nations naturally does not contain any rules concerning the intercourse with and treatment of such States as are outside that circle. That this intercourse and treatment ought to be regulated by the principles of

Christian morality is obvious. But actually a practice frequently prevails which is not only contrary to Christian morality, but arbitrary and barbarous. Be that as it may, it is discretion, and not International Law, according to which the members of the Family of Nations deal with such States as still remain outside that family. . . .

§169. The territory of a State may consist of one piece of the surface of the globe only, such as that of Switzerland, [or it] may also be dismembered and consist of several pieces, such as that of Great Britain. All States with colonies have a "dismembered territory." . . . Colonies rank as territory of the motherland, although they may enjoy complete self-government and therefore be called Colonial States. . . .

§211. States as living organisms grow and decrease in territory. If the historical facts are taken into consideration, different reasons may be found to account for the exercise of sovereignty. . . . One section may have been ceded by another State, another section may have come into possession of the owner in consequence of accretion, a third through subjugation, a fourth through occupation of no State's land. As regards a fifth section, a State may say that it has exercised its sovereignty over the same for so long a period that the fact of having had it in undisturbed possession is a sufficient title of ownership. . . . Most writers recognise these five modes. . . .

Consider the following two perspectives on the history of international law and the state of that law by the nineteenth century.

R.P. Anand, *The Influence of History on the Literature of International Law*

The Structure and Process of International Law 342-43 (R.St.J. MacDonald and D.M. Johnston eds., 1983)

There is little doubt that in some form or another, rules of inter-state conduct or what we now call international law can be traced to some of the most ancient civilizations, like China, India, Egypt and Assyria. Apart from just and humane rules of war and peace, one can find numerous rules and regulations on the law of treaties, right of asylum, treatment of aliens and foreign nationals, the immunities and privileges of ambassadors, modes of acquiring territory, and even glimpses of the law of the sea and maritime belt. . . . As Majid Khadduri points out: "In each civilization the population tended to develop within itself a community of political entities—a family of nations—whose interrelationships were regulated by a set of customary rules and practices, rather than being a single nation governed by a single authority and a single system of law. Several families of nations existed or coexisted in areas such as the ancient Near East, Greece and Rome, China, Islam and Western Christiandom, where at least one distinct civilization had developed in each of them. Within each civilization a body of principles and rules developed for regulating the conduct of states with one another in peace and war."

Although many of these systems of inter-state rules and practices were confined to one or two civilizations, and disappeared with the disappearance of those civilizations, it would be wrong to dismiss them as not international law or as of no consequence and merely "religious precepts" or moral obligations. Apart from the fact that even the so-called modern system of international law was sought to be based by classical jurists on Christian theology and natural law, it is recognized that necessities in intercourse between nations in different civilizations probably provoked similar responses and similar rules and institutions, such as the immunity of foreign envoys and the establishment of durable treaty relationships. . . .

[L]ong before the emergence of Europe as the center of the world stage, relations between Europe and Asia were conducted on the basis of well-recognized rules of inter-state conduct which were supposed to be universally applicable to all states. [W]hen European adventurers arrived in Asia in the fifteenth century "they found themselves in the middle of a network of states and inter-state relations based on traditions which were more ancient than their own and in no way inferior to notions of European civilization." . . . European sovereign or semi-sovereign agencies which appeared on the Asian scene were automatically drawn into the Asian legal system and influenced by its rules. The confrontation of the Asian and European states "took place on a footing of equality and the ensuing commercial and political transactions, far from being in a legal vacuum, were governed by the law of nations as adjusted to local inter-state custom." The East Indies constituted the meeting ground of the Dutch, English, French and other European East India companies, on the one hand, and Asian sovereigns on the other. The more these contacts became intensified, the more they affected each other's practices with a common framework of diplomatic exchanges and treaty making.

Anthony Anghie, *Finding the Peripheries: Sovereignty and Colonialism in Nineteenth-Century International Law*

40 Harv. Intl. L.J. 1, 22, 25, 29, 30, 49, 69, 79, 80 (1999)

. . . A central feature of positivism was the distinction it made between civilized and uncivilized states. The naturalist notion that a single, universally applicable law governed a naturally constituted society of nations was completely repudiated by jurists of the mid-nineteenth century. Instead, nineteenth-century writers such as Wheaton claimed that international law was the exclusive province of civilized societies. . . .

. . . [T]he distinction between the civilized and uncivilized was a fundamental tenet of positivist epistemology and thus profoundly shaped the concepts constituting the positivist framework. The racialization of positivist law followed inevitably from these premises—as demonstrated, for example, by the argument that law was the creation of unique, civilized, and social institutions and that only states possessing such institutions could be members of "international society." . . .

The concept of society enabled positivists to develop a number of strategies for explaining further why the non-European world was excluded from international law. One such strategy consisted of asserting that no law existed in certain non-European, barbaric regions. A second strategy used to distinguish the civilized from the uncivilized consisted of asserting the fact that while certain societies may have had their own systems of law these were of such an alien character that no proper legal relations could develop between European and non-European states.

The problem of the legal personality of non-European peoples could be most simply resolved by the actual act of colonization, which effectively extinguished this personality. Once colonization took place, the colonizing power assumed sovereignty over the non-European territory, and any European state carrying on business with that territory would deal with the colonial power. In this way, legal relations would once again take place between two European powers. . . .

Sovereignty manifested itself quite differently in the non-European world than in the European world. First, since the non-European world was not "sovereign," virtually no legal restrictions were imposed on the actions of European states with respect to non-European peoples. European states could engage in massive violence, invariably justified as necessary to pacify the natives and followed by the project of reshaping those societies in accordance with their particular vision of the world. Sovereignty was therefore aligned with existing European ideas of social order, political organization, progress, and development. . . . [Second,] lacking sovereignty, non-European states exercised no rights recognizable by international law over their own territory. Any legal restrictions on the actions of European states towards non-European states resulted from contentions among European states regarding the same territory, not from the rights of the non-European states. This is evident in the partition of Africa, which was determined in accordance with the needs of the major European states. . . .

. . . [T]he nineteenth century offers us an example of a much broader theme: the importance of the existence of the "other" for the progress and development of the discipline itself. Seen from this perspective, the nineteenth century is both distinctive and conventional. Its method, focus, and techniques are in many ways unique. But in another respect, the nineteenth century is simply one example of the nexus between international law and the civilizing mission. The same mission was implemented by the vocabulary of naturalism in sixteenth-century international law. Furthermore, the succeeding paradigm of pragmatism, which developed in the inter-war period, was similarly preoccupied with furthering the civilizing mission even as it condemned nineteenth-century positivism for being formalist and colonial. Thus, the only thing unique about the nineteenth century is that it explicitly adopted the civilizing mission and reflected these goals in its very vocabulary. The more alarming and likely possibility is that the civilizing mission is inherent in one form or another in the principal concepts and categories that govern our existence: ideas of modernity, progress, development, emancipation, and rights. The enormous task of identifying these biases and ridding the discipline of them continues, as does the related task of constructing an international law that fulfils its promise of advancing the cause of justice.

International law by the nineteenth century had developed an entire doctrine to justify acquisition of territory by colonial powers. That law recognized, for instance, that European states could acquire so-called empty land or *terra nullius*, or land not already under the control of another state—based on its purported discovery by Europeans, notwithstanding its prior discovery, so to speak, by indigenous peoples who may have been living on the territory for thousands of years. It also justified the colonial presence by placing great weight on treaties of cession whereby indigenous peoples signed over control of their land to colonial powers, despite the coerced nature of many of these agreements. Colonial powers could divide their possessions as they saw fit, a process that reached its apogee in the Congress of Berlin in 1884-1885, when the European imperial powers drew up legal spheres of influence for most of Africa, and continued with numerous bilateral agreements setting individual frontiers, such as those cited by Chad and Libya in the Aouzou Strip controversy.

In the case of territorial disputes between colonial powers not resolved by treaty, arbitral tribunals recognized by the end of the century that effective control over the territory—in terms of constant, peaceful, and acknowledged use—more than the original form of acquisition, was the key to title. Sometimes the law would accept title over hinterlands adjacent to those under clear control. Again, however, the views of the local populations played little if any role. The centrality of these colonial treaty arrangements, notwithstanding their historical context, ultimately proved decisive to the ICJ in adjudicating the boundary dispute.

B. Resolution of the Chad-Libya Conflict

On February 3, 1994, three and a half years after Chad and Libya submitted the case, the ICJ ruled 16-1 (the sole dissenter was the judge that Libya was allowed to appoint under the Court's rules) that the Aouzou Strip in its entirety, as well as all lands south of it claimed by Libya, belonged to Chad. The Court first examined the text and context of the 1955 Treaty and concluded that, contrary to Libya's assertions, it "was aimed at settling all the frontier questions, and not just some of them." It then closely examined the various colonial agreements incorporated into the 1955 Treaty; these included agreements between Britain and France from 1898, 1899, and 1919, and between France and Italy from 1900 and 1902. The Court relied extensively on and even reprinted, a French colonial map from 1899 (see next page) that showed the border agreed to by France and Britain that year, although the Court ultimately concluded that France and Britain adopted a slightly different line (more favorable to Chad) in their 1919 agreement. The line from the 1919 France-Britain agreement, combined with the line resulting from the France-Italy agreements, determined the border, as Chad had claimed. The Court continued:

Case Concerning the Territorial Dispute (Libya/Chad)

1994 I.C.J. 6 (Feb. 3)

66. Having concluded that a frontier resulted from the 1955 Treaty, and having established where that frontier lay, the Court is in a position to consider the subsequent attitudes of the Parties to the question of frontiers. No subsequent agreement, either between France and Libya, or between Chad and Libya, has called in question the frontier in this region deriving from the 1955 Treaty. On the contrary, if one considers treaties subsequent to the entry into force of the 1955 Treaty, there is support for the proposition that after 1955, the existence of a determined frontier was accepted and acted upon by the Parties. The Treaty between Libya and Chad of 2 March 1966 . . . deals with frontier questions. Articles 1 and 2 mention "the frontier" between the two countries, with no suggestion of there being any uncertainty about it. . . . If a serious dispute had indeed existed regarding frontiers, eleven years after the conclusion of the 1955 Treaty, one would expect it to have been reflected in the 1966 Treaty. . . .

68. The Court now turns to the attitudes of the Parties, subsequent to the 1955 Treaty, on occasions when matters pertinent to the frontiers came up before international fora. Libya achieved its independence nearly nine years before Chad; during that period, France submitted reports on this territory to the United Nations General Assembly. The report for 1955 . . . shows the area of Chad's territory as 1,284,000 square kilometres, which expressly includes [the Aouzou Strip]. . . .

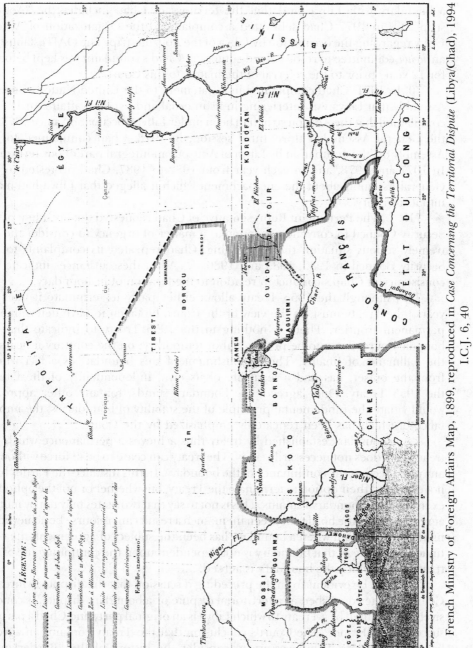

French Ministry of Foreign Affairs Map, 1899, reproduced in *Case Concerning the Territorial Dispute (Libya/Chad)*, 1994
I.C.J. 6, 40

Moreover United Nations publications from 1960 onward continued to state the area of Chad as 1,284,000 square kilometres. . . . Libya did not challenge the territorial dimensions of Chad as set out by France.

69. As for Chad, it has consistently adopted the position that it does have a boundary with Libya, and that the territory of Chad includes the "Aouzou strip". . . . In 1977 Chad submitted a complaint to the Organization of African Unity regarding the occupation by Libya of the Aouzou strip. The OAU established an *ad hoc* committee to resolve the dispute. . . . Chad's complaint was kept before it for 12 years prior to the referral of the matter to this Court. . . .

70. In 1971, Chad complained in a statement to the United Nations General Assembly that Libya was interfering in its internal and external affairs. In 1977 it complained that the Aouzou strip had been under Libyan occupation since 1973. At the General Assembly's thirty-third session, in 1978, Chad complained to the Assembly of "the occupation by Libya of Aouzou, an integral part of our territory." In 1977 and 1978, and in each year from 1982 to 1987, Chad protested to the General Assembly about the encroachment which it alleged that Libya had made into its territory.

71. . . . The Permanent Representative of Chad requested the President of the Security Council to convene a meeting as a matter of urgency to consider the extremely serious situation then prevailing. Chad repeated its complaints to the Security Council in 1983, 1985 and 1986. . . . All of these instances indicate the consistency of Chad's conduct in relation to the location of its boundary. . . .

72. [Although the 1955 Treaty allows either party to terminate it after 20 years,] the Treaty must, in the view of the Court, be taken to have determined a permanent frontier. There is nothing in the 1955 Treaty to indicate that the boundary agreed was to be provisional or temporary; on the contrary it bears all the hallmarks of finality. The establishment of this boundary is a fact which, from the outset, has had a legal life of its own, independently of the fate of the 1955 Treaty. Once agreed, the boundary stands, for any other approach would vitiate the fundamental principle of the stability of boundaries, the importance of which has been repeatedly emphasized by the Court. . . .

73. A boundary established by treaty thus achieves a permanence which the treaty itself does not necessarily enjoy. The treaty can cease to be in force without in any way affecting the continuance of the boundary. In this instance the Parties have not exercised their option to terminate the Treaty, but whether or not the option be exercised, the boundary remains. This is not to say that two States may not by mutual agreement vary the border between them; such a result can of course be achieved by mutual consent, but when a boundary has been the subject of agreement, the continued existence of that boundary is not dependent upon the continuing life of the treaty under which the boundary is agreed. . . .

75. It will be evident from the preceding discussion that the dispute before the Court, whether described as a territorial dispute or a boundary dispute, is conclusively determined by a Treaty to which Libya is an original party and Chad a party in succession to France. The Court's conclusion that the Treaty contains an agreed boundary renders it unnecessary to consider the history of the "Borderlands" claimed by Libya on the basis of title inherited from the indigenous people, the Senoussi Order, the Ottoman Empire and Italy. . . .

76. Likewise, the effectiveness of occupation of the relevant areas in the past, and the question whether it was constant, peaceful and acknowledged, are not matters for determination in this case. . . . The concept of *terra nullius* and the nature of . . . Ottoman or French administration are likewise not germane to

the issue. For the same reason, the concepts of spheres of influence and of the hinterland doctrine do not come within the ambit of the Court's enquiry in this case. . . . The 1955 Treaty completely determined the boundary between Libya and Chad.

Within weeks of the ICJ's decision, Libya and Chad agreed to abide by it; in April 1994, they reached an agreement on the practicalities of the Libyan withdrawal, removal of mines, and demarcation of the border. They called for the United Nations to send a team of monitors to observe the withdrawal. In May, the UN Security Council established the United Nations Aouzou Strip Observer Group for this purpose. The team consisted of 15 military and civilian observers and cost the United Nations just over $67,000. On May 30, in accordance with the withdrawal schedule previously agreed upon, Libya completed its withdrawal, and the United Nations certified the result. Both governments consider the matter of the Strip's territorial sovereignty closed, though there is some evidence that Libya has continued to support a Chadian rebel movement in the Strip.

Notes and Questions

1. Why do you suppose that Libya and Chad considered the Aouzou Strip of such importance as to justify the use of armed force? Who would benefit from title over the Strip?

2. Why do you think the Court does not consider the historical circumstances surrounding the colonial agreements to which it refers? What are the differences among the ways that Oppenheim, Anand, and Anghie view the relationships between the European powers and local populations in Africa?

3. If there had been no treaties between the colonial powers on the location of the border, what factors should the Court have considered in arriving at its outcome? Would these factors be different from those a similar court would have examined a hundred years ago?

4. Why do you think the losing party—Libya—complied so readily with the ICJ's decision?

5. Do the facts and outcome represent a victory for the rule of law in international relations or simply a political loss for Libya?

C. International Law Moves into the Twentieth Century

The twentieth century brought about sea changes in the entire field of international law. As a historical matter, most originate in the gradual global transformation that began with World War I, as the populations of European states—and of some of their colonies—decimated themselves in bloody combat over control of small pieces of land. As a result of that war, at least three constitutive changes in the international legal order began. First, European states began to accept that unlimited recourse to war for the settlement of disputes was counterproductive to their national interests and that armed conflict should be regulated through some legal arrangements. (The states of Europe and Latin America had already agreed, at key international conferences in The Hague in 1899 and 1907, that the *methods* by which wars were conducted should also be limited, leading to the development of the modern law of war.) By 1928, European and American governments had agreed upon the Treaty Providing for the Renunciation of War as an Instrument of National Policy, the so-called Kellogg-Briand Pact.

Second, in the territorial shakeup that ended World War I, European and U.S. leaders concluded that some ethnic groups in Europe that lacked their own state were entitled to determine their own political future. As a result, the victorious World War I Allies carved new states out of the defeated Central Powers based in significant part on the principle of national self-determination, which was included in several of American President Woodrow Wilson's Fourteen Points (announced in January 1918 as the U.S. goals in the war). In addition, European leaders agreed on a network of treaties and other arrangements aimed at protecting ethnic minority groups within both new and newly enlarged states. This concern with self-determination and minority rights remained, however, quite circumscribed, most significantly in that the European states did not recognize their application to any of their colonies nor to minorities within the Allied states.

Third, after World War I the independent states agreed upon a fundamental institutional arrangement not only to address questions of war and peace and human rights but to develop legal norms in other areas, such as labor, health, and communications. This organization, the League of Nations, was created by the Versailles Treaty ending World War I. The League transcended prior forms of international cooperation by representing a true international organization, with decision-making bodies and a large, permanent Secretariat. Along with its specialized bodies, such as the International Telecommunication Union and the International Labour Office, the League studied and promoted international cooperation on numerous issues of transnational interest. The result was a shift in the way much international law was made, as the League took the lead in preparing multilateral treaties on many subjects, encouraged states to reach bilateral agreements, and drafted many nontreaty instruments that came to be influential among states. In addition, the world's first standing global court—the Permanent Court of International Justice—began to decide a handful of cases, leading some to believe that the future for the peaceful settlement of disputes through international law and adjudication was bright indeed.

In fact, the prospects for legal arrangements to regulate international affairs were soon overshadowed by the sequential aggression of the fascist states—Japan, Italy, and Germany—in China, Ethiopia, and central Europe. The League's members showed no political will to enforce by economic sanctions or military force the various legal commitments states had undertaken in the areas of recourse to force or protection of minorities, and America's absence from the League due to the U.S. Senate's rejection of the Versailles Treaty only worsened matters. Much of the apparent progress of international law proved to be illusory during the dark years of the 1930s. The cataclysm that followed—50 million dead, Germany's deliberate effort to exterminate European Jews and others, the obliteration of cities by both sides, the use of nuclear weapons, and the continued subjugation of colonial peoples—left little room for optimism about the possibility for the role, let alone the rule, of law in international relations.

Yet in the end, World War II proved the catalyst for the acceleration of the major trends that began before it started, as well as for the participation of new actors in the international legal process. Thus, states oversaw the change in substantive law with respect to the two core issues that had proved significant before the war—the use of force and human rights. (The role of new actors is discussed after the next problem in this chapter.) With respect to the first issue, governments agreed in the UN Charter to ban the use of force against the territorial integrity or political independence of states except in two situations—when a state was responding in self-defense and when the United Nations itself authorized force against a state. Wars hardly ceased as a result of the UN Charter, but states did begin to refrain from the sort of aggression against neighboring states, followed by annexation, that had characterized earlier years. The limits of the ban on the use of force, however, quickly became clear as powerful governments, principally the United States and the USSR, resorted to more subtle tactics to extend their spheres of influence, such as fomenting civil wars and carrying out covert actions against uncooperative political leaders abroad.

World War II and events after it also brought renewed attention to the issue of self-determination and human rights. Because the war exacted such a large human and financial toll on the European powers, their grip on colonial possessions significantly weakened. By the late 1940s, two of the largest—British India and the Dutch East Indies—had achieved independence (in the former case through civil disobedience; in the latter through armed conflict) as India, Pakistan, and Indonesia. Most of the rest of Africa and Asia followed suit within a dozen years, usually without significant violence. The independence of these new states vastly changed the legal landscape, as they came to have a significant role in the development of international norms. Their perspectives, molded by centuries of colonial domination, exerted a major influence on the process of law making and its outcomes.

With respect to human rights, the human tragedy of World War II led governments, both those of older states and those emerging from colonial rule, to devote significant resources to the creation of a corpus of law aimed at protecting individuals from their own governments. In December 1948, the UN General Assembly proclaimed the Universal Declaration of Human Rights, which sets out a wide variety of civil and political rights as well as various economic, social, and cultural rights. While the Universal Declaration was not a treaty and was not intended to be legally binding, many states consider it an authoritative interpretation of the Charter, setting forth in considerable detail the "human rights and fundamental freedoms" that UN members agreed in the Charter to promote and observe. States prepared and signed onto treaties covering genocide, civil and political rights, economic rights, racial discrimination, women's rights, apartheid, torture, and children's rights. Clearly, some states took this process, and human rights generally, more seriously than others; indeed, for most of the period after World War II, most governments merely paid lip service to the concept of human rights as a way of influencing or currying favor with others. Nevertheless, the growth of the human rights movement fundamentally challenged the notion that states were free to do what they wanted within their own borders.

In another important development related to human rights, the trials of German and Japanese political and military leaders after World War II helped solidify the notion of individual duties under international law. Many defendants argued that, because they were following superiors' orders, their activities were "acts of state," and they were therefore immune under international law. Instead, at Nuremberg, Tokyo, and in other post-war trials, thousands of individuals were tried and convicted, and hundreds were executed, dramatically demonstrating, as the Nuremberg Tribunal stated, that "crimes against international law are committed by men, not by abstract entities, and only by punishing individuals who commit such crimes can the provisions of international law be enforced." A number of the human rights treaties, including the 1948 Genocide Convention, make individuals, rather than just states, responsible for violations. In the 1990s, the UN Security Council established ad hoc tribunals with jurisdiction to try individuals for genocide, crimes against humanity, and war crimes. In July 1998, a treaty to establish an International Criminal Court (ICC) was concluded in Rome. The Rome treaty provides that the Court has jurisdiction over "the most serious crimes of concern to the international community as a whole," including those same three offenses.

New attitudes about the use of force and human rights were, in fact, only the beginning of the story of how government attitudes changed after the war, for beyond new outlooks on the core ingredients for a stable world order, the participants in defining that order were themselves increasing in number and taking on new roles. As we appraise these other developments in international law of the last 60 years, consider the following modern dispute of a type that has become more and more common in international relations.

II. THE *RAINBOW WARRIOR* AFFAIR

In 1978, the international non-governmental organization (NGO) Greenpeace purchased a converted research trawler, which it named the *Rainbow Warrior*. Over the next several years, Greenpeace used the *Rainbow Warrior* to publicize its protests against commercial whaling practices, the dumping of nuclear waste in the oceans, and offshore oil and gas operations. In July 1985, Greenpeace sent the *Rainbow Warrior* to the South Pacific to support New Zealand's decision to close its ports to ships carrying nuclear weapons. The vessel was then scheduled to proceed to France's nearby Mururoa Atoll to protest upcoming French underground nuclear testing in the atoll. On July 10, 1985, while the *Rainbow Warrior* was docked in Auckland Harbor, New Zealand, members of the French Directorate General of External Security (DGSE) placed a bomb aboard the vessel; the ensuing explosion resulted in the sinking and total destruction of the ship and the death of Fernando Pereira, a Dutch crew member.

Although most members of the French team quickly fled New Zealand, two agents—Major Alain Mafart and Captain Dominique Prieur—were arrested and charged with murder and arson under New Zealand law. While France initially denied any role in the bombing, in September 1985, France's Prime Minister admitted DGSE's involvement in the attack. At the same time, the French Defense Minister resigned, and the head of the DGSE was fired. In November, Mafart and Prieur pleaded guilty to charges of manslaughter and wilful damage to a ship by means of explosives and were each sentenced to ten years' imprisonment. The French Defense Minister informed the agents that the government would work for their release. At the same time, New Zealand informed France that it would seek compensation for damages caused by France's illegal actions. New Zealand also insisted that France compensate Greenpeace and Pereira's family.

Thereafter, France placed considerable pressure on New Zealand to release the two agents. France argued that the agents had been obeying superior orders and that, because France was prepared to assume responsibility, the agents should not be individually liable. New Zealand replied that neither New Zealand law nor

July 10, 1985: The Greenpeace Flagship *Rainbow Warrior* in Auckland Harbor after bombing by French secret service agents.
SOURCE: Greenpeace NZ © Greenpeace

international law excuse criminal acts on the grounds that they were committed pursuant to official orders. New Zealand was also reluctant to release the agents to France because French law did not authorize the serving out of a New Zealand sentence in France, and because the agents' acts were not illegal under French law, which provides that when a "homicide, wounding or striking [was] ordered by law or lawfully ordered authority, no felony or misdemeanor has been committed."

In early 1986, France began to restrict certain New Zealand exports to France and French territories. France also began to link the *Rainbow Warrior* dispute to the question of future access to the European Community of New Zealand exports, including butter, which is vital to the New Zealand economy. In response, New Zealand filed a formal complaint with the Organization for Economic Co-Operation and Development (OECD), an international organization promoting dialogue and open markets among wealthy states, and initiated nonbinding consultation procedures under the General Agreement on Tariffs and Trade (GATT), a multilateral treaty governing international trade. In the meantime, bilateral negotiations continued.

Notes and Questions

1. On the merits, how do you think the various disputes between France and New Zealand should have been resolved? How would you have predicted, in 1986, that they would be resolved?

2. As a matter of process, how do you think the disputes between France and New Zealand should be resolved? How would you have predicted they would be resolved?

On June 19, 1986, France and New Zealand agreed to submit all issues between them arising out of this episode to UN Secretary-General Javier Perez de Cuellar (of Peru) for a binding ruling. Once this agreement was reached, New Zealand withdrew its GATT and OECD complaints. Both sides submitted written statements to Perez de Cuellar, who, on July 6, issued the following decision:

Ruling Pertaining to the Differences between France and New Zealand Arising from the *Rainbow Warrior* Affair

26 I.L.M. 1349 (1987)

The issues that I need to consider are limited in number. I set out below my ruling on them which takes account of all the information available to me. My ruling is as follows:

1. APOLOGY

New Zealand seeks an apology. France is prepared to give one. My ruling is that the Prime Minister of France should convey to the Prime Minister of New Zealand a formal and unqualified apology for the attack, contrary to international law, on the *"Rainbow Warrior"* by French service agents which took place on 10 July 1985.

2. COMPENSATION

New Zealand seeks compensation for the wrong done to it and France is ready to pay some compensation. The two sides, however, are some distance apart on quantum. New Zealand has said that the figure should not be less than US Dollars 9 million, France that it should not be more than US Dollars 4 million. My ruling is that the French Government should pay the sum of US Dollars 7 million to the Government of New Zealand as compensation for all the damage it has suffered.

3. THE TWO FRENCH SERVICE AGENTS

It is on this issue that the two Governments plainly had the greatest difficulty in their attempts to negotiate a solution to the whole issue on a bilateral basis before they took the decision to refer the matter to me.

The French Government seeks the immediate return of the two officers. It underlines that their imprisonment in New Zealand is not justified, taking into account in particular the fact that they acted under military orders and that France is ready to give an apology and to pay compensation to New Zealand for the damage suffered.

The New Zealand position is that the sinking of the *"Rainbow Warrior"* involved not only a breach of international law, but also the commission of a serious crime in New Zealand for which the two officers received a lengthy sentence from a New Zealand court. The New Zealand side states that their release to freedom would undermine the integrity of the New Zealand judicial system. In the course of bilateral negotiations with France, New Zealand was ready to explore possibilities for the prisoners serving their sentences outside New Zealand.

But it has been, and remains, essential to the New Zealand position that there should be no release to freedom, that any transfer should be to custody, and that there should be a means of verifying that.

The French response to that is that there is no basis either in international law or in French law on which the two could serve out any portion of their New Zealand sentence in France,* and that they could not be subjected to new criminal proceedings after a transfer into French hands.

On this point, if I am to fulfil my mandate adequately, I must find a solution in respect of the two officers which both respects and reconciles these conflicting positions.

My ruling is as follows:

(a) The Government of New Zealand should transfer Major Alain Mafart and Captain Dominique Prieur to the French military authorities. Immediately thereafter, Major Mafart and Captain Prieur should be transferred to a French military facility on an isolated island outside of Europe for a period of three years.

(b) They should be prohibited from leaving the island for any reason, except with the mutual consent of the two Governments. They should be isolated during their assignment on the island from persons other than military or associated personnel and immediate family and friends. . . . These conditions should be strictly complied with and appropriate action should be taken under the rules governing military discipline to enforce them.

(c) The French Government should every three months convey to the New Zealand Government and to the Secretary-General of the United Nations, through diplomatic channels, full reports on the situation of Major Mafart and Captain Prieur in terms of the two preceding paragraphs in order to allow the New Zealand Government to be sure that they are being implemented.

(d) If the New Zealand Government so requests, a visit to the French military facility in question may be made, by mutual agreement by the two Governments, by an agreed third party.

(e) I have sought information on French military facilities outside Europe. On the basis of that information, I believe that the transfer of Major Mafart and Captain Prieur to the French military facility on the isolated island of Hao in French Polynesia would best facilitate the enforcement of the conditions which I have laid down in paragraphs (a) to (d) above. My ruling is that that should be their destination immediately after their transfer.

4. TRADE ISSUES

The New Zealand Government has taken the position that trade issues have been imported into the affair as a result of French action, either taken or in prospect. The French Government denies that, but it has indicated that it is willing to give some undertakings relating to trade, as sought by the New Zealand Government. I therefore rule that France should:

(a) Not oppose continuing imports of New Zealand butter into the United Kingdom in 1987 and 1988 at levels proposed by the Commission of the European Communities . . . ;

*In fact, many states have entered into treaties that permit the return of foreign convicts to their home state to serve out their sentence—EDS.

and

(b) Not take measures that might impair the implementation of the agreement between New Zealand and the European Economic Community on Trade in Mutton, Lamb and Goatmeat which entered into force on 20 October 1980. . . .

5. ARBITRATION

The New Zealand Government has argued that a mechanism should exist to ensure that any differences that may arise about the implementation of the agreements concluded as a result of my ruling can be referred for binding decision to an arbitral tribunal. The Government of France is not averse to that. My ruling is that an agreement to that effect should be concluded and provide that any dispute concerning the interpretation or application of the other agreements, which it has not been possible to resolve through the diplomatic channel, shall, at the request of either of the two Governments, be submitted to an arbitral tribunal. . . . The decisions of the tribunal . . . shall be binding on the two Governments.

6. The two Governments should conclude and bring into force as soon as possible binding agreements incorporating all of the above rulings. These agreements should provide that the undertaking relating to an apology, the payment of compensation and the transfer of Major Mafart and Captain Prieur should be implemented at the latest on 25 July 1986.

Three days later, France and New Zealand concluded agreements incorporating the substance of the Secretary-General's ruling. One agreement provided that Mafart and Prieur were to be "transferred to a French military facility on the island of Hao for a period of not less than three years. They will be prohibited from leaving the island for any reason, except with the mutual consent of the two governments." Major Mafart and Captain Prieur were transferred to French custody on the island of Hao on July 23, 1986. In addition, France reached a settlement with the family of Fernando Pereira that included a formal apology and payment of compensation totaling 2.3 million francs. France admitted that it was legally liable to Greenpeace, but these parties were unable to agree on appropriate compensation. After Greenpeace threatened to sue France in a New Zealand court, the parties agreed to submit the matter to binding international arbitration. After full briefing and argument, an ad hoc international arbitral tribunal consisting of a former New Zealand judge and two distinguished law professors awarded Greenpeace $5 million for the loss of the *Rainbow Warrior* and an additional $1.2 million "for aggravated damages," plus expenses, interest, and legal fees. Greenpeace representatives hailed the decision and stated that the precedent "will hold state security and intelligence agencies to account in the future."

On its face, the processes and outcome of the *Rainbow Warrior* affair seem to demonstrate international law's relevance, flexibility, and efficacy in the resolution of international disputes. Two states used independent third-party dispute resolution that upheld the norm against the use of force, one of the core principles of international law. In addition, a powerful state paid compensation to the family of a foreign national whose human rights had been violated and accepted legal responsibility for the damage its actions caused an international NGO.

But the *Rainbow Warrior* affair can also be understood as a much more nuanced and ambiguous tale about the relevance and effectiveness of international law. In fact, France and New Zealand had previously agreed to most of the Secretary-General's rulings during secret negotiations in Switzerland. However, given the high political visibility of this dispute, neither state was willing to take the domestic political risks associated with a compromise reached through bilateral negotiations. Both governments believed that a compromise agreement would be politically insulated if it had the imprimatur of an independent and neutral third party. The Secretary-General's prestige and authority made it easier for each government to persuade domestic constituencies to accept those elements of the compromise that were contrary to their interests.

Moreover, neither of the French agents spent three years on Hao island. On December 11, 1987, the French government was advised that Mafart's medical condition required "an emergency return to a hospital in mainland France." The following day, France sought New Zealand's permission to evacuate Mafart and, at the same time, stressed that the only available means of transport was by military aircraft leaving Hao the next morning. New Zealand sought to have one of its doctors examine Mafart; France refused but offered to have a doctor designated by New Zealand examine Mafart as soon as he arrived in France. On December 14, without New Zealand's consent, Mafart was flown to Paris and given medical treatment. The same day, New Zealand delivered a note to France stating that it "regards this action as a serious breach of both the letter and the spirit of the obligations undertaken pursuant to the [Secretary-General's ruling]." The New Zealand doctor who examined Mafart in Paris later that day reported that, although he needed medical treatment unavailable on Hao, "it is . . . highly arguable whether an emergency evacuation as opposed to a planned urgent evacuation was necessary." Mafart never returned to Hao. France insisted that, for medical reasons, he was to remain in France.

On May 3, 1988, France advised New Zealand that Prieur was pregnant and in need of special medical attention unavailable on Hao. This time, France agreed that a New Zealand doctor could travel to Hao to examine Prieur. But on the following day, before the New Zealand doctor could arrive in Hao, France advised New Zealand that Prieur's father was dying of cancer in Paris and that she was needed at his bedside. On May 5, three days before French presidential elections, France informed New Zealand that "[t]he French Government considers it impossible, for obvious humanitarian reasons, to keep Mrs. Prieur on Hao while her father is dying in Paris. [She] will therefore immediately depart for Paris." Prieur arrived in Paris on May 6 without New Zealand's consent. Four days later, New Zealand sent a note to the French Foreign Ministry to "protest these actions in the strongest possible terms." Calling the actions "a further serious violation of the legal obligations under the Agreement," it offered to allow medical treatment for both agents in Tahiti (the capital of French Polynesia) or to send the dispute to arbitration under the terms of the Secretary-General's decision.

Prieur's father died on May 16. France argued that Prieur could not be sent back to Hao as long as her pregnancy continued; after her child was born, France asserted that she could not be sent back to Hao with a baby. After negotiations over the return of the agents proved inconclusive, New Zealand requested the establishment of an arbitral tribunal as provided in paragraph 5 of the Secretary-General's ruling. The panel, chaired by a former president and judge of the ICJ, ruled in favor of New Zealand. In the case of Major Mafart, the tribunal unanimously declared that France had breached its obligations to New Zealand by failing to order his return to Hao, although a majority held that his initial removal was not wrongful.

In the case of Captain Prieur, the tribunal unanimously held that France committed a breach by not endeavoring in good faith to obtain New Zealand's consent to her removal from Hao, by subsequently removing her from Hao, and by failing to return her to Hao. A majority held, however, that as the three-year period that Mafart and Prieur were to serve on Hao had now passed, France's obligations were at an end, and accordingly the tribunal declined to order the agents' return. The tribunal unanimously declared "that the condemnation of the French Republic for its breaches of its treaty obligations to New Zealand, made public by the decision of the Tribunal, constitutes in the circumstances appropriate satisfaction for the legal and moral damage caused to New Zealand." Finally, although New Zealand had expressly rejected the award of monetary damages, the tribunal "recommended" that the two governments create a fund to promote close and friendly relations between the citizens of the two states and that the French government make an initial contribution of $2 million to the fund. Almost immediately after this award was issued, France contributed $2 million to a fund to promote friendly bilateral relations.

The *Rainbow Warrior* affair can also be understood to be part of a larger struggle by many states and NGOs against French nuclear testing in the South Pacific. While France's first nuclear tests were in the French Sahara in 1960, France shifted its testing site to the Mururoa Atoll after Algeria achieved independence. This decision and subsequent nuclear tests prompted a series of legal and political disputes between France and the region's states. Concern over French nuclear testing was also a major factor in the adoption of the South Pacific Nuclear Free Zone (SPNFZ) Treaty in 1985. The treaty establishes a nuclear free zone; states party to the treaty undertake not to possess or permit in their territory the testing of nuclear devices. This treaty was open only to members of the South Pacific Forum (SPF), a regional organization consisting of 15 South Pacific states. Thus, France was not a party to the treaty, and French testing continued until 1992, when France and other nuclear powers announced a moratorium on nuclear testing.

In June 1995, France announced that it would break this moratorium and conduct a final series of eight nuclear tests in the South Pacific. After France resumed testing in October 1995, the SPF suspended official links with France, and the European Parliament condemned the testing; the UN General Assembly urged the immediate cessation of the tests, and Greenpeace and other NGOs strongly protested the tests. France announced that it would conduct only six tests and that it would then shut down its testing site in the South Pacific. Finally, on March 25, 1996, France signed three SPNFZ Treaty protocols that were open to nuclear powers, including a protocol that prohibits nuclear testing in the South Pacific. New Zealand proclaimed that "France's signature [brought] an end to French nuclear testing in the South Pacific for all time." The SPF Chairman stated that these signings "mark the end of a tense and uncertain period when the region was a testing ground, and in certain respects a battleground, for nuclear testing by the nuclear powers."

Notes and Questions

1. Why did France agree to submit its disputes with New Zealand and Greenpeace to binding, third-party dispute resolution? What was the basis of the

Secretary-General's ruling? Was the ruling something other than a form of political theater? What was the basis of the rulings by the various arbitral tribunals? Why did France agree to compensate Pereira's family and Greenpeace?

2. Who won here? Does the *Rainbow Warrior* affair represent a victory for the rule of law in international relations? Can you identify specific points in this incident where international law made a difference?

A. New Actors, New Issues, New Processes

The *Rainbow Warrior* affair illustrates some of the ways that the traditional understanding of international law reflected in the Chad-Libya dispute—as a body of rules binding upon states in their relations—has been supplemented by a new international legal process characterized by new actors, issues, and modalities of prescription and enforcement. Notably, this new international law has not replaced traditional international law; indeed, the "contemporary" *Rainbow Warrior* affair preceded the ICJ decision in the "traditional" dispute between Chad and Libya by nearly a decade. Rather, as we shall see throughout this book, international law is a complex and constantly evolving field; in some areas, traditional norms continue to operate relatively untouched by new norms and processes; in other areas there are deep tensions between the old and the new norms; and in yet other areas new legal principles have emerged and occupy the field. A few of the most notable features of contemporary international law are outlined below.

1. International Institutions

The institutionalization of international law that began in significant part with the League of Nations accelerated in the postwar era. The three bodies that considered disputes arising out of the *Rainbow Warrior* affair—the United Nations, the GATT, and the OECD—represent three of the most important types of international bodies that states create. The United Nations, formed when 51 states signed the UN Charter in 1945, is the paradigmatic example of a multilateral body formed to address a diverse set of issues. Like other international organizations, the UN acts through a number of organs. The UN Security Council has primary responsibility for maintaining international peace and security and was intended to oversee a charter-based collective security system. But Cold War rivalries quickly undermined this system, and the UN enjoyed only mixed success in efforts to maintain international peace and security. While the Security Council acted more assertively in the aftermath of the Cold War, it soon found itself confronting new types of security challenges. As the UN Secretary-General noted in his 2000 Report on the Work of the Organization:

> The [new] demands made on the United Nations reflect a shift in the nature of the threats to peace and security since the end of the cold war: from inter-State conflict to intra-State conflict; from the violation of borders to a much greater emphasis on the violation of people.
> Where conflicts were once driven by the ideological divisions of a bipolar world, they are now fuelled by ethnic and religious intolerance, political ambition and greed, and are often exacerbated by the illicit traffic in arms, gems and drugs.

The demands we face also reflect a growing consensus that collective security can no longer be narrowly defined as the absence of armed conflict, be it between or within States. Gross abuses of human rights, the large-scale displacement of civilian populations, international terrorism, the AIDS pandemic, drug and arms trafficking and environmental disasters present a direct threat to human security, forcing us to adopt a much more coordinated approach to a range of issues. Such an approach . . . requires us, above all, to understand that the various elements that contribute to human security must be addressed in a comprehensive way if we are to sustain durable peace in the future.

While the United Nations is often judged on its ability to maintain international peace and security, the organization was also charged with promoting the peaceful settlement of international disputes. The UN Secretariat, headed by the Secretary-General, has helped to resolve a variety of international disputes, including *Rainbow Warrior*, through neutral fact finding, mediation, and other settlement-inducing activities. The ICJ, the UN's principal judicial organ, provides another possible forum for dispute resolution, as was seen in the Chad-Libya dispute. Ironically, the Court was not available in the *Rainbow Warrior* affair because France withdrew its consent to the Court's jurisdiction in response to a 1974 suit by New Zealand and Australia challenging French nuclear testing in the South Pacific. The General Assembly, composed of representatives of all member states, is the UN's main deliberative organ. Its resolutions, while not binding on states, have had a formative influence in the development of international law in many areas.

As governments and other international actors have come to regard more and more issues as requiring some form of international regulation, they have created specialized organizations. Thus, the trade disputes arising out of the *Rainbow Warrior* affair were submitted to the GATT, which eventually evolved into the World Trade Organization (WTO), whose rules now govern over $9 trillion per year in international trade. It, along with the International Monetary Fund and the International Bank for Reconstruction and Development (World Bank), were the primary international bodies created in the postwar era to address international economic issues. Other international organizations address aviation (International Civil Aviation Organization), intellectual property (World Intellectual Property Organization), and health (World Health Organization). The decisions to create these bodies followed from technological developments that made interstate borders more permeable and the actions of one state more likely to influence others, a process labeled today as "globalization" but that has been occurring, in various forms, for centuries.

States have also created numerous regional organizations, such as the Organization of American States, to coordinate policies, including through legal instruments, at a subglobal level. Of these regional bodies, the European Economic Community—now the European Union (EU)—has emerged as the most powerful and fully developed. European Union members delegate authority for certain matters to independent EU institutions that represent the interests of the Union, its member countries, and its citizens. These institutions have generated a dense system of EU law that is separate from, and superior to, the domestic law of EU members. Other organizations that have assumed particular importance to interstate interactions include the Organization of American States, the North Atlantic Treaty Organization, the Organization of African Unity, the Organization for Security and Cooperation in Europe, and the Association of Southeast Asian Nations.

2. Non-State Actors

Actors other than states and organizations of states have come to play a critical role in the creation and enforcement of international law. Non-state actors have been integrally involved in international relations for many hundreds of years—whether as organized religions such as the Catholic Church or the large trading companies of the colonial area—and non-governmental organizations have had an influence in international law making at least since the time of the antislavery movement in the nineteenth century. Yet the twentieth century saw these entities play a much more prominent role in international legal arenas.

NGOs—private, voluntary citizens' groups—today help frame agendas, mobilize constituencies, attend intergovernmental conferences to lobby governments, and even provide key staff delegations to such conferences. In one particularly dramatic example of NGO influence on law making processes, a coalition of 1,200 NGOs from more than 60 states initiated, and then convinced governments to negotiate, the 1997 Convention on the Prohibition of the Use, Stockpiling, Production, and Transfer of Anti-Personnel Mines and on their Destruction (the Landmines Convention). In addition to their enhanced roles in law making, NGOs also play a critical role in enforcing and promoting compliance with international legal norms. NGOs frequently investigate and publicize state violations of international law in order to shame states and build domestic constituencies for compliance. Although the ICJ and the WTO's Dispute Settlement Body only entertain state-to-state disputes, in many recently created dispute resolution fora, particularly in the human rights area, NGOs can institute cases or intervene as parties. For example, under amendments to the treaty creating the European Court of Human Rights, victims and NGOs can bring proceedings directly before the court. Similarly, NGOs can initiate proceedings before the World Bank Inspection Panel, which reviews complaints that the World Bank failed to comply with its own operational policies and procedures in the design, appraisal, or implementation of projects financed by the Bank.

The role of the individual in international law has also undergone significant development. As noted above, during the postwar era states have recognized an increasing number of international legal rights and obligations that individuals possess. Indeed, individual rights (of Pereira, the *Rainbow Warrior*'s Dutch crew member) and duties (of Mafart and Prieur) were both arguably in play in the *Rainbow Warrior* affair. Individuals also play enhanced roles in the implementation and enforcement of international law, in part through their increased access to international dispute resolution bodies—including, particularly, human rights bodies.

Finally, beyond NGOs and individuals, a number of other non-state actors, including indigenous peoples, ethnic minorities, subnational units in federal states, and business enterprises, now contribute to the creation and implementation of international law. At the same time, violent non-state actors, frequently labeled terrorists, have forced upon others their own notions of international order. The enhanced activities of all these groups, along with the development of individual rights and duties discussed above, has transformed the traditional "law of nations"—with states as the exclusive law makers and participants—into a dynamic discipline that touches on virtually all human relationships and transactions.

3. Non-Traditional Law Making and Enforcement

The rise of new actors has led to diverse and imaginative ways of both making and enforcing international law. The treaty remains the clearest expression of the expectations of states. But international organizations have served as the arenas for new forms of law making, including a form of administrative law making by executive bodies on which only some of the organization's members sit. When governments have been unwilling to agree on treaties, they have nonetheless prepared important instruments that are meant to, and in fact do, influence governmental behavior. These instruments, sometimes referred to as "soft law," cover areas ranging from foreign investment to telecommunications to human rights.

States, international organizations, NGOs, and others have also agreed on new methods for securing compliance with the law. Thematically, these ideas date back to the creation of the United Nations itself, as its members gave the Security Council the authority to order all states to carry out its directives on peace and security matters. Over the years, the Council has, in fact, ordered economic sanctions against a variety of states and non-state entities for committing acts that constitute threats to or breaches of international peace and security. In the trade arena, states gave the WTO the authority both to adjudicate disputes between member states and to allow the winner in the adjudication process to raise tariffs as a means of sanctioning the loser. Even criminal law, with the prospect of sanctions against individuals, has been enforced at the international level. The United Nations has created special criminal courts for the former Yugoslavia and Rwanda, a conference of states concluded a treaty to create a permanent international criminal court, and states have asserted unusual forms of jurisdiction to try foreign criminals for acts committed abroad. International organizations have also used new methods for monitoring state performance and inducing compliance with international legal norms, including reporting mechanisms that may embarrass a state into complying, and capacity building, technical assistance, and, less frequently, diplomatic, economic, and military sanctions.

Much of the impetus for these developments arose out of the end of the Cold War. During the years of intense Soviet-American ideological and military confrontation, opportunities for global cooperation on all areas of international concern were limited. Both superpowers and their allies used international fora as much to score points against the other side as to advance international cooperation. Each side viewed proposals for legal cooperation, however legitimate, with suspicion. During these years, international organizations were often polarized along East-West lines, included members of only one bloc (for instance, NATO had only U.S. allies), or excluded members of another (for example, the Association of Southeast Asian Nations and the Organization of American States excluded Communist states). As a result, their ability to address major areas of international concern was limited to areas where ideology played a relatively small role, such as health or telecommunications, or where East-West interests happened to coincide (such as with the creation of certain UN peacekeeping operations to stabilize regional conflicts).

The end of the Cold War drastically changed the situation, as an enormous obstacle to the development and implementation of international law disappeared. The opening up of the Soviet bloc also allowed the populations of those states to exert a greater influence on foreign policy, and NGOs began to become influential as well. These developments were no panacea for the rule of law, however. The termination of superpower support that had kept many world leaders in power led some to respond by playing parts of their populations against each other, with catastrophic consequences for human rights in Rwanda, Congo, the former Yugoslavia, and elsewhere. In addition, the weakness or complicity of some central governments resulted in havens for terrorist networks. But the end of the Cold War makes the international law of the twenty-first century work from a fundamentally different starting point from that which characterized much of the last century.

B. Conceptual Challenges

In the aggregate, the dramatic changes outlined above raise a number of practical, doctrinal, and conceptual challenges to those who seek to understand, practice, or improve international law. These challenges arise in part from the uneasy juxtaposition of the traditional understanding of international law and more recent processes; in part from increased global interdependence and the heightened need for international cooperation to solve transnational problems; and in part from changing conceptions of the power of the state. Below, we briefly introduce two conceptual challenges that speak to the place and meaning of international law today and that are relevant to all of the subsequent chapters of this book.

1. Legalization and Its Limits

Traditionally, scholars understood international law to address a narrow range of issues; today international law addresses almost every type of human activity. The *Rainbow Warrior* affair implicates just a few of the numerous fields that have either been created or expanded since 1945, including international environmental law, international trade law, international law on decolonization, and the international law of terrorism. Other recently developed areas, including human rights law, international criminal law, and international humanitarian law, receive extended treatment elsewhere in this text. The sheer increase in the kinds of issues and numbers of international agreements and bodies, standing alone, capture only part of the story. As we shall see throughout this text, many recent agreements and rules tend to be significantly more detailed and reach much more deeply into what was previously considered to be the domestic jurisdiction of states. Thus, both the *breadth* and *depth* of international law have increased, as the law regulates more areas than ever before and does so through processes and mechanisms that challenge a state's interest in keeping others out of its affairs—in a word, its sovereignty.

The result of these developments is, in essence, the increased legalization of international relations. Nevertheless, the move to law on the international plane is hardly uniform. While legalization has increased in some areas, such as international trade, in others, such as international monetary issues, legalization seems to ebb and flow. One goal of this book is to understand better this variation in the uses and effects of international law in different issue areas. In addition, through the problems examined in subsequent chapters, we explore the implicit claim that legalization encourages greater cooperation, the more effective and efficient resolution of international disputes, and a more equitable resolution of claims between parties of unequal bargaining power.

Moreover, increasing legalization has itself generated new issues and challenges. The staggering growth in international bodies and rules has started to produce phenomena that international elites call "institution fatigue" and "treaty congestion." Developing states experience great difficulties in finding the human, technical, administrative, and financial resources required to meet their multiple international commitments. More dramatically, states are increasingly discovering that different international regimes impose conflicting substantive obligations, such as when environmental treaties restrict trade in environmentally harmful products with certain states, while trade treaties require that states treat all their trade partners alike.

At a deeper level, the proliferation of subject areas, rules, and institutions; the lack of coordination or a formal structure of relations among them; and real and potential conflicts all raise the question of whether international law as it now exists is sufficiently coherent to constitute a "system." Does international law define comprehensively the rights and duties of states, or are there important areas of international life beyond or outside international law's domain? Are the various doctrines of international law oriented toward a common set of goals or objectives? Are there general themes that unite various bilateral, regional, and global rules? Or is an international legal "system" either unrealistic or undesirable given nonhierarchical and decentralized processes of law making, interpretation, and application?

2. The Persistent Puzzle of Compliance

Second, the *Rainbow Warrior* episode highlights another series of questions central to discussions of international law: do nations comply with their international legal obligations and, if so, why? We consider these questions in some detail in Chapter 14, after the reader has had a chance to gauge how and whether international law actually works. For now, we simply identify several of the compliance theories that international relations scholars and international lawyers have developed.

For many years, the field of international relations was dominated by the so-called realists. Realists focus on the distribution of power and resources in the international arena as well as on its anarchic nature. They argue that nations comply with international law only when it is in their interests to do so; when interests conflict with norms, interests will prevail. Compliance thus depends on the most powerful states deciding to comply and ensuring that weaker states comply. Iraq violated international law when it invaded Kuwait; it only "complied" with international law and withdrew from Kuwait in response to enforcement actions by a coalition of stronger states.

So-called institutionalists agree that nations obey international law when it is in their interests to do so; however, they stress that states have both conflicting and mutual interests. Hence international regimes, comprised of institutions and norms on a particular subject (although not always what lawyers would consider law) serve as mechanisms for restraining states and for achieving common aims. Regimes and their norms promote compliance by reducing transaction costs, providing information and dispute-resolution procedures, and providing a trigger and a focus for negative responses to noncompliance.

Finally, a so-called constructivist school argues that in an anarchic international order, states have no preexisting interests or identity; rather, their interests and identities are created—and changed—by and through their interactions with other states. Under this view, participation in international institutions helps states achieve shared understandings. These understandings, in turn, alter a state's perception of its own interests.

International lawyers have developed their own explanations for compliance. A "Kantian" strand of thought asserts that compliance is a function of international law's legitimacy vis-à-vis its targets. Some scholars see such legitimacy as deriving from those targets' sense that an international rule or institution has been created by and operates under fair procedures. Others suggest that the key to compliance is found at the domestic level. They argue that so-called liberal states, with representative governments, independent judiciaries, and guarantees of political and civil rights, rely more heavily on legal rules in their international relations, and on international adjudication in resolving international disputes—at least in their relations with other liberal states. This would explain why, for example, compliance with the European human rights system (largely by liberal democracies) is stronger than it is with the developing African human rights system, which addresses a collection of democratic and authoritarian states.

Yet another set of legal scholars have identified a "managerial" model, where states induce compliance not through coercion but rather through cooperative, interactive processes of justification, discourse, and persuasion. Through these processes, legal norms are invoked, interpreted, and elaborated in ways that generate pressure for compliance. Managerialists share much in common with institutionalists, but, like scholars focusing on international legitimacy, they place a heavier reliance on the norms themselves rather than on institutions. More recently, a related "transnational legal process" school has added a domestic law element to the horizontal, interstate focus of the managerialists. They believe that state compliance occurs when international legal norms "come home"—that is, when they are debated, interpreted, and ultimately internalized by domestic legal systems.

Of course, compliance questions are hardly new to international law. One of the most compelling explanations was formulated nearly a half century ago by French scholar Georges Scelle. Scelle observed that governmental officials play a dual function (*dédoublement fonctionnel*) in that they both make claims on behalf of their state and respond to the claims of other states against their state. Because any outrageous or illegal claims or acts governmental officials make or take will erode a legal norm and create precedents that another state might in the future use against their state, governments will restrain their behavior to conform to international law. Thus, for example, state A will respect the limits of the territorial sea of state B even if state B were too weak militarily to prevent state A from violating that norm, so that state C will likewise respect these limits vis-à-vis state A. This dynamic differs somewhat from reciprocity, another method of self-enforcement long understood by international lawyers, in that Scelle was concerned broadly with the precedential effect of illegal acts and not merely with whether the particular recipient of an illegal claim might be able to take action against the claimant.

As you study the materials that follow, consider how states might increase compliance, whether there is an optimal rate of compliance, and which—if any—of the above explanations ring true, or if different theories are relevant in different issue areas. Consider also whether compliance is even the correct issue on which to focus. High compliance rates may not prove that an international rule is effective, in the sense that it causes or even affects state behavior. For example, high compliance rates may reflect that international agreements simply codify the lowest common denominator among the parties. Thus, it is necessary to identify not only the reasons for compliance and the processes that induce compliance, but the types of rules, institutions, and processes that enable international law to produce effective change.

C. Ways of Understanding International Law

The exceedingly brief historical overview presented above describes a process of great change over the centuries both in terms of the areas ripe for regulation by international law and in the process by which international law is made and implemented—the participants, the arenas, the outcomes. At the same time, the study of international law—the intellectual task of conceptualizing, describing, and evaluating international law—has also changed fundamentally. The excerpts above describe what was perhaps the most fundamental shift, from the natural-law approach that dominated the early years of European international law to the positive-law approach that gained ascendancy in the nineteenth century. Positivism— put simply, the theory that international law is no more nor less than the rules to which states have consented—remains the lingua franca of most international lawyers, especially in continental Europe.

But legal scholars in the twentieth century also developed alternative methodologies for understanding or "doing" international law. In the 1940s and 1950s, Myres McDougal and Harold Lasswell of Yale Law School created a school of policy-oriented jurisprudence based on tenets of American legal realism. They saw international law not as a set of rules but as a process of decision making by which various actors (not just states) clarify and implement their common interests in accordance with their expectations of appropriate processes and of effectiveness in controlling behavior. They placed particular emphasis on the distinction between rules and operations, or between law as written down and law as actually observed. This so-called New Haven School remains influential in both the United States and abroad. In the 1960s, Abram Chayes, Thomas Ehrlich, and Andreas Lowenfeld helped develop an approach, since known as international legal process, which focuses on law as a constraint on international decision makers and events in international affairs. They developed a variety of case studies to show how government officials did or did not take international law into account in various crises.

The 1960s and 1970s also saw the increased influence of scholars with a decidedly post-colonial perspective on international law. Hailing primarily from former colonial countries, these scholars questioned the legitimacy of much of international law as emanating from the profound injustices of the colonial system and sought to develop ways for the law to rectify North-South inequities. Some, like Georges Abi-Saab and C.A. Amerasinghe, were particularly concerned with issues of sovereignty over natural resources and exploitation of the South by Northern investors, but this new generation addressed numerous other issues too. These scholars, and their current protégés, would find allies in the 1970s and 1980s in American and European scholars seeking to apply the methodology of critical legal studies to international law. This self-described "New Stream" has focused on the contradictions, hypocrisies, and failings not only of the rules themselves but of the ways actors invoke and talk about international law. Like the deconstructionist movement of literary theory and philosophy to which they owe great homage, the New Stream advocates place great emphasis on the use and misuse of language and culture in international legal discourse. In the 1980s, a related critical methodology emerged from scholars seeking to apply tools of feminist jurisprudence to international law. Many scholars are now examining how international norms reflect the domination of men in the international system. Although they are particularly concerned about issues of women's rights, they seek to uncover deep structural challenges to international law as insufficiently attentive to the interests and roles of women.

Last, the 1990s saw many scholars apply distinctively interdisciplinary methodologies to international law. Scholars initiated a movement to incorporate into international law the insights of international relations theory. This scholarship has encouraged inquiry into questions such as compliance with norms, the stability and effectiveness of international institutions, and causal mechanisms explaining how international actors react to particular rules. In a similar vein, other scholars began to explore whether economic analysis could usefully be applied to international law problems, while still others applied game theoretic insights and public choice theory to international legal issues.

The proliferation of methodologies means, of course, that each could form the basis for its own casebook. Positivism dominates most casebooks, but the founders of the policy-oriented jurisprudence and international legal process schools developed their own, admittedly idiosyncratic, teaching materials as well. This book adopts a more eclectic approach, not seeing these methods as inconsistent but rather as providing different lenses through which to examine the problems— and the opportunities—that those who practice international law confront.

2

Making Law
in a Decentralized System

The status of international law as "law" is often contested. In part, skepticism concerning international law stems from the way in which it is made, interpreted, and enforced. The international system lacks a central legislature to enact legislation; there is no executive to apply or enforce the law that is made; and there is no centralized judiciary to interpret the law and adjudicate disputes. Nonetheless, international lawyers, diplomats, government policy makers, representatives of international organizations, non-governmental actors, and others routinely invoke international law to justify, insist upon, or limit particular courses of action; individuals frequently rely on international law to assert claims in national and international fora; and international and domestic tribunals regularly apply international law to decide disputes. In short, as international lawyers frequently point out, international law is made, applied, interpreted, and (sometimes) enforced through a variety of processes that will be explored throughout this volume.

This chapter introduces the primary ways in which international law is made. Article 38 of the Statute of the International Court of Justice, which forms part of the United Nations Charter, provides the traditional starting point. It describes the law that the International Court of Justice (ICJ), the UN's principal judicial organ, should apply to resolve disputes:

Statute of the International Court of Justice, Article 38

1. The Court, whose function is to decide in accordance with international law such disputes as are submitted to it, shall apply:

   a. international conventions, whether general or particular, establishing rules expressly recognized by the contesting states;

   b. international custom, as evidence of a general practice accepted as law;

   c. the general principles of law recognized by civilized nations;

   d. . . . judicial decisions and the teachings of the most highly qualified publicists of the various nations, as subsidiary means for the determination of rules of law.

Article 38, though helpful, is only a starting point in two important respects. First, it suggests that courts and other decision makers simply find existing international law in one of several predefined "sources" and then apply it as appropriate to a given dispute. This reflects an unduly static and impoverished description of international law, which can also be understood in many other ways. Some scholars, for example, see international law as a process of decision making, a form of communication, or a mask for political power, among other things. These and various other approaches to international law are considered more fully in other chapters of this book.

Second, although treaties and custom, which are listed first in Article 38, remain the principal means by which international law is made, they are increasingly supplemented by alternative forms of law, which stem from the law-making and standard-setting activities of international organizations, regional bodies, multinational enterprises, and non-governmental organizations. The role of these actors in law making will become increasingly apparent as you study subsequent chapters. In particular, the law-making function of international organizations is considered in Chapters 3, 11, and 12.

The order of the sources of law listed in Article 38 does not reflect a formal hierarchy but is nonetheless suggestive. Article 38 is a directive to the judges on the ICJ. For a court faced with a legal dispute, treaties may be a preferred form of law for several reasons. First, despite issues of interpretation, their content is relatively easy to determine. Second, treaties in most cases reflect the formal consent of the states that ratified them to be bound by their terms. Third, treaties may be a more familiar source of law to national policy makers and their constituents than other sources of international law, and decisions based on a treaty may therefore find greater acceptance by those to whom the decisions are addressed.

Nonetheless, treaties may also have disadvantages in relation to other forms of law. In some situations, for example, a state's assertion of jurisdiction over acts or persons abroad, custom may prove to have broader applicability than a treaty. Customary international law evolves from state practice. It does not require the formal negotiation and express consent associated with treaties. A rule of customary international law binds all states that have not objected to the rule while it is in the process of formation. Despite the proliferation of treaties in recent years, custom continues to govern many issues that are not regulated by treaty; on other issues, custom and treaties may to a large extent coincide.

In some situations, the informality of so-called "soft" law may prove preferable to utilization of a treaty or custom. "Soft law" may be loosely defined as declared norms of conduct understood as legally nonbinding by those accepting the norms. Soft law instruments assume innumerable forms, ranging from declarations of international organizations, to industry codes of conduct, to experts' reports. Soft law instruments, though not enforceable by legal sanction, are often framed in legal language and in many respects may exhibit an authority comparable to that of treaties or custom. Soft law is not mentioned in Article 38 of the ICJ's Statute, which derives from a similar provision in the 1929 Statute of the Permanent Court of International Justice. But soft law instruments have proliferated in recent years and must be considered a vital part of the international law-making process.

In other instances, issues may arise that cannot be resolved by application of either treaty or custom. There are gaps in the coverage of these forms of international law, which courts and other decision makers sometimes attempt to fill by reliance on general principles common to most national legal systems. Thus, decision makers sometimes borrow from national legal systems principles such as *res judicata* or estoppel to resolve international disputes.

This chapter examines treaties, custom, soft law, and general principles in turn, although, as the following materials make clear, different sources of international law are often interrelated and simultaneously applicable to a given situation. Judicial decisions and the teachings of publicists, mentioned in Article 38 as "subsidiary means for the determination of rules of law," are not considered separately, but their role should become evident as you examine them in connection with the other forms of law described above.

I. CREATING AND USING TREATIES: THE CYPRUS CONFLICT

In recent years, bilateral and multilateral treaties have multiplied at an almost exponential pace. The United Nations Treaty Series, which includes all treaties deposited with the UN Secretary-General, now fills more than 2,000 volumes, with 100 or more new volumes published every year. The series contains over 40,000 treaties and related instruments, covering almost every conceivable subject. Most treaties are bilateral, but many involve dozens of states. Increasingly, treaties are being used to codify existing international law and to develop new law. Treaties also serve as the constitutive instruments of international organizations, such as the United Nations and the European Union, which often engage in their own law-making activities. The complexity and diversity of contemporary treaties, their multiple forms, and the different approaches to their conclusion and implementation will become increasingly evident as you consider the role of treaties in connection with different problems presented throughout this volume.

Like contracts in municipal legal systems, treaties create rights and obligations for the parties to them. In many cases, treaties specify particular quid pro quo arrangements relating to narrow or specific interests of the parties, such as a treaty allocating fishing rights in a particular area or one defining the terms by which individuals accused of crimes may be extradited from one country to another. In other cases, treaties may take on some of the characteristics of general legislation by establishing broad rules to govern state conduct in areas such as human rights, trade, or the environment.

The formation and vicissitudes of the modern state of Cyprus illustrate some of the legal issues that may arise in connection with treaties and their interrelation with other legal and political issues. Many of those related issues—including sovereignty, self-determination, statehood, recognition, and use of force—will be explored in greater detail in later chapters. As you read the following materials, consider the role of consent in treaty formation; the legal effect of differences in the bargaining power of the parties; the extent to which international public policy does or should preclude certain kinds of treaty arrangements; how ambiguities in a treaty should be resolved; the grounds available for invalidating or terminating treaties; the means open to a dissatisfied party to a treaty to seek renegotiation or modification of a treaty's terms; and the mechanisms available for dealing with disputes over treaty obligations.

A. The Problem

Throughout most of its history, Cyprus has been occupied, in whole or in part, by one or another foreign power. In 1878, Turkey transferred administrative control of the island to Great Britain in return for a British commitment to assist Turkey in its defense against Russia. When Turkey sided with Germany at the start of World War I, Britain declared the 1878 agreement void and claimed legal title to Cyprus. Turkey and Greece accepted British sovereignty over the island in 1923 under the terms of the Treaty of Lausanne. Two years later Cyprus became a British Crown colony. It retained that status until independence in August 1960. At that time, the Cypriot population was approximately 80 percent Greek Cypriot and 18 percent Turkish Cypriot, with various other minorities making up the remainder.

1. The Evolution of the 1960 Accords*

In the years leading up to independence, Greek Cypriots seeking self-determination in the form of union with Greece ("*enosis*") waged a guerilla war against the British. The Turkish Cypriot minority, fearing domination by the Greek Cypriot majority, argued that Cyprus should be partitioned and that the Turkish portion of Cyprus should be permitted to merge with Turkey.

In the 1950s, the government of Greece began to espouse the Greek Cypriot claim for *enosis* and to urge its acceptance by the United Nations as an appropriate expression of self-determination for Cyprus. In turn, Turkey became increasingly active in support of the Turkish Cypriots. In 1959, following a series of preliminary contacts and proposals, the prime ministers of Greece and Turkey met in Zurich to determine the island's fate.

At this summit meeting, the two leaders agreed on the essentials of a final settlement, and initialed drafts of three agreements: a Basic Structure of the Republic of Cyprus, a Treaty of Guarantee Between the Republic of Cyprus and Greece, the United Kingdom, and Turkey, and a Treaty of Alliance Between the Republic of Cyprus, Greece, and Turkey. The Basic Structure agreement was designed to create a constitutional system that would establish an immutable internal balance of power between the two communities on Cyprus and thereby protect the rights of the Turkish Cypriot minority. The Treaties of Guarantee and Alliance were designed to protect that constitutional balance against internal and external threats.

No Cypriot representatives participated in the drafting of these agreements. Shortly after the agreements were initialed, however, representatives of the two Cypriot communities were invited to join representatives of Greece, Turkey, and Britain at a meeting in London held to finalize the Zurich settlement. With only minor modifications, the treaties were accepted by all parties. Dr. Fazil Kutchuk, the Turkish Cypriot representative, signed readily; Archbishop Mikhail Makarios, the Greek Cypriot representative, also signed, albeit reluctantly.

As a result of the London accords, Cyprus became an independent state. Its new constitution carefully balanced power between the two ethnic communities. Executive power was divided between a Greek Cypriot president and a Turkish Cypriot vice president, each with similar powers and a capacity to frustrate the actions of his counterpart. Power in the legislature was similarly divided. Although representatives of the Greek community received a substantial majority of the seats in the legislature, separate majorities of Greek and Turkish Cypriot legislators were required for legislation pertaining to elections, municipalities, and taxes. Moreover, the vice president was entitled to veto legislation in the areas of foreign affairs, defense, and security. The Supreme Constitutional Court reflected similar checks

---

*Much of the following background information is drawn from David Wippman, *International Law and Ethnic Conflict in Cyprus*, 31 Tex Intl. L.J. 141 (1996).

and balances: a neutral judge presided, assisted by one Greek Cypriot and one Turkish Cypriot. The civil service also had to reflect a rough balance (in this case a 70-30 ratio) between the two communities. All of the principal provisions of this constitutional structure were incorporated into basic articles that could not be amended or repealed without the approval of all parties to the accords.

Under the Treaty of Guarantee, Cyprus agreed to ensure "respect for its Constitution" and to eschew any activity tending either to promote union with any other country or partition; in turn, Greece, Turkey, and the United Kingdom agreed to "recognize and guarantee the independence, territorial integrity and security of the Republic of Cyprus, and also the state of affairs established by the Basic Articles of its Constitution." Article IV of the Treaty of Guarantee provided further that:

> In the event of a breach of the provisions of the present Treaty, Greece, Turkey and the United Kingdom undertake to consult together with respect to the representations or measures necessary to ensure observance of those provisions. Insofar as common or concerted action may not prove possible, each of the three guaranteeing Powers reserve [sic] the right to take action with the sole aim of re-establishing the state of affairs created by the present Treaty.

2. Turkish Intervention and Its Aftermath

The accords worked for over two years but then fell apart. Greek Cypriots, convinced that the constitution conferred disproportionate benefits on the Turkish population, objected to rigid application of the mandatory 70-30 ratio for filling civil service positions; Turkish Cypriots responded by blocking passage of important legislation, including extension of the income tax. Similar conflicts surfaced in other areas. The resulting governmental stalemate prompted President Makarios to propose substantial revisions to the constitution that would have diluted the ability of the Turkish community to block action by the majority. Civil disorder erupted shortly thereafter, just before Christmas 1963.

Invoking Article IV of the Treaty of Guarantee, Turkey staged warning flights over Greek Cypriot positions. Turkish members of the Cypriot government abandoned or were forced from their positions, thereby leaving Greek Cypriots in full control of the government. Both communities stockpiled arms from abroad, and paramilitary groups in each community organized into defensive enclaves. As the fighting threatened to spread, the three Guarantor Powers, with the consent of the government of Cyprus, deployed peacekeeping troops to calm the situation. In March 1964, the United Nations Security Council authorized the deployment of a UN peacekeeping force. Both sides claimed victory.

Violence erupted again briefly in late 1964, when Turkish planes attacked advancing Greek Cypriot forces, and then again in 1967. But the next major crisis did not occur until 1974, when the military government of Greece engineered a coup in Cyprus that temporarily replaced President Makarios with a staunchly pro-*enosis* leader. Days later, Turkey invaded Cyprus and quickly occupied the northern third of the island. The line of demarcation established then still holds.

Condemnation of the Turkish invasion (and the coup in Cyprus that prompted the invasion) was widespread and swift. Turkey again relied on the Treaty of Guarantee to justify its actions. Most states, concerned about further violence on Cyprus and the possibility of war between Greece and Turkey, urged a prompt restoration of the preexisting constitutional order. Accordingly, the UN Security Council

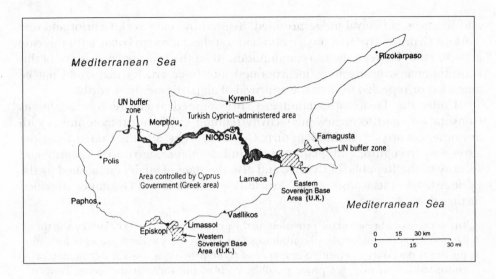

Cyprus Divided
SOURCE: CIA World Factbook 2001

demanded "an immediate end to foreign military intervention" in Cyprus, and called upon the three Guarantor Powers "to enter into negotiations without delay for the restoration of peace in the area and constitutional government. . . ." S.C. Res. 353 (1974).

Negotiations have continued on and off ever since. Over time, the Turkish Cypriots established their own autonomous administration over northern Cyprus. In 1983, they proclaimed the territory under their control to be an independent state, the Turkish Republic of Northern Cyprus. Turkey immediately recognized the self-proclaimed republic, but no other state followed suit. The United Nations Security Council denounced the declaration and adopted a resolution declaring the purported secession illegal. Nonetheless, Turkish Cypriots, supported by Turkey, still control the northern third of Cyprus, while UN peacekeepers continue to patrol the line dividing the two communities.

B. Why Do States Enter into Treaties?

Treaties figure prominently in the history of Cyprus. British sovereignty over Cyprus was confirmed by the 1923 Treaty of Lausanne, and the 1960 accords leading to Cypriot independence established a constitution for the new state, conferred rights on the Guarantor Powers, and afforded the United Kingdom indefinite rights to maintain military bases on Cyprus. The parties to these treaties, as well as other states, spent substantial time and energy at the highest levels negotiating these treaties and later arguing over their validity and interpretation. Why? For lawyers, the answer might at first seem obvious. Treaties are by definition legally binding. States must enter into treaties, then, to obtain binding commitments from other states; such legally binding commitments may assist the parties in pursuing their interests for the same reasons that legally binding contracts assist private parties in pursuing their interests. But what does it mean to say that treaties are legally binding? And why should states prefer treaties to other forms of commitment, such as informal agreements among governments?

International lawyers recognize, of course, that the international legal system does not have enforcement mechanisms comparable to those of effective national legal systems. There is a significant and increasing number of international courts and arbitral bodies but none with overarching general compulsory jurisdiction. There are various bodies with executive powers, such as the UN Security Council, but no international police force. As a result, states usually cannot count on outside actors to interpret agreements, decide on their validity, or enforce them in case of dispute. Yet international lawyers note, as Professor Louis Henkin famously observed, that "almost all nations observe . . . almost all of their [international] obligations almost all of the time." Louis Henkin, How Nations Behave 47 (1979). Some of the reasons why states often comply with their international legal obligations were identified in Chapter 1 and will be explored in subsequent chapters. But even if states often fulfill their treaty obligations, that still leaves open the question of why they enter into those obligations in the first place.

Political scientists who adhere to realist theories of international relations largely discount treaties—and international law generally. In their view, the international system is anarchic, in the sense that no central authority exists over states with power to compel compliance with international rules. As a result, treaties and international law generally exert little influence over state behavior. Instead, states pursue their interests, with outcomes of state interactions determined by the relative power of the states involved. States will enter into a treaty when convenient, interpret a treaty as they wish, and break a treaty when changing interests render it inconvenient.

Many political scientists, especially those of the so-called institutionalist school, accept some of the premises of the realists but reach quite different conclusions. In general, institutionalists accept the realist claim that the international system is anarchic, but they argue that states nonetheless have powerful incentives for entering into treaties beyond the simple pursuit of interests through power. The institutionalists, drawing on economics and game theory, suggest that states often enter into treaties to achieve mutually beneficial outcomes, forsaking short-term efforts to maximize power in favor of pursuing long-term goals. As Professors Kenneth Abbott and Duncan Snidal put it, "rationalists . . . view international agreements as 'contracts' created to resolve problems of coordination, collaboration, or domestic politics. . . ." Kenneth Abbott & Duncan Snidal, *Hard and Soft Law in International Governance*, 54 Intl. Org. 421, 424 (2000).

From this standpoint, one advantage of treaties is that they may enable states to make their commitments credible. Professor Charles Lipson offers the following account.

Charles Lipson, *Why Are Some International Agreements Informal?*

45 Intl. Org. 495, 508-512 (1991)

The decision to encode a bargain in treaty form is primarily a decision to highlight the importance of the agreement and, even more, to underscore the durability and significance of the underlying promises. The language of "binding commitments," in other words, is a diplomatic communication aimed at other signatories and, often, at third parties. In the absence of international institutions that permit effective self-binding or offer external guarantees for promises, treaties use conventional forms to signify a seriousness of commitment. By making that commitment both solemn and public, the parties indicate their intention, at least, to adhere to a particular bargain.

The effect of treaties, then, is to raise the political costs of noncompliance. That cost is raised not only for others but also for oneself. The more formal and public the agreement, the higher the reputational costs of noncompliance. . . . States deliberately choose to impose these costs on themselves in order to benefit from the counterpromises (or actions) of others. Given the inherent constraints of international institutions, these formal pledges are as close as states can come to precommitment—to a contractual exchange of promises. . . .

In a world of imperfect information, where others' current and future preferences cannot be known with certainty, reputation has value. . . . The threat of such loss [of reputational capital] promotes compliance, although it cannot guarantee it. Whether it succeeds depends on (1) the immediate gains from breaking an agreement, (2) the lost stream of future benefits and the rate of discount applied to that stream, and (3) the expected costs to reputation from specific violations.

Not all violations discredit equally. First, not all are witnessed. Some that are seen may be considered justifiable or excusable, perhaps because others have already violated the agreement, because circumstances have changed significantly, because compliance is no longer feasible, or because the contracted terms appear ambiguous. Thus, memory, inference, and context—social learning and constructed meaning—all matter. Second, not all actors have a reputation worth preserving. Some simply do not have much to lose, whether their violations are visible or not. Moreover, they may not choose to invest in reputation, presumably because the costs of building a good name outweigh the incremental stream of rewards. Sovereign debtors, for example, value their reputation least when they do not expect to borrow again. Alternatively, actors with poor reputations (or little track record) may choose to invest in them precisely to create expectations about future performance. . . . Thus, the value of reputation lost depends on the visibility and clarity of both promises and performance, on the value of an actor's prior reputation, and on the perceived usefulness of reputation in supporting other agreements. . . .

The price of noncompliance takes several forms. First, there is loss of reputation as a reliable partner. A reputation for reliability is important in reaching other cooperative agreements where there is some uncertainty about compliance. Second, the violation or perceived violation of a treaty may give rise to specific, costly retaliation, ranging from simple withdrawal of cooperation in one area to broader forms of noncooperation and specific sanctions. Some formal agreements, such as the General Agreement on Tariffs and Trade (GATT), even establish a limited set of permissible responses to violations, although most treaties do not. Finally, treaty violations may recast national reputation in a still broader and more dramatic way, depicting a nation that is not only untrustworthy but is also a deceitful enemy, one that makes promises in order to deceive.

Professor Lipson's account identifies some of the ways in which treaties assist states in making credible commitments. As Kenneth Abbott and Duncan Snidal point out, treaties may also enhance the credibility of states by "constraining self-serving auto-interpretation" of commitments, "mobiliz[ing] legally oriented interest and advocacy groups, such as the organized bar," "expand[ing] the role of legal bureaucracies within foreign offices and other government agencies," and modifying domestic actors' "plans and actions in reliance on such commitments, increasing the audience costs of violations." In addition, treaties may "reduce[] the transaction costs of subsequent interactions among states" as they seek to apply and elaborate agreed rules and enforce commitments. Abbott & Snidal, *supra*, 427-28, 430.

Further, Abbott and Snidal note that treaties may also serve the interests of private actors, who may organize within and across states to pursue shared objectives and values through interstate agreements. Alternatively, treaties may serve the interests of government officials, who may support particular agreements "as a way of making credible commitments to influential private actors in return for electoral support." *Id.* at 453.

International lawyers and political scientists have developed a variety of other theories to explain why states enter into international agreements and why they prefer some types of agreements to others. The latter question is considered later in this chapter. In other chapters we consider alternative theories concerning the motivations of states and other actors for reaching international agreements in different issue areas, and their incentives for compliance with those agreements.

Notes and Questions

1. What might have motivated the parties to the 1960 Cyprus accords to enter into them? What alternatives might they have considered? Would public statements by each government concerning their intentions regarding the future of Cyprus have served just as well as a formal treaty?

2. Do you agree with Professor Lipson that treaties raise the political costs of noncompliance? What other advantages might treaties have over less formal interstate agreements?

C. Applying Treaty Law to the Cyprus Dispute

Over time, states and other actors have agreed upon norms to govern treaty formation, validity, interpretation, breach, and termination. Each of these issues is considered below in connection with one or another aspect of the Cyprus dispute.

1. Background on Treaty Law

Most of the international law norms applicable to treaties have been codified in the Vienna Convention on the Law of Treaties, which was adopted by states at an international conference in 1969. As of January 2006, 105 states are parties to the Convention. The Vienna Convention reflects two decades of study and deliberation by members of the International Law Commission, a body of independent experts operating under UN auspices. Many of the Vienna Convention's provisions restate or codify customary international law already in place prior to the treaty's adoption. As a result, many tribunals and states relied on the Vienna Convention as an accurate statement of the law even prior to the treaty's entry into force. Other Convention provisions reflect a deliberate effort to modify existing law or to create new law, a process referred to as progressive development.

The Vienna Convention's rules are now so widely accepted that even some provisions that might have constituted "progressive development" when the treaty was drafted have acquired the status of custom. The United States is not a party to the treaty, but the executive branch has described the Convention as "the authoritative guide to current treaty law and practice."

The Vienna Convention provides the following definition of a treaty:

Vienna Convention on the Law of Treaties

1155 U.N.T.S. 331 (1969)

Article 2
Use of Terms

1. For purposes of the present Convention: (a) "treaty" means an international agreement concluded between States in written form and governed by international law, whether embodied in a single instrument or in two or more related instruments and whatever its particular designation. . . .

Article 3
International Agreements Not
Within the Scope of the Present Convention

The fact that the present Convention does not apply to international agreements concluded between States and other subjects of international law or between such other subjects of international law, or to international agreements not in written form, shall not affect: (a) the legal force of such agreements. . . .

As suggested in Article 2 of the Convention, treaties take many forms and can be denominated by many different terms, including "agreement," "protocol," "concordat," "pact," "accord," and "charter." Treaties may be written or oral, bilateral or multilateral, for a fixed term or indefinite. The limitations on the scope of the Convention contained in Article 3 reflect the desire of the Convention's drafters to facilitate agreement on the rules applicable to the most common kinds of international agreements. The commentary to the International Law Commission's final draft of the Convention makes clear that the Vienna Convention rules may be relevant to international agreements involving parties other than states (e.g., insurgent groups, international organizations) and to oral agreements.

Notes and Questions

1. States often enter into formal agreements that by their terms expressly disavow the creation of any legal obligations. The Final Act of the Conference on Security and Cooperation in Europe, signed in Helsinki in 1975, set out the terms of an agreement between the Eastern and Western blocs on a wide range of security and human rights issues. The Final Act was understood and intended to be politically but not legally binding. Agreements of this sort are considered more fully below.

States also frequently enter into informal and usually unwritten "gentlemen's agreements" to govern matters such as the nationality of the individual who heads a particular international agency or the regions to be represented in subsidiary bodies of international organizations. In 1999, for example, U.S. objections to the

European Union candidate for executive director of the International Monetary Fund were viewed by some states as a violation of such an agreement. What is the legal status of these "gentlemen's agreements"? Do they qualify as treaties under the Vienna Convention definition? Does the intention of the parties determine whether such agreements are legally binding? If so, how do you ascertain the intention of the parties?

Several states urged that the intent to create rights and obligations under international law be included in the Convention's definition of "treaty." The commentary to the final draft explained that "the Commission concluded that . . . the element of intention is embraced in the phrase 'governed by international law,' and it decided not to make any mention of the element of intention in the definition."

2. Can unilateral statements create binding international legal obligations equivalent to a treaty? In 1919, the Norwegian Minister of Foreign Affairs, speaking for his government, declared that Norway would not interfere with Danish plans concerning Greenland, an assurance sought by Denmark. The declaration was made in the course of negotiations over Greenland's status, which included a statement by Denmark that it would not press any claim to Spitzbergen, an archipelago claimed by Norway. In *The Legal Status of Eastern Greenland* (Nor. v. Den.), P.C.I.J. Rep. Series A/B, No. 53 (1933), the Permanent Court of International Justice (the predecessor to the ICJ), referring to the Norwegian foreign minister's statement, concluded that "a reply of this nature given by the Minister of Foreign Affairs on behalf of his government in response to a request by the diplomatic representative of a foreign Power, in regard to a question falling within his province, is binding upon the country to which the Minister belongs." In subsequent cases, the ICJ made clear that the effect of a unilateral statement depends upon the intention of the state in question. Speaking of a unilateral declaration by the government of France that it would halt nuclear tests in the South Pacific, the ICJ stated:

> When it is the intention of the State making the declaration that it should become bound according to its terms, that intention confers on the declaration the character of a legal undertaking. . . . In these circumstances, nothing in the nature of a *quid pro quo*, nor any subsequent acceptance of the declaration, nor even any reply or reaction from other States, is required for the declaration to take effect. . . .

Nuclear Tests (Austl. v. France), 1974 I.C.J. 253, 267. The Court did not decide whether unilateral engagements should be treated as the equivalent of treaty obligations but noted that all international legal obligations, from whatever source, should be governed by the principle of good faith. For a more recent example of a case in which a unilateral statement was given legal effect in an adjudicatory proceeding, see the discussion of the European Community's challenge to a U.S. trade law in Chapter 12.

Under what circumstances, if any, are unilateral statements enforceable under domestic law? Should unilateral declarations by governments be treated as the equivalent of treaty obligations? Should such declarations be deemed legally binding on some other ground, such as estoppel?

2. Making Treaties: Who Speaks for the State?

The onset of intercommunal fighting in Cyprus in 1963 triggered a variety of challenges to the validity of the 1960 accords. As an initial matter, Greek Cypriots questioned whether Dr. Kutchuk and Archbishop Makarios possessed sufficient legal authority in 1960 to bind Cyprus in the absence of a referendum. When Kutchuk and Makarios attended the London Conference and initialed the texts of the 1960 accords, they were unelected leaders of political communities that themselves had no standing under international law. Formally, the accords did not come into force until after Makarios and Kutchuk had been elected president and vice president of Cyprus and had signed the accords as the highest officials of the state of Cyprus. Still, the process leading to the final signature of the accords, including the elections that transformed Makarios and Kutchuk from leaders of subnational communities into elected leaders of the state of Cyprus, arguably derived its legitimacy in substantial part from the prior consent of the two communities as manifested by Makarios and Kutchuk.

The Vienna Convention contains several articles relating to the capacity of states to enter into treaties and the authority of particular individuals to represent and commit their states. In evaluating the arguments of the parties to the 1960 accords, consider the following provisions of the Vienna Convention:

Article 6
Capacity of States to Conclude Treaties

Every State possesses capacity to conclude treaties.

Article 7
Full Powers

1. A person is considered as representing a State for the purpose of adopting or authenticating the text of a treaty or for the purpose of expressing the consent of the State to be bound by a treaty if:

(a) he produces appropriate full powers; or (b) it appears from the practice of the States concerned or from other circumstances that their intention was to consider that person as representing the State for such purposes and to dispense with full powers.

2. In virtue of their functions and without having to produce full powers, the following are considered as representing their State:

(a) Heads of State, Heads of Government and Ministers for Foreign Affairs, for the purpose of performing all acts relating to the conclusion of a treaty; . . . (c) representatives accredited by States to an international conference or to an international organization or one of its organs, for the purpose of adopting the text of a treaty in that conference, organization or organ.

Article 8
Subsequent Confirmation of an Act Performed Without Authorization

An act relating to the conclusion of a treaty performed by a person who cannot be considered under article 7 as authorized to represent a State for that purpose is without legal effect unless afterwards confirmed by that State.

The early drafts of Article 6 of the Vienna Convention provided that some entities other than states also possessed the capacity to enter into treaties, and specifically identified international organizations and member states of federal unions, depending on the provisions of the federal constitution at issue. During the debate on Article 6, the United States argued that

To limit the scope of the term "other subjects of international law" to international organizations, the Holy See and cases such as an insurgent community would . . . be too restrictive; for colonies and similar entities given some measure of authority in foreign relations, especially when approaching statehood, should not have to be in a state of insurgency to be capable of concluding a valid international agreement. . . . [S]o far as such a colony or entity is entrusted with a measure of authority by the parent State in the conduct of its foreign relations, it necessarily becomes a subject of international law [and] it would be paradoxical if at the present time areas approaching independence could not be encouraged by being entrusted with authority to conclude agreements in their own name.

Article 6 was eventually reduced to its present form in keeping with the decision of the International Law Commission to confine the Vienna Convention to treaties between states.

Consider also Professor Oliver Lissitzyn's comments on capacity:

It may, indeed, be doubted that international law contains any objective criteria of international personality or treaty-making capacity. The very act or practice of entering into international agreements is sometimes the only test that can be applied to determine whether an entity has such personality or capacity, or, indeed, "statehood." For example, India had come to be regarded as an international person possessed of treaty-making capacity long before independence because, beginning with the Treaty of Versailles in 1919, there had developed a practice of India's becoming a separate party to international agreements. [After citing further examples, Lissitzyn continues:] Perhaps the only limitation on the possession and exercise of treaty-making capacity by a political subdivision is lack of consent to the exercise of such capacity by the dominant (or "sovereign") entity to which the subdivision is subordinate. Once such consent has been given, the capacity comes into being or is exercised whenever another entity is willing and able to enter into an agreement with the subdivision that is intended to be governed by international law. The very exercise of treaty-making capacity by a subordinate entity endows it with legal personality under international law. It makes little sense, therefore, to make possession of such personality a prerequisite to the conclusion of treaties.

Oliver J. Lissitzyn, *Efforts to Codify or Restate the Law of Treaties*, 62 Colum. L. Rev. 1166, 1183-84 (1962).

Notes and Questions

1. Did Cyprus, as an emerging state, have the capacity to enter into treaties independently of the United Kingdom? Could it have done so even against the wishes of the United Kingdom?

2. Under the facts of the Cyprus case, should Makarios and Kutchuk be viewed as possessing sufficient legal authority to enter into the 1960 treaties on behalf of Cyprus? Was it essential that both agree to the treaties?

3. If Makarios and Kutchuk lacked sufficient authority to commit Cyprus to the 1960 accords, did the later conduct of Cyprus amount to confirmation of their authority within the meaning of Article 8 of the Vienna Convention?

3. Invalidating Treaties: Coercion and Consent

Greek Cypriots and their supporters questioned the validity of Cypriot consent to the 1960 treaties. At various points in the 1964 UN debates over Cyprus, the

Greek Cypriots suggested that the treaties were "imposed" on Cyprus, that Makarios, as the Greek Cypriot representative, had no choice but to accept the treaties, and that the treaties were "unequal, inequitable and unjust."

According to Cyprus's UN representative:

108. Both of these treaties may fairly be described as having been arrived at in circumstances precluding free choice. Their basic articles were agreed upon in Zurich between the Greek and Turkish Governments in the absence of the representatives of the people of Cyprus. . . . The circumstances which compelled Archbishop Makarios, the leader then of the Greek majority of the people of Cyprus at the London Conference, to sign these Agreements are best described by him in a document dated 30 November 1963. . . .

> At the Conference at Lancaster House on 5 February 1959, which I was invited to attend as leader of the Greek Cypriots, I raised a number of objections and expressed strong misgivings regarding certain provisions of the agreement arrived at in Zurich between the Greek and the Turkish Governments and adopted by the British Government. I tried very hard to bring about the change of at least some of those provisions. I failed, however, in that effort and I was faced with the dilemma either of signing the agreement as it stood or of rejecting it with all the grave consequences which would have ensued. In the circumstances, I had no alternative but to sign the agreement. This was the course dictated to me by necessity. . . .

109. The parties were in an unequal bargaining position and the Greek Cypriot side did not give its consent freely. In this respect, may I remind the members that when we speak of the Greek Cypriot side it is 80 per cent of the population. These treaties which contained onerous provisions were thus imposed on the majority of the people of Cyprus making the doctrine of unequal, inequitable and unjust treaties relevant.

110. Thus a Constitution was foisted on Cyprus. . . . The combined effect of the Constitution and the Treaty of Guarantee is that a situation has been created whereby the constitutional and political development of the Republic has been arrested in its infancy and the Republic as a sovereign State has been placed in a strait jacket.

U.N. SCOR, 19th Sess., 1098th mtg. at 19, U.N. Doc. S/PV.1098 (1964).

The representative of the Soviet Union, criticizing the efforts of "certain specific Powers . . . to force upon the people and Government of Cyprus a solution agreeable" to NATO, concurred:

16. . . . The Cypriots themselves were not, of course, even allowed to participate in the talks held at Zurich and in London in 1959, when a constitution was drawn up for Cyprus by strangers and when foreigners also laid the foundations for the inequitable agreements which were then presented to Cyprus in the form of an ultimatum. Hence it is quite clear . . . that these agreements were imposed on the people of Cyprus. . . .

18. The unprecedented infringement of the sovereignty of Cyprus, which has led to the maintenance of foreign military bases in its territory and to the deployment on this island of thousands of soldiers belonging to the armed forces of members of the NATO military bloc, was intended from the very beginning, not to ensure the independence of Cyprus, but to accomplish something quite the opposite of this. The dangerous actions of the NATO

Powers in Cyprus are aimed with cynical frankness at nullifying the independence of the Republic of Cyprus, tying Cyprus to NATO and converting it into
one of their military bridgeheads.

U.N. SCOR, 19th Sess., 1096th mtg. at 3-4, U.N. Doc. S/PV.1096 (1964).
    Turkey's representative defended the adoption of the treaties:

> 192. It should be borne in mind that these treaties and the basic articles of
> the Constitution represented a compromise formula acceptable to all the
> parties and constituted the very *raison d'être* of the independence of Cyprus.
> Without these safeguards and without the basic articles of the Constitution the
> independence of Cyprus would have been unthinkable. . . .
> 193. This compromise arrangement was arrived at after long and bitter
> debates in the United Nations, as well as in international conferences, and
> convinced everyone of the necessity to establish a system which would take into
> consideration the rights and the legitimate interests of all concerned.

U.N. SCOR, 19th Sess., 1095th mtg. at 35, U.N. Doc. S/PV.1095 (1964).
    In support of his position, Turkey's representative quoted a statement made
by the Greek foreign minister, Mr. Averoff, shortly after the signing of the
agreements:

> We signed these Agreements because this is in the common interest of our
> countries in the middle of a world which is full of dangers. . . . We signed these
> Agreements because we felt that they cover relatively and absolutely satisfac-
> torily the interests of the people of Cyprus as a whole. We also signed these
> agreements because the respected man—and here he pointed to President
> Makarios—at the head of the Greek community in Cyprus and whom we
> considered in all our deliberations as representing the will of the Greeks of
> Cyprus, having been informed by us, said that he was in agreement with these
> Agreements.

U.N. SCOR, 19th Sess., 1098th mtg. at 35, U.N. Doc. S/PV.1098 (1964).
    To this point, the representative of Cyprus replied:

> 186. . . . What the representative of Turkey has proved, I submit—and it
> is not denied—is that the Agreements were signed by Archbishop Makar-
> ios. . . . But the problem is: how did he come to sign them? He signed
> them because at that time he had no choice. That is the reality.

Id. at 36.
    The Vienna Convention on the Law of Treaties contains a number of provisions
pursuant to which a treaty may be held invalid. Many of those provisions, including
provisions relating to error, fraud, and the corruption of a representative of a state,
relate to the validity of a state's consent to the treaty at issue. Consider the following
articles, and in particular, Article 52:

Article 42
Validity and Continuance in Force of Treaties

    1. The validity of a treaty or of the consent of a State to be bound by a
treaty may be impeached only through the application of the present
Convention.
    2. The termination of a treaty, its denunciation or the withdrawal of a
party, may take place only as a result of the application of the provisions of the

treaty or of the present Convention. The same rule applies to suspension of the operation of a treaty.

Article 45
Loss of a Right to Invoke a Ground for Invalidating, Terminating, Withdrawing from or Suspending the Operation of a Treaty

A State may no longer invoke a ground for invalidating, terminating, withdrawing from or suspending the operation of a treaty under articles 46 to 50 or articles 60 and 62 if, after becoming aware of the facts:

(a) it shall have expressly agreed that the treaty is valid or remains in force or continues in operation, as the case may be; or (b) it must by reason of its conduct be considered as having acquiesced in the validity of the treaty or in its maintenance in force or in operation, as the case may be.

Article 51
Coercion of a Representative of a State

The expression of a State's consent to be bound by a treaty which has been procured by the coercion of its representative through acts or threats directed against him shall be without any legal effect.

Article 52
Coercion of a State by the Threat or Use of Force

A treaty is void if its conclusion has been procured by the threat or use of force in violation of the principles of international law embodied in the Charter of the United Nations.

In the course of the negotiations over the Vienna Convention on the Law of Treaties, many socialist and developing states favored inclusion of an article that would invalidate "unequal treaties." Treaties might be deemed unequal either because one party is in a position to dictate terms to the other party by applying economic or political pressure or because the terms of the treaty greatly favor one party at the expense of the other. As a practical matter, these two forms of inequality go together, because almost by definition, states that are in an equal bargaining position will not reach one-sided agreements.

Those who supported a provision on the invalidity of unequal treaties relied in part on the principle of the sovereign equality of states, one of the core principles of international law embodied in Article 2(1) of the UN Charter. Of course, the equality of states is juridical only. As a practical matter, states vary enormously in size, resources, population, military capacity, and economic strength. These disparities necessarily place some states in stronger bargaining positions than others in the negotiation of particular treaties. As a general matter, such inequalities do not preclude the conclusion of a valid treaty any more than similar inequalities in the bargaining positions of private parties preclude the formation of valid private contracts.

On the other hand, there are doctrines in the municipal law of many states that invalidate contracts procured through pressure, even when such pressure falls short of coercion, or that invalidate contracts that are unduly onerous to one of the parties. States that challenged the validity of "unequal treaties" focused on colonial-era treaties, especially those granting metropolitan states extensive trade, mineral, or other rights in their former colonies as an implicit condition of independence, and on neocolonial treaties viewed by some as perpetuating colonialism through economic domination.

By contrast, most Western states viewed the notion of unequal treaties as vague, easily manipulated, and likely to jeopardize the stability of treaty relations. The issue came to a head in connection with the drafting of Article 52. States sympathetic to the notion of unequal treaties urged a broad definition of "coercion," one that would encompass political and economic pressure and permit the invalidation of imposed or "unequal" treaties.

Two U.S. government participants in the Vienna Convention negotiations describe the debate and its outcome:

> Afghanistan, Algeria, Bolivia, Congo (Brazzaville), Ecuador, Ghana, Guinea, India, Iran, Kenya, Kuwait, Mali, Pakistan, Sierra Leone, Syria, United Arab Republic, United Republic of Tanzania, Yugoslavia and Zambia proposed that the International Law Commission text . . . be amended by defining force to include any "economic or political pressure."
>
> The nineteen-state amendment was vociferously supported and vehemently attacked in the committee debate. . . .
>
> The proponents of the amendment made it quite clear in the committee of the whole that their amendment was directed toward "economic needs." . . . The Algerian representative advanced the thesis:
>
>> . . . the era of the colonial treaty was past or disappearing, but there was no overlooking the fact that some countries had resorted to new and more insidious methods, suited to the present state of international relations, in an attempt to maintain and perpetuate bonds of subjection. Economic pressure, which was a characteristic of neo-colonialism, was becoming increasingly common in relations between certain countries and the newly independent States.
>>
>> Political independence could not be an end in itself; it was even illusory if it was not backed by genuine economic independence. That was why some countries had chosen the political, economic and social system they regarded as best calculated to overcome under-development as quickly as possible. That choice provoked intense opposition from certain interests which saw their privileges threatened and then sought through economic pressure to abolish or at least restrict the right of peoples to self-determination. Such neo-colonialist practices . . . should therefore be denounced with the utmost rigour.
>
> Statements of this character reinforced the already deep misgivings as to the effect of the amendment held by the states concerned with the stability of treaties . . .
>
> The course of the debate had made it clear that if the amendment were put to the vote it would carry by quite a substantial majority. On the other hand, in private discussions it had been made quite clear to the proponents that adoption could wreck the conference because states concerned with the stability of treaties found the proposal intolerable.
>
> To reduce tension, discussion of the article was adjourned and private negotiations resorted to. A compromise solution was reached after some days of cooling off. The amendment was withdrawn. In its place, a draft declaration condemning threat or use of pressure in any form by a state to coerce any other state to conclude a treaty was unanimously adopted by the committee. Although at one point during the plenary it appeared that the compromise might be unraveling, it was adhered to by both sides. The declaration finally approved by the conference in 1969 is annexed to the Final Act.

Richard Kearney & Robert Dalton, *The Treaty on Treaties*, 64 Am. J. Intl. L. 495, 533-535 (1970).

Notes and Questions

1. Was Makarios subject to coercion within the meaning of Article 51 of the Vienna Convention? What type of pressure would amount to coercion for purposes of this article? Given that states are abstract entities that can only act through representatives, in what respects is coercion of a state's representative different from coercion of the state itself?

2. What "grave consequences . . . would have ensued" if Makarios had refused to sign the agreement? Does the possibility of such consequences amount to coercion?

3. Under Article 45 of the Vienna Convention, did Cyprus forfeit any claim of coercion by carrying out the terms of the 1960 accords for two and one-half years?

4. Which state or states might be viewed as having imposed the 1960 accords on Cyprus? Are the accords invalid under Article 52 of the Vienna Convention? Who decides whether coercion invalidates a treaty? Note that the government of Cyprus never formally claimed that the accords were coerced within the meaning of Article 52. What would have been the legal consequences of such a claim if it prevailed?

5. Does Archbishop Makarios's claim that the 1960 treaties were "unequal, inequitable, and unjust" raise a ground for invalidity recognized in any of the relevant articles of the Vienna Convention?

6. In 1995, representatives of Bosnia, Croatia, and the Federal Republic of Yugoslavia (FRY) met in Dayton, Ohio, to negotiate over the future status and political organization of Bosnia. The United States and its European allies used economic and political pressure to convince the FRY to participate; NATO, relying on UN Security Council resolutions authorizing the use of force in Bosnia for certain limited objectives, used air strikes to compel Bosnian Serbs to come to the bargaining table. The negotiations resulted in an agreement, the General Framework for Peace in Bosnia and Herzegovina (the Dayton Agreement), that rejected Bosnian Serb claims to independence and established power-sharing arrangements among the Bosnian Serbs, Croats, and Muslims. Bosnian Serbs initially rejected the results of the negotiations but ultimately acquiesced at the insistence of the FRY. The government of Bosnia also accepted the Dayton Agreement with reluctance. The Bosnian government felt it had no choice if it wished to avoid losing more people and territory in a war that it regarded as an international conflict launched by the FRY. Could any of the parties to the Dayton Agreement (FRY, Croatia, or Bosnia) refuse to carry out its terms on the ground that the agreement is invalid under Article 52 of the Vienna Convention?

In March 1999, NATO forces starting bombing targets in the FRY to force it to end human rights abuses in Kosovo and to accept a political settlement on the future status of Kosovo. (Further background on NATO's action and discussion of related legal issues appear in Chapters 8 and 13.) After an extensive air campaign lasting several months, the FRY signed an agreement accepting NATO's terms for ending the conflict. Could the FRY later declare that agreement void under Article 52?

4. Evaluating and Interpreting Treaties

The Cyprus government's principal objection to the 1960 accords was that the Treaty of Guarantee, as interpreted by Turkey, could be construed to permit military intervention. In the UN Security Council, the government of Cyprus and its allies argued repeatedly that Turkey's reading of the treaty conflicted with certain fundamental norms of international law, including the principles of sovereign equality and the non-use of force in international relations. Cyprus also argued that any treaty obligation inconsistent with the UN Charter's prohibition on the use of force would violate Article 103 of the UN Charter, which provides that "[i]n the event of a conflict between the obligations of the Members of the United Nations under the present Charter and their obligations under any other international agreement, their obligations under the present Charter shall prevail." Accordingly, in the initial UN debates in late 1963 and early 1964, the government of Cyprus urged the UN Security Council to pass a resolution "which would call upon all States to respect the political independence and territorial integrity of the Republic of Cyprus and refrain from any use or threat of force against it. . . ."

By contrast, Turkey emphasized the plight of the Turkish Cypriots and its obligation as a Guarantor Power to come to their aid. Turkey opposed any use of Security Council resolutions as a vehicle to override its rights and obligations under the Treaty of Guarantee. Turkey framed the legal issue as compliance with the basic principle that treaty obligations are binding and must be carried out in good faith. According to Turkey,

> 215. [W]hat they [the leaders of the Greek Cypriot community] would like is some kind of United Nations resolution, which they think they could pretend to interpret as though international treaties had been abrogated, as though commitments no longer exist—some formula which would eliminate their obligations not only to the guarantor Powers but also to all the civilized world, so that they could proceed without interference to the final extermination of the Turkish Cypriots. . . .
>
> [R]espect for pledges and commitments embodied in international treaties is the only foundation upon which stability in international relations can be achieved. The opposite would result in utter chaos, which in this atomic age would be disastrous for all humanity. It follows that the Security Council in all the questions submitted to it must show scrupulous care in respecting treaty rights and obligations.

U.N. SCOR, 19th Sess., 1095th mtg. at 39-40, U.N. Doc. S/PV.1095 (1964).

The following exchange between the Cypriot and Turkish UN representatives took place in December 1963:

> 19. Mr. ROSSIDES (Cyprus) . . . [Cyprus's] sovereignty and independence cannot be violated by any other Member State or non-member State, on whatever grounds or whatever excuses. If there was a dangerous situation on the island and Turkey thought that the security of the Turkish people on the island was threatened, they could very well have complained to the Security Council, and within an hour or two the Security Council would meet and there could be a collective decision, a fair decision, a straightforward and honest decision, for the protection of whoever is in danger on the island. But to find excuses in order to attack, in order to threaten, in order to use

force, that is a negation of the United Nations. If that were recognized we would then be returning to the period when force and nothing else prevailed in the world. . . . This is why we have the provisions of Article 2, paragraph 4, of the Charter, which not merely abolish war but forbid the use of force, in whatever manner, against any State, no matter how small. . . . One cannot say: I am a Member of the United Nations, but I will make a private agreement so that I can boss another country, use force against it, fly over its territory and terrorize its people, encourage one side, and create strife and trouble . . .

U.N. SCOR, 18th Sess., 1085th mtg. at 5-6, U.N. Doc. S/PV.1085 (1963).

37. Mr. KURAL (Turkey) The representative of Cyprus has just delivered a long tirade regarding his desire and that of the Greek leaders of Cyprus to see the constitutional rights of the Turks of the island denied. These rights were established in order to guarantee the existence and life of the Turks in Cyprus after the painful events of a few years ago. The President of Cyprus himself had acknowledged the need to recognize these rights and the Constitution had been drawn up accordingly. Today we are told that these rights are excessive. There is an obvious intention to be free to exterminate the Turkish population of Cyprus.

43. As a signatory State of the agreements on Cyprus and as a guarantor—even without regard to the fact that Turks are being massacred in Cyprus—my Government cannot remain indifferent to these events. . . .

Id. at 10-11.

63. Mr. ROSSIDES (Cyprus) I understood the representative of Turkey to refer to the Treaty of Guarantee as giving to Turkey the right to use force in Cyprus. I say that if the Treaty of Guarantee can be interpreted as giving Turkey, or any other country, the right to use force in Cyprus, then the Treaty itself is invalid under Article 103 of the Charter. . . .

Id. at 15.

The Soviet Union, echoed by several other socialist states, sided with the government of Cyprus. The United States expressed the hope that the legal issues raised by the Treaty of Guarantee could simply be avoided but also appeared to agree with Turkey that no action of the Security Council could abrogate the 1960 treaties:

74. I think we all know that the Treaty of Guarantee forms an integral part of the organic arrangements that created the Republic of Cyprus. . . . That Treaty assures the independence, territorial integrity and security of the Republic, as well as respect for its Constitution. It assigns to the Guarantor Powers certain responsibilities regarding the maintenance of the Constitution and of the Treaty itself, including the carefully negotiated balance and protection of the two Cypriot communities. It was signed after literally years of soul-searching negotiation and approved by all of the parties. This Treaty or any international treaty cannot be abrogated, cannot be nullified, cannot be modified either in fact or in effect by the Security Council of the United Nations. The Treaty can be abrogated or altered only by agreement of all of the signatories themselves or in accordance with its terms.

75. No one is threatening to take the territory of Cyprus, no one is threatening its independence—Turkey or Greece or anyone else. What is possible

is—and I quote the language of the Treaty: "action" expressly authorized by article IV of the Treaty "with the sole aim of re-establishing the state of affairs created by the present Treaty". . . .

U.N. SCOR, 19th Sess., 1096th mtg. at 13, U.N. Doc. S/PV.1096 (1964).

Privately, however, the United States strongly opposed a Turkish invasion of Cyprus. In early 1964, President Lyndon Johnson wrote a letter to the Turkish Prime Minister:

> I am gravely concerned by the information that the Turkish Government is contemplating a decision to intervene by military force to occupy a portion of Cyprus. It is my impression that you believe that such intervention by Turkey is permissible under the provisions of the Treaty of Guarantee of 1960. I must call your attention, however, to our understanding that the proposed intervention by Turkey would be for the purpose of effecting a form of partition of the island, a solution which is specifically excluded by the Treaty of Guarantee.
>
> Further, that Treaty requires consultation among the guarantor Powers. It is the view of the United States that the possibilities of such consultation have by no means been exhausted in this situation and that therefore the reservation of the right to take unilateral action is not yet applicable. There can be no question in your mind that a Turkish intervention in Cyprus would lead to a military engagement between Turkish and Greek forces. Adhesion to NATO in its very essence means that NATO countries will not wage war on each other. Furthermore, a military intervention in Cyprus by Turkey could lead to direct involvement by the Soviet Union. . . .
>
> I feel obligated to call to your attention the fact that such a Turkish move could lead to the slaughter of tens of thousands of Turkish Cypriots on the island. Such an action on your part would unleash the furies and there is no way by which military action on your part could be sufficiently effective to prevent wholesale destruction of many of those whom you are trying to protect.

Closely connected to the issue of the validity of the Treaty of Guarantee was the question whether its Article IV should be construed as permitting military intervention. The representative of Cyprus argued that the Turkish interpretation of the Treaty of Guarantee conflicted with Articles 2(4) and 103 of the UN Charter and demanded to know the views of the Guarantor Powers.

> 139. . . . I should like, with permission, to put a simple question to the Members signatories to the Treaty of Guarantee. . . . Is it the view of the Governments of Greece, Turkey and the United Kingdom that they have the right of military intervention under the Treaty of Guarantee, particularly, in view of the Charter? On this I must insist upon having an answer.

U.N. SCOR, 19th Sess., 1097th mtg., at 28, U.N. Doc. S/PV.1097 (1964).

Turkey's representative gave the following reply:

> 158. Mr. MENEMENCIOGLU (Turkey): We were asked some questions here. But the situation is too tragic to use that kind of stratagem. As all the world knows, we are here because very tragic events have taken place in Cyprus—and they can start again at any moment. World opinion is asking many questions and is awaiting the answers. Unfortunately, those answers have not been given until now by the Cypriot Greek delegation. There are questions such as this: Do they give assurances that they will not start again what they did during the Christmas week? Can they give assurances that they will accept an international investigation of who started these things?

. . . How is it possible that a State's police forces joined the bandits of that Government to try to exterminate one part of its own population? . . . Are the guilty going to be punished? Are there going to be damages paid for all the thousands of animals killed, of lands devastated, of houses burned, and so on?

[At this point there were interruptions from the public gallery.]

159. Mr. President, will you please throw these savages out. This is not Limassol [a town on the southern coast of Cyprus where Turkish Cypriots suffered heavy losses in fighting with Greek Cypriots].

160. The PRESIDENT: The public should refrain from any sort of manifestation during the Council's proceedings. Will the representative of Turkey please continue?

162. These are the questions which world opinion is waiting to have answered—and not other questions, which are only a smoke-screen. . . .

Id.

But the Representative of Cyprus was not to be put off.

165. . . . [L]et us not deviate from the issue. My question was quite simple, and it has not been answered. . . . Is it the position of the three other countries, the signatories to the Treaty of Guarantee—namely, Turkey, the United Kingdom and Greece—that the said Treaty confers upon them the right of military intervention?

Id. at 31.

Greece then gave its answer:

168. The question put to us by the Minister for Foreign Affairs of Cyprus is a critical and important one; it is, indeed, the question of all questions. Do we—the Greek Government—think that this article gives us the right to intervene militarily and unilaterally without the authorization of the Security Council? The answer is "no." At Zurich, where I was present, our intention was not to create a situation in which, for one reason or another, one of us might be able, one fine day, to put troops aboard warships and dispatch them to Cyprus. To do what? To change the situation created by the treaties? In the first place, I cannot see how the situation created by the treaties has been changed. There have been tragic events, and I was one of the first to deplore them and condemn violence, but legally speaking there has been no change in the position created by the treaties.

169. The representative of Turkey has said that it is not Turkey which is insisting that the Treaty be mentioned in any draft resolution. It is Cyprus which is asking for its independence and territorial integrity to be recognized. There lies the problem. The question is addressed to the Council, not to us. Can the independence, territorial integrity, security, sovereignty and unity of a State be subject to a treaty which may be interpreted as granting a right of unilateral military intervention without any other condition? The Greek Government's answer is clearly: "No."

Id.

The United Kingdom expressed its position as follows:

65. The first point I should like to make in answering the question put by the Foreign Minister of Cyprus is to emphasize that whether or not the use of

force is permissible under the existing rules of international law and, in particular, under the United Nations Charter must always depend on the circumstances in which and the purposes for which it is used. It is undeniable that the Charter itself contemplates the lawful use of force in certain circumstances. Article 51 is one clear example of this.

66. Secondly . . . [t]he right which is reserved to the guarantor Powers under the second paragraph of Article IV [of the Treaty of Guarantee] is not, as it appears to have been considered by some of the preceding speakers, an unlimited right of unilateral action, but—and here I quote—"the right to take action with the sole aim of re-establishing the state of affairs created by the present Treaty".

67. The purposes of the Treaty are, I would emphasize, entirely in accordance with the obligation contained in Article 2(4) of the Charter of the United Nations. Furthermore, the action provided for in Article IV(2) of the Treaty can only be taken in the event of a breach of the provisions of the Treaty, that is, in circumstances in which there is a threat to the independence, territorial integrity or security of the Republic of Cyprus as established by the Basic Articles of its Constitution; and, as I have already said, it must be limited to such action as is necessary to re-establish this state of affairs. . . . But the question of military intervention under Article IV of the Treaty of Guarantee would never arise if all concerned played their part as they have undertaken to do. The Government of Cyprus like any other Government—and I am sure the Foreign Minister of Cyprus will agree with what I am saying—is under a duty to maintain security within its country and to observe the Constitution under which it is created and which authorizes its representatives to speak on behalf of the Republic. Furthermore, it has undertaken by treaty to carry out these duties in the Treaty of Guarantee. So long as it does so, no question of an intervention can arise.

68. The legal effect of the provisions of Article IV of the Treaty of Guarantee, as in the case of other legal provisions, will depend on the facts and circumstances of the situation in which they are invoked, and there is nothing in Article IV to suggest that action taken under it would necessarily be contrary to the United Nations Charter. . . .

71. . . . As we all know, legal arguments can continue for a very long time, and this Council is not, and was never intended to be, a legal forum. We are here for one main purpose only, and that is to deal with a difficult and dangerous situation which, if allowed to continue, could threaten the peace.

U.N. SCOR, 19th Sess., 1098th mtg., at 11-12, U.N. Doc. S/PV.1098 (1964).

The Representative of Cyprus then offered an answer to his own question.

106. The Treaty of Guarantee provides that in case of a breach of its provisions, the guarantors—that is to say, Greece, Turkey and the United Kingdom—shall consult together with regard to "the representations or measures necessary to ensure observance of those provisions." And that if concerted action is not possible, separate action by any one of them could be taken. "Action" here obviously refers to "representations or necessary measures," as expressly stated in that very same article. The word "measures" could only mean the use of peaceful means, particularly in regard to the provisions of the Charter which I mentioned above. Any other interpretation involving the use of force would be in direct conflict with the cardinal principle

of the Charter contained in Article 2, paragraph 4. And in that respect, I repeat, the treaty would be void by virtue of the aforementioned Article 103 of the Charter.

Id. at 19.

a. Good Faith Compliance

As noted above, Turkey sought to frame the issue before the Security Council in terms of the basic duty of all states to carry out their treaty obligations in good faith. That principle, often referred to by the phrase *pacta sunt servanda*, has been described by the International Law Commission as "the fundamental principle of the law of treaties." It is enshrined in Article 26 of the Vienna Convention, which provides that "[e]very treaty in force is binding upon the parties to it and must be performed by them in good faith." An earlier draft of Article 26 added that "good faith, *inter alia*, requires that a party to a treaty shall refrain from any acts calculated to prevent the due execution of the treaty or otherwise to frustrate its objects." This addition was ultimately dropped on the ground that it was implicit in the notion of good faith.

b. Can a Treaty Violate International Law?

Cyprus did not deny that *valid* treaties are to be performed in good faith. Rather, it questioned the validity of the Treaty of Guarantee as interpreted by Turkey. Although the Vienna Convention provisions on peremptory norms (also referred to as *jus cogens*) were not in effect at the time of Turkish military intervention, those provisions embody customary international law that arguably dates back to 1945 and the adoption of the UN Charter. The relevant articles of the Vienna Convention provide:

Article 53
Treaties Conflicting with a Peremptory Norm of General International Law
(jus cogens)

A treaty is void if, at the time of its conclusion, it conflicts with a peremptory norm of general international law. For the purposes of the present Convention, a peremptory norm of general international law is a norm accepted and recognized by the international community of States as a whole as a norm from which no derogation is permitted and which can be modified only by a subsequent norm of general international law having the same character.

Article 64
Emergence of a New Peremptory Norm of General International Law
(jus cogens)

If a new peremptory norm of general international law emerges, any existing treaty which is in conflict with that norm becomes void and terminates.

Articles 53 and 64 of the Vienna Convention suggest the existence of a hierarchy of norms in international law. By definition, *jus cogens* norms are deemed to be so fundamental to the existence of a just international legal order that states cannot derogate from them, even by agreement. By contrast, other norms of general international law may be modified by agreement, at least with respect to the relations of the parties to the agreement.

The inclusion of provisions on *jus cogens* in the Vienna Convention generated considerable debate. Some states, including the United States, expressed concern about the possible disruption to treaty relations such provisions might permit; others disagreed on whether to include a list of peremptory norms in Article 53, and on which norms such a list might encompass. Luxembourg raised a more fundamental objection, one in keeping with the view of many positivist lawyers:

> [Luxembourg] interprets the Commission's object as being to introduce as a cause of nullity criteria of morality and "public policy" such as are used in internal law to determine the compatibility of private contracts with fundamental concepts of the social order; and it questions whether such concepts are suitable for transfer to international relations which are characterized by the lack of any authority, political or judicial, capable of imposing on all States standards of international justice and morality.

The commentary on the International Law Commission's final draft of Article 53 defended the inclusion of provisions on *jus cogens* in the Convention:

> (1) The view that in the last analysis there is no rule of international law from which States cannot at their own free will contract out has become increasingly difficult to sustain. . . . [T]he law of the Charter concerning the prohibition of the use of force in itself constitutes a conspicuous example of a rule in international law having the character of *jus cogens*. . . . [O]nly one [government has] questioned the existence of rules of *jus cogens* in the international law of today. Accordingly, the Commission concluded that in codifying the law of treaties it must start from the basis that today there are certain rules from which States are not competent to derogate at all by a treaty arrangement, and which may be changed only by another rule of the same character.
>
> (2) The formulation of the article is not free from difficulty, since there is no simple criterion by which to identify a general rule of international law as having the character of *jus cogens*. Moreover, the majority of the general rules of international law do not have that character, and States may contract out of them by treaty. It would therefore be going much too far to state that a treaty is void if its provisions conflict with a rule of general international law. Nor would it be correct to say that a provision in a treaty possesses the character of *jus cogens* merely because the parties have stipulated that no derogation from that provision is to be permitted, so that another treaty which conflicted with that provision would be void. Such a stipulation may be inserted in any treaty with respect to any subject-matter for any reasons which may seem good to the parties. . . .
>
> (3) The emergence of rules having the character of *jus cogens* is comparatively recent, while international law is in process of rapid development. The Commission considered the right course to be to provide in general terms that a treaty is void if it conflicts with a rule of *jus cogens* and to leave the full content of this rule to be worked out in State practice and in the jurisprudence of international tribunals. Some members of the Commission felt that there might be advantage in specifying, by way of illustration, some of the most obvious and best settled rules of *jus cogens* in order to indicate by these examples the general nature and scope of the rule contained in the article. Examples suggested included (*a*) a treaty contemplating an unlawful use of force contrary to the principles of the Charter, (*b*) a treaty contemplating the performance of any other act criminal under international law, and (*c*) a treaty contemplating or conniving at the commission of acts, such as trade in slaves, piracy or genocide, in the suppression of

which every State is called upon to co-operate. . . . [T]reaties violating human rights, the equality of States or the principle of self-determination were mentioned as other possible examples.

Notes and Questions

1. Is Cyprus correct in arguing that Article IV of the Treaty of Guarantee, if read to permit military intervention, violates a peremptory norm? Cyprus relies principally on the prohibition on the use of force contained in Article 2(4) of the UN Charter, which provides that "[a]ll Members shall refrain in their international relations from the threat or use of force against the territorial integrity or political independence of any state, or in any other manner inconsistent with the Purposes of the United Nations." Although this prohibition is framed in absolute terms, it is widely accepted that states may use force in the territory of another state with the consent of that state, provided that the use of force is consistent with other principles of international law. Thus, states may, for example, authorize international peacekeeping forces to use coercion to fulfill their mandate or seek external military assistance in putting down a limited rebellion. Could the Treaty of Guarantee itself constitute the requisite consent to Turkish military intervention? If so, with what limitations? If Article IV of the Treaty can be properly read to permit military intervention, is and should Cyprus be free to revoke that consent at any time? For the purpose of expressing or revoking consent, who should be able to express the will of Cyprus?

2. Should international law recognize peremptory norms? What norms should qualify? As a practical matter, how can a peremptory norm, once established, be modified?

3. Note that under Article 53 of the Vienna Convention, a treaty that conflicts with a peremptory norm is void in its entirety. Treaties obtained by coercion in violation of Articles 51 and 52 are also void. By contrast, other grounds for invalidating a treaty—for example, fraud or corruption of a state's representative—do not necessarily render the entire treaty void. In some cases, only a particular clause of the treaty is treated as invalid. What might explain the difference?

4. In Annex IA, one of 11 separate agreements appended to the 1995 General Framework Agreement for Peace in Bosnia and Herzegovina (the Dayton Agreement), the parties authorized the establishment of an international military force (IFOR) to supervise and help implement the overall peace settlement. In addition, "to provide for the effective implementation of the provisions of this Annex," the agreement invites the UN Security Council "to authorize Member States or regional organizations and arrangements to establish the IFOR acting under Chapter VII of the United Nations Charter." The agreement also provides that "[t]he Parties understand and agree that the IFOR Commander shall have the authority, without interference or permission of any Party, to do all that the Commander judges necessary and proper, including the use of military force, to protect the IFOR and to carry out" IFOR's responsibilities under the agreement. The Republic of Bosnia and Herzegovina, the Federation of Bosnia and Herzegovina, and the Republika Srpska (the latter two entities constituting political subdivisions of the state of Bosnia) signed the agreement; Croatia and the Federal Republic of Yugoslavia endorsed it. The agreement entered into force upon signature on

December 14, 1995. On the following day, the UN Security Council adopted Resolution 1031, which authorized member states to form IFOR and in connection with it "to take all necessary measures to effect the implementation of and to ensure compliance with Annex IA of the Peace Agreement." Is Annex IA valid in light of Article 53 of the Vienna Convention? From a legal standpoint, how does the authorization to use force in Annex IA differ from the authorization to "take action" in Article IV of the Treaty of Guarantee?

In the years following the adoption of the Dayton Agreement, IFOR used force on a number of occasions, to maintain order, to arrest suspected war criminals, and for other similar purposes. Would such uses of force be valid in the absence of Security Council Resolution 1031? Does your answer depend on the attitude of the government of Bosnia toward the use of force at issue?

5. In 1998, the Economic Community of West African States (ECOWAS), a regional group of 15 states founded in 1975, adopted a Protocol Relating to the Mechanism for Conflict Prevention, Management, Resolution, Peacekeeping and Security. The Protocol established a nine-member Mediation and Security Council, empowered to decide by a 2/3 vote on ECOWAS responses to conflicts in member states. Among other things, the Mediation and Security Council shall "decide on all matters relating to peace and security"; and shall "authorise all forms of intervention and decide particularly on the deployment of political and military missions" pursuant to triggering conditions that include "serious and massive violation of human rights and the rule of law"; "an overthrow or attempted overthrow of a democratically elected government"; and "[a]ny other situation as may be decided by the Mediation and Security Council." Member states are to designate military units to be available to carry out missions mandated by the Mediation and Security Council. Should the ECOWAS protocol be treated as void for purporting to authorize military intervention in ECOWAS member states without Security Council authorization?

c. Interpreting Treaties

The arguments of the parties described earlier rest to some extent on ambiguities in the Treaty of Guarantee. Consider those arguments in light of the following Vienna Convention articles:

Article 31
General Rule of Interpretation

  1. A treaty shall be interpreted in good faith in accordance with the ordinary meaning to be given to the terms of the treaty in their context and in the light of its object and purpose.

  2. The context for the purpose of the interpretation of a treaty shall comprise, in addition to the text, including its preamble and annexes:

> (a) any agreement relating to the treaty which was made between all the parties in connexion with the conclusion of the treaty; (b) any instrument which was made by one or more parties in connexion with the conclusion of the treaty and accepted by the other parties as an instrument related to the treaty.

  3. There shall be taken into account, together with the context:

> (a) any subsequent agreement between the parties regarding the interpretation of the treaty or the application of its provisions; (b) any subsequent practice in the application of the treaty which establishes the

agreement of the parties regarding its interpretation; (c) any relevant rules of international law applicable in the relations between the parties.

4. A special meaning shall be given to a term if it is established that the parties so intended.

Article 32
Supplementary Means of Interpretation

Recourse may be had to supplementary means of interpretation, including the preparatory work of the treaty and the circumstances of its conclusion, in order to confirm the meaning resulting from the application of article 31, or to determine the meaning when the interpretation according to article 31:

(a) leaves the meaning ambiguous or obscure; or (b) leads to a result which is manifestly absurd or unreasonable.

The Vienna Convention's articles on treaty interpretation were adopted by unanimous vote and largely reflect preexisting customary international law. Nonetheless, there was extensive discussion at the drafting conference both on the formulation of Articles 31 and 32 and whether to include them at all. The principal issue to be resolved was whether and to what extent the intentions of the parties and the object and purpose of an agreement should supplement consideration of the text of the treaty in the process of interpretation. The final commentary to Articles 31 and 32 notes:

(2) Jurists also differ to some extent in their basic approach to the interpretation of treaties according to the relative weight which they give to:

(a) The text of the treaty as the authentic expression of the intentions of the parties;

(b) The intentions of the parties as a subjective element distinct from the text; and.

(c) The declared or apparent objects and purposes of the treaty.

Some place the main emphasis on the intentions of the parties and in consequence admit a liberal recourse to the *travaux préparatoires* [the preparatory work of the treaty] and to other evidence of the intentions of the contracting States as means of interpretation. Some give great weight to the object and purpose of the treaty and are in consequence more ready, especially in the case of general multilateral treaties, to admit teleological interpretations of the text which go beyond, or even diverge from, the original intentions of the parties as expressed in the text. The majority, however, emphasizes the primacy of the text as the basis for the interpretation of a treaty, while at the same time giving a certain place to extrinsic evidence of the intentions of the parties and to the objects and purposes of the treaty as means of interpretation.

Notes and Questions

1. Should the phrase "take action" in Article IV of the Treaty of Guarantee be construed to include the use of force? On this point, is the meaning of Article IV "ambiguous or obscure"?

2. What aspects of the context and the object and purpose of the Treaty of Guarantee are relevant to an interpretation of Article IV? Do the other agreements concluded along with the Treaty of Guarantee shed any light on its proper interpretation?

3. If Article IV is construed to permit only peaceful measures, does it add anything to the rights already possessed by the Guarantor Powers under international law?

4. Is Cyprus's argument that to construe Article IV to permit the use of force would render it incompatible with a peremptory norm persuasive? Dispositive? Would your answer be different if there was clear evidence that the parties intended to permit the use of force when they signed the agreement?

5. In the UN debates, none of the parties made reference to the *travaux préparatoires* of the 1960 accords. Does this suggest that the parties did not address the issue of the proper interpretation of Article IV at the time it was drafted? Why might they have failed to address that issue?

5. Treaties and Sovereignty

Sovereignty is a concept regularly invoked in international discourse, but its meaning is notoriously difficult to pin down. In many instances, sovereignty is used as shorthand for a particular legal principle or a subset of the attributes associated with statehood. Sovereignty is often invoked in opposition to a state's participation in various treaty regimes, usually by domestic groups who object to what they perceive as a loss of national decision-making authority over the areas subject to regulation by the treaty.

Sovereignty was frequently invoked in the UN debates over Cyprus, usually as a ground for attacking the validity of the constraints placed upon Cyprus by the 1960 accords. For example, the representative of Morocco argued that:

> 18. . . . . [T]he concept of sovereignty must at the very least include the total freedom of a free and independent country to be the sole architect of its constitution and to ensure that its content reflects, in the best possible way, the rights and guarantees of communities and private citizens alike— this, of course, in the absence of any kind of constraint or interference from abroad.

U.N. SCOR, 19th Sess., 1097th mtg., at 4, U.N. Doc. S/PV.1097 (1964).

To this line of argument, Turkey responded:

> 94. . . . . We are all sovereign countries here in the United Nations, but all of us have international commitments and we do not consider that to be a curtailment of sovereignty. We all have treaties by which we have accepted certain principles; we have treaties that give particular access to ships, for instance, in my country, to the [Black Sea] Straits. In other places there are minority rights protected by treaties. There is the Convention on Genocide to which we all must adhere. There are all sorts of commitments in international life which do not curtail sovereignty. There are also commitments to international morality and decency, and these are no curtailment of sovereignty, as we all know.

Id. at 19.

Notes and Questions

1. Inevitably, every treaty limits a state's freedom to act to some degree, just as a private contract constrains the behavior of the parties to it. Why then do states enter into treaties, and to what extent, if at all, should treaties be viewed as infringements on sovereignty? Does the subject matter of the treaty affect your answer?

2. In the *S.S. Wimbledon* (U.K., France, Italy, Japan, Germ.), 1923 P.C.I.J., (Ser. A), No.1, the Permanent Court of International Justice in 1923 discussed Germany's reliance on sovereignty as a reason to escape limitations placed on Germany by the Treaty of Versailles. Under the treaty, Germany accepted a permanent right of passage through the Kiel Canal for vessels of all nationalities. Following the outbreak of war between Russia and Poland, however, Germany sought to protect its neutral status by denying transit to a ship carrying arms for one of the belligerents. When charged with a breach of the treaty, Germany argued that a state's ability to declare itself neutral was "an essential part of her sovereignty," and that by signing the Versailles Treaty, Germany "neither could nor intended to renounce by anticipation" what it described as the "inalienable right of states to liberty of action." The Permanent Court held that "the right of entering into international engagements is an attribute of State sovereignty," and that therefore the limitations a state accepts under a treaty cannot later be renounced as impermissible infringements on that state's sovereignty. *Id.* at 25.

3. The meaning of the term "sovereignty" has varied widely since medieval times. A common understanding of the term in modern public international law is that it entails "the whole body of rights and attributes which a State possesses in its territory, to the exclusion of all other States, and also in its relations with other States." *Corfu Channel Case* (U.K. v. Alb.), 1949 I.C.J. 39, 43 (opinion of Judge Alvarez). Similarly, Professor Helmut Steinberger defines "sovereignty" as "the basic international legal status of a State that is not subject, within its territorial jurisdiction, to the governmental, executive, legislative, or judicial jurisdiction of a foreign State or to foreign law other than public international law." Helmut Steinberger, *Sovereignty, in* Encyclopedia of Public International Law 500, 512 (1992). But as Professor Louis Henkin points out in the following excerpt, the term "sovereignty" often obscures more than it reveals:

Louis Henkin, *International Law: Politics and Values*

8-10 (1995)

States are commonly described as "sovereign," and "sovereignty" is commonly noted as an implicit, axiomatic characteristic of statehood. The pervasiveness of that term is unfortunate, rooted in mistake, unfortunate mistake. Sovereignty . . . is often a catchword, a substitute for thinking and precision. It means many things, some essential, some insignificant; some agreed, some controversial; some that are not warranted and should not be accepted. . . .

Sovereignty, strictly, is the locus of ultimate legitimate authority in a political society, once the Prince or "the Crown," later parliament or the people. It is an internal concept and does not have, need not have, any implication for relations between one state and another.

Sovereignty, a conception deriving from the relations between a prince and his/her subjects, is not a necessary or appropriate external attribute for the abstraction we call a state. Nor is it the appropriate term or concept to define the relation between that abstraction and its counterpart abstractions, other states. For international relations, surely for international law, it is a term largely unnecessary and better avoided.

One can more meaningfully describe the state system—without invoking or implying "sovereignty"—as a social contract among entities which come together to establish a system of law and institutions for their governance, ceding some of their original autonomy, retaining the rest. What they retain is not "sovereignty" but the remainder of what they ceded to the needs of governance.

For legal purposes at least, we might do well to relegate the term sovereignty to the shelf of history as a relic from an earlier era. To this end, it is necessary to analyse, "decompose," the concept; to identify the elements that have been deemed to be inherent in, or to derive from, "sovereignty"; and to determine which of them are appropriate and desirable for a "state" in a system of states at the turn of the twenty-first century. As applied to a state, elements long identified with "sovereignty" are inevitably only metaphors, fictions, fictions upon fictions; some of them, however, do constitute essential characteristics and indicia of statehood today. These include principally: independence, equality, autonomy, "personhood," territorial authority, integrity and inviolability, impermeability and "privacy."

If Professor Henkin is correct that the term "sovereignty" is ambiguous and "better avoided," why do states so often invoke it? Are states likely to invoke the term for different purposes for different audiences?

6. The Consequences of Denouncing or Breaching a Treaty

During the course of the 1963-1964 debates, Turkey and Turkish Cypriots accused Greece and Greek Cypriots of breaching the 1960 accords, and vice versa, but each side drew different conclusions as to the effects of a breach. Turkey argued that Greek Cypriot breaches of the provisions protecting Turkish Cypriots entitled and obligated Turkey to "take action" to protect Turkish Cypriots, in accordance with Article IV of the Treaty of Guarantee. By contrast, Greek Cypriots suggested that Turkish actions, and what Greek Cypriots viewed as the unworkable provisions of an imposed Constitution, entitled them to terminate the 1960 accords:

> 112. Mr. Rossides (CYPRUS). . . . [B]oth the Treaty of Guarantee and the Treaty of Alliance had been materially violated by Turkey in a number of ways. . . . Turkey has broken its obligation to respect the independence and territorial integrity of Cyprus, and has acted in direct contravention of its specific obligation under Article II of the Treaty of Guarantee by pursuing itself the policy of partition and by violating the territorial integrity of Cyprus. The imposition on the people of Cyprus of the Treaty of Guarantee and the Treaty of Alliance, the arbitrary interpretation of the Treaty of Guarantee by Turkey and the use made by Turkey of both Treaties are the sources of the trouble which has been threatening and is threatening the peace in that area of the world.
>
> 113. . . . I wish to inform the Council that it is the intention of my Government to take all appropriate steps in accordance with international law and practice to rectify the intolerable and unacceptable situation caused by the Treaty of Guarantee and the Treaty of Alliance. . . .

136. . . . Our intention to terminate the Treaties of Guarantee and Alliance . . . should not be interpreted as in any way a desire on our part to do harm to the Turkish minority, or indeed to any other minority.

U.N. SCOR, 19th Sess., 1098th mtg., at 21, 26, U.N. Doc. S/PV.1098 (1964).
    Turkey vigorously contested the proposed termination of the treaties:

45. . . . [T]he Archbishop, by an unlawful act, has attempted to set aside unilaterally a valid international engagement, thereby also attempting to leave . . . the Security Council before [sic] a fait accompli. . . . I have termed this attempt as unlawful because it is not only contrary to the basic international law principles of *pacta sunt servanda*, but it is also in direct violation of the Constitution of the Republic . . .
    86. . . . Let there be no doubt in anyone's mind that, no sooner would the island of Cyprus achieve an independence free of the carefully worked-out safeguards of the Zurich and London Agreements, than it would hasten to accede to Greece, dragging with it the Turkish community against its will and irreparably upsetting the delicate balance between Greece and Turkey.

U.N. SCOR, 19th Sess., 1136th mtg., at 8, 20 U.N. Doc. S/PV.1136 (1964).
    Most treaties specify their duration or the conditions under which they may be terminated. Article 54 of the Vienna Convention provides that termination or withdrawal may take place "(a) in conformity with the provisions of the treaty; or (b) at any time by consent of all the parties after consultation with the other contracting States." But many treaties, including the Treaty of Guarantee, do not contain any specific provisions regarding their duration or termination. With respect to such treaties, the Vienna Convention provides:

Article 56
Denunciation of or Withdrawal from a Treaty Containing No Provision Regarding Termination, Denunciation or Withdrawal

1. A treaty which contains no provision regarding its termination and which does not provide for denunciation or withdrawal is not subject to denunciation or withdrawal unless:
        (a) it is established that the parties intended to admit the possibility of denunciation or withdrawal; or (b) a right of denunciation or withdrawal may be implied by the nature of the treaty.
    2. A party shall give not less than twelve months' notice of its intention to denounce or withdraw from a treaty under paragraph 1.

At the United Nations, Cyprus invoked Turkey's alleged breach of the Treaty of Guarantee as a basis for terminating the treaty. In evaluating this claim, consider the following Vienna Convention provisions:

Article 60
Termination or Suspension of the Operation of a Treaty as a Consequence of Its Breach

1. A material breach of a bilateral treaty by one of the parties entitles the other to invoke the breach as a ground for terminating the treaty or suspending its operation in whole or in part.
    2. A material breach of a multilateral treaty by one of the parties entitles:

(a) the other parties by unanimous agreement to suspend the operation of the treaty in whole or in part or to terminate it either: (i) in the
relations between themselves and the defaulting State, or (ii) as between
all the parties;

(b) a party specially affected by the breach to invoke it as a ground
for suspending the operation of the treaty in whole or in part in the relations between itself and the defaulting State;

(c) any party other than the defaulting State to invoke the breach as
a ground for suspending the operation of the treaty in whole or in part
with respect to itself if the treaty is of such a character that a material
breach of its provisions by one party radically changes the position of
every party with respect to the further performance of its obligations
under the treaty.

3. A material breach of a treaty, for the purposes of this article, consists in:
(a) a repudiation of the treaty not sanctioned by the present Convention; or (b) the violation of a provision essential to the accomplishment
of the object or purpose of the treaty.

4. The foregoing paragraphs are without prejudice to any provision in
the treaty applicable in the event of a breach.

5. Paragraphs 1 to 3 do not apply to provisions relating to the protection
of the human person contained in treaties of a humanitarian character, in
particular to provisions prohibiting any form of reprisals against persons protected by such treaties.

Notes and Questions

1. Under Article 56, did Cyprus have a valid ground for denouncing the Treaty
of Guarantee?

2. How should one determine whether a right of denunciation is implicit in the
nature of a treaty? An early draft of Article 56 listed treaties "effecting a final settlement of an international dispute" as among the kinds of treaties that should
ordinarily be viewed as continuing indefinitely. Does the Treaty of Guarantee fall
within that category? As a general matter, what other kinds of treaties should presumptively be viewed as continuing indefinitely? As permitting a right of denunciation by their nature?

3. Which state or states could have reasonably invoked breach as a valid ground
for terminating the Treaty of Guarantee in 1964? In 1974? What remedies would
have been available to the aggrieved state?

4. Turkey and Turkish Cypriots view the Treaty of Guarantee as a protection
against discrimination and even the destruction of the Turkish Cypriot community.
Does the treaty therefore qualify as a treaty of a humanitarian character within the
meaning of Article 60(5)?

5. Why do you think Cyprus never carried through on its threat to terminate
the Treaty of Guarantee? Most Security Council members opposed unilateral
denunciation or modification of the 1960 treaties. The United States, for example,
took the position that the Treaty of Guarantee "can be abrogated or altered only by
agreement of all of the signatories themselves or in accordance with its terms." At
the same time, many Council members were sympathetic to the argument of Greek
Cypriots that the treaty prohibition on the amendment of the Constitution's basic

articles put Cyprus in a constitutional "straitjacket." Accordingly, many states urged the parties to negotiate modifications to the 1960 accords, although nothing in the Vienna Convention on the Law of Treaties expressly requires modification or renegotiation of a treaty, even when circumstances suggest the desirability of changes to the treaty's terms.

Under sustained international pressure, negotiations over the adaptation of the 1960 treaties to current realities have proceeded intermittently since the 1970s. In 1992, UN Secretary-General Perez de Cuellar drafted a detailed "set of ideas" calling for establishment of a bi-communal, bi-zonal federal state, with politically equal Greek and Turkish Cypriot federated substates.

Both parties acknowledge that the 1960 accords continue in force, even though the constitutional structure they were designed to preserve has not functioned in over 30 years and cannot function as long as the de facto partition of Cyprus continues. The set of ideas expressly states that the treaties "continue in force" but suggests that they "will be supplemented" as part of a final agreement. The set of ideas also states that the Treaty of Guarantee will continue to "ensure against the unilateral change of the new constitutional order of the federal republic by either community."

On November 11, 2002, UN Secretary-General Kofi Annan presented a comprehensive plan (the "Annan plan") for the resolution of the Cyprus dispute to Greek and Turkish Cypriot leaders, and to the three guarantor powers under the 1960 Treaty of Guarantee. The plan called for the creation of a "common state" composed of two politically equal "component states," one Greek Cypriot and the other Turkish Cypriot. In April 2003, Greek Cypriot authorities signed an accession agreement with the European Union on behalf of Cyprus, although Turkish Cypriots will not benefit unless the island is reunited. As the May 1, 2004 date for accession of Cyprus to the European Union drew near, pressure intensified on both sides to reach an agreement that would permit Cyprus as a whole to join the EU. On April 24, 2004, the Annan Plan was put to simultaneous votes in the Greek and Turkish Cypriot communities. The overwhelming majority of Greek Cypriots—over 75 percent, according to the final tally—voted against the plan. Approximately 65 percent of Turkish Cypriots voted in favor. Since the plan required majority approval from both communities in order to go forward with reunification, the island remains divided. As a result, only the Greek Cypriot side of the island joined the European Union on May 1, 2004.

Notes and Questions

1. In *Gabčíkovo-Nagymaros Dam Project*, (Hung./Slovak.), 1997 I.C.J. 7, the ICJ confronted a complex set of treaty arrangements concerning the construction and operation of a Danube river watercourse project. The Court noted the parties' failure to comply with the terms of their treaty, but found that the treaty continued in force and that it expressly contemplated efforts by the parties to modify their project as necessary to conform to evolving standards and norms governing the protection of the environment. According to the Court, the parties therefore had a duty to negotiate in good faith:

133. The Court, however, cannot disregard the fact that the Treaty has not been fully implemented by either party for years, and indeed that their acts of commission and omission have contributed to creating the factual situation that now exists. Nor can it overlook that factual situation—or the practical possibilities and impossibilities to which it gives rise—when deciding on the legal requirements for the future conduct of the Parties.

This does not mean that facts—in this case facts which flow from wrongful conduct—determine the law. The principle *ex injuria jus non oritur* is sustained by the Court's finding that the legal relationship created by the 1977 Treaty is preserved and cannot in this case be treated as voided by unlawful conduct.

What is essential, therefore, is that the factual situation as it has developed since 1989 shall be placed within the context of the preserved and developing treaty relationship, in order to achieve its object and purpose in so far as that is feasible. For it is only then that the irregular state of affairs which exists as the result of the failure of both Parties to comply with their treaty obligations can be remedied. . . .

141. It is not for the Court to determine what shall be the final result of these negotiations to be conducted by the Parties. It is for the Parties themselves to find an agreed solution that takes account of the objectives of the Treaty, which must be pursued in a joint and integrated way, as well as the norms of international environmental law and the principles of the law of international watercourses . . .

142. What is required in the present case by the rule *pacta sunt servanda*, as reflected in Article 26 of the Vienna Convention of 1969 on the Law of Treaties, is that the Parties find an agreed solution within the co-operative context of the Treaty.

Article 26 combines two elements, which are of equal importance. It provides that "Every treaty in force is binding upon the parties to it and must be performed by them in good faith". This latter element, in the Court's view, implies that, in this case, it is the purpose of the Treaty, and the intentions of the parties in concluding it, which should prevail over its literal application. The principle of good faith obliges the Parties to apply it in a reasonable way and in such a manner that its purpose can be realized.

For a more detailed discussion of this case, see Chapter 11.

2. Do or should the parties to the 1960 Cyprus accords have a duty to negotiate in good faith? What use might a mediator make of such a duty?

3. Who decides whether parties are negotiating in good faith, and how? What are the legal implications of failing to negotiate in good faith? The practical implications?

4. The Annan plan described above contains a draft Additional Protocol to the Treaty of Guarantee, which provides that the treaty shall apply not only to Cyprus but also to "the territorial integrity, security and constitutional order" of the proposed component states. What would be the effect of that Protocol, if adopted?

D. Reservations to Treaties

The 1960 Cyprus accords provide an example of treaties for which acceptance of all terms by all parties was essential to the conclusion of an agreement. This uniform acceptance of all of the provisions of a treaty by all of the parties to it is the norm for most treaties. In some cases, however, one or more states wishes to become a party to a multilateral treaty but refuses to accept one or more of the treaty's provisions. In such cases, states may seek to enter a reservation to the treaty to limit or exclude the application of one or more of the treaty's terms to the reserving state, provided that the treaty does not expressly prohibit the reservation at issue.

Although reservations to certain multilateral treaties, especially human rights treaties, are now common, for many years states assumed that all parties had to agree to all terms of a treaty. The issue came to a head following promulgation of the Genocide Convention in 1948. By the end of 1950, eight states had indicated their intent to ratify the Convention with reservations concerning various articles, especially Article 9, which provided for reference of disputes to the ICJ. In an advisory opinion issued in 1951 on the permissibility of reservations to the Genocide Convention, the Court articulated reasons for moving away from the old rule, at least with regard to human rights treaties.

Reservations to the Convention on the Prevention and Punishment of the Crime of Genocide

1951 I.C.J. 15 (May 28)

It is well established that in its treaty relations a State cannot be bound without its consent, and that consequently no reservation can be effective against any State without its agreement thereto. It is also a generally recognized principle that a multilateral convention is the result of an agreement freely concluded upon its clauses and that consequently none of the contracting parties is entitled to frustrate or impair, by means of unilateral decisions or particular agreements, the purpose and *raison d'être* of the convention. To this principle was linked the notion of the integrity of the convention as adopted, a notion which in its traditional concept involved the proposition that no reservation was valid unless it was accepted by all the contracting parties without exception, as would have been the case if it had been stated during the negotiations.

This concept, which is directly inspired by the notion of contract, is of undisputed value as a principle. However, as regards the Genocide Convention, it is proper to refer to a variety of circumstances which would lead to a more flexible application of this principle. . . .

The Genocide Convention was . . . intended by the General Assembly and by the contracting parties to be definitely universal in scope. It was in fact approved on December 9th, 1948, by a resolution which was unanimously adopted by fifty-six States.

The objects of such a convention must also be considered. The Convention was manifestly adopted for a purely humanitarian and civilizing purpose. . . . In such a convention the contracting States do not have any interests of their own; they merely have, one and all, a common interest, namely, the accomplishment of those high purposes which are the *raison d'être* of the convention. Consequently, in a convention of this type one cannot speak of individual advantages or disadvantages to States, or of the maintenance of a perfect contractual balance between rights and duties. The high ideals which inspired the Convention provide, by virtue of the common will of the parties, the foundation and measure of all its provisions.

The foregoing considerations, when applied to the question of reservations, and more particularly to the effects of objections to reservations, lead to the following conclusions.

The object and purpose of the Genocide Convention imply that it was the intention of the General Assembly and of the States which adopted it that as many States as possible should participate. The complete exclusion from the Convention of one or more States would not only restrict the scope of its application, but would detract from the authority of the moral and humanitarian principles which are its basis. It is inconceivable that the contracting parties readily contemplated that an objection to a minor reservation should produce such a result. But even less could the contracting parties have intended to sacrifice the very object of the Convention in favour of a vain desire to secure as many participants as possible. The object and purpose of the Convention thus limit both the freedom of making reservations and that of objecting to them. It follows that it is the compatibility of a reservation with the object and purpose of the Convention that must furnish the criterion for the attitude of a State in making the reservation on accession as well as for the appraisal by a State in objecting to the reservation. Such is the rule of conduct which must guide every State in the appraisal which it must make, individually and from its own standpoint, of the admissibility of any reservation. . . .

. . . [E]ach State which is a party to the Convention is entitled to appraise the validity of the reservation, and it exercises this right individually and from its own standpoint. As no State can be bound by a reservation to which it has not consented, it necessarily follows that each State objecting to it will or will not, on the basis of its individual appraisal within the limits of the criterion of the object and purpose stated above, consider the reserving State to be a party to the Convention. . . .

The disadvantages which result from this possible divergence of views—which an article concerning the making of reservations could have obviated—are real; they are mitigated by the common duty of the contracting States to be guided in their judgment by the compatibility or incompatibility of the reservation with the object and purpose of the Convention. . . .

For these reasons,

THE COURT IS OF OPINION, . . .

by seven votes to five,

(a) that if a party to the Convention objects to a reservation which it considers to be incompatible with the object and purpose of the Convention, it can in fact consider that the reserving State is not a party to the Convention;

(b) that if, on the other hand, a party accepts the reservation as being compatible with the object and purpose of the Convention, it can in fact consider that the reserving State is a party to the Convention. . . .

Dissenting Opinion of Judges Guerrero, Sir Arnold McNair, Read, Hsu Mo

. . . [W]e have difficulty in seeing how the new rule can work. When a new rule is proposed for the solution of disputes, it should be easy to apply and calculated to produce final and consistent results. We do not think that the rule under examination satisfies either of these requirements.

(i) It hinges on the expression 'if the reservation is compatible with the object and purpose of the Convention'. What is the 'object and purpose' of the Genocide Convention? To repress genocide? Of course; but is it more than that? Does it comprise any or all of the enforcement articles of the Convention? That is the heart of the matter. One has only to look at them to realize the importance of this question. As we showed at the beginning of our Opinion, these are the articles which are causing trouble.

(ii) It is said that on the basis of the criterion of compatibility each party should make its own individual appraisal of a reservation and reach its own conclusion. Thus, a reserving State may or may not be a party to the Convention according to the different view-points of States which have already become parties. Under such a system, it is obvious that there will be no finality or certainty as to the status of the reserving State as a party as long as the admissibility of any reservation that has been objected to is left to subjective determination by individual States. It will only be objectively determined when the question of the compatibility of the reservation is referred to judicial decision; but this procedure, for various reasons, may never be resorted to by the parties. If and when the question is judicially determined, the result will be, according as the reservation is judicially found to be compatible or incompatible, either that the objecting State or States must, for the first time, recognize the reserving State as being also a party to the Convention, or that the reserving State ceases to be a party in relation to those other parties which have accepted the reservation. Such a state of things can only cause the utmost confusion among the interested States. . . .

. . . [W]hen a common effort is made to promote a great humanitarian object, as in the case of the Genocide Convention, every interested State naturally expects every other interested State not to seek any individual advantage or convenience, but to carry out the measures resolved upon by common accord. Hence, each party must be given the right to judge the acceptability of a reservation and to decide whether or not to exclude the reserving State from the Convention, and we are not aware of any case in which this right has been abused. It is therefore not universality at any price that forms the first consideration. It is rather the acceptance of common obligations—keeping step with like-minded States—in order to attain a high objective for all humanity, that is of paramount importance. Such being the case, the conclusion is irresistible that it is necessary to apply to the Genocide Convention with even greater exactitude than ever the existing rule which requires the consent of all parties to any reservation to a multilateral convention. In the interests of the international community, it would be better to lose as a party to the Convention a State which insists in face of objections on a modification of the terms of the Convention, than to permit it to become a party against the wish of a State or States which have irrevocably and unconditionally accepted all the obligations of the Convention. . . .

Notwithstanding the concerns of the dissenters, the drafters of the Vienna Convention on Treaties eventually adopted much of the majority's approach to treaty reservations, in language that applies to all treaties, not just to humanitarian treaties:

Article 20
Acceptance of and Objection to Reservations

1. A reservation expressly authorized by a treaty does not require any subsequent acceptance by the other contracting States unless the treaty so provides.

2. When it appears from the limited number of the negotiating States and the object and purpose of a treaty that the application of the treaty in its entirety between all the parties is an essential condition of the consent of each

one to be bound by the treaty, a reservation requires acceptance by all the parties.

3. When a treaty is a constituent instrument of an international organization and unless it otherwise provides, a reservation requires the acceptance of the competent organ of that organization.

4. In cases not falling under the preceding paragraphs and unless the treaty otherwise provides:

(a) acceptance by another contracting State of a reservation constitutes the reserving State a party to the treaty in relation to that other State if or when the treaty is in force for those States; (b) an objection by another contracting State to a reservation does not preclude the entry into force of the treaty as between the objecting and reserving States unless a contrary intention is definitely expressed by the objecting State; (c) an act expressing a State's consent to be bound by the treaty and containing a reservation is effective as soon as at least one other contracting State has accepted the reservation. . . .

Article 21
Legal Effects of Reservations and of Objections to Reservations

1. A reservation established with regard to another party . . .

(a) modifies for the reserving State in its relations with that other party the provisions of the treaty to which the reservation relates to the extent of the reservation; and (b) modifies those provisions to the same extent for that other party in its relations with the reserving State.

2. The reservation does not modify the provisions of the treaty for the other parties to the treaty *inter se*.

3. When a State objecting to a reservation has not opposed the entry into force of the treaty between itself and the reserving State, the provisions to which the reservation relates do not apply as between the two States to the extent of the reservation.

For discussion of the problems raised by reservations to multilateral treaties, see Chapter 7.

Notes and Questions

1. The Statute of the ICJ permits it to render advisory opinions at the request of the Security Council, or as in the above case, the General Assembly. The General Assembly may also authorize other UN organs or specialized agencies to request advisory opinions on "legal questions arising within the scope of their activities." Advisory opinions are not legally binding but nonetheless have substantial persuasive value. The Court's opinion in the Genocide Convention case contributed directly to the adoption of the Vienna Convention articles on reservations quoted above.

2. The ICJ decision and the Vienna Convention both declare that reservations incompatible with the object and purpose of a treaty are impermissible. Is each state free to decide whether a reservation is incompatible with the object and purpose of a treaty? What is the effect of a decision by a state that objects to a reservation but

accepts the reserving state as a party? Is the outcome different when a state accepts a reservation?

3. If a state makes a reservation that a body created pursuant to the treaty determines to be incompatible with the object and purpose of the treaty, is the reserving state still a party to the treaty? See the discussion of reservations to human rights treaties in Chapter 7.

II. CUSTOM AND SOFT LAW: REGULATING FOREIGN DIRECT INVESTMENT

In its list of the sources of international law, Article 38 of the Statute of the International Court of Justice includes "international custom, as evidence of a general practice accepted as law." Although listed after treaties, custom was, at least until World War II, widely viewed as equal to or more important than treaties in the development of international law. In recent years, treaties have overtaken custom for many purposes, and they are often preferred as a form of lawmaking because of their relative specificity. Nonetheless, many areas of international relations are not covered by treaties, and even in areas that are regulated by treaty, many states are not parties to the relevant instruments. Accordingly, custom continues to play a vital role in international law.

Increasingly, states are also using nontraditional forms of law making to supplement treaties and custom as means for the regulation of international activities and relations. This trend is most evident in the promulgation in recent years of a wide variety of quasi-legal instruments, from industry codes of conduct to guidelines issued by international organizations, to achieve multiple and varied purposes, which have collectively fallen under the general rubric of soft law. As you read the materials below, consider the ways in which different actors contribute to the formation of custom and soft law; the differences among treaties, custom, and soft law; the role soft law plays in enabling international actors to pursue their interests and to resolve disputes; and the factors that might lead different actors to prefer one type of law over another.

A. The Problem

Foreign direct investment—the transfer of capital by an investor from one country to another, accompanied by a claim to the income produced by the assets acquired or generated with that capital—takes many forms. It may involve the establishment of a foreign company or subsidiary or the purchase of shares in a foreign corporation. As discussed more fully in Chapter 12, global foreign direct investment has increased substantially over the last 15 years.

In many developing countries, foreign direct investment provides an important source of capital. But foreign direct investment has also proven highly controversial; some governments have tried to restrict it, and some non-governmental organizations (NGOs) have argued that in countries with inadequate financial controls and problems of official corruption, it may do more harm than good.

Many countries, including developed countries, restrict foreign investment for political and economic reasons. Often investment in particular sectors of the economy deemed essential to national security, such as telecommunications and defense-related industries, is restricted or even precluded altogether. In some developing countries, foreign investors may not purchase more than 50 percent of the stock of some domestic enterprises.

Disputes between foreign investors and their host states arise with some frequency, but the legal principles applicable to these disputes, and the political environment within which these disputes have been settled, have varied dramatically. During the colonial era, international law supported the political dominance generally enjoyed by the developed world vis-à-vis the developing world. The colonial powers enjoyed complete freedom to exploit the economic resources of their colonies as they saw fit, and this pattern of economic exploitation came to characterize the relations between developed and developing countries generally. Commercial enterprises based in developed countries could generally count on the political support of their home states in securing access to the wealth of the developing world on inordinately favorable terms. The developing states received little if any economic benefit from western investment and had little or no legal basis for pursuing claims against western companies. By virtue of "concession" agreements with host states, western companies gained control over much of the oil wealth of the Middle East, the mineral wealth of Africa, and the agricultural and other resources of Latin America.

Following World War II, however, the relationships between developed and developing countries changed dramatically. The Western states accepted that relations with developing countries had to be based on the principle of sovereign equality. As decolonization progressed, developing states joined international organizations, including the United Nations, in numbers large enough to pass numerous resolutions demanding greater economic equality with developed states. This process peaked in the 1970s, when the UN General Assembly passed a series of resolutions intended to establish a "New International Economic Order." These resolutions included the Charter of Economic Rights and Duties of States, excerpted below.

As part of this process of demanding economic and political equality with the developed world, developing states began to engage in large-scale expropriations of certain assets belonging to foreign investors. The best-known set of expropriations occurred in the Middle East, where host states nationalized the holdings of many Western oil companies. These nationalizations triggered vigorous debate on the applicable law. Developed states insisted on compensation for the full economic value of their investments; developing states denied that full compensation was required under international law and insisted that such issues should be governed by domestic law.

This debate harkened back to an earlier dispute between the United States and Mexico. Between 1915 and the late 1930s, Mexico expropriated numerous properties owned by U.S. nationals, including agricultural lands and petroleum concessions. In the lengthy diplomatic exchange that followed, Mexico denied that it was under any international legal obligation to pay compensation. It insisted instead that Mexican law (which did require some compensation) applied. United States Secretary of State Cordell Hull, in what came to be known as the Hull doctrine, insisted that Mexico was obligated to pay prompt, adequate, and effective compensation.

The Mexican Minister of Foreign Affairs to the American Ambassador, August 3, 1938:

My government maintains . . . that there is in international law no rule universally accepted in theory nor carried out in practice, which makes obligatory the payment of immediate compensation nor even of deferred compensation, for expropriations of a general and impersonal character like those which Mexico has carried out for the purpose of redistribution of the land. . . .

Secretary of State Hull to the Mexican Ambassador, August 22, 1938:

The government of the United States merely adverts to a self-evident fact when it notes that the applicable precedents and recognized authorities on international law support its declaration that, under every rule of law and equity, no government is entitled to expropriate private property, for whatever purpose, without provision for prompt, adequate, and effective payment therefor. In addition, clauses appearing in the constitutions of almost all nations today, and in particular in the constitutions of the American republics, embody the principle of just compensation. These, in themselves, are declaratory of the like principle in the law of nations.

The universal acceptance of this rule of the law of nations, which, in truth, is merely a statement of common justice and fair-dealing, does not in the view of this Government admit of any divergence of opinion. . . .

The Mexican Minister of Foreign Affairs to the American Ambassador:

This attitude of Mexico is not, as Your Excellency's Government affirms, either unusual or subversive. Numerous nations, in reorganizing their economy, have been under the necessity of modifying their legislation in such manner that the expropriation of individual interests nevertheless does not call for immediate compensation and, in many cases, not even subsequent compensation; because such acts were inspired by legitimate causes and the aspirations of social justice, they have not been considered unusual or contrary to international law.

Green Hackworth, 3 Digest of International Law 660-665 (1942).

The United States-Mexico dispute replayed itself many times in later years, as radical changes in the political administration of developing states often translated into abrupt policy changes regarding the role of foreign investors in the local economy. In a number of countries, revolutions were followed by the wholesale nationalization of particular industries, especially those related to mineral extraction. In many of these cases, enterprises owned in whole or in substantial part by foreign nationals were the primary targets of nationalization.

The UN General Assembly debated the legal principles relating to nationalization of foreign investment on many occasions. In 1962, the General Assembly adopted the following resolution, supported by both developed and developing countries.

Permanent Sovereignty over Natural Resources

G.A. Res. 1803 (1962)

4. Nationalization, expropriation or requisitioning shall be based on grounds or reasons of public utility, security or the national interest which are recognized as overriding purely individual or private interests, both domestic and foreign. In such cases the owner shall be paid appro-

priate compensation in accordance with the rules in force in the State
taking such measures in the exercise of its sovereignty and in accordance
with international law. In any case where the question of compensation
gives rise to a controversy, the national jurisdiction of the State taking such
measures shall be exhausted. However, upon agreement by sovereign
States and other parties concerned, settlement of the dispute should be
made through arbitration or international adjudication. . . .

Decent

In the early 1970s, as the movement to establish the New International
Economic Order was in full swing, the General Assembly adopted a different
approach to nationalizations, as reflected in the following resolutions:

Permanent Sovereignty over Natural Resources

G.A. Res. 3171 (1973)

The General Assembly . . .
1. *Strongly reaffirms* the inalienable rights of States to permanent sovereignty over all their natural resources. . . .
3. *Affirms* that the application of the principle of nationalization carried
out by States, as an expression of their sovereignty in order to safeguard their
natural resources, implies that each State is entitled to determine the amount of
possible compensation and the mode of payment, and that any disputes which
might arise should be settled in accordance with the national legislation of each
State carrying out such measures. . . .

Flexible

Charter of the Economic Rights and Duties of States (CERDS)

G.A. Res. 3281 (1974)

1. Every State has and shall freely exercise full permanent sovereignty,
including possession, use and disposal, over all its wealth, natural resources and
economic activities.
2. Each State has the right . . .
   c) To nationalize, expropriate or transfer ownership of foreign
property, in which case appropriate compensation should be paid by
the State adopting such measures, taking into account its relevant laws
and regulations and all circumstances that the State considers pertinent.
In any case where the question of compensation gives rise to a controversy,
it shall be settled under the domestic law of the nationalizing State and by
its tribunals, unless it is freely and mutually agreed by all States concerned
that other peaceful means be sought on the basis of the sovereign equality
of States and in accordance with the principle of free choice of means.

Weak!

In the years that followed, the international legal principles applicable to
nationalizations continued to generate vigorous dispute. Developing countries
usually acknowledged that some compensation was owed for expropriated foreign
investments, but they differed sharply with Western, capital-exporting countries on

the means for valuing the investments at issue and the form compensation should take. Both sets of countries invoked international law and pointed to resolutions of the General Assembly and various indicators of state practice in support of their positions.

These disputes have often been resolved through negotiated settlements. In some cases, those settlements take the form of agreements between the host state and the expropriated investors. In such cases, the value of the settlement depends on the relative bargaining power of the parties. In other cases, the host state and the home state of the investors agree on a lump sum to be paid over to the home state and later distributed by the home state to individual investors in accordance with particular criteria and claims-resolution procedures. In most lump-sum settlement arrangements, claimants receive only a modest amount in relation to the actual economic value of their loss. Developed countries accept such arrangements as the best available outcome, given the limited capacity of developing states to pay foreign investors' claims and the desire of developed countries to maintain or restore acceptable diplomatic relations with expropriating states. At the same time, to protect the interests of their investors, developed states increasingly entered into Friendship, Commerce, and Navigation treaties, and later, bilateral investment treaties (BITS) with developing states. These treaties included guarantees of fair and equitable treatment for foreign investors, as determined by international law. Among other things, the treaties required the payment of the full economic value of expropriated investments.

Despite these various means of resolving host state-investor disputes, a number of important cases were referred to international arbitration. Two of those cases are excerpted in Part C below.

B. Background on the Formation of Customary International Law

Custom has served as a form of law since ancient times. Common practices among the Greek city states gave rise to rules governing war, trade, and other relations. Similarly, Roman law recognized custom as a source. In theory, usage or repeated state acts become custom over time, as divergent practices of various states converge and achieve a level of uniformity, consistency, and regularity that in turn generates a sense of legal obligation, often referred to as *opinio juris*. The drafters of the Restatement (Third) of the Foreign Relations Law of the United States therefore describe custom as law that "results from a general and consistent practice of states followed by them from a sense of legal obligation."

Many scholars describe custom as based on implicit state consent. Rules form because states engage in or acquiesce in particular practices and eventually recognize them as obligatory. In keeping with positivist notions that states can only be bound by their consent, international law permits states to opt out of an emerging customary international law rule by objecting to the rule as it develops. As a practical matter, however, states rarely exercise this right of persistent objection. Moreover, a rule once formed is binding on states that did not object, even if they did not have the opportunity to object. Thus, new states, including those that emerged from decolonization, are bound by all general customary international law in effect at the time they achieve statehood.

1. State Practice

State practice takes numerous forms. These forms include diplomatic contacts and correspondence, public statements of government officials, legislative and executive acts, military manuals and actions by military commanders, treaties and executive agreements, decisions of international and national courts and tribunals, and decisions, declarations, and resolutions of international organizations, among many others. State practice also includes inaction, at least in circumstances in which a state's failure to object to actions by another state may imply acquiescence in those actions. The significance of any particular evidence of state practice may vary enormously depending on the circumstances. In the case of resolutions of international organizations, for example, much will depend on whether the resolution purports to declare existing law or simply recommends a particular course of action. It will also depend on the number of states voting for and against, as well as the extent to which the states involved are directly affected by the subject matter of the resolution.

The extent to which practice must be uniform and the time required for practice to result in custom varies with the circumstances. In 2000, the International Law Association's Committee on the Formation of Customary (General) International Law issued a Statement of Principles Applicable to the Formation of General Customary International Law. (The International Law Association (ILA) is a distinguished organization of international lawyers and academics founded in 1873). The statement noted:

(a) In the North Sea Continental Shelf cases the ICJ observed that "Although the passage of only a short period of time is not necessarily, or of itself, a bar to the formation of a new rule of customary international law on the basis of what was originally a purely conventional rule, an indispensable requirement would be that within the period in question, short though it might be, State practice, including that of States whose interests are specially affected, should have been both extensive and virtually uniform in the sense of the provision invoked. . . . "

(b) The quotation from the ICJ just cited makes it clear that . . . there is no specific time requirement: it is all a question of accumulating a practice of sufficient density, in terms of uniformity, extent and representativeness. Some customary rules have sprung up quite quickly: for instance, sovereignty over air space, and the régime of the continental shelf, because a substantial and representative quantity of State practice grew up rather rapidly in response to a new situation.

(c) However, in the nature of things some time will normally need to elapse before a practice matures into a rule. The development of the continental shelf is an example of how the process often works. In 1945, President Truman proclaimed the "jurisdiction and control" of the USA over the adjacent continental shelf. Other States with important interests in their own continental shelf, such as the United Kingdom, followed suit. Some others, though their own interests were affected, failed to object. What started out as, first, a unilateral claim and undertaking, next a bilateral set of obligations, and then a body of particular customary law restricted to a confined (though not regionally defined) group of States, gradually ramified into a rule of general law. The process took several years to be completed. Even in the present era of easy and instantaneous communications, if a State or group of States adopts a practice, others will need to consider how (if at all) they wish to respond. These responses may give rise to further responses, and so on. All of this will usually involve some delay.

The *North Sea Continental Shelf* cases and the evolution of the continental shelf legal regime are discussed in more detail in Chapter 10.

2. *Opinio Juris*

Not all state practice results in customary law. Indeed, there are many instances of repeated state practice that reflect simply convenience or courtesy—for example, the forms of address used for ambassadors or other government officials—but not law. Consistent state practice becomes law when states follow the practice out of a sense of legal obligation encapsulated in the phrase *opinio juris sive necessitatis*. Unfortunately for international lawyers, however, states often act without express reference to rules of international law. Accordingly, the subjective element implicit in customary international law, the belief that a practice is in fact binding, must often be inferred from the nature and circumstances of the practice itself. In many cases, judges and international law scholars may help identify and establish such inferences through careful review of the relevant practice and their work is therefore listed in Article 38 of the Statute of the International Court of Justice as a subsidiary means for determining the law.

Whether proof of *opinio juris* is essential to the recognition of a new rule of customary international law is controversial. The International Law Association's Committee on Formation of Customary (General) International Law concluded in 2000 that "it is not necessary to the formation of such a rule that such a belief exists, either generally or on the part of any particular State":

> (c) It may well be true (though trivial) to observe that States will usually or always hold an *opinio juris* about an established rule of law. . . . [T]herefore . . . where it can be shown that an *opinio juris* exists about a practice, that will be sufficient [to prove the existence of a rule of customary international law]. But this tells us nothing about the necessity of this subjective state for the formation of a new rule of customary law. . . . And in fact, it is hard to see how a State, if properly advised, could entertain the belief that its conduct is permitted (or required) by existing law when that conduct is, by definition, a departure from it. States actively engaged in the creation of a new customary rule may well wish or accept that the practice in question will give rise to a legal rule, but it is logically impossible for them to have an *opinio juris* in the literal and traditional sense, that is, a belief that the practice is already legally permissible or obligatory. This is true both individually and collectively.
>
> (d) This latter statement is contrary to a substantial body of doctrine and, more importantly, appears to be contrary to a number of dicta of the International Court. However, . . . these dicta have been taken out of context and . . . most or all of them relate to special situations where *opinio juris* is relevant, especially in preventing practice counting towards the formation of a customary rule.
>
> Those special, and comparatively unusual, cases [in which states express the belief that particular practice does not count towards formation of customary law] do not provide guidance on whether, in the more typical instance of a constant and uniform practice by several States, unopposed by others (including those directly affected by the practice), it is necessary to demonstrate some sort of *opinio juris*. Of course, in such a case it might often be relatively easy to infer the existence of the subjective element from the practice, if one so desired. But this begs the question why it is necessary to look for it at all. In practice international tribunals and, it seems, States, do not specifically look for evidence of *opinio juris* unless there is reason to believe . . . that practice otherwise satisfying the criteria of [consistent state practice] does not "count" towards the formation of customary law.

3. From Practice to Law

Determining the point at which a consistent practice becomes law is more a matter of art than of science. It requires a careful but necessarily subjective weighing of all the various indicators of practice and *opinio juris* noted above. Similarly, determining whether state practice that is inconsistent with an already existing rule of customary international law is simply a violation of that law, a contribution to the formation of new law, or both, is equally difficult. In other cases, state practice may be so inconsistent or incomplete that decision makers must look to other sources of law for guidance. As you read the following cases, consider what kinds of practice count toward the creation of custom, the extent to which practice must be widespread and consistent, the time period over which the practice at issue extends, the point at which emerging custom can be properly described as binding law, the relationship between custom and treaties, and the means by which customary law once established may be changed.

In 1900, the U.S. Supreme Court had to determine the validity of the condemnation of two Spanish fishing vessels as prizes of war. The Court's decision illustrates some of the issues involved in identifying and applying a rule of customary international law.

The Paquete Habana

175 U.S. 677 (1900)

MR. JUSTICE GRAY delivered the opinion of the court.

There are two appeals from decrees of the District Court of the Southern District of Florida, condemning two fishing vessels and their cargoes as prize of war.

Each vessel was a fishing smack, running in and out of Havana, and regularly engaged in fishing on the coast of Cuba; [each] sailed under the Spanish flag. . . . Until stopped by the blockading squadron, [the *Paquete Habana*] had no knowledge of the existence of the war, or of any blockade. She had no arms or ammunition on board, and made no attempt to run the blockade after she knew of its existence, nor any resistance at the time of the capture. . . .

Both the fishing vessels were brought by their captors into Key West. . . . [A] final decree of condemnation and sale was entered, "the court not being satisfied that as a matter of law, without any ordinance, treaty or proclamation, fishing vessels of this class are exempt from seizure."

Each vessel was thereupon sold by auction; the Paquete Habana for the sum of $490; and the Lola for the sum of $800. . . .

We are then brought to the consideration of the question whether, upon the facts appearing in these records, the fishing smacks were subject to capture by the armed vessels of the United States during the recent war with Spain.

By an ancient usage among civilized nations, beginning centuries ago, and gradually ripening into a rule of international law, coast fishing vessels, pursuing their vocation of catching and bringing in fresh fish, have been recognized as exempt, with their cargoes and crews, from capture as prize of war.

This doctrine, however, has been earnestly contested at the bar; and no complete collection of the instances illustrating it is to be found, so far as we are aware, in a single published work, although many are referred to and discussed by the writers on international law. . . . It is therefore worth the while to trace the history of the rule, from the earliest accessible sources, through the increasing recognition of it, with occasional setbacks, to what we may now justly consider as its final establishment in our own country and generally throughout the civilized world.

The earliest acts of any government on the subject, mentioned in the books, either emanated from, or were approved by, a King of England. [The Court then reviews orders issued by King Henry IV in 1403 and 1406, pursuant to a treaty with France, directing that fishermen from France, Flanders, and Brittany be permitted to carry out their trade without hindrance, provided they should not "do or attempt, or presume to do or attempt, anything that could prejudice the King, or his kingdom of England, or his subjects." The Court next describes a 1521 treaty between the Emperor Charles V and Francis I of France, pursuant to which subjects of either sovereign could "safely and freely, everywhere in the sea, take herrings and every other kind of fish, the existing war by land and sea notwithstanding," for a limited period. The Court then notes French and Dutch edicts issued in 1536 to permit herring fishing during wartime, and describes the early authority of French admirals to grant "fishing truces" in time of war, a custom that continued until late in the seventeenth century, when France abandoned it in the face of a refusal by other states to extend reciprocal treatment to French fishermen. The Court then turned to a review of eighteenth century practice.]

The doctrine which exempts coast fishermen with their vessels and cargoes from capture as prize of war has been familiar to the United States from the time of the War of Independence.

On June 5, 1779, Louis XVI, our ally in that war, addressed a letter to his admiral, informing him that the wish he had always had of alleviating, as far as he could, the hardships of war, had directed his attention to that class of his subjects which devoted itself to the trade of fishing, and had no other means of livelihood; that he had thought that the example which he should give to his enemies, and which could have no other source than the sentiments of humanity which inspired him, would determine them to allow to fishermen the same facilities which he should consent to grant; and that he had therefore given orders to the commanders of all his ships not to disturb English fishermen, nor to arrest their vessels laden with fresh fish, even if not caught by those vessels; provided they had no offensive arms, and were not proved to have made any signals creating a suspicion of intelligence with the enemy; and the admiral was directed to communicate the King's intentions to all officers under his control. By a royal order in council of November 6, 1780, the former orders were confirmed; and the capture and ransom, by a French cruiser, of The John and Sarah, an English vessel, coming from Holland, laden with fresh fish, were pronounced to be illegal.

[The Court then reviews British practice and treaties between the United States and Prussia exempting fishermen from molestation during war, and concludes that: "Since the United States became a nation, the only serious interruptions, so far as we are informed, of the general recognition of the exemption of coast fishing vessels from hostile capture, arose out of the mutual suspicions and recriminations of England and France during the wars of the French Revolution." The Court describes at some length the disputes between England and France over the treatment of fishermen, and the occasions on which each captured fishermen of the other, and then comments upon Lord Stowell's judgment upholding a British seizure of a Dutch fishing vessel in 1798.]

[Lord Stowell's] opinion begins by admitting the known custom in former wars not to capture such vessels—adding, however, "but this was a rule of comity only, and not of legal decision." . . . The word "comity" was apparently used by Lord Stowell as synonymous with courtesy or good will. But the period of a hundred years which has since elapsed is amply sufficient to have enabled what originally may have rested in custom or comity, courtesy or concession, to grow, by the general assent of civilized nations, into a settled rule of international law. As well said by Sir James Mackintosh: "In the present century a slow and silent, but very substantial mitigation has taken place in the practice of war; and in proportion as that mitigated practice has received the sanction of time, it is raised from the rank of mere usage, and becomes part of the law of nations." Discourse on the Law of Nations, 38; 1 Miscellaneous Works, 360.

The French prize tribunals, both before and after Lord Stowell's decision, took a wholly different view of the general question. [The Court cites decisions finding the capture of English and Portuguese fishing vessels to be in violation of international law.]

The English government . . . more than once unqualifiedly prohibited the molestation of fishing vessels employed in catching and bringing to market fresh fish. [The Court cites English orders in council of 1806 and 1810 relating to Prussia and France, respectively.] In the war with Mexico in 1846, the United States recognized the exemption of coast fishing boats from capture. . . . [According to Navy Department records,] Commodore Conner, commanding the Home Squadron blockading the east coast of Mexico, on May 14, 1846, . . . [instructed] "commanders of the vessels of the Home Squadron, showing the principles to be observed in the blockade of the Mexican ports," one of which was that "Mexican boats engaged in fishing on any part of the coast will be allowed to pursue their labors unmolested;" and that on June 10, 1846, those instructions were approved by the Navy Department. . . .

[After further discussion of British, French, Mexican, and U.S. practice, the Court continues:] Since the English orders in council of 1806 and 1810 . . . in favor of fishing vessels employed in catching and bringing to market fresh fish, no instance has been found in which the exemption from capture of private coast fishing vessels, honestly pursuing their peaceful industry, has been denied by England, or by any other nation. . . .

International law is part of our law, and must be ascertained and administered by the courts of justice of appropriate jurisdiction, as often as questions of right depending upon it are duly presented for their determination. For this purpose, where there is no treaty, and no controlling executive or legislative act or judicial decision, resort must be had to the customs and usages of civilized nations; and, as evidence of these, to the works of jurists and commentators, who by years of labor, research and experience, have made themselves peculiarly well acquainted with the subjects of which they treat. Such works are resorted to by judicial tribunals, not for the speculations of their authors concerning what the law ought to be, but for trustworthy evidence of what the law really is. *Hilton v. Guyot*, 159 U.S. 113, 163, 164, 214, 215 [1895]. . . .

[The Court then reviews in detail the works of commentators from England, France, Argentina, Germany, Netherlands, Portugal, Spain, Austria, Italy, and other states.]

[The Court concludes:] This review of the precedents and authorities on the subject appears to us abundantly to demonstrate that at the present day, by the general consent of the civilized nations of the world, and independently of any express treaty or other public act, it is an established rule of international law, founded on considerations of humanity to a poor and industrious order of men, and of the mutual convenience of belligerent States, that coast fishing vessels, with their implements and supplies, cargoes and crews, unarmed, and honestly pursuing their peaceful calling of catching and bringing in fresh fish, are exempt from capture as prize of war. . . .

This rule of international law is one which prize courts, administering the law of nations, are bound to take judicial notice of, and to give effect to, in the absence of any treaty or other public act of their own government in relation to the matter. . . .

[In rejecting the argument that "a distinct exemption in a treaty or other public act of the Government," was necessary to exempt coastal fishing vessels from seizure, the Court noted:] To this subject, in more than one aspect, are singularly applicable the words uttered by Mr. Justice Strong, speaking for this court: "Undoubtedly, no single nation can change the law of the sea. That law is of universal obligation, and no statute of one or two nations can create obligations for the world. Like all the laws of nations, it rests upon the common consent of civilized communities. It is of force, not because it was prescribed by any superior power, but because it has been generally accepted as a rule of conduct. Whatever may have been its origin, whether in the usages of navigation, or in the ordinances of maritime States, or in both, it has become the law of the sea only by the concurrent sanction of those nations who may be said to constitute the commercial world. Many of the usages which prevail, and which have the force of law, doubtless originated in the positive prescriptions of some single State, which were at first of limited effect, but which, when generally accepted, became of universal obligation." "This is not giving to the statutes of any nation extra-territorial effect. It is not treating them as general maritime laws; but it is recognition of the historical fact that by common consent of mankind these rules have been acquiesced in as of general obligation. Of that fact, we think, we may take judicial notice. Foreign municipal laws must indeed be proved as facts, but it is not so with the law of nations." *The Scotia*, 14 Wall. 170, 187, 188 [1871].

The position taken by the United States during the recent war with Spain was quite in accord with the rule of international law, now generally recognized by civilized nations, in regard to coast fishing vessels.

. . . On April 22, the President issued a proclamation, declaring that the United States had instituted and would maintain [its] blockade, "in pursuance of the laws of the United States, and the law of nations applicable to such cases." . . .

On April 28, 1898 (after the capture of the two fishing vessels now in question,), Admiral Sampson telegraphed to the Secretary of the Navy as follows: "I find that a large number of fishing schooners are attempting to get into Havana from their fishing grounds near the Florida reefs and coasts. They are generally manned by excellent seamen, belonging to the maritime inscription of Spain, who have already served in the Spanish navy, and who are liable to further service. As these trained men are naval reserves, have a semi-military character, and would be most valuable to the Spaniards as artillerymen, either afloat or ashore, I recommend that they should be detained as prisoners of war, and that I should be authorized to deliver them to the commanding officer of the army at Key West." To that communication the Secretary of the Navy, on April 30, 1898, guardedly answered: "Spanish fishing vessels attempting to violate blockade are subject, with crew, to capture, and any such vessel or crew considered likely to aid enemy may be detained." Bureau of Navigation Report of 1898, appx. 178. The Admiral's despatch assumed that he was not authorized, without express order, to arrest coast fishermen peaceably pursuing their calling; and the necessary implication and evident intent of the response of the Navy Department were that Spanish coast fishing vessels and their crews should not be interfered with, so long as they neither attempted to violate the blockade, nor were considered likely to aid the enemy. . . .

Upon the facts proved in either case, it is the duty of this court, sitting as the highest prize court of the United States, and administering the law of nations, to declare and adjudge that the capture was unlawful, and without probable cause; and it is therefore, in each case,

Ordered, that the decree of the District Court be reversed, and the proceeds of the sale of the vessel, together with the proceeds of any sale of her cargo, be restored to the claimant, with damages and costs.

Notes and Questions

1. The Court describes the formation of a customary international law rule against confiscation of fishing vessels as the "ripening" of an "ancient usage among civilized nations." What does the Court mean by "ripening," and how can such a process give rise to a rule of international law? How much time must elapse before a usage can be deemed to have "ripened" into a rule of customary international law, and how can one ascertain when that has happened? Why should states rely on rules of international law derived from practice that may be ambiguous or conflicting? Wouldn't it be preferable to rely only on treaties?

2. What indicators of state practice support the Court's conclusion? Are these indicators consistent? The Court notes that France temporarily discontinued its practice of exempting fishing vessels from seizure in the late seventeenth century in response to the refusal of other states to exempt French fishermen. What is the effect of this interruption in the "ripening" of the rule at issue? How uniform must state practice be to support the formation of a rule of custom? Does it matter if a few countries fail to follow a practice generally followed by most other states?

3. Which countries' practice does the Court examine in attempting to determine the existence and content of a rule governing the treatment of fishing vessels during wartime? Is it reasonable to assume that most other countries acquiesced in the practice of a handful of dominant maritime powers? Does a state's silence on an issue indicate acquiescence? Note that a rule of customary international law binds all states that do not object to the rule as it is forming. By contrast, states that do not affirmatively ratify a treaty are not bound by it, even if it is a general multilateral treaty.

4. Do different forms of state practice carry different weight in assessing the existence or content of a customary international law rule? Note the variety of practice referred to by the Court. Do treaties between sovereigns carry more weight than orders issued by military commanders in the field? Is either more important than a decision by a municipal court? Do the acts of any government official relating to the subject of the rule constitute evidence of state practice, or only acts by senior government officials?

5. Is customary international law based on state consent? If not, why is it binding? Would states generally better satisfy their law-making objectives by negotiating multilateral treaties instead of waiting for customary rules to develop and crystallize into law?

6. Why is *opinio juris* often considered a necessary element for the formation of a rule of customary international law? Do you agree with the ILA Committee on Formation of Customary (General) International law that *opinio juris* should not be

deemed a necessary element in the formation of a new rule of customary international law? Is there any discussion of *opinio juris* in the *Paquete Habana*? Is there any evidence in the Court's opinion to suggest that the practice it was considering was being carried out under a sense of legal obligation? Can *opinio juris* be inferred from statements of writers on international law who opine that a particular rule has attained the status of custom? Determining the existence of *opinio juris* with regard to a particular state practice can be extremely difficult. For an opinion of the ICJ discussing this issue, see *The North Sea Continental Shelf* case, discussed in Chapter 10.

7. As a general matter, why might states refrain from the seizure of coastal fishing vessels in the absence of an applicable legal rule? Two commentators, after reviewing state practice on this issue, conclude that state behavior in this regard can best be explained as a "coincidence of interest":

> The most parsimonious explanation for the evidence is that states seized fishing vessels when they had a military reason to do so, whether the reason was to reward sailors under the rules of prize, to clear away obstructions or spies, or to terrorize the population—and they did not seize fishing vessels when they had a military reason not to do so, for example, to avoid the trouble or to maintain naval discipline. One might conjecture that a few cases, perhaps some of the interactions between France and England, are attributable to the solution of bilateral repeated prisoner's dilemmas. Most cases, however, are best attributable to simple lack of anything to cooperate about. If one insists on looking for a general pattern, one might conclude that most of the time states did not seize fishing vessels after the Napoleonic Wars because most of the time they were not at war, and when they were at war, their navies had better uses. One may dignify this pattern of behavior with the CIL [customary international law] label, if one wants, as long as one understands that it hardly reflects international cooperation or anything that is noteworthy or desirable, and it is certainly not the result of states acting out of a sense of legal or moral obligation.

Jack Goldsmith & Eric Posner, *A Theory of Customary International Law*, Chicago Working Paper in Law and Economics 69-70 (1999). As you study the role of custom in this and later chapters, consider why rules of custom form and whether and to what extent they influence state behavior.

8. What happens when states broadly subscribe to a norm in their public declarations but frequently violate the norm in practice? In a 1984 suit in which Nicaragua accused the United States of illegally assisting rebel forces seeking to overthrow the Nicaraguan government, the ICJ considered that question in its discussion of customary international law governing the use of force. The Court opined:

> It is not to be expected that in the practice of States the application of the rules in question should have been perfect, in the sense that States should have refrained, with complete consistency, from the use of force or from intervention in each other's internal affairs. The Court does not consider that, for a rule to be established as customary, the corresponding practice must be in absolutely rigorous conformity with the rule. In order to deduce the existence of customary rules, the Court deems it sufficient that the conduct of States should, in general, be consistent with such rules, and that instances of State conduct inconsistent with a given rule should generally have been treated as breaches of that rule, not as indications of the recognition of a new rule. If a State acts in a way prima facie incompatible with a recognized rule, but defends its conduct by appealing to exceptions or justifications contained within the rule itself, . . . the significance of that attitude is to confirm rather than to weaken the rule.

Case Concerning Military and Paramilitary Activities In and Against Nicaragua (Nicar. v. U.S.), 1986 I.C.J. 14.

Do you find the Court's reasoning persuasive? What would be the consequences of the view that a rule of customary international law retains its validity despite frequent violations? Should the extent to which inconsistent practice is viewed as insufficient to vitiate a rule turn on the norm at issue?

C. Discerning and Applying Custom: Foreign Direct Investment (FDI) and Expropriation

In the two cases that follow, international arbitrators apply customary international law to determine the standard of compensation to be paid for the expropriation of foreign enterprises. In attempting to identify the relevant customary norms, the arbitrators consider, among other things, the UN General Assembly resolutions excerpted in Section A above.

The first case arose in the aftermath of the Iranian revolution, when the Islamic Republic of Iran expropriated numerous foreign enterprises. Among other things, the Iranian government expropriated the interest held by SEDCO, the subsidiary of a U.S. corporation, in the SEDIRAN drilling company. Under the subsequently negotiated Algiers Accords, the United States and Iran agreed to resolve this and other commercial disputes through arbitration before a special arbitral tribunal created by the Accords—the Iran-U.S. Claims Tribunal. In the decision excerpted below, the Tribunal considers "the standard of compensation to be applied in determining any compensable damages resulting from" the expropriation of SED-CO's interest in SEDIRAN.

Interlocutory Award in Case Concerning SEDCO, Inc. v. National Iranian Oil Company and the Islamic Republic of Iran

Iran-United States Claims Tribunal, 10 Iran-U.S. Cl. Rep. 180 (1986)

II. CONTENTIONS OF THE PARTIES

. . . SEDCO claims to be entitled to full ("prompt, adequate and effective") compensation by virtue of customary international law. SEDCO contends that in the case of an ongoing business enterprise like SEDIRAN the full market value means going concern value including not only net assets but also goodwill and anticipated future earnings. . . .

The standard of "full" (or "prompt, adequate and effective") compensation in fact has never been the standpoint of international law, Respondents assert. Customary international law, according to Respondents, requires "appropriate" compensation to be measured in the light of all the circumstances of the case, and assessed with "unjust enrichment" as the guiding principle. Should any enrichment on the part of Respondents entitling Claimant to compensation be found, such compensation should be calculated according to the net book value of the company, a valuation basis allegedly widely used in compensation settlements in the oil industry.

III. CONCLUSIONS OF THE TRIBUNAL

. . . Although Respondents argue otherwise, it is the Tribunal's conclusion that "the overwhelming practice and the prevailing legal opinion" before World War II supported the view that customary international law required compensation equivalent to the full value of the property taken. . . . It is only since those days that this traditional legal standpoint has been challenged by a number of States and commentators.

Assessment of the present state of customary law on this subject on the basis of the conduct of States in actual practice is difficult, *inter alia*, because of the questionable evidentiary value for customary international law of much of the practice available. This is particularly true in regard to "lump sum" agreements between States (a practice often claimed to support the position of less than full compensation), as well as to compensation settlements negotiated between States and foreign companies. Both types of agreements can be so greatly inspired by non-judicial considerations—e.g., resumption of diplomatic or trading relations—that it is extremely difficult to draw from them conclusions as to *opinio juris*, i.e., the determination that the content of such settlements was thought by the States involved to be required by international law. . . . The bilateral investment treaty practice of States, which much more often than not reflects the traditional international law standard of compensation for expropriation, more nearly constitutes an accurate measure of the High Contracting Parties' views as to customary international law, but also carries with it some of the same evidentiary limitations as lump sum agreements. Both kinds of agreements involve in some degree bargaining in a context to which "*opinio juris* seems a stranger."

Those arguing that there has been an erosion of the traditional international law standard of full compensation often cite also resolutions and declarations of the United Nations General Assembly. Respondents in this case, for example, refer in particular to the Declaration on the Establishment of a New International Economic Order and the Charter of Economic Rights and Duties of States ("Charter") as well as the earlier Resolution 1803, of 14 December 1962, on Permanent Sovereignty over Natural Resources.

United Nations General Assembly Resolutions are not directly binding upon States and generally are not evidence of customary law. Nevertheless, it is generally accepted that such resolutions in certain specified circumstances may be regarded as evidence of customary international law or can contribute—among other factors—to the creation of such law.

There is considerable unanimity in international arbitral practice and scholarly opinion that of the resolutions cited above, it is Resolution 1803, and not either of the two later resolutions, which at least reflects, if it does not evidence, current international law. . . .

. . . [Resolution 1803] has been argued, on the one hand, to express the traditional standard of compensation with different words and, on the other hand, to signify an erosion of this standard.

Those learned writers who have argued, however, that the adoption of Resolution 1803, against the background of general recognition of the permanent sovereignty of States over natural resources, evidenced or brought about a change in customary international law so that less than full compensation should be the applicable standard, have focused mainly on the possible impact of the Resolution on the issue of compensation in the context of a formal systematic large-scale nationalization, e.g., of an entire industry or a natural resource, a circumstance not argued by either of the Parties to have been present in the instant case.

Opinions both of international tribunals and of legal writers overwhelmingly support the conclusion that under customary international law in a case such as here presented—a discrete expropriation of alien property—full compensation should be awarded for the property taken. This is true whether or not the expropriation itself was otherwise lawful. . . .

The Tribunal thus holds that Claimant must receive compensation for the full value of its expropriated interest in SEDIRAN, as claimed, whether viewed as an application of the Treaty of Amity or, independently, of customary international law, and regardless of whether or not the expropriation was otherwise lawful.

The second case involved Libya's nationalization of various Western oil properties. When Libya became an independent state in 1951, its economic prospects were bleak. But the discovery of large oil deposits in 1959 soon transformed Libya from a poverty-stricken country to a wealthy one. To achieve this transformation, Libya granted deeds of concession to Western oil companies to encourage them to undertake the costly and risky efforts necessary to find and develop Libya's oil deposits. The concessions conferred broad rights on the oil companies, enabling them to earn substantial profits on their investments. In the early 1970s, Libya began to insist on substantial equity participation in the Western oil company concessions, anywhere from 51 to 100 percent. In 1973 and 1974, Libya nationalized the interests and properties in Libya of nine international oil companies, including Texaco Overseas Petroleum Company (TOPCO), a Texaco subsidiary, and California Asiatic Oil Company (CAOC), a Standard Oil subsidiary. The timing was dictated in part by Libya's desire to retaliate for U.S. support for Israel and U.S. efforts to coordinate opposition to the 1973 Arab oil embargo. TOPCO and CAOC invoked the arbitration clauses in their deeds of concession. They sent notices to the Libyan government requesting arbitration and appointed their arbitrator. When Libya responded by denying that there was any arbitrable dispute, TOPCO and CAOC requested Manfred Lachs, the President of the ICJ, to appoint a sole arbitrator, as provided for in the deeds of concession. Lachs appointed René-Jean Dupuy, Professor of Law at the University of Nice. In the following excerpt, Dupuy considers the effect of General Assembly resolutions on the customary international law relating to expropriation.

Award on the Merits in Dispute Between Texaco Overseas Petroleum Company/California Asiatic Oil Company and the Government of the Libyan Arab Republic

17 I.L.M. 1 (1978)

. . . Substantial differences . . . exist between Resolution 1803 (XVII) and the subsequent Resolutions as regards the role of international law in the exercise of permanent sovereignty over natural resources. . . . [T]his Tribunal is obligated to consider the legal validity of the above-mentioned Resolutions and the possible existence of a custom resulting therefrom.

83. . . . This Tribunal will recall first that, under Article 10 of the U.N. Charter, the General Assembly only issues "recommendations", which have long appeared to

be texts having no binding force and carrying no obligations for the Member States. . . .

Refusal to recognize any legal validity of United Nations Resolutions must, however, be qualified according to the various texts enacted by the United Nations. These are very different and have varying legal value, but it is impossible to deny that the United Nations' activities have had a significant influence on the content of contemporary international law. In appraising the legal validity of the above-mentioned Resolutions, this Tribunal will take account of the criteria usually taken into consideration, i.e., the examination of voting conditions and the analysis of the provisions concerned.

84. (1) With respect to the first point, Resolution 1803 (XVII) of 14 December 1962 was passed by the General Assembly by 87 votes to 2, with 12 abstentions. It is particularly important to note that the majority voted for this text, including many States of the Third World, but also several Western developed countries with market economies, including the most important one, the United States. The principles stated in this Resolution were therefore assented to by a great many States representing not only all geographical areas but also all economic systems.

From this point of view, this Tribunal notes that the affirmative vote of several developed countries with a market economy was made possible in particular by the inclusion in the Resolution of two references to international law, and one passage relating to the importance of international cooperation for economic development.

85. On the contrary, it appears to this Tribunal that the conditions under which Resolutions 3171 (XXVII) . . . and 3281 (XXIX) (Charter of the Economic Rights and Duties of States) [were adopted] were notably different:

—Resolution 3171 (XXVII) was adopted by a recorded vote of 108 votes to 1, with 16 abstentions, but this Tribunal notes that a separate vote was requested with respect to the paragraph in the operative part mentioned in the Libyan Government's Memorandum whereby the General Assembly stated that the application of the principle according to which nationalizations effected by States as the expression of their sovereignty implied that it is within the right of each State to determine the amount of possible compensation and the means of their payment, and that any dispute which might arise should be settled in conformity with the national law of each State instituting measures of this kind. As a consequence of a roll-call, this paragraph was adopted by 86 votes to 11 (Federal Republic of Germany, Belgium, Spain, United States, France, Israel, Italy, Japan, The Netherlands, Portugal, United Kingdom), with 28 abstentions (South Africa, Australia, Austria, Barbados, Canada, Ivory Coast, Denmark, Finland, Ghana, Greece, Haiti, India, Indonesia, Ireland, Luxembourg, Malawi, Malaysia, Nepal, Nicaragua, Norway, New Zealand, Philippines, Rwanda, Singapore, Sri Lanka, Sweden, Thailand, Turkey). This specific paragraph concerning nationalizations, disregarding the role of international law, not only was not consented to by the most important Western countries, but caused a number of the developing countries to abstain. . . .

—The conditions under which Resolution 3281 (XXIX), proclaiming the Charter of Economic Rights and Duties of States, was adopted also show unambiguously that there was no general consensus of the States with respect to the most important provisions and in particular those concerning nationalization. Having been the subject matter of a roll-call vote, the Charter was adopted by 118 votes to 6, with 10 abstentions. The analysis of votes on specific sections of the Charter is most significant insofar as the present case is concerned. From this point of view, paragraph 2 (c) of Article 2 of the Charter, which limits consideration of the characteristics of compensation to the State and does not refer to international law, was voted by 104 to 16, with 6 abstentions, all of the industrialized countries with market economies having abstained or having voted against it. . . .

86. . . . [T]he absence of any binding force of the resolutions of the General Assembly of the United Nations implies that such resolutions must be accepted by the members of the United Nations in order to be legally binding. In this respect, the Tribunal notes that only Resolution 1803 (XVII) of 14 December 1962 was supported by a majority of Member States representing all of the various groups. By contrast, the other Resolutions mentioned above . . . were supported by a majority of States but not by any of the developed countries with market economies which carry on the largest part of international trade.

87. . . . [I]t appears essential to this Tribunal to distinguish between those provisions stating the existence of a right on which the generality of the States has expressed agreement and those provisions introducing new principles which were rejected by certain representative groups of States and having nothing more than a *de lege ferenda* [the law as it should be] value only in the eyes of the States which have adopted them; as far as the others are concerned, the rejection of these same principles implies that they consider them as being *contra legem*. With respect to the former, which proclaim rules recognized by the community of nations, they do not create a custom but confirm one by formulating it and specifying its scope, thereby making it possible to determine whether or not one is confronted with a legal rule. . . .

On the basis of the circumstances of adoption mentioned above and by expressing an *opinio juris communis*, Resolution 1803 (XVII) seems to this Tribunal to reflect the state of customary law existing in this field. Indeed, on the occasion of the vote on a resolution finding the existence of a customary rule, the States concerned clearly express their views. The consensus by a majority of States belonging to the various representative groups indicates without the slightest doubt universal recognition of the rules therein incorporated, i.e., with respect to nationalization and compensation the use of the rules in force in the nationalizing State, but all this in conformity with international law.

88. While Resolution 1803 (XVII) appears to a large extent as the expression of a real general will, this is not at all the case with respect to the other Resolutions mentioned above. . . . In particular, as regards the Charter of Economic Rights and Duties of States, several factors contribute to denying legal value to those provisions of the document which are of interest in the instant case.

—In the first place, Article 2 of this Charter must be analyzed as a political rather than as a legal declaration concerned with the ideological strategy of development and, as such, supported only by non-industrialized States.

—In the second place, this Tribunal notes that in the draft submitted by the Group of 77 [a grouping of developing states formed in 1964 to promote the collective economic interests of its now 133 members] . . . the General Assembly was invited to adopt the Charter "as a first measure of codification and progressive development" within the field of the international law of development. However, because of the opposition of several States, this description was deleted from the text submitted to the vote of the Assembly. . . .

89. Such an attitude is further reinforced by an examination of the general practice of relations between States with respect to investments. This practice is in conformity, not with the provisions of Article 2 (c) of the above-mentioned Charter conferring exclusive jurisdiction on domestic legislation and courts, but with the exception stated at the end of this paragraph. Thus a great many investment agreements entered into between industrial States or their nationals, on the one hand, and developing countries, on the other, state, in an objective way, the standards of compensation and further provide, in case of dispute regarding the level of such compensation, the possibility of resorting to an international tribunal. . . .

Some eight months after Dupuy rendered his award on the merits, finding Libya obligated to carry out the terms of the deeds of concession, TOPCO, CAOC, and Libya reached a settlement. In return for Libyan oil valued at $152 million, delivered over the course of the next 15 months, TOPCO and CAOC terminated the arbitration proceedings.

Notes and Questions

1. Why does the SEDCO tribunal majority consider bilateral investment treaties better evidence of custom than lump-sum settlements and other indicators?

2. Do you agree with the two tribunals' assessments of customary international law? Of the significance of the pertinent General Assembly resolutions? Even if Resolution 3281 did not suffice to evidence a new rule of custom, should the lopsided vote in its favor be treated as evidence that the *opinio juris* necessary to support the prompt, adequate, and effective standard had ceased to exist as of the 1970s?

3. Is voting in the General Assembly state practice, *opinio juris*, both, or neither?

4. Note that a significant number of states abstained during the votes on the various resolutions discussed by Dupuy. What considerations might induce a state to abstain? What effect, if any, should such abstentions have on a decision maker's effort to determine whether *opinio juris* exists with respect to a given practice?

5. Notwithstanding the decisions in *Sedco* and *Topco*, controversy continued to surround the law governing compensation for expropriation of foreign investments. In a subsequent decision by the Iran-U.S. Claims Tribunal, the majority noted that

> [t]he rules of customary international law relating to the determination of the nature and amount of the compensation to be paid, as well as of the conditions of its payment . . . were, and still are, the object of heated controversies, the outcome of which is rather confused. Terms such as "prompt, adequate and effective," "full," "just," "adequate," "adequate in taking account of all pertinent circumstances," "equitable," and so on, are currently used in order to qualify the compensation due, and are construed with broadly divergent meanings.

Amoco International Finance Corporation v. Islamic Republic of Iran, 27 I.L.M. 1320 (1988).

D. The Soft Law Alternative

Treaties and custom, the two principal and traditional forms of international law recognized in the ICJ's statute, retain their preeminent position in contemporary

international law. But many issues, including the treatment of foreign direct investment, have not proven amenable to satisfactory or exclusive regulation by treaty or
custom.

In some instances, traditional forms of international legal regulation are seen as
too rigid; treaty and custom form through deliberate state action, which may be slow
to respond to the rapidly shifting needs of an increasingly interdependent world.
Moreover, treaties and custom, precisely because they are legally binding, may
sometimes preclude more flexible but technically nonbinding approaches to particular issues or problems. Further, treaties and custom are limited in that they are
(for the most part) formed by and binding upon states; while they are also applicable
to international organizations and, particularly in the area of humanitarian law, to
individuals, they were not traditionally associated with the regulation of non-state
actors and activities. But many non-state actors now play vital roles together with
states in developing international standards and regulations to apply to a whole
range of issues, and in many cases those standards and regulations apply to non-
state actors as well as to states. Finally, formal "hard law" instruments such as treaties
may trigger politically contentious or cumbersome national law procedures for
approval and ratification, which can sometimes be circumvented through the use
of technically nonbinding alternatives.

To some extent, states and international organizations have responded to the
changing international environment by including non-state actors of various kinds,
especially non-governmental interest and advocacy groups, in traditional law-
making activity. Thus, for example, human rights groups and other non-state actors
figured prominently in the recent negotiations on the creation of a permanent
International Criminal Court (ICC), even though the final vote leading to the adoption of the ICC statute was limited to states.

But even more striking, and more by evolution than by design, states have
accommodated and to some extent embraced a broad range of regulatory activity
in the international sphere that differs in important respects from traditional international law making. Such activity has yielded a wide variety of quasi-legal instruments, ranging from pronouncements of international organizations to standards
and codes of conduct promulgated by industry groups; these diverse instruments
are often referred to as "soft law." Formally, soft law instruments are not legally
binding, but as indicated below, the line between binding and nonbinding may be
both harder to draw and less significant than one might expect.

Perhaps the best known example of soft law is the Helsinki Final Act of 1975 and
its progeny. In the 1960s, the Soviet Union proposed a pan-European security
conference to negotiate a treaty that would confirm existing borders and permit
East-West economic cooperation. After preliminary discussions resolved a number
of important obstacles, the Conference on Security and Cooperation in Europe
(CSCE) opened in Helsinki in 1973 and eventually produced a document known
as the Helsinki Final Act. This document, signed by 35 heads of state and government, contained three sets (or "baskets") of principles relating to the political-
military aspects of security, economic cooperation, and human rights. These
principles were expressly understood to be legally nonbinding, but participating
states have routinely invoked them to challenge nonconforming behavior by
other participating states. When challenged, no state has attempted to evade
responsibility on the ground that the Final Act was not legally binding.

The CSCE has held many follow-up meetings to build on the Helsinki outcome
and has produced many successor instruments similar to the Helsinki Final Act. In

the early 1990s, the CSCE was converted from a "conference" to a permanent international organization with 53 member states and a confusingly similar title—the Organization on Security and Cooperation in Europe (OSCE). As the OSCE handbook notes, although the legal status of OSCE pronouncements differs significantly from treaties, the difference does not render OSCE instruments ineffective:

> Most [OSCE] instruments, decisions and commitments are framed in legal language and their interpretation requires an understanding of the principles of international law and of the standard techniques of the law of treaties. Furthermore, the fact that OSCE commitments are not legally binding does not detract from their efficacy. Having been signed at the highest political level, they have an authority that is arguably as strong as any legal statute under international law.

OSCE instruments reflect just one of the many forms in which soft law now appears. General Assembly resolutions, examined in Section C above, and similar pronouncements by other international bodies can also serve as soft law. Other forms of soft law may include administrative decisions by agencies of international organizations, joint communiques and other instruments expressing shared political commitments of particular states, "gentlemen's agreements" on the composition of international bodies and tribunals, codes of conduct such as those proposed by the apparel industry to regulate working conditions in foreign-owned garment factories, interpretive statements regarding treaties and other international instruments, programs of action for multilateral conferences, guidelines and reports prepared by expert groups, and countless others.

Many of these soft-law instruments are controversial with respect to their legal status, their impact, and their legitimacy. For some international lawyers, soft-law instruments, because they are not legally binding, are by definition not law. The multiplicity of these instruments, their often vague and general terms, and the doubtful law-making authority of some of the actors who participate in their creation render their normative status variable and elusive. Insofar as they conflict with each other, they may simply create confusion; insofar as they diverge significantly from existing customary and treaty norms, they may undermine those norms without establishing new norms to replace them. Soft-law instruments may sometimes relieve states of the burden of creating "hard law" but in the process may also sacrifice some of the benefits, which may include the enhanced status, clarity, and pressures for compliance associated with treaties in particular.

At the same time, it is easy to overstate the differences between hard and soft law. Indeed, it may be questioned whether any meaningful line can be drawn to separate them. Treaties often contain vague language, and many treaties are not subject to any meaningful enforcement mechanism. Conversely, soft law instruments often contain precise language with strong incentives and in some cases institutional mechanisms for compliance. Some scholars, such as Professors Michael Reisman and Kenneth Abbott, argue that all forms of law making exhibit three characteristics that vary, making the binding character of every law-making instrument a matter of degree. First, instruments vary in terms of their *precision*. Some obligations are clear; others confer substantial discretion on those who are to implement the obligations. Second, legal instruments differ in the extent to which they are viewed as *authoritative*. The more those to whom the instruments are addressed view the instruments as products of a legitimate process and reflective of their own views of appropriate conduct, the more they are likely to see the instruments as binding. Third, law-making instruments vary in the degree to which they are likely to be the subject of effective *enforcement* mechanisms. Thus, "[d]etermining the softness or hardness of an instrument with respect to these criteria demands an examination of the form, subject matter, and content of a document, as well as the intention of the parties." Steven Ratner, *Does International Law Matter in Preventing Ethnic Conflict?*, 32 N.Y.U. J. Intl. L. & Pol. 591, 613 (2000).

To complicate matters, treaties and soft-law instruments often complement each other, and both may be used by the same actors dealing with the same subject matter. In some cases, treaties and state practice give rise to soft law that supplements and advances treaty and customary norms; in other cases, soft-law instruments are consciously used to generate support for the promulgation of treaties or to help generate customary international law norms.

In the following excerpt, Professor Christine Chinkin elaborates further on the ambiguous status of soft law.

Christine Chinkin, *Normative Development in the International Legal System*

Commitment and Compliance: The Role of Non-Binding Norms in the International Legal System 21, 23-25 (Dinah Shelton ed., 2000)

A range of opinion exists on the theoretical and practical desirability of soft law. Some authors have long rejected formal distinctions between international law and policy; others acknowledge that the contemporary international law-making process is complex and deeply layered, that there is a "brave new world of international law" where "transnational actors, sources of law, allocation of decision function and modes of regulation have all mutated into fascinating hybrid forms. International law now comprises a complex blend of customary, positive, declarative and soft law." From this perspective, drawing a formal distinction between hard and soft obligations is less important than understanding the processes at work within the law-making environment and the products that flow from it.

In an impassioned backlash to the perceived blurring of the binary (positivist) division between law and non-law, other theorists reject outright the notion of law-making through non-binding instruments. The idea of different categories of law is seen to weaken the objectives of stability and certainty, creating a "gliding binding-ness" and even undermining the international rule of law. They uphold the exclusive criteria of formal legal validity listed in Article 38(1) of the Statute of the ICJ . . . strongly reiterating that they are not "some esoteric invention but rather they provide criteria by which the actual expectations and commitments of States can be tested." Klabbers [one of the critics of soft law as a distinct category of international law] argues for the redundancy concept of soft law, asserting that to denote an instrument as "soft law" is to impute legal character to it, albeit of a different nature (or degree) than that of hard law. This necessarily raises difficult questions about further legal consequences, such as whether violation of a principle of soft law amounts to an internationally wrongful act and thus incurs responsibility that can be imputed to the state, or whether it has some other "softer" consequence? Klabbers asserts that:

> . . . [I]f it could be claimed that soft law leads, in its application, to either hard law (hard responsibility, hard sanctions) or to non-law (no responsibility and no sanctions), soft law loses its distinctiveness, and therewith its reason of existence.

. . . [Klabbers considers that]

Our binary law is well capable of handling all kinds of subtleties and sensitivities; within the binary mode, law can be more or less specific, more or less exact, more or less determinate, more or less serious, more or less far-reaching; the only thing it cannot be is more or less binding.

. . . The concept of international soft law thus remains controversial. On an overtly political level, acceptance of normative standards articulated through soft forms of law-making entails recognition that the rigid control of states over that process is weakening. Yet public international law is not alone in seeking a variety of techniques and devices for changing, predicting, and monitoring behavior. Social systems utilize both binding principles and substrata of non-binding principles that are not and need not be incorporated within formal law-making processes, but still create normative standards and expectations of appropriate behavior. Indeed the priority accorded to law and legal sanction by western societies is not universal; other cultures readily employ non-legal forms of social control. Domestic legal systems avail themselves of diverse means of regulating conduct. Some are widely applicable, others appertain to societal sub-groups, often in forms of self-regulation, for example through codes of conduct of professional associations. Similar distinctions are inherent in European Community law-making. That international law has progressed in a similar fashion may be a sign of a maturing system breaking free of the limitations of exclusive law-making through treaty and custom and recognizing a decline of the consensual system.

In Section I of this chapter, Professor Lipson outlined some of the reasons states might prefer treaties to less formal agreements. In the following excerpt, Professor Dinah Shelton suggests some of the reasons why actors may prefer soft law over treaties or other forms of hard law.

Dinah Shelton, *Law, Non-Law and the Problem of "Soft Law"*

Commitment and Compliance: The Role of Non-Binding Norms in the International Legal System 1, 12-13 (Dinah Shelton ed., 2000)

(1) Bureaucratization of international institutions has led to law that is "deformalized" through programs of action and other policy instruments . . . . Technical details, need for flexibility, and rapid response necessitate permanent institutions with the competence and mandate to initiate norm-creation, monitor and assist performance, and secure compliance. Where institutions can assess performance, hard law may not be necessary because state behavior is likely to change in response to the assessments. Moreover, international institutions generally lack the power to adopt binding instruments and can only have recourse to soft law.

(2) The choice of non-binding norms and instruments may reflect respect for hard law, which states and other actors view cautiously. They may use the soft law form when there are concerns about the possibility of non-compliance, either because of domestic political opposition, lack of ability or capacity to comply, uncertainty about whether compliance can be measured, or disagreement with aspects of the proposed norm. . . .

(3) Soft law instruments may be intended to induce states to participate or to pressure non-consenting states to conform. Some environmental treaties . . . have sought to influence the behavior of non-parties, but, in general, treaty rules preclude binding non-consenting states. . . .

(7) Soft law generally can be adopted more rapidly because it is non-binding. It can also be quickly amended or replaced if it fails to meet current challenges. Its flexibility extends to implementation and compliance where the dynamic interaction of the various actors can play a crucial role. It may be that an increased number of negotiating states makes it more likely that there will be few hard law agreements in the global setting. If this is the case, we would expect to see more soft law on the global than the regional level, and that appears to be the case.

Notes and Questions

1. In what sense can an instrument that is not legally binding qualify as a form of law? Is the very concept of "soft law" a contradiction in terms? Are there any legal consequences to the failure to comply with the terms of a soft law instrument? Does it depend on the specific instrument?

2. Do you agree with critics who argue that blurring the distinction between law and nonlaw through the proliferation of quasi-legal instruments undermines efforts to use law to promote stability and certainty in international relations, and possibly undermines the rule of law itself? What countervailing benefits does soft law offer?

3. Would you expect soft law to be more common in certain issue areas than others? Or is the use of soft law a function of the level of consensus that states share on a particular issue? Or might it depend on the "structure" of the problem states face? Game theory, a form of rational choice analysis that is frequently applied to international relations, suggests that states often encounter both "coordination" and "collaboration" problems. In coordination problems—such as the language airline pilots and air traffic controllers should use in international flights—it is often difficult to reach an agreement. But once an agreement has been reached there are few incentives not to follow the rule. In collaboration problems—such as arms control—there are benefits from following agreed rules, but often potentially greater benefits from noncompliance. Does this suggest a way of understanding when states are more likely to use soft law, and the conditions under which soft law will be as effective as other forms of international law?

4. Are developed and developing countries likely to have different attitudes toward soft law? Consider the following excerpt, written in 1988:

> The rapid growth of soft law and complaints about it are, in large part, a concern of the developed countries. Part of it has to do with the deep dissatisfaction that we [in developed countries] feel at the shift of power within formal lawmaking arenas, in which we are a numerical minority. We discover that many of these fora make law we do not like. This law, we insist derisively, is soft. This may be a valid complaint, but those who are making this soft law also have a valid complaint. From their perspective, customary law, which we would consider very hard, is in fact law that is created primarily because of the great power that we in the industrial world exercise over others. There are really two sides to the controversy over soft law. It is important, when we criticize it, to appreciate that there are others on the other side of the mirror who are looking at it quite differently.

A Hard Look at Soft Law, Remarks by W. Michael Reisman, 82 Proc. Am. Socy. Intl. L. 373, 377 (1988).

E. The World Bank Guidelines on the Treatment of Foreign Direct Investment

The following materials continue the story of international efforts to regulate foreign direct investment and illustrate the ways in which soft law has interacted with both treaties and custom, and in the process contributed to the evolution of legal norms in that area. As you read these materials, consider the role played by each form of international law in dealing with the disputes at issue, the reasons why a particular form seemed appropriate at a particular time, and the interests of the actors involved in emphasizing one form of law over another.

In the late 1970s, the United Nations initiated a series of efforts to generate an international consensus on the treatment of foreign direct investment. But the divergence in views between the capital importing and capital exporting countries was then too large to surmount. In 1985, the World Bank considered the possibility of incorporating standards for the treatment of foreign investors into its draft convention for the creation of the Multilateral Investment Guarantee Agency, but again the subject proved too controversial to articulate detailed and meaningful standards.

In 1991, the World Bank decided to try again. The first issue to decide was whether to pursue a convention or a set of nonbinding guidelines. Ibrahim Shihata, Vice President and General Counsel of the Bank and head of the relevant Working Group, describes the options and the Bank's approach.

Ibrahim Shihata, *The Legal Treatment of Foreign Investment*
40-43, 63-64, 55, 88-90, 110-112 (1993)

The difference between the two approaches is clear. A convention requires elaborate negotiations and must be signed and ratified before it enters into force in respect of a given country. While it is legally binding, it can only reflect the common denominator, that is what is acceptable to the potential contracting parties. Recommendations or guidelines issued by the World Bank could not have this binding effect since they would not be subject to the same process involved in the preparation of a draft convention and would not be ratified. However, they would not necessarily represent the lowest common denominator.

The proposed work plan envisaged, as a first step, a survey of all existing instruments dealing with foreign investments including bilateral investment treaties, multilateral conventions and other multilateral instruments (such as declarations, resolutions and draft conventions), international arbitral awards, writings of international law writers, and national investment codes. Such a survey was needed for two basic reasons. First, it was hoped originally that certain general trends could be drawn out from the survey, which could be used as the basis for guidelines to be developed by the Working Group. While some additions representing the progressive development of these general trends were always envisaged, the product was intended to be perceived as based largely on international practice and not simply representing the preferences of its authors or the institutions they work for. Second, the survey would provide valuable evidence of what member states have already accepted, either unilaterally in their national laws, bilaterally with another state, or on a multilateral level, and this knowledge could facilitate the working group's subsequent efforts in persuading members to accept the guidelines. . . .

The approach which was proposed in the work plan, which is akin to the so-called "soft law" approach, has become widespread in the international law-making process. . . .

As is well known, the concept of soft law is generally used to refer to non-binding, declaratory common rules of conduct. "Their recognized practical advantage is that since they are not subject to national ratification, they can take instant effect." While clearly not legally binding, soft law may harden into legally binding rules through a variety of processes which indicate general compliance by states. These include simultaneous or successive behavior by individual states, or the cross-referencing and repetition of soft law concepts in various bilateral and multilateral instruments. . . . In the actual practice of states, some instruments which started as non-binding declarations, such as the United Nations General Assembly's 1948 resolution incorporating the Universal Declaration of Human Rights, are now considered by many international law writers not only as legally binding but as *jus cogens*, that is peremptory law that cannot be derogated from by the mutual agreement of states.

The process described in my memorandum to the Bank's President did not involve the preparation of a draft convention which would codify existing law and represent the lowest common denominator acceptable to the totality of the Bank's almost universal membership. Rather, the intention was to produce a set of rules which would be based generally on existing trends in international law but would attempt to develop progressively the content of such law in order to serve the purpose of promoting FDI. This purpose, it was thought, would be better served if part descriptive, part normative principles were developed, which, given their preparation by international organizations of near universal membership and the broad consultations we intended to undertake, could receive broad acceptance in practice. If the consistent practice of states so indicated, such guidelines could evolve over time into generally accepted practice and might acquire a legally binding nature with the possible evolution of the required *opinio juris*. Alternatively, they could pave the way for the preparation of a universal convention on the subject. . . .

[With respect to the content of the guidelines, Shihata outlined the Bank's aims:]

If the guidelines were to be useful, they would need to go beyond the mere restatement of generalities. This was particularly important in disputed areas such as state obligations regarding compensation for expropriated property and transfer of funds. For instance, it was felt that a guideline which referred to "fair" or "appropriate" or even "prompt, adequate and effective" compensation, without detailing the manner in which such compensation would be determined, could not be of much practical value. Also, one of the principal aims of the Working Group was to go beyond a mere restatement of the minimum accepted principles of international law. When dealing with the issue of expropriation and compensation, most legal instruments refer to "fair treatment" or "market value." In drafting the guidelines, it was important that the Working Group go beyond this conclusion to the actual meaning that should be given to these words, drawing upon the substance of the background studies, for instance by examining more closely how arbitral awards have defined these terms in actual cases and what comments international law writers in different countries have made on such awards. . . .

. . . The studies of the various multilateral instruments showed that the most vocal objections to earlier attempts at codification were voiced by developing countries. Not only did they see in this exercise an attempt to impose on them rules which reflected what they perceived to be the interests of foreign investors and their home states; some of them probably felt that their own interests would be better served in this particular area if no hard and fast rules representing a binding law were in place. It was therefore important, in drafting the guidelines, to do so in a manner that would lessen rather than aggravate the concerns of developing countries. A sensitive approach to the position of developing countries would stress the relevance of the guidelines to the promotion of FDI in these countries and the developmental importance of FDI in the current climate of reduced commercial loans to developing countries. Moreover, if the text of the guidelines was to receive general approval, it was important that it would not be perceived to deviate significantly from existing generally accepted standards of international law. . . . [I]f the guidelines were to receive the wide acceptance needed for them to be issued at all, they should be related to principles which could be demonstrated to have a strong basis in state practice, not to principles favored by a small group of countries, be they developed or developing. Yet, for the exercise to serve the purpose defined by the [Bank's] Development Committee, "so as to promote FDI," the guidelines clearly had to go beyond what was commonly reflected in state practice. The task was not simple.

[Shortly after the surveys of state practice were completed, the Working Group drew on them to complete a first draft of its proposed guidelines. As in the past, the most controversial issue related to the amount of compensation to be paid following expropriation of a foreign national's investment. Shihata summarizes the approach adopted in the Bank's draft guidelines:]

More than any of the other four draft guidelines, the intent of the Working Group with respect to the issue of compensation for expropriation was to provide practical details which could be used by host states in determining whether to resort to expropriation and what compensation to pay in such cases. By making these details known in advance as acceptable international standards, it was hoped that disputes over this matter could be avoided or, that if disputes arose, they would be more amenable to amicable settlement. . . .

In keeping with the provisions found in most bilateral investment treaties, relevant multilateral instruments and many national investment codes . . . section 1 of draft guideline IV permitted states to expropriate in full or partially, or to take measures which have an equivalent effect on foreign investment, only if such expropriation was effected in accordance with a number of conditions. These included that the taking of property had to take place (1) under applicable legal procedures, (2) in good faith pursuit of the public interest, (3) in a nondiscriminatory manner, and (4) against payment of appropriate compensation. . . .

As mentioned above, the principal controversy focused on the standard to be used in assessing the amount of compensation due. The use of the compromise term "appropriate" does not necessarily conflict with the better-known formula of "prompt, adequate and effective." The latter term is preferred by governments of developed countries and many western international law writings, and is also used in many bilateral investment treaties. The approach adopted in the draft guideline set the general standard of compensation as "appropriate," but immediately defined this term in the following section of the guideline, by stating that compensation which was adequate, effective and paid without undue delay would be deemed generally to be appropriate. This approach tried to accommodate the seemingly conflicting views on this matter and accepted the Hull formula as a general standard, thereby encouraging its use without requiring it in all circumstances.

[After completing its initial draft guidelines, the Working Group circulated them to numerous governments and a variety of business groups for comment. The United States and some of the business groups were sharply critical of a number of the draft guidelines and, in particular, draft guideline IV, relating to expropriation. Shihata describes the U.S. reaction:]

[The U.S.] argued that the standard of compensation should be the Hull formula, in other words, that the compensation should be "prompt, adequate and effective," without any qualification, as opposed to the standard adopted in the guidelines which was that compensation should be "appropriate." In fact, the draft guidelines, as explained earlier, clearly provided that compensation would generally be deemed to be appropriate if it was adequate, effective and paid without undue delay. But the U.S. wanted the deletion of all the qualifications in the draft allowing for exceptional deviations from the Hull doctrine, such as where the host country faced foreign exchange stringencies or in the case of large scale, non-discriminatory nationalizations taken in the context of broad social reforms or in other exceptional cases of war and the like (draft guideline IV, sections 8 and 10). . . .

Following the informal meeting of the [Bank's] Executive Directors, the U.S. Executive Director arranged for a meeting between the members of the Working Group and a high level U.S. delegation to discuss the substance of the U.S. comments. In this meeting it became clear that the U.S. was objecting to the idea of preparing any guidelines that would provide standards less favorable to investors than those provided for in the most recent bilateral investment treaties concluded by the U.S. At that time, the U.S. was heavily involved in negotiating such bilateral treaties with the Russian Federation and a number of other former Soviet Republics and was also involved with Canada and Mexico in the completion of the North American Free Trade Agreement (NAFTA). In the judgement of the Working Group, a set of guidelines addressing the world community and submitted for issuance by a world forum could not be identical to the bilateral investment treaties concluded by a few countries which, to a large extent, follow the lines of a standard text prepared by one party. In fact, the number of U.S. bilateral investment treaties was small compared to the number of treaties concluded by other major industrial countries which should also be taken into account, along with other sources. . . .

More generally, the U.S. delegation indicated that the proposed guidelines represented, in their view, the lowest common denominator. . . . The Working Group responded to this comment by stating that the guidelines, far from representing the lowest common denominator, were in fact based on a combination of existing principles and commendable practices identified with a view to their usefulness and acceptability. In many respects, the draft guidelines constituted a progressive development of customary international law and presented a set of liberal recommendations on the subject compared to the practice of many countries, including developed countries. They could not, however, ignore general trends in state practice without risking becoming an academic exercise with little practical value from a legal viewpoint.

Other developed countries had a variety of criticisms but were generally more positive than the United States. Developing countries provided relatively little input.

The Working Group revised the guidelines on the basis of comments received, with some last-minute changes to accommodate some proposed amendments offered by the United States. The revised version, excerpted below, was unanimously endorsed by the Bank's Development Committee and published in 1992.

Guidelines on the Treatment of Foreign Direct Investment

31 I.L.M. 1379 (1992)

The Development Committee
   Recognizing
   that a greater flow of foreign direct investment brings substantial benefits to bear on the world economy and on the economies of developing countries in particular, . . .
   [t]hat these guidelines are not ultimate standards but an important step in the evolution of generally acceptable international standards which complement, but do not substitute for, bilateral investment treaties,
   therefore *calls the attention* of member countries to the following Guidelines as useful parameters in the admission and treatment of private foreign investment in their territories, without prejudice to the binding rules of international law at this stage of its development. . . .

IV EXPROPRIATION AND UNILATERAL ALTERATIONS OR TERMINATION OF CONTRACTS

   1. A State may not expropriate or otherwise take in whole or in part a foreign private investment in its territory, or take measures which have similar effects, except where this is done in accordance with applicable legal procedures, in pursuance in good faith of a public purpose, without discrimination on the basis of nationality and against the payment of appropriate compensation.
   2. Compensation for a specific investment taken by the State will, according to the details provided below, be deemed "appropriate" if it is adequate, effective and prompt.
   3. Compensation will be deemed "adequate" if it is based on the fair market value of the taken asset as such value is determined immediately before the time at which the taking occurred or the decision to take the asset became publicly known.
   4. Determination of the "fair market value" will be acceptable if conducted according to a method agreed by the State and the foreign investor (hereinafter referred to as the parties) or by a tribunal or another body designated by the parties.
   5. In the absence of a determination agreed by, or based on the agreement of, the parties, the fair market value will be acceptable if determined by the State according to reasonable criteria related to the market value of the investment, i.e., in an amount that a willing buyer would normally pay to a willing seller after taking into account the nature of the investment, the circumstances in which it would operate in the future and its specific characteristics. . . .
   6. Without implying the exclusive validity of a single standard for the fairness by which compensation is to be determined and as an illustration of the reasonable

determination by a State of the market value of the investment under Section 5 above, such determination will be deemed reasonable if conducted as follows:

(i) for a going concern with a proven record of profitability, on the basis of the discounted cash flow value;

(ii) for an enterprise which, not being a proven going concern, demonstrates lack of profitability, on the basis of the liquidation value;

(iii) for other assets, on the basis of (a) the replacement value or (b) the book value in case such value has been recently assessed or has been determined as of the date of the taking and can therefore be deemed to represent a reasonable replacement value. . . .

7. Compensation will be deemed "effective" if it is paid in the currency brought in by the investor where it remains convertible, in another currency designated as freely usable by the International Monetary Fund or in any other currency accepted by the investor.

8. Compensation will be deemed to be "prompt" in normal circumstances if it is paid without delay. In cases where the State faces exceptional circumstances, as reflected in an arrangement for the use of the resources of the International Monetary Fund or under similar objective circumstances of established foreign exchange stringencies, compensation . . . may be paid in installments within a period which will be as short as possible and which will not in any case exceed five years from the time of the taking, provided that reasonable, market-related interest applies to the deferred payments in the same currency. . . .

10. In case of comprehensive non-discriminatory nationalizations effected in the process of large scale social reforms under exceptional circumstances of revolution, war and similar exigencies, the compensation may be determined through negotiations between the host State and the investors' home State and failing this, through international arbitration. . . .

The World Bank Guidelines have had a mixed reception. On the one hand, the Guidelines have contributed to an evolving consensus in favor of strengthened protections for investors. They have influenced national legislation and bilateral treaties relating to the treatment of foreign direct investment, and have been cited in arbitration decisions.

On the other hand, the Guidelines have been partly superseded by the same forces that helped create the conditions making the Guidelines possible. The types of nationalizations and expropriations that fueled debate over the customary international law obligations governing foreign direct investment peaked in the 1970s, declined sharply in the 1980s, and have now largely disappeared. With the collapse of socialism as a possible economic alternative to capitalism, developing countries throughout the world increasingly find themselves in competition with each other to attract foreign direct investment. Accepting treaty conditions favorable to investors is one way to compete. Accordingly, despite U.S. fears that the World Bank Guidelines might impede the negotiation of bilateral investment treaties, such treaties have proliferated. As of 2004, there were over 2,000 BITs in place. Most developing countries, and virtually all developed states, continue to enter into new BITs. Where such treaties are in force, they take precedence over the Bank Guidelines.

Notwithstanding the proliferation of BITs, many states, including the United States, continued to favor the promulgation of a comprehensive, multilateral treaty governing foreign direct investment. Supporters sought a uniform set of rules to govern foreign investment comparable to the rules on trade associated with the World Trade Organization. In particular, supporters hoped for liberal rules on admission of investments, treatment for all foreign investors equivalent to that given to nationals or most favored nations, whichever was more favorable, strong legal protections in cases of expropriations, including the prompt, adequate, and effective standard for compensation, and effective dispute settlement procedures.

The OECD began to draft such an agreement, the proposed MAI, in 1995, building on existing BITs, the World Bank Guidelines, NAFTA, and various other multilateral agreements with investment provisions. Initially, it appeared that the MAI was headed for rapid completion and broad acceptance. But the MAI soon ran into major obstacles. The United States insisted on investor protections comparable to those in the typical U.S. BIT; other states feared that developing countries would not accept investor protections stronger than those contained in most European BITs, which are generally less favorable to investors than U.S. BITs. Participants in the negotiations disagreed on the nature and extent of possible exceptions to the general principles of the treaty, including exceptions for public order, culture, and regional economic integration organizations. Perhaps most important, MAI supporters encountered unexpectedly strong opposition from environmental and labor groups, who feared the new treaty would impair national efforts at strengthening environmental and labor standards. As a result, the effort to create the MAI has largely ground to a halt. Similar efforts to create a comprehensive set of investment rules in the WTO and elsewhere have met with only limited success.

Notes and Questions

1. What role should the World Bank Guidelines play in a dispute over the compensation to be paid to a foreign investor for the expropriation of the investor's property, assuming no BIT or other treaty is directly on point?

2. Did the World Bank Guidelines fulfill the role envisioned for them by their drafters? How should one judge the effectiveness of soft-law instruments? What are the advantages and disadvantages of such instruments in comparison to treaties or custom?

3. How would a decision maker know whether the World Bank Guidelines are becoming or have become hard law in the sense of conferring legally binding rights on investors? If the guidelines are becoming hard law, might one expect the Guidelines to be invoked in international arbitrations? In other fora?

4. Recall the discussion at the beginning of this section on the ways in which different legal instruments may be hard or soft on various criteria. How hard or soft are the World Bank Guidelines? Note that the Guidelines are not legally binding, but they do help to clarify the meaning of "appropriate compensation," a previously vague concept in customary international law. What are the implications of failure to comply with soft-law instruments such as the Guidelines?

5. Do the World Bank Guidelines favor the interests of a particular group of states? Which states could be expected to press for a more comprehensive and binding instrument, such as the MAI?

6. As Shihata points out, BITs generally "follow the lines of a standard text prepared by one party." The United States essentially follows a "take it or leave it" policy with regard to its BITs. Why might developing countries accept agreements tendered to them without opportunity for meaningful negotiation?

F. Note on Incorporating Principles from Domestic Law

Article 38 of the Statute of the International Court of Justice identifies "general principles of law recognized by civilized nations" as a source of law separate from (and therefore implicitly independent of) treaties and custom. As a source of law, general principles are the subject of considerable debate, with respect to both their content and their jurisprudential underpinnings. Some positivist scholars maintain that general principles can be treated as binding only when states manifest their consent through widespread recognition of such principles as international law. Other scholars suggest general principles can be derived in part from natural law, without reference to state consent. Most scholars, however, regard general principles as those principles so basic to developed legal orders that they arise in most national legal systems and can therefore be ascertained through an objective, comparative assessment of municipal law in the relevant states.

In practice, courts and other tribunals rely on general principles largely as an adjunct to treaties and custom, to be invoked sporadically and only as necessary to supplement or extend those other forms of law or to fill gaps created when treaty and custom fail to supply all of the relevant rules for decision of a particular dispute. Principles invoked are usually very general rules of procedure, evidence, or liability. For example, the Permanent Court of International Justice announced in the *Chorzow Factory* case that "it is a general conception of law that every violation of an engagement involves an obligation to make reparation." *Chorzow Factory* (Ger. v. Pol.), 1928 P.C.I.J. (Ser. A., No. 17) at 29. Other tribunals have relied on general principles for such basic precepts of law as *res judicata*, estoppel, that "a party cannot take advantage of his own wrong," that no one shall judge his or her own case, that the passage of time may bar a claim through prescription or laches, and that circumstantial evidence may be probative. Similarly, general principles have been accepted as sources for rules viewed as intrinsic to the logical function of a legal system, such as the rule that a law later in time takes precedence over an earlier law if both are from the same source.

PART II

Participants in the International Legal Process

Treaties, custom, soft law, and other outcomes of the international law-making process result from the interaction of diverse participants, each making claims about the lawfulness of its own conduct or that of another actor. Identifying these participants more explicitly and understanding the roles they play in the international legal process is essential and is the goal of the following two chapters. Chapter 3 addresses states and organizations of states, entities that orthodox international law regards as the principal, if not sole, relevant actors. Chapter 4 examines entities other than states that contemporary international law treats as key participants, namely non-governmental organizations (NGOs), corporations, and substate entities—both states of the United States and various territories with autonomy in their international relations.

Both particip*ants* and particip*ation* come in a variety of forms. The actors themselves may be territorially organized, as are states, subfederal entities (such as U.S. states), or autonomous units within states (such as Hong Kong). Indeed, the notion that states possess unique authority and control over territory has served as the foundation for their predominant—though far from exclusive—role in international law. International organizations start as an agent of the states that create them (usually via treaty), but can come to take on an identity separate from their members, as their organs or officials implement the organization's goals. Still, other key participants lack such a nexus to territory. NGOs are principally entities based on shared agendas, comprised of like-minded individuals within one or more states. Business entities are organized for an economic goal. And all these actors are, in a sense, the result of decisions by individuals to combine their talents in different spheres and for various purposes.

Why pursue international law's treatment of these participants as a discrete subject of inquiry rather than merely the substantive norms they eventually agree upon? First, the norms resulting from law making very much reflect who is involved in that law making. It is thus critical to understand what access to law-making arenas the international legal process provides. Second, international legal norms themselves address the question of participation. That is, international law has rules as to which entities are entitled to take part in different stages of the legal process. Third, to comprehend the meaning of international norms (or any norms for that matter) requires examining who exactly has rights

107

and duties. International law has recognized many rights and duties for states, but fewer for non-state actors. Finally, the implementation of norms depends very much upon different roles played by various actors. Thus, international organizations and NGOs will have significant roles in securing compliance with international law.

THE STATE AND BEYOND

The very term "law of nations" captured the idea that international law was for much of its history a law by and about states. As Stephen Krasner explains, a community that has achieved statehood (as opposed to the other ways in which actors might participate) has a special place in international law and relations. It possesses a bundle of attributes he calls (in a term that might make international lawyers cringe a bit) "international legal sovereignty":

Stephen D. Krasner, *Sovereignty: Organized Hypocrisy*
14-20 (1999)

. . . [I]nternational legal sovereignty has been concerned with establishing the status of a political entity in the international system. Is a state recognized by other states? Is it accepted as a juridical equal? Are its representatives entitled to diplomatic immunity? Can it be a member of international organizations? Can its representatives enter into agreements with other entities? . . .

Almost all rulers have sought international legal sovereignty, the recognition of other states, because it provides them with both material and normative resources. Sovereignty can be conceived of as "a ticket of general admission to the international arena." All recognized states have juridical equality. International law is based on the consent of states. Recognized states can enter into treaties with each other, and these treaties will generally be operative even if the government changes. Dependent or subordinate territories do not generally have the right to conclude international agreements (although, as with everything else in the international system, there are exceptions), giving the central or recognized authority a monopoly over formal arrangements with other states. . . .

By facilitating accords, international legal sovereignty offers the possibility for rulers to secure external resources that can enhance their ability to stay in power and to promote the security, economic, and ideational interests of their constituents. The rulers of internationally recognized states can sit at the table. Entering into certain kinds of contracts, such as alliances, can enhance security by reducing uncertainty about the commitment of other actors. Membership in international financial institutions opens the possibility, although not the assurance, of securing foreign capital. Even if rulers have entered into accords that have far-reaching effects on their domestic autonomy, such as the European Union, they have nothing to lose by retaining their international legal sovereignty, including their formal right to withdraw from any international agreements. . . .

. . . The attractiveness of international legal sovereignty can also be understood from a more sociological or cognitive perspective. Recognition as a state is a widely, almost universally understood construct in the contemporary world. . . . Recognition gives the ruler the opportunity to play on the international stage; even if it is only a bit part, parading at the United Nations or shaking hands with the president of the United States or the chancellor of Germany, can enhance the standing of a ruler among his or her own followers. . . .

In light of this special role for states, Chapter 3 seeks to elaborate how international law has regulated the creation, transformation, and institutionalized cooperation of states.

Notwithstanding the many advantages of statehood on the global plane, individuals and groups seeking a place in making and applying international law have never assumed that only the state should possess rights (substantive or participatory) or duties. As discussed in Chapter 1, other organized entities have long played a role in international affairs. Although states have resisted recognizing these other entities as bona fide international actors and have preferred to see them as creatures of a particular state, these entities have continued to pursue their own interests independently. They have appraised the behavior of other actors and responded to attempts by those actors to judge their actions. This participation began long ago but accelerated in the second half of the twentieth century. Jessica Matthews has written:

Jessica Matthews, *Power Shift*

For. Aff. 50, 50-51 (Jan./Feb. 1997)

The end of the Cold War has brought no mere adjustment among states but a novel redistribution of power among states, markets, and civil society. National governments are not simply losing autonomy in a globalizing economy. They are sharing powers . . . with businesses, with international organizations, and with a multitude of citizens groups, known as nongovernmental organizations (NGOs). . . .

The absolutes of the Westphalian system—territorially fixed states where everything of value lies within some states' borders; a single, secular authority governing each territory and representing it outside its borders; and no authority above states—are all dissolving. Increasingly, resources and threats that matter, including money, information, pollution, and popular culture, circulate and shape lives and economies with little regard for political boundaries. . . . Even the most powerful states find the marketplace and international public opinion compelling them more often to follow a particular course. . . .

The most powerful engine of change in the relative decline of states and the rise of nonstate actors is the computer and telecommunications revolution. . . . Widely accessible and affordable technology has broken governments' monopoly on the collection and management of large amounts of information and deprived governments of the deference they enjoyed because of it. In every sphere of activity, instantaneous access to information and the ability to put it to use multiplies the number of players who matter and reduces the number who command great authority. . . .

In a similar vein, the political scientist Susan Strange has found corporations and market forces so powerful and impervious to government control as to speak of the "retreat of the state," and Peter Spiro has questioned whether non-governmental organizations constitute a new form of "global potentates."

Formal doctrine has nonetheless been slow to accept this reality, but the trend toward increased participation by these non-state actors seems irreversible. Chapter 4 thus examines how these actors have managed to achieve an independent voice on the international stage. In particular, it focuses upon the tensions between the strategies these actors undertake and the paradigm that grants certain roles only to states. The result is, if not a full-fledged "retreat" of the state, an undeniable challenge to its hitherto dominant role in international law.

3

The Traditional Actors: States and International Organizations

The organization of human communities into states remains a principal fact of political life in the international arena. States have been the dominant unit in international relations since at least the Peace of Westphalia in 1648, and much legal regulation of international relations still centers on the resolution of claims by states. Orthodox international law doctrine has regarded states as the primary, or even sole, actors in international law—the only entities that scholars considered to enjoy full "international legal personality," meaning that they could create and be the direct subject of international legal obligations. This view has meshed with the dominant view of international relations theory as well as diplomacy—realism—that regards states as the critical actors in, and state interests as the paramount determinants of, international relations.

In this chapter, we seek to gain an understanding of the state as a participant in the legal process. The chapter begins by analyzing how states are formed and whether international norms have emerged to regulate or constrain that process. We then turn to the process by which states change, whether through disintegration, secession, or other means. Third, we turn to the institutions within states that have legal authority and control—namely, governments—and consider the extent to which international law concerns itself with such internal matters. Finally, this chapter considers the formation of international institutions composed of states and how such organizations can become independent players in the inter-state system. As we examine these norms of participation, the basic assumption that states are the primary actors in international law and international relations itself becomes the subject of scrutiny.

I. THE FORMATION PROCESS: NEW STATES FROM THE FORMER YUGOSLAVIA

To those whose focus of attention does not extend past the United States and Western Europe, the world may seem like a system of old and stable states. But much of the contemporary state system is very recent. Much of Africa, Asia, and even

Eastern Europe is composed of relatively new, and in some cases unstable, states as a result of decolonization and the upheavals since 1990 in southeastern Europe and the former Soviet Union. The recent vintage and potential evanescence of the contemporary makeup of states means that legal issues constantly arise regarding the formation of states. The extent to which law actually controls or affects decision makers involved in the process of state formation—whether those within a putative state or those outside it deciding how to react to it—remains a central concern in the international legal process.

For at least the last 50 years, states have emerged on the global stage through the following processes:

1. Decolonization: This refers to the process by which states became independent from self-identified colonial empires, principally those of the United Kingdom and France, but also those of Spain and Portugal (principally in Latin America), Belgium, the Netherlands, Germany, the Ottoman Empire, and, to some extent, the United States. Independence might have resulted from the peaceful transfer of power (as with much of the British Empire) or wars of independence (as with French Indochina). Decolonization is virtually complete today in that nearly all colonial territories seeking independence from their metropolitan power have attained it. The United Nations has taken an active role in promoting and supervising decolonization.

2. Secession: With secession, one territory breaks off from a nonimperial state to form a new state, either peacefully or as a result of armed conflict. Since World War II, successful secession has been rare, but not nonexistent. Bangladesh (East Pakistan) seceded from Pakistan (though its inhabitants formed the majority of Pakistan's population) after a short but bloody war in 1971; and Eritrea seceded from Ethiopia in 1993 after a conflict lasting more than 30 years. The departure of the three Baltic states—Estonia, Latvia, and Lithuania—from the Soviet Union in 1990 may also be seen as a secession, although all three were, in fact, independent states from the end of World War I until their forced annexation by the Soviet Union in 1940, and the Soviet Union was in the process of dissolution at the time of their separation.

3. Dissolution: Dissolution is the process by which a state dissolves into two or more states, with the former state ceasing to exist. The most significant dissolutions in recent years have been those of Yugoslavia, the USSR, and Czechoslovakia, although other states (for instance, Somalia) may also be in the midst of such processes as well.

4. Merger: This is the creation of one state by the union of two states. The merger of North and South Yemen in 1990 and the merger of the Federal Republic of Germany and the German Democratic Republic in 1990 are prime examples. The two states may create an entirely new entity (Yemen), or one state may be absorbed into the second (Germany).

5. Peace Treaties: Historically, states have also emerged from peace settlements after major wars, such as the creation of new states in Eastern Europe after World War I.

In examining the formation of states as a result of the violent breakup of Yugoslavia, we confront the greatest human tragedy in Europe since World War II. This episode also challenged fundamental assumptions in international law about the nature of statehood, the meaning of self-determination, and the role of recognition of a state by other states. As you read the following materials, consider who the decision makers are concerning the formation of new states; to what extent preexisting legal texts provided useful guidance to them; to what extent did and could they base their decisions on law at all; how different fact patterns give rise to different legal consequences; and whether there are any clear norms regarding self-determination and the formation of new states.

A. The Problem

The state once known as Yugoslavia was a product of the Allied victory of World War I. Created in 1919 in the Treaty of Saint-Germain-en-Laye as the Kingdom of the Serbs, Croats, and Slovenes, or the South Slav State, its territory consisted of the pre-World War I Serbian state and a chunk of land carved out of the Austro-Hungarian empire containing the historic territories of Croatia, Slovenia, and Bosnia-Herzegovina. Yugoslavia represented an experiment for the victorious allies and a variant on President Woodrow Wilson's idea of self-determination of peoples: instead of giving each ethnic group its own state where it would be clearly dominant—as was done, for instance, in creating the new states of Estonia, Latvia, Lithuania, and Poland—the Allies combined several groups into one state. The challenge of Yugoslavia became making that entity function.

Before World War II, the monarchs in Yugoslavia divided it for governance purposes into 22 regions, then reallocated it into nine provinces. After World War II, the partisan leader Josip Broz (Tito) assumed power and declared a Socialist Federal Republic of Yugoslavia (SFRY). The SFRY had six republics that closely corresponded to the pre-1918 political units—Serbia, Montenegro, Macedonia, Croatia, Bosnia-Herzegovina, and Slovenia. Only Slovenia was close to ethnically uniform; each of the others contained significant minorities. Bosnia-Herzegovina did not contain a majority of any ethnic group but rather a plurality of Muslims and large populations of Serbs and Croats. Tito, an ethnic Croat, used his authoritarian rule to create a Yugoslav state and identity by suppressing nationalist or secessionist tendencies in the republics and creating structures at the national and regional level that would balance the power of the Serbs (the largest ethnic group) with those of the other ethnic groups. (See map of the former Yugoslavia.)

Upon Tito's death in 1980, these structures began to weaken and fall prey to nationalist leaders in Serbia, in particular Slobodan Milosevic, who sought to ensure Serb dominance of the SFRY. Nationalist sentiments grew correspondingly in two of Yugoslavia's republics, Slovenia and Croatia, the latter under the leadership of another ultranationalist, Franjo Tudjman. In late 1990, Slovenia and Croatia declared that SFRY law would no longer apply in their territories; in June 1991 both declared independence. The Yugoslav federal army responded immediately in Slovenia by leaving its bases and attacking the Slovene militia, though the SFRY agreed under international pressure to withdraw its army from Slovenia a few weeks later. In Croatia, ethnic Serbs in the Krajina region (bordering northwestern Bosnia) and the federal Yugoslav army took up arms in the summer of 1991, with the former claiming they wished to ensure that Serb-inhabited areas would remain part of the SFRY.

The Former Yugoslavia
SOURCE: CIA World Factbook

Both the European Community (EC)—the 12 member regional organization in Western Europe*—and the Conference on Security and Cooperation in Europe—an informal organization then consisting of 33 European states as well as the United States and Canada—were caught unprepared. In August 1991, the EC announced that it would not "recognize changes of frontiers which have not been brought about by peaceful means and by agreement," and called the Yugoslav army's support of Serbs in Croatia "illegal." The EC set up a Conference on Yugoslavia as a negotiation forum that would include the SFRY federal government, the presidents of the republics, and EC representatives. The Conference also created a five-person arbitration commission to address legal questions. The latter, known as the Badinter Commission, included the heads of the constitutional courts of France, Germany, Italy, Spain, and Belgium, and was chaired by Judge Robert Badinter of

*Through the Treaty on European Union, the EC became part of a broader European Union after 1993. It currently has 25 members.

France. On September 17, Macedonia declared its independence, and on October 14, Bosnia-Herzegovina followed suit. In response, on November 10, Serbs in Serb-dominated parts of Bosnia held a referendum for a "common Yugoslav state." On September 25, the UN Security Council, noting that the UN Charter "enshrined" the principle that territorial gains could not be brought about by force, agreed to impose an arms embargo on all of Yugoslavia.

Despite these actions and intermittent cease-fires brokered by the EC, the fighting in Yugoslavia quickly accelerated. Yugoslav National Army (JNA) forces, composed principally of Serbs, laid siege to numerous cities and towns in Croatia, including the ancient port city of Dubrovnik. JNA forces worked with Croatian Serbs to gain control of Serb-majority parts of Croatia, including the Krajina region and Eastern Slavonia (along the eastern border with Serbia). The JNA levelled the Croat city of Vukovar in Eastern Slavonia, killing 2,300 civilians. By early 1992, the war risked spreading to Bosnia.

Beyond a call to end the fighting, the EC and other key actors could not immediately agree on policy toward Yugoslavia. Germany and Austria favored quick recognition of the new entities, but other states, including the United States, as well as the UN Secretary-General, favored delaying recognition at least until all sides could accept certain basic principles of a future settlement. On December 16, 1991, the EC agreed on guidelines for recognition of the new states in Yugoslavia as well as the then-disintegrating USSR and invited claimants to submit requests for recognition by December 23. Immediately after Bosnia submitted its request, a self-proclaimed Assembly of the Serbian People of Bosnia-Herzegovina resolved to create a Serbian Republic of Bosnia-Herzegovina if the Bosnian government insisted on independence; in January 1992, these Bosnian Serbs declared the independence of the Serbian Republic of Bosnia-Herzegovina. Ethnic Croats also declared two new entities in Bosnia without explicitly seeking statehood.

B. Requisites of Statehood

The decision by various actors within Yugoslavia to form new states raised at least two key legal questions: did international law specify the criteria any new entities must meet to constitute a new state, and what did the formation of these entities mean for Yugoslavia's status as a state? The very actors that prescribe law have attempted to make law regarding the grounds for participation in that law making—for who may join the club or lose membership in it and how the obligations of membership might change if the member itself undergoes changes. In the past, international law offered a deceptively simple answer to these questions. As stated in the 1933 Convention on the Rights and Duties of States (the Montevideo Convention), concluded among 16 states in the Western hemisphere:

> The state as a person of international law should possess the following qualifications:
> a) a permanent population; b) a defined territory; c) government; d) capacity to enter into relations with the other states.

In practice, global elites have interpreted these criteria quite flexibly. As for "permanent population," some entities recognized as states have very small populations, such as the Pacific Island state of Nauru (10,000), or the city-state of San Marino (24,000). The requirement of "a defined territory" has not prevented the international community from regarding as states entities with disputed or even unknown boundaries, such as Israel, with its half-century dispute with its Arab neighbors; the two Koreas, with their claims to each other's territory; or the states of the Arabian peninsula, whose desert borders were often unknown. New states have emerged even without a full capacity to enter into foreign relations with other states. The national defense of Liechtenstein and Monaco, both regarded for many years as states (and both members of numerous international organizations), is the responsibility of Switzerland and France, respectively. Micronesia, Palau, the Cook Islands, and Niue are termed "freely associated states": the defense of Micronesia and Palau is controlled by the United States under agreements of free association that accompanied their independence; the foreign and defense relations of the Cook Islands and Niue are controlled by New Zealand. The first two are members of the UN; the last two are not.

Equally important, what has been the reaction of the international community when a state loses one of the traits listed in the Montevideo Convention? This issue has arisen most visibly with respect to the third criterion, when a government has fled or been disbanded due to military occupation or when internal strife has eliminated any effective power of the central government. During World War II, states did not regard the occupation of most countries in Western Europe as eliminating their legal status as states; rather, such states were regarded as occupied nations. Similarly, Kuwait did not lose its legal status despite Iraq's occupation from August 1990 to April 1991. During much of the Cold War, the states of Eastern Europe effectively lost their ability to conduct foreign and defense relations independent of the USSR and yet continued to be regarded as states. Today, certain states remain under the firm control of neighbors, such as Lebanon vis-à-vis Syria or Bhutan vis-à-vis India. As for collapsed governments, no state has claimed that the collapse of central government control in Somalia and Afghanistan during most of the 1990s has deprived them of statehood.

Notes and Questions

1. What underlying purposes do the traditional criteria advance? Is it possible to imagine an entity that fulfills the purposes of statehood but lacks some of these attributes?

2. What would be the consequence of the view that entities that cease to fulfill all of the traditional criteria are no longer states with respect to the integrity of land, sea, and air boundaries, treaty relations, the holders of the entity's passports, and the assets of the entity in foreign lands?

C. Separation Anxiety: Self-Determination and Its Limits

Statehood is not a static condition. As noted above, states are born (and disappear) through a variety of processes, both peaceful and violent. In the case of Yugoslavia, constituent groups and territories attempted to secede from their state to create a new one. Does international law have norms regarding the legitimacy of separation from states? On the one hand, the traditional criteria suggest that statehood is about effective power: a state exists and enjoys all the benefits of statehood as long as the government enjoys effective control over the territory. States have generally recognized the right of a state to defend itself against internal threats to its unity, including through armed force (subject to compliance with the law of war, as discussed in

Chapter 8). International law thus has a strong presumption in favor of the continuity of states. On the other hand, groups within a state might conceivably have legitimate reasons to separate from the state, including repression by the central government. Does international law make an ex ante choice between the existing state and those attempting to secede from it, or does it simply ratify the outcome of a civil war, whether victory for the government or for those seceding?

In the case of Yugoslavia, the claimants to statehood invoked the "principle of equal rights and self-determination of peoples" in Article 1 of the United Nations Charter. The federal authorities in Belgrade—the capital of both Serbia and the SFRY—denied the applicability of self-determination to this situation. Serbs in Croatia invoked self-determination as a basis for remaining part of Yugoslavia; and the Bosnian Serbs invoked it as a basis for remaining part of Yugoslavia or, as a last resort, for obtaining *their* own state independent of Bosnia. These claims inherently raised a second question: if the republics (or the Croatian or Bosnian Serbs) had such a right, how would their new state be defined territorially? To help answer these questions, self-determination must be considered in its historical context.

1. The Pre-UN Charter Era

The primarily Eurocentric form of international law that emerged in the seventeenth century did not generally regard communities other than states as participants in the process of making international law. Instead, the law of nations became the handmaiden of the policies of many states to expand their spheres of influence through acquisition of lands inhabited by non-European peoples. Lands not under the control of any state were termed *terra nullius* (empty land), subject to legal acquisition by states through a variety of methods. The peoples living in those lands were treated, for most purposes, no differently from the flora and fauna. Governments argued over title to land, which often depended on the mode of acquisition and evidence of control, but the basic starting point that land beyond state control could be acquired and maintained was well accepted. Imperial powers typically differentiated between their core territory inhabited by their citizens—the metropolitan area—and additional lands under their control but whose inhabitants were subjugated peoples rather than full members of the state: colonial territories. These colonies might be contiguous to the metropole, as they were in the Austro-Hungarian, Russian, and Chinese empires, or far away, as in the "blue water" colonies of European states in Africa, Latin America, and Asia.

International law indeed developed an entire doctrine surrounding colonies. For example, a territory became a so-called protectorate if its leaders—or, in some cases, those without any internal authority—had concluded some form of agreement with the metropole giving the latter certain authority over it, although in many cases these agreements were coerced. Regardless of the locutions used, at the core of international law's approach to colonialism was the legal responsibility of the metropole over the territory and the corresponding right of the metropole to govern the colony as it saw fit (eventually subject to some modest limitations such as the ban on the slave trade). States were free to swap, combine, or divide up colonies as they might choose as a matter of power politics. This practice reached its apogee in the Berlin West Africa Conference of 1884 and 1885, where 13 European states agreed upon a division of much of the continent through a formal international agreement.

The Treaty of Versailles ending World War I constituted a significant shift in international law's treatment of colonial lands and peoples. The losing powers—Germany, Austria-Hungary, and the Ottoman Empire—were stripped of their colonies. Their overseas colonies were not transferred to the victorious powers, as would have been typical after previous wars, but instead were placed under a new legal regime, the Mandates system of the League of Nations. The Covenant of the League provided, in now somewhat haunting language, that

> [for] peoples not yet able to stand by themselves under the strenuous conditions of the modern world, there should be applied the principle that the well-being and development of such peoples form a sacred trust of civilisation and that securities for the performance of this trust should be embodied in this Covenant. . . . [As a result,] the tutelage of such peoples should be entrusted to advanced nations who by reason of their resources, their experience or their geographical position can best undertake this responsibility.

Covenant of the League of Nations, art. XXII.

The Mandatory powers assumed a more or less de facto colonial control over the new territories but had international obligations under the Covenant regarding the treatment of the inhabitants. These included duties to "endeavour to secure and maintain fair and humane conditions of labour," "secure just treatment of the native inhabitants," and allow the League to supervise international arrangements regarding traffic in women and children, drug trafficking, and arms transfers. *Id.*, art. XXIII. The League concluded detailed agreements with the Mandatory powers and established an elaborate oversight mechanism at its headquarters in Geneva, which had some positive effects on the treatment by some Mandatory states of some of their new territories. From the perspective of international law, the Mandate territories and peoples had a new status as a subject of direct concern to the League. Yet from the perspective of the inhabitants, the Mandates system seemed a continuation of the status quo—only with a new set of colonizers. Moreover, the victorious powers were not willing to place any of their own colonies under the Mandates system.

Although the impact of the Treaty of Versailles may not have been of great import to the lives of people living in colonies, it did have a more significant impact for those in Europe. President Wilson had spoken during the war of the need for self-government. In a February 11, 1918, speech to Congress, he stated: "Self-determination is not a mere phrase; it is an imperative principle of action which statesmen will henceforth ignore at their peril." The Allies adopted this position at their peace conferences in their treatment of the Central Powers—though not, as noted, with respect to either their colonies or disgruntled minorities within their metropolitan territories. As a result, the Austro-Hungarian and Ottoman Empires were dissolved, leaving only the relatively small states of Austria, Hungary, and Turkey; Germany and Russia lost parts of their territory as well. The result was the creation of new states: Czechoslovakia, Yugoslavia, Finland (which actually emerged prior to the end of the war), Estonia, Latvia, Lithuania, and Poland. Under Wilson's idea, new states should enable a people in Europe to govern itself. Yet each state also had its own minorities, and two of the states, Czechoslovakia and Yugoslavia, combined different groups in a way that, 70 years later, would eventually prove impossible to sustain.

Even after the World War I peace treaties were concluded, the new League of Nations faced a number of self-determination claims. Among the claimants were the people of the Aland Islands, an archipelago of about 300 small islands situated between southern Finland and southern Sweden. From the middle of the seventeenth century, the islands were administered as part of Finland, which was then a province in the Swedish kingdom. In the early nineteenth century, as a result of various wars between Sweden and Russia, Sweden ceded Finland, including the islands, to Russia. In 1917, after the outbreak of the Russian Revolution, Finland itself declared independence from Russia. The Alanders, who were nearly all Swedish in familial origin and used Swedish as their language of communication, seized the opportunity to seek unification with their kin in Sweden. They insisted on a plebiscite, which Finland refused to authorize. Finland and Sweden then brought the issue before the League of Nations, which first created an International Committee of Jurists to determine whether the League had competence over the issue or whether it was solely within the domestic jurisdiction of Finland (which, under the Covenant of the League, would deny it the ability to act). The Committee's report included the following passages:

Report of the International Committee of Jurists Entrusted by the Council of the League of Nations with the Task of Giving an Advisory Opinion upon the Legal Aspects of the Aaland Islands Question

League of Nations Official Journal, Special Supp. No. 3, at 5-10 (1920)

OCTOBER,
1920.

League of Nations–Official Journal.

THE PRINCIPLE OF SELF-DETERMINATION AND THE RIGHTS OF PEOPLES.

Although the principle of self-determination of peoples plays an important part in modern political thought, especially since the Great War, it must be pointed out that there is no mention of it in the Covenant of the League of Nations. The recognition of this principle in a certain number of international treaties cannot be considered as sufficient to put it upon the same footing as a positive rule of the Law of Nations.

On the contrary, in the absence of express provisions in international treaties, the right of disposing of national territory is essentially an attribute of the sovereignty of every State. Positive International Law does not recognise the right of national groups, as such, to separate themselves from the State of which they form part by the simple expression of a wish, any more than it recognises the right of other States to claim such a separation. Generally speaking, the grant or refusal of the right to a portion of its population of determining its own political fate by plebiscite or by some other method, is, exclusively, an attribute of the sovereignty of every State which is definitively constituted. A dispute between two States concerning such a question, under normal conditions therefore, bears upon a question which International Law leaves entirely to the domestic jurisdiction of one of the States concerned. Any other solution would amount to an infringement of sovereign rights of a State and would involve the risk of creating difficulties and a lack of stability which would not only be contrary to the very idea embodied in the term "State," but would also endanger the interests of the international community. . . .

The Commission, in affirming these principles, does not give an opinion concerning the question as to whether a manifest and continued abuse of sovereign power, to the detriment of a section of the population of a State, would, if such circumstances arose, give to an international dispute, arising therefrom, such a character that its object should be considered as one which is not confined to the domestic jurisdiction of the State concerned, but comes within the sphere of action of the League of Nations. . . .

DE FACTO AND DE JURE CONSIDERATIONS. THEIR INTERNATIONAL CHARACTER.

3. It must, however, be observed that all that has been said concerning the attributes of the sovereignty of a State, generally speaking, only applies to a nation which is definitively constituted as a sovereign State and an independent member of the international community and so long as it continues to possess these characteristics. From the point of view of both domestic and international law, the formation, transformation and dismemberment of States as a result of revolutions and wars create situations of fact which, to a large extent, cannot be met by the application of the normal rules of positive law. . . . [I]f the essential basis of these rules, that is to say, territorial sovereignty, is lacking, either because the State is not yet fully formed or because it is undergoing transformation or dissolution, the situation is obscure and uncertain from a legal point of view, and will not become clear until the period of development is completed and a definite new situation, which is normal in respect to territorial sovereignty, has been established.

This transition from a *de facto* situation to a normal situation *de jure* cannot be considered as one confined entirely within the domestic jurisdiction of a State. It tends to lead to readjustments between the members of the international community and to alterations in their territorial and legal status; consequently, this transition interests the community of States very deeply both from political and legal standpoints.

SELF-DETERMINATION AS APPLIED TO *DE FACTO* SITUATIONS. ITS FORMS.

Under such circumstances, the principle of self-determination of peoples may be called into play. New aspirations of certain sections of a nation, which are sometimes based on old traditions or on a common language and civilisation, may come to the surface and produce effects which must be taken into account in the interests of the internal and external peace of nations. . . .

HISTORICAL DEVELOPMENT OF FINLAND.

In the light of the foregoing, the question has to be decided as to whether, from the standpoint of territorial sovereignty, the situation of the Aaland Islands in the independent State of Finland is of a definite and normal character, or whether it is a transitory or not fully developed situation. . . .

THE PURPORT OF THE FINNISH DECLARATION OF INDEPENDENCE.

The Aaland Islands were undoubtedly part of Finland during the period of Russian rule. Must they, for this reason alone, be considered as definitely incorporated *de jure* in the State of Finland which was formed as a result of the events described above ?

The Commission finds it impossible to admit this. The extent and nature of the political changes, which take place as facts and outside the domain of law, are necessarily limited by the results actually produced. . . . If one part of a State actually separates itself from that State, the separation is necessarily limited in its effect to the population of the territory which has taken part in the act of separation. . . . It may even be said that if a separation occurs from a political organism which is more or less autonomous, and which is itself *de facto* in process of political transformation, this organism cannot at the very moment when it transforms itself outside the domain of positive law invoke the principles of this law in order to force upon a national group a political status which the latter refuses to accept.

By the application of a purely legal method of argument it might be said that a kind of acquired right exists in favour of the Aaland Islands which would be violated if Finland were allowed to suppress it retrospectively. . . .

For these reasons, Finland cannot claim that the future of the Aaland Islands should be the same as hers simply because of the one fact that the Islands formerly formed part of the Finnish political organisation in the Russian Empire.

Based on these views, the Committee decided that the question of the islands' status was not solely within the domestic jurisdiction of Finland and that the League's Council was competent to make a recommendation. The League then appointed a Commission of Rapporteurs (representatives of member states) to recommend a solution to the problem. Its report from 1921 included the following:

The Aaland Islands Question: Report Submitted to the Council of the League of Nations by the Commission of Rapporteurs

League of Nations Doc. B7/21/68/106 (1921)

First of all, we must eliminate an analogy which cannot be pleaded justly.

The Aalanders and the Swedes are wrong in citing the example of Finland, which, in determining her own fate, has succeeded, thanks to the results of the great war, in freeing herself from her dependence on Russia. As we think we have fully proved, Finland has been an autonomous State since long before the war, i.e. from 1809. . . . [N]o one will dispute the natural right of the Finns, born of inherent justice, to proclaim their independence; but this right which Finland possessed does not provide any evidence in support of the demand of the Aalanders. The Aaland Archipelago is only a small part of the Finnish territory, and the Aaland population a small fraction of the Finnish nation. Now, it is evident that one cannot treat a small minority, a small fraction of a people, in the same manner and on the same footing as a nation taken as a whole.

. . . [Moreover,] Finland has been oppressed and persecuted, her tenderest feelings have been wounded by the disloyal and brutal conduct of Russia. The Aalanders have neither been persecuted nor oppressed by Finland. . . . It is true that, as a result of quite exceptional conditions, the Aaland population is threatened in its language and its culture. But this is not the result of a policy of oppression; on the contrary, we feel certain that it is possible to appeal to the good will of the

Finnish Government to preserve and protect the language and the culture which are so precious to the Aalanders. . . .

. . . Is it possible to admit as an absolute rule that a minority of the population of a State, which is definitely constituted and perfectly capable of fulfilling its duties as such, has the right of separating itself from her in order to be incorporated in another State or to declare its independence? The answer can only be in the negative. To concede to minorities, either of language or religion, or to any fractions of a population the right of withdrawing from the community to which they belong, because it is their wish or their good pleasure, would be to destroy order and stability within States and to inaugurate anarchy in international life; it would be to uphold a theory incompatible with the very idea of the State as a territorial and political unity. . . .

The separation of a minority from the State of which it forms a part and its incorporation in another State can only be considered as an altogether exceptional solution, a last resort when the State lacks either the will or the power to enact and apply just and effective guarantees.

In the case of the Aalanders, the important question is the protection of their language—the Swedish language. . . . We appreciate the ardent desire, the resolute wish of the Aaland population, proud in its democratic simplicity and eager for independence, to preserve intact the Swedish language and culture—their heritage from their ancestors. The conviction that their language is threatened and can only be saved by union with Sweden has profoundly moved this gallant little race, which inhabits, from an international point of view, one of the most interesting regions of Europe. . . .

We recognise that the Aaland population, by reason of its insular position and its strong tradition, forms a group apart in Finland, not only distinct from the Finnish population, but also in certain respects distinct from the Swedish-speaking population. . . . We admit also that the fear fostered by the Aalanders of being little by little submerged by the Finnish invasion has good grounds . . . . If it were true that incorporation with Sweden was the only means of preserving its Swedish language for Aaland, we should not have hesitated to consider this solution. But such is not the case. There is no need for a separation. The Finnish State is ready to grant the inhabitants satisfactory guarantees and faithfully observe the engagement which it will enter into with them: of this we have no doubt. . . .

[The Commission recommended strengthening the existing Finnish statute that gave autonomy to the islands regarding schools and language.]

. . . [I]t is necessary that the Government and Parliament of Finland on their side consent to make some steps on the road towards pacification, by adopting the international guarantees which we consider indispensable. They will certainly do this if they recognise, as do we, that . . . Aaland deserves a place apart in the midst of the other Finnish provinces. . . .

However, in the event that Finland . . . refused to grant the Aaland population the guarantees which we have just detailed, there would be another possible solution, and it is exactly the one which we wish to eliminate. The interest of the Aalanders, the interests of a durable peace in the Baltic, would then force us to advise the separation of the islands from Finland, based on the wishes of the inhabitants which would be freely expressed by means of a plebiscite. . . .

In the end, the League of Nations recommended that the islands remain part of Finland, but be subject to a special regime providing for their demilitarization and a special autonomy regime that included, for instance, the teaching of Swedish in schools. The parties accepted the recommendation, and this regime, which has been amended several times, survives to the present day.

2. Self-Determination After the UN Charter

In the years leading up to World War II, the notion of self-determination received a significant blow, as Adolf Hitler invoked it as an excuse for unifying German-speaking peoples in Austria, Czechoslovakia (the Sudetenland), France (Alsace-Lorraine), and western Poland into one Reich. Moreover, after the war, when the victorious Allies came together to prepare the United Nations Charter, France, Britain, the Netherlands, and various other states still clung to their far-flung colonies. As a result, the Charter offered only the briefest provisions about self-determination and essentially saw the principle as limited to states as they currently existed, rather than as applying to colonies or minorities within states.

United Nations Charter

(1945)

Article 1

[The purposes of the United Nations are:] 2. To develop friendly relations among nations based on respect for the principle of equal rights and self-determination of peoples, and to take other appropriate measures to strengthen universal peace; . . .

Article 73

Members of the United Nations which have or assume responsibilities for the administration of territories whose peoples have not yet attained a full measure of self-government recognize the principle that the interests of the inhabitants of these territories are paramount, and accept as a sacred trust the obligation to promote to the utmost, within the system of international peace and security established by the present Charter, the well-being of the inhabitants of these territories, and, to this end:

a. to ensure, with due respect for the culture of the peoples concerned, their political, economic, social, and educational advancement, their just treatment, and their protection against abuses;

b. to develop self-government, to take due account of the political aspirations of the peoples, and to assist them in the progressive development of their free political institutions, according to the particular circumstances of each territory and its peoples and their varying stages of advancement;

c. to further international peace and security;

d. to promote constructive measures of development, to encourage research, and to co-operate with one another and, when and where appropriate, with specialized international bodies with a view to the practical achievement of the social, economic, and scientific purposes set forth in this Article. . . .

In addition to these provisions, the drafters did include in the Charter an International Trusteeship System under which the World War II Allies would administer former German, Italian, and Japanese colonies. Under the new system, the Administering states had more significant obligations than under the Mandates system, including "to promote the political, economic, social and educational advancement of the inhabitants of the trust territories, and their progressive development towards self-government or independence as may be appropriate" and "to encourage respect for human rights and for fundamental freedoms for all without distinction as to race, sex, language, or religion." UN Charter, art. 76. Most trust territories became independent in the 1950s and 1960s, with the trusteeship system shutting down following the independence of the U.S. Trust Territory of Palau in 1994.

Despite the absence of a call for decolonization in the Charter, the end of the Second World War exposed the weaknesses of all the colonial powers, and the system itself lost legitimacy among most members of the new United Nations. Colonial territories separated from their metropoles relatively peacefully, as in India and much of Africa, or through armed conflict with the colonial powers, as in Indochina and Indonesia. This process began shortly after the war and was largely complete by the mid-1970s. By 1960, the European colonial empires had receded, with most of their component parts independent states that increasingly became a dominant voice in the UN General Assembly. With support from the Soviet Union and its allies, they passed the following resolution. No states opposed the resolution, although nine (nearly all states with colonies) abstained.

Declaration on the Granting of Independence to Colonial Countries and Peoples

G.A. Res. 1514 (1960)

The General Assembly . . .

Declares that:

1. The subjection of peoples to alien subjugation, domination and exploitation constitutes a denial of fundamental human rights, is contrary to the Charter of the United Nations and is an impediment to the promotion of world peace and cooperation.

2. All peoples have the right to self-determination; by virtue of that right they freely determine their political status and freely pursue their economic, social and cultural development.

3. Inadequacy of political, economic, social or educational preparedness should never serve as a pretext for delaying independence.

4. All armed action or repressive measures of all kinds directed against dependent peoples shall cease in order to enable them to exercise peacefully and freely their right to complete independence, and the integrity of their national territory shall be respected.

5. Immediate steps shall be taken, in Trust and Non-Self-Governing Territories or all other territories which have not yet attained independence, to transfer

all powers to the peoples of those territories, without any conditions or reservations, in accordance with their freely expressed will and desire, without any distinction as to race, creed or colour, in order to enable them to enjoy complete independence and freedom.

6. Any attempt aimed at the partial or total disruption of the national unity and the territorial integrity of a country is incompatible with the purposes and principles of the Charter of the United Nations. . . .

In the 1970s, in anticipation of the twenty-fifth anniversary of the United Nations, the members of the General Assembly prepared a lengthy resolution to restate or proclaim basic principles of international law concerning various aspects of the Charter. The long-titled resolution, adopted by consensus and commonly known as the Friendly Relations Declaration, included the following section:

Declaration on Principles of International Law Concerning Friendly Relations and Co-operation Among States in Accordance with the Charter of the United Nations

G.A. Res. 2625 (1970)

The principle of equal rights and self-determination of peoples . . .

The establishment of a sovereign and independent State, the free association or integration with an independent State or the emergence into any other political status freely determined by a people constitute modes of implementing the right of self-determination by that people.

Every State has the duty to refrain from any forcible action which deprives peoples referred to above in the elaboration of the present principle of their right to self-determination and freedom and independence. In their actions against and resistance to such forcible action in pursuit of the exercise of their right to self-determination, such peoples are entitled to seek and to receive support in accordance with the purposes and principles of the Charter of the United Nations.

The territory of a colony or other non-self-governing territory has, under the Charter of the United Nations, a status separate and distinct from the territory of the State administering it; and such separate and distinct status under the Charter shall exist until the people of the colony or non-self-governing territory have exercised their right of self-determination in accordance with the Charter, and particularly its purposes and principles.

Nothing in the foregoing paragraphs shall be construed as authorizing or encouraging any action which would dismember or impair, totally or in part, the territorial integrity or political unity of sovereign and independent States conducting themselves in compliance with the principle of equal rights and self-determination of peoples as described above and thus possessed of a government representing the whole people belonging to the territory without distinction as to race, creed or colour.

Every state shall refrain from any action aimed at the partial or total disruption of the national unity and territorial integrity of any other State or country.

Notes and Questions

1. Why did states approve of decolonization as a method for creation of new states while adopting a more nuanced stance on secession?

2. What is a "people?" Why is the term undefined in the Aland Islands opinions, the UN Charter, and the Friendly Relations Declaration? To which sorts of peoples has international law afforded a right of self-determination?

3. Do the above instruments suggest any normative evolution since the United Nations Charter? What did the 1970 Friendly Relations Declaration contribute to the law on self-determination? How does the penultimate paragraph of the above excerpt address this issue?

4. Should any right to secede turn on the wishes of the seceding group or the whole state? Does the Friendly Relations Declaration create a huge new set of claimants for secession?

5. Despite their hesitation to approve of secession in international instruments in the years before the Yugoslavia conflict, states have accepted as states certain entities that have seceded from other states. These determinations were based, in essence, on whether those seceding proved able by force to control their territory, rather than whether it met certain legal criteria. Most notable is the decision by the United Nations to admit Bangladesh (former East Pakistan) as a new member in 1974, after it seceded from Pakistan in 1971 with the significant help of the Indian army. Does this suggest that law is ultimately irrelevant to the permissibility of secession?

D. The Badinter Commission Speaks

The EC's Badinter Commission faced the issue of self-determination in response to a series of questions posed to it in November 1991 by the President of the Conference on Yugoslavia. First, the Conference president asked whether the events in Yugoslavia were best viewed as the secession of entities from Yugoslavia, as Serbia insisted, or the dissolution of the state itself, as the other republics claimed. On December 7, the Commission published its opinion:

CONFERENCE ON YUGOSLAVIA ARBITRATION COMMISSION OPINION NO. 1

31 I.L.M. 1494 (1992)

```
1 - The Committee considers:

   a) that the answer to the question should be based on the
   principles of public international law which serve to de-
   fine the conditions on which an entity constitutes a State;
   that in this respect, the existence or disappearance of the
```

State is a question of fact; that the effects of recognition by other States are purely declaratory;

b) that the State is commonly defined as a community which consists of a territory and a population subject to an organized political authority; that such a State is characterized by sovereignty;

c) that, for the purpose of applying these criteria, the form of internal political organization and the constitutional provisions are mere facts, although it is necessary to take them into consideration in order to determine the Government's sway over the population and the territory;

d) that in the case of a federal-type State, which embraces communities that possess a degree of autonomy and, moreover, participate in the exercise of political power within the framework of institutions common to the Federation, the existence of the State implies that the federal organs represent the components of the Federation and wield effective power. . . .

2 – The Arbitration Committee notes that:

a) – although the SFRY has until now retained its international personality, notably inside international organizations, the Republics have expressed their desire for independence [by referenda in Slovenia, Croatia, and Macedonia in 1990 and 1991, and];

    – in Bosnia and Herzegovina, by a sovereignty resolution adopted by Parliament on October 14th, 1991, whose validity has been contested by the Serbian community of the Republic of Bosnia and Herzegovina.

b) – The composition and workings of the essential organs of the Federation, be they the Federal Presidency, the Federal Council, the Council of the Republics and the Provinces, the Federal Executive Council, the Constitutional Court or the Federal Army, no longer meet the criteria of participation and representativeness inherent in a federal State;

c) – The recourse to force has led to armed conflict between the different elements of the Federation which has caused the death of thousands of people and wrought considerable destruction within a few months. The authorities of the Federation and the Republics have shown themselves to be powerless to enforce respect for the succeeding ceasefire agreements concluded under the auspices of the European Communities or the United Nations Organization.

3 - Consequently, the Arbitration Committee is of the opinion:

- that the Socialist Federal Republic of Yugoslavia is in the process of dissolution;

- that it is incumbent upon the Republics to settle such problems of State succession as may arise from this process in keeping with the principles and rules of international law, with particular regard for human rights and the rights of peoples and minorities;

- that it is up to those Republics that so wish, to work together to form a new association endowed with the democratic institutions of their choice.

The second question asked of the Commission (originally posed by Serbia) was the following: "Does the Serbian population in Croatia and Bosnia-Herzegovina, as one of the constituent peoples of Yugoslavia, have the right to self-determination?" On January 11, 1992, the Commission responded.

CONFERENCE ON YUGOSLAVIA ARBITRATION COMMISSION OPINION NO. 2

31 I.L.M. 1497 (1992)

1. The Commission considers that international law as it currently stands does not spell out all the implications of the right to self-determination.

However, it is well established that, whatever the circumstances, the right to self-determination must not involve changes to existing frontiers at the time of independence (*uti possidetis juris*) except where the States concerned agree otherwise.

2. Where there are one or more groups within a State constituting one or more ethnic, religious or language communities, they have the right to recognition of their identity under international law.

As the Commission emphasized in its Opinion No 1 of 29 November 1991, published on 7 December, the now-peremptory-norms of international law require States to ensure respect for the rights of minorities. This requirement applies to all the Republics vis-à-vis the minorities on their territory.

The Serbian population in Bosnia-Hercegovina and Croatia must therefore be afforded every right accorded to minorities under international conventions as well as national and international guarantees consistent with the principles of international law. . . .

3. Article 1 of the two 1966 International Covenants on human rights establishes that the principle of the right to self-determination serves to safeguard human rights. By virtue of that right every individual may choose to belong to whatever ethnic, religious or language community he or she wishes.

In the Commission's view one possible consequence of this principle might be for the members of the Serbian population in Bosnia-Hercegovina and Croatia to be recognized under agreements between the Republics as having the nationality of their choice, with all the rights and obligations which that entails with respect to the States concerned.

4. The Arbitration Commission is therefore of the opinion:

(i) that the Serbian population in Bosnia-Hercegovina and Croatia is entitled to all the rights accorded to minorities and ethnic groups under international law . . . and

(ii) that the Republics must afford the members of those minorities and ethnic groups all the human rights and fundamental freedoms recognized in international law, including, where appropriate, the right to choose their nationality.

For nearly four years after the Badinter Commission's opinion, Serbs and Croats in Bosnia fought the Muslim-led government for independence, although the Muslims and Croats eventually formed an uneasy alliance. In Bosnia, the conflict exacted its largest toll—some 200,000 dead, including the war's worst single atrocity, the July 1995 massacre of 5,000 to 8,000 Bosnian Muslim men and boys at Srebrenica. As discussed in Chapter 2, the civil war ended with a Western-imposed peace treaty that left Bosnia formally united. But as a practical matter, Bosnia remained divided between the Muslim-Croat federation and the Serb-controlled Republika Srpska. Each had separate government structures, schools, and economies. The High Representative charged by the parties to the peace accords with overseeing implementation of their nonmilitary aspects has managed to achieve only a few trappings of a united state, such as common license plates, passports, and a national anthem.

In 1999, after years of atrocities by Serb forces against ethnic Albanians in Kosovo (part of Serbia, itself part of the FRY), the North Atlantic Treaty Organization (NATO), led by the United States, attacked the FRY to force it to withdraw its forces from Kosovo. The FRY was forced to accept significant autonomy for Kosovo, which was put under the administration of the United Nations, although it remained formally part of Serbia. The UN Mission in Kosovo (UNMIK) has governed the region since 1999, with the assistance of a significant international security presence (KFOR) (15,000 troops from NATO and other states as of 2006) and advisers from the EU, OSCE, and other international organizations. Though UNMIK had some significant achievements in returning refugees to their homes, setting up a local police force, and establishing indigenous political institutions, tensions between Albanians and Serbs in Kosovo remained strong and the economy weak, with periodic outbreaks of violence. In October 2005, UN Secretary-General Kofi Annan called for the beginning of international negotiations on the final status of the region.

In February 2003, the Assembly of the FRY adopted a new Constitutional Charter, changing the name of the state to Serbia and Montenegro. This marked the formal end to the state of Yugoslavia. Serbia and Montenegro's composition and boundaries remain in flux, not only because of the uncertain status of Kosovo, but because of the desire of many residents of Montenegro to separate. Only pressure from the European Union to keep the state together resulted in the 2003 compromise, which creates a loose confederation with weak central organs and allows for a referendum in either republic on the state's future in 2006.

Notes and Questions

1. In light of the many precedents where the absence of a government was not regarded as eliminating statehood, should the Commission have regarded Yugoslavia as dissolving due to the weakness of its federal government? What are the consequences of a view that a state is dissolving once its federal organs lack certain powers? How might Opinion No. 1 actually encourage secessions?

2. Why would the SFRY wish to view the situation as a secession rather than a dissolution? How does Opinion No. 1 legitimate the role of the EC in the conflict? Did it state a legal conclusion?

3. Why do you think that the Badinter Commission refused in Opinion No. 2 to state that the Serbs in Bosnia and Croatia were collectively entitled to self-determination? Who was the audience for the opinion?

4. How different are the Badinter Commission's views from those of the Commission of Rapporteurs in the Aland Islands case? Do the former correspond to the norms in the Friendly Relations Declaration?

5. Are minority rights a substitute for self-determination, or a form of it? Does the Badinter Commission's solution—a right to choose one's nationality—offer a satisfactory response to the minorities in Bosnia?

6. What do the wars in Yugoslavia and their outcome suggest about the views of the actors involved in the conflict regarding the right to self-determination?

E. Territory and Borders

As the above excerpts make clear, self-determination is not just about who peoples are, or what they may do, but where they may do it. The extent to which self-determination might change borders has occupied global actors since decolonization in Latin America in the early 1800s. The issue assumed particular importance in Africa, most of which had been decolonized by the mid-1960s. With a few exceptions, the territory of the new states was determined by their pre-independence colonial borders—borders between imperial domains and administrative borders within imperial domains—a principle known as *uti possidetis*. Thus, for example, the border between the central African states of Chad and Niger—two former French colonies—corresponded to a French colonial administrative line, whereas the border between the states of Niger and Nigeria corresponded to a French-British imperial border. These borders had, in most cases, been drawn a century or more earlier with no regard for the will of the people concerned and little regard for preexisting boundaries of tribal or other ethnic entities. To address the issue of borders, the Organization of African Unity (OAU) issued the following decision in 1964:

Border Disputes Among African States

O.A.U. Res. AGH/RES.16(I) (1964)

The Assembly of Heads of State and Government . . .
> Considering that the border problems constitute a grave and permanent factor of dissension;
> Conscious of the existence of extra-African maneuvers aiming at dividing the African States;
> Considering further that the borders of African States, on the day of their independence, constitute a tangible reality; . . .
> Recognizing the imperious necessity of settling, by peaceful means and within a strictly African framework, all disputes between African States; . . .
> 1. Solemnly reaffirms the strict respect by all Member States of the Organization for the principles laid down in Article III, paragraph 3 of the Charter of the Organization of African Unity [namely, "respect for the sovereignty and territorial integrity of each State and for its alienable right to independent existence"];
> 2. Solemnly declares that all Member States pledge themselves to respect the frontiers existing on their achievement of national independence.

Burkina Faso and Mali are two states in West Africa that, prior to independence, were separate colonies within French West Africa, known, respectively, as Upper Volta and French Sudan. Both states attained independence in 1960. They disagreed on the location of parts of their border, though they agreed that the dispute should be resolved according to the principle of *uti possidetis*. In 1983, they submitted their case to the International Court of Justice, which eventually drew a border between the two states. In the course of its opinion, it offered the following dictum:

Case Concerning the Frontier Dispute (Burkina Faso / Mali)

1986 I.C.J. 554 (Dec. 22)

20. . . . [T]he principle of *uti possidetis* seems to have been first invoked and applied in Spanish America, inasmuch as this was the continent which first witnessed the phenomenon of decolonization involving the formation of a number

of sovereign States on territory formerly belonging to a single metropolitan State. Nevertheless the principle is not a special rule which pertains solely to one specific system of international law. It is a general principle, which is logically connected with the phenomenon of the obtaining of independence, wherever it occurs. Its obvious purpose is to prevent the independence and stability of new States being endangered by fratricidal struggles provoked by the challenging of frontiers following the withdrawal of the administering power.

21. It was for this reason that, as soon as the phenomenon of decolonization characteristic of the situation in Spanish America in the 19th century subsequently appeared in Africa in the 20th century, the principle of *uti possidetis*, in the sense described above, fell to be applied. The fact that the new African States have respected the administrative boundaries and frontiers established by the colonial powers must be seen not as a mere practice contributing to the gradual emergence of a principle of customary international law, limited in its impact to the African continent as it had previously been to Spanish America, but as the application in Africa of a rule of general scope. . . .

23. There are several different aspects to this principle, in its well-known application in Spanish America. The first aspect . . . is found in the pre-eminence accorded to legal title over effective possession as a basis of sovereignty. Its purpose, at the time of the achievement of independence by the former Spanish colonies of America, was to scotch any designs which non-American colonizing powers might have on regions which had been assigned by the former metropolitan State to one division or another, but which were still uninhabited or unexplored. . . . [Moreover,] the essence of the principle lies in its primary aim of securing respect for the territorial boundaries at the moment when independence is achieved. Such territorial boundaries might be no more than delimitations between different administrative divisions or colonies all subject to the same sovereign . . . [as with] the States Parties to the present case, which took shape within the vast territories of French West Africa. *Uti possidetis*, as a principle which upgraded former administrative delimitations, established during the colonial period, to international frontiers, is therefore a principle of a general kind which is logically connected with this form of decolonization wherever it occurs.

24. The territorial boundaries which have to be respected may also derive from international frontiers which previously divided a colony of one State from a colony of another, or indeed a colonial territory from the territory of an independent State, or one which was under protectorate, but had retained its international personality. . . .

25. However, it may be wondered how the time-hallowed principle has been able to withstand the new approaches to international law as expressed in Africa, where the successive attainment of independence and the emergence of new States have been accompanied by a certain questioning of traditional international law. At first sight this principle conflicts outright with another one, the right of peoples to self-determination. In fact, however, the maintenance of the territorial status quo in Africa is often seen as the wisest course, to preserve what has been achieved by peoples who have struggled for their independence, and to avoid a disruption which would deprive the continent of the gains achieved by much sacrifice. The essential requirement of stability in order to survive, to develop and gradually to consolidate their independence in all fields, has induced African States judiciously to consent to the respecting of colonial frontiers, and to take account of it in the interpretation of the principle of self-determination of peoples.

Borders were a core element of the Yugoslavia debacle as well. Recall that the Security Council and the EC political bodies had issued statements in August and September 1991 reminding the parties that changes to existing borders could not come about by force. Yet Serbs in Bosnia and Croatia had control over certain parts of those republics and wanted to unify those parts with Serbia or attain independence. Indeed, the Serbs in Bosnia explicitly sought to unify disparate patches of Serb-controlled territory into a contiguous region, a policy that led to the "ethnic cleansing" of non-Serbs in those areas.

On January 11, 1992, the Badinter Commission issued an opinion in response to the following question from the chairman of the peace conference: "Can the internal boundaries between Croatia and Serbia and between Bosnia-Hercegovina and Serbia be regarded as frontiers in terms of public international law"?

CONFERENCE ON YUGOSLAVIA
ARBITRATION COMMISSION OPINION NO. 3

31 I.L.M 1499 (1992)

2. . . . [O]nce the process in the SFRY leads to the creation of one or more independent States, the issue of frontiers, in particular those of the Republics referred to in the question before it, must be resolved in accordance with the following principles:

First - All external frontiers must be respected in line with the principle stated in the United Nations Charter, in the Declaration on Principles of International Law concerning Friendly Relations and Cooperation among States in accordance with the Charter of the United Nations (General Assembly resolution 2625 (XXV)). . . .

Second - The boundaries between Croatia and Serbia, between Bosnia-Hercegovina and Serbia, and possibly between other adjacent independent States may not be altered except by agreement freely arrived at.

Third - Except where otherwise agreed, the former boundaries become frontiers protected by international law. This conclusion follows from the principle of respect for the territorial status quo and, in particular, from the principle of *uti possidetis*. *Uti possidetis*, though initially applied in settling decolonization issues in America and Africa, is today recognized as a general principle, as stated by the International Court of Justice in . . . the case between Burkina Faso and Mali. . . .

The principle applies all the more readily to the Republics since the second and fourth paragraphs of Article 5 of the Constitution of the SFRY stipulated that the Repub-

lics' territories and boundaries could not be altered
without their consent.

Fourth - According to a well-established principle of
international law the alteration of existing frontiers
or boundaries by force is not capable of producing any
legal effect. This principle is to be found, for instance,
in the Declaration on Principles of International Law concerning Friendly Relations. . . . It is . . . enshrined in
the draft Convention of 4 November 1991 [on a comprehensive peace] drawn up by the Conference on Yugoslavia.

Notes and Questions

1. Why would the OAU agree to respect the legacy of a system against which its members had fought? To whom was the OAU sending a message?

2. Is the Badinter Commission's analogy between the administrative borders within a colonial empire and the inter-republican lines within the SFRY persuasive? One scholar has written that the Commission's "neo-decolonization territorial approach can have troubling consequences if used to legitimize secession for groups possessing a distinct political status while denying the right of secession to territorially based ethnic communities not formally organized into political units." Hurst Hannum, *Rethinking Self-Determination*, 34 Va. J. Intl. L. 1, 38 (1993). Do you agree?

3. If you disagree with the Badinter Commission's approach, can you construct alternative solutions? What would be their costs and benefits?

4. Based on what you know of the outcome of the war in Yugoslavia, did the relevant decision makers enforce the decision of the Badinter Commission regarding borders?

F. Peaceful Secession? A Note on Quebec

For many years, many French-speaking residents of Quebec have called for greater independence, and even secession, from Canada. Referenda among Quebec's citizens on this question have not shown a majority in favor of secession, although a referendum in October 1995 resulted in only 50.6 percent of the population against independence compared to 49.4 percent in favor. In 1998, the Supreme Court of Canada, in response to a request by the Canadian Parliament, issued a lengthy opinion addressing the legality of unilateral secession under both the Canadian Constitution and international law.

Reference re Secession of Quebec

[1998] 2 S.C.R. 217

(ii) Scope of the Right to Self-Determination

The recognized sources of international law establish that the right to self-determination of a people is normally fulfilled through *internal* self-determination—a people's pursuit of its political, economic, social and cultural development within the framework of an existing state. A right to *external* self-determination (which in this case potentially takes the form of the assertion of a right to unilateral secession) arises in only the most extreme of cases and, even then, under carefully defined circumstances. . . .

The international law principle of self-determination has evolved within a framework of respect for the territorial integrity of existing states. The various international documents that support the existence of a people's right to self-determination also contain parallel statements supportive of the conclusion that the exercise of such a right must be sufficiently limited to prevent threats to an existing state's territorial integrity or the stability of relations between sovereign states. . . .

There is no necessary incompatibility between the maintenance of the territorial integrity of existing states, including Canada, and the right of a "people" to achieve a full measure of self-determination. A state whose government represents the whole of the people or peoples resident within its territory, on a basis of equality and without discrimination, and respects the principles of self-determination in its own internal arrangements, is entitled to the protection under international law of its territorial integrity. . . .

Accordingly, the general state of international law with respect to the right to self-determination is that the right operates within the overriding protection granted to the territorial integrity of "parent" states. . . .

A number of commentators have further asserted that the right to self-determination may ground a right to unilateral secession in a third circumstance [other than colonialism or foreign conquest]. Although this third circumstance has been described in several ways, the underlying proposition is that, when a people is blocked from the meaningful exercise of its right to self-determination internally, it is entitled, as a last resort, to exercise it by secession. . . .

Clearly, such a circumstance parallels the other two recognized situations in that the ability of a people to exercise its right to self-determination internally is somehow being totally frustrated. While it remains unclear whether this third proposition actually reflects an established international law standard, it is unnecessary for present purposes to make that determination. Even assuming that the third circumstance is sufficient to create a right to unilateral secession under international law, the current Quebec context cannot be said to approach such a threshold. As stated by the *amicus curiae* . . .

> [TRANSLATION] 15. The Quebec people is not the victim of attacks on its physical existence or integrity, or of a massive violation of its fundamental rights. The Quebec people is manifestly not, in the opinion of the *amicus curiae*, an oppressed people.
>
> 16. For close to 40 of the last 50 years, the Prime Minister of Canada has been a Quebecer. During this period, Quebecers have held from time to time all the most important positions in the federal Cabinet. During the 8 years prior to June 1997, the Prime Minister and the Leader of the Official Opposition in the House of Commons were both Quebecers. At present, the Prime Minister of Canada, the Right Honourable Chief Justice and two other members of the Court, the Chief of Staff of the Canadian Armed Forces and the Canadian ambassador to the United States, not to mention the Deputy Secretary-General of the United Nations, are all Quebecers. . . .

The population of Quebec cannot plausibly be said to be denied access to government. Quebecers occupy prominent positions within the government of Canada. Residents of the province freely make political choices and pursue economic, social and cultural development within Quebec, across Canada, and throughout the world. The population of Quebec is equitably represented in legislative, executive and judicial institutions. In short, to reflect the phraseology of the international documents that address the right to self-determination of peoples, Canada is a "sovereign and independent state conducting itself in compliance with the principle of equal rights and self-determination of peoples and thus possessed of a government representing the whole people belonging to the territory without distinction."

The continuing failure to reach agreement on amendments to the Constitution, while a matter of concern, does not amount to a denial of self-determination. In the absence of amendments to the Canadian Constitution, we must look at the constitutional arrangements presently in effect, and we cannot conclude under current circumstances that those arrangements place Quebecers in a disadvantaged position within the scope of the international law rule.

———————————

The Quebec secession debate has also included much discussion of the future of groups physically located in Quebec who oppose and fear a separate Quebec. The James Bay Crees are a nation of 12,000 aboriginal people who have lived in the area of the James and Hudson Bays for several thousand years. The Crees' homelands are primarily in Quebec, and they have been concerned that the independence of Quebec would not take into account their concerns for self-government. In 1992, the Crees submitted a statement to the UN Commission on Human Rights, and later they submitted a brief to the Canadian Supreme Court during its consideration of the legality of Quebec's secession. The latter included the following:

81. There is no generally accepted definition of "peoples" for purposes of self-determination under international law. However, the United Nations generally has taken a very broad view of the term. Without being exhaustive or essential, objective elements can include: common language, history, culture, race, or ethnicity, way of life, and territory. In addition, a subjective element is necessary, whereby a people identify itself as such. . . .

83. Under Canada's Constitution, Aboriginal peoples are recognized as "peoples" without qualification. This constitutional recognition of Aboriginal peoples as "peoples" and not simply minorities is relevant for international as well as domestic contexts. Moreover, the Quebec National Assembly expressly recognizes Aboriginal peoples in Quebec as distinct "nations" . . . .

84. Presently, the province of Quebec is made up of numerous peoples, including distinct Aboriginal peoples. It cannot be said by the National Assembly or government of Quebec that there is a single "people" within the province that is synonymous with the province or government of Quebec. Nor can it be suggested . . . that there is a single "people" in Canada under international law which can exercise rights of self-determination.

85. For purposes of self-determination and secession, it would appear that a "people" can be constituted of different peoples or different ethnic, linguistic, or religious groups—if there is a common will to constitute as a people. However, "common will" connotes an essential voluntariness among the different individuals and peoples involved. As emphasized in this [brief], there is clearly no such common will by the James Bay Cree people to identify, for purposes of self-determination or for secession, with Quebecers as a single "Quebec people" . . . .

87. To force the James Bay Cree and other Aboriginal peoples in Quebec to identify as a single people with Quebecers for the purposes of secession would effectively deny Aboriginal peoples not only their right to self-identification but also their right to self-determination. . . .

95. The James Bay Crees in Quebec are not claiming a right to secede. There is not and has never been any Cree secessionist movement in Canada. However, the Crees reserve the right to claim a right to secede, in conformance with international law, should the Cree people and Cree territory be forcibly included in a sovereign Quebec, in violation of their fundamental rights.

_____

The Canadian Supreme Court declined to decide the claims of the Crees in its opinion based on its holding that Quebec lacked a unilateral right to secede.

Notes and Questions

1. Does international law play a different role in the secession of entities from a stable state like Canada than from a dissolving one like Yugoslavia?

2. Would and should the decision of the Canadian Supreme Court influence outside decision makers in the event Quebec were unilaterally to secede? If you were the Legal Adviser to the U.S. Secretary of State, would you recommend recognition of an independent Quebec resulting from such a process?

3. Why are the Crees so concerned with the prospect of an independent Quebec? What options are available to the Crees in such an event?

4. In 1898 and 1912, the Canadian government transferred to Quebec from other parts of Canada much of Quebec's current territory, including most of the Cree territory, for the express purpose of keeping Quebec in Canada. Should Quebec be able to take these lands with it if the majority decides to leave Canada?

G. Recognition of New States by Outside Actors: Does It Matter?

Assuming the new entities in Yugoslavia eventually met the traditional criteria for statehood, was this the end of the matter regarding their entry into the community of nations? Was statehood purely a matter of meeting objective criteria, or did statehood itself depend upon the views of other states? International law's characterization of this practically metaphysical question has come under the rubric of the doctrine of recognition. Under one traditional theory, the declaratory view, recognition is a purely political act that states undertake for a variety of reasons—for example, to show support for a new state—but it is irrelevant for the legal determination of statehood. An entity that meets the criteria of statehood immediately enjoys all the rights and duties of a state regardless of the views of other states. States supporting this view codified it in the Montevideo Convention, which declares in Article 3: "The political existence of the state is independent of recognition by the other states." Recognition by one state of a new state is thus merely a declaration by the former of what is already the case; and if the entity is not yet a new state, recognition does not make it one.

The contrary position, known as the constitutive view, regards recognition as one of the elements of statehood—that is, regardless of its satisfaction of the objective criteria, a claimant to statehood is not itself a state until it has been recognized by others. Thus, the refusal by states to afford recognition would mean that the entity claiming statehood would not be entitled to the rights of a state. Indeed, the fear that powerful states, for political reasons, would refuse to recognize an entity meeting the criteria of statehood and thereby cut it off from interstate relations led the Latin American states to explicitly adopt the declaratory view in both the Montevideo Convention excerpt above and in the treaty creating the Organization of American States (OAS).

Most scholars have regarded the declaratory view as more consistent with the practice of states, which have viewed recognition as a discretionary and political act and treated many entities meeting the formal criteria as states without formally recognizing them. Thus, although most Arab states have not recognized the existence of Israel, they have not, for example, ignored rules prohibiting unauthorized overflight by civilian aircraft. Yet it is equally clear that the actual determination as to whether a state has met the criteria of statehood is made by other states, not some independent and wholly impartial body. Thus, if states refuse to acknowledge that an entity meets these criteria (even if it clearly does), they might continue to treat the claimant as something less than a state. For example, a state that is unrecognized may find that its passports are not accepted by immigration authorities in other states. This lends some credence to the constitutive view. As a leading treatise states, "Recognition, while declaratory of an existing fact, is constitutive in nature, at least so far as concerns relations with the recognising state." 1 Oppenheim's International Law 133 (Robert Jennings & Arthur Watts eds., 9th ed. 1992).

As support for the constitutive view, consider the 1965 decision of the UN Security Council following the unilateral declaration of independence from Britain by the white-dominated minority government of Southern Rhodesia (now Zimbabwe). Although the territory met all four criteria in the Montevideo Convention, the Security Council "[c]ondemn[ed] the usurpation of power by a racist settler minority in Southern Rhodesia and regard[ed] the declaration of independence by it as having no legal validity." S.C. Res. 217, Nov. 20, 1965. As a result, nearly all states refused to conclude treaties with Rhodesia. (The situation was resolved only in 1978 following a peace accord that led to a majority government in Zimbabwe.)

As a type of argument in the alternative to the declaratory view, some scholars and states concerned about politically driven refusals to recognize have sought to meld the declaratory and constitutive views. They have asserted that the existence of a state is determined by recognition, but that outside states have a duty to recognize entities meeting the criteria of statehood. Yet, as the Rhodesia case and others make clear, states do not seem to have based their recognition policies on such a duty, and most seem to consider recognition a discretionary act.

How, then, did the law on recognition affect decision making in the context of Yugoslavia? On December 16, 1991, the foreign ministers of the EC issued a document entitled Guidelines on the Recognition of New States in Eastern Europe and in the Soviet Union (the USSR was collapsing simultaneously), along with a Declaration on Yugoslavia.

DECLARATION ON THE ''GUIDELINES ON THE RECOGNITION OF NEW STATES IN EASTERN EUROPE AND IN THE SOVIET UNION''

31 I.L.M. 1486 (1992)

The Community and its Member States confirm their attachment to the principles of the Helsinki Final Act and the Charter of Paris [an important political declaration concluded among all European states in 1990], in particular the principle of self-determination. They affirm their readiness to recognise, subject to the normal standards of international practice and the political realities in each case, those new states which, following the historic changes in the region, have constituted themselves on a democratic basis, have accepted the appropriate international obligations and have committed themselves in good faith to a peaceful process and to negotiations.

Therefore, they adopt a common position on the process of recognition of these new states, which requires:

- respect for the provisions of the Charter of the United Nations and the commitments subscribed to in the Final Act of Helsinki and in the Charter of Paris, especially with regard to the rule of law, democracy and human rights;

- guarantees for the rights of ethnic and national groups and minorities in accordance with the commitments subscribed to in the framework of the CSCE;

- respect for the inviolability of all frontiers which can only be changed by peaceful means and by common agreement;

- acceptance of all relevant commitments with regard to disarmament and nuclear non-proliferation as well as to security and regional stability;

- commitment to settle by agreement, including where appropriate by recourse to arbitration, all questions concerning state succession and regional disputes.

The Community and its Member States will not recognise entities which are the result of aggression. They would take account of the effects of recognition on neighbouring states.

DECLARATION ON YUGOSLAVIA

31 I.L.M. 1485 (1992)

The Community and its member States agree to recognise the independence of all the Yugoslav Republics fulfilling all the conditions set out below. The implementation of this decision will take place on January 15, 1992.

They are therefore inviting all Yugoslav Republics to state by 23 December whether:

- they wish to be recognised as independent States;

- they accept the commitments contained in the above-mentioned guidelines;

- they accept the provisions laid down in the draft Convention-especially those in Chapter II on human rights and rights of national or ethnic groups-under consideration by the Conference on Yugoslavia [these explicit protections of human rights and minority rights were part of a draft treaty to end the conflict that never reached fruition];

- they continue to support the efforts of the Secretary-General and the Security Council of the United Nations, and the continuation of the Conference on Yugoslavia.

The applications of those Republics which reply positively will be submitted through the Chair of the Conference to the Arbitration Commission for advice before the implementation date. . . .

Slovenia, Croatia, Bosnia, and Macedonia immediately sent their applications for recognition to the EC, which passed them first to the Badinter Commission. In January 1992, the Commission issued opinions on each of the four claimants' applications. It approved those of Slovenia and Croatia. The applications from Bosnia and Macedonia, however, raised new issues.

**CONFERENCE ON YUGOSLAVIA
ARBITRATION COMMISSION OPINION NO. 4
ON INTERNATIONAL RECOGNITION OF THE
SOCIALIST REPUBLIC OF BOSNIA-HERZEGOVINA
BY THE EUROPEAN COMMUNITY AND ITS
MEMBER STATES**

31 I.L.M. 1501 (1992)

In a letter dated 20 December 1991 to the President of the Council of the European Communities, the Minister of Foreign Affairs of the Socialist Republic of Bosnia-Hercegovina [SRBH] asked the Member States of the Community to recognize the Republic. . . .

1. By an instrument adopted separately by the Presidency and the Government of Bosnia-Hercegovina on 20 December 1991 . . . these authorities accepted all the commitments indicated in the Declaration and the Guidelines of 16 December 1991. . . .

2. The Commission also noted that on 24 October 1991 the Assembly of the SRBH adopted a ''platform'' on future arrangements for the Yugoslav Community. According to this document the SRBH is prepared to become a member of a new Yugoslav Community on two conditions:

(i) the new Community must include Serbia and Croatia at least; and

(ii) a convention must be signed at the same time recognizing the sovereignty of the SRBH within its present borders; the Presidency of the SRBH has informed the Commission that this in no way affects its application for recognition of its sovereignty and independence.

3. The Commission notes:

(a) that the declarations and undertakings above were given by the Presidency and the Government of the Socialist Republic of Bosnia-Hercegovina, but that the Serbian members of the Presidency did not associate themselves with those declarations and undertakings. . . .

Outside the institutional framework of the SRBH, on 10 November 1991 the ''Serbian people of Bosnia-Hercegovina'' voted in a plebiscite for a ''common Yugoslav State''. On 21 December 1991 an ''Assembly of the Serbian people of Bosnia-Hercegovina'' passed a resolution calling for the formation of a ''Serbian Republic of Bosnia-Hercegovina'' in a federal Yugoslav State if the Muslim and Croat communities of Bosnia-Hercegovina decided to ''change their attitude towards Yugoslavia''. On 9 January 1992 this Assembly proclaimed the independence of a ''Serbian Republic of Bosnia-Hercegovina''.

4. In these circumstances the Arbitration Commission is of the opinion that the will of the peoples of Bosnia-Hercegovina to constitute the SRBH as a sovereign and independent State cannot be held to have been fully established.

This assessment could be reviewed if appropriate guarantees were provided by the Republic applying for recognition, possibly by means of a referendum of all the citizens of the SRBH without distinction, carried out under international supervision.

Macedonia sent its application for recognition to the EC despite objections by Greece to Macedonia's name and flag. Greece claimed that a new state of Macedonia would have territorial claims against the region of northern Greece also known as Macedonia. Indeed, before the creation of Yugoslavia, Macedonia had, at various times in its long history (whether as a state or part of another empire), included large areas of northern Greece and Bulgaria. The Commission's Opinion follows:

CONFERENCE ON YUGOSLAVIA
ARBITRATION COMMISSION OPINION NO. 6
ON THE RECOGNITION OF THE SOCIALIST
REPUBLIC OF MACEDONIA BY THE EUROPEAN
COMMUNITY AND ITS MEMBER STATES

31 I.L.M. 1507 (1992)

1. In his answers to the Commission's questionnaire the Minister of Foreign Affairs made the following statements on behalf of the Republic of Macedonia:

   [Macedonia responded positively to questions regarding respect for international law, protection of minorities, non-use of force, acceptance of the Yugoslavia Conference process, and protection of minorities.]

2. Following a request made by the Arbitration Commission on 10 January 1992 the Minister of Foreign Affairs of the Republic of Macedonia stated in a letter of 11 January that the Republic would refrain from any hostile propaganda against a neighbouring country which was a Member State of the European Community. . . .

4. On 6 January 1992 the Assembly of the Republic of Macedonia amended the Constitution of 17 November 1991 by adopting the following Constitutional Act:

``These Amendments are an integral part of the Constitution of the Republic of Macedonia and shall be implemented on the day of their adoption.

Amendment I

1. The Republic of Macedonia has no territorial claims against neighbouring states.

2. The borders of the Republic of Macedonia could be changed only in accordance with the Constitution, and based on the principle of voluntariness and generally accepted international norms. . . .''

5. The Arbitration Commission consequently takes the view:

— that the Republic of Macedonia satisfies the tests in the Guidelines on the Recognition of New States in Eastern Europe and in the Soviet Union and the Declaration on Yugoslavia adopted by the Council of the European Communities on 16 December 1991;

— that the Republic of Macedonia has, moreover, renounced all territorial claims of any kind in unambiguous statements binding in international law; that the use of the name ''Macedonia'' cannot therefore imply any territorial claim against another State. . . .

On April 6, 1992, the EC foreign ministers decided that, notwithstanding the opinion of the Commission and the opposition of Bosnian Serbs, they would recognize Bosnia; the United States followed the next day. As for Macedonia, the EC's members agreed in 1992 only that they were prepared to "recognize that republic within its present borders under a title which did not include the term Macedonia." The United Nations agreed to admit Macedonia under the provisional name of The Former Yugoslav Republic of Macedonia (alphabetically listed under "T") on April 8, 1993, pending settlement of the name issue with Greece. Greece rejected the EC's decision to recognize Macedonia, and on February 16, 1994, blocked transit of goods to or from landlocked Macedonia through Greece's port of Thessaloniki, with the exception of humanitarian goods. Greece withdrew the embargo the following year after reaching an agreement with Macedonia, in which, among other things, the latter agreed to redesign its flag and national symbol so as not to incorporate the star of Alexander the Great. In November 2004, the U.S. government announced it would refer to the country as the Republic of Macedonia, eliciting strong protest from Greece. The U.S. move was apparently meant as a gesture of support for Macedonia's government and, in particular, its legislation granting significant local autonomy for ethnic Albanians in the country.

Notes and Questions

1. Why did the Badinter Commission seek additional assurances from Macedonia beyond those in the Guidelines? Was this a legitimate request?

2. Does the practice of the EC support the declarative view or the constitutive view regarding recognition?

3. Did the EC follow the Montevideo Convention in formulating its recognition policies? Was it consistent with international law to inject other criteria? Were these other criteria applied consistently by the relevant decision makers?

4. What is the state of the law regarding the elements of statehood, or the criteria for recognition, after the Yugoslavia case?

II. THE SUCCESSION PROCESS: THE END OF THE USSR

In addition to questions of state formation and recognition, the emergence of new states, whether through decolonization, secession, dissolution, or merger, raises serious questions as to the relationship of the new entities to other states and international actors. In particular, do the new states assume the legal rights and obligations of the states from which they emerged? This question—that of state succession—remains central to evaluating the claims of states for participation in the international system.

In this context, decision makers, whether states, international organizations, or private entities, have faced three paramount issues. First, do new states assume the treaty obligations of the states of which they were a part? Second, do they assume the membership in international organizations of which their former state was a member? And third, what norms and processes govern the disposition of property owned by the former state? Underlying these questions will be the status of the state that formerly controlled the new entities: does it still exist, albeit without some of its constituent parts; or is the loss of those parts tantamount to its dissolution such that its remnant part is, like those that split from it, a new state as well? This issue was a central question for the Badinter Commission in Opinion Number 1 discussed above.

As a conceptual matter, international actors face two alternative starting points for an appraisal of options. First, they might adopt a course of action that severs all links between the new states and the old. Under such a "clean slate" position, a new state would assume none of the rights, obligations, memberships, assets, or debts of the predecessor state. Second, they could adopt the opposite course, sometimes referred to as "continuity," under which the new state assumes all the rights and obligations of the prior state, all its memberships in international organizations, and some pro rata share of its assets and debts. As the problem of the USSR below demonstrates, governments, international organizations, and other actors evaluating the claims of successor states have tended to adopt a course of action somewhere between these two extremes; indeed, one might ask whether they have adopted any discernibly consistent practice or have simply responded on a case-by-case basis.

As you read the following excerpts, consider the position of the states of the former USSR as shown on the map below as well as the position of other states; what values and interests these various positions advance; whether all the successor states were and should have been treated equally; whether the positions adopted conform to existing legal rules on the subject; and, perhaps most critically, how important the rules proved to be in the decision-making process.

A. The Problem

Until December 1991, the Union of Soviet Socialist Republics was a state comprised of 15 so-called Union Republics or Soviet Socialist Republics (SSRs). These Republics essentially fell into three groups. At the apex was the largest and most politically important republic, Russia, which contained the seat of government of both the Russian empire (Leningrad, now St. Petersburg) and the USSR (Moscow). Second were lands most of which had been part of the Russian Empire

Commonwealth of Independent States
SOURCE: CIA World Factbook

prior to the 1917 Bolshevik Revolution and which were absorbed by Soviet Russia in
the 1920s—those in Eastern Europe (the Ukrainian and Byelorussian SSRs), the
Caucasus region to the south (Armenian, Azerbaijani, and Georgian SSRs), and
Central Asia (Tadjik, Uzbek, Turkmen, Kazakh, and Kyrghiz SSRs). Third were
lands annexed by the USSR under the terms of a secret 1939 agreement between
Josef Stalin and Adolf Hitler—Romanian Bessarabia (which became the Moldavian
SSR), and three Baltic states that had been independent since the end of World War
I (Estonia, Latvia, and Lithuania). Some Western states did not recognize the
annexation of the Baltic states and even continued to host symbolic diplomatic
representatives of these states after 1940. When the United Nations was formed
in 1945, a political deal among the Allies gave separate membership to the USSR,
the Ukrainian SSR, and the Byelorussian SSR, although the latter two were for all
other purposes part of the USSR.

During the middle and late 1980s, the Soviet Union underwent enormous
internal change under General Secretary Mikhail Gorbachev's policies of *peres-
troika*, and the republics began to assert more distance from Moscow. In 1990,
Estonia, Latvia, and Lithuania declared their independence, and, under some
Western pressure, the government in Moscow eventually accepted their break-
away from the Union in 1991. The other republics also began to distance themselves from Moscow. When conservative communists attempted to seize power
from Gorbachev while he was on vacation in August 1991, the President of the
Russian Republic, Boris Yeltsin, played the leading role in mobilizing popular
opposition to, and eventually reversing, the coup. The result was greatly

enhanced credibility for Russia as an independent actor and its ability to lead the other republics toward a dissolution of the Union. The USSR officially ceased to exist on December 25, 1991, and the hammer and sickle flag was lowered from the Kremlin and replaced by the tricolor of the Russian Federation. The result was 12 completely new states, as well as the resumed independence of the three Baltic states. In December 1991, a few days before the formal dissolution of the USSR, 11 of the 12 non-Baltic states created a Commonwealth of Independent States—a loose political and economic alliance—and created a formal charter for that purpose that all 12 states had joined by 1994. They further agreed to respect the inter-republican borders of the former USSR. The three Baltic states did not join the CIS or any of the various legal regimes related to it, preferring to sever all ties from the remnants of the USSR.

B. Succeeding to Treaty Commitments: The Vienna Convention and Its Variants

Nearly every state in the world had had some political, economic, or cultural contact or relationship with the Soviet Union. But states deciding how to respond to the legal questions surrounding succession did not work in a legal vacuum. In 1978, a UN-sponsored multilateral conference completed the Vienna Convention on Succession of States in Respect of Treaties. The Convention was the product of long preparatory work in the UN's International Law Commission (ILC) beginning in 1962, as well as reconsideration by governments in 1977 and 1978. Drafters of the treaty considered some of it to codify customary international law, although significant parts of it represented new policy. The treaty had only 18 parties as of 2006; in 1991 and 1992, Estonia and Ukraine, respectively, became the only two former Soviet Republics to accede to the 1978 Vienna Convention. (The United States is not a party.) Yet governments have often invoked it as establishing default rules on the effect of state succession on treaty obligations—rules that apply unless the relevant states agree upon other approaches to govern a particular succession. Several articles are of particular importance:

Vienna Convention on Succession of States in Respect of Treaties

1946 U.N.T.S. 3 (1978)

Article 11. Boundary Regimes

A succession of States does not as such affect:
    (a) a boundary established by a treaty; or
    (b) obligations and rights established by a treaty and relating to the regime of a boundary.

Article 16. Position in Respect of the Treaties of the Predecessor State

A newly independent State [defined earlier as a state that used to be a dependent territory, i.e., a colony, of another state] is not bound to maintain in force, or to become a party to, any treaty by reason only of the fact that at the date of the succession of States the treaty was in force in respect of the territory to which the succession of States relates.

Article 34. Succession of States in Cases of Separation of Parts of a State

    1. When a part or parts of the territory of a State separate to form one or more States, whether or not the predecessor State continues to exist:

        (a) any treaty in force at the date of the succession of States in respect of the entire territory of the predecessor State continues in force in respect of each successor State so formed;

        (b) any treaty in force at the date of the succession of States in respect only of that part of the territory of the predecessor State which has become a successor State continues in force in respect of that successor State alone.

    2. Paragraph 1 does not apply if:

        (a) the States concerned otherwise agree; or

        (b) it appears from the treaty or is otherwise established that the application of the treaty in respect of the successor State would be incompatible with the object and purpose of the treaty or would radically change the conditions for its operation.

Article 35. Position if a State Continues After Separation of Part of Its Territory

    When, after separation of any part of the territory of a State, the predecessor State continues to exist, any treaty which at the date of the succession of States was in force in respect of the predecessor State continues in force in respect of its remaining territory unless:

        (a) the States concerned otherwise agree;

        (b) it is established that the treaty related only to the territory which has separated from the predecessor State; or

        (c) it appears from the treaty or is otherwise established that the application of the treaty in respect of the predecessor State would be incompatible with the object and purpose of the treaty or would radically change the conditions for its operation.

    In the 1970s and 1980s, legal scholars in the United States preparing the Restatement (Third) of the Foreign Relations Law of the United States adopted the following position regarding state succession and international agreements:

Restatement (Third) of the Foreign Relations Law of the United States §210 (1987)

    (1) When part of the territory of a state becomes territory of another state, the international agreements of the predecessor state cease to have effect in respect of that territory and the international agreements of the successor state come into force there.

    (2) When a state is absorbed by another state, the international agreements of the absorbed state are terminated and the international agreements of the absorbing state become applicable to the territory of the absorbed state.

    (3) When part of a state becomes a new state, the new state does not succeed to the international agreements to which the predecessor state was party, unless,

expressly or by implication, it accepts such agreements and the other party or parties thereto agree or acquiesce.

(4) Pre-existing boundary and other territorial agreements continue to be binding notwithstanding Subsections (1)-(3).

Notes and Questions

1. Compare the Vienna Convention and Restatement views regarding new states. Why might they have adopted different rules regarding new states? What were the interests of the drafters of each document regarding new states?

2. How would you determine which view, if either, represents customary international law regarding succession to treaties?

3. Why do you think so few states have become parties to the 1978 Vienna Convention?

C. The Commonwealth of Independent States' Approach to Succession

On December 21, 1991, in the waning days of the USSR, the members of the new CIS met in Alma Ata (now Almaty), Kazakhstan, and issued the following document:

Alma Ata Declaration

U.N. Doc. A/47/60-S/23329, Annex II (1991)

Recognizing and respecting each other's territorial integrity and the inviolability of existing borders . . . [the 12 republics]

Declare that:

Cooperation between the parties in the Commonwealth shall be conducted in accordance with the principle of equality through coordinating bodies constituted on a basis of parity and operating under a procedure to be determined by agreements between the parties in the Commonwealth, which is neither a State nor a supra-State entity. . . .

The Commonwealth of Independent States is open, with the consent of all its participants, to accession by other States members of the former Union of Soviet Socialist Republics, and also by other States sharing the purposes and principles of the Commonwealth. . . .

With the establishment of the Commonwealth of Independent States, the Union of Soviet Socialist Republics ceases to exist.

The States participating in the Commonwealth guarantee in accordance with their constitutional procedures the dis-

```
charge of the international obligations deriving from trea-
ties and agreements concluded by the former Union of Soviet
Socialist Republics.
```

At the same meeting, the heads of state declared that "[b]earing in mind that the Republic of Belarus, the Union of Soviet Socialist Republics and Ukraine were founding Members of the United Nations," they "support Russia's continuance of the membership of the Union of Soviet Socialist Republics in the United Nations, including permanent membership of the Security Council, and other international organizations. . . ."

Based on this decision, Russian President Yeltsin sent a letter to UN Secretary-General Javier Perez de Cuellar on December 24, 1991, stating:

> I have the honour to inform you that the membership of the Union of Soviet Socialist Republics in the United Nations, including the Security Council and all other organs and organizations of the United Nations system, is being continued by the Russian Federation (RSFSR) with the support of the countries of the Commonwealth of Independent States. In this connection, I request that the name "the Russian Federation" should be used in the United Nations in place of the name "the Union of Soviet Socialist Republics."

> The Russian Federation maintains full responsibility for all the rights and obligations of the USSR under the Charter of the United Nations, including the financial obligations. . . .

U.N. Doc. A/47/60-S/23329 (1991).

Notes and Questions

1. Which approach to succession of treaties did the CIS states endorse? Does their position suggest that a particular norm of succession is somehow achieving customary law status?

2. Why do you think the CIS heads of state agreed to support Russia's assumption of the permanent seat on the UN Security Council? Did the CIS and President Yeltsin characterize Russia as a new state, or the legal continuation of the USSR? What did they assume about the membership of Belarus and Ukraine?

3. Article 2(1) of the UN Charter states that the United Nations is based on the "sovereign equality of all its Members." As discussed in Chapter 2, the term "sovereign equality" refers to juridical or legal equality in the sense that all states as a formal matter enjoy equal rights and duties; states with larger populations, economies, or military resources do not, in theory, enjoy special legal rights by virtue of those capacities. Is the decision of the CIS states regarding the Security Council seat consistent with the notion of sovereign equality?

D. Governmental Reactions on Treaty Succession

Governments and international organizations faced with responding to the breakup of the USSR adopted different strategies regarding the continuation of treaty obligations. Consider the following account based on the records of a meeting of foreign ministry legal advisers of the Council of Europe, an organization of democratic states in Europe:

> Addressing the usefulness of the Vienna Convention, a majority of the Legal Advisers stated that the Vienna Convention could not be assumed to represent existing public international law. Particularly, the Legal Advisers found the distinction between continuation and dissolution unhelpful in determining the obligations of successor states under the treaty rights of the predecessor state. However, the Legal Advisers did indicate that the Vienna Convention contained many "useful elements" . . . .
>
> In summing up the discussion, the Chairman of the conference stated that bilateral agreements should "be dealt with in a practical way, irrespective of the theoretical point of departure (clean slate or succession). States should arrive at a common list containing agreements which should apply between them."
>
> The Legal Advisers found it difficult to establish a general rule concerning multilateral agreements. Some Legal Advisers supported the clean slate approach, while others were willing to accept the principle of succession but felt it necessary to require something more than a general declaration of succession. . . . A number of Legal Advisers noted that the nature of the treaty was important when considering continuity and that, in cases such as human rights and navigation treaties, every successor should be bound by the treaty obligations of the predecessor.
>
> Switzerland explained that it considered Russia to be the continuity of the former Soviet Union, so it had replaced the designation "USSR" with "Russia" on all multilateral treaties for which it was a depository. . . .
>
> . . . [T]he Chairman of the Conference stated that a "new State should make a declaration of succession in order to avoid a legal vacuum. States Parties to such a treaty should be able to oppose a declaration of succession."
>
> . . . [T]he General Consul of Russia, attending as an observer, stated that Russia was the continuity of the former Soviet Union, and the other former Republics "could be considered to be successor States." In support of this view, a number of states expressed the opinion that it was unnecessary to recognize Russia "as the international community considered that Russia was the continuity of the Soviet Union." In summing up the discussion on the former Soviet Union, the Chairman noted "that the Russian Federation had been considered as the continuing State of the Soviet Union in the United Nations. . . . With respect to the other former Soviet republics the question of succession had to be considered."

Paul R. Williams, *The Treaty Obligations of the Successor States of the Former Soviet Union, Yugoslavia, and Czechoslovakia: Do They Continue in Force?*, 23 Denv. J. Intl. L. & Poly. 1, 17-19 (1994).

The Legal Adviser of the U.S. Department of State later wrote:

> As a practical matter, given the unsettled nature of the governing legal rules and the diversity of agreements in question, we concluded that the only way to establish clearly what agreements would remain in force for the former Soviet Union would be an explicit, case-by-case review of outstanding agreements with each of the former republics. Beginning in mid-1992, the Bush Administration engaged in just such a process with the republics in order to confirm which of the bilateral agreements would continue in force, and to determine which should be modified or terminated. In the interim, the United States regards the various agreements as continuing in force with all of the republics, unless and until it makes a clear determination to the contrary.

Edwin D. Williamson & John E. Osborn, *A U.S. Perspective on Treaty Succession and Related Issues in the Wake of the Breakup of the USSR and Yugoslavia*, 33 Va. J. Intl. L. 261, 267 (1993).

In the State Department's official publication listing treaties in force for the United States as of 2005, the Department reprinted the statement from the Alma Ata Declaration regarding the successor states' intention to discharge their obligations under the USSR's treaties and stated that the United States "is reviewing the continued applicability" of pre-1992 agreements with the USSR, which were still listed in the publication.

Notes and Questions

1. How did European states and the United States respond to the question of the continued application of their treaties with the USSR? Did they follow the Vienna Convention, the Restatement, or neither?

2. If you were in the foreign ministry of one of these countries and believed that a particular treaty with the USSR was no longer in force by virtue of the dissolution, how would you address the problem with the successor states?

3. Is there any point in having rules of succession if key states simply resolve succession issues on a case-by-case basis? Economic analysis suggests that default rules will govern unless the parties' gains from bargaining around them exceed the costs of negotiations. When parties do negotiate, default rules help determine who will bargain and at what cost. From this perspective, default rules such as the Vienna Convention are not simply "neutral" background rules; they have potentially important distributional implications. What implications could they have?

4. Should international law recognize different succession rules for different sorts of treaties? For example, might a presumption of continuation in force make more sense for a human rights or arms control treaty compared to an economic development agreement?

5. On rare occasions, one part of a state has been transferred to another, as took place in 1997 when Britain returned Hong Kong to China under the terms of a 1984 agreement. (See Chapter 4.) In these cases, the Vienna Convention's default rule is that the treaty obligations of the predecessor state are replaced by those of the new state unless such replacement "would be incompatible with the object and purpose of the treaty or would radically change the conditions for its operation." (Article 15). Britain and China agreed that Hong Kong could, at the discretion of China, remain a party to some agreements to which the United Kingdom, but not China, was a party as of 1997. China eventually agreed that 87 such multilateral treaties would remain in force for Hong Kong, including the 1966 International Covenant on Civil and Political Rights, but not the 1984 Convention against Torture and Other Cruel, Inhuman or Degrading Treatment or Punishment. Two hundred thirty-one multilateral treaties to which the UK was a party as of 1997 were not applied to Hong Kong after the transfer of sovereignty.

E. The Response of International Institutions on Membership Questions

The Soviet Union was a member of many important international organizations. Most significantly, of course, it was a founding member of the United Nations and a permanent member of the Security Council. The most immediate question for these institutions regarding succession concerned whether some or all of the successor states to the USSR would need to apply for membership or could somehow automatically assume the seat of the USSR. As for the Baltic states, their formal independence from the USSR in 1991 was quickly followed by their application for admission to the United Nations and then entry on September 17, 1991. Regarding the successor states in the CIS, the Alma Ata Declaration above had made clear their position. After receiving President Yeltsin's December 24, 1991, letter, the UN Secretariat circulated the communication to all delegations the same day. Without any discussion in, or formal decision by, the Security Council or the General Assembly, Russia replaced the Soviet Union in all UN bodies and organizations. Belarus and Ukraine, which had been admitted separately to the United Nations in 1945 despite being republics of the USSR (as part of a compromise between the West and Josef Stalin during negotiations on setting up the United Nations), remained members, although the former notified the United Nations that it was changing its name from Byelorussia. Secretariat officials replaced flags and nameplates without fanfare. The other nine successor states applied for membership; all were admitted in 1992.

At the time, media reports stated that the United States, the United Kingdom, and France allowed Russia to assume the USSR's seat automatically, rather than applying for UN membership, as would be required under Article 4 of the Charter, in order to avoid encouraging any discussion within the United Nations over the appropriate composition of the Security Council. Since the 1980s, many developing world nations have been urging an increase in their representation on the Council, and have even proposed replacing Britain and France as permanent members with a European Union seat (an issue discussed in Chapter 14). Moreover, making the decision in late December meant that the General Assembly was not meeting at the time.

The response of the United Nations—both its members and its Secretariat—stands in some contrast to its response to the dissolution of Yugoslavia discussed in the first problem in this chapter. On April 27, 1992, after Slovenia, Croatia, Bosnia-Herzegovina, and Macedonia had declared independence from Belgrade, the national assemblies of the two remaining republics, Serbia and Montenegro, publicly proclaimed their policy to stay part of Yugoslavia, which they renamed the Federal Republic of Yugoslavia (FRY). They declared that the FRY "continues the State, international legal and political personality of the Socialist Federal Republic of Yugoslavia." The four new entities, for their part, all applied for UN membership, and on May 22, 1992, the General Assembly admitted all but Macedonia as new UN members (see the discussion in the previous problem regarding Macedonia's status).

On that day, the authorities in Belgrade circulated a document to the General Assembly stating that the admission of the three republics "in no way challenges the international legal personality and continuity of membership of the Federal Republic of Yugoslavia in the United Nations and its specialized agencies." The United States Representative to the United Nations stated publicly in the General Assembly on the same day that "if Serbia and Montenegro desire to sit in the U.N., they should be required to apply for membership and be held to the same standards as all other applicants."* On July 4, the Badinter Commission issued its Opinion No. 8, declar-

*This account is adapted in part from Michael P. Scharf, *Musical Chairs: The Dissolution of States and Membership in the United Nations,* 28 Cornell Intl. L.J. 29 (1995).

ing that the Socialist Federal Republic of Yugoslavia no longer existed and that the
FRY was a new state. The United States and EC states, intent on punishing the FRY
over the war in Bosnia, engaged in intensive discussions with UN members over an
approach to deny the FRY the seat once held by the SFRY.

On September 19, 1992, the Security Council passed the following resolution:

Security Council Resolution 777 (1992)

The Security Council . . .

Considering that the state formerly known as the Socialist
Federal Republic of Yugoslavia has ceased to exist,

Recalling in particular resolution 757 (1992) which notes
that ''the claim by the Federal Republic of Yugoslavia (Serbia and Montenegro) to continue automatically the membership
of the former Socialist Federal Republic of Yugoslavia in the
United Nations has not been generally accepted'',

1. Considers that the Federal Republic of Yugoslavia (Serbia
and Montenegro) cannot continue automatically the membership of
the former Socialist Federal Republic of Yugoslavia in the United Nations; and therefore recommends to the General Assembly
that it decide that the Federal Republic of Yugoslavia (Serbia
and Montenegro) should apply for membership in the United
Nations and that it shall not participate in the work of the General Assembly. . . .

At the Council's meeting at which the resolution was adopted, the Russian
delegate emphasized that the resolution was a compromise that rejects any notion
that the FRY "should be excluded formally or de facto from membership in the
United Nations," stated that it would still participate in the work of the Security
Council and circulate documents, and noted that the name "Yugoslavia" would still
appear on the nameplate in the General Assembly hall (although presumably with
nobody sitting behind it). The United States, on the other hand, stated that the
membership of the SFRY had "expired." The General Assembly adopted the
Council's recommendation three days later in Resolution 47/1, echoing the language of the Council's resolution. But the confusion over its interpretation
prompted several states to ask the UN's Legal Counsel for a formal opinion,
which he circulated ten days later. In it, he noted that the resolution "neither terminates nor suspends Yugoslavia's membership in the Organization." He then
stated that the nameplates would remain unchanged, the old SFRY flag would
continue to fly outside the United Nations, FRY representatives could participate
in organs other than the General Assembly, and the UN's specialized agencies could
make their own decisions on these issues (though a number of specialized agencies
decided to take the same steps as the General Assembly).

This state of affairs prevailed for over eight years. On October 27, 2000, following the replacement of the government of Slobodan Milosevic in an election, the
new government of Vojuslav Kostunica submitted an application for membership to

the United Nations "[i]n the wake of fundamental democratic changes that took place in the Federal Republic of Yugoslavia" and "in light of the implementation of Security Council resolution 777 (1992)." The Security Council endorsed the admission, which the General Assembly granted on November 1, 2000. In December 2004, the ICJ found that it lacked jurisdiction to rule on the merits of an April 1999 suit by the FRY against eight NATO states arising out of the 1999 Kosovo war (see Chapter 8, Section II.F and Chapter 13, Section IV). Eight of the Court's 15 judges concluded that the admission of Serbia and Montenegro to the UN in 2000 meant that it had not been a member of the UN and not a party to the ICJ's Statute in 1999, though the lack of reasoning on this conclusion was harshly criticized by the other seven judges. This conclusion could have a direct bearing on Bosnia's pending ICJ suit against Serbia-Montenegro for violations of the Genocide Convention during the Bosnian conflict.

Notes and Questions

1. Was the UN's procedure regarding the membership of the USSR's successor states consistent with the Vienna Convention or the Restatement? Did international law play a role in the action of the United Nations?

2. What decision did the Security Council make in 1992 regarding Yugoslavia's status as a state? Why do you think it did not adopt the same stance as it did toward Russia and the USSR's seat? To what extent did legal principles of state succession appear to influence the decision makers in this episode?

3. How does the identity of the decision maker on questions of succession—namely, legal advisers within foreign ministries, politicians, or international organizations like the United Nations—affect the extent to which law will play a role in those decisions?

F. Dividing Up Soviet Assets and Liabilities

The division of the USSR's financial and physical assets, as well as liabilities, proved quite contentious during the early years of the successor states. In the waning months of the Soviet Union, the republics desperately sought some financial relief from Western governments and banks, but those entities were concerned about responsibility for existing debts of the USSR. In October and November 1991, under pressure from creditors, eight of the twelve non-Baltic republics agreed to be jointly and severally liable for the debts of the Soviet Union, in exchange for which Western governments and banks agreed to defer repayment of much of the pre-1991 debt. On December 8, 1991, eight of the republics (though not all the same as those that were party to the earlier agreement) agreed to a treaty on the succession to the USSR's debts and assets. Under it, Russia assumed 61.34 percent, Ukraine 16.37 percent, Belarus 3.86 percent, Uzbekistan 3.27 percent, and all other states less than 2 percent of the USSR's debts and assets (down to Estonia, which would assume 0.62 percent). These shares were based upon the republics' population, national income, exports, and imports. Ten states eventually signed the agreement, but Ukraine, Georgia, and the three Baltic states did not. Nonetheless, disagreement continued even among the signatories on the implementation of the scheme, and the division did not work in practice.

In 1992, Russia announced the so-called zero-option, by which it would assume all the external liabilities—and assets—of the former republics. It eventually reached bilateral agreements to this effect with the other non-Baltic republics, with the exception of Ukraine, which would keep its share of the assets and pay Russia directly in exchange for Russia's assuming the liabilities. When it became clear that Ukraine could not pay these amounts, the two governments agreed in 1994 that Russia would take over all of Ukraine's share of the liabilities as well as assets. Ukraine's parliament refused to ratify the agreement, however, and the issue remained unresolved in 2006.

As with succession to treaties, international law offered some guidance on these issues, but neither a complete nor broadly accepted set of rules. Governments working through the United Nations had developed some norms to govern such situations in the Vienna Convention on Succession of States in Respect of State Property, Archives, and Debts, which was concluded in 1983 following extensive drafting by the ILC and a conference of governments. The treaty was not, however, in force during the dissolution of the USSR, although Ukraine, Estonia, and Georgia eventually became parties. (Only seven states are parties as of 2006.) It included the following provisions:

Article 11
Passing of State Property Without Compensation

Subject to the provisions of the articles in the present Part and unless otherwise agreed by the States concerned or decided by an appropriate international body, the passing of State property of the predecessor State to the successor State shall take place without compensation.

Article 18
Dissolution of a State

1. When a State dissolves and ceases to exist and the parts of the territory of the predecessor State form two or more successor States, and unless the successor States concerned otherwise agree:

   (a) immovable State property of the predecessor State shall pass to the successor State in the territory of which it is situated;
   (b) immovable State property of the predecessor State situated outside its territory shall pass to the successor States in equitable proportions;
   (c) movable State property of the predecessor State connected with the activity of the predecessor State in respect of the territories to which the succession of States relates shall pass to the successor State concerned;
   (d) movable State property of the predecessor State, other than that mentioned in subparagraph (c), shall pass to the successor States in equitable proportions.

2. The provisions of paragraph 1 are without prejudice to any question of equitable compensation among the successor States that may arise as a result of a succession of States.

Article 36
Absence of effect of a succession of States on creditors

A succession of States does not as such affect the rights and obligations of creditors.

Article 41
Dissolution of a State

When a State dissolves and ceases to exist and the parts of the territory of the predecessor State form two or more successor States, and unless the successor States otherwise agree, the State debt of the predecessor State shall pass to the successor States in equitable proportions, taking into account, in particular, the property, rights and interests which pass to the successor States in relation to that State debt.

The most contentious issue between Russia and Ukraine has been the status of Russia's Black Sea fleet, whose home port is in the Ukrainian city of Sevastopol, on the Crimean peninsula. For six years, Moscow and Kiev had sharp disagreements regarding the ownership and operation of the fleet, with officials of each side threatening various unilateral steps. Meanwhile, much of the fleet decayed due to lack of maintenance. In May 1997, Presidents Boris Yeltsin and Leonid Kuchma signed a treaty that affirmed Ukraine's territorial sovereignty over the area but allowed Russia to rent most of the base at a low cost and operate the fleet in Sevastopol for 20 years; Ukraine received ownership of only 17 percent of the fleet's ships. Nevertheless, the two sides still disagree on various implementation issues, and tensions increased after the election of Ukraine's new president in 2004.

Notes and Questions

1. Did the 1983 Vienna Convention provide any useful guidance to the USSR's successor states? Did it prove a useful tool for creditor states?

2. What is the likelihood that states will ever need default rules on division of property? Are not all these situations likely to be negotiated by bilateral or multilateral treaties?

3. Is succession to assets and liabilities likely to be more or less contentious than succession to treaties?

4. In the 1990s, the SFRY's successor states (with the exception of the FRY (Serbia-Montenegro)) reached various agreements with foreign creditors on the division of the debt of the former Yugoslavia. After the election of a democratic government in Serbia, all five successor states negotiated a complex agreement on remaining property and debts, including real property within their territories, diplomatic property abroad, and gold and money on deposit in foreign banks. (A leading British international law scholar, Arthur Watts, oversaw the talks.) Concluded in Vienna on June 29, 2001, it was the first agreement signed by all five successor states. Each state generally kept all Yugoslav property on its territories (with exceptions for military property and cultural property of particular importance to another state); foreign embassies and assets were to be divided roughly in the following ratio based on their market value: 15 percent for Bosnia; 23.5 percent for Croatia; 8 percent for Macedonia; 15 percent for Slovenia; and 38.5 percent for Serbia-Montenegro. These numbers were based on the International Monetary Fund's (IMF's) division of the former Yugoslavia's IMF debts and assets in 1993, which had taken into account each state's share of the economy and population of the former Yugoslavia but were adjusted during the negotiations. External debts were assumed by each state that benefitted from the underlying transaction. A joint committee is supposed to implement the accord.

III. THE PROCESS OF GOVERNMENTAL CHANGE: NEW GOVERNMENTS IN CAMBODIA

Despite the manifold legal questions that governments and other decision makers face due to the formation and transformation of states, the far more common phenomenon in international relations is the change of government or ruling elites within a state. Many such changes are routine matters according to constitutional procedures following an election. For instance, the government (in the continental sense, meaning the head of government and his or her cabinet) might change from Labor to Likud in Israel or from Social Democrats to Christian Democrats in Germany. Others, however, result from extraconstitutional situations, whether revolution, military coup, or civil war. When such changes take place, new governments are often tempted to renounce international commitments made by their predecessors. Moreover, external actors need to decide upon their attitude toward the new government—whether to approve it through, for instance, a formal act of recognition; disapprove it by, for example, continuing to deal only with the prior regime; transact interstate business with it without taking such a stance; or otherwise.

As a starting point, international law, at least in theory, provides a clear rule: a change in government in a state does not affect its international obligations. Moreover, traditional law also had strong views on the relevance of two other factors to the rights and duties of states with new governments: (1) the way in which the new government took power, and (2) the views of other states as to its legitimacy—often expressed in their decisions whether to recognize the new government. American Chief Justice William Howard Taft put forth the position of international law on these issues while he was acting as arbitrator in a dispute between Great Britain and Costa Rica. The issue was whether Costa Rica could nullify the financial obligations incurred by the previous government, led by Frederico Tinoco, which had come to power extraconstitutionally and not been recognized by the United Kingdom or the United States:

> . . . [W]hen recognition *vel non* of a government is by such nations determined by inquiry, not into its *de facto* sovereignty and complete governmental control, but into its illegitimacy or irregularity of origin, their non-recognition loses something of evidential weight on the issue with which those applying the rules of international law are alone concerned. . . . Such non-recognition for any reason . . . cannot outweigh the evidence disclosed by this record before me as to the *de facto* character of Tinoco's government, according to the standard set by international law. . . . The issue is not whether the new government assumes power or conducts its administration under constitutional limitations established by the people during the incumbency of the government it has overthrown. The question is, has it really established itself in such a way that all within its influence recognize its control, and that there is no opposing force assuming to be a government in its place? Is it discharging its functions as a government usually does, respected within its own jurisdiction?

Tinoco Arbitration (U.K. v. Costa Rica), 1 U.N.R.I.A.A. 369, 381-382 (1923).

The legal irrelevance of recognition of governments received further support in the so-called Estrada Doctrine, enunciated by the Mexican Foreign Minister in 1930:

[T]he Mexican government is issuing no declarations in the sense of grants of recognition, since that nation considers that such a course is an insulting practice and one which, in addition to the fact that it offends the sovereignty of other nations, implies that judgment of some sort may be passed upon the internal affairs of those nations by other governments, inasmuch as the latter assume, in effect, an attitude of criticism, when they decide, favorably or unfavorably, as to the legal qualifications of foreign régimes.

Marjorie Whiteman, 2 Digest of International Law 85 (1963).

Thus, international law would regard a change in government by coup or revolution as no different from, for example, the transfer of power from the Democratic Party to the Republican Party in the United States after an election. The Tinoco and Estrada positions were not completely unopposed at the time. Woodrow Wilson, for instance, had endorsed the so-called Tobar Doctrine, named for the Ecuadoran foreign minister. To promote democratic transfers of power, the Tobar Doctrine would deny recognition to governments resulting from extraconstitutional power struggles; the United States even applied it in the first part of the twentieth century to a handful of recognition decisions regarding Latin America and the Soviet Union.

But if governmental change does not alter a state's international obligations as a general matter, such change clearly affects other aspects of its international relations. As you read the following materials about Cambodia's changing governments, consider how the test of effective control enunciated in the *Tinoco* case has fared since that time; what political interests such a test serves; what the consequences of alternative tests are; how important the law was in dictating the decision making in Cambodia; to what extent the make-up of a state's government is solely a matter of its domestic jurisdiction; and to what extent states will and should take into account the method of governmental change in their international relations with a government.

A. The Problem

Cambodia, a country of some 12 million people in Southeast Asia, assumed its independence from France in 1953. Until 1970, Cambodia was a kingdom, with Norodom Sihanouk as the head of state or of the government for much of the period. In 1970, Sihanouk was overthrown by his prime minister, Lon Nol, who was backed by the Cambodian military and the United States, which saw him as an ally in the Vietnam War. The ouster of Sihanouk aggravated disagreements between the government and the Khmer Rouge, a local communist guerrilla insurgent movement that had been receiving support from Vietnam and China. A full-scale civil war ensued. After five years, Lon Nol's government fell, on April 17, 1975.

For the next three years and nine months, the Khmer Rouge governed Cambodia, renaming it Democratic Kampuchea. During this period, the government engaged in horrific violations of human rights, including the evacuation of Cambodia's cities, extermination of perceived political opponents, and subjection of much of the population to forced agrarian work under abysmal conditions. It is estimated that some one-fifth of Cambodia's 1975 population of 7.3 million perished under the Khmer Rouge.

In December 1978, following tensions between Cambodia and Vietnam, including fighting along their common border, Vietnam invaded Cambodia and ousted the Khmer Rouge. On January 7, 1979, the Vietnamese army took control of the capital and installed a new government consisting of a group of ex-Khmer Rouge who had left the movement and the country for Vietnam in the preceding years. The Khmer Rouge fled to the western part of the country, from which for the next decade they engaged in fighting the new government with assistance from China and other opponents of Vietnam. The conflict was, however, generally confined in scope; the new regime, which renamed the state the People's Republic of Kampuchea (PRK), controlled roughly 90 percent of Cambodia's territory. The PRK government also sought to represent Cambodia in international organizations and resume the relations with other countries that Cambodia had had prior to its civil war.

The reaction of outside states to the changes in government in Cambodia took place both in bilateral relations and in multilateral fora. Bilaterally, many states responded to the Khmer Rouge's victory in 1975 by breaking diplomatic relations, leaving the country politically isolated (and consequently leaving few diplomats in Cambodia to report on the atrocities). Democratic Kampuchea's principal diplomatic ally was China. When the new government took over in 1979, most Western states remained at a distance, although the Soviet-bloc states, in solidarity with Vietnam, and some others, resumed ties. Beyond the practice of individual states, the best single forum for observing decision making regarding the status of these new governments was the United Nations. While individual governments might choose to ignore Cambodia, the General Assembly had to decide who would occupy Cambodia's seat in the organization. The Khmer Rouge had quickly assumed Cambodia's seat upon its victory in 1975, but the PRK proved less successful at the UN after its conquest in 1979.

B. The China Precedent

The change in governments in Cambodia was hardly the first time the United Nations had to address the consequences of extraconstitutional change. The first significant challenge had come decades earlier, during and after the Chinese revolution. The Nationalist government in Beijing had governed the state, which it called the Republic of China (ROC), ever since it overthrew the Chinese empire in 1911; beginning in the 1930s, it engaged in a civil war with Mao Zedong's well-organized communist forces. As conditions worsened for the Nationalist cause after World War II, hundreds of thousands of its supporters fled to Taiwan, the large island off the coast of China. On October 1, 1949, with the Nationalists defeated, Mao declared the founding of the People's Republic of China (PRC). Many states immediately or shortly thereafter formally recognized Mao's government as the sole legitimate government of China. The Nationalist leaders who fled to Taiwan declared that they remained the government of all of China and promised to liberate the mainland. Taiwan retained diplomatic relations with the United States and many of its Western friends.

The Republic of China under the Nationalist government had been not only a founding member of the United Nations but a permanent member of the Security Council. The United Nations would thus have to decide which government would occupy China's seat at the organization. On March 8, 1950, Secretary-General Trygve Lie made public his views in a memorandum.

Legal Aspects of Problems of Representation in the United Nations

U.N. Doc. S/1466 (1950)

From the standpoint of legal theory, the linkage of representation in an international organization and recognition of a government is a confusion of two institutions which have superficial similarities but are essentially different.

The recognition of a new State, or of a new government of an existing state, is a unilateral act which the recognizing government can grant or withhold. It is true that some legal writers have argued forcibly that when a new government, which comes into power through revolutionary means, enjoys, with a reasonable prospect of permanency, the habitual obedience of the bulk of the population, other States are under a legal duty to recognize it. However, while States may regard it as desirable to follow certain legal principles in according or withholding recognition . . . [it] is still regarded as essentially a political decision, which each State decides in accordance with its own free appreciation of the situation. . . .

. . . It is a remarkable fact that, despite the fairly large number of revolutionary changes of government and the larger number of instances of breach of diplomatic relations among members, there was not one single instance of a challenge of credentials of a representative in the many thousands of meetings which were held during four years. On the contrary, whenever the reports of credentials committees were voted on (as in the sessions of the General Assembly), they were always adopted unanimously and without reservation by any Members. . . .

The practice which has been thus followed in the United Nations is not only legally correct but conforms to the basic character of the Organization. The United Nations is not an association limited to like-minded States and governments of similar ideological persuasion (as in the case in certain regional associations). As an Organization which aspires to universality, it must of necessity include States of varying and even conflicting ideologies.

The Chinese case is unique in the history of the United Nations, not because it involves a revolutionary change of government, but because it is the first in which two rival governments exist. It is quite possible that such a situation will occur again in the future and it is highly desirable to see what principle can be followed in choosing between the rivals. It has been demonstrated that the principle of numerical preponderance of recognition is inappropriate and legally incorrect. Is any other principle possible?

It is submitted that the proper principle can be derived by analogy from Article 4 of the Charter. This Article requires that an applicant for membership must be able and willing to carry out the obligations of membership. The obligations of membership can be carried out only by governments which in fact possess the power to do so. Where a revolutionary government presents itself as representing a State, in rivalry to an existing government, the question at issue should be which of these two governments in fact is in a position to employ the resources and direct the people of the State in fulfillment of the obligations of membership. In essence, this means an inquiry as to whether the new government exercises effective authority within the territory of the State and is habitually obeyed by the bulk of the population.

If so, it would seem to be appropriate for the United Nations organs, through their collective action, to accord it the right to represent the State in the Organization, even though the individual Members of the Organization refuse, and may continue to refuse, to accord it recognition as the lawful government for reasons which are valid under their national policies.

On December 14, 1950, the General Assembly, by a vote of 36-6-9, adopted a resolution stating that "whenever more than one authority claims to be the government entitled to represent a Member State in the United Nations and this question becomes the subject of controversy in the United Nations, the question should be considered in the light of the Purposes and Principles of the Charter and the circumstances of each case." G.A. Res. 396 (1950).

The United States continued to muster enough support in the General Assembly for its position to block the replacement of the ROC delegation by the PRC delegation throughout the 1950s and 1960s. In 1971, as part of Richard Nixon's opening of relations with the PRC as a lever against the USSR in the Cold War, the United States agreed to the seating of the PRC delegation. The PRC quickly assumed Taiwan's seat in nearly all international organizations. On January 1, 1979, the United States recognized the PRC regime as the sole legal government of China, and both states established diplomatic relations. The United States and a number of other states continued to maintain unofficial relations with Taiwan through government-controlled private bodies.

Notes and Questions

1. What would the UN's position on the seating of China call for with respect to the seating of a Cambodian delegation after the Vietnamese invasion and takeover in 1979?

2. Does the UN Secretary-General's reliance on the language of the UN Charter resolve the question of which governmental claimants should represent states at the United Nations?

3. What sort of arguments could the United States have made to the General Assembly to promote the continued seating of the delegation from Taiwan? How did law and politics interact to affect the outcome?

C. The 1979 Credentials Fight

Following the PRK's ouster of the Khmer Rouge in 1979, the new government sent a letter to the United Nations asking to be seated at the next session of the General Assembly. The issue first fell to the General Assembly's Credentials Committee, which determines whether a delegation may represent a member state in the

Assembly, which normally results in a routine approval. It discussed the issue on September 19, 1979, and by a vote of 6 (Belgium, China, Ecuador, Pakistan, Senegal, United States) to 3 (Congo, Panama, USSR) agreed to accept the credentials of the ousted government of Democratic Kampuchea and thereby reject those of the PRK. When the General Assembly debated the issue on September 21, various legal and political positions and options emerged:

26. Mr. MISHRA (India): . . .

31. It is our conviction that the General Assembly should not take a definitive position at this moment . . . . If we were to accept the report of the Credentials Committee as it stands, I have no doubt that we would get involved in a very acrimonious debate which might spill over from this meeting to other meetings of the Assembly, and to the Main Committees of the Assembly. We would like to try to have a solution, a temporary one, which would give this Assembly the opportunity to take stock of the situation, and if necessary, to reopen the question even at this very session. . . .

33. We must learn from our past experience. Year after year in this Assembly decisions have been taken which have had no relationship to the reality of the situation within the country concerned, and today we are again asked to choose between two positions and we are not sure what the actual situation is. Is it correct for us to pronounce ourselves in a definitive manner? I submit that that would be unwise, not only for the sake of the Assembly, but for the sake of the situation which is involved in this procedural question. . . .

58. Mr. ZAITON (Malaysia): . . .

62. As we all know, Democratic Kampuchea has been legally accredited to the United Nations in all its previous meetings. Its credentials were accepted by the United Nations as its thirty-third session [in 1978] and it has been participating in all meetings of the United Nations and its various agencies and organs. Its credentials have now been challenged by none other than the party which has used force of arms to intervene in the internal affairs of Kampuchea, overthrow an established Government and set up in its place an alien Government, backed by the huge and immense military force of the Government which has intervened.

63. As we all know, one of the sacred principles of the United Nations is that of non-interference and non-intervention in the internal affairs of another State. . . . Were we to accept the draft resolution and seat the People's Republic of Kampuchea, it would mean that we would be condoning armed intervention and aggression that is in direct violation of the various principles we are supposed to uphold.

64. Furthermore, if we accept the draft resolution it will mean that qualification for membership in this Assembly will be measured by the yardstick of a Government's internal policies. This is an argument difficult to accept, for if it is valid then the Credentials Committee will have to determine the credentials of all Member States on the basis of their internal policies.

65. It will be recalled that at the height of the atrocities committed by the Pol Pot Government, which we all deplore, no one in this Assembly voiced any objection to the credentials of Democratic Kampuchea. Yet now we are being asked to evaluate the credentials of a Government in the light of the record of its violations of human rights. . . . The very people who are today proposing that another delegation should be seated as the representative of that particular Government are

performing a flagrant *volte-face* based not on any principle, but merely on political expediency.

8. Mr. TROYANOVSKY (Union of Soviet Socialist Republics) (interpretation from Russian): . . .

14. There can be no doubt at all that the question as to who should represent the interests of a State in the United Nations is an important political issue, the solution of which is fraught with serious consequences. If any delegation should vote in favour of the Committee's report . . . then the position adopted by that delegation would be tantamount to support for the criminal Pol Pot clique, which has been condemned by the Kampuchean people.

15. The whole world knows the facts of the bloody misdeeds of the Pol Pot clique, which has slain 3 million Kampucheans—in other words, it is openly carrying out a policy of genocide vis-à-vis its own people. As representatives know, the crime of genocide, according to the Convention on the Prevention and Punishment of the Crime of Genocide . . . is severely condemned, and by no means can it be supposed that there is support in the United Nations for people who have committed that crime.

16. The only legitimate representative of Kampuchea is the People's Revolutionary Council of the People's Republic of Kampuchea. That Government is exercising full and stable control over the whole territory of the country and is effectively exercising State power. The People's Revolutionary Council is implementing energetic measures to bring the country back to normal, to revive the shattered economy and the culture, and to have families reunited. That policy conducted by the Government is supported by the absolute majority of the Kampuchean people. . . .

General Assembly Official Records, Thirty-Fourth Session, Records of the 3rd and 4th Plenary Meetings (1979).

After a long debate, the General Assembly voted with 71 in favor, 35 against, 34 abstaining, with 12 absences, to accept the Credentials Committee's report and thereby retain the seating of the delegation from the ousted Democratic Kampuchea government. The states voting yes were principally developing world states and Western states (e.g., Australia, Denmark, Germany, and the United States); those opposed were principally the Soviet Union and its allies; the abstentions consisted of a small number of Western states (e.g., Austria, France, Netherlands, and Sweden) and some developing world states. At the end of the debate, the delegate of Democratic Kampuchea, Ieng Thirith (the wife of Khmer Rouge leader Pol Pot), stated:

> [T]he delegation of Democratic Kampuchea would like to express, first of all, its deep gratitude to this honourable Assembly and to the peoples that love peace and justice, who by their vote just now have done an act of justice. They did this by saying "No" to aggression and "No" to violation of the United Nations Charter, and by recognizing the legitimate right of a victim of aggression in this Assembly.

Notes and Questions

1. Which of the three delegates had the best legal argument?
2. Should recognition decisions be made to protect other values, such as the ban on the use of force?

3. The PRK's supporters were all members of the Soviet bloc. Those calling for the continued seating of the DK were states in the Southeast Asian region fearful of Vietnam's power, as well as Western states allied against Vietnam and the USSR in the Cold War. Why would these groups want to make their arguments in legal terms? Who were the targets of these legal arguments?

4. Note the voting tally for seating of the DK delegation. Did it receive the support of a majority of the UN's members?

5. What role did the human rights abuses of the DK regime play in the decision regarding recognition?

6. The United States was part of the majority in both the Credentials Committee and the General Assembly, out of both opposition to Vietnam's invasion and solidarity with its new strategic partner, China. Robert Rosenstock, the U.S. delegate to the committee, later recalled that, after the vote, someone had grabbed his hand and shaken it in congratulations. "I looked up and saw it was Ieng Sary [the Khmer Rouge's number two official]. I felt like washing my hand." Gareth Porter, *Kampuchea's UN Seat: Cutting the Pol Pot Connection*, Indochina Issues, No. 8, July 1980, at 1.

D. The Next Stages

The delegation of Democratic Kampuchea continued to occupy Cambodia's UN seat throughout the 1980s, although in 1982, at the urging of China and other allies, it agreed to form, along with two noncommunist factions opposed to the Vietnamese regime, a Coalition Government of Democratic Kampuchea (CGDK) to represent Cambodia externally. In the late 1980s, diplomatic discussion among regional actors and the Cambodian factions began in earnest. The result was a multilateral conference on Cambodia in 1989, but one that did not achieve agreement. Following the conference, due to public outcry Western support for the CGDK waned to the point that CGDK did not send a delegation to the 1990 General Assembly.

In October 1991, after significant outside mediation, the PRK and the factions fighting it agreed upon a peace accord, which provided for a massive UN presence to demobilize troops and run elections. Officially, Cambodia was run by a Supreme National Council (SNC), with representatives of all the fighting factions included; foreign governments accredited their diplomats to the SNC, and a delegation from the SNC occupied Cambodia's UN seat during the transitional period. At the same time, the PRK continued to control most of the instrumentalities of government, despite a requirement in the peace accord that it allow the United Nations to ensure that these institutions were neutral. After United Nations-administered elections in 1993, the elected constituent assembly promulgated a new constitution. Cambodia became a kingdom again, with Sihanouk as its king and power shared by the party of the PRK's principal non-communist opponent, led by Norodom Ranariddh (a son of Sihanouk), as First Prime Minister, and the party of the former Vietnamese-installed government, led by Hun Sen, as Second Prime Minister. Representatives of the new government quickly assumed Cambodia's seat in international organizations and received congratulations from their colleagues.

Four years later, in July 1997, Hun Sen ousted Ranariddh as First Prime Minister in a violent coup and replaced him with an ally, Ung Huot. Following the coup, the General Assembly's Credentials Committee revisited the Cambodian question when it received two sets of credentials for attendance at the 52nd Session, one from the ousted First Prime Minister and the other from his replacement. Its report stated as follows:

Report of the Credentials Committee

U.N. Doc. A/52/719 (1997)

4. On 17 and 19 September, the Committee examined the situation with respect to the credentials of Cambodia. The Committee was informed that the following two sets of credentials had been received, presenting two delegations to represent Cambodia at the fifty-second session of the General Assembly:

(a) A letter dated 2 September 1997 signed by King Norodom Sihanouk, presenting a delegation headed by Mr. Ung Huot who was identified as ''First Prime Minister [and Minister] of Foreign Affairs and International Cooperation'';

(b) A facsimile letter dated 25 August 1997 addressed to the Secretary-General by Prince Norodom Ranariddh, presenting a delegation headed by Prince Norodom Ranariddh who was identified as ''First Prime Minister of the Kingdom of Cambodia''.

5. On 19 September, the Committee, having considered the question of the credentials of Cambodia, decided to defer a decision on the credentials of Cambodia on the understanding that, pursuant to the applicable procedures of the Assembly, no one would occupy the seat of that country at the fifty-second session.

With his grip on power secure, Hun Sen agreed to hold scheduled elections in July 1998. After a campaign characterized by numerous instances of official harassment and even attacks on opposition officials, Hun Sen emerged as the victor and sole Prime Minister. Although many NGO observers criticized the conduct of the election, the official UN delegation (whose visit to the country began only the week before the election) declared it "free and fair to an extent that enables it to reflect, in a credible way, the will of the Cambodian people." Following the election, the Credentials Committee agreed to accept the credentials of Cambodia—whose delegation would be staffed by the new government—at the fifty-third session of the General Assembly.

Notes and Questions

1. What factors do you think caused the Credentials Committee to act as it did at the UN's 1997 General Assembly? What happened to the Lie formula?

2. What is the meaning of the statement from the UN's election observer?

3. Should the fairness of an election determine whether the United Nations will seat a delegation or whether foreign states should interact with it?

E. An Alternative Path? A Note on the Haiti Episode

During the 1980s and 1990s, UN members faced other challenges regarding recognition of governments. During roughly the same years that governments were negotiating with the Cambodian factions on an end to the civil war, the United Nations agreed to work with the government of Haiti that had come to power following the fall of the Duvalier regime, a father-son dynasty of autocrats who had run the country since the 1940s. Under an agreement with Haiti, the United Nations sent a mission of several hundred civilians to the country to monitor the fairness of multiparty elections. These elections, which took place in December 1990 and were certified as free and fair by the United Nations, led to the election as president of Jean-Bertrand Aristide, a Catholic priest and opponent of the Duvaliers.

The election of Aristide ended one of the region's oldest dictatorships; it also enabled the Organization of American States (OAS) to claim with pride that all its members, many of which had once been military regimes, were now elected governments. (Cuba was excluded from the organization in January 1962.) In June 1991, the OAS General Assembly adopted the following resolution to address any future attempts at military coups:

Representative Democracy

O.A.S. Res. AG/RES 1080 (1991)

WHEREAS: . . .

Under the provisions of the Charter, one of the basic purposes of the OAS is to promote and consolidate representative democracy, with due respect for the principle of non-intervention. . . .

THE GENERAL ASSEMBLY

RESOLVES:

1. To instruct the Secretary General to call for the immediate convocation of a meeting of the Permanent Council in the event of any occurrences giving rise to the sudden or irregular interruption of the democratic political institutional process or of the legitimate exercise of power by the democratically elected government in any of the Organization's member states, in order, within the framework of the

Charter, to examine the situation, decide on and convene an ad hoc meeting of the Ministers of Foreign Affairs, or a special session of the General Assembly, all of which must take place within a ten-day period.

2. To state that the purpose of the ad hoc meeting of Ministers of Foreign Affairs or the special session of the General Assembly shall be to look into the events collectively and adopt any decisions deemed appropriate, in accordance with the Charter and international law. . . .

Just under four months later, however, on September 30, 1991, Aristide was ousted in a military coup. He fled to the United States, where, with U.S. support, he waged a lengthy diplomatic campaign to oust the military government. The OAS convened to condemn the coup, and on October 11, 1991, the UN General Assembly unanimously passed Resolution 46/7, which stated:

Given the importance of support from the international community for the development of democracy in Haiti by strengthening its institutions and giving high priority to the serious social and economic problems that it faces,

Aware that, in accordance with the Charter of the United Nations, the Organization promotes and encourages respect for human rights and fundamental freedoms for all, and that the Universal Declaration of Human Rights states that ''the will of the people shall be the basis of the authority of government'', . . .

1. Strongly condemns the attempted illegal replacement of the constitutional President of Haiti, the use of violence and military coercion and the violation of human rights in that country;

2. Affirms as unacceptable any entity resulting from that illegal situation and demands the immediate restoration of the legitimate Government of President Jean-Bertrand Aristide, together with the full application of the National Constitution and hence the full observance of human rights in Haiti. . . .

Delegations from Aristide's government continued to represent Haiti in the United Nations and other international organizations. Indeed, with encouragement from the United States, the UN Security Council imposed severe economic sanctions on the new government, pressured the military regime to sign an agreement returning power to Aristide, and, when the regime failed to comply with it, even authorized the use of force to return President Aristide to power. Only at the last minute, on September 19, 1994, with U.S. troops poised to invade under the cloak of UN authority, did the military agree to depart. Aristide returned to power on October 15, 1994.

Notes and Questions

1. Is the UN's and OAS's position on Haiti a victory for the Tobar Doctrine? The United Nations undertook a similar course of action in 1997. After the army seized power from the democratically elected president of Sierra Leone, the Security Council condemned the coup and the General Assembly continued to seat a delegation from the prior regime, which was restored to power the following year through military intervention by a Nigerian-led West African force. What might account for states' willingness to continue to recognize a government that was no longer in power?

2. In October 1991, the Conference (now Organization) for Security and Cooperation in Europe adopted a policy on extraconstitutional takeovers similar to that in OAS Resolution 1080, although it has not yet had to employ its procedures. The Organization of African Unity (OAU) adopted such policies beginning in the late 1990s; the Constitutive Act of its successor, the African Union (AU), lists the "condemnation and rejection of unconstitutional changes of governments" among its core principles and prohibits participation in Union activities of governments coming to power through such means. Are the developments in the United Nations, OAS, OSCE, and AU evidence that a new doctrine of recognition of governments is emerging that takes into account the process by which a new government assumes power? What additional evidence would you need to reach such a conclusion?

3. The United Nations faced other issues of rival governments into the twenty-first century. In Afghanistan, the Taliban movement gained control of the country in the late 1990s after a decade of civil war following nearly a decade of Soviet occupation of that country. The Taliban controlled over 90 percent of the territory, but its delegation was not seated due to allegations by the United States, Russia, and European states that it supported international terrorism and drug trafficking. Bilaterally, the Taliban was recognized only by Pakistan, the United Arab Emirates, and Saudi Arabia. Yet the regime defeated by the Taliban, the Northern Alliance, which controlled little territory, was seated at the United Nations. In late 2001, as result of U.S. and British military action against the Taliban, the Northern Alliance gained control of most of the country. Under the terms of the December 5, 2001, political settlement brokered by the United Nations among the Northern Alliance and other Afghan groups, a new "Interim Authority" was created as "the repository of Afghan sovereignty"; it gradually began taking over the reins of government in late 2001 and assumed the United Nations seat as well, with a new government installed in 2004 under the state's 2003 constitution.

F. Note on Consequences of State and Governmental Change in Domestic Law

The processes of state formation and transformation are not merely interstate issues. We have already seen, for instance, how state formation almost inevitably involves claims by groups of people, such as ethnic minorities or indigenous peoples, who might seek a new state or favor the status quo. State and governmental changes also affect private actors through the disruptions they create for those engaging in economic transactions in a territory undergoing such events. Contracts granting various enterprises rights to carry out business—from mineral extraction to service industries—become the subject of significant controversy should part of the affected territory become a new state. Or a business might seek to work with a government that is unrecognized by other states.

These and other situations may eventually come before national courts adjudicating controversies between private entities or between such entities and foreign states. In such cases, courts will typically face issues similar to those that governments face in deciding whether to recognize states or governments for purposes of diplomatic intercourse. Thus, for example, courts may have to determine whether a state or government unrecognized by the forum's government can sue or be sued, whether a citizen of such a state can sue or be sued, or whether the acts of an unrecognized government should be given effect or ignored. Should the state's or government's status be determined solely in terms of its de facto control of territory, or should other criteria, such as its democratic credentials, make a difference? Or should the possibility to sue or be sued turn on the attitude of the forum's government—thus, for example, denying access to the courts to states or governments simply by virtue of the foreign policy of the forum state?

The United States has frequently been the forum for litigation arising from governmental change. As a general matter, governments and states not recognized by the United States may not themselves sue in U.S. courts. On the other hand, U.S. courts have not challenged the validity of acts of unrecognized governments solely because they were unrecognized: in *Salimoff & Co. v. Standard Oil Co.*, 262 N.Y. 220 (1933), for example, the New York State Court of Appeals refused to strip Standard Oil of title to oil it drilled from plaintiff's land, which had been seized by the then-unrecognized Soviet government.

At the same time, with respect to governmental change, the State Department's practice for the last several decades has generally been to avoid either affirmatively recognizing or refusing to recognize a new government, a policy undertaken for the same reasons the United Nations has based most of its recognition decisions on effective control. Rather, the United States either continues or discontinues diplomatic relations, depending on the state of the bilateral relationship with the new government. On occasion, the United States has affirmatively announced that it does not recognize a government resulting from a coup (such as Haiti's).

The effect of the Executive Branch's recognition policy on a government's ability to sue in U.S. courts was at issue in *National Petrochemical Co. v. M/T Stolt Sheaf*, 860 F.2d 551 (2d Cir. 1988). In that case, Iran's governmentally owned oil company had contracted with and paid several foreign companies to purchase chemicals that it could not buy in the United States due to a U.S. embargo on trade with Iran. The foreign companies actually procured the chemicals in the United States but did not reveal this to Iran. When the companies eventually did not deliver the chemicals (not because of U.S. enforcement of the embargo, but because the defendants did not wish to ship to Iran once the Iran-Iraq war began in 1980), Iran sued the companies for fraud in Manhattan federal court (under the federal diversity statute) in 1986. The United States had severed diplomatic relations with Iran in 1980 as a result of the 1979-1981 seizure of American diplomats in Tehran and had not resumed relations due to severe foreign policy disagreements, though the United States had not formally stated that it did not recognize Iran's government. Indeed, the Secretary of State had said that the United States accepted the reality of the Iranian revolution and had concluded an agreement with that government for the release of the American diplomats. The district court dismissed the case based on lack of recognition of the new government, and National Petrochemical Company (NPC) appealed. The U.S. government agreed to file a brief urging that NPC be granted access to U.S. courts for this case. The court concluded as follows:

A break in diplomatic relations with another government does not automatically signify denial of access to federal courts. As the Supreme Court has observed, courts are hardly competent to assess how friendly or unfriendly our relationship with a foreign government is at any given moment, and absent some "definite touchstone for determination, we are constrained to consider any relationship, short of war, with a recognized sovereign power as embracing the privilege of resorting to United States courts." [Quoting Banco Nacional de Cuba v. Sabbatino, 376 U.S. 398, 410 (1964).]

. . . [A]ppellees urge that NPC must be denied access to federal court based on the President's failure to extend formal recognition to the Khomeini government. We disagree . . . . First, as this century draws to a close, the practice of extending formal recognition to new governments has altered: The United States Department of State has sometimes refrained from announcing recognition of a new government because grants of recognition have been misinterpreted as pronouncements of approval . . . . As a result, the absence of formal recognition cannot serve as the touchstone for determining whether the Executive Branch has "recognized" a foreign nation for the purpose of granting that government access to United States courts.

Second, the power to deal with foreign nations outside the bounds of formal recognition is essential to a president's implied power to maintain international relations. As part of this power, the Executive Branch must have the latitude to permit a foreign nation access to U.S. courts, even if that nation is not formally recognized by the U.S. government. This is because the president alone—as the constitutional guardian of foreign policy—knows what action is necessary to effectuate American relations with foreign governments . . . . It is evident that in today's topsy-turvy world governments can topple and relationships can change in a moment. The Executive Branch must therefore have broad, unfettered discretion in matters involving such sensitive, fast-changing, and complex foreign relationships . . . .

. . . The United States has submitted a Statement of Interest . . . stating that "it is the position of the Executive Branch that the Iranian government and its instrumentality should be afforded access to our courts for purposes of resolution of the instant dispute." . . . This is not a case where the Executive Branch is attempting to prohibit a formally recognized government from bringing a single suit in the United States courts, nor is it a case where the Executive is arbitrarily allowing some suits by an unrecognized nation while disallowing others. Rather, here the Executive Branch . . . expressly entered this case as Amicus requesting that Iran be given access to our courts. Under such circumstances, and as the sole branch authorized to conduct relations with foreign countries, the Executive clearly did not act arbitrarily. Accordingly, we hold that, for all the reasons stated, NPC must be permitted to proceed with its diversity suit in the Southern District of New York.

Id. at 554-555.

Notes and Questions

1. Are there any circumstances in which a foreign government not recognized by the United States should not have access to U.S. courts?

2. Why should this question be solely a matter for the Executive Branch and not the judiciary applying principles of international law?

3. Why would the Executive Branch want to allow Iran to sue in this case? At the time, the United States and Iran were participating in arbitration at The Hague under the terms of the 1981 agreement between them that ended the 1979-1981 hostage crisis. The Iran-U.S. Claims Tribunal was adjudicating the claims of the nationals of each country against the government of the other for expropriations arising out of the decline in U.S.-Iran relations during the Iranian hostage crisis (as well as government-to-government claims). (For further details, see Chapters 2, 5, and 12.) The vast majority of private claimants were American companies and individuals, though the Tribunal also had jurisdiction over counterclaims by Iran. Prevailing American claimants were paid from a "judgment fund" of monies contributed by Iran; if the counterclaim exceeded the claim, Iran would obtain its proceeds through a suit in U.S. courts; if the suit failed, Iran could have recourse to the Tribunal and force the U.S. government to pay. To avoid having to pay these counterclaim judgments itself, the U.S. government needed to assure Iran and the Tribunal that Iran would be able sue the American claimants in U.S. courts, and thus it filed a statement of interest on behalf of Iran each time it asserted a claim in U.S. courts (even if it was not a counterclaim based on an original claim against Iran).

4. Should U.S. courts be open to suits against unrecognized states or governments? If they are, should plaintiffs be given a default judgment or should those states or governments be able to defend themselves? Consider in this context the language of the Foreign Sovereign Immunities Act discussed in Chapter 6.

5. In *Kuwait Airways Corporation v. Iraqi Airways Co. (Nos. 4 and 5)*, [2002] UKHL 19, Kuwait's national airline sued Iraq's national airline for its seizure of KAC airplanes following Iraq's 1990 invasion and purported annexation of Kuwait and the subsequent destruction of the planes in Iraq by coalition bombing. Under British choice of law rules, British courts would normally apply Iraqi law as the law of the situs of the damage. The House of Lords upheld a lower court ruling refusing to apply the Iraqi official decree that dissolved KAC and took over the planes. It noted that Iraq's attempted annexation had not been recognized internationally, indeed had been explicitly rejected by the UN Security Council as a violation of the UN Charter (see Chapter 13, Section II), and was thus clearly contrary to British public policy. Is this case consistent with U.S. case law?

IV. INTERNATIONAL ORGANIZATIONS AS GLOBAL ACTORS: THE UNITED NATIONS AND APARTHEID

Over the past two centuries, states have formed hundreds of international organizations, from localized technical groups such as the Commission Internationale pour la Protection des Eaux du Léman (International Commission for the Protection of the Waters of Lake Geneva), through regional organizations such as the Association of Southeast Asian Nations or the OAU, to global specialized institutions such as the World Health Organization (WHO) or the WTO, to the largest and broadest in scope, the United Nations. Each of these organizations came about because governments and other international actors perceived a need to engage in some institutionalized form of cooperation. As discussed in Chapter 1, international organizations have proliferated considerably since World War II, and their areas of expertise cover all subject areas for transnational cooperation. Their actions have changed the planet in ways large and small. The WHO took the leading role in organizing a massive vaccination against smallpox, eradicating the disease; the International Telecommunication Union develops standards that allow telephones around the world to communicate and ensure that radio signals do not conflict with one another; and the International Civil Aviation Organization sets rules of aircraft and airport safety.

What forces drive states to create international organizations? Consider the following account of three perspectives from political science:

Harold K. Jacobson, *Networks of Interdependence: International Organizations and the Global Political System*

60-67 (2d ed. 1984)

FEDERALISM

. . . Federalism can be concerned with the expansion of the territorial domain of political authority, which is also the purpose of international governmental organizations. . . .

. . . The word "bargain" provides an equally apt description of what must occur for an international organization to be established. In forming an international organization, the constituent units, be they individuals, national associations, or governments, agree to give up some of their autonomy to achieve some purpose that can only be gained by aggregating their authority. . . . For an international organization to be created, those involved must perceive that in the relatively near term the benefits to be gained from membership will outweigh the costs. . . .

FUNCTIONALISM

Functionalism argues that two basic and observable trends in modern history are crucially important in shaping the domain and scope of political authority; they are the growth of technology and the spread and intensification of the desire for higher standards of material welfare. Technological developments both bring peoples closer together and make possible higher standards of material welfare . . . .

Functionalists feel that governments will be pressured by their citizens to engage in international cooperation to take advantage of technological developments. They maintain that people everywhere desire better material conditions, and they postulate that increasingly literate and urbanized populations will more and more be able to make governments respond to this desire. . . .

Functionalists applauded the fact that the specific purpose institutions that had been created were staffed by specialists in substantive fields rather than diplomats . . . . The functionalist strategy was based on the assumption that governments were not unitary actors but rather organizations of departments and individuals that often had different, and sometimes conflicting, interests. When it came to staffing the secretariats of international organizations, functionalists wanted career officials, and they postulated the creation of "a detached international civil service:" . . . .

THE THEORY OF PUBLIC GOODS

. . . The theory deals with a seeming paradox: contrary to the assumption that rational self-interest would lead the members of a group having a common interest to organize and to act collectively to promote their common interest, this does not happen.

. . . If the group is large, individual efforts will seem inconsequential and incapable of achieving the overall objective; hence the individual will concentrate on more proximate objectives even though their achievement may be counterproductive toward the group goal. An example is the individual who increases immediate income by increasing production even though the long-run effect of all producers doing this is to drive prices down and reduce the aggregate profits of the group. In world politics an individual state temporarily may increase security by increasing armaments, but all states may be less secure at the end of the resulting arms race.

. . . [Moreover], [s]ome services have the character of being public goods; that is, if they are available to anyone, they must be available to everyone. Thus, with large organizations, individual efforts will have no noticeable effect on the organization, and the individual will receive the benefits of the organization with or without contributing to it . . . .[I]n world politics, the benefits of general disarmament cannot be denied to the state that ignores the overall agreement and increases its own armaments. These properties of public goods are particularly relevant to international organizations since they are largely in the business of providing such goods.

Several ancillary arguments flow from these basic postulates. One is that to insure wide participation, large organizations must utilize coercive sanctions or benefits other than the public good that can be allocated selectively. Compulsory membership tends to be a corollary of the efficient production of the collective good by a large organization.

Another argument is that small groups operate according to fundamentally different principles than do large groups. In a small group it is likely that there will be at least a few members who would be better off if the public good were provided even if they had to provide it themselves. This is because the smaller the number of members that share in the benefits of the public good, the greater the proportion going to any individual. If the size of the members of the group is unequal, there will be a tendency for smaller members to rely on voluntary, self-interested actions of larger members. The largest member would receive the largest benefit, and consequently would be willing to make the largest contribution. The smallest member, since it would enjoy some of the benefits of the public good in any case, and since its contribution would make little difference to the total public good, would have little incentive to contribute even its proportional share. Consequently, in small groups there is a tendency for small members to exploit large members, to seek a free ride, and there is also a tendency toward suboptimal production of the public good. But small groups are much more likely to organize to provide public goods than are large groups. The larger the group, the less adequate the rewards for individual action, the less likely that any subset or individual will be willing to bear the entire or a substantial proportion of the burden of providing the public good, and the greater the initial costs of creating an organization.

The critical role of international organizations in the world raises important questions of how international law treats them. As you read the following materials, consider whether international organizations enjoy the same rights, obligations, and powers as states; at what stage a grouping of states becomes a bona fide international organization; how the organization's membership and functions affect its structure and decision-making process; how that process determines its powers as an independent actor; the extent to which international organizations are constrained by the legal instruments creating them; and whose policy interests international organizations advance.

A. The Problem

Nelson Mandela described apartheid as "the color line that all too often determines who is rich and who is poor . . . who lives in luxury and who lives in squalor . . . who shall get food, clothing, and health care . . . and who will live and who die." Apartheid was the system of racial separation and discrimination that prevailed in South Africa as a matter of governmental policy from 1948 until its abolition in the early 1990s. Building on years of discrimination against blacks, South Africa's National Party adopted apartheid as a model for the separate development of races, though it served only to preserve white superiority. It classified persons as either white, Bantu (black), coloured (mixed race), or Asian. Manifestations of apartheid included the denial of the right to vote, limitations on employment, separate living areas and schools, limits on ownership of property, prohibitions on intermarriage, internal pass laws limiting domestic travel of nonwhites, and white control of the legal system. The result was the legally mandated separation of the races and denial of basic human rights to the black population of South Africa, which made up approximately 90 percent of the population.

Apartheid was administered through a complex legal system, as described by South Africa's Truth and Reconciliation Commission (a panel appointed by the post-apartheid government to examine the apartheid era) in 1998.

Final Report of the Truth and Reconciliation Commission

Vol. 1, ch. 2 (1998)

[The Population Registration Act of 1950] formed the very bedrock of the apartheid state in that it provided for the classification of every South African into one of four racial categories. To achieve this end, it came up with definitions of racial groupings which were truly bizarre:

A White person is one who is in appearance obviously white—and not generally accepted as Coloured—or who is generally accepted as White—and is not obviously Non-White, provided that a person shall not be classified as a White person if one of his natural parents has been classified as a Coloured person or a Bantu . . . A Bantu is a person who is, or is generally accepted as, a member of any aboriginal race or tribe of Africa . . . a Coloured is a person who is not a white person or a Bantu.

Despite the crude and hopelessly imprecise wording of these definitions, the Act was imposed with vigour and determination.

President Nelson Mandela wrote:

Where was one was allowed to live and work could rest on such absurd distinctions as the curl of one's hair or the size of one's lips. . . .

[The Commission described other laws, including the 1950 Group Areas Act, which decided where blacks and whites could live; the 1949 Prohibition of Mixed Marriages Act and 1950 Immorality Amendment Act; the 1953 Separate Amenities Act, which divided up use of parks, libraries, beaches, and other public facilities; and the 1953 Bantu Education Act, which created a separate and inferior education system for blacks.]

The effects of apartheid legislation

Overall, what the National Party did in its first ten to twelve years of power amounted, in Leo Kuper's words, to "a white counter-revolution" to forestall the perceived (although, as will be noted later, misinterpreted and exaggerated) growing threat to white supremacy from both local forces and the rising tide of African nationalist sentiment on the continent. . . .

It was also a social engineering project of awesome dimensions through which, from about the mid-1950s and for the next thirty or so years, the inherited rural and urban social fabric of South Africa was torn asunder and recreated in the image of a series of racist utopias. In the process, as indicated earlier, millions of black people and a handful of mainly poor whites were shunted around like pawns on a chessboard. Forced to relocate to places that often existed only on the drawing boards of the architects of apartheid, entire communities were simply wiped out. These included urban suburbs and rural villages, traditional communities and homelands, schools, churches and above all people . . . .

———————————

During this period, South Africa maintained diplomatic relations with many states and was a member of the United Nations. Its gem and metal resources gave it significant economic ties with other states. During the Cold War, South Africa was allied with the West, though this alliance often proved embarrassing to Western governments and pushed some other African states closer to the Soviet Union. Indeed, the need to abolish apartheid was one of the few principles on which East and West could agree, though both sides took advantage of the South African situation for their own strategic ends. As a result of this basic consensus, as well as the increased control of the General Assembly by developing world states as a result of decolonization, the United Nations was able to engage in a sustained and proactive policy of placing pressure on the South African government.

The efforts to end apartheid had a normative and legal dimension as well. Apartheid violated one of the most fundamental prescriptions in the United Nations Charter and the Universal Declaration of Human Rights—the requirement that states respect human rights without distinction as to race. As a result, the UN's work to end apartheid can be viewed as an effort by its members to secure the compliance of South Africa with one of the most basic norms of international law. And although we discuss this problem in the context of international organizations, the anti-apartheid movement owed much of its power to non-state actors, in particular well mobilized non-governmental organizations, religious groups, and other components of civil society that put pressure on both their own governments and South Africa's for many years.

B. Background on the Structures and Decision-Making Processes of International Organizations

The multiplicity of forms of international organizations makes categorization somewhat elusive. In general, they might be organized along two axes—the breadth of their *participation*, from fairly regional (or subregional), to global; and the *issues* over which they have a mandate, from specialized (or highly technical), to those with a mandate to consider all issues. Examples of the combinations are:

Global and general: United Nations

Global and specialized: WTO, IMF, World Bank, ILO, International Telecommunication Union, Food and Agriculture Organization, and others; most such organizations are part of the UN system and adopt common practices regarding membership questions and management issues. Some global organizations are only open to states with a particular common interest, such as the International Coffee Organization, the International Whaling Commission, or the Commonwealth (comprised of Great Britain and most of its former colonies).

Regional and general: Organization of American States, OAU, Gulf Cooperation Council, Commonwealth of Independent States.

Regional and specialized: European Union (though its mandate is very large), North Atlantic Treaty Organization, Association of South East Asian Nations, Arctic Council, Inter-American Development Bank.

Of course, organizations differ in other ways. Some institutions are quite welcoming to non-state actors, at times allowing them significant rights of participation, while others relegate them to observer status at best. Most significantly, organizations differ with respect to their powers: they can serve merely as fora for dialogue, or they can possess decision-making powers that bind their members (including those members that may not have participated in the decision or that did and opposed it).

Despite these many differences, most international organizations share several core aspects. These are described below, with particular emphasis on the United Nations, the most significant organization in terms of breadth of responsibilities and legal effect of some of its decisions—as well as the organization most actively involved in the anti-apartheid movement. (See chart of the UN's components.)

Constitutive Instruments: International organizations are usually the creatures of treaties, though some, notably the Organization for Security and Coopera-

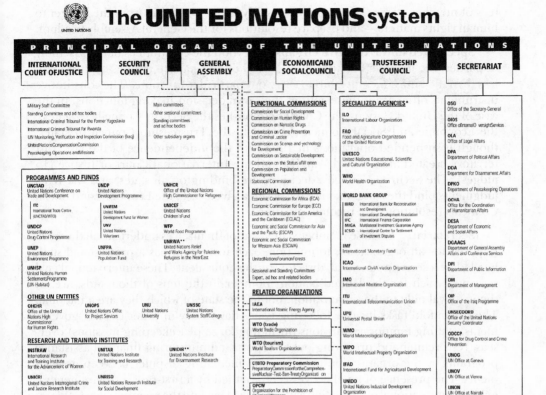

tion in Europe, are the products of political instruments. The United Nations Charter is the most significant document in this respect. Constitutive instruments describe the membership policies, powers of the organization, roles for different organs, and decision-making procedures. They often include, or are appended to, treaty provisions containing the respective obligations of states on the underlying substantive issues.

Assembly of Members: International organizations typically have one organ that includes all the members. These bodies are entrusted with broad policy questions as well as structural matters such as membership in the organization and in its various organs and committees, budget, personnel policy, and amendment of the constitutive instrument. Although generally each state has one vote in these organs, some institutions, typically in the financial arena, will allocate votes based on financial contributions. The General Assembly is the United Nation's assembly of all its members. Although it makes most key decisions regarding the internal functioning of the organization, under the terms of the Charter its resolutions on political and economic issues (outside the management of the United Nations itself) are generally only recommendations to states. The General Assembly, like other similar organs in other institutions, delegates certain responsibilities to standing and special committees of member states. The committees study issues—ranging from the budget to human rights matters—and prepare resolutions for the General Assembly to adopt.

Specialized and Executive Organs: Beyond the committees of the assembly of parties, the members of an institution will often establish entities composed of less than the entire membership to carry out particular functions. The constitutive instruments often grant these entities their own decision-making functions. In the case of the United Nations, the Charter establishes the Security Council (15 states), the Economic and Social Council (54 states), the Trusteeship Council (5 states, though it suspended operations in 1994 with the independence of the last trust territory created after World War II), and the International Court of Justice (15 judges). The Security Council's decisions are binding on all states, and the ICJ's judgments bind the states that are parties to a given case; the Economic and Social Council's resolutions are recommendations.

Secretariat: Because member states cannot themselves undertake all the work required for an organization to function, each institution has a professional staff, headed by a secretary-general, director, or the equivalent. These international civil servants, which for the United Nations number in the tens of thousands, are, in theory, loyal only to the organization, not to the state of which they are a national. Their manifold tasks include following issues day to day in order to brief governments, staffing temporary missions (including large peacekeeping missions) overseas, researching and preparing public reports, administering financial assistance programs by the organization to states, and mediating disputes between governments. The presence of an effective secretariat led by a first-rate secretary-general gives an international organization a life of its own beyond the member states. As long as they act within the terms of the constitutive instrument and are not challenged by too many member states, secretariat officials can significantly shape the agenda of the organization. Indeed, a secretariat may transform a treaty regime that does not itself create an international organization into a de facto international organization. (The name of the treaty is often used interchangeably to describe the de facto organization.) Thus, during the years before the creation of the World Trade Organization in 1994, the General Agreement of Tariffs and Trade was a de facto organization with its own building, a Director-General, and a large staff; the Convention on Trade in Endangered Species of Wild Fauna and Flora of 1973 has a large secretariat in Geneva that oversees the functioning of the treaty regime.

Much of the influence and power of any international organization turns upon the mechanisms it uses for making decisions, as well as the effect of those decisions upon member states. The extent to which organizations leave major decisions to the assembly of states parties or delegate them to specialized organs will affect the number and content of the decisions made. As an obvious example, the limited membership of the Security Council permits faster decisions than would be the case if the General Assembly, with its 191 members, had to agree on each issue. In addition, the International Civil Aviation Organization (with 187 members) delegates to its 33-member Council, which includes states with particular technical expertise on aviation matters, the authority to issue aviation regulations.

Moreover, states are usually quite explicit in the constitutive instrument regarding the decision-making processes within each organ. While some organizations make decisions by a simple majority of their members acting through the assembly of states parties, usually the situation is more complex—either because the key decisions are delegated to other, smaller organs or because special sorts of majorities are required for organs to make decisions (or both). Consider the following articles of the UN Charter regarding the Security Council.

Article 23

1. The Security Council shall consist of fifteen Members of the United Nations. The Republic of China, France, the Union of Soviet Socialist Republics, the United Kingdom of Great Britain and Northern Ireland, and the United States of America shall be permanent members of the Security Council. The General Assembly shall elect ten other Members of the United Nations to be non-permanent members of the Security Council, due regard being specially paid, in the first instance to the contribution of Members of the United Nations to the maintenance of international peace and security and to the other purposes of the Organization, and also to equitable geographical distribution.

2. The non-permanent members of the Security Council shall be elected for a term of two years. . . .

The drafters designated the five states noted in Article 23 as permanent members because they were the principal World War II victors. (For discussion as to whether developments since 1945 suggest a different group of permanent members, or the elimination of the category entirely, see Chapter 14.) By virtue of a 1963 General Assembly resolution, the nonpermanent seats are allocated as follows: three to Africa, two to Asia, two to Latin America, two to Western Europe "and other states" (for instance, Canada, Australia, New Zealand), and one to Eastern Europe. A so-called "gentlemen's agreement" among the UN's members ensures that certain particularly populated, wealthy, or otherwise influential nonpermanent members, such as Japan, Germany, and India, rotate on the Council with greater frequency than other states.

Article 24

1. In order to ensure prompt and effective action by the United Nations, its Members confer on the Security Council primary responsibility for the maintenance of international peace and security, and agree that in carrying out its duties under this responsibility the Security Council acts on their behalf.

Article 25

The Members of the United Nations agree to accept and carry out the decisions of the Security Council in accordance with the present Charter.

Article 27

1. Each member of the Security Council shall have one vote.

2. Decisions of the Security Council on procedural matters shall be made by an affirmative vote of nine members.

3. Decisions of the Security Council on all other matters shall be made by an affirmative vote of nine members including the concurring votes of the permanent members; provided that, in decisions under Chapter VI, and under paragraph 3 of Article 52, a party to a dispute shall abstain from voting.

By contrast, the Articles of Agreement of the IMF allocate votes based on each state's financial contribution to the IMF. The total number of votes as of 2006 was 2,176,037. Consider this sample of the number of votes of selected member states:

State	Number of votes	Percentage of total
Argentina	21,421	0.98
Botswana	880	.04
China	63,942	2.94
France	107,635	4.95
Germany	130,332	5.99
Indonesia	21,043	0.97
Japan	133,378	6.13
Marshall Islands	285	0.01
Russia	59,704	2.74
Saudi Arabia	70,105	3.22
United States	371,743	17.08

IMF Members' Quotas and Voting Power, and IMF Governors, *www.imf.org*.

As another example, the Organization for Security and Cooperation in Europe (OSCE) makes its decisions—none of which are legally binding on members—by consensus, either at annual summits of heads of government, regular meetings of foreign ministers (the Ministerial Council), or weekly meetings of diplomats (the Permanent Council). Each year one state serves as the Chairman-in-Office and convenes the various meetings and sets the agenda. The OSCE has established special procedures to make decisions by less than consensus: if one state is committing gross violations of the OSCE's commitments, the others may make a decision on that question; and if two states are having a dispute, the others may instruct them to seek mediation.

Notes and Questions

1. What factors would the founding states of an international organization consider in deciding which issues should be decided by the assembly of members and which should be delegated to smaller bodies?

2. Why do you think the founders of the United Nations allowed only the Security Council to make binding decisions regarding matters of international peace and security? How does this decision relate to the structure and voting requirements of the Council?

3. Do the Articles of the Charter making five states permanent members of the Security Council and requiring that any nonprocedural decision of the Council have

their assent violate the principle of the sovereign equality of states? How about the unequal voting in the Articles of Agreement of the IMF?

C. Legal "Personality"

The proliferation and power of international organizations leaves no doubt that they are major actors in the international legal process. Yet in the early years of the United Nations, some states and scholars still questioned just how much independent authority the United Nations and other organizations possessed in light of the traditional international law view that only states had rights and obligations. On the one hand, Article 104 of the Charter provided that the United Nations would have legal capacity within its member states (so that, for instance, it could hire plumbers and pay electricity bills); yet where the Charter was silent, what sorts of things could the organization do vis-à-vis its members, and who spoke for it—all of its members, some of them, or the Secretary-General? These questions are similar in a sense to questions faced in domestic systems long ago about the status of corporations as opposed to partnerships.

Decision makers within the United Nations faced this issue head on shortly after its creation. After the outbreak of war between Israel and the Arab states following Israel's declaration of independence in 1948, the Secretary-General appointed Count Folke Bernadotte of Sweden to mediate between the parties in the hopes of bringing about a cease-fire. On September 16, 1948, Bernadotte's car was blown up in Jerusalem, killing the mediator and a French observer. While Jewish extremists were suspected, none was ever tried by Israel. In traditional international law, a state whose national is injured in the territory of another state has the right to bring a claim against the latter for damages. In order to ascertain whether the United Nations had this right as well regarding one of its agents, the General Assembly asked the ICJ for an advisory opinion. Specifically, the Assembly asked, first, whether the United Nations could make a claim for damages to the organization (e.g., expenses of returning and burying the body), and second, whether the United Nations could make a claim for damages to the victim's heirs. The Charter was silent on both questions.

Reparation for Injuries Suffered in the Service of the United Nations

1949 I.C.J. 174 (Apr. 11)

Competence to bring an international claim is, for those possessing it, the capacity to resort to the customary methods recognized by international law for the establishment, the presentation and the settlement of claims . . . . In the international sphere, has the Organization such a nature as involves the capacity to bring an international claim? In order to answer this question, the Court must first enquire whether the Charter has given the Organization such a position that it possesses, in regard to its Members, rights which it is entitled to ask them to respect . . . .

The subjects of law in any legal system are not necessarily identical in their nature or in the extent of their rights, and their nature depends upon the needs of the community. Throughout its history, the development of international law has been influenced by the requirements of international life, and the progressive increase in the collective activities of States has already given rise to instances of action upon the international plane by certain entities which are not States. This development culminated in the establishment in June 1945 of an international organization whose purposes and principles are specified in the Charter of the United Nations. But to achieve these ends the attribution of international personality is indispensable.

The Charter has not been content to make the Organization created by it merely a centre 'for harmonizing the actions of nations in the attainment of these common ends' (Article I, para. 4). It has equipped that centre with organs, and has given it special tasks. It has defined the position of the Members in relation to the Organization by requiring them to give it every assistance in any action undertaken by it (Article 2, para. 5), and to accept and carry out the decisions of the Security Council; by authorizing the General Assembly to make recommendations to the Members; by giving the Organization legal capacity and privileges and immunities in the territory of each of its Members; and by providing for the conclusion of agreements between the Organization and its Members. Practice—in particular the conclusion of conventions to which the Organization is a party—has confirmed this character of the Organization, which occupies a position in certain respects in detachment from its Members . . . .

. . . [The United Nations exercises] functions and rights which can only be explained on the basis of the possession of a large measure of international personality and the capacity to operate upon an international plane. It is at present the supreme type of international organization, and it could not carry out the intentions of its founders if it was devoid of international personality. It must be acknowledged that its Members, by entrusting certain functions to it, with the attendant duties and responsibilities, have clothed it with the competence required to enable those functions to be effectively discharged.

Accordingly . . . the Organization is an international person. That is not the same thing as saying that it is a State, which it certainly is not, or that its legal personality and rights and duties are the same as those of a State. Still less is it the same thing as saying that it is 'a super-State', whatever that expression may mean. It does not even imply that all its rights and duties must be upon the international plane, any more than all the rights and duties of a State must be upon that plane. What it does mean is that it is a subject of international law and capable of possessing international rights and duties, and that it has capacity to maintain its rights by bringing international claims.

. . . The functions of the Organization are of such a character that they could not be effectively discharged if they involved the concurrent action, on the international plane, of fifty-eight or more Foreign Offices, and the Court concludes that the Members have endowed the Organization with capacity to bring international claims when necessitated by the discharge of its functions . . . .

. . . [As to whether the United Nations can bring a claim for damage to itself on account of the death of one of its agents,] [i]t is clear that the Organization has the capacity to bring a claim for this damage . . . .When the Organization has sustained damage resulting from a breach by a Member of its international obligations, it is impossible to see how it can obtain reparation unless it possesses capacity to bring an international claim. It cannot be supposed that in such an event all the Members of the Organization, save the defendant State, must combine to bring a claim against the defendant for the damage suffered by the Organization . . . .

[As to whether the United Nations can bring a claim for injury to the agent or his survivors,] [t]he Charter does not expressly confer upon the Organization the capacity to include, in its claim for reparation, damage caused to the victim or to persons entitled through him . . . .Under international law, the Organization must be deemed to have those powers which, though not expressly provided in the Charter, are conferred upon it by necessary implication as being essential to the performance of its duties . . . .

. . . [T]he Organization may find it necessary, and has in fact found it necessary, to entrust its agents with important missions to be performed in disturbed parts of the world. Many missions . . . involve the agents in unusual dangers to which ordinary persons are not exposed. For the same reason, [sometimes] their national State would not be justified in bringing a claim for reparation on the ground of diplomatic protection, or, at any rate, would not feel disposed to do so . . . .

In order that the agent may perform his duties satisfactorily, he must feel that this protection is assured to him by the Organization, and that he may count on it. To ensure the independence of the agent, and, consequently, the independent action of the Organization itself, it is essential that in performing his duties he need not have to rely on any other protection than that of the Organization (save of course for the more direct and immediate protection due from the State in whose territory he may be).

In particular, he should not have to rely on the protection of his own State. If he had to rely on that State, his independence might well be compromised, contrary to the principle applied by Article 100 of the Charter. And lastly, it is essential that— whether the agent belongs to a powerful or to a weak State; to one more affected or less affected by the complications of international life; to one in sympathy or not in sympathy with the mission of the agent—he should know that in the performance of his duties he is under the protection of the Organization . . . .

Upon examination of the character of the functions entrusted to the Organization and of the nature of the missions of its agents, it becomes clear that the capacity of the Organization to exercise a measure of functional protection of its agents arises by necessary intendment out of the Charter . . . .

. . . [As to whether the UN's power to make claims extended to a non-member state such as Israel then was,] the Court's opinion is that fifty States, representing the vast majority of the members of the international community, had the power . . . to bring into being an entity possessing objective international personality, and not merely personality recognized by them alone . . . .

After the ICJ issued its opinion, the General Assembly authorized the Secretary-General to make claims against states when UN agents are injured. In 1950, the Secretary-General wrote to the government of Israel demanding a formal apology, the prosecution of those responsible, and $54,628 in reparations to the United Nations for funeral and administrative expenses. (Count Bernadotte's widow was not interested in having the United Nations make a claim on her behalf.) Shortly thereafter, Israel paid the requested amount and issued a strong statement of regret (somewhat short of a full apology), but suggested that the crime was likely to remain unsolved. The Secretary-General told the General Assembly that he considered Israel's reply "substantial compliance" with his request. When the Secretary-General made a similar claim against the governments of Jordan and Egypt over the death of other UN officials by those states' soldiers, both disclaimed responsibility, and the United Nations never received reparations.

Notes and Questions

1. What would have been the consequence for the United Nations had the ICJ held that it lacked the capacity to assert claims for damage to itself or to its agents' families? Did the ICJ have a real choice in the *Bernadotte* case?

2. How would you determine whether other international organizations have the capacity to make claims, sign treaties, or undertake other sorts of activities that states do? What sort of international organization would not have the rights that the United Nations enjoys?

3. One scholar described the ICJ's views on the UN's capacity to make claims for injuries to its agents and their families as having "broken the exclusive fiduciary relationship between a citizen and his state in those cases where the citizen is working for the international organization . . . . International civil servants, thereafter, were to look to the Secretary-General, not to their governments, to protect them and safeguard their interests." Thomas Franck, Nation Against Nation 99 (1985). Yet officials of international organizations routinely seek the assistance of their home governments in obtaining promotions within the organization; and many receive de facto instructions from their governments, who may hold sway over their post-UN careers. In peacekeeping operations, although soldiers officially serve under the UN flag and are paid by the United Nations, they are typically deployed in contingents by state of origin, and their governments play a central role in deciding where and how they will undertake their duties (with avoidance of danger a priority for most states donating troops). What tools do international organizations have to ensure that international civil servants are independent of governments?

D. Condemnations of Apartheid

The UN's first foray into the racial system in South Africa began in response to a complaint by the government of India in 1946 regarding the treatment of Indians in South Africa. In a mildly worded resolution at its first session, the General Assembly simply stated its opinion that Indians should be treated according to agreements concluded between the two governments and requested that the two parties consult. G.A. Res. 44 (1946). Four years after the legal establishment of apartheid in South Africa, a group of developing states requested that the Secretary-General put apartheid per se on the agenda of the 1952 General Assembly. At the debate in the Assembly, South Africa objected that the United Nations lacked the competence to consider the internal affairs of one of its members. The Assembly nonetheless passed the following resolution:

General Assembly Resolution 616 B (1952)

The General Assembly . . .

Considering that one of the purposes of the United Nations is to achieve international co-operation in promoting and encouraging respect for human rights and fundamental freedoms for all, without distinction to race, sex, language or religion . . .

1. *Declares* that in a multi-racial society harmony and respect for human rights and freedoms and the peaceful development of a unified community are best assured when patterns of legislation and practice are directed towards ensuring equality before the law of all persons regardless of race, creed or colour, and when economic, social, cultural and political participation of all racial groups is on a basis of equality;

2. *Affirms* that governmental policies of Member States which are not directed towards these goals, but which are designed to perpetuate or increase discrimination, are inconsistent with the pledges of the Members under Article 56 of the Charter;

3. *Solemnly* calls upon all Member States to bring their policies into conformity with their obligation under the Charter to promote the observance of human rights and fundamental freedoms.

On March 21, 1960, in Sharpville, a township in northeastern South Africa, during a peaceful protest by blacks against the laws that restricted their movement and permissible habitations, government troops opened fire, killing 68 men, women, and children and injuring 180. Four days after the Sharpville Massacre, a group of 29 states from Africa and Asia asked the UN Security Council to hold a meeting to discuss this issue. (See accompanying photo of the debate.) The Council's members agreed quickly (though Britain and France abstained) on the following resolution:

Security Council Resolution 134 (1960)

The Security Council . . .

Recognizing that such a situation has been brought about by the racial policies of the government of the Union of South Africa and the continued disregard by that Government of the resolutions of the General Assembly calling upon it to revise its policies and bring them into conformity with its obligations and responsibilities under the Charter of the United Nations . . .

1. *Recognizes* that the situation in the Union of South Africa is one that has led to international friction and if continued might endanger international peace and security;

2. *Deplores* that the recent disturbances in the Union of South Africa should have led to the loss of life of so many Africans and extends to the families of the victims its deepest sympathies; . . .

South African Representative Bernardus Fourie addresses the Security Council,
March 30, 1960
SOURCE: United Nations Photo 65121

4. *Calls upon* the Government of the Union of South Africa to initiate measures aimed at bringing about racial harmony based on equality in order to ensure that the present situation does not continue or recur, and to abandon its policies of *apartheid* and racial discrimination . . . .

Notes and Questions

1. Under what provisions of the UN Charter did the Security Council take these actions?

2. Article 2(7) of the Charter states that nothing in the Charter "shall authorize the United Nations to intervene in matters which are essentially within the domestic jurisdiction of any state" (except when the Council is undertaking enforcement measures, e.g., sanctions, under Chapter VII of the Charter). As early as 1946 the General Assembly had condemned the Spanish regime of Generalissimo Francisco Franco as having been imposed upon Spain by the World War II Axis powers (during the Spanish civil war) and not "represent[ing] the Spanish people." It recommended that the Security Council consider how to remedy the situation if a new government did not come to power and urged states to withdraw their diplomats from Spain. Article 2(7) did not prevent the Assembly and Council from passing the two resolutions reprinted above, notwithstanding sustained legal argu-

mentation by the representatives of South Africa at the United Nations. But the vote on the 1952 resolution was 24 in favor, 1 opposed, and 34 abstentions; the abstentions included powerful Western states that opposed including apartheid on the UN's agenda as well as East bloc and developing states that favored stronger measures against South Africa. What does this practice suggest about member states' interpretation of Article 2(7)? Does the UN's refusal to condemn unrepresentative governments elsewhere change your answer?

3. What purpose do such condemnations serve? How can they affect the target states? How do they differ from condemnations by individual states? What incentives might South Africa have to comply with the resolutions? How could they make a difference to those within South Africa?

E. The UN's Sanctioning Processes

During the apartheid years, the United Nations and its specialized agencies utilized a variety of sanctioning mechanisms. These efforts began in the General Assembly, whose powers under the Charter are limited to recommendations, but eventually included the Security Council as well. In November 1962, the Assembly passed the following resolution by a vote of 67-16-23; nearly all the opposing states were wealthy Western states:

General Assembly Resolution 1761 (1962)

The General Assembly . . .

1. *Deplores* the failure of the Government of the Republic of South Africa to comply with the repeated requests and demands of the General Assembly and of the Security Council and its flouting of world public opinion by refusing to abandon its racial policies;

2. *Strongly deprecates* the continued and total disregard by the Government of South Africa of its obligations under the Charter of the United Nations and, furthermore, its determined aggravation of racial issues by enforcing measures of increasing ruthlessness involving violence and bloodshed;

3. *Reaffirms* that the continuance of those policies seriously endangers international peace and security;

4. *Requests* Member States to take the following measures, separately or collectively, in conformity with the Charter, to bring about the abandonment of those policies:

(a) Breaking off diplomatic relations with the Government of the Republic of South Africa or refraining from establishing such relations;

(b) Closing their ports to all vessels flying the South African flag;

(c) Enacting legislation prohibiting their ships from entering South African ports;

(d) Boycotting all South African goods and refraining from exporting goods, including all arms and ammunition, to South Africa;

(e) Refusing landing and passage facilities to all aircraft belonging to the Government of South Africa and companies registered under the laws of South Africa;

5. *Decides* to establish a Special Committee consisting of representatives of Member States [to review and report to the Assembly and Council on apartheid] . . .

8. *Requests* the Security Council to take appropriate measures, including sanctions, to secure South Africa's compliance with the resolutions of the General Assembly and of the Security Council on this subject and, if necessary, to consider action under Article 6 of the Charter [concerning expulsion].

The Special Committee created by the General Assembly operated for over 21 years, until the end of the apartheid regime in 1994. During that period, it contributed extensively to framing the international debate about South Africa and apartheid. Its work included elaborate reporting on apartheid; convening of conferences devoted to apartheid; and preparation and implementation of a program of action for the United Nations, its members, and other international organizations concerning South Africa (that included sports boycotts and other sanctions).

In 1963, Western nations, facing pressure from the developing world to take significant action against apartheid, announced that they would stop arms sales to South Africa. United States Ambassador Adlai Stevenson announced the U.S. policy as the Security Council was debating the South Africa issue in August 1963. Five days after his announcement, the Council passed the first arms embargo by the United Nations against a member state. It was adopted with no opposition, with Britain and France again abstaining, the former asserting that Britain's military cooperation with South Africa for the protection of sea routes prevented support for a full arms embargo. The resolution was not, however, adopted under Chapter VII of the UN Charter and was not considered at the time to be a legally binding decision:

Security Council Resolution 181 (1963)

The Security Council,

Having considered the question of race conflict in South Africa resulting from the policies of *apartheid* of the Government of the Republic of South Africa, as submitted by the thirty-two African Member States . . .

Noting with concern the recent arms build-up by the Government of South Africa, some of which arms are being used in furtherance of that Government's racial policies . . .

Being convinced that the situation in South Africa is seriously disturbing international peace and security,

1. *Strongly deprecates* the policies of South Africa in its perpetuation of racial discrimination as being inconsistent with the principles contained in the Charter of the United Nations and contrary to its obligations as a Member of the United Nations;

2. *Calls upon* the Government of South Africa to abandon the policies of *apartheid* and discrimination . . . and to liberate all persons imprisoned, interned or subjected to other restrictions for having opposed the policy of *apartheid*;

3. *Solemnly calls upon* all States to cease forthwith the sale and shipment of arms, ammunition of all types and military vehicles to South Africa . . . .

The U.S. delegate stated after the vote that U.S. support for the resolution was based on the resolution's sponsors' willingness to use the term "disturbing international peace and security" in the preamble, in lieu of the term "endangering international peace and security." He argued that the chosen language kept the embargo outside of Chapter VII, which he said was appropriate only to "a fully matured threat to, or breach of, the peace."

These resolutions notwithstanding, South Africa continued to practice—and indeed strengthen—apartheid during the 1960s and 1970s. It obtained arms clandestinely from some states, such as Israel, and developed an expensive domestic armaments industry. The Assembly, with its majority of developing world states, responded with numerous strongly worded resolutions, including some singling out three permanent members of the Security Council—France, the United Kingdom, and the United States—for their economic ties with South Africa.

In the early 1970s, a coalition of states opposed to apartheid sought to devise yet a new sanction—removal of South Africa from the United Nations itself. Article 6 of the Charter gives the General Assembly the right to expel a member that "has persistently violated the Principles" of the Charter, but only upon the recommendation of the Security Council; Article 5 allows the General Assembly to suspend any privileges of a member state that has been the subject of Security Council "preventive or enforcement action," but also only upon the Council's recommendation. These anti-apartheid states began this process in the Credentials Committee in September 1974.

First Report of the Credentials Committee

U.N. Doc. A/9779 (1974)

7. The representative of Senegal stated that his delegation objected to the acceptance of the credentials of the representatives of South Africa . . . . The representatives of South Africa to the General Assembly had been appointed by a Government which was the product of racial criteria and, as an institution, represented only a very small fraction of the South African population . . . . [T]hat country would certainly not have been admitted as a Member of the United Nations in 1945 had the policy of *apartheid* been put into law at the time. Furthermore, the question under consideration was to exclude not South Africa as a State Member of the United Nations, but solely the South African delegation, as it could not be considered that the latter represented the country . . . .

9. The representative of the United States of America declared that the Credentials Committee . . . was to examine whether the credentials of representatives had been issued in conformity with rules 27 and 28 of the rules of procedure. [Note: These rules address the form of the credentials submitted by governments.] The Committee's function was to verify the execution of the administrative duties that the Secretary-General had been entrusted with in relation to credentials, and

was therefore much akin to that of a parliamentary body . . . . [T]he Committee was not in a position to make a decision in that matter . . . . [F]or the Committee to decide on the basis of domestic policies would constitute a dangerous precedent for all. Furthermore, there was much to be gained by the continued participation of South Africa in the activities of the United Nations . . . .

11. The representative of Costa Rica felt that the Committee should not go beyond its limited competence. As to the question of *apartheid* itself, the Government of Costa Rica was in complete agreement with the Government of Senegal . . . . However, the Committee was not in a position to suspend or expel a Member State since that action, under Article 6 of the Charter, could be taken only by the General Assembly upon the recommendation of the Security Council. His delegation accepted the credentials submitted on behalf of South Africa as valid . . . .

The Credentials Committee decided by a vote of 5-3-1 to accept the credentials of all states except South Africa. Two days later, the General Assembly approved the report of the Credentials Committee, as well as a resolution asking the Security Council to "review the relationship between the United Nations and South Africa in the light of the constant violation by South Africa of the principles of the Charter and the Universal Declaration of Human Rights." G.A. Res. 3207 (1974). When the Council accordingly took up the matter in October 1974, it debated for 11 meetings whether to expel South Africa. Ultimately, a resolution to expel South Africa was vetoed by France, the United Kingdom, and the United States. After this defeat for the states seeking South Africa's removal, the General Assembly decided the next month to consider explicitly the effect of the rejection of the credentials by the Credentials Committee.

Official Records of 2281st Plenary Meeting of the General Assembly

U.N. Doc. A/PV.2281 (1974)

53. Mr. RICHARD (United Kingdom): . . .

55 . . . .We are either a law-abiding, law-respecting body or we are nothing, a mere talking shop. If we put aside the Charter whenever its provisions may seem to a majority of us—even, indeed, to a preponderant majority of us—to be inconvenient, then we lose all claim to authority and to credence . . . .

56. The Charter requires . . . that certain decisions have to be taken by the Security Council. Sometimes the Security Council operates alone; sometimes it operates in conjunction with the Assembly in the sense that a decision by the Security Council to make a certain recommendation to the Assembly is the necessary pre-condition for the Assembly to take action.

57. The Charter also provides—and again this is no incidental provision but goes to the heart of the way in which this Organization was conceived and in which therefore it must function—that certain decisions of the Security Council require not merely the support of the prescribed majority of members of the Council, but also the concurrence of all the permanent members. By concurrence we mean of course

the absence of a negative vote. This in turn casts a heavy responsibility on those permanent members . . . .

58. We must therefore reject . . . any argument that in discharging this important function under the Charter we ought to abandon our own judgement in deference to the views urged upon us by other delegations, even a majority of them, or indeed by other organs of the United Nations . . . . The Charter imposes a responsibility on each of the members of the Security Council, and each of them in turn must discharge it as it sees fit, conscientiously, honourably and in good faith . . . .

59. I turn now to the . . . argument that, despite the fact that the Security Council has not made a recommendation to the Assembly under Article 5 or Article 6 of the Charter, it is nevertheless open to the Assembly today by its own decision to exclude the delegation of a Member State.

60 . . . .[This argument] flies in the face of the Charter . . . . That Charter provides explicitly and exhaustively in Article 5 how a Member State may be suspended from the exercise of its rights and privileges of membership . . . .

62. It seems to me to be unarguable, therefore, as a matter of law—as a matter of the fundamental constitutional law of this Organization—that if we purport to exclude the delegation of a Member State, any Member State, from participating in our proceedings, and if we do so by a simple decision of the Assembly itself and not in the circumstances and in the manner provided for in Article 5, we are acting improperly, unconstitutionally and illegally . . . .

64. Mr. JAIPAL (India): . . .

67. No amount of pressure, influence and persuasion has so far deflected the white régime from its chosen doctrine of racial supremacy over the blacks, the browns and the Coloured people . . . .

68 . . . .What, then, are the options open to us? The expulsion of the white régime in terms of Article 6 of the Charter is certainly one of the options; but, unfortunately, three permanent members of the Security Council have vetoed such a course of action. One may expect a similar decision in regard to action to suspend South Africa in terms of Article 5 of the Charter.

69. In vetoing expulsion, those three Member States have . . . condemned those policies, and yet they remain hopeful of bringing about a change in the policy of the Pretoria regime. This is a hope which we do not share. In our opinion, there is little evidence in support of such a hopeful posture . . . .

74 . . . .[I]t is anomalous—that the representatives of a Member State whose credentials have been rejected should be allowed to participate in the work of this session . . . .Surely this decision is within our competence . . . .

76. In rejecting the credentials of the representatives of South Africa, we are in fact acting in accordance with our rules of procedure and also in conformity with the Charter; and I say that in deciding not to admit the representatives of South Africa . . . we shall be acting in conformity with our rules of procedure, and certainly with their spirit, and in doing so we shall certainly not be acting contrary to the Charter, because we shall not be expelling or suspending South Africa. We shall only be deciding not to allow the representatives of South Africa to participate in this session of the General Assembly—and that does not need the recommendation of the Security Council . . . .

153. The PRESIDENT [of the General Assembly, Abdelaziz Bouteflika of Algeria] *(interpretation from French)*. . .

155 . . . .[T]he absence of a decision by the Security Council [due to the veto] in no way affects the General Assembly's rejection of the credentials of the delegation of South Africa. Since its twenty-fifth session the General Assembly has been regularly rejecting, each year, the credentials of that delegation. It did so until last year by adopting an amendment to the report of the Credentials Committee . . . .

159. It would therefore be a betrayal of the clearly and repeatedly expressed will of the General Assembly to understand this to mean that it was merely a procedural method of expressing its rejection of the policy of *apartheid*. On the basis of the consistency with which the General Assembly has regularly refused to accept the credentials of the South African delegation, one may legitimately infer that the General Assembly would in the same way reject the credentials of any other delegation authorized by the Government of the Republic of South Africa to represent it, which is tantamount to saying in explicit terms that the General Assembly refuses to allow the South African delegation to participate in its work.

160. Thus it is, as President of the twenty-ninth session of the General Assembly, that I interpret the decision of the General Assembly, leaving open the question of the status of the Republic of South Africa as Member of the United Nations which, as we all as all know, is a matter requiring a recommendation from the Security Council . . . .

Compared to the actions in the General Assembly, the Security Council, by virtue of the veto power of three states with economic ties to South Africa, adopted far fewer, and much narrower resolutions; these urged South Africa to cease specific policies, such as imprisonment and execution of political opponents and indiscriminate attacks on peaceful protesters, and emphasized the need for dialogue between the races. Yet in November 1977, the Security Council unanimously, with no abstentions, tightened the arms embargo on South Africa. Its new embargo was taken under Chapter VII of the Charter, the first time the Council had imposed such sanctions against a UN member state. (The Council had acted under Chapter VII in authorizing the United States and its allies to use military force against North Korea in 1950 and in imposing economic sanctions against Rhodesia in 1962, but those states were not UN members.)

Security Council Resolution 418 (1977)

The Security Council, . . .

Recognizing that the military build-up by South Africa and its persistent acts of aggression against the neighbouring States seriously disturb the security of those States . . . .

Acting therefore under Chapter VII of the Charter of the United Nations,

1. *Determines*, having regard to the policies and acts of the South African Government, that the acquisition by South Africa of arms and related *matériel* constitutes a threat to the maintenance of international peace and security;

2. *Decides* that all States shall cease forthwith any provision to South Africa of arms and related *matériel* of all types, including the sale or transfer of weapons and ammunition, military vehicles and equipment, paramilitary police equipment . . . .

In 1985, the Council urged member states to suspend new investment, prohibit the sale of South African gold coins (krugerrands), restrict sport and cultural relations, and prohibit sales of nuclear and computer technology and equipment.

Ultimately, domestic and international pressure led the Nationalist Party to select F. W. DeKlerk, a moderate party member, as President of South Africa in 1989. DeKlerk began a four-year process that would lead to the end of apartheid. Following free and open elections in April 1994, a nonracial government, led by Nelson Mandela, took office on May 10, 1994. In a speech to the General Assembly in October 1994, President Mandela stated:

> We stand here today to salute the United Nations Organization and its Member States, both singly and collectively, for joining forces with the masses of our people in common struggle that has brought about our emancipation and pushed back the frontiers of racism. The millions of our people say "thank you" and "thank you again" because the respect for your own dignity as human beings inspired you to act to ensure the restoration of our dignity as well.

Notes and Questions

1. The arms embargo began in the General Assembly, then moved into the Security Council, first in the form of a strong recommendation and then in the form of a binding decision. What would explain this progression?

2. What are the respective roles of the General Assembly and the Security Council in sanctioning South Africa for apartheid? Did their actions appear to complement or conflict with one another? Should they act together or separately? Does Article 12 of the Charter, which bars the Assembly from making any recommendations on an issue "while the Security Council is exercising . . . the functions assigned to it" with respect to that issue, seem to have influenced the Assembly? How might the different legal effects of their decisions account for the outcomes in each body?

3. Which side had the better legal argument in the 1974 credentials battle? How much do you think law influenced the decision making of the General Assembly?

4. Did the permanent members of the Security Council influence the decision making of the United Nations too much regarding South Africa?

5. How would we know if President Mandela was right that the UN's sanctions were effective in promoting human rights compliance by ending apartheid? Consider the following perspective from international relations theory.

> Sanctions changed the balance of normative power among the key parties, the National Party and the ANC . . . .In the 1980s, domestic and international pressures mounted, and the NP's apartheid policies unraveled. Both inside and outside the NP, the hand of those whites who favored abolishing apartheid and entering into negotiations with the ANC (and other banned organizations) was strengthened . . . .Various sanctions packages had defined steps that the South Africa government needed to follow to

give clear evidence of its intent to dismantle apartheid . . . .During 1990 to 1991, de Klerk carefully followed these steps [and in] response to the government's move, Britain, the European Community, and the United States all moved to reward the NP by lifting their sanctions . . . .

While most of the groups in the anti-apartheid movement had an expansive socio-economic conception of the post-apartheid transformation, the official sanctions packages explicitly promoted the more narrow goals of political democratization, particularly universal suffrage . . . .The "international community," led by its leading Western members, demanded only political reform and juridical non-racialism, as reflected in the demands of the sanctions, and welcomed South Africa back into the fold following its universal-suffrage elections.

David Black, *The long and winding road: International norms and domestic political change in South Africa, in* The Power of Human Rights: International Norms and Domestic Change 78, 98-103 (Thomas Risse, Stephen C. Ropp & Kathryn Sikkink eds., 1999).

6. The Irish author and sometime diplomat Conor Cruise O'Brien wrote the following about the United Nations in a compelling 1968 book titled *United Nations, Sacred Drama* (pp. 9-11). Consider its relevance to the role of the UN in South Africa.

Why, men often ask, does the United Nations not *act*? The answer is that it seldom does anything else: it is acting all the time . . . .It has no power except the actor's power: the power to move, emotionally and morally. It has no *role* except a *role*; it plays the part of what men take it for. Its Council Chambers and Assembly Hall are stage sets for a continuous dramatisation of world history.

. . . Since the United Nations makes its impression on the imagination of mankind through a spectacle presented in an auditorium with confrontations of opposing personages, it may be said to belong to the category of *drama*. Since the personages . . . symbolise mighty forces . . . the drama may rightly be called *sacred*. . . .

. . . The "satisfaction" derived from the public offering of the "glowing phrases" [is] the same as that derived by the faithful from the public offering of a prayer: the sense of common aspiration; the appeal to a higher power, symbolised in this case by the Security Council and the General Assembly; the implied promise to meet again in continued acts of faith; the feeling that the thing feared may be averted, and the thing hoped for be won, by the solemn and collective use of appropriate words . . . .

F. The United Nations as a Forum for Treaty Making

The United Nations also became the forum for preparation of legal instruments against apartheid. The United Nations and other international organizations have become the primary arenas for the drafting of multilateral treaties. Typically, the United Nations will delegate preparatory work to one of two arenas: the International Law Commission, a 34-member body of independent legal experts created in 1947, or an intergovernmental conference process composed of numerous committees. Both will usually take a matter of years to complete their work. At times, the first process will flow into the second. The ILC's work has been critical to many conventions, such as the Vienna Convention on the Law of Treaties. Among the many treaties to emerge principally from the conference process is the 1982 Convention on the Law of the Sea.

In 1973, the USSR and Guinea mobilized a group of foes of South Africa at the United Nations to draft a multilateral treaty to criminalize apartheid—that is, to make individual officials criminally liable for carrying it out. The sponsors did not, however, want to wait for the more normal treaty-drafting processes to run their course. Instead, in a matter of weeks, states had negotiated and concluded a new convention.

International Convention on the Suppression and Punishment of the Crime of Apartheid

1015 U.N.T.S. 243 (1973)

Article I. 1. The States Parties to the present Convention declare that *apartheid* is a crime against humanity and that inhuman acts resulting from the policies and practices of *apartheid* and similar policies and practices of racial segregation and discrimination, as defined in article II of the Convention, are crimes violating the principles of international law . . . .

2. The States Parties to the present Convention declare criminal those organizations, institutions and individuals committing the crime of *apartheid*.

Article II. For the purpose of the present Convention, the term "the crime of *apartheid*", which shall include similar policies and practices of racial segregation and discrimination as practised in southern Africa, shall apply to the following inhuman acts committed for the purpose of establishing and maintaining domination by one racial group of persons over any other racial group of persons and systematically oppressing them:

(a) denial to a member or members of a racial group or groups of the right to life and liberty of person . . . ;
(b) deliberate imposition on a racial group or groups of living conditions calculated to cause its or their physical destruction in whole or in part;
(c) any legislative measures and other measures calculated to prevent a racial group or groups from participation in the political, social, economic and cultural life of the country and the deliberate creation of conditions preventing the full development of such a group or groups . . . ;

Article IV. The States Parties to the present Convention undertake:

(a) to adopt any legislative or other measures necessary to suppress as well as to prevent any encouragement of the crime of *apartheid* and similar segregationist policies or their manifestations and to punish persons guilty of that crime;
(b) to adopt legislative, judicial and administrative measures to prosecute, bring to trial and punish in accordance with their jurisdiction persons responsible for, or accused of, the act defined in article II of the present Convention, whether or not such persons reside in the territory of the State in which the acts are committed or are nationals of that State or of some other State or are stateless persons.

Article V. Persons charged with the acts enumerated in article II of the present Convention may be tried by a competent tribunal of any State Party to the Convention which may acquire jurisdiction over the person of the accused or by an international penal tribunal having jurisdiction with respect to those States Parties which shall have accepted its jurisdiction.

Western states sought to block or alter the convention for a number of reasons. They viewed the entire drafting process as an opportunity by the USSR and its allies to embarrass the West for its commercial dealings with South Africa, rather than a useful contribution to ending apartheid. They also expressed concerns that many provisions were too broadly worded for a criminal law instrument, in particular Article III's conferral of criminal responsibility on all persons who "commit, participate in, directly incite or conspire in the commission of," and "directly abet, encourage or co-operate" in apartheid, irrespective of motive, which might include Western business executives. As a result, none ever signed or ratified the Convention. As of 2006, the Convention had 106 parties, nearly all of them developing world states that became parties in the 1970s and 1980s. Only seven states have joined the Convention since Mandela assumed office.

Notes and Questions

1. What did the drafters of the Apartheid Convention accomplish? No person has ever been charged in a domestic or international court with the crime of apartheid. In that light, was the treaty a success?

2. The drafting of treaties under the auspices of international organizations is no guarantee that states will in fact become parties to them. In many cases, when national governments closely consider agreements that their delegations to international conferences have voted to adopt, they do not in the end become parties to them. This has proven a particular problem with the conventions of the International Labor Organization (ILO). Since the days of the League of Nations, it has served as an arena for governments, business, and labor groups to negotiate standards regulating all aspects of the workplace. Yet of the over 180 treaties that the ILO General Conference (its plenary assembly) has adopted, only a relatively small number have garnered widespread ratification. For more on the ILO, see Chapter 4. On the other hand, states may ratify agreements concluded long ago — such as, for example, when the United States ratified the 1948 Genocide Convention in 1988.

3. International organizations may engage in law making not only through the preparation of conventions like the Apartheid Convention, but through decision making that their members accept as having certain legal effects. This process represents a form of international administrative law making, as the members of the organization delegate responsibility to bodies within it to respond to different issues and make decisions that carry more weight than mere expressions of government sentiments.

For example, as noted earlier, the International Civil Aviation Organization (ICAO) delegates significant authority over civil aviation to its 33-member Council, which alone is empowered to pass International Civil Aviation Standards. These govern manifold issues of civil aviation, from airport safety to airplane communications to search-and-rescue operations. Under the ICAO's constitutive instrument, after the Council passes a standard (a two-thirds majority is required), ICAO states can register their objection; if a majority do so, it will not enter into force. This, however, has never happened in the ICAO's history. In addition, individual states can object to a new standard because compliance would be "impracticable"; if they do not, the most common view among ICAO member states and scholars is that the standard is binding on that state. Opt-outs tend to be unusual, and compliance with

ICAO standards is very high. The ICAO Council also promulgates recommendations, with which most states generally comply as well. Consider why a state would
avoid opting out of an ICAO Standard, for example, on the required length of a
runway to accept long-range aircraft.

G. Judicial and Quasi-Judicial Settlement of Disputes

The UN's involvement in the apartheid issue—and numerous other problems in
this book—demonstrate how international organizations can play an active role in
the settlement of disputes between actors in the international arena, whether states,
international organizations, or the nonstate actors discussed in the next chapter.
Chapter VI and other parts of the Charter specify the role of the Security Council,
the General Assembly, and other organs in facilitating settlements of disputes
between states. Chapter VI's first provision, Article 33, calls on all states whose
disputes might create international friction to settle them by peaceful means, offering an illustrative list of now-classic techniques:

— negotiation: direct discussion between the parties
— enquiry: neutral fact-finding by a third party
— mediation: third-party attempts to bridge differences with its own proposals
  and possibly incentives
— conciliation: a combination of enquiry and mediation
— arbitration: a binding solution devised by a third party
— judicial settlement: a binding solution devised by an international court
— resort to regional agencies or arrangements.

Though disputes arise between numerous actors in international law and can be
resolved through many techniques, many international law texts have used the term
"dispute settlement" to mean only arbitration and judicial settlement—and only of
disputes between states—and sometimes only judicial settlement. This usage
remains even though the vast majority of disputes among international actors
never reach international tribunals and even though the effect of the decisions of
international tribunals on the parties to a case and other actors remains empirically
contested.

Arbitral and judicial settlement began long before the United Nations and
League of Nations, e.g., in bilateral commissions resolving economic claims
between states or third-party heads of states serving as arbitrators in boundary
disputes. A major impetus toward institutionalization of arbitration was the creation
in 1900 of the Permanent Court of Arbitration, which, despite its name, is not a
court but rather a mechanism for the creation of ad hoc arbitral tribunals to resolve
disputes that states wish to send to arbitration. A second major impetus was the
establishment in 1921 of the Permanent Court of International Justice (PCIJ) under
the terms of a treaty prepared by the League of Nations. The PCIJ was based in The
Hague, Netherlands, and its jurisdiction resembled that of the International Court
of Justice, discussed below. It ruled on various disputes, mostly among European
states, and its jurisprudence remains relevant for international lawyers, though
neither it nor the League could prevent the catastrophes that soon overwhelmed
Europe.

When the UN Charter was drafted at San Francisco, the states involved decided to create the International Court of Justice (ICJ), which, like its predecessor, is a permanent court that sits in The Hague. Its Statute is appended to and part of the UN Charter. It is comprised of 15 permanent judges of different nationalities, elected by the General Assembly and the Security Council for nine-year renewable terms. The Court has at times sat in smaller chambers of five judges. In cases where a national of a litigating party is not on the Court, that party may appoint a judge *ad hoc*, a process meant to ensure that that state's views will receive ample consideration in the ICJ's deliberations. By informal agreement, a national from each of the five permanent members of the Security Council is always on the Court.

The Court hears two kinds of cases: (1) advisory proceedings, where it provides nonbinding but authoritative answers to specific legal questions posed to it by a UN organ or agency; and (2) contentious cases between states that are parties to the Statute (and only states), where it rules on a dispute between them. Contentious cases often begin with a request to the Court by one state for provisional measures (i.e., a temporary injunction) pending its determination of the merits. Provisional measures and judgments of the Court are binding on the parties to a contentious case, the latter explicitly so under Article 94 of the Charter and the former as a result of recent ICJ jurisprudence (see Chapter 5, Section III). The Security Council has the authority to enforce decisions of the ICJ, though it has rarely taken measures to do so.

Unlike domestic courts, the ICJ is not a court of mandatory jurisdiction with the ability to hear a case simply because a state is party to its Statute or a member of the UN. It is critical to remember that the ICJ can only hear cases where the states have consented in advance through some other instrument—not just ratification of the Charter—to its jurisdiction. The details of this jurisdictional regime are spelled out in its Statute:

Statute of the International Court of Justice Art. 36 (1945)

1. The jurisdiction of the Court comprises all cases which the parties refer to it and all matters specially provided for in the Charter of the United Nations or in treaties and conventions in force.

2. The states parties to the present Statute may at any time declare that they recognize as compulsory ipso facto and without special agreement, in relation to any other state accepting the same obligation, the jurisdiction of the Court in all legal disputes concerning:

a. the interpretation of a treaty;

b. any question of international law;

c. the existence of any fact which, if established, would constitute a breach of an international obligation;

d. the nature or extent of the reparation to be made for the breach of an international obligation.

3. The declarations referred to above may be made unconditionally or on condition of reciprocity on the part of several or certain states, or for a certain time . . . .

In effect, Article 36 means that the ICJ can hear three sorts of contentious cases: (a) those arising from treaties to which both states are parties that provide for settlement of disputes in the ICJ; (b) those arising from a special agreement of the parties to send a dispute to the ICJ (a *compromis*); and (c) those covered by declarations given by both parties in which they accept the compulsory jurisdiction of the Court. As of 2006, 68 states have consented to such jurisdiction, many with various qualifications and exceptions to their consent. (The United States withdrew its declaration, originally filed in 1946, in 1985, after Nicaragua instituted proceedings against it arising out of U.S. aid to the *contras*. See Chapter 13, Section III.)

Yet, except in contentious cases where both parties have signed a *compromis*, the state against which a suit is brought typically will contest the jurisdiction of the Court or, somewhat relatedly, the admissibility of the case. Among the many issues that have been the subject of decisions on jurisdiction and admissibility are: (1) whether both states were parties to a treaty conferring jurisdiction under Article 36(1) before the dispute arose; (2) whether both states had filed declarations under Article 36(2) before the dispute arose; (3) whether the dispute fits within the description of cases for which the parties accept the Court's jurisdiction under those treaties or declarations; and (4) whether there is really an ongoing legal dispute between the parties, e.g., whether it is moot, and whether the parties have a legal interest in the dispute (i.e., standing).

As a result of these issues and numerous others, the ICJ has frequently found a reason not to rule on the merits of a contentious case. In some situations, this has meant that a UN organ has instead asked the ICJ for an advisory opinion on a related issue. In the case of apartheid, this problem manifested itself with respect to South Africa's western neighbor, Namibia (Southwest Africa). Namibia had been a German colony before World War I; after the war, the victorious powers placed it under the League of Nations' Mandates system. South Africa concluded an agreement with the League with various commitments regarding the governance of the territory but nonetheless began to extend racially discriminatory policies to Namibia. After World War II, South Africa asserted that the Mandate had expired with the League. The General Assembly asked the ICJ for an advisory opinion on this question, and the Court replied in 1950 that the Mandate and South Africa's duties continued in force. South Africa rejected the opinion.

In 1960, Ethiopia and Liberia sued South Africa in the ICJ for violating the Mandate. Although the ICJ rejected South Africa's preliminary objections concerning the applicant states' standing and jurisdiction in an 8-7 opinion in 1962, in 1966, it essentially reversed itself and ruled by 8-7 (due to changes in membership) that the applicants did not have a legal interest in the claims. The decision proved the low point for the ICJ's international reputation. For many years thereafter, developing states were reluctant to include ICJ dispute settlement clauses in treaties, conclude *compromis* sending disputes to the ICJ, or issue declarations under Article 36(2).

The UN's political actors then took stronger measures, though the ICJ remained peripherally involved. In 1966, the General Assembly unilaterally terminated the Mandate and created a new body, the Council for South West Africa, to administer the territory. South Africa again rejected the UN action. In 1970, the Security Council declared South Africa's presence illegal and "call[ed] upon" all states to "refrain from any dealings" with South Africa that suggested otherwise. A 1970 ICJ advisory opinion clarified that these actions were within the Council's power and binding on member states, even though they were not taken under Chapter VII. South Africa again refused to comply. South Africa's grip on Namibia only loosened in the late 1980s, when the United States and the Soviet Union oversaw the negotiation of a complex agreement under which South Africa agreed to withdraw from Namibia in exchange for the withdrawal of Cuban troops from Angola, which had accepted such troops in the 1970s. The United Nations deployed a peacekeeping mission to oversee elections, which took place in November 1989. In 1990, Namibia achieved independence.

The Namibia case demonstrates the many barriers to a major role for the ICJ in the settlement of disputes between states. Most states are simply unwilling to entrust major matters of foreign policy to international judges; as a result, most bilateral and multilateral treaties do not include clauses in which the parties consent to ICJ jurisdiction over disputes under Article 36(1); most states do not conclude a *compromis* on matters they view as of vital interest unless they are pressured from outside to do so; declarations under Article 36(2) are the exception rather than the norm, and many are highly conditioned; and, as noted above, jurisdiction is typically contested by the respondent state. Moreover, the pace of ICJ proceedings is remarkably slow, as the Court can do nothing to require states to file pleadings on time. Though provisional measures may be issued very quickly, rulings on jurisdiction and admissibility, and then the merits, which are typically issued sequentially, can drag on for years, or even more than a decade. As a result, on matters of great urgency, the ICJ can only have a limited role.

The largest single type of case decided by the ICJ has been land and maritime boundary disputes, like the Libya-Chad *Territorial Dispute* in Chapter 1, the Burkina Faso-Mali *Frontier Dispute* in Chapter 3, or various maritime cases discussed in Chapter 10, where the parties seek the political cover of a third-party decision-maker to avoid painful concessions to the other side. Compliance with such decisions has generally been high. When states have attempted to use the ICJ for more controversial issues, in particular, the use of force, jurisdiction has been hotly contested, the ICJ itself has sought ways to avoid offending states, and compliance has been more problematic. This pattern can be seen in the *Avena* case on consular notification in Chapter 5, the *NATO Use of Force* and *Nicaragua* cases in Chapter 13, and the *Lockerbie Incident* case in Chapter 14.

Nonetheless, the end of the Cold War and the willingness of developing governments to look past the 1966 *Namibia* judgment seem to have reduced the reluctance of states to use the ICJ, and its caseload has significantly increased from a handful of contentious cases under consideration at any one time in the 1970s and 1980s to 10 on the docket in mid 2006. And the Court has issued some significant advisory opinions, including the *Legality of the Threat or Use of Nuclear Weapons* and the *Israeli Wall* opinions, discussed in Chapter 9.

Despite, or perhaps because of, these limitations on the ICJ, the last part of the twentieth century was marked by an increased willingness of states to entrust certain issues—not merely interstate disputes—to highly specialized tribunals. These include human rights courts in Europe and Latin America (which hear individual complaints against states), the WTO's Dispute Settlement Body, ad hoc tribunals for investment disputes (which hear business complaints against governments), the International Tribunal for the Law of the Sea, and international criminal courts (where a prosecutor institutes cases against individuals). The caseload of these courts has greatly increased, indeed exploded in the case of the European Court of Human Rights, suggesting that judicial settlement is on the rise, even if the ICJ itself is not the major actor in this process. Yet international law disputes are still and will likely always be resolved outside of any international court.

4

The Challenge
of Non-State Actors

The international legal process has never been the province of states—or of organizations composed of states—alone. Actors unaffiliated with governments have long played a role in the prescription, invocation, and application of international norms. Non-governmental actors range from large, territorially organized communities without state status, to organized religions, to groups of individuals sharing a dedication to a particular political cause, to business entities seeking a profit, to individual human beings. Men and women organized themselves into tribes, both stationary and roaming, millennia before any notion of a state; and religious institutions, such as the Catholic Church, have long had a global presence that permeated various communities, both state and non-state. These agglomerations of people are based upon certain organizing principles and structures, though different from those of the state. Whether their members are from one state or spread across many states, they are capable of action at the international level, action that inevitably affects the functioning of international law.

Despite the importance of such actors, traditional international lawyers and scholars rejected the notion that they could ever be true subjects of international law, for only states enjoyed rights and duties directly under international law. States alone created law, they created it for each other, and all other international actors were mere objects of that law. This mythical construct, while convenient as a matter of doctrine, never really corresponded with the way non-state actors and states interacted. Instead, non-state actors have repeatedly made claims under international law—for themselves qua entities, for their members, or for others for whom they are concerned. States have long endorsed many of these claims, whether by granting groups special rights in international agreements (as was done for the Catholic Church or ethnic minorities), including them in law making (as was done with antislavery groups), or even defending their interests militarily (as was done for domestic business interests operating abroad).

In this chapter, we explore four of the most significant non-state actors: non-governmental organizations, corporations, states of the United States, and special territories and organized communities within states. A fifth — the individual — is the subject of Part IV of this book. This list of non-state actors is hardly exhaustive — one might include organized crime syndicates, sporting federations, organized religions, and international terrorists as well (the last of which are discussed in

Chapter 14). In focusing on these four actors in this chapter, we hope to provide an understanding of their place in the international legal process in several senses: whether international norms recognize rights and duties for such entities; what sort of capacity they can and do enjoy to act independently of states in global arenas; and what sorts of effects they have had upon the international legal process.

I. NON-GOVERNMENTAL ORGANIZATIONS AND THE STRUGGLE FOR INCLUSION: THE CAIRO POPULATION CONFERENCE

Interest groups whose organization is based on a shared commitment to a particular cause have assumed a great voice in the international legal process. The entities most actively seeking and playing a direct role in the international legal process are the non-governmental organizations (NGOs), a term of art used to describe groups of individuals united to advocate a particular agenda on the domestic or international stage. The majority of NGOs are national in both their composition and their project; indeed, most are hardly known outside their home state. Others, however, are transnational in their membership, agenda, or both. As much as some might think that the telecommunications revolution is responsible for such transnational NGOs, they long predate it. One of the most significant NGOs in the nineteenth century was the Anti-Slavery League, which lobbied governments to eliminate the African slave trade. Today, NGOs have so proliferated that new acronyms have sprung up to describe them, including GONGOs (government-organized NGOs), BINGOs (business and industry NGOs), and DONGOs (donor-organized NGOs).

The era where NGOs focused on lobbying only their own governments to take positions in international legal fora is long gone. Today, NGOs actively participate in such arenas. They may prepare studies for wide dissemination, engage the media in an attempt to influence public opinion, attend international conferences as observers or lobbyists, contribute expertise to governmental delegations and thereby gain a seat at intergovernmental negotiations, or even co-opt delegations through promises of various assistance. The power of these groups, whose memberships can be anonymous or whose internal decision making may lack transparency or accountability compared to that of governments — both democratic and nondemocratic — has become one of the central issues in understanding the international legal process. As you read the following problem, consider what interests and constituencies NGOs can represent better than states; to whom NGOs might constitute a threat; what participatory rights NGOs ought to have in international conferences, organizations, and dispute resolution processes; and whether NGOs are accountable to their members or others in the international system.

A. The Problem

In mid-2006, world population stood at 6.5 billion, double that of 1960. The United Nations Population Fund has estimated that global population will increase to 9 billion by 2050. The distribution of the population increase, and its effects, are hardly uniform across the planet. All of the projected increase to 2050 is expected to take place in the developing world, which will constitute 85 percent of the world's population by that year. Indeed, the world's poorest nations will triple in size, from

668 million to 1.86 billion. The fertility rate (the average number of children per woman) in the developing world is currently just under 3, whereas in the developed world it stands at 1.6, below what demographers refer to as the "replacement level."

Population experts have long studied the links between population growth and economic development. Until recently, the conventional wisdom, based on research by major American demographers in the 1950s, was that population growth affirmatively impeded economic growth. As a result, many developing states engaged in, and placed significant reliance upon, inexpensive family planning programs, and industrialized states encouraged such programs through their foreign aid policies. In the 1980s, however, in part because many of these states remained desperately poor, demographers and other social scientists began to reconsider the causal link between population growth and poverty. As two experts have written:

> The new model asserts that programs that are demographically driven, and are intended to act directly on fertility, are inherently coercive and abusive of women's right to choose the number and timing of their children. Such programs should be replaced by others that "empower" women by increasing their educational levels, providing them with satisfying jobs, lightening their domestic responsibilities, and otherwise raising their status in the family and community. While family planning services should be provided, they should be only one element in comprehensive programs of reproductive health services, designed and managed with intensive inputs from women. Feminists advocating this agenda assert that once women become more empowered and development advances, women will opt to have fewer children and population growth will slow . . . .

C. Alison McIntosh & Jason L. Finkle, *The Cairo Conference on Population and Development: A New Paradigm?*, 21 Population & Dev. Rev. 223, 226-227 (1995).

The United Nations has long been interested in population issues. The UN Population Fund began operations in 1969, dispensing over $5 billion in assistance to developing states since that time. To highlight the population issue, the United Nations convened in 1994 the International Conference on Population and Development (ICPD) at Cairo. The Cairo Conference was the UN's third such conference on population following summits at Bucharest in 1974 and Mexico City in 1984. Among the most important issues for the conference was the relationship between family planning and population growth.

The Cairo Conference was the third in a series of seven "world conferences" convened by the United Nations from 1992 to 2001 to provide a forum for governments to meet and discuss some of the world's most pressing problems. The others were the UN Conference on Environment and Development in Rio de Janeiro in 1992; the World Conference on Human Rights in Vienna in 1993; the Fourth World Conference on Women in Beijing in 1995; the World Summit for Social Development in Copenhagen in 1995; the Second United Nations Conference on Human Settlements in Istanbul in 1996; and the World Conference Against Racism, Racial Discrimination, Xenophobia and Related Intolerance in Durban, South Africa, in 2001. All UN member states were invited to participate in the conferences, along with various non-state entities (such as dependent territories) and international organizations specializing in the particular issue discussed. In addition, the United Nations accredited various non-governmental organizations to the conferences, although the participatory rights of the NGOs varied at each conference. Each conference was typically preceded by a year or more of preparatory work; delegates from governments, international organizations, and NGOs met in both regional groupings and plenary sessions to argue out their differences and draft the lengthy policy documents that would be issued at the end of each conference.

B. The Process: A New Place for NGOs

The Cairo Conference demonstrated a major shift in the role for non-governmental organizations as participants in the international legal process. Although NGOs had long lobbied governments behind the scenes, their direct involvement in international negotiations had been in many ways limited. Article 71 of the UN Charter authorizes the Economic and Social Council (ECOSOC) to make "suitable arrangements for consultation" with NGOs. ECOSOC has an special 19-member Committee on Non-Governmental Organizations, which considers applications from NGOs for so-called consultative status, which gives them access to UN documents and public meetings and limited privileges to speak or circulate statements in ECOSOC. Some 2,700 NGOs had such status as of 2006. But beyond this participation, states generally expected NGOs to stay in the background during actual negotiations over new international agreements or other instruments. NGOs, for their part, continually sought ways to have a seat at the table of conferences, a more influential role behind the scenes, or both.

For the ICPD, NGOs played a major role in the preparatory proceedings; at the actual conference, 4,000 representatives from 1,500 NGOs based in 133 states attended the NGO Forum, housed at a remodeled stadium complex a half-mile from the conference venue.

Rules of Procedure of the International Conference on Population and Development

U.N. Doc. A/CONF.171/2 (1994)

Representatives of non-governmental organizations

Rule 65

1. Non-governmental organizations accredited to participate in the Conference may designate representatives to sit as observers at public meetings of the Conference and the Main Committee.

2. Upon the invitation of the presiding officer of the conference body concerned and subject to the approval of that body, such observers may make oral statements on questions in which they have special competence. If the number of requests to speak is too large, the non-governmental organizations shall be requested to form themselves into constituencies, such constituencies to speak through spokespersons.

Written Statements
Rule 66

Written statements submitted by the designated representatives referred to in rules 59 to 65 shall be distributed by the secretariat to all delegations in the quantities and in the language in which the statements are made available to it at the site of the Conference, provided that a statement submitted on behalf of a non-governmental organization is related to the work of the Conference and is on a subject in which the organization has a special competence. Written statements shall not be made at United Nations expense and shall not be issued as official documents.

At the conference itself, women's NGOs proved influential and very busy. Rather than allowing governments to take the lead in setting the agenda, exchange drafts of various documents, and negotiate, as would be typical of most UN conferences, the NGOs became direct participants. Consider the following two accounts:

C. Alison McIntosh & Jason L. Finkle, *The Cairo Conference on Population and Development: A New Paradigm?*

21 Population & Dev. Rev. 223, 238-239, 241-242 (1995)

In March 1993, just before Prepcom II [i.e., the second preparatory commission before the conference], a Women's Declaration on Population Policies was circulated by the International Women's Health Coalition (IWHC), a feminist health organization based in New York City. This document, calling for a broad range of reproductive health and development issues to be incorporated into population policies, had been prepared by some 24 "initiators" representing women's organizations in all five continents. The document was circulated around the world and received the endorsement of numerous organizations and individuals. The acceptance of the Women's Declaration by feminist activists and some family planning agencies notwithstanding, tensions between feminists and family planners were clearly visible at Prepcom II in May 1993. At this meeting, which presented to country delegations the ICPD Secretariat's proposed "outline" of the Cairo document, concerns were expressed by orthodox "populationists" about what they feared would be a serious dilution of population objectives by the women's agenda (Population Action International 1994). Nevertheless, the meeting ended with what the State Department called a "fragile consensus" on the scope and structure of the recommendations yet to be drafted for Cairo. It was decided to accommodate the women's demands by including two new chapters, on "Gender Equality, and the Empowerment of Women" and "Reproductive Rights, Reproductive Health, and Family Planning." Language recognizing that there are "various concepts of the family" was included in a chapter "The Family, Its Roles, Composition and Structure."

In the ensuing 11 months prior to Prepcom III, at which time it was hoped that the draft document would be approved by consensus, feminist activists undertook an energetic and sophisticated campaign to gain acceptance for their position. Women worked hard to bring other women together; they sidelined radical feminist views that they judged to have little chance of winning approval; they worked intensively with sympathetic population/family planning agencies to find language that might be acceptable to both sides. Feminists gave lectures, appeared on panels, lobbied the ICPD Secretariat, gave briefings to State Department officials and members of Congress, participated in numerous intersessional meetings (between prepcoms) where they helped draft language for the document, and secured a significant number of places on the US delegation.

Feminists in IWHC and the Women's Environment and Development Organization (WEDO) . . . banded together to form the Women's Caucus with a membership, by Prepcom III, of over 300 individuals, many of them members of NGOs from both developed and developing countries. At the Prepcom, the Women's Caucus organized workshops and meetings, formulated lengthy resolutions for the consideration of delegates, issued informative updates on the proceedings on the floor, and drafted new language on issues that were proving difficult. Although not all NGOs, especially some from developing countries, were in agreement with the women's position, there was a strong tendency to close ranks in the face of the intense attack mounted by the Holy See against a list of feminist issues. Where Prepcom II had ended with a "fragile consensus," by the end of Prepcom III only one position seemed to be open to a large majority of participants, that of the feminist agenda . . . .

From the moment the Clinton administration took office [in January 1993], AID [the Agency for International Development]'s Office of Population had started to consider how best to respond to the new directions that were emerging from the ICPD preparations. . . . As part of the process, AID held discussions with women's groups in an effort to identify parts of the women's agenda that could be incorporated incrementally into its ongoing programs . . . .

In elaborating the US position, Under Secretary [of State Timothy] Wirth decided to canvass public opinion in a manner more typical of elected political leaders on Capitol Hill than of officials at the State Department. . . . Environmentalists, health organizations, religious leaders of many denominations, pro-life and pro-choice groups, family planning agencies, and foundations made their way to Washington to present their views . . . . Back in Washington, negotiations were entered into with the major proponents of the women's agenda. The one constituency that does not seem to have been seriously consulted was the community of demographers and other academic social scientists who have provided the theoretical and analytical underpinnings of US international population policy for nearly 30 years . . . .

Once formed, the US position was advanced with determination and skill through every available channel. Collaboration with the ICPD Secretariat, as with women's organizations and other NGOs, was close, with exchanges taking place daily . . . . In the judgment of most seasoned observers, the United States, the Holy See, and the women's movement were the three most organized, best disciplined, and effective participants in the conference.

Ethan Bronner, *Population Talks: The Flip Side; Unofficial Groups Get Chance to Tell World Their Views*

The Boston Globe, Sept. 8, 1994, at 2

When they are not hovering around the conference center seeking to influence the wording of the document on abortion, the environment or female circumcision, NGOs are handing out paper about themselves, listening to one another's concerns, playing videos and gathering into caucuses—youth caucuses, women's caucuses, "pro-life" caucuses and "progressive religious" caucuses.

There are booths where Englishwomen who have converted to the Sikh faith make full physical diagnoses based on examination of tongue and pulse. There are daily yoga sessions at 1 P.M. There are Nigerian women in "gele" headties and stunningly colorful dresses and Indians in saris and Americans in Earth shoes.

What is perhaps most striking is how many women there are, about 70 percent by official estimates. While the gray-suited men at the UN conference debate words, the brightly dressed women at the NGO Forum seem to represent the link to real work on the ground. They are the ones who train villagers in contraception.

At their summit, dozens of events compete for attention. Sessions with titles such as "Women in Livestock Development—a panel discussion" sponsored by Heifer Project International are up against others like "Sex and Sexuality: Do You Know the Difference?"

Press conferences spill into one another. Some are packed, others thinly attended. Yesterday, Benton Musslewhite, a Texas lawyer who is founder of One World Now, lectured to a huge room with seven people in it, saying that if people band together, they can remake the United Nations into a democratic world government.

The NGO Forum is being held inside a vast converted athletic stadium complete with pizza and Chinese restaurants, multimedia displays and banks of telephones and computers. About 4,000 NGO representatives have come to Cairo.

Some are among the most established in population activities, groups such as International Planned Parenthood, the Population Council, CARE and Oxfam.

Another established group, Pathfinder International of Watertown, Mass., which does family planning in nearly 30 countries, sponsored a play by a dozen teen-agers from around the world who sang and performed skits about peer pressure, teen pregnancy and parental abuse.

The International Right to Life Federation has a leaflet with a photo of a 19-week old fetus and the words, "When they tell you that abortion is a matter just between a woman and her doctor, they're forgetting someone."

The group has its booth right next to Marie Stopes International, a British family planning agency, a neighborly match that is almost as good as the All-China Women's Federation and the Street Food Vendors Organization.

Some groups rely extensively on initials, expecting people to remember that IIASA stands for the International Institute for Applied Systems Analysis and that EGJMDA is the Egyptian General Junior Medical Doctors Association.

But the prize for alphabetical obscurity surely goes to the NCPDZDPI. So marginal is it that its leaders failed to show up; the booth has been empty all week. None of the activists nearby seems to know the first thing about it.

Notes and Questions

1. How did women's groups shape—or capture—the agenda of the population conference? What strategies did they use? Who were the targets of their lobbying activities?

2. How much participation did the rules of the ICPD allow NGOs? How were they able to convince delegates to accept their positions? Should the involvement of NGOs depend upon the final product of the international forum, for example, a treaty versus a softer instrument?

3. If you were chair of a body of the Cairo Conference, how would you decide which of the many NGOs at Cairo to allow to make an oral statement under the Rules

of Procedure? If you were a governmental delegate, how would you decide whose policy papers to read? Consider also the readings on NGO accountability below.

4. Does the influence of American (and other Western) NGOs at the ICPD due to their funding, political connections, and expertise suggest that increased NGO participation can exacerbate North-South tensions? Does their involvement further tilt the playing field away from developing world perspectives?

5. At the 1995 World Conference on Women, the Chinese government located the NGO Forum some miles away from the main conference center. Why are different governments likely to have different attitudes about the involvement of NGOs?

6. The Holy See — the supreme organ of the Catholic Church — participated extensively at the Cairo conference, emphasizing on many occasions Church positions on family planning and dissenting from much of the final conference document. In the end, it issued a lengthy statement opposing key portions of that document. Though not legally a state itself, the Holy See enjoys diplomatic relations with over 100 states, has membership or observer status in international organizations, and has signed treaties. (Under the 1929 Lateran Treaty between Italy and the Holy See, the latter has territorial sovereignty over the tiny State of Vatican City within Rome, but it is the Holy See, rather than Vatican City, that engages in diplomatic relations.) At Cairo, as in other venues, its representatives were treated like governmental delegates, and the Holy See was listed as a state in the list of delegations. In light of the functions of the Holy See, should it instead be treated as an NGO?

C. The Product: The Programme of Action

At the end of the nine-day conference, the ICPD issued the lengthy Programme of Action. The document was adopted without a vote, although some two dozen states issued statements or reservations interpreting or objecting to parts of the Programme.

Programme of Action of the International Conference on Population and Development

U.N. Doc. A/CONF.171/13 (1994)

Principle 4

Advancing gender equality and equity and the empowerment of women, and the elimination of all kinds of violence against women, and ensuring women's ability to control their own fertility, are cornerstones of population and development-related programmes. . . .

Chapter IV
GENDER EQUALITY, EQUITY AND EMPOWERMENT OF WOMEN

A. Empowerment and Status of Women

Basis for Action

4.1. . . . In all parts of the world, women are facing threats to their lives, health and well-being as a result of being overburdened with work and of their lack of power and influence. In most regions of the world, women receive less formal education than men, and at the same time, women's own knowledge, abilities and coping mechanisms often go unrecognized . . . . [I]mproving the status of women also enhances their decision-making capacity at all levels in all spheres of life, especially in the area of sexuality and reproduction. This, in turn, is essential for the long-term success of population programmes. . . .

Actions

4.4. Countries should act to empower women and should take steps to eliminate inequalities between men and women as soon as possible by:

(a) Establishing mechanisms for women's equal participation and equitable representation at all levels of the political process and public life in each community and society and enabling women to articulate their concerns and needs;

(b) Promoting the fulfilment of women's potential through education, skill development and employment, giving paramount importance to the elimination of poverty, illiteracy and ill health among women;

(c) Eliminating all practices that discriminate against women; assisting women to establish and realize their rights, including those that relate to reproductive and sexual health;

(d) Adopting appropriate measures to improve women's ability to earn income beyond traditional occupations, achieve economic self-reliance, and ensure women's equal access to the labour market and social security systems; . . .

4.12. Every effort should be made to encourage the expansion and strengthening of grass-roots, community-based and activist groups for women. Such groups should be the focus of national campaigns to foster women's awareness of the full range of their legal rights, including their rights within the family, and to help women organize to achieve those rights. . . .

Chapter VII
REPRODUCTIVE RIGHTS AND REPRODUCTIVE HEALTH

A. Reproductive Rights and Reproductive Health

Basis for Action

7.2. Reproductive health is a state of complete physical, mental and social well-being and not merely the absence of disease or infirmity, in all matters relating to the reproductive system and to its functions and processes. Reproductive health therefore implies that people are able to have a satisfying and safe sex life and that they have the capability to reproduce and the freedom to decide if, when and how often to do so. Implicit in this last condition are the right of men and women to be informed and to have access to safe, effective, affordable and acceptable methods of family planning of their choice, as well as other methods of their choice for regulation of fertility which are not against the law, and the right of access to appropriate health-care services . . . .

Actions

7.6. All countries should strive to make accessible through the primary health-care system, reproductive health to all individuals of appropriate ages as soon as possible and no later than the year 2015. Reproductive health care in the context of primary health care should, inter alia, include: family-planning counselling . . . ; education and services for prenatal care, safe delivery and post-natal care . . . ; prevention and appropriate treatment of infertility; abortion as specified in paragraph 8.25 [This paragraph stated, ''Any measures or changes related to abortion within the health system can only be determined at the national or local level according to the national legislative process. In circumstances in which abortion is not against the law, such abortion should be safe.''], including prevention of abortion and the management of the consequences of abortion.

B. Family Planning

Actions

7.15. Governments and the international community should use the full means at their disposal to support the principle of voluntary choice in family planning . . .

7.18. Non-governmental organizations should play an active role in mobilizing community and family support, in increasing access and acceptability of reproductive health services including family planning, and cooperate with Governments in the process of preparation and provision of care, based on informed choice, and in helping to monitor publicand private-sector programmes, including their own.

Since the Cairo Conference, the UN Population Fund has structured much of its activity and development assistance to promote the goals of the Programme of Action. By 2006, population experts were attributing a greater than expected decline in fertility rates in some developing world nations to the implementation of many of the plans in the Programme of Action. The United Nations has also involved numerous NGOs in that process. In addition, from June 30-July 2, 1999, the General Assembly convened a follow-up conference to the Cairo meeting, known as "ICPD+5." The organizers encouraged NGO participation at a variety of preparatory meetings as well as the conference itself. NGOs with consultative status to ECOSOC were automatically accredited to the Special Session. Others were asked to submit to the UN Secretariat documentation regarding their purpose, annual reports, financial statements (including lists of contributors), lists of the members of the governing body, a description of the membership, and a copy of the bylaws before accreditation. None, however, was granted the right to make a formal statement in the plenary session of the conference.

Notes and Questions

1. How do these excerpts reflect the influence of women's organizations? How do they reflect a change in thinking about population issues from the traditional paradigm discussed earlier?

2. Has the NGO community placed unrealistic goals upon governments? What can NGOs do after the Cairo Conference to assist governments with carrying out the mandate from the ICPD?

D. Accountability of NGOs

The participation of NGOs in international law-making fora has accelerated since the Cairo Conference. NGOs now routinely observe and participate in major international and regional conferences, lobbying governments behind the scenes. Their influence extends well beyond conferences preparing political documents to more direct forms of law making. The World Wide Web has enabled these organizations to transmit the proceedings of the conferences, including official drafts of treaties and other documents, along with NGO commentary, around the world, and to urge their members to lobby governments to take various positions.

For example, the International Campaign to Ban Landmines (ICBL), which began with six NGOs and grew to include over 1,200 NGOs from 60 countries, lobbied governments intensively in the 1990s to enact a global prohibition on landmines. The movement gained additional momentum when another NGO, the International Committee of the Red Cross (a century-old Swiss organization that works with governments on protecting victims of armed conflict), opened a worldwide campaign in the fall of 1995. When a UN conference to look at the problem reached an impasse in 1995-1996, ICBL, other NGOs, and some mid-size states collaborated to create an alternative negotiating forum, which came to be known as the Ottawa process. With strong NGO support, in just over a year the Ottawa process produced a new Landmines Treaty. The treaty, with 154 parties by 2006, prohibits the production or use of landmines and requires parties to destroy stockpiled and buried landmines. It represents the first time that an active weapons system has been banned outright (and not simply regulated) since poison gas was outlawed after World War I. In 1997, the ICBL received the Nobel Peace Prize. NGOs were also major players during the negotiations in the mid-1990s for the Statute of the International Criminal Court, which is discussed in Chapter 9.

NGOs also play an active role in judicial processes. They have represented individuals before human rights tribunals in Europe and Latin America. The International Court of Justice's (ICJ's) important advisory opinion on the legality of nuclear weapons, discussed in Chapter 8, resulted from a ten-year effort by an NGO, the World Court Project, to persuade the World Health Organization and the

General Assembly to request the ICJ for an opinion on the legality of nuclear weapons. The Project lobbied national leaders, sponsored academic meetings and publications, and collected 3.8 million signatures from citizens opposed to nuclear weapons. Another NGO provided pro bono legal assistance to the Solomon Islands, Samoa, and the Marshall Islands, which enabled these states to participate fully before the ICJ in this case.

NGOs have also demonstrated the ability to disrupt law-making processes instituted by governments. Environmental and anti-corporate NGOs chalked up a major victory in 1998 when they were able to convince governments in the Organization for Economic Co-operation and Development, the 30-nation organization of mostly rich states, to abandon negotiations on a Multilateral Agreement on Investment (MAI) that aimed at safeguarding foreign investment against discriminatory practices by host states. The NGOs accomplished this after they obtained a confidential copy of the draft agreement, posted it on the Internet along with their commentary, and mobilized members throughout the world to lobby their governments to change course. In 1999, a similar coalition organized significant demonstrations at a major meeting of the World Trade Organization (WTO) in Seattle that sought to set an agenda for a new trade round. These protests, however, also attracted small groups of violent demonstrators, who vandalized stores seen as symbols of capitalism and engaged in limited, but bloody, skirmishes with police.

Yet who or what are these increasingly powerful actors in the international arena? Non-governmental organizations come in all shapes and sizes. They may be formed and funded by individuals, corporations, religious organizations, or even governments. Some have worldwide memberships in the tens of thousands; others are just a handful of volunteer activists dedicated to a particular cause. Some work by lobbying governments or corporations directly or through their members (whether through letter-writing campaigns or economic boycotts); others take direct action to advance their cause, such as Greenpeace's dispatch of dinghies to separate whales from whaling ships, or Medecins Sans Frontières' provision of doctors to war-torn areas of the world. Members of NGOs may even serve on official governmental delegations to conferences that prepare international agreements or nonbinding documents (such as the Cairo Programme of Action). Such participation may stem from a decision by the government to include NGO perspectives in the official positions — perhaps as a way of co-opting the NGO to cooperate with the government — or because the government itself lacks expertise on a particular issue. Several Pacific Island nations have staffed their delegations to environmental conferences with experts from Western environmental NGOs.

The increased power of NGOs raises critical questions regarding the appropriate level of participation of these entities in the international legal process. Whereas the international community routinely accepts governmental delegations as representatives of a state — even if the government is autocratic and not based on the will of the people — there is less consensus on the degree to which NGOs should be accepted, given their vastly different constituencies and relationships with constituencies.

For one perspective on this issue, consider the work of Global Trade Watch (GTW), a division of Public Citizen, a consumer advocacy NGO created in 1972 by Ralph Nader. Public Citizen created GTW in 1993 "to promote government and corporate accountability in an area on which few public interest groups were focused: the international commercial agreements shaping the current version of globalization." GTW, along with other NGOs, played a central role in the successful derailing of the MAI in 1998 and the demonstrations at the WTO ministerial meeting in Seattle in 1999. Its media-savvy director offered the following perspective:

"Lori's War": Interview with Lori Wallach, Director, Global Trade Watch

Foreign Policy 38-39, 40-41, 46-47 (Spring 2000)

MN *[Moises Naim, Editor of Foreign Policy]*: If Lori Wallach had her way, would she like the United States to pull out of the WTO?

LW: . . . From my perspective, it has given every indication that it is an institution that will break itself by its inability to bend . . . . And where the international activists, the network that brought you Seattle, is going, on consensus, is to say all right, Seattle was the wake-up call of all time . . . . Between now and the next meeting of the world's trade ministers, there is a list of things the WTO must do-[t]hings that must be accomplished . . . . And if those changes aren't made at the end of those 18 months or so before the next ministerial, then, not only should the United States get out, but, in fact, all of the country-based campaigns, and there are 30 of them at least, will launch campaigns either to get their countries out or to withdraw their funding. . . .

MN: You have put together a very odd coalition of labor, Greens, environmentalists, Gray Panthers, progressives . . .

LW: Church groups, Tibetan monks, small businesses . . .

MN: What holds that coalition together?

LW: I would say two things. One, philosophically, the notion that the democracy deficit in the global economy is neither necessary nor acceptable. The second is that they're all directly damaged by the actual outcomes of the status quo, in different ways. And so you have family farmers, for instance, who've seen a huge increase in the volume of exports of U.S. agricultural commodities, in the exact same decade that farm income has crashed.

MN: How many countries are members of this coalition?

LW: Well, there are country-based campaigns, and there are basically 30 of them, 25 of which are really quite operational.

MN: You had a year of preparation or more [for the demonstrations in Seattle in 1999]?

LW: Yeah, it wasn't the week on the ground, it was the work that happened beforehand. Perhaps there was an enzymatic effect, where all of the work to that point was cooked, ultimately, by some reaction that was sparked by what was going on on the ground. But that was just the final stop. As soon as the European Union and Japan announced their agreement in 1999 to push for a millennium round [of trade talks], the NGOs around the world that had . . . come out of the campaign against the Multilateral Agreement on Investment, basically said, "Listen, we sort of thought maybe the MAI would send the message that we are not going down that road anymore." But it's like that shell game in a carnival. With the MAI, we smashed the shell that was the OECD. So they just took the pea and put it in another shell. And now it's in the WTO shell, and we're going to just have to smash that one. . . .

MN: What is your annual budget?

LW: I believe the total budget of Public Citizen is slightly less than $11 million. I think this year's Global Trade Watch budget is about $760,000.

MN: Where does the money come from?

LW: The vast majority of Public Citizen's funding is from our members.

MN: How many members do you have?

LW: I believe right now, 150,000. They pay minimally $20 a year to be a member; they get a magazine, and other benefits. And some people give extra for extra campaigns. For Global Trade Watch, another important source is foundation funding. For instance, the Foundation for Deep Ecology supports our work on the implications of globalization for the environment. And the Ford Foundation has funded us to look at democratic accountability in an era of globalization.

MN: Is the list of your funders available?

LW: Yes. . . .

MN: Are there professional associations that fund Ralph Nader? Like lawyers, tort lawyers, and —

LW: No. Any time we do something successful, we're always accused of taking some bagman's money. And we jokingly say, considering how poor our institution is, and how much hell we get about this, it's a shame we don't just get the goddamned money. But, in fact, our terms of incorporation prohibit corporate or government funds.

MN: Who are you accountable to?

LW: Our members.

MN: How do they express their oversight?

LW: Well, a couple of different things, not the least of which is their checkbooks. The times that we've gone off on issues that they didn't find important or valuable, they stopped being members.

Consider the following academic commentary on the issue:

Peter J. Spiro, *New Global Potentates: Nongovernmental Organizations and the "Unregulated" Marketplace*

18 Cardozo L. Rev. 957, 963-966 (1996)

. . . With very few exceptions, NGO leaders are not elected by memberships, nor are their memberships likely to scrutinize particular policy positions closely. Indeed, members may maintain their affiliation with an organization even though they disagree with some of its stances; in this respect, international NGOs profit by the phenomenon of "packaged preferences" enjoyed by domestic political parties by which the party is, in effect, trusted to formulate certain policy choices on the member's behalf. As a result, however, the leadership is afforded tremendous discretion in deciding what policies it will pursue and with what level of vigor. At the same time, NGO decision-making need be only as open as the organization itself so mandates.

. . . Non-profit corporate law is . . . unlikely in any jurisdiction to constrain NGO executives to the extent that public officials routinely are constrained by ethics legislation and regulations. The absence of standard public law safeguards concentrates significant power in NGO secretariats. Armed with the leverage of large memberships, and knowing that those members are likely to be a docile herd, NGO leaders have emerged as a class of modern day, nonterritorial potentates, a position rather like that commanded by medieval bishops.

Good governance (if one can call it governance) does not always result . . . . The Brent Spar [oil rig] episode is in this respect instructive. Greenpeace evidently saw an excellent publicity (and fundraising) opportunity in opposing the proposed scuttling of a decommissioned oil rig in the North Sea. The context supplied a visible adversary, one against whom Greenpeace members and other environmentalists could be and were mobilized. The problem: the scuttling posed a trivial environmental threat. Indeed, Greenpeace was working from incorrect information as to the volume of hazardous wastes that would go down with the rig. But even after acknowledging the error, and notwithstanding independent analyses establishing the inconsequence of sending the rig to the ocean floor, Greenpeace kept at it — and Shell relented, at great cost. Greenpeace continues to oppose the scuttling of rigs in the North Sea. Shell has gone so far as to meet with Greenpeace representatives to seek its approval of plans to decommission other rigs. Disposing of the platforms at sea would violate no domestic law or international accord, notwithstanding the fact that hazardous waste disposal is at the center of an area of relatively refined international regulation. Greenpeace, in effect, has created and enforced a new norm of international environmental law. By way of entrenching it, the organization is now moving to have intergovernmental bodies adopt the prohibition, but regardless of that effort's success, one might doubt that oil companies will dare undertake scuttlings so long as Greenpeace maintains its vigilance on the issue.

Over the medium to long term, two developments may be posited which would change this dynamic of NGO-corporate (or NGO-state) interplay. First, one might suppose that competition among NGOs would correct the excesses of any single organization. If Greenpeace expends too high a level of resources on matters that are in fact marginal to the effective protection of the environment, then other groups could be expected to make light of this in soliciting members and funds . . . . On the other hand . . . some groups (such as Greenpeace and Amnesty International) have established themselves as institutional behemoths in such a way as to obstruct true competition . . . .

Second, it is possible that the targets of NGO activity will move to buy them off. NGOs can do nothing without money. Fundraising is notoriously difficult in a crowded field . . . . At the same time, it may make good business sense for corporations to start writing checks to their would-be adversaries (or related laudable causes), with a quid pro quo, stated or not. Freeport-McMoRan has become a major underwriter of CARE at the same time as it has come under increasing fire from human rights groups for its activities in Indonesia. Reebok funds a human rights award, all the better to insulate itself with respect to employment practices in the third world that could otherwise generate negative publicity . . . . NGOs now routinely accept government funds, potentially compromising their ability to bite the hands that feed them.

Notes and Questions

1. What models of participation by NGOs address the need for inclusion of non-governmental perspectives but take account of the accountability concerns raised by Spiro? Was the involvement of NGOs in the preparations for and negotiations at the Cairo conference enough? Too much?

2. What is the rationale for direct NGO participation if they can already participate in domestic debates on international issues? Do NGOs foster the democratization of international processes by injecting citizen voices into intergovernmental decision making? Is their increased involvement an indictment of the state, or do they themselves lack legitimacy and simply represent self-appointed international elites?

3. Should NGOs have to make public their sources of funding in order to be able to participate in international conferences? In determining whether to grant consultative status to an NGO, the UN's Economic and Social Council requires that the NGO "have a democratic decision making mechanism" and that the "major portion of the organization's funds should be derived from contributions from national affiliates, individual members, or other non-governmental components."

4. NGOs have, at times, used troubling tactics. For example, in order to obtain the three-fourths majority vote of states party to the International Whaling Convention (IWC) necessary to adopt a moratorium on commercial whaling, NGOs mounted a "membership drive" to get developing states, many with little interest in whales, to join the IWC. To encourage these states to join, NGOs paid the annual dues and expenses of attending IWC meetings; in some instances they even drafted and submitted the required membership documents for states to join the IWC.

II. CORPORATIONS AS INTERNATIONAL ACTORS: WORKPLACE CONDITIONS IN SOUTHEAST ASIAN APPAREL FACTORIES

Corporations have long been major actors on the international scene. During the colonial era, charter companies, such as the Dutch East India Company, served as proxies for governments in gaining European domination over overseas territories and were given significant powers in governing certain colonies. The twentieth century brought the rise of the multinational corporation, with shareholders, offices, and facilities in many countries. The economic power of business enterprises (including their ability to provide or withhold funds to politicians seeking election) has given them great influence over governmental policy on international issues such as trade, investment, antitrust, intellectual property, and telecommunications. They frequently prod governments to make claims against each other regarding treatment of businesses — leading to diplomatic negotiations, new international agreements, or invocation of formal dispute resolution procedures such as those in the WTO. Corporations can also provide experts to sit on governmental teams at intergovernmental negotiations. Indeed, at one conference of the International Telecommunication Union, the American delegation had so many representatives from Motorola — seeking special frequencies for (an eventually failed form of) satellite telephones — that it became known as the "delegation from Motorola." The success of corporations in shaping the international legal process to advance their economic agenda has offered many lessons to NGOs seeking a greater role in law making and enforcement.

As a result of corporate influence, it is now common for international legal instruments to effectively grant business entities certain rights. For example, bilateral investment treaties and regional economic agreements, such as the North American Free Trade Agreement (NAFTA) and the treaties establishing the European Union, require states to allow foreign corporations to set up investments on a nondiscriminatory basis; some also require countries hosting foreign corporations to accede to international arbitration if the corporation prefers that option to the host state's local courts in the event of a dispute. As for duties on corporations, international labor treaties emerging from the International Labor Organization (ILO) have long required governments to enact domestic legislation affecting private businesses; and some environmental treaties require that states impose civil liability on corporations for accidents in the course of certain dangerous activities, such as transportation of hazardous wastes. Legal scholars differ as to whether these sorts of provisions in treaties confer "international legal personality" on corporations.

Whatever the significance of such doctrinal disagreements, serious disagreements remain among governments, international organizations, corporations, and non-governmental organizations about the proper role for international law in regulating corporate behavior and the proper role for corporations in prescribing international law. As you read the following problem, consider how corporations affect the content of international norms; how much influence they should have over the international legal process; for which issues their contributions are helpful; and how corporations can further or undermine the implementation of certain norms.

A. The Problem

One of the most significant trends in international commerce in the last half of the twentieth century was the shift in production of many different products from rich, Northern states to developing world states. From a time when developing countries depended almost exclusively upon exports of raw materials for production in the North, many states in the South have now developed significant manufacturing capabilities. Some rely heavily on relatively simple skills, such as the manufacture of clothing and toys; but others produce cars and computer chips for export.

The clothing industry has taken a major role in this transformation, as less developed country workers offer inexpensive labor and high-quality products that sell well in the richer states. The clothing industry has tended to operate in developing states in several ways, including direct investment in production facilities and contractual relationships with locally owned factories. These local factories often farm out part of the production process to subcontractors, which may themselves be smaller factories or simply individuals working out of their own homes.

The following description of Nike's operations in Southeast Asia in the late 1990s is typical of much of the industry:

> Nike does not own the factories producing Nike goods . . . . [I]t has determined that contractors can do so more efficiently and less expensively. Virtually all of Nike's shoes and half its clothing line are assembled outside the United States by contractors, who — for the most part — have dedicated factories solely to the manufacture of Nike products . . . . Nike has footwear contractors in Indonesia, China, Vietnam, Thailand, the Philippines, South Korea and Taiwan, although it says it is cutting back on operations in Korea and Taiwan because workers in these quickly developing economies are no longer interested in working in low-paying shoe and textile factories.
>
> Indonesia is Nike's biggest production center, with 17 footwear factories that employ 90,000 workers and produce about 7 million pairs of shoes each month . . . . Each Nike apparel contractor in Indonesia employs anywhere from 400 to

2,000 workers, totaling about 30,000 apparel workers in Indonesia. Indonesian factories account for 37 percent of Nike products manufactured in the Asia-Pacific Region; in turn, Nike products comprise 40 percent of Indonesia's exported brand name footwear — more than $1 billion worth in 1997 . . . .

    Tony Nava, Nike's general manager in Indonesia . . . says 80 to 85 percent of the factory employees are women, because of the heavy amount of sewing required. He says it is commonly accepted that men would not do as good a job on the stitching. . . .

Investor Responsibility Research Center, The Sweatshop Quandary: Corporate Responsibility on the Global Frontier 256-257 (1998).

    Although conditions of employment in the apparel industry in the Northern states received significant attention in the early twentieth century and proved a major impetus for the labor movement, working conditions in the developing world have long evaded effective action at home and abroad. Local governments have lacked the resources and, at times, the will to enforce domestic or international labor standards; domestic producers have been content with the guaranteed business from foreign importers; Northern corporations have welcomed the profits from the cheaply produced clothing; consumers have enjoyed the low prices; and governments in the North have claimed that the matter was beyond their jurisdiction to regulate.

    Conditions, of course, have varied depending upon the factory, the foreign importer, the commodity produced, and the country of origin. For example, in Indonesia, Nike paid the legal minimum wage of $2.60 per day, but labor activists claimed this was not sufficient to meet basic subsistence levels. Nike has responded by pointing out that farmers make about $1 per day and that employees get free meals and basic health care, though labor groups pointed to the higher cost of living in the cities where factories are located. Workers have also been pressured to work overtime, including Saturdays and Sundays. Female employees have also accused some Nike managers in Vietnam and Taiwan of physically abusing them, including hitting workers whom the managers believed were not working hard enough. More common are complaints of verbal abuse. Workers who have complained about abuses have been fired, and factory managers have blocked efforts of unions to organize workers. At one point Nike came under criticism when it was discovered that a contractor making soccer balls in Pakistan had relied on ten- and eleven-year-old children to work at $1 a day, but Nike corrected the problem by moving such production from scattered family and village settings to a centralized, supervised factory where age could be verified.

    International scrutiny of the apparel industry began to change in the 1980s and 1990s, however, as NGOs in both the developing and developed worlds began to mobilize international attention to the issue. NGOs also focused attention on labor conditions in other industries, such as use of child labor in the production of handmade carpets, as well as on environmental damage traceable to investment by Northern companies. Western media eventually picked up the story, leading to revelations of employment conditions, such as the soccer ball issue, that often embarrassed major Western apparel manufacturers. Consumer groups threatened boycotts; and shareholder groups put pressure on corporate officers as well.

B. Attempts at Multilateral Regulation

Corporate activity has long been a subject for regulation by international law. Treaties between states on trade directly affect the way companies do business, as do agreements on myriad other subjects such as telecommunications, intellectual property, taxation, and investment. International decision makers have also relied upon various forms of law making to regulate corporate treatment of employees and others directly affected by corporate activity.

The oldest regime specifically governing employment conditions is that of the ILO, which has been developing a vast international labor code, composed of treaties and recommendations, since the days of the League of Nations. As of 2006, the ILO had promulgated over 180 conventions and over 190 recommendations. In creating the ILO, states sought to develop international standards for laborers and thereby avoid a situation where each state would cut back on worker protections in order to make its exports more competitive — the so-called "race to the bottom."

The ILO has sought to regulate the activities at issue in the apparel industry controversy. Among the treaties on workplace conditions is the following agreement from 1981:

Convention Concerning Occupational Safety and Health and the Working Environment

ILO Convention No. 155 (1981), http://www.ilolex.ilo.ch

Article 4

1. Each Member shall, in the light of national conditions and practice, and in consultation with the most representative organisations of employers and workers, formulate, implement and periodically review a coherent national policy on occupational safety, occupational health and the working environment. . . .

Article 8

Each Member shall, by laws or regulations or any other method consistent with national conditions and practice and in consultation with the representative organisations of employers and workers concerned, take such steps as may be necessary to give effect to Article 4 of this Convention. . . .

Article 13

A worker who has removed himself from a work situation which he has reasonable justification to believe presents an imminent and serious danger to his life or health shall be protected from undue consequences in accordance with national conditions and practice. . . .

Article 16

1. Employers shall be required to ensure that, so far as is reasonably practicable, the workplaces, machinery, equipment and processes under their control are safe and without risk to health. . . .

Article 19

There shall be arrangements at the level of the undertaking under which —
   (a) workers, in the course of performing their work, co-operate in the fulfilment by their employer of the obligations placed upon him;

(b) representatives of workers in the undertaking co-operate with the employer in the field of occupational safety and health;

(c) representatives of workers in an undertaking are given adequate information on measures taken by the employer to secure occupational safety and health and may consult their representative organisations about such information provided they do not disclose commercial secrets;

(d) workers and their representatives in the undertaking are given appropriate training in occupational safety and health;

(e) workers or their representatives and, as the case may be, their representative organisations in an undertaking, in accordance with national law and practice, are enabled to enquire into, and are consulted by the employer on, all aspects of occupational safety and health associated with their work . . . .

As of 2006, this treaty had only 45 parties. Indeed, most of the ILO conventions have relatively few ratifications. In an effort to encourage states to ratify the most important conventions, the ILO's Governing Body identified eight so-called fundamental conventions, covering freedom of association, forced labor, equal pay, and child labor. Each of these conventions has been ratified by well over 100 countries. (Convention 155 is not one of the fundamental conventions.)

During the 1970s and 1980s, many states in the United Nations undertook to develop a binding code of conduct for corporations. This effort followed disclosures of corporate involvement in U.S. government efforts to destabilize regimes in Iran, Guatemala, and Chile in the 1950s and 1970s. The General Assembly created the Commission on Transnational Corporations (CTC) within the UN Conference on Trade and Development, the UN unit responsible for studying the effect of international economic trends on less developed states. The Commission became a venue for bitter debates between Northern and Southern governments over the responsibilities of corporations. Over the objections of many Western states, the CTC issued the following draft in June 1990, hoping for formal adoption by the General Assembly:

Draft Code of Conduct on Transnational Corporations

U.N. Conference on Trade and Development, U.N. Doc. E/1990/94 (1990)

The General Assembly . . .

Convinced that a universally accepted, comprehensive and effective Code of Conduct on Transnational Corporations is an essential element in the strengthening of international economic and social co-operation and, in particular . . . to maximize the contributions of transnational corporations to economic development and growth and to minimize the negative effects of the activities of these corporations.

Decides to adopt the following Code of Conduct on Transnational Corporations: . . .

7. Transnational corporations shall respect the national sovereignty of the countries in which they operate and the right of each State to exercise its permanent sovereignty over its natural wealth and resources.

Obex national laws

8. An entity of a transnational corporation is subject to the laws, regulations and established administrative practices of the country in which it operates. . . .

10. Transnational corporations should carry out their activities in conformity with the development policies, objectives and priorities set out by the Governments of the countries in which they operate and work seriously towards making a positive contribution to the achievement of such goals at the national and, as appropriate, the regional level, within the framework of regional integration programmes. . . .

13. Transnational corporations should respect the social and cultural objectives, values and traditions of the countries in which they operate. While economic and technological development is normally accompanied by social change, transnational corporations should avoid practices, products or services which cause detrimental effects on cultural patterns and socio-cultural objectives as determined by Governments. . . .

Respect Culture

14. Transnational corporations shall respect human rights and fundamental freedoms in the countries in which they operate. In their social and industrial relations, transnational corporations shall not discriminate on the basis of race, colour, sex, religion, language, social, national and ethnic origin or political or other opinion. Transnational corporations shall conform to government policies designed to extend equality of opportunity and treatment. . . .

16. Without prejudice to the participation of transnational corporations in activities that are permissible under the laws, regulations or established administrative practices of host countries . . . transnational corporations shall not interfere in the internal affairs of host countries. . . .

what does this mean?

23. Transnational corporations should carry out their personnel policies in accordance with the national policies of each of the countries in which they operate which give priority to the employment and promotion of its nationals at all levels of management and direction of the affairs of each entity so as to enhance the effective participation of its nationals in the decision-making process. . . .

36. (a) Transnational corporations shall conform to the transfer of technology laws and regulations of the countries in which they operate. They shall co-operate with the competent authorities of those countries in assessing the impact of international transfers of technology in their economies and consult with them regarding the various technological options which might help those countries, particularly developing countries, to attain their economic and social development. . . .

The Draft Code of Conduct was never adopted by the General Assembly. Instead, political support for attempted UN regulation of corporations dissipated with the end of the Cold War. Developing states, increasingly desperate for foreign investment, acceded to Western demands that the United Nations drop the Draft Code. Indeed, in 1994, the United Nations dissolved the CTC and created a smaller and downgraded Commission on International Investment and Transnational Corporations. The UN's focus in this area is now primarily on encouraging foreign investment by corporations as a way of fostering free trade and development.

Nonetheless, the global interest in corporate conduct beginning in the 1970s prompted a response from rich nations through the Organization for Economic Co-operation and Development (OECD), the organization of 30 economically wealthy states that offers a forum for their governments to discuss and coordinate economic policy. In 1976, the OECD promulgated a set of nonbinding guidelines for multi-national corporations, but they were fairly brief and general. The principal implementation mechanism for the guidelines were the so-called National Contact Points(NCPs), whereby each member would designate one official or office within a particular ministry to promote awareness of the guidelines and receive any domestic complaints about their nonimplementation. The NCPs, typically obscure offices whose work did not gain the attention of domestic political leaders and which had little independent funding, were generally ineffective. In addition, the OECD created a committee composed of representatives of OECD members to hear complaints from labor unions and others alleging violations. In response, the committee could and did issue nonbinding interpretations of the guidelines that clarified the obligations of corporations. These interpretations could be adopted only by consensus, and they did not directly declare whether the particular enterprise had complied with the guidelines; consequently, they ultimately had little effect on OECD members or their companies.

In the mid-1990s, as NGOs and other groups emphasized the need for stronger global norms on corporate conduct, the OECD's members began discussions on a new nonbinding code. After several years of negotiations, governments agreed in 2000 upon a fuller set of principles in the OECD Guidelines for Multinational Enterprises. According to the Guidelines' preface,

> They provide voluntary principles and standards for responsible business conduct consistent with applicable laws. The Guidelines aim to ensure that the operations of these enterprises are in harmony with government policies, to strengthen the basis of mutual confidence between enterprises and the societies in which they operate, to help improve the foreign investment climate and to enhance the contribution to sustainable development made by multinational enterprises.

The Guidelines were appended to a declaration on investment adopted by all OECD countries the same day, in which they "jointly recommend to multinational enterprises operating in or from their territories the observance of the Guidelines."

OECD Guidelines for Multinational Enterprises

(2000), www.oecd.org/daf/investment/guidelines

General Policies

Enterprises should take fully into account established policies in the countries in which they operate, and consider the views of other stakeholders. In this regard, enterprises should:

1. Contribute to economic, social and environmental progress with a view to achieving sustainable development.

2. Respect the human rights of those affected by their activities consistent with the host government's international obligations and commitments. . . .

9. Refrain from discriminatory or disciplinary action against employees who make *bona fide* reports to management or, as appropriate, to the competent public authorities, on practices that contravene the law, the *Guidelines* or the enterprise's policies.

10. Encourage, where practicable, business partners, including suppliers and sub-contractors, to apply principles of corporate conduct compatible with the *Guidelines*. . . .

IV. Employment and Industrial Relations

Enterprises should, within the framework of applicable law, regulations and prevailing labour relations and employment practices:

1. (a) Respect the right of their employees to be represented by trade unions . . . ;

   (b) Contribute to the effective abolition of child labour;

   (c) Contribute to the elimination of all forms of forced or compulsory labour;

   (d) Not discriminate against their employees with respect to employment or occupation on such grounds as race, colour, sex, religion, political opinion, national extraction or social origin, unless selectivity concerning employee characteristics furthers established governmental policies which specifically promote greater equality of employment opportunity or relates to the inherent requirements of a job. . . .

4. (a) Observe standards of employment and industrial relations not less favourable than those observed by comparable employers in the host country;

   (b) Take adequate steps to ensure occupational health and safety in their operations.

   [Other provisions addressed transparency, the environment, bribery, consumer interests, and competition.]

The 2000 OECD Guidelines appear to be receiving more serious treatment by OCED member states than did their predecessor. NCPs have been more active in publicizing the Guidelines, and the OECD itself has opened its consultation processes to NGOs. Nonetheless, at a 2001 conference organized by the OECD to review the guidelines, business leaders, trade unions, and NGOs differed over the future of the Guidelines. Business leaders emphasized their voluntary character and their subordination to domestic law; unions lamented what they considered the continued lack of effectiveness of NCPs.

The OECD Guidelines are now supplemented by other guidelines. Among the most significant are the Global Sullivan Principles, issued in 1999 by an American minister who some 20 years earlier had prepared principles for involvement by foreign companies in apartheid-era South Africa; Social Accountability 8000, a set of standards issued by Social Accountability International, an NGO that relies on authorized monitors to certify labor conditions worldwide; and the UN Global Compact, a joint project of the United Nations and various business leaders that sets forth nine basic principles of corporate practice and urges business leaders to adopt them.

In August 2003, the UN Commission on Human Rights' Sub-Commission on the Promotion and Protection of Human Rights, a body of 26 independent human rights experts, adopted and passed on to the full Commission a set of proposed human rights norms for corporations, drafted principally by Professor David Weissbrodt:

Norms on the responsibilities of transnational corporations and other business enterprises with regard to human rights

UN Comm'n on Human Rights, Sub-Commission on the Promotion and Protection of Human Rights, UN Doc. E/CN.4/Sub.2/2003/12/Rev.2 (2003)

A. General obligations

1. States have the primary responsibility to promote, secure the fulfilment of, respect, ensure respect of and protect human rights . . . including ensuring that transnational corporations and other business enterprises respect human rights. Within their respective spheres of activity and influence, transnational corporations and other business enterprises have the obligation to promote, secure the fulfilment of, respect, ensure respect of and protect human rights recognized in international as well as national law . . . .

broad.

B. Right to equal opportunity and non-discriminatory treatment

2. Transnational corporations and other business enterprises shall ensure equality of opportunity and treatment, as provided in the relevant international instruments and national legislation . . . for the purpose of eliminating discrimination . . . or of complying with special measures designed to overcome past discrimination against certain groups.

C. Right to security of persons

3. Transnational corporations and other business enterprises shall not engage in nor benefit from war crimes, crimes against humanity, genocide, torture, forced disappearance, forced or compulsory labour, hostage-taking, extrajudicial, summary or arbitrary executions, other violations of humanitarian law and other international crimes against the human person . . . .

D. Rights of workers

5. Transnational corporations and other business enterprises shall not use forced or compulsory labour as forbidden by the relevant international instruments and national legislation . . . .

6. Transnational corporations and other business enterprises shall respect the rights of children to be protected from economic exploitation as forbidden by the relevant international instruments and national legislation . . . .

7. Transnational corporations and other business enterprises shall provide a safe and healthy working environment as set forth in relevant international instruments and national legislation . . . .

8. Transnational corporations and other business enterprises shall provide workers with remuneration that ensures an adequate standard of living for them and their

families. Such remuneration shall take due account of their needs for adequate living conditions with a view towards progressive improvement.

9. Transnational corporations and other business enterprises shall ensure freedom of association and effective recognition of the right to collective bargaining by protecting the right to establish and . . . to join organizations of their own choosing without distinction, previous authorization, or interference, for the protection of their employment interests . . . .

E. Respect for national sovereignty and human rights

10. Transnational corporations and other business enterprises shall recognize and respect applicable norms of international law, national laws and regulations, as well as administrative practices, the rule of law, the public interest, development objectives, social, economic and cultural policies including transparency, accountability and prohibition of corruption, and authority of the countries in which the enterprises operate.

12. Transnational corporations and other business enterprises shall respect economic, social and cultural rights as well as civil and political rights and contribute to their realization, in particular the rights to development, adequate food and drinking water, the highest attainable standard of physical and mental health, adequate housing, privacy, education, freedom of thought, conscience, and religion and freedom of opinion and expression . . . .

H. General provisions of implementation

15. As an initial step towards implementing these Norms, each transnational corporation or other business enterprise shall adopt, disseminate and implement internal rules of operation . . . . Each transnational corporation or other business enterprise shall apply and incorporate these Norms in their contracts . . . with contractors, subcontractors, suppliers, licensees, distributors, or natural or other legal persons . . . .

16. Transnational corporations and other business enterprises shall be subject to periodic monitoring and verification by United Nations, other international and national mechanisms already in existence or yet to be created. . . .

Reactions to the draft norms were mixed. The United States and some other industrialized governments, as well as some BINGOs, opposed the entire project on the basis that human rights norms should apply to states, not corporations; other states and numerous NGOs found the Norms a useful starting point for discussion. Within the Commission on Human Rights, the intergovernmental body to which the Sub-Commission reports, behind-the-scenes discussions began on how to bridge the differences between the two sides. In 2004, the Commission asked the UN High Commissioner on Human Rights to study the issue further while affirming that the Sub-Commission's document "has no legal standing." In 2005, the Commission, over the objections of the United States, South Africa, and Australia, adopted a resolution establishing a new Special Rapporteur to, among other things, "clarify standards of corporate responsibility and accountability" and "compile a compendium of best practices." The Special Rapporteur was instructed to work with all interested international organizations, transnational business, labor groups, and other interested constituencies. The future trajectory of the process of drafting norms for corporations within the UN thus seems very uncertain.

Notes and Questions

1. Whom does the ILO Convention regulate—states or companies? Does it matter from the perspective of the target of these norms? Should corporations be directly liable for human rights violations under international law?

2. How much flexibility does the Convention afford a state in addressing worker safety? Why do you think that only 45 states are parties to the Convention?

3. Who was the intended beneficiary of the UN's Draft Code of Conduct? Consider in this context the debates in the 1970s between North and South regarding sovereignty over natural resources, discussed in Chapter 2.

4. How do the OECD Code, the Draft UN Code, and the Sub-Commission's Norms differ? What would explain the difference?

5. How useful are these documents to workers in the apparel industry? Do they provide meaningful guidelines to corporations regarding conditions of labor for employees?

6. Since the mid-1990s, groups claiming to be victims of various forms of corporate misconduct have filed suit against corporations under the Alien Tort Claims Act, 28 U.S.C. §1350, which gives U.S. courts jurisdiction over "any civil action by an alien for a tort only, committed in violation of the law of nations." (The Act is discussed in detail in Chapter 5.) Defendants have tended to be companies in the extractive industries, such as oil and minerals. Most of the suits have alleged that the companies aided and abetted in human rights abuses by governmental agents, e.g., by providing agents with equipment or otherwise working with them in order to suppress opposition to the defendant's projects or to other governmental policies. No plaintiff has prevailed on the merits, although in 2004, the oil company Unocal settled a law suit by Burmese villagers over the company's alleged complicity with the Burmese government in human rights abuses, in particular forced labor and relocation, associated with the construction of a gas pipeline. The settlement reportedly included both monetary compensation and the creation of various programs in Burma to improve the welfare of those affected by the pipeline. Is the United States the right forum for complaints of human rights abuses by corporations committed abroad? Consider that, since 1977, the United States has forbidden, indeed criminalized, a form of corporate activity abroad—the giving of bribes by American corporate officials to foreign governmental officials (under the Foreign Corrupt Practices Act). In the 1990s, after European companies continued to benefit from the tolerance of their governments for such bribegiving, the United States convinced the other members of the OECD to criminalize such activity by treaty.

C. Options for Direct Participation of Corporations in Law Making

What is the role for the corporation in the prescription of hard and soft law affecting it? For traditional international lawyers, only states can make international law, as it is clear for such scholars that the very nature of a treaty and custom requires certain activities by states. But just as the material above regarding NGOs suggests that the conclusion of international instruments by states does not preclude the participation of NGOs, corporate actors can have a role to play in law making. Consider the following two examples:

Structure of the International Labor Organization

www.ilo.org

The ILO accomplishes its work through three main bodies, all of which encompass the unique feature of the Organization: its tripartite structure (government, employers, workers).

1. International Labour Conference: The member States of the ILO meet at the International Labour Conference in June of each year, in Geneva. Each member State is represented by two government delegates, an employer delegate and a worker delegate. They are accompanied by technical advisors. It is generally the Cabinet Ministers responsible for labour affairs in their own countries who head the delegations, take the floor and present their governments' points of view.

Employer and worker delegates can express themselves and vote according to instructions received from their organizations. They sometimes vote against each other or even against their government representatives.

The Conference plays a very important role. It establishes and adopts international labour standards. It acts as a forum where social and labour questions of importance to the entire world are discussed. The Conference also adopts the budget of the Organization and elects the Governing Body.

2. The Governing Body is the executive council of the ILO and meets three times a year in Geneva. It takes decisions on ILO's policy. It establishes the programme and the budget which it then submits to the Conference for adoption. It also elects the Director-General.

It is composed of 28 government members, 14 employer members and 14 worker members. Ten of the government seats are permanently held by States of chief industrial importance. Representatives of other member countries are elected at the Conference every three years, taking into account geographical distribution. The employers and workers elect their own representatives respectively.

International Telecommunication Union, Explanation of Membership Policies

www.itu.int

Note: The ITU is the UN's specialized agency responsible for the international regulation of telecommunications, including the radio spectrum, telephone equipment, and satellite communication. The ITU is divided into three sectors—one that allocates use of the radio-frequency spectrum (the Radiocommunications Sector), one that sets technical standards for telecommunication equipment (the Standardization Sector), and one that assists developing world nations (the Development Sector). These Sectors work through periodic conferences and assemblies of all states, as well as smaller study groups composed of experts on particular topics. Study groups can issue recommendations that effectively become standards for various telecommunications equipment. 190 states are members of the organization, while some 590 private enterprises are members of the Sectors. The ITU's Web site invites private enterprises to: "Shape the future. Join the ITU and help build tomorrow's Information Society." It continued:

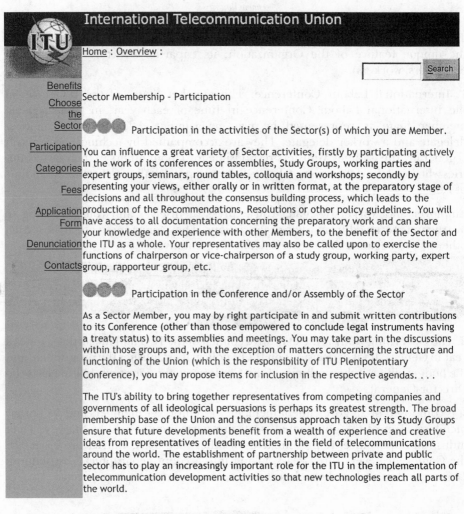

International Telecommunication Union

Home : Overview :

Search

Benefits
Choose the Sector

Sector Membership - Participation

Participation in the activities of the Sector(s) of which you are Member.

Participation
Categories
Fees
Application Form
Denunciation
Contacts

You can influence a great variety of Sector activities, firstly by participating actively in the work of its conferences or assemblies, Study Groups, working parties and expert groups, seminars, round tables, colloquia and workshops; secondly by presenting your views, either orally or in written format, at the preparatory stage of decisions and all throughout the consensus building process, which leads to the production of the Recommendations, Resolutions or other policy guidelines. You will have access to all documentation concerning the preparatory work and can share your knowledge and experience with other Members, to the benefit of the Sector and the ITU as a whole. Your representatives may also be called upon to exercise the functions of chairperson or vice-chairperson of a study group, working party, expert group, rapporteur group, etc.

Participation in the Conference and/or Assembly of the Sector

As a Sector Member, you may by right participate in and submit written contributions to its Conference (other than those empowered to conclude legal instruments having a treaty status) to its assemblies and meetings. You may take part in the discussions within those groups and, with the exception of matters concerning the structure and functioning of the Union (which is the responsibility of ITU Plenipotentiary Conference), you may propose items for inclusion in the respective agendas. . . .

The ITU's ability to bring together representatives from competing companies and governments of all ideological persuasions is perhaps its greatest strength. The broad membership base of the Union and the consensus approach taken by its Study Groups ensure that future developments benefit from a wealth of experience and creative ideas from representatives of leading entities in the field of telecommunications around the world. The establishment of partnership between private and public sector has to play an increasingly important role for the ITU in the implementation of telecommunication development activities so that new technologies reach all parts of the world.

Approximately 119 of the Sector Members are U.S.-based companies. They include AT&T, Cisco Systems, Hewlett Packard, Intel, MCI, Microsoft, Nokia USA, and Sprint.

Notes and Questions

1. What sorts of corporate participation might address the problems faced by apparel industry workers in the developing world? If you were the general counsel of Nike, in which venues, domestic and international, would you want a presence?

2. The ILO and the ITU are among the most welcoming of organizations with respect to direct corporate participation. What might account for this? Is direct corporate involvement especially conducive to good law making in certain subject areas?

3. Why have corporations and business and industry NGOs (BINGOs) proved more successful at integrating themselves in the prescription process than other non-state actors?

4. Corporate participation in setting international labor standards has not prevented corporations from evading those standards. How can corporate participation in law making be structured to promote corporate cooperation in implementation of norms?

5. Corporate involvement in international organizations extends beyond the prescriptive process to dispute resolution as well. For example, the 1965 Convention on the Settlement of Investment Disputes allows corporations from one state party to institute arbitration against any other state party if the latter has violated an investment commitment toward the company and consents to the arbitration. Even where a dispute resolution process formally concerns two or more states, such as the WTO, the real parties in interest and moving parties may be corporations. Thus, for example, the real economic actors in the dispute in the mid-1990s between the United States and Japan over access to Japan's market for film products were film manufacturers Kodak and Fuji. Kodak strongly lobbied both the Executive branch and Congress to take action against Japan; at one point, Japan refused to negotiate over the issue, and, in its place, Fuji's lawyers engaged in extensive negotiations with the office of the U.S. Trade Representative in the hopes of averting a formal state-to-state case in the WTO; both companies attempted to persuade foreign governments to back their side (Kodak's success leading to an EU endorsement of the U.S. position); and both worked side by side with their governments during the entire WTO dispute settlement process—for example, by drafting briefs and providing legal and economic analysis (which led to a 1997 ruling for Fuji—or was it Japan?).

6. Transnational corporations have been very active in international environmental law issues. In the case of acid rain, British, French, and Italian opposition to decreases in nitrogen oxide emissions was determined by the positions of their car makers, while Germany's position in favor stemmed from the ability of German makers to incorporate catalytic converters. Food and drug companies in the United States, Canada, and elsewhere that export genetically modified organisms influenced the position of those states on trade in GMOs during talks on the 2000 Cartagena Protocol on Biosafety and in limiting its scope. Much, but not all, U.S. industry has lobbied the U.S. Administration and Congress against binding standards on greenhouse gases. Business participation can be still more direct. Representatives of the pesticide and chemical industries have served on expert panels of the Food and Agriculture Organization and the UN Environmental Programme that determined the substances to be covered by various agreements requiring the prior informed consent of importing states before exportation of hazardous chemicals could proceed. The Conference of Parties to the Biodiversity Convention created expert panels, including industry representatives, to address bioprospecting, namely access to, and sharing of the scientific and monetary benefits from, plant and animal genetic resources. The groups worked closely with the Swiss government and Swiss companies to create the 2002 Bonn Guidelines, a key step to a regime on bioprospecting.

D. Corporate Self-Regulation: Codes of Conduct

Beyond participation in law making alongside states, corporations have engaged in a form of self-regulation through enactment of codes of conduct.

These codes are voluntary commitments made by companies, business associations, or other entities, that put forth standards and principles for the conduct of business. Although they date back at least to the beginning of the twentieth century, they have proliferated in the last 20 years due to shareholder, consumer, and NGO interest in corporate behavior. Now numbering in the hundreds, they generally focus on the same sorts of issues found in the OECD Code.

Nike has had a code of conduct in place since 1992. As shown on its Web page *www.nike.com*, its current version states:

NIKE Inc. was founded on a handshake.

Implicit in that act was the determination that we would build our business with all of our partners based on trust, teamwork, honesty and mutual respect. We expect all of our business partners to operate on the same principles.

At the core of the Nike corporate ethic is the belief that we are a company comprised of many different kinds of people, appreciating individual diversity, and dedicated to equal opportunity for each individual. . . .

Wherever Nike operates around the globe, we are guided by this Code of Conduct. We bind our manufacturing partners to these principles. Our manufacturing partners must post this Code in all major workspaces, translated into the language of the worker, and must endeavor to train workers on their rights and obligations as defined by this Code and applicable labor laws.

While these principles establish the spirit of our partnerships, we also bind these partners to specific standards of conduct. These standards are set forth below.

1. Forced Labor: The manufacturer does not use forced labor in any form — prison, indentured, bonded or otherwise.

2. Child labor: The manufacturer does not employ any person below the age of 18 to produce footwear. The manufacturer does not employ any person below the age of 16 to produce apparel, accessories or equipment. Where local standards are higher, no person under the legal minimum age will be employed.

3. Compensation: The manufacturer provides each employee at least the minimum wage, or the prevailing industry wage, whichever is higher; provides each employee a clear, written accounting for every pay period; and does not deduct from worker pay for disciplinary infractions, in accordance with the Nike Manufacturing Leadership Standard on financial penalties.

4. Benefits: The manufacturer provides each employee all legally mandated benefits. Benefits vary by country, but may include meals or meal subsidies; transportation or transportation subsidies; other cash allowances; health care; child care; emergency, pregnancy or sick leave; vacation, religious, bereavement or holiday leave; and contributions for social security and other insurance, including life, health and worker's compensation.

5. Hours of Work/Overtime: The manufacturer complies with legally mandated work hours; uses overtime only when each employee is fully compensated according to local law; informs each employee at the time of hiring if mandatory overtime is a condition of employment; and, on a regularly scheduled basis, provides one day off in seven, and requires no more than 60 hours of work per week, or complies with local limits if they are lower. . . .

In August 1996, in response to public attention regarding conditions in foreign factories contracting with American apparel manufacturers, these companies joined forces with human rights NGOs, labor unions, consumer advocates, religious groups, and the U.S. government to form the Apparel Industry Partnership (AIP) (now called the Fair Labor Association). Among their tasks was to draft a set of guidelines for corporations to endorse voluntarily. In April 1997, the AIP announced the following Code of Conduct to guide the operation of its members (available at *www.fairlabor.org*):

Workplace Code of Conduct

The Apparel Industry Partnership has addressed issues related to the erad-ication of sweatshops in the United States and abroad. On the basis of this examination, the Partnership has formulated the following set of standards defining decent and humane working conditions. The Partnership believes that consumers can have confidence that products that are manufactured in compliance with these standards are not produced under exploitative or inhu-mane conditions.

[The AIP Code prohibits forced labor, child labor (defined as younger than 15 unless local law allows for age 14), harassment, and discrimination. It also calls for "a safe and healthy working environment to prevent accidents and injury to health." Regarding wages, it calls for "at least the minimum wage required by local law or the prevailing industry wage, whichever is higher." Hours of work are limited, "[e]xcept in extraordinary business circumstances," to "the lesser of (a) 48 hours per week and 12 hours overtime or (b) the limits on regular and over-time hours allowed by [local] law" or, where local law is silent, "the regular work week in such country plus 12 hours overtime"; and one day off every seven. Overtime pay must also follow local law or, if no law exists, at least the regular hourly rate.]

Any Company that determines to adopt the Workplace Code of Conduct shall, in addition to complying with all applicable laws of the country of manufacture, comply with and support the Workplace Code of Conduct . . . and shall apply the higher standard in cases of differences or conflicts. Any Company that deter-mines to adopt the [Code] also shall require its licensees and contractors and, in the case of a retailer, its suppliers to comply with applicable local laws and with this Code. . . .

Principles of Monitoring

I. OBLIGATIONS OF COMPANIES

A. Establish Clear Standards

- Establish and articulate clear, written workplace standards
- Formally convey those standards to Company factories as well as to licen-sees, contractors and suppliers
- Receive written certifications . . . from Company factories as well as contrac-tors and suppliers that standards are being met, and that employees have been informed about the standards
- Obtain written agreement of Company factories and contractors and suppliers to submit to periodic inspections and audits, including by accredited external monitors, for compliance with the workplace standards

B. Create an Informed Workplace

Ensure that all Company factories as well as contractors and suppliers inform their employees about the workplace standards orally and through the posting of standards in a prominent place . . . and undertake other efforts to educate employees about the standards on a regular basis. . . .

E. Conduct Periodic Visits and Audits

- Have trained Company monitors conduct periodic announced and unannounced visits to an appropriate sampling of Company factories and facilities of contractors and suppliers to assess compliance with the workplace standards
- Have Company monitors conduct periodic audits of production records and practices and of wage, hour, payroll and other employee records and practices of Company factories and contractors and suppliers. . . .

G. Establish Relationships with Labor, Human Rights, Religious or Other Local Institutions

- Consult regularly with human rights, labor, religious or other leading local institutions that are likely to have the trust of workers . . . and utilize, where companies deem necessary, such local institutions to facilitate communication with Company employees. . . .
- Consult periodically with legally constituted unions representing employees at the worksite regarding the monitoring process and utilize, where companies deem appropriate, the input of such unions. . . .

Some of the union participants in the AIP negotiations, including the AFL-CIO and the Union of Needletrades, Industrial and Textile Employees (the largest union in the U.S. apparel industry), refused to accept the Code of Conduct because it failed to mandate a so-called "living wage" to workers, had insufficient rights to unionize, and included weak enforcement provisions. In 2000, a new NGO, the Workers Rights Consortium (WRC), was formed by university administrators, students, and labor experts to promote worker rights. As of 2006, it included over 150 colleges and universities. The WRC's Model Code of Conduct contains the following principles on wages and benefits and collective bargaining (available at *www.workersrights.org*):

Wages and Benefits: Licensees recognize that wages are essential to meeting employees' basic needs. Licensees shall pay employees, as a floor, wages and benefits which comply with all applicable laws and regulations, and which provide for essential needs and establish a dignified living wage for workers and their families. [A living wage is a "take home" or "net" wage, earned during a country's legal maximum workweek, but not more than 48 hours. A living wage provides for the basic needs (housing, energy, nutrition, clothing, health care, education, potable water, childcare, transportation and savings) of an average family unit of employees in the garment manufacturing employment sector of the country divided by the average number of adult wage earners in the family unit of employees in the garment manufacturing employment sector of the country.]

Freedom of Association and Collective Bargaining: Licensees shall recognize and respect the right of employees to freedom of association and collective bargaining.

No employee shall be subject to harassment, intimidation or retaliation in their efforts to freely associate or bargain collectively. Licensees shall not cooperate with governmental agencies and other organizations that use the power of the State to prevent workers from organizing a union of their choice. Licensees shall allow union organizers free access to employees. Licensees shall recognize the union of the employees' choice.

In January 2001, the WRC sent a delegation to an apparel factory in Puebla, Mexico, that manufactures for Nike and Reebok various sweatshirts with the names of many American colleges and universities. It revealed violations of child labor laws, physical abuse, serving of rotten food in the company cafeteria, and firing of hundreds of employees who had gone on strike over these conditions. Nike criticized the report but nonetheless pledged to end the practices.

Many companies participating in the Fair Labor Association Code of Conduct have retained Price Waterhouse Coopers Lybrand, a multinational accounting firm, to monitor their factories for violations. In 2000, an MIT professor claimed that Price Waterhouse missed numerous violations and limited much of its detailed interviewing to plant managers rather than a range of employees.

Notes and Questions

1. How does the participation of corporations in drafting codes of conduct affect their contents? What effect might this participation have in the implementation of a code?

2. Are these codes international law? Soft law? How do they contribute to the law-making process?

3. In 1935, the ILO concluded the Forty Hour Week Convention, which requires states generally to utilize a 40-hour work week. In 1962, the ILO approved a detailed recommendation to states on various methods to attain that goal. The Convention has been ratified by only 14 countries. What will be the likely impact of the Nike or Fair Labor Association Codes of Conduct on prospects for further ratification? Are Codes of Conduct that contain standards different from those in international instruments detrimental or constructive to the promotion of human and labor rights? Is self-enforcement an alternative to standards from outside of the industry or a complement to them?

4. Consider the following position from the United States Council on International Business, a BINGO:

The supply chain—unmanageable expectations: **The preponderance of the business community rejects the notion that companies can be held responsible for . . . their subcontractors and suppliers throughout the supply chain. . . .** This degree of responsibility is unrealistic, overly simplistic, and legally dubious. . . .

Standardizing codes—conflicting priorities: **The business community rejects the notion that standardization is necessary or desirable.** Proposals for codes have come from a wide variety of sources, including governments, labor organizations, and a broad array of other non-governmental organizations. Each has different priorities and goals. Various codes and their requirements could conflict with one another. A one-size-fits-all approach is bound to conflict with the company's policies and practices, based on its history, culture, philosophy, and the laws and regulations of the countries of its operations.

Independent monitoring—lack of accountability: Corporations recognize their responsibility to stakeholders, their communities, and society at large. Cooperation between corporations and a variety of groups can be a positive force for competitive and profitable companies, and for the communities in which they do business. **However, business overwhelmingly rejects demands by outside groups that seek to impose codes and assert the right to independently audit companies' compliance.** Company practice varies. Some rely on internal monitoring or audits. Others retain outside firms to assist them in assuring that their internal guidelines are implemented throughout the corporation. . . .

USCIB Position Paper on Codes of Conduct, Dec. 21, 1998, *www.uscib.org*.

5. The overall effectiveness of codes of conduct in actually changing corporate behavior is the subject of much debate. Consider the following argument:

In the end, for optimal effect, corporations will need to internalize [human rights] norms in their decisionmaking. This point resonates with the key insight from international relations theorists and others that internalization is critical to successful implementation of international norms, whether in human rights or other areas of the law. . . .

. . . The overall impact of such codes on corporate behavior is . . . unclear, with different companies and industries adopting stronger or weaker codes, each of which is observed with varying degrees of seriousness. The route of corporate-initiated codes of conduct nonetheless seems useful in the process of addressing violations of human rights, as it will at least raise corporate awareness of these issues and permit the possibility of monitoring (either by independent monitors paid by the industry or by NGOs). Undoubtedly, corporations will adopt various, even inconsistent, codes as a substantive matter, and human rights NGOs will object to that inconsistency. But the process of international lawmaking often begins with such private codes, which create expectations of appropriate conduct among diverse actors and can lead over time to other forms of lawmaking.

Steven R. Ratner, *Corporations and Human Rights: A Theory of Legal Responsibility*, 111 Yale L.J. 443, 531, 532-533 (2001).

6. One offshoot of the corporate code of conduct is social labeling, whereby industry groups agree, often in cooperation with NGOs, to certify products as resulting from processes that do not involve certain deleterious practices. The most prominent examples are "dolphin-safe" tuna (discussed in more detail in Chapter 12) and the Rugmark label on carpets from the Indian subcontinent that are not produced with child labor. Do these responses to consumer pressures represent forms of international law?

III. STATES OF THE UNITED STATES IN THE INTERNATIONAL ARENA: MASSACHUSETTS'S SANCTIONS ON BURMA

Beyond non-state actors such as NGOs and corporations, certain territorially organized communities can be active participants in the international legal process. One situation of particular importance to the United States concerns the role for territorial units in federal states. In such states, the constitutional order is designed so that the national government cannot make all decisions. The territorial units are not merely administrative divisions of a central government but are actors in their own right. The organizing principle of such states is that the best governance is that as close as possible to those affected by particular decisions, a principle Europeans refer to as "subsidiarity."

Typically, units within a federal structure primarily exercise authority in a way that affects those within the unit or, perhaps in addition, those in neighboring units. But what happens when the units within a federal state become involved in an international matter? States have accepted as a matter of customary law, under the doctrine of state responsibility, that a state is responsible for all acts of its political units. Article 27 of the Vienna Convention on the Law of Treaties makes clear that a state is responsible for violations of treaties by a substate entity, regardless of the legality of the action under either the law of the substate unit or of the state as a whole. For instance, if a Swiss canton were to pollute a lake along the border with Germany in violation of a Swiss treaty with Germany on the protection of the lake, international law makes Switzerland responsible for the breach.

Yet such a simple starting point obscures much of the contemporary situation regarding entities within federal states. What if these entities seek their own role in international affairs by trying to play a part in the international legal process? This is the problem increasingly facing the United States and other federal states, where subnational actors (states, länder, cantons, or provinces) adopt a stance on various international issues independent of that of the central government. As you read the following problem, consider whether the participation of subnational actors helps in the development and implementation of international norms (such as those of human rights) or confuses the process; whether international law should impose limits on the ability of these units to act internationally; how (or perhaps whether) international organizations and other legal regimes should ensure that subnational units comply with treaties to which the state is a party; who should decide these questions, domestic or international decision makers; how states that oppose involvement by such actors can register their opposition — to the subnational entity alone or to the national government; and whether joint action by subnational units and the central government is possible or even desirable.

A. The Problem

Over the last 45 years of military rule, Myanmar, the southeast Asian state known more commonly as Burma, has compiled one of the more deplorable human rights records on the planet. Violations include killing and torture of political opponents, arbitrary arrest, denial of fair trial, and forced labor. Myanmar is also desperately poor, with GDP per capita of about $1,600, despite impressive natural resources, including mineral and petroleum wealth. In 1988, the military agreed to hold elections, which the opposition National League for Democracy overwhelmingly won; but the military regime refused to abide by the results and instead clamped down further on domestic opponents. The United Nations and many states (principally Western states) have regularly condemned Myanmar for its failure to abide by the 1988 elections and its human rights abuses.

Non-governmental organizations in the United States and elsewhere have actively lobbied governments to impose economic and political sanctions on Myanmar as an expression of opposition to Myanmar's practices and as a way of putting pressure on the regime to carry through on the aborted process of democratic reform. In the United States, these NGOs have approached both the federal government and various state governments. In response to these efforts, in

June 1996 the state of Massachusetts enacted An Act Regulating Contracts with Companies Doing Business with or in Burma (Myanmar), 1996 Mass. Acts 239, ch. 130. Under the law, the state is generally barred from buying goods or services from any person or business doing business with Burma, which the act defines as:

> (a) having a principal place of business, place of incorporation or its corporate headquarters in Burma (Myanmar) or having any operations, leases, franchises, majority-owned subsidiaries, distribution agreements, or any other similar agreements in Burma (Myanmar), or being the majority-owned subsidiary, licensee or franchise of such a person;
>
> (b) providing financial services to the government of Burma (Myanmar), including providing direct loans, underwriting government securities, providing any consulting advice or assistance, providing brokerage services, acting as a trustee or escrow agent, or otherwise acting as an agent pursuant to a contractual agreement;
>
> (c) promoting the importation or sale of gems, timber, oil, gas or other related products, commerce in which is largely controlled by the government of Burma (Myanmar), from Burma (Myanmar);
>
> (d) providing any goods or services to the government of Burma (Myanmar).

The only exceptions are if the procurement is essential for Massachusetts and there are no other bids; if it is for medical supplies; or if no other bid is less than 10 percent higher than that of the company doing business with Burma. As a result, the state established a list of companies with which it would not conduct business. More than 20 other local, county, and state governments have restrictive purchasing laws related to Burma as well.

Federal policy on Myanmar has originated in both the State Department and Congress. Since the early 1990s, the State Department has worked for resolutions in the UN Commission on Human Rights and the International Labor Organization condemning Burma; successfully urged its allies and international financial institutions to cut back on assistance to Burma; and sought to convince members of the Association of Southeast Asian Nations (which includes Burma) to confront the Burmese government over its abuses. In addition, the Department engaged in various unilateral actions, such as a downgrade in diplomatic relations with Burma by removing its ambassador, prohibition on sales of arms, and denials of visas to senior officials.

In 1996, Congress passed a comprehensive set of sanctions that wrote into law some of the Department's policies and added others. The statute banned foreign aid (except for humanitarian assistance, counternarcotics efforts, and promotion of human rights and democracy), required the United States to oppose loans to Burma in international financial institutions, denied visas to Burmese officials, and authorized the President to prohibit new investment in — but not trade in goods or services with — Burma. In May 1997, President Clinton issued an Executive Order imposing the ban on new investment.

B. State and Local Foreign Policy Making: Some Precedents

The Massachusetts Burma law was hardly the first attempt by a U.S. state or city to play an active role in foreign policy. Hundreds of municipalities have established sister-city relationships with communities overseas; many pass nonbinding resolutions on issues of foreign policy; states and cities routinely send trade missions to other countries to encourage investment in their local economy; and most states have at least one permanent trade office in a foreign country. In the 1980s over two dozen communities declared themselves sanctuaries for refugees from the Cold War conflicts in Central America.

The most ambitious attempt by municipalities to play a role in foreign policy took place over South Africa's policies of apartheid. Apartheid had long elicited the condemnation of most countries, through, for example, resolutions of international organizations and limitations on participation in such institutions. (See Chapter 3.) In the United States, state and local governments enacted a variety of sanctions, including selective purchasing laws and divestment of public funds (especially pension funds) from companies doing business in South Africa. These acts generally originated from sentiments in these communities that federal policy was too lax toward South Africa, and that, if the federal government would not impose sanctions, the municipalities would step in. For example, in 1985 New York City passed a law banning city agencies from purchasing goods or services from any company that did business with the South African police or military as long as another company could provide those goods or services "at a comparable price."

The U.S. Department of Justice's Office of Legal Counsel issued an opinion in April 1986 finding that state and local anti-apartheid divestment laws did not violate the Commerce Clause or conflict with any federal laws. With regard to interference in federal supremacy over foreign affairs, the Opinion stated:

Constitutionality of South African Divestment Statutes Enacted by State and Local Governments

10 U.S. Op. Off. Legal Counsel 49, 61-62 (1986)

The [Supreme] Court has only once employed this general power to strike down an exercise of state police power that affected foreign affairs. In *Zschernig v. Miller*, 389 U.S. 429 (1968), the Court invalidated an Oregon statute as an unconstitutional intrusion into the federal field of foreign affairs, even though . . . the statute did not conflict with any federal treaty or statute. The state statute at issue provided that a nonresident alien could not inherit property from an Oregon decedent unless three conditions were satisfied: (1) the alien's government must accord Americans the right to inherit on equal terms with its citizens; (2) the alien's government must give Americans the right to receive payment in the United States of funds from foreign estates; and (3) the nonresident alien must be able to receive "the benefit, use or control" of the proceeds of the Oregon estate "without confiscation" by his government. The Court concluded that this type of probate law *as enforced in the Oregon courts* had "a direct impact on foreign relations and may well adversely affect the power of the central government to deal with those problems." . . .

Zschernig stands for the proposition that the Court will scrutinize state statutes to determine whether such statutes have a direct impact on foreign relations; the case may not fairly be interpreted to mean that the court will strike down any state exercise of authority that has some indirect impact on foreign affairs or that is intended to affect the behavior of foreign governments. *Zschernig* did not overrule *Clark v. Allen*, 331 U.S. 503 (1947), in which the Court . . . upheld the facial validity of a California statute similar to the first two sections of the Oregon law. Although the California statute was clearly designed to influence foreign countries to change their laws to allow Americans to inherit, the Court dismissed the challenge to the statute as "farfetched." . . .

Read together, *Zschernig* and *Clark* suggest that even in scrutinizing state statutes that have an impact on foreign affairs, the Court will balance the degree to which the statute intrudes on foreign affairs against the degree to which the exercise of the state power falls within traditional state powers. In both *Clark* and *Zschernig*, states were performing a traditional state function in establishing a rule of inheritance. What distinguished the cases was that the California statute had only an indirect influence on foreign affairs because the state legislature's judgment could be implemented simply through the "routine reading of foreign law" . . . [whereas the] Oregon statute . . . allowed state courts to evaluate the credibility of foreign representatives and engage in persistent "judicial criticism" of foreign states . . . .

Application of such a balancing test to divestment statutes yields the conclusion that they do not impermissibly encroach into the realm of foreign affairs. First . . . the implementation of the South African divestment statute would require no investigation by state officials into the operation of South African law and require no assessment of the credibility of South African officials. Second, the statute would fall directly on American companies and only indirectly on South Africa. . . .

Finally, in evaluating the impact of state investment decisions on foreign policy, it should be noted that a state is necessarily involved in the investment of state funds. . . . A state for instance, may decide not to invest in a company doing business in South Africa because it believes that there is a large risk of revolution and, thus, of expropriation in that country. The decision would have an impact on South Africa and on national policy toward that country identical to a decision to divest on the basis of moral opposition to South Africa's system of apartheid. But surely no one would suggest that states are constitutionally forbidden from making such investment decisions. We therefore question the proposition that state divestment statutes should be subject to challenge simply because they have some impact on South Africa and our foreign policy toward that country. If state investment decisions are subject to invalidation for intrusion into foreign policy, we perceive no limiting principle to prevent constant judicial scrutiny of those decisions for consistency with some perceived foreign policy.

Congress eventually imposed sanctions on South Africa in the Comprehensive Anti-Apartheid Act of 1986. The law prohibited the importation of arms, minerals, textiles, agricultural goods, and other commodities and the exportation of fuel, computers, most nuclear-related materials, and munitions for the police forces. The law contained numerous financial sanctions, including a ban on loans to South Africa and the holding of new deposits by the South African government. It did not, however, prohibit U.S investment — new or old — in South Africa. In the only court case to address the consistency of local sanctions with the 1986 federal law, the Maryland Court of Appeals upheld Baltimore's city statute requiring public pension funds to divest from companies doing significant business in South Africa. The court found no conflict between Congress's policy toward South Africa and the city's divestment law and no evidence that Congress meant to preempt local sanctions; the Maryland court further found that the law did not unconstitutionally impinge on the federal government's power over foreign affairs, as the sanctions were aimed at American companies and not relations with South Africa per se; it also found no violation of the Commerce Clause. *Board of Trustees of the Employees' Retire-*

ment System of the City of Baltimore v. Mayor and City Council of Baltimore City, 562 A.2d 720 (Md. Ct. App. 1989).

Notes and Questions

1. Is there a difference in the extent to which the federal government — or other nations — should tolerate sister city relationships as compared to disinvestment of public pension funds or selective purchasing laws by localities?

2. Does the Justice Department effectively make the case that local anti-apartheid sanctions do not intrude on federal power over foreign affairs? What would be the perspective of a foreign governmental official on this question?

3. Does the type of human rights violations distinguish the South African case from the Myanmar case in terms of the extent to which subnational actors should be able to participate in the legal process?

C. International Reactions

U.S. allies, principally the European Union (EU) and Japan, protested the Massachusetts law from the outset, as it resulted in the exclusion from bidding of many European and Japanese companies (or their subsidiaries) that conducted business in Burma, a practice perfectly permissible in Europe and Japan. Indeed, many European companies without any business in Massachusetts were sent questionnaires by the state government regarding their ties to Burma; if they responded that they did business with Burma, Massachusetts put their names on its "blacklist" as well — a list publicly available on the World Wide Web.

The EU and Japan based much of their legal argument on the view that the Massachusetts law violated a multilateral agreement on government procurement concluded in 1994 as part of the so-called Uruguay Round of trade talks that created the World Trade Organization (WTO). Under the Government Procurement Agreement (GPA), WTO members are supposed to ensure that governmental entities procure goods and services on a nondiscriminatory basis vis-à-vis companies of the other parties (subject to numerical thresholds and numerous exceptions). During the negotiations for the Agreement, the United States delegation had originally proposed that subnational units such as U.S. states (which were excluded from a predecessor procurement agreement) be able to submit voluntarily to the new code; at the request of the U.S. Trade Representative, the federal government's chief trade official, some 24 states agreed to be bound by the code. However, the EU found the U.S. proposal inadequate and threatened to limit access by U.S. companies to EU telecommunications procurement unless the United States offered more. The U.S. Trade Representative returned to the states, and eventually 37 states, including Massachusetts, agreed to abide by the provisions with respect to some or all of their government procurement. The vast majority of state procurement was thus covered.

The states, however, exacted a price for their acceptance of the GPA and their willingness to endorse the "fast track" procedure by which the Uruguay Round agreements would be approved by Congress without the possibility of amendment. First, the GPA exempted particular forms of government procurement for which existing state law required domestic preferences — that is, the states agreed to allow foreign suppliers to bid on projects only to the extent state law as of 1994 did not require otherwise. Second, in the U.S. domestic legislation implementing the Uruguay Round, Congress barred federal suits against states based on violations of the Uruguay Round agreements and stated its intention to occupy the field and thereby preclude such suits in state courts. Thus, European companies excluded from state government procurement could not sue those U.S. states in the United States. Third, when the Executive Branch submitted the Uruguay Round accords (including the GPA) to Congress, it promised: (a) if a foreign state brought an action against the United States at the WTO alleging that one of its companies had faced discrimination by a U.S. state in a manner inconsistent with the GPA, the federal government would involve the state in any defenses; and (b) that the Executive Branch would use its authority under the implementing legislation to force a state to change its law to comply with the Uruguay Round agreements only as a last resort, meaning that the federal government might well tolerate sanctions against the United States (which a prevailing party in the WTO may impose on the losing party) before it seeks to remedy its violation.

Japanese and EU officials raised the Massachusetts law repeatedly with U.S. federal officials as well as directly with Massachusetts authorities. On September 8, 1998, the EU asked for the formation of a panel of the WTO's Dispute Settlement Body to adjudicate the responsibility of the United States for noncompliance with the Government Procurement Agreement.

Request for Establishment of a Panel by the European Communities

www.wto.org

My authorities have instructed me to request the establishment of a panel pursuant to Article 6 of the Understanding on Rules and Procedures Governing the Settlement of Disputes, and Article XXII of the Agreement on Government Procurement (GPA) with respect to the Massachusetts Act of 25 June, 1996. . . .

The Law forbids State agencies, State authorities and other State entities from procuring goods and services from any person currently doing business with the Union of Myanmar (formerly known as the Nation of Burma). In practice, this is achieved by applying an automatic price penalty of 10% on bids from companies which are deemed to be doing business in or with the Union of Myanmar (as set out in a restricted purchase list which contains the names of such companies, although companies which are not on the list but which are deemed to meet the criteria for inclusion in the list are similarly affected).

In doing so, the Law attaches conditions for the participation of suppliers in tendering procedures which violate the requirement set out in Article VIII(b) of the GPA [which requires government entities engaged in procurement to limit any conditions on participation in procurement to those "essential to ensure the firm's capability to fulfil the contract in question."]. Furthermore, by imposing a 10% price increase on the basis of whether or not a company does business in or with Myanmar, the Law violates the basic GPA requirement embodied inter alia in Article XIII.4(b) [which generally requires procuring entities to award contracts to the qualified bidder with the lowest offer]. . . .

The Law also nullifies or impairs the benefits accruing to the European Communities ("EC") under this Agreement, particularly as it limits the access of EC suppliers to procurement by a sub-federal authority covered by the Government Procurement Agreement in such a way as to result in a de facto reduction of the US sub-federal offer under the GPA.

On October 21, 1988, the WTO's Dispute Settlement Body established a panel to consider the EU's complaint and a similar complaint filed by Japan.

Notes and Questions

1. The above petition assumes that the United States is legally responsible for the actions of U.S. states. Is there some way by which the United States might distance itself from the activities of its states? What would be the reaction of other governments? In 1994 the UN's Human Rights Committee, which monitors compliance with the International Covenant on Civil and Political Rights (ICCPR), considered a complaint brought against Australia by Nicholas Toonen, a gay rights advocate from the state of Tasmania. Toonen asserted that a Tasmanian law criminalizing male homosexual sex violated the ICCPR's prohibition against "arbitrary or unlawful interference with . . . privacy, family, home or correspondence." Australia appeared before the Committee to respond to the complaint but essentially conceded that the Tasmanian law violated the ICCPR. The Committee ruled for Toonen and requested that Australia rescind the Tasmanian law, but Tasmanian authorities refused to comply. In response, the federal government enacted a new privacy law in 1994 meant to override the Tasmanian law. After Tasmanian advocates sued Tasmania in Australia's High Court to enforce the new law, the Tasmanian legislature finally repealed the offending law in 1997.

2. Why would the federal government compromise with the states rather than override their concerns? Was the compromise effective given Massachusetts' decision to violate it? How would foreign governments react to this compromise?

3. Why do you think U.S. states would have an interest in becoming party to the GPA?

4. What should the federal government do vis-à-vis Massachusetts in response to a claim of illegal action by foreign governments? Should it matter that the complaining states are political or military allies of the United States or major economic partners?

D. Domestic Reactions

In 1998, the National Foreign Trade Council (NFTC), an industry group that included companies on Massachusetts's no-purchase list, sued Massachusetts in federal district court, arguing that the statute unconstitutionally infringed on the federal government's foreign affairs power. The district court agreed and enjoined enforcement of the statute, a position affirmed by the U.S. Court of Appeals for the First Circuit. Massachusetts appealed to the U.S. Supreme Court.

The EU filed amicus briefs at each stage of the litigation in support of the NFTC, alleging that the law had created a significant irritant in EU-U.S. relations.

Within the U.S. Executive Branch, the Departments of State, Justice, Treasury, and Commerce, and the U.S. Trade Representative engaged in a vigorous inter-agency debate on whether the United States should file an amicus brief, and if so, what position it should take. The debate centered on the domestic political costs to challenging the Massachusetts law and the constitutional and foreign policy arguments against that law. In the end, the U.S. filed a brief in the Supreme Court that supported the NFTC, emphasizing the foreign policy ramifications. Congress was similarly divided: 78 members filed an amicus brief urging reversal, arguing that Congress did not intend to preempt the Massachusetts law, while 20 members filed a brief urging affirmance and calling on the court to declare all state and local sanctions law unconstitutional.

Crosby, Secretary of Administration and Finance of Massachusetts v. National Foreign Trade Council

530 U.S. 363 (2000)

SOUTER, J., delivered the opinion of the Court, in which REHNQUIST, C.J., and STEVENS, O'CONNOR, KENNEDY, GINSBURG, and BREYER, JJ., joined. SCALIA, J., filed an opinion concurring in the judgment, in which THOMAS, J., joined.

The issue is whether the Burma law of the Commonwealth of Massachusetts, restricting the authority of its agencies to purchase goods or services from companies doing business with Burma, is invalid under the Supremacy Clause of the National Constitution owing to its threat of frustrating federal statutory objectives. We hold that it is . . . .

III

A fundamental principle of the Constitution is that Congress has the power to preempt state law. Art. VI, cl. 2; *Gibbons v. Ogden*, 9 Wheat. 1 [1824]. . . . Even without an express provision for preemption, we have found that state law must yield to a congressional Act in at least two circumstances. When Congress intends federal law to "occupy the field," state law in that area is preempted. . . . And even if Congress has not occupied the field, state law is naturally preempted to the extent of any conflict with a federal statute. . . . We will find preemption where it is impossible for a private party to comply with both state and federal law . . . and where "under the circumstances of [a] particular case, [the challenged state law] stands as an obstacle to the accomplishment and execution of the full purposes and objectives of Congress." [Hines v. Davidowitz, 312 U.S. 52, 67 (1941)]. . . .

A

First, Congress clearly intended the federal Act to provide the President with flexible and effective authority over economic sanctions against Burma. Although Congress immediately put in place a set of initial sanctions prohibiting bilateral aid . . . , support for international financial assistance . . . , and entry by Burmese officials into the United States . . . , it authorized the President to terminate any and all of those measures upon determining and certifying that there had been progress in human rights and democracy in Burma. . . . It invested the President with the further power to ban new investment by United States persons, dependent only on specific Presidential findings of repression in Burma. . . . And, most significantly, Congress empowered the President "to waive, temporarily or permanently, any sanction [under the federal act] . . . if he determines and certifies to Congress that the application of such sanction would be contrary to the national security interests of the United States."

This express investiture of the President with statutory authority to act for the United States in imposing sanctions with respect to the Government of Burma, augmented by the flexibility to respond to change by suspending sanctions in the interest of national security, recalls Justice Jackson's observation in *Youngstown Sheet & Tube Co. v. Sawyer*, 343 U.S. 579, 635 (1952): "When the President acts pursuant to an express or implied authorization of Congress, his authority is at its maximum, for it includes all that he possesses in his own right plus all that Congress can delegate." . . . Within the sphere defined by Congress, then, the statute has placed the President in a position with as much discretion to exercise economic leverage against Burma, with an eye toward national security, as our law will admit. And it is just this plenitude of Executive authority that we think controls the issue of preemption here. The President has been given this authority not merely to make a political statement but to achieve a political result, and the fullness of his authority shows the importance in the congressional mind of reaching that result. It is simply implausible that Congress would have gone to such lengths to empower the President if it had been willing to compromise his effectiveness by deference to every provision of state statute or local ordinance that might, if enforced, blunt the consequences of discretionary Presidential action.

And that is just what the Massachusetts Burma law would do in imposing a different, state system of economic pressure against the Burmese political regime. As will be seen, the state statute penalizes some private action that the federal Act (as administered by the President) may allow, and pulls levers of influence that the federal Act does not reach. But the point here is that the state sanctions are imme-diate . . . and perpetual, there being no termination provision. . . . This unyielding application undermines the President's intended statutory authority by making it impossible for him to restrain fully the coercive power of the national economy when he may choose to take the discretionary action open to him. . . .

B

Congress manifestly intended to limit economic pressure against the Burmese Government to a specific range. The federal Act confines its reach to United States persons, . . . imposes limited immediate sanctions, . . . places only a conditional ban on a carefully defined area of "new investment," . . . and pointedly exempts contracts to sell or purchase goods, services, or technology. . . .

The State has set a different course, and its statute conflicts with federal law at a number of points by penalizing individuals and conduct that Congress has explicitly exempted or excluded from sanctions. . . . It restricts all contracts between the State and companies doing business in Burma . . . and thus prohibits contracts between the State and United States persons for goods, services, or technology, even though those transactions are explicitly exempted from the ambit of new investment prohibition when the President exercises his discretionary authority to impose sanctions under the federal Act. . . .

As with the subject of business meant to be affected, so with the class of companies doing it: the state Act's generality stands at odds with the federal discreteness. . . . The state Act . . . penalizes companies with pre-existing affiliates or investments, all of which lie beyond the reach of the federal Act's restrictions on "new investment" in Burmese economic development. . . . The state Act, moreover, imposes restrictions on foreign companies as well as domestic, whereas the federal Act limits its reach to United States persons.

The conflicts are not rendered irrelevant by the State's argument that there is no real conflict between the statutes because they share the same goals and because some companies may comply with both sets of restrictions. . . . The fact of a common end hardly neutralizes conflicting means, . . . and the fact that some companies may be able to comply with both sets of sanctions does not mean that the state Act is not at odds with achievement of the federal decision about the right degree of pressure to employ. . . . "'[C]onflict is imminent'" when "'two separate remedies are brought to bear on the same activity,'" *Wisconsin Dept. of Industry v. Gould Inc.*, 475 U.S. 282, 286 (1986). . . . Sanctions are drawn not only to bar what they prohibit but to allow what they permit, and the inconsistency of sanctions here undermines the congressional calibration of force.

C

Finally, the state Act is at odds with the President's intended authority to speak for the United States among the world's nations in developing a "comprehensive, multilateral strategy to bring democracy to and improve human rights practices and the quality of life in Burma." . . . As with Congress's explicit delegation to the President of power over economic sanctions, Congress's express command to the President to take the initiative for the United States among the international community invested him with the maximum authority of the National Government . . . in harmony with the President's own constitutional powers, U.S. Const., Art. II, §2, cl. 2 ("[The President] shall have Power, by and with the Advice and Consent of the Senate, to make Treaties" and "shall appoint Ambassadors, other public Ministers and Consuls"); §3 ("[The President] shall receive Ambassadors and other public Ministers"). . . .

Again, the state Act undermines the President's capacity, in this instance for effective diplomacy. It is not merely that the differences between the state and federal Acts in scope and type of sanctions threaten to complicate discussions; they compromise the very capacity of the President to speak for the Nation with one voice in dealing with other governments. [T]he President's maximum power to persuade rests on his capacity to bargain for the benefits of access to the entire national economy without exception for enclaves fenced off willy-nilly by inconsistent political tactics. . . .

While the threat to the President's power to speak and bargain effectively with other nations seems clear enough, the record is replete with evidence to answer any skeptics. First, in response to the passage of the state Act, a number of this country's allies and trading partners filed formal protests with the National Government, see [the court of appeals opinion] (noting protests from Japan, the European Union (EU), and ASEAN). . . . EU officials have warned that the state Act "could have a damaging effect on bilateral EU-US relations." [*Citing* a 1997 letter from the EU to the Massachusetts governor.]

Second, the EU and Japan have gone a step further in lodging formal complaints against the United States in the World Trade Organization (WTO) . . . . In their brief before this Court, EU officials point to the WTO dispute as threatening relations with the United States . . . and note that the state Act has become the topic of "intensive discussions" with officials of the United States at the highest levels, those discussions including exchanges at the twice yearly EU-U.S. Summit.

Third, the Executive has consistently represented that the state Act has complicated its dealings with foreign sovereigns and proven an impediment to accomplishing objectives assigned it by Congress. Assistant Secretary of State Larson, for example, has directly addressed the mandate of the federal Burma law in saying that the imposition of unilateral state sanctions under the state Act "complicate[s] efforts to build coalitions with our allies" to promote democracy and human rights in Burma. . . .

IV

The State's remaining argument is unavailing. It contends that the failure of Congress to preempt the state Act demonstrates implicit permission. The State points out that Congress has repeatedly declined to enact express preemption provisions aimed at state and local sanctions, and it calls our attention to the large number of such measures passed against South Africa in the 1980s, which various authorities cited have thought were not preempted. The State stresses that Congress was aware of the state Act in 1996, but did not preempt it explicitly when it adopted its own Burma statute. . . .

The argument is unconvincing on more than one level. A failure to provide for preemption expressly may reflect nothing more than the settled character of implied preemption doctrine that courts will dependably apply, and in any event, the existence of conflict cognizable under the Supremacy Clause does not depend on express congressional recognition that federal and state law may conflict. . . . The State's inference of congressional intent is unwarranted here, therefore, simply because the silence of Congress is ambiguous. . . .

V

Because the state Act's provisions conflict with Congress's specific delegation to the President of flexible discretion, with limitation of sanctions to a limited scope of actions and actors, and with direction to develop a comprehensive, multilateral strategy under the federal Act, it is preempted, and its application is unconstitutional, under the Supremacy Clause.

Notes and Questions

1. Does the Massachusetts statute conflict with federal law? Do not both seek to put pressure on Burma to improve its human rights practices?

2. What sorts of participation by states in foreign policy would the Supreme Court tolerate under the reasoning in *Crosby*? How does the Massachusetts law differ from the anti-apartheid statutes that the Office of Legal Counsel found constitutional in 1986?

3. How important to the Court's reasoning was the position of the Executive Branch that the law complicated multilateral efforts on Burma? What does this suggest about the Court's approach to the role of states?

4. Which was the better forum for the resolution of this matter — the WTO (through its three-person dispute resolution panel) or the U.S. Supreme Court? In February 1999, two months after the federal district court in Boston first struck down the Massachusetts law as unconstitutional, the EU and Japan asked the WTO to suspend its proceedings. Under the WTO's rules the authority for the panel lapsed one year later. Should America's trading partners be satisfied with the Supreme Court's decision in light of their complaint to the WTO?

E. State Prerogatives in the Absence of Congressional Action

In many situations where states seek an independent voice, Congress has not passed legislation addressing the same general area. As discussed in the 1986 Department of Justice opinion excerpted above, this was the issue in *Zschernig v. Miller*. In 2003, this issue again reached the Supreme Court in litigation over California's response to claims by Holocaust survivors that European governments had looted their families' assets and insurance companies had failed to pay survivors who were beneficiaries of pre-war insurance policies. In the mid-1990s, the U.S. and German governments negotiated the German Foundation Agreement, whereby Germany and German companies set up a 10-billion Deutschmark foundation to compensate Holocaust victims. That foundation worked with a private organization, the International Commission on Holocaust Era Insurance Claims (ICHEIC), comprised of various Holocaust survivor groups, European insurance companies, U.S. state insurance commissioners, and the government of Israel. ICHEIC negotiated with European insurance companies to get access to information on unpaid policies and settled claims of some survivors. The U.S. subsequently concluded similar agreements with Austria and France. As part of these undertakings, it promised to use its "best efforts" to ensure that U.S. state and local governments would allow the foundation to serve as the exclusive mechanism for resolution of these claims.

In 1999, California passed the Holocaust Victim Insurance Relief Act (HVIRA), which requires any insurer doing business there to disclose information about insurance policies issued "to persons in Europe, which were in effect between 1920 and 1945." This covers policies by any "related company," including parents, subsidiaries, and affiliates. If a company refuses to do so, it cannot do business in California. The legislature claimed the Act was needed "to protect the claims and interests of California residents." Senior U.S. government officials protested the action as undermining the ICHEIC process, and an insurance industry association sued the state.

American Insurance Association v. Garamendi, Insurance Commissioner, State of California

539 U.S. 396 (2003)

SOUTER, J., delivered the opinion of the Court, in which REHNQUIST, C.J., and O'CONNOR, KENNEDY, and BREYER, JJ., joined. GINSBURG, J., filed a dissenting opinion, in which STEVENS, SCALIA, and THOMAS, JJ., joined.

The issue here is whether HVIRA interferes with the National Government's conduct of foreign relations. We hold that it does, with the consequence that the state statute is preempted. . . .

III

The principal argument for preemption made by petitioners and the United States as amicus curiae is that HVIRA interferes with foreign policy of the Executive Branch, as expressed principally in the executive agreements with Germany, Austria, and France. . . . There is, of course, no question that at some point an exercise of state power that touches on foreign relations must yield to the National Government's policy, given the "concern for uniformity in this country's dealings with foreign nations" that animated the Constitution's allocation of the foreign relations power to the National Government in the first place. *Banco Nacional de Cuba v. Sabbatino*, 376 U.S. 398, 427, n. 25 (1964). . . .

[After discussing the facts in *Zschernig* noted in the 1986 Justice Department opinion excerpted above, the Court stated:] The *Zschernig* majority relied on statements in a number of previous cases open to the reading that state action with more than incidental effect on foreign affairs is preempted, even absent any affirmative federal activity in the subject area of the state law, and hence without any showing of conflict. . . . Justice Harlan . . . disagreed with the *Zschernig* majority on this point, arguing that its implication of preemption of the entire field of foreign affairs was at odds with some other cases suggesting that in the absence of positive federal action "the States may legislate in areas of their traditional competence even though their statutes may have an incidental effect on foreign relations." Thus, for Justice Harlan it was crucial that the challenge to the Oregon statute presented no evidence of a "specific interest of the Federal Government which might be interfered with" by the law. He would, however, have found preemption in a case of "conflicting federal policy." . . . [E]ven on Justice Harlan's view, the likelihood that state legislation will produce something more than incidental effect in conflict with express foreign policy of the National Government would require preemption of the state law. And since on his view it is legislation within "areas of . . . traditional competence" that gives a State any claim to prevail, it would be reasonable to consider the strength of the state interest, judged by standards of traditional practice, when deciding how serious a conflict must be shown before declaring the state law preempted. . . .

IV

A

. . . The exercise of the federal executive authority means that state law must give way where, as here, there is evidence of clear conflict between the policies adopted by the two. The foregoing account of negotiations toward the three settlement agreements is enough to illustrate that the consistent Presidential foreign policy has been to encourage European governments and companies to volunteer settlement funds in preference to litigation or coercive sanctions. . . .

California has taken a different tack of providing regulatory sanctions to compel disclosure and payment, supplemented by a new cause of action for Holocaust survivors if the other sanctions should fail. The situation created by the California legislation calls to mind the impact of the Massachusetts Burma law [in] *Crosby v. National Foreign Trade Council*, 530 U.S. 363 (2000). HVIRA's economic compulsion to make public disclosure, of far more information about far more policies than ICHEIC rules require, employs "a different, state system of economic pressure," and in doing so undercuts the President's diplomatic discretion and the choice he has made exercising it. *Id.*, at 376. Whereas the President's authority to provide for settling claims in winding up international hostilities requires flexibility in wielding "the coercive power of the national economy" as a tool of diplomacy, *id.*, at 377, HVIRA denies this, by making exclusion from a large sector of the American insurance market the automatic sanction for noncompliance with the State's own policies on disclosure. "Quite simply, if the [California] law is enforceable the President has less to offer and less economic and diplomatic leverage as a consequence." *Ibid.* The law thus "compromise[s] the very capacity of the President to speak for the Nation with one voice in dealing with other governments" . . . 530 U.S., at 381.

Crosby's facts are replicated again in the way HVIRA threatens to frustrate the operation of the particular mechanism the President has chosen. The letters from [the State Department] to California officials show well enough how the portent of further litigation and sanctions has in fact placed the Government at a disadvantage in obtaining practical results from persuading "foreign governments and foreign companies to participate voluntarily in organizations such as ICHEIC." . . . California's indiscriminate disclosure provisions [also] place a handicap on the ICHEIC's effectiveness (and raise a further irritant to the European allies) by undercutting European privacy protections. . . .

B

The express federal policy and the clear conflict raised by the state statute are alone enough to require state law to yield. If any doubt about the clarity of the conflict remained, however, it would have to be resolved in the National Government's favor, given the weakness of the State's interest, against the backdrop of traditional state legislative subject matter, in regulating disclosure of European Holocaust-era insurance policies in the manner of HVIRA. . . .

[T]he state interest actually underlying HVIRA is concern for the several thousand Holocaust survivors said to be living in the State. . . . But this fact does not displace general standards for evaluating a State's claim to apply its forum law to a particular controversy or transaction, under which the State's claim is not a strong one. . . . But should the general standard not be displaced, and the State's interest recognized as a powerful one, by virtue of the fact that California seeks to vindicate the claims of Holocaust survivors? The answer lies in recalling that the very same objective dignifies the interest of the National Government in devising its chosen mechanism for voluntary settlements, there being about 100,000 survivors in the country, only a small fraction of them in California. As against the responsibility of the United States of America, the humanity underlying the state statute could not give the State the benefit of any doubt in resolving the conflict with national policy.

C

The basic fact is that California seeks to use an iron fist where the President has consistently chosen kid gloves. We have heard powerful arguments that the iron fist would work better, and it may be that if the matter of compensation were considered in isolation from all other issues involving the European allies, the iron fist would be the preferable policy. But our thoughts on the efficacy of the one approach versus the other are beside the point, since our business is not to judge the wisdom of the National Government's policy; dissatisfaction should be addressed to the President or, perhaps, Congress . . . .

[The Court also rejected plaintiff's claim that Congress had implicitly authorized the California law by statute.]

JUSTICE GINSBURG, with whom JUSTICE STEVENS, JUSTICE SCALIA, and JUSTICE THOMAS join, dissenting . . . .

Although the federal approach differs from California's, no executive agreement or other formal expression of foreign policy disapproves state disclosure laws like the HVIRA. Absent a clear statement aimed at disclosure requirements by the "one voice" to which courts properly defer in matters of foreign affairs, I would leave intact California's enactment. . . .

At least until very recently . . . ICHEIC's progress has been slow and insecure . . . . Initially, ICHEIC's insurance company members represented little more than one-third of the Holocaust-era insurance market . . . . Moreover, ICHEIC has thus far settled only a tiny proportion of the claims it has received. Evidence submitted in a series of class actions filed against Italian insurer Generali indicated that by November 2001, ICHEIC had resolved only 797 of 77,000 claims. . . . Finally, although ICHEIC has directed its members to publish lists of unpaid Holocaust-era policies, that non-binding directive had not yielded significant compliance at the time this case reached the Court . . . .

We have not relied on *Zschernig* since it was decided, and I would not resurrect that decision here. The notion of "dormant foreign affairs preemption" with which *Zschernig* is associated resonates most audibly when a state action "reflect[s] a state policy critical of foreign governments and involve[s] 'sitting in judgment' on them." L. Henkin, Foreign Affairs and the United States Constitution 164 (2d ed. 1996); see Constitutionality of South African Divestment Statutes Enacted by State and Local Governments, 10 Op. Off. Legal Counsel 49, 50 (1986) ("[W]e believe that [*Zschernig*] represents the Court's reaction to a particular regulatory statute, the operation of which intruded extraordinarily deeply into foreign affairs."). The HVIRA . . . takes no position on any contemporary foreign government and requires no assessment of any existing foreign regime. It is directed solely at private insurers doing business in California, and it requires them solely to disclose information. . . .

[N]one of the executive agreements extinguish any underlying claim for relief. The United States has agreed to file precatory statements advising courts that dismissing Holocaust-era claims accords with American foreign policy, but the German Foundation Agreement confirms that such statements have no legally binding effect. It remains uncertain, therefore, whether even *litigation* on Holocaust-era insurance claims must be abated in deference to the German Foundation Agreement . . . . If it is uncertain whether insurance *litigation* may continue given the executive agreements on which the Court relies, it should be abundantly clear that those agreements leave *disclosure* laws like the HVIRA untouched . . . . Here, the Court invalidates a state disclosure law on grounds of conflict with foreign policy "embod[ied]" in certain executive agreements, although those agreements do not refer to state disclosure laws . . . . To fill the agreements' silences, the Court points to statements by individual members of the Executive Branch . . . . [N]o authoritative text accords such officials the power to invalidate state law simply by conveying the Executive's views on matters of federal policy . . . .

Sustaining the HVIRA would not compromise the President's ability to speak with one voice for the Nation. To the contrary, by declining to invalidate the HVIRA in this case, we would reserve foreign affairs preemption for circumstances where the President, acting under statutory or constitutional authority, has spoken clearly to the issue at hand. . . . As I see it, courts step out of their proper role when they rely on no legislative or even executive text, but only on inference and implication, to preempt state laws on foreign affairs grounds.

Notes and Questions

1. After *Garamendi*, what sorts of international relations may U.S. states practice without fear of preemption? How can state and local officials determine whether their policies conflict with federal policy?

2. Does the slow pace of proceedings under the German Foundation agreement provide a justification for California's actions? Are the objections of the State Department and foreign governments a sufficient ground for preemption in the absence of federal law?

3. In October 2003, the Attorney General of Texas issued a legal opinion concluding that two Texas statutes from 2001 and 2003 modeled on the California law struck down in *Garamendi* were unconstitutional. The statutes gave Holocaust victims or their heirs in Texas who bought insurance before 1946 a right of action against their insurance companies and required companies to publish the names of policyholders and the status of their payments. Relying on *Garamendi*, the Attorney-General found that the revision to the Texas insurance code created by the laws "interferes with the President's conduct of foreign affairs, and is thus preempted by the United States Constitution."

4. In January 2001, Missouri and the Canadian province of Manitoba concluded a Memorandum of Understanding addressing the transfer of water from the Missouri River watershed (Missouri's water supply) to the Hudson Bay watershed (Manitoba's water supply). The two jurisdictions agreed to work together to oppose water transfers between the two watersheds by sharing information and working with their respective national governments. At the request of North Dakota Senator Byron Dorgan, the Department of State's Legal Adviser examined the agreement for its consistency with the Constitution's Compact Clause and Supremacy Clause and the federal power over foreign affairs. His November 20, 2001, legal memorandum highlighted potential conflicts between the agreement and the Dakota Waters Resources Act of 2000, which gave the federal government authority over the water resources issues addressed in the agreement. As the *Garamendi* decision had not yet been issued, the Legal Adviser examined the agreement under *Zschernig* and concluded that the agreement's "actual interference with U.S. foreign policy efforts in managing the water resources of the Hudson Bay watershed shared with Canada" would determine its constitutionality. The Legal Adviser nonetheless abstained from any formal opinion as to the agreement's constitutionality under the various doctrines.

IV. ASCRIBING INTERNATIONAL STATUS TO TERRITORIES AND GROUPS: THE HONG KONG SPECIAL ADMINISTRATIVE REGION

Beyond units in federal states, other communities within states may seek a role independent of the state itself in the international legal arena. Chapter 3 describes international law's treatment of such entities during the colonial era as well as the dismantling of that system after the First and Second World Wars. With the near end of the formal colonial system, one might conclude that international law had returned to the paradigm of an international community of states, although a much larger community and one where those states had also agreed on norms to protect individual rights within states as well.

Yet such a simple way of looking at the world—as composed of states, with individuals protected through human rights law—has proved incapable of grappling with developments since the end of colonialism and, later, the end of the Cold War. Substate communities have sought their own international standing, but the option of creating a new state, discussed in Chapter 1, is not always realistic or desirable. Contemporary events have forced decision makers to consider communities within states as actors meriting some form of autonomy. We thus focus here on the extent to which global actors have allowed substate entities—communities organized along territorial or ethnic lines—to participate as actors *themselves* in the prescription, invocation, and application of international law. Just as this issue lay at the heart of the last problem, concerning Massachusetts's attempt to sanction a foreign nation notwithstanding federal government policy, so it is central to understanding other attempts to grant special international status to substate territories. As you read the following short problem, consider how international law has afforded some international status to substate communities; why some territories and groups have enjoyed such status and not others; the differences between such status and full statehood in terms of participatory rights; and the prospects for increased participation by such entities in the future.

A. The Problem

Hong Kong is a territory consisting of a small portion of the southeast Chinese mainland along with more than two hundred islands off the coast of China. In 1842, following China's defeat by Britain in the Opium War, China was forced in the Treaty of Nanking to cede in perpetuity the most important of the islands, Hong Kong island, to Britain. In 1860 China ceded the southernmost part of the Kowloon peninsula on the Chinese mainland to Britain in perpetuity, and in 1898 China agreed to lease to Britain for 99 years a large area north of Kowloon known as the New Territories. Britain soon established colonial administrative control over Hong Kong, and over the next century Hong Kong became one of the world's most important commercial centers. Its large harbor proved a natural base for transoceanic shipping, and Hong Kong island became the financial and banking center of East Asia. Its proximity to the PRC during the decades in which that state was closed to most Western commerce and influence also made it an important locus for Western intelligence-gathering.

Nonetheless, British colonial dominion over Hong Kong had long been the most serious irritant to British-Chinese relations. China had always regarded the treaties on Hong Kong as imposed on China and thus void, but neither the Chinese empire, the Chinese republic (1911-1949), nor the People's Republic of China had used military force to restore Chinese sovereignty. With the lease on the New Territories (comprising 90 percent of the area of Hong Kong and supplying much of its water and power) due to expire in 1997, Britain and China began intensive negotiations in the early 1980s aimed at resolving the future of the entire territory. The result was the Joint Declaration of 1984, a treaty between the two states.

In the treaty the United Kingdom agreed to restore Chinese sovereignty effective July 1, 1997, and China agreed to a special regime for the territory. The Joint Declaration was implemented by China in the 1990 Basic Law for Hong Kong, a Chinese statute that is essentially a constitution for the territory. Most of the Joint Declaration and Basic Law address the relationship of Hong Kong to the PRC. Hong Kong became the "Hong Kong Special Administrative Region" (HKSAR), which was to "enjoy a high degree of autonomy, except in foreign and defence affairs which are the responsibilities of the Central People's Government." (Joint Declaration, art. 3(2).) China pledged to leave existing laws "basically unchanged" and to respect Hong Kong's free-market economy as well as the existing rights and freedoms of its inhabitants. (*Id.*, arts. 3(3), 3(5).) Hong Kong would have a local legislature, although the Chief Executive would be appointed by Beijing. China's National People's Congress could invalidate (but not amend) any Hong Kong law it believed was not in accordance with the Basic Law. Hong Kong courts would, in theory, remain independent. These policies would remain unchanged for 50 years.

B. Hong Kong's International Status

Both the Joint Declaration and the Basic Law also addressed the international status of the HKSAR:

Joint Declaration of the Government of the United Kingdom of Great Britain and Northern Ireland and the Government of the People's Republic of China on the Question of Hong Kong

23 I.L.M. 1366 (1984)

3(7) The Hong Kong Special Administrative Region will retain the status of an international financial centre, and its markets for foreign exchange, gold, securities and futures will continue. There will be free flow of capital. The Hong Kong dollar will continue to circulate and remain freely convertible. . . .

3(9) The Hong Kong Special Administrative Region may establish mutually beneficial economic relations with the United Kingdom and other countries, whose economic interests in Hong Kong will be given due regard.

3(10) Using the name of "Hong Kong, China", the Hong Kong Special Administrative Region may on its own maintain and develop economic and cultural relations and conclude relevant agreements with states, regions and relevant international organisations.

Basic Law of the Hong Kong Special Administrative Region of the People's Republic of China

www.info.gov.hk

Article 13

The Central People's Government shall be responsible for the foreign affairs relating to the Hong Kong Special Administrative Region.

Article 116

The Hong Kong Special Administrative Region shall be a separate customs territory.

The Hong Kong Special Administrative Region may, using the name "Hong Kong, China," participate in relevant international organizations and international trade agreements (including preferential trade arrangements), such as the General Agreement on Tariffs and Trade and arrangements regarding international trade in textiles.

Export quotas, tariff preferences and other similar arrangements, which are obtained or made by the Hong Kong Special Administrative Region or which were obtained or made and remain valid, shall be enjoyed exclusively by the Region.

Article 150

Representatives of the Government of the Hong Kong Special Administrative Region may, as members of delegations of the Government of the People's Republic of China, participate in negotiations at the diplomatic level directly affecting the Region conducted by the Central People's Government.

Article 151

The Hong Kong Special Administrative Region may on its own, using the name "Hong Kong, China", maintain and develop relations and conclude and implement agreements with foreign states and regions and relevant international organizations in the appropriate fields, including the economic, trade, financial and monetary, shipping, communications, tourism, cultural and sports fields.

Article 152

Representatives of the Government of the Hong Kong Special Administrative Region may, as members of delegations of the People's Republic of China, participate in international organizations or conferences in appropriate fields limited to states and affecting the Region, or may attend in such other capacity as may be permitted by the Central People's Government and the international organization or conference concerned, and may express their views, using the name "Hong Kong, China". . . .

Article 154

The Central People's Government shall authorize the Government of the Hong Kong Special Administrative Region to issue, in accordance with law, passports of the Hong Kong Special Administrative Region of the People's Republic of China to all Chinese citizens who hold permanent identity cards of the Region, and travel documents of the Hong Kong Special Administrative Region of the People's

Republic of China to all other persons lawfully residing in the Region. The above passports and documents shall be valid for all states and regions and shall record the holder's right to return to the Region.

The Government of the Hong Kong Special Administrative Region may apply immigration controls on entry into, stay in and departure from the Region by persons from foreign states and regions.

Article 157

The establishment of foreign consular and other official or semi-official missions in the Hong Kong Special Administrative Region shall require the approval of the Central People's Government.

Consular and other official missions established in Hong Kong by states which have formal diplomatic relations with the People's Republic of China may be maintained.

According to the circumstances of each case, consular and other official missions established in Hong Kong by states which have no formal diplomatic relations with the People's Republic of China may be permitted either to remain or be changed to semi-official missions.

States not recognized by the People's Republic of China may only establish nongovernmental institutions in the Region.

As of 2006, Hong Kong had ten official governmental offices in foreign states. Nearly 100 states had official representatives based in Hong Kong. At the same time, China's willingness to allow Hong Kong to develop some independent foreign relations, as contemplated in Article 3(10) of the Joint Declaration, remains unclear. On the one hand, Hong Kong hosted meetings of the World Bank and the International Monetary Fund in 1997 that included 25 states that have diplomatic relations with the Republic of China (which governs Taiwan). Yet in 1999 China refused to allow Pope John Paul II to visit Hong Kong because of the Vatican's diplomatic relations with Taiwan.

Notes and Questions

1. Why would China agree to such significant external autonomy for Hong Kong?

2. United States-Hong Kong policy is governed by the 1992 United States Hong Kong Policy Act, 22 U.S.C. §5701. Section 102 of that Act states:

> It is the sense of the Congress that the following, which are based in part on the relevant provisions of the Joint Declaration, should be the policy of the United States with respect to Hong Kong after June 30, 1997:
>
> > (1) The United States should support Hong Kong's participation in all appropriate multilateral conferences, agreements, and organizations in which Hong Kong is eligible to participate.
> >
> > (2) The United States should continue to fulfill its obligations to Hong Kong under international agreements, so long as Hong Kong reciprocates, regardless of whether the People's Republic of China is a party to the particular international agreement. . . .

(3) The United States should respect Hong Kong's status as a separate customs territory, and as a WTO member country . . . whether or not the People's Republic of China participates in the World Trade Organization. . . .

How do the reactions of other states to the terms of Hong Kong's external autonomy defined in the Joint Declaration and Basic Law affect Hong Kong's status as an international actor? Consider in this context the declaratory and constitutive theories of recognition discussed in Chapter 3.

3. Is the Hong Kong case completely sui generis, or could such extensive external autonomy arrangements apply to other territories within states? What would have to be the dynamic between a region and the central government for other states to allow such independent international status for their territories?

C. Participation in International Organizations

Members of international organizations have shown significant flexibility in affording some participatory rights to territories and groups within states. Some international organizations allow full membership. Thus, Hong Kong is a full member of the Asian Development Bank (as is the Republic of China on Taiwan), the WTO, the Asia Pacific Economic Cooperation Forum, the Bank for International Settlements, the International Olympic Committee, and others. Indeed, Hong Kong joined the WTO, whose constitutive instrument allows for the membership of any "customs territory possessing full autonomy in the conduct of its external commercial relations," upon the WTO's formal creation in 1995, whereas the PRC did not become a member until December 2001. It is also an associate member of other organizations and participates in the Chinese delegation to other institutions.

Short of full membership, international organizations have afforded substate actors other rights. In 1974 the majority of states in the UN General Assembly sought to invite a number of "liberation movements" — movements they concluded were fighting colonial domination — to participate in the organization's work. The first to be invited was the Palestine Liberation Organization (PLO).

Observer Status for the Palestine Liberation Organization

G.A. Res. 3237 (1974)

The General Assembly, . . .
Taking into consideration the universality of the United Nations prescribed in the Charter. . . .
Noting that the Diplomatic Conference on the Reaffirmation and Development of International Humanitarian Law Applicable in Armed Conflicts, the World Population Conference and the World Food Conference have in effect invited the Palestine Liberation Organization to participate in their respective deliberations,
Noting also that the Third United Nations Conference on the Law of the Sea has invited the Palestine Liberation Organization to participate in its deliberations as an observer,
1. *Invites* the Palestine Liberation Organization to participate in the sessions and the work of the General Assembly in the capacity of observer;

2. *Invites* the Palestine Liberation Organization to participate in the sessions and the work of all international conferences convened under the auspices of the General Assembly in the capacity of observer;

3. *Considers* that the Palestine Liberation Organization is entitled to participate as an observer in the sessions and the work of all international conferences convened under the auspices of other organs of the United Nations. . . .

The United Nations subsequently invited the South West Africa People's Organization (SWAPO), the main opposition group to South African control of Namibia, as well as two of the leading opposition groups to the government of South Africa, to participate in debates on Namibia and apartheid, respectively. While Namibia is now independent and South Africa is no longer under apartheid, the PLO — since 1988 behind the nameplate "Palestine" — continues to participate in UN agencies and meetings.

In 1996 the eight states whose territories touch the Arctic Circle — Canada, Denmark (including Greenland), Finland, Iceland, Norway, Russia, Sweden, and the United States — agreed to establish a new international organization, the Arctic Council, as a forum for cooperation on issues related to that area. The founding document included the following provisions:

Joint Communique and Declaration on the Establishment of the Arctic Council

35 I.L.M. 1382 (1996)

1. The Arctic Council is established as a high level forum to:

    (a) provide a means for promoting cooperation, coordination and interaction among the Arctic States, with the involvement of the Arctic indigenous communities and other Arctic inhabitants on common Arctic issues [a footnote here stated that the Council "should not deal with matters related to military security"], in particular issues of sustainable development and environmental protection in the Arctic.

    (b) oversee and coordinate the programs established under the AEPS [Arctic Environmental Protection Strategy, a comprehensive 1991 policy document on environmental issues in the region]. . . .

2. Members of the Arctic Council are: Canada, Denmark, Finland, Iceland, Norway, the Russian Federation, Sweden and the United States of America (the Arctic States).

    The Inuit Circumpolar Conference, the Saami Council and the Association of Indigenous Minorities of the North, Siberia and the Far East of the Russian Federation are Permanent Participants in the Arctic Council. Permanent participation equally is open to other Arctic organizations of indigenous peoples [a footnote here stated that "[t]he use of the term 'peoples' in this Declaration shall not be construed as having any implications as regard the rights which may attach to the term under international law."] with majority Arctic indigenous constituency, representing:

(a) a single indigenous people resident in more than one Arctic State; or

(b) more than one Arctic indigenous people resident in a single Arctic state.

The determination that such an organization has met this criterion is to be made by decision of the Council. The number of Permanent Participants should at any time be less than the number of members.

The category of Permanent Participation is created to provide for active participation and full consultation with the Arctic indigenous representatives within the Arctic Council.

3. Observer status in the Arctic Council is open to:

(a) non-Arctic states;

(b) inter-governmental and inter-parliamentary organizations, global and regional; and

(c) non-governmental organizations that the Council determines can contribute to its work. . . .

7. Decisions of the Arctic Council are to be by consensus of the Members.

Notes and Questions

1. Why do you think the PLO, SWAPO, and the anti-apartheid groups were given extensive participatory rights in the United Nations but not other groups within states?

2. How important a role were the states willing to give the indigenous peoples in the Arctic Council?

3. Are these cases sui generis or do they represent precedents for guaranteed participation by substate actors in other international organizations?

4. Do you think that participation by substate ethnic groups in a separate "General Assembly of Peoples" within the United Nations would help address their concerns? How would you design such a chamber to be acceptable to states and substate actors? In 1991 a group of delegates from a variety of substate communities created the Unrepresented Nations and Peoples Organization (UNPO). According to its Web page (*www.unpo.org*), UNPO is "an international forum for occupied nations, indigenous peoples, minorities, and even oppressed majorities who currently struggle to regain their lost countries, preserve their cultural identities, protect their basic human and economic rights, and safeguard the natural environment." Its more than 50 members include Abkhazia, the Aboriginals of Australia, Crimea, the Hungarian Minority in Romania, Kosovo, Kurdistan, Tibet, and Taiwan.

D. The Internationalization Option

Independence as a separate state and autonomy within an existing state represent the two major forms by which substate entities have attained separate recognition in international arenas. Yet a third possibility remains — direct governance by an international organization as an internationalized territory not under the sovereignty of any state. As audacious as the notion might sound, both the League of Nations and the United Nations have prepared detailed plans for such governance, some of which were implemented. Some of these efforts were aimed at permanent internationalization; others imposed a temporary internationalization.

1. Permanent Internationalization

In the early years of the United Nations, its members crafted two regimes for internationalization of disputed territories. The first concerned Trieste, a densely populated port city and territory on the Italian-Yugoslav (now Slovenian) border. The 1947 peace treaty between the Allies and Italy made Trieste a "Free Territory," and the UN was to assume governance through the approval by the Security Council of a statute for the territory and the appointment of its governor. The governor could override any laws, regulations, or treaties incompatible with the statute and appoint certain officials. Only the Security Council could review the governor's decisions. The plan, however, never achieved fruition because U.S.-Soviet rivalries prevented the appointment of a governor; in 1954 a treaty among Yugoslavia, Italy, the United States, and the United Kingdom split the territory between Yugoslavia and Italy along the lines of occupation of their armies.

The second proposed permanent internationalization proposal was for Jerusalem. The General Assembly's 1947 plan for the partition of Palestine called for making Jerusalem "a *corpus separatum* under a special international regime . . . administered by the United Nations." The UN Trusteeship Council adopted a statute in April 1948 with provisions on the appointment by the Trusteeship Council of a powerful governor, guarantees of human rights to all inhabitants, and special protections of religious sites. Yet with the outbreak of the 1948 Israeli war of independence, the UN could not prevail on either Israel or its neighbors to accept the plan. Israel and Jordan refused to surrender control over their respective halves of Jerusalem between 1949 and 1967, and since that time Israel has ruled out any internationalization. Some actors, such as the Vatican, continue to propose such an option, especially with respect to the religious sites in the Old City of Jerusalem.

2. Temporary Internationalization

Although permanent internationalization of territory has never materialized, international organizations have implemented various temporary internationalization schemes. In general, their purpose has been to provide a breathing spell for a territory's inhabitants pending some final settlement of its status by incorporation in one state or another. The first such plan was the League of Nation's governance after World War I of the Saar Basin, a coal-rich area in Germany on its border with France that was inhabited by ethnic Germans. Although Germany was forced to surrender the coal deposits as war damages, the territory itself was not ceded to France. It remained under German sovereignty but was placed under the direct governance of the League of Nations, which would, after 15 years, conduct a plebiscite. The League carried out its governance with general acceptance by both states; in the plebiscite, 90 percent of the inhabitants voted for integration into Germany, which the League authorized in 1935.

The United Nations has engaged in at least four forays into direct governance. In 1962-1963, under the terms of a Netherlands-Indonesia treaty, it governed Irian Jaya, the western half of the island of New Guinea, during a six-month transition from Dutch colonial rule to Indonesian control. (The plan called for an "act of self-determination" for the territory's final status, but the consultation of the population in 1969, six-years *after* the territory had been retuned to Indonesia, was rigged in favor of permanent incorporation into Indonesia.) From 1995 to 1998, the United Nations administered Eastern Slavonia, a small region on Croatia's border with Serbia that Serbia had occupied during the wars in the former Yugoslavia. The Dayton Agreement had specified that the territory would be reintegrated into Croatia; during the transitional period, the United Nations assumed major responsibilities concerning police, disarmament, return of refugees, and economic reconstruction. The war in Yugoslavia also led to the agreement by Muslim and Croat officials in Bosnia-Herzegovina to allow the EU to govern the city of Mostar, a city without a functional government because neither ethnic group was willing to govern the city as a whole with the other. (The two communities were separated by a river traversed by a medieval bridge, which was destroyed during the Bosnian war.) The European Union Administration of Mostar restored basic infrastructure to the city and governed it until municipal elections were held in 1996.

In 1999 the United Nations assumed its two most significant governance roles. After NATO's war with Serbia over Kosovo in 1999, the United Nations assumed direct administration of the territory. Under Security Council Resolution 1244 of June 10, 1999, the United Nations created an "interim administration for Kosovo under which the people of Kosovo can enjoy substantial autonomy within the Federal Republic of Yugoslavia, and which will provide transitional administration while establishing and overseeing the development of provisional democratic self-governing institutions." Kosovo's final status was deliberately left unaddressed, as the relevant actors could simply not agree.

Later that year, the United Nations assumed direct governance of East Timor, a former Portuguese colony annexed by Indonesia in 1975 when Portugal was unilaterally withdrawing from most of its colonial possessions. Indonesian occupation had been brutal: it led to hundreds of thousands of deaths. Only after its long-time president, Suharto, left the political stage under pressure in 1998 did Indonesia show some willingness to allow the East Timorese a voice in their future. The negotiations that followed led to the UN's conduct of a referendum in 1999 that overwhelmingly endorsed independence. After the vote, pro-Indonesia militias went on a rampage, killing approximately 1,000 civilians; the United Nations and Indonesia eventually authorized Australia to send in its forces to restore order pending the arrival of a UN administration.

Security Council Resolution 1272 (1999)

The Security Council . . .

Reiterating its welcome for the successful conduct of the popular consultation of the East Timorese people of 30 August 1999, and *taking note* of its outcome through which the East Timorese people expressed their clear wish to begin a process of transition under the authority of the United Nations towards independence, which it regards as an accurate reflection of the views of the East Timorese people . . .

Reaffirming respect for the sovereignty and territorial integrity of Indonesia . . .

Acting under Chapter VII of the Charter of the United Nations,

1. Decides to establish, in accordance with the report of the Secretary-General, a United Nations Transitional Administration in East Timor (UNTAET), which will be endowed with overall responsibility for the administration of East Timor and will be empowered to exercise all legislative and executive authority, including the administration of justice;

2. Decides also that the mandate of UNTAET shall consist of the following elements:

(a) To provide security and maintain law and order throughout the territory of East Timor;

(b) To establish an effective administration;

(c) To assist in the development of civil and social services;

(d) To ensure the coordination and delivery of humanitarian assistance, rehabilitation and development assistance;

(e) To support capacity-building for self-government;

(f) To assist in the establishment of conditions for sustainable development;

3. Decides further that UNTAET['s] . . . main components will be:

(a) A governance and public administration component, including an international police element with a strength of up to 1,640 officers;

(b) A humanitarian assistance and emergency rehabilitation component;

(c) A military component, with a strength of up to 8,950 troops and up to 200 military observers;

4. Authorizes UNTAET to take all necessary measures to fulfil its mandate;

5. Recognizes that, in developing and performing its functions under its mandate, UNTAET will need to draw on the expertise and capacity of Member States, United Nations agencies and other international organizations, including the international financial institutions;

6. Welcomes the intention of the Secretary-General to appoint a Special Representative who, as the Transitional Administrator, will be responsible for all aspects of the United Nations work in East Timor and will have the power to enact new laws and regulations and to amend, suspend or repeal existing ones; . . .

By 2002, UNTAET had generally succeeded in carrying out its extensive mandate of essentially creating a self-sustaining government where none had existed and where infrastructure was in a deplorable condition. Staffed by 8,000 peacekeeping troops and some 2,500 civilians, it recruited and trained a nascent local civil service, including a judicial and police system; organized successful elections for a constituent assembly that drafted a constitution; rehabilitated schools; and improved health conditions. On May 20, 2002, East Timor became an independent state; the United Nations replaced UNTAET with a smaller support mission to continue to assist the new government with law and order and other security functions. In Kosovo, the United Nations has enjoyed some success in setting up many institutions of governance, but tensions between the majority ethnic Albanians and the small Serb minority have greatly hindered its work; negotiations began in 2006 on Kosovo's final status.

Notes and Questions

1. What purposes does internationalization serve? Did the League of Nations and United Nations engage in internationalization in response to claims of the inhabitants of the disputed territory or claims of the affected states?

2. How did the United Nations address the status of the territories during the period of transitional administration? How strong was the paradigm of statehood?

3. The agreements and arrangements for internationalization offered different plans for the final status of the territory — permanent internationalization in the cases of Trieste and Jerusalem; a plebiscite for the Saar; an "act of self-determination" for Irian Jaya (though only once it had been handed over to Indonesia); reintegration into Croatia for Eastern Slavonia; deliberate ambiguity for Kosovo; and independence for East Timor. How important a factor in the acceptance by the state to which the territory belonged legally was the issue of the final status? How might this explain the absence of any successful permanent internationalizations? Should internationalization still be an option for Jerusalem?

PART III

International Law and Domestic Law

Having studied the ways international law is made and the participants in the international legal system, we now turn to the relationships between international and domestic law. This topic is of particular importance because, as discussed in Parts I and II above, the international system lacks a central law-making body, an executive to enforce the law, and a centralized judiciary to interpret the law and adjudicate disputes. As a result, international law is frequently interpreted, applied, and enforced in domestic political and legal systems. For example, executive branch officials may invoke international law to augment their power, or to limit the power of other branches or actors, and legislatures may pass statutes specifically designed to implement, change, or violate international legal norms.

Domestic courts, as well, frequently address the relationships between international and domestic law. Private parties often ask courts to decide whether the jurisdictional reach of domestic statutes violates international legal norms, to enforce treaty or customary international law obligations, and to resolve conflicts between international and domestic legal obligations. In these actions, courts often look to both international and domestic legal norms; in addition, domestic or foreign political actors may ask courts to consider the laws and public policies of foreign states, and to minimize judicial interference with the conduct of national foreign relations by the political branches.

Part III begins with a short overview of theoretical debates over the relationship between international and domestic law. These debates provide a useful framework for approaching the materials in Chapters 5 and 6. However, as a World Court judge explains, how a domestic legal system treats the relationships between international and domestic law turns, in part, on that system's particular "legal culture":

> In some jurisdictions international law will be treated as a familiar topic, one that both judge and the counsel before him will expect to deal with on a routine basis, the introduction of which occasions no special comment or interest. . . . But I speak of very practical matters: the judge and lawyer in his court will have studied international law and be familiar with it, just as they are familiar with other everyday branches of the law. But there is another culture that exists, in which it is possible to become a practising lawyer without having studied international law, and indeed to become a judge knowing no

international law. Psychologically that disposes both counsel and judge to treat international law as some exotic branch of the law, to be avoided if at all possible, and to be
looked upon as if it is unreal, of no practical application in the real world.

Rosalyn Higgins, Problems and Process: International Law and How We Use It 206
(1995).

Chapters 5 and 6 are an exploration of the ways that political actors and courts
incorporate — or fail to incorporate — international law into domestic law and activities.
While many national constitutions address the status of international law on the domestic
plane, these provisions are often phrased at a sufficiently high level of generality that they
fail to resolve concrete controversies, and many international law questions are resolved
through domestic political processes or through domestic court litigation. In Chapter 5,
we focus on these processes — on how domestic systems create rules regarding the
hierarchy of international law sources, particularly treaty and custom, in relation to
domestic law; and on how these systems make and apply rules concerning the ways
that states can enter into — or violate — international legal norms. We also look at how
and when courts and legislatures enable private parties to rely upon international legal
norms in domestic litigation.

Chapter 6 addresses the issues raised when domestic law reaches beyond national
borders. As we will see, international law provides general principles that purport to
govern the ability of states to regulate conduct and persons outside their borders, as
well as their ability to enforce their laws outside their borders. Nevertheless, controversies over the extraterritorial reach of domestic jurisdiction arise with some frequency.
These controversies are, at times, resolved in international fora, but more frequently are
settled in domestic arenas. In Chapter 6, we explore the resolution of such jurisdictional
conflicts, as well as the various types of jurisdiction recognized by international law.

A number of important themes that build on the materials presented in Parts I and II
run through all of the problems in Part III. Chapter 1 introduced the idea of the *dédoublement fonctionnel*, the dual function of state authorities as representatives of specific
states and, at times, as agents of the broader international community. Chapters 5
and 6 provide a series of case studies that test whether this is an accurate characterization of the role that domestic actors play, or whether it conceals the tensions between the
policy and legal orientations (and obligations) of domestic political actors and judges, on
the one hand, and the political and legal pull of international legal norms, which frequently
require some degree of subordination of national policies to international law, on the
other. The problems that follow also explore the ways that national bias and interests
affect the resolution of international legal problems on the domestic plane, and permit you
to test the various approaches to international law discussed in Chapter 1. In addition, the
problems in this part show how the various actors described in Part II — states, international organizations, non-governmental organizations and multinational corporations —
participate in a dynamic process of interpreting and applying international law on the
domestic plane. Moreover, each of the problems reveals how the relationships between
international and domestic law are complex and subtle, and blur what were once considered to be the bright lines that distinguish international from domestic law.

Finally, the problems in this part of the book raise the larger question of whether
international legal norms addressing the relationships between international and

domestic law strike an appropriate "balance between the inclusive competence of the general community of states and the exclusive competence [that is, jurisdiction] of particular states which best promotes the greatest total production, at least cost, of their shared values." Myres S. McDougal, *The Impact of International Law Upon National Law: A Policy-Oriented Perspective, in* International Law Essays 437, 438 (Myres S. McDougal & W. Michael Reisman eds., 1981). In considering whether the right balance has been struck, Professor McDougal identified the following "important questions":

> [H]ow, and with what access to decision by interested participants, are [international legal norms], purporting to express a common interest, actually prescribed . . . for regulating the practices of states and the exclusive competence of particular states; what balance between the inclusive competence of the general community of states and the exclusive competence of particular states . . . is in fact established by such prescription; in what degree, and by what practices, are [internationally] prescribed practices effectively applied in action . . . to regulate states both in their external strategies and in their internal policies; and, finally, how compatible are the aggregate effects achieved, by the impact of international upon national processes of authority, with shared values of human dignity?

Id. at 447.

At bottom, norms governing the role of international law in the domestic plane (Chapter 5), and norms governing the exercise of jurisdiction (Chapter 6), are really norms governing the exercise of state power. Thus, the materials that follow are, in part, an examination of the international and domestic processes for defining and limiting state power and, in part, an inquiry into whether current international norms appropriately define and limit the exercise of state power.

5

International Law in the Domestic Arena

International law frequently says little about how governments should implement their international legal obligations. As a result, domestic actors, including legislatures, courts, and individuals, confront a number of complex conceptual and doctrinal questions regarding the role and status of international law on the domestic plane. In the United States and many other states a constitution addresses the relationships between international and domestic law and explicitly allocates authority over specific international legal issues to one or another branch of government. However, most international legal questions are resolved in the United States and other domestic legal systems through the interactions of different branches of government.

In this chapter, we will explore a variety of ways that courts and political actors address international legal issues, including the ways that international law is incorporated into and made part of domestic law, whether and when international legal norms are judicially enforceable by individuals, and whether domestic law treats treaties and customary international law the same or differently. Stated less formally, in this chapter we explore many of the techniques and doctrines that domestic courts and political actors use to make, break, interpret, incorporate, or fail to incorporate international law. While our focus will be on the U.S. legal system, similar issues arise in virtually all domestic legal systems. From time to time, reference will be made to some of these other systems.

I. THE MONIST-DUALIST DEBATE

Understanding the relationships between domestic and international law begins with the question of whether these legal systems are part of a single, universal legal order (the "monist" position) or form two distinct systems of law (the "dualist" position). For monists, international law is automatically part of a state's domestic legal system and is just as much domestic law as is contract or tax law. In addition, international law is superior to domestic law (as a constitution is superior to a statute) in the case of a conflict. Under the monist view, the national legislature is bound to respect international law when passing legislation; the executive is obliged to follow international law, even in the face of contrary domestic law; and the judiciary is bound to give effect to international law.

For dualists, as Professor Lassa Oppenheim explained, "International Law and Municipal Law are in fact two totally and essentially different bodies of law which have nothing in common except that they are both branches—but separate branches—of the tree of law." That is, for dualists, international and domestic law govern different actors and issues. International law governs relations among states, while domestic law governs relations between a state and its citizens and among citizens. Under the dualist view, each state determines for itself whether, when, and how international law is "incorporated" into domestic law, and the status of international law in the domestic system is determined by domestic law.

In part, the monist-dualist debate turns on how to determine the status of international law in the domestic legal system. Monists would argue that international law provides the answer to this question; dualists counter that domestic legal norms answer this question. Of course, as is true of many idealized analytic dichotomies, pure forms of monism or dualism are rarely encountered in practice. Instead, different states tend to fall along a continuum between pure monism and total dualism in their approach to international law. The constitutional provisions reproduced below illustrate the diversity of approaches that states can take regarding the relationships between international and domestic law.

France

Article 54

If the Constitutional Council, on a reference from the President of the Republic, from the Prime Minister, from the President of one or the other Assembly, or from sixty deputies or sixty senators, has declared that an international commitment contains a clause contrary to the Constitution, authorization to ratify or approve the international commitment in question may be given only after amendment of the Constitution.

Article 55

Treaties or agreements duly ratified or approved upon publication, prevail over Acts of Parliament, subject, in regard to each agreement or treaty, to its application by the other party.

Haiti

Article 276

The National Assembly may not ratify any international treaty, convention or agreement containing clauses contrary to this Constitution. . . .

Article 276-2

Once international treaties or agreements are approved and ratified in the manner stipulated by the Constitution, they become part of the legislation of the country and abrogate any laws in conflict with them.

The Netherlands

Article 91

(1) The Kingdom shall not be bound by treaties, nor shall such treaties be denounced, without the prior approval of the Parliament. The cases in which approval is not required shall be specified by Act of Parliament.

(2) The manner in which approval shall be granted shall be laid down by Act of Parliament, which may provide for the possibility of tacit approval.

(3) Any provisions of a treaty that conflict with the Constitution or which lead to conflicts with it may be approved by the Chambers of the Parliament only if at least two-thirds of the votes cast are in favor.

Article 94

Statutory regulations in force within the Kingdom shall not be applicable if such application is in conflict with provisions of treaties that are binding on all persons or of resolutions by international institutions.

South Africa

Section 231 International Agreements

(4) Any international agreement becomes law in the Republic when it is enacted into law by national legislation; but a self-executing provision of an agreement that has been approved by Parliament is law in the Republic unless it is inconsistent with the Constitution or an Act of Parliament.

Section 232 Customary International Law

Customary international law is law in the Republic unless it is inconsistent with the Constitution or an Act of Parliament.

Section 233 Application of International Law

When interpreting any legislation, every court must prefer any reasonable interpretation of the legislation that is consistent with international law over any alternative interpretation that is inconsistent with international law.

United States of America

Article VI

[2] This Constitution, and the Laws of the United States which shall be made in Pursuance thereof; and all Treaties made, or which shall be made, under the Authority of the United States, shall be the supreme Law of the Land; and the Judges in every State shall be bound thereby, any Thing in the Constitution or Laws of any State to the Contrary notwithstanding.

The European Union (EU) provides an important example of how international law can be directly applicable on the domestic plane. The Union is a unique, treaty-based institutional framework that defines and manages economic and political cooperation among its 25 member states. The Union is the result of a process that began in the wake of World War II. At that time, as a devastated Western Europe sought ways to rebuild its economy and prevent future wars, Jean Monnet and Robert Schuman proposed placing German and French coal and steel production under a common high authority. The integration of these two industries was intended to make future war on the continent impossible, and to set the stage for future forms of economic and political integration. The 1951 Treaty of Paris, establishing the European Coal and Steel Community, was signed by the three Benelux countries, France, Germany, and Italy. Coal and steel trade among these six nations increased by 129 percent in the first five years that this treaty was in force.

Encouraged by this success, European leaders decided to pursue additional efforts at economic integration. In 1957, the two so-called Rome treaties were ratified. One created the European Economic Community to merge the separate national markets into a single market that would ensure the free movement of goods, people, capital, and services. The other created the European Atomic Energy Community (Euratom) to further the peaceful use of nuclear energy.

Progress in European integration slowed considerably in the 1970s and early 1980s. The Single European Act, signed in 1986, amended the three original treaties by, inter alia, changing the Community's decision-making processes and bringing new areas, such as the environment, within the scope of Community law. The Treaty on European Union, signed in Maastricht, Netherlands, in December 1991, created the European Union, which encompasses the existing European Community and two new "pillars" — Common Affairs and Security Policy as well as Justice and Home Affairs (addressing, inter alia, crime and immigration issues). The June 1997 Treaty of Amsterdam paved the way for the introduction of the single currency and the enlargement of EU membership. The 2001 Treaty of Nice reformed the Union's institutions to enable them to function efficiently after the enlargement of the EU from 15 to 25 member states.

Through a variety of different processes, the EU produces several different types of legislation. The Rome Treaty creating the Community provides that regulations "are binding in their entirety and directly applicable in all Member States." They can be analogized to federal laws in the United States. Directives are binding with respect to "the results to be achieved." They are addressed to the member states, which are free to choose the best "form and methods" of implementation. Decisions are binding in their entirety upon those to whom they are addressed. Recommendations and opinions are not binding.

The development of a substantial body of Community law gave rise to a number of questions about the relationship between Community law and national law. Does Community law create rights that private parties can enforce against member states or that member states can enforce against private parties? When is a member state adequately enforcing or implementing Community law? Who makes this determination? As the relevant treaties did not expressly address many of the fundamental questions involving the relationship between Community and member state law, the European Court of Justice (ECJ), the EU's judicial organ, took the initiative in defining this relationship.

In *Van Gend en Loos v. Nederlandse Administratie Der Belastingen*, [1963] E.C.R. 3, the court considered whether provisions of the Rome Treaty "have direct application within the territory of a Member State, in other words, whether nationals of such State can, on the basis of the Article in question, lay claim to an individual right which the courts must protect."

The Court reasoned that:

> The objective of the EEC [Rome] Treaty, which is to establish a Common Market, the functioning of which is of direct concern to interested parties in the Community, implies that this Treaty is more than an agreement which merely creates mutual obligations between the contracting states. This view is confirmed by the preamble to the Treaty which refers not only to governments but to peoples. It is also confirmed more specifically by the establishment of institutions endowed with sovereign rights, the exercise of which affects Member States and also their citizens. . . .
>
> . . . The Community constitutes a new legal order of international law for the benefit of which the states have limited their sovereign rights, albeit within limited fields, and the subjects of which comprise not only the Member States but also their nationals. Independently of the legislation of Member States, Community law therefore not only imposes obligations on individuals but is also intended to confer upon them rights which become part of their legal heritage.

The Court held that the treaty provision at issue had a "direct effect" in domestic law that individuals could rely upon in national courts.

A year after *Van Gend en Loos*, the ECJ considered whether a directly applicable treaty provision prevails over conflicting domestic law in national courts. In *Costa v. Ente Nazionale per l'Energia Ellettrica*, [1964] E.C.R. 585, a customer and shareholder of a power company challenged an Italian law nationalizing the electric industry as inconsistent with the Italian Constitution and the Rome Treaty. The Italian Corte Costituzionale (constitutional court) ruled that, as the nationalization law was adopted after the law approving the Rome Treaty, the domestic law was "last in time" and therefore controlling. The ECJ disagreed:

> By contrast with ordinary international treaties, the [Rome Treaty] has created its own legal system which, on the entry into force of the Treaty, became an integral part of the legal systems of the Member States and which their courts are bound to apply.
>
> By creating a Community of unlimited duration, having its own institutions, its own personality, its own capacity and capacity of representation on the international plane, and more particularly, real powers stemming from a limitation of sovereignty or a transfer of powers from the States to the Community, the Member States have limited their sovereign rights, albeit within limited fields, and have thus created a body of law which binds both their nationals and themselves.
>
> The integration into the laws of each Member State of provisions which derive from the Community and more generally the terms and the spirit of the Treaty, make it impossible for the States, as a corollary, to accord precedence to a unilateral and subsequent measure over a legal system accepted by them on a basis of reciprocity. . . .
>
> The obligations undertaken under the Treaty establishing the [European] Community would not be unconditional, but merely contingent, if they could be called in question by subsequent legislative acts of the signatories. . . .
>
> The precedence of Community law is confirmed by Article 189 [of the Rome Treaty], whereby a regulation 'shall be binding' and 'directly applicable in all Member States'. This provision, which is subject to no reservation, would be quite meaningless if a State could unilaterally nullify its effects by means of a legislative measure which could prevail over Community law.
>
> It follows from all these observations that the law stemming from the Treaty, an independent source of law, could not, because of its special and original nature, be overriden by domestic legal provisions, however framed, without being deprived of its

character as Community law and without the legal basis of the Community itself being called into question.

In later cases, the Court expanded these principles. First, the court applied the direct effects principle not only in cases where an individual invokes Community law against a member state (the "vertical" dimension) but also to cases where Community law is invoked by one individual against another (the "horizontal" dimension). Second, the court applied the principle not only in the context of treaty law but also in the context of secondary community legislation, such as directives and decisions.

It is difficult to overestimate the impact of these cases on the development of the Community. The following extract captures something of this impact:

The implications of [the judicial doctrine of direct effect] were and are far reaching. The European Court reversed the normal presumption of public international law whereby international legal obligations are result-oriented and addressed to states. Public international law typically allows the internal constitutional order of a state to determine the method and extent to which international obligations may, if at all, produce effects for individuals within the legal order of the state. Under the normal canons of international law, even when the international obligation itself, such as a trade agreement or a human rights convention, is intended to bestow rights (or duties) on individuals within a state, if the state fails to bestow the rights, the individual cannot invoke the international obligation before national courts, unless internal constitutional or statutory law, to which public international law is indifferent, provides for such a remedy. The typical remedy under public international law in such a case would be an inter-state claim. The main import of the Community doctrine of direct effect was not simply the conceptual change it ushered forth. In practice direct effect meant that Member States violating their Community obligations could not shift the locus of dispute to the inter-state or Community plane. They would be faced with legal actions before their own courts at the suit of individuals within their own legal order.

Individuals (and their lawyers) noticed this practical implication, and the number of cases brought on the basis of this doctrine grew exponentially. Effectively, individuals in real cases and controversies (usually against state public authorities) became the principal "guardians" of the legal integrity of Community law within Europe similar to the way that individuals in the United States have been the principal actors in ensuring the vindication of the Bill of Rights and other federal law.

. . . The full impact of direct effect is realized in combination with the second "constitutionalizing" doctrine, supremacy. Unlike some federal constitutions, the Treaty does not include a specific "supremacy clause." However, in a series of cases starting [with *Costa*] the Court has pronounced an uncompromising version of supremacy: in the sphere of application of Community law, any Community norm, be it an article of the Treaty (the Constitutional Charter) or a minuscule administrative regulation enacted by the Commission, "trumps" conflicting national law whether enacted before or after the Community norm. . . .

In light of supremacy the full significance of direct effect becomes transparent. Typically, in monist or quasi-monist states . . . [treaties are] equivalent to national legislation. Thus the normal rule of "later in time" (*lex posteriori derogat lex anteriori*) governs the relationship between the treaty provision and conflicting national legislation. A national legislature unhappy with an internalized treaty norm simply enacts a conflicting national measure and the transposition will have vanished for all internal practical effects. By contrast, in the Community, because of the doctrine of supremacy, the E.C. norm, which by virtue of the doctrine of direct effect must be regarded as part of the Law of the Land, will prevail even in these circumstances. The combination of the two doctrines means that Community norms that produce direct effects are not merely the Law of the Land but the "Higher Law" of the Land. Parallels to this kind of constitutional architecture may, with very few exceptions, be found only in the internal constitutional order of federal states.

J.H.H. Weiler, *The Transformation of Europe,* 100 Yale L.J. 2403, 2413-2415 (1991).

II. MAKING INTERNATIONAL LAW: IS NAFTA CONSTITUTIONAL?

The United States uses at least three different methods to enter into international agreements. Article II of the United States Constitution provides that the President "shall have power, by and with the advice and consent of the Senate to make treaties, provided that two thirds of the Senate present concur. . . ." These agreements are often called "Article II treaties." While the U.S. Constitution does not explicitly grant Presidents the ability to conclude international agreements other than by an Article II treaty, since the early days of the republic the United States has also entered into congressional-executive agreements. The Executive Branch enters into these agreements with either the prior authorization or the subsequent approval of a simple majority of both Houses of Congress. Finally, Presidents from George Washington onward have entered into sole executive agreements, or agreements without congressional participation, on the basis of inherent constitutional authority. Since World War II, the use of such congressional-executive and sole executive agreements has greatly expanded.

At various times in the nation's history, controversy has raged over the nature and scope of the government's power to enter into international agreements. The Constitution does not define the term "treaty," prompting debate over whether certain issues, such as racial discrimination, are appropriate topics for international agreements. As you read the materials that follow, consider whether the federal government can enter into international agreements on matters that the Constitution otherwise leaves to the states. Consider also whether there are circumstances in which the federal government is constitutionally obligated to use a particular method for entering into an international agreement, or whether the various methods are interchangeable. This issue came to the fore during the 1990s when the United States entered into the North American Free Trade Agreement and the Uruguay Round Agreements creating the World Trade Organization (WTO).

A. The Problem

In February 1991, the presidents of Mexico and the United States, and the prime minister of Canada endorsed the idea of negotiating a trilateral North American Free Trade Agreement (NAFTA). On March 1, 1991, President George Bush requested a two-year extension of "fast track" authority from the U.S. Congress. Under "fast track" legislation, now called "trade promotion authority," Congress authorizes the President to negotiate trade agreements with other nations; the agreements and implementing legislation are then submitted to Congress under an accelerated timetable that limits floor debate and the ability to introduce amendments. In return for this expedited consideration, the President consults with relevant congressional committees throughout the negotiating process. If Congress approves the implementing legislation, the result is a congressional-executive agreement that incorporates the United States's obligations under the international agreement into domestic law.

After Congress passed fast track legislation, formal NAFTA negotiations began in June 1991 and, following intense and difficult bargaining, were completed in August 1992. In relatively short order, the parties negotiated one of the most important and comprehensive regional trade agreements in history. The treaty created a massive open market, with over 360 million consumers and over $6 trillion in annual output. Like other trade agreements, NAFTA provides for the progressive phaseout of tariffs on goods traded among the parties. However, NAFTA also includes a number of other provisions not common to most trade agreements.

For example, the treaty includes detailed provisions on foreign investment, addressing issues such as expropriation and domestic content requirements. NAFTA also provides that private investors of one party can directly seek relief from another party for certain NAFTA violations. That is, if a Mexican investor believes that, for example, a U.S. environmental regulation constitutes an impermissible expropriation of his U.S. investment, the investor can seek monetary damages from the United States in international arbitration. These provisions also cover, with some exceptions, actions taken by state and provincial governments. The NAFTA investor-state dispute resolution provisions are examined in more detail in Chapter 12. In addition to the investor-state dispute resolution provisions, NAFTA includes a few state-to-state dispute resolution processes. The treaty also contains extremely detailed provisions on trade in services (including banking, securities, insurance, and telecommunications), intellectual property, permissible federal and state food safety standards, government procurement, and certain immigration law matters.

On November 4, 1993, the President submitted to Congress the NAFTA draft implementing legislation. At the same time, he submitted supplemental side agreements on labor and the environment.

B. Are There Limits to the U.S. Government's Power to Make International Agreements?

Article VI of the U.S. Constitution declares that, along with the Constitution and federal law, "all Treaties made, or which shall be made, under the Authority of the United States, shall be the supreme Law of the Land," and that they prevail over inconsistent state laws. However, neither the Supremacy Clause nor any other constitutional provisions define or limit the scope of the treaty power. As a result, since the founding there has been debate among politicians and scholars over the appropriate limits to this power. The following two cases address these issues.

Missouri v. Holland

252 U.S. 416 (1920)

MR. JUSTICE HOLMES delivered the opinion of the court.

This is a bill in equity brought by the State of Missouri to prevent a game warden of the United States from attempting to enforce the Migratory Bird Treaty Act of July 3, 1918, and the regulations made by the Secretary of Agriculture in pursuance of the same. The ground of the bill is that the statute is an unconstitutional interference with the rights reserved to the States by the Tenth Amendment, and that the acts of the defendant done and threatened under that authority invade the sovereign right of the State and contravene its will manifested in statutes. . . .

On December 8, 1916, a treaty between the United States and Great Britain was proclaimed by the President. It recited that many species of birds in their annual migrations traversed certain parts of the United States and of Canada . . . but were in danger of extermination through lack of adequate protection. It therefore provided for specified closed seasons and protection in other forms, and agreed that the two powers would take or propose to their law-making bodies the necessary measures for carrying the treaty out. The . . . Act of July 3, 1918 . . . prohibited . . . killing, capturing or selling any of the migratory birds included in the terms of the treaty. . . . [T]he question raised is the general one whether the treaty and statute are void as an interference with the rights reserved to the States.

To answer this question it is not enough to refer to the Tenth Amendment, reserving the powers not delegated to the United States, because by Article II, §2, the power to make treaties is delegated expressly, and by Article VI treaties made under the authority of the United States, along with the Constitution and laws of the United States made in pursuance thereof, are declared the supreme law of the land. If the treaty is valid there can be no dispute about the validity of the statute under Article I, sec. 8, as a necessary and proper means to execute the powers of the Government. The language of the Constitution as to the supremacy of treaties being general, the question before us is narrowed to an inquiry into the ground upon which the present supposed exception is placed.

It is said that a treaty cannot be valid if it infringes the Constitution, that there are limits, therefore, to the treaty-making power, and that one such limit is that what an act of Congress could not do unaided, in derogation of the powers reserved to the States, a treaty cannot do. An earlier act of Congress that attempted . . . to regulate the killing of migratory birds within the States had been held bad in the District Court. *United States* v. *Shauver*, 214 Fed. Rep. 154. *United States* v. *McCullagh*, 221 Fed. Rep. 288. Those decisions were supported by arguments that migratory birds were owned by the States in their sovereign capacity for the benefit of their people, and that . . . this control was one that Congress had no power to displace. The same argument is supposed to apply now with equal force.

Whether the two cases cited were decided rightly or not they cannot be accepted as a test of the treaty power. Acts of Congress are the supreme law of the land only when made in pursuance of the Constitution, while treaties are declared to be so when made under the authority of the United States. It is open to question whether the authority of the United States means more than the formal acts prescribed to make the convention. We do not mean to imply that there are no qualifications to the treaty-making power; but they must be ascertained in a different way. It is obvious that there may be matters of the sharpest exigency for the national well being that an act of Congress could not deal with but that a treaty followed by such an act could, and it is not lightly to be assumed that, in matters requiring national action, "a power which must belong to and somewhere reside in every civilized government" is not to be found. . . . [W]e may add that when we are dealing with words that also are a constituent act, like the Constitution of the United States, we must realize that they have called into life a being the development of which could not be foreseen completely by the most gifted of its begetters. It was enough for them to realize or to hope that they had created an organism; it has taken a century and has cost their successors much sweat and blood to prove that they created a nation. The case before us must be considered in the light of our whole experience and not merely in that of what was said a hundred years ago. The treaty in question does not contravene any prohibitory words to be found in the Constitution. The only question is whether it is forbidden by some invisible radiation from the general terms of the Tenth Amendment. We must consider what this country has become in deciding what that Amendment has reserved.

The State as we have intimated founds its claim of exclusive authority upon an assertion of title to migratory birds, an assertion that is embodied in statute. No doubt it is true that as between a State and its inhabitants the State may regulate the killing and sale of such birds, but it does not follow that its authority is exclusive of paramount powers. To put the claim of the State upon title is to lean upon a slender reed. . . . The whole foundation of the State's rights is the presence within their jurisdiction of birds that yesterday had not arrived, tomorrow may be in another State and in a week a thousand miles away. If we are to be accurate we cannot put the case of the State upon higher ground than that the treaty deals with creatures that for the moment are within the state borders, that it must be carried out by officers of the United States within the same territory, and that but for the treaty the State would be free to regulate this subject itself. . . .

Here a national interest of very nearly the first magnitude is involved. It can be protected only by national action in concert with that of another power. The subject-matter is only transitorily within the State and has no permanent habitat therein. But for the treaty and the statute there soon might be no birds for any powers to deal with. We see nothing in the Constitution that compels the Government to sit by while a food supply is cut off and the protectors of our forests and our crops are destroyed. . . . We are of the opinion that the treaty and statute must be upheld.

Notes and Questions

1. Does *Missouri* mean that Congress can, if acting to implement a treaty, pass a statute otherwise in excess of its constitutional authority?

2. Justice Holmes states that the limits to the treaty-making power "must be ascertained in a different way." Does he identify that "different way"? Does this opinion impose any limits on the treaty-making power?

Missouri has proved to be one of the most important, and controversial, decisions in the foreign affairs area. In the 1950s in particular there were efforts to amend the Constitution, in effect to overrule *Missouri*. These efforts, collectively known as the Bricker Amendment after Senator John Bricker of Ohio, grew out of conservative senators' concerns over the UN Charter and early human rights treaties, such as the Genocide Convention. Some Bricker Amendment supporters feared that the Charter's human rights provisions would give Congress power to enact civil rights legislation otherwise beyond its constitutional powers. In addition, many amendment supporters, including conservative Southern Democrats, believed that the Genocide Convention and other human rights treaties could be interpreted in a way that could override racially discriminatory state laws. Other amendment supporters, including a former president of the American Bar Association, argued that the Charter and human rights treaties would intrude upon domestic jurisdiction and diminish U.S. sovereignty, expand the power of the federal government at the expense of states' rights, strengthen Communist influence, and enhance the prospects of world government.

The most widely debated version of the Bricker Amendment was that reported out by the Senate Judiciary Committee in 1953. It provided:

> 1. A provision of a treaty which conflicts with this Constitution shall not be of any force or effect.
>
> 2. A treaty shall become effective as internal law in the United States only through legislation which would be valid in the absence of a treaty.
>
> 3. Congress shall have power to regulate all executive and other agreements with any foreign power or international organization. All such agreements shall be subject to the limitations imposed on treaties by this article.

The Eisenhower Administration strongly opposed the Bricker Amendment on the grounds that it would encroach on the President's foreign affairs powers. To help defeat the amendment, the administration stated that it would not seek to become a party to any more human rights treaties. The Secretary of State testified, in 1953, that

> [t]he present administration intends to encourage the promotion everywhere of human rights and individual freedoms, but to favor methods of persuasion, education and example rather than formal undertakings. . . . Therefore, while we shall not withhold our counsel from those who seek to draft a treaty or covenant on human rights, we do not ourselves look upon a treaty as the means which we would now select as the proper and most effective way to spread throughout the world the goals of human liberty to which this Nation has been dedicated since its inception. We therefore do not intend to become a party to any such covenant or present it as a treaty for consideration by the Senate.

Treaties and Executive Agreements: Hearings Before a Subcomm. of the Senate Judiciary Comm. on S.J. Res. 1, and S.J. Res. 43, 83d Cong. 824 (1953).

For many years thereafter, Presidents did not submit major human rights treaties to the Senate (although they did continue to seek the Senate's advice and consent to the Genocide Convention submitted by President Truman to the Senate in 1949). This changed under President Carter, who submitted several major human rights treaties to the Senate in 1978. However, each was accompanied by a package of reservations, understandings, and declarations (RUDs) that, in effect, provided that adherence to these treaties would not effect changes in U.S. law or practice. We examine the use of RUDs to human rights treaties in more detail in Chapter 7.

The Supreme Court's next major discussion of the treaty power helped to defuse some of the political pressure in support of the Bricker Amendment.

Reid v. Covert

354 U.S. 1 (1957)

MR. JUSTICE BLACK announced the judgment of the Court and delivered an opinion, in which the CHIEF JUSTICE, MR. JUSTICE DOUGLAS, and MR. JUSTICE BRENNAN join.

These cases raise basic constitutional issues of the utmost concern. . . . Mrs. Clarice Covert killed her husband, a sergeant in the United States Air

Force, at an airbase in England. . . . She was tried by a court-martial for murder under Article 118 of the Uniform Code of Military Justice (UCMJ). . . . The court-martial asserted jurisdiction over Mrs. Covert under Article 2(11) of the UCMJ, which provides:

> The following persons are subject to this code:
>
> (11) Subject to the provisions of any treaty or agreement to which the United States is or may be a party or to any accepted rule of international law, all persons serving with, employed by, or accompanying the armed forces without the continental limits of the United States. . . .

[Mrs. Covert was found guilty and sentenced to life imprisonment. She sought a writ of habeas corpus to set her free on the ground that the Constitution forbade her trial by military authorities.]

I

At the beginning we reject the idea that when the United States acts against citizens abroad it can do so free of the Bill of Rights. The United States is entirely a creature of the Constitution. Its power and authority have no other source. It can only act in accordance with all the limitations imposed by the Constitution. When the Government reaches out to punish a citizen who is abroad, the shield which the Bill of Rights and other parts of the Constitution provide to protect his life and liberty should not be stripped away just because he happens to be in another land. . . .

Among those provisions, Art. III, §2 and the Fifth and Sixth Amendments are directly relevant to these cases. Article III, §2 lays down the rule that:

> "The Trial of all Crimes, except in Cases of Impeachment, shall be by Jury; and such Trial shall be held in the State where the said Crimes shall have been committed; but when not committed within any State, the Trial shall be at such Place or Places as the Congress may by Law have directed."

The Fifth Amendment declares:

> "No person shall be held to answer for a capital, or otherwise infamous crime, unless on a presentment or indictment of a Grand Jury, except in cases arising in the land or naval forces, or in the Militia, when in actual service in time of War or public danger; . . ."

And the Sixth Amendment provides:

> "In all criminal prosecutions, the accused shall enjoy the right to a speedy and public trial, by an impartial jury of the State and district wherein the crime shall have been committed. . . ."

The language of Art. III, §2 manifests that constitutional protections for the individual were designed to restrict the United States Government when it acts outside of this country, as well as here at home. After declaring that *all* criminal trials must be by jury, the section states that when a crime is 'not committed within any State, the Trial shall be at such Place or Places as the Congress may by Law have directed.' If this language is permitted to have its obvious meaning, §2 is applicable to criminal trials outside of the States as a group without regard to where the offense is committed or the trial held. . . . The Fifth and Sixth Amendments, like Art. III,

§2, are also all inclusive with their sweeping references to 'no person' and to 'all criminal prosecutions. . . .'

II

At the time of Mrs. Covert's alleged offense, an executive agreement was in effect between the United States and Great Britain which permitted United States' military courts to exercise exclusive jurisdiction over offenses committed in Great Britain by American servicemen or their dependents. . . . Even though a court-martial does not give an accused trial by jury and other Bill of Rights protections, the Government contends that article 2(11) of UCMJ, insofar as it provides for the military trial of dependents accompanying the armed forces in Great Britain . . . can be sustained as legislation which is necessary and proper to carry out the United States' obligations under the international agreements made with those countries. The obvious and decisive answer to this, of course, is that no agreement with a foreign nation can confer power on the Congress, or on any other branch of Government, which is free from the restraints of the Constitution.

Article VI, the Supremacy Clause of the Constitution, declares:

> This Constitution, and the Laws of the United States which shall be made in Pursuance thereof; and all Treaties made, or which shall be made, under the Authority of the United States, shall be the supreme Law of the Land; . . .

There is nothing in this language which intimates that treaties and laws enacted pursuant to them do not have to comply with the provisions of the Constitution. . . . It would be manifestly contrary to the objectives of those who created the Constitution, as well as those who were responsible for the Bill of Rights — let alone alien to our entire constitutional history and tradition — to construe Article VI as permitting the United States to exercise power under an international agreement without observing constitutional prohibitions. . . . The prohibitions of the Constitution were designed to apply to all branches of the National Government and they cannot be nullified by the Executive or by the Executive and the Senate combined.

There is nothing new or unique about what we say here. This Court has regularly and uniformly recognized the supremacy of the Constitution over a treaty. . . .

This Court has also repeatedly taken the position that an Act of Congress, which must comply with the Constitution, is on a full parity with a treaty, and that when a statute which is subsequent in time is inconsistent with a treaty, the statute to the extent of conflict renders the treaty null. It would be completely anomalous to say that a treaty need not comply with the Constitution when such an agreement can be overridden by a statute that must conform to that instrument.

There is nothing in *Missouri v. Holland* . . . which is contrary to the position taken here. There the Court carefully noted that the treaty involved was not inconsistent with any specific provision of the Constitution. The Court was concerned with the Tenth Amendment which reserves to the States or the people all power not delegated to the National Government. To the extent that the United States can validly make treaties, the people and the States have delegated their power to the National Government and the Tenth Amendment is no barrier. . . .

Notes and Questions

1. Can *Missouri* and *Reid* be harmonized? Is it relevant that *Reid* involves individual rights and *Missouri* involves states' rights?

2. What are the limits on the federal government's power to make international agreements?

3. In his separate opinion in *Reid*, Justice Harlan wrote that:

> Decision is easy if one adopts the constricting view that these constitutional guarantees as a totality do or do not "apply" overseas. But, for me, the question is *which* guarantees of the Constitution *should* apply in view of the particular circumstances, the practical necessities, and the possible alternatives which Congress had before it. The question is one of judgment, not of compulsion . . . .

Justice Harlan was persuaded that requiring a full Article III trial for "run of the mill cases" was both "impractical" and "anomalous." However, "for capital offenses . . . special considerations apply," and therefore Justice Harlan concurred in the result.

Later cases have made clear that the protections in the Bill of Rights do not always apply abroad. For example, in *United States v. Verdugo-Urquidez*, 494 U.S. 259 (1990), the Supreme Court held that the Fourth Amendment, which protects "the right of the people to be secure in their persons [and] houses . . . against unreasonable searches and seizures," was inapplicable to searches by U.S. agents of property outside the United States owned by an alien. We explore the extraterritorial reach of domestic law in greater detail in Chapter 6.

4. *Missouri* seemed less important during the many years that courts understood the Commerce Clause to be an extremely broad grant of legislative authority to Congress. However, in *United States v. Lopez*, 514 U.S. 549 (1995), the Supreme Court struck down, for the first time since the New Deal era, a federal statute as not within Congress's Commerce Clause powers.

The Court's more restrictive reading of the Commerce Clause may raise anew the question of when legislation otherwise outside Congress's powers is constitutionally permissible under the Treaty Clause; it may also alter U.S. positions in international negotiations. For example, during negotiations over the Framework Convention on Tobacco Control, a draft treaty provision would have prohibited the distribution of free tobacco samples to children. The United States opposed this provision on the grounds that free samples were not in "interstate commerce" because they were not sold, and therefore the federal government lacked authority to regulate in this area. The treaty was revised to provide that parties "shall prohibit or promote the prohibition" of the distribution of free tobacco products to minors. The United States has signed, but not ratified, this treaty.

Assuming that the United States becomes a party to this treaty, and that distributing free tobacco products does not constitute interstate commerce, should Congress have constitutional authority to pass a statute prohibiting distribution of free tobacco products?

C. Are There Limits to the Use of Congressional-Executive Agreements?

As noted above, the United States often makes and implements international law through sole executive and congressional-executive agreements. As the chart below indicates, the United States has greatly expanded its use of sole executive and congressional-executive agreements and has used the Article II process relatively less often over time.

Years	Article II Treaties	Sole Executive and Congressional-Executive Agreements
1789-1839	60	27
1839-1889	215	238
1889-1939	524	917
1940-1949	116	919
1950-1959	138	2,229
1960-1969	114	2,324
1970-1979	173	3,039
1980-1989	166	3,524
1990-1999	249	2,857
Totals	1,755	16,074

Figures derived from Committee on Foreign Relations, Treaties and Other International Agreements: The Role of the United States Senate, S. Rpt. 106-71, 106th Congress, 2d Sess. (2001).

The trend toward executive agreements is not uniform across all issue areas. For example, every arms control agreement since 1972 has been approved as a treaty, and human rights conventions have only been submitted as treaties. However, the political branches increasingly use congressional-executive agreements for many of the nation's most important international agreements, particularly in the economic area. For example, both the NAFTA and the Uruguay Round Agreements creating the WTO were approved via congressional-executive agreements. It is therefore important to examine why congressional-executive agreements have become so prominent, and whether there are constitutional limitations on their use.

Debates over the use of congressional-executive agreements arose as a number of international agreements were negotiated and institutions were created in the aftermath of World War II. In this context, with fresh memories that an isolationist minority in the Senate had rejected the Versailles Treaty and kept the United States out of the League of Nations, many believed that Article II's super-majority requirement was antidemocratic, unwise, or both. New Deal era scholars argued that a minority of senators should not be able to impose their isolationist preferences on a majority committed to U.S. engagement in international affairs.

In May 1945, the House approved a proposed constitutional amendment that provided for treaty approval by majority vote in both Houses of Congress. As the Senate sought to maintain its constitutional prerogative, the executive branch engineered a compromise by submitting the Bretton Woods Agreement establishing the World Bank and the International Monetary Fund as a congressional-executive agreement and submitting the more important UN Charter as a treaty.

Thereafter, the interchangeability thesis — the claim that congressional-executive agreements were legally equivalent to Article II treaties and that one was interchangeable with the other — gained currency. The conventional wisdom on this issue is captured by a comment to the Restatement (Third) of the Foreign Relations Law of the United States §303(e):

> Since any agreement concluded by Congressional-Executive Agreement could also be concluded by treaty . . . [t]he prevailing view is that the Congressional-Executive agreement can be used as an alternative to the treaty method in every instance. Which procedure should be used is a political judgment, made in the first instance by the President, subject to the possibility that the Senate might refuse to consider a joint resolution of Congress to approve an agreement, insisting that the President submit the agreement as a treaty.

For nearly half a century, this conventional wisdom was largely unquestioned in Congress. However, NAFTA opponents argued that this agreement could not properly be treated as a congressional-executive agreement and had to be submitted to the Senate as an Article II treaty. The ensuing debate raised the more general question of whether congressional-executive agreements were interchangeable with Article II treaties.

Harvard Law School Professor Laurence Tribe summarized the arguments against the interchangeability thesis in Senate testimony:

> In countering the claims of those who argue that congressional-executive agreements and treaties are wholly interchangeable, I find support in a variety of sources:
>
> In the leading Supreme Court case on treaties, *Missouri v. Holland*, the Court made clear — as everyone understands — that the treaty power and Congress's legislative power are not coextensive. The Constitution permits treaties to accomplish things that cannot be achieved through mere legislation. It necessarily follows that the treaty form and the congressional-executive agreement are not wholly interchangeable. . . .
>
> The State Department has issued guidelines for deciding whether a particular agreement should properly be negotiated and approved as a treaty. See 11 Foreign Affairs Manual, Chapter 700, 721.3 (codifying State Department Circular 175, December 13, 1955, as amended). [Circular 175 is a State Department document identifying "treaties" and "international agreements other than treaties" as the "two procedures under the Constitution through which the United States becomes a party to international agreement." Circular 175 lists a number of factors to be considered to determine which procedure to follow for any particular international agreement, including the extent to which the agreement involves commitments or risks affecting the nation as a whole; whether the agreement is intended to affect State laws; whether the agreement can be given effect without the enactment of subsequent legislation by the Congress; past U.S. practice as to similar agreements; Congressional preferences; and general international practice as to similar agreements.]
>
> All these sources support a conclusion that should be obvious from the mere existence of the Treaty Clause: the content and import of certain international agreements require that they be approved by two-thirds of Senators present. . . .
>
> The Constitution does not permit the Senate simply to abandon its constitutional role. . . . Those who would read the Treaty Clause out of the Constitution by appealing to past congressional practice (no matter how questionable that practice) essentially suggest that a period of disregard for constitutional text and structure may suffice in large part to erase the disregarded constitutional text or structure from the Constitution. If this becomes the accepted wisdom, then the Constitution will have failed in its central mission — to establish a framework for government that would outlast those who hold office at any given time. . . .
>
> State sovereignty concerns find special protection in the Treaty Clause because the Senate is the only body that represents the states as states, and the only body in which every state, from the smallest to the largest, is guaranteed equal representation. It is the

only national body in which all members are politically accountable to all the voters in their respective states. . . . [T]he Treaty Clause's provision for supermajority approval is an independent guarantee that particularly important international agreements — those that very significantly constrain U.S. sovereignty by seriously implicating normal state and federal lawmaking process — will be subject to especially serious deliberation and will be based upon especially strong national consensus.

GATT Implementing Legislation: Hearings Before the Senate Comm. on Commerce, Science, and Transportation on S. 2467, 103d Cong. 285 (1994).

The Clinton Administration responded to Professor Tribe's arguments in a memorandum prepared by the Justice Department:

As Secretary of State Dulles explained in testimony before the Senate Judiciary Committee in 1953, there is an

undefined, and probably undefinable, borderline between international agreements which require two-thirds Senate [c]oncurrence, but no House concurrence, as in the case of treaties, and agreements which should have the majority concurrence of both Chambers of Congress. . . . This is an area to be dealt with by friendly cooperation between the three departments of Government which are involved, rather than by attempts at constitutional definition, which are futile, or by the absorption, by one branch of Government, of responsibilities which are presently and properly shared.

. . . [T]he Constitution on its face permits foreign commerce to be regulated either through the Treaty Clause or through the Foreign Commerce Clause [which grants Congress power "to regulate Commerce with foreign Nations"]. Nothing in the language of the Constitution privileges the Treaty Clause as the "sole" or "exclusive" means of regulating such activity. In actual practice, Congress and the President, understanding that nothing in the Constitution constrained them to choose one procedure rather than the other, have followed different procedures on different occasions. . . .

In general, these inter- and intra-branch disputes over the scope of the Treaty Clause have been resolved through the political process, occasionally with marked departures from prior practices. . . .

The existence of such recurring disputes over the scope and meaning of the Treaty Clause undermines any dogmatic claim that a major trade agreement such as the Uruguay Round Agreements, which stands at the intersection of the foreign affairs, revenue raising and commerce powers, *must* be ratified as a treaty and *cannot* be implemented by the action of both Houses of Congress. The distinctions between the Federal government's treaty power and the other constitutional powers in play are simply too fluid and dynamic to dictate the conclusion that one method must be followed to the complete exclusion of the other. Here, if anywhere, is an area where the sound judgment of the political branches, acting in concert and accommodating the interests and prerogatives of one another, should be respected. . . .

18 Opinions of the Office of Legal Counsel, 232, 237, 239, 240 (1994).

Less than two weeks after the President submitted the NAFTA implementing legislation to Congress, the House of Representatives passed it by a vote of 234 to 200. Shortly thereafter, by a vote of 61-38, the Senate also passed the implementing legislation and resolved that "Congress approves . . . the North American Free Trade Act." On December 8, 1993, President Clinton signed the implementing legislation into law.

A group of national and local labor organizations and an NGO that promotes the purchase of American-made products challenged the constitutionality of

NAFTA. The district court in *Made in the USA Foundation v. United States*, 56 F. Supp. 2d 1226 (N.D. Ala. 1999), did not determine whether NAFTA was a full-fledged "treaty" for constitutional purposes. Rather, the court held that even if NAFTA is a "treaty," the Treaty Clause does not constitute the exclusive means of enacting international commercial agreements, given Congress's plenary powers to regulate foreign commerce under Art. I, §8, and the President's inherent authority under Article II to manage the nation's foreign affairs. Accordingly, the district court held that NAFTA's passage by simple majorities of both Houses of Congress was constitutionally sound.

On appeal, the 11th Circuit Court of Appeals affirmed the result, but on different grounds:

Made in the USA Foundation v. United States

242 F.3d 1300 (11th Cir. 2001)

The Constitution confers a vast amount of power upon the political branches of the federal government in the area of foreign policy — particularly foreign commerce. The breadth of the President's inherent powers in foreign affairs arises from his role as Chief Executive, U.S. Const. Art. II, §1, cl. 1, and as Commander in Chief, U.S. Const. Art. III, §2, cl. 1. In addition to his power to "make Treaties" with the advice and consent of two-thirds of the Senators present, the President's authority in foreign affairs is further bolstered by his power to "appoint Ambassadors . . . and Consuls," U.S. Const. Art. II, §2, cl. 2, and "to receive Ambassadors and other public Ministers," U.S. Const. Art. II, §3. Meanwhile, Congress's enumerated powers in the realm of external affairs include its power "to declare war," U.S. Const., Art. I, §8, cl. 11; "to raise and support armies," U.S. Const., Art. I, §8, cl. 12; "to provide and maintain a navy," U.S. Const., Art. I, §8, cl. 13; and the Senate's advice-and-consent role in the treaty-making process. Most significantly, the Constitution also confers on the entire Congress (and not just the Senate) authority "to regulate commerce with foreign nations," U.S. Const. Art. I, §8, cl. 3 — an express textual commitment that is directly relevant to international commercial agreements such as NAFTA. . . . .

These . . . broad textual grants of authority to the President and Congress in the areas of foreign affairs leave only a narrowly circumscribed role for the Judiciary. As the Supreme Court stated in *Oetjen v. Central Leather Co.*, 246 U.S. 297, 302 (1918), "[t]he conduct of the foreign relations of our government is committed by the Constitution to the executive and legislative — 'the political' — departments of the government, and the propriety of what may be done in the exercise of this political power is not subject to judicial inquiry or decision." . . .

. . . [I]n *Goldwater v. Carter*, [444 U.S. 996 (1979),] members of Congress challenged the President's unilateral termination of a mutual defense treaty with Taiwan (formerly known as the Republic of China). As in the present case, the crux of the challenge centered on the allegedly unconstitutional procedures used to abrogate the treaty, and not on the treaty's substantive provisions. A plurality of the Court determined that the case was nonjusticiable because the text of the Constitution failed to provide any guidance on the issue; joined by three other members of the Court, Justice Rehnquist noted that "while the Constitution is express as to the manner in which the Senate shall participate in the ratification of a treaty, it is silent as to the body's participation in the abrogation of a treaty." Justice Rehnquist thus concluded that "in light of the absence of any constitutional provision governing the termination of a treaty, and the fact that different termination procedures may be appropriate for different treaties . . . the instant case . . . must surely be controlled by political standards" rather than by judicial standards. . . .

While the nature of the issue presented in *Goldwater* differs somewhat from the present case, we nonetheless find the disposition in *Goldwater* instructive, if not controlling, for our purposes, in that the Supreme Court declined to act because the constitutional provision at issue does not provide an identifiable textual limit on the authority granted by the Constitution. Indeed, just as the Treaty Clause fails to outline the Senate's role in the abrogation of treaties, we find that the Treaty Clause also fails to outline the circumstances, if any, under which its procedures must be adhered to when approving international commercial agreements. . . .

In dismissing this case as a political question, we do not mean to suggest that the terms of the Treaty Clause effectively allow the political branches to exercise unfettered discretion in determining whether to subject a particular international agreement to the rigors of that Clause's procedural requirements; to state as much would be tantamount to rendering the terms of Art. II, §2, cl. 2 a dead letter. . . . We only conclude that in the context of international commercial agreements such as NAFTA—given the added factor of Congress's constitutionally-enumerated power to regulate commerce with foreign nations, as well as the lack of judicially manageable standards to determine when an agreement is significant enough to qualify as a "treaty"—the issue of what kinds of agreements require Senate ratification pursuant to the Art. II, §2 procedures presents a nonjusticiable political question.

Notes and Questions

1. The court says that its decision does not "allow the political branches unfettered discretion" in deciding whether or not to use the Article II treaty process. What limits does the decision impose upon the political branches?

2. Should there be different standards for judicial review of governmental actions in domestic and in foreign affairs cases? If so, what is different about governmental actions in the foreign relations area that justifies a reduced judicial role?

3. Are you more persuaded by Tribe's testimony or the administration's response? When determining the constitutionality of congressional-executive agreements, should more weight be given to constitutional text or to historical practice? Should it matter, for constitutional purposes, whether congressional approval is given ex ante, as is frequently the case for congressional-executive agreements, or ex post, as in the NAFTA case? Should courts or the political branches decide when Article II processes must be followed? For detailed treatments of the constitutional issues raised, see Bruce Ackerman & David Golove, *Is NAFTA Constitutional?*, 108 Harv. L. Rev. 799 (1995); Laurence H. Tribe, *Taking Text and Structure Seriously: Reflections on Free-Form Method in Constitutional Interpretation*, 108 Harv. L. Rev. 1221 (1995).

4. Who is advantaged and who disadvantaged by the diminished use of Article II processes and the increased use of congressional-executive agreements? Is one process more democratic than the other?

D. Are There Limits to the President's Power to Make International Agreements?

Many of the issues that NAFTA raises in the context of congressional-executive agreements also arise in the context of sole executive agreements. These are international agreements that presidents make on the basis of their constitutional authority, including their authority as chief executive to represent the nation in foreign affairs. Important sole executive agreements include the accords that ended the Spanish-American War and the destroyer-bases deal of 1940 with the United Kingdom, whereby the United States sent destroyers to the United Kingdom in exchange for the use of British military bases. In practice, issues regarding the scope and limits of presidential authority are commonly resolved through political processes, with courts rarely intervening. However, from time to time, the courts are asked to rule on the scope of the President's foreign affairs authority.

1. Resolving the Iran Hostage Crisis

On November 4, 1979, 52 Americans were taken hostage at the U.S. embassy in Tehran, Iran. This event sparked an extraordinary series of legal and diplomatic developments, some of which are explored elsewhere in this book. For present purposes, we focus on the President's legal authority to enter into an international agreement to end the hostage crisis.

For much of the postwar era, oil politics dominated U.S.-Iran relations. In 1951, a nationalist government led by Dr. Mohammed Mossadegh was elected to replace a government led by Shah Mohammed Reza Pahlavi. Mossadegh nationalized the oil industry in Iran and, facing strong opposition from the West, allied himself with the Tudeh (Communist) Party. In 1953, with strong U.S. support, the Shah led a coup that returned him to power. Thereafter, the United States provided economic and military assistance to the Shah's government. However, the Shah's attempts to "modernize" Iran, along with his increasingly authoritarian rule, sparked a strong backlash. By 1978 Iran was convulsed by riots, demonstrations, and strikes. Facing increasing domestic discontent and dwindling support from Iran's military, on January 16, 1979, the Shah fled Iran for Egypt.

Shortly thereafter, the U.S. government learned that the Shah had cancer and decided, on humanitarian grounds, to permit him to enter the United States for medical treatment.* Ironically, before admitting the Shah, the State Department feared that Americans in Iran might be taken hostage if the Shah were admitted into the United States; the Department requested, and received, assurances from the Iranian government that it would protect the U.S. Embassy from any attacks. On October 22, 1979, the Shah entered a New York City hospital. Two weeks later, a group of several hundred Iranian students seized the U.S. Embassy in Tehran and took hostage all diplomatic and consular personnel present. They demanded the Shah's extradition to Iran in return for the hostages' release.

On November 12, President Carter halted all oil imports from Iran, while keeping open the possibility of additional economic sanctions. On November 14, in response to reports that Iran would soon remove all its dollar deposits from U.S.

---

*The account that follows is drawn in part from American Hostages in Iran: The Conduct of a Crisis (Warren Christopher et al, eds. 1985); Jimmy Carter, Keeping the Faith: Memoirs of a President (1982); Hamilton Jordan, Crisis: The Last Year of the Carter Presidency (1982); and Cyrus Vance, Hard Choices: Critical Years in America's Foreign Policy (1983).

banks, President Carter froze all Iranian assets in U.S. banks. U.S. officials worried that U.S. businesses harmed by the deteriorating relations might sue Iran in U.S. courts and seek to satisfy any judgments out of the frozen funds. The freeze order thus prohibited any action that would affect title to the frozen Iranian assets. Regulations implementing the freeze order permitted the preliminary phases of litigation against Iran to proceed — including the filing of prejudgment attachments — while prohibiting the entry of final judgments.

In late November, the United States filed suit against Iran at the ICJ and sought an interim order that Iran release the hostages. On December 15, 1979, the ICJ issued a provisional order that Iran should immediately release the hostages and that neither government should take any action that might "aggravate the tension between the two countries or render the existing dispute more difficult" to resolve. Iran failed to release the hostages.

On April 11, 1980, President Carter approved plans for a military rescue operation. On April 24, eight U.S. military helicopters took off from the USS *Nimitz*. Due to mechanical problems, three of the helicopters were unable to continue, and the mission commander aborted the operation. During refueling operations in Iranian territory preparatory to withdrawal, one of the remaining helicopters collided with a C-130 refueling aircraft, which immediately burst into flames. Eight crew members died and five were injured. The remaining helicopters were abandoned, and the force withdrew on board the C-130s.

After the failed rescue mission, secret discussions began between U.S. bank lawyers and Iranian representatives. During extensive negotiating sessions, the banks proposed a plan where the United States would lift the freeze on overseas Iranian assets — totaling approximately $5.6 billion — upon the release of the hostages, and Iran would pay its dollar debts to U.S. banks from these funds. The banks would then release their attachments on domestic deposits, thus freeing them up for satisfaction of non-bank claims. These negotiations continued through the fall and winter of 1980.

On September 9, 1980, the government of Iran, acting through German intermediaries, for the first time expressed a desire to open negotiations with the U.S. government, and secret meetings began. On September 19, the Iran-Iraq war began, greatly increasing the cost of Iran's diplomatic isolation, its inability to obtain spare military parts, and the various economic sanctions. At this point, in return for the hostages, Iran sought a return of the Shah's property, return of the frozen assets, cancellation of all claims against Iran, and a U.S. pledge not to intervene in Iranian affairs.

However, Iran refused to negotiate with the United States directly and designated the Algerian government as the official intermediary through which negotiations would be conducted. Thereafter, a series of proposals and counter-proposals were conveyed through Algerian diplomats. The pace of negotiations quickened in late November and early December and, by early January 1981, the banks, the U.S. government, the Iranian government, and the Algerian government were engaged in round-the-clock negotiations in Washington, London, New York, Algiers, and Tehran. By January 6, the gap between the parties' proposals had narrowed considerably, with Iran demanding $9.5 billion and the United States offering $7.3 billion. On January 11, President-elect Reagan announced that if the hostage crisis was not resolved by the time he took office, he would approach the situation with a "clean slate," meaning that any prior agreements would be off the table. On January 15, Iran reduced the amount of cash it demanded be returned and committed to paying off certain international loans. With these concessions and with round-the-clock work by bankers, accountants, lawyers, and government officials, a series of complex agreements — the Algiers Accords — were completed a day before President Reagan assumed office. Because Iran would not sign an agreement with the United States, the Algiers Accords consist of "Declarations" by the Algerian government to be "adhered to" by Iran and the United States.

The Algiers Accords provide, in relevant part, that:

> On the basis of formal adherences received from Iran and the United States, the Government of Algeria now declares that the following interdependent commitments have been made by the two Governments: . . .
> A. . . . [T]he United States will restore the financial position of Iran, insofar as possible, to that which existed prior to November 14, 1979. In this context, the United States commits itself to insure the mobility and free transfer of all Iranian assets within its jurisdiction. . . .
> B. It is the purpose of both parties . . . to terminate all litigation as between the government of each party and the nationals of the other, and to bring about the settlement and termination of all such claims through binding arbitration. Through the procedures provided in the Declaration relating to the Claims Settlement Agreement, the United States agrees to terminate all legal proceedings in United States courts involving claims of United States persons and institutions against Iran and its state enterprises, to nullify all attachments and judgments obtained therein, to prohibit all further litigation based on such claims, and to bring about the termination of such claims through binding arbitration. . . .

Nullification of Sanctions and Claims

> 10. Upon [Algeria's certification that the U.S. hostages have safely departed Iran,] the United States will revoke all trade sanctions which were directed against Iran in the period Nov. 4, 1979, to date.

Through a separate document, entitled Settlement of Claims, the United States and Iran agreed to create an international arbitral tribunal (the Iran-U.S. Claims Tribunal) to decide "claims of nationals of the United States against Iran and claims of nationals of Iran against the United States" as well as "official claims of the United States and Iran against each other arising out of contractual arrangements between them for the purchase and sale of goods and services."

The Algiers Accords provided for a complex series of fund transfers and creation of various escrow accounts. Pursuant to the Accords, on January 20, 1981, in excess of $8 billion held by the Federal Reserve Bank and overseas branches of U.S. banks was transferred to escrow accounts at the Central Bank of Algiers and, minutes after President Reagan assumed office, Iran released the hostages. After the hostages were released, over $3 billion of the escrow funds were used to pay off in full all syndicated Iranian loans in which U.S. banks participated. One billion dollars was transferred to a separate escrow account, established in the Netherlands, to be used to secure the payment by Iran of awards rendered by the Claims Tribunal in favor of the U.S. government or its nationals. Under the Accords, Iran is obligated to replenish this account "promptly" if it falls below $500 million.

2. Challenging the President's Authority

In December 1979, Dames & Moore, a U.S. company, filed suit in federal district court against the government of Iran for breach of a contract to perform site studies for a proposed nuclear power plant in Iran. Dames & Moore obtained a pre-judgment attachment against Iranian property. On January 27, 1981, less than two weeks after the Algiers Accords were signed and President Carter had issued executive orders transferring the frozen assets pursuant to the Accords, Dames & Moore moved for summary judgment. The district court granted this motion and awarded Dames & Moore $3.4 million in damages plus interest. The government of Iran appealed, and the district court stayed execution of its judgment and vacated all pre-judgment attachments. Dames & Moore then filed an action for declaratory and injunctive relief against the United States to prevent enforcement of the executive orders implementing the Algiers Accords. The case quickly made its way to the Supreme Court, which, eight days after oral argument, issued a unanimous opinion on the President's ability to suspend claims against Iran pending in U.S. courts.

Dames & Moore v. Regan

453 U.S. 654 (1981)

JUSTICE REHNQUIST delivered the opinion of the Court.

The questions presented by this case touch fundamentally upon the manner in which our Republic is to be governed. . . .

On February 24, 1981, President Reagan issued an Executive Order in which he "ratified" [President Carter's] January 19th Executive Orders [implementing the terms of the Algiers Accords]. Moreover, he "suspended" all "claims which may be presented to the . . . Tribunal" and provided that such claims "shall have no legal effect in any action now pending in any court of the United States." The suspension of any particular claim terminates if the Claims Tribunal determines that it has no jurisdiction over that claim; claims are discharged for all purposes when the Claims Tribunal either awards some recovery and that amount is paid, or determines that no recovery is due. . . .

II

[Dames & Moore argued that the President's executive orders implementing the Algiers Accords exceeded his statutory and constitutional powers.] The parties and the lower courts, confronted with the instant questions, have all agreed that much relevant analysis is contained in *Youngstown Sheet & Tube Co.* v. *Sawyer*, 343 U.S. 579 (1952). . . . Justice Jackson's concurring opinion elaborated in a general way the consequences of different types of interaction between the two democratic branches in assessing Presidential authority to act in any given case. When the President acts pursuant to an express or implied authorization from Congress, he exercises not only his powers but also those delegated by Congress. In such a case the executive action "would be supported by the strongest of presumptions and the widest latitude of judicial interpretation, and the burden of persuasion would rest heavily upon any who might attack it." When the President acts in the absence of congressional authorization he may enter "a zone of twilight in which he and Congress may have concurrent authority, or in which its distribution is uncertain." In such a case the analysis becomes more complicated, and the validity of the President's action, at least so far as separation-of-powers principles are concerned, hinges on a consideration of all the circumstances which might shed light on the views of the Legislative Branch toward such action, including "congressional

inertia, indifference or quiescence." Finally, when the President acts in contravention of the will of Congress, "his power is at its lowest ebb," and the Court can sustain
his actions "only by disabling the Congress from acting upon the subject."

Although we have in the past found and do today find Justice Jackson's classification of executive actions into three general categories analytically useful, we
should be mindful of Justice Holmes' admonition . . . that "[t]he great ordinances
of the Constitution do not establish and divide fields of black and white." Justice
Jackson himself recognized that his three categories represented "a somewhat over-
simplified grouping," and it is doubtless the case that executive action in any particular instance falls, not neatly in one of three pigeonholes, but rather at some point
along a spectrum running from explicit congressional authorization to explicit
congressional prohibition. . . .

IV

[The Court examined the International Emergency Economic Powers Act
(IEEPA), which authorizes the President to "nullify" or "void" transactions involving "property in which any foreign country" or national has an interest, and found
that it constitutes specific congressional authorization to the President to nullify the
attachments and order the transfer of Iranian assets.] [T]here remains the question
of the President's authority to suspend claims pending in American courts. Such
claims have, of course, an existence apart from the attachments which accompanied
them. In terminating these claims through Executive Order, the President purported to act under authority of both the IEEPA and the so-called "Hostage Act."

We conclude that . . . the IEEPA . . . cannot be read to authorize the suspension of the claims. The claims of American citizens against Iran are not in themselves transactions involving Iranian property or efforts to exercise any rights with
respect to such property. An *in personam* lawsuit, although it might eventually be
reduced to judgment and that judgment might be executed upon, is an effort to
establish liability and fix damages and does not focus on any particular property
within the jurisdiction. The terms of the IEEPA therefore do not authorize the
President to suspend claims in American courts. . . .

[The Court also analyzed the Hostage Act, which provides that when "any citizen of the United States has been unjustly deprived of his liberty by or under the
authority of any foreign government, . . . the President shall use such means . . . as
he may think necessary and proper to obtain or effectuate [their] release." Relying
upon legislative history, the Court concluded that this Act also does not authorize
the President to suspend the claims.]

Concluding that neither the IEEPA nor the Hostage Act constitutes specific
authorization of the President's action suspending claims, however, is not to say
that these statutory provisions are entirely irrelevant to the question of the validity
of the President's action. We think both statutes highly relevant in the looser sense
of indicating congressional acceptance of a broad scope for executive action in
circumstances such as those presented in this case. . . . [T]he IEEPA delegates
broad authority to the President to act in times of national emergency with respect
to property of a foreign country. The Hostage Act similarly indicates congressional
willingness that the President have broad discretion when responding to the hostile
acts of foreign sovereigns. . . .

Although we have declined to conclude that the IEEPA or the Hostage Act
directly authorizes the President's suspension of claims for the reasons noted, we

cannot ignore the general tenor of Congress' legislation in this area in trying to determine whether the President is acting alone or at least with the acceptance of Congress. As we have noted, Congress cannot anticipate and legislate with regard to every possible action the President may find it necessary to take or every possible situation in which he might act. Such failure of Congress specifically to delegate authority does not, "especially . . . in the areas of foreign policy and national security," imply "congressional disapproval" of action taken by the Executive. On the contrary, the enactment of legislation closely related to the question of the President's authority in a particular case which evinces legislative intent to accord the President broad discretion may be considered to "invite" "measures on independent presidential responsibility," *Youngstown*, 343 U.S., at 637 (Jackson, J., concurring). At least this is so where there is no contrary indication of legislative intent and when, as here, there is a history of congressional acquiescence in conduct of the sort engaged in by the President. It is to that history which we now turn.

Not infrequently in affairs between nations, outstanding claims by nationals of one country against the government of another country are "sources of friction" between the two sovereigns. To resolve these difficulties, nations have often entered into agreements settling the claims of their respective nationals. . . . Consistent with that principle, the United States has repeatedly exercised its sovereign authority to settle the claims of its nationals against foreign countries. Though those settlements have sometimes been made by treaty, there has also been a longstanding practice of settling such claims by executive agreement without the advice and consent of the Senate. Under such agreements, the President has agreed to renounce or extinguish claims of United States nationals against foreign governments in return for lump-sum payments or the establishment of arbitration procedures. . . . It is clear that the practice of settling claims continues today. Since 1952, the President has entered into at least 10 binding settlements with foreign nations, including an $80 million settlement with the People's Republic of China.

Crucial to our decision today is the conclusion that Congress has implicitly approved the practice of claim settlement by executive agreement. This is best demonstrated by Congress' enactment of the International Claims Settlement Act of 1949. The Act had two purposes: (1) to allocate to United States nationals funds received in the course of an executive claims settlement with Yugoslavia, and (2) to provide a procedure whereby funds resulting from future settlements could be distributed. To achieve these ends Congress created the International Claims Commission, now the Foreign Claims Settlement Commission, and gave it jurisdiction to make final and binding decisions with respect to claims by United States nationals against settlement funds. By creating a procedure to implement future settlement agreements, Congress placed its stamp of approval on such agreements. . . .

Over the years Congress has frequently amended the International Claims Settlement Act to [implement settlement agreements with other states] thus demonstrating Congress' continuing acceptance of the President's claim settlement authority. . . .

In light of all of the foregoing — the inferences to be drawn from the character of the legislation Congress has enacted in the area, such as the IEEPA and the Hostage Act, and from the history of acquiescence in executive claims settlement — we conclude that the President was authorized to suspend pending claims pursuant to Executive Order No. 12294. As Justice Frankfurter pointed out in *Youngstown*, "a systematic, unbroken, executive practice, long pursued to the knowledge of the Congress and never before questioned . . . may be treated as a gloss on

'Executive Power' vested in the President by §1 of Art. II." Past practice does not, by itself, create power, but "long-continued practice, known to and acquiesced in by Congress, would raise a presumption that the [action] had been [taken] in pursuance of its consent. . . ." *United States v. Midwest Oil Co.*, 236 U.S. 459, 474 (1915). Such practice is present here and such a presumption is also appropriate. In light of the fact that Congress may be considered to have consented to the President's action in suspending claims, we cannot say that action exceeded the President's powers.

Our conclusion is buttressed by the fact that the means chosen by the President to settle the claims of American nationals provided an alternative forum, the Claims Tribunal, which is capable of providing meaningful relief. The Solicitor General also suggests that the provision of the Claims Tribunal will actually *enhance* the opportunity for claimants to recover their claims, in that the Agreement removes a number of jurisdictional and procedural impediments faced by claimants in United States courts. Although being overly sanguine about the chances of United States claimants before the Claims Tribunal would require a degree of naiveté which should not be demanded even of judges, the Solicitor General's point cannot be discounted. Moreover, it is important to remember that we have already held that the President has the *statutory* authority to nullify attachments and to transfer the assets out of the country. The President's power to do so does not depend on his provision of a forum whereby claimants can recover on those claims. The fact that the President has provided such a forum here means that the claimants are receiving something in return for the suspension of their claims, namely, access to an international tribunal before which they may well recover something on their claims. Because there does appear to be a real "settlement" here, this case is more easily analogized to the more traditional claim settlement cases of the past.

Just as importantly, Congress has not disapproved of the action taken here. Though Congress has held hearings on the Iranian Agreement itself, Congress has not enacted legislation, or even passed a resolution, indicating its displeasure with the Agreement. Quite the contrary, the relevant Senate Committee has stated that the establishment of the Tribunal is "of vital importance to the United States." We are thus clearly not confronted with a situation in which Congress has in some way resisted the exercise of Presidential authority.

Finally, we re-emphasize the narrowness of our decision. We do not decide that the President possesses plenary power to settle claims, even as against foreign governmental entities. . . . But where, as here, the settlement of claims has been determined to be a necessary incident to the resolution of a major foreign policy dispute between our country and another, and where, as here, we can conclude that Congress acquiesced in the President's action, we are not prepared to say that the President lacks the power to settle such claims.

Notes and Questions

1. Given the express terms of the Algiers Accords, is the Court correct that the plaintiff's claims were simply "suspend[ed]"?

2. Is the Court correct to read congressional silence as acquiescence? Is the Court in effect granting the President plenary discretion over foreign affairs as long as Congress lacks the votes to override a presidential veto of restrictive legislation?

3. Was the President's action upheld as part of his inherent foreign affairs power, or on the basis of congressional authorization? Could a sole executive agreement override an earlier federal statute?

4. What would have happened if the Court had found in favor of Dames & Moore? Would this have undermined the Algiers Accords? By the time the case was decided, the hostages had, of course, already returned home, and the assets had already been released.

5. Following this decision, Dames & Moore pursued its claims at the Iran-U.S. Claims Tribunal and was awarded $208,435, plus interest. The Iran-U.S. Claims Tribunal is discussed in Chapter 12.

6. In late 2000, a suit was filed on behalf of the 52 embassy employees who had been taken hostage in Tehran. The district court entered a default judgment in favor of the plaintiffs. Shortly thereafter, the U.S. government intervened to request that the judgment be vacated and the case dismissed on the grounds that the suit was barred by the Algiers Accords. While this motion was pending, Congress passed an appropriations bill that included a provision addressing this specific case. P.L. 107-77, Sec. 626(c). A conference committee statement explained that this provision "acknowledges that notwithstanding any other authority, the American citizens who were taken hostage by Iran . . . have a claim against Iran." In signing the bill, President Bush noted this provision and stated that "[t]o the extent permitted by applicable law, the executive branch will act, and will encourage the courts to act . . . in a manner consistent with the obligations of the United States under the Algiers Accords. . . ." Thereafter, the district court granted the government's motion and dismissed the suit, relying in part on the Algiers Accords. *Roeder v. Iran*, 195 F. Supp. 2d 140 (D.D.C. 2002), *aff'd*, 333 F.3d 228 (D.C. Cir. 2003), *cert. denied*, 542 U.S. 915 (2004). The mixed legacy of efforts to sue states involved in terrorist activities is discussed in Chapter 6.

7. The IEEPA was amended after the September 11, 2001, attacks to authorize the President to "confiscate" any property of a foreign entity or state that has attacked or is engaged in armed hostilities against the United States. In March 2003, President George W. Bush used this authority to confiscate approximately $1.7 billion in Iraqi assets that had previously been frozen under IEEPA. Some of these assets were to be used for the reconstruction of Iraq.

III. BREAKING INTERNATIONAL LAW: CONSULAR NOTIFICATION AND THE ARREST OF FOREIGN NATIONALS

What should happen if a state's domestic law conflicts with its international legal obligations? Article 27 of the Vienna Convention on the Law of Treaties provides that a state "may not invoke the provisions of its internal law as justification for its failure to perform a treaty." Domestic law may, however, suggest a different approach to conflicting domestic and international legal obligations. While the Supremacy Clause of the U.S. Constitution states that both statutes and treaties are the supreme law of the land, it is silent on how to resolve a conflict between these two sources of law (and on the status of custom as domestic law). In the treaty context, the Supreme Court has long applied the "later in time" rule, meaning that "[a] treaty may supersede a prior act of Congress, and an act of Congress may supersede a prior treaty." *The Cherokee Tobacco,* 78 U.S. (11 Wall.) 616, 621 (1870).

Of course, a subsequent federal statute does not extinguish the nation's international legal obligation. As Secretary of State Charles Evans Hughes wrote, "Congress has the power to violate treaties, but if they are violated, the Nation will be none the less exposed to all the international consequences of such a violation because the action is taken by the legislative branch of the Government." As a result, courts have often sought to minimize the conflict between U.S. law and international law. Over two centuries ago, the Supreme Court stated that, "an Act of Congress ought never to be construed to violate the law of nations if any other possible construction remains." *Murray v. Schooner Charming Betsy,* 6 U.S. (2 Cranch) 64, 118 (1804). In the materials that follow, we examine how courts respond when confronted with international legal norms and apparently inconsistent federal law.

A. The Problem

On the evening of June 24, 1993, Jose Ernesto Medellín participated in the brutal rape and murder of two teenage girls in Houston, Texas. Shortly thereafter, Medellín and other gang members were arrested by Texas police. Medellín is a Mexican citizen. Mexico, the United States, and 165 other states are parties to the Vienna Convention on Consular Relations, 596 U.N.T.S. 261, which expressly provides that foreign nationals have the right, upon arrest, to contact their consulate and to have consular officials notified of the arrest. (Consular officials are employed by foreign governments to provide assistance on behalf of that government to that government's citizens in a foreign country.) As Texas officials would later concede, Medellín was not advised of his Vienna Convention rights at the time of his arrest.

At trial, Medellín's confession to the crime was admitted into evidence. On September 16, 1994, Medellín was convicted of capital murder and, upon the jury's recommendation, on October 11, 1994, the trial court sentenced Medellín to death. On March 16, 1997, the Texas Court of Criminal Appeals affirmed Medellín's conviction and sentence. Medellín did not raise a claim based on Texas's failure to advise him of his treaty rights at trial or on appeal. In April 1997, some six weeks after the affirmance of his death sentence on direct appeal, Mexican consular officials first learned of Medellín's arrest, detention, trial, conviction, and sentence.

On March 26, 1998, Medellín filed a state habeas corpus petition, alleging for the first time the violation of his Vienna Convention rights. In January 2001, the state trial-level habeas court recommended to the Texas Court of Criminal Appeals that Medellín's application be denied on the grounds that Medellín's Vienna Convention claim was barred because it had not been raised at trial. In October 2001, the Texas Court of Criminal Appeals denied Medellín's petition.

In November 2001, Medellín filed a federal habeas corpus petition, again raising a Vienna Convention claim. On June 26, 2003, the district court denied relief; the court held that Medellín had defaulted his Vienna Convention claim under the procedural default rule* used by the Texas state system and, in any event, that the Vienna Convention did not create judicially enforceable rights.

---

*Under procedural default rules applied in state and federal courts, a criminal defendant who could have raised, but fails to raise, a legal issue at trial will generally not be permitted to raise it in future proceedings, including on appeal or in a habeas corpus petition.

On January 9, 2003, while Medellín's federal habeas petition was pending, Mexico filed suit against the United States in the International Court of Justice (ICJ), alleging violations of the Vienna Convention in the cases of Medellín and 53 other Mexican nationals who had been sentenced to death in state criminal proceedings in the United States. *Avena and other Mexican Nationals (Mexico v. United States of America).* ICJ jurisdiction was based upon Article I of the Optional Protocol to the Vienna Convention, which provides that "[d]isputes arising out of the interpretation or application of the [Vienna Convention on Consular Relations] shall lie within the compulsory jurisdiction of the [ICJ]." Both Mexico and the United States were parties to the Optional Protocol at the time Mexico initiated this suit.

Mexico requested, among other relief, the annulment of the convictions and sentences of the 54 Mexicans and a declaration that procedural default rules may not be applied to prevent redress of Vienna Convention violations. Mexico also sought provisional measures, a form of interim relief akin to a preliminary injunction, preventing the execution of Mexican nationals pending the Court's final judgment.

B. Addressing Conflicts Between International and Domestic Legal Obligations

Mexico's suit was the third in a trilogy of ICJ cases involving United States breaches of the Vienna Convention. Domestic court litigations involving U.S. breaches of the Vienna Convention squarely raise questions regarding conflicting domestic and international legal norms, and related questions concerning the status of ICJ orders as a matter of domestic law.

1. The Execution of Angel Breard

The first ICJ action against the United States for noncompliance with the Vienna Convention involved Angel Breard, a Paraguayan citizen who was convicted of capital murder. At the time of his arrest, Virginia authorities failed to advise Breard of his Vienna Convention rights. Breard testified at his trial, against the advice of his court-appointed attorneys. Breard admitted that he committed the murder, but claimed he did so under the influence of a satanic curse placed on him by his ex-wife's father. The jury found Breard guilty of capital murder and attempted rape, and Breard was sentenced to death.

Breard did not raise his Vienna Convention claim at trial, on appeal, or in state habeas corpus proceedings. He raised his treaty claim for the first time in a federal habeas petition filed three years after his conviction. His petition was denied, and Virginia set an execution date of April 14, 1998.

On April 3, 1998, Paraguay filed suit against the United States in the ICJ, requesting that Breard's conviction and sentence be voided. Paraguay also requested that the Court indicate provisional measures directing the United States to ensure that Breard not be executed pending the Court's determination of the case. Six days later, the ICJ unanimously indicated that "[t]he United States should take all measures at its disposal to ensure that [Breard] is not executed pending the final decision in these proceedings. . . ." Immediately thereafter, both Breard and Paraguay sought relief from the U.S. Supreme Court.

On April 13, the U.S. Secretary of State wrote to Virginia's Governor, request-ing that Virginia stay the execution:

> In light of the [International] Court's request, the unique and difficult foreign policy issues, and other problems created by the Court's provisional measures, I . . . request that you exercise your powers as Governor and stay Mr. Breard's execution. . . .
> I am particularly concerned about the possible negative consequences for the many U.S. citizens who live and travel abroad. The execution of Mr. Breard in the present circumstances could lead some countries to contend incorrectly that the U.S. does not take seriously its obligations under the Convention. The immediate execution of Mr. Breard in the face of the Court's April 9 action could be seen as a denial by the United States of the significance of international law and the Court's processes in its international relations and thereby limit our ability to ensure that Americans are pro-tected when living or traveling abroad.

At the same time, the Departments of State and Justice submitted an amicus brief to the Supreme Court urging the Court to deny Breard's petition. After arguing that provisional measures orders are not binding, the brief stated:

> Finally, even if [ICJ provisional measures are binding], the ICJ's order in this case does not require *this Court* to stop Breard's execution. That order states that the United States "should" take all measures "at its disposal" to ensure that Breard is not executed.
> . . . [T]he "measures at [the Government's] disposal" are a matter of domestic United States law, and our federal system imposes limits on the federal government's ability to interfere with the criminal justice systems of the States. The "measures at [the United States'] disposal" under our Constitution may in some cases include only per-suasion — such as the Secretary of State's request to the Governor of Virginia to stay Breard's execution — and not legal compulsion through the judicial system. That is the situation here. Accordingly, the ICJ's order does not provide an independent basis for this Court either to grant certiorari or to stay the execution.

On April 14, 1998 — less than one hour before the scheduled execution — the Supreme Court issued its opinion:

Breard v. Greene, The Republic of Paraguay v. Gilmore

523 U.S. 371 (1998)

PER CURIAM.

It is clear that Breard procedurally defaulted his claim, if any, under the Vienna Convention by failing to raise that claim in the state courts. Nevertheless . . . both Breard and Paraguay contend that Breard's Vienna Convention claim may be heard in federal court because the Convention is the "supreme law of the land" and thus trumps the procedural default doctrine. This argument is plainly incorrect for two reasons.

First, while we should give respectful consideration to the interpretation of an international treaty rendered by an international court, . . . it has been recognized in international law that . . . the procedural rules of the forum State govern the implementation of the treaty in that State. This proposition is embodied in [Article 36(2) of] the Vienna Convention itself, which provides that the rights expressed in the Convention "shall be exercised in conformity with the laws and regulations of the receiving State," provided that "said laws and regulations must enable full effect to be given to the purposes for which the rights accorded under this Article are intended." It is the rule in this country that assertions of error in criminal proceedings must first be raised in state court in order to form the basis for relief in habeas. Claims not so raised are considered defaulted. By not asserting his Vienna Convention claim in state court, Breard failed to exercise his rights under the Vienna Convention in conformity with the laws of the United States and the Commonwealth of Virginia. Having failed to do so, he cannot raise a claim of violation of those rights now on federal habeas review.

Second, although treaties are recognized by our Constitution as the supreme law of the land . . . [w]e have held "that an Act of Congress . . . is on a full parity with a treaty, and that when a statute which is subsequent in time is inconsistent with a treaty, the statute to the extent of conflict renders the treaty null." *Reid v. Covert*, 354 U.S. 1, 18 (1957). The Vienna Convention — which arguably confers on an individual the right to consular assistance following arrest — has continuously been in effect since 1969. But in 1996, before Breard filed his habeas petition raising claims under the Vienna Convention, Congress enacted the Antiterrorism and Effective Death Penalty Act (AEDPA), which provides that a habeas petitioner alleging that he is held in violation of "treaties of the United States" will, as a general rule, not be afforded an evidentiary hearing if he "has failed to develop the factual basis of [the] claim in State court proceedings." Breard's ability to obtain relief based on violations of the Vienna Convention is subject to this subsequently-enacted rule, just as any [other] claim . . . would be. This rule prevents Breard from establishing that the violation of his Vienna Convention rights prejudiced him. . . .

It is unfortunate that this matter comes before us while proceedings are pending before the ICJ that might have been brought to that court earlier. Nonetheless, this Court must decide questions presented to it on the basis of law. . . . Last night the Secretary of State sent a letter to the Governor of Virginia requesting that he stay Breard's execution. If the Governor wishes to wait for the decision of the ICJ, that is his prerogative. But nothing in our existing case law allows us to make that choice for him.

Immediately after the Court's decision was issued, Virginia's Governor released the following statement:

> I am concerned that to delay Mr. Breard's execution so that the International Court of Justice may review this matter would have the practical effect of transferring responsibility from the courts of the Commonwealth and the United States to the International Court. . . .
>
> [T]he International Court of Justice has no authority to interfere with our criminal justice system. Indeed, the safety of those residing in the Commonwealth of Virginia is not the responsibility of the International Court of Justice. It is my responsibility and the responsibility of law enforcement and judicial officials throughout the Commonwealth. I cannot cede such responsibility to the International Court of Justice.

Breard was executed later that evening. The following day, the State Department's Legal Adviser wrote to the International Court of Justice, stating that "[t]hrough its actions, culminating in the Secretary of State's April 13 request to the Governor of Virginia to stay Mr. Breard's execution on account of this Court's indication of provisional measures, the United States took all measures lawfully at its disposal to do what the Court requested." In November 1998, Paraguay withdrew its request that the ICJ issue a final ruling on the merits, and the case was removed from the ICJ's docket. Contemporaneous press reports suggest that the United States withdrew a threat to impose trade sanctions on Paraguay for its alleged failure to protect intellectual property in exchange for Paraguay's decision to discontinue the ICJ action, although officials from both the United States and Paraguay publicly denied any linkage.

Notes and Questions

1. Given Breard's decision to testify at his trial, against the advice of counsel, what harm resulted from the failure to notify Breard of his Vienna Convention rights?

2. When the Supreme Court states in *Breard* that it "must decide questions presented on the basis of law," which law should it use — the Vienna Convention on Consular Relations, or the domestic "last in time" rule? Under the "last in time" rule, should the 1996 AEDPA trump the 1969 Vienna Convention, or should the ICJ's 1998 order in the *Paraguay* case trump the AEDPA?

3. Did the *Breard* Court adequately address the competing foreign relations and domestic federalism interests at stake? Is the Court the appropriate body to engage in this balancing process? Why did the executive branch, in effect, concede to state officials, such as Virginia's Governor, power to breach the United States' international legal obligations?

4. Do you think that the United States took "all measures . . . at is disposal" to comply with the ICJ order in the *Paraguay* case, or, more broadly, with the Vienna Convention? In an October 2005 report, the U.S. State Department stated that, since 1998, it had distributed to federal, state and local law enforcement over 1,000,000 training videos, booklets and pocket cards that provide instructions for arrests and detentions of foreign nationals, and conducted over 350 training seminars on consular notification and access throughout the United States and its territories. Do these acts satisfy U.S. obligations under the Convention? Should Congress act in this area?

2. The *LaGrand* Case

In January 1982, Karl and Walter LaGrand were arrested in Arizona for committing murder and other crimes in connection with an attempted bank robbery. Both were German citizens, but neither was advised of his Vienna Convention rights at the time of the arrest. The LaGrands were subsequently convicted and sentenced to death. Invoking the procedural default doctrine, courts rejected Karl LaGrand's efforts to raise a Vienna Convention claim in collateral attacks upon his conviction and sentence. On February 24, 1999, Karl LaGrand was executed.

Walter LaGrand's execution was scheduled for March 3, 1999. On March 2, 1999, Germany filed an action in the ICJ and sought provisional measures against the United States. On March 3, the Court indicated provisional measures ordering the United States to "take all measures at its disposal to ensure that Walter LaGrand is not executed pending the final decision in these proceedings" and to "transmit this Order to the Governor of the State of Arizona." Later that same day, the U.S. Supreme Court rejected efforts by Germany and LaGrand to enforce compliance with the ICJ order, *Germany v. U.S.*, 526 U.S. 111 (1999), and Walter LaGrand was executed.

Unlike Paraguay, Germany did not discontinue its ICJ action and, in June 2001, the Court issued a final judgment on the merits. *LaGrand Case (Germany v. United States)*, 2001 I.C.J. 466. The Court held that the failure to notify the LaGrands of their Vienna Convention rights violated U.S. obligations under the treaty to Germany and the LaGrand brothers. Turning to the "procedural default" rule, the Court emphasized that "a distinction must be drawn between the rule as such and its specific application in the present case." The Court determined that on the facts of this case, the "procedural default" rule prevented U.S. courts from "attaching any legal significance" to the treaty violation, and therefore that application of the rule itself violated the Vienna Convention.

In addition, the Court decided, for the first time ever, that an order indicating provisional measures is "binding" and, in this case, "created a legal obligation for the United States." The Court held that the government's actions of (a) simply forwarding the Court's order to Arizona's governor, "without even so much as a plea for a temporary stay," (b) stating to the U.S. Supreme Court that "an order of the [ICJ] indicating provisional measures is not binding," and (c) the Supreme Court's summary rejection of Germany's application for a stay of execution constituted a failure by "the various competent United States authorities . . . to take all the steps they could have taken to give effect to the Court's Order."

Notes and Questions

1. What is an appropriate remedy for a breach of the Vienna Convention? In oral arguments in *LaGrand*, Germany asked for "an adequate assurance that [the United States] will not repeat its unlawful acts, and that in the future it will ensure in law and practice the effective exercise of the rights under Article 36 of the Vienna Convention. . . ." The United States replied that it had conveyed to Germany "the apologies and regrets of the United States" regarding the treaty breach, that it had taken efforts to improve compliance with the treaty, and that these acts were adequate satisfaction. Do you agree that these acts by the United States are sufficient? If not, what else should the United States do?

2. *LaGrand* explicitly states that the right to consular notification and access is an individual right. In a case decided a month after *LaGrand*, the Tenth Circuit stated that "it remains an open question whether the Vienna Convention gives rise to any individually enforceable rights"; three months later, the Second Circuit opined that the Vienna Convention does not create judicially enforceable rights. Can these opinions be reconciled with *LaGrand*? If aggrieved individuals lack judicially enforceable rights, what incentive do federal or state officials have to advise foreign nationals of their Vienna Convention rights?

3. *LaGrand*'s holding that provisional measures impose binding legal obligations is one of the most significant parts of the Court's judgment. Do you think this holding will lead to increased compliance with provisional measures? Or might the relatively poor record of compliance with provisional measures prompt the Court to become less willing to grant requests for provisional measures?

3. *Avena* and Its Aftermath

On February 5, 2003, a unanimous ICJ granted Mexico's request for provisional measures and ordered the United States to "take all measures necessary" to prevent the executions of three Mexican nationals who were "at risk of execution in the coming months." On March 31, 2004, the Court issued a final judgment in *Avena*.

Case Concerning Avena and Other Mexican Nationals (Mexico v. United States of America)

2004 I.C.J. 1 (Mar. 31)

[The Court held that, in cases of 51 of the Mexican nationals, the United States had breached its obligation under Article 36(1)(b) of the Vienna Convention "to inform detained Mexican nationals of their rights under that paragraph" and in 49 of those cases "to notify the Mexican consular post of the[ir] detention." The ICJ also held that in 49 cases, the United States had breached its obligation under Article 36(1)(a) "to enable Mexican consular officers to communicate with and have access to their nationals, as well as its obligation under paragraph 1(c) of that Article regarding the right of consular officers to visit their detained nationals." Jose Ernesto Medellín was expressly included in each of these holdings of breach. The Court then discussed "what remedies are required in order to redress the injury done to Mexico and to its nationals by the United States."]

119. The general principle on the legal consequences of the commission of an internationally wrongful act was stated by the Permanent Court of International Justice . . . as follows: "It is a principle of international law that the breach of an engagement involves an obligation to make reparation in an adequate form." (*Factory at Chorzów, Jurisdiction, 1927, P.C.I.J., Series A, No. 9*, p. 21.) What constitutes "reparation in an adequate form" clearly varies depending upon the concrete circumstances surrounding each case and the precise nature and scope of the injury. . . .

121. . . . It should be clear from what has been observed above that the internationally wrongful acts committed by the United States were the failure of its competent authorities to inform the Mexican nationals concerned, to notify Mexican consular posts and to enable Mexico to provide consular assistance. It follows that the remedy to make good these violations should consist in an obligation on the United States to permit review and reconsideration of these nationals' cases by the United States courts . . . with a view to ascertaining whether in each case the violation of Article 36 . . . caused actual prejudice to the defendant in the process of administration of criminal justice.

123. It is not to be presumed, as Mexico asserts, that partial or total annulment of conviction or sentence provides the necessary and sole remedy. . . . [I]n the present case it is not the convictions and sentences of the Mexican nationals which are to be regarded as a violation of international law, but solely certain breaches of treaty obligations which preceded them.

133. However, the Court wishes to point out that the current situation in the United States criminal procedure, as explained by the [U.S.] Agent at the hearings, is that . . . *"If the foreign national did not raise his Article 36 claim at trial, he may face procedural constraints* [i.e., the application of the procedural default rule] on raising that particular claim in direct or collateral judicial appeals" (emphasis added). As a result, a claim based on the violation of Article 36, paragraph 1, of the Vienna Convention, however meritorious in itself, could be barred in the courts of the United States by the operation of the procedural default rule. . . .

136. . . . [T]he United States claims that it "gives 'full effect' to the 'purposes for which the rights accorded under [Article 36, paragraph 1,] are intended' through executive clemency." . . .

137. Specifically in the context of the present case, the United States contends that . . . "clemency officials are not bound by principles of procedural default, finality, prejudice standards, or any other limitations on judicial review. They may consider any facts and circumstances that they deem appropriate and relevant, including specifically Vienna Convention claims."

138. The Court would emphasize that the "review and reconsideration" prescribed by it . . . should be effective. Thus it should "tak[e] account of the violation of the rights set forth in [the] Convention" and guarantee that the violation and the possible prejudice caused by that violation will be fully examined and taken into account in the review and reconsideration process. . . .

140. As has been explained . . . the Court is of the view that, in cases where the [Vienna Convention has been breached], the legal consequences of this breach have to be examined and taken into account in the course of review and reconsideration. The Court considers that it is the judicial process that is suited to this task.

The *Avena* decision has had a dramatic and substantial impact on several cases proceeding through courts in the United States.

a. The Torres Litigation

Osbaldo Torres is one of the Mexicans covered by the ICJ's provisional measures. He was arrested by Oklahoma police in July 1993 and charged with having committed two murders during the course of a burglary. He was not advised of his rights under the Vienna Convention; subsequently he was convicted of murder and sentenced to death.

After the *Avena* judgment, the U.S. State Department wrote to the Oklahoma Board of Pardon and Parole, "request[ing]" that the Board "give careful consideration" to Torres' request for clemency, "including by considering the failure to provide Mr. Torres with consular information and notification pursuant to [the Vienna Convention] and whether that failure should be regarded as having ultimately led to his conviction and sentence." The State Department also urged the Board to "give particular attention to the representations of the Government of Mexico on Mr. Torres' behalf." On May 7, 2004, the Oklahoma Board of Pardon and Parole held a hearing on a clemency petition filed by Torres; the Mexican Ambassador to the United States testified and urged the Board to grant clemency. Later that day, the Board recommended, in a 3-2 vote, that the Governor grant clemency. Shortly thereafter, Mexico's President and Foreign Minister sent letters urging the Governor to grant clemency. The State Department sent a letter to the Governor similar to the one it sent the Board of Pardon and Parole.

On May 13, 2004, the Oklahoma Court of Criminal Appeals ordered that Torres' execution date be stayed pending an evidentiary hearing on "(a) whether Torres was prejudiced by the State's violation of his Vienna Convention rights in failing to inform Torres, after he was detained, that he had the right to contact the Mexican consulate; and (b) ineffective assistance of counsel." *Torres v. Oklahoma*, No. PCD-04-442 (Okla. Crim. App. May 13, 2004). In a concurrence, Judge Charles S. Chapel cited the Supremacy Clause and stated that "[t]here is no question that this Court is bound by the Vienna Convention. . . ." Judge Chapel continued:

> At its simplest, this is a matter of contract. A treaty is a contract between sovereigns. The notion that contracts must be enforceable against those who enter into them is fundamental to the Rule of Law. This case is resolved by that very basic idea. The United States voluntarily and legally entered into a treaty, a contract with over 100 other countries. The United States is bound by the terms of the treaty and the State of Oklahoma is obligated by virtue of the Supremacy Clause to give effect to the treaty.
>
> As this Court is bound by the treaty itself, we are bound to give full faith and credit to the *Avena* decision. I am not suggesting that the International Court of Justice has jurisdiction over this Court — far from it. However . . . the issue of whether this Court must abide by [the ICJ's] opinion in [*the Avena*] case is not ours to determine. The United States Senate and the President have made that decision for us. . . . [T]he State Department has . . . consistently turned to the International Court of Justice to provide a binding resolution of disputes under the Vienna Convention, and has relied on the binding nature of International Court of Justice decisions to enforce United States rights under the Convention. The *Avena* decision mandates a remedy for a particular violation of Torres's, and Mexico's rights under the Vienna Convention. . . .
>
> *Avena* directs the United States to review and reconsider Torres' conviction and sentence in light of the consequences of the treaty violation. That review and reconsideration falls to this Court. . . . In order to give full effect to *Avena*, we are bound by its holding to review Torres's conviction and sentence in light of the Vienna Convention violation, without recourse to procedural bar. . . .

On the same day that this opinion was issued, Oklahoma's Governor commuted Torres' death sentence to life imprisonment without the possibility of parole. The Governor noted that Torres had been denied his consular rights under the Vienna Convention and that "that treaty is also important in protecting the rights of American citizens abroad."

In November 2004, a trial court held the evidentiary hearing ordered by the Court of Criminal Appeals. The trial judge found that the treaty violation did not result in "actual prejudice" to Torres. The court reasoned, however, that this finding "could lead some in the international community to believe that the United States does not take seriously" its Vienna Convention obligations, and could encourage some foreign officials to ignore the Vienna Convention when U.S. citizens are detained abroad. As a result, the trial court found that Torres was prejudiced as a result of the treaty violation.

On appeal, the Court of Criminal Appeals set out a three-pronged test for finding prejudice: "(1) whether the defendant did not know he had a right to contact his consulate for assistance; (2) whether he would have availed himself of the right had he known of it; and (3) whether it was likely that the consulate would have assisted the defendant." The court expressly rejected a suggestion that a defendant needs to demonstrate that consular assistance "would, or could, have made a difference in the outcome of a trial." A Mexican diplomat stated that "all" of Mexico's consular efforts on behalf of accused citizens "are focused on trying to avoid the imposition of the death penalty"; Torres introduced no evidence regarding how consular assistance would have assisted in the guilt phase of the trial. The court reasoned that:

> [i]f Torres were still under a capital sentence, [the evidence] would indeed amount to a showing of prejudice. However, the Governor's grant of clemency in Torres's case ensures that Torres is not subject to the death penalty. Any assistance Mexico could

have given in this regard has become moot. . . . Under these circumstances, Torres is not entitled to relief from his convictions, and has already received relief from his capital sentences. No further relief is required.

Torres v. State, 120 P.3d 1184 (Okla. Crim. App. 2005).

b. The Medellín *Litigation*

The *Avena* judgment also sparked an extraordinary series of events in the *Medellín* litigation. On October 24, 2003, while *Avena* was pending before the ICJ, Medellín sought relief from the Fifth Circuit Court of Appeals on several grounds including his Vienna Convention claim. On May 20, 2004, after the ICJ had rendered its judgment in *Avena*, the Court of Appeals denied Medellín's application. The Fifth Circuit reasoned that it was bound by the Supreme Court's opinion in *Breard*, notwithstanding the fact that subsequent ICJ decisions "contradict" *Breard*. *Medellín v. Dretke*, 371 F.3d 270, 279 (5th Cir. 2004).

Medellín then filed a petition for a writ of certiorari with the United States Supreme Court. The Court granted the writ on the following questions:

1. In a case brought by a Mexican national whose rights were adjudicated by the International Court of Justice . . . must a court in the United States apply as the rule of decision the holding in *Avena* that the United States courts must review and reconsider the national's conviction and sentence taking account of the violation of his rights under the Vienna Convention on Consular Relations without resort to procedural default doctrines?
2. In the alternative . . . should a court in the United States give effect to the [*Avena*] judgment . . . in the interest of judicial comity and uniform treaty interpretation?

After the Supreme Court issued a writ of certiorari, the executive branch submitted an amicus brief arguing that the Vienna Convention does not provide judicially enforceable private rights: "It is for the President, not the courts, to determine whether the United States should comply with the [ICJ] decision, and, if so, how." The brief went on to state that the United States has a treaty obligation to comply with the *Avena* decision and that, on February 28, 2004 (one day before the brief was filed), the President had issued a memorandum to the Attorney General making the following determination:

I have determined . . . that the United States will discharge its international obligations under the [*Avena* decision] by having state courts give effect to the decision in accordance with general principles of comity in cases filed by the 51 Mexican nationals addressed in that decision.

Relying upon the President's memorandum and the *Avena* judgment as separate bases for relief that were not available at the time of his first state habeas corpus action, Medellín filed a new state habeas petition four days before oral argument at the Supreme Court. On May 23, 2005, the Supreme Court issued a decision in Medellín's case.

Medellín v. Dretke

125 S. Ct. 2088 (2005)

PER CURIAM.
After we granted certiorari, Medellín filed an application for a writ of habeas corpus in the Texas Court of Criminal Appeals, relying in part upon a

memorandum from President George W. Bush that was issued after we granted certiorari. . . .

In light of the possibility that the Texas courts will provide Medellín with the review that he seeks pursuant to the *Avena* judgment and the President's memorandum, and the potential for review in this Court once the Texas courts have heard and decided Medellín's pending action, we think it would be unwise to reach and resolve . . . the questions here presented. Accordingly, we dismiss the writ [of certiorari] as improvidently granted.

JUSTICE O'CONNOR, with whom JUSTICE STEVENS, JUSTICE SOUTER, and JUSTICE BREYER join, dissenting.

[These justices would remand to the Fifth Circuit Court of Appeals for consideration of "(1) whether the International Court of Justice's judgment in Medellín's favor is binding on American courts; (2) whether Article 36(1)(b) of the Convention creates a judicially enforceable individual right; and (3) whether Article 36(2) of the Convention sometimes requires state procedural default rules to be set aside so that the treaty can be given 'full effect.'"]

At every step, the federal courts must evaluate Medellín's Vienna Convention claim through the framework of the Antiterrorism and Effective Death Penalty Act of 1996 (AEDPA), which controls the process by which a state prisoner may obtain federal habeas relief. And wherever the Convention, which has been in continuous force since 1969, conflicts with this subsequently enacted statute, the statute must govern. . . .

If Medellín is right to say that [American courts are bound by *Avena*], then the District Court's resolution of his Vienna Convention claim is not merely debatable, but wrong in result and in reasoning. In terms of result, the ICJ made clear that it would be improper to dismiss Medellín's claim, for once the United States had committed "internationally wrongful acts," the necessary "remedy to make good these violations should consist in an obligation on the United States to permit review and reconsideration of [the 51 Mexican] nationals' cases by the United States courts." *Avena*, 2004 I.C.J. No. 128, ¶121. The ICJ's reasoning is also irreconcilable with the District Court's. The ICJ specified that the Convention confers rights on individual defendants, and that applying state procedural default rules to prevent them from vindicating their rights violates the treaty, for the treaty requires that its purposes be given "'full effect.'" *Id.*, ¶¶106, 113.

Medellín argues that once the United States undertakes a substantive obligation (as it did in the Vienna Convention), and at the same time undertakes to abide by the result of a specified dispute resolution process (as it did by submitting to the ICJ's jurisdiction through the Optional Protocol), it is bound by the rules generated by that process no less than it is by the treaty that is the source of the substantive obligation. In other words, . . . Medellín asserts, at bottom, that *Avena*, like a treaty, has the status of supreme law of the land.

On the other hand, Texas and the United States argue that the issue turns in large part on how to interpret Article 94(1) of the United Nations Charter, which provides that "[e]ach Member of the United Nations undertakes to comply with the decision of the International Court of Justice in any case to which it is a party." They maintain that the charter imposes an international duty only on our political branches. A contrary result could deprive the Executive of necessary discretion in foreign relations, and may improperly displace this Court's responsibilities to an international body. . . .

Reasonable jurists can vigorously disagree about whether and what legal effect ICJ decisions have in our domestic courts, and about whether Medellín can benefit from such effect in this posture. The Court of Appeals should have . . . given the issue further consideration. . . .

[Justice O'Connor then reviews, without deciding, the question of whether Article 36 confers rights on individuals.] Of course, even if the Convention does confer individual rights, there remains the question of whether such rights can be forfeited according to state procedural default rules. . . . In *Breard*, in the course of denying a stay of imminent execution and accompanying petitions, we concluded that the petitioner had defaulted his Article 36 claim by failing to raise it in state court prior to seeking collateral relief in federal court. Subsequently in *Avena* . . . the International Court of Justice interpreted Article 36(2) differently. In the past the Court has revisited its interpretation of a treaty when new international law has come to light. Even if *Avena* is not itself a binding rule of decision in this case, it may at least be occasion to return to the question of Article 36(2)'s implications for procedural default. . . .

Notes and Questions

1. Who won? What did Medellín seek from the Supreme Court? What did Texas seek? What did the executive branch seek? Is *Breard* still good law?

2. On March 7, 2004, the United States sent a letter to the UN Secretary General stating that the United States "hereby withdraws" from the Optional Protocol to the Vienna Convention and, as a result, that "the United States will no longer recognize the jurisdiction of the International Court of Justice reflected in that Protocol." The Optional Protocol supplied the basis for ICJ jurisdiction in the *Paraguay*, *LaGrand*, and *Avena* cases. The withdrawal from the Optional Protocol removes the basis for ICJ jurisdiction over the U.S. in actions arising out of alleged Vienna Convention violations. The President's authority to withdraw from a treaty is discussed in Section IV of this chapter.

3. What is the status of procedural default rules in cases alleging breaches of the Vienna Convention? In its amicus brief to the Supreme Court in *Medellín*, the Executive Branch claimed that, as a result of the President's memorandum, state courts "may not . . . interpose procedural default to prevent review and reconsideration." Is the Executive Branch's position in *Medellín* consistent with its position in *Breard*? Is it compelled by *Avena*? In its Supreme Court brief, the Administration argued that:

> The President's determination, which means that procedural default rules may not prevent review and reconsideration of the 51 individuals identified in *Avena*, is emphatically not premised on a different interpretation of the Vienna Convention [than that found in *Breard*]. To the contrary . . . the Executive Branch regards the Court's holding in *Breard* as controlling. . . . Nonetheless, pursuant to his authority under the U.N. Charter and Article II of the Constitution, the President has determined that the foreign policy interests of the United States in meeting its international obligations and protecting Americans abroad require the ICJ's decision to be enforced without regard to the merits of the ICJ's interpretation of the Vienna Convention. Just as *Breard* would not stand in the way of legislation that provided for the implementation of the *Avena* decision, it does not stand in the way of the President's determination that the *Avena* decision should be given effect.

4. Texas questioned the President's constitutional authority to issue a determination directing state courts to take a particular action and whether the determination "is somehow sufficiently authoritative to preempt longstanding state criminal laws of general applicability." In its brief, the Administration relied upon *Garamendi, Dames & Moore,* and other cases to argue that, if the President can "enter into an executive agreement to resolve a dispute with a foreign government, the President should be equally free to resolve a dispute with a foreign government by determining how the United States will comply with a decision reached after the completion of formal dispute-resolution procedures with that foreign government." Should the President have unilateral authority to "interfere" with state criminal proceedings to further compliance with international law? Is the state (or federal) interest here greater than the state (or federal) interest in *Garamendi*?

What theory would support the Administration's argument that the President's determination "has independent legal force and effect, and contrary state rules must give way under the Supremacy Clause" while the relevant treaties and ICJ judgments lack this quality?

5. Do you interpret President Bush's memorandum directing state courts to give effect to *Avena* as a matter of comity as evidencing a greater respect for international law than that found in the other Vienna Convention cases discussed above? What does the memorandum suggest about the status of ICJ judgments as law in courts in the United States? The Administration urged the Court to "reject petitioner's reliance on international treaties and the ICJ's decision as free-standing sources of law under which he can obtain judicial review and reconsideration," and argued that "[i]t is for the President, not the courts, to determine whether the United States should comply with the decision, and, if so, how."

6. What are *Avena*'s implications for non-capital defendants who were not advised of their Vienna Convention rights at the time of their arrest? Why has the litigation around Vienna Convention violations focused on death penalty cases? There is substantial evidence that numerous states violate Article 36 of the Vienna Convention. Why has the United States been the only country to be sued at the ICJ over this issue?

7. In the Uruguay Round of trade negotiations, the United States and other countries agreed to the creation of the World Trade Organization (WTO) and a legally binding dispute settlement system with compulsory jurisdiction over trade disputes. In the legislation implementing the Uruguay Round Agreements, Congress provided that no person can rely in U.S. courts upon WTO or Appellate Body reports, and a federal court has stated that "WTO decisions are not binding on the United States, much less this court." Why would Congress enact such a provision? Why is there great public concern when U.S. courts fail to follow ICJ decisions, but little public concern when U.S. courts fail to follow decisions resulting from WTO dispute settlement proceedings?

C. An Alternative Approach to Conflicts Between International and Domestic Law

United States courts faced with apparent conflicts between treaties and domestic statutes do not always adopt the approach of the *Breard* court. Consider the case of the Palestine Liberation Organization (PLO) Mission to the United Nations. In

1947, the United States entered into an international agreement with the United Nations known as the Headquarters Agreement. This agreement provides that federal and state authorities "shall not impose any impediments to transit to or from the headquarters district [of the United Nations] of . . . persons invited to the headquarters district by the United Nations . . . on official business. . . ."

In 1974, the United Nations invited the PLO to "participate in the sessions and the work of the General Assembly in the capacity of observer." In the years that followed, the PLO participated without interruption as a permanent observer and maintained a mission to the United Nations in New York City.

In 1987, Congress passed the Anti-Terrorism Act (ATA), which found that "the PLO and its affiliates are a terrorist organization." The ATA provided that:

> It shall be unlawful, if the purpose be to further the interests of the Palestine Liberation Organization or any of its constituent groups . . . on or after [March 21, 1988]— . . .
>
> > (3) notwithstanding any provision of law to the contrary, to establish or maintain an office, headquarters, premises or other facilities or establishments within the jurisdiction of the United States at the behest or direction of, or with funds provided by the Palestine Liberation Organization or any of its constituent groups, any successor to any of those, or any agents thereof.

After the ATA was passed, the UN General Assembly adopted Resolution 42/229A, stating that the United States was "under a legal obligation" to enable the PLO Mission to maintain its premises and carry out its official functions and calling upon the United States "to abide by its treaty obligations." The U.S. Representative to the UN advised the Secretary-General that under the ATA, the U.S. Attorney General was "required" to close the PLO Mission, "irrespective of any obligations the United States may have under the [Headquarters Agreement]." On March 22, the day after the ATA took effect, the federal government filed a federal court action seeking injunctive relief to accomplish the closing of the mission. The court considered the relationship between the apparently conflicting international and domestic legal obligations.

United States of America v. Palestine Liberation Organization

695 F. Supp. 1456 (S.D. N.Y. 1988)

V

The Anti-Terrorism Act and the Headquarters Agreement

If the ATA were construed as the government suggests, it would be tantamount to a direction to the PLO Observer Mission at the United Nations that it close its doors and cease its operations *instanter*. Such an interpretation would fly in the face of the Headquarters Agreement, a prior treaty between the United Nations and the United States, and would abruptly terminate the functions the Mission has performed for many years. This conflict requires the court to seek out a reconciliation between the two.

Under our constitutional system, statutes and treaties are both the supreme law of the land, and the Constitution sets forth no order of precedence to differentiate between them. Wherever possible, both are to be given effect. Only where a treaty is irreconcilable with a later enacted statute and Congress has clearly evinced an intent to supersede a treaty by enacting a statute does the later enacted statute take precedence. *E.g., The Chinese Exclusion Case*, 130 U.S. [581,] 599-602 [1889] (finding clear intent to supersede); *Edye v. Robertson (The Head Money Cases)*, 112 U.S. 580, 597-99 (1884) (same, decided on the same day as *Chew Heong [v. United States*, 112 U.S. 536(1884),] which found no such intent). . . .

A. The Obligations of the United States under the Headquarters Agreement

The obligation of the United States to allow transit, entry and access stems not only from the language of the Headquarters Agreement but also from forty years of practice under it. Section 11 of the Headquarters Agreement reads, in part,

> The federal, state or local authorities of the United States shall not impose any impediments to transit to or from the headquarters district of: (1) representatives of Members . . . , (5) other persons invited to the headquarters district by the United Nations . . . on official business.

These rights could not be effectively exercised without the use of offices. The ability to effectively organize and carry out one's work, especially as a liaison to an international organization, would not be possible otherwise. . . .

After the United Nations invited the PLO to participate as a permanent observer, the Department of State took the position that it was required to provide access to the U.N. for the PLO. The State Department at no time disputed the notion that the rights of entry, access and residence guaranteed to invitees include the right to maintain offices.

. . . The United States has, for fourteen years, acted in a manner consistent with a recognition of the PLO's rights in the Headquarters Agreement. This course of conduct under the Headquarters Agreement is important evidence of its meaning. . . .

Shortly before the adoption of the ATA, . . . the United States' representative [to the United Nations] noted "that the United States Secretary of State had stated that the closing of the mission would constitute a violation of United States obligation under the Headquarters Agreement." He had previously stated that "closing the mission, in our view, and I emphasize this is the executive branch, is not consistent with our international legal obligations under the Headquarters Agreement." . . .

Thus the language, application and interpretation of the Headquarters Agreement lead us to the conclusion that it requires the United States to refrain from interference with the PLO Observer Mission in the discharge of its functions at the United Nations.

B. Reconciliation of the ATA and the Headquarters Agreement

. . . *Chew Heong* concerned the interplay of legislation regarding Chinese laborers with treaties on the same subject. During the passage of the statute at issue in *Chew Heong*, "it was objected to the legislation sought that the treaty of 1868 stood in the way, and that while it remained unmodified, such legislation would be a breach of faith to China. . . ." In spite of that, and over Justice Field's dissent, the Court, in Justice Field's words, "narrow[ed] the meaning of the act so as measurably to frustrate its intended operation." Four years after the decision in

Chew Heong, Congress amended the act in question to nullify that decision. With the amended statute, there could be no question as to Congress' intent to supersede the treaties, and it was the later enacted statute which took precedence. *The Chinese Exclusion Case, supra*, 130 U.S. at 598-99 (1889).

The principles enunciated and applied in *Chew Heong* and its progeny require the clearest of expressions on the part of Congress. We are constrained by these decisions to stress the lack of clarity in Congress' action in this instance. Congress' failure to speak with one clear voice on this subject requires us to interpret the ATA as inapplicable to the Headquarters Agreement. This is so, in short, for the reasons which follow.

First, neither the Mission nor the Headquarters Agreement is mentioned in the ATA itself. Such an inclusion would have left no doubt as to Congress' intent on a matter which had been raised repeatedly with respect to this act, and its absence here reflects equivocation and avoidance, leaving the court without clear interpretive guidance in the language of the act. Second, while the section of the ATA prohibiting the maintenance of an office applies "notwithstanding any provision of law to the contrary," 22 U.S.C. §5202(3), it does not purport to apply notwithstanding any *treaty*. The absence of that interpretive instruction is especially relevant because elsewhere in the same legislation Congress expressly referred to "United States law (including any treaty)." 101 Stat. at 1343. Thus Congress failed, in the text of the ATA, to provide guidance for the interpretation of the act, where it became repeatedly apparent before its passage that the prospect of an interpretive problem was inevitable. Third, no member of Congress expressed a clear and unequivocal intent to supersede the Headquarters Agreement by passage of the ATA. In contrast, most who addressed the subject of conflict denied that there would be a conflict: in their view, the Headquarters Agreement did not provide the PLO with any right to maintain an office. Here again, Congress provided no guidance for the interpretation of the ATA in the event of a conflict which was clearly foreseeable. . . .

In sum, the language of the Headquarters Agreement, the long-standing practice under it, and the interpretation given it by the parties to it leave no doubt that it places an obligation upon the United States to refrain from impairing the function of the PLO Observer Mission to the United Nations. The ATA and its legislative history do not manifest Congress' intent to abrogate this obligation. We are therefore constrained to interpret the ATA as failing to supersede the Headquarters Agreement and inapplicable to the Mission.

Notes and Questions

1. Are you persuaded that the court correctly interpreted the ATA? If the court's interpretation of the ATA seems strained as a matter of statutory interpretation, is the decision defensible on other grounds? Why was no member of Congress willing to state explicitly that the ATA was designed to override the Headquarters Agreement?

2. The Reagan Administration was split on whether to appeal this decision. The Justice Department strongly urged appeal, while the State Department was on the other side of the issue. Ultimately, the President had to mediate this dispute and decided not to appeal. The Justice Department explained the decision as follows: "It is the Administration's normal policy to appeal adverse District Court decisions

of this kind. But it was decided, in light of foreign policy considerations . . . not to appeal in this instance." Was it wise not to follow normal policy in this case?

3. On several occasions, the Supreme Court has interpreted acts of Congress so as to avoid conflict with earlier treaty provisions. Most recently, in *Spector v. Norwegian Cruise Line*, 125 S. Ct. 2169 (2005), the Court held that Title III of the Americans with Disabilities Act applied to foreign flag vessels in U.S. waters. Title III bans discrimination against disabled persons and requires covered entities to remove architectural barriers where doing so is "readily achievable." The *Spector* plaintiffs alleged that ship coamings—the raised edges around vessel doors—make many areas of ships inaccessible to mobility-impaired passengers, and that Title III may require removal of these and other access barriers. Defendants argued that the International Convention for the Safety of Life at Sea requires coamings on certain doors to ensure that they will be watertight. The Court ruled that removal of a structural barrier is not "readily achievable" if it "would bring a vessel into non-compliance with the International Convention for the Safety of Life at Sea or any other international legal obligation."

How does the Court's treatment of the relationship between international and statutory norms in *Spector* differ from its treatment of this relationship in *Breard*?

D. May the President Violate International Law?

In both *Breard* and *PLO*, the courts were asked to rule upon apparent conflicts between international legal norms and domestic legislation. But the President also has independent constitutional authority—as treaty maker, as "sole organ" of the state in foreign affairs, and as commander-in-chief. What should happen if the President acts in a way that conflicts with international law? Should courts use the same principles when evaluating congressional and presidential actions? In *The Paquete Habana*, 175 U.S. 677, 700 (1900), the Court declared that:

> International law is part of our law, and must be ascertained and administered by the courts of justice of appropriate jurisdiction, as often as questions of right depending upon it are duly presented for their determination. For this purpose, where there is no treaty, and no controlling executive or legislative act or judicial decision, resort must be had to the customs and usages of civilized nations; and, as evidence of these, to the works of jurists and commentators, who by years of labor, research and experience, have made themselves peculiarly well acquainted with the subjects of which they treat. Such works are resorted to by judicial tribunals, not for the speculations of their authors concerning what the law ought to be, but for trustworthy evidence of what the law really is.

The Court went on to hold that the Navy's capture of a fishing smack was contrary to customary international law and hence unlawful.

A more recent case purported to apply *Paquete Habana* in an immigration law context. Congress has broad constitutional authority to refuse to admit certain classes of aliens to the United States, and the U.S. immigration laws provide that inadmissible aliens should be removed. However, before removal, inadmissible aliens usually have a right to a hearing to determine their admissibility before an immigration judge. The immigration laws also give the U.S. Attorney General authority to grant parole to an alien, pending a hearing on removal. Parole allows aliens to be in the United States temporarily until the immigration authorities determine whether the alien may remain in the country.

The case below arose out of the detention of Cuban citizens who came to the United States during a massive 1980 boatlift originating from the port of Mariel, Cuba. Plaintiffs consisted of two classes of Mariel Cubans. The first group included those who were guilty of crimes committed in Cuba before the boatlift or who were deemed mentally incompetent. This group was never paroled into the country. The second group consists of all other Mariels who were paroled into the country, but whose paroles were subsequently revoked. At the time of the opinion, both the first and second groups were being detained in the Atlanta penitentiary.

Garcia-Mir v. Meese

788 F.2d 1446 (11th Cir. 1986)

II

B. International Law

The public law of nations was long ago incorporated into the common law of the United States. *The Paquete Habana*, 175 U.S. 677 (1900); *Restatement of the Law of Foreign Relations Law of the United States (Revised)* §131 comment d (Tent. Draft No. 6, 1985) [hereinafter cited as Restatement 6]. To the extent possible, courts must construe American law so as to avoid violating principles of public international law. But public international law is controlling only "where there is no treaty and no controlling executive or legislative act or judicial decision. . . ." 175 U.S. at 700. Appellees argue that, because general principles of international law forbid prolonged arbitrary detention, we should hold that their current detention is unlawful.

We have previously determined that the general deportation statute, 8 U.S.C.A. §1227(a) (1985), does not *restrict* the power of the Attorney General to detain aliens indefinitely. But this does not resolve the question whether there has been an *affirmative legislative grant* of authority to detain. As to the First Group there is sufficiently express evidence of congressional intent as to interdict the application of international law. . . .

The trial court found, correctly, that there has been no affirmative legislative grant to the Justice Department to detain the Second Group without hearings because 8 U.S.C.A. §1227(c) does not expressly authorize indefinite detention. Thus we must look for a controlling executive act. The trial court found that there was such a controlling act in the Attorney General's termination of the status review plan and in his decision to incarcerate indefinitely pending efforts to deport. The appellees and the *amicus* challenge this by arguing that a controlling executive act can only come from an act by or expressly sanctioned by the President himself, not one of his subordinates. They rely for that proposition upon *The Paquete Habana* and upon the *Restatement of the Law of Foreign Relations Law of the United States (Revised)* §131 comment c (Tent. Draft No. 1, 1980) [hereinafter cited as Restatement 1].

As to *The Paquete Habana*, that case involved the capture and sale as war prize of several fishing boats during the Spanish-American War. The Supreme Court found this contrary to the dictates of international law. The *amicus* characterizes the facts of the case such that the Secretary of the Navy authorized the capture and that the Supreme Court held that this did not constitute a controlling executive act because it was not ordered by the President himself. This is a mischaracterization. After the capture of the two vessels at issue, an admiral telegraphed the Secretary for permission to seize fishing ships, to which the Secretary responded that only those vessels "likely to aid enemy may be detained." Seizing fishing boats aiding the enemy would be in obvious accord with international law. But the facts of *The Paquete Habana* showed the boats in question to be innocent of aiding the Spanish. The Court held that the ships were seized in violation of international law because they were used solely for fishing. It was the *admiral* who acted in excess of the clearly delimited authority granted by the Secretary, who instructed him to act only consistent with international law. Thus *The Paquete Habana* does not support the proposition that the acts of cabinet officers cannot constitute controlling executive acts. At best it suggests that lower level officials cannot by their acts render international law inapplicable. That is not an issue in this case, where the challenge is to the acts of the Attorney General.

As to the Restatement 1, the provision upon which *amicus* relies has been removed in subsequent drafts. The most recent version of that provision notes that the President, "acting within his constitutional authority, may have the power under the Constitution to act in ways that constitute violations of international law by the United States." The Constitution provides for the creation of executive departments, *U.S. Const.* art. 2, §2, and the power of the President to delegate his authority to those departments to act on his behalf is unquestioned. Likewise, in Restatement 6, §135 Reporter's Note 3, the power of the President to disregard international law in service of domestic needs is reaffirmed. Thus we hold that the executive acts here evident constitute a sufficient basis for affirming the trial court's finding that international law does not control.

Notes and Questions

1. In October 2000, the Inter-American Commission on Human Rights adopted Report 85/00, which found that the deprivation of liberty suffered by the Mariel Cubans violated several provisions of the American Declaration of the Rights and Duties of Man. Although the United States vigorously objected to the Commission's rationale and conclusions, in April 2001, the Commission ratified its finding that the United States's treatment of the Mariel Cubans violated the American Declaration.

2. The President has the constitutional obligation to "take Care that the Laws be faithfully executed," and international law is, according to *Paquete*, part of U.S. law. So why does the *Garcia-Mir* court in effect endorse executive branch lawlessness? Would the United States be handicapped in the process of making customary international law if courts enjoined the President from violating customary international law?

3. Should the courts treat executive branch action that is inconsistent with a treaty differently from legislation that is inconsistent with customary international law?

4. The question whether the President is bound by customary international law arose in the context of debates over the legal norms applicable to al Qaeda and Taliban detainees. A 2002 memorandum from the Justice Department's Office of Legal Counsel to the Defense Department's General Counsel argued that "customary international law, whatever its source and content, does not bind the President . . . because it does not constitute federal law recognized under the Supremacy

Clause of the Constitution." The debate over the applicability of customary international legal norms to these detainees is discussed in Chapter 14.

E. Note on Self-Executing Treaties

The constitutional provision that treaties are, like federal statutes, the supreme law of the land might suggest that all treaties should be enforceable in U.S. courts to the same extent as federal statutes. Since early in the nation's history, however, the Supreme Court has distinguished between "self-executing" and "non-self-executing" treaties. While courts have characterized this distinction as the "most confounding" in the U.S. law of treaties, as a general matter individuals can invoke self-executing treaties in domestic court proceedings without the need for domestic legislation implementing the treaty. That is, these treaties are automatically incorporated into domestic law. Non-self-executing treaties, by contrast, can only be invoked by individuals in domestic courts to the extent that Congress has implemented the treaty provisions by federal statute.

While the Supreme Court did not use the phrase "self-executing" until 1887, the roots of this distinction are found in an earlier opinion by Chief Justice Marshall. In *Foster and Elam v. Neilson*, 27 U.S. 253 (1829), the plaintiffs claimed title to property in Florida on the basis of a grant from Spain. The treaty that transferred the disputed land from Spain to the United States provided, according to the English-language text, that the Spanish grants "shall be ratified and confirmed to the persons in possession of the lands." Plaintiffs argued that the treaty confirmed their title to the property. The Court decided that the Spanish grants were not valid as domestic law until Congress passed legislation confirming the grants:

> A treaty is in its nature a contract between two nations, not a legislative act. It does not generally effect, of itself, the object to be accomplished, especially so far as its operation is infra-territorial; but is carried into execution by the sovereign power of the respective parties to the instrument.
>
> In the United States a different principle is established. Our constitution declares a treaty to be the law of the land. It is, consequently, to be regarded in courts of justice as equivalent to an act of the legislature, whenever it operates of itself without the aid of any legislative provision. But when the terms of the stipulation import a contract, when either of the parties engages to perform a particular act, the treaty addresses itself to the political, not the judicial department; and the legislature must execute the contract before it can become a rule for the Court.

The Court thus distinguished between treaties that "operate of themselves" and are therefore applicable by the courts without legislative action, and those that are not judicially applicable unless and until implementing legislation is enacted. However, this distinction has proved easier to state than to apply. For example, the treaty provision at issue in *Foster* was also central to a case decided by the Court only four years later. In that case, *United States v. Percheman*, 32 U.S. 51 (1833), the Court relied upon the Spanish language version of the treaty, translated as stating that the land grants "shall remain ratified and confirmed to the persons in possession [of the lands]," and held the treaty to be self-executing.

In a more recent case, *United States v. Postal*, 589 F.2d 862 (5th Cir. 1979), U.S. Coast Guard officials boarded a foreign vessel outside of a 12-mile limit set by a treaty ratified by the United States. The officials arrested members of the ship's crew, who were later convicted for conspiring to import marijuana into the

United States. On appeal, the defendants argued that the breach of the treaty divested the court of jurisdiction over the defendants. The court wrote:

> The question whether a treaty is self-executing is a matter of interpretation for the courts when the issue presents itself in litigation and, as in the case of all matters of interpretation, the courts attempt to discern the intent of the parties to the agreement so as to carry out their manifest purpose. The parties' intent may be apparent from the language of the treaty, or, if the language is ambiguous, it may be divined from the circumstances surrounding the treaty's promulgation. . . .
>
> . . . In the specific context of determining whether a treaty provision is self-executing, we may refer to several factors:
>
>> the purposes of the treaty and the objectives of its creators, the existence of domestic procedures and institutions appropriate for direct implementation, the availability and feasibility of alternative enforcement methods, and the immediate and long-range consequences of self- or non-self-execution.
>
> With these principles in mind, we proceed to examine the treaty provision in issue here, article 6 of the [1958] Convention on the High Seas.
>
> Article 6 declares the exclusivity of a nation's jurisdiction over the vessels entitled to fly its flag: "Ships shall sail under the flag of one State only and, save in exceptional cases expressly provided for in international treaties or in these articles, shall be subject to its exclusive jurisdiction on the high seas." On its face, this language would bear a self-executing construction because it purports to preclude the exercise of jurisdiction by foreign states in the absence of an exception embodied in treaty. We are admonished, however, to interpret treaties in the context of their promulgation, and we think the context of article 6 compels the conclusion that it is not self-executing.
>
> We start with the observation that the Convention . . . is intended to be "generally declaratory of established principles of international law." Indeed, that a state enjoys exclusive jurisdiction over its flag vessels, in the absence of an exception sanctioned under customary international law, is just such a principle. But the question we must answer is whether by ratifying the Convention on the High Seas the United States undertook to incorporate the restrictive language of article 6, which limits the permissible exercise of jurisdiction to those provided by treaty, into its domestic law and make it available in a criminal action as a defense to the jurisdiction of its courts. There is nothing in the circumstances surrounding the formulation and adoption of the Convention that would support the conclusion that it did.
>
> The Convention on the High Seas is a multilateral treaty which has been ratified by over fifty nations, some of which do not recognize treaties as self-executing. It is difficult therefore to ascribe to the language of the treaty any common intent that the treaty should of its own force operate as the domestic law of the ratifying nations. This is not to say that by entering into such a multilateral treaty the United States cannot without legislation execute provisions of it, but one would expect that in these circumstances the United States would make that intention clear. The lack of mutuality between the United States and countries that do not recognize treaties as self-executing would seem to call for as much. Here there was no such manifestation. . . .

Id. at 876-878.

Notes and Questions

1. In what sense are non-self-executing treaties law? Does the judicial creation of the doctrine of non-self-executing treaties undermine the intent of the Framers who drafted the Supremacy Clause? Does it contradict the plain language of the

Supremacy Clause — or do such arguments mistakenly conflate the "law of the land" with judicial enforcement?

2. Courts have repeatedly declared that whether a treaty is self-executing is largely, if not entirely, a matter of intent. Whose intent counts? What must the relevant actors have intended? How is this intent to be determined?

3. Professor Carlos Vazquez has identified four situations in which a treaty is likely to be deemed non-self-executing. *See* Carlos Vázquez, *The Four Doctrines of Self-Executing Treaties*, 89 Am. J. Intl. L. 695 (1995). First, courts will deem a treaty to be non-self-executing when the parties intended that the treaty's purpose be accomplished through domestic legislation. Second, courts will hold treaties non-self-executing when they address an issue that, as a constitutional matter, requires domestic implementing legislation (for example, criminalizing certain conduct). Third, courts will find treaties or treaty provisions that are precatory or hortatory to be non-self-executing. The UN Charter, for example, calls upon its members to cooperate to promote human rights, and this provision has been held to be non-self-executing. A final category of non-self-executing treaties consists of treaties that are deemed not to create a private right of action. In Section V of this chapter, we shall see a court discussing whether international legal instruments create private rights of action.

4. Is the Vienna Convention provision at issue in *Breard* self-executing? At the time of the Senate's advice and consent to the treaty, the Executive Branch stated that the treaty was "entirely self-executing and [did] not require any implementing or complementing legislation."

IV. INTERPRETING INTERNATIONAL LAW: MISSILE DEFENSE AND THE ANTI-BALLISTIC MISSILE TREATY

As we saw in Chapter 2, the basic international legal norms governing treaty interpretation are set out in the Vienna Convention on the Law of Treaties, which is frequently invoked when states disagree on these questions. But questions of treaty interpretation also arise frequently in domestic legal systems. Should the same rules apply in domestic settings? What should happen, as a matter of domestic law, if two branches of government adopt different views of a treaty?

In the United States, some questions of treaty law are governed by the Constitution. As noted above, the President is constitutionally authorized to enter into treaties, provided that two-thirds of the Senate concurs. But what happens when the Senate and the President disagree over a treaty's meaning? Is the President bound by the Senate's understanding of a treaty's meaning? If so, how can one determine what a collective body like the Senate understood a treaty to mean, and what happens if the Senate's understanding differs from that of this country's treaty partners? These, and related questions, were raised in the 1980s when the Executive branch announced a controversial "reinterpretation" of the Treaty on the Limitation of Anti-Ballistic Missile Systems (the ABM treaty).

A. The Problem

The United States and the USSR concluded and ratified the ABM Treaty in 1972. The treaty is premised upon the strategy of mutual assured destruction (MAD) — the theory that neither superpower would launch a first strike if it lacked a defense to enable it to survive a retaliatory second strike. Thus, the two sides entered into a treaty to restrict the ability to develop or deploy anti-missile systems. Relevant provisions of the treaty follow:

Treaty on the Limitation of Anti-Ballistic Missile Systems

23 U.S.T. 3435

Article I

2. Each Party undertakes not to deploy ABM systems for a defense of the territory of its country and not to provide a base for such a defense, and not to deploy ABM systems for defense of an individual region except as provided for in Article III of this Treaty.

Article II

1. For the purposes of this Treaty an ABM system is a system to counter strategic ballistic missiles or their elements in flight trajectory, currently consisting of:

(a) ABM interceptor missiles, which are interceptor missiles constructed and deployed for an ABM role, or of a type tested in an ABM mode;

(b) ABM launchers, which are launchers constructed and deployed for launching ABM interceptor missiles; and

(c) ABM radars. . . .

Article III

[Article III permits each Party to deploy, inter alia, an ABM system to protect its national capital.]

Article V

1. Each Party undertakes not to develop, test, or deploy ABM systems or components which are sea-based, air-based, space-based, or mobile land-based. . . .

Pursuant to the Senate's advice-and-consent role, the Foreign Relations Committee and the Armed Services Committee held extensive hearings on the ABM treaty during the summer of 1972. The Secretary of State testified that "the parties have agreed that future exotic types of ABM systems, i.e., systems depending on such devices as lasers, may not be deployed, even in permitted areas." The chief U.S. treaty negotiator confirmed that "both sides have agreed that they will not deploy future type ABM technology unless the treaty is amended." One of the two senators who voted against the ABM treaty complained that "Article V of the ABM Treaty . . . would have the effect, for example[,] of prohibiting the development and testing of a laser-type system based in space. . . . The technological possibility has been formally excluded by this agreement. . . ."

In August 1972, the Treaty received the Senate's advice and consent to ratification by a vote of 88-2. President Nixon ratified the Treaty on September 30, and, upon the formal exchange of instruments of ratification, the ABM Treaty entered into force on October 3, 1972. Over the following decade, many argued that the ABM Treaty was at the very center of the effort to limit the strategic arms race by international agreements, and leading commentators characterized the Treaty as the "most important single arms control agreement" that the United States and Soviet Union entered into.

However, on March 23, 1983, President Ronald Reagan stunned the American people — and many of his own advisors — by proposing a Strategic Defense Initiative (SDI) designed to render incoming ballistic missile warheads "impotent and obsolete." Administration briefings after the speech made clear that the goal was to develop means to destroy enemy missiles — meaning, primarily, Soviet missiles — by a series of attacks along their flight path. Ever since, fierce disagreements have raged over the technical feasibility, fiscal practicality, and effect upon the strategic balance of missile defense. Another highly contentious issue has been whether such a missile defense is consistent with the ABM Treaty and whether the Executive Branch has the authority to change its interpretation of the Treaty to permit development or deployment of this technology.

SDI's critics immediately argued that the program would force the United States either to withdraw from or abrogate the ABM Treaty. However, the President countered that SDI would initially be only a research program and would therefore be "consistent with our obligations [under] the ABM Treaty." However, as research progressed, the Treaty's terms became a more significant constraint to advanced development and testing of system components.

On October 6, 1985, during an appearance on the TV show *Meet the Press*, National Security Adviser Robert McFarlane announced that the Administration was about to adopt a new interpretation of the Treaty. He said that the Treaty "make[s] clear that on research involving new physical concepts, that activity, as well as testing, as well as development, indeed, are approved and authorized by the Treaty. Only deployment is foreclosed. . . ." Under this new, broader interpretation, the treaty ban on development and testing of ABM systems was considered to apply only to "current" (that is, 1972) technologies. Space-based and other so-called "exotic" systems, based on "future" (i.e., post-1972) technologies were not so limited. Under this new reading, not simply research, but also development and testing of space-based SDI systems would be permitted. This view, which came to be known as the "broad" interpretation, was based on a preliminary legal opinion written the preceding week by Abraham Sofaer, the State Department Legal Adviser and a former federal judge and law professor.

B. The Reinterpretation Debate: Who Decides?

The Reagan Administration's proposed reinterpretation of the Treaty to permit development and testing of ABM systems sparked a political firestorm. Former ABM negotiators, members of Congress, and allied and Soviet leaders argued that the broad interpretation misread the Treaty's text and negotiating history. Others questioned the Executive Branch's authority to implement such a "reinterpretation" of the established meaning of a treaty.

Sofaer's report, submitted during Senate hearings on May 19, 1987, asserted that the broad interpretation was "wholly justified" by the Treaty's language and drafting history:

The restrictive interpretation [of the Treaty] rests on the language of Article V(1), which on its face unqualifiedly prohibits the development, testing, or deployment of mobile "ABM systems or components." But this language does not settle the issue of the Article's applicability to ABM devices other than missiles, launchers, and radars that could serve the same functions as ABM systems and components in use when the Treaty was drafted. That issue depends on whether the term "ABM systems and components" is limited in Article V(1) to systems and components based on physical principles then in use or also includes substitutes based on other physical principles.

In attempting to answer this question, one must turn to the definition of "ABM system" in Article II(1). Proponents of the restrictive view contend that the definition in Article II(1) is purely functional, and includes all components ever created that could serve the function of countering strategic missiles in flight. They argue that the three components identified in that paragraph — ABM missiles, launchers, and radars — are merely listed as the elements of current ABM system, and that all future components of a system that satisfies the functional definition are also covered by Article II(1). . . .

This reading of the Treaty is plausible, but it has shortcomings. . . . The Treaty's other provisions consistently use "ABM system" and "components" in contexts that reflect that the Parties were referring in the Treaty text to systems and components based on known physical principles then in use.

133 Cong. Rec. 12839, 12840-12841 (1987).

In essence, the Administration argued that Article II's definition of the term "ABM system" was a definition of limitation — that is, an "ABM system" was only a system consisting of ABM interceptor missiles, launchers, and radars using then-existing technology. Sofaer testified that this reading of the Treaty was made necessary by the language of "Agreed Statement D," an agreement that accompanies the Treaty. It provides:

> In order to insure fulfillment of the obligation not to deploy ABM systems and their components except as provided in Article III of the Treaty, the Parties agree that in the event ABM systems based on other physical principles . . . are created in the future, specific limitations on such systems and their components would be subject to discussion in accordance with Article XIII [creating a standing consultative commission] and agreement in accordance with Article XIV [regarding amendments] of the Treaty.

Sofaer argued that this agreement permitted the development and testing of ABM systems based on "other physical principles" — that is, future technology other than ABM interceptor missiles, launchers, and radars available in 1972. In short, Sofaer contended that if Article II banned future technologies, there would have been no need for Agreed Statement D.

Sofaer also argued that the Treaty's drafting history supported the broad reinterpretation:

> The entire negotiating record is classified, and I, therefore, cannot reveal any detail in open session. . . . [Having reviewed these documents], I reached the firm conclusion that, although the U.S. delegates initially sought to ban development and testing of nonland-based systems or components based on future technology, the Soviets refused to go along, and no such agreement was reached. . . .
> . . . Treaties, like other agreements, are enforceable only to the extent they create mutual rights and duties. In effect, because the Soviets succeeded in avoiding a broad, binding commitment regarding the development and testing of mobile systems and components based on future technology, we cannot properly be said to be bound by such a commitment.

Thereafter, State Department Legal Adviser Sofaer released a series of reports. The first, which was submitted to the Senate as a classified memorandum, relied upon the Treaty's drafting history to support the broad interpretation. The report was widely criticized for failing to consider the ratification record. Thereafter, Sofaer released two unclassified studies, one on the Treaty's drafting history and one on the Treaty's ratification record. Finally, he released a report on the subsequent practice of the parties. In each case, Sofaer found that these histories supported the broad interpretation.

While the Administration was constructing the legal case for the "broader" interpretation of the Treaty, the President insisted during 1985 and 1986 that the SDI program was being conducted in a manner consistent with the traditional "restrictive" interpretation of the Treaty and promised to consult with Congress and U.S. allies before making any change in that policy. In February 1987, the Administration "began to seriously consider the possibility of restructuring the SDI program" and engaged in consultations with Congress and European allies.

In response, on March 11, 1987, Senator Joseph Biden introduced the ABM Treaty Interpretation Resolution (S. Res. 167). This provided that "during the period in which a treaty is in force, the meaning of that treaty is what the Senate understands the treaty to mean when it gives its advice and consent. . . ." Later that month, Senator Biden chaired a joint hearing of the Foreign Relations and Judiciary Committees. In his opening statement, Biden explained that "during the life of the Treaty, the Constitution permits . . . only that interpretation [as presented by the Executive Branch and as understood by the Senate], unless the treaty is formally amended with the advice and consent of the Senate."

In his testimony, Legal Adviser Sofaer introduced what came to be known as the Sofaer Doctrine. Sofaer stated that "[w]hen [the Senate] gives its advice and consent to a treaty, it is to the treaty that was made, irrespective of the explanations [the Senate] is provided." Sofaer elaborated this view in a detailed study concluding that the President is free to depart from a previously held treaty interpretation unless several conditions were met. A particular interpretation would be binding if it were "authoritatively communicated to the Senate by the Executive and clearly intended, generally understood and relied upon by the Senate in its advice and consent to ratification." The Administration argued that it was free to adopt the broad interpretation of the ABM Treaty because the restrictive interpretation failed to meet each of these criteria.

Senator Biden spoke for many senators when he called the Sofaer Doctrine "absolutely staggering." Senator Carl Levin, for example, asked:

> What is the importance of the advice and consent process if the executive can redefine the terms of treaties at will? If we allow this administration to reinterpret the ABM Treaty the Senate will have written itself out of the treatymaking process altogether. . . .

The Foreign Relations Committee, controlled by Democrats, favorably reported an amended version of Senate Resolution 167, stating that the meaning of a treaty provision "is to be determined in light of what the Senate understands the treaty to mean when it gives its advice and consent." The Resolution also said that "the contents of the secret negotiating record, not brought to the attention of the Senate, cannot be a part of the Senate's understanding of the treaty." Not all committee members shared this view. Republican Senator Jesse Helms, for example, characterized this portion of the report as an effort to "rewrite constitutional history" and argued that "subsequent practice gives to the Chief Executive the right to adjust the implementation of a treaty."

The full Senate never took action on this resolution. Nevertheless, the Congress did — indirectly — frustrate the Reagan reinterpretation of the ABM Treaty by enacting the Nunn-Levin amendment to the National Defense Authorization Act for Fiscal Years 1988 and 1989. This provided that no funds from the 1988-1989 fiscal year defense authorization could be used for new SDI projects that were inconsistent with the traditional interpretation of the Treaty. This was apparently part of a political compromise where the administration agreed to accept the narrow interpretation of the Treaty and the Senate agreed, for the time being, to forgo legislation endorsing the restrictive view of the Treaty.

C. The INF Treaty

Less than one year later, the Senate considered the Treaty on the Elimination of Intermediate Range and Shorter Range Missiles (INF Treaty). This treaty required the United States and the USSR to eliminate their stockpiles (principally in Europe) of ground-based missiles capable of reaching distances between approximately 300 and 3,500 miles. A number of senators sought administration assurances that the INF Treaty would not be subject to the same type of reinterpretation as the ABM Treaty. When such assurances were not forthcoming, the Foreign Relations Committee revised Senate Resolution 167, now called the Biden Condition, to "reaffirm the long-standing practice and the long-standing principle that the 'shared understanding' of the Executive and Senate, as reflected in the Executive's formal representations, is indeed fully binding."

A revised version of the Biden Condition was approved by the Foreign Relations Committee. It provided:

> That this Treaty shall be subject to the following principles, which derive, as a necessary implication, from the provisions of the Constitution for the making of treaties:
>
>> (a) the United States shall interpret this Treaty in accordance with the understanding of the Treaty shared by the Executive and the Senate at the time the Senate gave its advice and consent to ratification;
>> (b) such common understanding is:
>>> (i) based on the text of the Treaty; and
>>> (ii) reflected in the authoritative representations provided by the Executive branch to the Senate and its committees . . . ; [and]
>> (c) the United States shall not agree to or adopt an interpretation different from that common understanding except pursuant to Senate advice and consent to a subsequent treaty or protocol, or the enactment of a statute. . . .

This revised Biden Condition was approved by a vote of 72 to 27. After the exchange of instruments of ratification with the USSR, President Reagan wrote to the Senate:

> . . . The Senate Condition related to the Treaty Clauses of the Constitution apparently seeks to alter the law of treaty interpretation. The accompanying report

of the [Foreign Relations Committee] accords primacy, second only to the Treaty text, to all Executive branch statements to the Senate above all other sources which international forums or even U.S. courts would consider in interpreting treaties. It subordinates fundamental and essential treaty interpretative sources such as the treaty parties' intent, the treaty negotiating record and the parties' subsequent practices.

Treaties are agreements between sovereign states and must be interpreted in accordance with accepted principles of international law. . . . As a practical matter, the Senate condition can only work against the interests of the United States by creating situations in which a treaty has one meaning under international law and another under domestic law. . . .

. . . [T]he principles of treaty interpretation . . . may not be limited or changed by the Senate alone. . . . Accordingly, I am compelled to state that I cannot accept the proposition that a condition in a resolution to ratification can alter the allocation of rights and duties under the Constitution, nor could I . . . accept any diminution claimed to be effected by such a condition in the constitutional powers and responsibilities of the Presidency.

Public Papers of the Presidents of the United States: Ronald Reagan, 1988, Book I, 760-761.

In response, the Chair of the Foreign Relations Committee quoted from the Committee's report:

. . . [T]he [Biden] Condition is binding under domestic law, and obtains its binding effect because the President, in the absence of the resolution of ratification, lacks authority to participate in the treaty's ratification. He obtains such authority through the resolution of ratification and is governed by any stipulations by which the Senate conditions its consent.

In sum, the President may not act upon the Senate's consent without honoring this Condition. Nothing that he or his Administration does . . . whether before or after the act of ratification, can alter the binding effect of any condition which the Senate places upon its consent to treaty ratification. . . .

134 Cong. Rec. 14603 (1988).

Notes and Questions

1. Much of the debate turned on whether the phrase "currently consisting of" in Article II of the ABM Treaty defines prohibited systems in terms of their performance (i.e., a system that counters ballistic missiles during their flight), or in terms of their technology (i.e., using interceptor missiles, launchers, and radars). What interpretive method(s) should be used to answer these questions? Which branch of government is best placed to use these methods?

2. As a matter of international law, what is the status of statements made by executive branch officials during domestic deliberations over treaty ratification? Article 31 of the Vienna Convention precludes the use of such statements unless "accepted by the other parties as an instrument related to the treaty." Does this support Sofaer's contention that "when [the Senate] gives its advice and consent to a treaty, it is to the treaty that was made, irrespective of the explanations [the Senate] is provided"?

3. What weight should a treaty's negotiating record have? Recall that Article 31 of the Vienna Convention on the Law of Treaties provides that a treaty is to be interpreted "in good faith in accordance with the ordinary meaning to be given to

the terms of the treaty in their context and in light of its object and purpose." The Vienna Convention also provides that "[r]ecourse may be had to supplementary means of interpretation, including the preparatory work of the treaty" to confirm the meaning resulting from the application of Article 31, or to determine a treaty's meaning when the interpretation according to Article 31 is "ambiguous or obscure," or leads to a "manifestly absurd or unreasonable" result.

Consider Senator Sam Nunn's report on his review of the ABM negotiating history:

> . . . [I]t is important to note that the "negotiating record" . . . consists of a disjointed collection of cables, internal working documents, prepared talking points, [and memoranda].
>
> There is no single document or even set of documents that constitutes an official negotiating history. There is no verbatim transcript of the proceedings. Instead, we have a variety of documents of uneven quality. . . . [Some] are quite detailed . . . others contain nothing more than cryptic comments.

133 Cong. Rec. 13143, 13144 (1987).

Does Senator Nunn's report suggest a rationale for the Vienna Convention's treatment of "the preparatory work of the treaty"?

4. Which is fairer to U.S. treaty partners, the Biden Condition or the Sofaer Doctrine? Can the Biden Condition be implemented in a practical way? Are you persuaded by the following argument:

> . . . In more than a figurative sense, performance constantly becomes part of the [treaty] agreement. Documents uttered in solemn fashion, let us say, by hearings and advice and consent, continue to evolve in the course of their performance. . . .
>
> . . . In fact, appliers have no choice but to interpret and reinterpret in all treaty performance. There is simply no practical alternative to this reinterpretation. . . .
>
> Our own system would grind to a halt if, in each instance in which courts were faced with instruments that required input from them, they suspended operations and referred the matter back to Congress. The system would grind to a halt if, in cases in which executive agents had to interpret or had to respond to another party's performance-interpretation, they got in line on the Hill for additional legislation, which would, in its performance-interpretation, require additional instruction ad infinitum. . . .

W. Michael Reisman, *Necessary and Proper: Executive Competence to Interpret Treaties*, 15 Yale. J. Intl. L. 316 (1990).

5. In December 2001, the United States gave Russia, Belarus, Kazakhstan, and Ukraine formal notice that it was withdrawing from the ABM Treaty. Article XV of the Treaty provides that "[e]ach Party shall, in exercising its national sovereignty, have the right to withdraw from this Treaty if it decides that extraordinary events related to the subject matter of this Treaty have jeopardized its supreme interests." Russian President Vladimir Putin stated that the U.S. withdrawal "does not pose a threat to the national security of the Russian Federation."

In May 2002, the United States and Russia signed a Treaty on Strategic Offensive Reductions, which provides that each state "shall reduce and limit strategic nuclear warheads" so that, by December 31, 2012, the aggregate number of such warheads "does not exceed 1700-2200 for each party."

6. Should the President have the unilateral ability to terminate international agreements? This issue has reached the Supreme Court only once, in *Goldwater v.*

Carter, 444 U.S. 996 (1979). The case arose out of President Carter's unilateral termination of the United States-Republic of China [Taiwan] Defense Treaty in connection with U.S. recognition of the People's Republic of China (PRC). Thereafter, in the federal courts, nine senators and sixteen members of the House of Representatives challenged President Carter's right to do so. The district court reasoned that, as treaties are the "law of the land," it is inappropriate for a President to be able unilaterally to repeal them. The court concluded, on the basis of constitutional text and history, that the treaty power was a shared power. The Court of Appeals reversed, relying upon the President's broad foreign affairs powers. The Supreme Court granted the legislators' petition for a writ of certiorari, and, without issuing an opinion, vacated the judgment of the Court of Appeals and directed that the complaint be dismissed. Justice Powell concurred on the grounds that the case was not ripe for judicial review, because Congress had not officially responded to the President's termination of the treaty. Justice Rehnquist, writing for himself and three other Justices, concurred on the grounds that the case presented a nonjusticiable political question. Three Justices dissented. Justice Brennan argued that abrogation of the treaty was "a necessary incident" to executive recognition of the PRC and that the President has "exclusive power to recognize, and withdraw recognition from, foreign regimes."

After President Bush announced his intention to withdraw from the ABM treaty, and two days before the termination of the treaty became effective, 32 members of the House of Representatives challenged the President's ability unilaterally to withdraw from the treaty. A federal court granted defendants' motion to dismiss on the grounds that (1) the members of Congress lacked standing to pursue this action and (2) the "treaty termination issue is a nonjusticiable political question that cannot be resolved by the courts." *Kucinich v. Bush*, 236 F. Supp. 2d 1 (D.D.C. 2002).

Are the principles from treaty creation and treaty interpretation relevant to issues of treaty termination? Or is each a separate and distinct function with the executive branch playing a different role in each? What, if anything, can Congress do if it disagrees with a President's decision to terminate or withdraw from a treaty?

7. Questions regarding the executive branch's unilateral authority to change, or reinterpret, traditional U.S. understandings of the country's treaty obligations under the Convention Against Torture (CAT) arose in the context of debates over various interrogation techniques used on Taliban and al Qaeda detainees; a discussion of Administration memoranda interpreting U.S. obligations under the CAT can be found in Chapter 7, Section II.

D. Note on the Relevance of International and Foreign Law to the Interpretation of Constitutional Provisions

Courts in many states have struggled with questions of when, if ever, they should use international or comparative law to interpret constitutional language. As we saw in Section I of this chapter, many domestic constitutions explicitly refer to international law; for example, the U.S. Constitution authorizes Congress to "define offenses against the law of nations" and extends the judicial power to certain cases involving "foreign states." Reference to international law in the interpretation of these and similar constitutional clauses is relatively uncontroversial.

However, the postwar development of international human rights law described in Chapter 7 has widened the field for potential interaction between international law and constitutional interpretation. In recent years, the U.S. Supreme Court has referred to the opinions of foreign or international courts in several of its most controversial cases. The practice of using international or comparative law in these contexts to interpret the Constitution is highly contested; some, such as Justice Breyer, argue that comparative material "emphatically is relevant" to determining the meaning of constitutional provisions; others, such as former Judge Robert Bork, argue that the Court's citations to foreign and international law to the context of constitutional interpretation are "risible," "absurd," and "flabbergasting."

In *Bowers v. Hardwick*, 478 U.S. 186 (1986), the Supreme Court rejected a constitutional challenge to Georgia's law criminalizing sodomy. In a separate concurrence, Chief Justice Burger noted that "the proscriptions against sodomy have very 'ancient roots'" and that "[c]ondemnation of those practices is firmly rooted in Judeao-Christian moral and ethical standards." After reviewing Roman law, English law, and early American law, Chief Justice Burger argued that "[t]o hold that the act of homosexual sodomy is somehow protected as a fundamental right would be to cast aside millennia of moral teaching."

In *Lawrence v. Texas*, 539 U.S. 558 (2003), the Court overruled *Bowers* and held that a Texas statute criminalizing homosexual conduct was unconstitutional. Writing for the Court, Justice Kennedy stated:

> The sweeping references by Chief Justice Burger to the history of Western civilization and to Judeo-Christian moral and ethical standards did not take account of other authorities pointing in an opposite direction. A committee advising the British Parliament recommended in 1957 repeal of laws punishing homosexual conduct [and] Parliament enacted the substance of those recommendations 10 years later. Of even more importance, almost five years before *Bowers* was decided the European Court of Human Rights . . . held that the [Northern Ireland] laws proscribing [consensual homosexual] conduct were invalid under the European Convention on Human Rights. *Dudgeon v. United Kingdom*, 45 Eur. Ct. H.R. (1981) & ¶ 52. Authoritative in all countries that are members of the Council of Europe (21 nations then, 45 nations now), the decision is at odds with the premise in *Bowers* that the claim put forward was insubstantial in our Western civilization.

The Court noted that "[o]ther nations, too, have taken action consistent with an affirmation of the protected right of homosexual adults to engage in intimate, consensual conduct" and concluded that: "The right the petitioners seek in this case has been accepted as an integral part of human freedom in many other countries. There has been no showing that in this country the governmental interest in circumscribing personal choice is somehow more legitimate or urgent."

Lawrence marked the first time that a Supreme Court majority relied on the decision of an international tribunal to interpret the scope of the individual liberties found in the U.S. Constitution, and the decision revived a debate among judges, scholars, and practitioners over the use of international and foreign law materials by U.S. courts engaged in constitutional interpretation. Dissenting in *Lawrence*, Justice Scalia argued that "[c]onstitutional entitlements do not . . . spring into existence . . . because *foreign nations* decriminalize conduct." He argued that "[t]he Court's discussion of these foreign views (ignoring, of course, the many countries that have retained criminal prohibitions on sodomy) is therefore meaningless dicta. Dangerous dicta, however, since 'this Court . . . should not impose foreign moods, fads, or fashions on Americans.'"

The Court revisited this debate in *Roper v. Simmons*, 543 U.S. 551 (2005), a case involving a constitutional challenge to execution of a juvenile who was under the age of 18 when he committed his crime. After reviewing a trend among U.S. states to reject the juvenile death penalty, the diminished culpability of juveniles, and the absence of evidence that the death penalty deters juveniles, the Court stated:

> Our determination that the [juvenile] death penalty is [unconstitutional] . . . finds confirmation in the stark reality that the United States is the only country in the world that continues to give official sanction to the juvenile death penalty. This reality does not become controlling, for the task of interpreting the Eighth Amendment remains our responsibility. Yet . . . the Court has [long] referred to the laws of other countries and to international authorities as instructive for its interpretation of the Eighth Amendment's prohibition of "cruel and unusual punishments." . . .
>
> Article 37 of the United Nations Convention on the Rights of the Child, which every country in the world has ratified save for the United States and Somalia, contains an express prohibition on capital punishment for crimes committed by juveniles under 18. . . . Parallel prohibitions are contained in other significant international covenants. See [International Covenant on Civil and Political Rights, Art. 6(5)] (prohibiting capital punishment for anyone under 18 at the time of offense) (signed and ratified by the United States subject to a reservation regarding Article 6(5)). . . .
>
> [O]nly seven countries other than the United States have executed juvenile offenders since 1990: Iran, Pakistan, Saudi Arabia, Yemen, Nigeria, the Democratic Republic of Congo, and China. Since then each of these countries has either abolished capital punishment for juveniles or made public disavowal of the practice. . . . The opinion of the world community, while not controlling our outcome, does provide respected and significant confirmation for our own conclusions. . . .

Justice Scalia opposed the use of international and foreign materials:

> The Court begins by noting that "Article 37 of the United Nations Convention on the Rights of the Child, which every country in the world has ratified *save for the United States* and Somalia, contains an express prohibition on capital punishment for crimes committed by juveniles under 18." The Court also discusses the International Covenant on Civil and Political Rights (ICCPR), which the Senate ratified only subject to a reservation [reserving the right to impose capital punishment on juveniles].
>
> Unless the Court has added to its arsenal the power to join and ratify treaties on behalf of the United States, I cannot see how this evidence favors, rather than refutes, its position. That the Senate and the President — those actors our Constitution empowers to enter into treaties, see Art. II, §2 — have declined to join and ratify treaties prohibiting execution of under-18 offenders can only suggest that *our country* has either not reached a national consensus on the question, or has reached a consensus contrary to what the Court announces. . . .
>
> [T]he basic premise of the Court's argument — that American law should conform to the laws of the rest of the world — ought to be rejected out of hand. In fact the Court itself does not believe it. In many significant respects the laws of most other countries differ from our law — including not only such explicit provisions of our Constitution as the right to jury trial and grand jury indictment, but even many interpretations of the Constitution prescribed by this Court itself. . . .
>
> The Court has been oblivious to the views of other countries when deciding how to interpret [a number of constitutional provisions, including the First Amendment and the due process clause in abortion cases]. . . .

Notes and Questions

1. What is the strongest argument for citing to foreign or international law when interpreting constitutional provisions? In public comments off the bench,

Justice Breyer has suggested that U.S. and foreign judges address common issues and that U.S. judges can benefit from learning how foreign courts address these issues. Is this argument persuasive?

2. Some judges and scholars suggest that when courts in different jurisdictions cite to each other's opinions, they are engaged in a form of transjudicial conversation. Former Canadian Supreme Court Justice Claire L'Heureux-Dubé argues that "as courts look all over the world for sources of authority, the process of international influence has changed from reception to dialogue. . . . [C]ross-pollination and dialogue between jurisdictions is increasingly occurring." Does such a "dialogue" presuppose that courts in different states are engaged in a common enterprise? Would it be desirable for courts in different jurisdictions to understand themselves as being part of a larger judicial community? Some Justices have suggested that foreign courts will be more likely to cite U.S. Supreme Court opinions if the Court is more willing to cite foreign opinions. Is this a legitimate reason for the Court to refer to foreign precedent?

3. Justice Scalia argued that the *Lawrence* majority was selective in its use of international and comparative legal materials. If a U.S. court is to consider non-U.S. decisions, is there any principled justification for relying upon jurisprudence from some, but not all, foreign or international tribunals? If U.S. court is to consider international or foreign decisions in death penalty cases, should it also consider international or foreign decisions in abortion cases? Is there a difference between using international law and using comparative law when interpreting constitutional provisions? If so, which is more appropriate, and why?

4. Following the *Lawrence* decision, Congressman Tom Feeney introduced a resolution "[e]xpressing the sense of the House of Representatives that judicial determinations regarding the meaning of the Constitution of the United States should not be based on judgments, laws, or pronouncements of foreign institutions. . . ." Should Congress through legislation tell judges what legal materials they can or cannot rely upon in constitutional litigation?

V. OPENING AND CLOSING THE COURTHOUSE DOOR TO INTERNATIONAL LAW CLAIMS: PURSUING FERDINAND MARCOS IN U.S. COURTS

States have a number of reasons for accepting and for rejecting international legal claims in their domestic court systems. While many of the problems explored above can be understood in this light, we now turn to some specific statutes and doctrines that explicitly either open or close U.S. courts to international law claims. As you read these materials, consider the political and institutional forces that tend to support or oppose the use of international law norms in U.S. courts. Consider also how courts explicitly struggle with the appropriate relationship between international and domestic law — and with the appropriate role of courts in determining this relationship.

A. The Problem

Ferdinand Marcos was elected president of the Philippines in 1965 and re-elected in 1969. The Philippine constitution limited presidents to two four-year terms.

However, in September 1972, shortly before he was to leave office, Marcos suspended the constitution and declared martial law. In January 1973, Marcos ordered ratification of a new constitution eliminating term limits for the president and, in effect, granting Marcos sole authority to rule the Philippines. Marcos then named himself Commander-in-Chief of the Philippine Armed Forces and proclaimed that he would direct the operation of the entire government, including all its agencies and instrumentalities.

Political dissent was harshly repressed after martial law was imposed. Marcos ordered the arrest of thousands of persons because of their real or apparent opposition to his government. Some arrestees were beaten and tortured. Torture methods included electric shock, "games" of Russian roulette, and rape or other forms of sexual assault.

Marcos also engaged in the widespread and systematic theft of funds and properties belonging to the Philippine government and people. Marcos accomplished this by accepting payments in exchange for government contracts and other public benefits, taking private property for the benefit of persons beholden to or fronting for him, diverting loans and credits from other governments intended for use by the Philippine government, and creating public monopolies, which were given to his cronies and friends.

In 1986, as part of a "People Power" revolution, Marcos was deposed as president. Marcos, his family, and members of his inner circle flew to Hickam Air Force Base in Hawaii, taking with them dozens of crates filled with gold, jewelry, and cash. Within a month after his arrival in the United States, half a dozen lawsuits were filed against Marcos in U.S. courts for human rights violations that occurred in the Philippines during Marcos's rule.

Several different types of actions were filed. Approximately 30 suits were filed on behalf of named individuals. These included, for example, *Trajano v. Marcos*. On August 31, 1977, Imee Marcos-Manotoc, President Marcos's daughter, was the featured speaker at a university forum. After posing a question to Marcos-Manotoc at the forum, Archimedes Trajano was kidnaped, interrogated, and tortured to death by military intelligence personnel acting under Marcos-Manotoc's authority. The *Trajano* suit sought damages for false imprisonment, kidnaping, wrongful death, and deprivation of rights.

In addition, a series of class action suits were filed. One was filed on behalf of Philippine torture and summary execution victims. Two others were brought by victims of arbitrary detention and, in some cases, torture. Another was filed on behalf of "all civilian citizens of the Philippines who, between 1972 and 1986, were tortured, summarily executed, or 'disappeared' by Philippine military or paramilitary groups." These suits were consolidated and involved classes consisting of approximately 10,000 persons. Finally, the Republic of the Philippines filed actions in state and in federal courts in California and in federal courts in New York, New Jersey, and Texas in an attempt to recover $1.55 billion that Marcos allegedly stole from the national treasury.

Should U.S. courts hear these suits?

B. Opening the Door to International Law Claims? The Alien Tort Statute

Some of the claims against Marcos were filed under the Alien Tort Statute (ATS), 28 U.S.C. §1350. This provision, originally passed as part of the Judiciary Act of 1789, provides that "[t]he district courts shall have original jurisdiction of any civil action by an alien for a tort only, committed in violation of the law of nations or of a treaty of the United States." This statute was rarely used for nearly two hundred years. However, in 1980, the Second Circuit decided *Filartiga v. Pena-Irala* under the ATS. The decision was hailed by human rights advocates, and sparked a flurry of human rights litigation in U.S. courts. As we will see, these cases have, in turn, sparked a reaction from courts and commentators highly critical of the adjudication of international human rights claims in U.S. courts.

Filartiga v. Pena-Irala

630 F.2d 876 (2d Cir. 1980)

I

The appellants, plaintiffs below, are citizens of the Republic of Paraguay. Dr. Joel Filartiga, a physician, [is] . . . a longstanding opponent of the government of President Alfredo Stroessner, which has held power in Paraguay since 1954. [Plaintiff Dolly Filartiga is his daughter.] . . . The Filartigas brought this action in the Eastern District of New York against Americo Norberto Pena-Irala (Pena), also a citizen of Paraguay, for wrongfully causing the death of Dr. Filartiga's seventeen-year old son, Joelito. . . .

[O]n March 29, 1976, Joelito Filartiga was kidnapped and tortured to death by Pena, who was then Inspector General of Police in Asuncion, Paraguay. . . . The Filartigas claim that Joelito was tortured and killed in retaliation for his father's political activities and beliefs.

[The Filartigas' efforts to obtain justice in Paraguay were unsuccessful. In 1978, Pena entered the United States on a visitor's visa. Dolly Filartiga learned that Pena was in Brooklyn and had a summons and complaint served on Pena. The complaint invoked the ATS as a basis for jurisdiction. The District Court dismissed the complaint on the grounds that "the law of nations" as used in the ATS does not govern a state's treatment of its own citizens].

II

[T]he Alien Tort Statute . . . provides: "The district courts shall have original jurisdiction of any civil action by an alien for a tort only, committed in violation of the law of nations or a treaty of the United States." Since appellants do not contend that their action arises directly under a treaty of the United States, a threshold question on the jurisdictional issue is whether the conduct alleged violates the law of nations. . . .

The Paquete Habana, 175 U.S. 677 (1900), reaffirmed that

> where there is no treaty, and no controlling executive or legislative act or judicial decision, resort must be had to the customs and usages of civilized nations; and, as evidence of these, to the works of jurists and commentators, who by years of labor, research and experience, have made themselves peculiarly well acquainted with the subjects of which they treat. . . .

Habana is particularly instructive for present purposes, for it held that the traditional prohibition against seizure of an enemy's coastal fishing vessels during wartime, a standard that began as one of comity only, had ripened over the preceding century into "a settled rule of international law" by "the general assent of civilized nations." Thus it is clear that courts must interpret international law not as it was in 1789, but as it has evolved and exists among the nations of the world today. . . .

The United Nations Charter . . . makes it clear that in this modern age a state's treatment of its own citizens is a matter of international concern. It provides:

> With a view to the creation of conditions of stability and well-being which are necessary for peaceful and friendly relations among nations . . . the United Nations shall promote . . . universal respect for, and observance of, human rights and fundamental freedoms for all. . . .

[A]lthough there is no universal agreement as to the precise extent of the "human rights and fundamental freedoms" guaranteed to all by the Charter, there is at present no dissent from the view that the guaranties include, at a bare minimum, the right to be free from torture. This prohibition has become part of customary international law, as evidenced and defined by the Universal Declaration of Human Rights, which states, in the plainest of terms, "no one shall be subjected to torture." The General Assembly has declared that the Charter precepts embodied in this Universal Declaration "constitute basic principles of international law."

Particularly relevant is the [General Assembly] Declaration on the Protection of All Persons from Being Subjected to Torture . . . [which] expressly prohibits any state from permitting the dastardly and totally inhuman act of torture. . . . This Declaration, like the Declaration of Human Rights before it, was adopted without dissent by the General Assembly. . . .

Turning to the act of torture, we have little difficulty discerning its universal renunciation in the modern usage and practice of nations. The international consensus surrounding torture has found expression in numerous international treaties and accords. E.g., American Convention on Human Rights, Art. 5 ("No one shall be subjected to torture or to cruel, inhuman or degrading punishment or treatment"); International Covenant on Civil and Political Rights (identical language). The substance of these international agreements is reflected in modern municipal — i.e., national — law as well. Although torture was once a routine concomitant of criminal interrogations in many nations, during the modern and hopefully more enlightened era it has been universally renounced. According to one survey, torture is prohibited, expressly or implicitly, by the constitutions of over fifty-five nations, including both the United States and Paraguay. . . .

We have been directed to no assertion by any contemporary state of a right to torture its own or another nation's citizens. Indeed, United States diplomatic contacts confirm the universal abhorrence with which torture is viewed:

> In exchanges between United States embassies and all foreign states with which the United States maintains relations, it has been the Department of State's general experience that no government has asserted a right to torture its own nationals. Where reports of torture elicit some credence, a state usually responds by denial or, less frequently, by asserting that the conduct was unauthorized or constituted rough treatment short of torture.[15]

Memorandum of the United States as *Amicus Curiae* at 16 n.34.

[15]The fact that the prohibition of torture is often honored in the breach does not diminish its binding effect as a norm of international law. As one commentator has put it, "The best evidence for the existence of international law is that every actual State recognizes that it does exist and that it is itself under an obligation to observe it. States often violate international law, just as individuals often violate

Having examined the sources from which customary international law is derived — the usage of nations, judicial opinions and the works of jurists — we conclude that official torture is now prohibited by the law of nations. The prohibition is clear and unambiguous, and admits of no distinction between treatment of aliens and citizens. Accordingly, we must conclude that the dictum in [earlier cases] to the effect that "violations of international law do not occur when the aggrieved parties are nationals of the acting state," is clearly out of tune with the current usage and practice of international law. . . .

Filartiga sparked a number of ATS suits, often by plaintiffs with human rights claims against foreign states or officials and, later, against multinational corporations. One of the most controversial of these cases was *Tel-Oren v. Libyan Arab Republic,* which arose out of an attack by 13 armed PLO members on cars and buses traveling along a main highway in Israel. The PLO members took the passengers hostage, shot them, tortured them, and murdered them. Most of the victims were Israeli citizens; a few were American and Dutch citizens. The victims filed suit in federal district court under the ATS. The district court dismissed the complaint for lack of jurisdiction and, in a series of splintered opinions, the Court of Appeals affirmed.

Tel-Oren v. Libyan Arab Republic

726 F.2d 774 (D.C. Cir. 1984)

BORK, CIRCUIT JUDGE, concurring:

II.

The question in this case is whether appellants have a cause of action in courts of the United States for injuries they suffered in Israel. . . . [T]he Second Circuit in *Filartiga* assumed [] that Congress' grant of jurisdiction [in the ATS] also created a cause of action. That seems to me fundamentally wrong and certain to produce pernicious results. For reasons I will develop, it is essential that there be an explicit grant of a cause of action before a private plaintiff be allowed to enforce principles of international law in a federal tribunal. It will be seen below, however, that no body of law expressly grants appellants a cause of action; the relevant inquiry, therefore, is whether a cause of action is to be inferred. . . .

An analysis of the appropriateness of providing appellants with a cause of action must take into account the concerns that are inherent in and peculiar to the field of international relations. . . . The factors counseling hesitation [in inferring a cause of action] are constitutional; they derive from principles of separation of powers.

The crucial element of the doctrine of separation of powers in this case is the principle that "[t]he conduct of the foreign relations of our Government is committed by the Constitution to the Executive and Legislative — 'the political' — Departments." *Oetjen v. Central Leather Co.*, 246 U.S. 297, 302 (1918). That principle

----

municipal law; but no more than individuals do States defend their violations by claiming they are above the law." J. Brierly, The Outlook for International Law 4-5 (Oxford 1944).

has been translated into a limitation on judicial power in the international law area principally through the act of state and political question doctrines. Whether or not this case falls within one of these categories, the concerns that underlie them are present and demand recognition here. . . .

[Judge Bork then determined that none of the treaties appellants invoked granted them a cause of action for a violation of their provisions]. . . .

IV.

[A]ppellants . . . contend that federal common law automatically provides a cause of action for international law violations, as it would for violations of other federal common law rights. I cannot accept this conclusion.

Appellants' argument reflects a confusion of two distinct meanings of "common law." That term has long referred to the body of court-made law whose origins can be traced to the medieval English legal system. It has also come to refer generally to law (mostly court-made) not based on a statute or constitution. "Federal common law," in particular, has been used "to refer generally to federal rules of decision where the authority for a federal rule is not explicitly or clearly found in federal statutory or constitutional command." P. Bator, P. Mishkin, D. Shapiro & H. Wechsler, *Hart and Wechsler's The Federal Courts and the Federal System* 770 (2d ed. 1973). To say that international law is part of federal common law is to say only that it is nonstatutory and nonconstitutional law to be applied, in appropriate cases, in municipal courts. It is not to say that, like the common law of contract and tort, for example, by itself it affords individuals the right to ask for judicial relief.

Thus, the step appellants would have us take — from the phrase "common law" to the implication of a cause of action — is not a simple and automatic one. Neither is it advisable. The considerations of separation of powers rehearsed above provide ample reason for refusing to take a step that would plunge federal courts into the foreign affairs of the United States. . . .

What little relevant historical background is now available to us indicates that those who drafted the Constitution and the Judiciary Act of 1789 wanted to open federal courts to aliens for the purpose of avoiding, not provoking, conflicts with other nations. A broad reading of section 1350 runs directly contrary to that desire. . . .

Judge Bork's argument that ATS plaintiffs need a separate cause of action was not widely accepted and, after *Tel-Oren*, most courts to consider the issue, including the Second, Ninth and Eleventh Circuits, found that the ATS provides a cause of action. In addition, in 1991, Congress responded to *Tel-Oren* by enacting the Torture Victim Protection Act (TVPA). This act provides that "[a]n individual who, under actual or apparent authority, or color of law, of any foreign nation" subjects an individual to torture or extrajudicial killing shall be liable in a civil action to that individual or the individual's legal representative.

Thereafter, the number of cases under the ATS and TVPA grew in number and expanded in scope. A number of suits were filed against government officials for human rights abuses, including the former Guatemalan Defense Minister, the former Chinese Prime Minister, and the President of Zimbabwe. Other suits were filed

lots or law suits,

against U.S. and foreign companies, often on a theory that the corporation had aided and abetted the unlawful acts of a foreign government. For example, after the Nigerian government executed human rights activist Ken Saro-Wiwa, his son and others sued Royal Dutch Shell under the ATS; Burmese plaintiffs sued Unocal for human rights abuses associated with the construction of a gas pipeline project in Burma; and Holocaust survivors sued German companies and their U.S. parent companies for slave labor during World War II. More recently, plaintiffs have sought redress under the ATS for violations of international environmental law.

These suits proved highly controversial. Some commentators argued that ATS cases interfered with executive branch prerogatives in foreign affairs and threatened U.S. foreign policy interests. Some business groups argued that imposing corporate liability for human rights violations abroad would chill international trade and investment as multinationals would be reluctant to do business in states with poor records of respecting human and labor rights. A narrower and more technical critique echoed Judge Bork's arguments that the ATS is purely jurisdictional and that Congress must adopt legislation implementing an international norm before it can becomes actionable under Section 1350.

Notes and Questions

1. Judge Bork argues that ATS plaintiffs must show that the "law of nations" grants them a cause of action. Other appellate courts found that the ATS "creates a cause of action for violations of specific, universal and obligatory human rights standards." Reviewing the language of the statute, who has the better of the argument?

2. In *Filartiga*, the Second Circuit stated that "[w]e believe it is sufficient here to construe the Alien Tort Statute, not as granting new rights to aliens, but simply as opening the federal courts for adjudication of the rights already recognized by international law." Is the court suggesting that international law provides a cause of action? If international law provides an independent cause of action, would international law claims be covered by the general grant of federal jurisdiction over claims "arising under" federal law, thereby obviating the need for the ATS?

3. Although Libya was named as a defendant in *Tel-Oren*, plaintiffs cannot sue a foreign state under the ATS. In *Argentine Republic v. Ameranda Hess*, 488 U.S. 428 (1989), the Supreme Court held that the Foreign Sovereign Immunities Act (FSIA) provides the sole basis for obtaining jurisdiction over foreign states and their instrumentalities in U.S. courts. The FSIA is explored in Chapter 6.

4. What interest does the United States have in the adjudication in U.S. courts of claims by foreign plaintiffs against foreign defendants over events that happened outside the United States?

C. The Supreme Court Weighs In: "The Door Is Still Ajar"

In June 2004, the U.S. Supreme Court addressed the scope of the ATS for the first time. The case involved a Mexican national, Humberto Alvarez-Machain, whom the U.S. government believed to be an accomplice in the murder of an undercover Drug Enforcement Administration (DEA) agent. The DEA approved the abduction of Alvarez-Machain from Mexico to the United States to stand trial. As discussed in

Chapter 6, the U.S. Supreme Court rejected the argument that the kidnaping divested U.S. courts of jurisdiction over Alvarez-Machain. After Alvarez-Machain was acquitted at his murder trial, he filed suit to recover damages from his abductors under the ATS. The district court awarded the plaintiff $25,000 in damages, and the Ninth Circuit affirmed.

Sosa v. Alvarez-Machain

542 U.S. 692 (2004)

JUSTICE SOUTER delivered the Court's opinion; he wrote for a unanimous Court in Part III of his opinion, and was joined by JUSTICES STEVENS, O'CONNER, KENNEDY, GINSBURG and BREYER in Part IV of his opinion. JUSTICE SCALIA filed an opinion concurring in part and concurring in the judgement, in which JUSTICES REHNQUIST and THOMAS joined.

III

A

Ats does not provide a new cause of action.

Alvarez says that the ATS was intended not simply as a jurisdictional grant, but as authority for the creation of a new cause of action for torts in violation of international law. We think that reading is implausible. As enacted in 1789, the ATS gave the district courts "cognizance" of certain causes of action, and the term bespoke a grant of jurisdiction, not power to mold substantive law. The fact that the ATS was placed in §9 of the Judiciary Act, a statute otherwise exclusively concerned with federal-court jurisdiction, is itself support for its strictly jurisdictional nature. . . . In sum, we think the statute was intended as jurisdictional in the sense of addressing the power of the courts to entertain cases concerned with a certain subject.

But holding the ATS jurisdictional raises a new question, this one about the interaction between the ATS at the time of its enactment and the ambient law of the era. . . .

1

In the years of the early Republic, [the] law of nations comprised two principal elements, the first covering the general norms governing the behavior of national states with each other. . . . This aspect of the law of nations thus occupied the executive and legislative domains, not the judicial.

The law of nations included a second, more pedestrian element, however, that did fall within the judicial sphere, as a body of judge-made law regulating the conduct of individuals situated outside domestic boundaries and consequently carrying an international savor. To Blackstone, the law of nations in this sense was implicated "in mercantile questions, such as bills of exchange and the like; in all marine causes, relating to freight, average, demurrage, insurances, bottomry . . . ; [and] in all disputes relating to prizes, to shipwrecks, to hostages, and ransom bills." 4 W. Blackstone, Commentaries on the Laws of England 67 (1769). . . .

There was, finally, a sphere in which these rules binding individuals for the benefit of other individuals overlapped with the norms of state relationships. Blackstone referred to it when he mentioned three specific offenses against the law of nations addressed by the criminal law of England: violation of safe conducts, infringement of the rights of ambassadors, and piracy. An assault against an ambassador, for example, impinged upon the sovereignty of the foreign nation and if not adequately redressed could rise to an issue of war. It was this narrow set of violations of the law of nations, admitting of a judicial remedy and at the same time threatening serious consequences in international affairs, that was probably on the minds of the men who drafted the ATS with its reference to tort.

2

Before there was any ATS, a distinctly American preoccupation with these hybrid international norms had taken shape owing to the distribution of political power from independence through the period of confederation. The Continental Congress was hamstrung by its inability to "cause infractions of treaties, or of the law of nations to be punished," J. Madison, Journal of the Constitutional Convention 60, and in 1781 the Congress implored the States to vindicate rights under the law of nations. In words that echo Blackstone, the congressional resolution called upon state legislatures to "provide expeditious, exemplary, and adequate punishment" for "the violation of safe conducts or passports, . . . of hostility against such as are in amity, . . . with the United States, . . . infractions of the immunities of ambassadors and other public ministers . . . [and] infractions of treaties and conventions to which the United States are a party." The resolution recommended that the States "authorise suits . . . for damages by the party injured, and for compensation to the United States for damage sustained by them from an injury done to a foreign power by a citizen." *Id.*, at 1137 . . . .

Appreciation of the Continental Congress's incapacity to deal with this class of cases was intensified by the so-called Marbois incident of May 1784, in which a French adventurer, Longchamps, verbally and physically assaulted the Secretary of the French Legion in Philadelphia. See *Respublica v. De Longchamps*, 1 Dall. 111 (O.T. Phila. 1784). Congress called again for state legislation addressing such matters. . . .

The Framers responded by vesting the Supreme Court with original jurisdiction over "all Cases affecting Ambassadors, other public ministers and Consuls." U.S. Const., Art. III, §2, and the First Congress followed through [by enacting the ATS]. . . .

3

There is no record of congressional discussion about private actions that might be subject to the [ATS's] jurisdictional provision, or about any need for further legislation to create private remedies; there is no record even of debate on the section. . . . [D]espite considerable scholarly attention, it is fair to say that a consensus understanding of what Congress intended has proven elusive.

[Nonetheless] there is every reason to suppose that the First Congress did not pass the ATS as a jurisdictional convenience to be placed on the shelf for use by a future Congress or state legislature that might, some day, authorize the creation of causes of action or itself decide to make some element of the law of nations actionable for the benefit of foreigners. The anxieties of the preconstitutional period cannot be ignored easily enough to think that the statute was not meant to have a practical effect. . . . It would have been passing strange for . . . Congress to vest federal courts expressly with jurisdiction to entertain civil causes brought by aliens alleging violations of the law of nations, but to no effect whatever until the Congress should take further action. . . .

The second inference to be drawn from the history is that Congress intended the ATS to furnish jurisdiction for a relatively modest set of actions alleging violations of the law of nations. Uppermost in the legislative mind appears to have been offenses against ambassadors, violations of safe conduct were probably understood to be actionable, and individual actions arising out of prize captures and piracy may well have also been contemplated. But the common law appears to have understood only those three of the hybrid variety as definite and actionable, or at any rate, to have assumed only a very limited set of claims. . . .

IV

We think it is correct, then, to assume that the First Congress understood that the district courts would recognize private causes of action for certain torts in violation of the law of nations, though we have found no basis to suspect Congress had any examples in mind beyond . . . violation of safe conducts, infringement of the rights of ambassadors, and piracy. We assume, too, that no development in the two centuries from the enactment of §1350 to the birth of the modern line of cases beginning with *Filartiga v. Pena-Irala,* has categorically precluded federal courts from recognizing a claim under the law of nations as an element of common law; Congress has not in any relevant way amended §1350. . . . Still, there are good reasons for a restrained conception of the discretion a federal court should exercise in considering a new cause of action of this kind. Accordingly, we think courts should require any claim based on the present-day law of nations to rest on a norm of international character accepted by the civilized world and defined with a specificity comparable to the features of the 18th-century paradigms we have recognized. . . .

A

A series of reasons argue for judicial caution when considering the kinds of individual claims that might implement the jurisdiction conferred by the early statute. First, the prevailing conception of the common law has changed since 1789 in a way that counsels restraint in judicially applying internationally generated norms. When §1350 was enacted, the accepted conception was of the common law as "a transcendental body of law outside of any particular State but obligatory within it unless and until changed by statute." *Black and White Taxicab & Transfer Co. v. Brown and Yellow Taxicab & Transfer Co.,* 276 U.S. 518, 533 (1928) (Holmes, J., dissenting). Now, however, in most cases where a court is asked to state or formulate a common law principle in a new context, there is a general understanding that the law is not so much found or discovered as it is either made or created. . . .

Second, along with, and in part driven by, that conceptual development in understanding common law has come an equally significant rethinking of the role of the federal courts in making it. *Erie R. Co. v. Tompkins,* 304 U.S. 64 (1938), was the watershed in which we denied the existence of any federal "general" common law, *id.,* at 78, which largely withdrew to havens of specialty, some of them defined by express congressional authorization to devise a body of law directly. . . . And although we have . . . assumed competence to make judicial rules of decision of particular importance to foreign relations, such as the act of state doctrine, the general practice has been to look for legislative guidance before exercising innovative authority over substantive law. . . .

Third, . . . [the] decision to create a private right of action is one better left to legislative judgment in the great majority of cases. The creation of a private right of

Congress has to create a cause of action

action raises issues beyond the mere consideration whether underlying primary conduct should be allowed or not, entailing, for example, a decision to permit enforcement without the check imposed by prosecutorial discretion. . . .

Courts Should be careful not to interfere with foreign relations

Fourth, . . . the potential implications for the foreign relations of the United States of recognizing such causes should make courts particularly wary of impinging on the discretion of the Legislative and Executive Branches in managing foreign affairs. It is one thing for American courts to enforce constitutional limits on our own State and Federal Governments' power, but quite another to consider suits under rules that would go so far as to claim a limit on the power of foreign governments over their own citizens, and to hold that a foreign government or its agent has transgressed those limits. Yet modern international law is very much concerned with just such questions, and apt to stimulate calls for vindicating private interests in §1350 cases. Since many attempts by federal courts to craft remedies for the violation of new norms of international law would raise risks of adverse foreign policy consequences, they should be undertaken, if at all, with great caution.

Don't encroach on Congress where they haven't given authority.

[Fifth, we] have no congressional mandate to seek out and define new and debatable violations of the law of nations, and modern indications of congressional understanding of the judicial role in the field have not affirmatively encouraged greater judicial creativity. It is true that a clear mandate appears in the [TVPA] . . . [b]ut that affirmative authority is confined to specific subject matter, and although the legislative history includes the remark that §1350 should "remain intact to permit suits based on other norms that already exist or may ripen in the future into rules of customary international law," Congress as a body has done nothing to promote such suits. Several times, indeed, the Senate has expressly declined to give the federal courts the task of interpreting and applying international human rights law, as when its ratification of the International Covenant on Civil and Political Rights declared that the substantive provisions of the document were not self-executing. . . .

C

Don't interpret more than was meant when Statute was enacted.

. . . [W]e are persuaded that federal courts should not recognize private claims under federal common law for violations of any international law norm with less definite content and acceptance among civilized nations than the historical paradigms familiar when §1350 was enacted. And the determination whether a norm is sufficiently definite to support a cause of action[20] should (and, indeed, inevitably must) involve an element of judgment about the practical consequences of making that cause available to litigants in the federal courts.[21]

[20]A related consideration is whether international law extends the scope of liability for a violation of a given norm to the perpetrator being sued, if the defendant is a private actor such as a corporation or individual.

[21]This requirement of clear definition is not meant to be the only principle limiting the availability of relief in the federal courts for violations of customary international law, though it disposes of this case. For example, the European Commission argues as *amicus curiae* that basic principles of international law require that before asserting a claim in a foreign forum, the claimant must have exhausted any remedies available in the domestic legal system, and perhaps in other fora such as international claims tribunals. We would certainly consider this requirement in an appropriate case.

Another possible limitation that we need not apply here is a policy of case-specific deference to the political branches. For example, there are now pending in federal district court several class actions seeking damages from various corporations alleged to have participated in, or abetted, the regime of apartheid that formerly controlled South Africa. The Government of South Africa has said that these

Alvarez's detention claim must be gauged against the current state of international law, looking to those sources we have long, albeit cautiously, recognized. . . .

To begin with, Alvarez . . . says that his abduction by Sosa was an "arbitrary arrest" within the meaning of the Universal Declaration of Human Rights (Declaration), . . . article nine of the International Covenant on Civil and Political Rights (Covenant), to which the United States is a party, and to various other conventions to which it is not. But the Declaration does not of its own force impose obligations as a matter of international law. And, although the Covenant does bind the United States as a matter of international law, the United States ratified the Covenant on the express understanding that it was not self-executing and so did not itself create obligations enforceable in the federal courts. Accordingly, Alvarez cannot say that the Declaration and Covenant themselves establish the relevant and applicable rule of international law. He instead attempts to show that prohibition of arbitrary arrest has attained the status of binding customary international law.

Here, it is useful to examine Alvarez's complaint in greater detail. As he presently argues it, the claim does not rest on the cross-border feature of his abduction. . . . Instead, it relied on the conclusion that the law of the United States did not authorize Alvarez's arrest, because the DEA lacked extraterritorial authority under [federal law]. . . .

Alvarez thus invokes a general prohibition of "arbitrary" detention defined as officially sanctioned action exceeding positive authorization to detain under the domestic law of some government. . . . Alvarez cites little authority that a rule so broad has the status of a binding customary norm today. He certainly cites nothing to justify the federal courts in taking his broad rule as the predicate for a federal lawsuit, for its implications would be breathtaking. His rule would support a cause of action in federal court for any arrest, anywhere in the world, unauthorized by the law of the jurisdiction in which it took place . . . .

Whatever may be said for the broad principle Alvarez advances, in the present, imperfect world, it expresses an aspiration that exceeds any binding customary rule having the specificity we require. Creating a private cause of action to further that aspiration would go beyond any residual common law discretion we think it appropriate to exercise.[30] It is enough to hold that a single illegal detention of less than a day, followed by the transfer of custody to lawful authorities and a prompt arraignment, violates no norm of customary international law so well defined as to support the creation of a federal remedy.

[Holding.]

---

cases interfere with the policy embodied by its Truth and Reconciliation Commission, which [is] . . . "based on confession and absolution, informed by the principles of reconciliation, reconstruction, reparation and goodwill." The United States has agreed. In such cases, there is a strong argument that federal courts should give serious weight to the Executive Branch's view of the case's impact on foreign policy.

[30]Alvarez also cites a finding by a United Nations working group that his detention was arbitrary under the Declaration, the Covenant, and customary international law. See Report of the United Nations Working Group on Arbitrary Detention, U.N. Doc. E/CN.4/1994/27, pp. 139-140 (Dec. 17, 1993). That finding is not addressed, however, to our demanding standard of definition, which must be met to raise even the possibility of a private cause of action. If Alvarez wishes to seek compensation on the basis of the working group's finding, he must address his request to Congress.

JUSTICE SCALIA, with whom THE CHIEF JUSTICE and JUSTICE THOMAS join, concurring in part and concurring in the judgment.

III

The analysis in the Court's opinion departs from my own in this respect: After concluding in Part III that "the ATS is a jurisdictional statute creating no new causes of action," the Court addresses at length in Part IV the "good reasons for a restrained conception of the *discretion* a federal court should exercise in considering a new cause of action" under the ATS. By framing the issue as one of "discretion," the Court skips over the antecedent question of authority. This neglects the "lesson of *Erie*," that "grants of jurisdiction alone" (which the Court has acknowledged the ATS to be) "are not themselves grants of law-making authority." On this point, the Court observes only that no development between the enactment of the ATS (in 1789) and the birth of modern international human rights litigation under that statute (in 1980) "has categorically *precluded* federal courts from recognizing a claim under the law of nations as an element of common law." This turns our jurisprudence regarding federal common law on its head. The question is not what case or congressional action *prevents* federal courts from applying the law of nations as part of the general common law; it is what *authorizes* that peculiar exception from *Erie's* fundamental holding that a general common law *does not exist.* . . .

* * *

We Americans have a method for making the laws that are over us. We elect representatives to two Houses of Congress, each of which must enact the new law and present it for the approval of a President, whom we also elect. For over two decades now, unelected federal judges have been usurping this lawmaking power by converting what they regard as norms of international law into American law. Today's opinion approves that process in principle, though urging the lower courts to be more restrained. . . .

Notes and Questions

1. Are you persuaded by the court's discussion of (a) congressional intent behind the passage of the ATS, (b) the judiciary's ability to recognize claims under common law, or (c) the role of the courts in cases involving foreign relations? Which seems most important to the Court?

2. The *Sosa* majority stated that "the door is still ajar [to further independent judicial recognition of actionable international norms] subject to vigilant doorkeeping, and thus [U.S. courts remain] open to a narrow class of international norms today." Compare the sources that the *Filartiga* court used to find the existence of a customary norm prohibiting official torture and the sources that the *Sosa* court found insufficient to establish a customary norm prohibiting arbitrary detention. What sources should future ATS plaintiffs rely upon to establish the existence of a customary norm actionable in ATS litigation? After *Sosa*, would any of the following claims be actionable: genocide, kidnaping, extrajudicial killing, forced labor, ethnic or religious discrimination, sexual violence, environmental degradation?

3. In *Sosa*, the Court stated that it would "welcome any congressional guidance in exercising jurisdiction with such obvious potential to affect foreign relations." What significance, if any, attaches to the fact that Congress has not amended the ATS since *Filartiga* was decided and, following *Tel-Oren*, enacted the TVPA?

4. In footnote 21, the Court referred to "a policy of case-specific deference to the political branches." Under what doctrine, and under what standard of review, should courts evaluate executive branch views? Should parties be permitted to challenge the factual basis of executive branch submissions?

In *Doe v. Unocal*, an ATS case alleging that a multinational corporation had aided and abetted human rights abuses in Burma, the Clinton Administration advised the district court that "adjudication of the claims based on allegations of torture and slavery would not prejudice or impede the conduct of U.S. foreign relations with the current government of Burma." After *Sosa* was decided, the Bush Administration filed a brief in the *Doe* case stating that "economic engagement" is a foreign policy tool for encouraging reform in oppressive regimes, and that recognition of "aiding and abetting" liability for ATS claims could diminish economic engagement and hence "depriv[e] the Executive of an important tactic of diplomacy and available tools for the political branches in attempting to induce improvements in foreign human rights practices." Do arguments supporting the policy of economic engagement constitute a "case-specific" rationale for refusing to permit the case to proceed? (The *Unocal* case was eventually settled, with Unocal paying the villagers an undisclosed amount of money to compensate plaintiffs and improve living conditions in the pipeline region.)

5. In *Presbyterian Church of Sudan v. Talisman Energy*, 347 F. Supp. 2d 331 (S.D.N.Y. 2005), plaintiffs alleged that they were victims of crimes against humanity committed by the Government of Sudan and Talisman Energy, a Canadian firm. The Canadian government submitted a letter stating that the exercise of jurisdiction over this case would interfere with its ability "to implement its foreign policy" vis-à-vis Sudan. Canada also objected to the exercise of jurisdiction over the "activities of Canadian corporations that take place entirely outside the US." What weight, if any, should U.S. courts give to statements by foreign governments? Does it matter whether or not the U.S. government agrees with the foreign government's assessment? In *Talisman*, the U.S. State Department stated that "when the government in question protests that the U.S. proceeding interferes with the conduct of its foreign policy in pursuit of goals that the United States shares, we believe that considerations of international comity and judicial abstention may properly come into play."

6. Would the President's authority to conduct operations against suspected terrorists be threatened if the *Sosa* court had found that the extraterritorial arrest of foreign suspects violated customary international law?

7. In recent years, there has been intense debate over the legitimacy of the use of customary international law in cases like *Filartiga*. Do you find the following critique of this line of cases persuasive?

> Since [World War II], international law has developed to regulate to some extent the ways in which nations treat their citizens. The principal sources of this change have been a series of multilateral human rights treaties and several non-binding United Nations General Assembly Resolutions. . . . Although the United States has voted in favor of most — but not all — of the resolutions, it has declined to ratify many of the treaties. Moreover, for the ones that it has ratified, it has generally insisted, through a series of reservations, understandings, and declarations . . . that the treaties not apply as domestic law and thus not preempt inconsistent state law. . . .
>
> We are now in a position to understand what is at stake in [cases like *Filartiga* and *Tel-Oren*]. What is at stake is the enforceability of international human rights law in the U.S. federal courts. . . . The [argument] that [customary international law] is to be applied as federal common law . . . permits federal courts to accomplish through the back door of [custom] what the political branches have prohibited through the front door of treaties. . . .

Curtis A. Bradley & Jack L. Goldsmith, *The Current Illegitimacy of International Human Rights Litigation*, 66 Fordham L. Rev. 319, 327-28, 330-31 (1997).

The *Marcos* complaints were, of course, filed long before *Sosa* was decided. In *Trajano*, defendant did not appear, and the district court entered a default judgment. The court applied Philippine law and awarded damages in an amount of $4.16 million, plus attorney fees. On appeal, the Ninth Circuit upheld the district court's determination that the ATS provided jurisdiction, and that "wrongful death statutes" and tort law provided plaintiffs with a cause of action. In the class action litigation, a six-member jury heard two weeks of testimony and awarded $1.2 billion in exemplary damages to a class of 10,000 Filipinos and 23 named plaintiffs on claims involving torture, summary execution, disappearance, and prolonged arbitrary detention.

Notes and Questions

1. Under the principles announced in *Sosa*, would the various claims advanced in the *Marcos* litigation proceed in U.S. courts? Should they?
2. Despite victories in the *Marcos* litigation and a relatively small number of other ATS actions, for the most part, victorious plaintiffs have not been able to collect on their judgments. What, then, is the point of these suits?

D. Closing the Door to International Legal Claims? Judging the Acts of Foreign Governments

Under what circumstances can, or should, the courts of one nation judge the legality of another government's actions? In particular, should domestic courts give effect to foreign government actions that violate international law? Courts in the United States, and elsewhere, have developed an "act of state" doctrine providing that domestic courts should generally refrain from judging the validity of another state's sovereign acts taken within its own territory, even if the acts violate international legal norms. Like the doctrine of foreign sovereign immunity discussed in Chapter 6, the act of state doctrine is premised, in part, upon the juridical equality of all states and the fear that having courts in one state judging the validity of of another state's acts would likely "imperil the amicable relations between governments and vex the peace of nations." *Oetjen v. Central Leather Co.*, 246 U.S. 297 (1918). However, while foreign sovereign immunity can only be invoked by sovereigns and provides a jurisdictional immunity, the act of state doctrine can be invoked by private parties and constitutes a defense on the merits.

In the United States, judicial application of this doctrine has its origins in *Underhill v. Hernandez*, 168 U.S. 250 (1897). Underhill, a U.S. citizen, had built a waterworks project for the Venezuelan government. He was living in Venezuela when, in 1892, a revolution began. Revolutionary forces, later recognized by the United States as Venezuela's government, placed Underhill under house arrest during the insurrection. After he was released and returned to the United States,

Underhill filed suit in federal court seeking damages for unlawful detention and assault and battery by the Venezuelan forces. The Supreme Court held that

> Every sovereign state is bound to respect the independence of every other sovereign state, and the courts of one country will not sit in judgment on the acts of the government of another, done within its own territory. Redress of grievances by reason of such acts must be obtained through the means open to be availed of by sovereign powers as between themselves.

The Supreme Court's seminal modern discussion of the act of state doctrine is found in the *Sabbatino* opinion:

Banco Nacional de Cuba v. Sabbatino

376 U.S. 398 (1964)

MR. JUSTICE HARLAN delivered the opinion of the Court.

[In July 1960, the United States reduced the amount of sugar that could lawfully be imported from Cuba. In response, Cuba enacted a law that granted the President authority to nationalize property in Cuba in which U.S. nationals had an interest. Pursuant to this law, the Cuban government expropriated property of certain companies owned by U.S. nationals, including Compania Azucarera Vertientes-Camaguey de Cuba (CAV).

Previously, Farr, Whitlock & Company, a U.S. commodity broker, had contracted to purchase sugar from CAV. After the expropriation, Farr, Whitlock entered into new contracts to purchase the sugar identical to those it had made with CAV, with an instrumentality of the Cuban government. The sugar was then shipped from Cuba.

Farr, Whitlock then paid the purchase price of the sugar to CAV's receiver, Sabbatino, rather than to the Cuban government. Banco Nacional de Cuba, which possessed the Cuban government's right to payment under the second sugar contract, filed suit against Sabbatino in a U.S. federal court. In response to the defendant's argument that the expropriation of the sugar was unlawful, Banco invoked the act of state doctrine.]

. . . While acknowledging the continuing vitality of the act of state doctrine, the [district] court believed it inapplicable when the questioned foreign act is in violation of international law. Proceeding on the basis that a taking invalid under international law does not convey good title, the District Court found the Cuban expropriation decree to violate such law in three separate respects: it was motivated by a retaliatory and not a public purpose; it discriminated against American nationals; and it failed to provide adequate compensation. Summary judgment against petitioner was accordingly granted.

The Court of Appeals, affirming the decision on similar grounds, relied on two letters (not before the District Court) written by State Department officers which it took as evidence that the Executive branch had no objection to a judicial testing of the Cuban decree's validity. The court was unwilling to declare that any one of the infirmities found by the District Court rendered the taking invalid under international law, but was satisfied that in combination they had that effect. We granted certiorari because the issues involved bear importantly on the conduct of the country's foreign relations and more particularly on the proper role of the Judicial

Branch in this sensitive area. . . . For reasons to follow we decide that the judgment below must be reversed. . . .

IV

In deciding the present case the Court of Appeals relied in part upon an exception to the unqualified teachings of *Underhill* . . . which that court had earlier indicated. In *Bernstein v. Van Heyghen Freres Societe Anonyme*, 163 F.2d 246 (2d Cir. 1947), suit was brought to recover from an assignee property allegedly taken, in effect, by the Nazi Government because plaintiff was Jewish. Recognizing the odious nature of this act of state, the court, through Judge Learned Hand, nonetheless refused to consider it invalid on that ground. Rather, it looked to see if the Executive had acted in any manner that would indicate that United States Courts should refuse to give effect to such a foreign decree. Finding no such evidence, the court sustained dismissal of the complaint. In a later case involving similar facts the same court again assumed examination of the German acts improper, *Bernstein v. N. V. Nederlandsche-Amerikaansche Stoomvaart-Maatschappij*, 173 F.2d 71 (2d Cir. 1949), but, quite evidently following the implications of Judge Hand's opinion in the earlier case, amended its mandate to permit evidence of alleged invalidity, subsequent to receipt by plaintiff's attorney of a letter from the Acting Legal Adviser to the State Department written for the purpose of relieving the court from any constraint upon the exercise of its jurisdiction to pass on that question.[18]

This Court has never had occasion to pass upon the so-called *Bernstein* exception, nor need it do so now. For whatever ambiguity may be thought to exist in the two letters from State Department officials on which the Court of Appeals relied is now removed by the position which the Executive has taken in this Court . . . that these letters were intended to reflect no more than the Department's then wish not to make any statement bearing on this litigation. . . .

V

Preliminarily, we discuss the foundations on which we deem the act of state doctrine to rest. . . .

We do not believe that this doctrine is compelled either by the inherent nature of sovereign authority, as some of the earlier decisions seem to imply, see *Underhill*, [168 U.S. 250 (1897)]; *American Banana, supra;* or by some principle of international law. . . .

---

[18]The letter stated:

> 1. This government has consistently opposed the forcible acts of dispossession of a discriminatory and confiscatory nature practiced by the Germans on the countries or peoples subject to their controls. . . .
> 3. The policy of the Executive, with respect to claims asserted in the United States for the restitution of identifiable property (or compensation in lieu thereof) lost through force, coercion, or duress as a result of Nazi persecution in Germany, is to relieve American courts from any restraint upon the exercise of their jurisdiction to pass upon the validity of the acts of Nazi officials.

State Department Press Release, April 27, 1949, 20 Dept. State Bull. 592.

That international law does not require application of the doctrine is evidenced by the practice of nations. Most of the countries rendering decisions on the subject fail to follow the rule rigidly.[21] . . . If international law does not prescribe use of the doctrine, neither does it forbid application of the rule even if it is claimed that the act of state in question violated international law. The traditional view of international law is that it establishes substantive principles for determining whether one country has wronged another. Because of its peculiar nation-to-nation character the usual method for an individual to seek relief is to exhaust local remedies and then repair to the executive authorities of his own state to persuade them to champion his claim in diplomacy or before an international tribunal. Although it is, of course, true that United States courts apply international law as a part of our own in appropriate circumstances, *The Paquete Habana*, 175 U.S. 677, 700, the public law of nations can hardly dictate to a country which is in theory wronged how to treat that wrong within its domestic borders.

Despite the broad statement in *Oetjen* that "The conduct of the foreign relations of our Government is committed by the Constitution to the Executive and Legislative . . . Departments," it cannot of course be thought that "every case or controversy which touches foreign relations lies beyond judicial cognizance." *Baker v. Carr*, 369 U.S. 186, 211 [(1962)]. The text of the Constitution does not require the act of state doctrine; it does not irrevocably remove from the judiciary the capacity to review the validity of foreign acts of state.

The act of state doctrine does, however, have "constitutional" underpinnings. It arises out of the basic relationships between branches of government in a system of separation of powers. It concerns the competency of dissimilar institutions to make and implement particular kinds of decisions in the area of international relations. The doctrine as formulated in past decisions expresses the strong sense of the Judicial Branch that its engagement in the task of passing on the validity of foreign acts of state may hinder rather than further this country's pursuit of goals both for itself and for the community of nations as a whole in the international sphere. . . .

VI

If the act of state doctrine is a principle of decision binding on federal and state courts alike but compelled by neither international law nor the Constitution, its continuing vitality depends on its capacity to reflect the proper distribution of functions between the judicial and political branches of the Government on matters bearing upon foreign affairs. It should be apparent that the greater the degree of codification or consensus concerning a particular area of international law, the

---

[21]In English jurisprudence, in the classic case of *Luther v. James Sagor & Co.*, [1921] 3 K. B. 532, the act of state doctrine is articulated in terms not unlike those of the United States cases. See *Princess Paley Olga v. Weisz*, [1929] 1 K. B. 718. But see *Anglo-Iranian Oil Co. v. Jaffrate*, [1953] 1 Weekly L. R. 246, [1953] Int'l L. Rep. 316 (Aden Sup. Ct.) (exception to doctrine if foreign act violates international law). Civil law countries, however, which apply the rule make exceptions for acts contrary to their sense of public order. See, e.g., *Ropit* case, Cour de Cassation (France), [1929] Recueil Général Des Lois et Des Arrêts (Sirey) Part I, 217; Domke, Indonesian Nationalization Measures Before Foreign Courts, 54 Am. J. Int'l L. 305 (1960) (discussion of and excerpts from opinions of the District Court in Bremen and the Hanseatic Court of Appeals in *N. V. Verenigde Deli-Maatschapijen v. Deutsch-Indonesische Tabak-Handelsgesellschaft m. b. H.*, and of the Amsterdam District Court and Appellate Court in *Senembah Maatschappij N. V. v. Republiek Indonesie Bank Indonesia*); 40 Blätter für Zürcherische Rechtsprechung No. 65, 172-173 (Switzerland). See also *Anglo-Iranian Oil Co. v. Idemitsu Kosan Kabushiki Kaisha*, [1953] Int'l L. Rep. 312 (High Ct. of Tokyo).

more appropriate it is for the judiciary to render decisions regarding it, since the courts can then focus on the application of an agreed principle to circumstances of fact rather than on the sensitive task of establishing a principle not inconsistent with the national interest or with international justice. It is also evident that some aspects of international law touch much more sharply on national nerves than do others; the less important the implications of an issue are for our foreign relations, the weaker the justification for exclusivity in the political branches. The balance of relevant considerations may also be shifted if the government which perpetrated the challenged act of state is no longer in existence . . . for the political interest of this country may, as a result, be measurably altered. Therefore, rather than laying down or reaffirming an inflexible and all-encompassing rule in this case, we decide only that the Judicial Branch will not examine the validity of a taking of property within its own territory by a foreign sovereign government, extant and recognized by this country at the time of suit, in the absence of a treaty or other unambiguous agreement regarding controlling legal principles, even if the complaint alleges that the taking violates customary international law.

There are few if any issues in international law today on which opinion seems to be so divided as the limitations on a state's power to expropriate the property of aliens. [The Court reviews the conflicting positions taken by developed, developing, and Communist states.] . . .

The disagreement as to relevant international law standards reflects an even more basic divergence between the national interests of capital importing and capital exporting nations and between the social ideologies of those countries that favor state control of a considerable portion of the means of production and those that adhere to a free enterprise system. It is difficult to imagine the courts of this country embarking on adjudication in an area which touches more sensitively the practical and ideological goals of the various members of the community of nations.

When we consider the prospect of the courts characterizing foreign expropriations, however justifiably, as invalid under international law and ineffective to pass title, the wisdom of the precedents is confirmed. While each of the leading cases in this Court may be argued to be distinguishable on its facts from this one . . . the plain implication of all these opinions . . . is that the act of state doctrine is applicable even if international law has been violated. . . .

The possible adverse consequences of a conclusion to the contrary of that implicit in these cases is highlighted by contrasting the practices of the political branch with the limitations of the judicial process in matters of this kind. Following an expropriation of any significance, the Executive engages in diplomacy aimed to assure that United States citizens who are harmed are compensated fairly. Representing all claimants of this country, it will often be able, either by bilateral or multilateral talks, by submission to the United Nations, or by the employment of economic and political sanctions, to achieve some degree of general redress. Judicial determinations of invalidity of title can, on the other hand, have only an occasional impact, since they depend on the fortuitous circumstance of the property in question being brought into this country. Such decisions would, if the acts involved were declared invalid, often be likely to give offense to the expropriating country; since the concept of territorial sovereignty is so deep seated, any state may resent the refusal of the courts of another sovereign to accord validity to acts within its territorial borders. Piecemeal dispositions of this sort involving the probability of affront to another state could seriously interfere with negotiations being carried on by the Executive branch and might prevent or render less favorable the terms of an agreement that could otherwise be reached. Relations with third countries which have engaged in similar expropriations would not be immune from effect.

The dangers of such adjudication are present regardless of whether the State Department has, as it did in this case, asserted that the relevant act violated international law. If the Executive branch has undertaken negotiations with an expropriating country, but has refrained from claims of violation of the law of nations, a determination to that effect by a court might be regarded as a serious insult, while a finding of compliance with international law would greatly strengthen the bargaining hand of the other state with consequent detriment to American interests. . . .

Against the force of such considerations, we find respondents' countervailing arguments quite unpersuasive. Their basic contention is that United States courts could make a significant contribution to the growth of international law, a contribution whose importance, it is said, would be magnified by the relative paucity of decisional law by international bodies. But given the fluidity of present world conditions, the effectiveness of such a patchwork approach toward the formulation of an acceptable body of law concerning state responsibility for expropriations is, to say the least, highly conjectural. Moreover, it rests upon the sanguine presupposition that the decisions of the courts of the world's major capital exporting country and principal exponent of the free enterprise system would be accepted as disinterested expressions of sound legal principle by those adhering to widely different ideologies. . . .

It is suggested that if the act of state doctrine is applicable to violations of international law, it should only be so when the Executive branch expressly stipulates that it does not wish the courts to pass on the question of validity. We should be slow to reject the representations of the Government that such a reversal of the *Bernstein* principle would work serious inroads on the maximum effectiveness of United States diplomacy. Often the State Department will wish to refrain from taking an official position, particularly at a moment that would be dictated by the development of private litigation but might be inopportune diplomatically. Adverse domestic consequences might flow from an official stand which could be assuaged, if at all, only by revealing matters best kept secret. . . . We do not now pass on the *Bernstein* exception, but even if it were deemed valid, its suggested extension is unwarranted.

However offensive to the public policy of this country and its constituent States an expropriation of this kind may be, we conclude that both the national interest and progress toward the goal of establishing the rule of law among nations are best served by maintaining intact the act of state doctrine in this realm of its application. . . .

MR. JUSTICE WHITE, dissenting:

I am dismayed that the Court has, with one broad stroke, declared the ascertainment and application of international law beyond the competence of the courts of the United States in a large and important category of cases. I am also disappointed in the Court's declaration that the acts of a sovereign state with regard to the property of aliens within its borders are beyond the reach of international law in the courts of this country. However clearly established that law may be, a sovereign may violate it with impunity, except insofar as the political branches of the government may provide a remedy. This backward-looking doctrine, never before declared in this Court, is carried a disconcerting step further: not only are the courts powerless

to question acts of state proscribed by international law but they are likewise powerless to refuse to adjudicate the claim founded upon a foreign law; they must render
judgment and thereby validate the lawless act. . . . No other civilized country has
found such a rigid rule necessary for the survival of the executive branch of its
government; the executive of no other government seems to require such insulation
from international law adjudications in its courts; and no other judiciary is apparently so incompetent to ascertain and apply international law. . . .

IV

The reasons for nonreview, based as they are on traditional concepts of territorial sovereignty, lose much of their force when the foreign act of state is shown to
be a violation of international law. All legitimate exercises of sovereign power,
whether territorial or otherwise, should be exercised consistently with rules of international law, including those rules which mark the bounds of lawful state action
against aliens or their property located within the territorial confines of the foreign
state. Although a state may reasonably expect that the validity of its laws operating
on property within its jurisdiction will not be defined by local notions of public
policy of numerous other states . . . , it cannot with impunity ignore the rules governing the conduct of all nations and expect that other nations and tribunals will
view its acts as within the permissible scope of territorial sovereignty. . . .

The Court puts these considerations to rest with the assumption that the decisions of the courts "of the world's major capital exporting country and principal
exponent of the free enterprise system" would hardly be accepted as impartial
expressions of sound legal principle. The assumption, if sound, would apply to
any other problem arising from transactions that cross state lines and is tantamount
to a declaration excusing this Court from any future consequential role in the
clarification and application of international law. This declaration ignores the historic role which this Court and other American courts have played in applying and
maintaining principles of international law. . . .

Notes and Questions

1. Should the *Sabbatino* court have applied the international legal norms on
expropriation, discussed in Chapter 2? Does the Court rest its decision not to
examine the international legality of the alleged expropriation on comity? Separation of powers? Or does the act of state doctrine act as a choice of law doctrine? If so,
why should the validity of Cuba's expropriation be governed by Cuban law, rather
than by international (or U.S.) law?

2. The *Sabbatino* decision was extremely unpopular. It prompted Congress to
pass what has become known as the Sabbatino or Second Hickenlooper Amendment to the Foreign Assistance Act of 1964. This amendment provides:

> Notwithstanding any other provision of law, no court in the United States shall
> decline on the ground of the federal act of state doctrine to make a determination on
> the merits giving effect to the principles of international law in a case in which a claim of
> title or other right to property is asserted by any party including a foreign state (or a
> party claiming through such state) based upon (or traced through) a confiscation or
> other taking after January 1, 1959, by an act of that state in violation of the principles of
> international law, including the principles of compensation. . . .

> *Provided*, That this subparagraph shall not be applicable . . . in any case with respect to which the President determines the application of the act of state doctrine is required in that particular case by the foreign policy interests of the United States and a suggestion to this effect is filed on his behalf in that case with the court.

22 U.S.C. §2370(e)(2). Courts have, in general, narrowly interpreted this Amendment. The Second Circuit, for example, held that the Amendment applies only when the expropriated property is found in the United States.

Cases following *Sabbatino* revealed considerable confusion over both the scope and underlying rationale for the act of state doctrine. Two sharply divided decisions, *First National City Bank v. Banco Nacional de Cuba*, 406 U.S. 759 (1972), and *Alfred Dunhill v. Republic of Cuba*, 425 U.S. 682 (1976), raised as many questions as they answered, as in neither case was any Justice's opinion able to garner a majority of the Court. For example, in *First National City Bank*, Justice Rehnquist's plurality opinion adopted the *Bernstein* exception to the act of state doctrine, although at least five Justices rejected the exception in a splintered series of opinions. Not surprisingly, lower courts have had difficulty determining whether a *Bernstein* exception exists and, if so, its scope.

In *Dunhill*, a four-Justice plurality held that the act of state doctrine applied only to "sovereign acts" and that "the concept of an act of state should not be extended to include the repudiation of a purely commercial obligation owed by a foreign sovereign or by one of its commercial instrumentalities." 425 U.S. at 695. Four other Justices rejected this so-called commercial activity exception, and one declined to address the issue. Lower courts have split on whether this exception exists, and the Supreme Court has not addressed the issue since *Dunhill*.

Finally, courts after *Sabbatino* also split over the question of whether to apply the act of state doctrine where the plaintiff's claim would require an examination of the motivations for a foreign state's act, as opposed to an inquiry into the validity of a foreign state's act. In its most recent act of state case, the Court addressed this question.

W. S. Kirkpatrick & Co. v. Environmental Tectonics Corp., International

493 U.S. 400 (1990)

In this case we must decide whether the act of state doctrine bars a court in the United States from entertaining a cause of action that does not rest upon the asserted invalidity of an official act of a foreign sovereign, but that does require imputing to foreign officials an unlawful motivation (the obtaining of bribes) in the performance of such an official act. . . .

[Plaintiff unsuccessfully sought a construction contract from the Republic of Nigeria. After the contract was awarded, the plaintiff learned that the defendants obtained the contract by paying a bribe to Nigerian officials. The plaintiff brought these allegations to the U.S. Attorney, who filed criminal charges against the defendants. After the defendants pleaded guilty to these charges, the plaintiff filed a civil action against the defendants in federal district court. The defendants argued that the act of state doctrine barred the suit.

The District Court held that the act of state doctrine applies "if the inquiry presented for judicial determination includes the motivation of a sovereign act which would result in embarrassment to the sovereign or constitute interference in the conduct of foreign policy of the United States." The court dismissed the complaint because, to prevail, the plaintiff would have to show bribery of a Nigerian governmental official. The Court of Appeals for the Third Circuit reversed, relying heavily upon a State Department letter stating that judicial inquiry into the purpose behind the act of a foreign sovereign would not produce the "unique embarrassment, and the particular interference with the conduct of foreign affairs, that may result from the judicial determination that a foreign sovereign's acts are invalid."]

II

This Court's description of the jurisprudential foundation for the act of state doctrine has undergone some evolution over the years. We once viewed the doctrine as an expression of international law, resting upon "the highest considerations of international comity and expediency," *Oetjen v. Central Leather*, 297, 303-04 (1918). We have more recently described it, however, as a consequence of domestic separation of powers, reflecting "the strong sense of the Judicial Branch that its engagement in the task of passing on the validity of foreign acts of state may hinder" the conduct of foreign affairs, *Banco Nacional de Cuba v. Sabbatino*, 376 U.S. 398, 423 (1964). Some Justices have suggested possible exceptions to application of the doctrine . . . , for example, for acts of state that consist of commercial transactions, since neither modern international comity nor the current position of our Executive Branch accorded sovereign immunity to such acts, or an exception for cases in which the Executive Branch has represented that it has no objection to denying validity to the foreign sovereign act, since then the courts would be impeding no foreign policy goals.

The parties have argued at length about the applicability of these possible exceptions, and, more generally, about whether the purpose of the act of state doctrine would be furthered by its application in this case. We find it unnecessary, however, to pursue those inquiries, since the factual predicate for application of the act of state doctrine does not exist. Nothing in the present suit requires the Court to declare invalid, and thus ineffective as "a rule of decision for the courts of this country," *Ricaud v. American Metal Co.*, 246 U.S. 304, 310 (1918), the official act of a foreign sovereign.

In every case in which we have held the act of state doctrine applicable, the relief sought or the defense interposed would have required a court in the United States to declare invalid the official act of a foreign sovereign performed within its own territory. In *Underhill v. Hernandez*, holding the defendant's detention of the plaintiff to be tortious would have required denying legal effect to "acts of a military commander representing the authority of the revolutionary party as government, which afterwards succeeded and was recognized by the United States." . . . In *Sabbatino*, upholding the defendant's claim to the funds would have required a holding that Cuba's expropriation of goods located in Havana was null and void. In the present case, by contrast, neither the claim nor any asserted defense requires a determination that Nigeria's contract with Kirkpatrick International was, or was not, effective.

Petitioners point out . . . that in order to prevail respondent must prove that petitioner Kirkpatrick made, and Nigerian officials received, payments that violate

Nigerian law, which would, they assert, support a finding that the contract is invalid under Nigerian law. Assuming that to be true, it still does not suffice. The act of state doctrine is not some vague doctrine of abstention but a *"principle of decision* binding on federal and state courts alike." *Sabbatino, supra*, at 427 (emphasis added). . . . Act of state issues only arise when a court *must decide* — that is, when the outcome of the case turns upon — the effect of official action by a foreign sovereign. When that question is not in the case, neither is the act of state doctrine. That is the situation here. Regardless of what the court's factual findings may suggest as to the legality of the Nigerian contract, its legality is simply not a question to be decided in the present suit, and there is thus no occasion to apply the rule of decision that the act of state doctrine requires. . . .

Petitioners insist, however, that the policies underlying our act of state cases — international comity, respect for the sovereignty of foreign nations on their own territory, and the avoidance of embarrassment to the Executive Branch in its conduct of foreign relations — are implicated in the present case because, as the District Court found, a determination that Nigerian officials demanded and accepted a bribe "would impugn or question the nobility of a foreign nation's motivations," and would "result in embarrassment to the sovereign or constitute interference in the conduct of foreign policy of the United States." The United States, as *amicus curiae*, favors the same approach to the act of state doctrine, though disagreeing with petitioners as to the outcome it produces in the present case. . . .

These urgings are deceptively similar to what we said in *Sabbatino*, where we observed that sometimes, even though the validity of the act of a foreign sovereign within its own territory is called into question, the policies underlying the act of state doctrine may not justify its application. We suggested that a sort of balancing approach could be applied — the balance shifting against application of the doctrine, for example, if the government that committed the "challenged act of state" is no longer in existence. But what is appropriate in order to avoid unquestioning judicial acceptance of the acts of foreign sovereigns is not similarly appropriate for the quite opposite purpose of expanding judicial incapacities where such acts are not directly (or even indirectly) involved. It is one thing to suggest, as we have, that the policies underlying the act of state doctrine should be considered in deciding whether, despite the doctrine's technical availability, it should nonetheless not be invoked; it is something quite different to suggest that those underlying policies are a doctrine unto themselves, justifying expansion of the act of state doctrine . . . into new and uncharted fields.

The short of the matter is this: Courts in the United States have the power, and ordinarily the obligation, to decide cases and controversies properly presented to them. The act of state doctrine does not establish an exception for cases and controversies that may embarrass foreign governments, but merely requires that, in the process of deciding, the acts of foreign sovereigns taken within their own jurisdictions shall be deemed valid. That doctrine has no application to the present case because the validity of no foreign sovereign act is at issue. . . .

Notes and Questions

1. Does the Court satisfactorily explain the distinction between an inquiry into the "motivation" for the acts of a foreign state and inquiry into the "validity" of the acts of a foreign state? Does the plaintiff's case require an inquiry into the validity of the Nigerian contract? Is "validity" the same as "legality"?

2. After *Kirkpatrick* (a unanimous opinion), does the act of state doctrine still rest upon a separation of powers rationale? What does the court mean when it says that the doctrine is not "some vague doctrine of abstention" but a "principle of decision"?

In the Republic of the Philippines' suit to recover public funds that Marcos allegedly stole, the district court issued an order enjoining defendants from disposing of any assets anywhere in the world. On appeal, a divided panel of the Ninth Circuit Court of Appeals held that the act of state doctrine bars consideration of the Republic's claims:

> Plaintiff's case implicates the act of state doctrine in its most fundamental sense. In order to resolve plaintiff's various claims against Marcos, the court will have to adjudicate whether Marcos' actions as President were lawful under Philippine law. A number of the acts plaintiff challenges are purely governmental ones, such as expropriation of property and creation of public monopolies. These were not merely the acts of Ferdinand Marcos, private citizen, while he happened to be president; they were an exercise of his authority as the country's head of state and, as such, were the sovereign acts of the Philippines.

A lengthy dissent argued that the majority failed to distinguish between Marcos' official acts, which may be insulated by the act of state doctrine, and his private acts, which are not acts of state. The Ninth Circuit then granted a rehearing en banc. Portions of the en banc opinion follow:

Republic of the Philippines v. Marcos

862 F.2d 1355 (9th Cir. 1988)

NOONAN, CIRCUIT JUDGE

Acts of State. The classification of certain acts as "acts of state" with the consequence that their validity will be treated as beyond judicial review is a pragmatic device, not required by the nature of sovereign authority and inconsistently applied in international law. The purpose of the device is to keep the judiciary from embroiling the courts and the country in the affairs of the foreign nation whose acts are challenged. Minimally viewed, the classification keeps a court from making pronouncements on matters over which it has no power; maximally interpreted, the classification prevents the embarrassment of a court offending a foreign government that is "extant at the time of suit." . . .

The classification might, it may be supposed, be used to prevent judicial challenge in our courts to many deeds of a dictator in power, at least when it is apparent that sustaining such challenge would bring our country into a hostile confrontation with the dictator. Once deposed, the dictator will find it difficult to deploy the defense successfully. The "balance of considerations" is shifted. *A fortiori*, when a ruler's former domain has turned against him and seeks the recovery of what it claims he has stolen, the classification has little or no applicability. The act of state doctrine is supple, flexible, ad hoc. The doctrine is meant to facilitate the foreign relations of the United States, not to furnish the equivalent of sovereign immunity to a deposed leader.

In the instant case the Marcoses offered no evidence whatsoever to support the classification of their acts as acts of state. The burden of proving acts of state rested upon them. . . . The United States, invited by the court to address this matter as an amicus, assures us that the Executive does not at present see the applicability of this defense. The act of state doctrine, the Executive declares, has "no bearing" on this case as it stands. As the doctrine is a pragmatic one, we cannot exclude the possibility that, at some later point in the development of this litigation, the Marcoses might produce evidence that would warrant its application. On the present record, the defense does not apply. . . .

SCHROEDER, CIRCUIT JUDGE, with whom CANBY, CIRCUIT JUDGE, joins concurring in part and dissenting in part:

The majority of our three-judge panel concluded that the act of state doctrine bars consideration of the plaintiffs' claims. I agree with the majority of this en banc court that such a holding is not appropriate on this record. I do not agree with the majority, however, that this injunction can be affirmed without any regard to the act of state doctrine.

The panel majority's use of the act of state doctrine as a threshold bar in the circumstances of this case is not consistent with the development of that doctrine under Supreme Court authority. . . . Rather, the doctrine involves the judiciary's prudential decision to refrain from adjudicating the legality of a foreign sovereign's public acts that were committed within its own territory. . . .

However, [the considerations identified by the *Sabbatino* court] are less compelling in the situation before us, where the foreign government has itself invoked our jurisdiction, and the challenged actions involve a government no longer in power. In *Sabbatino*, the Supreme Court observed that, "[t]he balance of relevant considerations may also be shifted if the government which perpetrated the challenged act of state is no longer in existence . . . for the political interest of this country may, as a result, be measurably altered." 376 U.S. at 428. "Moreover, the act of state doctrine reflects respect for foreign states, so that when a state comes into our courts and asks that our courts scrutinize its actions, the justification for application of the doctrine may well be significantly weaker." *Republic of the Philippines v. Marcos*, 806 F.2d 344, 359 (2d Cir. 1986).

Further, the Supreme Court has noted that for [the] doctrine to apply the acts in question must have involved public acts of the sovereign. The Court stated that in each of its act of state decisions, the facts were sufficient to demonstrate that

> the conduct in question was the public act of those with authority to exercise sovereign powers and was entitled to respect in our courts. . . .

Accordingly, the courts have insisted that the act of state doctrine precludes review of public acts of the sovereign.

As the dissenting opinion of Judge Nelson quite rightly pointed out, the act of state doctrine cannot bar the plaintiffs' action at this stage in the proceedings due to the distinction between the official acts and the private conduct of a former head of state. As Judge Nelson stated:

> Marcos and his agents no doubt exercised broad power, especially after the imposition of martial law in 1972. But the appropriate inquiry is not to invoke the talismanic label "dictator." The district court should determine which of the challenged acts were

official and which were not. Only by doing so can the court determine the extent to which the act of state doctrine may apply.

818 F.2d at 1494-95.

At this point, no determinations have been made regarding the capacity in which the Marcoses were acting when the alleged unlawful conduct occurred. Accordingly, the original panel majority erred in finding that, at this stage of the litigation, the act of state doctrine bars adjudication of the bulk of the Philippine government's pendent claims.

The majority decision here, however, goes much further. It declares that the injunction can be affirmed without regard to the act of state doctrine. In my view, we should instead instruct the district court to consider to what extent, if any, the doctrine applies in the circumstances of this case, and on the basis of the record which has developed more fully during the pendency of this interlocutory appeal. Until such consideration can be given, an injunction of this breadth is not appropriate.

This en banc court requested the amicus views of the Department of State on the act of state issues. Its brief concludes that the application of the act of state doctrine at this stage is speculative and the injunction premature. The majority's reliance upon the position of the United States as support for its holding is wholly misplaced. The government urges that an injunction should not have been entered on the basis of this record. The government amicus curiae brief states in appropriate context as follows:

> [T]he record before the district court, which did not include any detailed specification of the factual basis for the bulk of the nonfederal claims, did not make it possible even to analyze the extent to which those claims are properly before the court. . . .
>
> Even assuming jurisdiction, it is not clear at this stage that the district court should, as a prudential matter, undertake to adjudicate the bulk of the nonfederal claims. The court's capacity to do so fairly and expeditiously and without offending the sensibility of other nations cannot be resolved on this record. Adjudication in this district court may turn out to be barred by considerations of international comity and *forum non conveniens.*
>
> The act of state doctrine seems to us to have little or no bearing on this case at this stage of its development. The doctrine provides, in general, that the validity of specific acts of a foreign sovereign is not subject to challenge in our courts; the circumstances of a particular case may, however, make that general principle inapplicable. On the present record, it is not clear that any act of state — an act of a sovereign within its territorial jurisdiction on matters pertaining to its governmental sovereignty — is involved in this case. Nor is it clear that the case would require an adjudication of the validity of such an act, without which the case could not fairly proceed. Under these circumstances, the bearing, if any, of the act of state doctrine on this case should be determined only after further development of the case on the merits.

Amicus brief at 11-12.

The United States' views are wholly in accord with those expressed in this dissent and are in conflict with the majority. . . .

Notes and Questions

1. The various *Marcos* opinions, as well as the Executive Branch's amicus submission, emphasize that, on the present record, the act of state doctrine is

inapplicable. What type of evidence might be introduced that would change the court's opinion?

2. Note that this opinion was issued before *Kirkpatrick* was decided. How, if at all, does *Kirkpatrick* change the analysis?

3. *Sabbatino* involved an expropriation, and *Kirkpatrick* involved a contract obtained through bribery. Should the act of state analysis be different when a foreign government's acts allegedly violate international human rights norms?

6

The Reach of Domestic Law in the International Arena: Jurisdiction and Its Limits

I. LIMITING THE REACH OF DOMESTIC LAW

Many of the most difficult and controversial international legal disputes arise when states seek to assert authority over persons, property, or events abroad. These disputes often involve the extraterritorial application of domestic law in ways that harm the interests of other states and at times are contrary to international legal limits on the exercise of jurisdiction. Given the frequency with which these disputes arise, Rosalyn Higgins, now a judge of the International Court of Justice (ICJ), stated that "[t]here is no more important way to avoid conflict than by providing clear norms as to which state can exercise authority over whom, and in what circumstances. Without that allocation of competencies, all is rancor and chaos." Rosalyn Higgins, Problems and Process: International Law and How We Use It 57 (1994).

Litigants often ask domestic courts to address the international legality of extra-territorial assertions of jurisdiction. In addition, legislative and executive branches also address these issues as they consider whether and when to assert extraterritorial jurisdiction. The legal limits on a state's exercise of jurisdiction implicate both domestic and international legal norms—which may or may not be consistent with each other.

States assert their authority over people, things, and events in various ways. For international law purposes, these assertions of authority fall within one of three categories. The first is "jurisdiction to prescribe," which refers to a state's authority or competence to promulgate law applicable to persons or activities. As this jurisdiction is typically exercised by legislative bodies, it is sometimes called legislative jurisdiction. But because government authorities other than legislatures also prescribe laws and regulations, the broader term "prescriptive jurisdiction" is more accurate. In Section II of this chapter, we explore various bases upon which states can exercise jurisdiction to prescribe. The second type of jurisdiction is "jurisdiction to adjudicate," which refers to a state's authority or competence to subject persons or things to its judicial processes. The third type of jurisdiction is "jurisdiction to enforce," which refers to a state's authority or competence to induce or compel compliance with its law through its courts, as well as through executive, administrative, or police action. In Section III of this chapter, we explore these two types of jurisdiction. Finally, in Section IV, we examine an important immunity from jurisdiction, foreign sovereign immunity.

As you review the materials in this chapter, keep in mind that the norms governing jurisdiction are largely customary and hence not the result of deliberate and purposeful acts of assembled states at any one time. Consider why international law developed *any* limitations on the ability of autonomous states to exercise jurisdiction and why the particular limitations that exist were developed. What purposes are served, and what values are furthered, by these norms? Finally, consider how states deal with conflicting claims of jurisdiction and whether the "system" that exists produces an unacceptable level of "rancor and chaos."

A. *The* Lotus *Case*

On August 2, 1926, the *Lotus*, a French mail steamer, collided with the *Boz-Kourt*, a Turkish vessel. The collision sank the *Boz-Kourt* and caused the deaths of eight Turkish sailors and passengers. The accident was allegedly caused by the gross negligence of the *Lotus*'s watch officer, Lieutenant Demons. The day after the collision, the *Lotus* arrived in Constantinople, and Turkish authorities asked Lieutenant Demons to go ashore to give evidence. Following this examination, Lieutenant Demons was placed under arrest and later charged with manslaughter by the Public Prosecutor of Stamboul (now Istanbul). The Criminal Court of Stamboul rejected Demons's argument that it lacked jurisdiction over him. Following a trial, Demons was found guilty and sentenced to 80 days' imprisonment and fined 22 Turkish pounds. By special agreement, France and Turkey asked the Permanent Court of International Justice to determine whether Turkey "acted in conflict with the principles of international law" by instituting criminal proceedings against Demons.

The S.S. "Lotus" (France/Turkey)

P.C.I.J., Ser. A, No. 10, p. 4 (1927)

The Court . . . is confronted in the first place by a question of principle which . . . has proved to be a fundamental one. The French Government contends that the Turkish Courts, in order to have jurisdiction, should be able to point to some title to jurisdiction recognized by international law in favor of Turkey. On the other hand, the Turkish Government takes the view that [it can exercise] jurisdiction whenever such jurisdiction does not come into conflict with a principle of international law.

The latter view seems to be in conformity with the special agreement itself . . . which asks the Court to say whether Turkey has acted contrary to the principles of international law and, if so, what principles. . . .

This way of stating the question is also dictated by the very nature and existing conditions of international law.

International law governs relations between independent States. The rules of law binding upon States therefore emanate from their own free will as expressed in conventions or by usages generally accepted as expressing principles of law and established in order to regulate the relations between these co-existing independent communities or with a view to the achievement of common aims. Restrictions upon the independence of States cannot therefore be presumed.

Now the first and foremost restriction imposed by international law upon a State is that — failing the existence of a permissive rule to the contrary — it may not exercise its power in any form in the territory of another State. In this sense jurisdiction is certainly territorial; it cannot be exercised by a State outside its territory except by virtue of a permissive rule derived from international custom or from a convention.

It does not, however, follow that international law prohibits a State from exercising jurisdiction in its own territory, in respect of any case which relates to acts which have taken place abroad, and in which it cannot rely on some permissive rule of international law. . . . Far from laying down a general prohibition to the effect that States may not extend the application of their laws and the jurisdiction of their courts to persons, property and acts outside their territory, [international law] leaves them in this respect a wide measure of discretion which is only limited in certain cases by prohibitive rules; as regards other cases, every State remains free to adopt the principles which it regards as best and most suitable. . . .

It follows from the foregoing that the contention of the French Government to the effect that Turkey must in each case be able to cite a rule of international law authorizing her to exercise jurisdiction, is opposed to the generally accepted international law. . . .

[France argues that] international law does not allow a state to take proceedings with regard to offenses committed by foreigners abroad, simply by reason of the nationality of the victim. . . .

. . . Even if that argument were correct generally speaking — and in regard to this the Court reserves its opinion — it could only be used in the present case if international law forbade Turkey to take into consideration the fact that the offense produced its effects on the Turkish vessel and consequently in a place assimilated to Turkish territory in which the application of Turkish criminal law cannot be challenged. . . . But no such rule of international law exists. . . . On the contrary, it is certain that the courts of many countries . . . interpret criminal law in the sense that offenses, the authors of which at the moment of commission are in the territory of another state, are nevertheless to be regarded as having been committed in the national territory if one of the constituent elements of the offense, and more especially its effects, have taken place there. . . . Consequently, it becomes impossible to hold that there is a rule of international law which prohibits Turkey from prosecuting Lieutenant Demons because of the fact that . . . [Demons] was on board the French ship. . . .

The second argument put forward by the French Government is the principle that the State whose flag is flown has exclusive jurisdiction over everything which occurs on board a merchant ship on the high seas. . . .

. . . All that can be said is that . . . a ship is placed in the same position as national territory. . . . It follows that what occurs on board a vessel on the high seas must be regarded as if it occurred on the territory of the State whose flag the ship flies. If, therefore, a guilty act committed on the high seas produces its effects on a vessel flying another flag . . . the same principles must be applied as if the territories of two different States were concerned, and the conclusion must therefore be drawn that there is no rule of international law prohibiting the State to which the ship on which the effects of the offense have taken place belongs, from regarding the offense as having been committed in its territory. . . .

The offense . . . was an act . . . having its origin on board the *Lotus*, whilst its effects made themselves felt on board the *Boz-Kourt*. These two elements are, legally, entirely inseparable, so much so that their separation renders the offense nonexistent. Neither the exclusive jurisdiction of either State, nor the limitations of the jurisdiction of each of the occurrences which took place on the respective ships would appear calculated to satisfy the requirements of justice and effectively to protect the interests of the two States. It is only natural that each should be able to exercise jurisdiction and to do so in respect of the incident as a whole. It is therefore a case of concurrent jurisdiction. . . .

Notes and Questions

1. The Judges of the Permanent Court were evenly divided in *Lotus*; in these circumstances, the President of the Court breaks the tie by voting twice. In dissent, Judge Bernard Loder (Netherlands) argued:

> The fundamental consequence of the[] independence and sovereignty [of states] is that no municipal law, in the particular case under consideration no criminal law, can apply or have binding effect outside the national territory. . . .
>
> The criminal law of a State may extend to crimes and offenses committed abroad by its nationals, since such nationals are subject to the law of their own country; but it *cannot* extend to offenses committed by a foreigner in foreign territory, without infringing the sovereign rights of the foreign State concerned, since in that State the State enacting the law has no jurisdiction. . . .

2. Is *Lotus* about how to allocate the burden of proof on jurisdictional issues? Or does it stand for a more fundamental proposition about the international legal system? Is the Court suggesting, as Judge Loder charged elsewhere in his dissent, that "under international law everything which is not prohibited is permitted"? How could such a principle be justified?

3. How persuasive is the following critique:

> [T]he reasoning of the majority seems to imply that the process by which the international principles of penal jurisdiction have been formed is by the imposition of certain limitations on originally unlimited competence, and this is surely historically unsound. The original conception of law was personal, and it was only the rise of the modern territorial State that subjected aliens — even when they happened to be resident in a State not their own — to the law of that State. International law did not start as the law of a society of States each of omnicompetent jurisdiction, but of States possessing a personal jurisdiction over their own nationals and later acquiring a territorial jurisdiction over resident non-nationals. If it is alleged that they have now acquired a measure of jurisdiction over non-resident non-nationals, a valid international custom to that effect should surely be established by those who allege it.

J.L. Brierly, *The Lotus Case*, 44 L.Q. Rev. 154, 156 (1928).

4. What is the flaw in the following jurisdictional syllogism — (1) under international law, the extraterritorial exercise of jurisdiction is generally forbidden, save for a handful of exceptions; (2) Turkish jurisdiction in this case did not fall within any of these exceptions; (3) therefore, Turkey's exercise of jurisdiction violated international law norms.

5. Was the outcome of this case influenced by the fact that Demons had already been tried in Turkey?

B. *Creating International Law on Jurisdiction*

Lotus remains a landmark of twentieth-century international legal jurisprudence. But suppose that an individual, a group of individuals, a state, or a number of states disagreed with the Court's holding? What strategies might they pursue?

Shortly after the *Lotus* decision was rendered, the International Association of Mercantile Marine Officers expressed its concern that, under the Court's holding, masters (and shipowners) could be prosecuted by the state where the vessel put in as well as the flag state. The Association raised the issue before the League of Nations Advisory and Technical Committee for Communications and Transit. The Association also brought the issue to the Permanent Committee on Ports and Maritime Navigation, and to the International Labour Office's Bureau, Governing Body, and Joint Maritime Commission. Eventually, the issue was referred to the International Maritime Committee (IMC) — a private body organized by national groups of maritime lawyers in 1897 — which sent questionnaires to national committees of maritime counsel, seeking their input. The matter of concurrent jurisdiction was studied at the IMC's 1930 Antwerp Conference and its 1933 Oslo Conference. The Oslo Conference adopted a resolution stating:

> This Conference records its unanimous approval of the principle that in cases of a collision upon the high seas no criminal or disciplinary proceedings arising out of such collision should be permissible against [any person] in the service of the ship except in the ports of the State of which the [person] is a national or of which his ship was flying the flag at the moment of collision. . . .

Thereafter, regional and international negotiations continued for many years. In March 1940, at the Montevideo Conference, a number of Latin American states adopted an International Penal Law treaty, which provided that "crimes committed on the high seas . . . must be tried and punished according to the law of the State whose flag the vessel flies." Thereafter, the IMC's 1952 Brussels Conference adopted the International Convention for the Unification of Certain Rules Relating to Penal Jurisdiction in Matters of Collision or Other Incidents of Navigation, which provides in Article I:

> In the event of a collision or any other incident of navigation concerning a sea-going ship and involving the penal or disciplinary responsibility of [any person] in the service of the ship, criminal or disciplinary proceedings may be instituted only before the judicial or administrative authorities of the State of which the ship was flying the flag at the time of the collision or other incident of navigation.

Article 11(1) of the 1958 Convention on the High Seas, the first major effort to codify oceans law, and Article 97(1) of the 1982 United Nations Convention on the Law of the Sea, a treaty examined in detail in Chapter 10, provide that in the event of a high seas collision "involving the penal or disciplinary responsibility of [any person] in the service of the ship, no penal or disciplinary proceedings may be instituted against such persons except before the judicial or administrative authorities either of the flag State or of the State of which such person is a national."

These provisions, of course, effectively reverse the *Lotus* judgment for the parties to these treaties. For present purposes, consider the law-making process employed. International law was traditionally considered to be formed though state action, but here a complex legal process was set in motion by a high seas collision between vessels owned by two private parties. This was followed by a domestic court action, a bilateral agreement, and an authoritative pronouncement by an international tribunal. However, this judicial decision proved unsatisfactory to a directly affected group, which then sought to influence domestic and international law makers to adopt a rule other than that announced by the Court. After inconclusive consideration by a number of international bodies, the issue was picked up by the International Maritime Committee, a private body premised on the idea that shipowners, merchants, bankers, and other parties interested in the maritime trade should help shape the creation of international maritime law. At IMC urging, states eventually adopted, through a treaty, a jurisdictional rule preferred by IMC members.

Recalling the discussion of "public interest" NGOs and corporations in Chapter 4, consider whether it is appropriate to have "special interest" groups like the International Association of Mercantile Marine Officers and the IMC play such a central role in the law-making process.

II. JURISDICTION TO MAKE AND APPLY LAW: THE BOEING-McDONNELL DOUGLAS MERGER

States have claimed a number of bases for the exercise of jurisdiction to prescribe, with varying degrees of international acceptance. The most commonly used and accepted is the "territorial principle," under which a state has jurisdiction to make law applicable to all persons and property within its territory. As Chief Justice Marshall said in *Schooner Exchange v. McFaddon*, 7 U.S. 116, 136 (1812), "[t]he jurisdiction of the nation within its own territory is necessarily exclusive and absolute. It is susceptible of no limitation not imposed by itself."

During the nineteenth century, many states also understood the territorial principle to strictly limit the ability of states to regulate conduct outside their territory. In *The Apollon*, 22 U.S. 362 (1824), the Supreme Court held that U.S. customs laws did not reach foreign vessels outside of U.S. waters. The Court reasoned that "[t]he laws of no nation can justly extend beyond its own territories, except so far as regards its own citizens." The Court also observed that extraterritorial assertion of jurisdiction to prescribe would be "at variance with the independence and sovereignty of foreign nations," and that such extraterritorial claims had "never yet been acknowledged by other nations, and would be resisted by none with more pertinacity than by the American." Relying on this view of the "law of nations," the Court declared that "however general and comprehensive the phrases used in our municipal laws may be, they must always be restricted in construction, to places and persons, upon whom the Legislature have authority and jurisdiction."

Despite its historic importance, the presumption that domestic statutes have only territorial reach and its underlying rationale have significantly eroded over the last 60 years. The materials that follow illustrate the evolution of the territorial principle and the continuing debates over the international legal norms governing the extraterritorial reach of domestic legislation.

As you review these materials, consider whether international law should permit only the United States, for example, to regulate a merger between two U.S. companies? Or should international law reflect the principle articulated by a European Community spokesman: "If any deal has an effect on the European marketplace, then the jurisdiction is within our territory. We don't give a damn about extraterritoriality." Finally, consider whether it would be sensible for international law to authorize two or more jurisdictions each to have regulatory authority over a person or event.

A. The Problem

The end of the Cold War ushered in an era of declining defense budgets and sharply reduced expenditures for military procurement in the United States and elsewhere. This led, in turn, to a dramatic restructuring in the global defense industry. In short order, about a dozen leading U.S. military contractors quickly folded into only four. None of these consolidations attracted as much international diplomatic and legal attention as the merger between the Boeing Company (Boeing) and the McDonnell Douglas Corporation (MDC). As announced on December 15, 1996, this merger would have combined the last two remaining commercial jet airplane manufacturers in the United States and created the world's largest aerospace company and second largest defense supplier. The new company would have approximately 200,000 employees and annual sales of nearly $50 billion (about the size of New Zealand's economy). The company would also be the largest U.S. exporter and the leading supplier to both the Pentagon and NASA.

The merged company would have but one rival in the commercial aircraft industry, Airbus Industrie. Airbus is a four-nation manufacturing consortium based in Toulouse, France. It is owned by France's government-owned Aerospatiale (37.9 percent), Germany's DaimlerChrysler Aerospace (37.9 percent), British Aerospace (20 percent), and Spain's government-owned CASA (4.2 percent).

In February 1997, Boeing and MDC notified the U.S. Federal Trade Commission (FTC) and the European Community (EC) of the planned merger.[*] At the time, the EC's Merger Regulation required that it be notified of any merger that had a "community dimension." This was defined as a merger involving companies with combined worldwide sales of five billion ecus, a currency representing the weighted average of the currencies of EC member-states and combined European sales of 250 million ecus (about $270 million), regardless of where the merging firms were based (these threshold figures have since been changed). If the European Commission (the EC's executive body) decides that such a merger is not "compatible with the [European] common market," then the company must offer "remedies," typically the sale of some European production facilities or assets. Companies can appeal adverse findings to the European Court of Justice, an EC court that interprets and applies EC law.

While the EC did not claim the ability to halt the proposed merger, the EC did assert the authority to fine the new company up to 10 percent of its earnings, over $4 billion, or to fine any European airline that purchased Boeing jets. Such

---

[*]For a discussion of the relationship between the European Community and the European Union, see section 1 of Chapter 5.

actions would likely shut Boeing out of the European market for airliners, which constitutes approximately 26 percent of the world demand.

After the companies announced their intention to merge, both the FTC and the Commission began to investigate the proposed deal. Almost immediately thereafter, the EC Commission's Competition Minister, Karel Van Miert of Belgium, publicly characterized the transaction as "extremely problematic." In particular, Van Miert objected to contracts Boeing had with several U.S. airlines naming Boeing as their sole supplier as "totally unacceptable because they eliminate Airbus as a rival for at least the next 20 years." Merger supporters noted that the airlines themselves had proposed the sole-source contracts during intensive bidding between Boeing and Airbus, apparently concluding that these deals would produce valuable savings.

On May 21, 1997, the Commission issued a formal "statement of objections" to the merger, highlighting the sole-source contracts. This document also noted the Commission's concern that, by acquiring MDC's defense and space business, Boeing would enjoy the benefits of the billions of dollars of MDC research funded by the Pentagon and NASA. Finally, the Commission noted that the merger would increase Boeing's share of the world market from 64 percent to 70 percent, as against Airbus's 30 percent.

In the meantime, the FTC investigation was also proceeding. On July 1, 1997, after the most detailed and wide-ranging investigation in its history of merger enforcement, the FTC decided that the acquisition would not substantially lessen competition or create a monopoly in the global aircraft market. The FTC concluded that MDC, with only a 6 percent (and shrinking) share of the world market, was no longer an effective market player, and therefore that its acquisition by Boeing would have little impact upon competition. Moreover, according to the FTC, no companies other than Boeing were interested in purchasing MDC.

The Commission's investigation also proceeded, with a final vote scheduled for July 31. The Commission referred the matter to a special panel consisting of antitrust experts from each of the EC's 15 member nations. On July 4, 1997, the panel unanimously concluded that the merger would strengthen Boeing's "existent dominant position and therefore should be prohibited." The panel's recommendation was echoed by political leaders in Germany and France, with French President Chirac claiming that the merger would be "dangerous" to European industry. In response, the Clinton Administration dispatched its top antitrust and trade officials to meet with their EC counterparts to emphasize that the United States would not tolerate undue interference in an industry crucial to U.S. military and economic strength. Simultaneously, Boeing initiated behind-the-scenes negotiations with the Commission in an effort to meet the Commission's concerns.

By July 15, the negotiations between Boeing and the Commission had broken down. Later that day, the White House convened the Secretaries of Commerce and Transportation, U.S. trade officials, and top Pentagon and State Department officials to discuss possible retaliation if the EC disapproved of the merger. On July 16, antitrust regulators from all 15 EC members publicly reaffirmed their opposition to the merger. On July 17, President Clinton threatened trade sanctions against the EC if the merger was blocked. The U.S. Senate and House of Representatives passed resolutions denouncing the EC's "unwarranted and unprecedented interference in a United States business transaction."

B. Prescribing Law Based on Territorial Links

Courts in the United States and elsewhere are frequently asked to rule upon the scope and limits of the exercise of jurisdiction pursuant to the territorial principle. As we will see in the materials that follow, the principle has undergone considerable evolution over the last century. We begin by examining how, over time, U.S. courts have treated extraterritorial assertions of jurisdiction.

In 1903, Sam McConnell, an American businessman, bought a banana plantation in what is now Panama but was then part of Colombia. McConnell soon realized that the United Fruit Company controlled both the local banana industry and the local military. United Fruit threatened to put McConnell out of business if he did not sell his assets to United Fruit. McConnell refused. In November 1903, Panama revolted and achieved independence. McConnell then sold his plantation to American Banana, a U.S. corporation. Shortly thereafter, Costa Rican soldiers invaded Panama, allegedly at the behest of United Fruit, and seized American Banana's plantation. Through *ex parte* proceedings in a Costa Rican court, the plantation was transferred to an individual who then sold the land to United Fruit. American Banana filed a complaint in a U.S. court alleging that United Fruit's activities violated the Sherman Antitrust Act, which prohibits "[e]very contract, combination . . . or conspiracy, in restraint of trade or commerce." Justice Holmes, writing for the Supreme Court in *American Banana Co. v. United Fruit Co.*, 213 U.S. 347, 355-357 (1909), discussed whether U.S. antitrust laws governed United Fruit's conduct in Panama:

> It is obvious that, however stated, the plaintiff's case depends on several rather startling propositions. In the first place, the acts causing the damage were done, so far as appears, outside the jurisdiction of the United States, and within that of other states. It is surprising to hear it argued that they were governed by the act of Congress.
>
> . . . [T]he general and almost universal rule is that the character of an act as lawful or unlawful must be determined wholly by the law of the country where the act is done. . . . For another jurisdiction, if it should happen to lay hold of the actor, to treat him according to its own notions rather than those of the place where he did the acts, not only would be unjust, but would be an interference with the authority of another sovereign, contrary to the comity of nations, which the other state concerned justly might resent. . . .
>
> The foregoing considerations would lead in case of doubt to a construction of any statute as intended to be confined in its operation and effect to the territorial limits over which the lawmaker has general and legitimate power. "All legislation is prima facie territorial." Words having universal scope, such as "every contract in restraint of trade," "every person who shall monopolize," etc., will be taken, as a matter of course, to mean only everyone subject to such legislation, not all that the legislator subsequently may be able to catch. In the case of the present statute, the improbability of the United States attempting to make acts done in Panama or Costa Rica criminal is obvious. . . . We think it entirely plain that what the defendant did in Panama or Costa Rica is not within the scope of the statute so far as the present suit is concerned. . . .

Notes and Questions

1. Why should a court presume that domestic statutes do not regulate extraterritorial conduct?

2. Is *American Banana* an international law case, or is it about domestic law statutory presumptions or canons of construction? Or is it a case about choice of law rules?

3. What interests does the territoriality principle advance? What interests does it frustrate?

1. Extending the Reach of the Territorial Principle

As *American Banana* illustrates, the governing assumption in the early 1900s was that jurisdiction was territorial. However, with the increasing internationalization of commerce and industry, governments increasingly viewed the territorial test as overly restrictive. Courts in the United States and elsewhere replaced the territorial test with one that examined whether the foreign conduct had an effect in the forum state.

United States v. Aluminum Co. of America (Alcoa), remains a landmark in the U.S. development of the effects doctrine. The suit arose out of the government's attempts to break up Alcoa's aluminum holdings and to prohibit Alcoa and Aluminum Limited (Limited), a Canadian corporation, from engaging in an international cartel with several major European aluminum companies. The Second Circuit, sitting by certification as a court of final appeal because the Supreme Court lacked a quorum, addressed whether the Sherman Act reached Limited's participation in the cartel, even though most of Limited's cartel-related activities occurred outside the United States. The court, in an opinion by Judge Learned Hand, reasoned as follows:

United States v. Aluminum Co. of America (Alcoa)

148 F.2d 416 (2d Cir. 1945)

Whether "Limited" itself violated [the Sherman Act] depends upon the character of the "Alliance." It was a Swiss corporation, created [through an agreement among Limited and several European companies. The Alliance made agreements in 1931 and 1936 that governed the sale of aluminum by Limited and the European companies.] . . .

Did either the agreement of 1931 or that of 1936 violate §1 of the Act? . . . [We] are concerned only with whether Congress chose to attach liability to the conduct outside the United States of persons not in allegiance to it. That being so, the only question open is whether Congress intended to impose the liability, and whether our own Constitution permitted it to do so: as a court of the United States, we cannot look beyond our own law. Nevertheless, it is quite true that we are not to read general words, such as those in this Act, without regard to the limitations customarily observed by nations upon the exercise of their powers; limitations which generally correspond to those fixed by the "Conflict of Laws." We should not impute to Congress an intent to punish all whom its courts can catch, for conduct which has no consequences within the United States. *American Banana Co. v. United Fruit Co.* On the other hand, it is settled law — as "Limited" itself agrees — that any state may impose liabilities, even upon persons not within its allegiance, for conduct outside its borders that has consequences within its borders which the state reprehends; and these liabilities other states will ordinarily recognize. It may be argued that this Act extends further. Two situations are possible. There may be agreements made beyond our borders not intended to affect imports, which do affect them, or which affect exports. Almost any limitation of the supply of goods in Europe, for example, or in South America, may have repercussions in the United States if there is trade between the two. Yet when one considers the international complications likely to arise from an effort in this country to treat such agreements as unlawful, it is safe to assume that Congress certainly did not intend the Act to cover them. Such agreements may on the other hand intend to include imports into the United States, and yet it may appear that they have had no effect upon them. That situation might be thought to fall within the doctrine that intent may be a substitute for performance in the case of a contract made within the United States; or it might be thought to fall within the doctrine that a statute should not be interpreted to cover acts abroad which have no consequence here. We shall not choose between these alternatives; but for argument we shall assume that the Act does not cover agreements, even though intended to affect imports or exports, unless its performance is shown actually to have had some effect upon them. . . .

Both agreements would clearly have been unlawful, had they been made within the United States; and it follows from what we have just said that both were unlawful, though made abroad, if they were intended to affect imports and did affect them. . . . [The court went on to find that the 1936 agreement restricting production was intended to restrict imports into the United States, had such an effect, and therefore was in violation of U.S. antitrust laws.]

Notes and Questions

1. Do *American Banana* and *Alcoa* both purport to rely upon international legal principles to determine the extraterritorial reach of the Sherman Act? Why do these courts reach such different results?

2. Recall that *American Banana* and other early U.S. cases argued that strict application of the territoriality principle respected the authority and independence of other nations. Does the *Alcoa* effects test harm the interests of other states? What values or interests does the effects test advance?

3. Did the Swiss, Canadian, or other foreign governments have any interest in the outcome of the *Alcoa* case? Does the court consider these interests? Should it?

The *Alcoa* effects test quickly gained wide acceptance in U.S. courts, and U.S. government agencies and courts often applied federal antitrust laws to conduct taking place partially or wholly outside the United States. However, the extraterritorial assertion of U.S. law gave rise to considerable friction between the United States and other states. These tensions arose, in part, out of disagreements over the appropriate substantive content of antitrust law and in part out of a belief by other states that foreign law, rather than U.S. law, ought to regulate activity occurring on foreign territory. As the British Secretary of State for Trade stated during a 1979 parliamentary debate:

[W]e do not dispute the right of the United States or any other nation to pass and enforce what economic laws it likes to govern business operating fully within its own country. Our objection arises only at the point when a country attempts to achieve the maximum beneficial regulation of its own economic environment by ensuring that all those having any contact with it abide by its laws and legal principles.

In other words, there is an attempt to export economic policy and law to persons domiciled in countries that may have different legal systems and priorities, without recognizing that those countries have the right to lay down the standards to be observed by those trading within their jurisdiction.

Litigants continued to raise questions about the extraterritorial reach of the Sherman Act, and dissatisfaction with the *Alcoa* test, along with questions about the test's scope and limits, prompted judicial efforts to refine this test. One of the most influential attempts to do so was undertaken by the Ninth Circuit Court of Appeals in the *Timberlane* case.

Timberlane, a U.S. partnership, imported lumber into the United States from Central America and sought to establish operations in Honduras. Bank of America financed much of the Honduran lumber industry. A Honduran company financed by the bank went bankrupt. The company's assets passed to the company's creditors, who sold the assets to Timberlane. After Timberlane began operations in Honduras, the bank allegedly conspired with Honduran lumber companies to drive Timberlane out of business. The bank allegedly did so to enable other companies financed by the bank to continue to monopolize the Honduran lumber market. The district court dismissed the complaint for lack of subject matter jurisdiction and on act of state grounds (a doctrine explored in detail in Chapter 5). On appeal, the Ninth Circuit discussed the extraterritorial reach of U.S. antitrust laws:

Timberlane Lumber Co. v. Bank of America

549 F.2d 597 (9th Cir. 1976)

CHOY, CIRCUIT JUDGE.

There is no doubt that American antitrust laws extend over some conduct in other nations. . . .

That American law covers some conduct beyond this nation's borders does not mean that it embraces all, however. Extraterritorial application is understandably a matter of concern for the other countries involved. Those nations have sometimes resented and protested, as excessive intrusions into their own spheres, broad assertions of authority by American courts. . . . Our courts have recognized this concern and have, at times, responded to it, even if not always enough to satisfy all the foreign critics. In any event, it is evident that at some point the interests of the United States are too weak and the foreign harmony incentive for restraint too strong to justify an extraterritorial assertion of jurisdiction. . . .

American courts have, in fact, often displayed a regard for comity and the prerogatives of other nations and considered their interests as well as other parts of the factual circumstances, even when professing to apply an effects test. To some degree, the requirement for a "substantial" effect may silently incorporate these additional considerations, with "substantial" as a flexible standard that varies with other factors. The intent requirement suggested by *Alcoa* is one example of an attempt to broaden the court's perspective, as is drawing a distinction between American citizens and non-citizens. . . .

The failure to articulate these other elements in addition to the standard effects analysis is costly, however, for it is more likely that they will be overlooked or slighted in interpreting past decisions and reaching new ones. . . .

A tripartite analysis seems to be indicated. As acknowledged above, the antitrust laws require in the first instance that there be *some* effect — actual or intended — on American foreign commerce before the federal courts may legitimately exercise subject matter jurisdiction under those statutes. Second, a greater showing of burden or restraint may be necessary to demonstrate that the effect is sufficiently large to present a cognizable injury to the plaintiffs and, therefore, a civil *violation* of the antitrust laws. Third, there is the additional question which is unique to the international setting of whether the interests of, and links to, the United States — including the magnitude of the effect on American foreign commerce — are sufficiently strong, vis-à-vis those of other nations, to justify an assertion of extraterritorial authority.

It is this final issue which is both obscured by undue reliance on the "substantiality" test and complicated to resolve. An effect on United States commerce, although necessary to the exercise of jurisdiction . . . is alone not a sufficient basis on which to determine whether American authority *should* be asserted in a given case as a matter of international comity and fairness. In some cases, the application of the direct and substantial test in the international context might open the door too widely by sanctioning jurisdiction over an action when these considerations would indicate dismissal. At other times, it may fail in the other direction, dismissing a case for which comity and fairness do not require forbearance, thus closing the jurisdictional door too tightly — for the Sherman Act does reach some restraints which do not have both a direct and substantial effect on the foreign commerce of the United States. A more comprehensive inquiry is necessary. We believe that the field of conflict of laws presents the proper approach. . . .

The elements to be weighed include the degree of conflict with foreign law or policy, the nationality or allegiance of the parties and the locations or principal places of business or corporations, the extent to which enforcement by either state can be expected to achieve compliance, the relative significance of effects on the United States as compared with those elsewhere, the extent to which there is explicit purpose to harm or affect American commerce, the foreseeability of such effect, and the relative importance to the violations charged of conduct within the United States as compared with conduct abroad. A court evaluating these factors should identify the potential degree of conflict if American authority is asserted. A difference in law or policy is one likely sore spot, though one which may not always be present. Nationality is another; though foreign governments may have some concern for the treatment of American citizens and business residing there, they primarily care about their own nationals. Having assessed the conflict, the court should then determine whether in the face of it the contacts and interests of the United States are sufficient to support the exercise of extraterritorial jurisdiction. . . .

Timberlane has alleged that the complained of activities were intended to, and did, affect the export of lumber from Honduras to the United States — the flow of United States foreign commerce, and as such they are within the jurisdiction of the federal courts under the Sherman Act. Moreover, the magnitude of the effect alleged would appear to be sufficient to state a claim.

The comity question is more complicated. From Timberlane's complaint it is evident that there are grounds for concern as to at least a few of the defendants, for some are identified as foreign citizens. . . . Moreover, it is clear that most of the activity took place in Honduras, though the conspiracy may have been directed from San Francisco, and that the most direct economic effect was probably on Honduras. However, there has been no indication of any conflict with the law or policy of the Honduran government, nor any comprehensive analysis of the relative connections and interests of Honduras and the United States. Under these circumstances, the dismissal by the district court cannot be sustained on jurisdictional grounds.

Notes and Questions

1. The *Timberlane* court characterized its approach as a "jurisdictional rule of reason." What is the source of this rule of reason? Is the court inferring congressional intent? Applying a rule of statutory construction? Applying international law?

2. Has the *Timberlane* court properly identified the factors that should be balanced? Does the court give guidance as to the relative weight or importance of the various factors identified? How is a court to evaluate and properly balance the political factors included in *Timberlane*'s interest-balancing test?

3. How is a court to identify the foreign interests implicated by any particular litigation?

4. On remand, the district court in *Timberlane* concluded that the Sherman Act did not reach defendants' conduct. The Ninth Circuit affirmed, finding that virtually all the allegedly illegal activity occurred in Honduras; that the alleged conduct had an insignificant effect on the foreign commerce of the United States, but a substantial effect in Honduras; that the defendant had no intent to affect United States commerce; and that the application of United States antitrust law created a potential conflict with Honduran policy. *Timberlane v. Bank of America*, 749 F.2d 1378 (1984), *cert. denied*, 472 U.S. 1032 (1985).

The Supreme Court revisited the extraterritorial reach of the Sherman Act in *Hartford Fire v. California*. In this case, 19 U.S. states and numerous private plaintiffs alleged that certain London reinsurers, who sell insurance to primary insurers, conspired to coerce primary insurers in the United States to offer certain insurance coverage to consumers only if certain changes advantageous to the reinsurers were made in the insurance forms. The plaintiffs alleged that the reinsurers would boycott any insurance company that failed to make these changes, in violation of the Sherman Act. A central question was whether U.S. antitrust law governed British reinsurers concerning reinsurance written by them in London relating to primary insurance written by U.S. companies in the United States, where the British Parliament had established a comprehensive regulatory regime over the London reinsurance market. Relevant portions of the Court's opinion follow:

Hartford Fire Insurance Co. v. California

509 U.S. 764 (1993)

JUSTICE SOUTER, joined by JUSTICES WHITE, BLACKMUN, STEVENS, and REHNQUIST, delivered the opinion of the Court with respect to the extraterritorial reach of the Sherman Act.

III

At the outset, we note that the District Court undoubtedly had jurisdiction of these Sherman Act claims, as the London reinsurers apparently concede. . . . Although the proposition was perhaps not always free from doubt, see *American Banana Co. v. United Fruit Co.*, it is well established by now that the Sherman Act applies to foreign conduct that was meant to produce and did in fact produce some substantial effect in the United States. Such is the conduct alleged here: that the London reinsurers engaged in unlawful conspiracies to affect the market for insurance in the United States and that their conduct in fact produced substantial effect.

According to the London reinsurers, the District Court should have declined to exercise such jurisdiction under the principle of international comity. The Court of Appeals agreed that courts should look to that principle in deciding whether to exercise jurisdiction under the Sherman Act. . . .

When it enacted [amendments to the Sherman Act in 1982 addressing foreign trade,] Congress expressed no view on the question whether a court with Sherman Act jurisdiction should ever decline to exercise such jurisdiction on grounds of international comity. We need not decide that question here, however, for even assuming that in a proper case a court may decline to exercise Sherman Act jurisdiction over foreign conduct (or, as Justice Scalia would put it, may conclude by the employment of comity analysis in the first instance that there is no jurisdiction), international comity would not counsel against exercising jurisdiction in the circumstances alleged here.

The only substantial question in this litigation is whether "there is in fact a true conflict between domestic and foreign law." *Société Nationale Industrielle Aérospatiale v. United States District Court for Southern Dist. of Iowa*, 482 U.S. 522, 555 (1987) (Blackmun, J., concurring in part and dissenting in part). The London reinsurers contend that applying the Act to their conduct would conflict significantly with British law, and the British Government, appearing before us as *amicus curiae*, concurs. They assert that Parliament has established a comprehensive regulatory regime over the London reinsurance market and that the conduct alleged here was perfectly consistent with British law and policy. But this is not to state a conflict. "[T]he fact that conduct is lawful in the state in which it took place will not, of itself, bar application of the United States antitrust laws," even where the foreign state has a strong policy to permit or encourage such conduct. Restatement (Third) Foreign Relations Law §415, Comment *j*. No conflict exists, for these purposes, "where a person subject to regulation by two states can comply with the laws of both." Restatement (Third) Foreign Relations Law §403, Comment *e*. Since the London reinsurers do not argue that British law requires them to act in some fashion prohibited by the law of the United States, or claim that their compliance with the laws of both countries is otherwise impossible, we see no conflict with British law. We have no need in this litigation to address other considerations that might inform a decision to refrain from the exercise of jurisdiction on grounds of international comity. . . .

JUSTICE SCALIA, joined by JUSTICES O'CONNOR, KENNEDY, and THOMAS, dissented. . . .

II

. . . It is important to distinguish two distinct questions raised by this petition: whether the District Court had jurisdiction, and whether the Sherman Act reaches the extraterritorial conduct alleged here. On the first question, I believe that the District Court had subject-matter jurisdiction over the Sherman Act claims against all the defendants (personal jurisdiction is not contested). Respondents asserted nonfrivolous claims under the Sherman Act, and 28 U.S.C. §1331 vests district courts with subject-matter jurisdiction over cases "arising under" federal statutes. As precedents . . . make clear, that is sufficient to establish the District Court's jurisdiction over these claims. . . .

The second question — the extraterritorial reach of the Sherman Act — has nothing to do with the jurisdiction of the courts. It is a question of substantive law turning on whether, in enacting the Sherman Act, Congress asserted regulatory power over the challenged conduct. If a plaintiff fails to prevail on this issue, the court does not dismiss the claim for want of subject-matter jurisdiction — want of power to adjudicate; rather, it decides the claim, ruling on the merits that the plaintiff has failed to state a cause of action under the relevant statute.

There is, however, a type of "jurisdiction" relevant to determining the extra-territorial reach of a statute; it is known as "legislative jurisdiction," or "jurisdiction to prescribe." . . . There is no doubt, of course, that Congress possesses legislative jurisdiction over the acts alleged in this complaint: Congress has broad power . . . "[t]o regulate Commerce with foreign Nations," and this Court has repeatedly upheld its power to make laws applicable to persons or activities beyond our territorial boundaries where United States interests are affected. But the question in this litigation is whether, and to what extent, Congress *has* exercised that undoubted legislative jurisdiction in enacting the Sherman Act.

Two canons of statutory construction are relevant in this inquiry. The first is the "longstanding principle of American law 'that legislation of Congress, unless a contrary intent appears, is meant to apply only within the territorial jurisdiction of the United States.'" [*EEOC v. Arabian American Oil Co. [Aramco]* 499 U.S. 244, 248 (1991)]. Applying that canon in *Aramco*, we held that the version of Title VII of the Civil Rights Act of 1964 then in force did not extend outside the territory of the United States even though the statute contained broad provisions extending its prohibitions to, for example, "any activity, business, or industry in commerce." We held such "boilerplate language" to be an insufficient indication to override the presumption against extraterritoriality. The Sherman Act contains similar "boilerplate language," and if the question were not governed by precedent, it would be worth considering whether that presumption controls the outcome here. We have, however, found the presumption to be overcome with respect to our antitrust laws; it is now well established that the Sherman Act applies extraterritorially.

But if the presumption against extraterritoriality has been overcome or is otherwise inapplicable, a second canon of statutory construction becomes relevant: "[A]n act of congress ought never to be construed to violate the law of nations if any other possible construction remains." *Murray v. Schooner Charming Betsy*, 6 U.S. (2 Cranch) 64, 118 (1804) (Marshall, C.J.). This canon is "wholly independent" of the presumption against extraterritoriality. It is relevant to determining the substantive reach of a statute because "the law of nations," or customary international law, includes limitations on a nation's exercise of its jurisdiction to prescribe. Though it clearly has constitutional authority to do so, Congress is generally presumed not to have exceeded those customary international-law limits on jurisdiction to prescribe.

Consistent with that presumption, this and other courts have frequently recognized that, even where the presumption against extraterritoriality does not apply, statutes should not be interpreted to regulate foreign persons or conduct if that regulation would conflict with principles of international law. . . .

More recent lower court precedent has also tempered the extraterritorial application of the Sherman Act with considerations of "international comity." See *Timberlane Lumber Co. v. Bank of America, N. T. & S. A.*, 549 F.2d 597 (CA9 1976). The "comity" they refer to is . . . what might be termed "prescriptive comity": the respect sovereign nations afford each other by limiting the reach of their laws. That comity is exercised by legislatures when they enact laws, and courts assume it has been exercised when they come to interpreting the scope of laws their legislatures have enacted. . . . Comity in this sense includes the choice-of-law principles that, "in the absence of contrary congressional direction," are assumed to be incorporated into our substantive laws having extraterritorial reach. Considering comity in this way is just part of determining whether the Sherman Act prohibits the conduct at issue.

In sum, the practice of using international law to limit the extraterritorial reach of statutes is firmly established in our jurisprudence. In proceeding to apply that practice to the present cases, I shall rely on the Restatement (Third) for the relevant principles of international law. . . . Whether the Restatement precisely reflects international law in every detail matters little here, as I believe this litigation would be resolved the same way under virtually any conceivable test that takes account of foreign regulatory interests.

Under the Restatement, a nation having some "basis" for jurisdiction to prescribe law should nonetheless refrain from exercising that jurisdiction "with respect to a person or activity having connections with another state when the exercise of such jurisdiction is unreasonable." Restatement (Third) §403(1). The "reasonableness" inquiry turns on a number of factors including, but not limited to: "the extent to which the activity takes place within the territory [of the regulating state]," *id.*, §403(2)(a); "the connections, such as nationality, residence, or economic activity, between the regulating state and the person principally responsible for the activity to be regulated," *id.*, §403(2)(b); "the character of the activity to be regulated, the importance of regulation to the regulating state, the extent to which other states regulate such activities, and the degree to which the desirability of such regulation is generally accepted," *id.*, §403(2)(c); "the extent to which another state may have an interest in regulating the activity," *id.*, §403(2)(g); and "the likelihood of conflict with regulation by another state," *id.*, §403(2)(h). Rarely would these factors point more clearly against application of United States law. The activity relevant to the counts at issue here took place primarily in the United Kingdom, and the defendants in these counts are British corporations and British subjects having their principal place of business or residence outside the United States. Great Britain has established a comprehensive regulatory scheme governing the London reinsurance markets, and clearly has a heavy "interest in regulating the activity," *id.*, §403(2)(g). . . . Considering these factors, I think it unimaginable that an assertion of legislative jurisdiction by the United States would be considered reasonable, and therefore it is inappropriate to assume, in the absence of statutory indication to the contrary, that Congress has made such an assertion.

It is evident from what I have said that the Court's comity analysis, which proceeds as though the issue is whether the courts should "decline to exercise . . . jurisdiction," rather than whether the Sherman Act covers this conduct, is simply misdirected. I do not at all agree, moreover, with the Court's conclusion that the issue of the substantive scope of the Sherman Act is not in the case. . . . It is not realistic, and also not helpful, to pretend that the only really relevant issue in this litigation is not before us. In any event, if one erroneously chooses, as the Court does, to make adjudicative jurisdiction (or, more precisely, abstention) the vehicle for taking account of the needs of prescriptive comity, the Court still gets it wrong. It concludes that no "true conflict" counseling nonapplication of United States law (or rather, as it thinks, United States judicial jurisdiction) exists unless compliance with United States law would constitute a *violation* of another country's law. That breathtakingly broad proposition, which contradicts the many cases discussed earlier, will bring the Sherman Act and other laws into sharp and unnecessary conflict with the legitimate interests of other countries — particularly our closest trading partners. . . .

The most recent Supreme Court decision to address the extraterritorial reach of the Sherman Act is *F. Hoffman LaRoche v. Empagran*, 542 U.S. 155 (2004). *Empagran* involved a worldwide conspiracy to fix prices for vitamins that produced significant effects in the U.S. market and that independently harmed consumers outside the United States. Plaintiff was a foreign purchaser who brought suit in the United States based on harm in foreign markets. In analyzing whether the Sherman Act reached this claim, the Court stated that it "ordinarily construes ambiguous statutes to avoid unreasonable interference with the sovereign authority of other nations" and that this rule of construction "reflects principles of customary international law — law that (we must assume) Congress ordinarily seeks to follow." The Court reasoned that the exercise of Sherman Act jurisdiction where a foreign plaintiff's claim is based wholly on foreign harm is not "reasonable" because it "creates a serious risk of interference with a foreign nation's ability independently to regulate its own commercial affairs."

Notes and Questions

1. Do *Alcoa*, *Timberlane*, and *Hartford Fire* shed light on the international legality of the EC's assertion of jurisdiction over the Boeing-MDC merger?

2. Does *Hartford Fire* reject the *Timberlane* balancing approach? Does it mean that U.S. courts will, in effect, give greater respect to the laws of nations that require monopolistic and anti-competitive practices and less consideration to laws from nations that share the U.S.'s market-based principles?

3. Was there a conflict between U.S. antitrust laws and the English reinsurance regulations in *Hartford Fire*?

4. The U.S. Department of Justice and the Federal Trade Commission, in their 1995 Antitrust Enforcement Guidelines for International Operations, state that they will "take full account of comity factors beyond whether there is a conflict with foreign law" in their enforcement activities. The Guidelines also state:

> In cases where the United States decided to prosecute an antitrust action, such a decision represents a determination by the Executive Branch that the importance of antitrust enforcement outweighs any relevant foreign policy concerns. The Department does not believe that it is the role of the court to "second guess the executive branch's judgment as to the proper role of comity concerns under these circumstances." [*Quoting United States v. Baker Hughes, Inc.*, 731 F. Supp. 3, 6 n.5 (D.D.C. 1990)].

Should courts rely on comity factors when considering cases implicating foreign interests? If so, should a court's consideration of these factors differ in cases brought by the government and cases brought by private parties?

5. Similar issues arise outside of the antitrust field. The federal securities laws, for example, contain broad prohibitions against fraudulent conduct in the issuance and trading of securities. These prohibitions have frequently been applied to conduct occurring partially or totally outside the United States. But, unlike the Sherman Act cases, the securities cases have not sparked strong foreign protests. In addition, U.S. courts have often determined that Congress did not intend that "social" legislation, such as Title VII of the 1964 Civil Rights Act, reach overseas conduct. What might explain the different reactions of foreign governments in the antitrust and securities areas, and the greater judicial reluctance to find extraterritorial reach in social legislation?

2. A European Alternative?

European nations have been among the most vocal critics of the extraterritorial reach of U.S. legislation. The European Court of Justice has addressed whether EC laws apply to conduct outside the territory of the EC's member states. A leading case, *Wood Pulp*, involved alleged "concerted practices" by foreign wood pulp producers and trade associations outside of the EC that affected the prices for wood pulp within the EC. Defendants challenged the European Commission's attempt to assert jurisdiction over them. The Commission explained why it believed the exercise of jurisdiction was appropriate:

> . . . First, what is important from the point of view of jurisdiction is where the conduct of the parties which it is the object, or effect, of the agreement to influence occurred and not the place where the agreement was made. Secondly, the relevant conduct of the parties includes not only the conduct of the principals but also that of their subsidiaries, agents and others whose acts they direct. . . .
>
> The Commission acknowledges that it is not always easy to distinguish "the effects" of "conduct" from the conduct itself. In the context of the Court's question, however, the Commission defines the "effects" as the direct and perceivable consequences of certain "conduct". The distinction to be made is thus between "conduct" which distorts the competitive process in the Community and "conduct" which, though not itself distorting the competitive process within the Community, produces such consequences.
>
> Applying those principles to this case, the Commission considers that the different kinds of conduct penalized in this case did indeed take place in the Community.
>
> Thus the communication of announced prices was made in the Community. The transaction prices themselves were charged in the Community by the producers themselves, by their subsidiaries, branches or other establishments, or by their agents or employees.
>
> With regard to the exchange of information within KEA [a U.S.-based export association], the Commission considers that it must first of all be regarded as facilitating the concerted practices on prices. In those circumstances, the relevant conduct for that infringement is in substance the same as that for the concentration on prices. However, if that exchange of information is treated as a separate infringement, it may be presumed to have taken place in the United States so far as KEA is concerned. However, such conduct had certain effects within the Community inasmuch as it facilitated the concentration on prices and also strengthened the system of mutual solidarity between the members of KEA. . . .

[handwritten margin notes: "where effect seems. Conduct of associate"]

In this case, the Commission considers that if the Community's jurisdiction in this case is considered to be based on conduct which occurred within the Community, it is not in breach of any prohibitive rule of international law. The same holds true in so far as its jurisdiction is based on the effects within the Community of conduct which occurred elsewhere. . . .

———————————

The European Court of Justice upheld the extraterritorial assertion of EC competition law:

Re Wood Pulp Cartel

[1988] E.C.R. 5193

[T]he Commission [has] set out the grounds which in its view justify the Community's jurisdiction to apply Article 85 of the Treaty [of Rome, prohibiting agreements and concerted practices that prevent, restrict, or distort competition] to the concentration in question. It stated first that all the addressees of the decision were either exporting directly to purchasers within the Community or were doing business within the Community through branches, subsidiaries, agencies or other establishments in the Community. It further pointed out that the concentration applied to the vast majority of the sales of those undertakings to and in the Community. Finally it stated that two-thirds of total shipments and 60 per cent of consumption of the product in question in the Community had been affected by such concentration. The Commission concluded that "the effect of the agreements and practices on prices announced and/or charged to customers and on resale of pulp within the EEC was therefore not only substantial but intended, and was the primary and direct result of the agreements and practices". . . .

. . . The applicants have submitted that the decision is incompatible with public international law on the grounds that the application of the competition rules in this case was founded exclusively on the economic repercussions within the Common Market of conduct restricting competition which was adopted outside the Community.

. . . It should be observed that an infringement of Article 85, such as the conclusion of an agreement which has had the effect of restricting competition within the Common Market, consists of conduct made up of two elements, the formation of the agreement, decision or concerted practice and the implementation thereof. If the applicability of prohibitions laid down under competition law were made to depend on the place where the agreement, decision or concerted practice was formed, the result would obviously be to give undertakings an easy means of evading those prohibitions. The decisive factor is therefore the place where it is implemented.

. . . The producers in this case implemented their pricing agreement within the Common Market. It is immaterial in that respect whether or not they had recourse to subsidiaries, agents, sub-agents, or branches within the Community in order to make their contacts with purchasers within the Community.

. . . Accordingly the Community's jurisdiction to apply its competition rules to such conduct is covered by the territoriality principle as universally recognized in public international law. . . . As regards the argument based on the infringement of the principle of non-interference, it should be pointed out that the applicants who are members of KEA have referred to a rule according to which where two States have jurisdiction to lay down and enforce rules and the effect of those rules is that a person finds himself subject to contradictory orders as to the conduct he must adopt, each State is obliged to exercise its jurisdiction with moderation. . . .

. . . There is not, in this case, any contradiction between the conduct required by the United States and that required by the Community since [U.S. law] merely exempts the conclusion of export cartels from the application of United States antitrust laws but does not require such cartels to be concluded. . . .

Notes and Questions

1. Shortly after the *Wood Pulp* decision, the Assistant Attorney General in charge of the Antitrust Division of the U.S. Department of Justice argued that the *Wood Pulp* decision was, as a practical matter, "very close to, if not indistinguishable from, the so-called 'effects' test as applied by U.S. courts." However, the EC's Commissioner for Competition Policy sharply disagreed:

> [I]t is in my view unreasonable to assume unqualified espousal of a doctrine in a judgement which does not mention it by name, while those who urged its adoption accepted that it should be qualified. So the Court of Justice does not endorse the effects doctrine. . . . But the Court of Justice held the sale in the Community at a concerted price was implementation, and I find that conclusion thoroughly reasonable and appropriate. . . . Nevertheless, this specific use of the word "implementation" rather than "effects" suggests to me that implementing conduct perhaps has to be direct, substantial, and foreseeable for jurisdiction to be engaged.

As a doctrinal matter, which test makes more sense? In practice, would you expect the "implementation test" often to yield results different from the U.S. "effects test"?

2. By 1995, Austria, Canada, Denmark, Finland, France, Germany, Greece, Japan, Norway, Portugal, Spain, Sweden, and Switzerland, among others, had adopted jurisdictional approaches similar to the effects doctrine. Can you reconcile European and other governments' protests against the assertion of extraterritorial jurisdiction by the United States under the Sherman Act while at the same time interpreting their own antitrust laws to permit prescriptive jurisdiction over foreign conduct?

C. Resolving the Boeing Dispute

Transatlantic political tensions continued to mount as the EC vote on the Boeing-MDC merger approached. At least six U.S. government agencies prepared lists of retaliatory measures for the President should the EC not approve the merger. United States legislators declared that "any effort to block [the merger] is nothing short of a foreign government trying to dictate America's vital national security policy. As such, it is an assault on our national sovereignty." President Clinton called the Prime Ministers of Italy, Luxembourg, and Britain, and the Secretary of State called her European counterparts.

On July 23, 1997, after the President's personal intervention, Boeing and the Commission reached agreement. In exchange for the Commission's approval of the merger, Boeing agreed (1) not to enforce the exclusivity clauses in its airplane supply contracts with Delta, American, and Continental; (2) to keep MDC's commercial aircraft division a separate legal entity for ten years and to submit reports to the Europeans on its business; and (3) to license technology it might develop from the military contracts it takes over from MDC. The merger received final Commission endorsement on July 30.

EC Competition Minister Van Miert characterized these concessions as "spectacular." However, American and Continental airline officials said that they intended to continue making purchases from Boeing, and Boeing's Chairman said that the concessions would have "if not zero impact, minimal impact on the bottom line." Given the agreement between Boeing and the Commission, no court considered the EC's assertion of jurisdiction over this merger, nor the legitimacy of the Commission's focus on the sole-source contracts between Boeing and U.S. airlines.

Notes and Questions

1. Who won the dispute over the Boeing-MDC merger? Who lost? If there had been litigation over the Commission's jurisdiction in this matter, how would the issue likely have been resolved?

2. In July 2001, after U.S., Canadian, and other regulators had given their approval, the EU blocked a proposed $45 billion merger between U.S. companies Honeywell and General Electric. This prompted a relatively muted reaction from the U.S. government. How would you know if this reflects U.S. acquiescence in the European position?

3. Do the Boeing or Honeywell fact patterns suggest a need for an international antitrust body? European governments have long favored creation of an international antitrust regime. The United States has opposed this idea and instead has entered into a series of bilateral agreements with the EU, Japan, Canada, and other states. Under these agreements, either party can ask the other to take antitrust enforcement action against practices that harm the requesting party's interests. However, these agreements do not require any changes in the laws of the parties or require either party to surrender jurisdiction to the other on a matter affecting both; one even goes so far as to state that "[n]othing in this Agreement shall be construed to prejudice the policy or legal position of either party regarding any issue related to jurisdiction." Do you think these agreements will defuse or avoid the type of conflicts raised by the Boeing fact pattern? Why does the United States enter into these agreements?

4. The Boeing-Airbus rivalry continues to raise international legal issues. Lengthy negotiations between the United States and the EC led to a 1992 agreement in which each party agreed to limit its support to aircraft manufacturers. However, this agreement proved unsatisfactory, and extensive efforts to reach a new agreement proved unsuccessful. After negotiations broke down in the summer of 2005, the United States initiated dispute settlement proceedings at the World Trade Organization (WTO), challenging European aid to Airbus as an illegal export subsidy. The EC immediately retaliated by filing a WTO action claiming that U.S. government subsidies and research and development contracts give Boeing an unfair competitive advantage over Airbus. The WTO proceedings are expected

to continue into 2007. The WTO's dispute settlement system is examined in Chapter 12.

D. Note on Other Bases for Prescriptive Jurisdiction

States recognize several bases, in addition to territory, upon which to exercise jurisdiction. Some of the most important are outlined below.

1. The Nationality Principle

Under the nationality principle, states can exercise prescriptive jurisdiction over their own nationals, even when they are located outside national territory. A classic example of the exercise of nationality jurisdiction occurred in *Blackmer v. United States*, 284 U.S. 421 (1932), where the Supreme Court ruled that U.S. laws applied to a U.S. citizen resident in France: "By virtue of the obligations of citizenship, the United States retained its authority over him, and he was bound by its laws made applicable to him in a foreign country." The criminal laws of several states, including France, Germany, India, and the UK, cover the criminal acts of citizens committed while abroad. The nationality of natural persons can be based upon birth in a state's territory (*jus soli*) or birth to parents who are nationals (*jus sanguinis*).

While defining the nationality of natural persons is often relatively straightforward, determining the nationality of corporations and other legal entities raises a number of difficult problems. What is the nationality of a Polish subsidiary of a German multinational corporation? Or, more controversially, who can exercise nationality jurisdiction over, for example, a Euro-denominated bank account of a Canadian citizen located in the Geneva branch of a London-based bank? Who should make such determinations?

The United States has been relatively aggressive in asserting nationality jurisdiction in the corporate setting. For example, during the Iran hostage crisis in 1979, the United States froze all Iranian assets under its jurisdiction, which the United States interpreted to include all dollar-denominated accounts held by U.S. banks and their subsidiaries abroad. In the early 1980s, in response to the imposition of martial law in Poland, the United States prohibited foreign subsidiaries of U.S. corporations from delivering oil and gas equipment to the USSR. This sparked vigorous objections from a number of states. The EC issued a legal opinion concluding that the pipeline controls "were not in conformity with well-recognized principles of international law"; the British government prohibited British companies from complying with the U.S. law, and France directed its companies to honor their pipeline contracts. Most of the foreign subsidiaries honored their contracts; the United States eventually lifted the pipeline controls in exchange for a vague promise that the Europeans would study future limits on trade with the Soviets.

In the aftermath of this dispute, a former German diplomat offered the following observations:

> More in the United States than in any other country, international law in general and jurisdiction in particular is seen as a dynamic process rather than as a set of given rules. The view that rules of jurisdiction emanate from the process of action and reaction may be helpful as a political analysis of legal development. As a guide for

national decision makers to assert jurisdictional powers, however, such an approach invites a disregard for existing rules in the hope that other nations may tolerate the assertion either freely or be forced to by the existing power balance. This may serve a powerful nation well, and it might not even damage the stability of the international community so long as the acting state shows moderation and does not judge the reasonableness of its assertion entirely and persistently on national interests alone. But generally, this approach implies a risk of international conflict and creates uncertainty and unpredictability for international business and trade. . . . Moreover, it appears to be an inherent aspect of this approach that an affected country considers retaliation in order to prevent a repetition of the extraterritorial application of jurisdiction. . . .

The unwillingness of Europe to retaliate by asserting jurisdiction within the territory of the United States appears to have worked to its disadvantage. At least the European Communities and their member states have made it sufficiently clear that they consider the U.S. actions contrary to international law. This view is probably shared by a number of other nations friendly to the United States, not to speak of other parts of the international community. Even admitting a degree of uncertainty as to what the international law on jurisdiction was before the pipeline case, the answer to the question, "What is the law today?" should no longer be uncertain.

Extraterritorial Application of U.S. Export Controls — The Siberian Pipeline, Remarks by Werner Hein, 77 Proc. Am. Socy. Intl. L. 241, 247-278 (1983).

2. The Protective Principle

The French Napoleonic Code provided:

> Any foreigner who, outside the territory of France, shall be culpable, either as principal or as an accomplice, of a crime against the security of the state, or of counterfeiting the seal of the state or national moneys in circulation or national papers or bank notes authorized by law, shall be prosecuted and tried according to the provisions of French laws, if he is arrested in France or if the Government obtains his extradition.

This provision served as a model for the drafting of many criminal codes in Europe in the 1800s. Many Latin American nations have similar provisions in their domestic laws. More generally, states recognize the right to regulate conduct outside their territory by non-nationals that is directed against their security or a limited number of other important state interests. This is known as the "protective principle."

The House of Lords considered the protective principle for the first time in the *Joyce* case, which arose out of allegedly treasonous acts during World War II. William Joyce was born in Brooklyn, New York, in 1906, and moved to England in 1921. In 1933, he applied for a British passport, stating that he was a British subject by birth. Joyce received a British passport, which was renewed in 1939, ten days before the outbreak of World War II. He then left for Germany and, weeks after the war started, began broadcasting pro-German propaganda from Germany. Joyce broadcast until April 30, 1945. A month later, he encountered two British officers near the Danish frontier — one of whom shot him in the leg — and was arrested.

Joyce was tried in September 1945 and was convicted and sentenced to death. He appealed on the grounds, inter alia, that "the Court wrongly assumed jurisdiction to try an alien for an offense against British law committed in a foreign country." On December 18, the House of Lords dismissed the appeal, and, three weeks later, William Joyce was hanged before a crowd of approximately 300 people.

On February 1, 1946, the House of Lords issued an opinion containing the following passage:

> The second point of appeal . . . was that . . . no English court has jurisdiction to try an alien for a crime committed abroad and your Lordships heard an exhaustive argument upon the construction of penal statutes. There is, I think, a short answer to this point. The statute in question deals with the crime of treason committed within or . . . without the realm: it is general in its terms and I see no reason for limiting its scope. No principle of comity demands that a state should ignore the crime of treason committed against it outside its territory. On the contrary a proper regard for its own security requires that all those who commit that crime, whether they commit it within or without the realm should be amenable to its laws. . . .

[1946] A.C. 347, 372 (per Lord Jowett, L.C.).

The United States has at times exercised jurisdiction based upon the protective principle. For example, in *United States v. Pizzarusso*, 388 F.2d 8 (2d Cir. 1968), a Canadian citizen was tried and convicted for the crime of knowingly making a false statement under oath in a visa application to a U.S. official. In a case of first impression, the Second Circuit upheld the exercise of jurisdiction based upon the protective principle, stating that the government has a "legitimate interest" in information regarding persons seeking entry to the United States and that false statements in visa applications "constitute[ ] an affront to the very sovereignty of the United States."

Notes and Questions

1. How does a false statement on a visa application constitute "an affront to the very sovereignty of the United States"? May a state prosecute any act or statement by a non-national that affronts its sovereignty?

2. Does *Pizzarusso* suggest any limits to the use of the protective principle? Should it apply to drug cases? In *United States v. Romero-Galue*, 757 F.2d 1147 (11th Cir. 1985), the court stated that "the United States could, under the 'protective principle' of international law, prosecute foreign nationals on foreign vessels on the high seas for possession of narcotics."

3. The Passive Personality Principle

Under the passive personality principle, a state may apply its law — particularly criminal law — to an act committed outside its territory by a person not its national when a national is a victim of the act. Although this form of jurisdiction was traditionally disfavored, states provided for passive personality jurisdiction in a series of treaties on hijacking and other forms of terrorism. For example, the 1963 Convention on Offenses and Certain Other Acts Committed on Board Aircraft allowed states whose nationals had been victims to assert criminal jurisdiction over individuals who had committed offenses on board aircraft. More recently, the use of passive personality jurisdiction has expanded beyond the terrorism context; for example, the 2000 Transnational Organized Crime Convention, adopted in 2003, authorizes states to enact passive personality statutes in respect of transnational crimes covered by the treaty.

Over the past few decades, increasing numbers of countries began to incorporate the passive personality principle in domestic legislation, largely in response to increased terrorist activity. The United States, in particular, has moved away from its historic criticism of the principle and enacted a number of federal statutes that authorize passive personality jurisdiction. For example, in *United States v. Bin Laden*, 92 F. Supp. 2d 189 (S.D.N.Y. 2000), defendants were indicted, inter alia, for a conspiracy to kill U.S. nationals abroad. The court rejected a challenge to the indictment and noted, quoting the *Restatement*, that the passive personality principle is "increasingly accepted as applied to terrorist and other organized attacks on a state's nationals by reason of their nationality. . . . ."

4. Universal Jurisdiction

Under the universal jurisdiction principle, any state may exercise jurisdiction over an individual who commits certain heinous and widely condemned offenses, even when no other recognized basis for jurisdiction exists. The traditional rationale for universal jurisdiction is that the prohibited acts are of an international character and are of serious concern to the international community as a whole. States accept that piracy, war crimes, genocide, and slave trade give rise to universal jurisdiction. Debate on the universal principle tends to center on whether to extend universal jurisdiction to other categories of acts, such as certain acts of terrorism, assaults on diplomatic personnel, or kidnaping.

The classic modern example of a state exercising universal jurisdiction is the Eichmann episode. Adolf Eichmann was the senior German official responsible for organizing the arrest, deportation, internment, and extermination of Jews during World War II, as discussed further in Section III below. After the war, Eichmann stood trial in Israel for his wartime actions. The Israeli Supreme Court rejected Eichmann's challenge to Israel's jurisdiction.

Attorney-General of the State of Israel v. Adolf Eichmann

36 I.L.R. 277 (1962)

1. The Appellant, Adolf Eichmann, was found guilty by the District Court of Jerusalem of offenses of the most extreme gravity against the Nazis and Nazi Collaborators (Punishment) Law 5710-1950 (hereinafter — "the Law") and was sentenced to death. . . .

6. Most of the legal contentions of Counsel for the Appellant concentrate on the argument that the District Court, in assuming jurisdiction to try the Appellant, acted contrary to the principles of international law. . . .

(2) The offenses for which the Appellant was tried are in the nature of 'extra-territorial offenses,' that is to say, offenses that were committed outside the territory of Israel by a citizen of a foreign state; and even though the above-mentioned Law confers jurisdiction in respect of such offenses, it conflicts, in so doing, with the principle of territorial sovereignty, which postulates that only the country within whose territory the offense was committed, or to which the offender belongs-in this case, Germany — has jurisdiction to punish therefor. . . .

12. . . . [I]t is the universal character of the crimes in question which vests in every state the power to try those who participated in the perpetration of such crimes and to punish them therefor. . . .

(a) One of the principles whereby states assume, in one degree or another, the power to try and punish a person for an offense he has committed, is the principle of universality. Its meaning is, in essence, that that power is vested in every state regardless of the fact that the offense was committed outside its territory by a person who did not belong to it, provided he is in its custody at the time he is brought to trial. This principle has wide support and is universally acknowledged with respect to the offense of piracy *jure gentium*. But while there exists general agreement as to its application to this offense, there is a difference of opinion as to the scope of its application. Thus one school of thought holds that it cannot be applied to any offense other than the one mentioned above, lest this entail excessive interference with the competence of the state in which the offense was committed. . . .

A second school of thought . . . considers [universal jurisdiction] to be no more than an auxiliary principle, to be applied in circumstances in which no resort can be had to the principle of territorial sovereignty or to the nationality principle, both of which are universally agreed to. . . . [Under this theory,] the state contemplating the exercise of the power in question must first offer the extradition of the offender to the state within whose territory the offense was committed (*forum delicti commissi*). . . .

A third school of thought holds that the rule of universal jurisdiction, which is valid in cases of piracy, logically applies also to all such criminal acts of commission or omission which constitute offenses under the law of nations (*delicta juris gentium*). . . . This view has been opposed in the past because of the difficulty in securing general agreement as to the offenses to be included in the above-mentioned class. . . .

(b) This brief survey of views set out above shows that, notwithstanding the differences between them, there is full justification for applying here the principle of universal jurisdiction, since the international character of the "crimes against humanity" (in the wide meaning of the term) is, in this case, not in doubt, and the unprecedented extent of their injurious and murderous effects is not open to dispute at the present day. In other words, the basic reason for which international law recognizes the right of each state to exercise such jurisdiction in piracy offences — notwithstanding the fact that its own jurisdiction does not extend to the scene of the commission of the offense (the high seas) and the offender is a national of another state or is stateless — applies with all the greater force to the above-mentioned crimes. That reason is, it will be recalled, that the interest to prevent bodily and material harm to those who sail the seas, and to persons engaged in free trade between nations, is a vital interest, common to all civilized states and of universal scope. . . .

This means that it was not the recognition of the universal jurisdiction to try and punish the person who committed 'piracy' that justified the viewing of such an act as an international crime *sui generis*, but it was the agreed vital interest of the international community that justified the exercise of the jurisdiction in question. . . .

It follows that the state which prosecutes and punishes a person for that offense acts solely as the organ and agent of the international community, and metes out punishment to the offender for his breach of the prohibition imposed by the law of nations. . . .

The above explanation of the substantive basis underlying the exercise of universal jurisdiction in respect of the crime of piracy also justifies its exercise in regard to the crimes with which we are dealing in this case. . . .

(d) This is the place to discuss the limitation imposed by most of those who support this principle upon the exercise of universal jurisdiction, namely, that the state which has apprehended the offender must first offer his extradition to the state in which the offense was committed (see sub-paragraph (a) above). This means that only if the second state does not respond to the offer of extradition may the first state arrogate to itself the jurisdiction to try and punish. The above limitation is based upon the approach implicit in the maxim *aut dedere aut punire* [extradite or prosecute]. . . .

As to the limitation itself in the sense explained above, we are of the opinion that it has no place in the circumstances of this case. First . . . Counsel for the Appellant has himself admitted that his application to the Government of Western Germany to demand the extradition of his client was refused, and therefore an offer in this sense by the Government of Israel could be of no practical use. Secondly — and this is the principal reason for the rejection of his submission — the idea behind the above-mentioned limitation is not that the requirement to offer the offender to the state in which the offense was committed was designed to prevent the violation of its territorial sovereignty. Its reason is rather a purely practical one: The great majority of the witnesses and the greater part of the evidence are concentrated in that state, and it becomes, therefore, the most convenient place (*forum conveniens*) for the conduct of the trial. . . . [I]t must be said that the great majority of the witnesses who gave evidence here on the grave crimes attributed to the Appellant, especially those against the Jews, were residents of Israel, and, moreover, the bulk of the vast mass of documents produced was previously gathered and preserved (through Yad Vashem) [a Holocaust museum and research center] in the State of Israel. . . . It is clear, therefore, that it is the State of Israel — not the State of Germany — that must be regarded as the *forum conveniens* for the trial.

. . . (f) We sum up our views on this subject as follows: Not only are all the crimes attributed to the Appellant of an international character, but they are crimes whose evil and murderous effects were so widespread as to shake the stability of the international community to its very foundations. The State of Israel, therefore, was entitled, pursuant to the principle of universal jurisdiction, and acting in the capacity of guardian of international law and agents for its enforcement, to try the Appellant. This being the case, it is immaterial that the State of Israel did not exist at the time the offenses were committed. . . .

Notes and Questions

1. In upholding the exercise of universal jurisdiction, the Israeli Supreme Court draws an analogy between war crimes and crimes against humanity, on the one hand, and piracy, on the other. Are you persuaded by this analogy? Is it relevant that piracy is typically defined to include private acts but to exclude state acts?

2. What factors does the *Eichmann* court use to distinguish between those criminal acts that give rise to universal jurisdiction and those that do not? Should terrorism give rise to universal jurisdiction?

3. While the *Eichmann* case was for many years the preeminent example of the exercise of universal jurisdiction, in recent years criminal complaints or investigations based on universal jurisdiction have been instituted in a number of states, including Austria, Belgium, Canada, Denmark, France, Germany, the Netherlands, Senegal, Spain, Switzerland, and the United Kingdom. (A number of these cases

are discussed in Chapter 9.) Why would a state prosecute foreign nationals for human rights atrocities committed against other foreign nationals outside its territory? Why have such prosecutions become more prevalent in the last decade?

4. Where more than one state wishes to exercise jurisdiction over an individual, and where the state with custody of that individual has no basis for jurisdiction other than the principle of universality, who should decide which state will exercise jurisdiction? In November 2004, a U.S.-based NGO and four Iraqi citizens filed a criminal complaint with the German Federal Prosecutor's Office. The complaint alleged that U.S. Secretary of Defense Donald Rumsfeld and other current and former U.S. government officials were responsible for unlawful acts committed against detainees at Abu Ghraib and elsewhere. The complainants sought indictments under the German Code of Crimes Against International Law (CCAIL), which provides for jurisdiction over genocide, war crimes, and crimes against humanity "even when the offence was committed abroad and bears no relation to Germany."

In February 2005, the General Prosecuting Attorney dismissed the complaint. The prosecutor reasoned that the CCAIL does not "legitimize unlimited criminal prosecution." Rather, the purpose of the law is "to close gaps in punishability and criminal prosecution" and therefore CCAIL prosecutions "must . . . occur in the framework of non-interference in the affairs of foreign countries." The prosecutor noted that the United States is the "primary jurisdiction" for criminal prosecution of the crimes alleged and that "there are no indications that the authorities and courts of the [U.S.] are refraining, or would refrain, from penal measures as regards the violations described in the complaint."

Does the German prosecutor use a sensible framework for resolving conflicting jurisdictional claims? Is this a decision that is better made by prosecutors or by courts? Or are such decisions better made by political actors? Consider the case of Hissène Habré, who ruled Chad from 1982 until 1990, when he was deposed and fled to Senegal. In February 2000, a Senegalese court charged Habré with torture and crimes against humanity committed during his years in power; however, in March 2001, Senegal's highest court decided that he could not be tried in Senegal for crimes committed abroad. In September 2005, a Belgian judge issued an international arrest warrant for Habré under Belgium's universal jurisdiction law, and the following month Habré was arrested in Senegal. In November 2005, Senegal's Court of Appeals ruled that it could not decide whether Habré should be extradited to Belgium because of Habré's immunity as a former head of state. As a result, the decision to extradite shifted to Senegal's executive branch. Shortly thereafter, Senegal's Interior Minister issued an order placing Habré "at the disposition" of the Chairman of the African Union. Senegal's Foreign Minister stated that Senegal would ask a January 2006 African Union summit "to indicate the jurisdiction which is competent to hear the case." At the summit, AU leaders decided to create a Committee of Eminent African Jurists to recommend where Habré should be tried.

Is the African Union—an international organization designed to achieve greater unity and solidarity among African countries and the peoples of Africa, and to promote human rights and democratic principles—an appropriate body to decide where Habré should be tried? If not, what body or institution would be more appropriate?

The use of universal jurisdiction to address human rights abuses is discussed in Chapter 9.

5. Note on Jurisdiction Over Internet-Based Activities

The Internet makes possible vast new opportunities for interaction among parties located around the globe. Although some scholars have suggested that activities in cyberspace cannot legitimately be governed by territorially based sovereigns, over the last decade, states have enacted legislation purporting to regulate almost every conceivable form of Internet activity. These assertions of authority raise a number of difficult issues: What level of online commercial activity renders one "present" in a jurisdiction for tax purposes? Are national intellectual property laws sufficient when information can be transferred instantly around the planet? If a person uploads content that is lawful in her home jurisdiction, but unlawful in a state where it can be accessed, is the person liable in the second jurisdiction?

Courts in many states have struggled with these and related jurisdictional issues. For example, in *Dow Jones & Co. v. Gutnick*, [2002] HCA 56, a plaintiff who lived in Victoria, Australia, sued U.S.-based Dow Jones in Australian courts over an allegedly defamatory article posted on Dow Jones' U.S-based Web site. The lower court upheld jurisdiction on the theory that the defamation occurred at the time and place that the article was downloaded in Australia. On appeal to the High Court of Australia, Dow Jones claimed that this holding would have a "chilling effect" on publishers, who would face the possibility of lawsuits from around the globe. Dow Jones argued that an Internet publisher should only have to conform its conduct to the law of the place where it maintained its web servers, unless that place was merely "adventitious or opportunistic." The High Court disagreed, reasoning that Internet publishers knowingly make their materials available on a worldwide basis, and holding that Australian defamation law would govern this action.

In a concurrence, Justice Kirby noted that the legal issues raised by the Internet

> appear to warrant national legislative attention and to require international discussion in a forum as global as the Internet itself. In default of local legislation and international agreement, there are limits on the extent to which national courts can provide radical solutions that would oblige a major overhaul of longstanding legal doctrine in the field of defamation law. Where large changes to settled law are involved, in an area as sensitive as the law of defamation, it should cause no surprise when the courts decline the invitation to solve problems that others, in a much better position to devise solutions, have neglected to repair.

In a separate concurrence, Justice Callinan rejected Dow Jones' argument that, for purposes of defamation law, "publication occurs . . . [at] the place where the matter is [first] provided or first published." He wrote:

> What the appellant seeks to do, is to impose upon Australian residents for the purposes of this and many other cases, an American legal hegemony in relation to Internet publications. The consequence . . . would be to confer upon one country, and one notably more benevolent to the commercial and other media than this one, an effective domain over the law of defamation, to the financial advantage of publishers in the United States, and the serious disadvantage of those unfortunate enough to be reputationally damaged outside the United States. A further consequence might be to place commercial publishers in this country at a disadvantage to commercial publishers in the United States.

Following the High Court's decision, Dow Jones' attorneys filed a complaint before the United Nations Human Rights Committee on behalf of William Alpert, the journalist who wrote the story about Gutnick, and a co-defendant in the Australian litigation. The complaint alleged that the Australian litigation violated

Alpert's right of free speech guaranteed by the International Covenant on Civil and Political Rights (to which both Australia and the United States are parties). The Australian litigation was settled shortly after Alpert's complaint was filed, with Dow Jones reportedly paying plaintiff approximately $440,000 in damages and fees. After the settlement, a Dow Jones editor complained that Australia's libel law was "archaic and onerous" and stated that "[t]he verdict, had we gone to trial, would have been foregone. Result: a settlement. Kafka and Pirandello are alive and well and chuckling in Victoria."

Internet auctions are another form of web-based activity that have generated litigation with an international flavor. In *LICRA v. Yahoo!*, No. RG 00/05308 (Tribunal de Grande Instance de Paris, Nov. 20, 2000), French NGOs dedicated to eliminating anti-Semitism sued Yahoo! in a Paris court on the ground that the sale of Nazi and Third Reich-related goods through Yahoo!'s Web site violated French law. The French court found that Yahoo! had sufficient contacts with France to uphold the exercise of jurisdiction, and ordered Yahoo! to eliminate French citizens' access to any material on Yahoo!'s auction site that offers Nazi objects for sale. Yahoo! argued that it was technologically impossible to comply with this order. After receiving an expert opinion, the French court found that Yahoo! was capable of complying with the order and threatened a substantial fine against Yahoo! for each day that it failed to comply with the order.

Yahoo! then sought a declaratory judgment from a U.S. district court that the French order was neither cognizable nor enforceable under U.S. law. In particular, Yahoo! argued that it could not comply with the order without banning Nazi-related material from its website altogether, and that such a ban would violate Yahoo!'s First Amendment rights. While affirming France's right to ban the purchase and possession of Nazi memorabilia, the court framed the issue as "whether it is consistent with the Constitution and laws of the United States for another nation to regulate speech by a United States resident within the United States on the basis that such speech can be accessed by Internet users in that nation." The court reasoned that:

> The extent to which the United States, or any state, honors the judicial decrees of foreign nations is a matter of choice, governed by "the comity of nations." Hilton v. Guyot, 159 U.S. 113, 163 (1895). . . . United States courts generally recognize foreign judgments and decrees unless enforcement would be prejudicial or contrary to the country's interests. . . . [T]he French order's content and viewpoint-based regulation of the web pages and auction site on Yahoo.com . . . clearly would be inconsistent with the First Amendment if mandated by a court in the United States. What makes this case uniquely challenging is that the Internet in effect allows one to speak in more than one place at the same time. Although France has the sovereign right to regulate what speech is permissible in France, this Court may not enforce a foreign order that violates the protections of the United States Constitution by chilling protected speech that occurs simultaneously within our borders. . . . Absent a body of law that establishes international standards with respect to speech on the Internet and an appropriate treaty or legislation addressing enforcement of such standards to speech originating within the United States, the principle of comity is outweighed by the Court's obligation to uphold the First Amendment.

Accordingly, the court held that "the First Amendment precluded enforcement within the United States of a French order intended to regulate the content of its speech over the Internet." *Yahoo!, Inc. v. La Ligue Contre Le Racisme et l'Antisemitisme*, 169 F. Supp. 2d 1181 (N.D. Cal. 2001).

The Ninth Circuit, sitting en banc, reversed the district court and ordered that the case be dismissed. *Yahoo!, Inc. v. La Ligue Contre Le Racisme et l'Antisemitisme*, 433 F.3d 1199 (9th Cir. 2006). Three of the judges who thought the case should be dismissed argued that:

> The legal question presented by this case is whether the [French court orders] are enforceable in this country. These orders, by their explicit terms, require only that Yahoo! restrict access by Internet users located in France. The orders say nothing whatsoever about restricting access by Internet users in the United States. . . .
>
> The core of Yahoo!'s . . . argument may thus be that it has a First Amendment interest in allowing access by users in France. Yet under French criminal law, Internet service providers are forbidden to permit French users to have access to the materials specified in the French court's orders. French users . . . are criminally forbidden to obtain such access. In other words, as to the French users, Yahoo! is necessarily arguing that it has a First Amendment right to violate French criminal law and to facilitate the violation of French criminal law by others. . . .

These judges argued that the case was not ripe for adjudication as Yahoo! had not taken any material off its site as a result of the French court order, and as Yahoo! had not been found to be in violation of the French court order. Three other judges disagreed with this analysis and wrote:

> The issue is not . . . one of extra-territorial application of the First Amendment; if anything, it is the extra-territorial application of French law to the United States. We do not question the validity of the French orders on French soil. . . . Rather the question we face . . . is whether our own country's fundamental constitutional guarantee of freedom of speech protects Yahoo! (and, derivatively, at least its users in the United States) against some or all of the restraints the French defendants have deliberately imposed upon it within the United States. . . .
>
> We should not allow a foreign court order to be used as leverage to quash constitutionally protected speech by denying the United States-based target an adjudication of its constitutional rights in federal court. [The judges who invoke the doctrine of prudential ripeness] deny Yahoo! the only forum in which it can free itself of a facially unconstitutional injunction. Moreover, in doing so [these judges create] a new and troubling precedent for U.S.-based Internet service providers who may be confronted with foreign court orders that require them to police the content accessible to Internet users from another country. . . .

Finally, one judge argued that the French court orders constituted acts of state, and that the district court therefore should have abstained from deciding Yahoo!'s claims: "The criminal statutes of most nations do not comport with the U.S. Constitution. That does not give judges in this country the unfettered authority to pass critical judgement on their validity, especially where . . . the criminal statute embodies the determined will of a foreign sovereign to protect its borders from what it deems as morally reprehensible speech of the worst order."

Notes and Questions

1. Does *Gutnick* suggest that anyone who publishes material on a Web site is potentially liable for defamation in every jurisdiction in the world? *Bangoura v. Washington Post*, 2005 CarswellOnt 4343 (Ont. C.A.), involved a defamation action by a former UN employee against a U.S.-based newspaper that published and uploaded onto its Web site an article stating the plaintiff's co-workers had accused

him of sexual harassment, financial improprieties and nepotism during his work for the UN in the Ivory Coast. The Ontario Court of Appeal ruled in favor of the newspaper; the court distinguished *Gutnick* on the grounds that "Gutnick was a well-known businessman who resided in Victoria at the time of the impugned publication," whereas Bangoura did not live in Ontario at the time the article was published; that Dow Jones had "some 1,700 Internet subscribers in Australia," whereas there were only seven subscribers to the defendant paper in Ontario when the article was published and evidence that only one person (plaintiff's counsel) had accessed the article online; and that Gutnick undertook to "sue only in Victoria and only in respect of damages to his reputation in that state," whereas Bangoura made no similar undertaking. Should a plaintiff's ability to recover damages (as opposed to the amount of damages) turn on how many people accessed the relevant Web site?

2. In *Gutnick*, Justice Callinan objected to the idea of "an American legal hegemony" that would privilege an American understanding of the value of free speech over an Australian understanding. Does a holding that Australian law applies to statements on Dow Jones' website threaten to impose an Australian legal hegemony upon a U.S. entity? Why should a court favor one form of extraterritorial regulation over the other?

3. Is it appropriate to emphasize the physical location of an act, such as reading a Web site, when the underlying activity occurs in cyberspace? Should it matter in cases like *Gutnick* whether the defendant is a large multinational corporation or a local business?

4. Are France's interests in exercising jurisdiction over Yahoo!'s conduct stronger or weaker than the United States' interests in exercising jurisdiction over the activity of the British reinsurers at issue in *Hartford Fire*? Compare the U.S. interest in not having the *Yahoo!* litigation proceed in France with the UK's interest in not having the *Hartford Fire* litigation proceed in the United States. Are domestic courts well-positioned to evaluate these interests?

5. Is it sensible for domestic courts to decide when a particular state can regulate Internet-based activity, or should such activity be governed by international agreement? Alternatively, should the scope of government authority to regulate Internet-based activity be governed by international agreement? In June 2003, Antigua initiated World Trade Organization (WTO) dispute settlement proceedings against the United States on the grounds that several U.S. state and federal laws prohibiting the cross-border supply of gambling services (e.g., Internet and telephone gambling) were inconsistent with U.S. obligations under the General Agreement on Trade in Services (GATS). The WTO's Appellate Body found that several U.S. laws were inconsistent with GATS obligations, but that all but one of the laws fell within the scope of an exception for measures "necessary to protect public morals or maintain public order." *United States — Measures Affecting the Cross-Border Supply of Gambling and Betting Services*, WT/DS285/AB/R (2005). Should the ability to regulate Internet-based activity be limited by international trade norms?

E. Does the System Work? Containing and Resolving Conflict over the Helms-Burton Legislation

As demonstrated above, private actors sometimes challenge state assertions of prescriptive jurisdiction in domestic litigation. But conflicts over jurisdictional claims are more frequently addressed by states on the international plane. The controversy over the Cuban Liberty and Democratic Solidarity (Libertad) Act, also known as the Helms-Burton Act, reveals how states deal with contested jurisdictional claims and raises important questions as to whether the process for resolving conflicting claims over state assertions of jurisdiction is sufficient.

The Helms-Burton Act is best understood as a stage in the long history of contentious relations between the United States and Cuba. The United States occupied Cuba in 1898, during the Spanish-American War, and remained there for five years. In 1901, the United States prepared a set of principles, which were inserted into the Cuban Constitution the following year, conferring a right of intervention on the United States to preserve Cuban independence and to ensure "the maintenance of a government adequate for the protection of life, property, and individual liberty." The United States sent troops to Cuba several times in the following 30 years to establish friendly governments and to protect U.S. business interests. Although the Cuban government wrote a new constitution in 1940 that emphasized Cuban sovereignty and sought to make the country less dependent on the United States, on the eve of the 1959 Cuban Revolution most of Cuba's imports came from the United States, and the United States bought most of Cuba's exports.

On January 1, 1959, after a protracted guerilla conflict, Fidel Castro succeeded in overthrowing Fulgencio Batista, the dictator who had ruled Cuba for many years. Castro's government moved quickly to confiscate and redistribute all properties larger than 1,000 acres; it also expropriated billions of dollars worth of assets belonging to Cuban and foreign nationals. All U.S. businesses and properties in Cuba, valued in excess of $2 billion, were expropriated.

Alarmed at the prospect of a hostile government 90 miles from U.S. shores, the U.S. Central Intelligence Agency initiated a series of attempts to assassinate Castro, experimenting on various occasions with poison cigars, an exploding seashell, botulin pills, and organized crime hit men. In 1961, the United States supported a disastrous attempt by some 1,300 Cuban exiles to invade Cuba. Tensions between the United States and Cuba peaked when the Soviet Union began to construct nuclear missile bases in Cuba capable of striking targets in the United States. In 1962, the United States imposed a naval quarantine on Cuba, and for a brief period the world was poised on the brink of a nuclear war. Although the Soviet Union eventually backed down and agreed to remove its missiles from Cuba, the United States remained determined to undermine the Castro government. That same year, President Kennedy instituted an embargo on trade with Cuba. The United States has maintained that embargo ever since, though it has been tightened and loosened at various times and in various ways.

For many years the Soviet Union provided substantial economic assistance to Cuba. When the USSR disintegrated in 1991, Cuba lost the Soviet subsidies that had kept its economy afloat. Over the next five or six years, the Cuban economy declined by over 50 percent. Cuba was forced to solicit foreign investment to fill the gap left by the loss of Soviet support. In some cases, foreign companies began to invest in businesses or properties that had been confiscated from their original owners at the time of the Cuban Revolution. Some members of Congress feared that Cuba would start selling land expropriated from Americans to cure its financial crisis and in 1995 began drafting the Helms-Burton Act.

1. Discouraging Foreigners from Investing in Cuba: The Helms-Burton Act

The Helms-Burton Act was designed to strengthen existing legislation authorizing sanctions against Cuba and to create a cause of action in U.S. courts allowing U.S. nationals to sue foreign companies transacting business in Cuba involving those nationals' expropriated assets. Although large majorities in both Houses of Congress voted for this legislation, President Clinton initially indicated his intention to veto it. But on February 24, 1996, Cuban Air Force MiGs shot down two Cessna light civilian aircraft over international waters, killing four Cuban Americans. The planes, which were acting for Brothers to the Rescue, an anti-Castro Cuban exile group based in the United States, were seeking to drop anti-Castro leaflets over Cuba. Seventeen days after the planes were shot down, President Clinton signed the Helms-Burton Act into law, notwithstanding the vehement opposition of the United States's closest trading partners.

The Helms-Burton Act has four titles. Title I strengthens the U.S. economic sanctions against Cuba. It prohibits sugar imports from countries that purchased Cuban sugar intending to re-export it to the United States and directs the U.S. representative in each of the international financial institutions to continue to oppose Cuban membership in those institutions. Title II provides a framework for American assistance during a transition to a democratic government in Cuba and for generous aid to a democratically elected Cuban government. Title III is the most controversial part of the law. It allows American citizens (including naturalized Cuban refugees) to sue individuals or companies who "traffic" in property confiscated by the Cuban government after January 1, 1959. Title III also allows the President to suspend its enforcement for renewable six-month periods. This provision was not included in the legislation as originally passed by either the House or the Senate. However, the President threatened to veto the legislation if it did not include presidential authority to suspend Title III. Finally, Title IV prohibits the issuance of visas to key employees of foreign companies that "traffic" in confiscated assets, and also to their families, thus prohibiting them from entering the United States. Excerpts from the Helms-Burton law are reproduced below.

Cuban Liberty and Democratic Solidarity (Libertad) Act of 1996

22 U.S.C. §§6021-6091

SEC. 6023. DEFINITIONS

(13) TRAFFICS

(A) As used in title III . . . a person "traffics" in confiscated property if that person knowingly and intentionally —

> (i) sells, transfers, distributes, dispenses, brokers, manages, or otherwise disposes of confiscated property, or purchases, leases, receives, possesses, obtains control of, manages, uses, or otherwise acquires or holds an interest in confiscated property,
>
> (ii) engages in a commercial activity using or otherwise benefitting from confiscated property, or
>
> (iii) causes, directs, participates in, or profits from, trafficking (as described in clause (i) or (ii)) by another person, or otherwise engages in trafficking (as described in clause (i) or (ii)) through another person,

without the authorization of any United States national who holds a claim to the property.

(B) The term "traffics" does not include — . . .

(iv) transactions and uses of property by a person who is both a citizen of Cuba and a resident of Cuba, and who is not an official of the Cuban Government or the ruling political party in Cuba. . . .

Title III — Protection of Property Rights of United States Nationals

SEC. 6081. FINDINGS

The Congress makes the following findings: . . .

(5) The Cuban Government is offering foreign investors the opportunity to purchase an equity interest in, manage, or enter into joint ventures using property and assets some of which were confiscated from United States nationals. . . .

(8) The international judicial system, as currently structured, lacks fully effective remedies for the wrongful confiscation of property and for unjust enrichment from the use of wrongfully confiscated property by governments and private entities at the expense of the rightful owners of the property.

(9) International law recognizes that a nation has the ability to provide for rules of law with respect to conduct outside its territory that has or is intended to have substantial effect within its territory. . . .

(11) To deter trafficking in wrongfully confiscated property, United States nationals who were the victims of these confiscations should be endowed with a judicial remedy in the courts of the United States that would deny traffickers any profits from economically exploiting Castro's wrongful seizures.

SEC. 6082. LIABILITY FOR TRAFFICKING IN CONFISCATED PROPERTY CLAIMED BY UNITED STATES NATIONALS

(a) Civil Remedy. —

(1) Liability for Trafficking

(A) Except as otherwise provided in this section, any person that . . . traffics in property which was confiscated by the Cuban Government on or after January 1, 1959, shall be liable to any United States national who owns the claim to such property for money damages. . . .

[The Act further provides for treble damages in the event that a potential defendant continues to traffic in confiscated property 30 days after receipt of written notice of a potential claim under the Act.]

(6) Inapplicability of Act of State Doctrine. — No court of the United States shall decline, based upon the act of state doctrine, to make a determination on the merits in an action brought under paragraph (1). . . .

SEC. 6085. EFFECTIVE DATE

(b) Suspension Authority

(1) The President may suspend the [right to bring an action under this title with respect to confiscated property] for a period of not more than 6 months if the President determines . . . that such suspension is necessary to the national

interests of the United States and will expedite a transition to democracy in Cuba.

(2) Additional Suspensions. — The President may suspend the right to bring an action under this title for additional periods of not more than 6 months each. . . .

Notes and Questions

1. What are the purposes of the Helms-Burton legislation? By what means does the legislation seek to accomplish those purposes?

2. In the Helms-Burton Act, is the United States seeking to prescribe, adjudicate, or enforce its domestic law? Does the statute rest on a basis of jurisdiction recognized under international law?

3. Presidents Clinton and George W. Bush have both continually suspended enforcement of Title III. Does this frustrate congressional intent?

2. The International Response to the Helms-Burton Act

International reactions to the Helms-Burton Act were unanimous and condemnatory. Even before the legislation was adopted, the European governments issued a series of demarches criticizing the proposed legislation and indicating the EC's readiness to challenge it before the World Trade Organization (WTO). Shortly after the legislation was enacted, Canada, Mexico, several European states, and Argentina, among others, passed antidote laws prohibiting compliance with the provisions of the Act and providing monetary relief for companies sued under it. The Canadian Parliament considered a bill that would allow the descendants of British loyalists to claim compensation for property confiscated during the American Revolution, a half-serious effort that demonstrated the extent of Canadian resentment of the U.S. legislation. Cuba passed a law designed to restrict information regarding foreign investment primarily through punitive measures against Cuban citizens deemed to be assisting in the implementation of the Act. The UN General Assembly, which for many years had passed resolutions calling upon the United States to end its embargo of Cuba, passed a resolution, by a vote of 138 to 3 (with 25 abstentions) urging the United States to repeal or invalidate Helms-Burton. Canada and Mexico seriously considered challenging the law under the North American Free Trade Agreement's dispute resolution procedures.

In June 1996, the General Assembly of the OAS passed a resolution, over the lone U.S. dissent, directing the organization's Inter-American Juridical Committee "to examine and decide upon the validity under international law" of the Helms-Burton legislation. Excerpts from the Committee's legal opinion follow.

Opinion of the Inter-American Juridical Committee

5. [The Committee set forth relevant international legal norms regarding the protection of property rights of nationals]:

a) Any State that expropriates, nationalizes or takes measures tantamount to expropriation or nationalization of property owned by foreign nationals must respect the following rules: such action must be for a public purpose, nondiscriminatory, and accompanied by prompt, adequate and effective compensation, granting to the expropriated party effective administrative or judicial review of the measure and quantum of compensation. Failure to comply with these rules will entail State responsibility. . . .

c) When a national of a foreign State is unable to obtain effective redress in accordance with international law, the State of which it is a national may espouse the claim through an official State-to-State claim. . . .

d) Claims against a State for expropriation of the property of foreign nationals cannot be enforced against the property of private persons except where such property is itself the expropriated asset and within the jurisdiction of the claimant State. . . .

e) Any use by nationals of a third State of expropriated property located in the expropriating State where such use conforms to the laws of that State, as well as the use anywhere of products or intangible property not constituting the expropriated asset itself, does not contravene any norm of international law. . . .

6. In the light of the principles and norms set out in paragraph 5. above the Committee considers that the legislation under analysis does not conform to international law in each of the following respects:

a) The domestic courts of a claimant State are not the appropriate forum for the resolution of State-to-State claims. . . .

c) The claimant State does not have the right to attribute liability to nationals of third States for a claim against a foreign State.

d) The claimant State does not have the right to attribute liability to nationals of third States for the use of expropriated property located in the territory of the expropriating State where such use conforms to the laws of this latter State, nor for the use in the territory of third States of intangible property or products that do not constitute the actual asset expropriated.

e) The claimant State does not have the right to impose liability on third parties not involved in a nationalization through the creation of liability not linked to the nationalization or unrecognized by the international law on this subject, thus modifying the juridical bases for liability. . . .

h) Successful enforcement of such a claim against the property of nationals of a third State in a manner contrary to the norms of international law could itself constitute a measure tantamount to expropriation and result in responsibility of the claimant State. . . .

8. The Committee has also examined the applicable norms of international law in respect of the exercise of jurisdiction by States and its limits on such exercise. In the opinion of the Committee, these norms include the following: . . .

c) Except where a norm of international law permits, the State may not exercise its power in any form in the territory of another State. The basic premise under international law for establishing legislative and judicial jurisdiction is rooted in the principle of territoriality. . . .

e) A State may justify the application of the laws of its territory only insofar as an act occurring outside its territory has a direct, substantial and foreseeable effect within its territory and the exercise of such jurisdiction is reasonable.

f) A State may exceptionally exercise jurisdiction on a basis other than territoriality only where there exists a substantial or otherwise significant connection between the matter in question and the State's sovereign authority, such as in the case of the exercise of jurisdiction over acts performed abroad by its nationals and in certain specific cases of the protection objectively necessary to safeguard its essential sovereign interests.

9. [The Committee concluded that the exercise of jurisdiction over acts of "trafficking in confiscated property" was inconsistent with the norms established by international law for the exercise of jurisdiction in each of the following respects]:

a) A prescribing State does not have the right to exercise jurisdiction over acts of "trafficking" abroad by aliens unless specific conditions are fulfilled which do not appear to be satisfied in this situation.

b) A prescribing State does not have the right to exercise jurisdiction over acts of "trafficking" abroad by aliens under circumstances where neither the alien nor the conduct in question has any connection with its territory and where no apparent connection exists between such acts and the protection of its essential sovereign interests.

Thereafter, in October 1996, the EC formally began dispute resolution proceedings in the WTO. The EC's representative stated that "[t]he EC's problem with the U.S. legislation concerns not its objectives, but the extraterritorial means chosen to achieve those objectives and the adverse effect they have on EC trade in goods and services."

The United States responded that the dispute with the Europeans was not over a trade matter, but rather over a foreign policy designed to promote democracy in Cuba, and therefore an inappropriate dispute for WTO processes. The United States also indicated that, if the dispute moved forward, it would invoke the GATT's national security exception, which provides that nothing in the GATT "shall be construed . . . to prevent any party from taking any action which it considers necessary for the protection of its essential security interests . . . taken in time of war or other emergency in international relations."

Notes and Questions

1. How would you characterize the disagreement between the Inter-American Juridical Committee and the U.S. Congress over the permissible extraterritorial reach of domestic legislation? Which body has the better position on this issue?

2. Why did the Europeans institute WTO proceedings against the United States? Did they wish to support investors seeking to profit from illegally expropriated property? Do you agree with the United States that, as this is a conflict over foreign policy, the WTO is an inappropriate forum for this dispute? Would a WTO action by Cuba have more or less impact than an action initiated by the EC?

3. Does the disposition of assets located in Cuba threaten the United States's "essential security interests"? Does the Castro regime threaten these interests? Who should answer these questions?

3. A Defense of Helms-Burton?

Although most academics, like most governments, condemned the Helms-Burton legislation as an impermissible exercise of extraterritorial jurisdiction, the legislation does have its defenders. Consider the following arguments:

Brice M. Clagett, *Title III of the Helms-Burton Act Is Consistent with International Law*

90 Am. J. Intl. L. 434, 435-438 (1996)

Castro's strategy of involving foreign companies in confiscated properties threatens to place significant roadblocks in the path of claims resolution. If a property remains exclusively in the hands of the Cuban state, it will be readily available for restitution or substitution. If clouds on title have been created by purported transfers to traffickers of other nationalities who claim to be holders in due course, the problem becomes, in Secretary of State Warren Christopher's words, "far more difficult."

The need to resolve such issues would, at the least, delay and complicate the task of healing Castro's legacy. The victims' rights and interests would accordingly be prejudiced. To the extent they are U.S. citizens, the prejudice to them has a substantial effect on the United States. . . .

A state has jurisdiction to prescribe rules of law with respect to "conduct outside its territory that has or is intended to have substantial effect within its territory," at least when the exercise of that jurisdiction is reasonable in all the circumstances. . . .

. . . [E]ven if [a state] has jurisdiction to prescribe based on "substantial effects," [it] must balance its interests against those of other states, and refrain from applying its laws when the legitimate and reasonable interests of another state are greater. The appropriate question thus becomes: what other state is entitled to complain? What state can accuse the United States of an international delinquency against it?

If the "other state" is Cuba, Cuba has no legitimate interest, which other states need or should respect, in confiscating property without compensation and profiting from foreign investment in that property. Cuba's comprehensive violations of international law fully justify U.S. countermeasures such as title III, even if those measures would otherwise be unlawful.

If the "other state" is the state of which the trafficker is a national, that state's interest in protecting its national's ability to traffic in confiscated property in a third country is, at the most, no greater (let alone more legitimate) than the United States' interest in protecting the ability of *its* national — the rightful owner — to prevent further interference with his property and perhaps ultimately to recover it. The interests of both states are equally "extraterritorial," since the activity with which both are concerned is taking place in a third country, Cuba. Thus, title III does not fail a balancing test, even if such a test is deemed part of international law. . . .

A further reason for title III is the notorious weakness and ineffectiveness of international enforcement mechanisms. Because the jurisdiction of international tribunals is consensual, it is only rarely that a confiscation case can be brought in such a forum. Espousal of claims by the victims' government can take generations to bear any fruit at all and, even when it does, typically results in recovery by the victims of only a pathetically inadequate fraction of the just compensation to which international law entitles them. . . . Creation of such a remedy, far from violating international law, works toward rescuing that law from relative impotence.

Enactment of title III does no injustice to the "traffickers" who may become defendants. . . . Traffickers are fully aware that they are dealing in tainted property. It can be presumed that the culpability of dealing in stolen goods is a familiar concept to them from their own legal systems. Traffickers are knowingly taking the risk that the dispossessed owners or aggrieved states might take action against them. . . .

Thus, it seems difficult to make a serious argument that title III infringes international law to the extent that it permits suits by confiscation victims who were U.S. nationals at the time [of confiscation]. To the contrary, title III applies and vindicates international law. As to these lawsuits . . . the United States is not even exercising its jurisdiction to prescribe, but only its jurisdiction to adjudicate. It is applying international law, not just its own law.

Notes and Questions

1. Does Clagett persuade you that Helms-Burton is an appropriate assertion of jurisdiction under the effects test? Is Helms-Burton consistent with the approach to jurisdiction outlined in the *Hartford Fire* case?

Professor Andreas Lowenfeld has argued that the effort to rely upon the "effects doctrine" is "fundamentally flawed." He argues that

> the effect against which the legislation is directed—even if one can locate it in the United States—was caused by the Government of Cuba, not by the persons over whom jurisdiction is sought to be exercised. Thus, even leaving aside the thirty-six year interval between the conduct and the effect on the one hand, and the exercise of prescriptive jurisdiction on the other, the effort to place Helms-Burton within the effects doctrine is no more than a play on words. It does not withstand analysis, and it would carry the effects doctrine farther than it has ever been carried before.

Andreas Lowenfeld, *Congress and Cuba: The Helms-Burton Act*, 90 Am. J. Intl. L. 419, 431 (1996). Professor Lowenfeld added that "It would be very sad indeed if conflicts over an exorbitant and unreasonable piece of U.S. legislation were to divert attention from the deplorable events occurring in Cuba, and were even to attract sympathy for the Castro regime, once again arrayed against the big bully." *Id.* at 433.

2. Do you agree with Clagett that, in light of "the notorious weakness and ineffectiveness of international enforcement mechanisms," the legislation "far from violating international law, works toward rescuing that law from relative impotence"? Under this theory, would it be better if the law provided a remedy for anyone who had property confiscated, rather than only U.S. citizens? Would such a law be more or less acceptable to the Europeans?

4. Negotiating a Partial Resolution to the Jurisdictional Dispute

Since Helms-Burton came into effect, the United States has attempted to address international outrage in several ways. First, President Clinton repeatedly exercised his power to suspend civil lawsuits brought under title III, a policy the Bush Administration has thus far chosen to continue. Second, the Clinton Administration took a series of steps to loosen the embargo against Cuba, including streamlining visa procedures between Cuba and the United States, expanding direct licensed passenger flights, authorizing the sale of food and agricultural materials to private entities and farmers in Cuba, and restoring direct mail service between the United States and Cuba. In February 1997, the United States threatened to boycott the WTO proceedings on the grounds that the WTO lacked jurisdiction over national security matters and because the WTO had "no competence" to rule on U.S. foreign policy. Two months later — and three days before the European brief was due at the WTO — the United States and the EU reached a tentative understanding on Helms-Burton.

Understanding Between the United States and the European Union

36 I.L.M. 529 (1997)

The U.S. reiterates its presumption of continued suspension of Title III during the remainder of the President's term so long as the EU and other allies continue their stepped up efforts to promote democracy in Cuba. Each side will encourage other countries to promote democracy and human rights in Cuba.

The EU and the U.S. agree to step up their efforts to develop agreed [rules] and principles for the strengthening of investment protection, bilaterally and in . . . other appropriate international fora. Recognizing that the standard of protection governing expropriation and nationalization embodied in international law . . . should be respected by all States, these [rules] should inhibit and deter the future acquisition of investments from any State which has expropriated or nationalized such investments in contravention of international law, and subsequent dealings in covered investments. Similarly, and in parallel, the EU and U.S. will work together to address and resolve through agreed principles the issue of conflicting jurisdictions, including issues affecting investors of another party because of their investments in third countries. . . .

The U.S. Administration, at the same time as the above bilateral consultations commence, will begin to consult with Congress with a view to obtaining an amendment providing the President with the authority to waive Title IV of the Act once the bilateral consultations are completed and the EU has adhered to the agreed [rules] and principles. In the circumstances of such adherence it is expected that such a waiver would be granted.

In the meantime, the U.S. notes the President's continuing obligation to enforce Title IV. Consistent with the guidelines for implementation, the U.S. will apply rigorous standards to all evidence submitted to the Department of State for use in enforcing Title IV. The U.S. is committed to a thorough, deliberate process in order to ensure careful implementation of Title IV. This will involve discussions with all affected parties in order to consider all relevant information prior to Title IV actions.

In the light of all of the above, the EU agrees to the suspension of the proceedings of the WTO panel. The EU reserves all rights to resume the panel procedure, or begin new proceedings, if action is taken against EU companies or individuals under Title III or Title IV of [Helms-Burton]. . . .

On May 18, 1998, the United States and the European Union reached an Understanding on Expropriated Property, which is described in the following congressional testimony by Under Secretary of State Stuart Eisenstat:

As part of the May 18 Understanding, the Europeans have acknowledged that Castro's expropriation of U.S. property "appears to be contrary to international law." This conclusion, and the rest of the Understanding, represent the first such collective acknowledgment by the Europeans since the Cuban revolution that Cuba has engaged in illegal expropriations of U.S. property. It says clearly that it is no longer business as usual with respect to these properties. . . .

Let me outline for you the key elements of the Understanding.

Where states expropriate property inconsistent with international law in the future, investment in such property will be barred.

A Registry of Claims will be established to warn . . . that a property has a troubled past. It will be open to any claimant who alleges that its property was expropriated in contravention of international law. If basic information is provided by the claimant, the claim will be included. There will be no screening out of claims.

Where illegal expropriations have already taken place, government support or commercial assistance for transactions related to such properties will be denied. . . . Lists of expropriated properties will be published and investment actively discouraged.

Not only will the disciplines apply to cases of future acquisitions from the expropriating state, but they will apply to transactions with respect to existing investments that involve the acquisition of new rights, including the renewal of leases or management contracts, or the acquisition of new mineral rights. This will fence off existing investments and severely limit new transactions by those investors.

International financial institutions such as the IMF and the World Bank will be urged to adopt programs and policies to discourage investment in illegally expropriated properties. . . .

To realize all the gains provided by the Understanding, we need Congressional support. The EU will begin to implement these strong disciplines simultaneously with the receipt of a waiver from the provisions of Title IV of the Libertad Act. . . . We believe that such a waiver should benefit only countries that are implementing the Understanding . . . [and] I can assure you that the Administration would be prepared to revoke such a waiver should a participant fail to implement it faithfully.

Both the United States and the EU emphasized that they considered this agreement to be a political, rather than a legal, commitment. As of December 2005, the United States had not enacted legislation to waive Title IV of Helms-Burton nor created a registry of claims, and the Europeans had not revived their WTO complaint.

Moreover, the United States continues to use, or threaten to use, the authority to deny visas granted by Title IV. As of December 2005, the State Department had used Title IV to ban from the United States a number of executives (and their families) because of their firms' investment in confiscated U.S. property in Cuba, including individuals associated with Grupos Domos, a Mexican telecommunications company; Sherritt International, a Canadian mining company; and BM Group, an Israeli-owned citrus company. In 1997, Grupos Domos disinvested from U.S.-claimed property in Cuba, and as a result, its executives were again eligible to enter the United States. Threatened actions against executives from STET, an Italian telecommunications company, were averted when the company agreed to pay U.S.-based ITT Corporation $25 million for the use of ITT-claimed property in Cuba for ten years; threatened actions against executives from Super-Clubs, a Jamaican hotel chain, were averted when the company disinvested from two Cuban hotels.

Notes and Questions

1. Who won the dispute over Helms-Burton? What consession(s) did the United States and the EU actually gain from the other in the 1997 and 1998 Under-

standings? What does this dispute teach about the international legal limits on the exercise of prescriptive jurisdiction and about the process of creating new jurisdictional norms?

2. Does Helms-Burton suggest that powerful states can unilaterally violate international legal norms with minimal adverse consequences? Or, considering the U.S. response to Cuban and European objections to Helms-Burton, does it matter whether such a violation harms the interests of relatively powerful, as opposed to relatively weak, states?

3. How should states resolve conflicts over the exercise of jurisdiction of the sort at issue in this case? Is there a viable international forum for resolution of claims that an assertion of jurisdiction violates international law?

4. In August 2005, the U.S. Department of Justice created a "Cuban Claims Program" to receive claims of U.S. citizens or corporations against the Government of Cuba for previously unadjudicated losses of real and personal property taken after May 1, 1967. The Justice Department announced that "[a]lthough there are no funds currently available to make payment on any American claims," its findings "will be used as a basis for future negotiation of a claims settlement with the Government of Cuba." Does this program serve the same purposes as the Helms-Burton legislation? Does the creation of this program, along with the continued suspension of Title III, suggest that the United States has abandoned the jurisdictional theory supporting the litigation contemplated by Title III?

III. CAPTURING CRIMINALS ABROAD: THE ARREST OF SLAVKO DOKMANOVIC

We now turn our attention to jurisdiction to adjudicate and jurisdiction to enforce. States have long accepted the general norm that one state cannot exercise its judicial functions within the territory of another state without that state's consent. They have also accepted that international law prohibits the agents of one state from enforcing, without permission, their criminal law within the territory of another state. Nevertheless, from time to time, a state or some of its citizens may undertake to enforce its laws through direct actions in another state's territory. One dramatic example is the abduction or luring of a suspect from one state to another to stand trial.

In this section, we focus on whether and how international law bears on the permissibility of, and exercise of jurisdiction after, an abduction, luring, or other irregular rendition of a suspect from one state to another. Consider whether, if these actions violate international law, that should disbar a court in the receiving state from exercising personal jurisdiction over the defendant. Or should jurisdiction nevertheless be exercised, at least against those who have allegedly committed the most horrible crimes?

A. The Problem

In June 1991, Croatia declared independence from the Federal Republic of Yugoslavia (FRY). Shortly thereafter, many Croatian Serbs, supported by the federal Yugoslav National Army (JNA), rose up against the Croatian government. By August 1991, the JNA had surrounded Vukovar, Croatia, and was laying siege to it. Vukovar is located on the bank of the Danube River, which marks the boundary between Serbia (part of the FRY) and Croatia.

In November 1991, several hundred people sought refuge at Vukovar Hospital. On November 18, the JNA and the Croatian government agreed that the hospital would be evacuated in the presence of international observers. The next day, JNA units took control of Vukovar Hospital. JNA soldiers hurriedly removed about 400 men from the hospital, including wounded patients, hospital staff, Croatian political activists, and other civilians. The men were loaded onto buses and driven to a site outside of Vukovar. There JNA soldiers beat the men for several hours. The men were then divided into groups of ten to twenty, loaded onto a truck, and transported to the edge of a nearby ravine. There JNA and Serb paramilitary troops under the command of Slavko Dokmanovic, a Croatian Serb and President of the Vukovar Municipality, shot and killed approximately 260 men. A bulldozer pushed the bodies into a mass grave at the site. These events constituted the greatest single massacre of the 1991 war in Croatia.

In April 1996, Dokmanovic was secretly indicted by the Prosecutor of the International Criminal Tribunal for the Former Yugoslavia (ICTY) for his role in the Vukovar massacre. At the same time, an order for Dokmanovic's arrest was secretly transmitted to the UN Transitional Administration for Eastern Slavonia (UNTAES),* directing the UN forces to search for, arrest, and surrender Dokmanovic to the ICTY. However, by the time UNTAES received the order for Dokmanovic's arrest, he had moved from Eastern Slavonia to the Federal Republic of Yugoslavia.

In January 1997, ICTY investigators traveled to UNTAES headquarters in Vukovar to develop a plan to entice Dokmanovic to leave the FRY and enter the UNTAES region where he could be arrested. United Nations Secretary-General Kofi Annan and UN legal authorities in New York approved the plan.

During the first half of 1997, investigators from the Office of the Prosecutor (OTP) made several attempts to arrange meetings with Dokmanovic. Finally, a meeting was held in Dokmanovic's home on June 24. The ostensible purpose of the meeting was for Dokmanovic to assist ICTY officials in their investigation of Croatian war crimes. During the meeting, Dokmanovic raised the issue of compensation for property in Croatia that he lost. The OTP investigator suggested that Dokmanovic raise this issue with Transitional Administrator Jacques Klein and offered to arrange a meeting between Dokmanovic and Klein. On June 25, the investigator urged Dokmanovic to call Klein's office to confirm a meeting time. Dokmanovic did so, and Klein's office offered to send an UNTAES vehicle to collect Dokmanovic from the Bogojevo-Erdut bridge over the Danube river.

On the afternoon of June 27, Dokmanovic arrived at the border post on the FRY side of the Danube River. Walking onto the Bogojevo-Erdut bridge and past the FRY checkpoint, he entered an UNTAES vehicle. Soon after crossing the bridge, the vehicle abruptly departed the road and sped into a secured area. UNTAES troops quickly removed Dokmanovic from the vehicle at gunpoint. Within minutes, ICTY agents appeared and placed Dokmanovic under arrest. The speed of the

---

*As discussed in Chapter 4, UN Security Council Resolution 1037 temporarily placed the administration of Eastern Slavonia, a part of Croatia that the Serbs occupied during the war, under UNTAES control, pending its return to Croatian control. The resolution also gave UN peacekeeping forces the right to exercise police powers in that region of Croatia.

maneuver prevented Dokmanovic from removing a loaded .357 Magnum Zastafa hand pistol from his briefcase. Within an hour of his arrest, Dokmanovic was driven to an airfield and placed on an airplane bound for The Hague. On July 7, 1997, Dokmanovic filed a preliminary motion for release on the grounds that his arrest had been unlawful and that the ICTY therefore lacked jurisdiction over him.

B. Seizing War Criminals: The Eichmann Precedent

The Dokmanovic case was not the first time that a suspected war criminal argued that he had been unlawfully brought before a court. During World War II, Adolf Eichmann was in charge of Jewish Affairs and Evacuation in the Gestapo and was responsible for the arrest, deportation, internment, and extermination of Jews. After the war, Eichmann fled to Argentina, where he lived under an assumed name. In 1960, Israeli agents kidnaped Eichmann and forcibly brought him to Israel to stand trial for his actions during the war. Earlier in this chapter we explored Eichmann's challenge to Israel's jurisdiction to prescribe. Eichmann also argued that due to the kidnaping, the Israeli courts lacked jurisdiction to adjudicate. Excerpts from the Jerusalem district court's opinion follow.

Attorney-General of the Government of Israel v. Eichmann

36 I.L.R. 5 (1961)

1. Adolf Eichmann has been arraigned before this Court on charges of unsurpassed gravity — crimes against the Jewish people, crimes against humanity, and war crimes. . . .

40. . . . Counsel argued that the accused, who had resided in Argentina under an assumed name, was kidnaped on May 11, 1960, by agents of the State of Israel and forcibly brought . . . [to Israel] in violation of international law. He summed up his submission by contending that the Court ought not to lend its support to an illegal act of the State, and that in these circumstances the State of Israel has no jurisdiction to try the accused.

On the other hand, the learned Attorney-General pleaded that . . . it is the duty of the Court simply to try such crimes; and that in accordance with established judicial precedents in England, the United States and Israel, the Court is not to enter into the circumstances of the arrest of the accused and of his transfer to the area of jurisdiction of the State, these questions having no bearing on the jurisdiction of the Court to try the accused for the offenses for which he is being prosecuted, but only on the foreign relations of the State. The Attorney-General added that, with reference to the circumstances of the arrest of the accused and his transfer to Israel, the Republic of Argentina had lodged a complaint with the Security Council of the United Nations, which resolved on June 23, 1960, as follows (Doc. S/4349):

> *The Security Council,*
>   Having examined the complaint that the transfer of Adolf Eichmann to the territory of Israel constitutes a violation of the sovereignty of the Argentine Republic, . . .
>   *Noting* that the repetition of acts such as that giving rise to this situation would involve a breach of the principles upon which international order is founded, creating an atmosphere of insecurity and distrust incompatible with the preservation of peace,

Eichmann in the dock at the district court in Jerusalem, 1961
SOURCE: Library of Congress

Mindful of the universal condemnation of the persecution of the Jews under the Nazis and the concern of people in all countries that Eichmann should be brought to appropriate justice for the crimes of which he is accused,

Noting at the same time that this resolution should in no way be interpreted as condoning the odious crimes of which Eichmann is accused,

1. *Declares* that acts such as that under consideration, which affect the sovereignty of a Member State and therefore cause international friction, may, if repeated, endanger international peace and security;

2. *Requests* the Government of Israel to make appropriate reparation in accordance with the Charter of the United Nations and the rules of international law;

3. *Expresses* the hope that the traditionally friendly relations between Argentina and Israel will be advanced.

Pursuant to this Resolution the two Governments reached agreement on the settlement of the dispute between them, and on August 3, 1960, issued the following joint communiqué:

The Governments of Argentina and Israel, animated by a desire to give effect to the resolution of the Security Council of June 23, 1960, in so far as the hope was expressed that the traditionally friendly relations between the two countries will be advanced, resolve to regard as closed the incident which arose out of the action taken by citizens of Israel, which infringed the fundamental rights of the State of Argentina. . . .

41. It is an established rule of law that a person being tried for an offense against the laws of a State may not oppose his trial by reason of the illegality of his arrest or of the means whereby he was brought within the jurisdiction of that State. The courts in England, the United States and Israel have constantly held that the

circumstances of the arrest and the mode of bringing of the accused into the territory of the State have no relevance to his trial, and they have consistently refused in all instances to enter upon an examination of these circumstances. . . .

42. That principle is also acknowledged in Palestine case law. . . .

43. . . . The question which poses itself from this point of view is — whether the principle . . . that the accused may not challenge his trial by reason of the illegality of his arrest or of the means whereby he was brought into the jurisdiction, is limited to the illegality of those means in the sense of the municipal law of the country in question, or whether the principle is general and also applies to the use of means which are a violation of international law, namely, a violation of the sovereignty of a foreign State. . . .

44. . . . American precedents expressly establish that it makes no difference whether or not the measures whereby the accused was brought into the jurisdiction were unlawful in point of municipal law or of international law and they are all unanimous that the Court will not enter into an examination of this question, which is not relevant to the trial of the accused. The *ratio* of this rule is that the right to plead violation of the sovereignty of a State is the exclusive right of that State. Only a sovereign State may raise the plea or waive it, and the accused has no right to take over the rights of that State. . . .

Considerable importance attaches to this [principle] in the present case, in view of the settlement of the dispute between Argentina and Israel. . . . The indictment in this case was filed after Argentina had exonerated Israel of violation of her sovereignty and there was no longer any breach of international law. In these circumstances the accused cannot presume to speak, as it were, on behalf of Argentina and claim rights which that sovereign State had waived. . . .

48. The Anglo-Saxon rule has been accepted by Continental jurists as well. . . .

50. Indeed, there is no escaping the conclusion that the question of the violation of international law by the manner in which the accused was brought into the territory of a country arises at the international level, namely, the relations between the two countries concerned alone, and must find its solution at such level. A violation of international law of this order constitutes an "international tort" to which the usual rules of current international law apply. . . .

Notes and Questions

1. Immediately after learning of the abduction, Argentina demanded "the restitution of Eichmann" and "the punishment of the individuals guilty of the violation of Argentine territory" and recalled its ambassador to Israel. As noted above, the June 1960 Security Council resolution on this matter requested that Israel make "appropriate reparation" to Argentina. In response, Israel stated that "the expressions of regret which we have already made directly to the Argentine Government constitute adequate reparations." Two weeks later, Argentina declared itself "not satisfied" with Israel's expressions of regret, and reserved the right to take appropriate action. Argentina then expelled the Israeli Ambassador to Argentina. In August 1960, the two states issued their joint communiqué declaring the incident "closed."

What, if anything, does the Security Council's failure to demand Eichmann's return suggest about international attitudes toward kidnaping? Might the international community react differently if the kidnaped person was not a notorious war criminal? Should it?

2. Would returning Eichmann have been appropriate in this case? Shortly after his capture, Eichmann wrote, in German, "I, the undersigned, Adolf Eichmann, state herewith of my own free will: Since my true identity has now been revealed, I realize that there is no point in my continuing to try to evade justice. I declare myself willing to proceed to Israel and to stand trial there before a competent court." Is Eichmann's statement relevant?

In considering what would constitute "appropriate reparation," note that in the *Rainbow Warrior* affair, an arbitral panel stated that "the condemnation of the French Republic for its breaches of its treaty obligations to New Zealand, made public by the decision of the Tribunal, constitutes in the circumstances appropriate satisfaction for the legal and moral damage caused to New Zealand." In the *Corfu Channel* case, 1949 I.C.J. 4, the ICJ held that the entry of British minesweepers into Albanian territorial waters to remove undersea mines violated Albania's sovereignty. It then stated that "this declaration by the Court constitutes in itself appropriate satisfaction." Is the Security Council statement that Israel had violated Argentina's sovereignty "appropriate reparation" in this case?

3. In her controversial report on the Eichmann trial, Hannah Arendt argued that the kidnaping was justified:

> This, unhappily, was the only almost unprecedented feature in the whole Eichmann trial, and certainly it was the least entitled ever to become a valid precedent. . . . Its justification was the unprecedentedness of the crime and the coming into existence of a Jewish State. There were, however, important mitigating circumstances in that there hardly existed an alternative if one indeed wished to bring Eichmann to justice. . . . In short, the realm of legality offered no alternative to kidnaping. Those who are convinced that justice, and nothing else, is the end of law will be inclined to condone the kidnaping act, though not because of precedents.

Hannah Arendt, Eichmann in Jerusalem: A Report on the Banality of Evil 264-265 (1963).

However, Arendt went on to argue that the Israeli Attorney General's explicit use of the trial as a pedagogic device to educate Israelis and the world about the Holocaust undermined its legal function: "the purpose of a trial is to render justice, and nothing else; even the noblest of ulterior purposes . . . can only detract from the law's main business: to weigh the charges brought against the accused, to render judgment, and to mete out due punishment." *Id*. at 233.

The *Eichmann* court stated:

> In this maze of insistent questions, the path of the Court was and remains clear. It must not allow itself to be enticed to stray into provinces which are outside its sphere. The judicial process has ways of its own, laid down by law and immutable, whatever the subject-matter of the trial. . . . The purpose of every criminal trial is to investigate the truth of the prosecutor's charges against the accused who is on trial, and, if the accused is convicted, to mete out due punishment to him.

Is it appropriate for the prosecution to pursue extralegal goals through the vehicle of a criminal trial? May the prosecution avoid doing so in cases involving events as momentous as those at issue in the Eichmann case? Do such extralegal goals undermine the court's legal role?

C. Kidnaping or Extradition?: The Alvarez-Machain Case

One way that states can avoid disputes like those arising out of the *Eichmann* case is by entering into extradition treaties. These treaties set forth the procedures by which one state can request another state to send it individuals charged with a crime in the first state. However, extradition treaties do not solve all problems in this area, as the case of *United States v. Alvarez-Machain* illustrates.

Humberto Alvarez-Machain is a Mexican citizen and a medical doctor. He was indicted in the United States for his alleged participation in the February 1985 torture and murder of Enrique Camarena-Salazar, a special agent of the U.S. Drug Enforcement Agency (DEA) who was working in Mexico. On April 2, 1990, Alvarez-Machain was forcibly kidnaped from his office in Mexico and flown by private plane to Texas, where he was arrested by DEA agents. The DEA approved the use of Mexican nationals to apprehend Alvarez-Machain. Alvarez-Machain moved to dismiss the complaint on the grounds that the abduction violated an extradition treaty between the United States and Mexico and divested the court of jurisdiction over him.

United States v. Alvarez-Machain

504 U.S. 655 (1992)

CHIEF JUSTICE REHNQUIST delivered the opinion of the Court.

Although we have never before addressed the precise issue raised in the present case, we have previously considered proceedings in claimed violation of an extradition treaty and proceedings against a defendant brought before a court by means of a forcible abduction. We addressed the former issue in *United States v. Rauscher*, 119 U.S. 407 (1886); more precisely, the issue whether the Webster-Ashburton Treaty of 1842, which governed extraditions between England and the United States, prohibited the prosecution of defendant Rauscher for a crime other than the crime for which he had been extradited. Whether this prohibition, known as the doctrine of specialty, was an intended part of the treaty had been disputed between the two nations for some time. Justice Miller delivered the opinion of the Court, which carefully examined the terms and history of the treaty; the practice of nations in regards to extradition treaties; the case law from the States; and the writings of commentators, and reached the following conclusion:

> "[A] person who has been brought within the jurisdiction of the court *by virtue of proceedings under an extradition treaty*, can only be tried for one of the offenses described in that treaty, and for the offense with which he is charged in the proceedings for his extradition, until a reasonable time and opportunity have been given him, after his release or trial upon such charge, to return to the country from whose asylum he had been forcibly taken under those proceedings." . . .

In *Ker v. Illinois*, 119 U.S. 436 (1886), also written by Justice Miller and decided the same day as *Rauscher*, we addressed the issue of a defendant brought before the court by way of a forcible abduction. Frederick Ker had been tried and convicted in an Illinois court for larceny; his presence before the court was procured by means of forcible abduction from Peru. A messenger was sent to Lima with the proper warrant to demand Ker by virtue of the extradition treaty between Peru and the United States. The messenger, however, disdained reliance on the treaty processes, and instead forcibly kidnaped Ker and brought him to the United States. We distinguished Ker's case from *Rauscher*, on the basis that Ker was not brought into the United States by virtue of the extradition treaty between the United States and Peru, and rejected Ker's argument that he had a right under the extradition treaty to be returned to this country only in accordance with its terms. We rejected Ker's due process argument more broadly, holding . . . that "such forcible abduction is no sufficient reason why the party should not answer when brought within the jurisdiction of the court which has the right to try him for such an offense, and presents no valid objection to his trial in such court." . . .

The only differences between *Ker* and the present case . . . are that *Ker* was decided on the premise that there was no governmental involvement in the abduction, and Peru, from which Ker was abducted, did not object to his prosecution. Respondent finds these differences to be dispositive, as did the Court of Appeals . . . contending that they show that respondent's prosecution, like the prosecution of Rauscher, violates the implied terms of a valid extradition treaty. The Government, on the other hand, argues that *Rauscher* stands as an "exception" to the rule in *Ker* only when an extradition treaty is invoked, and the terms of the treaty provide that its breach will limit the jurisdiction of a court. Therefore, our first inquiry must be whether the abduction of respondent from Mexico violated the Extradition Treaty between the United States and Mexico. If we conclude that the Treaty does not prohibit respondent's abduction, the rule in *Ker* applies, and the court need not inquire as to how respondent came before it.

In construing a treaty, as in construing a statute, we first look to its terms to determine its meaning. The Treaty says nothing about the obligations of the United States and Mexico to refrain from forcible abductions of people from the territory of the other nation, or the consequences under the Treaty if such an abduction occurs. . . .

. . . Article 9 of the Treaty . . . provides:

> 1. Neither Contracting Party shall be bound to deliver up its own nationals, but the executive authority of the requested Party shall, if not prevented by the laws of that Party, have the power to deliver them up if, in its discretion, it be deemed proper to do so.
> 2. If extradition is not granted pursuant to paragraph 1 of this Article, the requested Party shall submit the case to its competent authorities for the purpose of prosecution, provided that Party has jurisdiction over the offense.

According to respondent, Article 9 embodies the terms of the bargain which the United States struck: If the United States wishes to prosecute a Mexican national, it may request that individual's extradition. Upon a request from the United States, Mexico may either extradite the individual or submit the case to the proper authorities for prosecution in Mexico. In this way, respondent reasons, each nation preserved its right to choose whether its nationals would be tried in its own courts or by the courts of the other nation. This preservation of rights would be frustrated if either nation were free to abduct nationals of the other nation for the purposes of prosecution. More broadly, respondent reasons, as did the Court of Appeals, that all the processes and restrictions on the obligation to extradite established by the Treaty would make no sense if either nation were free to resort to forcible kidnaping to gain the presence of an individual for prosecution in a manner not contemplated by the Treaty.

We do not read the Treaty in such a fashion. Article 9 does not purport to specify the only way in which one country may gain custody of a national of the other country for the purposes of prosecution. In the absence of an extradition treaty, nations are under no obligation to surrender those in their country to foreign authorities for prosecution. Extradition treaties exist so as to impose mutual obligations to surrender individuals in certain defined sets of circumstances, following established procedures. The Treaty thus provides a mechanism which would not otherwise exist, requiring, under certain circumstances, the United States and Mexico to extradite individuals to the other country, and establishing the procedures to be followed when the Treaty is invoked.

The history of negotiation and practice under the Treaty also fails to show that abductions outside of the Treaty constitute a violation of the Treaty. As the Solicitor General notes, the Mexican Government was made aware, as early as 1906, of the *Ker* doctrine, and the United States' position that it applied to forcible abductions made outside of the terms of the United States-Mexico Extradition Treaty. Nonetheless, the current version of the Treaty, signed in 1978, does not attempt to establish a rule that would in any way curtail the effect of *Ker*. . . .

Thus, the language of the Treaty, in the context of its history, does not support the proposition that the Treaty prohibits abductions outside of its terms. The remaining question, therefore, is whether the Treaty should be interpreted so as to include an implied term prohibiting prosecution where the defendant's presence is obtained by means other than those established by the Treaty.

Respondent contends that the Treaty must be interpreted against the backdrop of customary international law, and that international abductions are "so clearly prohibited in international law" that there was no reason to include such a clause in the Treaty itself. The international censure of international abductions is further evidenced, according to respondent, by the United Nations Charter and the Charter of the Organization of American States. Respondent does not argue that these sources of international law provide an independent basis for the right respondent asserts not to be tried in the United States, but rather that they should inform the interpretation of the Treaty terms.

The Court of Appeals deemed it essential, in order for the individual defendant to assert a right under the Treaty, that the affected foreign government had registered a protest. Respondent agrees that the right exercised by the individual is derivative of the nation's right under the Treaty, since nations are authorized, notwithstanding the terms of an extradition treaty, to voluntarily render an individual to the other country on terms completely outside of those provided in the treaty. The formal protest, therefore, ensures that the "offended" nation actually objects to the abduction and has not in some way voluntarily rendered the individual for prosecution. Thus the Extradition Treaty only prohibits gaining the defendant's presence by means other than those set forth in the Treaty when the nation from which the defendant was abducted objects.

This argument seems to us inconsistent with the remainder of respondent's argument. The Extradition Treaty has the force of law, and if, as respondent asserts, it is self-executing, it would appear that a court must enforce it on behalf of an individual regardless of the offensiveness of the practice of one nation to the other nation. In *Rauscher*, the Court noted that Great Britain had taken the position in other cases that the Webster-Ashburton Treaty included the doctrine of specialty, but no importance was attached to whether or not Great Britain had protested the prosecution of Rauscher for the crime of cruel and unusual punishment as opposed to murder.

More fundamentally, the difficulty with the support respondent garners from international law is that none of it relates to the practice of nations in relation to extradition treaties. In *Rauscher*, we implied a term in the Webster-Ashburton Treaty because of the practice of nations with regard to extradition treaties. In the instant case, respondent would imply terms in the Extradition Treaty from the practice of nations with regards to international law more generally. Respondent would have us find that the Treaty acts as a prohibition against a violation of the general principle of international law that one government may not "exercise its police power in the territory of another state." There are many actions which could be taken by a nation that would violate this principle, including waging war, but it cannot seriously be contended that an invasion of the United States by Mexico would violate the terms of the Extradition Treaty between the two nations.

. . . In *Rauscher*, the implication of a doctrine of specialty into the terms of the Webster-Ashburton Treaty, which, by its terms, required the presentation of evidence establishing probable cause of the crime of extradition before extradition was required, was a small step to take. By contrast, to imply from the terms of this Treaty that it prohibits obtaining the presence of an individual by means outside of the procedures the Treaty establishes requires a much larger inferential leap, with only the most general of international law principles to support it. The general principles cited by respondent simply fail to persuade us that we should imply in the United States-Mexico Extradition Treaty a term prohibiting international abductions.

Respondent and his *amici* may be correct that respondent's abduction was "shocking," and that it may be in violation of general international law principles. Mexico has protested the abduction of respondent through diplomatic notes, and the decision of whether respondent should be returned to Mexico, as a matter outside of the Treaty, is a matter for the Executive Branch. We conclude, however, that respondent's abduction was not in violation of the Extradition Treaty between the United States and Mexico, and therefore the rule of *Ker v. Illinois* is fully applicable to this case. The fact of respondent's forcible abduction does not therefore prohibit his trial in a court in the United States for violations of the criminal laws of the United States.

JUSTICE STEVENS, with whom JUSTICE BLACKMUN and JUSTICE O'CONNOR join, dissenting:

I

The extradition treaty with Mexico is a comprehensive document containing 23 articles and an appendix listing the extraditable offenses covered by the agreement. The parties announced their purpose in the preamble: The two governments desire "to cooperate more closely in the fight against crime and, to this end, to mutually render better assistance in matters of extradition." From the preamble, through the description of the parties' obligations with respect to offenses committed within as well as beyond the territory of a requesting party, the delineation of the procedures and evidentiary requirements for extradition, the special provisions for political offenses and capital punishment, and other details, the Treaty appears to have been designed to cover the entire subject of extradition. . . . Article 9 expressly provides that neither contracting party is bound to deliver up its own nationals, although it may do so in its discretion, but if it does not do so, it "shall submit the case to its competent authorities for purposes of prosecution."

The Government's claim that the Treaty is not exclusive, but permits forcible governmental kidnaping, would transform these, and other, provisions into little more than verbiage. For example, provisions requiring "sufficient" evidence to grant extradition (Art. 3), withholding extradition for political or military offenses (Art. 5), withholding extradition when the person sought has already been tried (Art. 6), withholding extradition when the statute of limitations for the crime has lapsed (Art. 7), and granting the requested country discretion to refuse to extradite an individual who would face the death penalty in the requesting country (Art. 8), would serve little purpose if the requesting country could simply kidnap the person. . . . In addition, all of these provisions "only make sense if they are understood as *requiring* each treaty signatory to comply with those procedures whenever it wishes to obtain jurisdiction over an individual who is located in another treaty nation."

It is true, as the Court notes, that there is no express promise by either party to refrain from forcible abductions in the territory of the other nation. Relying on that omission, the Court, in effect, concludes that the Treaty merely creates an optional method of obtaining jurisdiction over alleged offenders, and that the parties silently reserved the right to resort to self-help whenever they deem force more expeditious than legal process. If the United States, for example, thought it more expedient to torture or simply to execute a person rather than to attempt extradition, these options would be equally available because they, too, were not explicitly prohibited by the Treaty. That, however, is a highly improbable interpretation of a consensual agreement, which on its face appears to have been intended to set forth comprehensive and exclusive rules concerning the subject of extradition. In my opinion, "the manifest scope and object of the treaty itself," *Rauscher*, 119 U.S. at 422, plainly imply a mutual undertaking to respect the territorial integrity of the other contracting party. . . .

III

A critical flaw pervades the Court's entire opinion. It fails to differentiate between the conduct of private citizens, which does not violate any treaty obligation, and conduct expressly authorized by the Executive Branch of the Government, which unquestionably constitutes a flagrant violation of international law, and in my opinion, also constitutes a breach of our treaty obligations. Thus, at the outset of its opinion, the Court states the issue as "whether a criminal defendant, abducted to the United States from a nation with which it has an extradition treaty, thereby acquires a defense to the jurisdiction of this country's courts." That, of course, is the question decided in *Ker v. Illinois*; it is not, however, the question presented for decision today. . . .

The same reasoning was employed by Justice Miller to explain why the holding in *Rauscher* did not apply to the *Ker* case. The arresting officer in *Ker* did not pretend to be acting in any official capacity when he kidnaped Ker. . . . The exact opposite is true in this case. . . .

Notes and Questions

1. The *Alvarez-Machain* ruling provoked a strong international reaction. China, Colombia, Costa Rica, Cuba, Denmark, Ecuador, Guatemala, Honduras, Jamaica,

Malaysia, and Venezuela all filed formal diplomatic protests with the United States in the months following the decision. Several governments also expressed their disapproval in more public forms. The Colombian government, for example, stated that it "energetically rejects the judgment issued by the United States Supreme Court," and that "its substance threatens the legal stability of [all] public treaties." Venezuela's Foreign Relations Legislative Commission asked President Carlos Andres Perez to revise its extradition treaty with the United States as a result of the decision.

The opinion also prompted actions in several multilateral fora. For example, in 1992, the UN Working Group on Arbitrary Detention determined that "the object and purpose of the Treaty, and an analysis of the context, lead to the unquestionable conclusion that abduction for the purpose of bringing someone in Mexico or in the United States before a court of the requesting party is a breach of the 1978 Treaty."

The Permanent Council of the Organization of American States (OAS) expressed concern about the decision and asked the Inter-American Juridical Committee to render an opinion on the legality of the decision. The Committee, an OAS advisory body on juridical matters, issued the following legal opinion:

9. [T]he Committee considers that it cannot be disputed or is not in doubt that the abduction in question was a serious violation of public international law since it was a transgression of the territorial sovereignty of Mexico. . . .

10. Pursuant to the rules governing state responsibility in international law, any state that violates an international obligation must make reparations for the consequences of the violation. The reparation has the purpose of returning, to the extent possible, the situation to the way it was before the transgression occurred. Only to the extent that this would prove impossible, or that the aggrieved party would so agree, could there be room for any substitute reparation.

11. In accordance with these statements, it is clear that the United States of America, as the party responsible for violating the sovereignty of Mexico by abducting a Mexican citizen, Humberto Alvarez Machain, is obligated to repatriate him, without prejudice to any other reparations that its conduct might give rise to. . . .

13. Finally, the Committee observes that if the principles involved in the decision in question were taken to their logical consequences, international juridical order would be irreversibly damaged by any state that attributes to itself the power to violate with impunity the territorial sovereignty of another state. The Committee should likewise underscore the incompatibility of the practice of abduction with the right of due process to which every person is entitled, no matter how serious the crime they are accused of, a right protected by international law. . . .

Legal Opinion on the Decision of the Supreme Court of the United States of America, CJI/Res. II-15/92. Why did the international community react so differently to the abductions of Eichmann and Alvarez-Machain?

2. In 1992, President George H.W. Bush wrote to Mexican President Carlos Salinas to assure him that the United States would neither "conduct, encourage, nor condone" the abduction of criminal suspects from Mexican territory. In November 1994, the United States and Mexico concluded the Treaty to Prohibit Transborder Abductions. Under this treaty, both parties agreed to "not conduct transborder abductions." The treaty provides in such cases for repatriation of the abducted individual and prosecution of those individuals responsible for the abduction. As of February 2006, the treaty had not been submitted to the Senate for advice and

consent. Should other governments that have extradition treaties with the United States seek to negotiate similar non-abduction treaties?

3. After the Supreme Court's ruling, Alvarez-Machain was tried in federal district court in Los Angeles. After the prosecution concluded its case, the trial judge granted Alvarez-Machain's motion for acquittal and stated that the case against Alvarez-Machain had been based on "hunches" and the "wildest speculation." After the acquittal, Alvarez-Machain filed suit in federal district court against the United States, several DEA agents, and several individuals who participated in his abduction. Alvarez-Machain's suit eventually reached the U.S. Supreme Court, and is discussed in Chapter 5.

D. Challenging Irregular Renditions in Other Jurisdictions

Domestic courts in several other states have considered whether to exercise jurisdiction over criminal defendants who were irregularly brought into the territory of the prosecuting state. For example, in *R. v. Horseferry Road Magistrates' Court, Ex Parte Bennett*, [1993] 3 All E.R. 138, the English police located the defendant, a New Zealand citizen, in South Africa. After consulting with the Crown Prosecution Service, the police decided not to seek formal extradition. Instead, they persuaded the South African police to arrest the defendant and return him forcibly to England under the pretext of deporting him to New Zealand via London's Heathrow Airport. Bennett was arrested by the English police upon arrival at Heathrow.

By a 4-to-1 vote, the Law Lords held that English courts have discretion not to exercise jurisdiction over a criminal defendant where English police have disregarded the protections of formal extradition procedures and have had the defendant seized abroad by illegal means.

Lord Griffiths wrote:

> Extradition procedures are designed not only to ensure that criminals are returned from one country to another but also to protect the rights of those who are accused of crimes by the requesting country. . . . If a practice developed in which the police or prosecuting authorities of this country ignored extradition procedures and secured the return of an accused by a mere request to police colleagues in another country they would be flouting the extradition procedures and depriving the accused of the safeguards built into the extradition process for his benefit. It is to my mind unthinkable that in such circumstances the court should declare itself to be powerless and stand idly by. . . .

Lord Lowry wrote:

> [I]f British officialdom at any level has participated in or encouraged the kidnaping, it seems to represent a grave contravention of international law, the comity of nations and the rule of law generally if our courts allow themselves to be used by the executive to try an offense which the courts would not be dealing with if the rule of law had prevailed.

Lord Oliver argued, in dissent, that courts should not concern themselves with pre-trial police impropriety that does not affect the fairness of the trial itself. In his view, the proper remedy for executive branch unlawfulness is civil or criminal proceedings against the wrongdoers, not the denial of criminal jurisdiction. Lord Oliver rejected the argument that English courts should act to protect the rights of foreign states:

> An English criminal court is not concerned nor is it in a position to investigate the legality under foreign law of acts committed on foreign soil and in any event any complaint of an invasion of the sovereignty of a foreign state is, as it seems to me, a matter which can only properly be pursued on a diplomatic level between the government of the United Kingdom and the government of that state.

Australian courts have held that judges have discretion to refuse to exercise jurisdiction over defendants who have been irregularly brought into the jurisdiction. For example, in *Levinge v. Director of Custodial Services*, 9 N.S.W.L.R. 546 (1987), the New South Wales court of appeals considered the *Eichmann* case and relevant Anglo-American precedents and stated:

> Where a person, however unlawfully, is brought into the jurisdiction and is before a court in this State, that court has undoubted jurisdiction to deal with him or her. But it also has discretion not to do so, where to exercise its discretion would involve an abuse of the court's process. . . . [S]uch conduct may exist, including wrongful and even unlawful involvement in bypassing the regular machinery for extradition and participation in unauthorized and unlawful removal of criminal suspects from one jurisdiction to another.

The New Zealand courts have also adopted a discretionary approach to jurisdiction in such cases.

The South African Supreme Court adopted a different approach in *State v. Ebrahim*, 1991 (2) SALR 553. In *Ebrahim*, two men identifying themselves as South African police officers seized a South African member of the military wing of the anti-apartheid African National Congress in Swaziland in December 1986. Ebrahim was bound, gagged, blindfolded, and brought to Pretoria and charged with treason. Swaziland did not protest this abduction. Ebrahim argued that his abduction and rendition violated international law, and that the trial court was thus incompetent to try him because international law was a part of South African law.

Invoking Roman-Dutch common law, the Court concluded that it lacked jurisdiction to try a person brought before it from another state by means of state-sponsored abduction. These common law rules embodied fundamental legal principles, including "the preservation and promotion of human rights, friendly international relations, and the sound administration of justice." The Court continued:

> The individual must be protected from unlawful arrest and abduction, jurisdictional boundaries must not be exceeded, international legal sovereignty must be respected, the legal process must be fair towards those affected by it and the misuse thereof must be avoided in order to protect and promote the dignity and integrity of the judicial system. This applies equally to the State. When the State is itself party to a dispute, as for example in criminal cases, it must come to court "with clean hands" as it were. When the State is itself involved in an abduction across international borders as in the instant case, its hands cannot be said to be clean.

The Court also noted that "the abduction was a violation of the applicable rules of international law, that these rules are part of [South African] law, and that this violation of these rules deprived the trial court of competence to hear the matter."

In a subsequent civil proceeding, Ebrahim was awarded compensation for the kidnaping.

In *State v. Beahan*, 103 I.L.R. 203 (1991), the Zimbabwe Supreme Court found that the act of bringing the defendant into Zimbabwe from abroad did not involve "force or deception." The Court nevertheless opined:

> it is essential that, to promote confidence in and respect for the administration of justice and preserve the judicial process from contamination, a court should decline to compel an accused person to undergo trial in circumstances where his appearance before it has been facilitated by an act of abduction undertaken by the prosecuting State. There is an inherent objection to such a course both on grounds of public policy pertaining to international ethical norms and because it imperils and corrodes the peaceful coexistence and mutual respect of sovereign nations. For abduction is illegal under international law, provided the abductor was not acting on his own initiative and without the authority or connivance of his government. A contrary view would amount to a declaration that the end justifies the means, thereby encouraging States to become law-breakers in order to secure the conviction of a private individual.

What bearing, if any, do these cases have on the question before the court in *Dokmanovic*?

E. The ICTY Opines, Eventually

Dokmanovic argued that his arrest violated international law and divested the ICTY of jurisdiction to try him. After hearing testimony from Dokmanovic and UNTAES officials, the ICTY Trial Chamber concluded that Dokmanovic entered into Croatia "of his own free will" on the basis of his belief that he would be meeting with Transitional Administrator Klein to discuss his property in Croatia. As a result, the court determined that the prosecutor's "ruse" did not constitute a "forcible abduction or kidnaping." The court then examined judicial decisions from several states and concluded that, absent an extradition treaty, "luring a suspect into another jurisdiction in order to effect his arrest is not an abuse of the suspect's rights or an abuse of process." The Trial Chamber found that as "the particular method used to arrest and detain Mr. Dokmanovic was justified and *legal*, we need not decide at this time whether the International Tribunal has the authority to exercise jurisdiction over a defendant *illegally* obtained from abroad." *Prosecutor v. Mrskic, et al.*, Case No. IT-95-13a-PT (1997). Shortly after the close of evidence at his trial, but before a verdict was rendered, Dokmanovic committed suicide in his cell, and the ICTY Appeals Chamber had no occasion to consider the legality of Dokmanovic's arrest.

Another case involving an alleged abduction was resolved before the issue reached the Appeals Chamber. *Prosecutor v. Todorovic* involved a Bosnian Serb indicted on 28 counts of crimes against humanity, grave breaches, and war crimes arising out of acts of rape, murder, torture, sexual humiliation, and other cruelty. The defendant alleged that he had been abducted from his home in Serbia by four armed, masked men who smuggled him into Bosnia and Herzegovina, where he was transferred to the NATO-led stabilization force (SFOR).

Todorovic's informal efforts to obtain information from SFOR about his arrest were unsuccessful; a motion requesting evidence related to his arrest from the Office of the Prosecutor was denied. However, a subsequent habeas corpus motion led to the scheduling of an evidentiary hearing. The trial chamber ordered the prosecutor to turn over all relevant reports and materials related to Todorovic's arrest, including information regarding the steps it had taken to obtain relevant information from SFOR; the prosecutor produced a one page "report" and stated that no other information was within its custody and control. The trial chamber then ordered SFOR and the 33 states participating in SFOR to provide Todorovic with evidence relating to his arrest. Almost immediately thereafter, the prosecutor entered into a plea agreement with Todorovic. The agreement provided that Todorovic would plead guilty to one count of crimes against humanity and the other 27 counts against him would be dropped. In addition, Todorovic would withdraw all motions related to the circumstances of his arrest and "withdraw the allegations that his arrest was unlawful and that SFOR or NATO was involved in any unlawful activity in relation to his arrest." The trial chamber accepted Todorovic's guilty plea and sentenced him to ten years imprisonment. No appeal was filed.

In the case of *Prosecutor v. Nikolic*, the Appeals Chamber did address the question of whether the ICTY could exercise personal jurisdiction over a defendant who had been kidnapped. The defendant in this action was abducted by the NATO-led stabilization force in Bosnia, acting in collusion with unknown individuals from Serbia and Montenegro.

Prosecutor v. Nikolic, Decision on Interlocutory Appeal Concerning Legality of Arrest

Case No. IT-94-2-AR73 (2003)

20. The impact of a breach of a State's sovereignty on the exercise of jurisdiction is a novel issue for this Tribunal. There is no case law directly on the point, and the [ICTY's] Statute and the Rules provide little guidance. . . . [As a result,] the Appeals Chamber will seek guidance from national case law, where the issue at hand has often arisen, in order to determine state practice on the matter.

21. In several national cases, courts have held that jurisdiction should not be set aside, even though there might have been irregularities in the manner in which the accused was brought before them. [The court discussed a French case that upheld jurisdiction over a defendant kidnaped in Germany, a German court that upheld jurisdiction over a defendant improperly brought into Germany, and *Alvarez-Machain*.]

22. On the other hand, there have been cases in which the exercise of jurisdiction has been declined. [The court reviewed an incident in the 1930s when Germany released a suspect who it had kidnapped from Switzerland, and decisions by the Supreme Court of South Africa and the UK House of Lords where courts declined to exercise jurisdiction over defendants.]

23. With regard to cases concerning the same kinds of crimes as those falling within the jurisdiction of the [ICTY], reference may be made to *Eichmann* and *Barbie*. In *Eichmann*, the Supreme Court of Israel decided to exercise jurisdiction over the accused, notwithstanding the apparent breach of Argentina's sovereignty involved in his abduction. . . . In *Barbie*, the French Court of Cassation (Criminal Chamber) asserted its jurisdiction over the accused, despite [an irregular rendition], on the basis, *inter alia*, of the special nature of the crimes ascribed to the accused, namely, crimes against humanity.

24. Although it is difficult to identify a clear pattern in this case law . . . two principles seem to have support in State practice as evidenced by the practice of their courts. First, in cases of crimes such as genocide, crimes against humanity and war crimes . . . ("Universally Condemned Offenses"), courts seem to find in the special character of these offenses and, arguably, in their seriousness, a good reason for not setting aside jurisdiction. Second, absent a complaint by the State whose sovereignty has been breached or in the event of a diplomatic resolution of the breach, it is easier for courts to assert their jurisdiction. . . .

25. Universally Condemned Offenses are a matter of concern to the international community as a whole. There is a legitimate expectation that those accused of those crimes will be brought to justice swiftly. Accountability for these crimes is a necessary condition to the achievement of international justice, which plays a critical role in the reconciliation and rebuilding based on the rule of law of countries and societies torn apart by international and internecine conflicts.

26. . . . In the opinion of the Appeals Chamber, the damage caused to international justice by not apprehending fugitives accused of serious violations of international humanitarian law is comparatively higher than the injury, if any, caused to the sovereignty of a State by a limited intrusion in its territory. . . . Therefore, the Appeals Chamber does not consider that in cases of universally condemned offenses, jurisdiction should be set aside on the ground that there was a violation of the sovereignty of a State, when the violation is brought about by the apprehension of fugitives from international justice, whatever the consequences for the international responsibility of the State or organisation involved. . . .

[The tribunal then considered whether the violation of the accused's human rights divest the court of jurisdiction.]

30. . . . Although the assessment of the seriousness of the human rights violations depends on the circumstances of each case and cannot be made *in abstracto*, certain human rights violations are of such a serious nature that they require that the exercise of jurisdiction be declined. It would be inappropriate for a court of law to try the victims of these abuses. Apart from such exceptional cases, however, the remedy of setting aside jurisdiction will . . . usually be disproportionate. The correct balance must therefore be maintained between the fundamental rights of the accused and the essential interests of the international community in the prosecution of persons charged with serious violations of international humanitarian law.

[The Appeals Chamber concluded that the kidnapping of the accused did not divest the court of jurisdiction.]

Notes and Questions

1. How does the Appeals Chamber know that the "damage caused to international justice" by not apprehending individuals accused of serious violations of international humanitarian law is "comparatively higher" than the injury caused by violations of state sovereignty? Does *Eichmann* or state practice support this claim?

2. Is the Appeals Chamber suggesting that a suspect accused of universally condemned offenses somehow enjoys fewer rights than one accused of lesser crimes? What justification would there be for such a position?

3. Why did the Appeals Chamber rely upon the decisions of national tribunals? Is an irregular rendition to an international tribunal more justifiable than an irregular rendition to a national court?

4. In June 2005, an Italian judge issued arrest warrants for 13 CIA officials and operatives allegedly involved in the kidnapping of Iman Hassan Mustafa Osama Nasr in Italy in February 2003. Nasr was flown to a U.S. base in Ramstein, Germany, and then imprisoned in Egypt. Nasr was allegedly tortured in Egypt during interrogations concerning his alleged involvement in terrorist activities. Assuming Nasr is put on trial for terrorist activities, should a court decline to exercise jurisdiction over him? The international norms concerning torture are discussed in Chapter 7.

IV. SOVEREIGN IMMUNITY: SUING NIGERIA IN U.S. COURTS

Having examined the various ways that states assert authority, or jurisdiction, over people or activities, we now turn to certain situations where states have refrained from applying the general norms governing jurisdiction. As we shall see, states have excluded classes of entities — including foreign states; certain government officials, such as heads of state and diplomats; and international organizations — from the exercise of their jurisdiction in certain circumstances. Our focus will be on foreign state immunities, as this is the immunity most frequently raised in domestic court litigation.

The concept of state immunity from jurisdiction originated at a time when kings were considered to be the embodiment of a state's sovereignty, and when diplomatic envoys were considered to be rulers' personal representatives. The prevailing view was that, because they were of equal standing, one sovereign monarch could not be subject to the jurisdiction of another sovereign monarch: *par in parem non habet imperium*. Moreover, just as a king would not be subject to jurisdiction while visiting another state, so too the monarch's representatives were granted immunity.

Over time, the idea of an identity between state and ruler faded away, but states continued to extend to other states an absolute immunity from jurisdiction to adjudicate and jurisdiction to enforce. Governments justified these broad immunities by reference to the dignity, equality, and independence of states. However, pressures to limit various immunities grew as states and state instrumentalities became increasingly involved in international transactions. While recent developments have restricted traditional notions of sovereign immunity, the concept and policies underlying sovereign immunity remain important in much transnational litigation.

The materials that follow examine the historical development of the doctrine of sovereign immunity and its application in the United States. As you read these materials, consider the appropriate role of domestic courts in determining foreign sovereign immunity; how well current doctrine serves the purposes underlying sovereign immunity; and whether current doctrine appropriately balances the interests of sovereigns and the non-state actors who deal with foreign state entities.

A. The Problem

The Nigerian Airports Authority (NAA), a corporation wholly owned and operated by the Federal Republic of Nigeria (FRN), is responsible for the operation and management of all airports in Nigeria. Under Nigerian law, the NAA is responsible for generating its own funds to operate and manage airports in Nigeria. Thus, the NAA imposes landing fees, parking fees, car park fees, concession fees, and other airport user fees. Nigerian law provides that every civilian aircraft that uses an airport managed by the NAA must pay parking and landing fees to the NAA.

Antares Aircraft, L.P., is a Delaware limited partnership that owned a DC-8-55 aircraft. In February 1988, Antares leased the plane to Gam Air, a Gambian corporation, but Gam Air soon defaulted on its obligations under the lease. Gam Air also failed to pay the plane's pilot and crew in a timely fashion. To recover their wages, the pilots and crew filed an action in Nigeria against Gam Air. In connection with that action, a Nigerian court issued an order of attachment covering the aircraft, which was then at the Murtala Muhammed Airport in Lagos, Nigeria. Antares successfully moved to intervene in the Nigerian action and persuaded the Nigerian court to lift the order of attachment. However, the NAA refused to release the plane to Antares until various parking and landing fees, allegedly incurred by Gam Air and owed to the NAA, were paid.

Lengthy negotiations ensued between Antares and the NAA. Antares claims that between January and May 1989 it made a series of payments to the NAA. Several times Antares believed that its payments would enable it to recover the plane. However, on each occasion the NAA increased its demands. Antares eventually paid approximately $100,000 to the NAA. Most of these payments were wired from Antares's New York bank account to the NAA in Nigeria.

In October 1989, Antares sued the NAA and the FRN in the U.S. District Court for the Southern District of New York to recover damages resulting from the detention and alleged conversion of the aircraft in Nigeria. Antares claimed that the plane's detention was part of a scheme to extort payments from Antares. The FRN and the NAA moved to dismiss the complaint on the grounds that the court lacked subject matter jurisdiction over the action by virtue of the defendants' sovereign immunity.

B. Development of Foreign Sovereign Immunity

In determining whether U.S. courts should exercise jurisdiction over the FRN and the NAA, it is important to consider how the doctrine of sovereign immunity has evolved over time.

1. The Classical View of Sovereign Immunity

The seminal U.S. case on sovereign immunity is *The Schooner Exchange v. McFaddon*, 11 U.S. 116 (1812). This case involved a vessel owned by two U.S. citizens that, while en route from the United States to Spain, was captured by the French Navy. The French Navy took the vessel to a French port, where it was converted into a French warship. Several months later, inclement weather forced the *Schooner Exchange* into port in Philadelphia, where its original owners filed a libel action against the ship in U.S. district court for the return of their property. The case eventually reached the Supreme Court, which upheld a claim of sovereign immunity.

The Schooner Exchange v. McFaddon

11 U.S. 116 (1812)

MARSHALL, CH. J. delivered the opinion of the Court as follows:

This case involves the very delicate and important inquiry, whether an American citizen can assert, in an American court, a title to an armed national vessel, found within the waters of the United States. . . .

The jurisdiction of the nation within its own territory is necessarily exclusive and absolute. It is susceptible of no limitation not imposed by itself. Any restriction upon it, deriving validity from an external source, would imply a diminution of its sovereignty to the extent of the restriction, and an investment of that sovereignty to the same extent in that power which could impose such restriction.

All exceptions, therefore, to the full and complete power of a nation within its own territories, must be traced up to the consent of the nation itself. They can flow from no other legitimate source. . . .

This full and absolute territorial jurisdiction being alike the attribute of every sovereign, and being incapable of conferring extra-territorial power, would not seem to contemplate foreign sovereigns nor their sovereign rights as its objects. One sovereign being in no respect amenable to another; and being bound by obligations of the highest character not to degrade the dignity of his nation, by placing himself or its sovereign rights within the jurisdiction of another, can be supposed to enter a foreign territory only under an express license, or in the confidence that the immunities belonging to his independent sovereign station . . . are reserved by implication, and will be extended to him.

This perfect equality and absolute independence of sovereigns, and this common interest impelling them to mutual intercourse, have given rise to a class of cases in which every sovereign is understood to waive the exercise of a part of that complete exclusive territorial jurisdiction, which has been stated to be the attribute of every nation. . . .

When private individuals of one nation spread themselves through another as business or caprice may direct, mingling indiscriminately with the inhabitants of that other, or when merchant vessels enter for the purposes of trade, it would be obviously inconvenient and dangerous to society, and would subject the laws to continual infraction, and the government to degradation, if such individuals or merchants did not owe temporary and local allegiance, and were not amenable to the jurisdiction of the country. . . .

But in all respects different is the situation of a public armed ship. She constitutes a part of the military force of her nation; acts under the immediate and direct command of the sovereign; is employed by him in national objects. He has many and powerful motives for preventing those objects from being defeated by the interference of a foreign state. Such interference cannot take place without affecting his power and his dignity. The implied license therefore under which such vessel enters a friendly port, may reasonably be construed . . . as containing an exemption from the jurisdiction of the sovereign, within whose territory she claims the rites of hospitality. . . .

It seems then to the Court, to be a principle of public law, that national ships of war, entering the port of a friendly power open for their reception, are to be considered as exempted by the consent of that power from its jurisdiction. . . .

The arguments in favor of this opinion which have been drawn from the general inability of the judicial power to enforce its decisions in cases of this description, from the consideration, that the sovereign power of the nation is alone competent to avenge wrongs committed by a sovereign, that the questions to which such wrongs give birth are rather questions of policy than of law, that they are for diplomatic, rather than legal discussion, are of great weight, and merit serious attention. But the argument has already been drawn to a length, which forbids a particular examination of these points. . . .

If the preceding reasoning be correct, the Exchange, being a public armed ship, in the service of a foreign sovereign, with whom the government of the United States is at peace, and having entered an American port open for her reception, on the terms on which ships of war are generally permitted to enter the ports of a friendly power, must be considered as having come into the American territory, under an implied promise, that while necessarily within it, and demeaning herself in a friendly manner, she should be exempt from the jurisdiction of the country.

Notes and Questions

1. Does *The Schooner Exchange* rest upon the application of international or domestic law?

2. Is the immunity granted in *The Schooner Exchange* a function of the juridical equality of all states? Or does the immunity granted here reflect an understanding that domestic courts can do little that is useful in such cases?

3. The U.S. Attorney argued that *The Schooner Exchange* was immune from the jurisdiction of U.S. courts. Was this an important element in the Court's analysis? Would, or should, the case come out differently if the Executive Branch argued against a grant of immunity?

While *The Schooner Exchange* by its terms applies only to warships, subsequent English and American cases extended the rule of immunity to other vessels owned by foreign sovereigns and, eventually, to other kinds of property as well. For example, *Berizzi Bros. Co. v. S.S. Pesaro*, 271 U.S. 562 (1926), involved an ordinary commercial claim arising out of an Italian government-owned merchant vessel's delivery of damaged cargo in New York. The Supreme Court upheld dismissal of the action on immunity grounds. In reaching this conclusion, the Court did not refer to the position of the Executive Branch.

In *Ex Parte Peru*, 318 U.S. 578 (1943), the Court affirmed its holding that vessels owned by foreign governments were immune from suit in courts in the United States, even if both the vessel and the claim were commercial. In this case, however, the State Department had formally "recognized and allowed" Peru's claim of immunity. The Court held that the State Department's determination "must be accepted by the courts as a conclusive determination by the political arm of the Government that the continued retention of the vessel interferes with the proper conduct of our foreign relations."

Two years later, the Supreme Court considered a case involving a merchant vessel owned by, but not in the possession of, the Mexican government. In *Republic of Mexico v. Hoffman*, 324 U.S. 30 (1944), the Justice Department presented the courts with a State Department communication accepting Mexico's claim of ownership but expressing no opinion as to Mexico's claim of immunity. The Court stated that:

> Every judicial action exercising or relinquishing jurisdiction over the vessel of a foreign government has its effect upon our relations with that government. Hence it is a guiding principle in determining whether a court should exercise or surrender its jurisdiction in such cases, that the courts should not so act as to embarrass the executive arm in its conduct of foreign affairs. . . .

Id. at 35. For this reason, the Court concluded that the judiciary should not "deny an immunity which our government has seen fit to allow, or to allow an immunity on new grounds which the government has not seen fit to recognize."*Id.*

2. The Tate Letter

Ex Parte Peru and *Hoffman* granted the State Department considerable leeway in developing the doctrine of sovereign immunity and determining its application in particular cases. But scholars and practitioners criticized an approach that appeared to turn on concepts such as the distinction between government ownership and possession of a vessel and argued that there was little justification for extending immunity to foreign governments when they engaged in commercial activity akin to that conducted by private parties.

As a result, the absolute theory of sovereign immunity articulated in *The Schooner Exchange* came under significant diplomatic and theoretical attack, and state practice moved away from the absolute theory during the 1940s and 1950s. During this period, the State Department conducted a study of the relevant practices of other states and reached the conclusion that immunity should not be granted in cases involving private, as contrasted with sovereign, acts. The Department set forth its position and reasoning in a May 1952 letter to the Department of Justice:

Letter from State Department Acting Legal Adviser Jack B. Tate

26 Dep't State Bull. 984-985 (1952)

MY DEAR MR. ATTORNEY GENERAL:

The Department of State has for some time had under consideration the question whether the practice of the Government in granting immunity from suit to foreign governments made parties defendant in the courts of the United States without their consent should not be changed. The Department has now reached the conclusion that such immunity should no longer be granted in certain types of cases. . . .

A study of the law of sovereign immunity reveals the existence of two conflicting concepts of sovereign immunity, each widely held and firmly established. According to the classical or absolute theory of sovereign immunity, a sovereign cannot, without his consent, be made a respondent in the courts of another sovereign. According to the newer or restrictive theory of sovereign immunity, the immunity of the sovereign is recognized with regard to sovereign or public acts (*jure imperii*) of a state, but not with respect to private acts (*jure gestionis*). . . .

The classical or virtually absolute theory of sovereign immunity has generally been followed by the courts of the United States, the British Commonwealth, Czechoslovakia, Estonia, and probably Poland. . . .

The decisions of the courts of Brazil, Chile, China, Hungary, Japan, Luxembourg, Norway, and Portugal may be deemed to support the classical theory of immunity if one or at most two old decisions anterior to the development of the restrictive theory may be considered sufficient on which to base a conclusion. . . .

The newer or restrictive theory of sovereign immunity has always been supported by the courts of Belgium and Italy. It was adopted in turn by the courts of Egypt and of Switzerland. In addition, the courts of France, Austria, and Greece, which were traditionally supporters of the classical theory, reversed their position in the 20's to embrace the restrictive theory. Rumania, Peru, and possibly Denmark also appear to follow this theory. . . .

Of related interest . . . is the fact that ten of the thirteen countries which have been classified above as supporters of the classical theory have ratified the Brussels Convention of 1926 under which immunity for government owned merchant vessels is waived. In addition the United States, which is not a party to the Convention, some years ago announced and has since followed, a policy of not claiming immunity for its public owned or operated merchant vessels. . . .

It is thus evident that with the possible exception of the United Kingdom little support has been found except on the part of the Soviet Union and its satellites for continued full acceptance of the absolute theory of sovereign immunity. . . . The reasons which obviously motivate state trading countries in adhering to the theory with perhaps increasing rigidity are most persuasive that the United States should change its policy. Furthermore, the granting of sovereign immunity to foreign governments in the courts of the United States is most inconsistent with the action of the Government of the United States in subjecting itself to suit in these same courts in both contract and tort and with its long established policy of not claiming immunity in foreign jurisdictions for its merchant vessels. Finally, the Department feels that the widespread and increasing practice on the part of governments of engaging in commercial activities makes necessary a practice which will enable persons doing business with them to have their rights determined in the courts. For these reasons it will hereafter be the Department's policy to follow the restrictive theory of sovereign immunity in the consideration of requests of foreign governments for a grant of sovereign immunity.

It is realized that a shift in policy by the executive cannot control the courts but it is felt that the courts are less likely to allow a plea of sovereign immunity where the executive has declined to do so. . . .

In order that your Department, which is charged with representing the interests of the Government before the courts, may be adequately informed it will be the Department's practice to advise you of all requests by foreign governments for the grant of immunity from suit and of the Department's action thereon.

The State Department's efforts to apply the principles set forth in the Tate Letter proved unsatisfactory. First, the Letter made no attempt to define the critical distinction between a state's "public" and "private" acts. Was the purchase of boots for a state's army a private or a public act? What about the purchase of bullets? In addition, the restrictive theory of immunity adopted in the Tate Letter depends less on foreign relations concerns than on an analysis of the particular activity on which the claim is based. This would seem to call for a legal, rather than a political, determination. But in the Letter the Executive Branch apparently asserts authority to decide this issue, and in practice, the State Department faced pressure from foreign governments to request immunity in cases where immunity was not warranted, placing the Department in difficult positions. Litigants quickly sensed that foreign policy considerations seemed to influence the Department's immunity determinations, and similar situations yielded different outcomes. Moreover, the courts lacked clear rules to apply when a foreign state did not request immunity or the State Department chose not to intervene. As a result, immunity determinations were made by different branches based on varying standards that were neither clearly articulated nor uniformly applied. Dissatisfaction with the perceived politicization of the process for deciding immunity and a desire for greater predictability led practitioners, scholars, and the State Department itself to urge reforms that would remove the Department from the process of determining immunity.

3. Codification of the Restrictive Theory: The Foreign Sovereign Immunities Act

Reform efforts bore fruit as Congress passed the Foreign Sovereign Immunities Act (FSIA) in 1976. This statute essentially codifies the U.S. view of the restrictive theory of sovereign immunity and is the exclusive means for obtaining jurisdiction over foreign states and their instrumentalities in courts in the United States. The statute provides that foreign states are immune from the jurisdiction of federal and state courts unless one or more of the FSIA's exceptions to immunities is applicable.

Foreign Sovereign Immunities Act of 1976

28 U.S.C. §§1602-1605

§1602. *Findings and Declaration of Purpose*

The Congress finds that the determination by the United States courts of the claims of foreign states to immunity from the jurisdiction of such courts would serve the interests of justice and would protect the rights of both foreign states and litigants in United States courts. Under international law, states are not immune from the jurisdiction of foreign courts insofar as their commercial activities are concerned, and their commercial property may be levied upon for the satisfaction of judgments rendered against them in connection with their commercial activities. Claims of foreign states to immunity should henceforth be decided by courts of the United States and of the States in conformity with the principles set forth in this Chapter.

§1603. *Definitions*

For purposes of this chapter—

(a) A "foreign state" . . . includes a political subdivision of a foreign state or an agency or instrumentality of a foreign state. . . .

(d) A "commercial activity" means either a regular course of commercial conduct or a particular commercial transaction or act. The commercial character of an activity shall be determined by reference to the nature of the course of conduct or particular transaction or act, rather than by reference to its purpose.

(e) A "commercial activity carried on in the United States by a foreign state" means commercial activity carried on by such state and having substantial contact with the United States.

§1604. Immunity of a Foreign State from Jurisdiction

Subject to existing international agreements to which the United States is a party at the time of enactment of this Act a foreign state shall be immune from the jurisdiction of the courts of the United States and of the States except as provided in sections 1605 to 1607 of this chapter.

§1605. General Exceptions to the Jurisdictional Immunity of a Foreign State

(a) A foreign state shall not be immune from the jurisdiction of courts of the United States or of the States in any case —

(1) in which the foreign state has waived its immunity either explicitly or by implication . . . ;

(2) in which the action is based upon a commercial activity carried on in the United States by the foreign state; or upon an act performed in the United States in connection with a commercial activity of the foreign state elsewhere; or upon an act outside the territory of the United States in connection with a commercial activity of the foreign state elsewhere and that act causes a direct effect in the United States;

(3) in which rights in property taken in violation of international law are at issue and that property or any property exchanged for such property is present in the United States in connection with a commercial activity carried on in the United States by the foreign state; . . .

(4) in which rights in property in the United States acquired by succession or gift or rights in immovable property situated in the United States are in issue; or

(5) not otherwise encompassed in paragraph (2) above, in which money damages are sought against a foreign state for personal injury or death, or damage to or loss of property, occurring in the United States and caused by the tortious act or omission of that foreign state or of any official or employee of that foreign state while acting within the scope of his office or employment; except this paragraph shall not apply to —

(A) any claim based upon the exercise or performance or the failure to exercise or perform a discretionary function regardless of whether the discretion be abused. . . .

Notes and Questions

1. Is the statutory language in the FSIA consistent with the restrictive theory of sovereign immunity as articulated in the Tate Letter?

2. Note the statute's definition of "commercial activity." Do you see any problems with this definition? Can you draft better statutory language? Or should Congress leave the definition of this term to the courts?

3. In *Republic of Austria v. Altmann*, 541 U.S. 677 (2004), the Supreme Court ruled that the FSIA can apply retroactively to actions taken before the passage of the FSIA.

4. On December 2, 2004, the UN General Assembly adopted the UN Convention on Jurisdictional Immunities of States and Their Property. The treaty reflects more than two decades of negotiations and is the first modern multilateral instrument comprehensively to address immunity issues. The treaty provides, in general, that a state is immune from the jurisdiction of another state unless an enumerated exception to immunity applies. With respect to commercial transactions, the Convention states:

> If a State engages in a commercial transaction with a foreign . . . person and, by virtue of the applicable rules of private international law, differences relating to the commercial transaction fall within the jurisdiction of a court of another State, the State cannot invoke immunity from that jurisdiction in a proceeding arising out of that commercial transaction.

In determining whether a particular transaction is a "commercial transaction," the Convention provides that "reference should be made primarily to the nature of the contract or transaction, but its purpose should also be taken into account if the parties to the contract or transaction have so agreed, or if, in the practice of the State of the forum, that purpose is relevant to determining the non-commercial character of the contract or transaction." The Convention was opened for signature on January 17, 2005, and will enter into force when 30 states have deposited their instruments of ratification, acceptance, approval or accession with the UN Secretary-General.

C. What Is Commercial Activity?

Despite codification, sovereign immunity cases continue to raise difficult issues. One recurring issue is determining when an activity is commercial and when it causes a direct effect in the United States for purposes of the commercial activity exception set forth in §1605(a)(2). Several early commercial activity cases involved tort actions where U.S. citizens were injured while abroad. For example, in *Martin v. Republic of South Africa*, 836 F.2d 91 (2d Cir. 1987), an African American was injured in a car accident while traveling in South Africa. A state-owned ambulance and two state-owned hospitals refused to give Martin prompt medical attention, allegedly because of his race. These actions aggravated Martin's injuries, and when he returned to the United States he incurred significant medical expenses. Courts in the United States rejected jurisdiction in this and similar cases, on the grounds that the direct effect of the defendant's actions — the plaintiff's injuries — occurred where the injury took place. The medical expenses and other damages suffered thereafter in the United States were the indirect effects of defendant's actions.

Other cases involved breach of contract claims filed by U.S. corporations. In these cases, courts often reasoned that a corporation can suffer only financial injury, and where U.S. firms had not been paid in the United States, they suffered a direct effect in the United States, triggering the commercial activity exception. Thus, as the *Antares* case worked its way through the courts, it was unclear how courts would treat tort claims brought by corporations or whether the direct effect clause would be satisfied when a defendant failed to pay a foreign corporation in the United States or a U.S. corporation abroad.

The *Weltover* case, excerpted below, was decided while the *Antares* litigation was pending. *Weltover* arises out of Argentina's foreign exchange crisis of the 1980s. To deal with this crisis, the Argentine Government entered into contracts to exchange local currency for U.S. dollars with domestic borrowers to enable these borrowers to pay their foreign debts. However, by 1982, Argentina's dollar reserves were insufficient to cover these contracts. As a result, Argentina refinanced these contracts by issuing government bonds, called Bonods, to the creditors. The Bonods provided that payment with specified interest would be made in dollars on scheduled dates in 1986 and 1987 into the holder's account in either New York, Frankfurt, Zurich, or London. Foreign creditors were given the option of either accepting the Bonods in satisfaction of the original debt or maintaining their relationship with the original Argentine debtor with the Bonods serving as a guarantee.

When the Bonods began to mature in May 1986, Argentina again lacked sufficient foreign currency reserves to retire the Bonods. The Argentine government then unilaterally rescheduled repayment of the Bonods. Two Panamanian corporations and a Swiss bank insisted on full payment into their New York accounts under the Bonods' terms. Argentina did not pay, and the three plaintiffs brought suit in the federal district court.

Republic of Argentina v. Weltover, Inc.

504 U.S. 607 (1992)

JUSTICE SCALIA delivered the opinion of the [unanimous] Court.

II

In the proceedings below, respondents relied only on the third clause of §1605(a)(2) [which removes immunity in actions based "upon an act outside the territory of the United States in connection with a commercial activity of the foreign state elsewhere and that act causes a direct effect in the United States."] . . . The dispute pertains to whether the unilateral refinancing of the Bonods was taken "in connection with a commercial activity" of Argentina, and whether it had a "direct effect in the United States." We address these issues in turn.

A

The FSIA defines "commercial activity" to mean:

"[E]ither a regular course of commercial conduct or a particular commercial transaction or act. The commercial character of an activity shall be determined by reference to the nature of the course of conduct or particular transaction or act, rather than by reference to its purpose."

This definition, however, leaves the critical term "commercial" largely undefined: The first sentence simply establishes that the commercial nature of an activity does *not* depend upon whether it is a single act or a regular course of conduct; and the second sentence merely specifies what element of the conduct determines commerciality (*i.e.*, nature rather than purpose), but still without saying what "commercial" means. Fortunately, however, the FSIA was not written on a clean slate. As we have noted, the Act (and the commercial exception in particular) largely codifies the so-called "restrictive" theory of foreign sovereign immunity first endorsed by the State Department in 1952. The meaning of "commercial" is the meaning generally attached to that term under the restrictive theory at the time the statute was enacted.

This Court did not have occasion to discuss the scope or validity of the restrictive theory of sovereign immunity until our 1976 decision in *Alfred Dunhill of London, Inc. v. Republic of Cuba*, 425 U.S. 682. . . . The plurality stated that . . . [a] foreign state engaging in "commercial" activities "do[es] not exercise powers peculiar to sovereigns"; rather, it "exercise[s] only those powers that can also be exercised by private citizens." *Id.* at 704. The dissenters did not disagree with this general description. . . .

In accord with that description, we conclude that when a foreign government acts, not as regulator of a market, but in the manner of a private player within it, the foreign sovereign's actions are "commercial" within the meaning of the FSIA. Moreover, because the Act provides that the commercial character of an act is to be determined by reference to its "nature" rather than its "purpose," the question is not whether the foreign government is acting with a profit motive or instead with the aim of fulfilling uniquely sovereign objectives. Rather, the issue is whether the particular actions that the foreign state performs (whatever the motive behind them) are the *type* of actions by which a private party engages in "trade and traffic or commerce." Thus, a foreign government's issuance of regulations limiting foreign currency exchange is a sovereign activity, because such authoritative control of commerce cannot be exercised by a private party; whereas a contract to buy army boots or even bullets is a "commercial" activity, because private companies can similarly use sales contracts to acquire goods.

The commercial character of the Bonods is confirmed by the fact that they are in almost all respects garden-variety debt instruments: They may be held by private parties; they are negotiable and may be traded on the international market (except in Argentina); and they promise a future stream of cash income. . . .

Argentina contends that, although the FSIA bars consideration of "purpose," a court must nonetheless fully consider the *context* of a transaction in order to determine whether it is "commercial." Accordingly, Argentina claims that the Court of Appeals erred by defining the relevant conduct in what Argentina considers an overly generalized, acontextual manner and by essentially adopting a *per se* rule that all "issuance of debt instruments" is "commercial." We have no occasion to consider such a *per se* rule, because it seems to us that even in full context, there is nothing about the issuance of these Bonods (except perhaps its purpose) that is not analogous to a private commercial transaction. . . .

Argentina argues that the Bonods differ from ordinary debt instruments in that they "were created by the Argentine Government to fulfill its obligations under a foreign exchange program designed to address a domestic credit crisis, and as a component of a program designed to control that nation's critical shortage of foreign exchange." . . . Indeed, Argentina asserts that the line between "nature" and "purpose" rests upon a "formalistic distinction [that] simply is neither useful nor warranted." We think this line of argument is squarely foreclosed by the language of the FSIA. However difficult it may be in some cases to separate "purpose" (*i.e.*, the *reason* why the foreign state engages in the activity) from "nature" (*i.e.*, the outward form of the conduct that the foreign state performs or agrees to perform), the statute unmistakably commands that to be done. . . . [I]t is irrelevant *why* Argentina participated in the bond market in the manner of a private actor; it matters only that it did so. We conclude that Argentina's issuance of the Bonods was a "commercial activity" under the FSIA.

B

The remaining question is whether Argentina's unilateral rescheduling of the Bonods had a "direct effect" in the United States. In addressing this issue, the Court of Appeals rejected the suggestion in the legislative history of the FSIA that an effect is not "direct" unless it is both "substantial" and "foreseeable." . . . As the Court of Appeals recognized, an effect is "direct" if it follows "as an immediate consequence of the defendant's . . . activity." . . .

We . . . have little difficulty concluding that Argentina's unilateral rescheduling of the maturity dates on the Bonods had a "direct effect" in the United States. Respondents had designated their accounts in New York as the place of payment, and Argentina made some interest payments into those accounts before announcing that it was rescheduling the payments. Because New York was thus the place of performance for Argentina's ultimate contractual obligations, the rescheduling of those obligations necessarily had a "direct effect" in the United States: Money that was supposed to have been delivered to a New York bank for deposit was not forthcoming. We reject Argentina's suggestion that the "direct effect" requirement cannot be satisfied where the plaintiffs are all foreign corporations with no other connections to the United States. . . .

We conclude that Argentina's issuance of the Bonods was a "commercial activity" under the FSIA; that its rescheduling of the maturity dates on those instruments was taken in connection with that commercial activity and had a "direct effect" in the United States; and that the District Court therefore properly asserted jurisdiction, under the FSIA, over the breach-of-contract claim based on that rescheduling. . . .

The Supreme Court's most recent examination of the commercial activity exception occurred in *Saudi Arabia v. Nelson,* 507 U.S. 349 (1993). Nelson, a U.S. citizen, was recruited in the United States to work in a government-owned hospital in Saudi Arabia. Nelson repeatedly advised hospital officials of certain defects in hospital equipment that endangered patients' lives. Hospital officials told Nelson to ignore these problems. In September 1984, hospital employees summoned Nelson to the hospital's security office, where Saudi government agents arrested him. The agents transported Nelson to a jail cell, where they allegedly tortured and beat him and kept him for four days without food. Nelson was then transferred to an overcrowded, rat-infested cell in another prison. At no time did Nelson learn the nature of the charges, if any, against him. For several days, the Saudi government failed to advise Nelson's family of his whereabouts, though a Saudi official eventually told Nelson's wife that he could arrange for her husband's release in exchange for sexual favors.

After the intercession of Senator Edward Kennedy, Nelson was freed and, after returning to the United States, in 1988 he and his wife sued Saudi Arabia in federal court. The key legal issue was whether Nelson's claims fell within the commercial activity exception. Justice Souter delivered the opinion of the court:

Saudi Arabia v. Nelson

507 U.S. 349 (1993)

Unlike Argentina's activities that we considered in *Weltover*, the intentional conduct alleged here (the Saudi Government's wrongful arrest, imprisonment, and torture of Nelson) could not qualify as commercial under the restrictive theory. The conduct boils down to abuse of the power of its police by the Saudi Government, and however monstrous such abuse undoubtedly may be, a foreign state's exercise of the power of its police has long been understood for purposes of the restrictive theory as peculiarly sovereign in nature. Exercise of the powers of police and penal officers is not the sort of action by which private parties can engage in commerce. "[S]uch acts as legislation, or the expulsion of an alien, or a denial of justice, cannot be performed by an individual acting in his own name. They can be performed only by the state acting as such." Lauterpacht, *The Problem of Jurisdictional Immunities of Foreign States*, 28 Brit. Y.B. Int'l L. 220, 225 (1951).

The Nelsons and their *amici* urge us to give significance to their assertion that the Saudi Government subjected Nelson to the abuse alleged as retaliation for his persistence in reporting hospital safety violations, and argue that the character of the mistreatment was consequently commercial. One *amicus*, indeed, goes so far as to suggest that the Saudi Government "often uses detention and torture to resolve commercial disputes." But this argument does not alter the fact that the powers allegedly abused were those of police and penal officers. In any event, the argument is off the point, for it goes to purpose, the very fact the Act renders irrelevant to the question of an activity's commercial character. Whatever may have been the Saudi Government's motivation for its allegedly abusive treatment of Nelson, it remains the case that the Nelsons' action is based upon a sovereign activity immune from the subject-matter jurisdiction of United States courts under the Act.

[Justice White, joined by Justice Blackmun, wrote:]

To run and operate a hospital, even a public hospital, is to engage in a commercial enterprise. . . . By the same token, warning an employee when he blows the whistle and taking retaliatory action, such as harassment, involuntary transfer, discharge, or other tortious behavior, although not prototypical commercial acts, are certainly well within the bounds of commercial activity. . . .

Indeed, I am somewhat at a loss as to what exactly the majority believes petitioners have done that a private employer could not. As countless cases attest, retaliation for whistle-blowing is not a practice foreign to the marketplace. Congress passed a statute in response to such behavior, see Whistleblower Protection Act of 1989, as have numerous States. . . .

At the heart of the majority's conclusion . . . is the fact that the hospital in this case chose to call in government security forces. I find this fixation on the intervention of police officers, and the ensuing characterization of the conduct as "peculiarly sovereign in nature," to be misguided. To begin, it fails to capture respondents' complaint in full. Far from being directed solely at the activities of the Saudi police, it alleges that agents of the *hospital* summoned Nelson to its security office because he reported safety concerns and that the *hospital* played a part in the subsequent beating and imprisonment. Without more, that type of behavior hardly qualifies as sovereign. Thus, even assuming for the sake of argument that the role of the official police somehow affected the nature of petitioners' conduct, the claim cannot be said to "res[t] entirely upon activities sovereign in character." At the very least it "consists of both commercial and sovereign elements," thereby presenting the specific question the majority chooses to elude. The majority's single-minded focus on the exercise of police power, while certainly simplifying the case, thus hardly does it justice.

Reliance on the fact that Nelson's employer enlisted the help of public rather than private security personnel is also at odds with Congress' intent. The purpose of the commercial exception being to prevent foreign states from taking refuge behind their sovereignty when they act as market participants, it seems to me that this is precisely the type of distinction we should seek to avoid. Because both the hospital and the police are agents of the state, the case in my mind turns on whether the sovereign is acting in a commercial capacity, not on whether it resorts to thugs or government officers to carry on its business. That, when the hospital calls in security to get even with a whistle-blower, it comes clothed in police apparel says more about the state-owned nature of the commercial enterprise than about the noncommercial nature of its tortious conduct. . . .

Nevertheless, I reach the same conclusion as the majority because petitioners' commercial activity was not "carried on in the United States." . . . Neither the hospital's employment practices, nor its disciplinary procedures, has any apparent connection to this country. On that basis, I agree that the Act does not grant the Nelsons access to our courts.

Notes and Questions

1. Both *Weltover* and *Nelson* present questions of statutory interpretation. Why would Congress enact a statute that, in effect, provides Swiss and Panamanian corporations suing the Argentine government access to U.S. courts but does not permit an American citizen, allegedly beaten by foreign government agents while working overseas, to pursue claims in U.S. courts?

2. Is the *Nelson* Court correct that torture and arbitrary detention are sovereign activities? Should it matter whether the activity alleged was unlawful under Saudi law? If a federal or state policeman is sued for beating a criminal suspect, do U.S. courts consider this a sovereign activity?

Courts outside the United States have considered whether sovereign immunity applies to acts of torture. In *Al Adsani v. Kuwait*, the UK courts held that Kuwait enjoyed sovereign immunity in a suit alleging torture. The European Court of Human Rights rejected plaintiff's claim that by granting Kuwait immunity, the UK courts failed to secure plaintiff's right not to be tortured under the European Convention on Human Rights. *Al-Adsani v. the United Kingdom*, ECHR 35763/97 (Eur. Ct. H.R. 2001). In *Jones v. Saudi Arabia*, [2005] Q.B. 699 (CA (Civ. Div.)), the United Kingdom Court of Appeal ruled that a torture victim could not sue Saudi Arabia, on grounds of state immunity, but could sue three Saudi officials implicated in the alleged torture. The relationship between immunity for foreign states and for public officials regarding acts of torture is discussed in Chapter 9.

3. An activity — such as operating the railroads or providing medical care — may be performed by private parties in one state and by the government in another state. In some states, the same activity may be carried out by both the government and private parties. In determining whether an act is commercial activity, should

the court look to the law and practice of the state engaged in the activity in question, or to the law and practice of the state where the suit has been filed?

4. A number of other states, including Canada and the United Kingdom, have codified the restrictive theory of sovereign immunity. As in the United States, however, codification has not eliminated the difficulty of distinguishing between the commercial and noncommercial acts of foreign sovereigns. Courts in various jurisdictions have struggled, in particular, with whether commercial activity should be defined by its nature or its purpose.

For example, Canada's State Immunity Act removes foreign sovereign immunity "in any proceedings that relate to any commercial activity of the foreign state." The Act defines "commercial activity" as "any particular transaction, act or conduct or any regular course of conduct that by reason of its nature is of a commercial character." Canada's Supreme Court first considered the commercial activity exception in *The United States of America v. The Public Service Alliance of Canada*, [1992] 2 S.C.R. 50. This case arose out of a union's effort to organize Canadian civilians who performed maintenance work at a U.S. naval base in Newfoundland, Canada. The union sought certification to bargain on behalf of the civilian personnel under the provisions of the Canada Labour Code. The United States objected on the grounds that it was immune from the jurisdiction of the Canada Labour Relations Board. In deciding whether the certification proceeding involved sovereign or commercial acts, Justice LaForest wrote:

> I find it difficult if not impossible to distinguish in a principled manner between the nature and purpose of employment relationships, and I would thus decline to follow this approach. Nature and purpose are interrelated, and it is impossible to determine the former without considering the latter. I do not accept that the definition of "commercial activity" in the Act precludes consideration of its purpose. . . . In many cases, it may be unnecessary to delve into metaphysical distinctions between the ontology and teleology of the activity in question. However, if consideration of purpose is helpful in determining the nature of an activity, then such considerations should be and are allowed under the Act.

Id. at 70.

Finding that the employment relationships at the base were both commercial and sovereign, the Court considered whether the certification effort at issue was "related to" the commercial or sovereign aspects of the employment relationships. The union was seeking to replace a series of private contractual relationships with a collective bargaining agreement governed by Canadian labor law. The Court held that such an agreement would involve decisions about

> what work will be done, when and by whom. Traditionally, decisions regarding this aspect of employment are reserved for management — in this case, the base commander. This aspect of the employment relationship will, in most instances, be "sovereign" in character since it goes to the heart of the operation of the base.

Id. at 77. For this reason, the Court held that the United States enjoyed sovereign immunity.

Do you agree that "it is impossible to distinguish in a principled manner between the nature and purpose" of the employment relationships at issue here? Would the U.S. courts decide a similar case in the same way? Should courts be focused on the nature of the activity or on whether removing immunity would interfere with the sovereign activities of a foreign state?

5. Does the difficulty in defining and identifying commercial activity suggest a deeper difficulty with the restrictive theory of immunity? Professor (later ICJ Judge) Hersch Lauterpacht argued:

> [I]t is no longer generally accepted that the economic activities of the state — such as state management of industry, state buying, and state selling — are necessarily of a purely 'private-law' nature . . . and that in engaging in them a state acts like a private person. In these and similar cases ostensibly removed from the normal field of its political and administrative activities, the state nevertheless acts as a public person for the general purposes of the community as a whole. . . . [T]he state always acts as a public person. It cannot act otherwise.

Hersch Lauterpacht, *The Problem of Jurisdictional Immunities of Foreign States*, 28 Brit. Y.B. Intl. L. 220, 224 (1951). Is there a persuasive response to this argument?

————————————

In the *Antares* action, the district court granted Nigeria's motion to dismiss for lack of subject matter jurisdiction, and the Second Circuit Court of Appeals affirmed in an opinion by Judge Altimari. Antares petitioned the Supreme Court for a writ of certiorari. The Supreme Court vacated the Second Circuit decision and remanded for further consideration in light of *Weltover*. How should the case now be decided?

Antares Aircraft, L.P. v. Federal Republic of Nigeria

999 F.2d 33 (2d Cir. 1993)

WINTER, CIRCUIT JUDGE
    . . . The following is not in dispute. The "act outside the territory of the United States" was the allegedly wrongful detention of the plane in Nigeria. The detention of the aircraft and collection of fees were "in connection with a commercial activity of the foreign state." The final element of the "commercial activity" exception poses the issue remaining on this remand, namely, in light of *Weltover*, did the detention of the aircraft cause "a direct effect in the United States"?
    In *Weltover*, the Court endorsed our view that "an effect is 'direct' if it follows 'as an immediate consequence of the defendant's . . . activity.'" . . . The Court also rejected as "too remote and attenuated," any suggestion that the ground for the "direct effect in the United States" was a diminution in New York's status as "a world financial leader." Nevertheless, the Court had "little difficulty concluding that Argentina's unilateral rescheduling of the maturity dates on the [bonds] had a 'direct effect' in the United States" because New York was the contractually designated "place of performance."
    Although the Court did not expressly adopt our "legally significant acts" test [for determining where the "direct effect" occurs], it used a similar analysis. *Weltover* involved a breach of contract, and the Court found decisive the fact that the contractually designated place of performance was New York. The "legally significant" act was thus the breach that occurred in the United States. In tort, the analog to contract law's place of performance is the locus of the tort, here Nigeria. However, the analogy is not precise. Although a contractual provision designating the United States as the place of performance is sufficient to *vest* jurisdiction under the FSIA, a foreign tort is not necessarily sufficient to *deprive* federal courts of

jurisdiction because the foreign tort may have had sufficient contacts with the United States to establish the requisite "direct effect" this country.

However, in the instant matter, all legally significant acts took place in Nigeria. The aircraft was registered in Nigeria. There is no evidence that the use of the aircraft was related to substantial commerce with the United States. The detention of, and physical damage to, the plane happened in Nigeria. The alleged conversion thus occurred in Nigeria. Moreover, the negotiations over, and the payment of, the outstanding fees occurred in Nigeria and utilized Nigerian currency.

That the money came from a bank account in New York is a fact but one without legal significance to the alleged tort. The Nigerian authorities were indifferent to the geographic location of the source of the money used to pay the fees. Their demands would have been satisfied had Antares paid from a London checking account or borrowed the funds from a bank in Lagos. Wherever the source of the money, payment had to be in Nigeria, just as the payment in *Weltover* had to be in New York. The tort thus began in Nigeria with the detention of the aircraft and ended in Nigeria with the payment of the money. Unlike *Weltover*, where the parties had agreed that performance was to occur in New York, the sole act connected to the United States in the instant matter, the drawing of a check on a bank in New York, was entirely fortuitous and entirely unrelated to the liability of the appellees.

Antares argues that a "direct effect" of the tort occurred in the United States because an American partnership suffered a financial loss. We are unpersuaded. To be sure, the detention of Antares' sole asset affected the financial well-being of the American partnership. However, the fact that an American individual or firm suffers some financial loss from a foreign tort cannot, standing alone, suffice to trigger the exception.

If a loss to an American individual and firm resulting from a foreign tort were sufficient standing alone to satisfy the direct effect requirement, the commercial activity exception would in large part eviscerate the FSIA's provision of immunity for foreign states. Many commercial disputes, like the present one, can be pled as the torts of conversion or fraud and would, if appellant is correct, result in litigation concerning events with no connection with the United States other than the citizenship or place of incorporation of the plaintiff. Similarly, personal injury actions based on torts with no connection with this country, except for the plaintiff's citizenship, might be brought under appellant's theory. For example, an American citizen injured in a foreign city by a government-owned bus company might sue here if the commercial activity exception is triggered solely by the fact that the citizen's wealth is diminished by the accident. We find it difficult to characterize such an effect, standing alone, as "direct" or to read into this otherwise somewhat restrictive legislation an all-encompassing jurisdiction for foreign torts.

We therefore reaffirm our prior decision.

ALTIMARI, CIRCUIT JUDGE, dissenting:

Because I believe that the Supreme Court's affirmance of this Court's decision in *Weltover* coupled with the Court's decision to vacate and remand the instant case for further consideration in light of *Weltover*, indicates that the Court believes that an American firm suffers a direct effect in the United States as a result of the expropriation of its property by a foreign sovereign, I must respectfully dissent.

Antares Aircraft, L.P. is an American limited partnership, whose legal status is not unlike that of a corporation. As we noted in *Weltover*, "[w]here the plaintiff is a corporation, 'the relevant inquiry under the direct effect clause . . . is whether the corporation has suffered a "direct" financial loss.'" In *Weltover* we found it clear that "a foreign sovereign's improper commercial acts cause an effect to the foreign corporate plaintiff in that plaintiff's place of incorporation or principal place of business." Such must also hold true for an American firm seeking an assertion of jurisdiction under the Foreign Sovereign Immunities Act in order to recover a plane seized by a foreign sovereign.

Obviously corporations and limited partnerships are not natural persons, and consequently can only suffer financial rather than physical injuries. As noted above, in *Weltover* we concluded that these financial injuries are directly felt where a firm was organized or where its principal place of business is located. By contrast, an individual suffers a physical injury at the location where the mishap occurs. Therefore, especially given the Supreme Court's affirmance of our analysis in *Weltover*, I find the majority's reliance on personal injury cases to be unpersuasive. . . . Accordingly, upon further reflection in light of the Supreme Court's affirmance of our decision in *Weltover* and its subsequent remand of the instant case in light of *Weltover*, I conclude that the American partnership suffered a direct effect in the United States within the meaning of §1605(a)(2) of the Foreign Sovereign Immunities Act.

Notes and Questions

1. Does either the text of the commercial activity exception or the underlying purposes of the exception suggest that the NAA should be immune from suit in U.S. courts?

2. Is *Antares* consistent with *Weltover*? Why does the failure to make payment in the United States to a foreign firm create a "direct effect in the United States," but the payment of money by a U.S. firm from a U.S. bank account not create a "direct effect in the United States"?

D. Note on Litigating State-Sponsored Terrorism in U.S. Courts

Although a central purpose of the FSIA was to remove sovereign immunity from certain types of commercial disputes, litigants soon attempted to bring a broader set of claims under the statute. For example, after the downing of Pan Am flight 103 over Lockerbie, Scotland, an incident discussed in detail in Chapter 14, representatives of the victims sued Libya in federal court. They argued that Libya had violated a *jus cogens* norm by participating in the bombing and thereby waived its immunity under the FSIA. In *Smith v. Socialist People's Libyan Arab Jamahiriya*, 101 F.3d 239 (2d Cir.), *cert. denied*, 520 U.S. 1204 (1997), the court found this argument "appealing" but unsupported by the statute or its legislative history and dismissed the action for lack of subject matter jurisdiction. The plaintiffs' plight in *Smith*, along with those of similarly situated plaintiffs in other suits, provided the political momentum that led Congress to add a "terrorism exception" to the FSIA. This provision removes sovereign immunity for cases

> in which money damages are sought against a foreign state for personal injury or death that was caused by an act of torture, extrajudicial killing, aircraft sabotage, hostage taking, or the provision of material support or resources . . . for such an act. . . .

28 U.S.C. §1605(a)(7). The statutory phrase "provision of material support or resources" is defined broadly to include provision of monies, lodging, training, weapons, personnel, and the like. Congress expressly directed that this provision apply retroactively. This amendment removes immunity only from a foreign state identified by the U.S. State Department as a "state sponsor of terrorism." As of May 2006, Cuba, Iran, North Korea, Sudan, and Syria had been designated as terrorist states. (Iraq was removed from the list in 2003, and in 2006 the United States announced its intent to remove Libya from the list.) In addition, either the claimant or the victim must have been a national of the United States when the act occurred, and, if the act occurred in the foreign state against which the claim is brought, the claimant must afford the foreign state a reasonable opportunity to resolve the claim. Shortly thereafter, Congress adopted a further amendment to the FSIA (the "Flatow amendment") creating a private right of action against officials, employees, and agents of foreign states for the conduct identified in §1605(a)(7).

In several cases brought against foreign states, the defendant state has refused to participate and default judgments were entered; a number of these actions have resulted in substantial damage awards. See, e.g., *Alejandre v. Cuba*, 996 F. Supp. 1239 (S.D. Fla. 1997) ($190 million); *Sutherland v. Iran*, 151 F. Supp. 2d 27 (D.D.C. 2001) ($350 million). However, the continued viability of civil suits against states that sponsor terrorism has recently been thrown into question. In *Cicippio-Puleo v. Iran*, 353 F.3d 1024 (D.C. Cir. 2004), the court held that "neither 28 U.S.C. Sec. 1605(a)(7) nor the Flatow amendment, nor the two considered in tandem, creates a private right of action against a foreign government. Section 1605(a)(7) merely waives the immunity of a foreign state without creating a cause of action against it, and the Flatow Amendment only provides a private right of action against officials, employees, and agents of a foreign state, and not against the foreign state itself. . . ."

Those plaintiffs who have obtained judgments have found it difficult to collect. Almost all of the assets owned by states designated as sponsors of terrorism have been frozen by the Treasury Department. In October 2000, Congress passed a law permitting certain individuals who had obtained judgments against Iran and Cuba—but not other states—to obtain compensation. The United States will pay those who have judgments against Cuba from frozen Cuban assets under control of the U.S. government; those with judgments against Iran will be paid from the U.S. Treasury (as there no longer are frozen Iranian assets under the control of the U.S. government), and the U.S. will then seek to recover the funds through the U.S.-Iran Claims Tribunal or through negotiations with Iran.

Between 2000 and 2004, U.S. courts continued to issue judgments against terrorist states, and during this time a number of proposals to facilitate payment to certain classes of plaintiffs were introduced in Congress. In June 2003, Senator Richard Lugar introduced an Administration-backed proposal that would establish an administrative procedure to provide compensation to victims of state terrorism as an alternative to suits under the FSIA's terrorism exception. At a hearing on this proposal, the State Department Legal Adviser stated that "[t]he current litigation-based system of compensation is inequitable, unpredictable, occasionally costly to the U.S. taxpayer, and damaging to foreign policy and national security goals of this country." Plaintiff's lawyers countered that the proposal would deny victims their day in court and fail to hold terrorist states accountable for their actions. As of December 2005, no further action had been taken on this proposal.

Notes and Questions

1. How can one determine whether the FSIA's terrorism exception is a valuable tool in the fight against terrorism? Is it likely to deter future acts of terrorism? To punish guilty parties? To provide relief for injured parties? Should cases like these be litigated in U.S. courts?

2. Why might a Member of Congress vote against amending the FSIA to add the terrorism exception? Would you expect the State Department to support this amendment? In testimony before Congress, a State Department lawyer argued:

> [The terrorism exception] would permit actions in the United States against certain foreign states for terrorist acts committed anywhere in the world. Not only does such a provision extend well beyond the reach of our existing statute, but it also diverges significantly from the general practice of states. . . . We fully share the concerns over terrorism that underlie this proposal, but we do not believe such an expansion of the jurisdiction of our courts would be prudent.
>
> Consistency of the FSIA with established international practice is important. If we deviate from that practice and assert jurisdiction over foreign states for acts that are generally perceived by the international community as falling within the scope of immunity, this would tend to erode the credibility of the FSIA. We have made substantial efforts over the years to persuade foreign states to participate in our judicial system — to appear and defend in actions against them under the FSIA. That kind of broad participation serves the interests of all. If we expand our jurisdiction in ways that cause other states to question our statute, this could undermine the broad participation we seek. It could also diminish our ability to influence other countries to abandon the theory of absolute immunity and adopt the restrictive view of sovereign immunity, which the United States has followed for over forty years.
>
> These problems could be exacerbated where the divergence from state practice concerned alleged deliberate governmental wrongdoing. Domestic judicial proceedings designed to respond to such action would necessarily involve particular sensitivity, especially when a violation of important rules of international or domestic law was alleged. States are generally reluctant to enter into the domestic courts of another state to defend themselves against charges of serious violations of law.
>
> This bill could also lead to other undesirable consequences for our foreign relations. Current U.S. law allows the U.S. Government to fine-tune the application of sanctions against state-sponsors of terrorism, increasing them or decreasing them when in the national interest. In addition, the U.S. Government frequently coordinates closely with other nations at the UN and elsewhere on the imposition of sanctions and the development of joint positions vis-à-vis acts of terrorism. The possibility of civil suits and potential judgments against state-sponsors of terrorism would inject a new unpredictable element in these very delicate relationships. Such proceedings could in some instances interfere with U.S. counter-terrorism objectives. . . .
>
> Finally, . . . [i]f the United States extends the jurisdiction of its courts to embrace cases involving alleged wrongdoing by a foreign state outside the United States, we would have to expect that some other states could do likewise. However, there is of course no guarantee that any action taken by other states would precisely mirror our own. If other states were to expand the jurisdiction of their own courts, they might not limit such action to terrorism, for example, but could seek to include as well other kinds of alleged wrongdoing that could be of concern to us. . . .

Testimony of Jamison S. Borek before the Subcommittee on Courts and Administrative Practice of the Senate Committee on the Judiciary, June 21, 1994.

Are these arguments persuasive?

3. Other United States statutes may also be used to address international acts of terrorism. Under 18 U.S.C. §2333, which was enacted in 1992, any United States national "injured in his or her person, property, or business by reason of an act of international terrorism . . . may sue therefor in [federal district court] and shall recover threefold the damages he or she sustains." In a case of first impression, the Seventh Circuit held that this statute does not impose liability upon those who fund terrorist organizations without knowing or suspecting that the funds will be used in a terrorist act. However, funding that meets traditional tort definitions of "aiding and abetting" an act of terrorism will give rise to liability under section 2333. *Boim v. Quranic Literacy Institute*, 291 F.3d 1000 (7th Cir. 2002). Do you think civil actions against those who fund terrorist acts will prove an effective tool against terrorism? Or will terrorist organizations simply move assets and money-laundering operations into other states?

PART IV

The Protection of Human Dignity

Over the last several centuries, the formation and evolution of the modern, centralized, bureaucratic state has facilitated enormous economic growth, dramatic technological innovation, and lasting cultural and other forms of human achievement. But the unparalleled power of the modern state has also often been directed against individuals, and wars between states or struggles for power within states have cost at least 100 million lives in the last 60 years alone.

Modern international law emerged in tandem with the emergence of states as the eminent form of political organization. In keeping with that history, international law until relatively recently focused almost exclusively on the rights and responsibilities of states. To the extent that individuals had rights in international law, they were derivative of the rights of the individual's state of nationality.

The status of the individual in international law has changed substantially in recent years, as states and other actors have increasingly sought to protect the basic human dignity of all individuals through law. In this regard, three rapidly developing, related, and to some extent overlapping bodies of law are relevant: international human rights, international humanitarian law, and international criminal law.

International humanitarian law is the oldest of the three bodies of law. As Professor Yoram Dinstein observes,

> Whereas the development of the international human rights of peacetime began in earnest only after Word War II, some fundamental freedoms of wartime had a seminal existence even before World War I. Insofar as many peacetime human rights are concerned, 1948—the year in which the U.N. General Assembly adopted the Universal Declaration of Human Rights—was the *die a quo* from which they first started to crystallize in international law. By contrast, as regards numerous wartime human rights, 1949—the year in which the Geneva Conventions were opened for ratification—was the *dies ad quemi* which finalized their consolidation as binding legal norms . . . . [H]istorically the law of war is the most ancient part of international law.

Yoram Dinstein, *Human Rights in Armed Conflict: International Humanitarian Law,* in Human Rights in International Law 345, 347 (Theodor Meron ed., 1984).

The International Committee of the Red Cross (ICRC), a non-governmental organization (NGO) that has played a major role in the development of international humanitarian law, offers the following description of the relationship between international
human rights and international humanitarian law:

> Both seek to protect the individual, though they do so in different circumstances and
> in different ways.
> Humanitarian law applies in situations of armed conflict, whereas human rights, or at
> least some of them, protect the individual at all times, in war and peace alike.
> While the purpose of humanitarian law is to protect victims by endeavouring to limit
> the suffering caused by war, human rights seek to protect the individual and further his
> development.
> Humanitarian law is primarily concerned with the treatment of persons who have
> fallen into the hands of the adverse party, and with the manner in which hostilities are
> conducted, whereas by limiting the power of the State over individuals, human rights
> essentially seek to prevent arbitrary behaviour. It is not the aim of human rights to regulate
> the ways in which military operations are conducted.
> In order to ensure that it is respected, humanitarian law establishes mechanisms that
> institute a form of ongoing control over its implementation; it places the emphasis on
> cooperation between the parties to the conflict and a neutral intermediary with a view to
> preventing violations . . . .
> The mechanisms for monitoring human rights are extremely varied. In many cases,
> the appropriate institutions are required to establish whether or not a State has respected
> the law. For instance, the European Court of Human Rights may, upon completion of
> proceedings brought by an individual, declare that the European Convention on Human
> Rights has been violated by a national authority. The latter is then obliged to take the steps
> necessary to ensure that the internal situation meets the requirements of the Convention.
> The mechanisms for implementing human rights are essentially intended to make good
> any damage sustained . . . .
> The international human rights instruments contain clauses that authorize States
> confronted by a serious public threat to suspend the rights enshrined by them. An excep-
> tion is made for certain fundamental rights provided for in each treaty, which must be
> respected in all circumstances and can never be waived regardless of the treaty that
> contains them. In particular, these include the right to life, the prohibition of torture and
> inhuman punishment or treatment, slavery and servitude, and the principle of legality and
> non-retroactivity of the law . . . .
> Since humanitarian law applies precisely to the exceptional situations which con-
> stitute armed conflicts, the content of human rights law that States must respect in all
> circumstances . . . tends to converge with the fundamental and legal guarantees provided
> by humanitarian law, e.g. the prohibition of torture and summary executions.

International Humanitarian Law: Answers to Your Questions, *www.icrc.org*.
There is also a close relationship between international humanitarian law and international criminal law. As the ICRC explains, states have an obligation to prosecute
individuals who commit certain violations of the laws of war:

> On becoming party to the Geneva Conventions, States are obliged to take the legislative
> measures necessary to punish persons guilty of grave breaches of the Conventions.
> States are also bound to prosecute in their own courts any person suspected of having
> committed a grave breach of the Conventions, or to hand them over for judgment to

another State. In other words, the perpetrators of grave breaches, i.e. war criminals, must be prosecuted at all times and in all places, and States are responsible for ensuring that this is done.

Generally speaking, a State's criminal laws apply only to crimes committed on its territory or by its own nationals. International humanitarian law goes further in that it requires States to seek out and punish any person who has committed a grave breach, irrespective of his nationality or the place where the offence was committed. This principle of universal jurisdiction is essential to guarantee that grave breaches are effectively repressed.

Such prosecutions may be brought either by the national courts of the different States or by an international authority. In this connection, the International Criminal Tribunals for the former Yugoslavia and Rwanda were set up by the UN Security Council in 1993 and 1994, respectively, to try those accused of war crimes committed during the conflicts in those countries.

Id.

But not all violations of international humanitarian law are subject to criminal prosecution. Moreover, international criminal law permits or requires prosecution of many offenses that are not part of the corpus of international humanitarian law—for example, drug trafficking, piracy, and aircraft hijacking. Accordingly, although there is a considerable overlap between these two bodies of law, they nonetheless differ in many ways.

Much has changed in international law since World War II. Perhaps most striking is the rapid development of legal norms and institutions intended to protect basic human dignity. As Nobel laureate Elie Wiesel notes:

> The defense of human rights has, in the last fifty years, become a kind of worldwide secular religion . . . . Statesmen, high officials, and diplomats serve as moral watchmen . . . . They make it their business to know and let other people know each time an opposition member is punished, a journalist stifled, a prisoner tortured . . . . Crimes against humanity are part of the public domain.

Elie Wiesel, *A Tribute to Human Rights, in* The Universal Declaration of Human Rights 2 (Yael Danieli, Elsa Stamatopoulou & Clarence Dias eds., 1999).

At the same time, efforts to render effective existing human rights, humanitarian law, and international criminal law are fraught with difficulty. Chapters 7, 8, and 9 examine the issues raised by each of these different but related areas.

7

The Claims of Individuals on States: International Human Rights

In the seventeenth and eighteenth centuries, there was no sharp distinction between international and national law. Individuals possessed legal personality—and with it the ability to assert legal rights—under both bodies of law. But the positivists who came to dominate legal theory in the nineteenth century viewed the law applicable to sovereign states in their interactions with each other as distinct from the law that applied to individuals. In this conception, only states could be viewed as subjects of international law, only states could participate in law making, and only states could possess and assert rights under international law. Thus, for example, the Statute of the Permanent Court of International Justice (PCIJ), and the statute of its successor, the International Court of Justice (ICJ), both provided that only states may be parties to cases before those courts. Individuals might be able to assert rights under municipal law in connection with international transactions, but they could not bring claims against states, at least not in international fora. Moreover, how a state treated its own nationals was viewed largely as an internal matter. Individuals could not assert rights against their own state on the international plane.

International law did take cognizance of the ways in which a state treated foreign nationals present in the state's territory, but in a strained and artificial way. Under the traditional law of state responsibility, all states have an obligation to treat foreign nationals within their jurisdiction in accordance with an ill-defined minimum standard of justice. Absent special agreements, states ordinarily have no obligations to admit foreign nationals to their territory, but if they do admit them, they must act toward them in ways consistent with those minimum international standards.

Foreign nationals, in turn, must ordinarily accept the legal regime of the state in which they find themselves. If a state injures a foreign national in a way that violates an international legal obligation—if, for example, a state unjustly expropriates a foreign national's property or deliberately or recklessly causes physical injury to a foreign national (whether the national is an individual or a corporation)—then the state may incur responsibility under international law. But under the traditional law of state responsibility, the responsibility of the state at issue does not extend directly to the injured foreign national. Instead, responsibility exists vis-à-vis the national's state, which may in its own discretion decide to assert a claim against the state responsible for the injury, provided the injured national has first exhausted local remedies. By espousing the claim of its national, the offended state exercises its own right of diplomatic protection. It is under no obligation to exercise that right, and if it succeeds in obtaining compensation from the offending state, it has no obligation to share that compensation with its injured national.

The traditional approach to state responsibility and diplomatic protection proceeded from the assumption that only states were subjects of international law and thus capable of exercising rights and accepting responsibilities under it. From this perspective, injuries to individuals could only be deemed violations of international law if viewed as an injury to their state. As the PCIJ put it,

> It is an elementary principle of international law that a State is entitled to protect its subjects, when injured by acts contrary to international law committed by another State, from whom they have been unable to obtain satisfaction through ordinary channels. By taking up the case of one of its subjects and by resorting to diplomatic action or international judicial proceedings on his behalf, a State is in reality asserting its own rights . . . to ensure, in the person of its subjects, respect for the rules of international law.

Mavrommatis Palestine Concessions (Greece v. United Kingdom), P.C.I.J. Ser. A, No. 2, at 12 (1924).

In some issue areas, states did manifest a concern for human welfare that extended beyond the treatment of their own nationals abroad. As early as the seventeenth century, states in Europe entered into treaties designed to confer limited protections on religious minorities in other states. In the nineteenth century, states in Europe (and eventually in the Americas) worked to outlaw slavery and the international trade in slaves through international conventions. And as we consider more fully in Chapter 8, modern international humanitarian law, the body of rules designed to render the conduct of warfare more humane, had its origins in the mid-nineteenth century.

The aftermath of World War I generated innovative experiments in the international legal treatment of minorities through the League of Nations minorities treaty system. Concerned about the possible destabilizing influence of national minorities, the victors in World War I imposed treaties on certain states in Eastern and Central Europe designed to guarantee fair treatment to members of ethnic, linguistic, or religious minorities. Moreover, international efforts to improve the lot of workers began around the same time, with the establishment of the International Labour Office (now the International Labour Organization (ILO)) in 1919. Since its formation, the ILO has promulgated numerous treaties, reports, and other instruments designed to improve the condition of workers and their families. But both the League treaties and the ILO's work were limited in their subject matter focus, and the former were also limited in their application to particular states. In general, most states continued to regard their treatment of their own nationals as largely their own affair.

The atrocities of World War II forced a reassessment of the position of individuals under international law. Reliance on the doctrine of state responsibility was clearly insufficient to deal with abuses committed by a state against its own nationals, since no state could be expected to bring an action against itself. Recognizing this, the Allied Powers during World War II—the United States, the United Kingdom, France, and the Soviet Union—pledged to prosecute individuals responsible for atrocities committed during the course of the war. This decision, and the Nuremberg and related trials that followed the war, marked a turning point in attitudes toward the individual's status in international law. Under the Nuremberg Charter, which is discussed in greater detail in Chapter 9, individuals could be prosecuted for crimes against peace, war crimes, and crimes against humanity. The last category was broad enough to encompass certain crimes committed by a state against its own nationals.

During and immediately after World War II, widespread revulsion at the Holocaust prompted civic and religious groups in many countries to call for inclusion of an international bill of rights in the UN Charter. Many organizations and individuals, including the American Law Institute, the ILO, the American Jewish Committee, and the American Bar Association, prepared draft bills of rights. At the Inter-American Conference on War and Peace, held in Mexico in early 1945, 21 Latin American states joined in the call for a bill of rights in the UN Charter, and three of those states later prepared a draft. Ultimately, other issues dominated the discussions in San Francisco during which the UN Charter was prepared, and no bill of rights was included in it. But the Charter contains multiple references to human rights. The Preamble to the Charter states the determination of the peoples of the United Nations "to reaffirm faith in international human rights," and Article 55 commits UN members to promote "universal respect for, and observance of, human rights and fundamental freedoms for all . . . ." Similarly, Article 56 of the UN Charter requires UN member states to cooperate in promoting human rights.

Moreover, Article 68 of the UN Charter contemplated the formation of a UN Commission on Human Rights to conduct research on human rights and to draft treaties and other instruments for the articulation and promotion of human rights. Indeed, as President Truman told the delegates to the San Francisco conference, the UN Charter provided "good reason to expect the framing of an international bill of rights, acceptable to all the nations involved," and one that "will be as much a part of international life as our own Bill of Rights is a part of our Constitution." The Human Rights Commission was formed in 1946.

In the years that followed, individual states, the United Nations, and various regional organizations, including the Council of Europe, the Organization of American States, and the Organization of African Unity, working with countless non-governmental human rights organizations, scholars, and lawyers, have developed an extensive body of human rights treaties, declarations, and related instruments in an effort to develop and clarify international human rights norms. These same actors have also developed a complex system of institutions designed to monitor and to some extent to implement existing norms. These institutions include regional human rights courts, treaty bodies, groups of experts, and more.

The following sections of this chapter illustrate the development and application of human rights law by looking at several illustrative problems. In Section I we consider the application of universal instruments designed to protect fundamental liberty and personal security interests, by examining efforts to regulate Israel's interrogation practices and the controvery surounding recent U.S. interrogation policies. Section II examines disagreements over states' freedom to limit the scope of their obligations under human rights treaties through reservations. Section III examines economic, social, and cultural rights. As indicated in that section, the line between the two categories of rights is often hard to draw, and the principal international human rights treaties often include both types of rights. Nonetheless, the theoretical and practical problems associated with each set of rights differ sufficiently to warrant separate consideration. Section IV of this chapter examines efforts to protect the rights of women through the development of group-specific norms and processes.

I. PROTECTING POLITICAL AND CIVIL RIGHTS: ISRAEL'S USE OF "MODERATE PHYSICAL PRESSURE"

Contemporary articulations of political and civil rights, as claims of individuals on their society and government, find their principal historical roots in seventeenth and eighteenth century European political philosophy, though one can find related ideas in many cultures and periods. John Locke's insistence on rights to life, liberty, and property, and Jean Jacques Rousseau's proclamation that "man is born free," resonate in the 1776 American Declaration of Independence and its "self-evident" truth that "all men are created equal." Following the American Declaration, the newly proclaimed independent American states began drafting individual bills of rights, which influenced the 1789 French Declaration of the Rights of Man and the virtually contemporaneous Bill of Rights familiar to all American law students as the first ten amendments to the U.S. Constitution. The political philosophy animating these various instruments, and the instruments themselves, serve as the principal antecedents to contemporary international human rights treaties dealing with civil and political rights. In general, such instruments seek to guarantee everyone physical security and integrity through, for example, protections against torture and the arbitrary deprivation of life; equal treatment, through norms mandating nondiscrimination and the equal protection of the law; and basic liberties, such as the freedom to practice one's religion or express one's political views. In this section we seek to illustrate the development and application of political and civil rights through an examination of efforts to eliminate one of the most fundamental assaults on human dignity: torture.

In reviewing the materials below, consider whether international human rights have a coherent philosophical and jurisprudential basis; whether state or societal interests should ever be balanced against an individual's rights to liberty and personal integrity, and, if so, in what circumstances; what role international human rights norms should play in shaping decisions by governments and private actors; and what strategies states and other actors should pursue to see human rights norms more effectively implemented.

A. The Problem

The modern state of Israel was founded in 1948. From the outset, Israel has had to struggle for its survival. It has fought a series of wars with neighboring Arab states and has engaged in a low-intensity but persistent conflict with Palestinians seeking to establish their own state on territory claimed by Israel. Since its founding, Israel has been the target of frequent terrorist attacks. To combat such attacks, Israel has adopted a number of stringent measures, which until recently included the use of what Israel terms "moderate physical pressure" in the interrogation of individuals suspected of involvement in terrorist acts. The legitimacy of such methods has been hotly contested.

Primary responsibility for combating terrorist attacks within Israel rests with the General Security Service (GSS). In 1987, a special Commission of Inquiry appointed by the government issued a report (the Landau Report) examining the authority of the GSS to investigate and interrogate those suspected of terrorist acts. The Report concluded that GSS investigators were entitled to apply "a moderate degree of physical pressure" in order to elicit information required to save human lives, subject to certain restrictions. Among other things, the Report stated that such pressure "must not reach physical torture, ill-treatment of the interogee or severe harm to his honour which deprives him of human dignity."

In ensuing years the GSS was the subject of frequent complaints by detainees, Israeli human rights groups, and international human rights advocates, who charged that the GSS routinely used interrogation methods amounting to torture against a large number of Palestinian detainees. According to the Israeli human rights group B'Tselem, such methods were employed against "thousands" of detainees since the Landau Report, even though "some were innocent of any offense and many were released without being indicted or administratively detained."

The methods used by the GSS to elicit information included severe shaking, prolonged interrogation in awkward and painful positions, excessive tightening of handcuffs, and prolonged sleep deprivation. The Israeli government denied that these methods amounted to torture and justified its practices as necessary to save lives and to protect Israel's national security.

Israel's law pertaining to torture is set out below.

Israeli Penal Code (1977)

Article 277

A public servant who commits one of the following is liable to imprisonment for three years:

(1) uses or directs the use of force or violence against a person for the purpose of extorting from him or from anyone in whom he has an interest a confession of an offense or information relating to an offense;

(2) threatens any person, or directs any person to be threatened, with injury to his person or property, or to the person or property of anyone in whom he has an interest, for the purpose of extorting from him a confession of an offense or information relating to an offense.

Article 34 (ii)

A person shall not bear criminal liability for an act which was immediately necessary in order to save a life, freedom, person or property, be it his own or that of another, from a concrete danger of severe harm stemming from the conditions existing at the time of the act, and having no other way but to commit it.

B. International Human Rights Law and Torture

The UN Charter, to which almost all states are party, commits all UN members to cooperate in the promotion of human rights. But the Charter does not enumerate or define what is meant by human rights; it does not identify a particular philosophical basis for human rights; and it does not give human rights priority over the right of a state to be free, in the words of Article 2(7) of the Charter, from intervention "in matters which are essentially within the domestic jurisdiction of any state." As Professor Louis Henkin explains:

> Perhaps because we now wish to, we tend to exaggerate what the Charter did for human rights. The Charter made the promotion of human rights a purpose of the United Nations; perhaps without full appreciation of the extent of the penetration of statehood that was involved, it thereby recognized and established that relations between a state and its own inhabitants were a matter of international concern. But the Charter did not erode state autonomy and the requirement of state consent to new human rights law. The purpose which the Charter declared for the United Nations was only "[t]o achieve international co-operation [i.e., consenting co-operation] . . . in promoting and encouraging [not mandating] respect for human rights. . . ." (Art. 1 (3)). The Charter lodged overall responsibility for achieving that purpose in the General Assembly which has authority only to "make recommendations" for the purpose of "assisting in the realization of human rights" (Art. 13). The Charter gave direct responsibility for human rights to the Economic and Social Council (ECOSOC), which "may make recommendations for the purpose of promoting respect for, and observance of, human rights and fundamental freedoms for all" (Art. 62 (2)), and "may prepare draft conventions" (for voluntary adherence) (Art. 62 (3)). The Charter directed ECOSOC to establish a commission "for the *promotion* of human rights" (Art. 68) (emphasis added.)
>
>   . . . Surely, the Charter did not provide, clearly and explicitly, that every state party to the Charter assumes legal obligations not to violate the human rights, or some human rights, of persons subject to its jurisdiction.
>
>   In 1945, the principal Powers were not prepared to derogate from the established character of the international system by establishing law and legal obligation that would penetrate statehood in that radical way. . . .

Louis Henkin, International Law: Politics and Values 174-175 (1995).

When the Human Rights Commission was formed in 1946, its principal initial role was to prepare an international bill of rights that would flesh out the human rights commitments of the UN Charter. Eleanor Roosevelt, as Chair of the Human Rights Commission, asked John Humphrey, director of the UN Secretariat's Human Rights Division, to prepare an initial draft. He did so, coming up with 48 articles that he intended to cover the most basic human rights in a way that would be short, clear, and acceptable to all UN member states. Humphrey's draft went through numerous revisions, prompted by discussion among the Human Rights Commission delegates and comments received from many countries and dozens of non-governmental organizations.

For much of the two-year drafting period, the Human Rights Commission debated whether its mandate from the UN's Economic and Social Council (ECO-SOC) was to prepare a declaration or a treaty. Most of the members, Australia and the United Kingdom in particular, with support from Belgium, China, France, India, and Panama, interpreted the direction to prepare an international bill of rights as implying preparation of a draft treaty. In their view, only a treaty with enforcement provisions would be effective in preventing a recurrence of the kinds of discriminatory acts that contributed to World War II. A few states, led by Australia, went so far as to propose an international court to adjudicate treaty violations, but most viewed that proposal as utopian. The Soviet Union insisted that the Human Rights Commission's mandate was limited to the preparation of a declaration, with no associated implementation mechanism. The United States favored the preparation of a declaration, though it was willing to see the Commission prepare a draft convention at some later time. Ultimately, the Commission decided to go ahead with a nonbinding declaration, while simultaneously working on a subsequent binding convention.

In 1948, the General Assembly of the United Nations adopted Resolution 217A, the Universal Declaration of Human Rights (UDHR). Forty-eight states voted to adopt the Declaration; eight states—Saudi Arabia, South Africa, and six Communist states, including the Soviet Union—abstained. Saudi Arabia objected to provisions in the Declaration dealing with equal marriage rights and the right to change one's religion or beliefs. South Africa abstained because it knew the Declaration would be used to condemn its system of apartheid. The six Communist states abstained because, in their view, the Declaration assumed a tension between the individual and the state that did not exist in a communist society in which there were no rival classes and in which the interests of the state and the individual coincided.

At the same time it adopted the Universal Declaration, the General Assembly called for speedy completion of the convention the Human Rights Commission was still drafting. The Human Rights Commission continued its work on a convention, but growing Cold War tensions impeded the process. The Council of Europe, relying in part on Human Rights Commission drafts, completed its own human rights convention in 1950. That convention, the European Convention on Human Rights, focused on undue state interference with political and civil liberties and included strong implementation mechanisms. Western states in the Human Rights Commission wanted to follow the European model in preparing a UN convention, but socialist states wanted to place equal emphasis on economic, social, and cultural rights. They also opposed any international supervision of a state's implementation of its convention obligations, which they viewed as an impermissible intervention in a state's internal affairs. In 1950 the General Assembly urged the Human Rights Commission to prepare a single convention including both sets of rights, but Western states on the Commission managed, by a small majority, to prevail in their demand for two separate covenants. In 1954 the Human Rights Commission prepared two draft conventions, each with its own distinct approach to implementation. The Third Committee of the General Assembly (which deals with social, humanitarian, and cultural issues) debated and revised the draft conventions between 1954 and 1966, and in 1966 the General Assembly adopted both conventions, which did not come into force until 1976. Although states have drafted numerous subsequent human rights conventions and declarations, the Universal Declaration and the two covenants together make up what is often referred to as the International Bill of Rights.

The Universal Declaration articulates a wide variety of basic civil and political rights, including the rights to life, security of one's person, fair trial, nationality, freedom of movement, and freedom of religion and expression. The economic, social, and cultural rights that also appear in the Declaration are examined in Section III below. Although governments intended the Universal Declaration to serve principally as an intermediate step toward the preparation of a binding international human rights treaty, delays in the preparation of the two subsequent International Covenants left the Universal Declaration for many years as the primary and most heavily invoked international human rights instrument. Excerpts from the Universal Declaration pertinent to Israel's interrogation practices follow.

Universal Declaration of Human Rights
G.A. Res. 217A (1948)

Whereas recognition of the inherent dignity and of the equal and inalienable rights of all members of the human family is the foundation of freedom, justice and peace in the world,

Whereas disregard and contempt for human rights have resulted in barbarous acts which have outraged the conscience of mankind, and the advent of a world in which human beings shall enjoy freedom of speech and belief and freedom from fear and want has been proclaimed as the highest aspiration of the common people, ...

ARTICLE 1

All human beings are born free and equal in dignity and rights. They are endowed with reason and conscience and should act towards one another in a spirit of brotherhood.

ARTICLE 2

Everyone is entitled to all the rights and freedoms set forth in this Declaration, without distinction of any kind, such as race, colour, sex, language, religion, political or other opinion, national or social origin, property, birth or other status. . . .

ARTICLE 4

Everyone has the right to life, liberty and security of person. . . .

ARTICLE 5

No one shall be subjected to torture or to cruel, inhuman or degrading treatment or punishment. . . .

ARTICLE 7

All are equal before the law and are entitled without any discrimination to equal protection of the law. All are entitled to equal protection against any discrimination in violation of this Declaration and against any incitement to such discrimination.

ARTICLE 8

Everyone has the right to an effective remedy by the competent national tribunals for acts violating the fundamental rights granted him by the constitution or by law.

ARTICLE 9

No one shall be subjected to arbitrary arrest, detention or exile. . . .

ARTICLE 30

Nothing in this Declaration may be interpreted as implying for any State, group or person any right to engage in any activity or to perform any act aimed at the destruction of any of the rights and freedoms set forth herein.

In many respects, the International Covenant on Civil and Political Rights (ICCPR) closely resembles the first half of the Universal Declaration. Many of the political and civil rights in the Universal Declaration appear in almost identical form in the ICCPR; others are similar in substance though expressed in greater detail in the Covenant. In a few instances, political and civil rights found in one document are not included in the other. The Covenant, for example, does not include the right to own property, found in Article 17 of the UDHR, which became contentious due to the ideological conflict associated with the expropriation of foreign-owned assets, described in Chapter 2.

Despite the essential similarities between the ICCPR and the UDHR, there are also some significant differences. First, the Covenant is a formally binding treaty, not an aspirational declaration. Second, the Covenant establishes a formal international institution—the Human Rights Committee, a body of international human rights experts—to assist parties with the interpretation and implementation of the treaty's provisions. Among other things, the Human Rights Committee receives and reviews reports from parties concerning their compliance with the treaty's provisions. The Committee also issues periodic general comments articulating its interpretation of various treaty articles. Perhaps most significant, the Committee receives complaints from individuals concerning violations of the treaty with respect to states that have accepted the Committee's competence under the First Optional Protocol to the ICCPR, and transmits its views concerning those complaints to the affected state and the complainant. Third, the UDHR and the Covenant differ in their approach to articulating the circumstances under which specified rights and freedoms may be properly limited. The UDHR contains a single, general article on this issue.

Article 29

1. Everyone has duties to the community in which alone the free and full development of his personality is possible.

2. In the exercise of his rights and freedoms, everyone shall be subject only to such limitations as are determined by law solely for the purpose of securing due recognition and respect for the rights and freedoms of others and of meeting the just requirements of morality, public order and the general welfare in a democratic society.

3. These rights and freedoms may in no case be exercised contrary to the purposes and principles of the United Nations.

By contrast, the Covenant contains specific provisions applicable to specific rights. Some articles of the Covenant include limitations provisions. For example, Article 18 of the Covenant, which protects (among other things) the freedom to manifest one's religion or beliefs, provides that such freedom "may be subject only to such limitations as are prescribed by law and are necessary to protect public safety, order, health, or morals or the fundamental rights and freedoms of others." In addition, and more broadly, the Covenant permits the limitation—or derogation—of most rights during times of public emergency:

Article 4

1. In time of public emergency which threatens the life of the nation and the existence of which is officially proclaimed, the States Parties to the present Covenant may take measures derogating from their obligations under the present Covenant to the extent strictly required by the exigencies of the situation, provided

that such measures are not inconsistent with their other obligations under international law and do not involve discrimination solely on the ground of race, colour, sex, language, religion or social origin.

2. No derogation from articles 6 [right to life], 7 [ban on torture], 8 (paragraphs 1 and 2) [ban on slavery], 11 [ban on imprisonment for debt], 15 [ban on ex post facto crimes], 16 [recognition as a person before the law] and 18 [freedom of thought, conscience, and religion] may be made under this provision.

3. Any State Party to the present Covenant availing itself of the right of derogation shall immediately inform the other States Parties to the present Covenant, through the intermediary of the Secretary-General of the United Nations, of the provisions from which it has derogated and of the reasons by which it was actuated. A further communication shall be made, through the same intermediary, on the date on which it terminates such derogation.

As indicated in Article 4(2) above, the Covenant specifies which rights may *not* be subject to derogation under any circumstances.

Israel became a party to the Covenant in 1991. For present purposes, note that Article 7 of the Covenant, which provides that "no one shall be subjected to torture or to cruel, inhuman or degrading treatment or punishment," is listed among the nonderogable articles.

In 1975, the UN General Assembly adopted a declaration calling for an end to torture and other cruel, inhuman, and degrading treatment. Thereafter, human rights NGOs such as the International Commission of Jurists pressed for the preparation of a binding convention that would expand on the obligation not to torture contained in Article 7 of the ICCPR. In 1984, the UN General Assembly adopted the Convention Against Torture and Other Cruel, Inhuman or Degrading Treatment or Punishment. The Convention strengthens existing norms against torture in a number of ways. Among other things, the Convention requires state parties to present reports focused explicitly on torture, and creates an expert committee to review those reports and make recommendations. The Convention also includes an optional individual complaints procedure. Perhaps most important, the Convention requires states either to prosecute anyone who has committed torture and is found within their jurisdiction or to extradite such persons to another state for prosecution. While most states were not prepared to accept such obligations with regard to the full spectrum of political and civil rights, they were prepared to accept such obligations with regard to torture. As of May 2006, 141 states were party to the Convention. Israel ratified the Convention Against Torture on October 3, 1991. Particularly relevant are the following provisions:

Convention Against Torture and Other Cruel, Inhuman or Degrading Treatment or Punishment

1465 U.N.T.S. 85 (1984)

Article 1

1. For the purposes of this Convention, the term "torture" means any act by which severe pain or suffering, whether physical or mental, is intentionally inflicted on a person for such purposes as obtaining from him or a third person

information or a confession, punishing him for an act he or a third person has committed or is suspected of having committed, or intimidating or coercing him or a third person, or for any reason based on discrimination of any kind, when such pain or suffering is inflicted by or at the instigation of or with the consent or acquiescence of a public official or other person acting in an official capacity. It does not include pain or suffering arising only from, inherent in or incidental to lawful sanctions. . . .

Article 2

1. Each State Party shall take effective legislative, administrative, judicial or other measures to prevent acts of torture in any territory under its jurisdiction.

2. No exceptional circumstances whatsoever, whether a state of war or a threat of war, internal political instability or any other public emergency, may be invoked as a justification of torture.

3. An order from a superior officer or a public authority may not be invoked as a justification of torture. . . .

Article 4

1. Each State Party shall ensure that all acts of torture are offences under its criminal law. The same shall apply to an attempt to commit torture and to an act by any person which constitutes complicity or participation in torture.

2. Each State Party shall make these offences punishable by appropriate penalties which take into account their grave nature. . . .

Article 10

1. Each State Party shall ensure that education and information regarding the prohibition against torture are fully included in the training of law enforcement personnel, civil or military, medical personnel, public officials and other persons who may be involved in the custody, interrogation or treatment of any individual subjected to any form of arrest, detention or imprisonment.

2. Each State Party shall include this prohibition in the rules or instructions issued in regard to the duties and functions of any such person.

Article 11

Each State Party shall keep under systematic review interrogation rules, instructions, methods and practices as well as arrangements for the custody and treatment of persons subjected to any form of arrest, detention or imprisonment in any territory under its jurisdiction, with a view to preventing any cases of torture. . . .

Article 14

1. Each State Party shall ensure in its legal system that the victim of an act of torture obtains redress and has an enforceable right to fair and adequate compensation, including the means for as full rehabilitation as possible. In the event of the death of the victim as a result of an act of torture, his dependants shall be entitled to compensation.

2. Nothing in this article shall affect any right of the victim or other persons to compensation which may exist under national law. . . .

Article 16

1. Each State Party shall undertake to prevent in any territory under its jurisdiction other acts of cruel, inhuman or degrading treatment or punishment which do not amount to torture as defined in article 1, when such acts are committed by or at the instigation of or with the consent or acquiescence of a public official or other person acting in an official capacity. . . .

2. The provisions of this Convention are without prejudice to the provisions of any other international instrument or national law which prohibits cruel, inhuman or degrading treatment or punishment or which relates to extradition or expulsion.

Notes and Questions

1. Why do you think the United States and the Soviet Union initially preferred a nonbinding declaration of human rights to a treaty?

2. What is the current legal status of the rights contained in the Universal Declaration? When promulgated, it was expressly understood that the Declaration was not itself legally binding, but some academics have argued that the Declaration constitutes an elaboration of the human rights referred to in the UN Charter. The UDHR has been cited with approval in countless successor treaties, declarations, and resolutions by the UN and regional organizations, and many of its provisions have been incorporated into the constitutions and laws of individual states. At least some of its provisions are now part of customary international law.

3. After the UN Charter, the Universal Declaration is often considered to be the most influential international law instrument of the twentieth century. It helped transform attitudes toward the place of the individual in the international order, and undermined notions that sovereignty should shield states from criticism for their mistreatment of their own nationals. Why might it have taken so long for most governments to accept that individuals have rights that can be asserted even against their own state?

4. Why do the UDHR and the ICCPR take different approaches to the circumstances under which particular rights and freedoms may be limited? How should states determine whether a particular limitation is justified by morality, public order, or the general welfare? What might explain the selection of the particular articles listed as nonderogable in Article 4 of the ICCPR?

5. Who is protected under the ICCPR? Note that under Article 2 of the ICCPR, a state must respect and ensure the rights of all individuals "within its territory and subject to its jurisdiction." When a state's officials act on the high seas, or abroad, should the provisions of the ICCPR still apply to that state? The Human Rights Committee has stated that "it would be unconscionable to so interpret the responsibility under article 2 of the Covenant as to permit a State Party to perpetrate violations of the Covenant on the territory of another State, which violations it could not perpetrate on its own territory." *Cox v. Canada*, Report of the Human Rights Committee, U.N. Doc. A/50/40 (1994), vol. 2, at 105. Similarly, in its General Comment No. 31, the Human Rights Committee stated that "a State Party must respect and ensure the rights laid down in the Covenant to anyone within the power or effective control of that State Party, even if not situated within the territory of that State party." The European Court of Human Rights, however, has decided that the European Convention on Human

Rights applies extraterritorially only in exceptional circumstances, such as when a state exercises "effective control of the relevant territory and its inhabitants as a consequence of military occupation," or "exercises all or some of the public powers normally to be exercised by" the government of the territory. *Bankovic and Others v. Belgium and 16 Other Contracting States*, Decision on Admissibility, Dec. 19, 2001, *www.echr.coe.int*. Accordingly, the Court declared inadmissible a claim that NATO members violated the right to life in a bombing attack on a Federal Republic of Yugoslavia radio and television station during the Kosovo conflict. In *Al Skeini v. Secretary of State for Defence*, [2004] EWHC 2911, the British High Court of Justice considered whether the European Convention applied to five instances in which British soldiers in Iraq killed civilians, and a sixth case in which an Iraqi civilian died in a British prison in Iraq. The court held that jurisdiction under the Convention is "essentially territorial," and that "since Iraq is not within the regional sphere of the Convention," the "effective control of an area" exception referenced in *Bankovic* did not apply. However, the court concluded with reference to the sixth case "that a British military prison, operating in Iraq with the consent of the Iraqi sovereign authorities, and containing arrested suspects, falls within . . . a narrowly limited exception [to the exclusion of extraterritorial jurisdiction] exemplified by embassies, consulates, vessels and aircraft. . . . "

6. Unlike the UDHR, the ICCPR includes implementation mechanisms that consist of state reporting requirements, Human Rights Committee comments and recommendations, and an optional protocol permitting the Committee to consider individual complaints. As of December 2005, 105 states were parties to that optional protocol. This implementation machinery has often been contrasted unfavorably with the adjudicatory procedures available in the European and, to a lesser extent, the Inter-American regional human rights systems. Under the ICCPR procedures, states are often late, sometimes many years late, in submitting reports, and they often pay relatively little attention to the recommendations of the Human Rights Committee. Moreover, decisions of the Committee under the optional protocol are not officially binding, though they have considerable persuasive value to many governments. To date there has been little enthusiasm among governments for a global international human rights court of the sort suggested in 1947, though an international criminal court, as described in Chapter 9, has been established in The Hague. Why do you think governments in Europe and Latin America were willing to establish regional human rights courts, but governments generally are not yet ready to establish a global human rights tribunal?

7. In recent years, the Human Rights Commission, formed in 1946, came under increasing criticism for being political and ineffective. States often sought membership to shield themselves and allies from criticism rather than to promote human rights, and the UN General Assembly periodically elected to the Commission states with poor human rights records, such as Sudan, Zimbabwe, Pakistan, Libya, and Saudi Arabia. In March 2005, UN Secretary-General Kofi Annan called for the abolition of the Commission and the creation of a smaller, more effective body. On March 15, 2006, the General Assembly voted 170-4, with three abstentions, to create a new Human Rights Council. The Council will meet year-round. The General Assembly now approves new members individually (rather than as members of a regional group), and members are subject to a mandatory review of their human rights record. The United States, which voted against the resolution creating the Council, argued that it did not represent a sufficient improvement over the

Commission. However, the United States stated that it would be willing to work with other states to make the new Council as effective as possible. The Human Rights Commission ceased operating in spring 2006.

C. Applying the Law on Torture to "Moderate Physical Pressure"

The Torture Convention establishes several mechanisms for promoting compliance. Like most other UN human rights conventions, states parties are required to prepare periodic reports specifying the steps they are taking to give effect to the treaty's provisions. The Torture Convention also establishes a special committee of experts—the Committee Against Torture—to review those reports and to make observations and recommendations to the state party whose report is under consideration. In 1994 the Committee Against Torture offered the following observations and recommendations to Israel.

Consideration of Reports Submitted by States Parties under Article 19 of the Convention: Israel

U.N. Doc. A/49/44 (1994)

C. Subjects of Concern

165. There is real concern that no legal steps have been taken to implement domestically the Convention against Torture. Thus, the Convention does not form part of the domestic law of Israel and its provisions cannot be invoked in Israeli courts.

166. The Committee regrets the clear failure to implement the definition of torture as contained in article 1 of the Convention.

167. It is a matter of deep concern that Israeli law pertaining to the defences of "superior orders" and "necessity" are in clear breach of that country's obligations under article 2 of the Convention.

168. The Landau Commission Report, permitting as it does "moderate physical pressure" as a lawful mode of interrogation, is completely unacceptable to this Committee:

> (a) As for the most part creating conditions leading to the risk of torture or cruel, or inhuman or degrading treatment or punishment; . . .

169. The Committee is greatly concerned at the large number of heavily documented cases of ill-treatment in custody that appear to amount to breaches of the Convention, including several cases resulting in death that have been drawn to the attention of the Committee and the world by such reputable non-governmental organizations as Amnesty International, Al Haq (the local branch of the International Commission of Jurists) and others.

D. Recommendations

170. The Committee recommends:

> (a) That all the provisions of the Convention against Torture be incorporated by statute into the domestic law of Israel;

(b) That interrogation procedures be published in full so that they are both transparent and seen to be consistent with the standards of the Convention;

(c) That a vigorous programme of education and re-education of the General Security Service, the Israel Defence Forces, police and medical profession be undertaken to acquaint them with their obligations under the Convention;

(d) That an immediate end be put to current interrogation practices that are in breach of Israel's obligations under the Convention;

(e) That all victims of such practices should be granted access to appropriate rehabilitation and compensation measures.

Israel disagreed with the Committee's views of its interrogation practices and continued to employ "moderate physical pressure" against detainees. Excerpts of Israel's 1997 report to the Committee Against Torture follow.

Second Periodic Reports of States Parties Due in 1996: Israel

U.N. Doc. CAT/C/33/Add.2/Rev. 1 (1997)

I. Israel's Interrogation Policies and Practices

2. We would like to emphasize that Israeli law strictly forbids all forms of torture or maltreatment. . . .

3. The State of Israel maintains that the basic human rights of all persons under its jurisdiction must never be violated, regardless of the crimes that the individual may have committed. Israel recognizes, however, its responsibility to protect the lives of both Jews and Arabs from harm at the hands of terrorist organizations active throughout the world. To prevent terrorism effectively while ensuring that the basic human rights of even the most dangerous of criminals are protected, the Israeli authorities have adopted strict rules for the handling of interrogations. These guidelines are designed to enable investigators to obtain crucial information on terrorist activities or organizations from suspects who, for obvious reasons, would not volunteer information on their activities, while ensuring that the suspects are not maltreated.

II. The Landau Commission

4. The basic guidelines on interrogation were set by the Landau Commission of Inquiry. . . . In order to compile its recommendations, the Landau Commission examined international human rights law standards, existing Israeli legislation prohibiting torture and maltreatment, and guidelines of other democracies confronted with the threat of terrorism.

5. . . . The Commission determined that in dealing with dangerous terrorists who represent a grave threat to the State of Israel and its citizens, the use of a moderate degree of pressure, including physical pressure, in order to obtain crucial information, is unavoidable under certain circumstances. Such circumstances include situations in which information sought from a detainee believed to be personally involved in serious terrorist activities can prevent imminent murder, or

where the detainee possesses vital information on a terrorist organization which could not be uncovered by any other source (for example, location of arms or caches of explosives for planned acts of terrorism).

6. The Landau Commission recognized the danger posed to the democratic values of the State of Israel should its agents abuse their power by using unnecessary or unduly harsh forms of pressure. As a result, the Commission recommended that psychological forms of pressure be used predominantly and that only "moderate physical pressure" (not unknown in other democratic countries) be sanctioned in limited cases where the degree of anticipated danger is considerable.

7. It should be noted that the use of such moderate pressure is in accordance with international law. For example, when asked to examine certain methods of interrogation used by Northern Ireland police against IRA terrorists, the European Court of Human Rights ruled that "ill-treatment must reach a certain severe level in order to be included in the ban [of torture and cruel, inhuman or degrading punishment] contained in Article 3 [of the European Convention on Human Rights]". In its ruling, that Court disagreed with the view . . . that the above-mentioned methods could be construed as torture, though it ruled that their application *in combination* (emphasis added) amounted to inhuman and degrading treatment. The question whether each of these measures separately would amount to inhuman and degrading treatment was therefore left open by the Court. . . .

[Israel's report goes on to detail the safeguards adopted to ensure that pressure does not escalate into torture, including internal GSS investigations, external Ministry of Justice responsibility for investigation of complaints, and an agreement with the International Committee of the Red Cross for monitoring the conditions of detentions.]

24. In conclusion, we would like first to note that as a result of GSS investigations of terrorist organizations' activists during the last two years, some 90 planned terrorist attacks have been foiled. Among these planned attacks are some 10 suicide bombings; 7 car-bombings; 15 kidnappings of soldiers and civilians; and some 60 attacks of different types including shootings of soldiers and civilians, hijacking of buses, stabbing and murder of Israelis, placing of explosives, etc.

Notes and Questions

1. Is the Committee Against Torture correct in stating that Israel's laws on superior orders and necessity are incompatible with its treaty obligations? Does the Committee's position suggest that the rights at issue are absolute?

2. Does the Committee provide much in the way of specific guidance to Israel? How could Israel accomplish its security objectives consistent with its treaty obligations?

3. Does Israel's report suggest that human rights and state security must be balanced against each other? Or simply that its guidelines for the application of moderate physical pressure are sufficient to ensure that investigators do not cross the line prohibiting torture or other cruel, inhuman, or degrading treatment?

4. Many countries use physical coercion in the interrogation of suspects. As a democracy, Israel may be more candid in its reporting to the Committee Against Torture than many other governments that engage in the practice. What is the status of the norm against torture if many countries in fact engage in it? Is Israel being unfairly singled out for condemnation simply because it has been more candid than most other states in admitting its use of physical coercion in interrogation?

Israel's defense of its actions in the addendum to its report to the Committee Against Torture quoted above refers approvingly to the decision by the European Court of Human Rights in *Ireland v. United Kingdom*. The European Court adjudicates cases brought under the European Convention on Human Rights, the world's first general human rights treaty. As you read the excerpt below, consider whether and to what extent it supports Israel's position with respect to "moderate physical pressure."

Republic of Ireland v. United Kingdom

2 E.C.H.R. (Ser. A) at 25 (1978)

[The United Kingdom acknowledged that in combating terrorism in Northern Ireland, British security forces employed a number of methods that violated international human rights law. By the time of the decision, the UK had already taken steps to eliminate the use of those methods. Nonetheless, the Court felt obliged to consider their legality under article 3 of the European Convention on Human Rights, which prohibits torture and inhuman or degrading treatment or punishment. The interrogation techniques at issue included: "forcing the detainees to remain for periods of some hours in a 'stress position'"; "putting a black or navy coloured bag over the detainees' heads and, at least initially, keeping it there all the time except during interrogation"; "holding the detainees in a room where there was a continuous loud and hissing noise"; sleep deprivation; and deprivation of food and drink.]

C. QUESTIONS CONCERNING THE MERITS

162. As was emphasised by the Commission, ill-treatment must attain a minimum level of severity if it is to fall within the scope of Article 3. The assessment of this minimum is, in the nature of things, relative; it depends on all the circumstances of the case, such as the duration of the treatment, its physical or mental effects and, in some cases, the sex, age and state of health of the victim, etc.

163. The Convention prohibits in absolute terms torture and inhuman or degrading treatment or punishment, irrespective of the victim's conduct. Unlike most of the substantive clauses of the Convention and of Protocols 1 and 4, Article 3 makes no provision for exceptions and, under Article 15 (2), there can be no derogation therefrom even in the event of a public emergency threatening the life of the nation. . . .

167. The five techniques were applied in combination, with premeditation and for hours at a stretch; they caused, if not actual bodily injury, at least intense physical and mental suffering to the persons subjected thereto and also led to acute psychiatric disturbances during interrogation. They accordingly fell into the category of inhuman treatment within the meaning of Article 3. The techniques were also degrading since they were such as to arouse in their victims feelings of fear, anguish and inferiority capable of humiliating and debasing them and possibly breaking their physical or moral resistance. . . .

In the Court's view, [the] distinction [between torture and cruel, inhuman and degrading treatment] derives principally from a difference in the intensity of the suffering inflicted.

The Court considers in fact that, whilst there exists on the one hand violence which is to be condemned both on moral grounds and also in most cases under the domestic law of the Contracting States but which does not fall within Article 3 of the Convention, it appears on the other hand that it was the intention that the Convention, with its distinction between 'torture' and 'inhuman or degrading treatment', should by the first of these terms attach a special stigma to deliberate inhuman treatment causing very serious and cruel suffering. . . .

Although the five techniques, as applied in combination, undoubtedly amounted to inhuman and degrading treatment, although their object was the extraction of confessions, the naming of others and/or information and although they were used systematically, they did not occasion suffering of the particular intensity and cruelty implied by the word torture as so understood.

In 1999 the Israeli Supreme Court directly confronted the question whether the GSS interrogation methods constituted either torture or cruel, inhuman, or degrading treatment in a case brought by several Israeli human rights groups, including the Public Committee Against Torture, on behalf of Palestinian interrogees.

Public Committee Against Torture in Israel v. State of Israel

38 I.L.M. 1471 (1999)

Background:

1. The State of Israel has been engaged in an unceasing struggle for both its very existence and security, from the day of its founding. Terrorist organizations have established as their goal Israel's annihilation. Terrorist acts and the general disruption of order are their means of choice. In employing such methods, these groups do not distinguish between civilian and military targets. They carry out terrorist attacks in which scores are murdered in public areas, public transportation, city squares and centers, theaters and coffee shops. They do not distinguish between men, women and children. They act out of cruelty and without mercy. . . .

The purpose of [the GSS] interrogations is, among others, to gather information regarding terrorists and their organizing methods for the purpose of thwarting and preventing them from carrying out these terrorist attacks.

[The Court's opinion describes in considerable detail the challenged interrogation practices, which include "the forceful shaking of the suspect's upper torso," prolonged sitting on a low, tilted chair, with hands tied behind the back and head covered by an opaque sack, excessive tightening of handcuffs, and sleep deprivation.]

15. . . . With respect to the physical means employed by the GSS, the State argues that these do not violate International Law. . . .

In support of their position, the State notes that the use of physical means by GSS investigators is most unusual and is only employed as a last resort in very extreme cases. Moreover, even in these rare cases, the application of such methods is subject to the strictest of scrutiny and supervision, as per the conditions and restrictions set forth in the Commission of Inquiry's Report. This having been said, when the exceptional conditions requiring the use of these means are in fact present, the above described interrogation methods are fundamental to saving human lives and safeguarding Israel's security. . . .

22. . . . In crystallizing the interrogation rules, two values or interests clash. *On the one hand*, lies the desire to uncover the truth, thereby fulfilling the public interest in exposing crime and preventing it. *On the other hand*, is the wish to protect the dignity and liberty of the individual being interrogated. This having been said, these interests and values are not absolute. A democratic, freedom-loving society does not accept that investigators use any means for the purpose of uncovering the truth. . . . At times, the price of truth is so high that a democratic society is not prepared to pay it. To the same extent, however, a democratic society, desirous of liberty, seeks to fight crime and to that end is prepared to accept that an interrogation may infringe upon the human dignity and liberty of a suspect provided it is done for a proper purpose and that the harm does not exceed that which is necessary. . . . Our concern, therefore, lies in the clash of values and the balancing of conflicting values. The balancing process results in the rules for a "reasonable interrogation". . . .

23. . . . The "law of interrogation," by its very nature, is intrinsically linked to the circumstances of each case. This having been said, a number of general principles are nonetheless worth noting:

> *First,* a reasonable investigation is necessarily one free of torture, free of cruel, inhuman treatment of the subject and free of any degrading handling whatsoever. . . . This conclusion is in perfect accord with (various) International Law treaties—to which Israel is a signatory—which prohibit the use of torture, "cruel, inhuman treatment" and "degrading treatment". These prohibitions are "absolute". There are no exceptions to them and there is no room for balancing. Indeed, violence directed at a suspect's body or spirit does not constitute a reasonable investigation practice. . . .

> *Second,* a reasonable investigation is likely to cause discomfort; It may result in insufficient sleep; The conditions under which it is conducted risk being unpleasant. Indeed, it is possible to conduct an effective investigation without resorting to violence. Within the confines of the law, it is permitted to resort to various machinations and specific sophisticated activities which serve investigators today (both for Police and GSS); . . . . In the end result, the legality of an investigation is deduced from the propriety of its purpose and from its methods. Thus, for instance, sleep deprivation for a prolonged period, or sleep deprivation at night when this is not necessary to the investigation time wise may be deemed a use of an investigation method which surpasses the least restrictive means.

From the General to the Particular

24. . . . Plainly put, shaking is a prohibited investigation method. It harms the suspect's body. It violates his dignity. It is a violent method which does not form part of a legal investigation. It surpasses that which is necessary. . . .

[Reviewing the other interrogation methods at issue, the Court finds that each has elements that may be permissible when carried out humanely (e.g., handcuffing) but that when carried out unreasonably "impinge upon the suspect's dignity, his bodily integrity, and his basic rights" and cannot then "be deemed as included within the general power to conduct interrogations."]

Physical Means and the "Necessity" Defence

33. . . . As noted, an explicit authorization permitting GSS to employ physical means is not to be found in our law. An authorization of this nature can, in the State's opinion, be obtained in specific cases by virtue of the criminal law defense of "necessity", prescribed in the Penal Law. . . . The State's position is that by virtue of this "defence" to criminal liability, GSS investigators are also authorized to apply physical means, such as shaking, in the appropriate circumstances, in order to prevent serious harm to human life or body, in the absence of other alternatives. The State maintains that an act committed under conditions of "necessity" does not constitute a crime. Instead, it is deemed an act worth committing in such circumstances in order to prevent serious harm to a human life or body. . . . Not only is it legitimately permitted to engage in the fighting of terrorism, it is our moral duty to employ the necessary means for this purpose. . . . In the course of their argument, the State's attorneys submitted the "ticking time bomb" argument. A given suspect is arrested by the GSS. He holds information respecting the location of a bomb that was set and will imminently explode. There is no way to defuse the bomb without this information. If the information is obtained, however, the bomb may be defused. If the bomb is not defused, scores will be killed and maimed. Is a GSS investigator authorized to employ physical means in order to elicit information regarding the location of the bomb in such instances? . . .

36. In the Court's opinion, a general authority to establish directives respecting the use of physical means during the course of a GSS interrogation cannot be implied from the "necessity" defence. The "necessity" defence does not constitute a source of authority, allowing GSS investigators to make use of physical means during the course of interrogations. . . . This defence deals with deciding those cases involving an individual reacting to a given set of facts; It is an ad hoc endeavour, in reaction to an event. . . . Thus, the very nature of the defence does not allow it to serve as the source of a general administrative power. The administrative power is based on establishing general, forward looking criteria. . . .

Moreover, the "necessity" defence has the effect of allowing one who acts under the circumstances of "necessity" to escape criminal liability. The "necessity" defence does not possess any additional normative value. In addition, it does not authorize the use of physical means for the purposes of allowing investigators to execute their duties in circumstances of necessity. The very fact that a particular act does not constitute a criminal act (due to the "necessity" defence) does not in itself authorize the administration to carry out this deed, and in doing so infringe upon human rights. The Rule of Law (both as a formal and substantive principle) requires that an infringement on a human right be prescribed by statute, authorizing the administration to this effect. . . .

37. If the State wishes to enable GSS investigators to utilize physical means in interrogations, they must seek the enactment of legislation for this purpose. . . .

A Final Word

39. This decision opens with a description of the difficult reality in which Israel finds herself security wise. . . . We are aware that this decision does not ease dealing with that reality. This is the destiny of democracy, as not all means are acceptable to it, and not all practices employed by its enemies are open before it. Although a democracy must often fight with one hand tied behind its back, it nonetheless has

the upper hand. Preserving the Rule of Law and recognition of an individual's liberty constitutes an important component in its understanding of security. At the end of the day, they strengthen its spirit and its strength and allow it to overcome its difficulties. This having been said, there are those who argue that Israel's security problems are too numerous, thereby requiring the authorization to use physical means. If it will nonetheless be decided that it is appropriate for Israel, in light of its security difficulties to sanction physical means in interrogations (and the scope of these means which deviate from the ordinary investigation rules), this is an issue that must be decided by the legislative branch which represents the people. . . .

40. Deciding these applications weighed heavy on this Court. True, from the legal perspective, the road before us is smooth. We are, however, part of Israeli society. Its problems are known to us and we live its history. We are not isolated in an ivory tower. We live the life of this country. We are aware of the harsh reality of terrorism in which we are, at times, immersed. Our apprehension is that this decision will hamper the ability to properly deal with terrorists and terrorism, disturbs us. We are, however, judges. Our brethren require us to act according to the law. This is equally the standard that we set for ourselves. When we sit to judge, we are being judged. . . .

The Court's opinion was unanimous, but Justice Kedmi, although he accepted the Court's holding, wrote separately to express his view that the judgment should be suspended for one year to allow the Knesset, the Israeli legislature, to consider the issue. Justice Kedmi concluded that in "those rare emergencies that merit being defined as 'ticking time bombs,'" states may "order the use of exceptional interrogation methods" as part of the right of every state to defend itself and its citizens.

Notes and Questions

1. Did the Israeli Supreme Court conclude that GSS interrogation practices amount to torture? Does the relevant international law compel that conclusion?

2. Shortly after the Court reached its decision, the Israeli Government's Ministerial Committee for GSS Matters established a commission to consider whether legislation should be passed to permit the GSS to continue to use physical pressure in interrogating suspects. No legislation has been passed, but the issue remains open. Supporters of legislation argue that there are times when force in the interrogation of suspects is the only way to obtain information necessary to save lives, and justify it as the lesser of two evils. Do you agree? Does international human rights law permit this sort of utilitarian analysis, or are the prohibitions at issue absolute? In its Concluding Observations on Israel's Report, the Committee Against Torture stated:

> The Committee acknowledges the terrible dilemma that Israel confronts in dealing with terrorist threats to its security, but as a State party to the Convention Israel is precluded from raising before this Committee exceptional circumstances as justification for acts prohibited by article 1 of the Convention. This is plainly expressed in article 2 of the Convention.

U.N. Doc. A/52/44, para. 258 (1997). Similarly, the European Court of Human Rights has held that

[e]ven in the most difficult circumstances, such as the fight against terrorism and organised crime, [Article 3 of] the [European] Convention [on Human Rights] prohibits in absolute terms torture and inhuman or degrading treatment or punishment. Unlike most of the substantive clauses of the Convention . . . Article 3 makes no provision for exceptions and no derogation from it is permissible . . . even in the event of a public emergency threatening the life of the nation. . . .

Selmouni v. France, 1109 E.C.H.R. Rep. 149, 181 (1999).

3. Human Rights Watch has criticized Israel's "ticking bomb" argument on pragmatic grounds. Do you agree with its analysis below?

There are practical as well as moral reasons for not permitting a "ticking bomb"—or terrorist attack—exception to the ban on torture. Although such an exception might appear to be highly limited, experience shows that the exception readily becomes the standard practice. . . . Under the utilitarian logic that the end (saving many innocent lives) justifies the means, torture should be permitted even if the disaster might not occur until some point in the future, and it should be permitted against as many people as is necessary to secure the information that could be used to avert the disaster.

Israel provides a good example of how this logic works in practice. For years Israel justified its use of torture—what it called "moderate physical force"—by citing the "ticking bomb" scenario. But despite a genuine security threat, Israeli security forces rarely if ever were able to identify a particular suspect with knowledge about a particular bomb set to explode imminently. Rather, they ended up applying the scenario metaphorically to justify torturing virtually every Palestinian security detainee—thousands of people—on the theory that they might know something about some unspecified, future terrorist act. . . .

In addition, the ticking bomb scenario offers no logical limitations on how much or what kind of torture would be permitted. If the detainee does not talk when shaken or hit, why shouldn't the government move on to more severe measures, such as the application of electric shocks? Why not threaten to rape the suspect's wife or to torture his children? Once torture is allowed, setting limits is extraordinarily difficult.

Human Rights Watch, *The Legal Prohibition Against Torture,*
www.hrw.org/press/2001/11/TortureQandA.htm

4. According to the Public Committee Against Torture in Israel, the named plaintiff in the case before the Israel High Court, torture and ill treatment of detainees in Israel has accelerated since early 2003.

D. Applying the Law on Torture to Detainees in the "Global War on Terrorism"

In the aftermath of the U.S. military campaign in Afghanistan following the attacks of September 11, 2001, the United States detained thousands of suspected Taliban and al Qaeda members in Afghanistan, at Guantanamo Bay, Cuba, and at a number of other locations, some of them secret. Thousands more have been detained in connection with the conflict in Iraq. As of June 2005, approximately 68,000 people had been taken into U.S. custody, though many were held only briefly. Beginning in 2002, media accounts and later official investigations revealed that many detainees had been subjected to harsh interrogation techniques.

1. U.S. Interrogation Methods

The official interrogation policy in place when the detentions began in 2001 was contained in Army Field Manual 34-52. The Manual permitted the use of psychological ploys, such as shouting at a detainee or banging on the table to invoke a sense of fear, but expressly prohibited the use of "force, mental torture, threats, insults, or exposure to unpleasant and inhumane treatment of any kind." However, interrogators claimed that permitted methods were ineffective against the Taliban and al Qaeda detainees, and sought more aggressive methods of interrogation.

In October 2002, the Commanding Officer of Joint Task Force 170 (JTF 170), the division in charge of interrogations at Guantanamo Bay, Cuba, requested permission to use interrogation techniques not contained in Army Field Manual 34-52. The request came in a cover letter to a memorandum on "counter-resistance strategies" prepared by a lieutenant commander of JTF 170. That memorandum divided the new interrogation techniques into three categories, from the least aggressive to the most aggressive. Interrogation techniques in Category I included yelling at detainees, deceiving detainees, and using multiple interrogators, techniques similar to those already permitted under Army Field Manual 34-52. The interrogation methods in Category II included the use of stress positions, such as forcing the detainee to stand for up to four hours, isolating the detainee for up to 30 days (with medical and psychological supervision), placing a hood over the detainee's head during transportation and questioning, depriving the detainee of light and auditory stimuli, and "[u]sing detainees' individual phobias (such as fear of dogs) to induce stress." The interrogation methods in Category III included "[u]se of a wet towel and dripping water to induce the misperception of suffocation," exposing the detainee to cold weather or water, and using "mild, non-injurious physical contact such as grabbing, poking in the chest with the finger, and light pushing."

After extensive discussion by high-ranking military personnel about the legality of the proposed interrogation methods, on November 27, 2002, Department of Defense General Counsel William Haynes advised the Commander of the U.S. Southern Command that it was permissible "to employ, in his discretion, only Categories I and II and the fourth technique listed in Category III ('Use of mild, non-injurious physical contact such as grabbing, poking in the chest with the finger, and light pushing.')." While Haynes did not find that the other techniques listed in Category III were illegal, he determined that "a blanket approval of Category III techniques [was] not warranted." Secretary Rumsfeld approved Haynes's recommendations.

On December 26, 2002, the *Washington Post* published a detailed account of "stress and duress" interrogation tactics used to elicit information from suspected terrorists. According to the report, suspects were "sometimes kept standing or kneeling for hours, in black hoods or spray-painted goggles," and "at times they [were] held in awkward, painful positions and deprived of sleep with a 24-hour bombardment of lights." Shortly after publication of this account, Secretary Rumsfeld rescinded his approval of the additional interrogation techniques, and directed Haynes to establish a working group within the Department of Defense to assess interrogation techniques. On April 4, 2003, the Working Group issued its Report on Detainee Interrogations in the Global War on Terrorism. After reviewing the relevant international and domestic law, the report recommended that Secretary Rumsfeld approve the 17 interrogation techniques already in use in accordance with Army Field Manual 34-52 and 18 new, more aggressive techniques.

On April 16, 2003, Secretary Rumsfeld approved the use of some of the psychological techniques recommended in the Working Group Report, such as "change of scenery up/down" (removing the detainee from the standard interrogation setting to a setting that is more or less comfortable), "dietary manipulation," and isolation. Rumsfeld did not approve the harsher techniques, such as prolonged standing, sleep deprivation, slapping, or removal of clothing. As of January 2006, Secretary Rumsfeld's guidance remained in effect, though discussions on revised interrogation policies were in progress.

Notwithstanding the changes in U.S. interrogation policy, physical abuse by interrogators continued. On June 26, 2003, newspapers reported that the deaths of two Afghan detainees in U.S. custody at Bagram Air Force base in Afghanistan were probably homicides, resulting from the use of excessive force by U.S. interrogators. In response, on June 27, 2003, the United States formally pledged that it would not subject terrorism suspects to cruel, inhumane, or degrading treatment. Despite this pledge, CIA and military interrogators continued to use aggressive interrogation techniques. According to an April 2005 Human Rights Watch statement, detainees held at military bases in Afghanistan in 2002 and 2003 described being "beaten severely by both guards and interrogators, deprived of sleep for extended periods, and intentionally exposed to extreme cold, as well as other inhumane and degrading treatment." Former detainees at Guantanamo Bay, Cuba, reported "the use of painful stress positions, use of military dogs to threaten detainees, threats of torture and death, and prolonged exposure to extremes of heat, cold and noise," in addition to "weeks and even months in solitary confinement."

In late April 2004, television stations around the world broadcast shocking pictures showing American soldiers abusing Iraqi prisoners in Baghdad's infamous Abu Ghraib prison. In response to earlier reports, the U.S. Army directed Major General Antonio M. Taguba to investigate the allegations. His report, completed in February 2004, concluded that from October to December 2003, there were "numerous instances of sadistic, blatant, and wanton criminal abuses" at Abu Ghraib, and that "[t]his systemic and illegal abuse of detainees was intentionally perpetrated by several members of the military police guard force." (See Chapter 9, Section II.) Subsequent military investigations and reports by respected human rights organizations have documented similar patterns of abuse at other U.S.-run detention facilities. According to Human Rights First, at least 141 detainees have died in U.S. custody in Afghanistan and Iraq; at least 28 of these deaths are confirmed or suspected homicides.

Since 2001, the United States has also maintained a number of secret detention facilities in Asia, North Africa, on U.S. naval vessels, and elsewhere. To maintain the secrecy of these operations, the United States provides no notice to the detainees' families, no access to the ICRC, and, in the majority of cases, no acknowledgement that the detainees are even being held. In late 2005, news reports suggested that the U.S. Central Intelligence Agency held some of these "ghost detainees" in facilities in Eastern Europe before transferring them to North Africa and elsewhere, prompting widespread criticism within Europe, an investigation by the Council of Europe and the European Union into possible violations of the European Convention on Human Rights, and denials from countries suspected of cooperating with the United States. News accounts also suggest that the CIA has transferred some detainees—approximately 100 to 150—to countries in the Middle East, particularly Egypt and Syria, that are known to engage in torture, in a practice known as rendition. Individuals who have been subject to such renditions describe repeated torture in the receiving country, including the use of beatings and electric shocks.

2. U.S. Interrogation Policy and International Law

As explored more fully in Chapter 14, Part II, the Bush Administration decided after September 11, 2001, that the United States was in a "new kind of war," and that aspects of the Geneva Conventions of 1949 and their 1977 protocols were ill-suited to the conduct of this new war. To prevail in the "global war on terrorism," the Bush Administration believed it vital to be able to obtain useful intelligence quickly from individuals suspected of possible terrorist activities directed against the United States. With this in mind, Bush Administration lawyers crafted a series of memoranda intended in part to preserve flexibility for U.S. interrogators in determining which techniques to employ in order to elicit information from suspected terrorists.

a. Applicability of the Geneva Conventions and the Convention Against Torture

On January 9, 2002, John Yoo, Deputy Assistant Attorney General, and Robert J. Delahunty, Special Counsel of the Department of Justice's Office of Legal Counsel (OLC), wrote a memorandum to William J. Haynes II, the General Counsel of the Department of Defense, arguing that the Geneva Conventions do not apply to members of al Qaeda or the Taliban militia. The OLC memorandum concluded that the United States therefore would not violate the War Crimes Act, 18 U.S.C. §2441, which criminalizes grave breaches of the Conventions, if it chose not to afford al Qaeda and Taliban detainees all the protections—including the right to be free from "inhumane or degrading treatment"—owed to prisoners of war under the Geneva Conventions. The OLC memorandum further concluded that customary international law governing the treatment of detainees would have "no binding legal effect on either the President or the military because it is not federal law, as recognized by the Constitution." However, Secretary Rumsfeld advised combat commanders that they should still treat all detainees "humanely, and to the extent appropriate and consistent with military necessity, in a manner consistent with the principles of the Geneva Conventions."

The Bush Administration also considered whether the Convention Against Torture and accompanying U.S. implementing legislation limited U.S. interrogation practices. The United States ratified the Torture Convention in 1994, with various reservations and understandings. In a reservation, the United States stated that it would accept the obligation "to prevent" cruel, inhuman or degrading treatment or punishment "only insofar" as that language means "the cruel, unusual and inhumane treatment or punishment prohibited by the Fifth, Eighth, and/or Fourteenth Amendments to the Constitution of the United States." The United States also included an understanding with respect to the definition of torture:

> [T]he United States understands that, in order to constitute torture, an act must be specifically intended to inflict severe physical or mental pain or suffering and that mental pain or suffering refers to prolonged mental harm caused by or resulting from: (1) the intentional infliction or threatened infliction of severe physical pain or suffering; (2) the administration or application, or threatened administration or application, of mind altering substances or other procedures calculated to disrupt profoundly the senses or the personality; (3) the threat of imminent death; or (4) the threat that another person will imminently be subjected to death, severe physical pain or suffering, or the administration or application of mind altering substances or other procedures calculated to disrupt profoundly the senses or personality.

Following its ratification of the Convention, the United States enacted 18 U.S.C. §§2340-2340A to give effect to its obligations under the Convention. Section

2340A makes it a criminal offense for any person "outside of the United States [to] commit[ ] or attempt[ ] to commit torture." Section 2340(1) defines the act of torture as an "act committed by a person acting under the color of law specifically intended to inflict severe physical or mental pain or suffering (other than pain or suffering incidental to lawful sanctions) upon another person within his custody or physical control." Section 2340(2) defines "severe mental pain or suffering" in terms consistent with the understanding quoted above.

On August 1, 2002, Assistant Attorney General Bybee provided a lengthy OLC memorandum to White House Counsel Alberto Gonzalez, arguing that the definition of torture provided in §2340 proscribed only acts "that are specifically intended to inflict[ ] severe pain or suffering, whether mental or physical." Thus, according to the OLC analysis, to violate 18 U.S.C. §§2340-2340A, an interrogator must have the specific intent of inflicting "severe physical or mental pain or suffering" upon the detainee. Knowing that the interrogator's conduct would likely cause "severe physical or mental pain or suffering" is not sufficient to meet the specific intent requirement set out in §2340(1). Further, "a showing that an individual acted with a good faith belief that his conduct would not produce the result that the law prohibits negates specific intent."

The August 1 OLC memorandum further advised that "acts must be of an extreme nature to rise to the level of torture within the meaning of Section 2340A and the Convention. . . . [A]cts may be cruel, inhuman, or degrading, but still not produce pain and suffering of the requisite intensity to fall within §2340A's proscription against torture." The memorandum concluded, drawing in part on an analysis of "statutes defining an emergency medical condition for the purpose of providing health benefits" in which the term "severe pain" is used, that:

> Each component of the definition [of torture contained in 18 U.S.C. §2340] emphasizes that torture is not the mere infliction of pain or suffering on another, but is instead a step well removed. The victim must experience intense pain or suffering of the kind that is equivalent to the pain that would be associated with serious physical injury so severe that death, organ failure, or permanent damage resulting in a loss of significant body function will likely result. If that pain or suffering is psychological, that suffering must result from one of the acts set forth in the statute. In addition, these acts must cause long-term mental harm.

The August 1 OLC memorandum concluded that the Torture Convention "confirms [the OLC's] conclusion that Section 2340A was intended to proscribe only the most egregious conduct. CAT not only defines torture as involving severe pain and suffering, but also it makes clear that such pain and suffering is at the extreme end of the spectrum of acts by reserving criminal penalties solely for torture." According to the OLC's analysis, the Convention's "text, ratification history and negotiating history all confirm that Section 2340A reaches only the most heinous acts." The OLC also concluded that international decisions, including *Ireland v. United Kingdom* and *Public Committee Against Torture v. Israel*, further support a narrow definition of what constitutes torture, "permit[ting], under international law, an aggressive interpretation as to what amounts to torture, leaving that label to be applied only where extreme circumstances exist."

b. The Necessity Defense

The OLC memorandum also contended that it would be unconstitutional to apply §2340A to interrogations undertaken pursuant to the President's Commander- in-Chief power:

Congress may no more regulate the President's ability to detain and interrogate enemy combatants than it may regulate his ability to direct troop movements on the battlefield. Accordingly, we would construe Section 2340A to avoid this constitutional difficulty, and conclude that it does not apply to the President's detention and interrogation of enemy combatants pursuant to his Commander-in-Chief authority.

The memorandum added that:

Even if an interrogation method, however, might arguably cross the line drawn in Section 2340, and application of the statute was not held to be an unconstitutional infringement of the President's Commander-in-Chief authority, [the Office of Legal Counsel] believe[s] that under the current circumstances . . . [the s]tandard criminal law defenses of necessity and self-defense could justify interrogation methods needed to elicit information to prevent a direct and imminent threat to the United States and its citizens.

On the necessity defense, the memorandum stated:

We believe that a defense of necessity could be raised, under the current circumstances, to an allegation of a Section 2340A violation. Often referred to as the "choice of evils" defense, necessity has been defined as follows:

Conduct that the actor believes to be necessary to avoid a harm or evil to himself or to another is justifiable, provided that:
(a) the harm or evil sought to be avoided by such conduct is greater than that sought to be prevented by the law defining the offense charged;

. . . .

It appears to us that under the current circumstances the necessity defense could be successfully maintained in response to an allegation of a Section 2340A violation. On September 11, 2001, al Qaeda launched a surprise covert attack on civilian targets in the United States that led to the deaths of thousands and losses in the billions of dollars. According to public and governmental reports, al Qaeda has other sleeper cells within the United States that may be planning similar attacks. Indeed, al Qaeda plans apparently include efforts to develop and deploy chemical, biological and nuclear weapons of mass destruction. Under these circumstances, a detainee may possess information that could enable the United States to prevent attacks that potentially could equal or surpass the September 11 attacks in their magnitude. Clearly, any harm that might occur during an interrogation would pale to insignificance compared to the harm avoided by preventing such an attack, which could take hundreds or thousands of lives.

Under this calculus, two factors will help indicate when the necessity defense could appropriately be invoked. First, the more certain that government officials are that a particular individual has information needed to prevent an attack, the more necessary interrogation will be. Second, the more likely it appears to be that a terrorist attack is likely to occur, and the greater the amount of damage expected from such an attack, the more that an interrogation to get information would become necessary. Of course, the strength of the necessity defense depends on the circumstances that prevail, and the knowledge of the government actors involved, when the interrogation is conducted. While every interrogation that might violate Section 2340A does not trigger a necessity defense, we can say that certain circumstances could support such a defense.

c. U.S. Obligations Under the Torture Convention

In a subsequent memorandum, the Office of Legal Counsel concluded that "interrogation methods that comply with §2340 would not violate [the

United States's] international obligations under the Torture Convention." The memorandum explained that when the United States ratified the Convention Against Torture, the first Bush Administration submitted a memorandum of understanding "that defined torture in the exact terms used by §2340." Since "[t]he Senate approved the Convention based on this understanding, and the United States included the understanding in its instrument of ratification," no other state party to the Convention could hold the United States to a different definition of torture than the one outlined in the memorandum of understanding. Thus, the United States's obligations under the Convention Against Torture are identical to the prohibitions against torture outlined in 18 U.S.C. §2340A.

Notes and Questions

1. Is the definition of torture contained in the U.S. understanding attached to its ratification of the Torture Convention consistent with the Convention? Is the definition of torture in the Bybee memorandum consistent with the Convention? Under the Bybee memorandum definition, do any of the interrogation practices described in part D.1. above amount to torture? The Bybee memorandum attempts at considerable length to draw a sharp distinction between torture and cruel, inhuman, and degrading treatment; since both forms of conduct are prohibited by the Torture Convention, why is it important to distinguish between the two?

2. Compare the discussion of necessity in the Bybee memorandum with the discussion of necessity in *Public Committee against Torture in Israel v. Israel*. In either case, can "necessity" justify a government policy of coercive interrogations?

3. Many aspects of the Bybee memorandum proved highly controversial even within the Bush administration. Lawyers in both the State Department and the Defense Department took issue with key aspects of the memorandum for both legal and policy reasons. For example, the Army Judge Advocate General, Major General Thomas Romig, wrote in a March 2003 memorandum for the Defense Department General Counsel:

> While the OLC analysis speaks to a number of defenses that could be raised on behalf of those who engage in interrogation techniques later perceived to be illegal, the "bottom line" defense proffered by OLC is an exceptionally broad concept of "necessity." This defense is based upon the premise that any existing federal statutory provision or international obligation is unconstitutional per se, where it otherwise prohibits conduct viewed by the President, acting in his capacity as Commander-in-Chief, as essential to his capacity to wage war. I question whether this theory would ultimately prevail in either the U.S. courts or in any international forum. If such a defense is not available, soldiers ordered to use otherwise illegal techniques run a substantial risk of criminal prosecution or personal liability arising from a civil lawsuit.

> The OLC opinion states further that customary international law cannot bind the U.S. Executive Branch as it is not part of the federal law. As such, any presidential decision made in the context of the ongoing war on terrorism constitutes a "controlling" Executive act; one that immediately and automatically displaces any contrary provision of customary international law. This view runs contrary to the historic position taken by the United States Government concerning such laws and, in our opinion, could adversely impact DOD interests worldwide. On the one hand, such a policy will open us to international criticism that the "U.S. is a law unto itself." On the other, implementation of questionable techniques will very likely establish a new baseline for

acceptable practice in this area, putting our service personnel at far greater risk and vitiating many of the POW/detainee safeguards the U.S. has worked hard to establish over the past five decades.

Why might lawyers in the Defense and State Departments view these issues differently than lawyers in the Justice Department?

4. The OLC and White House Counsel legal memoranda excerpted above attracted broad criticism from international and constitutional law experts for misstating the law, omitting countervailing authorities and arguments, and relying on outcome-oriented analysis. Some experts argue that the memoranda created a permissive legal climate that facilitated the mistreatment of detainees, and that in fact the memoranda were designed "to provide legal cover—something akin to immunity—for U.S. soldiers and other officials who might subsequently be accused of criminal misconduct in the war on terrorism." David Bowker, *Unwise Counsel*, in The Torture Debate in America 183, 196 (Karen Greenberg ed., 2006). Bowker suggests a number of reasons why the lawyers involved in the preparation of these memoranda may have acted as they did: "their desire to help the President win the war on terrorism," their academic or political convictions, an unduly broad view of presidential power in wartime, a preoccupation with avoiding judicial review, and "groupthink" stemming from the narrow circle of insiders permitted to review the memoranda. What are the ethical responsibilities of government lawyers in this context? Who is their client?

When the memoranda described above were leaked to the press, a storm of criticism ensued, much of it focused on the August 2002 Bybee memorandum. On December 30, 2004, the Office of Legal Counsel issued a new memorandum, which declared torture "abhorrent both to American law and values and to international norms." Referring to the August 2002 memorandum, the December 30 memorandum stated:

> This memorandum supersedes the August 2002 Memorandum in its entirety. Because the discussion in that memorandum concerning the President's Commander-in-Chief power and the potential defenses to liability was—and remains—unnecessary, it has been eliminated from the analysis that follows. Consideration of the bounds of any such authority would be inconsistent with the President's unequivocal directive that United States personnel not engage in torture.
>
> We have also modified in some important respects our analysis of the legal standards applicable under 18 U.S.C. §§2340-2340A. For example, we disagree with statements in the August 2002 Memorandum limiting "severe" pain under the statute to "excruciating and agonizing" pain, or to pain "equivalent in intensity to the pain accompanying serious physical injury, such as organ failure, impairment of bodily function, or even death."

On the issue of specific intent, the new memorandum provides:

> We do not believe it is useful to try to define the precise meaning of "specific intent" in section 2340. In light of the President's directive that the United States not engage in torture, it would not be appropriate to rely on parsing the specific intent element of the statute to approve as lawful conduct that might otherwise amount to torture. Some observations, however, are appropriate. It is clear that the specific intent element of section 2340 would be met if a defendant performed an act and "consciously desire[d]" that act to inflict severe physical or mental pain or suffering. 1 LaFave, Substantive

Criminal Law §5.2(a), at 341. Conversely, if an individual acted in good faith, and only after reasonable investigation establishing that his conduct would not inflict severe physical or mental pain or suffering, it appears unlikely that he would have the specific intent necessary to violate sections 2340-2340A. Such an individual could be said neither consciously to desire the proscribed result, nor to have "knowledge or notice" that his act "would likely have resulted in" the proscribed outcome.

After the Abu Ghraib abuses came to light, the Department of Defense commissioned a number of investigations to examine the treatment of detainees in U.S. custody. The August 2004 final report of the Schlesinger Commission, assigned by Secretary Rumsfeld to review Department of Defense detention operations, found that the Abu Ghraib abuses were rooted in the sadism and brutality of a few individuals, rather than in any authorized policy. The Schlesinger Report did acknowledge, however, that failures in training and command contributed to the abuses, and that better guidance from the top could likely have avoided the incidents. Similarly, after five months of investigation, Army Inspector General Lt. Gen. Paul T. Mikolashek concluded that the abuses at Bagram and Abu Ghraib "were not the result of any widespread systemic failure, but . . . the result of an individual's failure to adhere to known standards of discipline, training or Army values." Like the Schlesinger Report, the 300-page Mikolashek Report did find that inadequate training and supervision of soldiers serving as interrogators and prison guards added to the abuse.

As discussed further in Chapter 9, Part II, an April 2005 investigation by Army Inspector General Stanley E. Green cleared the top-ranking officers involved in the Abu Ghraib scandal of any charges related to the abuses committed at the prison. Most notably, Lt. Gen. Ricardo Sanchez, the former senior U.S. commander in Iraq, who was criticized in Pentagon reports for allowing torture to continue under his command, was exonerated of any wrongdoing. Brigadier General Janice Karpinski, the officer in charge of Abu Ghraib prison, was demoted and relieved of command of the 800th Military Police brigade. A small number of enlisted personnel—most notably Pfc. Lynndie R. England and Spc. Charles A. Graner Jr.—have been prosecuted for their role in the Abu Ghraib torture. Graner received the heaviest sentence, ten years; England was sentenced to three years in prison, and the other reservists received sentences of under one year. Marine Major Clarke Paulus, who was convicted of the strangulation death of a non-Abu Ghraib prisoner, is to date the highest ranking officer to be successfully prosecuted for any of the known detainee abuses. Major Paulus was dismissed from service without jail time.

In late 2005, Senator John McCain, who was tortured as a prisoner of war in Vietnam, introduced an amendment to a 2006 Department of Defense Appropriations bill providing that "no person in the custody or under the effective control of the Department of Defense . . . shall be subject to any treatment or technique of interrogation not authorized by and listed in the United States Army Field Manual on Intelligence Interrogation." The amendment provided further:

(a) In General—No individual in the custody or under the physical control of the United States Government, regardless of nationality or physical location, shall be subject to cruel, inhuman, or degrading treatment or punishment.
(b) Construction—Nothing in this section shall be construed to impose any geographical limitation on the applicability of the prohibition against cruel, inhuman, or degrading treatment or punishment under this section.

The amendment added that "'cruel, inhuman, or degrading treatment or punishment' means the cruel, unusual, and inhumane treatment or punishment prohibited by the Fifth, Eighth, and Fourteenth Amendments to the Constitution of the United States, as defined in" the U.S. understanding to the Torture Convention.

Senator McCain argued that the legislation was essential to provide military personnel with clear guidance on permissible interrogation practices and to reverse the Administration's position that the restrictions in the Convention Against Torture did not apply to foreign nationals held outside the United States. The Bush Administration initially opposed the legislation, and later sought an exception for CIA personnel; however, after both houses of Congress voted overwhelmingly to support the legislation, the Bush Administration dropped its opposition, and the amendment became part of the Detainee Treatment Act of 2005.

President Bush signed the legislation on December 30, 2005. In a signing statement, Bush declared:

> The executive branch shall construe [Title X, the portion of the Act relating to detainees], in a manner consistent with the constitutional authority of the President to supervise the unitary executive branch and as Commander in Chief and consistent with the constitutional limitations on the judicial power, which will assist in achieving the shared objective of the Congress and the President, evidenced in Title X, of protecting the American people from further terrorist attacks. Further, in light of the principles enunciated by the Supreme Court . . . , and noting that the text and structure of Title X do not create a private right of action to enforce Title X, the executive branch shall construe Title X not to create a private right of action.

Shortly after the President's signing statement was released, Senator McCain and Senator John Warner released the following joint statement:

> We believe the President understands Congress's intent in passing by very large majorities legislation governing the treatment of detainees included in the 2006 Department of Defense Appropriations and Authorization bills. The Congress declined when asked by administration officials to include a presidential waiver of the restrictions included in our legislation. Our Committee intends through strict oversight to monitor the Administration's implementation of the new law.

In addition to the McCain amendment, the Detainee Treatment Act contains new protections for U.S. personnel engaged in interrogations. Among other things, the Act provides that "in any civil action or criminal prosecution" against such personnel in connection with

> specific operational practices, that involve detention and interrogation of aliens who the President or his designees have determined are believed to be engaged in or associated with international terrorist activity that poses a serious, continuing threat to the United States, its interests, or its allies, and that were officially authorized and determined to be lawful at the time that they were conducted, it shall be a defense that such officer, employee, member of the Armed Forces, or other agent did not know that the practices were unlawful and a person of ordinary sense and understanding would not know the practices were unlawful. Good faith reliance on advice of counsel should be an important factor, among others, to consider in assessing whether a person of ordinary sense and understanding would have known the practices to be unlawful.

Finally, the Detainee Treatment Act also contains language proposed by Senator Lindsey Graham, a former Air Force lawyer. The Graham amendment outlines procedures for reviewing the status of detainees at Guantanamo and for hearing charges against them in military commissions, a topic discussed in greater detail in Chapter 14, Part II. The Graham amendment also provides that "[n]o court, justice, or judge shall have jurisdiction to hear or consider" habeas petitions from detainees at Guantanamo or "any other action against the United States or its agents relating to any aspect of the detention" of detainees at Guantanamo. The amendment also limits the authority of the federal courts to review decisions of the Guantanamo status review tribunals and military commissions.

Notes and Questions

1. Do the Graham amendment and the President's signing statement effectively take away the legal protections the McCain amendment sought to provide detainees? Why might the President have sought a waiver for CIA interrogators?

2. Steven Hadley, the President's National Security Adviser, stated in a press conference that the protections for U.S. personnel in the Detainee Treatment Act emerged through negotiations between Senator McCain and the executive branch on how to achieve "three things: reaffirm our values and principles, aggressively pursue the war on terror and protecting the country, and protecting, through legal protections, our men and women engaged in that fight." Does the Detainee Treatment Act strike the right balance among those objectives? Is it consistent with international law?

3. Should evidence obtained through torture ever be admissible in court? In December 2005, the United Kingdom's highest court, the House of Lords, considered this issue in depth. The British government argued that although evidence procured by torture carried out by or with the complicity of British authorities should not be deemed admissible, evidence procured without any taint of complicity should not be excluded. The Law Lords, however, ruled unanimously that evidence procured by torture may not be admitted into evidence in British courts, regardless of its source. The Law Lords differed as to the precise rationale for excluding such evidence, the definition of torture, and the burden of proof to be met in establishing that evidence in fact was procured by torture. Consider the remarks of Lord Hope of Craighead:

> The use of such evidence is excluded not on grounds of its unreliability—if that was the only objection to it, it would go to its weight, not to its admissibility—but on grounds of its barbarism, its illegality and its inhumanity. The law will not lend its support to the use of torture for any purpose whatever. It has no place in the defence of freedom and democracy, whose very existence depends on the denial of the use of such methods to the executive.

A and Others v. Secretary of State for the Home Department, [2005] UKHL 71. Should state authorities be allowed to use information procured through torture for any purpose? The Law Lords generally agreed that while information procured through torture was not admissible in court, the executive could utilize such information to avert an attack or make an arrest.

II. NARROWING HUMAN RIGHTS TREATIES: THE UNITED STATES AND THE INTERNATIONAL COVENANT ON CIVIL AND POLITICAL RIGHTS

As discussed in Chapter 2, states may make reservations to treaties in order to modify or exclude the application to the reserving state of a particular provision or provisions of the treaty, provided that the reservation is not prohibited by the treaty and is compatible with its object and purpose. In its Advisory Opinion concerning reservations to the Genocide Convention, the ICJ suggested that it was particularly important to permit reservations to human rights and humanitarian law treaties—that is, to treaties "adopted for a purely humanitarian and civilizing purpose," for which the contracting parties desired that "as many States as possible should participate." Reservations to the Convention on the Prevention and Punishment of the Crime of Genocide, 1951 I.C.J. 15, 24.

Most multilateral treaties are ratified with few or no reservations. When states do make reservations to multilateral treaties, the reservations usually relate to the dispute settlement provisions of the treaty or other matters that do not go to the substantive heart of the treaty. By contrast, reservations to multilateral human rights treaties are frequent, and often apply to important substantive provisions of the treaties. As a result, human rights NGOs and treaty bodies frequently argue that the reservations significantly impair the protective purposes of the treaties. Yet only rarely do states object to reservations to human rights treaties. Even less often do states insist that a reservation is incompatible with the object and purpose of the treaty. The U.S. reservations to the ICCPR illustrate some of the issues associated with reservations to human rights treaties.

A. The Problem

The United States played a leading role in the drafting of the ICCPR, and the provisions of that treaty fit comfortably within the liberal political tradition of the U.S. Bill of Rights. Yet the United States did not ratify the ICCPR until 1992, more than 25 years after the Covenant was first opened for signature. Reluctance by the United States to ratify the ICCPR is part of a larger pattern. Although the United States has long supported the development of human rights treaties and routinely presses other countries to ratify and abide by them, the United States has long been reluctant to accept international scrutiny of its own human rights practices.

Several reasons help explain the U.S. attitude to human rights treaties. As discussed in Section I of Chapter 5, conservatives in the United States in the 1950s feared that rapidly developing international human rights norms would threaten segregation and other racially discriminatory practices then prevalent in the United States, expand the power of the federal government at the expense of the states, and undermine the latters' constitutional authority to regulate matters previously considered "local." These concerns drove support for a proposed constitutional amendment, the Bricker Amendment, that would sharply limit the reach of the federal government's treaty power. To defeat this proposed amendment, the Eisenhower Administration announced in 1953 that it did not view human rights treaties "as the proper and most effective way to spread throughout the world the goals of human liberty," and that it would not in the future support ratification of any human rights treaty.

Although subsequent administrations disavowed the Eisenhower Administration's blanket opposition to all human rights treaties, many conservatives in and out of government continue to resist their ratification. In their view, such treaties inappropriately transfer decision-making authority from the Congress and the states to international bodies. Accordingly, the United States to date has ratified only a handful of major human rights treaties, usually long after most other developed Western states. President Truman submitted the Genocide Convention to the

Senate for its advice and consent in 1949, but the United States did not ratify it until 1988. The United States did not ratify the Convention Against Torture or the International Convention on the Elimination of All Forms of Racial Discrimination until 1994. The United States has not ratified the International Covenant on Economic, Social and Cultural Rights or the Convention on the Elimination of Discrimination Against Women; and only the United States and Somalia have failed to ratify the Convention on the Rights of the Child.

Moreover, when the United States does ratify an international human rights treaty, it typically attaches to its instrument of ratification a detailed list of reservations, understandings, and declarations (RUDs) designed to limit the extent of U.S. obligations under the treaty. These RUDs have generated considerable controversy. Critics generally view the RUDs as a means to undercut the utility of treaties as a vehicle for encouraging states to improve their domestic human rights practices. The U.S. RUDs to the ICCPR are a case in point.

B. The Effects of U.S. Reservations

As you review the excerpts of the ICCPR set out below, consider which, if any, of the ICCPR's articles might be viewed as problematic by the U.S. government.

International Covenant on Civil and Political Rights

999 U.N.T.S. 171 (1966)

Article 2

1. Each State Party to the present Covenant undertakes to respect and to ensure to all individuals within its territory and subject to its jurisdiction the rights recognized in the present Covenant, without distinction of any kind, such as race, colour, sex, language, religion, political or other opinion, national or social origin, property, birth or other status. . . .

3. Each State Party to the present Covenant undertakes:

(a) To ensure that any person whose rights or freedoms as herein recognized are violated shall have an effective remedy, notwithstanding that the violation has been committed by persons acting in an official capacity;. . . .

Article 6

1. Every human being has the inherent right to life. This right shall be protected by law. No one shall be arbitrarily deprived of his life.

2. In countries which have not abolished the death penalty, sentence of death may be imposed only for the most serious crimes in accordance with the law in force at the time of the commission of the crime. . . .

5. Sentence of death shall not be imposed for crimes committed by persons below eighteen years of age and shall not be carried out on pregnant women.

6. Nothing in this article shall be invoked to delay or to prevent the abolition of capital punishment by any State Party to the present Covenant. . . .

Article 9

1. Everyone has the right to liberty and security of person. No one shall be subjected to arbitrary arrest or detention. No one shall be deprived of his liberty

except on such grounds and in accordance with such procedure as are established by law. . . .

Article 14

1. All persons shall be equal before the courts and tribunals. In the determination of any criminal charge against him, or of his rights and obligations in a suit at law, everyone shall be entitled to a fair and public hearing by a competent, independent and impartial tribunal established by law. . . .

3. In the determination of any criminal charge against him, everyone shall be entitled to the following minimum guarantees, in full equality:

(a) To be informed promptly and in detail in a language which he understands of the nature and cause of the charge against him;

(b) To have adequate time and facilities for the preparation of his defence and to communicate with counsel of his own choosing;

(c) To be tried without undue delay;

(d) To be tried in his presence, and to defend himself in person or through legal assistance of his own choosing; to be informed, if he does not have legal assistance, of this right; and to have legal assistance assigned to him, in any case where the interests of justice so require, and without payment by him in any such case if he does not have sufficient means to pay for it;

(e) To examine, or have examined, the witnesses against him and to obtain the attendance and examination of witnesses on his behalf under the same conditions as witnesses against him;

(f) To have the free assistance of an interpreter if he cannot understand or speak the language used in court;

(g) Not to be compelled to testify against himself or to confess guilt.

4. In the case of juvenile persons, the procedure shall be such as will take account of their age and the desirability of promoting their rehabilitation.

5. Everyone convicted of a crime shall have the right to his conviction and sentence being reviewed by a higher tribunal according to law. . . .

7. No one shall be liable to be tried or punished again for an offence for which he has already been finally convicted or acquitted in accordance with the law and penal procedure of each country. . . .

Article 17

1. No one shall be subjected to arbitrary or unlawful interference with his privacy, family, home or correspondence, nor to unlawful attacks on his honour and reputation.

2. Everyone has the right to the protection of the law against such interference or attacks.

Article 18

1. Everyone shall have the right to freedom of thought, conscience and religion. . . .

3. Freedom to manifest one's religion or beliefs may be subject only to such limitations as are prescribed by law and are necessary to protect public safety, order, health, or morals or the fundamental rights and freedoms of others.

Article 19

1. Everyone shall have the right to hold opinions without interference.

2. Everyone shall have the right to freedom of expression; this right shall include freedom to seek, receive and impart information and ideas of all kinds, regardless of frontiers, either orally, in writing or in print, in the form of art, or through any other media of his choice.

3. The exercise of the rights provided for in paragraph 2 of this article carries with it special duties and responsibilities. It may therefore be subject to certain restrictions, but these shall only be such as are provided by law and are necessary:

(a) For respect of the rights or reputations of others;

(b) For the protection of national security or of public order (*ordre public*), or of public health or morals.

Article 20

1. Any propaganda for war shall be prohibited by law.

2. Any advocacy of national, racial or religious hatred that constitutes incitement to discrimination, hostility or violence shall be prohibited by law.

Article 23

1. The family is the natural and fundamental group unit of society and is entitled to protection by society and the State.

2. The right of men and women of marriageable age to marry and to found a family shall be recognized.

3. No marriage shall be entered into without the free and full consent of the intending spouses.

4. States Parties to the present Covenant shall take appropriate steps to ensure equality of rights and responsibilities of spouses as to marriage, during marriage and at its dissolution. In the case of dissolution, provision shall be made for the necessary protection of any children. . . .

Article 25

Every citizen shall have the right and the opportunity, without any of the distinctions mentioned in article 2 and without unreasonable restrictions:

(a) To take part in the conduct of public affairs, directly or through freely chosen representatives;

(b) To vote and to be elected at genuine periodic elections which shall be by universal and equal suffrage and shall be held by secret ballot, guaranteeing the free expression of the will of the electors;

(c) To have access, on general terms of equality, to public service in his country.

The Carter Administration announced in 1977 that it would make the promotion of respect for human rights an important component of U.S. foreign policy. In keeping with that pledge, President Carter submitted both the ICCPR and the International Covenant on Economic, Social and Cultural Rights (ICESCR) to the Senate for its advice and consent in 1978. The Carter Administration prepared a package of RUDs to accompany each treaty. As President Carter told the Senate in his ICCPR transmittal message, "whenever a provision is in conflict with United States law, a reservation, understanding or declaration has been submitted." But the Senate took no action on the treaties, and the Reagan Administration, which was critical of Carter's human rights policy for allegedly undermining friendly authoritarian regimes in Latin America and elsewhere, did not pursue ratification. In August 1991, however, the first Bush Administration reformulated the package of RUDs originally prepared by the Carter Administration and asked the Senate Foreign Relations Committee to renew its consideration of the ICCPR. Following Senate approval, the United States ratified the ICCPR in June 1992.

The U.S. acceptance of the ICCPR is qualified by five reservations, four understandings, and four declarations. The reservations limit the effect of ICCPR provisions dealing with war propaganda and hate speech (Article 20), capital punishment (Article 6), the definition of "cruel, inhuman or degrading treatment" (Article 7), reduction of penalties for criminal offenses (Article 15(1)), and segregation of juvenile and adult offenders (Articles 10(2) and 14(4)). The understandings state U.S. interpretations of ICCPR provisions dealing with nondiscrimination (Articles 2 and 26), compensation for unlawful arrest (Articles 9(5) and 14(6)), segregation of accused and convicted persons (Article 10(2)), the purposes of incarceration (Article 10(3)), the rights to counsel, compelled attendance of witnesses, the prohibition of double jeopardy (Article 14(3)), and federal-state relations (Article 50). The U.S. declarations deal primarily with the means by which states implement their obligations under the ICCPR. Most important are the first declaration, which declares provisions 1-27 of the Covenant to be non-self-executing, and the third declaration, which "accepts the competence of the Human Rights Committee to receive and consider communications under Article 41 in which a State Party claims that another State Party is not fulfilling its obligations under the Covenant."

The Senate Foreign Relations Committee Report explains the U.S. approach to the ICCPR and includes the Bush Administration's explanation for its proposed reservations, understandings, and declarations.

Senate Committee on Foreign Relations, Report on the International Covenant on Civil and Political Rights

Senate Executive Rep. 102-123 (102d Cong. 2d Sess. 1992)

. . . The overwhelming majority of the provisions in the Covenant are compatible with existing U.S. domestic law. In those few areas where the two diverge, the Administration has proposed a reservation or other form of condition to clarify the nature of the obligation being undertaken by the United States. This approach has caused concern among some private groups and individuals in the human rights field who argue that U.S. law should be brought into conformance with international human rights standards in those areas where the international standards are superior.

The Committee recognizes the importance of adhering to internationally recognized standards of human rights. Although the U.S. record of adherence has been good, there are some areas in which U.S. law differs from the international standard. For example, the Covenant prohibits the imposition of the death penalty for crimes committed by persons below the age of eighteen but U.S. law allows it for juveniles between the ages of 16 and 18. In areas such as these, it may be appropriate and necessary to question whether changes in U.S. law should be made to bring the United States in to full compliance at the international level. However, the Committee anticipates that changes in U.S. law in these areas will occur through the normal legislative process.

The approach taken by the Administration and the Committee in its resolution of ratification will enable the United States to ratify the Covenant promptly and to participate with greater effectiveness in the process of shaping international norms and behavior in the area of human rights. It does not preclude the United States from modifying its obligations under the Covenant in the future if changes in U.S. law allow the United States to come into full compliance. In view of this situation, ratification with the Administration's proposed reservations, understandings, and declarations is supported by a broad coalition of human rights and legal groups and scholars in the United States, notwithstanding concerns any of them may have with respect to particular conditions. . . .

VII. EXPLANATION OF BUSH ADMINISTRATION CONDITIONS

The Bush Administration . . . submitted the following explanation of its proposals. . . .

FORMAL RESERVATIONS

1. Free Speech (Article 20)

Although Article 19 of the Covenant specifically protects freedom of expression and opinion, Article 20 directly conflicts with the First Amendment by requiring the prohibition of certain forms of speech and expression which are protected under the First Amendment to the U.S. Constitution (i.e., propaganda for war and advocacy of national, racial or religious hatred that constitutes incitement to discrimination, hostility or violence). The United States cannot accept such an obligation. . . .

2. Article 6 (Capital Punishment)

Article 6, paragraph 5 of the Covenant prohibits imposition of the death sentence for crimes committed by persons below 18 years of age and on pregnant women. In 1978, a broad reservation to this article was proposed in order to retain the right to impose capital punishment on any person duly convicted under existing or future laws permitting the imposition of capital punishment. The Administration is now prepared to accept the prohibition against execution of pregnant women. However, in light of the recent reaffirmation of U.S. policy towards capital punishment generally, and in particular the Supreme Court's decisions upholding state laws permitting the death penalty for crimes committed by juveniles aged 16 and 17, the prohibition against imposition of capital punishment for crimes committed by minors is not acceptable. . . .

3. Article 7 (Torture/Punishment)

Article 7 provides that no one shall be subjected to torture or to cruel, inhuman or degrading treatment or punishment or be subjected without his free consent to medical or scientific experimentation. . . . Because the Bill of Rights already contains substantively equivalent protections, and because the Human Rights Committee (like the European Court of Human Rights) has adopted the view that prolonged judicial proceedings in cases involving capital punishment could in certain circumstances constitute such treatment, U.S. ratification of the Covenant should be conditioned upon a reservation limiting our undertakings in this respect to the prohibitions of the Fifth, Eighth and/or Fourteenth Amendments. This would also have the effect of excluding such other practices as corporal punishment and solitary confinement, both of which the Committee has indicated might, depending on the circumstances, be considered contrary to Article 7. . . .

UNDERSTANDINGS

1. Article 2(1), 4(1) and 26 (non-discrimination)*

The very broad anti-discrimination provisions contained in the above articles do not precisely comport with long-standing Supreme Court doctrine in the equal protection field. In particular, Articles 2(1) and 26 prohibit discrimination not only on the basis of "race, colour, sex, language, religion, political or other opinion, national or social origin, property, birth" but also on any "other status." Current U.S. civil rights law is not so open-ended; discrimination is only prohibited for specific statuses, and there are exceptions which allow for discrimination. For example, under the Age Discrimination Act of 1975, age may be taken into account in certain circumstances. In addition, U.S. law permits additional distinctions, for example between citizens and non-citizens and between different categories of non-citizens, especially in the context of the immigration laws. . . .

DECLARATIONS

1. Non-self-executing treaty

For reasons of prudence, we recommend including a declaration that the substantive provisions of the Covenant are not self-executing. The intent is to clarify that the Covenant will not create a private cause of action in U.S. courts. As was the case with the Torture Convention, existing U.S. law generally complies with the Covenant; hence, implementing legislation is not contemplated. . . .

Notes and Questions

1. To what extent are the U.S. RUDs compelled by the U.S. Constitution? What effect do they have on U.S. legal obligations under the ICCPR? Are any of the RUDs unnecessary or undesirable?

2. What changes, if any, should the United States make to its laws to bring them into conformity with the ICCPR? When the Committee suggests such changes should take place through "the normal legislative process," does it mean that such changes should not be made through legislation designed specifically to implement the ICCPR?

3. By ratifying the ICCPR, the United States obtains the benefits of participation in the Convention, including a U.S. national on the Human Rights Committee. Did the United States take on any corresponding obligations by virtue of ratification or does its package of RUDs render illusory any obligations it might otherwise have had under the ICCPR?

---

*The U.S. understanding on nondiscrimination provided in part that the "United States understands distinctions based upon race, colour, sex, language, religion, political or other opinion, national or social origin, property, birth or any other status—as those terms are used in Article 2, paragraph 1 and Article 26—to be permitted when such distinctions are, at minimum, rationally related to a legitimate governmental, objective."—EDS.

C. Reactions to the U.S. RUDs

Following U.S. ratification of the ICCPR, many international law scholars and human rights NGOs criticized the United States for attaching RUDs to the ICCPR and to other human rights treaties to ensure that the treaties would have no effect on U.S. law or practice. Further, a number of states already party to the ICCPR objected to one or more of the U.S. reservations. In particular, many European states objected to the U.S. reservation to Article 6(5), which prohibits capital punishment for crimes committed by persons under 18. In most instances, however, the objecting states indicated that they did not wish to exclude the United States as a party to the Convention, even though they considered some of the U.S. reservations to be incompatible with the object and purpose of the treaty.

In considering the effect of these objections, and the materials that follow, you may wish to review the Vienna Convention provisions on reservations reprinted at pages 72-73. Note that under those provisions, if a state does not object to a reservation made by another state, the treaty enters into force between them, as modified by the reservation. As a practical matter, the outcome is the same if a state objects to a reservation but does not oppose "the entry into force of the treaty between itself and the reserving State." In that case also, "the provisions to which the reservation relates do not apply as between the two States to the extent of the reservation." However, if an objecting state "definitely expresses" its intention not to be bound, the treaty does not enter into force between the objecting and the reserving state. Of course, a particular treaty may contain its own treaty-specific rules regarding the acceptability of reservations.

Although the ICCPR itself contains no provisions dealing with reservations, the Human Rights Committee issued the following general comment on reservations.

Human Rights Committee, General Comment 24

U.N. Doc. A/50/40, Vol. 1, at 119 (1995)

1. As of 1 November 1994, 46 of the 127 States parties to the International Covenant on Civil and Political Rights had, between them, entered 150 reservations of varying significance to their acceptance of the obligations of the Covenant. Some of these reservations exclude the duty to provide and guarantee particular rights in the Covenant. Others are couched in more general terms, often directed to ensuring the continued paramountcy of certain domestic legal provisions. Still others are directed at the competence of the Committee. The number of reservations, their content and their scope may undermine the effective implementation of the Covenant and tend to weaken respect for the obligations of States Parties. . . .

4. The possibility of entering reservations may encourage States which consider that they have difficulties in guaranteeing all the rights in the Covenant nonetheless to accept the generality of obligations in that instrument. . . . However, it is desirable in principle that States accept the full range of obligations, because the human rights norms are the legal expression of the essential rights that every person is entitled to as a human being. . . .

8. Reservations that offend peremptory norms would not be compatible with the object and purpose of the Covenant. Although treaties that are mere exchanges

of obligations between States allow them to reserve *inter se* application of rules of general international law, it is otherwise in human rights treaties, which are for the benefit of persons within their jurisdiction. Accordingly, provisions in the Covenant that represent customary international law (and *a fortiori* when they have the character of peremptory norms) may not be the subject of reservations. Accordingly, a State may not reserve the right to engage in slavery, to torture, to subject persons to cruel, inhuman or degrading treatment or punishment, to arbitrarily deprive persons of their lives, to arbitrarily arrest and detain persons, to deny freedom of thought, conscience and religion, to presume a person guilty unless he proves his innocence, to execute pregnant women or children, to permit the advocacy of national, racial or religious hatred, to deny to persons of marriageable age the right to marry, or to deny to minorities the right to enjoy their own culture, profess their own religion, or use their own language. And while reservations to particular clauses of Article 14 may be acceptable, a general reservation to the right to a fair trial would not be. . . .

10. The Committee has further examined whether categories of reservations may offend the "object and purpose" test. In particular, it falls for consideration as to whether reservations to the non-derogable provisions of the Covenant are compatible with its object and purpose. While there is no hierarchy of importance of rights under the Covenant, the operation of certain rights may not be suspended, even in times of national emergency. This underlines the great importance of non-derogable rights. But not all rights of profound importance, such as articles 9 and 27 of the Covenant, have in fact been made non-derogable. One reason for certain rights being made non-derogable is because their suspension is irrelevant to the legitimate control of the state of national emergency (for example, no imprisonment for debt, in article 11). Another reason is that derogation may indeed be impossible (as, for example, freedom of conscience). At the same time, some provisions are non-derogable exactly because without them there would be no rule of law. A reservation to the provisions of article 4 itself, which precisely stipulates the balance to be struck between the interests of the State and the rights of the individual in times of emergency, would fall in this category. And some non-derogable rights, which in any event cannot be reserved because of their status as peremptory norms, are also of this character—the prohibition of torture and arbitrary deprivation of life are examples. While there is no automatic correlation between reservations to non-derogable provisions, and reservations which offend against the object and purpose of the Covenant, a State has a heavy onus to justify such a reservation.

11. The Covenant consists not just of the specified rights, but of important supportive guarantees. These guarantees provide the necessary framework for securing the rights in the Covenant and are thus essential to its object and purpose. Some operate at the national level and some at the international level. Reservations designed to remove these guarantees are thus not acceptable. Thus, a State could not make a reservation to article 2, paragraph 3, of the Covenant, indicating that it intends to provide no remedies for human rights violations. Guarantees such as these are an integral part of the structure of the Covenant and underpin its efficacy. . . .

12. . . . Of particular concern are widely formulated reservations which essentially render ineffective all Covenant rights which would require any change in national law to ensure compliance with Covenant obligations. No real international rights or obligations have thus been accepted. And when there is an absence of provisions to ensure that Covenant rights may be sued on in domestic courts,

and, further, a failure to allow individual complaints to be brought to the Committee under the first Optional Protocol, all the essential elements of the Covenant guarantees have been removed. . . .

17. As indicated above, it is the Vienna Convention on the Law of Treaties that provides the definition of reservations and also the application of the object and purpose test in the absence of other specific provisions. But the Committee believes that its provisions on the role of State objections in relation to reservations are inappropriate to address the problem of reservations to human rights treaties. Such treaties, and the Covenant specifically, are not a web of inter-State exchanges of mutual obligations. They concern the endowment of individuals with rights. The principle of inter-State reciprocity has no place, save perhaps in the limited context of reservations to declarations on the Committee's competence under article 41. And because the operation of the classic rules on reservations is so inadequate for the Covenant, States have often not seen any legal interest in or need to object to reservations. The absence of protest by States cannot imply that a reservation is either compatible or incompatible with the object and purpose of the Covenant. Objections have been occasional, made by some States but not others, and on grounds not always specified; when an objection is made, it often does not specify a legal consequence, or sometimes even indicates that the objecting party nonetheless does not regard the Covenant as not in effect as between the parties concerned. In short, the pattern is so unclear that it is not safe to assume that a non-objecting State thinks that a particular reservation is acceptable. In the view of the Committee, because of the special characteristics of the Covenant as a human rights treaty, it is open to question what effect objections have between States *inter se.* . . .

18. It necessarily falls to the Committee to determine whether a specific reservation is compatible with the object and purpose of the Covenant. This is in part because, as indicated above, it is an inappropriate task for States parties in relation to human rights treaties, and in part because it is a task that the Committee cannot avoid in the performance of its functions. In order to know the scope of its duty to examine a State's compliance under article 40 or a communication under the first Optional Protocol, the Committee has necessarily to take a view on the compatibility of a reservation with the object and purpose of the Covenant and with general international law. Because of the special character of a human rights treaty, the compatibility of a reservation with the object and purpose of the Covenant must be established objectively, by reference to legal principles, and the Committee is particularly well placed to perform this task. The normal consequence of an unacceptable reservation is not that the Covenant will not be in effect at all for a reserving party. Rather, such a reservation will generally be severable, in the sense that the Covenant will be operative for the reserving party without benefit of the reservation.

The United States and the United Kingdom objected to various aspects of General Comment 24. Portions of the U.S. response follow:

1. Role of the Committee

The last sentence of paragraph 11 states that "a reservation that rejects the Committee's competence to interpret the requirements of any provisions of the Covenant would also be contrary to the object and purpose of that treaty."

In this regard, the analysis in paragraphs 16-20 regarding which body has the legal authority to make determinations concerning the permissibility of specific reservations, is of considerable concern. Here the Committee appears to reject the established rules of interpretation of treaties as set forth in the Vienna Convention on the Law of Treaties and in customary international law. . . .

Moreover, the Committee appears to dispense with the established procedures for determining the permissibility of reservations and to divest States Parties of any role in determining the meaning of the Covenant, which they drafted and joined, and of the extent of their treaty obligations. In this view, "[i]t necessarily falls to the Committee to determine whether a specific reservation is compatible with the object and purpose of the Covenant".

The Committee's position, while interesting, runs contrary to the Covenant scheme and international law.

2. Acceptability of reservations: governing legal principles

. . . It is clear that a State cannot exempt itself from a peremptory norm of international law by making a reservation to the Covenant. It is not at all clear that a State cannot choose to exclude one means of enforcement of particular norms by reserving against inclusion of those norms in its Covenant obligations.

The proposition that any reservation which contravenes a norm of customary international law is *per se* incompatible with the object and purpose of this or any other convention, however, is a much more significant and sweeping premise. It is, moreover, wholly unsupported by and is in fact contrary to international law. As recognized in the paragraph 10 analysis of non-derogable rights, an "object and purpose" analysis by its nature requires consideration of the particular treaty, right, and reservation in question.

Observations by the United States of America on General Comment No. 24 (52), U.N. Doc. A/50/40, vol. 1, at 126-127 (1996), Annex VI.

The International Law Commission has been studying the subject of reservations since December 1993, and the Commission's special rapporteur has produced a series of reports and draft guidelines that have been the subject of extensive discussion within the Commission and among interested states. In 1997, the Commission, after considerable debate, offered the following observations concerning the competence of treaty monitoring bodies to assess the validity of a state's reservation:

> 5. The Commission also considers that where these treaties are silent on the subject, the monitoring bodies established thereby are competent to comment upon and express recommendations with regard, *inter alia*, to the admissibility of reservations by States, in order to carry out the functions assigned to them;
>
> 6. The Commission stresses that this competence of the monitoring bodies does not exclude or otherwise affect the traditional modalities of control by the contracting parties, on the one hand, in accordance with [the rules regarding reservations established in the Vienna Convention on the Law of Treaties] and, where appropriate, by the organs for settling any dispute that may arise concerning the interpretation or application of the treaties;
>
> 8. The Commission notes that the legal force of the findings made by monitoring bodies in the exercise of their power to deal with reservations cannot exceed that resulting from the powers given to them for the performance of their general monitoring role. . . .

Report of the International Law Commission on the work of its forty-ninth session, U.N. Doc. A/52/10, at 126-127 (1997).

In 1995, the Human Rights Committee considered the initial report of the United States pursuant to Article 40 of the ICCPR. The Committee offered various criticisms of U.S. law and practice, noting problems with the persistence of racial and gender discrimination and with the application of criminal and family law, among other things. The Committee also again criticized the extent of the U.S. reservations to the ICCPR, noting that "taken together, they are intended to ensure that the United States has accepted what is already the law of the United States." The Committee objected in particular to the U.S. reservation to the prohibition on the execution of juveniles as "incompatible with the object and purpose of the Covenant" and urged the United States to "review its reservations, declarations and understandings with a view to withdrawing them, in particular reservations to article 6, paragraph 5, and article 7 of the Covenant." Human Rights Committee, Comments on United States of America, U.N. Doc. A/50/40, at 48-50 (1995).

The Human Rights Committee again had an opportunity to address the effect of an invalid reservation in *Kennedy v. Trinidad & Tobago* (1999), in connection with Trinidad and Tobago's reservation to the First Optional Protocol to the ICCPR. The reservation provided:

> Trinidad and Tobago re-accedes to the Optional Protocol to the International Covenant on Civil and Political Rights with a Reservation to article 1 thereof to the effect that the Human Rights Committee shall not be competent to receive and consider communications relating to any prisoner who is under sentence of death in respect of any matter relating to his prosecution, his detention, his trial, his conviction, his sentence or the carrying out of the death sentence on him and any matter connected therewith.

Kennedy, who was in prison awaiting execution, claimed that the circumstances of his trial and the death penalty as applied to him violated various provisions of the ICCPR, including the right to life. Trinidad and Tobago argued that in light of its reservation, the Human Rights Committee lacked jurisdiction to consider Kennedy's petition. The Committee decided that the reservation was invalid and severable:

> [T]he Committee cannot accept a reservation which singles out a certain group of individuals for lesser procedural protection than that which is enjoyed by the rest of the population. In the view of the Committee, this constitutes a discrimination which runs counter to some of the basic principles embodied in the Covenant and its Protocols, and for this reason the reservation cannot be deemed compatible with the object and purpose of the Optional Protocol. The consequence is that the Committee is not precluded from considering the present communication. . . .

In subsequent proceedings, the Committee found Trinidad and Tobago in violation of the ICCPR. Four Committee members dissented. They disagreed with the majority's view that a refusal to consider communications from a particular class of individuals constituted impermissible discrimination. They also disagreed in part with the majority's view on severability. Although noting that, in most cases, an invalid reservation "will not vitiate the reserving state's agreement to be a party to the Covenant" under the analysis of General Comment 24, the dissenters argued that "this assumption cannot apply when it is abundantly clear that the reserving state's agreement to becoming a party to the Covenant is *dependent* on the acceptability of the reservation." In this case, the dissenters went on, Trinidad and Tobago denounced the Optional Protocol and immediately reacceded with the reservation. It also explained why it could not accept the Committee's competence to deal with communications from persons under sentence of death. In these particular circumstances it is quite clear that Trinidad and Tobago was not prepared to be a party to the Optional Protocol without the particular reservation, and that its reaccession was dependent on acceptability of that reservation.

Notes and Questions

1. Which, if any, of the U.S. reservations to the ICCPR are incompatible with the object and purpose of that treaty? Is the package of RUDs, taken as a whole, incompatible with the object and purpose of the treaty?

2. What is the basis for the Human Rights Committee's claim that it is particularly well placed to assess the validity of reservations to the ICCPR? Should the Committee's assessment of reservations be treated as authoritative?

3. Do you agree with the Committee's assessment of the consequences of an unacceptable reservation? What would be the consequences for the United States under the Committee's approach? If the Committee's approach to unacceptable reservations becomes generally accepted, what changes might states make in their approach to ratification of human rights treaties?

4. Why would the United States ratify the Covenant if it was unwilling to change its laws? Critics charge that with its package of RUDs, the United States "is pretending to assume international obligations, but is in fact undertaking nothing," and seeks the benefits of participating in human rights treaties "without assuming any obligations or burdens." One critic suggests that "Senator Bricker lost his battle, but his ghost is now enjoying victory." Do you agree?

D. Litigating the U.S. Reservation on Execution of Juveniles

In 1999, Michael Domingues petitioned the U.S. Supreme Court for a writ of certiorari to challenge the death sentence imposed on him by the state of Nevada for a crime committed when he was 16 years old. Domingues argued that the sentence violated the ICCPR's prohibition on the execution of juveniles, and that the U.S. reservation to that provision was void. Domingues made a similar argument to the Nevada Supreme Court; although the majority rejected his argument, two judges dissented, one indicating that the ICCPR prohibited execution of juveniles, the other urging a full hearing on the issue. The following excerpt provides the U.S. response to Domingues's certiorari petition to the U.S. Supreme Court.

Michael Domingues, Petitioner v. State of Nevada, Brief for the United States as Amicus Curiae

4-5, 8-10 (1999)

1. Petitioner first contends that his death sentence contravenes Article 6(5) of the ICCPR. . . . Petitioner maintains . . . that the Senate's reservation [to Article 6(5)] is invalid [and] . . . that the United States is bound by all of Article

6(5), including the prohibition against capital punishment for 16-year-old offenders, and that the domestic courts of the United States must therefore apply Article 6(5) to invalidate his death sentence. Those contentions are incorrect. . . .

Even if there were merit to those arguments as a matter of international treaty law, that would not mean that Article 6(5) should be enforced by a domestic court in the face of the United States' reservation. A reservation in which the President and the Senate have concurred is controlling as a matter of domestic law, and prevents the provision of the treaty to which the reservation was taken from being part of the "Treat[y] made . . . under the authority of the United States" that would bind the States under the Supremacy Clause. U.S. Const. Art. VI, Cl. 2. . . . If other nations are dissatisfied with the reservations attached by the United States to its ratification of a treaty, they may present a diplomatic protest or may decline to recognize themselves as being in treaty relations with the United States, but that is a matter between states and not for judicial resolution. . . .

In any event, petitioner's challenges to the validity of the reservation fall wide of the mark. Petitioner argues that the reservation to Article 6(5) is invalid under the law of treaties because it is contrary to the "object and purpose" of the ICCPR. Of the 149 states that are parties to the ICCPR, 11 have objected to the United States' reservation to Article 6(5), and nine of the 11 have objected on the ground that the reservation violated the ICCPR's object and purpose. Not one of the states that lodged an objection stated that, because of the United States' reservation, it does not recognize the ICCPR as being in force between itself and the United States. State practice therefore supports the conclusion that the United States' reservation to Article 6(5) is valid as a matter of treaty law. See Vienna Convention, art. 20(4)(b) (objection by a contracting state to another state's reservation to part of a treaty does not prevent the treaty from entering into force unless such an intention "is definitely expressed by the objecting State").

Petitioner also argues that, because the ICCPR makes Article 6(5) nonderogable in times of emergency, see ICCPR art. 4(2), Article 6(5) must be so fundamental to the treaty that no reservation may be taken to it. There is no necessary correlation under the ICCPR, however, between the nonderogability of a right and its importance or centrality to the treaty. Several rights of profound importance, such as the right against arbitrary arrest and detention (protected by Article 9(1)) and the right to be informed of the nature of criminal charges brought against one (protected by Article 14(3)(a)), are not made nonderogable under the ICCPR. If the parties to the Covenant had intended to prohibit reservations to Article 6(5), they could have so provided explicitly, as authorized by Article 19(b) of the Vienna Convention, rather than doing so obliquely (as petitioner argues) by making the article nonderogable in times of national emergency. Accordingly, as a matter of treaty law, the United States' reservation to Article 6(5) is valid and effective.

The Supreme Court denied certiorari. On May 1, 2000, Domingues filed a petition with the Inter-American Commission on Human Rights, claiming that the application of the death penalty to him would violate U.S. treaty and customary international law obligations forbidding the execution of juveniles. In a report dated October 22, 2002, the Commission stated that [t]he overwhelming evidence of global state practice . . . displays a consistency and generality amongst world states indicating that the world community considers the execution of offenders aged below 18 years at the time of their offence to be inconsistent with prevailing standards of decency. The Commission is therefore of the view that a norm of international customary law has emerged prohibiting the execution of offenders under the age of 18 years at the time of their crime. The Commission went on to conclude that "this rule has been recognized as being of a sufficiently indelible nature to now constitute a norm of *jus cogens*," and that the execution of Domingues would be a "grave and irreparable violation of Mr. Domingues' right to life."

On March 1, 2005, in *Roper v. Simmons*, 543 U.S. 551 (2005), the Supreme Court held by a vote of 5-4 that the Eighth and Fourteenth Amendments to the U.S. Constitution prohibit the execution of offenders who were under 18 at the time of their offense. Writing for the majority, Justice Kennedy observed that it is necessary to refer to "'the evolving standards of decency that mark the progress of a maturing society' to determine which punishments are so disproportionate as to be cruel and unusual." Justice Kennedy noted "the rejection of the juvenile death penalty in the majority of States; the infrequency of its use even where it remains on the books; and the consistency in the trend toward abolition of the practice," as well as the fact that the United States was the only country in the world to "give official sanction to the juvenile death penalty," before concluding that the penalty was "disproportionate punishment for offenders under 18." For more on the Supreme Court's use of international law in interpreting provisions of the U.S. Constitution, see Chapter 5, Section IV.

Notes and Questions

1. Why might states be reluctant to challenge the U.S. reservations to the ICCPR? Does it follow that the U.S. reservations are compatible with the object and purpose of the treaty?

2. Why is Article 6(5) listed among the nonderogable provisions of the ICCPR? Does that offer any support for the proposition that the U.S. reservation to that article is incompatible with the object and purpose of the treaty?

3. Under the U.S. Constitution, treaties are the law of the land. Should the Senate be able to render U.S. courts unable to adjudicate claims under the ICCPR by declaring it to be non-self-executing?

III. GUARANTEEING ECONOMIC, SOCIAL, AND CULTURAL RIGHTS: A RIGHT TO FOOD?

The Universal Declaration of Human Rights sets out both civil and political rights and economic, social, and cultural rights. But the relationship and relative status of the two sets of rights has long been controversial. Some states, particularly socialist and developing countries, have taken the position that the achievement of a minimum standard of economic and social welfare is an essential precondition to the realization of political and civil rights. Other states have emphasized the importance of political and civil rights to economic progress; some have questioned whether economic and social rights can properly be considered rights at all.

These political and philosophical differences, exacerbated by Cold War politics, played out in the debates over a successor covenant to the Universal Declaration of Human Rights. In 1948, the UN General Assembly proposed the promulgation of a single covenant to give binding legal effect to the principles enunciated in the Universal Declaration. But when the time came to begin drafting such a covenant, some Western states questioned the desirability and feasibility of including economic and social rights. To those states, and to the United States in particular, the ICCPR appeared to fall far more comfortably within the Western tradition of respect for liberal democratic rights than did the companion International Covenant on Economic, Social, and Cultural Rights. The former was seen as a natural descendant of Western theories of political liberty and civil rights, as reflected in antecedents such as the French Declaration of the Rights of Man and the Citizen and the Bill of Rights to the U.S. Constitution; the latter as more recent successor to the early twentieth-century Constitutions of states such as the Soviet Union and Mexico. As a result, the first draft covenant prepared by the United Nations Human Rights Commission contained only political and civil rights.

But in 1950, developing and socialist states managed to push through the General Assembly a resolution urging the Human Rights Commission "to include in the draft covenant a clear expression of economic, social and cultural rights in a manner which relates them to the civil and political freedoms proclaimed by the draft covenant." Western states then insisted that the single Covenant contemplated by the Commission be split into two separate Covenants. After a long debate, the General Assembly reaffirmed that the two sets of rights are "interconnected and interdependent," and emphasized that "when deprived of economic, social and cultural rights, man does not represent the human person whom the Universal Declaration regards as the ideal of the free man." G.A. Res. 421 (1950).

In 1952, the General Assembly accepted the Western demand for two covenants, but stipulated that the two should be promulgated simultaneously to reaffirm their interdependence. The different views concerning the demand for two covenants are described in the following analysis prepared by the UN Secretariat in 1955:

8. Those who were in favour of drafting a single covenant maintained that human rights could not be clearly divided into different categories, nor could they be so classified as to represent a hierarchy of values. All rights should be promoted and protected at the same time. Without economic, social and cultural rights, civil and political rights might be purely nominal in character; without civil and political rights, economic, social and cultural rights could not be long ensured . . .

9. Those in favour of drafting two separate covenants argued that civil and political rights were enforceable, or justiciable, or of an 'absolute' character, while economic, social and cultural rights were not or might not be; that the former were immediately applicable, while the latter were to be progressively implemented; and that, generally speaking, the former were rights of the individual 'against' the State, that is, against unlawful and unjust action of the State, while the latter were rights which the State would have to take positive action to promote. Since the nature of civil and political rights and that of economic, social and cultural rights, and the obligations of the State in respect thereof, were different, it was desirable that two separate instruments should be prepared.

10. The question of drafting one or two covenants was intimately related to the question of implementation. If no measures of implementation were to be formulated, it would make little difference whether one or two covenants were to be drafted. Generally speaking, civil and political rights were thought to be 'legal' rights and could best be implemented by the creation of a good offices committee,

while economic, social and cultural rights were thought to be 'programme' rights and could best be implemented by the establishment of a system of periodic reports. Since the rights could be divided into two broad categories, which should be subject to different procedures of implementation, it would be both logical and convenient to formulate two separate covenants.

11. However, it was argued that not in all countries and territories were all civil and political rights 'legal' rights, nor all economic, social and cultural rights 'programme' rights. A civil or political right might well be a 'programme' right under one regime, an economic, social or cultural right a 'legal' right under another. A covenant could be drafted in such a manner as would enable States, upon ratification or accession, to announce, each in so far as it was concerned, which civil, political, economic, social and cultural rights were 'legal' rights, and which 'programme' rights, and by which procedures the rights would be implemented.

Annotations on the Text of the Draft International Covenants on Human Rights, U.N. Doc. A/2929 at 7 (1955).

As you read the following materials, consider whether there are meaningful differences between political and civil rights and economic, social, and cultural rights; the reasons behind the U.S. reluctance to ratify the Covenant on Economic, Social and Cultural Rights; and the nature and extent of any international legal obligations imposed on states in connection with the effort to combat hunger.

A. The Problem

Although considerable progress has been made over the last three decades toward meeting the world's basic food needs, as many as 800 million people, including 200 million children, are malnourished. Millions die of hunger every year. Although many lack food as the result of drought or war, most hunger-related deaths occur as the result of chronic malnutrition. The problem stems principally from the grinding poverty that affects large portions of the developing world, where almost a third of the population subsists on less than a dollar a day. As Professor Asbjørn Eide explains:

> The cause of hunger is generally not to be found in a lack of sufficient food on the world market, but in the inability of food-insecure groups to produce or procure food. Many living in the rural areas of developing countries are either landless or unable to produce enough, including food, to make a decent living. Their sources of livelihood are sometimes destroyed. The land rights of indigenous peoples have sometimes remained unrecognized and their land encroached upon by others.
>
> Part of the problem of hunger arises from discrimination against women. In sub-Saharan Africa, a large part of the small farmers are women. Their rights to land or their inheritance rights are precarious or non-existing. The HIV/AIDS epidemic has further weakened their possibility to make a living for themselves and their families, and made the lack of inheritance rights an even greater obstacle for widows. In South Asia, another factor underlying serious malnutrition is discrimination of women within the household, with particularly serious consequences for malnutrition in the poorer sections. Undernourished mothers give birth to undernourished children, whose learning capacities are thereby often weakened. These children are likely to fail in

the educational institutions and live a new generation of poverty, causing an intergenerational cycle of poverty and malnutrition.

Asbjørn Eide, *Time to Move From Generalities*, 38 U.N. Chronicle 42, 42-43 (Sept.-Nov. 2001).

Aggregate food consumption in some 50 countries currently falls below the average daily caloric intake set by the UN Food and Agriculture Organization (FAO). As grim as these statistics are, they represent a significant improvement over the recent past. The FAO notes that although the population of developing countries has nearly doubled in the last 30 years, the proportion of people suffering from chronic malnourishment has been cut almost in half, to about 18 percent.

Although the problem of hunger is greatest in the developing world, particularly in sub-Saharan Africa, many people in developed countries also go hungry. A September 2000 report by the U.S. Department of Agriculture found that 31 million Americans, including 12 million children, lacked an adequate diet. The problem was particularly acute among the black and Hispanic segments of the population.

George McGovern, a former U.S. presidential candidate, describes some of the costs associated with the continuing problem of world hunger.

> So what will it cost [to end hunger]? Beyond what the United States and other countries are now doing, it will take an estimated $5 billion a year, of which $1.2 billion would come from the United States. If this annual allocation were continued for fifteen years, until 2015, we could reduce the 800 million hungry people by half. To erase hunger for the remaining 400 million would cost about the same if it were to be accomplished in the fifteen years leading up to the year 2030. . . .
>
> What will it cost if we don't end the hunger that now afflicts so many of our fellow humans? The World Bank has concluded that each year malnutrition causes the loss of 46 million years of productive life, at a cost of $16 billion annually, several times the cost of ending hunger and turning this loss into productive gain.
>
> But victory over hunger will not come without the assistance of those countries able to help, including the European nations, Japan, Canada, Australia, Argentina and the OPEC oil States. And before the battle is over, perhaps it can be joined by China, India and Russia. Of equal or greater importance is the need for reform in the developing countries if hunger is to be ended. This means improved farming methods; the conservation and wiser use of the earth's limited water resources; more rights and opportunities, especially education, for the girls and women of the Third World; a greater measure of democratic government responsive to basic human needs, including food security; and a substitution of common-sense negotiation of differences instead of the murderous civil, ethnic and nationalistic conflicts that have torn up people, property and land across the Third World.

George McGovern, *The Real Cost of Hunger*, 38 U.N. Chronicle 24, 25-26 (Sept.-Nov. 2001).

B. Background on Economic, Social, and Cultural Rights

In some respects, the ICCPR and the ICESCR are obviously similar. The Preambles and articles 1 (self-determination), 3 (equal rights of men and women to enjoy Covenant rights), and 5 (prohibiting reliance on the Covenant as a ground for limiting rights) of the two covenants are essentially identical. In other respects the two covenants differ significantly, as will be evident when you review the following excerpts.

International Covenant on Economic, Social and Cultural Rights

993 U.N.T.S. 3 (1966)

The States Parties to the present Covenant, . . .

Recognizing that, in accordance with the Universal Declaration of Human Rights, the ideal of free human beings enjoying freedom from fear and want can only be achieved if conditions are created whereby everyone may enjoy his economic, social and cultural rights, as well as his civil and political rights. . . .

Agree upon the following articles:

Article 2

1. Each State Party to the present Covenant undertakes to take steps, individually and through international assistance and co-operation, especially economic and technical, to the maximum of its available resources, with a view to achieving progressively the full realization of the rights recognized in the present Covenant by all appropriate means, including particularly the adoption of legislative measures.

2. The States Parties to the present Covenant undertake to guarantee that the rights enunciated in the present Covenant will be exercised without discrimination of any kind as to race, colour, sex, language, religion, political or other opinion, national or social origin, property, birth or other status.

3. Developing countries, with due regard to human rights and their national economy, may determine to what extent they would guarantee the economic rights recognized in the present Covenant to non-nationals.

Article 4

The States Parties to the present Covenant recognize that, in the enjoyment of those rights provided by the State in conformity with the present Covenant, the State may subject such rights only to such limitations as are determined by law only in so far as this may be compatible with the nature of these rights and solely for the purpose of promoting the general welfare in a democratic society.

Article 6

1. The States Parties to the present Covenant recognize the right to work, which includes the right of everyone to the opportunity to gain his living by work which he freely chooses or accepts, and will take appropriate steps to safeguard this right.

2. The steps to be taken by a State Party to the present Covenant to achieve the full realization of this right shall include technical and vocational guidance and training programmes, policies and techniques to achieve steady economic, social and cultural development and full and productive employment under conditions safeguarding fundamental political and economic freedoms to the individual.

Article 7

The States Parties to the present Covenant recognize the right of everyone to the enjoyment of just and favourable conditions of work, which ensure, in particular:

(a) remuneration which provides all workers, as a minimum, with:

(i) fair wages and equal remuneration for work of equal value without distinction of any kind, in particular women being guaranteed conditions of work not inferior to those enjoyed by men, with equal pay for equal work;

(ii) a decent living for themselves and their families in accordance with the provisions of the present Covenant;

(b) safe and healthy working conditions;

(c) equal opportunity for everyone to be promoted in his employment to an appropriate higher level, subject to no considerations other than those of seniority and competence;

(d) rest, leisure and reasonable limitation of working hours and periodic holidays with pay, as well as remuneration for public holidays.

Article 9

The States Parties to the present Covenant recognize the right of everyone to social security, including social insurance.

Article 11

1. The States Parties to the present Covenant recognize the right of everyone to an adequate standard of living for himself and his family, including adequate food, clothing and housing, and to the continuous improvement of living conditions. The States Parties will take appropriate steps to ensure the realization of this right, recognizing to this effect the essential importance of international co-operation based on free consent.

2. The States Parties to the present Covenant, recognizing the fundamental right of everyone to be free from hunger, shall take, individually and through international co-operation, the measures, including specific programmes, which are needed:

(a) to improve methods of production, conservation and distribution of food by making full use of technical and scientific knowledge, by disseminating knowledge of the principles of nutrition and by developing or reforming agrarian systems in such a way as to achieve the most efficient development and utilization of natural resources;

(b) taking into account the problems of both food-importing and food-exporting countries, to ensure an equitable distribution of world food supplies in relation to need.

Article 12

1. The States Parties to the present Covenant recognize the right of everyone to the enjoyment of the highest attainable standard of physical and mental health. . . .

Notes and Questions

1. What steps are parties to the ICESCR required to take to combat hunger?

2. To what extent and in what ways are the rights enumerated different in kind from political and civil rights? Do you agree with the General Assembly that economic, social, and cultural rights and political and civil rights are "interconnected

and interdependent," or do you agree with Western states who argued in favor of two separate covenants?

3. The decision to promulgate two separate covenants turned in part on the question of implementation. How would states go about implementing, for example, the right to an "adequate standard of living"? Would implementation of economic, social, and cultural rights generally require an approach different from implementation of political and civil rights?

4. Compare Article 2 of the ICESCR with Article 2 of the ICCPR. What obligations does each article impose? Under Article 16 of the ICESCR, states are required to submit reports "on the measures they have adopted and the progress made in achieving observance of" ICESCR rights. In 1985, the UN Economic and Social Council set up a Committee on Economic, Social and Cultural Rights modeled on the Human Rights Committee established under Article 28 of the ICCPR. The Committee is to monitor state reports and issue comments and recommendations on state compliance with the ICESCR. How should the Committee ascertain whether a party to the ICESCR is taking steps to realize Covenant rights "to the maximum of its available resources"? Would a court be competent to determine whether a state is meeting its obligations under the ICESCR?

5. Many states routinely fail to comply with their reporting obligations under the ICESCR. They either fail to present their reports at all or present their reports years after they were due. The problem became so acute that in 1998 the Committee on Economic, Social, and Cultural Rights complained in its annual report to the United Nations that "a situation of persistent non-reporting by states parties risks bringing the entire supervisory procedure into disrepute, thereby undermining one of the foundations of the Covenant." Committee on Economic, Social and Cultural Rights, Report on the Sixteenth and Seventeenth Sessions, U.N. Doc. E/1998/22, para. 42. The Committee decided that it would schedule "very much overdue" reports for consideration at future sessions, notify the states involved, and if those states then failed to provide the required reports, proceed to consider their compliance with the ICESCR "in light of all the available information." *Id*. para. 44. As of 2001, 184 ICESCR reports were still overdue. (Some states had two or more overdue reports.) By way of comparison, 133 reports were overdue under the Torture Convention, 149 under the ICCPR, and 430 under the Convention on the Elimination of Racial Discrimination. Why might states routinely ignore their reporting obligations? How effective is reporting likely to be as an implementation mechanism?

6. Human rights advocates have long urged adoption of an optional protocol to the ICESCR to provide for an individual complaints procedure. The Economic, Social and Cultural Rights Committee prepared a draft protocol in 1996 and submitted it to the UN Human Rights Commission for its consideration. Despite extensive discussion within the Commission and receipt of comments by governments, no optional protocol has yet been adopted. Why might states be reluctant to adopt such a protocol?

C. The U.S. Position on Economic, Social, and Cultural Rights

The United States played a lead role in pressing for separate covenants and has expressed considerable skepticism regarding the status of economic, social, and cultural rights. But the U.S. position has varied considerably from administration to administration. In January 1941, President Franklin Roosevelt delivered his famous "Four Freedoms" speech, warning the country of the need to strengthen democracy and combat totalitarianism, in part by protecting "four essential human freedoms," among them "freedom from want—which, translated into world terms, means economic understandings which will secure to every nation a healthy peacetime life for its inhabitants—everywhere in the world." 87 Cong. Rec. 44, 46-47 (1941).

Roosevelt elaborated on the four freedoms theme in his 1944 State of the Union message:

> It is our duty now to begin to lay the plans and determine the strategy for the winning of a lasting peace and the establishment of an American standard of living higher than ever before known. We cannot be content, no matter how high that general standard of living may be, if some fraction of our people—whether it be one-third or one-fifth or one-tenth—is ill-fed, ill-clothed, ill-housed, and insecure. . . .
>
> We have come to a clear realization of the fact that true individual freedom cannot exist without economic security and independence. "Necessitous men are not free men." People who are hungry and out of a job are the stuff of which dictatorships are made.
>
> In our day these economic truths have become accepted as self-evident. We have accepted, so to speak, a second Bill of Rights under which a new basis of security and prosperity can be established for all—regardless of station, race, or creed.
>
> Among these are:
>
> > The right to a useful and remunerative job in the industries or shops or farms or mines of the Nation;
> > The right to earn enough to provide adequate food and clothing and recreation;
> > The right of every farmer to raise and sell his products at a return which will give him and his family a decent living;
> > The right of every businessman, large and small, to trade in an atmosphere of freedom from unfair competition and domination by monopolies at home or abroad;
> > The right of every family to a decent home;
> > The right to adequate medical care and the opportunity to achieve and enjoy good health;
> > The right to adequate protection from the economic fears of old age, sickness, accident, and unemployment;
> > The right to a good education.

90 Cong. Rec. 55, 57 (1944)

In 1966, the U.S. representative in the UN General Assembly voted in favor of the adoption of the International Covenant on Economic, Social and Cultural Rights. Although the Nixon and Ford Administrations took no action with respect to the Covenant, President Carter signed it in 1978 and sent it to the Senate for its advice and consent. The Covenant languished there, and the Reagan and first Bush Administrations both opposed its ratification. Indeed, the Reagan and Bush Administrations rejected the idea that economic and social rights could properly be considered rights at all.

In 1982, the Reagan Administration decided to de-emphasize economic, social, and cultural rights in the annual State Department Country Report on Human Rights Practices, which surveys the human rights situation in countries around the world. Elliott Abrams, then Assistant Secretary of State for Human Rights and Humanitarian Affairs, explained why:

The particular interpretation of economic and social rights that has become common in the last two decades creates two kinds of difficulties for anyone who is trying to do effective work to protect human rights against abuse.

First, there is a blurring of what is the vital core of human rights—the core that we must protect at all costs. I can use examples from the first drafts of the country reports that we recently worked on. One of these drafts referred to the fact that the inhabitants of a certain country suffer from an excessively starchy diet. This is not a question we should ignore. But I frankly feel there is an enormous disproportion between the issue of whether people are being tortured and murdered and the issue of whether their diet is too starchy. It is already a very difficult task for the United States Government to find effective ways of stopping torture and murder. We can carry out this task effectively only if we can continue to focus on the vital core of human rights. . . .

The second practical problem is that the current interpretation of economic and social rights is easily exploited to excuse violations of civil and political rights. Everyone who follows world politics has heard the argument that the rights Americans have must be postponed for other peoples while economic and social rights are achieved. For example, we hear many governments arguing against press freedom with this kind of excuse: just as we are too poor to respect "rights" such as good housing and good medical care that you respect in America, so we are too poor to respect other rights such as a free press. It is often added that the achievement of economic and social rights actually *requires* depriving people of the rights every American enjoys as his birthright. I do not believe those who genuinely care about human rights can accept these excuses. . . .

The great men who founded the modern concern for human rights . . . wanted to focus the idealism of mankind by defining very precisely the rights that are truly inalienable. They sought to do this by separating those goods the government ought to encourage over the long term from the rights the government *has an absolute duty to respect* at any time. In order to achieve this result, these thinkers established separate spheres of public and private life. No longer was the Government to minutely specify how people traded, worshipped, and conducted their ordinary life, social, economic and cultural life was left in the private sphere, and the task of the government was to provide appropriate conditions in which the social, economic and cultural freedom of the people could develop.

. . . [W]e must not blur the distinction between two categories. The rights that no government *can violate* should not be watered down to the status of rights that governments should *do their best* to secure. The right to be free from torture or to freedom of speech can and should be easily respected by every Government. No government has to torture or censor its people. But the rights to an adequate standard of living or to holidays with pay or to technical and professional education pose enormous challenges to desperately poor nations. The policies likely to produce conditions where those rights can be enjoyed are matters of intense debate and may require generations to take effect. We resist any effort to lower all individual rights to that level. And we resist any effort to reinterpret economic and social rights so that they belong to groups rather than individuals. We are unwilling to allow them to become demands for an international regime of restriction and redistribution that would obstruct the prospects for growth and the eventual enjoyment of economic and social rights by all people.

Review of State Department Country Reports on Human Rights Practices for 1981, Hearing Before the House Subcommittee on Human Rights and International Organizations, April 28, 1982, 97th Cong., 2d Sess., at 13-17.

In 1993, the Clinton Administration announced that it would support ratification of the ICESCR, but in the face of Senate reluctance, it did not press the issue.

Notes and Questions

1. Do you agree with Abrams's critique of economic, social, and cultural rights? Some scholars and policy makers argue that economic, social, and cultural rights entail large government assistance programs, which can only be designed by legislatures and should not be viewed as individual rights. In this view, economic, social, and cultural rights are positive, cost-intensive, and programmatic. They argue that, by contrast, civil and political rights can be implemented if governments simply refrain from taking the prohibited actions (e.g., torture) and that violations can be easily adjudicated by courts. Accordingly, they consider political and civil rights to be negative, cost-free, and justiciable. Does this comparison withstand analysis?

2. Note that Article 4 of the ICCPR permits states to derogate from their obligations under certain provisions of the Covenant, provided certain criteria are met. Does the ICESCR contain any comparable provisions? What might account for the difference in approach?

3. Does the ICESCR require wealthy states to provide assistance to less fortunate states? Should it?

4. Should the United States ratify the ICESCR? If so, with what reservations, if any?

D. The Right to Food

Although the Universal Declaration and the Covenant on Economic, Social and Cultural Rights do not use the precise term "right to food," a broad array of governments and human rights advocates argue that such a right flows from those instruments. In its General Comment 12, the Committee on Economic, Social and Cultural Rights, the treaty body charged with monitoring states parties' implementation of the Covenant, stated:

Economic, Social and Cultural Rights Committee, General Comment 12

U.N. Doc. E/C.12/1999/5 (1999)

The right to adequate food (art. 11)

Introduction and Basic Premises

1. The human right to adequate food is recognized in several instruments under international law. . . . Pursuant to article 11.1 of the [ICESCR], States parties recognize "the right of everyone to an adequate standard of living for himself and his family, including adequate food, clothing and housing, and to the continuous improvement of living conditions", while pursuant to article 11.2 they recognize that more immediate and urgent steps may be needed to ensure "the fundamental right to freedom from hunger and malnutrition". The human right to adequate food is of crucial importance for the enjoyment of all rights. . . .

5. Despite the fact that the international community has frequently reaffirmed the importance of full respect for the right to adequate food, a disturbing gap still

exists between the standards set in article 11 of the Covenant and the situation prevailing in many parts of the world. More than 840 million people throughout the world, most of them in developing countries, are chronically hungry; millions of people are suffering from famine as the result of natural disasters, the increasing incidence of civil strife and wars in some regions and the use of food as a political weapon. . . . Fundamentally, the roots of the problem of hunger and malnutrition are not lack of food but lack of *access to* available food, *inter alia* because of poverty, by large segments of the world's population.

8. The Committee considers that the core content of the right to adequate food implies:

> The availability of food in a quantity and quality sufficient to satisfy the dietary needs of individuals, free from adverse substances, and acceptable within a given culture;
> The accessibility of such food in ways that are sustainable and that do not interfere with the enjoyment of other human rights.

15. The right to adequate food, like any other human right, imposes three types or levels of obligations on States parties: the obligations to *respect*, to *protect* and to *fulfil*. In turn, the obligation to *fulfil* incorporates both an obligation to *facilitate* and an obligation to *provide*. The obligation to *respect* existing access to adequate food requires States parties not to take any measures that result in preventing such access. The obligation to *protect* requires measures by the State to ensure that enterprises or individuals do not deprive individuals of their access to adequate food. The obligation to *fulfil (facilitate)* means the State must pro-actively engage in activities intended to strengthen people's access to and utilization of resources and means to ensure their livelihood, including food security. Finally, whenever an individual or group is unable, for reasons beyond their control, to enjoy the right to adequate food by the means at their disposal, States have the obligation to *fulfil (provide)* that right directly. This obligation also applies for persons who are victims of natural or other disasters.

16. Some measures at these different levels of obligations of States parties are of a more immediate nature, while other measures are more of a long-term character, to achieve progressively the full realization of the right to food.

17. Violations of the Covenant occur when a State fails to ensure the satisfaction of, at the very least, the minimum essential level required to be free from hunger. In determining which actions or omissions amount to a violation of the right to food, it is important to distinguish the inability from the unwillingness of a State party to comply. Should a State party argue that resource constraints make it impossible to provide access to food for those who are unable by themselves to secure such access, the State has to demonstrate that every effort has been made to use all the resources at its disposal in an effort to satisfy, as a matter of priority, those minimum obligations. This follows from Article 2.1 of the Covenant, which obliges a State party to take the necessary steps to the maximum of its available resources. . . .

19. Violations of the right to food can occur through the direct action of States or other entities insufficiently regulated by States. These include: the formal repeal or suspension of legislation necessary for the continued enjoyment of the right to food; denial of access to food to particular individuals or groups, whether the discrimination is based on legislation or is pro-active; the prevention of access to humanitarian food aid in internal conflicts or other emergency situations; adoption of legislation or policies which are manifestly incompatible with pre-existing legal obligations relating to the right to food; and failure to regulate activities of

individuals or groups so as to prevent them from violating the right to food of others, or the failure of a State to take into account its international legal obligations regarding the right to food when entering into agreements with other States or with international organizations. . . .

Implementation at the National Level

21. The most appropriate ways and means of implementing the right to adequate food will inevitably vary significantly from one State party to another. Every State will have a margin of discretion in choosing its own approaches, but the Covenant clearly requires that each State party take whatever steps are necessary to ensure that everyone is free from hunger and as soon as possible can enjoy the right to adequate food. This will require the adoption of a national strategy to ensure food and nutrition security for all, based on human rights principles that define the objectives, and the formulation of policies and corresponding benchmarks. It should also identify the resources available to meet the objectives and the most cost-effective way of using them.

Remedies and Accountability

32. Any person or group who is a victim of a violation of the right to adequate food should have access to effective judicial or other appropriate remedies at both national and international levels. . . .

International Obligations

States Parties

36. . . . States parties should recognize the essential role of international cooperation and comply with their commitment to take joint and separate action to achieve the full realization of the right to adequate food. In implementing this commitment, States parties should take steps to respect the enjoyment of the right to food in other countries, to protect that right, to facilitate access to food and to provide the necessary aid when required. States parties should, in international agreements whenever relevant, ensure that the right to adequate food is given due attention and consider the development of further international legal instruments to that end.

37. States parties should refrain at all times from food embargoes or similar measures which endanger conditions for food production and access to food in other countries. Food should never be used as an instrument of political and economic pressure.

On April 17, 2000, the UN Human Rights Commission adopted a resolution "[e]ncourag[ing] all States to take steps with a view to achieving progressively the full realization of the right to food, including steps to promote the conditions for everyone to be free from hunger and as soon as possible enjoy fully the right to food";

"welcoming" General Comment 12 of the Committee on Economic, Social and Cultural Rights, and deciding to appoint "a special rapporteur, whose mandate will focus on the right to food." The resolution was adopted by a vote of 49 to 1, with 2 abstentions. The United States explained its vote in opposition by noting its endorsement of the "right to access to food," and its opposition to the view that there is a violation of the Covenant "if a state does not provide food to all" or denies "a remedy against the state to those individuals who believe their right has been denied."

In June 2002, officials from 182 countries participating in a UN Food and Agriculture Organization (FAO) summit meeting unanimously approved the World Food Summit: Five Years Later final declaration, renewing their commitment to reduce by half the number of hungry people in the world by 2015. Paragraph 10 of the declaration requests the FAO to set up an intergovernmental working group "to elaborate, in a period of two years, a set of voluntary guidelines to support Member States' efforts to achieve the progressive realisation of the right to adequate food in the context of national food security." The United States attached the following reservation to its vote in favor of the declaration:

> The United States believes that the issue of adequate food can only be viewed in the context of the right to a standard of living adequate for health and well-being, as set forth in the Universal Declaration of Human Rights, which includes the opportunity to secure food, clothing, housing, medical care and necessary social services. Further, the United States believes that the attainment of the right to an adequate standard of living is a goal or aspiration to be realized progressively that does not give rise to any international obligation or any domestic legal entitlement, and does not diminish the responsibilities of national governments towards their citizens. Additionally, the United States understands the right of access to food to mean the opportunity to secure food, and not a guaranteed entitlement. [W]e are committed to concrete action to meet the objectives of the World Food Summit, and are concerned that sterile debate over "Voluntary Guidelines" would distract attention from the real work of reducing poverty and hunger.

Notes and Questions

1. What is the difference between the "right to food" and the "right to access to food"? Why does the United States find the first formulation of the right unacceptable?

2. What is the legal significance of the Committee's General Comment? Should the Committee's definition of the right to food be considered authoritative?

3. Do the three levels of obligation referred to in paragraph 15 of General Comment 12 apply equally to political and civil rights and economic, social, and cultural rights?

4. Is the right to food implicit in other rights, such as the right to life? In *Social and Economic Rights Action Center v. Nigeria*, Comm. No. 155/96 (2001), the African Commission on Human and People's Rights examined claims that the Nigerian government had exploited "oil reserves in Ogoniland with no regard for the health or environment of the local communities." The Commission endorsed the view that states must "respect, protect, promote, and fulfil" economic, social, and cultural

rights and political and civil rights. With regard to the right to food, the Commission stated:

> 64. The Communication argues that the right to food is implicit in the African Charter, in such provisions as the right to life (Art. 4), the right to health (Art. 16) and the right to economic, social and cultural development (Art. 22). By its violation of these rights, the Nigerian Government trampled upon not only the explicitly protected rights but also upon the right to food implicitly guaranteed.
>
> 65. The right to food is inseparably linked to the dignity of human beings and is therefore essential for the enjoyment and fulfilment of such other rights as health, education, work and political participation. The African Charter and international law require and bind Nigeria to protect and improve existing food sources and to ensure access to adequate food for all citizens. [T]he minimum core of the right to food requires that the Nigerian Government should not destroy or contaminate food sources [nor] allow private parties to [do so, or] prevent peoples' efforts to feed themselves.
>
> 66. The government's treatment of the Ogonis has violated all three minimum duties of the right to food. The government has destroyed food sources through its security forces and State Oil Company; has allowed private oil companies to destroy food sources; and, through terror, has created significant obstacles to Ogoni communities trying to feed themselves. . . .

According to a November 2005 Amnesty International Report, "local human rights activists are unanimous that the Nigerian government has paid little serious attention" to the Commission's decision.

   5. What should be done to promote respect for the right to food in countries with closed political systems? Consider the comments of the UN Special Rapporteur on the Right to Food in his 2005 report to the Human Rights Commission:

> The Special Rapporteur is . . . concerned about the situation in the Democratic People's Republic of Korea, given reports that millions of people continue to suffer from a "silent famine"; people have been publicly executed for "economic crimes", such as stealing crops or cows for food; and that food aid has not always been distributed in accordance with the conditions of non-discrimination and transparency. He is also concerned at reports that the Government of China has forcibly repatriated people escaping hunger, and that these "refugees from hunger" have been sentenced to severe punishment on their return.

IV. WOMEN'S RIGHTS: FEMALE CIRCUMCISION OR FEMALE GENITAL MUTILATION?

Most human rights treaties and instruments expressly confer protections on men and women equally. The Universal Declaration, for example, declares that all human beings are equal in dignity and rights, and that the rights enumerated in the Declaration must be applied "without distinction of any kind, such as . . . sex. . . . " Similar language appears in most other general human rights instruments, including the two International Covenants, the European Convention on Human Rights, and the Inter-American Convention on Human Rights.

   Nonetheless, in many countries deeply ingrained social attitudes about the role of women are still reflected in national laws limiting women's rights in family matters, employment, and political and community life. In other countries, national laws mandate equality for women, at least in the public sphere, but such laws are often either not enforced or are interpreted restrictively, leaving women vulnerable to widespread mistreatment, especially in areas deemed to be within the "private sphere" of family, social life, and private economic relations. As a result, advocates of enhanced international legal protections for women have pressed, with increasing success, for additional instruments devoted explicitly to the protection of women's rights and extending beyond the general nondiscrimination provisions found in more general human rights covenants.

In this Section, we examine issues relating to women's rights by looking at a practice referred to as female circumcision or female genital mutilation. In particular, we consider whether that practice amounts to discrimination against women and whether it constitutes a form of violence against women. We also consider to what extent existing international law offers protection against discrimination or violence that may take place in the "private" sphere—that is, against acts detrimental to women committed by non-state actors in family life or other private relations. We also examine whether cultural differences may justify different approaches to women's rights in different parts of the world, and in particular, whether cultural differences may justify clitoridectomy and related practices. As you read the materials that follow, consider the similarities and differences between international approaches to the protection of women's rights, and international approaches to the protection of political and civil rights, and economic, social, and cultural rights. Consider also whether and to what extent international law should regulate private relations, and whether existing international human rights norms are universal or whether they reflect particular cultural or regional values.

A. The Problem

For over 2000 years, communities in parts of Africa and the Middle East have practiced a custom or ritual involving the cutting of female genitalia. This practice, sometimes referred to as female circumcision by defenders and female genital mutilation by critics, is most often performed on girls between the ages of four and twelve.* The cutting usually takes place with the consent (or at the insistence) of a parent or guardian, though it may also be performed on adult women. The cutting is usually done by a woman, often a respected member of the community who may be one of a long line of traditional practitioners. The form of the practice varies considerably: in some communities the cutting is extensive, entailing the partial or complete removal of the external genitalia; in others the cutting is much less extreme. UNICEF, the United Nations Children's Fund, estimates that as many as 135 million women have experienced genital cutting, and as many as 2 million girls are subjected to it every year.

The physical effects of genital cutting also vary, but many girls and women experience severe pain, bleeding, and sometimes life-threatening infections or other potentially fatal complications. Many women also experience a variety of other significant long-term complications, including decreased sexual sensitivity and pain during intercourse. Psychological harms, ranging from difficulty eating and sleeping to loss of self-esteem, are also common.

---

*This section is drawn in part from Female Genital Mutilation: A Guide to Laws and Policies Worldwide (Anika Rahman & Nahid Toubia eds., 2000).

At the same time, many women in countries that practice female genital circumcision/mutilation vigorously defend the practice as an important rite of passage and a central element of their culture. They view it as a means for socializing girls into their community and linking them to the roles expected of them as women. The ritual affirms their cultural identity and binds them to the past and future life of their group. For many, it is a joyous event, a time of celebration, festivities, and gift-giving.

Critics of the practice, however, condemn it for more than its adverse health effects. They see it as a way of controlling women's sexuality, promoting virginity and marital fidelity, and perpetuating women's subordination to men. Women who resist genital cutting may be seen as unfit for marriage; in communities where only men may earn income, such exclusion from marriage opportunities may be economically fatal. In some communities, especially in Muslim communities, the practice has been espoused by local religious leaders, even though the origins of the practice are cultural, not religious. As the negative consequences of resisting increase, the social pressures for conformity increase, in a self-reinforcing cycle.

The practice continues in at least 28 African countries, although increasingly African states are responding to pressures to ban it. These pressures have been generated in part by domestic activists—women's groups and local doctors and health officials—and in part by international actors, including organizations such as the World Health Organization, concerned states, Western feminists, and international human rights groups.

The following excerpt from the *New York Times* illustrates the disagreements that continue to surround the issue.

Howard W. French, *The Ritual: Disfiguring, Hurtful, Wildly Festive*
N.Y. Times, Jan. 31, 1997, at A4.

The women of the Grafton [Sierra Leone] displaced persons camp are in a festive mood these days. After years of fighting, the war that destroyed their villages and made them refugees has ended, and soon they will be returning home.

To celebrate this change of fortune, many felt, it was only proper that there should be a major ceremony marking what they hope will be a resumption of their normal lives. So, since Christmas, as many as 600 women from the camp have hiked off in groups of a dozen or more at a time to a clearing in the bush nearby.

There, the group members, ranging from 4-year-old girls to adult women, have stayed for a week or two at a time, dancing, feasting and sharing lessons about womanhood as part of an ancestral communal ritual known as Bondo, which culminates in having their external genitals cut off—a practice commonly referred to as female circumcision. . . .

While the ritual of female genital cutting is common within regions and ethnic groups in a number of countries in Africa, Sierra Leone stands out as a society where the practice is nearly universal.

In many other parts of Africa, the practice is in retreat, under the assault of laws prohibiting it, educational drives aimed at women and, in some places, even preaching against the ritual by Muslim clerics.

Top: Villagers Celebrating Female Circumcision in Kenya (1995)
Bottom: Razor Blade Coated with Goat Fat to Abate Flow of Blood During Circumcision,
Kenya (1995)
SOURCE: Getty Images

But in Sierra Leone, where by some estimates as many as 90 percent of women undergo the ritual, the tiny minority of people willing to take a stand against the practice are overwhelmed by militant, if defensive, advocates.

In the middle stand millions of women who are, for the most part, willing, and sometimes fervent adherents. . . .

Defenders of the ritual, who range from intellectuals in the capital to illiterate displaced women, talk of preserving a tradition against an onslaught of alien cultures. . . .

Critics here say the rituals of genital cutting persist because they are a rare female preserve in a society otherwise heavily dominated by men. . . .

In a recent United Nations study, Sierra Leone ranked second-to-last in the world in a measurement of quality of life. Among the country's lowest indicators are female literacy, and maternal and infant mortality rates.

For Dr. Kosso-Thomas, whose life was threatened by the advocates of genital cutting who marched last year, these two facts are closely bound up in the ritual.

Dr. Kosso-Thomas said that Sierra Leone had one of the highest rates of miscarriage and pregnancy-related deaths in the world, in large part because of infections, scarring and other damage brought on by mutilations carried out in primitive and unhygienic conditions.

But here, amid the closely-spaced tin-roofed mud huts that have housed most of the displaced residents for the last year, a group of women, some of whom recently had their genitals cut, stepped forward to defend the practice, making it clear that they were eager to continue the practice.

Although genital cutting is now viewed as a human rights issue, that has not always been the case. Consider the following explanation:

> Several factors prevented [FGM] from being seen as a human rights issue for many years. FGM is encouraged by parents and family members, who believe it will have beneficial consequences for the child in later life. Violence against women and girls in the home or in the community was seen as a "private" issue; the fact that perpetrators were private actors rather than state officials precluded FGM from being seen as a legitimate human rights concern. An additional barrier was the fact that FGM is rooted in cultural tradition. Outside intervention in the name of universal human rights risked being perceived as cultural imperialism.

Amnesty International, Female Genital Mutilation: A Human Rights Information Pack (1997).

Recent reports suggest that female genital mutilation is slowly losing favor in Africa. Nonetheless, millions of girls and women continue to face pressures to undergo circumcision. As you review the materials below, consider whether FGM violates women's rights, and if so, which specific rights are at issue.

B. Background on Women's Rights

Women's rights have long been on the UN's agenda. In 1946, the Commission on the Status of Women (CSW) was created as a subcommission of the Commission on Human Rights. At the urging of women's rights advocates, it was quickly turned into a full commission. CSW's mandate was to prepare recommendations dealing with pressing issues affecting women. Over the next 15 years, CSW prepared a series of conventions, adopted by the General Assembly, dealing with women's political rights, the nationality of married women, and consent to marriage. The Commission viewed these subjects as areas of particular vulnerability for women, but otherwise the UN system relied on general human rights instruments to address women's rights.

By the early 1960s, however, supporters of women's rights had concluded that the general human rights system was not adequately protecting women's interests, and that a more comprehensive approach was needed. In 1963, the UN Economic and Social Council invited CSW to prepare a draft declaration that would combine in a single instrument international standards relating to women's rights. The result was the Declaration on the Elimination of Discrimination Against Women, adopted by the General Assembly in 1967. Thereafter, CSW began work on a comprehensive treaty that would obligate states to eradicate discrimination against women. A draft text was prepared by CSW working groups in 1976 and discussed extensively in the UN's Third (Economic, Social and Cultural) Committee from 1977 to 1979, when the revised text was adopted by the General Assembly as the Convention on the Elimination of All Forms of Discrimination Against Women (CEDAW). The Convention entered into force two years later, faster than any other general human rights treaty. As of March 2006, 182 states were party to it.

The Convention on the Elimination of All Forms of Discrimination Against Women

1249 U.N.T.S. 13 (1979)

Article 1

For the purposes of the present Convention, the term "discrimination against women" shall mean any distinction, exclusion or restriction made on the basis of sex which has the effect or purpose of impairing or nullifying the recognition, enjoyment or exercise by women, irrespective of their marital status, on a basis of equality of men and women, of human rights and fundamental freedoms in the political, economic, social, cultural, civil or any other field.

Article 2

States Parties condemn discrimination against women in all its forms, agree to pursue by all appropriate means and without delay a policy of eliminating discrimination against women. . . .

Article 3

States Parties shall take in all fields, in particular in the political, social, economic and cultural fields, all appropriate measures, including legislation, to ensure the full development and advancement of women, for the purpose of guaranteeing them the exercise and enjoyment of human rights and fundamental freedoms on a basis of equality with men.

Article 4

1. Adoption by States Parties of temporary special measures aimed at accelerating de facto equality between men and women shall not be considered discrimination as defined in the present Convention, but shall in no way entail as a consequence the maintenance of unequal or separate standards; these measures shall be discontinued when the objectives of equality of opportunity and treatment have been achieved. . . .

Article 5

States Parties shall take all appropriate measures:

(a) To modify the social and cultural patterns of conduct of men and women, with a view to achieving the elimination of prejudices and customary and all other practices which are based on the idea of the inferiority or the superiority of either of the sexes or on stereotyped roles for men and women;

(b) To ensure that family education includes a proper understanding of maternity as a social function and the recognition of the common responsibility of men and women in the upbringing and development of their children, it being understood that the interest of the children is the primordial consideration in all cases.

Article 16

1. States Parties shall take all appropriate measures to eliminate discrimination against women in all matters relating to marriage and family relations and in particular shall ensure, on a basis of equality of men and women:

(a) The same right to enter into marriage;

(b) The same right freely to choose a spouse and to enter into marriage only with their free and full consent;

(c) The same rights and responsibilities during marriage and at its dissolution;

(d) The same rights and responsibilities as parents, irrespective of their marital status, in matters relating to their children; in all cases the interests of the children shall be paramount;

(e) The same rights to decide freely and responsibly on the number and spacing of their children and to have access to the information, education and means to enable them to exercise these rights;

(f) The same rights and responsibilities with regard to guardianship, wardship, trusteeship and adoption of children, or similar institutions where these concepts exist in national legislation; in all cases the interests of the children shall be paramount;

(g) The same personal rights as husband and wife, including the right to choose a family name, a profession and an occupation;

(h) The same rights for both spouses in respect of the ownership, acquisition, management, administration, enjoyment and disposition of property, whether free of charge or for a valuable consideration.

Most of the remainder of the Convention specifies areas in which equality between men and women is to be ensured, blending together civil and political rights and economic, social, and cultural rights.

Notes and Questions

1. How might human rights NGOs rely on CEDAW in opposing female circumcision? According to Amnesty International, "FGM is rooted in discrimination against women. It is an instrument for socializing girls into prescribed roles within the family and community. It is therefore intimately linked to the unequal position of women in the political, social, and economic structures of societies where it is

practised." Do you agree with Amnesty that female circumcision is a form of prohibited discrimination? Is it a social or cultural practice that states are required to take steps to modify?

2. To what extent and in what ways do the rights afforded to women by CEDAW differ from those accorded to women by the ICCPR?

3. Does the Convention require positive state action to ensure the advancement of women? If so, what sorts of actions are required?

C. Violence Against Women and the Public-Private Distinction

International lawyers have long distinguished between a "public" sphere of state action deemed appropriate for regulation by international law, and a "private" sphere of interpersonal relations deemed more suited to regulation by national law. In this framework, female circumcision/mutilation is generally viewed as a private sphere practice, something done by women to women without governmental involvement. In recent years, a growing number of scholars and NGOs have criticized the "public-private" distinction in international law as one that privileges men's concerns over those of women. The following excerpt spells out this critique.

> Historically, the formation of the state depended on a sexual division of labor and the relegation of women to a private, domestic, devalued sphere. Men dominated in the public sphere of citizenship and political and economic life. The state institutionalized the patriarchal family both as the qualification for citizenship and public life and also as the basic socio-economic unit. The functions of the state were identified with men. . . .
>
> The distinction between public and private spheres which is at the heart of the traditional notion of the state has had a defining influence on international law and tenacity in international legal doctrine. Thus the United Nations Charter makes the (public) province of international law distinct from the (private) sphere of domestic jurisdiction; the acquisition of statehood or international personality confers "public" status on an entity with consequences, for example, for jurisdiction, representation, and ownership. The law of state responsibility sorts out (public) actions for which the state is accountable from those "private" ones for which it does not have to answer internationally. Even international human rights law, which is regarded as radically challenging the traditional distinction between international and domestic concerns, targets "public," state-sanctioned violations rather than those that have no apparent direct connection to the state. [This public/private distinction in international law] . . . sustains women's oppression on a global level. For example, the traditional doctrine of state responsibility deems typical injuries women suffer as outside the scope of international law. And while international human rights law gives international status to individuals, the core human rights are defined to protect individuals from a variety of public actions. But the most pervasive harm against women tends to occur right within the inner sanctum of the private realm, within the family. As in domestic law, the non-regulation of the private realm legitimates self-regulation, which translates ultimately into male dominance.

Hilary Charlesworth, *Alienating Oscar? Feminist Analysis of International Law*, in Reconceiving Reality: Women and International Law 1, 9-11 (Dorinda Dallmeyer ed., 1993).

Though human rights law and institutions continue to focus on harm to individuals caused by state action, it is now well established that states can be held responsible not only for human rights violations directly perpetrated by state authorities, but also for failing to take appropriate action to prevent or punish rights violations committed by private actors. Thus, in its General Comment 31, the Human Rights Committee observed:

> The Covenant [on Civil and Political Rights] cannot be viewed as a substitute for domestic criminal or civil law. However the positive obligations on States Parties to ensure Covenant rights will only be fully discharged if individuals are protected by the State, not just against violations of Covenant rights by its agents, but also against acts committed by private persons or entities that would impair the enjoyment of Covenant rights in so far as they are amenable to application between private persons or entities. There may be circumstances in which a failure to ensure Covenant rights as required by article 2 would give rise to violations by States Parties of those rights, as a result of States Parties' permitting or failing to take appropriate measures or to exercise due diligence to prevent, punish, investigate or redress the harm caused by such acts by private persons or entities.

Along the same lines, the European Court of Human Rights has held that the Netherlands' failure to prosecute a private person's sexual abuse of a mentally handicapped ward violated the victim's right to privacy; that the United Kingdom's proposed deportation of an AIDS victim to St. Kitts, where he would be unable to obtain adequate medical treatment, violated his right to life; and that the United Kingdom's failure to protect two boys from child abuse violated their right to be free from cruel treatment. Similarly, the Inter-American Court of Human Rights, in its 1988 *Velásquez Rodríguez* decision, found the Honduran government responsible for the failure to use due diligence to prevent, investigate, and punish a forced disappearance committed by persons whose identity could not be positively established but who were probably state agents. The Court held that a human rights violation that cannot be directly imputed to a state because it was committed by a private actor can nonetheless lead to "international responsibility of the State, not because of the act itself, but because of the lack of due diligence to prevent the violation or to respond to it. . . . " Inter-Am. Ct. H.R., Ser. C, No. 4, para. 172, (1988). But the circumstances that amount to a lack of due diligence sufficient to render a state responsible for acts of private actors, including those who commit violence against women, are still much debated.

CEDAW is designed in significant part to oblige states to challenge private action that interferes with women's development and well-being. But the Convention itself is largely silent on the issue of violence against women. Nonetheless, the Committee on the Elimination of Discrimination Against Women, the treaty body established by CEDAW to review national reports and make recommendations regarding issues affecting women, adopted the following General Recommendation in 1992:

CEDAW Committee, General Recommendation No. 19

U.N. Doc. A/47/38 (1992)

Violence against women

6. The Convention in article 1 defines discrimination against women. The definition of discrimination includes gender-based violence, that is, violence that is directed against a woman because she is a woman or that affects women

disproportionately. It includes acts that inflict physical, mental or sexual harm or suffering, threats of such acts, coercion and other deprivations of liberty. Gender-based violence may breach specific provisions of the Convention, regardless of whether those provisions expressly mention violence. . . .

8. The Convention applies to violence perpetrated by public authorities. Such acts of violence may breach that State's obligations under general international human rights law and under other conventions, in addition to breaching this Convention.

9. It is emphasized, however, that discrimination under the Convention is not restricted to action by or on behalf of Governments (see articles 2(e), 2(f) and 5). For example, under article 2(e) the Convention calls on States parties to take all appropriate measures to eliminate discrimination against women by any person, organization or enterprise. Under general international law and specific human rights covenants, States may also be responsible for private acts if they fail to act with due diligence to prevent violations of rights or to investigate and punish acts of violence, and for providing compensation. . . .

11. Traditional attitudes by which women are regarded as subordinate to men or as having stereotyped roles perpetuate widespread practices involving violence or coercion, such as family violence and abuse, forced marriage, dowry deaths, acid attacks and female circumcision. Such prejudices and practices may justify gender-based violence as a form of protection or control of women. The effect of such violence on the physical and mental integrity of women is to deprive them of the equal enjoyment, exercise and knowledge of human rights and fundamental freedoms. While this comment addresses mainly actual or threatened violence the underlying consequences of these forms of gender-based violence help to maintain women in subordinate roles and contribute to their low level of political participation and to their lower level of education, skills and work opportunities.

The pervasiveness of the problem of violence against women, and an increasingly common critique of the public/private distinction, may be seen in the reports of the UN Human Rights Commission's Special Rapporteur on Violence Against Women, published annually since 1995. The 1999 report on violence in family life is illustrative:

Violence Against Women in the Family, Report of the Special Rapporteur on Violence Against Women, Its Causes and Consequences

U.N. Doc. E/CN.4/1999/68 (1999)

II. Family and Violence: Definitions

6. Defined in both international and national law as the natural and fundamental unit of society, the family has been the focus of very little scrutiny under international law. This is largely a consequence of the traditional division between the public and private spheres and the emphasis in human rights discourse on public sphere violations. Increasingly, however, this is changing. No longer are human

rights guarantees restricted solely to the public sphere. They likewise apply to the private realm, including within the family, and oblige the State to act with due diligence to prevent, investigate and punish violations therein.

7. The State, through legal and moral regulation, plays an important role in family life, as well as an important role in determining the status, rights and remedies of individual family actors. Women's traditional familial roles are enshrined in secular and religious laws on, *inter alia,* sexuality, violence (including marital rape or the lack thereof), privacy, divorce, adultery, property, succession, employment, and child custody. Such laws validate and entrench the dominant ideology of the traditional family and the woman's position within it. Familial ideology is often Janus faced. On the one hand, it offers private space for nurturing and intimacy. On the other hand, it is often the site of violence against women and social constructions of women's role in society that are disempowering. . . .

16. . . . The Special Rapporteur has adopted an expansive definition of violence in the family to include "violence perpetrated in the domestic sphere which targets women because of their role within that sphere or as violence which is intended to impact, directly and negatively, on women within the domestic sphere. Such violence may be carried out by both private and public actors and agents. This conceptual framework intentionally departs from traditional definitions of domestic violence, which address violence perpetrated by intimates against intimates, or equates domestic violence with woman-battering" (E/CN.4/1996/53, para. 28).

17. Violence within the family comprises, *inter alia,* woman-battering, marital rape, incest, forced prostitution, violence against domestic workers, violence against girls, sex-selective abortions and female infanticide, traditional violent practices against women including forced marriage, son preference, female genital mutilation and honour crimes. . . .

32. Increasingly, States are using cultural relativist claims to avoid responsibility for positive, anti-violence action. The recognition of heterogeneous or multicultural communities is not at odds with developing comprehensive and multifaceted strategies to combat domestic violence. In all communities, the root causes of domestic violence are similar, even when the justifications for such violence or the forms of such violence vary.

In recent years, an increasing number of women facing domestic violence in their home country have sought asylum abroad. Courts and other decision makers have gradually become more receptive to such claims. In 1996 the Board of Immigration Appeals of the U.S. Department of Justice had occasion to consider whether the practice of female genital mutilation constituted grounds for asylum. To qualify for asylum, an applicant must demonstrate a "well-founded fear of persecution on account of race, religion, nationality, membership in a particular social group, or political opinion." 8 U.S.C. §1101(a)(42)(A)(1994). (The standard is drawn from the UN Convention and Protocol that forbids states from forcibly returning refugees.) Among the issues before the Board was whether a practice carried out by private actors with a subjectively benign intent could be deemed persecution, and whether the persecution was "on account of" membership in a particular social group. The Immigration and Naturalization Service (INS) argued that female genital mutilation could qualify as persecution, but only if carried out in a manner that "shocks the conscience." The Board's decision follows:

In re Fauziya Kasinga

21 I.& N. Dec. 357 (1996)

The applicant is a 19-year-old native and citizen of Togo. . . . She is a member of the Tchamba-Kunsuntu Tribe of northern Togo. She testified that young women of her tribe normally undergo FGM [female genital mutilation] at age 15. However, she did not because she initially was protected from FGM by her influential, but now deceased, father.

The applicant stated that upon her father's death in 1993, under tribal custom her aunt, her father's sister, became the primary authority figure in the family. . . .

The applicant further testified that her aunt forced her into a polygamous marriage in October 1994, when she was 17. The husband selected by her aunt was 45 years old and had three other wives at the time of marriage. The applicant testified that, under tribal custom, her aunt and her husband planned to force her to submit to FGM before the marriage was consummated.

The applicant testified that she feared imminent mutilation. With the help of her older sister, she fled Togo for Ghana. . . . [Kasinga then made her way to the United States, where she applied for asylum.]

The applicant testified that the Togolese police and the Government of Togo were aware of FGM and would take no steps to protect her from the practice. She further testified that her aunt had reported her to the Togolese police. Upon return, she would be taken back to her husband by the police and forced to undergo FGM. . . .

According to the applicant's testimony, the FGM practiced by her tribe, the Tchamba-Kunsuntu, is of an extreme type involving cutting the genitalia with knives, extensive bleeding, and a 40-day recovery period. . . .

The FGM Alert, compiled and distributed by the INS Resource Information Center, notes that "few African countries have officially condemned female genital mutilation and still fewer have enacted legislation against the practice." Further, according to the FGM Alert, even in those few African countries where legislative efforts have been made, they are usually ineffective to protect women against FGM. The FGM Alert notes that "it remains practically true that [African] women have little legal recourse and may face threats to their freedom, threats or acts of physical violence, or social ostracization for refusing to undergo this harmful traditional practice or attempting to protect their female children." Togo is not listed in the FGM Alert as among the African countries that have made even minimal efforts to protect women from FGM. . . .

While a number of descriptions of persecution have been formulated in our past decisions, we have recognized that persecution can consist of the infliction of harm or suffering by a government, or persons a government is unwilling or unable to control, to overcome a characteristic of the victim. . . .

As observed by the INS, many of our past cases involved actors who had a subjective intent to punish their victims. However, this subjective "punitive" or "malignant" intent is not required for harm to constitute persecution. . . .

We therefore reach the conclusion that FGM can be persecution without passing on the INS's proposed "shocks the conscience" test.

To be a basis for a grant of asylum, persecution must relate to one of five categories described in section 101(a)(42)(A) of the Act. The parties agree that the relevant category in this case is "particular social group." . . .

In the context of this case, we find the particular social group to be the following: young women of the Tchamba-Kunsuntu Tribe who have not had FGM, as practiced by that tribe, and who oppose the practice. . . .

[T]he particular social group is defined by common characteristics that members of the group either cannot change, or should not be required to change because such characteristics are fundamental to their individual identities. The characteristics of being a "young woman" and a "member of the Tchamba-Kunsuntu Tribe" cannot be changed. The characteristic of having intact genitalia is one that is so fundamental to the individual identity of a young woman that she should not be required to change it. . . .

Both parties have advanced, and the background materials support, the proposition that there is no legitimate reason for FGM. . . .

Record materials state that FGM "has been used to control woman's sexuality." It also is characterized as a form of "sexual oppression" that is "based on the manipulation of women's sexuality in order to assure male dominance and exploitation." . . .

We agree with the parties that, as described and documented in this record, FGM is practiced, at least in some significant part, to overcome sexual characteristics of young women of the tribe who have not been, and do not wish to be, subjected to FGM. We therefore find that the persecution the applicant fears in Togo is "on account of" her status as a member of the defined social group.

[In a concurring opinion, two Board members addressed the INS's proposed "shocks the conscience" test:]

The Service points out that it is "estimated that over eighty million females have been subjected to FGM." It further notes that there is "no indication" that "Congress considered application of [the asylum laws] to broad cultural practices of the type involved here." The Service proceeds to argue that "the underlying purposes of the asylum system . . . are unavoidably in tension" in both providing protection for those seriously in jeopardy and in maintaining broad overall governmental control over immigration. The Service further argues that "the Board's interpretation in this case must assure protection for those most at risk of the harms covered by the statute, but it cannot simply grant asylum to all who might be subjected to a practice deemed objectionable or a violation of a person's human rights." It is from these underpinnings that the Service argues that the class of FGM victims who may be eligible for asylum "does not consist of all women who come from the parts of the world where FGM is practiced, nor of all who have been subjected to it in the past."

The Service then offers its "framework of analysis." That framework includes a new "shocks the conscience" test for persecution. The advantages seen by the Service of this test evidently include: 1) the ability to define FGM as "persecution" notwithstanding any lack of intent to "punish" FGM victims on the part of the victims' parents or tribe members who may well "believe that they are simply performing an important cultural rite that bonds the individual to the society"; 2) the ability to exclude other cultural practices, such as "body scarring," from the definition of persecution as these do not shock the conscience; and 3) the ability to exclude past victims of FGM from asylum eligibility if "they consented" to it or "at least acquiesced," as in the case of a woman who experienced FGM as "a small child," since FGM would not shock the conscience unless inflicted on "an unconsenting or resisting individual." . . .

But we are not fundamentally a policy-making body. There may be some unsettling or unsatisfying aspects to the slower and less predictable development of legal guidelines that inures in the Board's case adjudication system. But there are alternatives if resort to the Board's issuance of precedent is not satisfactory in a particular context. The Service can seek to have the Attorney General issue regulations that comprehensively address competing concerns, or it can work within the Administration for appropriate legislative action by Congress. The Service should not, however, expect the Board to endorse a significant new framework for assessing asylum claims in the context of a single novel case.

Notes and Questions

1. Do you agree with the characterization of female genital mutilation in *Kasinga* as persecution? Is it a form of violence against women? Should all women who have a well-founded fear of being subjected to female genital mutilation be eligible for asylum?

2. What duties should a state have to prevent violence by private actors? Recall the due diligence standard adopted by the Inter-American Court in *Velásquez Rodríguez*. Does that standard necessarily vary depending on the capacity of the government to enforce its laws?

3. If states fail to exercise due diligence to prevent private actors from committing spousal abuse and other forms of domestic violence against women, should such women qualify for asylum? In *In re R-A-*, 2001 B.I.A. LEXIS 1, the applicant was a Guatemalan woman subject to repeated "heinous abuse" by her husband. The immigration judge found that the applicant was subject to persecution on account of membership in a particular social group consisting of "Guatemalan women who have been involved intimately with Guatemalan male companions, who believe that women are to live under male domination." The majority agreed that the level of harm was sufficient to constitute persecution and that the Guatemalan government was unable or unwilling to prevent such persecution. The majority concluded, however, that the applicant's husband did not target her because she was a member of this particular group and noted, among other things, that he did not target other members of the group. The dissenting opinion argued:

> This is not merely a case of domestic violence involving criminal conduct. The respondent's husband engaged in a prolonged and persistent pattern of abuse designed to dominate the respondent and to overcome any effort on her part to assert her independence or to resist his abuse. His mistreatment and persecution of her in private and in public was founded, as the majority states, on his view that it was his right to treat his wife as "his property to do with as he pleased." He acted with the knowledge that no one would interfere. His horrific conduct, both initially and in response to her opposition to it, was not that of an individual acting at variance with societal norms, but one who recognized that he was acting in accordance with them.
>
> The harm to the respondent occurred in the context of egregious governmental acquiescence. When the respondent sought the aid and assistance of government officials and institutions, she was told that they could do nothing for her. This is not a case in which the government tried, but failed, to afford protection. Here the government made no effort and showed no interest in protecting the respondent from her abusive spouse. . . .

The record confirms the Immigration Judge's finding that in Guatemala there are "institutional biases against women that prevent female victims of domestic violence from receiving protection from their male companions or spouses." The Immigration Judge found that these institutional biases "appear to stem from a pervasive belief, common in patriarchal societies, that a man should be able to control a wife or female companion by any means he sees fit: including rape, torture, and beatings." . . .

The majority's insistence that the respondent's husband was not motivated to harm her, "even in part, because of her membership in a particular social group or because of an actual or imputed political opinion," cannot be reconciled either with the reality of the respondent's situation in Guatemala, or with United States law. . . .

Id. at 57-59.

The dissent went on to argue that respondent's husband sought to "dominate and subdue her, precisely because of her gender," and that domestic violence generally "is used to control women in the one space traditionally dominated by women, the home."

In *Aguirre-Cervantes v. INS*, 242 F.3d 1169 (9th Cir. 2001), the court considered a petition for asylum from a nineteen year old Mexican woman subject to repeated physical abuse by her father. The court held that she had a well-founded fear of persecution "on account of her membership in a particular social group consisting of her immediate family, all of whose members were abused by her father." The court concluded further that "Mexico was unable or unwilling to do anything about this abuse, and that if she returned to Mexico the abuse would likely continue." Accordingly, the court determined that she was eligible for asylum.

In response to the decision in *In re R-A-*, the INS issued a proposed rule offering guidance on the interpretation of "persecution," "membership in a particular social group," and "on account of" a protected characteristic. The proposed rule provides, among other things, that "evidence that the persecutor seeks to act against other individuals who share the applicant's protected characteristic is relevant and may be considered but shall not be required." In 2001, the Attorney General vacated the decision in *In re R-A-*, and in 2005, remanded the case to the Board of Immigration Appeals (BIA) for further consideration following final publication of the proposed rule. *Aguirre-Cervantes* was also vacated and remanded to the BIA for further administrative proceedings following a decision of the Ninth Circuit to consider the case en banc. How should these cases be decided?

4. In *Mohammed v. Gonzalez*, 400 F.3d 785 (9th Cir. 2005), the Ninth Circuit Court of Appeals stated that "we have no doubt that the range of procedures collectively known as female genital mutilation rises to the level of persecution within the meaning of our asylum law." The court disagreed, however, with part of *Kasinga's* definition of the relevant social group: "We believe that opposition is not required in order to meet the 'on account of' prong in female genital mutilation cases. The persecution at issue in these cases—the forcible, painful cutting of a female's body parts—is not a result of a woman's opposition to the practice but rather a result of her sex and her clan membership and/or nationality. That is, the shared characteristic that motivates the persecution is not opposition, but the fact that the victims are female in a culture that mutilates the genitalia of its females." The Court then considered whether a woman who had already been subjected to female genital mutilation might still qualify for asylum. The Court concluded that "female genital mutilation . . . must be considered a continuing harm," so that an individual who has already endured genital mutilation "does not need to have a fear of the same

persecution recurring in the future in order to be eligible for withholding of removal." Under the Ninth Circuit's analysis, would all of the 135 million women estimated to have undergone female genital circumcision worldwide qualify for asylum in the United States?

5. In *Abay v. Ashcroft*, 368 F.3d 634 (6th Cir. 2004), the Court of Appeals for the Sixth Circuit decided that the petitioner's fear that Amare, Abay's minor daughter, would be subjected to female genital mutilation if she returned to Ethiopia was sufficient to qualify both Amare and her mother as refugees eligible for asylum. Noting that over 90 percent of women in Ethiopia undergo female genital mutilation, the Court determined that Amare would probably have to undergo the procedure if she returned to Ethiopia and married, and that the choice between marriage and ostracism was sufficient to create a legitimate fear of persecution. The Court also held that Amare's mother qualified as a refugee in her own right based on her fear that her daughter would be forced to undergo the procedure. The Court stated that prior cases "suggest a governing principle in favor of refugee status in cases where a parent and protector is faced with exposing her child to the clear risk of being subjected against her will to a practice that is a form of physical torture causing grave and permanent harm."

D. Debating Cultural Relativism

As noted in the preceding materials, defenders of female genital cutting often accuse Western activists seeking to ban the practice of cultural imperialism. This claim is a reflection of a much broader debate between those who argue that human rights are universal and those who claim that they are culturally relative. Universalists insist that human rights derive from our common humanity and so should apply equally to all. Relativists deny that human rights can or should be universal. Instead, they argue, human rights norms must be adapted to reflect wide variations in culture, beliefs, and economic and political circumstances.

The question of the universality of human rights was raised during the drafting of the Universal Declaration of Human Rights, which claims to set a "common standard of achievement for all peoples and all nations." In 1947, the Executive Board of the American Anthropological Association sent a long memorandum to the UN Human Rights Commission stating that "standards are relative to the culture from which they derive." The memorandum argued that individuals from the moment of birth have their thoughts, hopes, aspirations, and values shaped by the customs of the group of which they become a member, and that there is no scientifically validated technique for qualitatively evaluating different cultures. The memorandum noted further that "what is held to be a human right in one society may be regarded as anti-social by another people, or by the same people in a different period of their history." The memorandum therefore questioned whether the Universal Declaration could be anything other than "a statement of rights conceived only in terms of the values prevalent in the countries of Western Europe and America." The concerns expressed by the American Anthropological Association have been echoed by philosophers, political scientists, and international lawyers in a long-running debate.

Formally, most international human rights instruments, such as the Universal Declaration and CEDAW, make no explicit concessions to cultural variation. All parties are expected to give full effect to all provisions, absent an applicable reservation, although as a practical matter there is considerable room for interpretation in the application of specific provisions. Thus, for example, the right to a fair trial may involve quite different procedures in different countries. Moreover, the European Court of Human Rights recognizes that states must have a "margin of appreciation" in applying some European Convention on Human Rights provisions to their particular circumstances. Still, most human rights advocates argue strongly that in substance human rights are universal and should be because they are not based on local values but, rather, in the words of the Universal Declaration, on the "recognition of the inherent dignity and of the equal and inalienable rights of all members of the human family." In that vein, Rosalyn Higgins, a Judge on the ICJ, offered the following assessment.

> It is sometimes suggested that there can be no fully universal concept of human rights. . . . In my view this is a point advanced mostly by states, and by liberal scholars anxious not to impose the Western view of things on others. It is rarely advanced by the oppressed, who are only too anxious to benefit from perceived universal standards. Individuals everywhere want the same essential things: to have sufficient food and shelter; to be able to speak freely; to practise their own religion or to abstain from religious belief; to feel that their person is not threatened by the state; to know that they will not be tortured, or detained without charge, and that, if charged, they will have a fair trial. I believe there is nothing in these aspirations that is dependent upon culture, or religion, or stage of development.

Rosalyn Higgins, Problems and Process: International Law and How We Use It 96-97 (1994).

In a somewhat different take, Professor Jack Donnelly suggests that international human rights should be seen as "relatively universal."

Jack Donnelly, *Cultural Relativism and Universal Human Rights*

6 Hum. Rts. Q. 400, 410-419 (1984)

Standard arguments for cultural relativism rely on examples such as the precolonial African village, Native American tribes, and traditional Islamic social systems. . . . [H]uman rights . . . are foreign to such communities, which instead employed other, often quite sophisticated, mechanisms for protecting and realizing defensible conceptions of human dignity. The claims of communal self-determination are particularly strong here, especially if we allow a certain moral autonomy to such communities and recognize the cultural variability of the social side of human nature. It is important, however, to recognize the limits of such arguments. . . .

In the Third World today, more often than not we see dual societies and patchwork practices that seek to accommodate seemingly irreconcilable old and new ways. Rather than the persistence of traditional culture in the face of modern intrusions, or even the development of syncretic cultures and values, we usually see instead a disruptive and incomplete westernization, cultural confusion, or the enthusiastic embrace of "modern" practices and values. In other words, the traditional culture advanced to justify cultural relativism far too often no longer exists.

Therefore, while recognizing the legitimate claims of self-determination and cultural relativism, we must be alert to cynical manipulations of a dying, lost, or even mythical cultural past. We must not be misled by complaints of the inappropriateness of "western" human rights made by repressive regimes whose practices have at best only the most tenuous connection to the indigenous culture. . . .

In traditional cultures—at least the sorts of traditional cultures that would readily justify cultural deviations from international human rights standards—people are not victims of the arbitrary decisions of rulers whose principal claim to power is their control of modern instruments of force and administration. In traditional cultures, communal customs and practices usually provide each person with a place in society and a certain amount of dignity and protection. Furthermore, there usually are well-established reciprocal bonds between rulers and ruled, and between rich and poor. . . .

[In addition,] there are substantive human rights limits on even well-established cultural practices, however difficult it may be to specify and defend a particular account of what those practices are. For example, while slavery has been customary in numerous societies, today it is a practice that no custom can justify. Likewise, sexual, racial, ethnic, and religious discrimination have been widely practiced, but are indefensible today. . . .

RESOLVING THE CLAIMS OF RELATIVISM AND UNIVERSALISM

. . . While human rights . . . have not been a part of most cultural traditions, or even the western tradition until rather recently, there is a striking similarity in many of the basic values that today we seek to protect through human rights. This is particularly true when these values are expressed in relatively general terms. Life, social order, protection from arbitrary rule, prohibition of inhuman and degrading treatment, the guarantee of a place in the life of the community, and access to an equitable share of the means of subsistence are central moral aspirations in nearly all cultures.

This fundamental unity in the midst of otherwise bewildering diversity suggests a certain core of "human nature"—for all its undeniable variability, and despite our inability to express that core in the language of science. And if human nature is relatively universal, then basic human rights must at least initially be assumed to be similarly universal. . . .

ASSESSING CLAIMS OF CULTURAL RELATIVISM

. . . [I]t is hard to imagine cultural arguments against recognition of the basic personal rights of Articles 3 through 11 [of the Universal Declaration]. Rights to life, liberty, and security of the person; the guarantee of legal personality; and protections against slavery, arbitrary arrest, detention, or exile, and inhuman or degrading treatment are so clearly connected to basic requirements of human dignity, and are stated in sufficiently general terms, that any morally defensible contemporary form of social organization must recognize them (although perhaps not necessarily as inalienable rights). In fact, I am tempted to say that conceptions of human nature or society incompatible with such rights would be almost by definition indefensible; at the very least, such rights come very close to being fully universal.

Civil rights such as freedom of conscience, speech, and association would be a bit more relative; as they assume the existence and a positive evaluation of relatively autonomous individuals, they are of questionable applicability in strong traditional communities. In such communities, however, they would rarely be at issue. If traditional practices truly are based on and protect culturally accepted conceptions of human dignity, then members of such a community simply will not have the desire or need to claim such civil rights. But in the more typical contemporary case, in which the relatively autonomous individual faces the modern state, they would seem to be close to universal rights; it is hard to imagine a defensible modern conception of human dignity that did not include at least most of these rights. A similar argument can easily be made for the basic economic and social rights of the Declaration.

The Declaration does list some rights that are best viewed as "interpretations," subject to much greater cultural relativity. For example, the already mentioned right of free and full consent of intending spouses not only reflects a specific cultural interpretation of marriage, but an interpretation that is of relatively recent origin and by no means universal today even in the West. . . .

Such cases, however, are the exception rather than the rule. And if my arguments above are correct, we can justifiably insist on some form of weak cultural relativism; that is, on a fundamental universality of basic human rights, tempered by a recognition of the possible need for limited cultural variations. Basic human rights are, to use an appropriately paradoxical phrase, relatively universal.

Critics often argue that Western insistence on the universality of international human rights norms implicitly devalues other cultures and sometimes masks Western economic and political interests. Debates on this issue often center on cultural differences deriving either from different religious traditions or from different regional traditions.

Many states have made reservations to CEDAW based explicitly on religious values. Egypt's reservation, for example, makes acceptance of Article 2 on nondiscrimination contingent on the extent to which "compliance does not run counter to the Islamic Sharia [religious law]." Many other Islamic countries have similar reservations. Indeed, CEDAW is plagued by substantive reservations to a much greater extent than any other general human rights treaty. Efforts to induce states to withdraw reservations to core provisions of CEDAW have been controversial. Although the concluding document of the 1993 UN World Conference on Human Rights called for the withdrawal of reservations contrary to the object and purpose of the treaty, discussions in UN fora have been contentious. Some Islamic states have accused Western states and CEDAW of cultural imperialism and hostility to Islam.

The CEDAW Committee offered the following observations on the problem on the fiftieth anniversary of the Universal Declaration:

2. The Committee has, on a number of occasions, expressed its views and concerns regarding the number and extent of reservations to the Convention. It has also noted that some States parties that enter reservations to the Convention do not enter reservations to analogous provisions in other human rights treaties. A number

of States enter reservations to particular articles on the ground that national law, tradition, religion or culture is not congruent with Convention principles, and purport to justify the reservation on that basis. Some States enter a reservation to article 2, although their national constitutions or laws prohibit discrimination. . . .

4. As of 1 July 1998, 161 States parties had ratified the Convention on the Elimination of All Forms of Discrimination against Women. Fifty-four States had entered reservations to one or more articles in the Convention including permissible reservations to article 29(1) and (2).

5. Articles 2 and 16 are considered by the Committee to be core provisions of the Convention. Although some States parties have withdrawn reservations to those articles, the Committee is particularly concerned at the number and extent of reservations entered to those articles.

7. Although the Convention does not prohibit the entering of reservations, those which challenge the central principles of the Convention are contrary to the provisions of the Convention and to general international law. As such they may be challenged by other States parties.

9. Reservations affect the efficacy of the Convention, whose objective is to end discrimination against women and to achieve *de jure* and de facto equality for them. . . . Some States are concerned about a perceived conflict between article 2 and the Islamic shariah law. In other instances, States have entered reservations, which, although unspecific, are broad enough to encompass article 2. These reservations pose an acute problem for the implementation of the Convention and for the Committee's ability to monitor compliance with it. Several have entered reservations to article 2 to protect rights of succession to the throne and to chiefly and other traditional titles. This too is discriminatory against women. . . .

11. The Committee has previously analysed article 16 in its general recommendation 21. In the course of the analysis of factors impeding compliance with article 16, it said:

> *"Reservations"*
>
> "The Committee has noted with alarm the number of States parties which have entered reservations to the whole or part of article 16, especially when a reservation has also been entered to article 2, claiming that compliance may conflict with a commonly held vision of the family, based, *inter alia*, on cultural or religious beliefs or on a country's economic or political status.
>
> "Many of these countries hold a patriarchal belief in the structure of a family which places a father, husband or son in a favourable position. In some countries where fundamentalist or other extremist views or economic hardship have encouraged a return to old values and traditions, women's place in the family has deteriorated sharply. . . .
>
> "Consistent with articles 2, 3 and 24 in particular, the Committee requires that all States parties gradually progress to a stage where, by their resolute discouragement of notions of the inequality of women in the home, each country will withdraw its reservation, in particular to articles 9 [nationality], 15 [equality before the law] and 16 [marriage and family relations] of the Convention.
>
> "States parties should resolutely discourage any notions of inequality of women and men which are affirmed by laws or by private law or custom, and progress to the stage where reservations, in particular to article 16, will be withdrawn." . . .

16. Neither traditional, religious or cultural practice nor incompatible domestic laws and policies can justify violations of the Convention. The Committee also remains convinced that reservations to article 16, whether lodged for national, traditional, religious or cultural reasons, are incompatible with the Convention and therefore impermissible and should be reviewed and modified or withdrawn.

Contribution to the Commemoration of the Fiftieth Anniversary of the Universal Declaration of Human Rights, *in* Status of the Convention on the Elimination of All Forms of Discrimination against Women, Report of the Secretary-General, Annex X, at 29, U.N. Doc. A/53/318 (1998).

Whether and to what extent religious values require Islamic states to make reservations to CEDAW and other human rights treaties is much debated. In the following excerpt, Professor An-Na'im outlines some of the potential conflicts between Islam and international human rights norms:

Abdullah Ahmed An-Na'im, *Human Rights in the Muslim World: Socio-Political Conditions and Scriptural Imperatives*

3 Harv. Hum. Rts. J. 13 (1990)

The basic premise of my approach is that human rights violations reflect the lack or weakness of cultural legitimacy of international standards in a society. Insofar as these standards are perceived to be alien to or at variance with the values and institutions of a people, they are unlikely to elicit commitment or compliance. While cultural legitimacy may not be the sole or even the primary determinant of compliance with human rights standards, it is, in my view, an extremely significant one. . . .

. . . Some authors have gone so far as to argue that inherent differences exist between the Western notion of human rights as reflected in the international instruments and non-Western notions of human dignity. In the Muslim world, for instance, there are obvious conflicts between Shari'a [which An Naim describes as a "particular historical version of Islam"] and certain human rights, especially of women and non-Muslims. . . .

I believe that a modern version of Islamic law can and should be developed. Such a modern 'Shari'a' could be, in my view, entirely consistent with current standards of human rights. These views, however, are appreciated by only a tiny minority of contemporary Muslims. To the overwhelming majority of Muslims today, Shari'a is the sole valid interpretation of Islam, and as such *ought* to prevail over any human law or policy. . . .

The most important general principle of Shari'a influencing the status and rights of women is the notion of *qawama*. *Qawama* has its origin in verse 4:34 of the Qur'an: "Men have *qawama* [guardianship and authority] over women because of the advantage they [men] have over them [women] and because they [men] spend their property in supporting them [women]." According to Shari'a interpretations of this verse, men as a group are the guardians of and superior to women as a group, and the men of a particular family are the guardians of and superior to the women of that family.

. . . For example, Shari'a provides that women are disqualified from holding general public office, which involves the exercise of authority over men, because, in keeping with the verse 4:34 of the Qur'an, men are entitled to exercise authority over women and not the reverse.

Another general principle of Shari'a that has broad implications for the status and rights of Muslim women is the notion of *al-hijab*, the veil. This means more than requiring women to cover their bodies and faces in public. According to Shari'a interpretations of verses 24:31, 33:33, 33:53, and 33:59 of the Qur'an, women are supposed to stay at home and not leave it except when required to by urgent necessity. When they are permitted to venture beyond the home, they must do so with their bodies and faces covered. *Al-hijab* tends to reinforce women's inability to hold public office and restricts their access to public life. They are not supposed to participate in public life, because they must not mix with men even in public places. . . .

But as Professor Ann Mayer argues, Islamic societies, and the individuals that comprise them, are by no means monolithic in their attitudes toward international human rights norms; moreover, attitudes have varied by time as well as by country:

Ann Mayer, *Universal Versus Islamic Human Rights: A Clash of Cultures or a Clash with a Construct?*

15 Mich. J. Int'l L. 307, 321-322, 401-402 (1994)

In the decades immediately following World War II, Muslim countries for the most part appeared to accept the international consensus on human rights. . . .

By the 1970s, assertions that international human rights norms were incompatible with adherence to Islamic law were being voiced more frequently, and after the 1979 Islamic Revolution in Iran, Iran became a vigorous advocate of the proposition that international human rights were at variance with Islamic norms. . . .

The most extensive conflicts between past interpretations of Islamic requirements and international human rights norms lie in the area of women's rights, although Muslim feminists argue that it is actually patriarchal attitudes and misreadings of Islamic sources, not Islamic tenets, that inspire the patterns of discrimination against women. . . .

[Mayer goes on to critique efforts by governments of predominantly Islamic countries to promote alternative Islamic human rights instruments either through multilateral declarations (for example, the 1990 Cairo Declaration on Human Rights in Islam) or through national legislation (for example, the 1992 Basic Law of Saudi Arabia). She concludes:]

. . . [T]he constructs of Islamic rights in the civil and political sphere, that one finds in schemes like the Cairo Declaration and the Saudi Basic Law, are designed to shore up the political interests of those promoting them and have only a tenuous connection to Islamic culture. They borrow extensively from Western rights models and mine the Islamic heritage only very selectively—shutting out the enlightened, modern perspectives of Muslims who are supportive of human rights. The features of Islamic human rights schemes sometimes clash with Islamic principles or set forth rules that represent nothing more than the authors' own policy preferences or political agendas. . . . In reality, the world's Muslims have never been consulted about what rights they would like to have or about whether they truly prefer to be governed by so called "Islamic" rights norms that fall far below the protections guaranteed to nonMuslims under international law. . . .

Critics of the view that human rights are universal often point to the different cultural values found in different parts of the world and emphasize in particular the differences between Asian and Western cultures. In 1993, Bilihari Kausikan, then director of the East Asian and Pacific Bureau of the Singapore Ministry of Foreign Affairs, challenged the universality ideal in the pages of *Foreign Policy*, a foreign affairs magazine. Kausikan may have been responding in part to western criticism of Singapore, an authoritarian but prosperous state.

Bilihari Kausikan, *Asia's Different Standard*

92 For. Pol'y 24, 27-28, 32-36, 39-40 (1993)

. . . The United States and many European countries increasingly emphasize human rights in their foreign policies. Of course, human rights are not, and are not likely to become, a primary issue in international relations. Their promotion by all countries will always be selective, even cynical, and concern for human rights will always be balanced against other national interests. Nevertheless, the Western emphasis on human rights will affect the tone and texture of post-Cold War international relations. . . .

. . . [R]elations among the United States, Europe, and Asia may lead the West to use human rights as an instrument of economic competition. As American and European apprehensions about their competitiveness rise, the West is emphasizing values like openness and equal opportunity and relating them to broader issues of freedom and democracy. . . .

. . . This is not to say that the West is insincere in its commitment to human rights. But . . . it is difficult to believe that economic considerations do not to some degree influence Western attitudes toward such issues as, say, the prison labor component of Chinese exports, child labor in Thailand, or some of the AFL-CIO complaints against Malaysian labor practices. . . .

For the first time since the Universal Declaration was adopted in 1948, countries not thoroughly steeped in the Judeo-Christian and natural law traditions are in the first rank: . . . [A] genuine and fruitful dialogue . . . [between Asia and the West] will require finding a balance between a pretentious and unrealistic universalism and a paralyzing cultural relativism. The myth of the universality of all human rights is harmful if it masks the real gap that exists between Asian and Western perceptions of human rights. The gap will not be bridged if it is denied. . . .

For many in the West, the end of the Cold War was not just the defeat or collapse of communist regimes, but the supreme triumph and vindication of Western systems and values. . . .

. . . But the Western approach is ideological, not empirical. The West needs its myths; missionary zeal to whip the heathen along the path of righteousness and remake the world in its own image is deeply ingrained in Western (especially American) political culture. It is entirely understandable that Western human rights advocates choose to interpret reality in the way they believe helps their cause most.

But that is not how most East and Southeast Asian governments view the world. Economic success has engendered a greater cultural self-confidence. . . . The self-congratulatory, simplistic, and sanctimonious tone of much Western commentary at the end of the Cold War and the current triumphalism of

Western values grate on East and Southeast Asians. It is, after all, a West that launched two world wars, supported racism and colonialism, perpetrated the Holocaust and the Great Purge, and now suffers from serious social and economic deficiencies. . . .

The hard core of rights that are truly universal is smaller than many in the West are wont to pretend. Forty-five years after the Universal Declaration was adopted, many of its 30 articles are still subject to debate over interpretation and application—not just between Asia and the West, but within the West itself. . . . It is not only pretentious but wrong to insist that everything has been settled once and forever. . . . All international norms must evolve through continuing debate among different points of view if consensus is to be maintained.

Most East and Southeast Asian governments are uneasy with the propensity of many American and some European human rights activists to place more emphasis on civil and political rights than on economic, social, and cultural rights. They would probably not be convinced, for instance, by a September 1992 report issued by Human Rights Watch [arguing] . . . that "political and civil rights, especially those related to democratic accountability," are basic to survival and "not luxuries to be enjoyed only after a certain level of economic development has been reached". . . . Such an argument does not accord with their own historical experience. That experience sees order and stability as preconditions for economic growth, and growth as the necessary foundation of any political order that claims to advance human dignity. . . .

At any rate, many East and Southeast Asians tend to look askance at the starkly individualistic ethos of the West in which authority tends to be seen as oppressive and rights are an individual's "trump" over the state. Most people of the region prefer a situation in which distinctions between the individual, society, and state are less clear-cut, or at least less adversarial. . . .

Future Western approaches on human rights will have to be formulated with greater nuance and precision. It makes a great deal of difference if the West insists on humane standards of behavior by vigorously protesting genocide, murder, torture, or slavery. Here there is a clear consensus on a core of international law that does not admit of derogation on any grounds. The West has a legitimate right and moral duty to promote those core human rights, even if it is tempered by limited influence. But if the West objects to, say, capital punishment, detention without trial, or curbs on press freedoms, it should recognize that it does so in a context where the international law is less definitive and more open to interpretation and where there is room for further elaboration through debate. The West will have to accept that no universal consensus may be possible and that states can legitimately agree to disagree without being guilty of sinister designs or bad faith. Trying to impose pet Western definitions of "freedom" and "democracy" is an incitement to destructive conflict, best foregone in the interest of promoting real human rights.

Notes and Questions

1. Do claims that female genital cutting constitutes a human rights violation entail an imposition of Western values on people from non-Western cultures?

2. Why do so many states attach substantive reservations to their ratification of CEDAW? Why might other states be reluctant to challenge those reservations?

3. Are reservations such as Egypt's, which exclude the application of Article 2 of the Convention where incompatible with Islamic law, compatible with the object and purpose of the Convention?

4. Compared to other human rights treaty bodies, such as the Human Rights Committee under the First Optional Protocol to the ICCPR, the CEDAW Committee, which is charged with monitoring state parties' compliance with CEDAW, met less often and had weaker procedures. In 1999, the UN General Assembly adopted an Optional Protocol, which entered into force in December 2000. Under the Optional Protocol, the CEDAW Committee can consider communications from individuals claiming to have experienced violations of the Convention, and the Committee can examine situations of grave or systematic Convention violations. As of September 2005, 72 countries had ratified the Optional Protocol.

5. CEDAW requires modification of cultural practices that discriminate against women. Would the Convention preclude the practice within certain monarchies of making the first-born son the heir to the throne? Would it require states parties to take action to modify religious practices of certain Christian or Jewish denominations that permit only men to be priests or rabbis? Are such distinctions "social and cultural patterns of conduct" within the meaning of Article 5 of the Convention? How should human rights bodies reconcile conflicts between women's rights and other human rights?

6. Consider the reservations to CEDAW discussed above. If a predominantly Islamic state party insists that women must wear veils when in public, what arguments can be made for and against the validity of such a requirement? In 1995, the U.S. Department of Defense required U.S. servicewomen stationed in Saudi Arabia, when off a U.S. military base, to wear an "abaya," a traditional head-to-toe covering, to ride only in the back seat of cars, and to be continuously accompanied by a man. In December 2001, Lieutenant Colonel Martha McSally, the highest-ranking female fighter pilot in the U.S. Air Force, brought suit against the Secretary of Defense and the U.S. Government over its policy. The policy is no longer required but is still "strongly encouraged." Colonel McSally argued that the law discriminates against women and violates her freedom of religion. In May 2002, the House of Representatives voted unanimously to approve a measure prohibiting the military from requiring or encouraging servicewomen to wear the abaya. McSally dropped her lawsuit in 2004.

7. The United States signed CEDAW in 1980 but has not ratified it. In 1994, a majority of the Senate Foreign Relations Committee reported favorably on the Convention, subject to a proposed package of reservations, understandings and declarations. Although that package was designed to ensure that the Convention as ratified would be consistent with existing U.S. law and practice, the Committee minority opposed ratification. The minority issued a statement arguing (among other things) that the evolution of human rights must "take place within an international system of sovereign nations with differing cultural, religious and political systems." Congress adjourned before the full Senate had an opportunity to consider the treaty, which was then returned to Committee. CEDAW, with 169 parties, is the most widely ratified human rights convention after the Convention on the Rights of the Child. Almost all developed Western states other than the United States have ratified it. Should the United States ratify also?

E. Strategies for Overcoming the Cultural Divide

Most Western feminists and human rights advocates unequivocally condemn female circumcision as a human rights violation, but their analyses differ. Professor Karen Engle identifies three different approaches to women's rights as international human rights—doctrinalist, institutionalist, and external—and describes how each would apply to the problem of female circumcision.

Karen Engle, *Female Subjects of Public International Law: Human Rights and the Exotic Other Female*

26 New Eng. L. Rev. 1509, 1513-1518 (1992)

I. THE DOCTRINALIST APPROACH

Doctrinalists generally approach international human rights law by focussing on one practice that they believe violates a particular right, here the practice of "female circumcision" (as they label it). They then attempt to demonstrate doctrinally how the practice ought to be eradicated on the basis of rights derived from international law. Because no legal provisions specifically mention clitoridectomy or female circumcision, those who advocate its end go through one human rights instrument after another to show that the practice is prohibited by the existence of rights such as "rights of the child," "the right to sexual and corporal integrity," and the "right to health."

. . . While those who take other approaches to women's human rights do not openly confront [the] counter-claim of cultural relativism, doctrinalists often do. Although in the end they reject a cultural relativist perspective as they argue for "universal" human rights, they are nevertheless acutely aware that disagreements about the scope and shape of women's rights exist, particularly in the case of clitoridectomy. These disagreements are not just between men and women or between cultures; they actually exist between women. The acknowledgement of disagreements among women . . . allows [doctrinalists] to engage women's differences to a greater extent than those who take the other approaches, which tend to assume, albeit to different degrees, a monolithic or essential "woman." . . .

II. THE INSTITUTIONALIST APPROACH

The institutionalist approach to women's human rights concentrates on the institutions that have been created by international law to enforce human rights. . . . They believe that if positive law or doctrine guaranteeing women's rights is to be meaningful, institutions must transform that law or doctrine into action, through pragmatic, meaningful enforcement mechanisms. To the extent that transformation has not occurred, they largely hold responsible the (primarily male) actors that deploy human rights discourse through international institutions. . . .

Applying their analysis to clitoridectomy, institutionalists would argue that . . . either mainstream institutions must expand their (presently male) focus or specialized women's institutions must be granted power equal to the mainstream ones. . . .

III. EXTERNAL CRITIQUES

Other women's human rights advocates begin by situating themselves outside the human rights system looking in at the discourse. From their (initial) external perches, they raise questions about whether human rights discourse can really assimilate women's issues/demands/rights. . . .

Engle goes on to discuss three different external approaches, all of which assume that "structural changes—whether in human rights theory, doctrine, institutions or language—are needed to accommodate women's concerns." The external approaches "critique the human rights system for the ways it perpetuates women's subordination," and "[t]o a certain extent, . . . approach women's human rights as if all women were essentially the same." Engle argues that "[t]he radical feminist positions of these critics do not . . . make them incapable of accepting that women disagree, even about clitoridectomy. Rather, they focus so much on the subordination of women by men that they tend to generalize the extent to which all women have an interest in overcoming men's power, the assumption here being that 'genital mutilation' (as they call the practice) is a clear exercise of male power." According to Engle, "integrationists" assume that the male-dominated human rights system fails to pay adequate attention to women's rights, and that cultural relativist claims concerning female circumcision are "made by those who simply want to exclude practices such as clitoridectomy from human rights analysis." Integrationists do not reject human rights discourse, only what they see as "its presently exclusive male focus." Others argue that international human rights law rests on a male conception of rights, and should be reconceptualized to permit women to define their own rights. For these theorists, "the human rights system has not begun to deal with the issue [of female genital mutilation] because women have not defined the rights necessary to end the practice." Reconceptualists assume that "clitoridectomy—because it is a 'private' (not officially state conducted) practice—cannot be seen as a violation of international human rights until the human rights field has been reconceptualized to include the private." Finally, Engle notes that "linguistic" critics assume "that there are certain essential values that are female and that cannot be realized through traditional rights discourse." They see rights discourse as unnecessarily adversarial, and exclusive of other values such as friendship, cooperation and fairness. Engle concludes:

> It appears, then, that even though each approach provides some valuable insights into the workings of the international human rights framework, none actively engages the Exotic Other Female [a term Engle uses to signify the assumption of feminists that a woman who condones clitoridectomy is "not totally accessible to someone outside her culture"]. Either the advocates maternalistically try to change her mind or they seem to ignore or not believe her desires, often dissipating her by attributing to her false consciousness. . . .
>
> The task ahead for women's human rights advocates is to acknowledge the presence of the Exotic Other Female . . . and to use some of those insights already provided by their varied approaches to begin to move from imagination to engagement.

Id. at 1526.

8

Mitigating the Harms of War: International Humanitarian Law

International law has long distinguished between *jus ad bellum*—the law governing the initiation of war—and *jus in bello*—the law governing the conduct of war once initiated. The *jus ad bellum,* which will be examined in detail in Chapter 13, determines when a state may legitimately use armed force in international affairs. The subject of this chapter is the *jus in bello*, commonly referred to either as the law of war or international humanitarian law.

International humanitarian law places limits on the treatment of individuals caught up in armed conflicts and the means by which armed conflicts are fought. Those limits apply without regard to whether someone protected by the law may be viewed as fighting a war of aggression or a war of self-defense. International humanitarian law now applies to states, insurgent groups, and individuals engaged in armed conflict.

The goal of international humanitarian law is to mitigate some of the more horrific aspects of organized violence. Humanitarian law recognizes that states cannot generally be expected to refrain from using weapons or tactics necessary to achieve legitimate military aims. But in the words of the 1868 St. Petersburg Declaration, one of the earliest intergovernmental declarations on the principles applicable in armed conflict, international humanitarian law is designed to "conciliate the necessities of war with the laws of humanity." Thus, international humanitarian law attempts to shield individuals from all harm that cannot be justified as necessary and proportionate to the successful pursuit of military objectives, and from some types of harm, such as torture, whatever their military utility.

Over time, states have developed a large body of rules to regulate the conduct of armed conflict. The laws and customs of war, as this body of law was commonly referred to in the past, has its origins in two separate strands that have now merged to form a single body of law. One body of law emerged from efforts to codify the rights and obligations of combatants in their conduct of hostilities. Primarily, it was designed to limit combatants choice of the means and methods used to injure the enemy in international armed conflicts. To this end, a series of conferences held in The Hague produced a set of declarations and conventions (most notably in 1899 and 1907) now loosely referred to as "Hague law." A second body of law emerged through a series of Geneva Conventions—those of 1864, 1906, 1929, and 1949, as well as the two 1977 Additional Protocols to the 1949 Conventions—designed to protect military personnel who are injured or otherwise rendered unable to fight and other non-combatants. These two strands are now simply referred to as international humanitarian law.

International humanitarian law is closely related to two other bodies of law. International human rights law, considered in the preceding chapter, also seeks to safeguard human dignity. It applies during periods of armed conflict as well as in peacetime, but human rights law is not directly aimed at regulating armed conflict. Moreover, as discussed in Chapter 7, the majority of state obligations pursuant to most human rights treaties, such as the International Covenant on Civil and Political Rights, are subject to derogation in times of emergency, and therefore may be subject to derogation during wartime. International criminal law, which shares many of the goals of international human rights and humanitarian law, deals with the establishment and enforcement of criminal liability for violations of certain international norms. Like human rights law, international criminal law applies in times of peace and war. Since many violations of international humanitarian law entail individual criminal responsibility, there is a substantial overlap between the two bodies of law. International criminal law, however, addresses many areas of conduct outside the realm of human rights and humanitarian law, such as narcotics trafficking and hijacking. Similarly, human rights and humanitarian law address many issues that do not implicate international criminal law. The relationship among the three branches of law will become clearer as you examine the materials in this and related chapters.

The first three problems in this chapter examine the role of international law in efforts to place limits on the means and methods of warfare in both international and non-international armed conflicts. The final problem considers the law applicable to the control and administration of captured enemy territory, a subject governed by the law of belligerent occupation.

I. PLACING LIMITS ON THE CONDUCT OF WAR: PREVENTING THE USE OF NUCLEAR WEAPONS

Efforts to limit the use of weapons deemed unnecessarily cruel or destructive have a long history. Some 2,000 years ago, the Code of Manu, a text from India, prohibited the use of barbed or poisoned weapons. Similar restrictions on the conduct of warfare can be found in many other cultures and from every epoch. In the Middle Ages, for example, the Catholic Church, during a gathering of some 1,000 prelates from most of the Christian states in Europe, prohibited the use of the crossbow. Subsequent decrees restricted the use of other weapons that could kill from a distance—weapons then seen as dishonorable.

Contemporary efforts to prohibit particular weapons date back to the middle of the nineteenth century. In 1868, a conference convened in St. Petersburg by the Czar of Russia declared that the only legitimate aim of war was to disable enemy combatants, and that it would be illegitimate to employ "arms which uselessly aggravate the sufferings of disabled men, or render their death inevitable." In 1874, Czar Alexander II invited 15 states to a conference in Brussels to confirm and expand the principles contained in the St. Petersburg Declaration. This conference paved the way for a meeting of 26 states in The Hague in 1899. At this conference, and at a subsequent conference in 1907, the participating states adopted a series of agreements and declarations concerning the laws and customs of war. Among other things, they codified the St. Petersburg principles by prohibiting the use of weapons that cause superfluous injury or unnecessary suffering, or weapons that are inherently incapable of discriminating between combatants and non-combatants. According to the International Court of Justice (ICJ) in *Nicaragua v. United States*, this principle now forms part of customary international law.

Over the course of the last century, states have prohibited the use of many weapons by specific treaties (for example, those outlawing the use of poison gas, chemical weapons, and biological weapons). Other weapons (for example, blinding lasers) are arguably prohibited by customary international law. But considerable controversy remains over precisely which weapons are or should be deemed impermissible. That controversy is particularly acute with respect to nuclear weapons.

As you read the following materials, consider the process by which the laws governing war are generated and clarified, who is advantaged or disadvantaged by such rules, whether the rules that exist should be modified or supplemented, and the likely effect of those rules on the behavior of combatants.

A. The Problem

During World War II, indiscriminate aerial bombardments of major population centers were frequent. Germany, for example, repeatedly attacked London with V-2 rockets. Similarly, the Allies engaged in a strategic bombing campaign against Dresden and other German cities, as well as Japanese cities, in an effort to destroy the enemy populations' will to fight. In this context, both Allied and Axis powers viewed the development of nuclear weapons as potentially crucial to winning the war.

1. Development and Initial Use of the Atomic Bomb

In 1941, the United States established a secret program, known as the Manhattan Project, with the goal of developing an atomic bomb before Germany did. But even after Germany surrendered on May 8, 1945, research on the atomic bomb continued. As the war in Germany was nearing an end, attacks against Japan intensified. The United States attacked Tokyo with incendiary bombs on March 9, 1945, burning 15 square miles of the city and killing over 80,000 people. The United States launched similar attacks on other Japanese cities, including Nagoya, Osaka, and Kobe. With these attacks, the United States tried to place enough pressure upon the Japanese government to compel it to surrender unconditionally.

When Japan refused, President Truman elected to use the atomic bomb. In his view, the only alternative would be to launch a ground invasion that would entail enormous Allied and Japanese casualties. Following the war, President Truman's Secretary of War, Henry L. Stimson, claimed that by dropping atomic bombs on Japan, Truman saved more than 1 million U.S. lives.

The United States chose Hiroshima, a city on the main Japanese island of Honshu, as the primary target. The official reason given was the presence of military factories and the headquarters for the Japanese Second Army. At 8:15 A.M. on August 6, 1945, the U.S. bomber *Enola Gay* flew over Hiroshima and dropped "Little Boy," the first atomic bomb. Sixty percent of Hiroshima was destroyed, and 150,000 individuals were killed. Over four square miles were demolished instantly. Two days later, the United States ratified the Charter of the United Nations.

When Japan still did not agree to unconditional surrender, President Truman decided to drop another atomic bomb on a second target. At 11:02 A.M. on August 9, 1945, the United States dropped "Fat Man," a more powerful plutonium bomb, on Nagasaki. Nagasaki was a primary seaport and a center for the production of ships, munitions, and other materials useful to the Japanese war effort. Casualty estimates range from 60,000 to 160,000. On August 14, 1945, Japan told the United States that it would surrender. The next day, Emperor Hirohito announced Japan's surrender to the people of Japan.

2. Post-War Developments

The U.S. monopoly on nuclear weapons did not last long. On August 2, 1949, the Soviet Union exploded its first atomic bomb. The Soviet test touched off a nuclear arms race. Both the United States and the Soviet Union rapidly escalated the size and destructive power of their nuclear arsenals. Other countries worked to develop a nuclear capacity, and Britain conducted its first nuclear test in 1952. Recognizing the dangers posed by the unchecked development of nuclear weapons, the United States proposed to transfer control of fissionable material to an international agency under the auspices of the United Nations. This proposal met with considerable resistance from a mistrustful Soviet Union, but President Eisenhower pressed ahead anyway. On December 8, 1953, President Eisenhower made his famous Atoms for Peace speech to the United Nations General Assembly:

Atoms for Peace: Address by Dwight D. Eisenhower

Reprinted in Public Papers of the Presidents of the United States 813 (1960)

87. On 16 July 1945, the United States set off the world's biggest atomic explosion. Since that date in 1945, the United States of America has conducted forty-two test explosions. Atomic bombs are more than twenty-five times as powerful as the weapons with which the atomic age dawned, while hydrogen weapons are in the ranges of millions of tons of TNT equivalent.

88. Today, the United States stockpile of atomic weapons, which, of course, increases daily, exceeds by many times the total equivalent of the total of all bombs and all shells that came from every plane and every gun in every theatre of war in all the years of the Second World War. A single air group, whether afloat or land based, can now deliver to any reachable target a destructive cargo exceeding in power all the bombs that fell on Britain in all the Second World War. . . .

90. But the dread secret and the fearful engines of atomic might are not ours alone.

91. In the first place, the secret is possessed by our friends and allies, the United Kingdom and Canada. . . .

92. The secret is also known by the Soviet Union. . . . During this period the Soviet Union has exploded a series of atomic devices, including at least one involving thermo-nuclear reactions.

93. . . . . [T]he knowledge now possessed by several nations will eventually be shared by others, possibly all others. . . .

94. . . . [L]et no one think that the expenditure of vast sums for weapons and systems of defence can guarantee absolute safety for the cities and citizens of any nation. The awful arithmetic of the atomic bomb does not permit of any such easy solution. Even against the most powerful defence, an aggressor in possession of the effective minimum number of atomic bombs for a surprise attack could probably place a sufficient number of his bombs on the chosen targets to cause hideous damage.

95. Should such an atomic attack be launched against the United States, our reactions would be swift and resolute. But for me to say that the defence capabilities of the United States are such that they could inflict terrible losses upon an aggressor, for me to say that the retaliation capabilities of the United States are so great that such an aggressor's land would be laid waste, all this, while fact, is not the true expression of the purpose and the hopes of the United States.

96. To pause there would be to confirm the hopeless finality of a belief that two atomic colossi are doomed malevolently to eye each other indefinitely across a trembling world. To stop there would be to accept helplessly the probability of civilization destroyed. . . . Surely no sane member of the human race could discover victory in such desolation.

Eisenhower concluded his Atoms for Peace speech with a proposal to create an international agency entrusted with responsibility for overseeing the development and peaceful use of nuclear energy. Despite initial Soviet opposition, the proposal resulted in the creation of the International Atomic Energy Agency (IAEA) in 1957. The IAEA, a UN agency, is now the principal inter-governmental forum for technical cooperation on nuclear energy. In addition, the IAEA monitors and verifies states' compliance with treaty commitments concerning non-proliferation of nuclear weapons and use of nuclear materials and facilities for peaceful purposes. Nevertheless, the creation of the IAEA did little to slow the nuclear arms race.

France joined the nuclear weapons club in 1960, followed by China in 1964. The increase in the number of nuclear powers prompted efforts among the nuclear powers to reach agreements to restrict or end the testing and proliferation of nuclear weapons. In the late 1950s, the United States and the Soviet Union discussed and briefly attempted a moratorium on nuclear testing, but this ended with the commencement of French nuclear tests in 1960. In 1961, the United States and the Soviet Union jointly proposed, and the General Assembly adopted, a Joint Statement of Agreed Principles for Disarmament Negotiations. The principles urged multilateral negotiations aimed at general and complete disarmament, leaving states only with such armed forces as are necessary to maintain internal order. The proposal envisioned the creation of an International Disarmament Organization to oversee the phased and coordinated dismantling of all weapons of mass destruction and all military units and facilities beyond those needed for domestic purposes. In addition, the principles recommended the creation of a standing UN peacekeeping force. This ambitious proposal came to naught, and the arms race continued.

Throughout the Cold War, the North Atlantic Treaty Organization (NATO) and the Warsaw Pact targeted each others' members with enough nuclear weapons to plunge the world into a perpetual "nuclear winter." Under a strategy known as mutual assured destruction (MAD), states on both sides believed that a credible threat of an overwhelming retaliatory strike would deter adversaries from using nuclear weapons in the first place. This strategy of deterrence proved successful, though at times disaster seemed perilously near, as it did, for example, during the 1962 Cuban Missile Crisis. With the breakup of the former Soviet Union, the risks of a global thermonuclear exchange diminished dramatically but the risks of a regional nuclear war remained and perhaps intensified.

3. The Nuclear Non-Proliferation Treaty

In the early 1960s, the UN General Assembly and individual states began to consider the possibility of a treaty designed to prevent the spread of nuclear weapons. By that time, there were five declared nuclear weapon states (the United States, the Soviet Union, France, the United Kingdom, and China), but many expected that number to grow quickly to 20 or 30. In 1967, the United States and the Soviet Union presented identical treaty drafts to the General Assembly for discussion. The resulting Treaty on the Non-Proliferation of Nuclear Weapons (NPT) entered into force in March 1970. As of December 2005, 189 states were party to the treaty.

The treaty obligates all parties "not to transfer to any recipient whatsoever nuclear weapons or other nuclear explosive devices" and "not in any way to assist, encourage, or induce any non-nuclear weapon State to manufacture or otherwise acquire nuclear weapons. . . ." Non-nuclear-weapon states are required not to produce or acquire nuclear weapons, and to enter into safeguard agreements designed to prevent the diversion of nuclear energy or materials from peaceful activities to nuclear weapons. In return, nuclear weapon states agreed to pursue negotiations on nuclear disarmament. The treaty permits each party to pursue peaceful uses of nuclear energy, and "to withdraw from the Treaty if it decides that extraordinary events, related to the subject matter of [the] Treaty, have jeopardized the supreme interests of its country."

Overall, the NPT has achieved widespread but not universal adherence, and can claim some notable recent additions. South Africa abandoned its nuclear weapons program and joined the treaty in 1991. Libya followed suit when it gave up its own program in December 2003, following months of negotiations with the United States and the United Kingdom. Libya's action helped it end years of international sanctions imposed following the destruction of Pan Am Flight 103 over Lockerbie, Scotland, an episode examined more fully in Chapter 14. Iraq's nuclear program was found in violation of the NPT in 1991, although no nuclear weapons were found in Iraq following the coalition invasion in 2003.

But the NPT continues to face serious challenges. Two recognized nuclear weapon states, India and Pakistan, have refused to ratify the treaty. Both have criticized the treaty for creating a small set of nuclear "haves" and a large set of nuclear "have-nots." On May 11, 1998, almost 25 years after conducting its first nuclear test, India carried out another set of five tests. Pakistan promptly responded with nuclear tests of its own, prompting fears of a regional nuclear arms race. Israel has also refused to ratify the treaty, and although it is not known to have carried out any nuclear weapons tests, it is widely thought to possess nuclear weapons.

In 1994, North Korea agreed to halt development of its nuclear program in return for a U.S. promise to provide North Korea with 500,000 tons of heavy oil and two light water nuclear reactors. But in 2002, the United States accused North Korea of continuing its efforts to develop nuclear weapons; in response, North Korea withdrew from the NPT (the first country ever to do so), expelled IAEA inspectors, and threatened to explode a nuclear device to test its arsenal. China, South Korea, Russia, Japan, and the United States have held on-again, off-again talks with North Korea since August 2003 in an effort to reach a diplomatic solution.

In 2003, the IAEA determined that Iran had not lived up to its reporting obligations, and called on Iran to stop all plans to enrich uranium and to allow international inspectors access to all nuclear facilities. Following meetings between senior Iranian officials and several European foreign ministers, Iran agreed to suspend its enrichment program and to permit IAEA inspectors to make unannounced visits, in return for technological and other assistance. But in August 2005, Iran broke off negotiations, and announced that it had resumed uranium enrichment activities, prompting the IAEA to call for an immediate suspension of the program and to refer the matter to the Security Council. As of May 2006, no action had been taken by the Council.

4. The Comprehensive Test Ban Treaty

In response to the 1998 nuclear tests, many countries called on both India and Pakistan to ratify the Comprehensive Test Ban Treaty (CTBT). This treaty is the latest in a long series of efforts to regulate and ultimately prohibit nuclear testing. Ironically, the effort to ban testing began with a proposal from Indian Prime Minister Jawaharwal Nehru in 1954. In 1963, the United States, Great Britain, and the Soviet Union agreed on a Limited Test Ban Treaty (LTBT), which confined the parties to underground tests. France and China refused to ratify the treaty, however, and continued testing. Nonetheless, the LTBT contributed to the eventual end of atmospheric testing and its related environmental threat. A series of subsequent treaties placed limits on the size of underground tests, and public and non-governmental organization (NGO) pressure gradually built for conclusion of a comprehensive test ban treaty to end all nuclear testing.

Until recently, concerns over verification blocked the conclusion of a general test ban. But in 1994, negotiations resumed in Geneva at the UN Conference on Disarmament, a standing forum for discussion of disarmament issues. In 1996, states agreed on the CTBT, and by late 2005, 176 states had signed the treaty, and 126 states had ratified it. The treaty will not come into force, however, until 44 specified states (that is, states with nuclear weapons or reactors) ratify. As of December 2005, 33 of the 44 states had ratified the treaty. The United States signed the treaty, but on October 13, 2000, the U.S. Senate voted 51 to 48 against ratifying it. Opponents of the treaty in the Senate expressed concern that the United States would be unable to maintain adequately its nuclear stockpile without testing, the treaty would undermine the U.S. nuclear deterrent, and secret low-yield tests by other states would be hard to detect. Supporters argued that computer modeling would maintain the reliability of the arsenal without actual testing, verification methods were adequate, and the treaty would hinder a nuclear buildup in other countries, thereby strengthening U.S. nuclear superiority.

India and Pakistan are the two other most notable holdouts. India has long been critical of the CTBT on the ground that it freezes in place the military advantage of states with large arsenals of tested nuclear weapons. Pakistan has indicated its unwillingness to ratify the treaty unless and until India does. Both states, however, have suggested that they might ratify the treaty at some point in the future.

B. The Evolution of International Humanitarian Law

Admonitions of restraint in the conduct of warfare date back at least to the fourth century B.C., when Sun Tzu wrote in *The Art of War* that attacks should be directed against an enemy's armies, and not its cities.* Similarly, the Bible contains passages urging mercy in the treatment of prisoners and captured women and children. Roman law contained many restrictions aimed at mitigating atrocities in war. Codes of chivalry governed armed conflict in much of Europe during the Middle Ages. As Professor Lawrence Wechsler has observed, such codes governed everything from treatment of noncombatants and prisoners of war to behavior on the battlefield and were "rigorously observed for fear of loss of knightly honor." By the middle of the fifteenth century, France had instituted trials for war crimes, and a character in Shakespeare's *Henry V* could plausibly say, "the boys and the luggage! 'Tis expressly against the laws of arms: 'tis as arrant a piece of knavery as can be offer'd." But as the crusades demonstrated, chivalric codes did not apply against non-Christian adversaries. Nor did they apply during the religious wars of the sixteenth and seventeenth centuries, when opponents were viewed as heretics. In any event, such codes, based on notions of face-to-face combat, could not survive the introduction of large standing armies equipped with more sophisticated weapons of destruction, including bombs and artillery.

While state practice in the sixteenth and seventeenth centuries, augmented by the writings of scholars, helped develop new laws and customs of war, the increasing destructiveness of warfare in the eighteenth and nineteenth centuries prompted states to begin the development of more detailed codes of conduct. The following excerpt picks up the story and explains why states pursued such codes:

> To many people it seems a paradox that war, the ultimate breakdown in law and order, should be fought in accordance with rules of law; why should a nation fighting for survival allow its struggle to be impeded by legal restrictions? Part of the answer lies in the fact that nations did not regard themselves as fighting for survival in the eighteenth and nineteenth centuries. Wars were seldom fought for ideological reasons and tended not to rouse the same intensity of passion as twentieth century wars. In an age when governments interfered little with the lives of their subjects, a change of sovereignty over territory had little effect on the way of life of the inhabitants, who consequently tended to be philosophical about the prospect of defeat in war. . . . The balance-of-power system . . . necessitated flexibility in political alignments and meant that a state's enemy today might be its ally tomorrow; this naturally had a restraining effect on the degree of brutality practised in wars. . . .
>
> Even more important than these political considerations was the fact that the laws of war were designed mainly to prevent unnecessary suffering. 'Unnecessary suffering' meant suffering which would produce no military advantage, or a military advantage which was very small in comparison with the amount of suffering involved. However, there were a few exceptions to this general rule; for instance, it was and still is forbidden to torture prisoners in order to obtain information, although the military advantage could be enormous in certain cases. Violations of the laws of war were therefore rare, because the military advantage to be gained by breaking those laws was almost always outweighed by disadvantages such as reprisals, loss of neutral goodwill, and so on.

---

*This brief account of the evolution of the laws of war is drawn in part from Leslie C. Green, The Contemporary Law of Armed Conflict 20-29 (2d ed. 2000); and Lawrence Wechsler, *International Humanitarian Law: An Overview, in* Crimes of War 19-21 (Roy Gutman and David Rieff eds., 1999).

Wars in the eighteenth and nineteenth centuries were wars between armed forces, rather than wars between peoples. . . . It was therefore easy for international law to protect civilians. But the protection was never absolute; for instance, an army besieging a town was entitled to hasten the fall of the town by preventing food from entering the town and by preventing civilian inhabitants from leaving. In other words, the army compelled the town to surrender by starving the civilian inhabitants. . . .

Peter Malanczuk, Akehurst's Modern Introduction to International Law 342-344 (7th ed. 1997).

In the second half of the nineteenth century states began to issue manuals of military law, containing a restatement of the laws of war, for use by their commanders in the field. A famous example is the Lieber Code excerpted below. It was prepared by Dr. Francis Lieber from Columbia University in 1863 as the "Instructions for the Government of Armies of the United States in the Field." Such manuals led to greater respect for the laws of war, as well as more precision in their formulation.

Instructions for the Government of Armies of the United States in the Field

Presidential General Orders No. 100 (1863)

14.

Military necessity, as understood by modern civilized nations, consists in the necessity of those measures which are indispensable for securing the ends of the war, and which are lawful according to the modern law and usages of war.

15.

Military necessity admits of all direct destruction of life or limb of *armed* enemies, and of other persons whose destruction is incidentally *unavoidable* in the armed contests of the war; it allows of the capturing of every armed enemy, and every enemy of importance to the hostile government, or of peculiar danger to the captor; it allows of all destruction of property, and obstruction of the ways and channels of traffic, travel, or communication, and of all withholding of sustenance or means of life from the enemy; of the appropriation of whatever an enemy's country affords necessary for the subsistence and safety of the army, and of such deception as does not involve the breaking of good faith either positively pledged, regarding agreements entered into during the war, or supposed by the modern law of war to exist. Men who take up arms against one another in public war do not cease on this account to be moral beings, responsible to one another and to God.

16.

Military necessity does not admit of cruelty—that is, the infliction of suffering for the sake of suffering or for revenge, nor of maiming or wounding except in fight, nor of torture to extort confessions. It does not admit of the use of poison in any way, nor of the wanton devastation of a district. It admits of deception, but disclaims acts of perfidy; and, in general, military necessity does not include any act of hostility which makes the return to peace unnecessarily difficult.

17.

War is not carried on by arms alone. It is lawful to starve the hostile belligerent, armed or unarmed, so that it leads to the speedier subjection of the enemy.

19.

Commanders, whenever admissible, inform the enemy of their intention to bombard a place, so that the noncombatants, and especially the women and children, may be removed before the bombardment commences. But it is no infraction of the common law of war to omit thus to inform the enemy. Surprise may be a necessity.

20.

Public war is a state of armed hostility between sovereign nations or governments. It is a law and requisite of civilized existence that men live in political, continuous societies, forming organized units, called states or nations, whose constituents bear, enjoy, suffer, advance and retrograde together, in peace and in war.

21.

The citizen or native of a hostile country is thus an enemy, as one of the constituents of the hostile state or nation, and as such is subjected to the hardships of the war.

22.

Nevertheless, as civilization has advanced during the last centuries, so has likewise steadily advanced, especially in war on land, the distinction between the private individual belonging to a hostile country and the hostile country itself, with its men in arms. The principle has been more and more acknowledged that the unarmed citizen is to be spared in person, property, and honor as much as the exigencies of war will admit.

23.

Private citizens are no longer murdered, enslaved, or carried off to distant parts, and the inoffensive individual is as little disturbed in his private relations as the commander of the hostile troops can afford to grant in the overruling demands of a vigorous war.

24.

The almost universal rule in remote times was, and continues to be with barbarous armies, that the private individual of the hostile country is destined to suffer every privation of liberty and protection, and every disruption of family ties. Protection was, and still is with uncivilized people, the exception.

29.

Modern times are distinguished from earlier ages by the existence, at one and the same time, of many nations and great governments related to one another in close intercourse.

Peace is their normal condition; war is the exception. The ultimate object of all modern war is a renewed state of peace.

The more vigorously wars are pursued, the better it is for humanity. Sharp wars are brief.

In subsequent years, conventional and customary law regulating the conduct of warfare, and the weapons to be used in warfare, expanded dramatically. To a surprising extent, a single individual and the organization he helped found drove much of the development of the law.* In 1859, Henry Dunant, a Swiss businessman, arrived in the town of Solferino, Italy, shortly after a battle between Franco-Italian and Austrian troops in which some 40,000 men died. For several days, Dunant worked with local women to provide assistance to the thousands of wounded left unattended in the aftermath of the battle. In 1862, he published a moving account of the battle and its aftermath entitled *A Memory of Solferino*. Dunant's book proved highly influential and led to the creation of what came to be known as the International Committee of the Red Cross (ICRC), an organization dedicated to providing humanitarian assistance to victims of armed conflict. In 1863, the ICRC convened an international conference in Geneva, attended by private individuals as well as representatives of states and international organizations, to consider ways to improve the provision of medical services to military personnel. A follow-on conference the next year gave rise to the Geneva Convention on the Amelioration of the Condition of the Wounded in Armies in the Field. Ever since, the ICRC has continued to play a key role in the development of draft conventions and in the convening of conferences to transform those drafts into binding treaties. The ICRC also provides neutral and independent assistance to victims of war and internal violence. Under the Geneva Conventions, it is accorded special responsibilities for the monitoring of humanitarian law compliance.

In the years following the first Geneva Convention of 1864, states gathered periodically in Geneva to produce numerous subsequent conventions. These conventions often dealt with specific issues, such as the use of poison gas, that had proven controversial in an immediately preceding war. In the aftermath of World War II, states adopted the four best-known of the Geneva Conventions. Each of these 1949 conventions deals with a specific category of persons who are not, or have ceased to be, combatants. The four conventions, now almost universally ratified, are designed to protect wounded and sick members of armed forces in the field; wounded, sick and shipwrecked members of armed forces at sea; prisoners of war; and civilian non-combatants.

In addition to the Geneva Conventions, a series of conferences in The Hague produced a closely related body of law on the means and methods of warfare, most notably the 1907 Hague Regulations Respecting the Laws and Customs of War on Land. At the same time, a substantial body of customary international law governing the conduct of armed conflict also emerged.

Nonetheless, as of the early 1970s, humanitarian law failed to address many important issues, including indiscriminate attacks on civilian populations through aerial bombardment and other means. Moreover, new technologies, the proliferation of internal armed conflicts, and shifting state attitudes toward wars of national

---

*The following account is derived in part from an ICRC account, *Founding and Early Years of the International Committee of the Red Cross* (1863-1914), available on the ICRC Web site, www.icrc.org.

liberation raised additional issues not considered in 1949. Accordingly, the ICRC convened a new diplomatic conference to work out two new treaties. After a hotly contested three-year drafting effort, states adopted two additional protocols to the Geneva Conventions in 1977. Additional Protocol I applies to international armed conflicts. It updates and significantly modifies the law in that area; among other things, it designates national liberation struggles conducted in the name of self-determination as international armed conflicts. Additional Protocol II applies to internal armed conflicts and increases the protections available to persons caught up in such conflicts.

Although the provisions of the various treaties comprising Geneva and Hague law are extensive and at times bewildering, the basic principles can be summarized in relatively simple terms:

> [S]ix major treaties with more than 600 articles and a fine mesh of customary law rules place restrictions on the use of violence in wartime. Such complexity should not, however, make us forget that the gist of humanitarian law can be summarized in a few fundamental principles:
>
> 1. Persons who are not, or are no longer, taking part in hostilities shall be respected, protected and treated humanely. They shall be given appropriate care, without any discrimination.
>
> 2. Captured combatants and other persons whose freedom has been restricted shall be treated humanely. They shall be protected against all acts of violence, in particular against torture. If put on trial they shall enjoy the fundamental guarantees of a regular judicial procedure.
>
> 3. The right of parties to an armed conflict to choose methods or means of warfare is not unlimited. No superfluous injury or unnecessary suffering shall be inflicted.
>
> 4. In order to spare the civilian population, armed forces shall at all times distinguish between the civilian population and civilian objects on the one hand, and military objectives on the other. Neither the civilian population as such nor individual civilians or civilian objects shall be the target of military attacks.

Hans-Peter Gasser, *International Humanitarian Law and the Protection of War Victims,* *www.icrc.org.*

Notwithstanding the substantial progress in the development and codification of the laws of international humanitarian law described above, the law in this area remains incomplete and in many respects ill-defined. More important, even in the midst of the trend toward the elaboration and codification of norms in this area, international humanitarian law has been and continues to be regularly violated. The following excerpt suggests some reasons for these continuing problems:

> The creation of new law by treaties has tended to lag far behind the development of military technology. For instance, until the First Protocol of 1977 there was no treaty dealing with the bombing of civilians. This would not have mattered much if the customary law on the subject had been clear, but it was not. State practice concerning the laws of war develops mainly during wartime, and therefore lacks continuity; major wars are infrequent, and nowadays technological changes occur so rapidly that each war differs radically from the previous war. It is also difficult to establish an *opinio juris,* because states seldom give legal reasons for what they do in wartime. Nor do war crimes trials do much to clarify the law. For instance, not a single German was prosecuted after the Second World War for organizing mass bombing raids; it is understandable that the Allies were reluctant to prosecute Germans for doing what the Allies had also done on

an even larger scale, but the result is that there is no judicial pronouncement on the legality of bombing. Meanwhile, the Hague Conventions of 1899 and 1907 are still technically in force, but the fact that many of their provisions are manifestly inappropriate to modern conditions has often tempted states to break them.

There are two further factors which have encouraged violations of the laws of war during the twentieth century. In the first place, the First and Second World Wars produced more bitter feelings than previous wars; they were fought for ideological reasons, and for virtually unlimited objectives. Belligerent states no longer sought to achieve a delicate adjustment to the balance of power, but adopted a policy of unconditional surrender, which naturally spurred on the other side to fight to the death. Second, economic and technological changes vastly increased the military advantage to be gained by breaking the laws of war. (There are exceptions, of course; for instance, killing prisoners of war still produces little military advantage, and the relevant rules of law therefore stand a good chance of surviving.) In particular, the distinction between the armed forces and civilians is largely illusory, now that the whole of a country's economy is geared to the war effort. Destruction of factories, and even the killing of factory workers, produces a military advantage which would have been inconceivable in earlier times; and the invention of the aircraft has given belligerent states the means to carry out such acts.

Peter Malanczuk, Akehurst's Modern Introduction to International Law 345-346 (7th ed. 1997).

The opinion of the ICJ excerpted below chronicles the legal status of efforts to outlaw the most dangerous of weapons, and provides further analysis of the legal restrictions placed on a belligerent's choice of means for conducting warfare.

C. The ICJ Opines on Nuclear Weapons

In 1992, a number of prominent NGOs committed to the elimination of nuclear weapons joined together to form the World Court Project. Their goal was to elicit an opinion from the ICJ declaring that the use of nuclear weapons would be illegal in all circumstances. In 1993, after a vigorous lobbying campaign, the World Court Project and its supporters persuaded the World Health Organization (WHO) to solicit an advisory opinion from the Court. The following year, in Resolution 49/75K, the UN General Assembly also requested an advisory opinion on the following question: "Is the threat or use of nuclear weapons in any circumstance permitted under international law?"

In 1996, the ICJ declined to answer the question posed by the WHO on the ground that it was outside the scope of the organization's activities. Judge Oda took the position that the Court should also decline to answer the General Assembly's request for an opinion, noting that the request had been generated by NGO activists working with states to obtain a particular result on a highly sensitive political issue. But most of the judges concluded that the motivations driving states to support the request for an advisory opinion were not the proper concern of the Court so long as the request fell within the scope of the General Assembly's authority and mandate. Accordingly, the ICJ issued the requested opinion, which has proven to be highly controversial. Excerpts of the Court's opinion, as well as excerpts of several of the dissenting opinions, follow.

Legality of the Threat or Use Of Nuclear Weapons

1996 I.C.J. 226 (July 8)

[Before addressing the application of international humanitarian law to the question posed, the Court considered the applicability of other bodies of international law, including the law on genocide. On that issue, the Court offered the following observations.]

26. Some States also contended that the prohibition against genocide, contained in the Convention of 9 December 1948 on the Prevention and Punishment of the Crime of Genocide, is a relevant rule of customary international law which the Court must apply. The Court recalls that, in Article II of the Convention genocide is defined as

"any of the following acts committed with intent to destroy, in whole or in part, a national, ethnical, racial or religious group, as such:
   (a) Killing members of the group;
   (b) Causing serious bodily or mental harm to members of the group;
   (c) Deliberately inflicting on the group conditions of life calculated to being about its physical destruction in whole or in part;
   (d) Imposing measures intended to prevent births within the group;
   (e) Forcibly transferring children of the group to another group."

It was maintained before the Court that the number of deaths occasioned by the use of nuclear weapons would be enormous; that the victims could, in certain cases, include persons of a particular national, ethnic, racial or religious group; and that the intention to destroy such groups could be inferred from the fact that the user of the nuclear weapon would have omitted to take account of the well-known effects of the use of such weapons.

The Court would point out in that regard that the prohibition of genocide would be pertinent in this case if the recourse to nuclear weapons did indeed entail the element of intent, towards a group as such, required by the provision quoted above. In the view of the Court, it would only be possible to arrive at such a conclusion after having taken due account of the circumstances specific to each case. . . .

[After discussion of other relevant bodies of law, including human rights and environmental law, the Court concluded that the issue before it had to be decided by reference to "the most directly relevant applicable law"—that is, by the law "relating to the use of force enshrined in the United Nations Charter and the law applicable in armed conflict which regulates the conduct of hostilities, together with any specific treaties on nuclear weapons that the Court might determine to be relevant. . . ." With regard to the UN Charter's rules governing the use of force, the Court concluded that "[t]he Charter neither expressly prohibits, nor permits, the use of any specific weapon, including nuclear weapons. A weapon that is already unlawful per se, whether by treaty or custom, does not become lawful by reason of its being used for a legitimate purpose under the Charter." The Court then discussed whether other treaties prohibit the threat or use of nuclear weapons.]

52. The Court notes . . . that international customary and treaty law does not contain any specific prescription authorizing the threat or use of nuclear weapons or any other weapon in general or in certain circumstances, in particular those of the exercise of legitimate self defence. Nor, however, is there any principle or rule of international law which would make the legality of the threat or use of nuclear

weapons or of any other weapons dependent on a specific authorization. State practice shows that the illegality of the use of certain weapons as such does not result from an absence of authorization but, on the contrary, is formulated in terms of prohibition.

54. In this regard, the argument has been advanced that nuclear weapons should be treated in the same way as poisoned weapons. In that case, they would be prohibited under [Hague and Geneva Convention provisions outlawing poisonous weapons].

55. The Court will observe that the Regulations annexed to the Hague Convention IV do not define what is to be understood by "poison or poisoned weapons" and that different interpretations exist on the issue. . . . The terms have been understood, in the practice of States, in their ordinary sense as covering weapons whose prime, or even exclusive, effect is to poison or asphyxiate. This practice is clear, and the parties to those instruments have not treated them as referring to nuclear weapons.

56. In view of this, it does not seem to the Court that the use of nuclear weapons can be regarded as specifically prohibited on the basis of the above-mentioned provisions. . . .

58. In the last two decades, a great many negotiations have been conducted regarding nuclear weapons; they have not resulted in a treaty of general prohibition of the same kind as for bacteriological and chemical weapons. However, a number of specific treaties have been concluded in order to limit:

(a) the acquisition, manufacture and possession of nuclear weapons . . .

(b) the deployment of nuclear weapons and . . .

(c) the testing of nuclear weapons. . . .

60. Those States that believe that recourse to nuclear weapons is illegal stress that the conventions that include various rules providing for the limitation or elimination of nuclear weapons in certain areas . . . or the conventions that apply certain measures of control and limitation to the existence of nuclear weapons . . . all set limits to the use of nuclear weapons. In their view, these treaties bear witness, in their own way, to the emergence of a rule of complete legal prohibition of all uses of nuclear weapons.

61. Those States who defend the position that recourse to nuclear weapons is legal in certain circumstances see a logical contradiction in reaching such a conclusion. According to them, those Treaties . . . cannot be understood as prohibiting the use of nuclear weapons, and such a claim is contrary to the very text of those instruments. . . . The very logic and construction of the Treaty on the Non-Proliferation of Nuclear Weapons, they assert, confirm this. This Treaty, whereby, they contend, the possession of nuclear weapons by the five nuclear-weapon States has been accepted, cannot be seen as a treaty banning their use by those States; to accept the fact that those States possess nuclear weapons is tantamount to recognizing that such weapons may be used in certain circumstances. . . .

62. The Court notes that the treaties dealing exclusively with acquisition, manufacture, possession, deployment and testing of nuclear weapons, without specifically addressing their threat or use, certainly point to an increasing concern in the international community with these weapons; the Court concludes from this that these treaties could therefore be seen as foreshadowing a future general prohibition of the use of such weapons, but they do not constitute such a prohibition by themselves. . . . [The Court states further that the treaties and declarations at issue indicate that:]

(a) a number of States have undertaken not to use nuclear weapons in specific zones (Latin America; the South Pacific) or against certain other States (non-nuclear-weapon States which are parties to the Treaty on the Non-Proliferation of Nuclear Weapons);

(b) nevertheless, even within this framework, the nuclear-weapon States have reserved the right to use nuclear weapons in certain circumstances; and

(c) these reservations met with no objection from [parties to the relevant treaties] or from the Security Council.

[The Court concludes that the relevant treaties and state practice do not amount "to a comprehensive and universal conventional prohibition on the use, or the threat of use, of [nuclear] weapons as such." It continues:]

65. States which hold the view that the use of nuclear weapons is illegal have endeavoured to demonstrate the existence of a customary rule prohibiting this use. They refer to a consistent practice of non-utilization of nuclear weapons by States since 1945 and they would see in that practice the expression of an *opinio juris* on the part of those who possess such weapons.

66. Some other States, which assert the legality of the threat and use of nuclear weapons in certain circumstances, invoked the doctrine and practice of deterrence in support of their argument. They recall that they have always, in concert with certain other States, reserved the right to use those weapons in the exercise of the right to self-defence against an armed attack threatening their vital security interests. In their view, if nuclear weapons have not been used since 1945, it is not on account of an existing or nascent custom but merely because circumstances that might justify their use have fortunately not arisen.

67. The Court does not intend to pronounce here upon the practice known as the "policy of deterrence". It notes that it is a fact that a number of States adhered to that practice during the greater part of the Cold War and continue to adhere to it. Furthermore, the Members of the international community are profoundly divided on the matter of whether non-recourse to nuclear weapons over the past fifty years constitutes the expression of an *opinio juris*. Under these circumstances the Court does not consider itself able to find that there is such an *opinio juris*. . . .

73. Having said this, the Court points out that the adoption each year by the General Assembly, by a large majority, of resolutions . . . requesting the member States to conclude a convention prohibiting the use of nuclear weapons in any circumstance, reveals the desire of a very large section of the international community to take, by a specific and express prohibition of the use of nuclear weapons, a significant step forward along the road to complete nuclear disarmament. The emergence, as *lex lata* [law as it exists], of a customary rule specifically prohibiting the use of nuclear weapons as such is hampered by the continuing tensions between the nascent *opinio juris* on the one hand, and the still strong adherence to the practice of deterrence on the other.

74. The Court not having found a conventional rule of general scope, nor a customary rule specifically proscribing the threat or use of nuclear weapons per se, it will now deal with the question whether recourse to nuclear weapons must be considered as illegal in the light of the principles and rules of international humanitarian law applicable in armed conflict and of the law of neutrality. . . .

78. The cardinal principles contained in the texts constituting the fabric of humanitarian law are the following. The first is aimed at the protection of the civilian population and civilian objects and establishes the distinction between

combatants and non-combatants; States must never make civilians the object of attack and must consequently never use weapons that are incapable of distinguishing between civilian and military targets. According to the second principle, it is prohibited to cause unnecessary suffering to combatants: it is accordingly prohibited to use weapons causing them such harm or uselessly aggravating their suffering. In application of that second principle, States do not have unlimited freedom of choice of means in the weapons they use. . . .

85. Turning now to the applicability of the principles and rules of humanitarian law to a possible threat or use of nuclear weapons, the Court notes that doubts in this respect have sometimes been voiced on the ground that these principles and rules had evolved prior to the invention of nuclear weapons and that the Conferences of Geneva of 1949 and 1974-1977 which respectively adopted the four Geneva Conventions of 1949 and the two Additional Protocols thereto did not deal with nuclear weapons specifically. Such views, however, are only held by a small minority. In the view of the vast majority of States as well as writers there can be no doubt as to the applicability of humanitarian law to nuclear weapons.

86. The Court shares that view. . . . [To conclude that humanitarian law does not apply to nuclear weapons] would be incompatible with the intrinsically humanitarian character of the legal principles in question which permeates the entire law of armed conflict and applies to all forms of warfare and to all kinds of weapons, those of the past, those of the present and those of the future. . . .

91. According to one point of view, the fact that recourse to nuclear weapons is subject to and regulated by the law of armed conflict does not necessarily mean that such recourse is as such prohibited. As one State put it to the Court. . . .

> The reality . . . is that nuclear weapons might be used in a wide variety of circumstances with very different results in terms of likely civilian casualties. In some cases, such as the use of a low yield nuclear weapon against warships on the High Seas or troops in sparsely populated areas, it is possible to envisage a nuclear attack which caused comparatively few civilian casualties. It is by no means the case that every use of nuclear weapons against a military objective would inevitably cause very great collateral civilian casualties. (United Kingdom, Written Statement)

92. Another view holds that recourse to nuclear weapons could never be compatible with the principles and rules of humanitarian law and is therefore prohibited. In the event of their use, nuclear weapons would in all circumstances be unable to draw any distinction between the civilian population and combatants, or between civilian objects and military objectives, and their effects, largely uncontrollable, could not be restricted, either in time or in space, to lawful military targets. Such weapons would kill and destroy in a necessarily indiscriminate manner, on account of the blast, heat and radiation occasioned by the nuclear explosion and the effects induced; and the number of casualties which would ensue would be enormous. The use of nuclear weapons would therefore be prohibited in any circumstance, notwithstanding the absence of any explicit conventional prohibition. . . .

94. The Court would observe that none of the States advocating the legality of the use of nuclear weapons under certain circumstances, including the "clean" use of smaller, low yield, tactical nuclear weapons, has indicated what, supposing such limited use were feasible, would be the precise circumstances justifying such use; nor whether such limited use would not tend to escalate into the all-out use of high yield nuclear weapons. This being so, the Court does not consider that it has a sufficient basis for a determination on the validity of this view.

95. Nor can the Court make a determination on the validity of the view that the recourse to nuclear weapons would be illegal in any circumstance owing to their inherent and total incompatibility with the law applicable in armed conflict. Certainly, as the Court has already indicated, the principles and rules of law applicable in armed conflict—at the heart of which is the overriding consideration of humanity —make the conduct of armed hostilities subject to a number of strict requirements. Thus, methods and means of warfare, which would preclude any distinction between civilian and military targets, or which would result in unnecessary suffering to combatants, are prohibited. In view of the unique characteristics of nuclear weapons, to which the Court has referred above, the use of such weapons in fact seems scarcely reconcilable with respect for such requirements. Nevertheless, the Court considers that it does not have sufficient elements to enable it to conclude with certainty that the use of nuclear weapons would necessarily be at variance with the principles and rules of law applicable in armed conflict in any circumstance.

96. Furthermore, the Court cannot lose sight of the fundamental right of every State to survival, and thus its right to resort to self-defence, in accordance with Article 51 of the Charter, when its survival is at stake. . . .

97. Accordingly, in view of the present state of international law viewed as a whole, as examined above by the Court, and of the elements of fact at its disposal, the Court is led to observe that it cannot reach a definitive conclusion as to the legality or illegality of the use of nuclear weapons by a State in an extreme circumstance of self-defence, in which its very survival would be at stake. . . .

98. . . . . In the long run, international law, and with it the stability of the international order which it is intended to govern, are bound to suffer from the continuing difference of views with regard to the legal status of weapons as deadly as nuclear weapons. It is consequently important to put an end to this state of affairs: the long-promised complete nuclear disarmament appears to be the most appropriate means of achieving that result.

99. In these circumstances, the Court appreciates the full importance of the recognition by Article VI of the Treaty on the Non-Proliferation of Nuclear Weapons of an obligation to negotiate in good faith a nuclear disarmament. . . . . The legal import of that obligation goes beyond that of a mere obligation of conduct; the obligation involved here is an obligation to achieve a precise result—nuclear disarmament in all its aspects—by adopting a particular course of conduct, namely, the pursuit of negotiations on the matter in good faith.

100. This twofold obligation to pursue and to conclude negotiations formally concerns the 182 States parties to the Treaty on the Non-Proliferation of Nuclear Weapons, or, in other words, the vast majority of the international community.

By a vote of 7 to 7, the Court held that:

the threat or use of nuclear weapons would generally be contrary to the rules of international law applicable in armed conflict, and in particular the principles and rules of humanitarian law; However, in view of the current state of international law, and of the elements of fact at its disposal, the Court cannot conclude definitively whether the threat or use of nuclear weapons would be lawful or unlawful in an extreme circumstance of self-defence, in which the very survival of a State would be at stake.

Because one of the Court's 15 judges died during the course of the proceedings in this case, the outcome of the case turned in part on a procedural rule permitting the vote of the President of the Court to determine the outcome in the event of a tie. As President of the Court, Algerian Judge Mohammed Bedjaoui therefore had the "casting vote." It should be noted, however, that three of the judges voting no on this issue did so only because they concluded that the threat or use of nuclear weapons should be deemed illegal in all circumstances. The judges voting for and against the Court's principal holding are listed below:

IN FAVOUR: President Bedjaoui (Algeria); Judges Ranjeva (Madagascar), Herczegh (Hungary), Shi (China), Fleischhauer (Germany), Vereschetin (Russian Federation), Ferrari Bravo (Italy);

AGAINST: Vice-President Schwebel (United States); Judges Oda (Japan), Guillaume (France), Shahabuddeen (Guyana), Weeramantry (Sri Lanka), Koroma (Sierra Leone), Higgins (United Kingdom).

The Court's holding that states must pursue negotiations leading to nuclear disarmament was unanimous, but opinions on the central issues in the case diverged dramatically. Judges from several developed Western states viewed the Court as going too far toward accepting the proposition that use of nuclear weapons would be illegal; judges from the developing world viewed the Court as not going far enough. Excerpts from two diametrically opposed dissenting opinions follow:

Dissenting Opinion of Vice-President Schwebel

1996 I.C.J. 311

[Judge Schwebel expressed the view that the manufacture and deployment of nuclear weapons by the nuclear powers and their allies for the past 50 years, and their affirmation that they were entitled to use such weapons in particular circumstances, demonstrated that states "that together represent the bulk of the world's military and economic and financial and technological power and a very large proportion of its population" viewed the threat or use of nuclear weapons as lawful in some instances. Moreover, Judge Schwebel viewed the Nuclear Non-Proliferation Treaty and other treaties governing the acquisition, manufacture, possession, deployment, and testing of nuclear weapons as implicitly acknowledging that the threat or use of such weapons would not be per se unlawful. Judge Schwebel then addressed the application of international humanitarian law.]

Principles of International Humanitarian Law

While it is not difficult to conclude that the principles of international humanitarian law—above all, proportionality in the application of force, and discrimination between military and civilian targets—govern the use of nuclear weapons, it does not follow that the application of those principles to the threat or use of nuclear weapons "in any circumstance" is easy. Cases at the extremes are relatively clear; cases closer to the centre of the spectrum of possible uses are less so.

At one extreme is the use of strategic nuclear weapons in quantities against enemy cities and industries. . . .

At the other extreme is the use of tactical nuclear weapons against discrete military or naval targets so situated that substantial civilian casualties would not ensue. For example, the use of a nuclear depth-charge to destroy a nuclear submarine that is about to fire nuclear missiles, or has fired one or more of a number of its nuclear missiles, might well be lawful. By the circumstance of its use, the nuclear depth-charge would not give rise to immediate civilian casualties. It would easily meet the test of proportionality; the damage that the submarine's missiles could inflict on the population and territory of the target State would infinitely outweigh that entailed in the destruction of the submarine and its crew. The submarine's destruction by a nuclear weapon would produce radiation in the sea, but far less than the radiation that firing of its missiles would produce on and over land. Nor is it as certain that the use of a conventional depth-charge would discharge the mission successfully; the far greater force of a nuclear weapon could ensure destruction of the submarine whereas a conventional depth-charge might not.

An intermediate case would be the use of nuclear weapons to destroy an enemy army situated in a desert. In certain circumstances, such a use of nuclear weapons might meet the tests of discrimination and proportionality; in others not. . . .

[Referring to the Court's principal holding, Judge Schwebel continues:]

. . . [F]ar from justifying the Court's inconclusiveness, contemporary events rather demonstrate the legality of the threat or use of nuclear weapons in extraordinary circumstances.

Desert Storm

The most recent and effective threat of the use of nuclear weapons took place on the eve of "Desert Storm." The circumstances merit exposition, for they constitute a striking illustration of a circumstance in which the perceived threat of the use of nuclear weapons was not only eminently lawful but intensely desirable.

Iraq, condemned by the Security Council for its invasion and annexation of Kuwait and for its attendant grave breaches of international humanitarian law, had demonstrated that it was prepared to use weapons of mass destruction. It had recently and repeatedly used gas in large quantities against the military formations of Iran, with substantial and perhaps decisive effect. It had even used gas against its own Kurdish citizens. There was no ground for believing that legal or humanitarian scruple would prevent it from using weapons of mass destruction—notably chemical, perhaps bacteriological or nuclear weapons—against the coalition forces arrayed against it. . . .

To exorcise that nightmare, the United States took action as described by then Secretary of State James A. Baker in the following terms, in which he recounts his climactic meeting of 9 January 1990 in Geneva with the then Foreign Minister of Iraq, Tariq Aziz:

"I then made a point 'on the dark side of the issue' that Colin Powell had specifically asked me to deliver in the plainest possible terms. 'If the conflict involves your use of chemical or biological weapons against our forces,' I warned, 'the American people will demand vengeance. We have the means to exact it. With regard to this part of my presentation, that is not a threat, it is a promise. If there is any use of weapons like that, our objective won't just be the liberation of Kuwait, but the elimination of the current Iraqi regime, and anyone responsible for using those weapons would be held accountable.'

"The President had decided, at Camp David in December, that the best deterrent of the use of weapons of mass destruction by Iraq would be a threat to go after the Ba'ath regime itself. He had also decided that U.S. forces would not retaliate with chemical or nuclear response if the Iraqis attacked with chemical munitions. There was obviously no reason to inform the Iraqis of this. In hope of persuading them to consider more soberly the folly of war, I purposely left the impression that the use of chemical or biological agents by Iraq could invite tactical nuclear retaliation. (We do not really know whether this was the reason there appears to have been no confirmed use by Iraq of chemical weapons during the war. My own view is that the calculated ambiguity how we might respond has to be part of the reason.)" (The Politics of Diplomacy—Revolution, War and Peace, 1989-1992 by James A. Baker III, 1995, p. 359.) . . .

Thus there is on record remarkable evidence indicating that an aggressor was or may have been deterred from using outlawed weapons of mass destruction against forces and countries arrayed against its aggression at the call of the United Nations by what the aggressor perceived to be a threat to use nuclear weapons against it should it first use weapons of mass destruction against the forces of the coalition. Can it seriously be maintained that Mr. Baker's calculated—and apparently successful—threat was unlawful? Surely the principles of the United Nations Charter were sustained rather than transgressed by the threat. . . .

Dissenting Opinion of Judge Weeramantry

1996 I.C.J. 429

I am of the view that the threat or use of nuclear weapons would not be lawful in any circumstances whatsoever, as it offends the fundamental principles of the *ius in bello.* . . . Principles relating to unnecessary suffering, proportionality, discrimination, non-belligerent states, genocide, environmental damage and human rights would all be violated, no less in self-defence than in an open act of aggression. The *ius in bello* covers all use of force, whatever the reasons for resort to force. There can be no exceptions, without violating the essence of its principles. . . .

1. Unnecessary Suffering

The harrowing suffering caused by nuclear weapons . . . is not confined to the aggressive use of such weapons. The lingering sufferings caused by radiation do not lose their intensity merely because the weapon is used in self-defence.

2. Proportionality / Error

The principle of proportionality may on first impressions appear to be satisfied by a nuclear response to a nuclear attack. Yet, viewed more carefully, this principle is violated in many ways. As France observed: "The assessment of the necessity and proportionality of a response to attack depends on the nature of the attack, its scope, the danger it poses and the adjustment of the measures of response to the desired defensive purpose."

For these very reasons, precise assessment of the nature of the appropriate and proportionate response by a nation stricken by a nuclear attack becomes impossible. If one speaks in terms of a nuclear response to a nuclear attack, that nuclear response will tend, as already noted, to be an all-out nuclear response which opens up all the scenarios of global armageddon which are so vividly depicted in the literature relating to an all-out nuclear exchange.

Moreover, one is here speaking in terms of measurement—measurement of the intensity of the attack and the proportionality of the response. But one can measure only the measurable. With nuclear war, the quality of measurability ceases. . . . We are in territory where the principle of proportionality becomes devoid of meaning.

It is relevant also, in the context of nuclear weapons, not to lose sight of the possibility of human error. However carefully planned, a nuclear response to a nuclear attack cannot, in the confusion of the moment, be finely graded so as to assess the strength of the weapons of attack, and to respond in like measure. . . .

It is thus no fanciful speculation that the use of nuclear weapons in self defence would result in a cataclysmic nuclear exchange. That is a risk which humanitarian law would consider to be totally unacceptable. It is a risk which no legal system can sanction.

3. Discrimination

. . . [N]uclear weapons violate the principle of discrimination between armed forces and civilians. True, other weapons also do, but the intensity of heat and blast, not to speak of radiation, are factors which place the nuclear weapon in a class apart from the others. When one speaks of weapons that count their victims by hundreds of thousands, if not millions, principles of discrimination cease to have any legal relevance.

4. Non-Belligerent States

. . . Self-defence is a matter of purely internal jurisdiction only if such defence can be undertaken without clearly causing damage to the rights of non-belligerent states. The moment a strategy of self-defence implies damage to a non-belligerent third party, such a matter ceases to be one of purely internal jurisdiction. It may be that the act of self-defence inadvertently and unintentionally causes damage to a third State. Such a situation is understandable and sometimes does occur, but that is not the case here.

5. Genocide

. . . Self defence, which will . . . result in all probability in all-out nuclear war, is even more likely to cause genocide than the act of launching an initial strike. If the killing of human beings, in numbers ranging from a million to a billion, does not fall within the definition of genocide, one may well ask what will.

No nation can be seen as entitled to risk the destruction of civilization for its own national benefit.

6. Environmental Damage

Similar considerations exist here, as in regard to genocide. The widespread contamination of the environment may even lead to a nuclear winter and to the destruction of the eco-system. These results will ensue equally, whether the nuclear weapons causing them are used in aggression or in self-defence. . . .

7. Human Rights

. . . The humanitarian principles discussed above have long passed the stage of being merely philosophical aspirations. They are the living law and represent the high watermark of legal achievement in the difficult task of imposing some restraints on the brutalities of unbridled war. . . .

It seems difficult, with any due regard to the consistency that must underlie any credible legal system, to contemplate that all these hard-won principles should bend aside in their course and pass the nuclear weapon by, leaving that unparalleled agency of destruction free to achieve on a magnified scale the very evils which these principles were designed to prevent. . . .

Limited or Tactical or Battlefield Nuclear Weapons

Reference has already been made to the contention . . . that the inherent dangers of nuclear weapons can be minimized by resort to "small" or "clean" or "low yield" or "tactical" nuclear weapons. . . .

(iv) with the use of even "small" or "tactical" or "battlefield" nuclear weapons, one crosses the nuclear threshold. The state at the receiving end of such a nuclear response would not know that the response is a limited or tactical one involving a small weapon and it is not credible to posit that it will also be careful to respond in kind, i.e., with a small weapon. The door would be opened and the threshold crossed for an all-out nuclear war.

———————

Several judges were sharply critical of the Court's conclusion that "in the present state of international law," and with "the elements of fact at its disposal," the Court "cannot reach a definitive conclusion as to the legality or illegality of the use of nuclear weapons by a State in an extreme circumstance of self-defence. . . ." Judge Schwebel declared it "astounding" that the Court should conclude "on the supreme issue of the threat or use of force of our age that it has no opinion," and suggested that the Court "would have done better to have drawn on its undoubted discretion not to render an opinion at all." Judge Higgins offered the following analysis on this issue:

Dissenting Opinion of Judge Higgins

1996 I.C.J. 583

29. What the Court has done is reach a conclusion of "incompatibility in general" with humanitarian law; and then effectively pronounce a *non liquet* [a refusal to decide based on the absence of clear legal rules] on whether a use of nuclear weapons in self-defence when the survival of a State is at issue might still be lawful, even were the particular use to be contrary to humanitarian law. Through this formula of non-pronouncement the Court necessarily leaves open the possibility that a use of nuclear weapons contrary to humanitarian law might nonetheless be lawful. This goes beyond anything that was claimed by the nuclear weapons States appearing before the Court, who fully accepted that any lawful threat or use of nuclear weapons would have to comply with both the *jus ad bellum* and the *jus in bello* (see para. 86). . . .

31. The [Court's opinion] refers also to "the current state of international law" as the basis for the Court's *non liquet*. I find it very hard to understand this reference. . . .

33. Perhaps the reference to "the current state of international law" is a reference to perceived tensions between the widespread acceptance of the possession of nuclear weapons (and thus, it may be presumed, of the legality of their use in certain circumstances) as mentioned by the Court in paragraphs 67 and 96 on the one hand, and the requirements of humanitarian law on the other. If so, I believe

this to be a false dichotomy. The pursuit of deterrence, the shielding under the nuclear umbrella, the silent acceptance of reservations and declarations by the nuclear powers to treaties prohibiting the use of nuclear weapons in certain regions, the seeking of possible security assurances—all this points to a significant international practice which is surely relevant not only to the law of self-defence but also to humanitarian law. If a substantial number of States in the international community believe that the use of nuclear weapons might *in extremis* be compatible with their duties under the Charter (whether as nuclear powers or as beneficiaries of "the umbrella" or security assurances) they presumably also believe that they would not be violating their duties under humanitarian law.

[After noting that the Court has always previously avoided a holding of *non liquet*, Higgins concluded:]

40. Nor is the situation changed by any suggestion that the problem is as much one as "antimony" [sic] or clashes between various elements in the law as much as alleged "vagueness" in the law. Even were there such an "antimony" (which, as I have indicated above, I doubt), the judge's role is precisely to decide which of two or more competing norms is applicable in the particular circumstances. The corpus of international law is frequently made up of norms that, taken in isolation, appear to pull in different directions—for example, States may not use force/States may use force in self-defence; *pacta sunt servanda* /States may terminate or suspend treaties on specified grounds. It is the role of the judge to resolve, in context, and on grounds that should be articulated, why the application of one norm rather than another is to be preferred in the particular case. . . .

41. One cannot be unaffected by the knowledge of the unbearable suffering and vast destruction that nuclear weapons can cause. And one can well understand that it is expected of those who care about such suffering and devastation that they should declare its cause illegal. It may well be asked of a judge whether, in engaging in legal analysis of such concepts as "unnecessary suffering", "collateral damage" and "entitlement to self-defence", one has not lost sight of the real human circumstances involved. The judicial lodestar, whether in difficult questions of interpretation of humanitarian law, or in resolving claimed tensions between competing norms, must be those values that international law seeks to promote and protect. In the present case, it is the physical survival of peoples that we must constantly have in view. We live in a decentralized world order, in which some States are known to possess nuclear weapons but choose to remain outside of the non-proliferation treaty system; while other such non-parties have declared their intention to obtain nuclear weapons; and yet other States are believed clandestinely to possess, or to be working shortly to possess nuclear weapons (some of whom indeed may be party to the NPT). It is not clear to me that either a pronouncement of illegality in all circumstances of the use of nuclear weapons or the answers formulated by the Court . . . best serve to protect mankind against that unimaginable suffering that we all fear.

Notes and Questions

1. The United States and a number of other governments urged the Court to reject the General Assembly's request for an advisory opinion, arguing that the

request presented a purely hypothetical question and that it was unduly vague, abstract, and political. In response to the argument that the question presented was unduly vague, the Court stated:

> The Court does not consider that, in giving an advisory opinion in the present case, it would necessarily have to write "scenarios", to study various types of nuclear weapons and to evaluate highly complex and controversial technological, strategic and scientific information. The Court will simply address the issues arising in all their aspects by applying the legal rules relevant to the situation.

The Court also rejected the claim that it should decline to issue an opinion because of political concerns: "the Court . . . considers that the political nature of the motives which may be said to have inspired the request and the political implications that the opinion given might have are of no relevance in the establishment of its jurisdiction to give such an opinion." Given the political sensitivities of this case and the political motivations driving many states to seek the Court's views, should the Court have declined to issue an advisory opinion, as suggested by Judge Oda?

2. Who won this case? Was the decision a victory for those seeking a declaration that any use of nuclear weapons would be illegal? Was it a victory for the nuclear-weapon states? Professor Roger Clark, who served as counsel to Samoa, observes that "[f]oes of nuclear weapons got more from the Court . . . than many people expected, but less than might have been hoped for." He concludes:

> The whole object of seeking an advisory opinion on nuclear weapons had been to delegitimize the bomb, to take away some of its mana. No one doubted that ultimately it would still be necessary to complete the disarmament negotiations. Even a unanimous opinion that the threat or use of nuclear weapons is illegal under any circumstances would not have magically waved away existing stockpiles of nuclear weapons. To the extent that the opinion . . . chips away at the acceptability of nuclear weapons, it is a little more likely that those negotiations will be completed sooner rather than later. The Court's opinion is surely a call to go urgently and with gusto into the next stage—the final negotiation of a comprehensive treaty, with ample safeguards, aimed at total abolition.
>
> Events since the Court's opinion suggest some movement in the abolitionist direction. Thus, in September 1996, the General Assembly adopted the text of a Comprehensive Nuclear Test Ban Treaty, which was quickly signed in New York by well over one hundred states. And the General Assembly, in December, expressing its appreciation to the Court for its efforts, emphasized the Court's insistence on the need to proceed with the negotiations.

Roger S. Clark, *International Court of Justice: Advisory Proceedings on the Legality of the Threat or Use of Nuclear Weapons (Question Posed by the General Assembly): The Laws of Armed Conflict and the Use or Threat of Use of Nuclear Weapons*, 7 Crim. L.F. 265, 267, 296 (1996).

By contrast, Professor W. Michael Reisman sees the Court's opinion as a serious impediment to non-proliferation efforts:

> The real issue, which the Court treated only glancingly and which counsel appear often to have obscured, is not over *who* is for or against nuclear weapons, but over *which* is the optimal realistic strategy for containing and finally eliminating those weapons. . . . It is here—in finding the best way to protect mankind against the unimaginable suffering that we all fear—that the opinion of 8 July 1996 failed. . . .

There are a number of states in the world whose elites and significant parts of whose populations have cause to believe that the price of a war that they might lose will not be in a boundary adjustment or the payment of some form of tribute or other concession. Rather, defeat will result in the extinction of their political identity and possibly the extermination of large parts of their populations. These are often people who, as the saying goes, have come by their paranoia honestly. Their impulse to acquire nuclear weapons is strong. Now . . . the principal judicial organ of the United Nations has said to factions within those states that have long agitated in their internal political processes for the acquisition of the ultimate weapon and until now have received no authoritative international support, that the use of nuclear weapons for self-defence cannot be said to be prohibited by international law. That, of course, is exactly what the pro-nuclear activists in those states have been saying all along. In strengthening the hands of nuclear proponents in states with justifiable security fears, the Court has also strengthened 'nuclearists' in other states, who may now point to the enhanced probability of nuclear weapons acquisition by others as justification and compulsion for their states, too, to acquire nuclear weapons. This is the essential scenario of proliferation.

W. Michael Reisman, *The Political Consequences of the General Assembly Advisory Opinion, in* The International Court of Justice and Nuclear Weapons 473, 475, 485-486 (Laurence Boisson de Chazournes & Philippe Sands eds., 1999).

3. What influence is the Court's decision likely to have on state behavior? Consider the following comments by the then-Deputy Legal Adviser to the U.S. State Department:

The Court expressly declined to pronounce on the legality of the use of nuclear weapons in two of the most likely scenarios in which that use might be considered: namely, in "extreme" self-defense, where the survival of the user or its ally as a state is threatened; or as a belligerent reprisal—for example, in response to the use of nuclear, chemical or biological weapons by an enemy. Beyond this, the Court obviously had serious concerns about the likelihood that other uses of nuclear weapons could be made in compliance with the rule of proportionality and other aspects of the law of armed conflict, but did not rule that possibility out. . . .

There was some debate among the judges as to whether the Court's abstention from pronouncing on these issues meant that states were therefore legally free to take the actions in question or, rather, that the issue of legality was simply unresolved. But either way one prefers to think about it, the practical result is the same. National authorities that believe their policy is lawful and vital to national security are unlikely to change important elements of it simply because legal issues have been raised but not resolved.

As to whether the Court's opinion will hasten the day when nuclear weapons are eliminated, as called for by Article VI of the NPT [Treaty on the Non-Proliferation of Nuclear Weapons], my belief is that it was never reasonable to think that the Court could do so. That result can only be reached through the process of negotiations among states, which will require the resolution of very difficult technical, political and security problems. None of these problems would have been solved or eased by an opinion from the Court that all uses of nuclear weapons are unlawful.

W. Michael J. Matheson, *The Opinions of the International Court of Justice on the Threat or Use of Nuclear Weapons*, 91 Am. J. Intl. L. 417, 434-435 (1997).

What changes, if any, would the nuclear-weapon states have made in their nuclear capabilities if the Court had declared that the threat or use of nuclear weapons was illegal in all circumstances? How would the non-nuclear states have reacted to a decision finding that nuclear weapons could be lawfully used in some cases?

4. Professor Paul Kahn suggests that the Court is unable to resolve the question put to it by the General Assembly because to do so "the Court would have to find a ground of normative priority between two distinct approaches to international law." One approach "understands international law as the product of consensual actions by states." The authority of international law arises out of the consent of states, and states cannot be understood to have consented to their own destruction. "The other approach locates the normative claim of international law in the expression of principles of moral behavior among states." This approach, pursued in different ways by NGOs and international law scholars, interprets the law to which states have consented in ways that further transnational interests in human rights and the preservation of the environment and that value those interests above the particular interests of individual states. Kahn argues that "neither approach . . . is more important, basic or essential than the other." Hence, the Court is drawn to both perspectives, and is therefore unable to decide the case:

> The Court's ultimate muteness in this case reflects the central dilemma of contemporary international law. This is the problem of understanding the place of the state in a system that simultaneously recognizes the state as the source of its norms and interprets those norms in a transnational, principled fashion. . . .
>
> It is not the form of legal argument, but the double character of the content of the law that causes the dilemma here. . . . If all law must be interpreted through the lens of state sovereignty, we get one answer to the nuclear weapons issue: the answer that protects deterrence and stumbles over an ultimate right of self-defense. If all law is interpreted through a transnational moral principle of justice, survival of mankind cannot be a value subordinate to state sovereignty. Contemporary international law is caught between these two quite different value schemes. . . . The nuclear weapons case brings these two different schemes into conflict, without offering any legal grounds for their reconciliation.
>
> In ordinary terms, what would it mean to say that the use or threat of use of nuclear weapons is legally prohibited in all circumstances? Most importantly, this would mean that a state may be legally barred from responding effectively to an attack—even a nuclear attack—upon itself. In the extreme case, a state might have to suffer military defeat, or perhaps annihilation, even when there are weapons available that might prevent this outcome. . . .
>
> Despite the risks to any particular state, the geopolitical logic of a legal prohibition on nuclear weapons is straightforward: nuclear weapons must be prohibited, even in cases of self-defense, because their use would impose costs on the rest of the world greater than the benefits that could be obtained by the individual state. Thus, a state may be required to sacrifice its interest in self-defense to an idea of the greater good of the international order. . . .

Paul Kahn, *Nuclear Weapons and the Rule of Law*, 31 N.Y.U. J. Intl. L. & Pol. 349, 373-374 (1999).

Does Professor Kahn accurately state the dilemma facing the Court? Is there any way out of this dilemma? Does international law require a state to accept its own destruction in extreme cases? Should it? Do the two approaches outlined by Professor Kahn—one focusing on international law as a product of state consent, the other focusing on international law as a means to further transnational interests in human rights and the environment—correspond to the opinions by Judges Schwebel and Weeramantry, respectively?

5. Recall the discussion of the *Lotus* case starting at page 356 of the text. Does the ICJ's opinion at paragraph 52 suggest that what is not prohibited is permitted?

II. PROTECTING NON-COMBATANTS: THE QANA INCIDENT

The nuclear weapons case deals with the legality of the threat or use of nuclear weapons, a potentially cataclysmic but still hypothetical problem. This section considers a far more common problem in the conduct of armed conflict. All too often, warring parties injure or kill civilian non-combatants. While non-combatants have always suffered in warfare, the problem has grown increasingly acute as advances in technology provide combatants with ever more destructive weaponry. Indeed, in contemporary armed conflicts, non-combatants typically die in far greater numbers than combatants. In some instances, non-combatants are the primary targets of warring parties, who may be pursuing a policy of genocide or ethnic cleansing.

In recognition of this problem, states have agreed that reasonable efforts should be made to minimize the harm to non-combatants in armed conflicts. Indeed, protecting non-combatants is the central aim of contemporary international humanitarian law. At the same time, states recognize and accept that non-combatant casualties are an unavoidable feature of efforts to achieve military objectives. As you read the following materials, consider how the tension between these two approaches is and should be dealt with in humanitarian law and state practice.

A. The Problem

On April 18, 1996, Israeli artillery shelled a UN compound in Qana, a village in southern Lebanon.* In just a few minutes, over 100 civilians who had entered the base seeking refuge from the ongoing conflict between Israel and Hezbollah, a paramilitary organization based in Lebanon (and identified by the U.S. government as a terrorist organization), were killed. Israel attributed the attack to a deplorable error stemming from a faulty map, inadequate information, and inadequately synchronized weapons. But a UN report suggested otherwise. Immediately after the incident, UN Secretary-General Boutros Boutros-Ghali directed his top military adviser, Major General Franklin van Kappen of the Netherlands, to conduct an investigation. Van Kappen's report, itself highly controversial, indicated that the shelling was probably not accidental.

The incident at Qana had its genesis in Israel's long struggle to secure its borders. In 1978, in response to frequent cross-border attacks, Israel invaded southern Lebanon and carved out a "security zone" approximately nine miles wide. By controlling this area, Israel hoped to force the locus of conflict away from Israeli territory and to minimize rocket and other attacks on Israeli population centers.

In the aftermath of the Israeli invasion, the United Nations established the UN Interim Force in Lebanon (UNIFIL). UNIFIL's original mandate included "confirming the withdrawal of Israeli forces . . . and assisting the Government of Lebanon in ensuring the return of its effective authority in the area." Although the failure of the parties to cooperate prevented UNIFIL from fulfilling its mandate, it continued to operate in Lebanon despite numerous incidents in which UNIFIL

---

*The following description of the Qana incident is based in part on W. Michael Reisman, *The Lessons of Qana*, 22 Yale J. Intl L. 381 (1997), and James Walsh, *Anatomy of a Tragedy: Did Israel Unwittingly Shell a U.N. Base in Qana?*, Time Intl. (Euro. ed.), May 20, 1996, at 26.

personnel and positions came under fire from one or more of the various armed groups operating in the area.

In the years leading up to the Qana incident, Israel's struggle against the guerrillas and other irregular forces based in Lebanon assumed a cyclical quality: cease-fires, followed by cease-fire violations, Israeli attacks on civilian targets used by irregular forces for cover, guerrilla attacks on Israeli civilians, and escalating violence leading up to the next cease-fire. In the early 1990s, Hezbollah and Israel both agreed not to target civilians. The agreement broke down when Hezbollah resumed rocket attacks on Israeli towns and settlements in the spring of 1996. Israel responded by launching Operation Grapes of Wrath, a military campaign against various Hezbollah targets in Lebanon. During the course of the campaign, Israel complained repeatedly that Hezbollah forces would launch attacks and then hide in civilian settlements or UN compounds. Israel also warned civilians living in or near the security zone to flee the area or risk getting caught up in the conflict. About 400,000 civilians did take refuge in the north, but many sought safety in the various UNIFIL compounds. Approximately 800 villagers took shelter in the UN compound at Qana, then under the control of Fijian UN peacekeepers.

Early in the afternoon of April 18, Hezbollah forces fired rockets and mortars from several locations within a few hundred meters of the UN compound (see diagram below). An Israeli ground patrol, operating north of the "red line" demarcating the outer boundary of the Israeli security zone, came under attack and requested assistance. Because Israeli rules of engagement precluded shelling within 300 meters of a UN compound, the Israeli commander of a nearby artillery unit had to seek permission to fire from the Israeli Northern Command. Permission was evidently granted in order to protect the Israeli patrol requesting assistance. The ensuing bombardment killed approximately 105 civilians in Qana and wounded four Fijian peacekeepers. Whether Israeli artillery deliberately targeted the UN compound has been hotly contested.

B. The UN Report

Report dated 1 May 1996 of the Secretary-General's Military Adviser concerning the shelling of the United Nations compound at Qana on 18 April 1996

U.N. Doc. S/1996/337, Annex

Introduction

1. On 18 April 1996, shortly after 1400 hours local time, the headquarters compound of the Fijian battalion of the United Nations Interim Force in Lebanon (UNIFIL) came under fire by Israeli artillery. . . .

Israeli account of events

6. On 21 April, I met with Major-General Vilnai at Tel Aviv and visited the artillery battalion. On both occasions, the Director of Israeli artillery, Brigadier-General Dan Harel, was also present. He, I was told, had investigated the shelling incident. The Israeli officers gave the following account of the incident:

(a) In the early afternoon of 18 April, an Israeli patrol had come under fire emanating from Qana. The precise location of the patrol was not given, except that it was close to the "red line", which is a line on Israeli maps that marks the northern edge of the Israeli-controlled areas in southern Lebanon. Mortar shells had fallen as close as 40 metres to the patrol, which had requested assistance. The Israeli forces had initiated rescue fire procedures.

(b) At 1352 and 1358 hours, respectively, Israeli locating radar had identified two separate targets in Qana from where fire had originated. The first target was located 200 metres or so south-west of the United Nations compound. The second target was located some 350 metres south-east of the compound. The data had been sent automatically to the Northern Command and to an artillery battalion located on the Israel-Lebanon border, about 12 kilometres from the sea. . . . When the battalion received the data, it checked the targets on a map and found that one of the two locations was between 200 to 300 metres from the United Nations position at Qana. The commanding officer had therefore sought instructions from Northern Command, which rechecked the data and gave permission to fire. This decision had not been taken lightly; officers of some seniority had been involved.

(c) When the order to fire came, the first target had been engaged by one battery, using all four guns. Thirty-eight shells (high-explosive) had been fired, about two thirds with impact fuses and one third with proximity fuses. (Proximity fuses cause a round to explode in the air above the target; they are often used for anti-personnel fire.) The two types of fuses had been employed in random order. Convergence fire had been used so that the impacts would be concentrated in the target area. Regrettably, a few rounds had overshot and hit the United Nations compound.

(d) The commanding officer of the artillery battalion had no satisfactory explanation why so many shells had fallen some 200 meters north of the intended target. . . . Asked if he had shifted fire during the shelling, he said he had not; he added that the mission had taken only three to four minutes (the time given by the Israeli forces was from 1407 to 1412 hours) and there would have been no time to change target data.

(e) We questioned the commanding officer about the procedures employed in the firing. His replies indicated a high professional standard.

(f) The second target had been engaged by another battery located in the same position. It had fired 40 rounds, from 1411 to 1417 hours.

(g) In response to repeated questions, the Israeli interlocutors stated that there had been no Israeli aircraft, helicopters or remotely piloted vehicles (RPV) in the air over Qana before, during or after the shelling. (These would have enabled the Israeli forces to observe the target area and adjust their fire.) . . .

7. The Israeli officers stated that the Israeli forces were not aware at the time of the shelling that a large number of Lebanese civilians had taken refuge in the Qana compound. I did not pursue this question since I considered it irrelevant because the United Nations compound was not a legitimate target, whether or not civilians were in it.

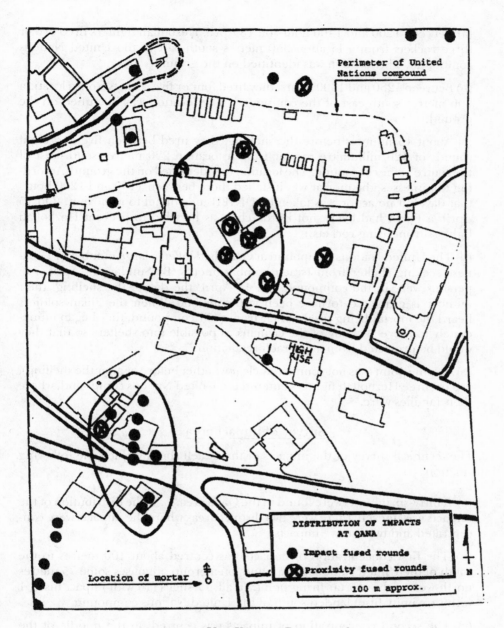

SOURCE: Van Kappen Report at 8

8. The Israeli officers emphasized that it was not Israeli policy to target civilians or the United Nations. On the contrary, the Israeli forces had made every effort to avoid the loss of innocent lives. The incident at Qana was therefore all the more deeply regretted.

Events prior to the shelling

9. My team and I questioned a number of witnesses on the activities of Hezbollah fighters in Qana prior to the incident. The following was found:

(a) Between 1200 and 1400 hours on 18 April, Hezbollah fighters fired two or three rockets from a location 350 metres south-east of the United Nations compound. The location was identified on the ground.

(b) Between 1230 and 1300 hours, they fired four or five rockets from a location 600 metres south-east of the compound. The location was identified on the ground.

(c) About 15 minutes before the shelling, they fired between five and eight rounds of 120 millimetre mortar from a location 220 metres south-west of the centre of the compound. The location was identified on the ground. According to witnesses, the mortar was installed there between 1100 and 1200 hours that day, but no action was taken by UNIFIL personnel to remove it. (On 15 April, a Fijian had been shot in the chest as he tried to prevent Hezbollah fighters from firing rockets.)

(d) The United Nations compound at Qana had taken a large number of Lebanese seeking shelter from Israeli bombardments. By Sunday, 14 April, 745 persons were in the compound. On 18 April, the day of the shelling, their number is estimated to have been well over 800. When the Fijian soldiers heard the mortar being fired not far from their compound, they began immediately to move as many of the civilians as possible into shelters so that they would be protected from any Israeli retaliation.

(e) At some point (it is not completely clear whether before or after the shelling), two or three Hezbollah fighters entered the United Nations compound, where their families were.

Survey of impact area

10. The technical survey of the impacts of the Israeli shells yielded the following information:

(a) Thirty-six impacts were found in the Qana area. . . . The distribution of the impacts was uneven; there were two distinct areas where the impacts were concentrated and two "stray" impacts.

(b) The first concentration of impacts was centred about 100 metres to the south of the United Nations compound, on a group of houses some 75 metres north-west of the mortar firing point. In all, 17 shells (16 with impact fuses, 1 with proximity fuse) landed south of the United Nations compound.

(c) The second concentration of impacts was centred on the middle of the United Nations compound. . . . [T]here was substantial evidence of multiple proximity-fused artillery ammunition detonating directly above the compound, covering a large portion of its area. . . . . In sum, evidence was found of 13 detonations inside or directly above the compound and 4 very close to it.

(d) Almost all the proximity fuses were used in the area of the United Nations compound. . . .

11. Several witnesses reported that during the shelling there had been a perceptible shift in the weight of fire from an area south-west of the compound (the mortar site) to the compound itself.

12. Several witnesses stated that they saw an RPV over the Qana area before, during and after the shelling. Two helicopters were seen 2 kilometres south-east of the United Nations compound during the shelling and one was observed close to the compound after the shelling had finished. The presence of one helicopter and an RPV was documented on a video tape, which covers the latter part of the shelling. . . . The RPV on the tape was of a type with a real-time data link capability.

Findings

13. The following are my findings:

(a) The distribution of impacts at Qana shows two distinct concentrations, whose mean points of impact are about 140 metres apart. If the guns were converged, as stated by the Israeli forces, there should have been only one main point of impact.

(b) The pattern of impacts is inconsistent with a normal overshooting of the declared target (the mortar site) by a few rounds, as suggested by the Israeli forces.

(c) During the shelling, there was a perceptible shift in the weight of fire from the mortar site to the United Nations compound.

(d) The distribution of point impact detonations and air bursts makes it improbable that impact fuses and proximity fuses were employed in random order, as stated by the Israeli forces.

(e) There were no impacts in the second target area which the Israeli forces claim to have shelled.

(f) Contrary to repeated denials, two Israeli helicopters and a remotely piloted vehicle were present in the Qana area at the time of the shelling.

While the possibility cannot be ruled out completely, it is unlikely that the shelling of the United Nations compound was the result of gross technical and/or procedural errors.

C. The Israeli Response and the UN Rejoinder

Israel vigorously denied what it saw as the implication of van Kappen's report: that Israel intentionally attacked civilians sheltered in a UN compound. Israel argued that its map was inaccurate and that it failed to take into account the extent of the compound's sprawl, leading planners to misjudge the precise location of the UN compound and to provide targeting coordinates to the artillery unit that were mistakenly closer to the UN compound than the soldiers involved understood at the time. Israel also argued that the helicopters and RPV in the area were not close enough to view Qana adequately until after the shelling stopped. General Harel stated further that the pattern of shells noted in van Kappen's report could be attributed to guns whose muzzle velocities were out of synch as a result of extensive recent use, causing shells with the same target to land in different locations. Further, Israel denied that it knew civilians had taken shelter at Qana, and criticized the United Nations for failing to provide a specific advance warning that it had admitted refugees into the compound.

In response to these and other criticisms of his report, van Kappen provided the following addendum:

Addendum Dated 7 May 1996 to the Report of the Secretary-General's Military Adviser Concerning the Qana Shelling

U.N. Doc. S/1996/337 (1996)

2. On 6 May . . . General Harel related the findings of an Israeli investigation which, he said, had been completed only the day before. He explained that, in their eagerness to cooperate with the United Nations, the Israeli forces had given me information during my visit before their own investigation was completed. Some of this information had turned out to be wrong. General Harel provided the following additions and corrections:

(a) Two errors had been discovered in the checking by Northern Command of the distance of the targets from the United Nations compound (see para. 6(b) of my report). First, the compound had been marked by a pin on a map (scale 1:20,000) about 100 metres north of its actual location. Secondly, in calculating the distance, the space covered by the compound had not been taken into account. As a result, the distance between the target and the compound (i.e., the edge of the compound—FVK) had been estimated at about 350 metres rather than the actual 180.

(b) The fuse mix ratio had been the reverse of what I was told, namely two thirds proximity fuses and one third impact fuses rather than the other way around.

(c) The second battery had missed the second target completely. General Harel showed me an aerial photograph on which a group of seven impacts was marked about 150 metres west of the rocket site (180 metres south of the mortar site). General Harel could not explain why the second battery missed its target; the data provided to the battery had been correct.

(d) General Harel could not explain why there were in Qana two distinct impact concentrations with main impact points 140 metres apart.

(e) It was now known that an RPV had in fact been operated over southern Lebanon. . . . It had been dispatched to Qana only at 1418 hours, that is, after the shelling ended, and arrived at its destination at 1431 hours. He pointed out that RPVs have a narrow field of view so that the presence of an RPV in the vicinity of Qana did not mean that Qana itself could be observed.

(f) Two helicopters had been sent north of the "red line" (see para. 6(a)) after the Israeli patrol came under attack in order to locate and attack the sources of fire. However, they could not find the target and left the area. . . .

(g) General Harel stressed that the Israeli forces were under strict instructions not to target the United Nations. Therefore, the shelling of the Qana compound could only be the result of a combination of technical and procedural errors and chance.

3. It will be noted that the additional explanations provided by General Harel address the question why the Israeli forces fired at a target close to a United Nations compound. They do not address the first four of my findings. . . . As I stated in my report, it is unlikely that gross technical and/or procedural errors led to the shelling of the United Nations compound. However, it cannot be ruled out completely.

Notes and Questions

1. The factual details concerning the incident at Qana are crucial to understanding what happened and why. What, for example, is the significance of the types of fuses used? The shift in the weight of fire described by some witnesses? The presence or absence of an RPV? The two distinct concentrations of impacts? Does it matter when the two or three Hezbollah fighters referred to in paragraph 9(e) of the initial UN report entered the UN compound? Why is it significant that there were no impacts in the second target area that Israel states it shelled?

2. Do you agree with General van Kappen's conclusions? Reading between the lines of his report, what do you think he believes actually happened? What, if anything, do you think Israel should have done differently?

3. Should the United Nations have provided a specific warning to Israel of the presence of civilians in the compound? Should the UN compound be exempt from attack if it is being used as a safe haven by combatants engaged in hit-and-run assaults on Israeli forces? Did the United Nations have a responsibility to prevent the compound from being used in that fashion?

D. The Geneva Conventions and Customary Law

It is not per se unlawful to kill civilians during wartime. As reflected in the *Nuclear Weapons Case* above, international law accepts the inevitability of "collateral damage"—civilian casualties and damage to civilian property. But international humanitarian law contains many provisions designed to minimize harm to non-combatants. The most important treaty in this regard is the 1977 Additional Protocol I to the Geneva Conventions of 1949, which applies to international armed conflicts. Protocol I reaffirms and elaborates on principles found in the Hague Conventions of 1899 and 1907 on the conduct of hostilities and customary international law; Protocol I also reaffirms and incorporates by reference the protections in the 1949 Geneva Conventions. Over 150 states are party to this Protocol. In a nutshell, Protocol I prohibits direct or indiscriminate attacks against civilians, and requires military forces to take all reasonable measures to avoid unnecessary civilian casualties. Although Israel is not a party to Protocol I, states generally regard its fundamental provisions as reflecting customary international law. In analyzing the Israeli and Hezbollah action at Qana, consider the following provisions of Protocol I.

Protocol Additional to the Geneva Conventions of 12 August 1949, and Relating to the Protection of Victims of International Armed Conflict (Protocol I)

1125 U.N.T.S. 3 (1977)

Article 48. Basic Rule

In order to ensure respect for and protection of the civilian population and civilian objects, the Parties to the conflict shall at all times distinguish between the civilian population and combatants and between civilian objects and military objectives and accordingly shall direct their operations only against military objectives.

Article 51. Protection of the Civilian Population

1. The civilian population and individual civilians shall enjoy general protection against dangers arising from military operations. To give effect to this protection, the following rules, which are additional to other applicable rules of international law, shall be observed in all circumstances.

2. The civilian population as such, as well as individual civilians, shall not be the object of attack. Acts or threats of violence the primary purpose of which is to spread terror among the civilian population are prohibited.

3. Civilians shall enjoy the protection afforded by this Section, unless and for such time as they take a direct part in hostilities.

4. Indiscriminate attacks are prohibited. Indiscriminate attacks are:

(a) Those which are not directed at a specific military objective;
(b) Those which employ a method or means of combat which cannot be directed at a specific military objective; or
(c) Those which employ a method or means of combat the effects of which cannot be limited as required by this Protocol; and consequently, in each such case, are of a nature to strike military objectives and civilians or civilian objects without distinction.

5. Among others, the following types of attacks are to be considered as indiscriminate:

(a) An attack by bombardment by any methods or means which treats as a single military objective a number of clearly separated and distinct military objectives located in a city, town, village or other area containing a similar concentration of civilians or civilian objects; and
(b) An attack which may be expected to cause incidental loss of civilian life, injury to civilians, damage to civilian objects, or a combination thereof, which would be excessive in relation to the concrete and direct military advantage anticipated.

6. Attacks against the civilian population or civilians by way of reprisals are prohibited.

7. The presence or movements of the civilian population or individual civilians shall not be used to render certain points or areas immune from military operations, in particular in attempts to shield military objectives from attacks or to shield, favour or impede military operations. The Parties to the conflict shall not direct the movement of the civilian population or individual civilians in order to attempt to shield military objectives from attacks or to shield military operations.

8. Any violation of these prohibitions shall not release the Parties to the conflict from their legal obligations with respect to the civilian population and civilians, including the obligation to take the precautionary measures provided for in Article 57.

Article 52. General Protection of Civilian Objects

2. Attacks shall be limited strictly to military objectives. In so far as objects are concerned, military objectives are limited to those objects which by their nature, location, purpose or use make an effective contribution to military action and whose total or partial destruction, capture or neutralization, in the circumstances ruling at the time, offers a definite military advantage.

3. In case of doubt whether an object which is normally dedicated to civilian purposes, such as a place of worship, a house or other dwelling or a school, is being

used to make an effective contribution to military action, it shall be presumed not to be so used.

Article 57. Precautions in Attack

1. In the conduct of military operations, constant care shall be taken to spare the civilian population, civilians and civilian objects.

2. With respect to attacks, the following precautions shall be taken:

    (a) Those who plan or decide upon an attack shall:

        (i) Do everything feasible to verify that the objectives to be attacked are neither civilians nor civilian objects and are not subject to special protection but are military objectives within the meaning of paragraph 2 of Article 52 and that it is not prohibited by the provisions of this Protocol to attack them;

        (ii) Take all feasible precautions in the choice of means and methods of attack with a view to avoiding, and in any event to minimizing, incidental loss of civilian life, injury to civilians and damage to civilian objects;

        (iii) Refrain from deciding to launch any attack which may be expected to cause incidental loss of civilian life, injury to civilians, damage to civilian objects, or a combination thereof, which would be excessive in relation to the concrete and direct military advantage anticipated;

    (b) An attack shall be canceled or suspended if it becomes apparent that the objective is not a military one or is subject to special protection or that the attack may be expected to cause incidental loss of civilian life, injury to civilians, damage to civilian objects, or a combination thereof, which would be excessive in relation to the concrete and direct military advantage anticipated;

    (c) Effective advance warning shall be given of attacks which may affect the civilian population, unless circumstances do not permit.

Notes and Questions

1. Protocol I to the Geneva Conventions prohibits indiscriminate attacks by requiring attackers to take all feasible measures to avoid hitting non-military targets. Did Israel's shelling of Qana amount to an indiscriminate attack? Consider the following excerpt.

> An indiscriminate attack is one in which the attacker does not take measures to avoid hitting non-military objectives, that is, civilians and civilian objects. . . .
>
> Military objectives are limited to "those objects which by their nature, location, purpose or use make an effective contribution to military action and whose total or partial destruction, capture or neutralization, in the circumstances ruling at the time, offers a definite military advantage." Although every instance of indiscriminate attack violates the law of armed conflict, it is equally the case where attacking a military target may cause collateral damage to civilians or civilian objects. If the harm to civilians is proportionate to the military advantage expected, the attack, other things being equal, is a legal act of war. If the harm is "excessive in relation to the concrete and direct military advantage anticipated," the attack is prohibited, whether or not indiscriminate. (Concrete means perceivable by the senses; direct means having no intervening factor.) . . .
>
> . . . In Operation Grapes of Wrath in April 1996, there was evidence [according to a Human Rights Watch report] that Israel had carried out "indiscriminate and disproportionate attacks against civilians in what had become virtual 'free-fire'

zones across large swaths of the south" of Lebanon, culminating in the shelling of a makeshift refugee compound at a UN post south of Tyre in which more than one hundred displaced civilians were killed. Israel said Hizbollah had fired mortars and Katyusha rockets from a position three hundred meters from the UN post. Locating military objectives near a concentration of civilians, known as shielding, is also a war crime, and the laws of armed conflict are clear that an attacker is not precluded from attacking a legitimate military target by the proximity of civilians or civilian objects. While acts of shielding did not render the zone immune from attack, neither did they "give Israel license to fire *indiscriminately* into a wide area that includes a UN base and concentrations of civilians," Human Rights Watch correctly noted (emphasis added). The International Committee of the Red Cross (ICRC) one day later issued a statement in which it "firmly condemned" the Israeli shelling at Qana and reiterated there was an "absolute ban" on indiscriminate attacks. However, a senior ICRC official said after an investigation that the real problem here was the fact that the Israeli system was designed to automatically fire back on the source of the original attack. Therefore Israel did not take sufficient precautions in their attack to ensure that it would not result in disproportionate civilian deaths.

Roy Gutman & Daoud Kuttab, *Indiscriminate Attack, in* Crimes of War 195-197 (Roy Gutman & David Rieff eds., 1999).

2. Does the legality of Israel's actions at Qana turn solely on whether Israel's shelling of the compound was intentional?

3. How should states such as Israel deal with irregular forces who seek shelter in protected places? Note that the Statute of the International Criminal Court, discussed in Chapter 9, lists among the acts constituting war crimes: "Utilizing the presence of a civilian or other protected person to render certain points, areas or military forces immune from military operations." During the conflict in Bosnia, Serb forces chained UN peacekeepers to artillery pieces to shield Serb gun emplacements from attack. In Iraq, Saddam Hussein temporarily detained foreign nationals to deter Western states from attacking Iraqi forces. How should international law respond to such actions? Does international humanitarian law confer an undue advantage on combatants willing to disregard the laws of war?

4. In many recent conflicts, soldiers have often found it difficult to distinguish between combatants and non-combatants. In the Korean conflict, for example, U.S. soldiers may have massacred civilians seeking shelter under a bridge at No Gun Ri for fear that combatants were mingled among the non-combatants and posed a risk to U.S. military personnel. Is it reasonable to expect soldiers to risk their own lives in order to avoid harm to non-combatants?

5. International humanitarian law demands that states attack only military objectives, and then only when doing so satisfies the principle of proportionality. But who determines whether a particular attack on a particular target is proportional? And what values are to be compared in making that assessment? Consider the following excerpt:

> As formulated in Additional Protocol I of 1977, attacks are prohibited if they cause incidental loss of civilian life, injury to civilians, or damage to civilian objects that is excessive in relation to the anticipated concrete and direct military advantage of the attack. This creates a permanent obligation for military commanders to consider the results of the attack compared to the advantage anticipated. The target list has to be continuously updated as the conflict develops with special attention given to the safe movement of civilians. . . .
>
> Some states ratifying Protocol I have stated that the concrete and direct military advantage anticipated from an attack can only be considered as a whole and not only

from isolated or particular parts of the attack. Article 85 defines an *indiscriminate attack* undertaken in the knowledge that it will cause excessive damage to the civilian population as a grave breach and therefore a war crime. The principle is hard to apply in war, still harder after an attack has occurred. But grossly disproportionate results will be seen as criminal by all belligerent parties and the world community.

Horst Fischer, *Proportionality, Principle of, in* Crimes of War 294 (Roy Gutman & David Rieff eds., 1999).

6. In October 2001, while U.S. forces were engaged in armed conflict with Taliban forces in Afghanistan, U.S. intelligence tracked a convoy of vehicles believed to be carrying Mullah Muhammad Omar, the leader of the Taliban, and some 100 of his guards, to a particular building. Journalist Seymour Hersh offers the following account of what happened:

> The precise sequence of events could not be fully learned, but intelligence officials told me that there was an immediate request for a full-scale assault by fighter bombers. At that point, however, word came from General Tommy R. Franks, the CENTCOM [Central Command] commander, saying, as the officials put it, "My JAG"—Judge Advocate General, a legal officer—"doesn't like this, so we're not going to fire." Instead, the Predator [a pilotless military aircraft] was authorized to fire a missile in front of the building—"bounce it off the front door," one officer said, "and see who comes out, and take a picture." CENTCOM suggested that the Predator then continue to follow Omar. The Hellfire [a missile carried by the Predator,] however, could not target the area in front of the building—in military parlance, it could not "get a signature" on the dirt there—and it was then agreed that the missile would attack a group of cars parked in front, presumably those which had carried Omar and his retinue. The missile was fired, and it "obliterated the cars," an official said. "But no one came out."
>
> It was learned later from an operative on the ground that Omar and his guards had indeed been in the convoy. . . .
>
> [After noting that Omar escaped before the building itself was hit, Hersh continues:] Days afterward, top Administration officials were still seething about the incident. "If it was a fuckup, I could live with it," one senior official said. "But it's not a fuckup—it's an outrage. This isn't like you're six years old and your mother calls you to come in for lunch and you say, 'Time out.' If anyone thinks otherwise, go look at the World Trade Center or the Pentagon." A senior military officer viewed the failure to strike immediately as a symptom of "a cultural issue"—"a slow degradation of the system due to political correctness: 'We want you to kill the guy, but not the guy next to him.' No collateral damage." Others saw the cultural problem as one of bureaucratic, rather than political, correctness. Either way, the failure to attack has left Defense Secretary Rumsfeld "kicking a lot of glass and breaking doors," the officer said. "But in the end I don't know if it'll mean any changes."

Seymour M. Hersh, *King's Ransom: How Vulnerable Are the Saudi Royals?*, The New Yorker (Oct. 22, 2001) at 35, 38.

Why might the JAG officer have opposed an immediate attack? Was it the right decision under international humanitarian law? What more would you need to know to answer that question? Does this incident demonstrate that the United States should change its practices in approving military attacks?

E. The Implications of Qana

Professor W. Michael Reisman offers the following observations on the events at Qana.

W. Michael Reisman, *The Lessons of Qana*

22 Yale J. Intl. L. 381, 395-397 (1997)

IV. Attacks on Civilians and the Requirement of Weapon Discrimination

UNIFIL has been fired upon hundreds of times in the course of its nineteen-year history. What was distinctive in the Qana incident was the large number of civilian casualties. Noncombatants are a key object of concern of contemporary humanitarian law, yet the law is proving ineffective for incidents like these because of intersecting technical and political factors. . . .

The ICRC Commentary [to Protocol I] makes clear that, though the law of war balances the necessities of war and humanitarian requirements, the principle of proportionality is secondary to the principles of protection: "[A]n attack cannot be justified only on grounds of proportionality if it contravenes the above-mentioned principles [i.e., articles 51-57]."

Many commentators and ICRC spokespersons suggest that proportionality should be a complex equation, taking into account factors such as the military importance or exigency of the target. A single sniper in the turret of a church or the top floor of a hospital will not justify destruction of the church or hospital; a highly destructive weapon placed there by an adversary may warrant it. In the first instance, the deployment of weapons that are more discriminating and less collaterally destructive is expected, even though the costs in terms of lives and casualties of the belligerent seeking to neutralize the sniper may be higher than would the use of a larger weapon, applied from a relatively safer remove.

How will that be applied to incidents like Qana? Assume the threatened destruction of part of a patrol of, let us say, twelve soldiers by mortar fire from the vicinity of a U.N. compound known to be sheltering more than 800 noncombatants. According to some commentators, knowledge of the presence of the noncombatants would severely restrict the choice of the weapons to be used to extricate the patrol because the application of a relatively undiscriminating weapon in this context, though it might be the only one that could be deployed rapidly enough to help the patrol, could cause great loss of civilian life. Even though the selection of a more discriminating weapon in this context—assuming that such weapons were available in real time—would probably increase the losses of the actor seeking to defend its unit, it is, according to this argument, legally required.

This agreement was unacceptable to Israel. . . . Israel was willing to defer to humanitarian considerations with respect to rockets emanating from the zone of the compound as long as there was no direct threat to its units. When such a threat eventuated, Israel responded vigorously in defense of the unit. . . .

In circumstances like these, any democratic polity engaged in elective conflict will insist on a comparable version of the law. Its elites will encounter two potentially conflicting imperatives: on the one hand, the imperative of using force in a limited fashion in an external arena and, on the other, the imperative of retaining the support of an internal constituency to whom the relation of such an operation to national interest may not appear vividly self-evident. For such actions, it is assumed that the public's tolerance for casualties is low, in contrast to circumstances in which national security or integrity are widely believed to be at stake, and in which tolerance for casualties may, for a time, be extremely high. Because some determinate casualty figure is believed, both by the democracy and its adversary, to be the cutoff point, the democracy's political-military leadership will make every effort to keep low or "zero" casualties as its adversaries try to push them up. To an extent, democratic leadership will seek to avoid elective military action. When it cannot, it will select and deploy weapons that provide maximum safety to its own forces.

Because of the increasing legal and moral force of humanitarian law, this strategy will be justified by a touting of "smart" weapons that are supposed to increase accuracy while reducing the exposure of the soldier operating them. The promise of these weapons is true—to an extent. Silicon chips may make a weapon more accurate, but that same weapon, corrected by an operator and intervisible with the target, will be even more accurate—meaning less injury to people with the misfortune to be in the way. Yet intervisibility means "retro-vulnerability": The operator is more vulnerable to injury by the adversary. Hence one may hypothesize that in order to minimize retro-vulnerability, human correction will be reduced or avoided in elective conflicts in which a democratic polity's tolerance of losses is expected to be inelastic. Unfortunately, in armed conflict, the safety equation is zero-sum: the more safety reserved for your forces, the more unintended and, of course, regrettable injury to civilians.

Notes and Questions

1. Does the principle of proportionality provide meaningful guidance to decision makers in situations such as the one Israel encountered at Qana?

2. Should Israel have to pay for damages incurred by the United Nations at Qana? The Group of 77, a loose coalition of developing countries, introduced a draft resolution in the General Assembly's Fifth Committee (Administration and Budgeting) seeking to have the General Assembly request that Israel pay approximately $1.7 million to cover costs associated with the incident. Israel has refused all such requests, stating that the responsibility for the incident rests with Hezbollah.

3. Do you agree with Professor Reisman that "any democratic polity engaged in elective conflict" will make decisions similar to those made by Israel at Qana? Might a democratic government's sensitivity to the adverse publicity associated with civilian casualties partly counteract the tendency to conduct military operations to minimize risks to its own forces even at the expense of heightening the risks to civilians? As you read the following materials on Kosovo, keep in mind Professor Reisman's argument that democracies engaged in elective military action will "select and deploy weapons that provide maximum safety to [their] own forces."

4. In December 2005, a U.S. and a Palestinian human rights organization filed suit against Lt. Gen. (ret.) Moshe Ya'alon, former Head of the Intelligence Branch and former Chief of Staff of the Israel Defense Forces (IDF), in connection with the shelling at Qana. The suit, brought under the Alien Tort Statute and the Torture Victim Protection Act, alleges that Ya'alon participated in the decision to shell the UN compound at Qana, and argues that he also had command responsibility for the attack. The suit accuses Ya'alon of war crimes, crimes against humanity, and other offenses. Are U.S. courts an appropriate forum for the issues raised by the shelling at Qana? For a discussion of the Alien

Tort Statute, see Chapter 5, Section V; for a discussion of command responsibility, see Chapter 9, Section II.

F. Applying the Lessons of Qana to the Bombing of Kosovo

As described more fully in Chapter 13, the North Atlantic Treaty Organization (NATO) conducted an extensive bombing campaign against the Federal Republic of Yugoslavia (FRY) during the spring of 1999 in an effort to force the FRY to confer autonomy on the province of Kosovo and to terminate human rights abuses directed against Kosovar Albanians. The campaign is described below.

Independent International Commission on Kosovo, The Kosovo Report

(2000), www.kosovocommission.org

CONDUCT OF THE NATO AIR CAMPAIGN

The NATO air campaign against Yugoslavia was conducted between March 24, 1999 and June 10, 1999. NATO aircraft from 13 countries flew 38,400 sorties in the campaign, including 10,484 strike sorties in which 26,614 air munitions were released.

The campaign was a complex, constantly evolving military operation. Decision-making throughout the campaign was influenced by micro-management and political judgment calls from several key NATO member governments. The need for consensus among all 19 members of the Alliance, including three new member states—Poland, Czech Republic, and Hungary—and those, like Greece, with close historical ties to Serbia, put additional constraints on the military decision-making process. . . .

In its first days, the bombing campaign struck military targets including air defense and communications installations. Though the bombing succeeded in completely grounding the Yugoslav air force it did not succeed in destroying its air defense, even though this was seriously damaged by the end of the war. NATO pilots were ordered to fly at altitudes above 15,000 feet to avoid the continuing threat of Yugoslav air defense systems. This decision has been criticized by opponents of the NATO campaign as limiting pilots' ability to positively establish the military nature of targets. The large number of decoy targets hit suggests that pilots were not able to make positive visual identification before attacking.

According to a number of reports, the NATO attacks in Kosovo did relatively little damage to FRY ground forces. In spite of the bombing, the FRY military forces attacked the KLA [Kosovo Liberation Army] rather successfully throughout Kosovo. It was also impossible for the NATO forces to stop the expulsion and killings of civilian Albanians.

After four weeks of bombing, the Yugoslav leadership still would not respond to negotiation proposals. At a NATO summit in Washington on April 23, 1999, Alliance leaders decided to further intensify the air campaign by expanding the target set to include military-industrial infrastructure, media, and other targets in Serbia itself. [See photo below.] 59 bridges (seven on the Danube), nine major highways (including Belgrade-Nis or Belgrade-Zagreb), and seven airports were destroyed. Most of the main telecommunications transmitters were damaged, two thirds of the main industrial plants were nearly destroyed. According to NATO, 70% of the electricity production capacity and 80% of the oil refinery capacity was knocked out. Hitting these targets, however, had significant political fallout: the consequent suffering of the Serbian civilian population contradicted initial NATO assurances that the war was not aimed at the Serbian people. . . .

There were very few military casualties in this war. There were no casualties at all on the NATO side, unique in any war. According to FRY sources, at least 600 FRY soldiers were killed in action; with about 300 of these killed in action with KLA. How many KLA soldiers who were killed is unknown.

CIVILIAN CASUALTIES OF THE NATO BOMBING CAMPAIGN

NATO made substantial efforts to avoid civilian casualties. In spite of these efforts there were some serious mistakes. The bombing of the Chinese embassy on May 7, had a significant political impact and most likely encouraged Milosevic to wait and see if he could profit from the error. Another catastrophic mistake was the bombing of Korishe/Korisa, with more than 80 Kosovars killed: There were a number of other instances during the NATO air campaign in which civilians were killed or injured by NATO bombs. These included two incidents on one day when many . . . convoys of internally displaced Kosovars were struck by NATO bombs, and another in which a passenger train was bombed.

In its report, Civilian Deaths in the NATO Air Campaign, Human Rights Watch (HRW) documented some 500 civilian deaths in 90 separate incidents. It concluded: "as few as 488 and as many as 527 Yugoslav civilians were killed as a result of NATO bombing. Between 62 and 66 percent of the total registered civilian deaths occurred in just twelve incidents."

During and after the Kosovo bombing campaign, numerous observers, including Amnesty International, Human Rights Watch, and the UN High Commissioner for Human Rights, Mary Robinson, raised questions concerning the legality of some of NATO's target selections and tactics. Amnesty International was particularly critical of NATO's "zero casualty war," charging that NATO's decision to limit itself to high-altitude bombing made it impossible in some instances to distinguish between civilian and military targets. Amnesty International also sharply criticized NATO's use of cluster bombs and depleted uranium shells (shells hardened to pierce armor by using a slightly radioactive heavy metal), and declared unlawful NATO's attacks on certain installations believed by Amnesty International to be predominantly civilian in nature. Amnesty called on the International Criminal Tribunal for the Former Yugoslavia (ICTY), whose statute gives it jurisdiction over all violations of the laws of war occurring in the territory of the former Yugoslavia from 1991 on, to investigate these and other allegations, and to prosecute if appropriate. (For further discussion of the Tribunal's Statute, see Section III below.)

In May 1999 the ICTY Office of the Prosecutor established a committee to review the NATO bombing campaign. The committee concluded that:

[O]n the basis of the information reviewed, . . . neither an in-depth investigation related to the bombing campaign as a whole nor investigations related to specific incidents are justified. In all cases, either the law is not sufficiently clear or investigations are unlikely to result in the acquisition of sufficient evidence to substantiate charges against high level accused or against lower accused for particularly heinous offenses.

Excerpts of the Committee's June 2000 report follow:

Final Report to the Prosecutor by the Committee Established to Review the NATO Bombing Campaign Against the Federal Republic of Yugoslavia

39 I.L.M. 1257 (2000)

c). The Military Objective

37. The definition [of "military objective" in Article 52 of Additional Protocol I to the Geneva Conventions] is supposed to provide a means whereby informed objective observers (and decision makers in a conflict) can determine whether or not a particular object constitutes a military objective. It accomplishes this purpose in simple cases. Everyone will agree that a munitions factory is a military objective and an unoccupied church is a civilian object. When the definition is applied to dual-use objects which have some civilian uses and some actual or potential military use (communications systems, transportation systems, petrochemical complexes, manufacturing plants of some types), opinions may differ. The application of the definition to particular objects may also differ depending on the scope and objectives of the conflict. Further, the scope and objectives of the conflict may change during the conflict. . . .

40. The Protocol I definition of military objective has been criticized by W. Hays Parks, the Special Assistant for Law of War Matters to the U.S. Army Judge Advocate General as being focused too narrowly on definite military advantage and paying too little heed to war sustaining capability, including economic targets such as export industries. . . . On the other hand, some critics of Coalition conduct in the Gulf War have suggested that the Coalition air campaign, directed admittedly against legitimate military objectives within the scope of the Protocol I definition, caused excessive long-term damage to the Iraqi economic infrastructure with a consequential adverse effect on the civilian population . . .

42. Although the Protocol I definition of military objective is not beyond criticism, it provides the contemporary standard which must be used when attempting to determine the lawfulness of particular attacks. That being said, it must be noted once again neither the USA nor France is a party to Additional Protocol I. The definition is, however, generally accepted as part of customary law.

43. To put the NATO campaign in context, it is instructive to look briefly at the approach to the military objective concept in the history of air warfare. The Protocol I standard was not applicable during World War II. The bomber offensives conducted during that war were conducted with technological means which rendered attacks on targets occupying small areas almost impossible. In general, depending upon the period in the conflict, bomber attacks could be relied upon, at best, to strike within 5 miles, 2 miles or 1 mile of the designated target . . .

. . . [F]or the most part World War II bombing campaigns were aimed at area targets and intended, directly or indirectly, to affect the morale of the enemy civilian population. It is difficult to describe the fire bombing of Hamburg, Dresden and Tokyo as anything other than attacks intended to kill, terrorize or demoralize civilians. Whether or not these attacks could be justified legally in the total war context of the time, they would be unlawful if they were required to comply with Protocol I.

44. Technology, law, and the public consensus of what was acceptable, at least in demonstrably limited conflicts, had evolved by the time of the 1990-91 Gulf Conflict. Technological developments, such as precision guided munitions, and the rapid acquisition of control of the aerospace by coalition air forces significantly enhanced the precision with which targets could be attacked . . .

[The report goes on to conclude that most of the targets described in various NATO reports were "clearly military objectives."]

d). The Principle of Proportionality

48. The main problem with the principle of proportionality is not whether or not it exists but what it means and how it is to be applied. It is relatively simple to state that there must be an acceptable relation between the legitimate destructive effect and undesirable collateral effects. For example, bombing a refugee camp is obviously prohibited if its only military significance is that people in the camp are knitting socks for soldiers. Conversely, an air strike on an ammunition dump should not be prohibited merely because a farmer is plowing a field in the area. Unfortunately, most applications of the principle of proportionality are not quite so clear cut. It is much easier to formulate the principle of proportionality in general terms than it is to apply it to a particular set of circumstances because the comparison is often between unlike quantities and values. One cannot easily assess the value of innocent human lives as opposed to capturing a particular military objective.

49. The questions which remain unresolved once one decides to apply the principle of proportionality include the following:

a) What are the relative values to be assigned to the military advantage gained and the injury to non-combatants and or the damage to civilian objects?

b) What do you include or exclude in totaling your sums?

c) What is the standard of measurement in time or space? and

d) To what extent is a military commander obligated to expose his own forces to danger in order to limit civilian casualties or damage to civilian objects?

50. The answers to these questions are not simple. It may be necessary to resolve them on a case by case basis, and the answers may differ depending on the background and values of the decision maker. It is unlikely that a human rights lawyer and an experienced combat commander would assign the same relative values to military advantage and to injury to noncombatants. Further, it is unlikely that military commanders with different doctrinal backgrounds and differing degrees of combat experience or national military histories would always agree in close cases. It is suggested that the determination of relative values must be that of the "reasonable military commander". Although there will be room for argument in close cases, there will be many cases where reasonable military commanders will agree that the injury to noncombatants or the damage to civilian objects was clearly disproportionate to the military advantage gained.

51. Much of the material submitted to the OTP [Office of the Prosecutor] consisted of reports that civilians had been killed, often inviting the conclusion to be drawn that crimes had therefore been committed. Collateral casualties to civilians and collateral damage to civilian objects can occur for a variety of reasons. Despite an obligation to avoid locating military objectives within or near densely populated

areas, to remove civilians from the vicinity of military objectives, and to protect civilians from the dangers of military operations, very little prevention may be feasible in many cases. Today's technological society has given rise to many dual use facilities and resources. City planners rarely pay heed to the possibility of future warfare. Military objectives are often located in densely populated areas and fighting occasionally occurs in such areas. Civilians present within or near military objectives must, however, be taken into account in the proportionality equation even if a party to the conflict has failed to exercise its obligation to remove them . . .

vi. General Assessment of the Bombing Campaign

. . . 55. The choice of targets by NATO . . . includes some loosely defined categories such as military-industrial infrastructure and government ministries and some potential problem categories such as media and refineries. All targets must meet the criteria for military objectives. . . . The targeted components of the military-industrial infrastructure and of government ministries must make an effective contribution to military action and their total or partial destruction must offer a definite military advantage in the circumstances ruling at the time. Refineries are certainly traditional military objectives but tradition is not enough and due regard must be paid to environmental damage if they are attacked . . . . The media as such is not a traditional target category. To the extent particular media components are part of the C3 (command, control and communications) network they are military objectives. . . . As a bottom line, civilians, civilian objects and civilian morale as such are not legitimate military objectives. The media does have an effect on civilian morale. If that effect is merely to foster support for the war effort, the media is not a legitimate military objective. If the media is used to incite crimes, as in Rwanda, it can become a legitimate military objective. If the media is the nerve system that keeps a war-monger in power and thus perpetuates the war effort, it may fall within the definition of a legitimate military objective. As a general statement, in the particular incidents reviewed by the committee, it is the view of the committee that NATO was attempting to attack objects it perceived to be legitimate military objectives.

56. The committee agrees there is nothing inherently unlawful about flying above the height which can be reached by enemy air defences. However, NATO air commanders have a duty to take practicable measures to distinguish military objectives from civilians or civilian objectives. The 15,000 feet minimum altitude adopted for part of the campaign may have meant the target could not be verified with the naked eye. However, it appears that with the use of modern technology, the obligation to distinguish was effectively carried out in the vast majority of cases during the bombing campaign.

Notes and Questions

1. The Report to the Prosecutor notes some of the difficulties in applying the principle of proportionality. To what extent can proportionality serve as a meaningful guide to decision makers in the course of a military conflict, or to prosecutors thereafter? Should prosecutors pursue close cases?

2. Many commentators have criticized NATO's refusal to introduce ground troops, arguing that the failure to do so enabled Serb forces to carry out a large-scale

campaign of ethnic cleansing. Did NATO have any obligation, legal or moral, to introduce ground troops?

3. The ICTY receives most of its political, financial, logistical, and intelligence support from the United States and other NATO countries. How might that have influenced the authors of the Report to the Prosecutor?

4. What is the significance of the conclusion that "it is the view of the committee that NATO was attempting to attack objects it perceived to be legitimate military objectives"? Does it matter for purposes of humanitarian law whether NATO's perception was reasonable?

5. Do you agree with the following critique of the Committee's report? As you read it, recall the discussion of *non liquet* in the *Nuclear Weapons* case above. Note also that ultimately the prosecutor's task is to determine whether to bring criminal charges. In making such determinations, the prosecutor must decide how best to use limited resources, and whether, among other things, the evidence will suffice to establish the requisite intent to commit an illegal act.

> The reason why the Committee did not recommend an investigation by the Office of the Prosecutor can be found in the penultimate paragraph of the Report. It says that it is not worth starting an investigation, since "the law is not sufficiently clear or investigations are unlikely to result in the acquisition of sufficient evidence to substantiate charges against high level accused or against lower accused for particularly heinous offences". Hence the Committee has given two reasons. . . .
>
> *The law is not sufficiently clear.*—This is equivalent to a non liquet. Difficulties in interpretation are not a good excuse for not starting an investigation. There are aspects of international humanitarian law, as in any body of law, which are not sufficiently clear. However, it is precisely the task of the Tribunal to interpret and "clarify" the law; it cannot therefore conclude by saying that it cannot adjudicate the case, since the "law is not clear". . . . [O]ne of the main achievements of the Tribunal has been the clarification of controversial rules of humanitarian law, taking into account State practice and developments in this field.
>
> *It is difficult to obtain sufficient evidence to substantiate an indictment.* —Evidence acquisition is undoubtedly a difficult and time-consuming task. Yet this is no excuse for not commencing an investigation. Article 18 of the ICTY Statute gives the Prosecutor the "power to question suspects, victims and witnesses" and to "collect evidence". Article 39 of the Rules of Procedure says that the Prosecutor may "summon and question suspects". He/she can "undertake such other matters as may appear necessary for completing the investigation . . ." and "request such orders as may be necessary from a Trial Chamber or a Judge". . . . [T]he Prosecutor enjoys substantial powers for collecting evidence and . . . the Committee's conclusion is unduly pessimistic.

Natalino Ronzitti, *Is the Non Liquet of the Final Report by the Committee Established to Review the NATO Bombing Campaign Against the Federal Republic of Yugoslavia Acceptable?* Intl. Rev. Red Cross No. 840, at 1017, 1020-1021 (2000).

III. PROTECTING NON-COMBATANTS IN INTERNAL CONFLICTS: THE *TADIC* CASE

Sections I and II of this chapter deal with limitations on the choice of means for injuring the enemy, and with protections afforded non-combatants in international armed conflicts. But the overwhelming majority of armed conflicts in the last

50 years have taken place within the territory of a given state, rather than between states. Moreover, the destructiveness of internal armed conflicts often rivals or exceeds that of international armed conflicts. In recognition of this shift in the frequency and destructiveness of civil wars, states and NGOs, led by the ICRC, have taken steps to expand the legal protections available to non-combatants in internal armed conflicts.

While the relevant treaty instruments distinguish between international and internal armed conflicts, it is often hard to discern in practice whether a particular conflict is truly internal, or whether outside states are so actively involved on one side or another as to render the conflict partially or even wholly international in character. As you read the following materials, consider the reasons for distinguishing between international and internal armed conflicts, the extent and significance of the differences in the legal regimes pertinent to both kinds of conflict, and whether the distinctions that exist make sense.

A. The Problem

The disintegration of the Socialist Federal Republic of Yugoslavia (SFRY) is chronicled in Chapter 3. The process of disintegration wreaked havoc in several of the former Yugoslav republics, but the republic that suffered the most was Bosnia. Prior to the collapse of the SFRY, Bosnia's population was approximately 44 percent Muslim, 33 percent Serb, and 17 percent Croat, with various other nationalities making up the balance.

As Yugoslavia broke apart, Muslims and Croats in Bosnia opposed remaining in a federation that would soon be dominated by Serbia. But Serbs within Bosnia rejected the idea of living as a minority within a Muslim-dominated independent state. In March 1992, Bosnia declared its independence following a referendum supported by most Muslims and some Croats, but opposed by Serbs. Shortly afterwards, Bosnian Serbs declared their own independent Republic of the Serbian People of Bosnia and Herzegovina, later known as the Republika Srpska. War in Bosnia broke out almost immediately thereafter.

During the first several years of the conflict, Bosnian Serbs held the upper hand and took control of large areas of Bosnia. The key factor in the Bosnian Serbs' initial military success was assistance from the national army of Yugoslavia, known as the Yugoslav National Army (the Jugoslovenska Narodna Armija or JNA). By tradition, the JNA was a multi-ethnic army, though its officer corps was dominated by Serbs. Prior to 1991, the JNA focused on defense of the whole of Yugoslavia. But as Yugoslavia disintegrated, the JNA began to withdraw units and equipment from the seceding republics and to shift its mission from the protection of Yugoslavia to the protection of Serbs and Serb territory in Croatia and Bosnia. Slobodan Milosevic and other Serb political and military leaders planned ultimately to create a new, Serb-dominated Yugoslavia consisting not only of Serbia and Montenegro but also of substantial parts of Bosnia and Croatia.

As the JNA gradually transformed into an army organized around a vision of creating a Greater Serbia, international pressure built for the removal of JNA forces from Bosnia. On May 15, 1992, the UN Security Council demanded that the JNA remove its units from Bosnia, submit them to the control of the Bosnian government, or disband. In response, Serbia transferred all Bosnian Serb soldiers in the JNA, wherever they were stationed, to JNA units in Bosnia, and simultaneously transferred non-Serb soldiers to JNA units outside Bosnia. The newly reorganized JNA units in Bosnia became the army of the Republika Srpska (the Vojska Republike Srpska or VRS). This new army retained all the equipment formerly belonging to the JNA in Bosnia and consisted of former JNA officers and enlisted men. Meanwhile, the JNA in Serbia and Montenegro became the army of the Federal Republic of Yugoslavia (consisting of Serbia and Montenegro), and renamed itself the Army of Yugoslavia (Vojska Jugoslavije or VJ). By this means, Serbia was able to appear to comply with international demands for the withdrawal of JNA forces from Bosnia, which it declared accomplished on May 19, 1992. Notwithstanding the reorganization and formal separation of the two armies, however, the VJ, the former national army, retained a major role in the operations of the VRS, the new Bosnian Serb army. Many of the officers of the VRS were former JNA officers who remained in place whether or not they were originally Bosnian Serbs. Moreover, the FRY continued to pay the salaries and pensions of VRS officers and to provide the VRS with military equipment and supplies.

The struggle for control of Bosnia was bitter and protracted. Bosnian Serb forces engaged in extensive ethnic cleansing of areas they captured or controlled, while Bosnian Muslim and Croat forces committed similar crimes but on a smaller scale. During the course of the fighting in early 1992, Bosnian Serb military and paramilitary forces took control of the district of Prijedor and imprisoned thousands of Muslim and Croat civilians in camps at Omarska and elsewhere. Prisoners were beaten, tortured, sexually assaulted, and in many instances killed.

One of the Bosnian Serbs accused of taking part in the attacks against civilians both in and outside of the camps in Prijedor was Dusko Tadic. In February 1994, Tadic was arrested in Germany, where he was living. Tadic was accused of committing torture and aiding in the commission of genocide, both crimes under German law. Shortly thereafter, the ICTY indicted Tadic, alleging numerous violations of international humanitarian law, and requested that Germany defer to the Tribunal's jurisdiction over the accused.

As detailed more fully in Chapter 9, the ICTY is the first international war crimes tribunal since Nuremberg. The UN Security Council established the Tribunal by a 1993 resolution finding the existence of widespread humanitarian law violations in the former Yugoslavia and directing the creation of the Tribunal as a means to contribute to the restoration of peace and stability in the region. The Tribunal was established under the Security Council's Chapter VII powers, which authorize the Council to deal with threats to international peace and security. The Tribunal's Statute provides that the Tribunal's jurisdiction is primary and that other states should defer to Tribunal prosecutions when requested. Accordingly, Germany agreed to transfer Tadic to the Tribunal for trial. As explained below, one of the major issues at trial and on appeal was whether Tadic's crimes took place in the context of an international or an internal armed conflict.

B. Background on Humanitarian Law in Civil Wars

In keeping with the traditional position that international law applies only in the relations between states, the laws of war historically applied only to international armed conflicts. Internal armed conflicts, between the government of a state and indigenous insurgent forces seeking to overthrow that government, or between a metropolitan state and one of its colonies, fell outside the purview of humanitarian law. In keeping with this historical division, the detailed provisions of the Geneva

Conventions of 1949 and Additional Protocol I apply almost exclusively to international armed conflicts. In many cases, however, it is difficult to determine whether a particular armed conflict is or is not international in character. The difficulty arises from the tendency of outside states to assist one side or another in what would otherwise be a purely internal armed conflict. Unless the assistance takes the form of the dispatch of troops or some other open act of war, it may be difficult to determine whether the level of foreign involvement in a conflict is sufficient to render it international for purposes of applying the Conventions or Protocol.

The difference is important. For example, the extensive provisions governing the status and treatment of prisoners of war in the Third Geneva Convention do not apply in internal armed conflicts; the Fourth Geneva Convention's rules on the rights and duties of an occupying power are similarly inapplicable. Instead, only a relatively simple set of basic principles apply in internal armed conflicts by virtue of Article 3 common to all of the 1949 Geneva Conventions. The protections of common Article 3 are supplemented by Additional Protocol II of 1977, but they are still considerably fewer in number and less comprehensive in scope than the protections available in the case of an international conflict. Moreover, as discussed in Chapter 9, neither Common Article 3 nor Additional Protocol II explicitly criminalizes serious violations of their provisions. By contrast, the 1949 Geneva Conventions expressly require prosecution of "grave breaches" of those conventions. Common article 3 provides:

Article 3

In the case of armed conflict not of an international character occurring in the territory of one of the High Contracting Parties, each Party to the conflict shall be bound to apply, as a minimum, the following provisions:

(1) Persons taking no active part in the hostilities, including members of armed forces who have laid down their arms and those placed "hors de combat" by sickness, wounds, detention, or any other cause, shall in all circumstances be treated humanely, without any adverse distinction founded on race, colour, religion or faith, sex, birth or wealth, or any other similar criteria.

To this end, the following acts are and shall remain prohibited at any time and in any place whatsoever with respect to the above-mentioned persons:

   (a)   violence to life and person, in particular murder of all kinds, mutilation, cruel treatment and torture;
   (b)   taking of hostages;
   (c)   outrages upon personal dignity, in particular humiliating and degrading treatment;
   (d)   the passing of sentences and the carrying out of executions without previous judgment pronounced by a regularly constituted court, affording all the judicial guarantees which are recognized as indispensable by civilized peoples.

(2) The wounded and sick shall be collected and cared for.

. . . The Parties to the conflict should further endeavour to bring into force, by means of special agreements, all or part of the other provisions of the present Convention.

> The application of the preceding provisions shall not affect the legal status of the Parties to the conflict.

The ICRC's Commentary on the Geneva Conventions describes the history and impetus behind the drafting of Common Article 3. During discussions on the adoption of the 1949 Geneva Conventions, the Red Cross proposed making all provisions of the Conventions applicable to internal conflicts. A modified set of proposals, known as the Stockholm Proposals, was considered at the 1949 Diplomatic Conference of States, convened by the ICRC. The Commentary describes governmental reactions to these proposals:

> From the very outset, in the course of the first discussions of a general character, divergences of view became apparent. A considerable number of delegations were opposed . . . to the unqualified application of the Convention to [internal] conflicts. The principal criticisms of the Stockholm draft may be summed up as follows. It was said that it would cover in advance all forms of insurrection, rebellion, anarchy, and the break-up of States, and even plain brigandage. Attempts to protect individuals might well prove to be at the expense of the equally legitimate protection of the State. To compel the Government of a State in the throes of internal conflict to apply to such a conflict the whole of the provisions of a Convention expressly concluded to cover the case of war would mean giving its enemies, who might be no more than a handful of rebels or common brigands, the status of belligerents, and possibly even a certain degree of legal recognition. There was also a risk of common or ordinary criminals being encouraged to give themselves a semblance of organization as a pretext for claiming the benefit of the Conventions, representing their crimes as "acts of war" in order to escape punishment for them. A party of rebels, however small, would be entitled under the Conventions to ask for the assistance and intervention of a Protecting Power. Moreover, it was asked, would not the *de jure* Government be compelled to release the captured rebels as soon as the troubles were over, since the application of the Convention would place them on the same footing as prisoners of war? Any such proposals giving insurgents a legal status, and consequently increased authority, would hamper and handicap the Government in its measures of legitimate repression.
>
> The advocates of the Stockholm draft, on the other hand, regarded the proposed text as an act of courage. Insurgents, said some, are not all brigands. It sometimes happens in a civil war that those who are regarded as rebels are in actual fact patriots struggling for the independence and the dignity of their country. Others argued that the behaviour of the insurgents in the field would show whether they were in fact mere brigands or, on the contrary, genuine soldiers deserving of the benefit of the Conventions. . . . It was not possible to talk of "terrorism", "anarchy" or "disorders" in the case of rebels who complied with humanitarian principles. Finally, the adoption of the Stockholm proposals would not in any way prevent a *de jure* Government from taking measures under its own laws for the repression of acts judged by it to be dangerous to the order and security of the State. . . .
>
> Faced with almost universal opposition to the application of the Convention, with all its provisions, to all cases of non-international conflict, the Committee had until then tried to solve the problem by limiting the number of cases in which the Convention was to be applicable. The French proposal now sought a solution in a new direction, namely in the limitation of the provisions applicable.

Commentary, I Geneva Convention for the Amelioration of the Condition of the Wounded and Sick in Armed Forces in the Field 43-46 (Jean Pictet ed., 1952).

The approach suggested by the French—limiting the number of Convention provisions applicable to internal conflicts—ultimately led to the adoption of

Common Article 3. Although its provisions are relatively basic, Common Article 3 has been described as a "convention in miniature" because it establishes the minimum obligations of parties to a non-international armed conflict without requiring application of the whole body of Geneva law. Over time, states accepted the provisions of Common Article 3 as customary international law. In that form, it is reflected in the Statute of the ICTY, as described below.

C. Applying International Humanitarian Law in the Tadic Case

The ICTY's prosecution of Tadic raised a number of important issues concerning the application of international humanitarian and criminal law. Two of those issues are considered here: what humanitarian law norms apply in internal conflicts, and how may such conflicts be distinguished from international armed conflicts when outside actors assist one or more parties to the conflict?

The Statute of the ICTY empowers it to prosecute genocide, crimes against humanity, grave breaches of the Geneva Conventions, and violations of the laws and customs of war. The latter two categories of crimes are specified, respectively, in Articles 2 and 3 of the Tribunal's Statute.

Both of these two categories of war crimes require proof of the existence of an armed conflict, but according to the trial chamber of the ICTY, Article 2 applies only to international armed conflicts, while Article 3 applies to internal conflicts as well:

> 559. Each of the relevant Articles of the Statute, either by its terms or by virtue of the customary rules which it imports, proscribes certain acts when committed "within the context of" an "armed conflict". Article 2 of the Statute directs the Trial Chamber to the grave breaches regime of the Geneva Conventions which applies only to armed conflicts of an international character and to offences committed against persons or property regarded as "protected", in particular civilians in the hands of a party to a conflict of which they are not nationals. Article 3 of the Statute directs the Trial Chamber to those sources of customary international humanitarian law that comprise the "laws or customs of war". Article 3 is a general provision covering, subject to certain conditions, all violations of international humanitarian law which do not fall under Article 2 or are not covered by Articles 4 [genocide] or 5 [crimes against humanity]. This includes violations of the rules contained in Article 3 common to the Geneva Conventions ("Common Article 3"), applicable to armed conflicts in general, with which the accused has been charged under Article 3 of the Statute.

Prosecutor v. Tadic, Judgment, Case No. IT-94-1-T (1997).

Tadic challenged the jurisdiction and competence of the Tribunal to try him, arguing (among other things) that the conflict in Yugoslavia was internal rather than international in nature and that violations of human dignity in such conflicts could not constitute either grave breaches of the Geneva Conventions under Article 2 of the Tribunal's statute or violations of the laws and customs of war entailing individual criminal responsibility under Article 3. To charge him with such crimes violated the principle of *nullum crimen sine lege*, which prohibits prosecution for an act not criminal when committed. The Appeals Chamber found that parts of the Yugoslavia conflict were international in character and parts domestic and left it to the trial chambers to make these determinations in each case based on the time and place of the alleged acts. It accepted Tadic's argument that, if the conflict were internal at the time and place of his acts, he could not be charged with grave breaches of the Geneva Conventions. The following is the Appeals Chamber's view as to whether he could be charged with violations of the laws and customs of war for atrocities in an internal conflict:

Prosecutor v. Tadic, Jurisdiction Appeal

Case No. IT-94-1-AR72 (1995)

(iii) CUSTOMARY RULES OF INTERNATIONAL HUMANITARIAN LAW GOVERNING INTERNAL ARMED CONFLICTS

a. General

96. . . . [Traditional] international law treated the two classes of conflict in a markedly different way: interstate wars were regulated by a whole body of international legal rules, governing both the conduct of hostilities and the protection of persons not participating . . . in armed violence (civilians, the wounded, the sick, shipwrecked, prisoners of war). By contrast, there were very few international rules governing civil commotion, for States preferred to regard internal strife as rebellion, mutiny and treason coming within the purview of national criminal law and, by the same token, to exclude any possible intrusion by other States into their own domestic jurisdiction. . . .

97. Since the 1930s, however, the aforementioned distinction has gradually become more and more blurred, and international legal rules have increasingly emerged or have been agreed upon to regulate internal armed conflict. There exist various reasons for this development. First, civil wars have become more frequent, not only because technological progress has made it easier for groups of individuals to have access to weaponry but also on account of increasing tension, whether ideological, inter-ethnic or economic. . . . Secondly, internal armed conflicts have become more and more cruel and protracted, involving the whole population of the State where they occur: the all-out resort to armed violence has taken on such a magnitude that the difference with international wars has increasingly dwindled. . . . Thirdly, the large-scale nature of civil strife, coupled with the increasing interdependence of States in the world community, has made it more and more difficult for third States to remain aloof: the economic, political and ideological interests of third States have brought about direct or indirect involvement of third States in this category of conflict. . . . Fourthly, the impetuous development and propagation in the international community of human rights doctrines, particularly after the adoption of the Universal Declaration of Human Rights in 1948, has brought about significant changes in international law. . . . A State-sovereignty-oriented approach has been gradually supplanted by a human-being-oriented approach. Gradually the maxim of Roman law *hominum causa omne jus constitutum est* (all law is created for the benefit of human beings) has gained a firm foothold in the international community as well. It follows that in the area of armed conflict the distinction between interstate wars and civil wars is losing its value as far as human beings are concerned. . . .

98. The emergence of international rules governing internal strife has occurred at two different levels: at the level of customary law and at that of treaty law. Two bodies of rules have thus crystallised, which are by no means conflicting or inconsistent, but instead mutually support and supplement each other. . . . [S]ome treaty rules have

gradually become part of customary law. This holds true for common Article 3 of the 1949 Geneva Conventions. . . .

99. Before pointing to some principles and rules of customary law that have emerged in the international community for the purpose of regulating civil strife, a word of caution on the law-making process in the law of armed conflict is necessary. When attempting to ascertain State practice with a view to establishing the existence of a customary rule or a general principle, it is difficult, if not impossible, to pinpoint the actual behaviour of the troops in the field for the purpose of establishing whether they in fact comply with, or disregard, certain standards of behaviour. This examination is rendered extremely difficult by the fact that not only is access to the theatre of military operations normally refused to independent observers (often even to the ICRC) but information on the actual conduct of hostilities is withheld by the parties to the conflict; what is worse, often recourse is had to misinformation with a view to misleading the enemy as well as public opinion and foreign Governments. In appraising the formation of customary rules or general principles one should therefore be aware that, on account of the inherent nature of this subject-matter, reliance must primarily be placed on such elements as official pronouncements of States, military manuals and judicial decisions.

b. Principal Rules

[The tribunal engaged in an exhaustive historical review of rules of warfare in internal conflicts, from the Spanish Civil War in the 1930s through the Yugoslavia conflict, examining domestic legislation, military manuals, statements of governments, and resolutions of international organizations. The tribunal noted that many principles applicable to international armed conflicts have been extended to internal conflicts, covering both the protection of civilians and the means and methods of warfare. For example, the tribunal cited as declaratory of customary law a 1970 General Assembly Resolution specifying the following principles as applicable to all armed conflicts:

1. Fundamental human rights . . . continue to apply fully in situations of armed conflict.
2. [A] distinction must be made at all times between persons actively taking part in the hostilities and civilian populations.
3. [E]very effort should be made to spare civilian populations from the ravages of war, and all necessary precautions should be taken to avoid injury, loss or damage to civilian populations.
4. Civilian populations as such should not be the object of military operations.
5. Dwellings and other installations that are used only by civilian populations should not be the object of military operations.
6. Places or areas designated for the sole protection of civilians, such as hospital zones or similar refuges, should not be the object of military operations.
7. Civilian populations, or individual members thereof, should not be the object of reprisals, forcible transfers or other assaults on their integrity.

The tribunal also observed that "elementary considerations of humanity and common sense make it preposterous that the use by States of weapons prohibited in armed conflicts between themselves be allowed when States try to put down rebellion by their own nationals on their own territory. What is inhumane, and consequently proscribed, in international wars, cannot but be inhumane and inadmissible in civil strife." The tribunal concluded:]

[I]t cannot be denied that customary rules have developed to govern internal strife. These rules . . . cover such areas as protection of civilians from hostilities, in particular from indiscriminate attacks, protection of civilian objects, in particular cultural property, protection of all those who do not (or no longer) take active part in hostilities, as well as prohibition of means of warfare proscribed in international armed conflicts and ban of certain methods of conducting hostilities.

The Court went on to conclude that under customary international law, the crimes of which Tadic was accused "entail individual criminal responsibility, regardless of whether they are committed in internal or international armed conflicts." This aspect of the Court's decision is discussed more fully in Chapter 9.

Following this decision, the trial chamber determined that there was an armed conflict between Bosnian Serb and government forces in Prijedor and elsewhere at the time of the acts of the accused, and that there was an adequate nexus between those acts and the armed conflict.

The trial chamber also found that until May 19, 1992, an international armed conflict existed in the relevant part of Bosnia. The issue then was whether the conflict continued to be international in character after that date, the day on which the JNA formally withdrew from Bosnia.

The trial chamber concluded that to impute responsibility to the FRY sufficient to treat the conflict as international following the formal withdrawal of the JNA, the prosecutor would have to show that the FRY exercised effective control over the acts of the Bosnian Serb forces. In the view of the trial chamber, the evidence established that "the JNA played a role of vital importance in the establishment, equipping, supplying, maintenance and staffing" of the VRS, but that it did not exercise effective control over it. Accordingly, the trial chamber held that "each of the victims of the acts ascribed to the accused . . . enjoy the protection of the prohibitions contained in Common Article 3, applicable as it is to all armed conflicts, rather than the protection of the more specific grave breaches regime applicable" in international armed conflicts. It thus acquitted him of the charges under Article 2 of the Statute. The trial chamber went on to convict Tadic of numerous violations of Article 3 of the Statute, though it also acquitted him on some counts under that article.

Notes and Questions

1. Why do states enter into treaties governing armed conflict, and why are the treaty provisions for international armed conflicts so much more extensive than those for internal armed conflicts? In the following excerpt, Professor Kenneth Abbott considers one possible explanation put forward by political scientist James Morrow:

> In this view, humanitarian law reflects a welfare-enhancing equilibrium: states obligate themselves to behave in specified ways, e.g., to protect prisoners of war, so that others will make the same commitments. The formality and legal character of the Geneva Conventions allow states unambiguously to signal their intentions and engage their reputations, making commitments more credible in a fundamentally anarchic setting. States revise the Conventions after major wars—and before new conflicts skew negotiating positions—to incorporate recent experience. The precision of the

Conventions creates common conjectures that limit mistakes and misperceptions. The Red Cross monitors compliance—forestalling both violations and erroneous retaliation—while aiding victims. For all this, Morrow views the Conventions as having little independent effect on behavior; they merely coordinate relations among states with preexisting cooperative interests. . . .

States comply with humanitarian law primarily because of expectations of reciprocity, though other considerations, including concern for their international reputation and domestic political support, also come into play. Even if national policy supports compliance, however, individual soldiers can violate the rules. Here it is dangerous to rely on reciprocity, which can easily get out of hand. Hence, the Conventions require parties to educate and supervise their own soldiers; that commitment is maintained by reciprocity. The "grave breaches" regime is a useful supplement. It applies mainly to high-level violators, who are unlikely to discipline themselves but highly likely to flee. The threat of prosecuting such individuals helps deter serious violations.

[After noting some empirical data in support of this account, Abbott continues:]

Symmetry and reciprocity help illuminate the legal distinction between international armed conflicts and other violent situations. In international conflicts, states can anticipate reasonable symmetry between opposing forces, facilitating tit-for-tat enforcement. Here the regime is strongest: the Geneva Conventions, Protocol I and their grave breaches regimes all apply. In internal conflicts, symmetry is less likely. Since insurrectionist groups cannot ratify the Conventions, they cannot clearly signal their intentions or formally engage their reputations. Such groups often operate anonymously, hampering verification and reciprocity. They may be unable to control their own fighters, creating noise. They may favor "dirty" tactics to counter superior forces. In these situations, states have been less willing to restrict their own operations, agreeing only to common Article 3 and Protocol II, with no grave breaches regime. (Apart from symmetry, governments may perceive internal conflicts as direct threats to survival, requiring maximum flexibility of response.) Finally, civil disturbances and terrorist actions are even more asymmetrical, and thus are not considered "armed conflicts" at all; even common Article 3 and Protocol II do not apply. Indeed, with low-level violence increasing worldwide, Protocol II actually narrowed the definition of "armed conflict" to situations involving organized dissident forces under "responsible command," where the logic of reciprocity can operate.

Kenneth Abbott, *International Relations Theory, International Law, and the Regime Governing Atrocities in Internal Conflicts*, 93 Am. J. Intl. L. 361, 369-370 (1999).

2. What is the current significance of the distinction between the two types of conflict? As noted in Chapter 9, the Statue of the International Criminal Court contains two different lists of acts constituting war crimes, one list for acts committed in international armed conflicts and another for acts committed in internal armed conflicts. Thus, employing certain weapons against combatants—for example, poisoned weapons or bullets that expand in the body—is prohibited only in international armed conflicts. Do such distinctions make sense? Are there good reasons for continuing to apply different rules to internal and international armed conflicts?

3. As the *Tadic* case makes clear, determining the existence and content of a customary international humanitarian law rule is often difficult. However, in 2004, the International Committee of the Red Cross released a 5,000-page study of the subject, identifying 161 rules of customary international law applicable to armed conflict. The study "focused on issues regulated by treaties that have not been universally ratified, in particular the Additional Protocols [to the Geneva

Conventions], the Hague Convention for the Protection of Cultural Property and a number of specific conventions regulating the use of weapons." According to the study, in international armed conflicts, "[e]xamples of rules found to be customary and which have corresponding provisions in Additional Protocol I include: the principle of distinction between civilians and combatants and between civilian objects and military objectives; the prohibition of indiscriminate attacks; the principle of proportionality in attack; [and] the obligation to take feasible precautions in attack and against the effects of attack." In non-international armed conflicts, "[e]xamples of rules found to be customary and which have corresponding provisions in Additional Protocol II include: the prohibition of attacks on civilians; . . . the prohibition of starvation; the prohibition of attacks on objects indispensable to the survival of the civilian population; [and] the obligation to respect the fundamental guarantees of civilians and persons hors de combat," among others.

To prepare the study, the ICRC engaged teams of experts to review state practice in nearly 50 countries over the last 30 years. The countries studied were selected to ensure geographic diversity and to cover different types of conflicts. According to its authors, the study "drew also on the military manuals, national legislation, national case-law and official statements of additional States not yet covered by an individual expert," as well as international sources and the ICRC archives.

The study has proven controversial in some circles. One expert has criticized the study for accepting the views and practice of small states that rarely fight wars as equivalent in importance to large states that do periodically engage in armed conflict. Some critics have suggested that the study sometimes reaches conclusions with little state practice to support them, and that it represents an effort to shape rather than simply reflect existing law. Others are more positive. Consider the following assessment of the difficulties inherent in the ICRC project:

> [C]ustomary IHL tends to develop during wartime, but wars are (relatively) infrequent, and the development is therefore non-continuous. In order to circumvent this difficulty, *usus* [state practice] was not defined for the purposes of the Study as "age-old" state practice but as practice during the last twenty years, with the caveat that sufficiently dense practice can accumulate over an even shorter period of time. In situations where relevant practice is sparse or ambiguous, *opinio juris* plays an important role, but it too proves elusive because States rarely provide reasons for what they do or do not do. The Study's editors were evidently tempted to adopt a teleological approach that international courts and tribunals have occasionally shown, namely that a rule of customary international law exists "when that rule is a desirable one for international peace and security or for the protection of the human person, provided that there is no important contrary *opinio juris*." Despite the attractiveness of this approach, the editors concluded that sufficient consistent support in the international community (including from so-called specially affected States) remains necessary to establish a customary international rule.
>
> In addition, the standards prescribed by IHL are, as noted, frequently disregarded. *Prima facie*, violations undermine the required uniformity of the practice concerned. The editors took the view that the contrary practice does not prevent the formation of a rule as long as this practice is condemned by other States or is denied by the perpetrator itself as not representing its *official* practice. Indeed, "[t]hrough such condemnation or denial, the original rule is actually confirmed." . . .
>
> Lastly, attempting to identify customary international law in areas like IHL that are heavily regulated by treaty can bring certain risks as well as the benefits outlined. For example, States that are not party to the treaties concerned may view the attempt to identify customary rules as an attempt to get around the express consent that is

required for them to be bound by the related treaty articles. These States will likely object to the application to them of any of the rules that are identified. Undertakings like the Study also run the risk of *in*creasing not *de*creasing legal uncertainty in the interpretation and application of the relevant standards. In IHL and other areas of international law where customary law is complex and imprecise, there is a natural tendency to rely on the wording of the treaty articles in the formulation of the customary rules. If the wording of the article and rule in question diverge for no apparent reason, the normative content of the standard will be brought into doubt, and legal protection may be undermined.

Malcolm MacLaren & Felix Schwendimann, *An Exercise in the Development of International Law: The New ICRC Study on Customary International Humanitarian Law*, 6 German Law Journal No. 9 (2005).

What use will likely be made of the ICRC study? Which states might be likely to be critical of the project?

————————————

Under the statute of the tribunal, both the prosecution and the defendant are entitled to appeal adverse rulings. Accordingly, the prosecution appealed the trial chamber's decision to dismiss all counts brought under Article 2 of the tribunal's statute (grave breaches). Excerpts of the Appeals Chamber's decision follow.

Prosecutor v. Tadic, Judgment

Case No. IT-94-1-A (1999)

83. The requirement that the conflict be international for the grave breaches regime to operate pursuant to Article 2 of the Statute has not been contested by the parties.

84. It is indisputable that an armed conflict is international if it takes place between two or more States. In addition, in case of an internal armed conflict breaking out on the territory of a State, it may become international (or, depending upon the circumstances, be international in character alongside an internal armed conflict) if (i) another State intervenes in that conflict through its troops, or alternatively if (ii) some of the participants in the internal armed conflict act on behalf of that other State.

85. In the instant case, the Prosecution claims that at all relevant times, the conflict was an international armed conflict between two States, namely Bosnia and Herzegovina ("BH") on the one hand, and the FRY on the other. Judge McDonald, in her dissent, also found the conflict to be international at all relevant times. . . .

91. . . . . [T]he Appeals Chamber will consider the conditions under which armed forces fighting against the central authorities *of the same State* in which they live and operate may be deemed to act on behalf of another State. In other words, the Appeals Chamber will identify the conditions under which those forces may be assimilated to organs of a State other than that on whose territory they live and operate.

92. A starting point for this discussion is provided by the criteria for lawful combatants laid down in the Third Geneva Convention of 1949. Under this Convention, militias or paramilitary groups or units may be regarded as

legitimate combatants if they form "part of [the] armed forces" of a Party to the conflict (Article 4A(1)) or "belong [. . .]" to a "Party to the conflict". . . . It is clear that this provision is primarily directed toward establishing the requirements for the status of lawful combatants. Nevertheless, one of its logical consequences is that if, in an armed conflict, paramilitary units "belong" to a State other than the one against which they are fighting, the conflict is international and therefore serious violations of the Geneva Conventions may be classified as "grave breaches".

93. The content of the requirement of "belonging to a Party to the conflict" is far from clear or precise. . . . The rationale behind Article 4 was that, in the wake of World War II, it was universally agreed that States should be legally responsible for the conduct of irregular forces they sponsor. . . .

94. In other words, States have in practice accepted that belligerents may use paramilitary units and other irregulars in the conduct of hostilities only on the condition that those belligerents are prepared to take responsibility for any infringements committed by such forces. In order for irregulars to qualify as lawful combatants, it appears that international rules and State practice therefore require control over them by a Party to an international armed conflict and, by the same token, a relationship of dependence and allegiance of these irregulars *vis-à-vis* that Party to the conflict. These then may be regarded as the ingredients of the term "belonging to a Party to the conflict".

95. The Appeals Chamber thus considers that the Third Geneva Convention, by providing in Article 4 the requirement of "belonging to a Party to the conflict," implicitly refers to a test of control. . . .

97. It is nevertheless imperative to *specify* what *degree of authority or control* must be wielded by a foreign State over armed forces fighting on its behalf in order to render international an armed conflict which is *prima facie* internal. Indeed, the legal consequences of the characterisation of the conflict as either internal or international are extremely important. Should the conflict eventually be classified as international, it would *inter alia* follow that a foreign State may in certain circumstances be held responsible for violations of international law perpetrated by the armed groups acting on its behalf.

(b) The Notion of Control: The Need for International Humanitarian Law to be Supplemented by General International Rules Concerning the Criteria for Considering Individuals to be Acting as De Facto State Organs

98. International humanitarian law does not contain any criteria unique to this body of law for establishing when a group of individuals may be regarded as being under the control of a State, that is, as acting as *de facto* State officials. Consequently, it is necessary to examine the notion of control by a State over individuals, laid down in general international law. . . .

(c) The Notion of Control Set Out By the International Court of Justice in *Nicaragua*

99. In dealing with the question of the legal conditions required for individuals to be considered as acting on behalf of a State, i.e., as *de facto* State officials, a high degree of control has been authoritatively suggested by the International Court of Justice in *Nicaragua*.

100. . . . The Court went so far as to state that in order to establish that the United States was responsible for "acts contrary to human rights and humanitarian law" allegedly perpetrated by the Nicaraguan contras, it was necessary to prove that the United States had specifically "directed or enforced" the perpetration of those acts.

[The Appeals Chamber concluded that the effective control test enunciated in the *Nicaragua* case and adopted by the Trial Chamber was not "persuasive." According to the Appeals Chamber, the logic of the law of state responsibility demanded a more flexible test aimed "at ensuring that States entrusting some functions to individuals or groups of individuals must answer for their actions." Moreover, the Appeals Chamber found that judicial and state practice "envisaged State responsibility in circumstances where a lower degree of control than that demanded by the Nicaragua test was exercised." The Appeals Chamber concluded that state practice "has upheld the Nicaragua test with regard to individuals or unorganised groups of individuals acting on behalf of States," but that it "has applied a different test with regard to military or paramilitary groups." After reviewing relevant cases, the Appeals Chamber continued:]

137. . . . [C]ontrol by a State over subordinate *armed forces* or *militias* or *paramilitary units* may be of an overall character (and must comprise more than the mere provision of financial assistance or military equipment or training). . . . The control required by international law may be deemed to exist when a State (or, in the context of an armed conflict, the Party to the conflict) *has a role in organising, coordinating or planning the military actions* of the military group, in addition to financing, training and equipping or providing operational support to that group. . . .

138. Of course, if, as in *Nicaragua*, the controlling State is *not the territorial State* where the armed clashes occur or where at any rate the armed units perform their acts, more extensive and compelling evidence is required to show that the State is genuinely in control of the units or groups not merely by financing and equipping them, but also by generally directing or helping plan their actions.

139. The same substantial evidence is required when, although the State in question is the territorial State where armed clashes occur, the general situation is one of turmoil, civil strife and weakened State authority.

140. Where the controlling State in question is an adjacent State with territorial ambitions on the State where the conflict is taking place, and the controlling State is attempting to achieve its territorial enlargement through the armed forces which it controls, it may be easier to establish the threshold.

The Court then found that even after the formal withdrawal of the JNA, the VJ "continued to control the Bosnian Serb Army" through the continuance in command of JNA officers who were not Bosnian Serbs, and the FRY's continuing payment of salaries for both the men and the officers of the VRS. According to the Appeals Chamber, the VRS and VJ did not in any real sense constitute two separate armies, their formal separation being in reality a device to conceal the FRY's continuing involvement in the conflict in pursuit of its own objectives. Accordingly, the Court concluded that "the relationship between the VJ and VRS cannot be characterised as one of merely coordinating political and military activities," as the trial chamber had concluded. Rather, "the renamed Bosnian Serb army still comprised one army under the command of the General Staff of the VJ in Belgrade." As a result, the conflict was international in character, and the "grave breaches" regime incorporated into Article 2 of the Tribunal's Statute could be applied.

Notes and Questions

1. Do you agree with the Appeals Chamber's test for determining whether a state exercises sufficient control over the acts of an armed group in another state to render the conflict international? Is the higher standard articulated by the ICJ in *Nicaragua v. United States* preferable? Under the reasoning of the Appeals Chamber, should the FRY be held responsible for some or all of the violations of international humanitarian law committed by Bosnian Serb forces?

2. What can be done to render the legal regulation of armed conflict more effective? Does it make sense to focus on the preparation of further legal instruments for ratification by states? Consider the following statement by UN Secretary-General Kofi Annan in his Millenium Report to the General Assembly:

> International conventions have traditionally looked at states to protect civilians, but today this expectation is threatened in several ways. First, states are sometimes the principal perpetrator of violence against the very citizens that humanitarian law requires them to protect. Second, non-state combatants, particularly in collapsed states, are often ignorant or contemptuous of humanitarian law. Third, international conventions do not adequately address the specific needs of vulnerable groups, such as internally displaced persons, or women and children in complex emergencies.

IV. OCCUPYING FOREIGN TERRITORY: ISRAEL'S WALL IN THE WEST BANK

The law of occupation is one of the most developed branches of international humanitarian law. International armed conflicts have declined in number since World War II, and instances of territorial conquest are now rare; as a result, states do not often seek to administer enemy territory. Nonetheless, the law of occupation remains an important part of international humanitarian law. It governs, for example, Israel's long-running control over territories seized in its 1967 war with neighboring states, Turkish control over northern Cyprus, Uganda's control of territory in the Democratic Republic of Congo in 1998-99, Ethiopian and Eritrean control over parts of each other's territory in 1998-2000, and the recent U.S. and British occupation of Iraq.

As you read the following materials, consider whether the law strikes the right balance between the security interests of the occupier and the rights of the population living in occupied territory, and the extent to which the law does or should permit an occupier to transform the economic, political, and legal rules and institutions of the occupied territory.

A. The Problem

Following World War II, the League of Nations allocated to particular member states certain territories of the Ottoman empire to govern under the League's mandate system. Palestine, which then consisted of territories that now constitute Israel, Jordan, the West Bank, and the Gaza Strip, became a British mandate. In 1947, the UN General Assembly proposed to partition Palestine into two separate states, one Jewish and the other Arab, with Jerusalem subject to a special international regime. Arab states and the Arab population of Palestine opposed the plan. On May 14, 1948, the day before Britain's scheduled withdrawal from the territory, Israel declared its independence on the basis of the General Assembly's partition resolution. The state of Israel was quickly recognized by the United States, the Soviet Union, and other states; however, a number of Arab states promptly invaded Israel, hoping to create a united state of Palestine.

In 1949, the United Nations brokered an armistice between Israel and its neighbors. The demarcation line between Israeli and Arab forces came to be known as the "Green Line" for the color used to indicate it on maps. The parties accepted the Green Line as a boundary, but without prejudice to future territorial settlements. Jordan, which had occupied East Jerusalem and the West Bank (part of the Palestine mandate territory lying to the west and southwest of the Jordan river) during the fighting, retained control of those territories, and formally annexed them in 1950.

In 1967, during the Six-Day War, Israel occupied the West Bank and the Gaza Strip, as well as the Sinai and the Golan Heights. In November 1967, the Security Council, in resolution 242, emphasized "the inadmissibility of the acquisition of territory by war," called upon Israel to withdraw "from territories occupied in the recent conflict," and called for "respect for and acknowledgment of the sovereignty, territorial integrity and political independence of every State in the area and their right to live in peace within secure and recognized boundaries free from threats or acts of force."

The territories in the West Bank and Gaza captured by Israel in 1967 are commonly referred to in UN discourse as the "occupied territories." They have generally been subject to Israeli military government. Moreover, Israel has built a large number of settlements in the occupied territories since 1967, prompting periodic condemnations by the General Assembly and individual states. At the same time, Palestinians, including (during the last decade) suicide bombers, have for many years periodically attacked Israel from the occupied territories.

In 1988, Jordan relinquished its claims to the West Bank. In 1994, Israel concluded a peace treaty, including a boundary agreement, with Jordan, but without prejudice to the status of the occupied territories. Beginning in 1993, Israel also entered into a series of agreements with the Palestine Liberation Organization concerning the administration of the occupied territories, and in August 2005, Israel evacuated its settlements in the Gaza Strip, turning control over to the Palestinian National Authority.

Israel has retained and in some places expanded its settlements elsewhere in the occupied territories. In June 2002, Israel began construction of a barrier expected to run over 400 miles through much of the West Bank. (A map of the barrier appears on page 592.) The barrier is intended to separate Israel proper, and many of the Israeli settlements in the West Bank, from most of the rest of the West Bank. Parts of the barrier run along the 1949 armistice line, but parts extend well into the West Bank. Israel contends that the barrier is a lawful response to Palestinian terrorism; Palestinians argue that it amounts to an unlawful confiscation of Palestinian land.

B. Background on the Law of Occupation

The law of occupation has been codified principally in the Hague Regulations of 1907, the Fourth Geneva Convention of 1949, and the 1977 Additional Protocol I to the Geneva Conventions. Customary international law is also well developed in this area. Some of the relevant treaties are excerpted below.

Hague Convention (IV) Respecting the Laws and Customs of War on Land and Its Annex: Regulations Concerning the Laws and Customs of War on Land

36 Stat. 2277 (1907)

Art. 42. Territory is considered occupied when it is actually placed under the authority of the hostile army.

The occupation extends only to the territory where such authority has been established and can be exercised.

Art. 43. The authority of the legitimate power having in fact passed into the hands of the occupant, the latter shall take all the measures in his power to restore, and ensure, as far as possible, public order and safety, while respecting, unless absolutely prevented, the laws in force in the country.

Art. 46. Family honour and rights, the lives of persons, and private property, as well as religious convictions and practice, must be respected.

Private property cannot be confiscated.

Art. 52. Requisitions in kind and services shall not be demanded from municipalities or inhabitants except for the needs of the army of occupation. They shall be in proportion to the resources of the country, and of such a nature as not to involve the inhabitants in the obligation of taking part in military operations against their own country.

Such requisitions and services shall only be demanded on the authority of the commander in the locality occupied.

Contributions in kind shall as far is possible be paid for in cash; if not, a receipt shall be given and the payment of the amount due shall be made as soon as possible.

Geneva Convention (IV) Relative to the Protection of Civilian Persons in Time of War

75 U.N.T.S. 287 (1949)

Art. 47. Protected persons who are in occupied territory shall not be deprived, in any case or in any manner whatsoever, of the benefits of the present Convention by any change introduced, as the result of the occupation of a territory, into the institutions or government of the said territory, nor by any agreement concluded between the authorities of the occupied territories and the Occupying Power, nor by any annexation by the latter of the whole or part of the occupied territory.

Art. 49. Individual or mass forcible transfers, as well as deportations of protected persons from occupied territory to the territory of the Occupying Power or to that of any other country, occupied or not, are prohibited, regardless of their motive.

Nevertheless, the Occupying Power may undertake total or partial evacuation of a given area if the security of the population or imperative military reasons so demand. Such evacuations may not involve the displacement of protected persons outside the bounds of the occupied territory except when for material reasons it is impossible to avoid such displacement. Persons thus evacuated shall be transferred back to their homes as soon as hostilities in the area in question have ceased. . . .

The Occupying Power shall not deport or transfer parts of its own civilian population into the territory it occupies.

Art. 53. Any destruction by the Occupying Power of real or personal property belonging individually or collectively to private persons, or to the State, or to other public authorities, or to social or cooperative organizations, is prohibited, except where such destruction is rendered absolutely necessary by military operations.

Art. 64. The penal laws of the occupied territory shall remain in force, with the exception that they may be repealed or suspended by the Occupying Power in cases where they constitute a threat to its security or an obstacle to the application of the present Convention.

Subject to the latter consideration and to the necessity for ensuring the effective administration of justice, the tribunals of the occupied territory shall continue to function in respect of all offences covered by the said laws.

The Occupying Power may, however, subject the population of the occupied territory to provisions which are essential to enable the Occupying Power to fulfil its obligations under the present Convention, to maintain the orderly government of the territory, and to ensure the security of the Occupying Power, of the members and property of the occupying forces or administration, and likewise of the establishments and lines of communication used by them.

Art. 78. If the Occupying Power considers it necessary, for imperative reasons of security, to take safety measures concerning protected persons, it may, at the most, subject them to assigned residence or to internment. . . .

Occupying powers in recent years have been reluctant to acknowledge the existence of a state of occupation, for a variety of reasons, including a reluctance to accept formally the extensive duties and restrictions the law imposes. Indeed, throughout most of the twentieth century, occupying powers denied that they exercised the requisite control over the occupied territory, claimed title to it, or denied that title rested with the prior sovereign.

A state's occupation of enemy territory does not effect a transfer of sovereignty, but does displace the authority of the indigenous government. As a result, the occupying forces must strike a difficult balance. They are expected to administer the occupied territory in lieu of national authorities, while still allowing life to continue in the occupied territory in a fashion as close to normal as feasible. Thus, the occupier must provide or at least allow for provision of the kinds of services ordinarily to be expected from a government, and may be required "to the fullest extent of the means available to it" to ensure that the local population has adequate food, medical supplies, clothing, shelter, and essential public services.

C. *The ICJ and the Israeli High Court Look at the Law of Occupation*

In October 2003, the UN General Assembly demanded that "Israel stop and reverse the construction of the wall in the Occupied Palestinian territory." On December 8, 2003, at the request of a group of Arab states, the General Assembly condemned Israeli settlements in the territories as a threat to peace and a violation of international law, and requested the ICJ to issue an advisory opinion on the following question:

> What are the legal consequences arising from the construction of the wall being built by Israel, the occupying Power, in the Occupied Palestinian Territory, including in and around East Jerusalem . . . considering the rules and principles of international law, including the Fourth Geneva Convention of 1949, and relevant Security Council and General Assembly resolutions?

The vote to request the advisory opinion was 90-8, with 74 abstentions. Australia, Ethiopia, the Federated States of Micronesia, Israel, the Marshall Islands, Nauru, Palau, and the United States voted against the resolution.

On December 19, 2003, the Court decided that Palestine could participate in the written and oral proceedings, noting that "the General Assembly has granted Palestine a special status of observer and that the latter is co-sponsor of the draft resolution requesting the advisory opinion." The Court eventually received 49 written statements, including statements from Israel, the Arab League, the Organization of the Islamic Conference, Palestine, and the United States. The submissions from Israel and the United States addressed only the jurisdictional issues raised by the request.

The Court issued its opinion finding the construction of the separation barrier illegal on July 9. On most issues, Judge Thomas Buergenthal, a U.S. national, was the sole dissenter.

Legal Consequences of the Construction of a Wall in the Occupied Palestinian Territory

2004 I.C.J. 131 (July 9)

67. [T]he "wall" in question is a complex construction, so that that term cannot be understood in a limited physical sense. However, the other terms used, either by Israel ("fence") or by the Secretary General ("barrier"), are no more accurate if understood in the physical sense. In this Opinion, the Court has therefore chosen to use the terminology employed by the General Assembly.

101. [T]he Court considers that the Fourth Geneva Convention is applicable in any occupied territory in the event of an armed conflict arising between two or more High Contracting Parties. Israel and Jordan were parties to that Convention when the 1967 armed conflict broke out. The Court accordingly finds that that Convention is applicable in the Palestinian territories which before the conflict lay to the east of the Green Line and which, during that conflict, were occupied by Israel, there being no need for any enquiry into the precise prior status of those territories.

105. In [the *Nuclear Weapons* case, the Court stated] that:

> the protection of the International Covenant of Civil and Political Rights does not cease in times of war, except by operation of Article 4 of the Covenant whereby certain

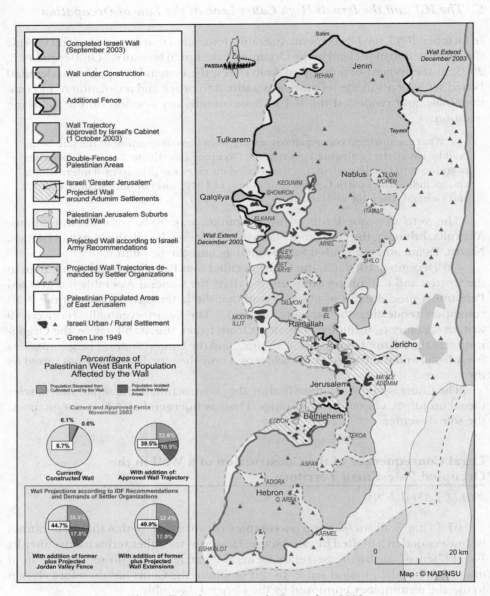

The Wall in the West Bank, December 2003
SOURCE: Negotiations Affairs Department (PLO)

provisions may be derogated from in a time of national emergency. . . . In principle, the right not arbitrarily to be deprived of one's life applies also in hostilities. The test of what is an arbitrary deprivation of life, however, then falls to be determined by the applicable *lex specialis*, namely, the law applicable in armed conflict which is designed to regulate the conduct of hostilities.

106. More generally, the Court considers that the protection offered by human rights conventions does not cease in case of armed conflict, save through the effect of provisions for derogation of the kind to be found in Article 4 of the International Covenant on Civil and Political Rights. . . .

[After concluding that the pertinent human rights treaties apply to Israel's conduct in the Occupied Territories, the Court continues:]

118. As regards the principle of the right of peoples to self determination, the Court observes that the existence of a "Palestinian people" is no longer in issue. Such existence has moreover been recognized by Israel in the exchange of letters of 9 September 1993 between Mr. Yasser Arafat, President of the Palestine Liberation Organization (PLO) and Mr. Yitzhak Rabin, Israeli Prime Minister. In that correspondence, the President of the PLO recognized "the right of the State of Israel to exist in peace and security" and made various other commitments. In reply, the Israeli Prime Minister informed him that, in the light of those commitments, "the Government of Israel has decided to recognize the PLO as the representative of the Palestinian people". . . .

119. The Court notes . . . that the wall's sinuous route has been traced in such a way as to include . . . the great majority of the Israeli settlements in the occupied Palestinian Territory (including East Jerusalem).

120. As regards these settlements, the Court notes that Article 49, paragraph 6, of the Fourth Geneva Convention . . . prohibits not only deportations or forced transfers of population such as those carried out during the Second World War, but also any measures taken by an occupying Power in order to organize or encourage transfers of parts of its own population into the occupied territory.

In this respect, the information provided to the Court shows that, since 1977, Israel has conducted a policy and developed practices involving the establishment of settlements in the Occupied Palestinian Territory, contrary to the terms of Article 49, paragraph 6, just cited.

The Security Council has thus taken the view that such policy and practices "have no legal validity". . . .

The Court concludes that the Israeli settlements in the Occupied Palestinian Territory (including East Jerusalem) have been established in breach of international law.

121. Whilst the Court notes the assurance given by Israel that the construction of the wall does not amount to annexation and that the wall is of a temporary nature . . . it nevertheless cannot remain indifferent to certain fears expressed to it that the route of the wall will prejudge the future frontier between Israel and Palestine, and the fear that Israel may integrate the settlements and their means of access. The Court considers that the construction of the wall and its associated régime create a "fait accompli" on the ground that could well become permanent, in which case, and notwithstanding the formal characterization of the wall by Israel, it would be tantamount to *de facto* annexation.

122. The Court recalls moreover that, according to the report of the Secretary-General, the planned route would incorporate in the area between the Green Line and the wall more than 16 per cent of the territory of the West Bank. Around 80 percent of the settlers living in the Occupied Palestinian Territory, that is 320,000 individuals, would reside in that area, as well as 237,000 Palestinians. Moreover, as a result of the construction of the wall, around 160,000 other Palestinians would reside in almost completely encircled communities.

In other terms, the route chosen for the wall gives expression *in loco* to the illegal measures taken by Israel with regard to Jerusalem and the settlements, as deplored by the Security Council. There is also a risk of further alterations to the demo-graphic composition of the Occupied Palestinian Territory resulting from the con-struction of the wall inasmuch as it is contributing . . . to the departure of Palestinian populations from certain areas. That construction, along with measures taken previously, thus severely impedes the exercise by the Palestinian people of its right to self-determination, and is therefore a breach of Israel's obligation to respect that right.

[The Court then reviews provisions of the Hague Regulations and the Fourth Geneva Convention which prohibit, among other things, "measures aim[ed] at creating unemployment or at restricting the opportunities offered to workers," and destruction of real or personal property "except where such destruction is rendered absolutely necessary by military operations," and which requires the occu-pying power to agree to outside relief assistance if needed. The Court also cites pertinent human rights provisions guaranteeing, among other things, freedom of movement, liberty and security of the person, and economic and social rights, such as the right to work. The Court describes various ways in which the barrier impedes agricultural production, and access to health care and education, and continues:]

132. From the information submitted to the Court, particularly the report of the Secretary-General, it appears that the construction of the wall has led to the destruc-tion or requisition of properties under conditions which contravene the require-ments of Articles 46 and 52 of the Hague Regulations of 1907 and of Article 53 of the Fourth Geneva Convention.

134. To sum up, the Court is of the opinion that the construction of the wall and its associated régime impede the liberty of movement of the inhabitants of the Occupied Palestinian Territory (with the exception of Israeli citizens and those assimilated thereto) as guaranteed under Article 12, paragraph 1, of the Interna-tional Covenant on Civil and Political Rights. They also impede the exercise by the persons concerned of the right to work, to health, to education and to an adequate standard of living as proclaimed in the International Covenant on Economic, Social and Cultural Rights and in the United Nations Convention on the Rights of the Child. Lastly, the construction of the wall and its associated régime, by contributing to the demographic changes referred to above contravene Article 49, paragraph 6, of the Fourth Geneva Convention.

135. The Court would observe, however, that the applicable international humanitarian law contains provisions enabling account to be taken of military exi-gencies in certain circumstances.

Neither Article 46 of the Hague Regulations of 1907 nor Article 47 of the Fourth Geneva Convention contain [sic] any qualifying provision of this type. With regard to forcible transfers of population and deportations, which are pro-hibited under Article 49, paragraph 1, of the Convention, paragraph 2 of that Article provides for an exception in those cases in which "the security of the popula-tion or imperative military reasons so demand." This exception however does not apply to paragraph 6 of that Article, which prohibits the occupying Power from deporting or transferring parts of its own civilian population into the territories it occupies. As to Article 53 concerning the destruction of personal property, it pro-vides for an exception "where such destruction is rendered absolutely necessary by military operations."

The Court considers that the military exigencies contemplated by these texts may be invoked in occupied territories even after the general close of the military operations that led to their occupation. However, on the material before it, the Court is not convinced that the destructions carried out contrary to the prohibition in Article 53 of the Fourth Geneva Convention were rendered absolutely necessary by military operations.

137. To sum up, the Court, from the material available to it, is not convinced that the specific course Israel has chosen for the wall was necessary to attain its security objectives. The wall, along the route chosen, and its associated régime gravely infringe a number of rights of Palestinians residing in the territory occupied by Israel, and the infringements resulting from that route cannot be justified by military exigencies or by the requirements of national security or public order. The construction of such a wall accordingly constitutes breaches by Israel of various of its obligations under the applicable international humanitarian law and human rights instruments.

138. . . . Israel's Permanent Representative to the United Nations . . . [stated that] Security Council resolutions [1368 and 1373] . . . "have clearly recognized the right of States to use force in self-defence against terrorist attacks," and therefore surely recognize the right to use non-forcible measures to that end.

139. . . . Article 51 of the Charter . . . recognizes the existence of an inherent right of self-defence in the case of armed attack by one State against another State. However, Israel does not claim that the attacks against it are imputable to a foreign State.

The Court also notes that Israel exercises control in the Occupied Palestinian Territory and that, as Israel itself states, the threat which it regards as justifying the construction of the wall originates within, and not outside, that territory. The situation is thus different from that contemplated by Security Council resolutions 1368 (2001) and 1373 (2001), and therefore Israel could not in any event invoke those resolutions in support of its claim to be exercising a right of self-defence.

Consequently, the Court concludes that Article 51 of the Charter has no relevance in this case.

140. The Court has, however, considered whether Israel could rely on a state of necessity which would preclude the wrongfulness of the construction of the wall. . . . One of [the conditions for invoking necessity] requires that the act being challenged be "the only way for the State to safeguard an essential interest against a grave and imminent peril" (Article 25 of the International Law Commission's Articles on Responsibility of States for Internationally Wrongful Acts). In the light of the material before it, the Court is not convinced that the construction of the wall along the route chosen was the only means to safeguard the interests of Israel against the peril which it has invoked as justification for that construction.

141. The fact remains that Israel has to face numerous indiscriminate and deadly acts of violence against its civilian population. It has the right, and indeed the duty, to respond in order to protect the life of its citizens. The measures taken are bound nonetheless to remain in conformity with applicable international law.

148. The Court will now examine the legal consequences resulting from the violations of international law by Israel by distinguishing between, on the one hand, those arising for Israel and, on the other, those arising for other States and, where appropriate, for the United Nations.

[After concluding that Israel must dismantle the wall, return confiscated land, and "compensate the persons in question for the damage suffered," the Court continues:]

159. Given the character and the importance of the rights and obligations involved, the Court is of the view that all States are under an obligation not to recognize the illegal situation resulting from the construction of the wall. . . . In addition, all the States parties to the [Fourth Geneva Convention] are under an obligation, while respecting the United Nations Charter and international law, to ensure compliance by Israel with international humanitarian law as embodied in that Convention.

160. Finally, the Court is of the view that the United Nations, and especially the General Assembly and the Security Council, should consider what further action is required to bring to an end the illegal situation resulting from the construction of the wall and the associated régime, taking due account of the present Advisory Opinion.

162. . . . The Court would emphasize that both Israel and Palestine are under an obligation scrupulously to observe the rules of international humanitarian law, one of the paramount purposes of which is to protect civilian life. Illegal actions and unilateral decisions have been taken on all sides, whereas, in the Court's view, this tragic situation can be brought to an end only through implementation in good faith of all relevant Security Council resolutions. . . .

Separate Opinion of Judge Higgins

2004 I.C.J. 207

. . .

15. [T]he Court states that it "is indeed aware that the question of the wall is part of a greater whole, and it would take this circumstance carefully into account in any opinion it might give."

16. In fact, it never does so. . . .

18. . . . It is true that in paragraph 162 the Court recalls that "Illegal actions and unilateral decisions have been taken on all sides" and that it emphasizes that "both Israel and Palestine are under an obligation scrupulously to observe the rules of international humanitarian law." But in my view much, much more was required to avoid the huge imbalance that necessarily flows from being invited to look at only "part of a greater whole," and then to take that circumstance "carefully into account." The call upon both parties to act in accordance with international humanitarian law should have been placed within the *dispositif*. . . . Further, the Court should have spelled out what is required of both parties in this "greater whole." This is not difficult—[since] Security Council resolution 242 . . . , the key underlying requirements have remained the same—that Israel is entitled to exist, to be recognized, and to security, and that the Palestinian people are entitled to their territory, to exercise self-determination, and to have their own State. . . .

19. I think the Court should also have taken the opportunity to say, in the clearest terms, what regrettably today apparently needs constant reaffirmation even among international lawyers, namely, that the protection of civilians remains an intransgressible obligation of humanitarian law, not only for the occupier but equally for those seeking to liberate themselves from occupation.

[Higgins concurs with the Court's finding that the construction of the wall violates Articles 49 and 53 of the Fourth Geneva Convention, and articles 46 and 52 of the Hague Regulations. On the issue of self-determination, however, Higgins disagrees with the majority:]

30. . . . As this Opinion observes (para. 118), it is now accepted that the Palestinian people are a "peoples" for purposes of self-determination. But it seems to me quite detached from reality for the Court to find that it is the wall that presents a "serious impediment" to the exercise of this right. The real impediment is the apparent inability and/or unwillingness of both Israel and Palestine to move in parallel to secure the necessary conditions—that is, at one and the same time, for Israel to withdraw from Arab occupied territory and for Palestine to provide the conditions to allow Israel to feel secure in so doing. The simple point is underscored by the fact that if the wall had never been built, the Palestinians would still not yet have exercised their right to self-determination. It seems to me both unrealistic and unbalanced for the Court to find that the wall (rather than "the larger problem", which is beyond the question put to the Court for an opinion) is a serious obstacle to self-determination.

[Higgins also takes issue with the majority's analysis of the law of self-defense:]

33. . . . There is, with respect, nothing in the text of Article 51 that *thus* stipulates that self defence is available only when an armed attack is made by a State. . . .

34. I also find unpersuasive the Court's contention that, as the uses of force emanate from occupied territory, it is not an armed attack "by one State against another." I fail to understand the Court's view that an occupying Power loses the right to defend its own civilian citizens at home if the attacks emanate from the occupied territory—a territory which it has found not to have been annexed and is certainly "other than" Israel. Further, Palestine cannot be sufficiently an international entity to be invited to these proceedings, and to benefit from humanitarian law, but not sufficiently an international entity for the prohibition of armed attack on others to be applicable. This is formalism of an unevenhanded sort. The question is surely where responsibility lies for the sending of groups and persons who act against Israeli civilians and the cumulative severity of such action.

35. In the event, however, these reservations have not caused me to vote against subparagraph (3) (A) of the *dispositif* [holding that the construction of the barrier violates international law], for two reasons. First, I remain unconvinced that non-forcible measures (such as the building of a wall) fall within self-defence under Article 51 of the Charter as that provision is normally understood. Second, even if it were an act of self-defence, properly so called, it would need to be justified as necessary and proportionate. While the wall does seem to have resulted in a diminution of attacks on Israeli civilians, the necessity and proportionality for the particular route selected, with its attendant hardships for Palestinians uninvolved in these attacks, has not been explained.

Dissenting Opinion of Judge Buergenthal

2004 I.C.J. 240

[Although Judge Buergenthal agrees with the majority that the construction of the wall raises important issues of humanitarian law, he argues that the Court "should have exercised its discretion and declined to render the requested advisory opinion":]

7. [I]n reaching [its conclusion that the wall violates international humanitarian law,] the Court fails to address any facts or evidence specifically rebutting Israel's claim of military exigencies or requirements of national security. It is true that in dealing with this subject the Court asserts that it draws on the factual summaries provided by the United Nations Secretary-General as well as some other United Nations reports. It is equally true, however, that the Court barely addresses the summaries of Israel's position on this subject that are attached to the Secretary-General's report and which contradict or cast doubt on the material the Court claims to rely on. Instead, all we have from the Court is a description of the harm the wall is causing and a discussion of various provisions of international humanitarian law and human rights instruments followed by the conclusion that this law has been violated. Lacking is an examination of the facts that might show why the alleged defences of military exigencies, national security or public order are not applicable to the wall as a whole or to the individual segments of its route. The Court says that it "is not convinced" but it fails to demonstrate why it is not convinced, and that is why these conclusions are not convincing.

8. It is true that some international humanitarian law provisions the Court cites admit of no exceptions based on military exigencies. Thus, Article 46 of the Hague Rules provides that private property must be respected and may not be confiscated. [T]he Secretary-General reports Israel's position on this subject in part as follows: "The Government of Israel argues: there is no change in ownership of the land; compensation is available for use of land, crop yield or damage to the land; residents can petition the Supreme Court to halt or alter construction and there is no change in resident status." The Court fails to address these arguments. While these Israeli submissions are not necessarily determinative of the matter, they should have been dealt with by the Court and related to Israel's further claim that the wall is a temporary structure. . . .

Notes and Questions

1. Why do you think the General Assembly asked for an advisory opinion? Why did it ask about the "legal consequences" of constructing a wall rather than whether construction of the wall was consistent with international law?

2. Should the Court have declined to issue an advisory opinion? Consider the following assessment:

> There was no shortage of "compelling reasons" that, both individually and certainly in combination, could and should have led the Court to desist from responding to the Assembly's request in this case. These included the formulation of the request; the transparent motives of its sponsors; the unprecedented number of states urging judicial restraint; the absence of an agreed factual basis for adjudication; the legitimacy and consequences of judicial intervention in an acute and ongoing conflict in which,

additionally, the Security Council was actively engaged; and, above all, the objection of Israel, the targeted state, to back-door nonconsensual adjudication of matters impinging so crucially on its existence, its territorial rights, and the defense of its citizens from a continuing daily terrorist onslaught.

Michla Pomerance, *The ICJ's Advisory Jurisdiction and the Crumbling Wall Between the Political and the Judicial*, 99 Am. J. Int'l L. 26, 31 (2005).

3. Why do you think Israel chose not to participate in the case? Does Israel's decision affect the strength of Judge Buergenthal's position?

4. Given the Court's analysis of the law of self-defense and necessity, what avenues remain open to Israel to protect itself against attacks launched from the occupied territories? Does a different analysis apply to acts taken to protect Israel's settlements in the West Bank, given the Court's determination that those settlements violate international law?

5. The Court concludes in paragraphs 135 and 137 that military exigencies do not justify Israel's destruction of property to build the separation barrier or its choice of route. Do you agree with the Court's analysis? What additional information might be useful in making such an assessment?

On June 30, 2004, just over a week before the ICJ issued its opinion, the Israeli Supreme Court issued its own opinion on the separation barrier. The case arose from a series of challenges to Israeli Defense Force (IDF) orders to seize certain plots of land in the West Bank (in an area Israel refers to as Judea and Samaria) in order to build the separation barrier. The Court's opinion, authored by Justice Aharon Barak, deals with a 25-mile section of the barrier being built around Jerusalem.

Beit Sourik Village Council v. Israel

HCJ 2056/04 (2004)

1. Since 1967, Israel has been holding the areas of Judea and Samaria [hereinafter the area] in belligerent occupation. . . .

In [a prior case], I described the security situation:

Israel's fight is complex. Together with other means, the Palestinians use guided human bombs. These suicide bombers reach every place that Israelis can be found (within the boundaries of the State of Israel and in the Jewish communities in Judea and Samaria and the Gaza Strip). They sew destruction and spill blood in the cities and towns. The forces fighting against Israel are terrorists: they are not members of a regular army; they do not wear uniforms; they hide among the civilian Palestinian population in the territories, including inside holy sites; they are supported by part of the civilian population, and by their families and relatives.

2. These terror acts have caused Israel to take security precautions on several levels. . . . This is the background behind the decision to construct the Separation Fence.

[The Court notes that the law of belligerent occupation applies, including the Hague Regulations as customary international law and, by agreement of the parties, the humanitarian provisions of the Fourth Geneva Convention. In response to petitioners' claim that the IDF Commander lacked legal authority to construct the fence because his decision was based on political rather than military considerations, the Court states:]

27. We accept that the military commander cannot order the construction of the Separation Fence if his reasons are political. . . . In [a prior case], this Court discussed whether it is possible to seize land in order to build a Jewish civilian town, when the purpose of the building of the town is not the security needs and defense of the area . . . but rather based upon a Zionist perspective of settling the entire land of Israel. . . . In his judgment, Justice Landau stated:

> . . . The answer to that depends upon the interpretation of article 52 of the Hague Regulations. It is my opinion that the needs of the army mentioned in that article cannot include, by way of any reasonable interpretation, national security needs in the broad meaning of the term. . . .

28. We examined petitioners' arguments, and have come to the conclusion, based upon the facts before us, that the Fence is motivated by security concerns. . . .

29. The Commander of the IDF Forces in the area of Judea and Samaria . . . stated that "the objective of the security Fence is to help contend with the threat of Palestinian terror. Specifically, the Fence is intended to prevent the unchecked passage of inhabitants of the area into Israel and their infiltration into Israeli towns located in the area. Based on this security consideration we determined the topographic route of the Fence." . . . He noted the necessity that the Fence pass through territory that topographically controls its surroundings, that, in order to allow surveillance of it, its route be as flat as possible, and that a "security zone" be established which will delay infiltration into Israel. These are security considerations par excellence. . . . We have no reason to give this testimony less than full weight, and we have no reason not to believe the sincerity of the military commander.

30. Petitioners, by pointing to the route of the Fence, attempt to prove that the construction of the Fence is not motivated by security considerations, but by political ones. They argue that if the Fence was primarily motivated by security considerations, it would be constructed on the "Green Line," that is to say, on the armistice line between Israel and Jordan after the War of Independence. We cannot accept this argument. The opposite is the case: it is the security perspective—and not the political one—which must examine a route based on its security merits alone, without regard for the location of the Green Line. The members of the Council for Peace and Security [a group of retired Israeli military officers], whose affidavits were brought before us by agreement of the parties, do not recommend following the Green Line. They do not even argue that the considerations of the military commander are political. Rather, they dispute the proper route of the Separation Fence based on security considerations themselves.

32. Petitioners' second argument is that the construction of the Fence in the area is based, in large part, on the seizure of land privately owned by local inhabitants, [and] that this seizure is illegal. . . . [O]ur opinion is that the military commander is authorized—by the international law applicable to an area under belligerent occupation—to take possession of land, if this is necessary for the needs of the army. . . .

33. The focus of this petition is the legality of the route chosen for the construction of the Separation Fence. This question stands on its own, and it requires a straightforward, real answer. It is not sufficient that the Fence be motivated by security considerations, as opposed to political considerations. . . .

34. The law of belligerent occupation recognizes the authority of the military commander to maintain security in the area and to protect the security of his country and her citizens. However, it imposes conditions on the use of this authority. This authority must be properly balanced against the rights, needs, and interests of the local population. . . .

[The Court notes that the requisite balance must be determined through application of the principle of proportionality, and identifies three subtests: a "rational means" test ("whether there is a rational connection between the route of the Fence and the goal of the construction of the Separation Fence"); a "least injurious means" test ("whether, among the various routes which would achieve the objective of the Separation Fence, is the chosen one the least injurious"); and a narrower "proportional means" test (whether the harm to individuals caused by the chosen route of the Separation Fence is proportionate to the security benefits provided by that route). The Court decides that whether the route of the Separation Fence is rational and whether it achieves its objectives better than alternative routes are fact questions calling for deference to "the military opinion of the official who is responsible for security," but that the question whether the route chosen is proportionate to the harm it causes is "a legal question, the expertise for which is held by the Court." The Court then examines the various segments of the barrier at issue, finding some proportionate, and others not. The Court's discussion of the third subtest as applied to one segment of the wall is excerpted below.]

59. The third subtest . . . weighs the costs against the benefits. According to this subtest, a decision of an administrative authority must reach a reasonable balance between communal needs and the damage done to the individual. . . . This judgment is made against the background of the general normative structure of the legal system, which recognizes human rights and the necessity of ensuring the provision of the needs and welfare of the local inhabitants, and which preserves "family honour and rights" (Regulation 46 of the Hague Regulations). All these are protected in the framework of the humanitarian provisions of the Hague Regulations and the Geneva Convention. . . .

60. [T]he route which the military commander established for the Security Fence—which separates the local inhabitants from their agricultural lands—injures the local inhabitants in a severe and acute way, while violating their rights under humanitarian international law. Here are the facts: more than 13,000 farmers (falahin) are cut off from thousands of dunams [a dunam is 1000 square meters] of their land and from tens of thousands of trees which are their livelihood, and which are located on the other side of the Separation Fence. . . . The route of the Separation Fence severely violates their right of property and their freedom of movement. Their livelihood is severely impaired. The difficult reality of life from which they have suffered (due, for example, to high unemployment in that area) will only become more severe.

61. These injuries are not proportionate. They can be substantially decreased by an alternate route. . . . The gap between the security provided by the military commander's approach and the security provided by the alternate route is minute, as compared to the large difference between a Fence that separates the local inhabitants from their lands, and a Fence which does not separate the two. . . . Indeed, we accept that security needs are likely to necessitate an injury to the lands of the local inhabitants and to their ability to use them. International humanitarian law on one hand, however, and the basic principles of Israeli administrative law on the other, require making every possible effort to ensure that injury will be proportionate.

Where construction of the Separation Fence demands that inhabitants be separated from their lands, access to these lands must be ensured, in order to minimize the damage to the extent possible.

Notes and Questions

1. Compare the Supreme Court's decision with that of the ICJ. What accounts for the difference in approach? Who are the likely audiences for each decision, and what is the likely impact of the two decisions on those audiences?

2. What influence should the ICJ's decision have on decisions by national courts? The Israeli courts have continued to hear challenges to segments of the separation barrier following the *Beit Sourik* decision, notwithstanding the Israeli government's decision to modify the route of the barrier in response to that decision. In one such case, the Israeli Supreme Court noted the common normative foundation to the *Beit Sourik* and ICJ decisions, and suggested that the principal reason for the different conclusions each court reached lay in the different factual records presented to each court. Against this backdrop, the Israeli Supreme Court decided the effect to be given to the ICJ decision:

> the Supreme Court of Israel shall give the full appropriate weight to the norms of international law, as developed and interpreted by the ICJ in its Advisory Opinion. However, the ICJ's conclusion, based upon a factual basis different than the one before us, is not *res judicata*, and does not obligate the Supreme Court of Israel to rule that each and every segment of the fence violates international law. The Israeli Court shall continue to . . . ask itself, regarding each and every segment, whether it represents a proportional balance between the security-military need and the rights of the local population.

Mara'abe v. Israel, HCJ 7957/04, Sept.15, 2005.

D. Note on "Transformative Occupation"

The law of occupation evolved at a time when central governments exercised less control over daily life than they do in most states today, and before the evolution of contemporary human rights and self-determination norms. As a result, the law of occupation envisioned occupiers as transient custodians with little interest in the long-term governance of the occupied territory. But much has changed. Since World War II, occupiers have sometimes sought the complete restructuring of the political, economic, and social life of the occupied territory, in what is sometimes called a "transformative occupation." The magnitude of change in a transformative occupation is best illustrated by the recent occupation of Iraq by the United States, the United Kingdom, and their coalition partners.

On April 9, 2003, Saddam Hussein's government collapsed as U.S. troops seized control of Baghdad. The United States declared major hostilities at an end on April 14, 2003. At that point, the United States and the United Kingdom became occupying powers, a status recognized by the Security Council in Resolution 1483. In the immediate aftermath of the war, the United States established the Coalition Provisional Authority (CPA) to administer Iraq. Under CPA Regulation 1, the CPA was "vested with all executive, legislative and judicial authority necessary to achieve its objectives, to be exercised under relevant

U.N. Security Council resolutions, including Resolution 1483 (2003), and the laws and usages of war."

Ordinarily, an occupying power is supposed to be only a temporary administrator pending the establishment of a lawful indigenous government. But the U.S.-led CPA wanted to convert Iraq from an authoritarian state into a free-market democracy. With this in mind, the CPA embarked on a comprehensive reform program. It "disestablished" the dominant Baath political party and barred senior members from government positions; created a new Iraqi army, intelligence service, and Ministry of Defense; adopted sweeping human rights regulations and created a new Ministry of Human Rights; revamped Iraq's criminal law and judicial institutions; moved Iraq from a state-dominated to a private sector economy; and partially restructured Iraq's political system.

The transformative program pursued by the United States and its allies in Iraq sparked a lively debate among international lawyers concerning the compatibility of the reforms with the law of occupation. In the nineteenth century, the public sphere of war was treated as separate from the private sphere of daily life under occupation. As Eyal Benvenisti observed:

> The separation of interests provided room for a simple balancing principle of disengagement: the occupant had no interest in the laws of the area under its control except for the security of its troops and the maintenance of order; the ousted sovereign was ready to concede this much in order to ensure maintenance of its bases of power in the territory against competing internal forces and in order to guarantee the humane treatment of its citizens. This solution was not only well founded in theory; it was supported by the practice of the nineteenth-century occupations. These occupations were of relatively short duration, during which occupants, by and large, retained existing legislation as much as possible.

Eyal Benvenisti, The International Law of Occupation 28 (1993). This approach was eventually codified in Article 43 of the Hague Regulations.

But as Professor Gregory Fox has observed,

> A literal interpretation of article 43 of the Hague Regulations, prohibiting change to the laws in force "unless absolutely prevented" from doing so, would likely find most of the CPA's reforms invalid. . . . While scholars have employed a remarkable range of linguistic constructions to shed light on when an occupier is "absolutely prevented" from respecting the laws in force, few propose justifications wholly divorced from military necessity.

Gregory Fox, *The Occupation of Iraq*, 36 Geo. J. Int'l L. 195, 240-41 (2005). Prior to the occupation of Iraq, the British Attorney General advised Prime Minister Tony Blair as follows:

> 2. In short, my view is that a further Security Council resolution is needed to authorise imposing reform and restructuring of Iraq and its Government. In the absence of a further resolution, the UK (and US) would be bound by the provisions of international law governing belligerent occupation. . . . [T]he general principle is that an Occupying Power does not become the government of the occupied territory. Rather, it exercises temporary de facto control in accordance with the defined rights and obligations under Geneva Convention IV and the Hague Regulations. These instruments are complex, but the following points give an indication of the limitations placed on the authority of an Occupying Power:
>
> (a) [W]hile some changes to the legislative and administrative structures of Iraq may be permissible [under Article 43 of the Hague Regulations] if they are necessary

for security or public order reasons, or in order to further humanitarian objectives, more wide-ranging reforms of governmental and administrative structures would not be lawful.

(b) Geneva Convention IV prohibits, subject to certain limited exceptions, any alteration in the status of public officials or judges (although officials may be removed from post in certain circumstances).

(c) Geneva Convention IV . . . [contains] limited exceptions allowing the Occupying Power to promulgate its own laws in order to fulfil its obligations under the Convention and to maintain security and public order, but in principle, the existing structures for the administration of justice must remain in place.

(d) [T]he general principle outlined in (a) above applies equally to economic reform, so that the imposition of major structural economic reforms would not be authorised by international law.

3. Different considerations could apply if it were suggested that the people of Iraq themselves were engaged in undertaking such governmental and administrative reform, but that is not what I understand is currently envisaged.

Memorandum of Lord Goldsmith to Prime Minister Blair, Mar. 26, 2003.

Security Council Resolution 1483, which as noted earlier recognized the United States and the United Kingdom as occupying powers, also calls upon them, "consistent with the Charter of the United Nations and other relevant international law, to promote the welfare of the Iraqi people through the effective administration of the territory, including in particular working towards the restoration of conditions of security and stability and the creation of conditions in which the Iraqi people can freely determine their own political future." Similarly, the Resolution "[s]upports the formation, by the people of Iraq with the help of the Authority [the occupying powers] and working with the Special Representative, of an Iraqi interim administration as a transitional administration run by Iraqis, until an internationally recognized, representative government is established by the people of Iraq and assumes the responsibilities of the Authority."

Although the occupation of Iraq formally ended in June 2004 following the election of an interim government, debate over the larger issues surrounding transformative occupation continues. Moreover, the underlying issue—the extent to which international human rights and humanitarian law permit external actors to restructure a state or territory undergoing some form of transition—is not confined to cases such as Iraq. Related questions also arise in the context of UN transitional administrations in territories such as Kosovo and East Timor. Administrators in these latter cases, however, can typically rely on the Security Council's Chapter VII authority for their actions, in much more explicit fashion than was possible for the United States and the United Kingdom in Iraq.

Notes and Questions

1. Is the law of occupation anachronistic? Should it be revised to permit occupiers to transform the legal and political institutions of occupied territories? If so, when and with what limits?

2. Consider the following view:

Occupation law . . . permits tinkering on the edges of societal reform, but it is not a license to transform. If it were, then the door would be wide open for abuse by aggressive and benevolent armies alike. . . .

But liberating armies that operate with international authority, advance democracy, and save civilian populations from atrocities should be regulated by a modern occupation regime that can be created under the UN Charter. Doing so puts those forces, their commanders, and the states deploying them at far less risk of legal liability than has been the case with respect to Iraq.

David Scheffer, *Beyond Occupation Law*, 97 Am. J. Intl. L. 842, 851 (2003). Do you agree with Scheffer that transformative occupation should generally require a UN mandate? Did Resolution 1483 provide such a mandate to the occupying powers in Iraq?

9

Individual Accountability for Violations of Human Dignity: International Criminal Law and Beyond

The previous two chapters show how participants in the international legal process have developed a set of norms and processes for the protection of the individual in peace and war. As we have seen, treaties and customary law typically place various duties on states, though they may also create obligations for certain non-state entities that have a significant potential to cause harm, such as opposition movements during a civil war. But societies around the world have long recognized, through the use of criminal law, that individuals must also be held accountable for harming human dignity. Individual responsibility through criminal law and procedures can—though it does not always—advance a number of societal goals, notably deterrence of future crime (whether by the particular criminal who is tried or by others), some form of spiritual reparation (the overused term "closure" for victims), rehabilitation of offenders, and validation of fundamental societal values.

Over the last several centuries, particularly as a result of several horrible episodes in human history, states and non-state actors have gradually accepted that individuals—not only states or insurgent groups—are responsible under international law for some acts against human dignity. Thus, international criminalization began in the era before modern human rights law. Indeed, the first international crime that states recognized—piracy—had little to do with human dignity at all; rather, states sought to punish pirates as individuals because they were not (by definition) the agents of any state. As early as the fifteenth century, states held trials for war crimes—namely, significant violations of international humanitarian law—and prescribed various legal codes in subsequent years. During the nineteenth century, various states concluded treaties making the slave trade—like piracy, an act carried out by private individuals (though clearly supported by many states)—a crime. With the advent of the modern human rights movement after World War II, states developed additional treaties providing for individual accountability for a variety of severe human rights abuses. For the sake of shorthand, we call these acts international crimes.

Geometrically, international human rights law, international humanitarian law, and international criminal law might be visualized as three circles or rings, each of which overlaps with the other two.

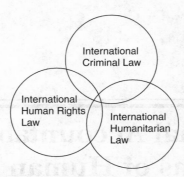

Thus, as will be seen, certain major human rights treaties and humanitarian law treaties contain penal provisions. In that sense, criminal processes are an alternative along a continuum to enforce human rights or humanitarian law. At the same time, and quite significantly, states do not regard most human rights and humanitarian law violations as entailing individual responsibility; international criminal law thus does not incorporate all humanitarian or human rights law. Moreover, although not discussed in this chapter, international criminal law addresses numerous acts beyond the area of human rights or the conduct of armed conflict, such as hijacking, sabotage of aircraft, narcotics offenses, and traffic in obscene publications.

International criminal law norms may be enforced at the national level or the international level, and through both traditional prosecutorial means as well as nonjudicial alternatives. Some states that have experienced horrendous human rights abuses will still have judicial systems capable of meting out justice; others, perhaps even most others, will fall prey to either lack of financial resources for effective trials or political forces that prevent or curtail such trials. In some situations, actors outside the state may be sufficiently interested to provide external support. Foreign states might even consider prosecuting individuals themselves under various jurisdictional principles. And, on rare occasions, states have acted together to set up international tribunals to try offenders. Some states and international organizations have tried to advance some of the goals of individual accountability through other fora, notably the truth commission, either in lieu of or in addition to criminal trials. However, truth commissions face problems of their own, including how deeply they should penetrate into the past and whether they should name offenders or merely focus on the fate of victims.

I. GOVERNMENTAL ATTACKS ON CIVILIAN POPULATIONS: THE KHMER ROUGE'S RULE OVER CAMBODIA

In the era before the development of human rights law, states generally saw international law as addressing violations by governments only when they were against citizens of *other* states—acts deemed an affront to those states and thus within the ambit of the law of nations. In doctrinal terms, these fell in two areas—the law of state responsibility for injury to aliens, which primarily dealt with disruption of property interests of aliens by foreign states but also included attacks on individuals; and the laws and customs of war, as discussed in Chapter 8. But international law was mostly silent in terms of mandating specific consequences for individuals who violated it. Nevertheless, some states developed sophisticated domestic codes punishing violations of the laws of war—among the most famous was the Lieber Code, developed by an American law professor during the American Civil War (excerpted in Chapter 8).

The scale of violence in World War I led to renewed emphasis on individual responsibility. The Allies in the Great War eventually inserted into the Treaty of Versailles four articles providing for the punishment by Allied military tribunals of persons accused of violating the laws and customs of war; in one, the Allies "publicly arraign William II of Hohenzollern, formerly German Emperor, for a supreme offence against international morality and the sanctity of treaties." However, the Allies never held any trials and did not insist on the Kaiser's removal from exile in the Netherlands, accepting instead that Germany's highest court, the Reichsgericht, prosecute based on a list of suspects provided by the Allies. A small number of trials began in 1921, but some of the key suspects were never arrested or they escaped, and the 12 who were tried were acquitted or received light sentences by a court sympathetic to the defendants. Under British pressure, the Ottoman Turks held trials of some officials responsible for the large-scale massacres against Armenians in 1915, as well as some wartime cabinet leaders; but the courts eventually released most of the accused to placate the nationalist movement that would eventually overthrow the Ottoman Empire.

The watershed for individual accountability was the exercise undertaken by the great powers after World War II. As early as 1943, the United States, the USSR, and the United Kingdom publicly declared that Nazi leaders would be held personally accountable for starting the war and committing atrocities during the war. As the Allied victory became certain, both Josef Stalin and Winston Churchill favored summary execution of the leading Nazis (with Stalin calling for execution of perhaps 100,000 men), but Franklin Roosevelt, after some initial hesitation, favored some sort of criminal trial. The British and Soviet leaders eventually acceded to American wishes, though the Soviets saw trials as mere preludes to executions of the defendants. In 1945, these three Allies, joined by France, negotiated the London Charter, providing for the establishment of an International Military Tribunal (IMT) to try the major German war criminals. It would have four judges, one from each Allied state. Twenty-one other states eventually became parties to the London Charter. The leading Allies would eventually set up a similar panel (including judges from other states), the International Military Tribunal for the Far East, to try Japanese leaders. They also agreed that lower-level officials would be tried by the domestic courts of the Allied states.

From November 1945 to September 1946, the IMT tried 22 defendants for crimes against peace—namely, for starting World War II; war crimes; and crimes against humanity. The accused included Hitler's chief deputy, Hermann Göring; his foreign minister, Joachim von Ribbentrop; and the chief of the military staff, Wilhelm Keitel. All but three were convicted of at least one charge; 11 were sentenced to death, with all but Göring (who managed to commit suicide in his cell) executed by hanging in October 1946.

In the years immediately following Nuremberg, governments held additional national trials, and, at the international level, states agreed to codify some of the crimes in the IMT Charter in additional treaties. For much of the postwar period, however, the Cold War prevented serious discussion of criminal accountability under international law. But atrocities continued to proliferate.

As you read the following materials, consider why states have recognized international crimes when the domestic laws of all states make most of these acts criminal anyway; under what circumstances international law will hold an individual criminally responsible for violations; why certain egregious acts against human dignity have become crimes but others have not; and how the historic calamities that led states and other actors to make certain violations of human rights international crimes have affected the contours of the law.

A. The Problem

In the late 1960s, the Communist Party of Kampuchea (CPK), popularly known as the Khmer Rouge (red Khmer), began an armed struggle against the Cambodian government of Prince Norodom Sihanouk. This struggle intensified after a 1970 coup overthrew Sihanouk and replaced him with a new regime, that of the Khmer Republic, a staunch supporter of the United States in the Vietnam War. Sihanouk soon joined forces with the Khmer Rouge, and thanks to his popularity and overseas communist support, the movement seized large amounts of territory. By April 1975, it had conquered the country and renamed it Democratic Kampuchea.

The CPK proclaimed its victory as ending 2,000 years of subjugation of the Khmer peasantry at the hands of foreign and class enemies. But it continued to see these enemies as a threat. It thus launched a revolution abolishing all existing societal institutions, expunging all foreign influences, and transforming the entire population into a collective workforce. It also acted ruthlessly against all elements suspected of being hostile to the new order. The human rights abuses of the period led to the deaths of 1.5 to 1.7 million of the April 1975 population of 7.3 to 7.9 million people. These atrocities fall into three main categories:

Forced Population Movements: Seeing the cities as the breeding grounds of the enemies of Cambodia, the government forced 2 to 3 million people of all ages out of urban areas and into the countryside. Many thousands died during the forced marches, and the Khmer Rouge continued to move people forcibly from village to village during its years in power.

Forced Labor and Inhumane Living Conditions: The bulk of the population was put onto work teams and forced to grow crops or construct large-scale infrastructure projects. Work hours were long and food rations meager. Starvation, disease, and physical exhaustion killed hundreds of thousands; Khmer Rouge overseers also killed many thousands who refused to or could no longer work.

Attacks on Enemies of the Revolution: Former government leaders, military officers, and bureaucrats of the Khmer Republic were summarily executed, some in front of their families. The Cham, a Muslim sect in Cambodia for 500 years, were forcibly dispersed, had their language and customs banned, and saw their leaders killed. Most ethnic Vietnamese, who played an important role in the economy, were expelled in 1975. Furthermore, the regime targeted for execution thousands of teachers, students, professionals, and anyone with foreign language skills or ties to foreign countries. The government attacked organized religion, including Buddhism, the religion of most Cambodians. Eventually, it looked for enemies within its own ranks and tortured and killed many thousands of officials and their families.

During this period, Democratic Kampuchea (DK) and Vietnam also engaged in a low-intensity border war. By 1977, Cambodia had massacred hundreds of Vietnamese in border villages. Vietnam eventually sent troops into Cambodia in late 1977 and launched a full-scale invasion in December 1978. Its army reached the capital in two weeks and installed in power a group of former Khmer Rouge officials who had previously fled to Vietnam. Ten years of low-level civil war followed between the

Khmer Rouge and the Vietnamese-installed regime, which occupied most of the country. The parties agreed on a foreign-brokered peace agreement in 1991, leading to the deployment of a large UN force and an eventual election in 1993, which the Khmer Rouge boycotted. (For the legal issues surrounding the various governments in Cambodia, see Chapter 3.) The new government encouraged the Khmer Rouge to surrender through offers of amnesty. By the mid-1990s, the group had effectively disbanded as a fighting force. Pol Pot, DK's former supreme leader, died in a reclusive mountain hideout in 1998, a prisoner of his own followers, and his remaining lieutenants pledged their loyalty to the government.

B. Retroactive Justice? The Contours of Nullum Crimen Sine Lege

In order to hold any Khmer Rouge defendant responsible for the atrocities discussed above, a court would need to take cognizance of the fundamental prohibition in international and domestic law on assigning guilt for acts not considered as crimes when committed. The maxim *nullum crimen sine lege, nulla poena sine lege*, or "no crime without law, no punishment without law," captures this notion, which finds different forms in various legal contexts. These include constitutional prohibitions on ex post facto laws, judicial rules of construction limiting the use of analogy in interpreting criminal laws, and provisions in international human rights instruments barring prosecutions for acts not criminal at the time of their commission. In the context of *international* criminal law, *nullum crimen* has a special dimension. Unlike the domestic criminal law of most countries, much of international criminal law is not codified in treaties or any other agreed code. The customary status of many norms creates dangers for defendants in criminal cases, who may face judges with different methodologies and approaches to the derivation of custom.

After World War II, when legal officials from the four victorious Allies drafted the Charter of the IMT at Nuremberg, they faced these issues in deciding the crimes for which the Nazi leaders should be tried. These officials, led by U.S. Supreme Court Justice Robert Jackson, who would become the Chief Prosecutor of the IMT, were keenly aware of the need to avoid accusations that the IMT was meting out retroactive justice. In August 1945, just as the war was ending, the Allies concluded the IMT Charter.

Charter of the International Military Tribunal at Nuremberg

82 U.N.T.S. 279 (1945)

II. Jurisdiction and General Principles

Article 6. The Tribunal . . . shall have the power to try and punish persons who, acting in the interests of the European Axis countries, whether as individuals or as members of organizations, committed any of the following crimes.

The following acts, or any of them, are crimes coming within the jurisdiction of the Tribunal for which there shall be individual responsibility:

(a) *Crimes against peace:* namely, planning, preparation, initiation or waging of a war of aggression, or a war in violation of international treaties, agreements or assurances, or participation in a common plan or conspiracy for the accomplishment of any of the foregoing;

(b) *War crimes:* namely, violations of the laws or customs of war. Such violations shall include, but not be limited to, murder, ill-treatment or deportation to slave labour or for any other purpose of civilian population of or in occupied territory, murder or ill-treatment of prisoners of war or persons on the seas, killing of hostages, plunder of public or private property, wanton destruction of cities, towns or villages, or devastation not justified by military necessity;

(c) *Crimes against humanity:* namely, murder, extermination, enslavement, deportation, and other inhumane acts committed against any civilian population, before or during the war, or persecutions on political, racial or religious grounds[,] in execution of or in connection with any crime within the jurisdiction of the Tribunal, whether or not in violation of the domestic law of the country where perpetrated. . . .

Article 7. The official position of defendants whether as Heads of State or responsible officials in Government Departments, shall not be considered as freeing them from responsibility or mitigating punishment.

Article 8. The fact that the Defendant acted pursuant to order of his Government or of a superior shall not free him from responsibility, but may be considered in mitigation of punishment if the Tribunal determines that justice so requires.

After the trial of the leading Nazi war criminals by the IMT, the Allies conducted individual trials of thousands of Nazis. Most of these were conducted in formerly occupied states, such as France, the Netherlands, and Poland, under the domestic law of those states. The United States, Britain, and France, however, organized trials in their zones of occupation in Germany. These courts generally had jurisdiction over the same crimes as the IMT. Many of the most significant cases were tried in the American zone under the terms of Law No. 10 promulgated by the Control Council that was officially governing occupied Germany. These courts were composed principally of state court judges from the United States; they tried groups of defendants, including the German high command, the leaders of the mobile execution squads (Einsatzgruppen), doctors organizing medical experiments, and leading industrialists. In the so-called *Justice Case,* excerpted below, the 14 defendants were leading Nazi judges and prosecutors accused of using the court system against political prisoners, Jews, and other targets, often leading to death sentences. They were prosecuted for war crimes and crimes against humanity.

United States v. Joseph Alstoetter et al.

3 Trials of War Criminals before the Neurenberg Tribunals under Control Council Law No. 10, at 954 (1948)

THE EX POST FACTO PRINCIPLE

The defendants claim protection under the principle *nullum crimen sine lege,* though they withheld from others the benefit of that rule during the Hitler regime. Obviously the principle in question constitutes no limitation upon the power or right of the Tribunal to punish acts which can properly be held to have been violations of international law when committed. . . .

[T]he *ex post facto* rule, properly understood, constitutes no legal nor moral barrier to prosecution in this case.

Under written constitutions the *ex post facto* rule condemns statutes which define as criminal, acts committed before the law was passed, but the *ex post facto* rule cannot apply in the international field as it does under constitutional mandate in the domestic field. Even in the domestic field the prohibition of the rule does not apply to the decisions of common law courts, though the question at issue be novel. International law is not the product of statute for the simple reason that there is as yet no world authority empowered to enact statutes of universal application. International law is the product of multipartite treaties, conventions, judicial decisions and customs which have received international acceptance or acquiescence. It would be sheer absurdity to suggest that the *ex post facto* rule, as known to constitutional states, *could* be applied to a treaty, a custom, or a common law decision of an international tribunal, or to the international acquiescence which follows the event. To have attempted to apply the *ex post facto* principle to judicial decisions of common international law would have been to strangle that law at birth. As applied in the field of international law, the principle *nullum crimen sine lege* received its true interpretation in the [1946] opinion of the IMT in the [case against the leading Nazi officials]. The question arose with reference to crimes against the peace [that is, the crime of starting World War II], but the opinion expressed is equally applicable to war crimes and crimes against humanity. The Tribunal said:

> "In the first place, it is to be observed that the maxim *nullum crimen sine lege* is not a limitation of sovereignty, but is in general a principle of justice. To assert that it is unjust to punish those who in defiance of treaties and assurances have attacked neighboring states without warning is obviously untrue, for in such circumstances the attacker must know that he is doing wrong, and so far from it being unjust to punish him, it would be unjust if his wrong were allowed to go unpunished." . . .

We quote with approval the words of Sir David Maxwell-Fyfe [a British prosecutor at the 1945-46 Nuremberg trial]:

> "With regard to "crimes against humanity," this at any rate is clear. The Nazis, when they persecuted and murdered countless Jews and political opponents in Germany, knew that what they were doing was wrong and that their actions were crimes which had been condemned by the criminal law of every civilized state. When these crimes were mixed with the preparation for aggressive war and later with the commission of war crimes in occupied territories, it cannot be a matter of complaint that a procedure is established for their punishment."

Concerning the mooted *ex post facto* issue, Professor [Herbert] Wechsler of Columbia University writes:

> " . . . [M]ost of those who mount the attack on one or another of these contentions hasten to assure us that their plea is not one of immunity for the defendants; they argue only that they should have been disposed of politically, that is, dispatched out of hand. This is a curious position indeed. A punitive enterprise launched on the basis of general rules, administered in an adversary proceeding under a separation of prosecutive and adjudicative powers is, in the name of law and justice, asserted to be less desirable than an *ex parte* execution list or a drumhead court martial constituted in the immediate aftermath of the war. . . . [H]istory will accept no conception of law, politics or justice that supports a submission in these terms." . . .

Many of the laws of the Weimar era which were enacted for the protection of human rights have never been repealed. Many acts constituting war crimes or crimes against humanity as defined in C.C. [Control Council] Law 10 were committed or permitted in direct violation also of the provisions of the German criminal law. It is true that this Tribunal can try no defendant merely because of a violation of the German penal code, but it is equally true that the rule against retrospective legislation, as a rule of justice and fair play, should be no defense if the act which he committed in violation of C.C. Law 10 was also known to him to be a punishable crime under his own domestic law.

As a principle of justice and fair play, the rule in question will be given full effect. As applied in the field of international law that principle requires proof before conviction that the accused knew or should have known that in matters of international concern he was guilty of participation in a nationally organized system of injustice and persecution shocking to the moral sense of mankind, and that he knew or should have known that he would be subject to punishment if caught. Whether it be considered codification or substantive legislation, no person who knowingly committed the acts made punishable by C.C. Law 10 can assert that he did not know that he would be brought to account for his acts. Notice of intent to punish was repeatedly given by the only means available in international affairs, namely, the solemn warning of the governments of the states at war with Germany. Not only were the defendants warned of swift retribution by the express declaration of the Allies at Moscow of 30 October 1943. Long prior to the Second World War the principle of personal responsibility had been recognized. [The court noted the provisions of the Versailles Treaty referred to above.]

The foregoing considerations demonstrate that the principle *nullum crimen sine lege*, when properly understood and applied, constitutes no legal or moral barrier to prosecution in the case at bar.

Notes and Questions

1. What theories of *nullum crimen sine lege* does the court endorse? What sort of view of *nullum crimen sine lege* do you believe a court should apply to Khmer Rouge defendants for their atrocities in the 1970s?

2. As the court notes, the IMT had justified charging and convicting the leading Nazis for crimes against peace by asserting that the war violated various treaties that Germany had signed, such as the Kellogg-Briand Pact, which had prohibited war as an instrument of national policy. Should the violation by a state of treaties it has signed translate into a crime for which the state's leaders may be held personally accountable? What would be the consequences of such a course of action for treaties addressing issues other than war and peace?

3. What proof of customary international law would you want to determine whether something is an international crime, as opposed to an illegal act for which a state can be held responsible?

4. At the opening of the Tribunal on November 21, 1945, Chief Prosecutor Robert Jackson stated:

> That four great nations, flushed with victory and stung with injury stay the hand of vengeance and voluntarily submit their captive enemies to the judgment of the law is one of the most significant tributes that Power has ever paid to reason. . . . The former high station of these defendants, the notoriety of their acts, and the adaptability of their

conduct to provoke retaliation make it hard to distinguish between the demand for a just and measured retribution, and the unthinking cry for vengeance which arises from the anguish of war. It is our task, so far as humanly possible, to draw the line between the two. . . . To pass these defendants a poisoned chalice is to put it to our own lips as well. We must summon such detachment and intellectual integrity to our task that this Trial will commend itself to posterity as fulfilling humanity's aspirations to do justice.

Yet the Nazi defendants challenged the legitimacy of the Allied tribunals by stating that they amounted to victor's justice. The defendants noted that only the losers were tried—by judges from the victorious states—and that the Allies had committed atrocities themselves, for example, the Soviet massacre of thousands of Polish officers at the Katyn Forest. Indeed, U.S. Chief Justice Harlan Fiske Stone said in 1946 that his colleague Jackson was "conducting his high-grade lynching party in Nuremberg . . . . I don't mind what he does to the Nazis, but I hate to see the pretense that he is running a court and proceeding according to common law. This is a little too sanctimonious a fraud to meet my old-fashioned ideas." How much do these criticisms of the trials undermine Nuremberg's contribution to establishing certain conduct as international crimes?

C. The Crime of Genocide

The Holocaust and the trials of the Nazi defendants spurred states after the war to criminalize some atrocities through the treaty process. During the war, Polish jurist Raphaël Lemkin had coined the term "genocide" to describe the Nazi actions against the Jews. He wrote of a unique crime characterized by a plan designed to eliminate the "essential foundations" of a particular group, adding: "Genocide is directed against the national group as an entity, and the actions involved are directed against individuals, not in their individual capacity, but as members of the national group." Raphaël Lemkin, Axis Rule in Occupied Europe 79 (1944).

By December 1948, the UN's members had agreed upon the Convention on the Prevention and Punishment of the Crime of Genocide. As of 2006, the Convention had 138 parties.

Convention on the Prevention and Punishment of the Crime of Genocide

78 U.N.T.S. 277 (1948)

Article I
The Contracting Parties confirm that genocide, whether committed in time of peace or in time of war, is a crime under international law which they undertake to prevent and to punish.

Article II
In the present Convention, genocide means any of the following acts committed with intent to destroy, in whole or in part, a national, ethnical, racial or religious group, as such:

  (a) Killing members of the group;
  (b) Causing serious bodily or mental harm to members of the group;

(c) Deliberately inflicting on the group conditions of life calculated to bring about its physical destruction in whole or in part;

(d) Imposing measures intended to prevent births within the group;

(e) Forcibly transferring children of the group to another group.

Article III

The following acts shall be punishable:

(a) Genocide;

(b) Conspiracy to commit genocide;

(c) Direct and public incitement to commit genocide;

(d) Attempt to commit genocide;

(e) Complicity in genocide.

Article IV

Persons committing genocide or any of the other acts enumerated in article III shall be punished, whether they are constitutionally responsible rulers, public officials or private individuals. *Jurisdiction over everyone*

Article V

non self-executing

The Contracting Parties ~~undertake to enact,~~ in accordance with their respective Constitutions, the necessary legislation to give effect to the provisions of the present Convention and, in particular, to provide effective penalties for persons guilty of genocide or any of the other acts enumerated in article III.

Article VI - *who has jurisdiction.*

Persons charged with genocide or any of the other acts enumerated in article III shall be tried by a competent tribunal of the State in the territory of which the act was committed, or by such international penal tribunal as may have jurisdiction with respect to those Contracting Parties which shall have accepted its jurisdiction.

Article IX

Disputes between the Contracting Parties relating to the interpretation, application or fulfilment of the present Convention, including those relating to the responsibility of a State for genocide or for any of the other acts enumerated in article III, shall be submitted to the International Court of Justice at the request of any of the parties to the dispute.

Did the acts of the Khmer Rouge against Cambodia's population constitute genocide? States, international organizations, and non-governmental organizations (NGOs) addressed this issue after the defeat of the Khmer Rouge (though they did little during its reign, in part because of the regime's effective closure of the country to most foreign observers). If the Khmer Rouge committed genocide, then Cambodia would presumably have an obligation to prosecute the offenders, and the state, even with its new government, would be responsible for a violation of the Convention as well.

One attempt to put this question on the international agenda took place in response to the decision by the United Nations to continue to allow the Khmer Rouge to hold Cambodia's UN seat following the regime's ouster by Vietnam in

1979. As a means of isolating the group diplomatically, several Western NGOs considered the possibility of a case in the International Court of Justice (ICJ) against Democratic Kampuchea. The case would be brought by an applicant state against the state of Democratic Kampuchea—Cambodia's name under the Khmer Rouge and at the time its official name at the United Nations. Two human rights activists, David Hawk and Hurst Hannum, prepared a detailed draft memorial, or ICJ brief, based on the facts known at that time of the Khmer Rouge's atrocities and circulated it to governments that might be willing to bring a case.

The draft memorial accused Democratic Kampuchea of violations of both the Genocide Convention and customary international human rights law. Jurisdiction would be based upon two provisions of the ICJ Statute. First, Article 36(1) of the Statute gives the Court jurisdiction over disputes relating to treaties providing for ICJ adjudication of disputes. The Genocide Convention, to which Cambodia has been a party since 1951, grants the ICJ jurisdiction over disputes relating to its application, thus allowing any other party to the Genocide Convention to sue Cambodia in the ICJ for a Convention violation. Second, Article 36(2) of the ICJ Statute gives the Court jurisdiction over *any* legal disputes if the two state parties have consented to such jurisdiction. Cambodia accepted ICJ jurisdiction under Article 36(2) in 1957, thus allowing any other state that had also accepted Article 36(2) jurisdiction to make claims against Cambodia for all violations of international law, including violations of the Genocide Convention.

Although the proposed ICJ suit addressed the accountability of a state for genocide (since the ICJ cannot hear cases against individuals), it also addressed definitional questions about genocide that apply in the case of individual prosecutions as well: in particular, whether the regime's acts against political opponents in the Khmer national group constituted genocide. Consider the draft memorial's interpretation of the Genocide Convention, as well as a different view from two scholars.

Hurst Hannum and David Hawk, The Case Against the Standing Committee of the Communist Party of Kampuchea

Draft ICJ Memorial at 133-150 (1986)

. . . [I]t is clear that a national group, such as the Khmer people of Kampuchea, falls within the ambit of article II of the Genocide Convention, whether or not such a group constitutes a majority or a minority within a particular State.

That the Khmer people decimated by the Government of Democratic Kampuchea constitute a ''national group'' within any accepted definition of that term cannot be doubted. The Khmers have a distinct language and a political and social history that spans centuries, and they are ethnically distinct from neighboring peoples . . . . [Hannum and Hawk further argue that nothing in the text of the Convention suggests that the victim group must be a minority group.]

In addition to the commission of acts which result in the physical destruction of a group protected under the Genocide Convention, Article II requires that to constitute genocide, the acts be ''committed with intent to destroy, in whole or in part, a . . . group as such.'' It is the intention to destroy the group, in whole or in part, which distinguishes the international crime of genocide from the domestic crime of murder.

Turning first to the text itself, the language seems plain and straightforward; there must be a specific intent to destroy wholly or partially a group qua group, but the particular motive or motives behind that destruction are immaterial. For example, destruction of a geographically distinct racial group as such in order to secure national borders would constitute genocide, as would destruction of a religious group because it was considered to wield too much economic power or because its members were considered heretics. . . .

. . . [T]he questions of intent and motive, and whether one or both should form part of an enumeration of acts which constitute genocide, were the subject of extensive debate [in the United Nations]. . . . The draft by the Ad Hoc Committee [the first draft of the Convention] included, after enumeration of the groups protected, the phrase ''on grounds of the national or racial origin, religious belief, or political opinion of its members;'' a Venezuelan amendment eventually adopted substituted the phrase ''as such'' for this specific listing of motives . . . .

The interpretation given to the words ''as such'' by the author of the amendment is perhaps the fullest explanation of their import and deserves to be cited at some length:

Mr. Perez Perozo (Venezuela) recalled . . . that an enumeration of motives was useless and even dangerous, as such a restrictive enumeration would be a powerful weapon in the hands of the guilty parties and would help them to avoid being charged with genocide. Their defenders would maintain that the crimes had been committed for other reasons than those listed in . . . article II . . . .

He felt that his amendment should meet the views of those who wished to retain a statement of motives; indeed, the motives were implicitly included in the words ''as such.'' . . . The purpose of [his amendment] was to specify that, for genocide to be committed, a group for instance, a racial group must be destroyed qua group. . . . The General Assembly had manifested its intention to suppress genocide as fully as possible. The adoption of the Venezuelan amendment would enable the Judges to take into account other motives than those listed in the Ad Hoc Committee's draft . . . .

In resolving the question of intent, therefore, the Court must determine whether the intent of the Government of DK was

to destroy, in whole or part, one or more of the groups enumerated and protected under Article II of the Convention. The
motivation, excuse or rationale which may have led to the
decision by DK authorities to destroy all or part of a
group is immaterial, as there can be no justification for
destruction of a protected group. . . .

With respect to the Khmer national group, there was obviously
no intention on the part of the Democratic Kampuchean authorities
to destroy the Khmer group ''in whole'' . . . . Nevertheless,
there was a clear intent to destroy the national group ''in
part,'' in order to purify to the Government of DK's satisfaction
the Khmer nation and eliminate perceived human causes of social
''contradictions'' . . . .

Steven R. Ratner & Jason S. Abrams, Accountability for Human Rights Atrocities in International Law: Beyond the Nuremberg Legacy

285-287 (2d ed. 2001)

The existing literature presents a strong *prima facie* case that the Khmer Rouge committed acts of genocide against the Cham minority group, the ethnic Vietnamese, Chinese, and Thai minority groups, and the Buddhist monkhood. . . .

A more complicated issue, however, is the characterization of atrocities committed against the general Cambodian population. Several observers have asserted that the Khmer Rouge committed genocide against the Khmer national group. . . . [O]ne line maintains that the Khmer Rouge committed genocide against that portion of the Khmer national group that did not conform to their notions of social and ideological purity. This portion transcended characterization as a political or economic group, neither of which is protected by the Convention. . . . Some have contended that the Khmer Rouge committed genocide against the urban Khmer population, the Khmer in the Eastern Zone . . . or both.

The Khmer people of Cambodia clearly constitute a national group within the meaning of the Convention. However, the question whether the Khmer Rouge committed genocide with respect to part of the Khmer national group turns on certain difficult interpretive issues, especially concerning the Khmer Rouge's intent with respect to its non-minority-group victims. While the drafters of the Convention eliminated any specific motive test, the requirement that intent be directed at a protected group 'as such' suggests that victims must have been targeted by virtue of their membership in a protected group. Accordingly, if the Khmer Rouge targeted these victims solely as members of political, professional, or economic groups, or they were victims of random violence or harsh conditions imposed on society at large, it would be difficult to conclude that acts committed against them constituted genocide under the Convention. . . .

The Convention's failure to address the type of situation that prevailed in Cambodia stems largely from the mindset that dominated its elaboration; the drafters did not appear to have contemplated the mass killing of one segment of a group by another segment of that same group. The paradigms that guided the drafting, primarily the Nazi genocide against the Jews, involved attempts to destroy groups that were distinct from the perpetrators, as opposed to the bulk of the atrocities committed by the Khmer Rouge. Thus, although arguments can be advanced that the Convention ought to be interpreted in light of its spirit and purpose to cover the mass killing of Cambodians by the Khmer Rouge, it is uncertain how a court would decide the issue. . . .

The argument that the Khmer Rouge committed genocide with respect to the Khmer national group appears to be relatively weak in light of the facts. Most of the literature suggests that the Khmer Rouge did not target their non-minority victims as members of the Khmer nation 'as such'. Rather, it indicates either that the regime targeted them as economic, social, or political elements whom the Khmer Rouge sought to eradicate but whom the Convention does not protect; or that they were victims of arbitrary violence and harsh conditions that the government imposed on virtually the entire country. Adoption of the alternative legal interpretation, though morally appealing, would, as a practical matter, enlarge the deliberately limited scope of the Convention's list of protected groups, insofar as almost any political, social, or economic element of a population can be viewed as a part of a larger national group. . . .

Notes and Questions

1. Who has the better argument—as a legal matter and a more general normative matter—about whether the Khmer Rouge committed genocide against the Khmer national group?

2. Do you think that the Genocide Convention should include political or social groups in its list of groups the attempted destruction of which constitutes genocide? What advantages and disadvantages would such an amendment to the Convention have? Given the involvement of the Soviet Union in the drafting of the Convention in the 1940s, what might explain the absence of these groups from the protected classes in the Convention?

3. In October 1998, the International Criminal Tribunal for Rwanda completed its first full trial, convicting a Rwandan regional official of genocide. In the course of its long opinion, it stated in dicta that "the intention of the drafters of the Genocide Convention . . . was patently to ensure the protection of any stable and permanent group," not only the four listed in the Convention. It defined such groups as those where "membership . . . would seem to be normally not challengeable by its members, who belong to it automatically, by birth, in a continuous and often irremediable manner." *Prosecutor v. Akayesu*, Judgment, Case No. ICTR-96-4-T (1998), paras. 511, 516. Do you agree with this view?

4. Could customary international law develop a broader definition of genocide than that in the Convention? How might that happen?

5. After Hannum and Hawk circulated their draft memorial, almost none of the many states that were party to the Genocide Convention expressed interest in proceeding, primarily because diplomatic allies of the Khmer Rouge, in particular China and the states of the Association of Southeast Asian Nations, opposed the suit. Officials in Australia, which was an ideal applicant state because it was party to the Genocide Convention and had accepted jurisdiction under Article 36(2) of the ICJ Statute, showed some initial interest in the application but in the end found the case too difficult to make politically and legally. United States government officials and Human Rights Watch, the American NGO, also discussed with various states in the

1990s the possibility of a suit in the ICJ against Iraq for genocide against Kurds in Northern Iraq during Saadam Hussein's 1987-1989 campaign that killed tens of thousands of civilians, including through poison gas attacks. As of 2006, no state has stepped forward for such a case.

6. Following Cambodia's 1993 elections, the new government did not prosecute any Khmer Rouge officials. In the late 1990s, under international pressure, Cambodia sought the UN's assistance in setting up a tribunal to prosecute the Khmer Rouge. The United States, for its part, considered the possibility of obtaining custody over Pol Pot, who was retired in a small part of western Cambodia controlled by his remaining followers, and sending him to another country for trial under the principle of universal jurisdiction (discussed in Chapter 6). No state expressed interest in such a prosecution. As discussed further in the next section of this chapter, the United Nations and Cambodia eventually conducted negotiations for a mixed foreign and domestic tribunal operating under Cambodian law, which was set to begin investigations in 2006.

7. Although Hannum and Hawk's plan to sue Democratic Kampuchea in the ICJ never achieved fruition, the Court is considering three cases concerning alleged violations of the Genocide Convention. In 1993 and 1999, Bosnia and Croatia, respectively, instituted proceedings against the Federal Republic of Yugoslavia, alleging genocide in the Balkan wars; and in 2002, the Democratic Republic of the Congo sued Rwanda, alleging genocide during the latter's incursions into the Congo since 1998. Like all ICJ cases, these concern alleged violations of the Convention by states, not individual criminal responsibility.

D. Crimes Against Humanity

Even if the Genocide Convention does not cover most of the Khmer Rouge's atrocities, Khmer Rouge leaders might still be held accountable for crimes against humanity. The Charter of the IMT recognized a broad set of atrocities against civilians as constituting crimes against humanity. Although the Genocide Convention codifies one subset of crimes against humanity—by focusing on particular groups—the broader definition from the IMT Charter has remained an important indicium of state practice for purposes of customary international law. Various other definitions of crimes against humanity appear in the domestic law of some states, the statutes of UN criminal tribunals prosecuting crimes in the former Yugoslavia and Rwanda, draft international criminal codes produced by the UN's International Law Commission, and, most recently, the Statute of the International Criminal Court.

These definitions assume great significance in determining the criminal responsibility of the Khmer Rouge. For example, Article 6(c) of the Nuremberg Charter defined crimes against humanity as various proscribed acts "in execution of or in connection with any crime within the jurisdiction of the Tribunal." This deliberate phrasing meant that the acts had to be related to crimes against peace or war crimes, and thus related to the armed conflict in that case (World War II). If this element were still part of the customary law of crimes against humanity during the time of the Khmer Rouge's atrocities, then principles of *nullum crimen sine lege* would require prosecutors to demonstrate a connection between their acts and an armed conflict—a connection that, for the most part, does not exist as a historical matter in that case. The UN Secretary-General's Group of Experts for Cambodia, charged with recommending options for trials of Khmer Rouge leaders following Cambodia's request for UN assistance, examined the state of customary law in its 1999 report and concluded that

> for the purpose of . . . the jurisdiction of any tribunal that would prosecute Khmer Rouge officials, the inclusion of crimes against humanity is legally justified. The bond between crimes against humanity and armed conflict appears to have been severed by 1975 [the year the Khmer Rouge took power, so] . . . that a prosecution of Khmer Rouge leaders for such violations would not violate a fair and reasonable reading of the *nullum crimen* principle.

When states and NGOs worked in the 1990s on the Statute of the International Criminal Court (discussed further in Section II below), they agreed upon detailed definitions of genocide, crimes against humanity, and war crimes, over which the Court would have jurisdiction. Consider the definition of crimes against humanity:

Statute of the International Criminal Court

U.N. Doc. A/CONF.183/9 (1998)

Article 7
Crimes Against Humanity

1. For the purpose of this Statute, "crime against humanity" means any of the following acts when committed as part of a widespread or systematic attack directed against any civilian population, with knowledge of the attack:

(a) Murder;

(b) Extermination;

(c) Enslavement;

(d) Deportation or forcible transfer of population;

(e) Imprisonment or other severe deprivation of physical liberty in violation of fundamental rules of international law;

(f) Torture;

(g) Rape, sexual slavery, enforced prostitution, forced pregnancy, enforced sterilization, or any other form of sexual violence of comparable gravity;

(h) Persecution against any identifiable group or collectivity on political, racial, national, ethnic, cultural, religious, gender as defined in paragraph 3, or other grounds that are universally recognized as impermissible under international law, in connection with any act referred to in this paragraph or any crime within the jurisdiction of the Court;

(i) Enforced disappearance of persons;

(j) The crime of apartheid;

(k) Other inhumane acts of a similar character intentionally causing great suffering, or serious injury to body or to mental or physical health.

2. For the purpose of paragraph 1:

(a) "Attack directed against any civilian population" means a course of conduct involving the multiple commission of acts referred to in paragraph 1 against any civilian population, pursuant to or in furtherance of a State or organizational policy to commit such attack; . . .

[Paragraphs (b), (c), (d), and (e) define extermination, enslavement, deportation or forcible transfer of population, and torture.]

(f) "Forced pregnancy" means the unlawful confinement of a woman forcibly made pregnant, with the intent of affecting the ethnic composition of any population or carrying out other grave violations of international law. This definition shall not in any way be interpreted as affecting national laws relating to pregnancy;

(g) "Persecution" means the intentional and severe deprivation of fundamental rights contrary to international law by reason of the identity of the group or collectivity;

(h) "The crime of apartheid" means inhumane acts of a character similar to those referred to in paragraph 1, committed in the context of an institutionalized regime of systematic oppression and domination by one racial group over any other racial group or groups and committed with the intention of maintaining that regime;

(i) "Enforced disappearance of persons" means the arrest, detention or abduction of persons by, or with the authorization, support or acquiescence of, a State or a political organization, followed by a refusal to acknowledge that deprivation of freedom or to give information on the fate or whereabouts of those persons . . . .

3. For the purpose of this Statute, it is understood that the term "gender" refers to the two sexes, male and female, within the context of society. The term "gender" does not indicate any meaning different from the above.

Notes and Questions

1. What is the practical difference between the definitions of genocide and crimes against humanity? What is the point of having a separate crime of genocide if the acts are already crimes against humanity?

2. The Iraqi Special Tribunal (IST), a domestic court established during the U.S. occupation of Iraq following the ouster of the Saddam Hussein regime, has jurisdiction under its statute to prosecute crimes against humanity taking place from July 1968, when Hussein assumed power, to May 2003. Does the IST Statute's use of the ICC Statute's definition of crimes against humanity create problems of retroactive justice?

3. The Genocide Convention's definition of genocide does not require that perpetrators have any connection to the state, whereas the definition of crimes against humanity requires an attack "pursuant to or in furtherance of a State or

organizational policy." Should the definition of crimes against humanity be read to cover wholly private attacks on civilians such as those by organized crime syndicates or drug cartels? Recall the public/private distinction in human rights law discussed in Chapter 7.

4. Was the attack on the World Trade Center on September 11, 2001, a crime against humanity?

5. The ICC Statute makes particular reference to gender-related crimes in Article 7(1)(g), partly as a result of highly successful consciousness-raising by women's rights NGOs. Islamic states and the Vatican, however, insisted upon the inclusion of the second sentence of Article 7(2)(f)'s definition of "forced pregnancy" as well as the definition of "gender" in Article 7(3). What do you think is the purpose of those qualifications? What sorts of persecutions are still not crimes against humanity under the ICC's Statute?

6. In September 2001, the United Nations convened the World Conference Against Racism, Racial Discrimination, Xenophobia, and Related Intolerance in Durban, South Africa. The Conference represented a major gathering of all the UN's members to debate racism and propose solutions to it. The Conference itself was plagued by disagreements between many Western states and much of the developing world, in particular as the latter sought to include in the Conference's final declaration an endorsement of reparations for slavery and a condemnation of Israel (but no other state) for racist policies. With respect to slavery, the final declaration stated:

> We acknowledge that slavery and the slave trade, including the transatlantic slave trade, were appalling tragedies in the history of humanity . . . and further acknowledge that slavery and the slave trade are crimes against humanity and should always have been so. . . .

U.N. Doc. A/CONF.189/12, at 10. Does the wording of this clause in the declaration reflect a victory for the Western states or for the African states?

7. Beginning in the spring and summer of 2004, international attention turned to the western Sudanese region of Darfur, where government-backed militias were waging a brutal campaign of repression, displacement, and murder against tribes seeking greater authority from the central government. The number of people killed or dead from starvation remained uncertain, with some estimates ranging from 70,000 to 200,000, with another 2 million displaced from their homes. The ethnic backgrounds and allegiances of the various groups are extraordinarily complex, though most public discussion characterized the dispute as one between pro-government Arab militias and non-Arab (but Muslim) tribes. The U.S. Department of State labeled the conduct genocide in September 2004; in January 2005, a UN commission of inquiry characterized the acts as crimes against humanity, stating that "the policy of attacking, killing and forcibly displacing members of some tribes does not evince a specific intent to annihilate, in whole or in part, a group distinguished on racial, ethnic, national or religious grounds." It nonetheless urged a full investigation and passed the names of key suspects to the International Criminal Court. As a legal or political matter, would the U.S. or UN determinations affect the international response to the Darfur crisis? Should they?

8. States have recognized a number of peacetime human rights abuses other than genocide and crimes against humanity as international crimes. The definitions of these crimes do not include the special elements of genocide and crimes against

humanity. Among the most significant are slavery, forced labor, torture, apartheid, and forced disappearances.

II. WARTIME ABUSES: U.S. TREATMENT OF PRISONERS AT ABU GHRAIB

War crimes are the oldest of international crimes other than piracy, and the oldest to concern violations of human dignity. As discussed in Chapter 8, norms for the conduct of war date back more than 2,000 years. The first trial for war crimes is generally considered to be that of Peter von Hagenbach, who was tried in 1474 before an ad hoc court of international jurists in Austria and sentenced to death for wartime atrocities. States have prosecuted enemy nationals for war crimes and, on occasion, their own soldiers, relying upon domestic law implementing the law of war. Among the most famous trials in the United States were those of William Calley and Ernest Medina for the 1968 massacre by American troops of at least 200 Vietnamese civilians at My Lai. At the international level, the Nuremberg Charter's inclusion of war crimes laid the groundwork for further efforts towards criminalization. Taking the lead on these issues was an NGO, the International Committee of the Red Cross (ICRC), which convened major conferences of states to prepare the 1949 Geneva Conventions and the 1977 Protocols to them.

The most comprehensive international judicial application of the modern law of war crimes has taken place in the International Criminal Tribunal for the Former Yugoslavia (ICTY), created by the UN Security Council to try individuals for atrocities committed in the Yugoslavia conflict. Its caselaw since 1995 has greatly enhanced the body of international criminal law by elaborating the elements of crimes, the extension of culpability to commanders, and the essential components of defenses to crimes. When governments in the late 1990s drafted the statute of the International Criminal Court, they relied extensively on the criminal provisions of the Geneva Conventions and Protocols, as well as the jurisprudence of both the ICTY and the International Criminal Tribunal for Rwanda.

Though conflicts in Yugoslavia, Rwanda, and elsewhere claimed huge numbers of victims, the culpability of soldiers for abuses of civilians received renewed attention with the publication in April 2004 of photographs showing abuses by U.S. service members at the Abu Ghraib prison in Baghdad following the ouster of the Ba'ath regime in 2003. The abuses triggered significant public discussion about the responsibility of both low-level enlisted personnel and their superiors for violations of the law of war. As you read the following problem, consider what sorts of violations of international humanitarian law trigger individual responsibility; the extent to which the law's recognition of the responsibility of superiors for the actions of subordinates is fair to a defendant; and whether defendants who commit atrocities in response to superior orders or coercion should be exculpated.

A. The Problem

Approximately 20 miles west of Baghdad lies the prison facility of Abu Ghraib, well known as a place of torture and execution under the regime of Saddam

Hussein. After Iraqi authorities abandoned the prison following the March 2003 U.S. invasion, the U.S. military renamed the prison the Baghdad Central Correctional Facility. In June 2003, Brigadier General Janis Karpinski was named the commanding officer of the 800th Military Police Brigade and placed in control of Iraqi military prisons, including Abu Ghraib. Karpinski, a reserve officer, had no prior experience working with prisoners, nor did most of the 3400 Army reservists under her command. The 372nd Military Police (MP) Company, an Army reserve unit, assumed responsibility for prison-guard duty at Abu Ghraib in October 2003. The unit, which had previously been assigned to traffic and police work, apparently was not given any specific guidelines for the operation of the prison and was left to rely on unit members with prior experience in civilian correctional facilities. Abu Ghraib housed as many as 7000 detainees in October 2003, despite having only 90 military prison guards. The 205th Military Intelligence (MI) Brigade, in charge of the Joint Intelligence Debriefing Center (JIDC), was charged with interrogating detainees, sometimes with the help of CIA officers and private contractors.

Mock electrocution, Abu Ghraib Prison, Baghdad, November 4, 2003

In October 2003, the International Committee of the Red Cross conducted an inspection of Abu Ghraib and submitted a confidential report to the U.S. military in Iraq outlining incidents of alleged abuse. The ICRC later said its numerous inspections from March to November 2003 had led to the discovery of "serious violations" and that it had warned U.S. officials for over a year about abuses at multiple prisons. A November 2003 investigation by Maj. Gen. Donald Ryder found that the units responsible for U.S.-run prisons in Iraq, including Abu Ghraib, had not been adequately trained to guard prisoners. His report concluded that there were human rights issues in need of immediate system-wide attention.

In January 2004, a military policeman, Sergeant Joseph Darby, alerted military investigators of prisoner abuse by anonymously leaving on the bed of a military investigator a CD of photographs depicting the abuse, which he had obtained when fellow soldiers distributed the pictures over computers in the unit. The photos triggered investigations within the U.S. government. Within several days, the commander of U.S. forces in Iraq (the forces were known as Combined Joint Task Force 7 (CJTF-7)), Lt. Gen. Ricardo Sanchez, ordered Maj. Gen. Antonio Taguba, a deputy commanding general of the U.S. Central Command, to conduct an investigation. In early February, President Bush was briefed by Secretary of Defense Donald Rumsfeld and Gen. Peter Pace, vice chairman of the Joint Chiefs of Staff, on the investigations.

General Taguba's report, completed in March 2004, found that American soldiers had committed "numerous incidents of sadistic, blatant and wanton criminal abuses" and "egregious acts and grave breaches of international law." The abuse was both "systemic and illegal." The individual abuses had been perpetrated by members of the 372nd MP Company as well as members of the U.S. intelligence services. The report detailed numerous acts of abuse, including:

— "Punching, slapping, and kicking detainees; jumping on their naked feet;"
— "Videotaping and photographing naked male and female detainees;"
— "Forcibly arranging detainees in various sexually explicit positions for photographing;"
— "Forcing groups of male detainees to masturbate themselves while being photographed and videotaped;"
— "Arranging naked male detainees in a pile and then jumping on them;"
— "Positioning a naked detainee on a MRE [Meals Ready-to-Eat] Box, with a sandbag on his head, and attaching wires to his fingers, toes, and penis to simulate electric torture;"
— "Placing a dog chain or strap around a naked detainee's neck and having a female Soldier pose for a picture;"
— "A male MP guard having sex with a female detainee;"
— "Using military working dogs (without muzzles) to intimidate and frighten detainees, and in at least one case biting and severely injuring a detainee."

Generally, the report was critical of the prison's organization, including its staffing, supervision, and prisoner screening systems. It noted that while "the average battalion size element should be able to handle approximately 4000 detainees at a time," the Abu Ghraib facility "normally housed between 6000 and 7000 detainees, yet it was operated by only one battalion" that suffered personnel shortages and very poor morale. The soldiers were found to be "poorly prepared and untrained . . . prior to deployment, at the mobilization site, upon arrival in theater, and throughout the mission."

April and May 2004 represented a crucial turning point in the abuse scandal. General Sanchez ordered another investigation of the facility, this time by Maj. Gen. George Fay, to examine the role of military intelligence personnel at Abu Ghraib. On April 28, the CBS news program, *60 Minutes II*, broadcast a feature on the abuses, showing several of the more graphic photos. In response to the broadcast, President Bush and Secretary Rumsfeld stated that they had not previously seen the photographs. On May 3, 2004, aides to Secretary Rumsfeld indicated that the Secretary had not yet read the Taguba report. Several days later, President Bush offered a formal apology for the abuses, and Rumsfeld accepted responsibility for them in testimony before congressional committees. In May 2004, the military convened yet another high-level investigation of Abu Ghraib, led by Lt. Gen. Anthony Jones, this time to focus on deficiencies outside and above the 205th MI Brigade, and Rumsfeld convened a three-person civilian investigatory panel led by former Defense Secretary James Schlesinger.

B. Prosecuting the Immediate Perpetrators at Abu Ghraib

As discussed in Chapter 8, the four Geneva Conventions of 1949 each place numerous obligations on states to protect people in international armed conflict who are not actively engaged in hostilities. These are the sick and wounded in armies (Convention I), the sick and wounded in navies (Convention II), prisoners of war (Convention III), and civilians, including those in occupied territories (Convention IV). In addition, the four Conventions—as well as Protocol I to the Geneva Conventions of 1977, which includes additional rules concerning international conflicts—contain a set of so-called grave breaches that states must prosecute. These grave breaches are the clearest treaty-based formulation of war crimes. Consider, for example, the obligations of the parties to the fourth Geneva Convention, which addresses situations of occupation such as that in Iraq:

Geneva Convention Relative to the Protection of Civilian Persons in Time of War

75 U.N.T.S. 287, 386-387 (1949)

ARTICLE 146

The High Contracting Parties undertake to enact any legislation necessary to provide effective penal sanctions for persons committing, or ordering to be committed, any of the grave breaches of the present Convention defined in the following Article.

Each High Contracting Party shall be under the obligation to search for persons alleged to have committed, or to have ordered to be committed, such grave breaches, and shall bring such persons, regardless of their nationality, before its own courts. It may also, if it prefers . . . hand such persons over for trial to another High Contracting Party concerned, provided such High Contracting Party has made out a prima facie case.

Each High Contracting Party shall take measures necessary for the suppression of all acts contrary to the provisions of the present Convention other than the grave breaches defined in the following Article. . . .

ARTICLE 147

Grave breaches to which the preceding Article relates shall be those involving any of the following acts, if committed against persons or property protected by the present Convention: wilful killing, torture or inhuman treatment, including biological experiments, wilfully causing great suffering or serious injury to body or health, unlawful deportation or transfer or unlawful confinement of a protected person, compelling a protected person to serve in the forces of a hostile Power, or wilfully depriving a protected person of the rights of fair and regular trial prescribed in the present Convention, taking of hostages and extensive destruction and appropriation of property, not justified by military necessity and carried out unlawfully and wantonly.

Beyond the treaty-based war crimes in the grave breaches provisions, customary law has recognized that certain violations of international humanitarian law concerning the conduct of hostilities also constitute war crimes. For instance, the Security Council gave the ICTY jurisdiction to try not only grave breaches of the Geneva Conventions but also customary law war crimes, including: (a) employment of poisonous weapons; (b) wanton destruction of cities, towns or villages; (c) attack on undefended towns or buildings; (d) seizure of or wilful damage done to institutions dedicated to religion, charity, education, the arts and sciences, and historic monuments; and (e) plunder of public or private property. At the same time, most governments would hold that many violations of international humanitarian law are not serious enough to incur individual responsibility, for example, failing to provide a prisoner of war with the required tobacco allowance.

In the case of Abu Ghraib, the United States government acknowledged that the Geneva Conventions applied to the war in Iraq and that the victims of the abuse were protected persons—civilians—under the Conventions. Even before the public disclosure of the abuses at Abu Ghraib, the U.S. military began various forms of disciplinary proceedings against those involved in the abuses. It first suspended 17 people in March 2003 and then brought criminal charges against some ten enlisted personnel in the 372nd MP Company, all at or below the rank of sergeant.

The military charged the personnel under the Uniform Code of Military Justice (UCMJ), a comprehensive U.S. federal statute that governs the courts martial process. The UCMJ gives courts martial jurisdiction to try military personnel (and other personnel associated with the military) for some 54 specific offenses—ranging from murder to rape to robbery to dereliction of duty—as well as any other violation of the law of war. The UCMJ does not specifically list the grave breaches of the Geneva Conventions or other war crimes recognized under customary international law under the enumerated offenses, but those suspected of war crimes can be charged with one of the listed offenses. Indeed, because the listed offenses include detailed elements for military prosecutors to prove, the Defense Department's policy is typically to charge those accused of all war crimes with one or more of the listed offenses, rather than war crimes per se. (Outside the military, the War Crimes Act of 1996 gave U.S. federal courts jurisdiction to try grave breaches, violations of Common Article 3, certain violations of the Hague Regulations, and some other offenses; unlike the courts martial, the federal courts have jurisdiction over both military personnel as well as retired military personnel and civilians.) Thus, the Abu Ghraib defendants were charged with mistreatment, assault, conspiracy to mistreat, dereliction of duty, and other offenses. During 2004-06, eight either pled guilty or were convicted of these charges; they were demoted in rank, dishonorably discharged, sentenced to prison, or some combination of these. Army Spc. Charles Graner, whom various media identified as the "ringleader" of the guards, was convicted of conspiracy, assault, maltreating prisoners, dereliction of duty, and committing indecent acts, and sentenced to ten years in prison. In addition, two soldiers from the 205th MI Brigade were convicted of abuses. At least seven other soldiers were convicted in 2005 of other abuses of civilians in Iraq. The Army reported in late May 2006 that some 270 personnel had been punished for detainee abuse in Iraq and elsewhere, although the vast majority of these were through internal disciplinary means.

Notes and Questions

1. How should a court decide whether a violation of international humanitarian law, other than those listed in the Geneva Conventions as grave breaches, is a war crime?

2. How close do you think domestic criminal law, including military criminal law, needs to correspond to the terms used in the Geneva Conventions in order for a state to satisfy its obligations to try those accused of war crimes?

3. As noted above, only two of the military intelligence personnel implicated in the Taguba, Jones, and Fay reports have been criminally prosecuted. The reports also noted the involvement in abuses of private military contractors working with the 205th MI Brigade. In 2000, Congress passed the Military Extraterritorial Jurisdiction Act, which makes a federal crime any action by a civilian employed by or accompanying U.S. military forces abroad (including dependents of military personnel and civilian contractors) if that action would be a crime in the United States punishable by at least one year in prison. No contractors have been indicted for the events at Abu Ghraib. What might explain the discrepancy between the punishment meted out to MP guards and the treatment given to MI personnel and contractors? Federal prosecutors have investigated, but not brought any charges against, CIA personnel for alleged abuses in Afghanistan and Iraq, although one CIA contractor was indicted in 2004 for the death of a detainee in Afghanistan.

C. Responsibility of Military and Civilian Commanders

Individuals such as the enlisted personnel at Abu Ghraib who commit war crimes or other violations of human dignity typically do so within some structure of authority, either military or civilian. In such situations, the superior who actually orders a subordinate to commit an atrocity is, under both domestic and international criminal law, as guilty as the person carrying it out. But does a superior have greater responsibilities? Does the mere existence of a hierarchical structure place certain duties upon superiors to know of the activities of subordinates and either prevent or punish them? In this case, the military chain of command of the prison guards ran to officers within the Company and then the Battalion, up to General Karpinski, then to General Sanchez; the chain of command of the military intelligence personnel ran to officers within the 205th Brigade, in particular its commander, Colonel Thomas Pappas, and then to General Sanchez. General Sanchez reported to the general in charge of the U.S. Central Command, then to the Secretary of Defense and the President.

1. International Standards on Command Responsibility

Military law has long accepted that commanders may be held responsible for the abuses committed by their subordinates as a result of the commander's failure to supervise their actions. The Nuremberg cases and their progeny, including domestic war crimes prosecutions and the statutes of the Yugoslavia and Rwanda Tribunals, have elaborated a number of formulations for this responsibility, all centering on the idea that a commander is responsible not merely if he or she ordered abuses, but if he or she knew or should have known that subordinates committed them and failed to prevent them or punish those responsible. In its 1998 ruling in *Prosecutor v. Mucic et al.*, the ICTY offered the following views on the doctrine, in particular the meaning of the requirement in the Tribunal's statute that a superior is guilty if he or she "knew or had reason to know" of actual or impending crimes:

> [T]he Trial Chamber takes as its point of departure the principle that a superior is not permitted to remain wilfully blind to the acts of his subordinates. There can be no doubt that a superior who simply ignores information within his actual possession compelling the conclusion that criminal offences are being committed, or are about to be committed, by his subordinates commits a most serious dereliction of duty for which he may be held criminally responsible under the doctrine of superior responsibility. Instead, uncertainty arises in relation to situations where the superior lacks such information by virtue of his failure to properly supervise his subordinates. . . .
>
> [A] superior can be held criminally responsible only if some specific information was in fact available to him which would provide notice of offences committed by his subordinates. This information need not be such that it by itself was sufficient to compel the conclusion of the existence of such crimes. It is sufficient that the superior was put on further inquiry by the information, or, in other words, that it indicated the need for additional investigation in order to ascertain whether offences were being committed or about to be committed by his subordinates.

Consider the standard for command responsibility in the ICC Statute, adopted at an intergovernmental conference in 1998, five years after the creation of the ICTY:

Article 28
Responsibility of commanders and other superiors

In addition to other grounds of criminal responsibility under this Statute for crimes within the jurisdiction of the Court:

(a) A military commander or person effectively acting as a military commander shall be criminally responsible for crimes within the jurisdiction of the Court committed by forces under his or her effective command and control, or effective authority and control as the case may be, as a result of his or her failure to exercise control properly over such forces, where:

(i) That military commander or person either knew or, owing to the circumstances at the time, should have known that the forces were committing or about to commit such crimes; and

(ii) That military commander or person failed to take all necessary and reasonable measures within his or her power to prevent or repress their commission or to submit the matter to the competent authorities for investigation and prosecution.

(b) With respect to superior and subordinate relationships not described in paragraph (a), a superior shall be criminally responsible for crimes within the jurisdiction of the Court committed by subordinates under his or her effective authority and control, as a result of his or her failure to exercise control properly over such subordinates, where:

(i) The superior either knew, or consciously disregarded information which clearly indicated, that the subordinates were committing or about to commit such crimes;

(ii) The crimes concerned activities that were within the effective responsibility and control of the superior; and

(iii) The superior failed to take all necessary and reasonable measures within his or her power to prevent or repress their commission or to submit the matter to the competent authorities for investigation and prosecution.

2. Governmental and NGO Views of Individual Responsibility at Abu Ghraib

Investigations commissioned by the Department of Defense addressed in differing levels of detail the responsibility of those beyond the immediate offenders, although these studies did not focus on criminal responsibility. Consider the following perspectives, three from official U.S. government inquiries and one from a human rights NGO:

Maj. Gen. George R. Fay, *Investigation of the Abu Ghraib Detention Facility and 205th Military Intelligence Brigade*

120 (2004)

Finding: COL Thomas M. Pappas, Commander, 205 MI BDE [Brigade]. A preponderance of evidence supports that COL Pappas did, or failed to do, the following:

- Failed to put the necessary checks and balances in place to prevent and detect abuses.
- Failed to ensure that his Soldiers and civilians were properly trained. . . .
- Improperly authorized the use of dogs during interrogations. Failed to properly supervise the use of dogs to make sure they were muzzled. . . .
- Failed to take appropriate action regarding the ICRC reports of abuse.

- Failed to take aggressive action against Soldiers who violated . . . the CJTF-7 interrogation and Counter-Resistance Policy and the Geneva Conventions.
- Failed to properly communicate to Higher Headquarters when his Brigade would be unable to accomplish its mission due to lack of manpower and/or resources. Allowed . . . the JIDC to be subjected to inordinate pressure from Higher Headquarters.
- Failed to establish appropriate MI and MP coordination at the brigade level which would have alleviated much of the confusion that contributed to the abusive environment. . . .
- The significant number of systemic failures documented in this report does not relieve COL Pappas of his responsibility as the Commander, 205th MI BDE for the abuses that occurred and went undetected for a considerable length of time.

Recommendation: This information should be forwarded to COL Pappas' chain of command for appropriate action.

Lt. Gen. Anthony R. Jones, *Investigation of the Abu Ghraib Prison and 205th Military Intelligence Brigade*

24 (2004)

RESPONSIBILITY ABOVE 205th MI BRIGADE

(a) I find that the chain of command above the 205th MI Brigade was not directly involved in any of the abuses that occurred at Abu Ghraib.

(b) I find that the chain of command above the 205th MI Brigade promulgated policy memoranda that, inadvertently, left room for interpretation and may have indirectly led to some of the non-violent and non-sexual abuse incidents.

(c) I find that [Lt. Gen.] Sanchez and his [deputy, Maj. Gen.] Wojdakowski, failed to ensure proper staff oversight of detention and interrogation operations. . . . Further, staff elements of the CJTF-7 reacted inadequately to some of the Indications and Warnings discussed above. However, in light of the operational environment, and CJTF-7's under-resourcing and unplanned missions, and the Commander's consistent need to prioritize efforts, I find that the CJTF-7 Commander and staff performed above expectations. . . .

(d) I find that the [tactical control] relationship of the 800th MP Brigade to the CJTF-7 created a dysfunctional relationship for proper oversight and effective detention operations in the Iraqi Theater of Operations. In addition, the relationship between leaders and staff of the 205th MI Brigade and 800th MP Brigade was ineffective as they failed to effect proper coordination of roles and responsibilities for detention and interrogation operations.

(e) I find that a number of causes outside of the control of CJTF-7 also contributed to the abuses at Abu Ghraib. These . . . include, individuals' criminal propensity; Soldier knowledge of interrogation techniques permitted in GTMO [Guantanamo] and Afghanistan and failure to distinguish between those environments and Iraq; interaction with [other government agencies] and other agency interrogators who did not follow the same rules as U.S. Forces; integration of some contractors without training, qualifications, and certification; underresourcing of personnel . . . , specifically in the interrogator, analyst, and linguist fields.

James Schlesinger, Harold Brown, Tillie Fowler, and Charles Horner, *Final Report of the Independent Panel to Review DoD Detention Operations*

43, 47 (2004)

Although the most egregious instances of detainee abuse were caused by the aberrant behavior of a limited number of soldiers and the predilections of the noncommissioned officers . . . commanding officers and their staffs at various levels failed in their duties and . . . such failures contributed directly or indirectly to detainee abuse. Commanders are responsible for all their units do or fail to do, and should be held accountable for their action or inaction. Command failures were compounded by poor advice provided by staff officers with responsibility for overseeing battlefield functions related to detention and interrogation operations. Military and civilian leaders at the Department of Defense share this burden of responsibility. . . .

Once it became clear in July 2003 there was a major insurgency growing in Iraq and the relatively benign environment projected for Iraq was not materializing, senior leaders should have adjusted the plan from what had been assumed to be a . . . benign handoff of detention operations to the Iraqis. If commanders and staffs at the operational level had been more adaptive in the face of changing conditions, a different approach to detention operations could have been developed by October 2003, as difficulties with the basic plan were readily apparent by that time. Responsible leaders who could have set in motion the development of a more effective course of action extend up the command chain (and staff) to include . . . Deputy Commanding General, CJTF-7 [Wojdakowski]; Commander, CJTF-7 [Sanchez]; . . . Commander, CENTCOM [U.S. Central Command, General Abizaid] . . . , the Chairman of the Joint Chiefs of Staff; and the Office of the Secretary of Defense. In most cases these were errors of omission, but they were errors that should not go unnoted.

Human Rights Watch, *Getting Away with Torture? Command Responsibility for the U.S. Abuse of Detainees*

39-40, 42-44, 48 (2005)

Secretary Rumsfeld reportedly initiated pressure on troops at Abu Ghraib to obtain "actionable intelligence"

In August 2003, with American troops facing a growing insurgency in Iraq, and frustration rising over the failure to uncover "weapons of mass destruction" or to capture deposed Iraqi President Saddam Hussein, Maj. Gen. Geoffrey D. Miller, who oversaw the interrogation efforts at the U.S. military base at Guantánamo Bay, Cuba, was sent to Iraq. In the words of Maj. Gen. Taguba, Gen. Miller's task was to "review current Iraqi Theater ability to rapidly exploit internees for actionable intelligence." As the Schlesinger report noted, Gen Miller brought with him the secretary of defense's April 16th memo (the final of three memos) outlining Guantánamo interrogation techniques and presented it as a possible model for interrogations in Iraq. As Gen. Taguba highlighted and criticized in his report, Gen. Miller recommended that "the guard force be actively engaged in setting the conditions for successful exploitation of the internees." . . .

At an intelligence briefing conducted in the summer of 2003 in the Pentagon for the benefit of Rumsfeld . . . Rumsfeld complained loudly about the quality of the intelligence which was being gathered from detainees in Iraq. He contrasted it with the intelligence which was being produced from detainees at Guantánamo following the institution there of new "extreme" interrogation practices. . . . *Rumsfeld gave an oral order to dispatch MG Miller to Iraq to "Gitmoize" the intelligence gathering operations there* . . . [citing a report based on discussions with a senior officer at the meeting].

On September 14, 2003, the top U.S. commander in Iraq, Lt. Gen. Ricardo Sanchez, implemented Gen. Miller's proposals by adopting a policy that brought back into play the techniques which Secretary Rumsfeld had approved in December 2002 for use at Guantánamo. Gen. Sanchez's memo authorized 29 interrogation techniques, including the "presence of military working dog: Exploits Arab fear of dogs while maintaining security during interrogations," and sleep deprivation, both approved by Secretary Rumsfeld for Guantánamo. . . .

Between three and five interrogation teams were sent in October from Guantánamo to the American command in Iraq "for use in the interrogation effort" at Abu Ghraib.

Beyond this, the Schlesinger report noted that "senior leaders expressed, forcibly at times, their needs for better intelligence." It also concluded that a number of high-level visits to Abu Ghraib contributed to this pressure, including those by Gen. Miller and "a senior member of the National Security Council Staff." This second visit, focused primarily on intelligence collection, led "some personnel at the facility to conclude, perhaps incorrectly, that even the White House was interested in the intelligence gleaned from their interrogation reports." . . .

Secretary Rumsfeld was personally warned about the abuse of detainees

- Throughout the period in question, Secretary Rumsfeld was personally notified about the mistreatment of detainees. . . .

The Defense Department was warned about the abuse of detainees

The ICRC delivered repeated warnings during the same period. The organization paid 29 visits to 14 detention centers in Iraq, delivering oral and written reports to U.S. officials in Iraq after each visit. . . .

Given the widespread nature of crimes against detainees, Secretary Rumsfeld should have known of them

The widespread nature of the abuses across three countries suggests that the Secretary of Defense should have been aware, through internal channels, that his subordinates were committing crimes.

Secretary Rumsfeld failed to intervene to prevent the commission of war crimes and torture by soldiers and officers under his command in Afghanistan and Iraq

During the entire period listed above Secretary Rumsfeld failed to intervene to prevent further commission of crimes. Even as he was being personally warned about abuses, even as the press and human rights groups were publicly denouncing abuses, even as the ICRC was complaining, Secretary Rumsfeld apparently never issued specific orders or guidelines to forbid coercive methods of interrogation, other than withdrawing his blanket approval for certain methods at Guantánamo in January 2003. . . .

[The report continued with similar discussions regarding the role of CIA Director George Tenet and Generals Sanchez, Miller, Wodjakowski, and Karpinski. It also urges inquiry into the roles of Colonel Pappas and others.]

_____

As of May 2006, only 11 soldiers had faced criminal proceedings for the events at Abu Ghraib. In April 2005, the Army Inspector-General found no wrongful conduct by General Sanchez and three of his deputies (including his legal adviser). In May 2005, Pappas was reprimanded and fined two months' pay ($8000) for dereliction of duty; Karpinski was demoted in rank to colonel after having been permanently relieved of command of the 800th MP Brigade; Miller and General Sanchez announced their retirement from the military. At the same time, the military instituted a number of important reforms to prevent the recurrence of those abuses, although, as discussed in Chapter 7, the United States government still faces serious and credible charges of abuse of detainees in other locations.

Notes and Questions

1. What more would you need to know about the roles of Colonel Pappas, General Karpinski, General Sanchez, and Secretary Rumsfeld to determine if their acts or omissions create criminal responsibility under international law?

2. Recall the discussion of the U.S. government legal memoranda on interrogations in Chapter 7, Section I. To what extent might the legal guidance in these memos have contributed to the abuses at Abu Ghraib?

3. Is the ICC's standard for military commanders too lenient? Too burdensome given the fog of war? Would strict liability ever be justifiable regarding the guilt of superior officials? In the fall of 1945, an American military tribunal prosecuted General Tomoyuki Yamashita, the Japanese commander of the Philippines in 1944-1945, a time during which the occupying Japanese army committed horrendous atrocities against the civilian population. In convicting Yamashita (and sentencing him to death), the tribunal did not discuss any specific knowledge by Yamashita of his forces' crimes. Its opinion, later upheld by the U.S. Supreme Court, stated:

> It is absurd . . . to consider a commander a murderer or rapist because one of his soldiers commits a murder or rape. Nevertheless, where murder and rape and vicious, revengeful actions are widespread offenses, and there is no effective attempt by a commander to discover and control the criminal acts, such a commander may be held . . . criminally liable for the lawless acts of his troops.

In re Yamashita, 4 Law Reports of Trials of War Criminals 1, 35 (1945). How does this compare to the ICC Statute?

4. Is the difference in the ICC Statute's standards for the responsibility of military commanders and civilian superior officials justifiable?

5. What factors might account for the U.S. prosecutions of only a relatively small number of enlisted personnel at the Abu Ghraib prison and no senior personnel?

6. The UN's tribunals for Yugoslavia and Rwanda have convicted a number of defendants based on command responsibility. These include Bosnian commanders of a concentration camp and a Croat general; the trial of former Yugoslav President Slobodan Milosevic examined his role not only in atrocities committed by the Yugoslav army within the province of Kosovo, but in acts committed by the Bosnian Serb army within Bosnia. The UN's Special Court for Sierra Leone indicted and is trying Charles Taylor, the former president of Liberia, for atrocities in his individual capacity and, in the alternative, under the court statute's provisions on command responsibility.

D. Defenses to War Crimes?

Defendants charged with war crimes and other crimes against human dignity often raise the same sorts of defenses as those charged with ordinary crimes. The most common defenses presented are mistaken identity or alibi. Yet two special sorts of defenses are often asserted by governmental officials involved in human rights abuses of the sort that took place in the former Yugoslavia.

1. Following Orders

A classic claim since the Nuremberg trials is that the defendant was merely following orders. American psychologist Stanley Milgram confirmed the relevance of such orders in the course of controversial experiments in 1960-1963. Subjects were told by researchers working with Milgram that they must apply an electrical current (which the subjects thought was genuine but was not) to an individual failing to answer certain questions (who was, unknown to the subjects, working with Milgram), and then did so despite feigned shrieks of pain from the perceived victim. Milgram wrote:

> [A]n act carried out under command is, psychologically, of a profoundly different character than action that is spontaneous. The person who, with inner conviction, loathes stealing, killing, and assault may find himself performing these acts with relative ease when commanded by authority. . . . A substantial portion of people do what they are told to do, irrespective of the content of the act and without limitations of conscience, so long as they perceive that the command comes from a legitimate authority.

Stanley Milgram, Obedience to Authority xi, 189 (1974).

In the case of Abu Ghraib, some of those investigated and prosecuted have claimed that the mistreatment they inflicted on prisoners was authorized or even ordered by those above them. Thus, Charles Graner stated to the Army court-martial before his sentencing, "We were called to violate the Geneva Convention"; "We were asked to do certain things I wasn't trained to do." "If [military intelligence] asks you to do this, it needs to be done. They're in charge, follow their orders." He testified that "at the time my understanding is that [the orders] were [lawful], or I wouldn't have done them." And, as noted in the excerpt above, Human Rights

Watch has suggested that Secretary Rumsfeld authorized harsh interrogation techniques, which effectively gave a green light to abuses by the guards as well.

Yet, as the excerpt from the IMT Charter on p. 612 makes clear, following orders is not per se a defense to international crimes: some defendants are more than willing to carry out atrocities and will simply use the existence of superior orders as a shield to immunize themselves from prosecution. The Nuremberg Charter and the cases based upon it require even subordinates who would *not* have committed the challenged acts except for the order to disobey it. This norm, now well-established, thus refuses to excuse subordinates for obeying such illegal orders even under the stressful, life-and-death circumstances of armed conflict. Consider the following excerpt from the Statute of the ICC, which generally reflects the case law from Nuremberg and subsequent courts. (This provision applies not merely to war crimes but also to the other crimes over which the Court has jurisdiction).

Article 33
Superior orders and prescription of law

1. The fact that a crime within the jurisdiction of the Court has been committed by a person pursuant to an order of a Government or of a superior, whether military or civilian, shall not relieve that person of criminal responsibility unless:

   (a) The person was under a legal obligation to obey orders of the Government or the superior in question;

   (b) The person did not know that the order was unlawful; and

   (c) The order was not manifestly unlawful.

2. For the purposes of this article, orders to commit genocide or crimes against humanity are manifestly unlawful.

Notes and Questions

1. Is it fair to convict subordinates of abuses ordered or authorized by superiors? Should it depend upon the education and training given to the subordinate, or the situation in which the subordinate finds himself or herself (e.g., combat vs. a prison)? What would you need to know about the Abu Ghraib situation to determine if any of those convicted should not have been found guilty?

2. Does the ICC Statute place too low a burden on subordinates? How much knowledge should be expected of subordinates?

3. The ICC has jurisdiction over genocide, crimes against humanity, and war crimes (and, perhaps at some point in the future, aggression). Article 33 makes clear that not all orders to commit war crimes are considered manifestly unlawful. Why would the drafters of the Statute make this distinction? Are any orders to commit war crimes not manifestly unlawful?

2. Duress

A defendant asserting that he is not guilty merely by virtue of an order to carry out crimes against humanity would find that claim rejected by a court applying international law. But what if he could argue that he was forced to carry out the atrocities, for example, on pain of death?

In 1997, the ICTY faced precisely this question. Drazen Erdemovic was part of a detachment of the Bosnian Serb Army that executed 1,200 men and boys outside the Bosnian town of Srebrenica on July 16, 1995. It is estimated that 5,000 to 8,000 people were executed there in the largest single atrocity in Europe since World War II. At the ICTY, where he was charged with crimes against humanity, he pled guilty, although he stated at the time of his plea: "Your Honour, I had to do this. If I had refused, I would have been killed together with the victims." He subsequently cooperated significantly with investigators. Based on his young age (23), remorse, and cooperation, the trial court sentenced him to ten years in prison. He appealed his sentence, arguing that the duress under which he committed the executions was a complete defense. The claim left the Tribunal sharply divided, with two judges joining the plurality opinion excerpted below and a third concurring in the result. Two judges wrote dissents, one of which is also excerpted below.

Prosecutor v. Erdemovic, Sentencing Appeal

Case No. IT-96-22 (1997)

III. CAN DURESS BE A COMPLETE DEFENCE IN INTERNATIONAL LAW TO THE KILLING OF INNOCENTS?

1. No customary international law rule can be derived on the question of duress as a defence to the killing of innocent persons

47. A number of war crimes cases have been brought to our attention as supporting the position that duress is a complete defence to the killing of innocent persons in international law [the Tribunal listed a number of cases from the post-World War I and post-World War II period]. . . .

49. Although some of the above mentioned cases may clearly represent the positions of national jurisdictions regarding the availability of duress as a complete defence to the killing of innocent persons, neither they nor the principles on this issue found in decisions of the post-World War Two military tribunals are, in our view, entitled to be given the status of customary international law. . . . To the extent that the domestic decisions and national laws of States relating to the issue of duress as a defence to murder may be regarded as state practice, it is quite plain that this practice is not at all consistent. The defence . . . surveys the criminal codes and legislation of 14 civil law jurisdictions [primarily in Europe] in which necessity or duress is prescribed as a general exculpatory principle applying to all crimes. . . . In stark contrast to this acceptance of duress as a defence to the killing of innocents is the clear position of the various countries throughout the world applying the common law. These common law systems categorically reject duress as a defence to murder. The sole exception is the United States where a few states have accepted Section 2.09 of the United States [Model] Penal Code which currently provides that duress is a general defence to all crimes. . . .

50. Not only is State practice on the question as to whether duress is a defence to murder far from consistent, this practice of States is not, in our view, underpinned by *opinio juris*. Again to the extent that state practice on the question of duress as a defence to murder may be evidenced by the opinions on this question in decisions of

national military tribunals and national laws, we find quite unacceptable any proposition that States adopt this practice because they "feel that they are conforming to what amounts to a legal obligation" at an international level [quoting the ICJ's *North Sea Continental Shelf Cases*— see Chapter 10.]. . .

[The court then reviews the approaches of different legal systems around the world to this issue.]

72. It is clear from the differing positions of the principal legal systems of the world that there is no consistent concrete rule which answers the question whether or not duress is a defence to the killing of innocent persons. It is not possible to reconcile the opposing positions and, indeed, we do not believe that the issue should be reduced to a contest between common law and civil law. . . .

D. The Rule Applicable to this Case

1. A normative mandate for international criminal law

75. . . . [T]he law should not be the product or slave of logic or intellectual hair-splitting, but must serve broader normative purposes in light of its social, political and economic role. . . . [W]e cannot but stress that we are not, in the International Tribunal, concerned with ordinary domestic crimes. The purview of the International Tribunal relates to war crimes and crimes against humanity committed in armed conflicts of extreme violence with egregious dimensions. . . .

78. We do not think our reference to considerations of policy are improper. It would be naive to believe that international law operates and develops wholly divorced from considerations of social and economic policy. . . . It is clear to us that whatever is the distinction between the international legal order and municipal legal orders in general, the distinction is imperfect in respect of the criminal law which, both at the international and the municipal level, is directed towards consistent aims. . . . It appears that the essence of this thesis is not that policy concerns dominate the law but rather, where appropriate, are given due consideration in the determination of a case. . . .

2. An exception where the victims will die regardless of the participation of the accused?

79. . . . [Defense counsel suggested that existing caselaw did not address] the situation in which the accused faced the choice between his own death for not obeying an order to kill or participating in a killing which was inevitably going to occur regardless of whether he participated in it or not. It has been argued that in such a situation where the fate of the victim was already sealed, duress should constitute a complete defence. This is because the accused is then not choosing that one innocent human being should die rather than another. . . . The argument, it is said, is vindicated in the [post-World War II] Italian case of *Masetti*. . . .

3. Rejection of utilitarianism and proportionality where human life must be weighed

80. The *Masetti* approach proceeds from the starting point of strict utilitarian logic based on the fact that if the victim will die anyway, the accused is not at all morally blameworthy for taking part in the execution; there is absolutely no reason why the accused should die as it would be unjust for the law to expect the accused to die for

nothing. . . . The approach we take does not involve a balancing of harms for and against killing but rests upon an application . . . of the rule that duress does not justify or excuse the killing of an innocent person. . . . In accordance with the spirit of international humanitarian law, we deny the availability of duress as a complete defence to combatants who have killed innocent persons. . . . [W]e give notice in no uncertain terms that those who kill innocent persons will not be able to . . . get away with impunity for their criminal acts in the taking of innocent lives. . . .

4. Mitigation of punishment as a clear, simple and uniform approach

[The Tribunal endorsed mitigation of punishment as an alternative to a complete defense of duress.]

85. . . . One cannot superficially gauge what the law "expects" by the existence of only two alternatives: conviction or acquittal. In reality, the law employs mitigation of punishment as a far more sophisticated and flexible tool for the purpose of doing justice in an individual case. The law, in our view, does not "expect" a person whose life is threatened to be a hero and to sacrifice his life by refusing to commit the criminal act demanded of him. The law does not "expect" that person to be a hero because in recognition of human frailty and the threat under which he acted, it will mitigate his punishment. In appropriate cases, the offender may receive no punishment at all. . . .

SEPARATE AND DISSENTING OPINION OF JUDGE CASSESE

2. . . . [L]egal constructs and terms of art upheld in national law . . . cannot be mechanically imported into international criminal proceedings. The International Tribunal, being an international body based on the law of nations, must first of all look to the object and purpose of the relevant provisions of its Statute and Rules.

3. This approach is dictated by three fundamental considerations. Firstly, the traditional attitude of international courts to national-law notions suggests that one should explore all the means available at the international level before turning to national law. . . .

4. The second consideration . . . is [that i]nternational criminal procedure results from the gradual decanting of national criminal concepts and rules into the international receptacle. . . . [I]t would be inappropriate mechanically to incorporate into international criminal proceedings ideas, legal constructs . . . unique, to a specific group of national legal systems, say, common-law or civil-law systems. . . .

5. . . . [Third], international trials exhibit a number of features that differentiate them from national criminal proceedings. . . . They discharge their functions in a community consisting of sovereign States. The individuals over whom these courts exercise their jurisdiction are under the sway and control of sovereign States. . . .

II. DURESS (OR: THE QUESTION OF WHETHER INTERNATIONAL CRIMINAL LAW UPHOLDS THE COMMON-LAW APPROACH TO DURESS IN CASE OF KILLING)

B. Notion And Requirements Of Duress

14. Duress, namely acting under a threat from a third person of severe and irreparable harm to life or limb, entails that no criminal responsibility is incurred by the person acting under that threat. . . .

16. . . . The relevant case-law is almost unanimous in requiring four strict conditions to be met for duress to be upheld as a defence, namely:

  i. the act charged was done under an immediate threat of severe and irreparable harm to life or limb;

  ii. there was no adequate means of averting such evil;

  iii. the crime committed was not disproportionate to the evil threatened (this would, for example, occur in case of killing in order to avert an assault). In other words, in order not to be disproportionate, the crime committed under duress must be, on balance, the lesser of two evils;

  iv. the situation leading to duress must not have been voluntarily brought about by the person coerced. . . .

4. Cases where courts upheld duress as a defence to war crimes or crimes against humanity involving unlawful killing

[Cassese summarizes a number of cases, including *Mazetti*, in which defendants were subordinates who were told to execute partisans upon pain of death, along with an assurance that the partisans would be executed even if the subordinates refused.]

5. The inferences to be drawn from the case-law on duress, with regard to war crimes and crimes against humanity involving the killing of persons

40. . . . [As to] the Prosecution's contention that an exception has evolved in customary international law excluding duress as an admissible defence in offences involving the taking of innocent lives [this] contention can only find support in one Canadian case . . . as well as the military regulations of the United Kingdom and the United States. . . . With these elements of practice one should contrast the contrary, copious case-law I have just surveyed as well as the legislation to the contrary of so many civil-law countries. . . . In my opinion, this manifest inconsistency of State practice warrants the dismissal of the Prosecution's contention: no special customary rule has evolved in international law on whether or not duress can be admitted as a defence in case of crimes involving the killing of persons.

41. . . . [The] majority does not draw from the absence of that special rule the only conclusion logically warranted: that one must apply, on a case-by-case basis, the general rule on duress to all categories of crime, whether or not they involve killing. . . .

42. The third criterion—proportionality (meaning that the remedy should not be disproportionate to the evil or that the lesser of two evils should be chosen)—will, in practice, be the hardest to satisfy where the underlying offence involves the killing of innocents. Perhaps . . . it will never be satisfied where the accused is saving his own life at the expense of his victim, since there are enormous . . . difficulties in putting one life in the balance against that of others in this way: how can a judge satisfy himself that the death of one person is a lesser evil than the death of another? Conversely, however, where it is not a case of a direct choice between the life of the person acting under duress and the life of the victim—in situations, in other words, where there is a high probability that the person under duress will not be able to save the lives of the victims whatever he does—then duress may succeed as a defence. . . .

43. These inferences, which I have drawn from the case-law, find support in the following considerations:

Firstly, it is extremely difficult to meet the requirements for duress where the offence involves killing of innocent human beings. . . . [C]ourts have very rarely allowed the defence of duress to succeed in cases involving unlawful killing even where they have in principle admitted the applicability of this defence. . . .

Secondly, it is a relevant consideration that the crime would have been committed in any case by a person other than the one acting under duress. . . . [W]here the accused has been charged with participation in a collective killing which would have proceeded irrespective of whether the accused was a participant, the defence has in principle been allowed. . . .

6. Concluding considerations

47. . . . Law is based on what society can reasonably expect of its members. It should not set intractable standards of behaviour which require mankind to perform acts of martyrdom, and brand as criminal any behaviour falling below those standards.

Consider the following example. A driver of a van unwittingly transporting victims to a place of execution, upon arrival is told by the executioners he must shoot one of the victims or he himself will be shot. This, of course, is done in order to assure his silence since he will then be implicated in the unlawful killing. The victims who are at the execution site will certainly die in any event. Can society reasonably expect the driver in these circumstances to sacrifice his life? In such situations it may be too demanding to require of the person under duress that they do not perpetrate the offence. . . .

48. . . . I do not see any point in contending that, since duress can be urged in mitigation, a court of law could . . . sentenc[e] the person who acted under duress to a minimum or token penalty. Any such contention would neglect . . . that the purpose of criminal law, including international criminal law, is to punish behaviour which is criminal, i.e., morally reprehensible or injurious to society. . . .

49. . . . I do not share the views of the majority . . . according to which, since international criminal law is ambiguous or uncertain on this matter, it is warranted to make a policy-directed choice and thus rely on "considerations of social and economic policy". [To have] recourse to a policy-directed choice is tantamount to running foul of the customary principle *nullum crimen sine lege*. An international court must apply *lex lata*, that is to say, the existing rules of international law as they are created through the sources of the international legal system. . . .

Notes and Questions

1. The Appeals Chamber also held, by four votes to one, that the accused's plea to crimes against humanity was not informed insofar as he did not understand the difference between crimes against humanity and violations of the laws and customs of war and the consequences of pleading guilty to the former. After the appeal, he pleaded guilty to the latter only. He was re-sentenced in March 1998 to five years imprisonment, with credit for time served since March 1996.

2. Which view of duress seems most appropriate to address crimes against humanity? Will the majority's opinion have the deterrent effect desired?

3. The author of the court's opinion was a former U.S. federal judge who had been active in the civil rights movement in the United States. The dissent was authored by an Italian professor of international law. How might the backgrounds of the two judges affect their approach to *nullum crimen sine lege?*

4. How relevant should the domestic laws of various states be to such determinations?

5. The Statute of the ICC adopts the following position with respect to duress:

Article 31
Grounds for excluding criminal responsibility

1. . . . [A] person shall not be criminally responsible if, at the time of that person's conduct: . . .

(d) The conduct . . . [was] caused by duress resulting from a threat of imminent death or of continuing or imminent serious bodily harm against that person or another person, and the person acts necessarily and reasonably to avoid this threat, provided that the person does not intend to cause a greater harm than the one sought to be avoided. Such a threat may either be:

(i) Made by other persons; or

(ii) Constituted by other circumstances beyond that person's control.

2. The Court shall determine the applicability of the grounds for excluding criminal responsibility provided for in this Statute to the case before it.

Why do you think the ICC Statute does not rule out the defense of duress to crimes against humanity and genocide despite the *Erdemovic* opinion?

E. Note on Criminalization of Atrocities in Civil Wars

As discussed in Chapter 8, international humanitarian law has different rules regarding the conduct of hostilities and the protection of victims in interstate conflicts compared to those in internal conflicts. As a result, decisionmakers involved in codifying and adjudicating war crimes have had to determine whether all the acts identified in treaty or custom as war crimes in interstate wars are also crimes in internal conflicts. The Security Council, for instance, intended the ICTY to have jurisdiction over war crimes even for those aspects of the Yugoslavia conflict that were purely internal (e.g., the conflict within Bosnia).

When the ICTY's first defendant, Dusko Tadic, was charged with a variety of offenses related to the conflict wholly within Bosnia—both grave breaches of the Geneva Conventions and the customary-law crimes—he claimed that such charges ran afoul of *nullum crimen sine lege* and constituted retroactive criminalization by the Security Council. In a long opinion, the ICTY Appeals Chamber accepted part of his argument and rejected part. It agreed that the Geneva Conventions themselves made clear that the grave breaches provisions applied only in the context of armed conflict between two states. As for the charges based on violations of customary international humanitarian law, the court found, as reprinted in Chapter 8, that "customary rules have developed to govern internal strife. These rules . . . cover such areas as protection of civilians from hostilities, in particular from indiscriminate attacks, protection of civilian objects, in particular cultural property, protection of all those who do not (or no longer) take active part in hostilities, as well as prohibition of means of warfare proscribed in international armed conflicts and ban of certain methods of conducting hostilities." It then found that states had indeed accepted that certain of these violations created individual responsibility:

128. . . . It is true that, for example, common Article 3 of the Geneva Conventions [containing a set of basic protections for individuals in situations other than interstate wars—see Chapter 8, Section III] contains no explicit reference to criminal liability for violation of its provisions. Faced with similar claims with respect to the various agreements and conventions that formed the basis of its jurisdiction, the International Military Tribunal at Nuremberg concluded that a finding of individual criminal responsibility is not barred by the absence of treaty provisions on punishment of breaches. . . . The Nuremberg Tribunal considered a number of factors relevant to its conclusion that the authors of particular prohibitions incur individual responsibility: the clear and unequivocal recognition of the rules of warfare in international law and State practice indicating an intention to criminalize the prohibition, including statements by government officials and international organizations, as well as punishment of violations by national courts and military tribunals. . . . Where these conditions are met, individuals must be held criminally responsible, because, as the Nuremberg Tribunal concluded:

> crimes against international law are committed by men, not by abstract entities, and only by punishing individuals who commit such crimes can the provisions of international law be enforced.

129. Applying the foregoing criteria to the violations at issue here, we have no doubt that they entail individual criminal responsibility, regardless of whether they are committed in internal or international armed conflicts. Principles and rules of humanitarian law reflect "elementary considerations of humanity" widely recognized as the mandatory minimum for conduct in armed conflicts of any kind. No one can doubt the gravity of the acts at issue, nor the interest of the international community in their prohibition.

[The Court then reviewed—rather cursorily—some statements, military instruction manuals, and laws of states criminalizing war crimes in internal conflicts, and noted the Security Council's views that individuals during Somalia's civil wars should be held accountable for violations of the law of armed conflict.]

134. All of these factors confirm that customary international law imposes criminal liability for serious violations of common Article 3, as supplemented by other general principles and rules on the protection of victims of internal armed conflict, and for breaching certain fundamental principles and rules regarding means and methods of combat in civil strife.

Prosecutor v. Tadic, Decision on the Defence Motion for Interlocutory Appeal on Jurisdiction, International Criminal Tribunal for the Former Yugoslavia, October 2, 1995.

Notes and Questions

1. If the Tribunal is correct in stating that protection of human dignity requires protection of civilians in internal conflicts through criminal sanctions on abusers, then why is the list of crimes it develops not simply identical to those considered

grave breaches of the Geneva Conventions? Are there crimes in international conflict that states might not be willing to view as crimes in civil wars?

2. Elsewhere in its opinion, the *Tadic* court stated, "elementary considerations of humanity and common sense make it preposterous that the use by States of weapons prohibited in armed conflicts between themselves be allowed when States try to put down rebellion by their own nationals on their own territory. What is inhumane, and consequently proscribed, in international wars, cannot but be inhumane and inadmissible in civil strife." The Statute of the International Criminal Court contains lengthy lists of war crimes over which the Court will have jurisdiction, separated based on the nature of the conflict. For international conflicts, the Court will have jurisdiction over grave breaches of the Geneva Conventions, as well as a list of 26 "other serious violations of the laws and customs of war applicable in international armed conflict." For civil wars, the Court will have jurisdiction over "serious violations" of Common Article 3, as well as a list of 12 "other serious violations of the laws and customs of war applicable in armed conflicts not of an international character." ICC Statute, Art. 8. Among the violations of the laws and customs of war that are listed for international conflict, but not domestic conflict, are: employing poison weapons, employing asphyxiating gases, employing bullets that expand or flatten in the body, and employing weapons that cause superfluous injury or unnecessary suffering. Why would these acts—many of which already violate widely ratified treaties—be made war crimes (making individuals, in addition to states, responsible for violations) in international conflicts but not domestic ones? Is this sort of bifurcation consistent with *Tadic*?

III. FORA FOR JUSTICE: THE RWANDAN GENOCIDE OF 1994

To hold individuals accountable for human rights abuses in a meaningful sense, rather than in a theoretical one, requires the creation and engagement of specific mechanisms for this purpose. Domestic and international decision makers have, over the years, created a variety of fora. National courts remain the principal venue for the administration of criminal justice. But in many societies, such courts may not be available due to a ruined infrastructure or the lack of judicial independence or political will. At times, and with greater frequency in recent years, states particularly concerned about punishing human rights abusers have tried offenders domestically for crimes that took place abroad under various theories of jurisdiction. Moreover, on occasion they have established international courts to address specific conflicts, such as the post-World War II tribunals, the UN's ad hoc tribunals, and the ICC. Criminal prosecution does not, however, exhaust the possibilities for individual accountability. In the last two decades, states emerging from political traumas have used truth commissions and other mechanisms as substitutes for or complements to trials (an issue discussed in the next problem).

The balancing act among the interests of the affected society, victims, perpetrators, and the international community has proved a great challenge for both domestic and international actors contemplating accountability options. These actors must consider the various purposes behind individual accountability noted at the beginning of this chapter, including a sense of justice, the possibility of some closure for victims, and repairing damage done to a society traumatized by victims.

They will have to decide which of these goals is most important and which methods of accountability best advance them. In doing so, they will have to make difficult choices between criminal and noncriminal forms of accountability; venues for accountability—namely, domestic, foreign, or international; and the number of targets to be included in any trial or other form of accountability. In the end, accountability often cannot be isolated from a political dynamic in which competing factions within states seek to gain power by manipulating the past for their own ends.

As you read the following materials, consider whether certain venues for justice advance the goals of individual accountability better than others; what arguments international actors have used to legitimize trials of human rights abusers outside the state where the acts took place and whether these arguments are convincing; whether the various possibilities for enforcement of international human rights and humanitarian norms through criminal processes add up to a comprehensive regime; and what standards of due process should apply at the domestic and international levels. Please note that one process of individual accountability, civil suits in the United States under the Alien Tort Claims Act, is discussed in Chapter 5.

A. The Problem

Since its days as a Belgian colony, Rwanda has fallen prey to tensions between Hutus and Tutsis. The two populations are not truly distinct physically or ethnically; rather, their separate identity and the eventual animosity between them owes most of its origins to the Belgian colonizers, who governed by creating an image of Tutsis (the minority) as a noble ruling class and Hutus as an inferior working class. Following decades of tensions and several years of civil war, Rwanda's Hutu-dominated government and the primarily Tutsi Rwandan Patriotic Front (RPF) insurgents agreed to a comprehensive peace plan in 1993. Extremists among the Hutus, however, opposed the plan and began to plan a campaign of massive killings of Tutsis and moderate Hutus. The mysterious downing of a plane carrying the Rwandan president in April 1994 gave them their excuse to begin. Journalist Philip Gourevitch describes what happened:

> With the encouragement of [radio propaganda] messages and of leaders at every level of society, the slaughter of Tutsis and the assassination of Hutu oppositionists spread from region to region. Following the militias' example, Hutus young and old rose to the task. Neighbors hacked neighbors to death in their homes, and colleagues hacked colleagues to death in their workplaces. Doctors killed their patients, and schoolteachers killed their pupils. Within days, the Tutsi populations of many villages were all but eliminated, and in Kigali prisoners were released in work gangs to collect the corpses that lined the roadsides. Throughout Rwanda, mass rape and looting accompanied the slaughter. Drunken militia bands, fortified with assorted drugs from ransacked pharmacies, were bused from massacre to massacre. Radio announcers reminded listeners not to take pity on women and children. . . .
>
> [Describing the scene at a church in the town of Nyarubuye, Gourevitch writes:]
> These dead and their killers had been neighbors, schoolmates, colleagues, sometimes friends, even in-laws. The dead had seen their killers training as militias in the weeks before the end, and it was well known that they were training to kill Tutsis; it was announced on the radio, it was in the newspapers, people spoke of it openly. The week before the massacre at Nyarubuye, the killing began in Rwanda's capital, Kigali. Hutus who opposed the Hutu Power ideology were publicly denounced as "accomplices" of

the Tutsis and were among the first to be killed as the extermination got under way. In Nyarubuye, when Tutsis asked the Hutu Power mayor how they might be spared, he suggested that they seek sanctuary at the church. They did, and a few days later the mayor came to kill them. He came at the head of a pack of soldiers, policemen, militiamen, and villagers; he gave out arms and orders to complete the job well. No more was required of the mayor, but he also was said to have killed a few Tutsis himself.

The killers killed all day at Nyarubuye. At night they cut the Achilles tendons of survivors and went off to feast behind the church, roasting cattle looted from their victims in big fires, and drinking beer. . . . And, in the morning, still drunk after whatever sleep they could find beneath the cries of their prey, the killers at Nyarubuye went back and killed again. Day after day, minute to minute, Tutsi by Tutsi: all across Rwanda, they worked like that.

Philip Gourevitch, We Wish to Inform You That Tomorrow We Will Be Killed with Our Families: Stories from Rwanda 115, 118-119 (1998).

Over the course of just a few months, between 500,000 and 1 million Rwandans were killed, representing at least three-quarters of the Tutsi population. By midsummer 1994, the RPF had defeated the government forces and established a new regime. It pledged to bring to justice all those who had participated in the genocidal violence and detained large numbers of suspects. While the Security Council established an international tribunal to try high-ranking offenders, the new Rwandan government maintained its intention to try all other offenders and enacted legislation for this purpose.

However, the destruction from the civil conflict and the flight of the former government left Rwanda without a functioning judicial system. In fact, the Rwandan government did not begin to try its first defendant until the last days of 1996. By 2002, some 5,000 had been tried, with several hundred sentenced to death and many more to life imprisonment. Twenty-two were executed in public in April 1998. Meanwhile, the government continued to detain over 100,000 suspects without charge in severely overcrowded facilities under appalling conditions.

B. The Domestic Option

National courts represent the logical first avenue of recourse for criminal proceedings against violators of human dignity. They have the closest relationship to the event, victims, defendants, evidence, and witnesses; and the results of such trials are likely to have an immediate impact on the public at large. As discussed in Chapter 6, international law clearly recognizes a state's jurisdiction over these offenses, whether on a territorial, nationality, or passive personality basis.

Yet in many situations of gross violations of human rights, national courts are not available or may have disadvantages in terms of their ability to mete out even a rough version of justice. First, the judicial system might be wholly inadequate in terms of physical resources or availability of trained judges and lawyers. Impoverished states attempting to prosecute past abusers will typically not have the resources to conduct fair trials. Second, the government in power might use the judicial system as a weapon against political enemies, with courts biased against potential defendants and unwilling to afford them rights of due process. Third, domestic prosecutors might refuse to prosecute, or judges might be afraid to hear cases against, powerful governmental officials, former officials, or their supporters; or the resulting trials might be shams leading to easy acquittals. The latter two problems are especially apparent in states undergoing transitions from authoritarian to democratic rule, an issue considered in Section III of this chapter. As for the issue of judicial resources, consider the following description of the situation in Rwanda:

Amnesty International, *Rwanda: Gacaca: A Question of Justice*

6, 8, 12, 14-16, 20-21, 36, 38, 40 (2002)

[T]he Rwandese judiciary became operational during the latter half of 1996. . . . The government frequently levied the charge of genocide in order to stifle dissent or dissatisfaction with its rule and policies. Following suit, Rwandese found it relatively easy to denounce individuals for a variety of personally motivated reasons and have an individual indefinitely detained with little or no investigation as to the validity of the accusation. Groups of individuals formed syndicates of denunciation, hiring themselves out to make accusations of genocide. These groups received a higher price if the accused was detained. . . .

III(2). Prison conditions

Between mid-1994 and mid-1996, the population in Rwandese detention facilities quintupled to slightly more than 90,000. By mid-1997 new prisons and extensions to the existing prisons had raised the capacity to 49,400. Nonetheless, the number of detainees continued to outstrip prison capacity. New facilities were overfilled as soon as they were constructed. The prison population levelled out at around 124,000 during 1997 and 1998. There have been annual, albeit slight, declines in the prison population since then. Rwanda today has a prison population of around 112,000.

The severe overcrowding and unsanitary conditions within Rwandese prisons amounts to cruel, inhuman and degrading treatment. Preventable diseases, malnutrition and the debilitating effects of overcrowding have resulted in a reported 11,000 deaths between the end of 1994 and end of 2001. There have also been reports of deaths in custody resulting from the physical abuse of detainees by prison officials. . . . Tens of thousands of detainees were also housed in district detention centres (cachots), [which] were originally constructed to temporarily hold detainees for up to 48 hours. . . . Physical conditions are far worse than those in the prisons. Detainees suffer from extreme overcrowding, unhygienic conditions and the lack of food. . . .

IV(3). Genocide trials within Rwanda

The Rwandese government, with considerable assistance from various United Nations agencies, foreign governments and nongovernmental organizations (NGOs) sought to materially reconstruct the judicial system's infrastructures and train the requisite judicial personnel. . . . Despite the accelerated recruitment and training of judicial personnel, the numbers fell far short of what was needed. The Ministry of Justice estimated that it needed a minimum of 694 magistrates to get the judicial system running. This was still less than the number of magistrates that existed prior to the genocide when there were far fewer than 90,000 individuals in detention facilities awaiting trial. Few of the magistrates were jurists, less than a quarter had adequate legal training. . . .

Rwandese genocide trials began in December 1996. . . . Amnesty International's concerns focused on four issues: the lack of defence counsel and witnesses for the vast majority of defendants; the lack of time and adequate facilities for defendants to prepare their defence; the competence, impartiality and independence of government and judicial officials, and the environment within the courtroom. International human rights instruments state that pro bono legal assistance is required "where the interests of justice so require" and all accused have the right "to enough time and [the] necessary facilities to prepare their defence." The Rwandese government['s] interpretation of Article 14(3)(d) is that legal assistance is required only where the death penalty was a possible punishment. The government has repeatedly maintained that the obligation to provide legal assistance was not absolute and could be derogated with respect to genocide.

The first cases in Kibungo, Kigali and Byumba in which defendants without counsel were sentenced to death led to considerable international criticism. Perhaps as a result, the Rwandese government rescinded its earlier decision and allowed foreign lawyers to represent genocide suspects. Avocats sans frontières (ASF), Lawyers Without Borders, began to represent defendants. . . . Observers noted a striking contrast in the fairness of trials where defendants had counsel. . . .

Although the overall quality of trials has improved, the complexity and gravity of the offences, the severity of the sentences and the political environment in which the courts were operating continue to cause problems. Numerous reports call into question the competence, impartiality and independence of judicial personnel. Court proceedings continue to reflect the hostile socio-political environment existing outside of the courtroom. . . . Defence counsel and witnesses are intimidated causing the former to withdraw from trials and the latter to refuse to testify. Some defense witnesses have been accused of complicity or involvement in the crimes committed by the defendant. Conviction sometimes rests more on public acclaim than on the incontrovertible evidence of guilt.

VI. Gacaca

Gacaca refers to a "traditional" Rwandese method of conflict resolution. When social norms were broken or disputes arose—land rights, property damage, marital disputes, inheritance rights, etc., meetings were convened between the aggrieved parties. Gacaca sessions were informal, non-permanent and ad hoc. They were presided over by community elders (inyangamugayo). The primary goal was to restore social order, after sanctioning the violation of shared values, through the re-integration of offender(s) into the community. . . . Contemporary Gacaca Jurisdictions deal, not with local disputes, but with a genocide organized and implemented by state authorities in which hundreds of thousands of individuals lost their lives. . . . The overall supervision of the Gacaca Jurisdictions and their coordination is under the control of . . . the Ministry of Justice. State authority—not local consensus—is the modus operandi of the new gacaca jurisdictions. . . . The significant differences existing between customary and contemporary forms of gacaca force the question of whether these differences negate the anticipated results: justice, the uncovering of truth and national reconciliation. If reconciliation is an essentially personal interaction between victim and perpetrator, [i]t is less clear that the state-mandated Gacaca Jurisdictions whose focus remains on retributive justice will achieve [it]. . . .

VII(2)(a). Minimum fair trial standards and the Gacaca Jurisdictions

[The report reviewed the various standards in key human rights instruments, notably the International Covenant on Civil and Political Rights.] There is no clear, definitive statement in the gacaca legislation that states when defendants are informed of the charges and case against them. Defendants require adequate time and facilities to prepare their defence, particularly as they are responsible for it. There is also no provision enabling the gacaca benches to adjourn proceedings if defendants have not been given sufficient time or the materials to prepare their case. . . .

The political sphere in contemporary Rwanda is both closed and exclusionary. The government is extremely intolerant of dissenters or those dissatisfied with its performance, too readily accusing such individuals of genocide or treason. . . . [A]n individual's willingness to testify for defendants who have been arrested and detained by the government is questionable. Some Rwandese fear that they would be arrested if they provide evidence in support of the defendant's innocence or if they demonstrate too much knowledge or information about the genocide. Genocide survivors are also afraid that their potential testimony puts their lives in danger. Information may not be forthcoming at the community level, given the limited enjoyment of freedom of expression and association or toleration of dissent at the national one. The intensified polarization of Rwandese communities and the increasing politicization of local community disputes into charges of genocide or treason raises further concerns regarding both the safety of gacaca participants as well as the overall fairness of gacaca proceedings. . . . The impartiality of appointed Gacaca Jurisdiction members cannot be assured in a socio-political environment characterized by the intense politicisation of personal disputes and dissatisfaction or dissent with the current government, transforming both into a vicious cycle of accusations and counter-accusations of genocide or treason.

The competence of the gacaca judges is questionable. Most of them have no legal or human rights background. The highly abbreviated training they have received is grossly inadequate to the task at hand, given the range, character and complexity of crimes committed during the genocide. . . .

[A]ppeal to a higher Gacaca Jurisdiction may not adequately address an individual's rights to have his or her conviction and sentence reviewed. . . . [H]uman rights concerns with the Gacaca Jurisdictions rise almost exponentially with the administrative move upwards from cell-level Gacaca Jurisdictions to provincial ones. Cell-level Gacaca Jurisdictions operate at an administrative level small enough to enable community debate to take place. . . . The same cannot be said for province-level Gacaca Jurisdictions where the conceptualization of gacaca as a community forum breaks down. There is also more room for intervention both from the state and various pressure groups.

Notes and Questions

1. Is the detention without trial of 112,000 Rwandans for eight years a justifiable response to genocide? Does a poor state have any other alternative?

2. To what extent should due process standards for criminal trials be applied flexibly to take account of the financial limitations of the state? Consider whether the full list of protections in Article 14 of the ICCPR (see Chapter 7) are necessary to fair trials.

3. As the gacaca process began, the Rwandan government released tens of thousands of prisoners from jails in a provisional release plan. Gacaca courts began their proceedings at a slow pace, originally as a pilot project, but extended to the whole country by 2005. Some 12,000 courts were set up, with hearings taking place in over 100 locations. Nonetheless, participation in the process was often below expectations as many witnesses could not afford to attend the proceedings. In February 2004, the government offered an amnesty from regular trials to those who had not taken a major role in the genocide in exchange for a confession of guilt and an apology. Those who take advantage of the amnesty could still face gacaca proceedings.

4. In postwar Iraq, the U.S. government considered a variety of options for trials of former regime officials, but eventually focused on two: military commissions led by American officers to try former officials for war crimes in the 1991 and 2003 Persian Gulf wars, and newly reconstituted Iraqi courts to try them for atrocities against the Iraqi people. In December 2003, with U.S. backing, the Iraqi Governing Council (a panel of Iraqis appointed by the occupational forces to decide on certain aspects of governance) adopted a statute creating the Iraqi Special Tribunal (IST). The IST may try "any Iraqi national or resident of Iraq accused of [genocide, crimes against humanity, war crimes, and certain crimes under Iraqi law] committed since July 17, 1968 and up until and including May 1, 2003, in the territory of the Republic of Iraq or elsewhere," including related to Iraq's wars with Iran and Kuwait. The court is comprised entirely of Iraqis, although non-Iraqis assist them in an advisory capacity. Human rights NGOs criticized the statute for, among other things, failing to specify the standard of guilt and not protecting defendants against forced confessions; NGOs and many governments also criticized the inclusion of the death penalty as a punishment option. Several days after the statute was promulgated, U.S. forces captured Saddam Hussein near his home town of Tikrit. After confusion within the IST regarding the charges against Hussein, he, along with seven others, was brought to trial in October 2005 for the murder of 150 residents of the town of Dujail in 1982. More significant charges, such as the gassing of thousands of Kurds, were deferred. In addition, in recent years, other states with underfunded or weak judiciaries, including Croatia, Bosnia, Serbia, and East Timor, have established special courts to try serious human rights abusers. What information would you need to evaluate the capacity of the IST and similar courts to conduct fair trials?

C. Going to the United Nations: Ad Hoc International Criminal Courts

When governments and NGOs interested in bringing to justice those responsible for human rights atrocities in Yugoslavia and Rwanda considered the various options for accountability, they concluded that domestic tribunals would be of limited utility for the reasons noted above—the destruction of the physical and human resources needed for trials, the prospect of a lack of due process for some defendants, and the likelihood that many defendants would be shielded from prosecutions by a sympathetic government. As a result, these international actors resurrected, for the first time in nearly 50 years, the idea of an international criminal tribunal.

Yet these actors did not pursue the process by which the IMT Charter was created—the negotiation of a treaty—but instead acted through the Security Council by invoking its power under Chapter VII of the Charter to respond to threats to the peace through economic, military, diplomatic, and other measures. They chose this option because they believed that negotiation of a treaty would have taken a long time and that states whose cooperation was needed—for the apprehension of suspects and for the provision of witnesses and evidence—would not ratify such a treaty. In the case of the former Yugoslavia, for instance, the Federal Republic of Yugoslavia (Serbia and Montenegro) and Croatia opposed a tribunal, both out of solidarity with their ethnic allies in the Bosnian war and out of fear that their own officials might be in the dock because of their involvement in the war in Bosnia (as well as the war in Croatia). In the case of Rwanda, the government, which was sitting on the Security Council at the time as part of the Council's rotation of the non-permanent seats, opposed the international tribunal because it could not impose the death penalty, whereas Rwandan law provided such a penalty for genocide.

Thus, in two critical resolutions, passed in 1993 and 1994, the Council set up two international tribunals, prescribing their structure and jurisdiction and requiring all states to cooperate with them regarding suspects, evidence, witnesses, and all other matters. Each court would try genocide, crimes against humanity, and war crimes; and each could prosecute anyone suspected of these crimes, from whatever side in the conflict. The Yugoslavia Tribunal could consider any covered crimes committed in the former Yugoslavia after 1991 (up to the present day); while the Rwanda Tribunal was confined to crimes in Rwanda in 1994. The Tribunals' judges would be elected by the General Assembly, and no two could be of the same nationality. The Yugoslavia Tribunal is based in The Hague, Netherlands, and the Rwanda Tribunal is based in Arusha, Tanzania. (The Security Council chose Arusha because it wanted a city near, but outside, Rwanda.) The Tribunals have a common Appeals Chamber.

Two years after the Yugoslavia Tribunal was created, when it began to prosecute its first defendant, Dusko Tadic, it came as little surprise that the defendant would challenge not only the law being applied to him (the issue considered in the previous problem), but also the legitimacy of the Tribunal itself. Tadic's lawyers alleged, on a variety of grounds, that the Security Council had acted *ultra vires* in creating the Tribunal.

Prosecutor v. Tadic, Jurisdiction Appeal

Case No. IT-94-1-AR72 (1995)

1. The Power Of The Security Council To Invoke Chapter VII

28. Article 39 opens Chapter VII of the Charter of the United Nations and determines the conditions of application of this Chapter. It provides:

> "The Security Council shall determine the existence of any threat to the peace, breach of the peace, or act of aggression and shall make recommendations, or decide what measures shall be taken in accordance with Articles 41 and 42, to maintain or restore international peace and security." (United Nations Charter, 26 June 1945, Art. 39.)

It is clear from this text that the Security Council plays a pivotal role and exercises a very wide discretion under this Article. But this does not mean that its powers are unlimited. The Security Council is an organ of an international organization, established by a treaty which serves as a constitutional framework for that organization. The Security Council is thus subjected to certain constitutional limitations, however broad its powers under the constitution may be. Those powers cannot, in any case, go beyond the limits of the jurisdiction of the Organization at large, not to mention other specific limitations or those which may derive from the internal division of power within the Organization. . . .

29. What is the extent of the powers of the Security Council under Article 39 and the limits thereon, if any?

     . . . The situations justifying resort to the powers provided for in Chapter VII are a "threat to the peace," a "breach of the peace" or an "act of aggression." While the "act of aggression" is more amenable to a legal determination, the "threat to the peace" is more of a political concept. But the determination that there exists such a threat is not a totally unfettered discretion, as it has to remain, at the very least, within the limits of the Purposes and Principles of the Charter. [The Tribunal found that the conflict in the former Yugoslavia was a threat to the peace.] . . .

2. The Range of Measures Envisaged Under Chapter VII

31. . . . [T]he Security Council has a broad discretion in deciding on the course of action and evaluating the appropriateness of the measures to be taken. The language of Article 39 is quite clear as to the channelling of the very broad and exceptional powers of the Security Council under Chapter VII through Articles 41 and 42. These two Articles leave to the Security Council such a wide choice as not to warrant searching, on functional or other grounds, for even wider and more general powers than those already expressly provided for in the Charter. . . .

3. The Establishment Of The International Tribunal As A Measure Under Chapter VII

32. In its resolution . . . [creating the Tribunal], the Security Council considers that "in the particular circumstances of the former Yugoslavia", the establishment of the International Tribunal "would contribute to the restoration and maintenance of peace" and indicates that, in establishing it, the Security Council was acting under Chapter VII. . . . However, it did not specify a particular Article as a basis for this action.

Appellant has attacked the legality of this decision at different stages before the Trial Chamber as well as before this Chamber on at least three grounds:

     a) that the establishment of such a tribunal was never contemplated by the framers of the Charter as one of the measures to be taken under Chapter VII; as witnessed by the fact that it figures nowhere in the provisions of that Chapter, and more particularly in Articles 41 and 42 which detail these measures;

     b) that the Security Council is constitutionally or inherently incapable of creating a judicial organ, as it is conceived in the Charter as an executive organ, hence not possessed of judicial powers which can be exercised through a subsidiary organ;

     c) that the establishment of the International Tribunal has neither promoted, nor was capable of promoting, international peace, as demonstrated by the current situation in the former Yugoslavia.

(a) <u>What Article of Chapter VII Serves As A Basis For The Establishment Of A Tribunal?</u>

33. The establishment of an international criminal tribunal is not expressly mentioned among the enforcement measures provided for in Chapter VII, and more particularly in Articles 41 and 42.

Obviously, the establishment of the International Tribunal is not a measure under Article 42, as these are measures of a military nature, implying the use of armed force. Nor can it be considered a "provisional measure" under Article 40. These measures, as their denomination indicates, are intended to act as a "holding operation," producing a "stand-still." . . . They are akin to emergency police action rather than to the activity of a judicial organ. . . .

34. Prima facie, the International Tribunal matches perfectly the description in Article 41 of "measures not involving the use of force." . . .

(b) <u>Can The Security Council Establish A Subsidiary Organ With Judicial Powers?</u>

38. The establishment of the International Tribunal by the Security Council does not signify . . . that the Security Council was usurping for itself part of a judicial function which does not belong to it but to other organs of the United Nations according to the Charter. The Security Council has resorted to the establishment of a judicial organ in the form of an international criminal tribunal as an instrument for the exercise of its own principal function of maintenance of peace and security, *i.e.*, as a measure contributing to the restoration and maintenance of peace in the former Yugoslavia. . . .

(c) <u>Was The Establishment Of The International Tribunal An Appropriate Measure?</u>

39. The third argument is directed against the discretionary power of the Security Council in evaluating the appropriateness of the chosen measure and its effectiveness in achieving its objective, the restoration of peace.

Article 39 leaves the choice of means and their evaluation to the Security Council, which enjoys wide discretionary powers in this regard; and it could not have been otherwise, as such a choice involves political evaluation of highly complex and dynamic situations.

It would be a total misconception of what are the criteria of legality and validity in law to test the legality of such measures *ex post facto* by their success or failure to achieve their ends (in the present case, the restoration of peace in the former Yugoslavia, in quest of which the establishment of the International Tribunal is but one of many measures adopted by the Security Council).

40. For the aforementioned reasons, the Appeals Chamber considers that the International Tribunal has been lawfully established as a measure under Chapter VII of the Charter.

After a shaky start, the Rwanda Tribunal eventually gained custody from other African states over most leaders of the Rwandan genocide. By early 2006, it had convicted 24 people and acquitted one, with some 40 others awaiting or under trial. Among those convicted have been Jean Kambanda, the prime minister of Rwanda during the massacres, as well as various regional leaders. Since its inception in 1993, the Yugoslavia Tribunal has convicted some 43 persons, with some 64 more in custody or provisionally released awaiting trial. For its first six years, the Tribunal enjoyed little cooperation from the Croatian and Yugoslav governments regarding arrests of suspects and access to evidence. NATO troops enforcing the Bosnian peace agreement of 1995 arrested relatively few suspects despite Security Council authority to do so. The Tribunal nonetheless had a few high-profile cases, including that of a leading Croatian general in Bosnia. The death of Croatian President Franjo Tudjman in 1999 and the election loss of Yugoslav President Slobodan Milosevic in 2000, both of whom led their nations during the atrocities under investigation by the Tribunal, led to the trials of more high-ranking officials, including Milosevic himself (until his death, during his trial, in March 2006), for genocide, crimes against humanity, and war crimes in Kosovo and Bosnia.

Following pressure from the United States government to wind up the operations of the ICTY and ICTR, the Tribunals' prosecutor, Carla del Ponte, announced a "Completion Strategy" for the ICTY, which the Security Council endorsed. Under that strategy, the ICTY would complete all investigations by the end of 2004, all trials at first instance by the end of 2008, and all activities by the end of 2010. As a result, the Prosecutor suspended a number of investigations and referred them to local prosecutors in the former Yugoslavia. Croatia, Serbia, and Bosnia all had laws in place for domestic trials, though actual trials proceeded very slowly in those venues. The ICTR has a similar strategy.

Notes and Questions

1. In what sense does the establishment of an international tribunal contribute to peace in Rwanda or in the Balkans? Did the political organs act *ultra vires*? And did the ICTY engage in judicial review of the Security Council's decision?

2. How do the Rwanda and Yugoslavia tribunals respond to concerns about victor's justice that surrounded the Nuremberg tribunal?

3. Are the Tribunals' legitimacy at all compromised by their creation by the 15-member Security Council rather than, for example, by the General Assembly? Why do you think advocates of accountability (as well as powerful states) did not opt to create the Tribunals through the General Assembly?

4. In the case of the Balkans, the ICTY seems to have helped jump-start some domestic trials in the affected states. Is this a useful goal for international courts? You may wish to consider this question later with respect to the ICC, discussed in the next section, and trials in other states, discussed in Section IV.

5. Although the Security Council has not created any additional ad hoc courts along the Yugoslavia and Rwanda models, the United Nations has endorsed the idea of so-called mixed or hybrid tribunals for addressing past atrocities in Sierra Leone and Cambodia. These courts are composed of both domestic and international judges working under the terms of a domestic statute and an agreement between the United Nations and the relevant government. With respect to Cambodia, after the Cambodian government rejected the idea of a new ad hoc UN tribunal, UN Secretariat officials began lengthy negotiations on a mixed tribunal. When the UN proposed a court with a majority of UN-appointed judges, Cambodia insisted on a majority of Cambodian judges. The UN eventually agreed to the majority-Cambodian court, but with a requirement that any decisions be

made by a supermajority of the court. The effect was that the Cambodian judges could not force an acquittal or conviction, but the possibility remained that the court would be unable to reach any decisions. After several years of foot-dragging by the Cambodian government, UN negotiators and Cambodia agreed in 2003 on the mixed tribunal plan, which the General Assembly endorsed. By early 2006, governments had provided to the tribunal most of the funding needed for its initial period of operation, though investigations had not commenced. The United Nations and the government of Sierra Leone signed an agreement in January 2002 to set up a war crimes tribunal there. The Special Court for Sierra Leone consists of eight judges, two Sierra Leonean and six foreigners. Although the court remains significantly underfunded compared to the UN's two ad hoc tribunals, the prosecutor issued a series of high-profile indictments, including against Charles Taylor, who at the time of his indictment was the president of neighboring Liberia. In August 2003, Taylor left office under pressure from the United States as part of a deal for the deployment of West African peacekeepers in Liberia; Nigeria offered him a safe haven and he flew there. In 2004, the Special Court ruled that Taylor did not enjoy immunity from prosecution as a former head of state. In the spring of 2006, a new government of Liberia asked Nigeria to return Taylor; after a brief escape by Taylor, Nigerian authorities delivered him to Liberia, which turned him over to the Special Court for trial.

6. How can we judge the effectiveness of the UN's tribunals? Consider the following perspective from international relations theory:

States find establishing a tribunal system appealing because it provides an economically and politically inexpensive means of responding to demands for international action; it enables states to commit at a level commensurate with their strategic interest in the region involved. From the standpoint of *realpolitik,* the regime is a success whether or not it succeeds in bringing justice or alleviating ethnic conflict. From the standpoint of *idealpolitik,* the measures of success—reducing human suffering, protecting human rights, and promoting regional stability—are certainly left wanting. Here we must assess the tribunal's success from another dimension—as a component of conflict management.

. . . For international lawyers the connection between a functioning legal regime and political order is clear: "There can be no peace without justice, no justice without law, and no meaningful law without a court to decide what is just and lawful under any given circumstance" [quoting a former Nuremberg prosecutor]. If peace is a function of law and justice, is an atrocities regime the panacea for the problem of ethnonationalist violence? Here, the current evidence is certainly not compelling. Effective deterrence requires three elements—commitment, capability, and credibility. The existence of war crimes tribunals and the successful prosecution of initial cases did little to curb actions in any of the cases examined. . . . Because of the rather spotty record of the West regarding intervention and the formidable institutional obstacles facing the fledgling tribunal system, perpetrators of brutality have had little reason to take UN commitment seriously. . . . [T]he difficulty of apprehending such people came at an unacceptably high logistical and political cost, considering that a large-scale military commitment would be necessary. . . . As one analyst noted, in the Bosnian case "U.S. and European (NATO) officials failed to satisfy even the most basic strategic requirements of deterrence. These conditions include definition of unacceptable behavior, clear communication of a commitment to punish transgressors, and demonstration of intent (that is, resolve) to carry out retaliation."

Preliminary evidence does not seem to support notions that decollectivization of guilt through war crimes adjudication is, on its own, an effective means to achieving national reconciliation. . . . In the former Yugoslavia, ethnic tensions remain high and are accompanied by sporadic violence and acts of retaliation on both sides. . . . Decollectivizing guilt is a curative measure taken by the state to break this historical cycle. However, the effectiveness of such a strategy is contingent on detaining high-level perpetrators and, presumably, giving amnesty to those at lower levels (perhaps in return for admitting guilt, fully disclosing events, and testifying at trials of political and military leaders, as has occurred in truth and reconciliation proceedings elsewhere). Yet early precedent set by the tribunals [of trying lower-level officials first] runs an opposite course.

Christopher Rudolph, *Constructing an Atrocities Regime: The Politics of War Crimes Tribunals*, 55 Intl. Org. 655, 684-685 (2001).

D. The International Criminal Court

The idea of a permanent international criminal court, with jurisdiction to consider atrocities anywhere, had long been proposed by advocates of human rights but had not advanced significantly for most of the twentieth century. In 1989, Trinidad and Tobago asked the General Assembly to consider such a tribunal for drug trafficking, and the General Assembly passed the issue to the International Law Commission (ILC) for study. Proponents of such a court favored creating it by a multilateral treaty rather than through the resolution of any UN body, arguing that participation should be voluntary and clearly based on consent. After the Security Council had established the two ad hoc tribunals, governments, in particular those in the West, proved much more interested in the proposal. The ILC offered a draft statute in 1994, after which the General Assembly convened a diplomatic conference of all states to draft a treaty. Negotiations took place throughout 1996 and 1997, culminating in a final, frenetic month of negotiations at Rome in July 1998. The result was the Statute of the International Criminal Court (the Rome Statute), a 128-article treaty creating a standing tribunal and providing in great detail for the jurisdiction of the Court, including definitions of the three crimes (genocide, war crimes, and crimes against humanity) over which the Court has jurisdiction. The Court has jurisdiction only over crimes committed after the Statute's entry into force.

1. Key Issues During the ICC Negotiations

The most contentious discussions during the drafting of the Rome Statute concerned the power that governments were willing to give the Court vis-à-vis individual states. Governments and NGOs sparred over three issues in particular.

• First, they disagreed on the extent to which certain states might need to consent to the jurisdiction of the Court before it could hear a case. Some states argued that once a state handed a defendant to the Court, it ought to be able to prosecute based on the international nature of the crime; others insisted that the state where the crime took place, the state of nationality of the defendant, or both, consent to the prosecution.

• Second, states and NGOs sparred over who could initiate an investigation and prosecution—states party to the Statute, the Security Council, the Court's Prosecutor, or some combination of these. In particular, disagreements centered on whether the Security Council alone should be able to initiate cases (originally favored by the United States), whether the Security Council ought to be able to halt a prosecution if it affected international peace and security, and whether the Prosecutor ought to be free to seek indictments on her own.

important to U.S.A

• Third, states and NGOs argued about the extent to which the Court could act in the face of ongoing domestic proceedings over the same facts—that is, whether it would work on the basis of primacy over national courts (as do the Yugoslavia and Rwanda Tribunals) or "complementarity"—namely, deference to national courts. Relevant provisions of the Statute are set forth below.

Statute of the International Criminal Court

U.N. Doc. A/CONF.183/9 (1998)

Article 12
Preconditions to the exercise of jurisdiction

1. A State which becomes a Party to this Statute thereby accepts the jurisdiction of the Court with respect to the crimes referred to in article 5 [that is, genocide, crimes against humanity, and war crimes].

2. In the case of article 13, paragraph (a) or (c), the Court may exercise its jurisdiction if one or more of the following States are Parties to this Statute or have accepted the jurisdiction of the Court in accordance with paragraph 3:

(a) The State on the territory of which the conduct in question occurred or, if the crime was committed on board a vessel or aircraft, the State of registration of that vessel or aircraft;

(b) The State of which the person accused of the crime is a national.

3. If the acceptance of a State which is not a Party to this Statute is required under paragraph 2, that State may, by declaration lodged with the Registrar, accept the exercise of jurisdiction by the Court with respect to the crime in question. . . .

Article 13
Exercise of jurisdiction

The Court may exercise its jurisdiction with respect to a crime referred to in article 5 in accordance with the provisions of this Statute if:

(a) A situation in which one or more of such crimes appears to have been committed is referred to the Prosecutor by a State Party in accordance with article 14;

(b) A situation in which one or more of such crimes appears to have been committed is referred to the Prosecutor by the Security Council acting under Chapter VII of the Charter of the United Nations; or

(c) The Prosecutor has initiated an investigation in respect of such a crime in accordance with article 15.

transogni
A 2,21 d

Article 14
Referral of a situation by a State Party

1. A State Party may refer to the Prosecutor a situation in which one or more crimes within the jurisdiction of the Court appear to have been committed requesting the Prosecutor to investigate the situation for the purpose of determining whether one or more specific persons should be charged. . . .

Article 15
Prosecutor

own authority

1. The Prosecutor may initiate investigations <u>proprio motu</u> on the basis of information on crimes within the jurisdiction of the Court. . . .

3. If the Prosecutor concludes that there is a reasonable basis to proceed with an investigation, he or she shall submit to the Pre-Trial Chamber a request for authorization of an investigation, together with any supporting material collected. . . .

4. If the Pre-Trial Chamber . . . considers that there is a reasonable basis to proceed with an investigation, and that the case appears to fall within the jurisdiction of the Court, it shall authorize the commencement of the investigation. . . .

Article 16
Deferral of investigation or prosecution

No investigation or prosecution may be commenced or proceeded with under this Statute for a period of 12 months after the Security Council, in a resolution adopted under Chapter VII of the Charter of the United Nations, has requested the Court to that effect; that request may be renewed by the Council under the same conditions.

Article 17
Issues of admissibility

A reason to join

1. . . . . [T]he Court shall determine that a case is inadmissible where:

    (a) The case is being investigated or prosecuted by a State which has jurisdiction over it, unless the State is unwilling or unable genuinely to carry out the investigation or prosecution;

    (b) The case has been investigated by a State which has jurisdiction over it and the State has decided not to prosecute the person concerned, unless the decision resulted from the unwillingness or inability of the State genuinely to prosecute;

    (c) The person concerned has already been tried for conduct which is the subject of the complaint, and a trial by the Court is not permitted under article 20, paragraph 3 [allowing retrial if the first trial was meant to shield the defendant];

(d) The case is not of sufficient gravity to justify further action by the Court.

2. In order to determine unwillingness in a particular case, the Court shall consider, having regard to the principles of due process recognized by international law, whether one or more of the following exist, as applicable:

(a) The proceedings were or are being undertaken or the national decision was made for the purpose of shielding the person concerned from criminal responsibility . . . ;

(b) There has been an unjustified delay in the proceedings which in the circumstances is inconsistent with an intent to bring the person concerned to justice;

(c) The proceedings were not or are not being conducted independently or impartially, and they were or are being conducted in a manner which, in the circumstances, is inconsistent with an intent to bring the person concerned to justice.

3. In order to determine inability in a particular case, the Court shall consider whether, due to a total or substantial collapse or unavailability of its national judicial system, the State is unable to obtain the accused or the necessary evidence and testimony or otherwise unable to carry out its proceedings.

The Rome Statute entered into force on July 1, 2002, after receiving its sixtieth ratification. As of May 2006, the ICC Statute had 100 parties. The parties have also adopted an agreement on the privileges and immunities of the staff, financial regulations, rules of procedure and evidence, and elements of the crimes. The parties held elections for judges in the spring of 2003, and 18 were elected. The first group of judges were nationals of Trinidad and Tobago, France, Cyprus, Costa Rica, Samoa, Republic of Korea, Ireland, Mali, United Kingdom, Brazil, South Africa, Germany, Italy, Ghana, Canada, Bolivia, Finland, and Latvia. The states parties subsequently elected Luis Moreno Ocampo, a prosecutor from Argentina, as the Court's first prosecutor. In a speech to the Assembly of States Parties after his election, the prosecutor Moreno Ocampo stated:

> [T]he principle of complementarity . . . represents the will of creating a global institution that is, at the same time, respectful of the member states' sovereignty. The primary responsibility to prevent, control, and prosecute those atrocious crimes belong to the states in which jurisdictions they are committed. The principle of complementarity established by the Statute compels the Prosecutor's office to collaborate with national jurisdictions in order to help them improve their efficiency. That is the first task of the Prosecutor's Office: make its best effort to help national jurisdictions fulfill their mission. The Prosecutor's Office can do this in different ways: in a cooperative way, by giving the state the information received from different sources or providing the state's personnel with training and technical support. Also, due to the dissuasive effect that the mere existence of the Court generates, the possibility of presenting a case at the International Criminal Court could convince some states with serious conflicts to take the appropriate action.

By 2006, after receiving hundreds of communications notifying him of events and urging investigations, Moreno Ocampo had initiated formal investigations into three situations: the human rights situation in the Ituri province in the Democratic Republic of the Congo; the activities in Uganda of the Lord's Resistance Army, a separatist group known for committing horrendous abuses, particularly against

children; and the Sudanese region of Darfur, following a formal referral of that
situation to the Prosecutor by the Security Council in March 2005.

Notes and Questions

1. If a slaughter resembling that which took place in Rwanda were to occur in the
future, what would have to happen for the ICC actually to try a defendant?

2. What is the effect of Article 12 on the functioning of the Court? What would be
the consequences if the Article were entirely removed from the Statute?

3. Why do you think Moreno Ocampo is emphasizing complementarity so
much in this speech to the parties to the ICC Statute?

2. United States Policy Toward the ICC

The United States was an active participant in the Rome negotiations, but in the
end refused to vote for the Statute. The United States originally envisioned the
Court as in essence a permanent version of the two existing ad hoc war crimes
tribunals, that is, as a forum to which the UN Security Council could refer situations
for investigation and prosecution. But most other states, and a small army of NGOs,
pressed for a Court that could act independently of the Security Council and the
veto exercised by its permanent members. During the Rome negotiations, the
United States pressed for adoption of several different provisions, each of which
would have eliminated the possibility that U.S. nationals could be prosecuted without U.S. consent. Unable to achieve its goals on this issue, the United States voted
against the treaty. In doing so, the United States found itself in a small minority. The
Statue was adopted by a vote of 120 to 7, with 21 abstentions. Because the vote was
not recorded, there is some uncertainty as to which states other than the United
States voted no, but most lists include China, Iraq, Israel, Libya, Qatar, and Yemen.
Consider the views of a military lawyer on the U.S. delegation to the Rome Conference and of Human Rights Watch.

William K. Lietzau, *The United States and the International Criminal Court: International Criminal Law After Rome: Concerns from a U.S. Military Perspective*

64 Law & Contemp. Probs. 119, 125-129 (2001)

Regarding jurisdiction over individuals whose state of nationality is party to the
treaty, the Rome negotiators settled on a regime that fell short of U.S. objectives to
maintain certain jurisdictional control over its own forces. The statute grants the
court "automatic" jurisdiction over the three categories of offenses for all states
parties. Referrals initiating such jurisdiction can derive from any of three sources:
the U.N. Security Council, a state party to the Statute, or the prosecutor. . . .

The U.S. military has been much criticized for its stance on this critical aspect
of the ICC Statute, but what the critics sometimes fail to recognize are the unique
and vital national security responsibilities of the U.S. armed forces and the
consequences of their front-line role in carrying out the nation's national
security strategy. Though some bristle at a description of the United States as

"the indispensable nation," it must be conceded that no other state regularly has nearly 200,000 troops outside its borders, either forward deployed or engaged in one of several operations designed to preserve international peace and security. . . .

. . . An ill-constituted ICC with the authority to make the final determination as to which cases will be investigated or come before it invites use of the court for political mischief. Those who would deny the possibility—even likelihood—of such ill-intended referrals overlook the natural trajectory of emotions stirred by the use of armed force. When the *jus ad bellum* basis for a particular military action is questioned, powerless victims of that application of force may seek redress by focusing on any *jus in bello* implementation issues raised by the actions of commanders and armed forces personnel.

Late in the Rome negotiations . . . the United States suggested a treaty regime in which states parties would accept the automatic jurisdiction of the court over the crime of genocide only. . . . As to the other core crimes, the United States attempted to facilitate participation in the treaty by proposing a ten-year transition period following entry into force of the treaty during which any state party could "opt-out" of the court's jurisdiction over war crimes and crimes against humanity. At the end of the ten-year opt-out period, several arrangements were proffered, including mechanisms whereby states could accept the automatic jurisdiction of the court over all of the core crimes, cease to be a party to the court (withdraw from the treaty), or extend the opt-out period. Even these modest suggestions were rejected. . . .

The ICC Statute creates automatic jurisdiction for states parties, even potentially withstanding a well-founded national decision not to prosecute. Though the United States would question the prudence of such a rubric, few would doubt a state's authority to consent to such an arrangement on behalf of its own citizens. Conversely, the statute's assertion of jurisdiction over non-party nationals is significantly more inimical to fundamental principles of international law. In cases not referred by the Security Council, the treaty specifies that a precondition to the jurisdiction of the court is consent by either the state of territory where the crime was committed *or* the state of nationality of the alleged perpetrator. . . . The United States sought an amendment to the text that would have required . . . that the consent of the state of nationality of the alleged perpetrator be obtained before the court could exercise jurisdiction. As a last resort, the United States recommended a provision that would discourage political manipulation of the court by excluding jurisdiction over non-party nationals when the conduct arose in the course of official acts of state. The United States was not successful, and the outcome threatens to undermine the credibility of the court. . . .

Ironically, while on one hand the court's jurisdiction is too independent and robust, inserted limitations went in the wrong direction. Most atrocities—and certainly such is the case in recent years—are committed internally. And most internal conflicts are between warring parties of the same nationality. Such internal crimes can easily escape the ICC's jurisdictional trigger of nationality *or* territory-based consent since the potentially relevant states are one and the same. Thus, the worst offenders of international humanitarian law can choose never to join the treaty and be fully insulated from its reach absent a Security Council referral. Recent events call our attention to . . . the crimes of Saddam Hussein, and the Kosovo atrocities perpetuated by the regime of Slobodan Milosevic. To bring such rogue leaders or their mercenary consorts to justice often requires some form of intervention, perhaps based on Security Council authorization. However, any peace-keeper or peace enforcer . . . would not enjoy the same ICC immunity as the rogue state actors themselves. . . .

Human Rights Watch, *The ICC Jurisdictional Regime: Addressing U.S. Arguments*

(1998), www.hrw.org/campaigns/icc/docs/icc-regime.htm

Since the diplomatic conference in Rome, U.S. representatives have made much of the claim that the International Criminal Court (ICC) is overreaching, asserting that it is based on "universal jurisdiction" and binds nonstate parties through the potential exercise of jurisdiction over their nationals. This has been used to support the position that some form of veto over the ICC's docket should be given to the state of nationality of the accused. These claims embody a misrepresentation both of the jurisdictional provisions of the ICC treaty and of existing state practice—including that of the United States—under general international law and international treaties. . . .

THE JURISDICTIONAL BASIS OF THE ICC TREATY

Before the ICC can act, the state of territory or nationality of the accused must be a party to the ICC treaty or accept the Court's jurisdiction (Article 12). . . .

The U.S. had insisted that the ICC's authority be yet more restrictive, depending solely on the acceptance of the Court's jurisdiction by the state of nationality of the accused. Assertions were made following the conference that any other approach violates international law. Yet requiring the consent of the state of nationality would be out of line with jurisdictional theory and state practice. The first and best established jurisdictional principle is "territoriality": when crimes are committed on the territory of a state, that state is entitled to exercise criminal jurisdiction, whatever the nationality of the accused. Insisting on the state of nationality as the essential nexus for prosecution contradicts even this most basic principle. It would be ludicrous to argue that the state of territory should require the consent of the state of nationality before prosecuting.

Moreover, the majority of the core crimes in the ICC treaty are crimes which, under general international law, any nation in the world has the authority to prosecute as crimes of universal jurisdiction. This principle has been applied as a basis for jurisdiction in a number of domestic cases, including in the U.S. Again, this jurisdiction could be exercised without requiring consent of the state of nationality of the accused, or any other state. The Article 12 requirement that the state of territory or nationality must have ratified the treaty or accepted its authority imposes preconditions on the exercise of ICC jurisdiction that would not be imposed on the exercise of universal jurisdiction by any state. . . .

EXISTING TREATY LAW AND PRACTICE

Many treaties, such as hijacking or anti-terrorism conventions, provide for states other than the state of nationality of the accused to exercise jurisdiction over persons accused of having committed the serious crimes within their scope. Those treaties provide—reflecting the states mentioned in the ICC treaty—firstly for the state of territory or secondly for the offender's state of nationality to exercise jurisdiction. In most cases they go beyond, providing that the state of nationality of the victim should also do so. And all contain provision for all state parties who find an offender on their territory to either prosecute or extradite. These treaties, like the ICC treaty, do not require that the state of nationality be a party to the treaty or consent to prosecution. This is unsurprising. It is hard to conceive of an anti-terrorism treaty, for example, that required ratification or consent by the state of nationality of the accused being acceptable to states, and certainly not to public opinion or to the government in the United States.

. . . [The United States] has in fact exercised jurisdiction over non-U.S. nationals in a number of cases, on the basis of the treaty provisions empowering it to do so. One example involved a Lebanese citizen suspected of hijacking a Jordanian aircraft in the Middle East. Based on domestic legislation implementing the International Convention Against the Taking of Hostages . . . , the U.S. exercised jurisdiction as the state of nationality of two U.S. passengers who were among the victims of the alleged crime. . . . U.S. Courts [did not consider] that the non-ratification of the relevant treaty by the suspect's state of nationality might somehow render "overreaching" or otherwise questionable the exercise of U.S. jurisdiction.

[handwritten margin note: us does what it doesn't want to be done]

On December 31, 2000, the last day possible for states to sign the ICC Statute, the United States did so (along with Iran and Israel, which for different reasons had opposed the Statute). At the same time, the Clinton Administration announced that it would not submit it to the Senate for advice and consent to ratification, but rather seek to amend it.

Beginning in 2002, the United States initiated a policy of active opposition to the International Criminal Court. This policy has a number of prongs:

First, on May 6, 2002, the United States sent a letter to the UN Secretary-General stating: "This is to inform you, in connection with the Rome Statute of the International Criminal Court adopted on July 17, 1998, that the United States does not intend to become a party to the treaty. Accordingly, the United States has no legal obligations arising from its signature on December 31, 2000. The United States requests that its intention not to become a party, as expressed in this letter, be reflected in the depositary's status lists relating to this treaty." (Israel sent a similar letter on August 28, 2002.)

Second, in the summer of 2002, in the course of the Security Council's consideration of the renewal of the mandate of the United Nations peacekeeping mission in Bosnia and Herzegovina (UNMIBH), the United States vetoed the renewal after the Council's other members refused to accept a U.S. proposal to exempt permanently all members of UN peacekeeping forces from the jurisdiction of the ICC through the form of a Security Council request under ICC Article 16. All the other members of the Council, as well as the Secretary-General (in a strong letter to the U.S. Secretary of State) opposed such an exemption on the grounds that it would undermine the object and purpose of the Rome Statute, and that it was practically meaningless because the ICTY continued to have jurisdiction over war crimes by any person in the former Yugoslavia. Britain eventually forged a compromise, under which the Council agreed to request the ICC Prosecutor to defer for one year (with the possibility of renewal) any investigation into crimes by members of UN operations who are nationals of states not party to the Rome Statute. (The same day, the Council extended UNMIBH's mandate until the end of 2002.) Many NGOs and other supporters of the ICC denounced the resolution.

The exemption resolution came up for reconsideration by the Council in the spring of 2004 shortly after the Abu Ghraib prison abuse scandal broke in the media. Despite attempts by the U.S. government to portray the renewal of the resolution as a "technical rollover," numerous governments resisted, noting privately that the United States could not claim that its troops were unlikely to commit war crimes. In June, as support within the Council evaporated, the United States announced that it would not press for a new resolution. It subsequently announced that it would withdraw nine peacekeepers from UN missions in Kosovo (Serbia) and the Ethiopia-Eritrea border, as those states had not signed Article 98 agreements with it (see below).

Third, during the summer of 2002, the United States began actively seeking agreements with states not to turn over U.S. nationals to the ICC. The United States argued that such agreements were specifically contemplated under Article 98(2) of the Rome Statute, which states: "The Court may not proceed with a request for surrender which would require the requested State to act inconsistently with its obligations under international agreements pursuant to which the consent of a sending State is required to surrender a person of that State to the Court, unless the Court can first obtain the cooperation of the sending State for the giving of consent for the surrender." The U.S. proposals to other states were very broad, covering current or former officials, employees (including contractors), military personnel, and all other U.S. nationals. By early 2006, some 100 states had signed such agreements with the United States, although some were subject to parliamentary approval; about 50 had announced that they would not sign such agreements.

Fourth, on August 3, 2002, President Bush signed into law the American Servicemembers Protection Act. Under the law, the United States will not cooperate with the work of the ICC, including by handing over suspects, evidence, or classified information to the ICC; will not participate in UN peacekeeping operations that might expose U.S. forces to ICC jurisdiction; will deny military aid to states that are parties to the ICC Statute (other than a list of NATO and other allied states) and have not signed an Article 98 agreement; and will take "necessary and appropriate action" to free any U.S. forces held in ICC custody. (The last section caused pro-ICC NGOs to dub the law the "Hague Invasion Act.") The law contains provisions for presidential waiver based on the national interest. In 2004, Congress added further restrictions on aid to ICC parties. In fiscal year 2005, prohibitions on military assistance or restrictions on economic aid applied, at some point, to approximately 60 countries that had not entered into Article 98 agreements.

Despite its continued strong opposition to the ICC, the United States chose to abstain (along with Algeria, Brazil, and China), rather than veto, the 2005 Security Council resolution that formally referred the situation in Darfur to the ICC Prosecutor for investigation. This followed an unsuccessful effort to convince other Council members to create a hybrid tribunal for Sudan. At U.S. insistence, the resolution included an exemption from ICC jurisdiction of all nationals of non-ICC parties participating in peacekeeping operations in Sudan and a clause recognizing that the investigation would be paid by the ICC's parties, not the UN.

Notes and Questions

1. If the United States had achieved the changes it sought to Article 12 and then ratified the treaty, would its troops be less exposed to ICC jurisdiction than under the Statute as it stands? Why, then, did the United States seek those changes?

2. How valid are the U.S. concerns about its forces? Does the complementarity regime protect the United States? What does the United States assume regarding the actual functioning of the Court and its Prosecutor? Why do you think that close U.S. allies that have ratified the Statute, such as the United Kingdom, do not share these concerns?

3. How might the absence of U.S. participation in, or overt hostility to, the Court affect its ability to function?

IV. SPECIAL DILEMMAS OF STATES IN TRANSITION: CHILE AFTER AUGUSTO PINOCHET

Among the many critical global developments of the last decade has been the burgeoning number of states undergoing some form of political transition from an authoritarian past to one dedicated, at least in principle, to human rights and democracy. In looking forward to solidifying the rule of law, these societies also face the question of how to deal with a legacy of human rights abuses. In principle, individual accountability can help repair the damage done to a society traumatized by massive human rights violations. Trials can promote national reconciliation by focusing on individual guilt, initiating a public dialogue about the past, and helping to solidify the rule of law. Yet domestic trials of past human rights violators might prove difficult in practice for the reasons discussed in the last problem—that is, structural incapacity, the possibility of show trials that ignore defendants' rights, or fear by prosecutors and judges of trying former public officials.

This last factor often proves especially important, for in many countries those who have committed the abuses not only remain in a nation's midst but, in many situations, retain some form of formal or informal power. Attempts to pierce the veil of impunity enjoyed by those associated with a previous regime might—although the causal link is often speculative—threaten the stability of the new political system. The larger and more powerful the segment of the population responsible for such abuses, the greater the potential link between any process of accountability and political or social upheaval. In Latin America, because successor regimes remain relatively weak and elements of the prior regime retain some power, efforts to pursue accountability have been half-hearted and incomplete; whereas in Eastern Europe, because successor regimes have inherited the strong governmental bureaucracies built up by the Communists, accountability has had a tendency to cross the line between justice and revenge. *See* Tina Rosenberg, The Haunted Land: Facing Europe's Ghosts After Communism (1995).

The perception that trials may foster instability has led many transitional governments to limit, or even abstain from, criminal proceedings in favor of some form of de facto or de jure amnesty. In some cases, states in transition have avoided trials in favor of commissions of inquiry, or truth commissions, empowered to uncover the scope of atrocities. Relying on expansive theories of jurisdicition, victims have sometimes turned to foreign tribunals for justice.

As you read the following problem, consider whether criminal trials of violators of human dignity are necessary for the protection of human rights; whether states other than those where the abuses took place should have jurisdiction to prosecute violators; whose interests—those of the victims, the new government, the population at large, or the population of the planet—should determine the path a transitional society should take after international crimes; how much deference outside actors, and thus international law, should give to domestic elites in determining the proper approach to accountability; and whether these global actors should adopt substantive norms limiting domestic options or process norms determining how states should arrive at certain outcomes.

A. *The Problem*

In 1970, Salvador Allende was elected President of Chile. Conservative elements in Chilean society, especially in the Chilean military, viewed Allende's election as a threat to Chilean stability and prosperity. On September 11, 1973, General Augusto Pinochet led a military coup against the Allende government. Scores of people died in the coup, including Allende, who was murdered in the presidential palace. Several months after the coup, Pinochet formally assumed the position of head of state.

Pinochet, whose photo appears on p. 668, maintained firm control over the country for the next 17 years. During that period, especially during the first five years of his rule, the Chilean government engaged in harsh repression of suspected leftists, Allende supporters, and opponents of military rule. Hundreds were tortured, and at least 3,000 political opponents were murdered or simply "disappeared." Most of the abuses of Pinochet's rule were carried out in Chile and against Chilean nationals. But in some cases, DINA, the Chilean intelligence agency, targeted foreign nationals, including several U.S. citizens, in Chile and abroad.

By 1978, Pinochet's government felt sufficiently secure, and deemed the threat of communism to be sufficiently under control, to relax its policies of repression. Human rights abuses declined significantly. The Pinochet government then issued Decree 2191, a general amnesty to immunize Pinochet and other government and military officials from prosecution for crimes committed between September 1973 and March 1978.

In 1990, Pinochet finally accepted a negotiated transition to democracy. In return for permitting democratic elections and accepting their outcome, Pinochet insisted on the adoption of a new constitution, which made him a member for life of the Chilean Senate. As such, Pinochet was rendered largely immune from legal process in Chile. Democratic elections were held in 1990. The new President, Patricio Aylwin, created a Truth and Reconciliation Commission to investigate the abuses committed during the Pinochet regime. The Commission detailed 3,197 cases of murder and disappearance, as well as thousands of cases of torture, but was precluded by its mandate from naming any individual offenders. Hundreds of criminal complaints were nonetheless filed by victims against Pinochet and other members of his government. The Chilean courts found that most of the cases were barred by the 1978 Amnesty Law. Some of the complaints filed alleged crimes against humanity, which are not covered by the Amnesty Law. Despite a number of victories in lower courts, most prosecutions for such crimes stalled through the 1990s.

B. *To Prosecute or to Pardon?*

Chile was one of many states that have passed amnesty laws since the late 1980s or honored those passed by their predecessor regimes. Other states, such as Russia

Messe de la junta, General Augusto Pinochet Santiago de Chile, September 19, 1973
SOURCE: Chas Gerretsen/The Netherlands Photo Archives

and some of the states of Eastern Europe, simply chose not to prosecute; and even Germany, which prosecuted officials, confined its trials to senior officials as well as a handful of youthful border guards. On the other hand, some of the above amnesties, such as those of Guatemala, Haiti, and South Africa, do contemplate at least the possibility of prosecutions for serious crimes or have been limited by executive or judicial interpretation. And a small number of states—Greece after the rule of a military junta in the late 1960s and early 1970s, Argentina, Bolivia, Ethiopia, Romania, Hungary, and Rwanda—have successfully prosecuted key officials of the prior regime for serious human rights abuses.

The decisions by most states to forego trials in favor of de facto or de jure amnesties and truth commissions have proved the source of claims at both the international and domestic level.

1. The View from International Human Rights Bodies

The treaty interpretation bodies set up under the International Covenant on Civil and Political Rights (ICCPR)—the UN's Human Rights Committee—and the American Convention on Human Rights—the Inter-American Commission and Court of Human Rights—have reviewed a variety of amnesty laws. Some opinions have resulted from periodic reviews of compliance reports filed by governments with these bodies; others have arisen after victims' groups instituted proceedings alleging that an amnesty law violated a particular treaty. Human rights NGOs have played particularly significant roles in the individual petitions brought to these bodies.

In the case of Chile, the Inter-American Commission, a panel of experts empowered to investigate and appraise human rights abuses, though without legally binding effect, reviewed a series of complaints filed by relatives of victims who had been arrested and then "disappeared" under General Pinochet. They alleged that the 1978 Amnesty Law violated three articles of the American Convention on Human Rights—Article 1.1, requiring states to "ensure to all persons subject to their jurisdiction" the various rights in the Convention; Article 8, granting all persons a fair trial; and Article 25, granting persons the right "to simple and prompt recourse . . . to a competent court or tribunal" in cases of violation of the Convention. They sought a Commission report that would urge Chile to identify the location of victims, punish those responsible for disappearances and executions, and provide compensation to the victims' families. In April 1998, three years after the first petition was filed, the Inter-American Commission issued its report.

Report No. 25/98: Alfonso René Chanfeau Orayce y otros

O.A.S. Doc. OEA/Ser.L/V/11.98, at 512 (1998)

VI. ALLEGATIONS PRESENTED BY THE STATE OF CHILE

12. The State of Chile alleges that it has not issued any amnesty law that is incompatible with the American Convention on Human Rights, as Decree Law 2191 was issued in 1978 under the de facto military regime. It requests that the Commission, in considering these cases, take into account the historical context surrounding the events and the special situation of the return of the country to a democratic regime which obliged the new government to accept the rules imposed by the de facto military regime, which could only be modified in accordance with the law and the Constitution.

13. The Government has sought to have the Decree Law repealed, but the relevant constitutional provision requires that any initiatives concerning matters of amnesty be tabled from the Senate (Article 62 (2) of the Constitution), where a majority in favor does not exist because of the number of persons in that Chamber who were not elected by popular vote [that is, military members, including General Pinochet]. Furthermore, the democratic government has called upon the Supreme Court to declare that the amnesty cannot be an obstacle to the investigation and punishment of crimes.

[The government also noted that it had established the National Truth and Reconciliation Commission and also passed legislation that gave family members of victims certain financial benefits, including a life-long pension.]

VII. OBSERVATIONS OF THE COMMISSION ON THE ALLEGATIONS OF THE PARTIES

A) Preliminary Considerations

a. Competence of the authorities which issued the amnesty

17. The Amnesty law 2191 of 1978 emanated from the military regime which overthrew the constitutional Government of President Salvador Allende in September, 1973. It emanates, therefore, from authorities which lack the credentials and right, as they were not elected or appointed in any way, but usurped power after deposing the legitimate Government, in violation of the Constitution. A de facto Government lacks the legal authority, for if a State has adopted a Constitution, anything which runs counter to it also runs counter to the Law. . . .

19. Those that benefited from the amnesty in the cases dealt with in this report were not disinterested parties, but the very accomplices of the acts perpetrated in keeping with the plans of the former military regime. It is one thing to have to legitimize acts of the society as a whole (so as to prevent chaos) and acts implying international responsibility, because obligations assumed in this area cannot be evaded. But it is an entirely different matter to grant equal treatment to those who acted with the illegitimate government, in violation of the Constitution.

[The commission then concluded that Chilean constitutional law also precluded the self-amnesty.]

B) General Considerations

a) The question of the Amnesty Decree Law

41. The problem of amnesties has been considered by the Commission on various occasions, in claims made against States parties to the American Convention which, seeking mechanisms to foster national peace and reconciliation, have resorted to amnesties. By so doing, they have abandoned an entire group, including many innocent victims of violence, who feel deprived of the right to seek remedy in their rightful claims against those who committed acts of barbarity against them. . . .

43. As the petitioners have clearly stated, their claims do not concern human rights violations resulting from the illegal detention and disappearance of the persons mentioned in their claims, acts which had been perpetrated by agents of the State of Chile during the former military regime, but rather the fact that Amnesty Decree Law 2191, which was enacted by the military government, has not been repealed and has consequently remained in effect under the democratic government, even after Chile has ratified the American Convention and acceded to its conditions. Their claims concern the fact that there has been neither trial nor identification of those responsible nor punishments meted out against the perpetrators of these acts and that this situation which began during the military regime still prevails under the rule of the democratic and constitutional government. . . .

47. The Commission recognizes and advocates the importance of the creation of the National Commission for Truth and Reconciliation and also the work which the latter has carried out in gathering antecedents on prior cases on human rights violations and detainees who disappeared, out of which came a report identifying individual victims—and among them cases of persons named in the claims—tried to establish their whereabouts and measures of compensation and redress for each

one. It recognized that the cases of these persons constitute serious violations of fundamental rights on the part of State agents. These victims, whose whereabouts have not been determined, are classified as "disappeared detainees". . . .

50. These measures, however, are not sufficient to guarantee the human rights of the petitioners . . . for as long as they continue to be denied the right to justice.

[The Commission found the refusal of the current government to repeal the amnesty "a violation of the obligations assumed by this State to ensure conformity of their laws with the precepts of the Convention," as well as a violation of the right to a fair trial and to effective recourse for violations of rights.]

e) Non-compliance with the obligation to investigate

66. In its interpretation of Article 1.1 of the American Convention on Human Rights, the Inter-American Court stipulates that "The second obligation of the States Parties is to "ensure" the free and full exercise of the rights recognized by the Convention to every person subject to its jurisdiction. . . . As a consequence of this obligation, the States must prevent, investigate and punish any violation of the rights recognized by the Convention. . . ." . . .

67. The National Truth and Reconciliation Commission established by the democratic Government to investigate human rights violations committed in the past, examined most of the total number of cases and granted reparation to the victims and their families. Nevertheless, the investigation carried out by the Commission . . . provided no legal recourse or any other type of compensation. . . .

70. The admission of responsibility by the Government, a partial investigation of the facts and the subsequent payment of compensation are not, in themselves, sufficient to fulfill the obligations provided for in the Convention. In accordance with the provisions of Article 1.1 of the Convention, the state has the obligation to investigate violations committed within its jurisdiction, in order to identify those responsible, to impose the necessary sanctions and ensure adequate reparation to the victim. . . .

The Right to Know the Truth

88. The right to truth constitutes both a right of a collective nature which allows society as a whole to have access to essential information on the development of the democratic system, and an individual right which allows the families of the victims to have access to some kind of reparation in those cases in which amnesty laws are in force. . . .

96. States which have resorted to the enactment of amnesty legislation while in search of mechanisms for national pacification and reconciliation, have abandoned the very part of their population which includes many of the innocent victims of violence. They have abandoned the victims who are denied the right to justice when claiming against those who have committed excesses and abhorrent acts of violence against them. . . . It constitutes a clear case of disregard of the obligation to effectively redress the rights that have been violated.

97. In the particular case of Chile, the Truth and Reconciliation Commission carried out a commendable task, by gathering information on human rights violations and on the situation of those "disappeared", with a view to establishing their

whereabouts, as well as the corresponding measures to redress their rights and clear their name. However, neither the investigation of the crimes committed by State agents nor their identification and punishment was allowed. Through the amnesty decree, the Chilean State impeded the realization of the right of the survivors and the families of the victims to know the truth.

The Commission then found the Amnesty Decree incompatible with the American Convention on Human Rights and recommended that Chile amend its legislation and provide damages to those who had instituted the proceedings.

In 2001, the Inter-American Court of Human Rights (whose rulings, unlike those of the Commission, are binding on the parties to a case) issued a broad ruling on the legality of amnesties in the case of *Chumbipuma Aguirre v. Peru*, in which the relatives of the victims of a 1991 massacre by Peruvian forces challenged Peru's 1995 law that immunized military and police from prosecution. The court wrote:

41. [A]ll amnesty provisions, provisions on prescription and the establishment of measures designed to eliminate responsibility are inadmissible, because they are intended to prevent the investigation and punishment of those responsible for serious human rights violations such as torture, extrajudicial, summary or arbitrary execution and forced disappearance, all of them prohibited because they violate non-derogable rights recognized by international human rights law.

42. [T]he amnesty laws adopted by Peru prevented the victims' next of kin and the surviving victims in this case from being heard by a judge, as established in Article 8(1) of the Convention; they violated the right to judicial protection embodied in Article 25 of the Convention; they prevented the investigation, capture, prosecution and conviction of those responsible for the events that occurred in Barrios Altos, thus failing to comply with Article 1(1) of the Convention, and they obstructed clarification of the facts of this case. . . .

In 2004, the Special Court for Sierra Leone, a hybrid tribunal created under a 2002 agreement between the UN and Sierra Leone, determined that the provision in that agreement allowing the court to prosecute despite any prior amnesties prevailed over a provision in a July 1999 (failed) peace accord whereby the government of Sierra Leone promised not to prosecute rebels for actions during Sierra Leone's brutal civil war. The court found that "a crystallizing norm that a government cannot grant amnesty for serious . . . crimes under international law."

Notes and Questions

1. What was the linchpin of the Inter-American Commission's decision? How do you think it would have ruled if Chile's elected legislature had decided upon an amnesty?

2. Do you agree with the Commission that the report of a truth commission is not a substitute for trials? How does the Commission address the interests of the victims and those of society as a whole? Does it see them as a trade-off?

3. In late 2001, Afghanistan's Taliban government fell to opposition forces aided by American bombing and ground operations. Afghanistan did not announce any plans for trials of former officials, either for human rights abuses or

international terrorism. Indeed, most Taliban officials were not detained, and the new government spoke of the need for national reconciliation. The United States did detain some senior Taliban officials, with the possibility of trials for terrorist acts. Who should decide whether Taliban officials should be put on trial—the United States or the government of Afghanistan?

4. Prosecutors at international tribunals have insisted that amnesties under domestic law cannot preclude proceedings by an international court. Do you agree? If so, should a prosecutor take such an amnesty into account in deciding whether to bring a case? The ICC Statute requires the Prosecutor to consider, in initiating an investigation, whether "[t]aking into account the gravity of the crime and the interests of victims, there are nonetheless substantial reasons to believe that an investigation would not serve the interests of justice." (Art. 53(1)(c).)

5. At what point can we say that the international legal process has created some duty on states to prosecute past abuses? If governments continue to defer to the decisions of states to choose amnesties over trials, what are the prospects for a firm norm requiring prosecution? Consider the following appraisal:

Steven R. Ratner, *New Democracies, Old Atrocities: An Inquiry in International Law*

87 Geo. L. J. 707, 720-729 (1999)

A. Treaty-Based Law

Most debate among states, NGOs, and observers over a generalized duty of accountability stems from a vacuum in treaty law—namely the absence of any specific state obligations in the . . . [ICCPR] to prosecute and punish abusers of human rights. Rather, the Covenant contains only less precise obligations, notably those to "respect and ensure to all individuals within its territory and subject to its jurisdiction the rights recognized [therein]," and to provide "an effective remedy". . . .

But while the treaty texts lack a generalized duty of accountability for serious abuses, the bodies charged by their parties with interpreting them have proclaimed such a norm. Thus, the UN Human Rights Committee . . . has repeatedly found that states have a duty to investigate and prosecute those committing disappearances, summary executions, ill-treatment, and arbitrary arrest and detention. . . .

. . . [But these rulings] have not been welcomed, or especially followed, by most states—transitional democracies all—to which they are directed. Thus, Argentina, Uruguay, Chile, Brazil, Peru, Guatemala, El Salvador, Honduras, Nicaragua, Haiti, Ivory Coast, Angola, and Togo have all passed broad amnesty laws in the last ten years—or honored amnesties of prior regimes—covering governmental atrocities; and South Africa is immersed in a long process of judgment of the past that includes, at its centerpiece, confession to a commission of inquiry in exchange for amnesty.

. . . How do we reconcile this practice with the purported duty to prosecute? . . .

. . . The views of the treaty implementation bodies are obviously important, but ultimately the contemporary meaning of a treaty depends as much, if not more, on what states do than on what such bodies say. In the end, it seems difficult to conclude that states are prepared to interpret [the ICCPR and the American Convention] to provide for a duty to prosecute all serious violations of human rights . . .

B. Customary Law

. . . Although governments and international organizations have condemned authoritarian states for failing to punish human rights abusers, they have, with the exception of those bodies responsible for interpreting treaties above, generally refrained from condemning those states for failure to prosecute past abuses once they adopt democratic systems of governance. . . .

As for the other element of custom as traditionally viewed, *opinio juris* . . . [t]hose states that routinely prosecute human rights abusers do not seem to claim they are required by international law to do so; and states that do not prosecute have advanced a number of arguments that international law permits, or at least does not prohibit, forms of impunity.

Some scholars have argued that in the context of deriving customary human rights norms, . . . one might focus on resolutions of international organizations, verbal statements of governments . . . and other professions of belief. But even this method yields at best mixed results about a duty of accountability. Undoubtedly, some resolutions of international organizations support a generalized duty of criminal accountability, [for example, the] 1993 World Conference on Human Rights called upon states to "abrogate legislation leading to impunity for those responsible for grave violations of human rights such as torture and prosecute such violations.". . .

But . . . one confronts the opinions of governments in transition that international law does not require them to punish prior offenders. . . . Thus the beliefs of governments in transition (regardless of their actions) contrast with the votes they pass in endorsing various resolutions. At a minimum, then, this suggests the absence of a sense of obligation to prosecute, at least in these cases of transition.

C. Some Tentative Judgments

. . . To adopt the insightful framework of the New Haven School . . . which views international law as a process of decisionmaking by global actors according to legitimate processes (authority) and with expectations of enforcement (control), one would say that states do not yet regard a generalized duty as accompanied by either an "authority signal" or a "control intention." It is not authoritative in that states do not appear to regard some of the fora that have asserted it (UN conferences, the UN Economic and Social Council, or Amnesty International) as capable of prescribing law. . . . More critically, perhaps, states do not yet regard any entity proclaiming the duty as in a position to enforce it.

2. The View from a Domestic Tribunal

The dilemmas of transitional states have also been the source of domestic litigation. Perhaps the most thoughtful exegesis on the question from a domestic court has come from South Africa's Constitutional Court. In South Africa's case, the leadership of the apartheid-era government began to negotiate a transition to majority rule in the early 1990s. (For details on apartheid and the UN's role in ending it, see Chapter 3.) Among the most significant issues was whether to prosecute those who had carried out apartheid and those who had committed violent acts to end it. Alex Boraine, a participant in the talks, describes the issues:

There were several choices open to South Africa as it sought to come to terms with its past. First, a blanket or general amnesty was proposed. This was strongly preferred by the former government, led by President Frederik W. de Klerk, as well as the security forces, including the military and the police. This option, however, was untenable for the African National Congress (ANC), representing the majority of people who had suffered gross human rights violations in the past.

The second option was that of calling to account those who were directly responsible for the gross human rights violations that took place and of putting them on trial and prosecuting them so that justice could be seen to be done. This approach, akin to the Nuremberg Trials, was for a very long period strongly supported by the members of the liberation movements while they were still in exile.

As Thabo Mbeki, then Deputy President of South Africa, put it, "Within the ANC the cry was to 'catch the bastards and hang them' but we realised that you could not simultaneously prepare for a peaceful transition. If we had not taken this route I don't know where the country would be today. Had there been a threat of Nuremberg-style trials over members of the apartheid security establishment we would never have undergone the peaceful change."

A third option was the one that gained majority support—to appoint a special commission that was at first referred to as a "truth commission" and was later introduced formally as a "truth and reconciliation commission." This commission would offer the possibility of truth relating to victims and perpetrators, the restoration of dignity for victims and survivors, a limited amnesty, and a search for healing and reconciliation. . . .

While there can be little doubt that Mbeki's commitment to "a peaceful transition" was a valid reason for not following the Nuremberg option, there can be no doubt that the strength of the right-wing and state military and security forces was a major factor that informed choices at the negotiating table. Mbeki made it absolutely clear, in a private interview with President Nelson Mandela, that senior generals of the security forces had personally warned him of dire consequences if members of the security forces had to face compulsory trials and prosecutions following the election. According to Mandela, they threatened to make a peaceful election totally impossible. Some compromise had to be made and, in the postamble [final section] of the Interim Constitution, provision was made for the granting of amnesty to advance reconciliation and reconstruction and for its legislative implementation.

Alex Boraine, *Truth and Reconciliation in South Africa: The Third Way, in* Truth v. Justice: The Morality of Truth Commissions 141, 143-144 (Robert I. Rotberg & Dennis Thompson eds., 2000).

To carry out the amnesty provisions of the 1993 Constitution, the Parliament adopted in 1995 the Promotion of National Unity and Reconciliation Act. It set up the Truth and Reconciliation Commission (TRC), and created three subcommissions — one to investigate the fate of the victims and issue an authoritative record; one to determine indemnification for the victims; and one to administer the amnesty. Shortly after passage of the Act, a group of victims of the apartheid period challenged the law's constitutionality in the South African Constitutional Court.

Azanian Peoples Organization (AZAPO) and Others v. President of the Republic of South Africa

[1996] 4 S.A.L.R. 671

[5] . . . The [TRC's Amnesty] Committee has the power to grant amnesty in respect of any act, omission or offence to which the particular application for amnesty relates, provided that the applicant concerned has made a full disclosure of all relevant facts and provided further that the relevant act, omission or offence is associated with a political objective committed in the course of the conflicts of the past. . . . [Sections 20(2) and (3) of the 1995 Act contain] very detailed provisions pertaining to what may properly be considered to be acts 'associated with a political objective'. . . . [The criteria include the person's motive, the act's connection to a political uprising, the act's gravity, the act's goal, whether it was carried out on behalf of the government or an opposition group, and the nexus between the political objective and the act in terms of proximity and proportionality; the definition excludes acts committed for personal gain or out of personal malice.]

[6] . . . [S]ection 20(7) (the constitutionality of which is impugned in these proceedings) provides [that persons granted amnesty will not be criminally or civilly liable and the state or organization to which they belonged shall also not be liable]. . . .

[8] The applicants [allege] that section 20(7) was inconsistent with section 22 of the Constitution, which provides that '[e]very person shall have the right to have justiciable disputes settled by a court of law or, where appropriate, another independent or impartial forum.' . . .

Amnesty in respect of criminal liability

[17] Every decent human being must feel grave discomfort in living with a consequence which might allow the perpetrators of evil acts to walk the streets of this land with impunity, protected in their freedom by an amnesty immune from constitutional attack, but the circumstances in support of this course require carefully to be appreciated. . . . Much of what transpired in this shameful period is shrouded in secrecy and not easily capable of objective demonstration and proof. . . . All that often effectively remains is the truth of wounded memories of loved ones sharing instinctive suspicions, deep and traumatising to the survivors but otherwise incapable of translating themselves into objective and corroborative evidence which could survive the rigours of the law. The Act seeks to address this massive problem by encouraging these survivors and the dependants of the tortured and the wounded, the maimed and the dead to unburden their grief publicly, to receive the collective recognition of a new nation that they were wronged, and, crucially, to help them to discover what did in truth happen to their loved ones, where and under what circumstances it did happen, and who was responsible. That truth, which the victims of repression seek so desperately to know is, in the circumstances, much more likely to be forthcoming if those responsible for such monstrous misdeeds are encouraged to disclose the whole truth with the incentive that they will not receive the punishment which they undoubtedly deserve if they do. Without that incentive there is nothing to encourage such persons to make the disclosures and to reveal the truth which persons in the positions of the applicants so desperately desire. With that incentive . . . the country begins the long and necessary process of healing the wounds of the past. . . .

[19] Even more crucially . . . [i]f the Constitution kept alive the prospect of continuous retaliation and revenge, the agreement of those threatened by its implementation might never have been forthcoming and, if it had, the bridge itself would have remained wobbly and insecure, threatened by fear from some and anger from others. It was for this reason that those who negotiated the Constitution made a deliberate choice, preferring understanding over vengeance, reparation over retaliation, ubuntu [Zulu for "humaneness" or generosity of spirit] over victimisation.

[20] Is section 20(7) . . . nevertheless objectionable on the grounds that amnesty might be provided in circumstances where the victims, or the dependants of the victims, have not had the compensatory benefit of discovering the truth at last or in circumstances where those whose misdeeds are so obscenely excessive as to justify punishment, even if they were perpetrated with a political objective during the course of conflict in the past? . . . The Amnesty Committee may grant amnesty in respect of the relevant offence only if the perpetrator of the misdeed makes a full disclosure of all relevant facts. If the offender does not, and in consequence thereof the victim or his or her family is not able to discover the truth, the application for amnesty will fail. Moreover, it will not suffice for the offender merely to say that his or her act was associated with a political objective. That issue must independently be determined by the Amnesty Committee pursuant to the criteria set out in section 20(3). . . .

[21] The result, at all levels, is a difficult, sensitive, perhaps even agonising, balancing act between the need for justice to victims of past abuse and the need for reconciliation and rapid transition to a new future. . . . We are not concerned with that debate or the wisdom of its choice of mechanisms but only with its constitutionality. That, for us, is the only relevant standard. Applying that standard, I am not satisfied that, in providing for amnesty for those guilty of serious offences associated with political objectives and in defining the mechanisms through which and the manner in which such amnesty may be secured by such offenders, the lawmaker, in section 20(7), has offended any of the express or implied limitations on its powers in terms of the Constitution. . . .

[24] [The court noted that Chile, Argentina, and El Salvador have faced similar issues and concluded:] What emerges from the experience of these and other countries that have ended periods of authoritarian and abusive rule is that there is no single or uniform international practice in relation to amnesty. Decisions of States in transition, taken with a view to assisting such transition, are quite different from acts of a State covering up its own crimes by granting itself immunity. In the former case, it is not a question of the governmental agents responsible for the violations indemnifying themselves, but rather one of a constitutional compact being entered into by all sides, with former victims being well-represented, as part of an ongoing process to develop constitutional democracy and prevent a repetition of the abuses.

[25] [The plaintiffs argue] that the State was obliged by international law to prosecute those responsible for gross human rights violations. . . . We were referred in this regard to . . . [the four Geneva Conventions of 1949]. . . .

[26] The issue which falls to be determined in this Court is whether section 20(7) of the Act is inconsistent with the Constitution. If it is, the enquiry as to whether or not international law prescribes a different duty is irrelevant to that determination. International law . . . [is] relevant only in the interpretation of the Constitution itself, on the grounds that the lawmakers of the Constitution should not lightly be presumed to authorise any law which might constitute a breach of the obligations

of the state in terms of international law. International conventions and treaties do not become part of the municipal law of our country, enforceable at the instance of private individuals in our courts, until and unless they are incorporated into the municipal law by legislative enactment.

[27] . . . [T]he Constitution makes it clear that when Parliament agrees to the ratification of or accession to an international agreement such agreement becomes part of the law of the country only if Parliament expressly so provides and the agreement is not inconsistent with the Constitution. . . . [A]n Act of Parliament can override any contrary rights or obligations under [prior] international agreements. . . .

[30] . . . [T]he international literature in any event clearly appreciates the distinction between the position of perpetrators of acts of violence in the course of war (or other conflicts between States or armed conflicts between liberation movements seeking self-determination against colonial and alien domination of their countries), on the one hand, and their position in respect of violent acts perpetrated during other conflicts which take place within the territory of a sovereign State in consequence of a struggle between the armed forces of that State and other dissident armed forces operating under responsible command, within such a State on the other. In respect of the latter category, there is no obligation on the part of a contracting state to ensure the prosecution of those who might have performed acts of violence or other acts which would ordinarily be characterised as serious invasions of human rights. On the contrary, article 6(5) of Protocol II to the Geneva Conventions of 1949 provides that

> '[a]t the end of hostilities, the authorities in power shall endeavour to grant the broadest possible amnesty to persons who participated in the armed conflict, or those deprived of their liberty for reasons related to the armed conflict, whether they are interned or detained.'

[31] The need for this distinction is obvious. It is one thing to allow the officers of a hostile power which has invaded a foreign State to remain unpunished for gross violations of human rights perpetrated against others during the course of such conflict. It is another thing to compel such punishment in circumstances where such violations have substantially occurred in consequence of conflict between different formations within the same State. . . . The erstwhile adversaries of such a conflict inhabit the same sovereign territory. They have to live with each other and work with each other. . . .

[32] Considered in this context, I am not persuaded that there is anything in the Act and more particularly in the impugned section 20(7) thereof, which can properly be said to be a breach of the obligations of this country in terms of the instruments of public international law. . . . The amnesty contemplated is not a blanket amnesty against criminal prosecution for all and sundry, granted automatically as a uniform act of compulsory statutory amnesia. . . . It is available only where there is a full disclosure of all facts to the Amnesty Committee and where it is clear that the particular transgression was perpetrated during the prescribed period and with a political objective committed in the course of the conflicts of the past. . . .

[The court also rejected arguments that the amnesty's elimination of the civil liability of offenders was unconstitutional.]

Chile and South Africa were two among some 20 states that used truth commissions as fora for addressing the past. Most commissions have been established by governments, but the United Nations set up two—in El Salvador and Guatemala—as part of a negotiated end to a civil war. In most cases, the governments that created these commissions saw them at the time as substitutes for trials of former governmental officials (although Argentina's 1983 commission immediately handed over its evidence to prosecutors, who later held trials). As noted earlier, Pinochet's democratically elected successor as president, Patricio Aylwin, organized an eight-person National Truth and Reconciliation Commission soon after assuming office. As for South Africa's TRC, it held numerous hearings throughout South Africa and received testimony from some 22,000 victims and witnesses, 2,000 of them in widely watched and highly emotional public proceedings. In October 1998, the TRC issued an enormous five-volume report (available at *www.truth.org.za*), which both former governmental and former ANC leaders criticized as being too favorable to the other. The TRC's amnesty committee received over 7,000 applications for amnesty from former governmental and resistance members. By the time the TRC closed down in March 2002, some 1,200 applications had been granted and 5,500 refused. The recommendations of the TRC regarding reparations for victims led to some small amounts for some victims, but the government generally showed an unwillingness to fund the program.

Notes and Questions

1. Was the South African Constitutional Court's opinion inevitable, given that the country's leaders had already agreed on the necessity of the amnesty? If so, what purpose did the opinion serve?

2. How important was it to the Court that the amnesty was selective, not blanket? Do you think the Court would have upheld a blanket amnesty of the sort General Pinochet gave himself?

3. How did the Court treat the question of international law? Did international norms seem to exert any effect on its decision? In a June 2005 ruling striking down Argentina's amnesty laws as violations of international law and unconstitutional exercises of legislative power, the Argentine Supreme Court relied extensively on the *Chumbipuma Aguirre v. Peru* case excerpted above, as well as other Inter-American Court and UN Human Rights Committee opinions on amnesties.

4. Should it matter for purposes of legal appraisal under international law which domestic authority approved the amnesty? Consider these possibilities: (a) a self-amnesty by an outgoing authoritarian regime (of the sort adopted by the Argentine military just before it handed over power to a democratically elected president in 1983); (b) a decision by a democratically elected president to respect a self-amnesty (as in Chile until recently); (c) an amnesty passed by the new parliament (as in South Africa); and (d) an amnesty approved by popular referendum (the case in Uruguay). Should the amount of public debate be relevant for determining whether international decision makers should regard the domestic decision as lawful?

5. What does a truth commission accomplish that trials do not, and vice versa? Can they work in tandem? Who should determine the mandate of the truth commission in terms of the events and time period it should examine? Who should serve on it? Should a truth commission name the names of offenders? Why might a government and opposition groups creating it want to keep the names of offenders out of a report?

6. How does the establishment of the International Criminal Court affect the debate over trials versus truth commissions? What advantages and disadvantages might newly democratic governments see in sending their former officials to the ICC if the person is overseas anyway (as was General Pinochet when he was arrested)?

7. Some transitional states have adopted yet another option for dealing with past human rights abusers—excluding them from governmental positions. This process, known as lustration, can entail the removal from public life of small numbers of leading suspected perpetrators, or far larger numbers. After the fall of communism in Czechoslovakia and the reunification of the two Germanys in 1989, the governments purged thousands from their jobs. A committee of the International Labor Organization found that many of the removals in Czechoslovakia violated the rights of workers under ILO Convention 111 not to be discriminated against based on political opinion. Western human rights groups also criticized much of the process as unfairly stigmatizing those (e.g., some informers) whose connection to the previous regime may have been minimal, coerced, or unintentional. The Czechoslovak Constitutional Court upheld most of that state's lustration law, but it found that the law was being administered in an arbitrary manner in many cases.

C. Prosecuting Pinochet Outside Chile

Frustrated by the difficulties in obtaining redress through the Chilean legal system, lawyers for Spanish victims of the Pinochet government shifted their efforts to the Spanish courts. In Spain, as in many civil law countries, individuals can initiate criminal investigations in cases deemed in the public interest. In 1996, a team of lawyers filed criminal complaints against the former military leaders of both Chile and Argentina. At the outset, their focus was on the more than 300 Spanish nationals injured in those countries as part of the so-called "dirty war" against Communism. Over time, however, the cases expanded to encompass crimes committed against Chilean nationals as well as foreign nationals.

How could a state other than the one where atrocities took place prosecute? First, the crimes might have been planned in another state, giving that state a territorial basis for jurisdiction, as discussed in Chapter 6. Second, nationals of another state might have committed the crime, allowing that state to prosecute its own nationals. Third, victims might include those with another nationality, permitting that state to prosecute under a theory of passive personality. The greatest number of fora, however, would be available if states could prosecute the crime based on universal jurisdiction. Under this principle, because certain offenses are so grave and affect humankind generally, any state is allowed to prosecute, even if the act took place abroad and was committed by foreign nationals against other foreign nationals. Spain's laws allowed for prosecutions of human rights abuses based on both passive personality and universality.

Although some of the states prosecuting World War II offenders relied on universal jurisdiction, for most of the last century universal jurisdiction was more a theory than a reality. The key exception, one still invoked by advocates of universal jurisdiction, was Israel's prosecution of Adolf Eichmann. For excerpts from the Israeli Supreme Court's decision in that case, see Chapter 6.

In September 1998, General Pinochet visited London on a Chilean diplomatic passport for treatment of a back ailment. Amnesty International's London office learned of the visit and alerted Spanish lawyers. On October 13, the two Spanish magistrates handling the cases against Pinochet requested Scotland Yard to detain him. They relied in part on the European Convention on the Suppression of Terrorism, which obligates parties to find and hold suspected terrorists at the request of another party. The initial request was followed by a "priority red" arrest warrant, issued by Spain through Interpol. Shortly before midnight on October 16, detectives from Scotland Yard entered Pinochet's room at an exclusive London clinic where Pinochet was recuperating from back surgery and placed him under arrest. On November 4, 1998, Spain formally requested Pinochet's extradition. Spain's request was followed by similar requests from Belgium, France, and Switzerland, where cases comparable to those in Spain had been filed by other victims of the Pinochet regime.

Pinochet's lawyers mounted a vigorous challenge to his arrest, claiming that as a former head of state, he was immune from legal process in Britain. A long, high-profile legal battle ensued. On October 28, the British High Court ruled in favor of Pinochet. The decision was appealed to a judicial panel of the House of Lords, Britain's highest court. The Law Lords reversed the holding of the lower court in a 3-2 decision, concluding that a former head of state's immunity from prosecution did not extend to the kinds of crimes with which Pinochet had been charged. This decision was later vacated because Lord Hoffman, who had voted to reject Pinochet's claim of immunity, had failed to disclose a connection with Amnesty International, one of the non-governmental organizations given special leave to intervene in the case against Pinochet.

The case was then reargued to a seven member judicial panel of the House of Lords. A majority of the judges found that many of Pinochet's alleged crimes did not satisfy the "dual criminality" requirement of Britain's 1989 Extradition Act. That requirement, common to the extradition laws of many countries, permits extradition only if the conduct at issue constituted a crime under the law of both Spain and the United Kingdom at the time the charged acts were committed. With respect to torture, a majority of the judges concluded that *extraterritorial* torture was not a crime that could be prosecuted in Britain prior to September 29, 1988. On that date, Britain passed legislation giving effect to its obligations under the UN's 1984 Convention Against Torture and Other Cruel, Inhuman or Degrading Treatment and Punishment by authorizing the prosecution in the United Kingdom of torture committed outside the United Kingdom. Since most of the acts with which Pinochet was accused took place in Chile and prior to 1988, the rulings effectively precluded Spain from trying Pinochet for the vast majority of the charges against him.

Nonetheless, several acts alleged to constitute torture satisfied the dual criminality requirement as interpreted by the judges of the House of Lords. Accordingly, the panel still had to consider whether Pinochet could claim immunity from UK and Spanish jurisdiction with respect to acts of torture because he had been a head of state at the time they were committed. Six of the panel members ruled, in a splintered set of opinions, that Pinochet could not avoid prosecution on the basis of head-of-state immunity.

Regina v. Bow Street Metropolitan Stipendiary Magistrate And Others, *Ex Parte* Pinochet Ugarte (No. 3)

[2000] 1 A.C. 147 (1999)

Lord Browne-Wilkinson

Torture

Apart from the law of piracy, the concept of personal liability under international law for international crimes is of comparatively modern growth. The traditional subjects of international law are states not human beings. But consequent upon the war crime trials after the 1939-45 World War, the international community came to recognise that there could be criminal liability under international law for a class of crimes such as war crimes and crimes against humanity. . . . Ever since 1945, torture on a large scale has featured as one of the crimes against humanity. . . .

Moreover, the Republic of Chile accepted before your Lordships that the international law prohibiting torture has the character of jus cogens or a peremptory norm, i.e. one of those rules of international law which have a particular status. . . .

The jus cogens nature of the international crime of torture justifies states in taking universal jurisdiction over torture wherever committed. . . . [O]ffences jus cogens may be punished by any state because the offenders are "common enemies of all mankind and all nations have an equal interest in their apprehension and prosecution:" *Demjanjuk v. Petrovsky* (1985) 603 F. Supp. 1468. . . .

But there was no tribunal or court to punish international crimes of torture. Local courts could take jurisdiction . . . [but] the fact that the local court had jurisdiction to deal with the international crime of torture was nothing to the point so long as the totalitarian regime remained in power. . . . What was needed therefore was an international system which could punish those who were guilty of torture and which did not permit the evasion of punishment by the torturer moving from one state to another. The Torture Convention was agreed not in order to create an international crime which had not previously existed but to provide an international system under which the international criminal—the torturer— could find no safe haven. . . .

The Torture Convention

Article 1 of the Convention defines torture as the intentional infliction of severe pain and of suffering with a view to achieving a wide range of purposes "when such pain or suffering is inflicted by or at the instigation of or with the consent or acquiescence of a public official or other person acting in an official capacity. . . ." [Other provisions require all states parties to extradite or prosecute any alleged offender found on their territory.]

State immunity

. . . The issue is whether international law grants state immunity in relation to the international crime of torture and, if so, whether the Republic of Chile is entitled to claim such immunity even though Chile, Spain and the United Kingdom are all parties to the Torture Convention and therefore "contractually" bound to give effect to its provisions from 8 December 1988 [the date that the last of these three states (the U.K.) ratified the Convention] at the latest.

It is a basic principle of international law that one sovereign state (the forum state) does not adjudicate on the conduct of a foreign state. . . . This immunity extends to both criminal and civil liability. . . . [T]he head of state is entitled to the same immunity as the state itself. The diplomatic representative of the foreign state in the forum state is also afforded the same immunity in recognition of the dignity of the state which he represents. This immunity enjoyed by a head of state in power and an ambassador in post is a complete immunity attaching to the person of the head of state or ambassador and rendering him immune from all actions or prosecutions whether or not they relate to matters done for the benefit of the state. Such immunity is said to be granted ratione personae.

What then when the ambassador leaves his post or the head of state is deposed? The position of the ambassador is covered by the Vienna Convention on Diplomatic Relations (1961) [which provides, in Article 39(2), that an ex-ambassador retains immunity only for acts "in the exercise of his functions as a member of the mission."] . . .

. . . [I]n order to preserve the integrity of the activities of the foreign state during the period when he was ambassador, it is necessary to provide that immunity is afforded to his *official* acts during his tenure in post. If this were not done the sovereign immunity of the state could be evaded by calling in question acts done during the previous ambassador's time. . . .

In my judgment at common law a former head of state enjoys similar immunities, ratione materiae, once he ceases to be head of state. . . . As ex-head of state he cannot be sued in respect of acts performed whilst head of state in his public capacity. . . .

. . . How can it be for international law purposes an official function to do something which international law itself prohibits and criminalises? . . . [A]n essential feature of the international crime of torture is that it must be committed "by or with the acquiesence of a public official or other person acting in an official capacity." As a result all defendants in torture cases will be state officials. Yet, if the former head of state has immunity, the man most responsible will escape liability while his inferiors (the chiefs of police, junior army officers) who carried out his orders will be liable. I find it impossible to accept that this was the intention [of the Torture Convention].

. . . [I]f the implementation of a torture regime is a public function giving rise to immunity ratione materiae, this produces bizarre results. Immunity ratione materiae applies not only to ex-heads of state and ex-ambassadors but to all state officials who have been involved in carrying out the functions of the state. Such immunity is necessary in order to prevent state immunity being circumvented by prosecuting or suing the official who, for example, actually carried out the torture when a claim against the head of state would be precluded by the doctrine of immunity. If that applied to the present case, and if the implementation of the torture regime is to be treated as official business sufficient to found an immunity for the former head of state, it must also be official business sufficient to justify immunity for his inferiors who actually did the torturing. Under the Convention the international crime of torture can only be committed by an official or someone in an official capacity. They would all be entitled to immunity. It would follow that there can be no case outside Chile in which a successful prosecution for torture can be brought unless the State of Chile is prepared to waive its right to its officials' immunity. Therefore the whole elaborate structure of universal jurisdiction over torture committed by officials is rendered abortive and one of the main objectives of the Torture

Convention—to provide a system under which there is no safe haven for torturers—will have been frustrated. In my judgment all these factors together demonstrate that the notion of continued immunity for ex-heads of state is inconsistent with the provisions of the Torture Convention. . . .

Lord Goff of Chiveley

. . . In broad terms I understand the argument to be that, since torture contrary to the Convention can only be committed by a public official or other person acting in an official capacity, and since it is in respect of the acts of these very persons that states can assert state immunity ratione materiae, it would be inconsistent with the obligations of state parties under the Convention for them to be able to invoke state immunity ratione materiae in cases of torture contrary to the Convention. . . . There can, however, be no doubt that, before the Torture Convention, torture by public officials could be the subject of state immunity. Since therefore exclusion of immunity is said to result from the Torture Convention and there is no express term of the Convention to this effect, the argument has, in my opinion, to be formulated as dependent upon an implied term in the Convention. . . .

. . . [Chile argues] that a state's waiver of its immunity by treaty must always be express. With that submission, I agree. . . .

. . . [I rely upon] the Report of the International Law Commission on the Jurisdictional Immunities of States and their Property. . . . Article 7 of the Commission's Draft Articles on this subject is entitled "*Express consent to exercise of jurisdiction.*" Article 7(1) provides:

> A state cannot invoke immunity from jurisdiction in a proceeding before a court of another state . . . if it has expressly consented to the exercise of jurisdiction by the court with regard to the matter or case: *(a)* by international agreement; *(b)* in a written contract; or *(c)* by a declaration before the court or by a written communication in a specific proceeding. . . .

[The commentary on this article provides that there is "no room for implying the consent of an unwilling state which has not expressed its consent in a clear and recognisable manner. . . ."]

In the light of the foregoing it appears to me to be clear that, in accordance both with international law, and with the law of this country which on this point reflects international law, a state's waiver of its immunity by treaty must . . . always be express. Indeed, if this was not so, there could well be international chaos as the courts of different state parties to a treaty reach different conclusions on the question whether a waiver of immunity was to be implied.

(c) *The function of public officials and others acting in an official capacity*

However it is, as I understand it, suggested that this well established principle can be circumvented in the present case on the basis that . . . for the purposes of the Convention, such torture does not form part of the functions of public officials or others acting in an official capacity including, in particular, a head of state. . . .

In my opinion, the principle which I have described cannot be circumvented in this way. I observe first that the meaning of the word "functions" as used in this context is well established. The functions of, for example, a head of state are governmental functions, as opposed to private acts; and the fact that the head of state performs an act, other than a private act, which is criminal does not deprive it of its governmental character. . . . If, however, a limit is to be placed on governmental functions so as to exclude from them acts of torture within the Torture Convention, this can only be done by means of an implication arising from the Convention itself. . . .

. . . Treaties are the fruit of long negotiation, the purpose being to produce a draft which is acceptable to a number, often a substantial number, of state parties. . . . In circumstances such as these, it is the text of the treaty itself which provides the only safe guide to its terms, though reference may be made, where appropriate, to the travaux préparatoires. But implied terms cannot, except in the most obvious cases, be relied on as binding the state parties who ultimately sign the treaty, who will in all probability include those who were not involved in the preliminary negotiations. . . .

The danger of introducing the proposed implied term in the present case is underlined by the fact that there is . . . nothing in the negotiating history of the Torture Convention which throws any light on the proposed implied term. Certainly the travaux préparatoires . . . reveal no trace of any consideration being given to waiver of state immunity. . . . It is surely most unlikely that during the [five] years in which the draft was under consideration no thought was given to the possibility of the state parties to the Convention waiving state immunity. Furthermore, if agreement had been reached that there should be such a waiver, express provision would inevitably have been made in the Convention to that effect. Plainly, however, no such agreement was reached. . . .

Lord Hope of Craighead

The Torture Convention and loss of immunity

. . . The Torture Convention does not contain any provision which deals expressly with the question whether heads of state or former heads of state are or are not to have immunity from allegations that they have committed torture.

But there remains the question whether the effect of the Torture Convention was to remove the immunity by necessary implication. . . .

. . . [The Convention's drafting history is silent on this issue, which] suggest[s] strongly that it would be wrong to regard the Torture Convention as having by necessary implication removed the immunity ratione materiae from former heads of state in regard to every act of torture of any kind which might be alleged against him falling within the scope of article 1. . . .

Nevertheless there remains the question whether the immunity can survive Chile's agreement to the Torture Convention if the torture which is alleged was of such a kind or on such a scale as to amount to an international crime. . . . The international agreements to which states have been striving in order to deal with this problem in international criminal courts have been careful to set a threshold for such crimes below which the jurisdiction of those courts will not be available. . . . Article 3 of the Statute of the International Criminal Tribunal for Rwanda (1994) included torture as one of the crimes against humanity "when committed as part of a widespread or systematic attack against any civilian population" on national, political, ethnic or other grounds. Article 7 of the Rome Statute contains a similar limitation to acts of widespread or systematic torture.

The allegations which the Spanish judicial authorities have made against Senator Pinochet fall into that category. . . . This is because he is said to have been involved in acts of torture which were committed in pursuance of a policy to commit systematic torture within Chile and elsewhere as an instrument of government. On the other hand it is said that, for him to lose his immunity, it would have to be established that there was a settled practice for crime[s] of this nature to be so regarded by customary international law at the time when they were committed. . . .

. . . I think that there are sufficient signs that the necessary developments in international law were in place by that date . . . [, including] the Torture Convention of 10 December 1984. Having secured a sufficient number of signatories, it entered into force on 26 June 1987. In my opinion, once the machinery which it provides was put in place to enable jurisdiction over such crimes to be exercised in the courts of a foreign state, it was no longer open to any state which was a signatory to the Convention to invoke the immunity ratione materiae in the event of allegations of systematic or widespread torture committed after that date. . . .

I would not regard this as a case of waiver. Nor would I accept that it was an implied term of the Torture Convention that former heads of state were to be deprived of their immunity ratione materiae with respect to all acts of official torture as defined in article 1. It is just that the obligations which were recognised by customary international law in the case of such serious international crimes by the date when Chile ratified the Convention [i.e., September 30, 1988] are so strong as to override any objection by it on the ground of immunity ratione materiae to the exercise of the jurisdiction over crimes committed after that date which the United Kingdom had made available.

. . . On the approach which I would take to this question the immunity ratione materiae was lost when Chile, having ratified the Convention to which section 134 gave effect and which Spain had already ratified, was deprived of the right to object to the extraterritorial jurisdiction which the United Kingdom was able to assert over these offences when the section came into force. . . .

The final decision whether to permit the extradition to proceed rested with Jack Straw, the British Home Secretary. Although Straw had earlier indicated that humanitarian concerns might persuade him to discontinue extradition proceedings, he authorized the proceedings to go forward, as he had after the first House of Lords' decision. Some months later, however, Pinochet suffered a stroke and related complications. After a medical assessment and further legal argument concerning Pinochet's health, Straw determined that Pinochet lacked the mental capacity to stand trial, and allowed him to return to Chile.

The proceedings in London riveted the Chilean public. Some victims' groups favored trial by Spain, but many of Pinochet's strongest domestic opponents argued against prosecution abroad in favor of domestic proceedings. As for trials in Chile, the public was sharply divided, with views often reflecting deep-seated differences over whether Pinochet had saved or destroyed Chile in 1973. Perhaps empowered by the British proceedings or by a sense that public opinion would support him, a Chilean investigating judge decided to consider various charges against the former general. The government remained ambivalent on the question, not wishing to directly confront Chile's military, which remained both powerful and respected. After Pinochet's return, the Chilean Supreme Court effectively stripped Pinochet of his immunity from prosecution. The Court ruled on August 9, 2000, that those who "disappeared" during Pinochet's rule and whose fate remains uncertain should be considered as kidnaping victims. Under Chilean law, the crime of kidnaping is considered in progress if the victims are still missing. Pinochet's amnesty does not apply to ongoing crimes. The Court's ruling provoked considerable controversy in Chile. Chilean courts struck down other claims of immunity brought by Pinochet in a series of rulings from 2001-2005, but as of 2006, he had not yet stood trial for any of his actions.

Notes and Questions

1. Lord Browne-Wilkinson suggests that torture could be considered an official function giving rise to immunity prior to the coming into force of the Torture Convention but not afterwards. Is Lord Browne-Wilkinson's position based on an implied term in the Convention, on the effect the Convention had on customary international law, or on something else?

2. Lord Goff contended that "if state immunity in respect of crimes of torture has been excluded at all in the present case, this can only have been done" by an implied term in the Torture Convention. He then concludes that no such term can reasonably be found. Do you agree with his analysis? Might the Convention's entry into force be viewed as the point at which an exclusion of immunity for torture crystallized as a rule of customary international law?

3. In 1999, the International Criminal Tribunal for the Former Yugoslavia indicted Slobodan Milosevic, the sitting President of Yugoslavia, for war crimes and crimes against humanity; in 2001, he was transferred to the Netherlands and put on trial, although he died in 2006 before proceedings concluded. What does the Pinochet case suggest about the immunity of sitting heads of state (as opposed to former ones like Pinochet) from trials abroad for international crimes? Does it matter that Milosevic appeared before an international court rather than a domestic court?

D. Beyond Chile

Cases based on universal jurisdiction extend well beyond *Pinochet*. Spain and Italy have initiated investigations against leaders of Argentina and Guatemala for human rights abuses associated with their regimes. Denmark, Germany, and Switzerland have tried individuals accused of war crimes in Bosnia. Switzerland and Belgium have already tried Rwandan officials for genocide associated with the 1994 events; in 2001, a Belgian jury convicted two nuns as accomplices to genocide. In February 2000, a Senegalese court indicted former Chadian head of state Hissene Habre, who was living in exile in Senegal, for large-scale torture and murder during his rule. Senegal's appellate court dismissed the case after it concluded that the absence of a domestic statute implementing Senegal's obligations under the Torture Convention precluded prosecution. In March 2001, the French Cour de Cassation held that the Libyan head of state, Muammar Qadhafi, could not be prosecuted in France for his alleged role in the bombing of a French airliner over Niger in 1989. The Court overturned a lower court and accepted the argument of French prosecutors that Qadhafi was entitled to head-of-state immunity.

Nonetheless, former dictators such as Idi Amin of Uganda and Mengistu Haile Mariam of Ethiopia have obtained refuge in other states, with guarantees of non-prosecution, and have even occasionally traveled to other states, which did not prosecute them. And, as mentioned in Section I, when, in 1997, the United States approached several states with statutes providing for universal jurisdiction and asked whether they might be willing to try former Khmer Rouge leaders for atrocities (assuming they were captured), all declined.

The Chilean government's opposition to a trial of Pinochet in Spain is not, moreover, the only example of objections by one state to the exercise of universal jurisdiction by another. In October 2000, the Democratic Republic of the Congo (DRC) sued Belgium in the ICJ after Belgium had issued an arrest warrant the previous spring for the DRC's acting Minister for Foreign Affairs, Abdoulaye Yerodia Ndombasi. Applyinging its universal jurisdiction statute, Belgium had sought Yerodia's arrest for war crimes and crimes against humanity in connection with his activities as an advisor to DRC President Laurent Kabila during the DRC's civil war. The DRC alleged that the arrest order constituted an illegal attempt by Belgium to exercise its law in the DRC, and violated the sovereign equality of states and the diplomatic immunity of Yerodia. Belgium sought to dismiss the case, asserting that because Yerodia was no longer the foreign minister, the DRC's suit was without merit. In February 2002, the Court ruled in favor of the DRC.

Case Concerning the Arrest Warrant of 11 April 2000 (Democratic Republic of the Congo v. Belgium)

2002 I.C.J. 121 (Feb. 14)

53. In customary international law, the immunities accorded to Ministers for Foreign Affairs are not granted for their personal benefit, but to ensure the effective performance of their functions on behalf of their respective States. . . . He or she is in charge of his or her Government's diplomatic activities and generally acts as its representative in international negotiations and intergovernmental meetings. . . . In the performance of these functions, he or she is frequently required to travel internationally. . . . He or she must also be in constant communication with the Government, and with its diplomatic missions around the world, and be capable at any time of communicating with representatives of other States. . . . [A] Minister for Foreign Affairs, responsible for the conduct of his or her State's relations with all other States, occupies a position such that, like the Head of State or the Head of Government, he or she is recognized under international law as representative of the State solely by virtue of his or her office. . . .

54. The . . . functions of a Minister for Foreign Affairs are such that, throughout the duration of his or her office, he or she when abroad enjoys full immunity from criminal jurisdiction and inviolability. That immunity and that inviolability protect the individual concerned against any act of authority of another State which would hinder him or her in the performance of his or her duties.

58. The Court has carefully examined State practice, including national legislation and those few decisions of national higher courts, such as the House of Lords or the French Court of Cassation. It has been unable to deduce from this practice that there exists under customary international law any form of exception to the rule according immunity from criminal jurisdiction and inviolability to incumbent Ministers for Foreign Affairs, where they are suspected of having committed war crimes or crimes against humanity.

The Court has also examined the rules concerning the immunity or criminal responsibility of persons having an official capacity contained in the legal instruments creating international criminal tribunals. . . . It finds that these rules likewise do not enable it to conclude that any such an exception exists in customary international law in regard to national courts.

Finally, none of the decisions of the Nuremberg and Tokyo international military tribunals, or of the International Criminal Tribunal for the former Yugoslavia, cited by Belgium, deal with the question of the immunities of incumbent Ministers for Foreign Affairs before national courts. . . .

60. The Court emphasizes, however, that the *immunity* from jurisdiction enjoyed by incumbent Ministers for Foreign Affairs does not mean that they enjoy *impunity* in respect of any crimes they might have committed, irrespective of their gravity. . . . Jurisdictional immunity may well bar prosecution for a certain period or for certain offences; it cannot exonerate the person to whom it applies from all criminal responsibility.

61. Accordingly, the immunities enjoyed under international law by an incumbent or former Minister for Foreign Affairs do not represent a bar to criminal prosecution in certain circumstances.

First, such persons enjoy no criminal immunity under international law in their own countries, and may thus be tried by those countries' courts in accordance with the relevant rules of domestic law.

Secondly, they will cease to enjoy immunity from foreign jurisdiction if the State which they represent or have represented decides to waive that immunity.

Thirdly, after a person ceases to hold the office of Minister for Foreign Affairs, he or she will no longer enjoy all of the immunities accorded by international law in other States. Provided that it has jurisdiction under international law, a court of one State may try a former Minister for Foreign Affairs of another State in respect of acts committed prior or subsequent to his or her period of office, as well as in respect of acts committed during that period of office in a private capacity.

Fourthly, an incumbent or former Minister for Foreign Affairs may be subject to criminal proceedings before certain international criminal courts, where they have jurisdiction. Examples include the [ICTY, ICTR, and ICC]. The latter's Statute expressly provides, in Article 27, paragraph 2, that "[i]mmunities or special procedural rules which may attach to the official capacity of a person, whether under national or international law, shall not bar the Court from exercising its jurisdiction over such a person." . . .

70. The Court notes that the *issuance*, as such, of the disputed arrest warrant represents an act by the Belgian judicial authorities intended to enable the arrest on Belgian territory of an incumbent Minister for Foreign Affairs on charges of war crimes and crimes against humanity. The fact that the warrant is enforceable is clearly apparent from the order given to "all bailiffs and agents of public authority . . . to execute this arrest warrant" . . . and from the assertion in the warrant that "the position of Minister for Foreign Affairs currently held by the accused does not entail immunity from jurisdiction and enforcement". . . . [G]iven the nature and purpose of the warrant, its mere issue violated the immunity which Mr. Yerodia enjoyed as the Congo's incumbent Minister for Foreign Affairs. The Court

accordingly concludes that the issue of the warrant constituted a violation of an obligation of Belgium towards the Congo, in that it failed to respect the immunity of that Minister and, more particularly, infringed the immunity from criminal jurisdiction and the inviolability then enjoyed by him under international law.

Regarding a remedy, the Court stated that it "considers that Belgium must, by means of its own choosing, cancel the warrant in question and so inform the authorities to whom it was circulated." The Court's vote on the underlying finding against Belgium was 13-3; the vote on the remedy was 10-6.

Beyond the Yerodia investigation, Belgium was the forum for a variety of human rights cases under its domestic universal jurisdiction law. In 2001 and 2005, the government prosecuted and courts convicted six Rwandans for complicity in the 1994 genocide. Most cases, however, were initiated by private individuals under the plaintiff-prosecutor model followed in many states, whereby crime victims can request criminal investigations. In June 2001, survivors of a 1982 massacre of Palestinians by Lebanese militiamen in refugee camps near Beirut that left 500-800 people dead filed a criminal complaint against Ariel Sharon, who was the Israeli defense minister in 1982—and in 2001 was the prime minister of Israel—and Amos Yaron, who had been the general in charge of Israeli forces in Beirut in 1982. In February 2003, the Belgian Supreme Court ruled that Belgian law did not require the accused to be present in Belgium for the case to proceed. Nonetheless, it found that sitting heads of government were immune from prosecution under customary international law. It thus dismissed the case against Sharon but allowed the investigation against Yaron to proceed. The tribunal left open the possibility that a sitting head of government could be tried after leaving office. In response, Israel withdrew its ambassador to Belgium.

In March 2003, seven Iraqi families requested an investigation against former U.S. President George H.W. Bush, U.S. Vice-President (and former Secretary of Defense) Dick Cheney, U.S. Secretary of State (and former Chairman of the Joint Chiefs of Staff) Colin Powell, and retired U.S. General Norman Schwarzkopf, for allegedly committing war crimes during the 1991 Gulf War. In response, Powell warned the Belgian government that it was risking its status as a diplomatic capital and the host state for NATO by allowing criminal investigations of those who might be visiting Belgium. The next month, the Belgian parliament amended the laws such that only the federal prosecutor could initiate cases if the violation was overseas, the offender was not Belgian or located in Belgium, and the victim was not Belgian or had not lived in Belgium for three years. Furthermore, the prosecutor could refuse to proceed if the complaint was "manifestly unfounded" or should be brought before an international tribunal or a competent and fair domestic tribunal. After passage of the amendments, Israel sent its ambassador back to Belgium.

But the amendment did not prove enough for U.S. officials. On June 12, 2003, U.S. Secretary of Defense Donald Rumsfeld told Belgium that the United States would refuse to fund a new headquarters building for NATO and would consider barring its officials from traveling to NATO meetings in Belgium unless Belgium rescinded its universal jurisdiction law. Rumsfeld stated, "Belgium appears not to respect the sovereignty of other countries." The Belgian government agreed within days to submit further amendments to limit the law's reach to cases with a direct link to Belgium. The prime minister stated, "Certain people and certain organizations, pursuing their own political agenda, systematically use this law in an abusive manner." Human Rights Watch announced that Belgium had "clearly capitulated to U.S. pressure." Under the new Belgian law passed in July 2003, Belgian courts can hear cases only if the victim or defendant is a citizen or long-term resident of Belgium at the time of the crime. It guarantees immunity to senior governmental leaders while in office and prohibits arrest of official visitors to Belgium.

In November 2004, the U.S.-based Center for Constitutional Rights and four Iraqi nationals who claimed to have been victims of abuse at Abu Ghraib prison filed charges against Rumsfeld in a German court under Germany's universal jurisdiction statute. In February 2005, shortly before a major conference in Munich to which Rumsfeld had been invited, the German federal prosecutor announced he would not investigate the allegations, stating that he could only proceed if the United States were unwilling to investigate, and that he had no evidence of such unwillingness.

Notes and Questions

1. Is the ICJ's ruling consistent with the House of Lords' ruling in *Pinochet*? How will the ICJ's ruling affect efforts to try current or former leaders for international crimes?

2. What interest did Spain have in prosecuting Pinochet for crimes committed in Chile against Chilean citizens? Consider that Spain has not prosecuted Spanish officials for human rights abuses committed during the Franco dictatorship. Is Spain's interest in prosecution greater than Chile's interest, expressed through Chilean law, in granting Pinochet amnesty? Who should judge the relative strength of these various interests—a Spanish magistrate, the Spanish government, the Chilean government, or someone else? Are these actions a welcome signal that tyrants can no longer violate human rights with impunity, or will these sorts of actions make it more difficult to persuade dictators to hand over power peacefully, as happened in the Philippines and Chile? Consider the following critique of universal jurisdiction from Henry Kissinger, former U.S. Secretary of State:

> Perhaps the most important issue is the relationship of universal jurisdiction to national reconciliation procedures set up by new democratic governments to deal with their countries' questionable pasts. One would have thought that a Spanish magistrate [that is, the one investigating General Pinochet] would have been sensitive to the incongruity of a request by Spain, itself haunted by transgressions committed during the Spanish Civil War and the regime of General Francisco Franco, to try in Spanish courts alleged crimes against humanity committed elsewhere.
>
> The decision of post-Franco Spain to avoid wholesale criminal trials for the human rights violations of the recent past was designed explicitly to foster a process of national reconciliation that undoubtedly contributed much to the present vigor of Spanish democracy. Why should Chile's attempt at national reconciliation not have been given the same opportunity? Should any outside group dissatisfied with the reconciliation procedures of, say, South Africa be free to challenge them in their own national courts or those of third countries? . . .
>
> Another grave issue is the use in such cases of extradition procedures designed for ordinary criminals. If the Pinochet case becomes a precedent, magistrates anywhere will be in a position to put forward an extradition request without warning to the accused and regardless of the policies the accused's country might already have in place for dealing with the charges. . . .
>
> Once extradition procedures are in train, they develop a momentum of their own. The accused is not allowed to challenge the substantive merit of the case and instead is

confined to procedural issues. . . . Meanwhile, while these claims are being considered by the judicial system of the country from which extradition is sought, the accused remains in some form of detention, possibly for years. Such procedures provide an opportunity for political harassment long before the accused is in a position to present any defense. . . .

The Pinochet precedent, if literally applied, would permit the two sides in the Arab-Israeli conflict, or those in any other passionate international controversy, to project their battles into the various national courts by pursuing adversaries with extradition requests. When discretion on what crimes are subject to universal jurisdiction and whom to prosecute is left to national prosecutors, the scope for arbitrariness is wide indeed. So far, universal jurisdiction has involved the prosecution of one fashionably reviled man of the right while scores of East European communist leaders—not to speak of Caribbean, Middle Eastern, or African leaders who inflicted their own full measures of torture and suffering—have not had to face similar prosecutions.

Henry A. Kissinger, *The Pitfalls of Universal Jurisdiction*, 80 For. Aff. 90, 90-92 (July/ Aug. 2001).

3. Does the Belgium story represent a defeat for human rights, as claimed by various NGOs? How much is a state with a universal jurisdiction law entitled to consider its own foreign policy interests, and the tensions that can arise from prosecutions, in deciding whether to permit prosecutions to proceed? What should be the role of private prosecutors in such situations?

4. Besides the Pinochet episode, Spain has also handled other cases under its universal jurisdiction statute. In February 2003, the Spanish Tribunal Supremo held that Spanish courts could hear cases brought by victims of atrocities during Guatemala's civil war against various Guatemalan officials, but limited the scope of Spain's statute to victims of Spanish nationality. In May 2003, the Tribunal Supremo decided that Spanish courts could not yet hear such claims against former Peruvian president Alberto Fujimori on the grounds that universal jurisdiction included a "principle of necessity of jurisdictional intervention." Because Peruvian courts were investigating him, Spanish courts need not yet do so.

In June 2003, Mexico extradited to Spain retired Argentine naval officer Ricardo Cavallo to face charges of terrorism and genocide in connection with his actions during Argentina's "dirty war" against political opponents from 1976-83. Cavallo stands accused of torturing people in Argentina's Naval Mechanical School, which was used to imprison and torture regime opponents. Cavallo had been living in Mexico, indeed running its national car registry, when he was indicted by the same Spanish investigating judge who initiated the proceedings against Pinochet. The event was the first time that one state had extradited a person to another state to face prosecution for atrocities committed in a third state.

PART V

Interdependence and Integration: The Challenge of Collective Action Problems

Economic and ecological interdependence challenge traditional conceptions of state authority and independence—as well as traditional forms of international law. National borders are routinely breached by pollution, international trade, financial flows, and refugees. These borders provide little protection against forces such as climate change or depletion of the earth's ozone layer. Indeed, no single nation can successfully address issues such as these. For this reason, state action on these issues often turns, in part, on how other states act. States may wait for other states to act first, or perhaps decide that they can maximize their gains by not incurring the costs of participation in efforts to address these problems while enjoying the benefits of efforts that other states make. Of course, if every state reasons in this way, there will be no collective response to these problems.

In recent years, new systems of international governance have emerged to address these so-called collective action problems. While management of different collective action problems is at different stages of development, in this part of the text we explore the norms and regimes that states have established to facilitate international cooperation; the international institutions that states have created, or need to create, to implement and enforce these rules; and the various political pressures that bear on the success or failure of these efforts. In this introduction, we explore some of the economic and political forces that complicate efforts to negotiate and implement international policies. While the readings focus on international environmental issues, they are relevant to other collective action problems as well. We then turn, in Chapters 10, 11, and 12, to an examination of three of the most important collective action problems facing states today—managing the oceans, the global environment, and the world economy.

AN ECONOMIC APPROACH TO COLLECTIVE ACTION PROBLEMS

States face a series of incentives and disincentives to international cooperation in various issue areas. The following reading provides a useful introduction to understanding the incentive structure that states confront:

There are many services that the general public desires, but for which it is very difficult to charge an appropriate price. An extreme case includes goods and services, called *pure public goods*, which if supplied to any one consumer are automatically provided to many others. A classic example is pesticide spraying to destroy malaria-bearing mosquitoes in a particular area. There is no way a mosquito-free neighborhood can be provided to some residents of the area without making it available, simultaneously, to everyone else who lives there. But if a profit-making business is to sell its product, it must be able to exclude nonpurchasers from the consumption of that product. In the case of malaria elimination, a pesticide spray company cannot charge individual residents since all the nonpayers in the region will also benefit from the spraying. For the same reason, no private business firm will undertake the supply of national defense, public health measures, the elimination of crime in a city, or any of the other services which can be considered public goods. There is simply (under existing institutions) no way to market such a good or service.

A less extreme version of this problem crops up in a much broader category of economic activities. These are activities that affect not only the welfare of the supplier and the purchaser of a product, but also (unintentionally) yield incidental benefits or cause incidental injuries to some third party or parties not directly involved in the exchange. These unintended side effects are called *externalities* or *spillovers*, that is, these activities spill over upon persons outside the immediate transaction . . . .

. . . A factory that pours smoke into the atmosphere does not do so as an end in itself, but as an incidental side effect of the process of production. The smoke that reduces the pleasure of living there, and that may constitute a health hazard is a spillover effect; it is omitted entirely from the firm's calculations of its receipts and costs. The fact that the business that causes a detrimental externality pays no part of its cost helps to explain why the market mechanism does such an imperfect job of protecting the environment. . . . The company has to pay for the steel and electricity it uses. But under most current arrangements, the use of the atmosphere is usually free of charge to the firm, and is not considered in its cost calculations.

We may, then, describe the externalities with which we are concerned to be products of an institutional arrangement under which a number of society's resources are given away free. . . . Fresh air, clean water, and attractiveness of the neighborhood are all available for the taking, and that is precisely where the difficulty lies, for a zero price is an invitation to the user to waste the resources for which he pays nothing.

William J. Baumol & Wallace E. Oates, Economics, Environmental Policy and the Quality of Life 75-76 (1979).

A GAME THEORETIC APPROACH TO COLLECTIVE ACTION PROBLEMS

When states act to address collective action problems, the consequences of their actions depend in part on choices that other states make. For example, whether one state's reductions of greenhouse gas emissions will help forestall global climate change will depend in part on whether other states increase or reduce their greenhouse gas emissions. In these contexts, the interests of individual states may conflict with those of all states in such a way that, when each state pursues individually rational strategies, collectively suboptimal results occur. Each fishing state may seek, for example, to increase its catch; but if all states act in this way the fishing stock may become depleted. Game theory can help illuminate the strategic environment that states confront in situations like these and can suggest ways to make it more likely that states will cooperate to their mutual advantage. The reading that follows explains some of the impediments to such cooperation.

The tragedy of the commons develops in this way. Picture a pasture open to all. It is to be expected that each herdsman will try to keep as many cattle as possible on the commons. Such an arrangement may work reasonably satisfactorily for centuries because tribal wars, poaching, and disease keep the numbers of both man and beast well below the carrying capacity of the land. Finally, however, comes the day of reckoning, that is, the day when the long-desired goal of social stability becomes a reality. At this point, the inherent logic of the commons remorselessly generates tragedy.

As a rational being, each herdsman seeks to maximize his gain. Explicitly or implicitly, more or less consciously, he asks, "What is the utility *to me* of adding one more animal to my herd?" This utility has one negative and one positive component.

1. The positive component is a function of the increment of one animal. Since the herdsman receives all the proceeds from the sale of the additional animal, the positive utility is nearly +1.

2. The negative component is a function of the additional overgrazing created by one more animal. Since, however, the effects of overgrazing are shared by all the herdsmen, the negative utility for any particular decision-making herdsman is only a fraction of −1.

Adding together the component partial utilities, the rational herdsman concludes that the only sensible course for him to pursue is to add another animal to his herd. And another. . . . But this is the conclusion reached by each and every rational herdsman sharing a commons. Therein is the tragedy. Each man is locked into a system that compels him to increase his herd without limit—in a world that is limited. Ruin is the destination toward which all men rush, each pursuing his own best interest in a society that believes in the freedom of the commons. Freedom in a commons brings ruin to all. . . .

In a reverse way, the tragedy of the commons reappears in problems of pollution. Here it is not a question of taking something out of the commons, but of putting something in — sewage, or chemical, radioactive, and heat wastes into water; noxious and dangerous fumes into the air. . . . The calculations of utility are much the same as before. The rational man finds that his share of the cost of the wastes he discharges into the commons is less than the cost of purifying his wastes before releasing them. Since this is true for everyone, we are locked into a system of "fouling our own nest. . . ."

The social arrangements that produce responsibility are arrangements that create coercion, of some sort. Consider bank robbing. The man who takes money from a bank acts as if the bank were a commons. How do we prevent such action? Certainly not by trying to control his behavior solely by a verbal appeal to his sense of responsibility. Rather than rely on propaganda we . . . insist that a bank is not a commons . . . . That we thereby infringe on the freedom of would-be robbers we neither deny nor regret.

The morality of bank robbing is particularly easy to understand because we accept complete prohibition of this activity. . . . When men mutually agreed to pass laws against robbing, mankind became more free, not less so. Individuals locked into the logic of the commons are free only to bring on universal ruin; once they see the necessity of mutual coercion, they become free to pursue other goals.

Garret Hardin, *The Tragedy of the Commons*, 162 Science 1243 (1968).

AN INSTITUTIONAL APPROACH TO COLLECTIVE ACTION PROBLEMS

In addition to the various economic and strategic impediments to cooperation, there are various institutional impediments. In recent years, international lawyers have paid increasing attention to the ways that the design of international institutions can enhance or impede cooperation. The extract that follows suggests why much of this attention has focused on decision-making procedures:

. . . National legislation, at least in democracies, employs a version of Majority rule. . . . By contrast, the voting rule for international treaty law is Voluntary Assent: Treaties bind only those who consent to be bound. . . . The fundamental difference between [domestic voting rules] on the one hand, and [international voting rules] on the other, is thus the ability to coerce dissenters. Under [domestic majoritarian processes] . . . losing dissenters never have the option to refuse to be bound by the law. Under a Voluntary Assent paradigm, dissenters cannot be coerced; rules are binding only on those who agree to be bound. . . .

. . . As the number of participants who must be consulted increases, the cost of multiple negotiations and the chance that a nation will act as a holdout, insisting on satisfaction of its interests as the price for its assent, rise as well. Even if all countries would reap net benefits from the treaty, uncertainty about others' likely cooperation may induce strategic noncooperation (free riding). Each party's perception of its own gain in turn depends partially on its perception of whether other parties are likely to keep their end of the deal; cooperation is thus endogenous, delicate, and potentially difficult to arrange. Even after becoming parties to the treaty, nation-states can withdraw or decide not to comply. Although such withdrawal or noncompliance might be made illegal under the terms of a treaty, the practical question is whether any enforceable sanctions could be brought to bear against the defector. The threat of withdrawal or noncompliance gives the nation a continuing ability to exact concessions from other parties to the treaty.

Thus, although the Voluntary Assent voting rule inhibits the tyranny of the majority — the ability to coerce dissenters — it also makes the adoption of new regulations more difficult to achieve. The costs to the entire group of negotiating a consensus treaty can be high in terms of the time and effort needed to craft a successful consensus, the side payments extracted by dissenters, and the collective gains forgone when individual countries delay or block action on parochial strategic grounds. . . .

Jonathan Baert Wiener, *Global Environmental Regulation: Instrument Choice in Legal Context*, 108 Yale L.J. 677, 737, 740, 741 (1999).

The materials in the next three chapters can be understood as an inquiry into various strategies to address the problems identified in the readings above, and as an implicit challenge to develop new strategies to address collective action problems. Underlying each of the problems is the question of whether a fragmented and conflictual political system of over 190 states can achieve the levels of cooperation and coordination necessary to manage pressing collective problems.

10

Responding to the First Global Commons Issue:
The Law of the Sea

Since the earliest days of travel by sea, individuals and societies have recognized the need for some regulation of shared bodies of water. Early on, states realized the importance of cooperation on the oceans and seas, whether with regard to navigation or the most classic issue of the global commons, fishing. As technology progressed and the seas were used for other purposes, both military and economic, states and other communities have asserted a variety of competing claims. States with merchant fleets and navies have sought rights of transit through waters close to land, while coastal states have wanted to protect their shores. States with long-distance fishing fleets sought access to fishing grounds that coastal states wanted to exploit. By the twentieth century, as technology permitted economic exploitation of resources under the sea, coastal states made claims to the continental shelf, and, by the 1960s, both wealthy and poor states began to contemplate how to share the minerals in the deep seabed. In general, the greatest tension has been between claims for treating the sea as common space and those for treating it as belonging to certain states.

As states made these claims and counterclaims, they eventually agreed on norms of customary law. Among the most important was the freedom of the high seas, such that all states could sail vessels and fish without interference in the waters between land masses. In addition, states drafted bilateral and multilateral treaties to provide a more comprehensive and detailed regime. Much of the relevant law formed during the classic or traditional phase of international law discussed in Chapter 1, which was dominated by states and traditional state interests—although private economic priorities, such as those of fishing and shipping businesses, always played a significant role as well. In the last quarter of the twentieth century, new claimants sought to participate in the legal process, in particular non-governmental organizations (NGOs) concerned with environmental degradation that governments were often slow to recognize.

As a result of this law making, states have effectively divided maritime spaces into a variety of zones, each subject to its own legal regime. For the water itself, the three most significant zones are the territorial sea, the 12-mile-wide band of water closest to a state's shores; the Exclusive Economic Zone (EEZ), stretching out to 200 miles from the coast and including most of the world's catches of fish; and the high seas, the areas beyond the EEZ. For the sea floor, the most significant zones are the continental shelf, the continuation of a state's landmass beneath the sea; and the deep seabed, the area beyond the continental shelf.

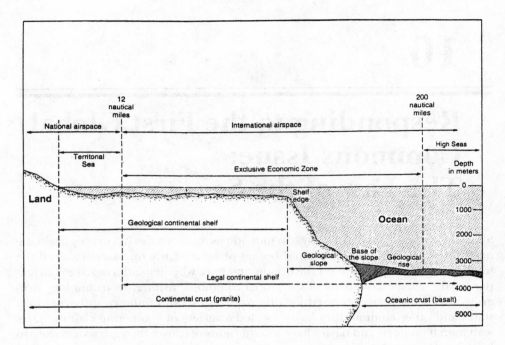

Major Maritime Spaces of the Law of the Sea Regime
SOURCE: U.S. Department of State

The long history of the law of the sea gives it two special characteristics worth highlighting. First, states have now codified much of the law of the sea in treaties, the centerpiece of which is the 1982 United Nations Convention on the Law of the Sea (UNCLOS), which had 149 parties as of 2006. That treaty addresses most of the key areas of the regime, although states have negotiated others to implement various aspects of it. Philip Allott has written of UNCLOS:

> It is comprehensive in dealing with the whole nonland area of the world. . . . It has a rule for everything. The rule may be a permissive rule. It may be an obligation. It may confer an explicit freedom or leave a residual liberty by not specifying a right or duty. But a Flying Dutchman wandering the sea areas of the world, carrying his copy of the Convention, would [find that] the Convention would never fail him.

Philip Allott, *Power Sharing in the Law of the Sea*, 77 Am. J. Intl. L. 1, 8 (1983).

The centrality of one treaty—akin to the Vienna Convention on Diplomatic Relations for the treatment of diplomats or the General Agreement on Tariffs and Trade for trade—makes discerning and applying the law easier than is the case in subject areas without such a focal point. But it does not eliminate areas of controversy between states bent on interpreting the law in their favor.

The negotiations leading up to the 1982 Convention took place under the auspices of the United Nations Conference on the Law of the Sea, which met from 1973 to 1982. The talks were long and arduous and covered a huge number of issues, including fishing, pollution, hydrocarbon exploration, criminal jurisdiction, seabed mining, marine scientific research, and passage for naval vessels. Moreover, they pitted manifold groupings of states (whose membership often overlapped) against each other: naval states, coastal states, shipping states, fishing states, land-locked states, nuclear weapons states, poor states, rich states, and many others. Each of the many issues became linked with the others, and the final package involved major trade-offs of seemingly unrelated issues, as one interest group lost on one issue but gained on another. These trade-offs proved necessary because the states agreed at the outset that the Conference would work by consensus. As Miles Kahler writes:

> Both the maritime and the developing countries had a strong interest in a legitimate global regime that was widely ratified. The conference was mandated to achieve one "package deal," not a series of separate treaties, and this linkage increased the leverage of developing countries . . . .
> . . . [T]he conference [was] governed by consensus; the search for consensus could be determined to have failed only by a two-thirds vote of those present and voting [with a quorum of a majority of participating states]. Although [this] formula . . . was believed to protect the interests of the developed and maritime powers, it also protected minority interests, including those of the landlocked and geographically disadvantaged states [namely, those with small coastlines, offshore fishing areas, or continental shelves], which possessed little leverage apart from their votes in the conference.

Miles Kahler, *Multilateralism with small and large numbers*, 46 Intl. Org. 681, 694 (1992).

Second, the law of the sea encompasses a complex set of norms and institutions that enjoy a very high degree of respect and compliance. The frequent invocation and observance of these norms by states challenges claims that international law is not law and that states freely ignore it (although observance alone does not equate with causation between law and outcome). Instead, a variety of states with differing interests have agreed on the advantages of adhering to the regime. As with many issues defined by game theory as cooperation problems, there would appear to be numerous incentives not to comply with parts of the regime—for example, the benefits that a state with a large fishing fleet achieves from fishing in another's exclusive economic zone. Yet compliance remains overall quite high. One explanation might be that of George Scelle's *dédoublement fonctionnel*, discussed in Chapter 1—the idea that states have accepted that the consequences for undercutting the regime would inure to their detriment, as other states would respond to violations in ways that would hurt the original violators. This explanation raises the question of why compliance is high for this set of cooperation problems but not for others.

In this chapter, we seek to provide an understanding of the law of the sea in terms of both the process and the product—how and why states agreed to resolve their claims through law, whether the law adequately solves those competing claims, and whether it adequately addresses the interests of other actors (as well as non-human interests) that may not have participated in the law's development. The interests of these claimants have centered principally on issues of *security, economics,* and the *environment*; the problems below seek to show how these interests have affected the debate and the law on four of the most important sea issues. The first concerns water areas near a state's shore (implicating all three interests); the second addresses exploitation of fishing grounds (implicating the second and third); and the third problem considers drilling in underground areas off a state's shore (implicating all three interests).

I. THE TERRITORIAL SEA AND INTERNATIONAL STRAITS: REGULATING THE PASSAGE OF NUCLEAR-ARMED SUBMARINES

Many law of the sea disputes relate to fundamental notions of national security. On the one hand, the sea is said to belong to no state; yet every state with a coast has an interest in protecting itself from a seaward invasion by its enemies as well as from other less immediate threats, such as offshore eavesdropping and military exercises, or pollution from sea-based sources. States with navies or large commercial fleets have another set of interests, based on security and economics, largely in unimpeded and expeditious passage. Yet the interests do not allocate themselves so simply. For one thing, most maritime and naval states are also coastal states. Moreover, all states have an interest in unimpeded passage to the extent that it promotes efficient movement of imports and exports.

In some cases, these interests will not conflict, such as when a ship need only traverse areas far from other states in moving from one destination to another (for example, from Cape Town, South Africa, to Colombo, Sri Lanka). But far more common are situations in which naval and commercial ships need to stay close to the coast of another state, in order, for instance, to save fuel or transit time or to pick up or drop off passengers or cargo at several destinations. In addition, at times geography may dictate that ships pass through narrow straits close to the coastline of one or more states to avoid having to expend large amounts of fuel and time to bypass these areas, or to avoid being trapped in certain bodies of water (such as the Black Sea). Such straits dot the world, creating key chokepoints. Straits also affect the movement of military aircraft, because such aircraft can bypass straits by flying over adjacent states only if they have those states' permission.

Claims regarding the right of foreign vessels to pass close to a nation's shores extend back centuries. The modern era, however, gave rise to new challenges and claims. As you read the following problem, consider the arenas in which claimants assert their concerns; which fora proved more hospitable to which groups; whether the process leading to UNCLOS treated all states in accordance with the UN Charter's basic principle of sovereign equality; whether the interests of certain states counted more than the interests of others; and what features of the solution achieved at UNCLOS might contribute to its stability and high degree of compliance.

A. The Problem

In the years after World War II, the United States and the Soviet Union developed a variety of weapons of mass destruction and doctrines for their use as part of an overall strategy of nuclear deterrence. The key to this strategy was "Mutually Assured Destruction"(MAD)—the idea, morally controversial to say the least, that neither side would start a nuclear war because the other side possessed enough weapons to survive the initial strike and destroy its adversary. Both sides realized that this strategy would be enhanced if the location of certain weapons were unknown to an adversary or if the weapons were otherwise impervious to destruction. By the 1950s, the superpowers had developed a nuclear strategy based on the idea of a triad of forces—land, sea, and air—as necessary for deterrence. The sea-based leg consisted of nuclear-powered submarines carrying long-range nuclear weapons. These submarines, which could spend months under water without surfacing, would be difficult to destroy in a nuclear attack by virtue of their stealth and mobility and would carry enough missiles to wreak havoc on the initiating party. Beyond nuclear deterrence, the superpowers also relied extensively on naval forces to project power in areas of crisis, whether by simply showing the flag or, in other circumstances, delivering sailors, aircraft, cruise missiles, and supplies to areas of operation.

Critical to the mobility of these navies was the ability to traverse large open spaces efficiently and to refuel at fueling stations as quickly as possible. To accomplish these goals, surface ships typically would often need to travel close to land; and both surface ships and submarines would need to cross international straits unencumbered by the coastal states. Such straits represent the sole or most efficient entry and exit points between key bodies of water—for example, the Strait of Gibraltar between the Atlantic Ocean and the Mediterranean Sea; the Strait of Hormuz between the Persian Gulf and the Indian Ocean; the Bab el Mandeb Strait between the Red Sea and the Indian Ocean; and the Straits of Malacca and Singapore between the Indian Ocean and the Pacific Ocean.

The states near whose coastline surface ships or submarines might pass did not, however, always share the political goals or philosophies of one or both superpowers. Some coastal states belonged to the East or West Bloc; most in the developing world professed political nonalignment. The idea that nuclear-powered submarines carrying a vast arsenal of weapons might be passing near their shores, submerged and undetected, alarmed politicians and the general public alike. This scenario especially concerned governments of states near straits, which knew that the superpowers saw unimpeded, undetected passage through those straits as critical to deterrence policy.

B. Regulating Offshore Waters

The competing claims of the superpowers and states near straits is simply the latest in a long historical process of confrontation and accommodation concerning areas close to a state's shore. As early as the thirteenth century, some European states asserted the concept of a band of sea at a fixed distance from the coastline known as the territorial sea. Within that band, the coastal state enjoyed most of the rights and powers that it enjoys with respect to its land territory and to generally enclosed bodies such as bays. Some states took advantage of the idea to impose fees on ships passing within the territorial sea. This band of waters stood in sharp contrast to areas outside it, known as the high seas. In accordance with Hugo Grotius's seventeenth-century idea of a *mare liberum* (free sea), this area would remain beyond the legal control of any state, and vessels could sail where, when, and how they chose. Nonetheless, over time coastal states accepted that maritime commerce required at least one significant right for maritime fleets even within the territorial sea—the right to navigate expeditiously through it, a practice that became known as innocent passage. Nearly all states eventually respected this practice and saw it as a duty on coastal states (and a right for maritime states), transforming it into a norm of customary international law.

At the same time, some states questioned whether such a right always extended to foreign military vessels and thus wanted to ensure some control over their passage. The International Law Commission studied this issue in the 1950s, and a regime was first codified in the 1958 Convention on the Territorial Sea. Governments preparing the 1982 Law of the Sea Convention codified much of the customary regime on the territorial sea, and compromised over some disagreements about it, as follows:

United Nations Convention on the Law of the Sea

1833 U.N.T.S. 3 (1982)

Article 2
Legal status of the territorial sea, of the air space
over the territorial sea and of its bed and subsoil

1. The sovereignty of a coastal State extends, beyond its land territory and internal waters and, in the case of an archipelagic State, its archipelagic waters, to an adjacent belt of sea, described as the territorial sea.

2. This sovereignty extends to the air space over the territorial sea as well as to its bed and subsoil.

3. The sovereignty over the territorial sea is exercised subject to this Convention and to other rules of international law.

Article 17
Right of innocent passage

Subject to this Convention, ships of all States, whether coastal or land-locked, enjoy the right of innocent passage through the territorial sea.

Article 18
Meaning of passage

1. Passage means navigation through the territorial sea for the purpose of:

   (a) traversing that sea without entering internal waters or calling at a roadstead or port facility outside internal waters; or

   (b) proceeding to or from internal waters or a call at such roadstead or port facility.

2. Passage shall be continuous and expeditious. However, passage includes stopping and anchoring, but only in so far as the same are incidental to ordinary navigation or are rendered necessary by force majeure or distress or for the purpose of rendering assistance to persons, ships or aircraft in danger or distress.

Article 19
Meaning of innocent passage

1. Passage is innocent so long as it is not prejudicial to the peace, good order or security of the coastal State. Such passage shall take place in conformity with this Convention and with other rules of international law.

2. Passage of a foreign ship shall be considered to be prejudicial to the peace, good order or security of the coastal State if in the territorial sea it engages in any of the following activities:

(a) any threat or use of force against the sovereignty, territorial integrity or political independence of the coastal State . . . ;

(b) any exercise or practice with weapons of any kind;

(c) any act aimed at collecting information to the prejudice of the defence or security of the coastal State;

(d) any act of propaganda aimed at affecting the defence or security of the coastal State;

(e) the launching, landing or taking on board of any aircraft. . . .

(h) any act of wilful and serious pollution contrary to this Convention;

(i) any fishing activities;

(j) the carrying out of research or survey activities. . . .

Article 20
Submarines and other underwater vehicles

In the territorial sea, submarines and other underwater vehicles are required to navigate on the surface and to show their flag.

Article 21
Laws and regulations of the coastal State relating to innocent passage

1. The coastal State may adopt laws and regulations, in conformity with the provisions of this Convention and other rules of international law, relating to innocent passage through the territorial sea, in respect of all or any of the following:

(a) the safety of navigation and the regulation of maritime traffic;

(b) the protection of navigational aids and facilities and other facilities or installations;

(c) the protection of cables and pipelines;

(d) the conservation of the living resources of the sea . . . ;

(f) the preservation of the environment of the coastal State . . . ;

(g) marine scientific research and hydrographic surveys. . . .

Article 24
Duties of the coastal State

1. The coastal State shall not hamper the innocent passage of foreign ships through the territorial sea except in accordance with this Convention. In particular, in the application of this Convention or of any laws or regulations adopted in conformity with this Convention, the coastal State shall not:

(a) impose requirements on foreign ships which have the practical effect of denying or impairing the right of innocent passage; or

(b) discriminate in form or in fact against the ships of any State or against ships carrying cargoes to, from or on behalf of any State. . . .

Article 25
Rights of protection of the coastal State

1. The coastal State may take the necessary steps in its territorial sea to prevent passage which is not innocent. . . .

2. In the case of ships proceeding to internal waters or a call at a port facility outside internal waters, the coastal State also has the right to take the necessary steps to prevent any breach of the conditions to which admission of those ships to internal waters or such a call is subject.

3. The coastal State may, without discrimination in form or in fact among foreign ships, suspend temporarily in specified areas of its territorial sea the innocent passage of foreign ships if such suspension is essential for the protection of its security, including weapons exercises. Such suspension shall take effect only after having been duly published.

The ability of states to agree on a regime governing the territorial sea stands in some contrast to sharp disagreements over the accepted width (or breadth) of the territorial sea. The origins and implications of this disagreement are considered further below. Suffice it to say for now that the Convention permits states to have a territorial sea of up to 12 miles. According to a 2004 UN report monitoring compliance with the 1982 Convention (U.N. Doc. A/59/62), fewer than 10 states continued to maintain a territorial sea claim greater than 12 miles. Of these, Benin (200 miles), Somalia (200 miles), and Togo (30 miles) are parties to the 1982 Convention.

Notes and Questions

1. Who benefits and who is harmed by the regime of innocent passage? Could the innocent passage of large warships in waters close to shore be very intimidating to coastal states? Consider in this context the relationship between the innocent passage provisions and Article 2(4) of the UN Charter banning the "threat" of force.

2. How much flexibility should a state have in interpreting Article 25 to allow it to suspend innocent passage?

3. The 12-mile limit is not always measured from the shore itself, but from so-called straight baselines that states may draw across certain irregularities in their shorelines to create straight lines—and thus straight lines for the limits of their territorial sea that are easier for navigators of vessels to understand. Not surprisingly, then, the practice by coastal states of drawing baselines has created its own set of disputes. Many states have drawn baselines not merely across small irregularities, but across large curved areas of their coastline. In one situation, when Norway drew straight baselines in 1935 that connected a set of outlying rocks, Britain sued in the International Court of Justice (ICJ). In the 1951 case of *Anglo-Norwegian Fisheries*, the Court upheld Norway's claim, in part based on the long-term economic ties between the coastal population and the islands.

The UN Conference on the Law of the Sea that prepared the 1958 Convention on the Territorial Sea and the Contiguous Zone (a predecessor to UNCLOS) was characterized by long, arduous negotiations on rules for straight baselines. States eventually accepted, and included in both the 1958 and 1982 Conventions, a regime based on the *Anglo-Norwegian Fisheries* holding, allowing such lines where the coastline is "deeply indented" or if there is a "fringe of islands along the coast in its immediate vicinity," although it required that the baselines "not depart to any appreciable extent from the general direction of the coast" and that the sea areas within the lines be "sufficiently closely linked" to the land. In addition, states drawing baselines can take account "of economic interests peculiar to the region concerned, the reality and the importance of which are clearly evidenced by long usage." UNCLOS, art. 7. Areas landward of straight baselines drawn in accordance with the Convention are internal waters (akin to lakes and rivers), except that there remains a right of innocent passage for foreign vessels. UNCLOS, art. 8. In a great victory for Indonesia, the Philippines, and other states whose landmass is an archipelago, the 1982 Convention allows archipelagic states to draw baselines across their outermost islands up to a maximum of 125 miles; the waters within are governed by a regime akin to the territorial sea. UNCLOS, arts. 46-49.

C. Developing a Regime for International Straits

The regime of the territorial sea seems at first glance to provide a compromise acceptable to both maritime and coastal states. But international straits raise particular questions, especially the following: What if a strait—the only practical way for a ship to move from one major body of water to another—lies within the territorial waters of one state? Would the coastal state be able to treat it like other territorial waters and suspend passage for national security reasons?

For some straits, states have agreed on specific international legal regimes to answer this question. In the nineteenth century, for instance, the Ottoman Empire and the major naval powers agreed on various treaties that prohibited foreign warships from traversing the Straits of Bosphorous and the Dardanelles that link the Mediterranean Sea with the Black Sea. The 1920 Treaty of Peace between the World War I Allies and Turkey proclaimed these areas open to all ships at all times. Subsequent treaties have given Turkey greater rights, including a ban on submarine passage (except for passage by Black Sea states) and on overflight of military aircraft, as well as Turkey's ability to halt passage if Turkey is at war.

Other states asserted unilateral rights to limit passage through international straits within their territorial waters. Maritime and coastal states did not negotiate any multilateral treaty on the issue, thus leaving room for significant disagreements. One led to both a military confrontation and an attempted clarification of customary law by the ICJ.

During the Greek civil war in the late 1940s, British warships in the eastern Adriatic and Ionian Seas engaged in extensive intelligence-gathering and other activities in support of their allies in the war. These vessels routinely passed through the Corfu Channel, a small strait between the Greek island of Corfu and the Albanian and Greek mainlands. (See map.) On May 15, 1946, an Albanian shore-based battery fired on two British cruisers as they passed through the northern part of the Corfu Channel. Neither ship was hit. After the United Kingdom protested the act and asserted that innocent passage through straits was a right under international law, Albania responded by insisting that naval states had to notify Albania in advance and seek its permission. Various diplomatic communications ensued, including a British note of August 2 that warned Albania that British ships would return any fire. In September of that year, London sent a cable to the head of the British fleet stating: "Establishment of diplomatic relations with Albania is again under consideration by His Majesty's Government who wish to know whether the Albanian Government have learnt to behave themselves. Information is requested whether any ships under your command have passed through the North Corfu Strait since August and, if not, whether you intend them to do so shortly." The British admiral said he planned to send four ships through the strait on October 22. On that day, one ship struck a mine, and a second, while towing it, also struck one. Forty-four people on board were killed and forty-two were injured. In November 1946, Britain, in defiance of Albanian policy, sent a large and imposing group of warships to the Channel to sweep for mines. Twenty-two were found.

In 1947, the UN Security Council asked the two states to refer their dispute to the International Court of Justice. After some procedural posturing, they concluded a special agreement on March 25, 1948, asking the Court first, whether Albania was responsible for the explosions and for the damage and loss of human life, and second, whether the United Kingdom violated Albania's rights by sailing through the Channel on October 22 and later sweeping for mines. The Court ruled for the

SOURCE: CIA World Factbook

United Kingdom on the first question; with respect to the passage on October 22, the Court's opinion was as follows:

The Corfu Channel Case (United Kingdom v. Albania)

1949 I.C.J. 4 (Apr. 9)

It is, in the opinion of the Court, generally recognized and in accordance with international custom that States in time of peace have a right to send their warships through straits used for international navigation between two parts of the high seas without the previous authorization of a coastal State, provided that the passage is *innocent*. Unless otherwise prescribed in an international convention, there is no right for a coastal State to prohibit such passage through straits in time of peace.

The Albanian Government does not dispute that the North Corfu Channel is a strait in the geographical sense; but it denies that this Channel belongs to the class of international highways through which a right of passage exists, on the grounds that it is only of secondary importance and not even a necessary route between two parts of the high seas, and that it is used almost exclusively for local traffic to and from the ports of Corfu and Saranda.

It may be asked whether the test is to be found in the volume of traffic passing through the Strait or in its greater or lesser importance for international navigation. But in the opinion of the Court the decisive criterion is rather its geographical situation as connecting two parts of the high seas and the fact of its being used for international navigation. Nor can it be decisive that this Strait is not a necessary route between two parts of the high seas, but only an alternative passage between the Ægean and the Adriatic Seas. It has nevertheless been a useful route for international maritime traffic. In this respect, the Agent of the United Kingdom Government gave the Court the following information relating to the period from April 1st, 1936, to December 31st, 1937: "The following is the total number of ships putting in at the Port of Corfu after passing through or just before passing through the Channel. During the period of one year nine months, the total number of ships was 2,884. The flags of the ships are Greek, Italian, Roumanian, Yugoslav, French, Albanian and British. . . ." There were also regular sailings through the Strait by Greek vessels three times weekly, by a British ship fortnightly, and by two Yugoslav vessels weekly and by two others fortnightly. The Court is further informed that the British Navy has regularly used this Channel for eighty years or more, and that it has also been used by the navies of other States.

One fact of particular importance is that the North Corfu Channel constitutes a frontier between Albania and Greece, that a part of it is wholly within the territorial waters of these States, and that the Strait is of special importance to Greece by reason of the traffic to and from the port of Corfu.

Having regard to these various considerations, the Court has arrived at the conclusion that the North Corfu Channel should be considered as belonging to the class of international highways through which passage cannot be prohibited by a coastal State in time of peace.

On the other hand, it is a fact that the two coastal States did not maintain normal relations, that Greece had made territorial claims precisely with regard to a part of Albanian territory bordering on the Channel, that Greece had declared that she considered herself technically in a state of war with Albania, and that Albania, invoking the danger of Greek incursions, had considered it necessary to take certain measures of vigilance in this region. The Court is of [the] opinion that Albania, in view of these exceptional circumstances, would have been justified in issuing regulations in respect of the passage of warships through the Strait, but not in prohibiting such passage or in subjecting it to the requirement of special authorization.

For these reasons the Court is unable to accept the Albanian contention that the Government of the United Kingdom has violated Albanian sovereignty by sending the warships through the Strait without having obtained the previous authorization of the Albanian Government. . . .

The Albanian Government has further contended that the sovereignty of Albania was violated because the passage of the British warships on October 22nd, 1946, was not an *innocent passage*. The reasons advanced in support of this contention may be summed up as follows: The passage was not an ordinary passage, but a political mission; the ships were manoeuvring and sailing in diamond combat formation with soldiers on board; the position of the guns was not consistent with innocent passage; the vessels passed with crews at action stations; the number of the ships and their armament surpassed what was necessary in order to attain their object and showed an intention to intimidate and not merely to pass; the ships had received orders to observe and report upon the coastal defences and this order was carried out.

It is shown by the Admiralty telegram of September 21st, cited above, and admitted by the United Kingdom Agent, that the object of sending the warships through the Strait was not only to carry out a passage for purposes of navigation, but also to test Albania's attitude. As mentioned above, the Albanian Government, on May 15th, 1946, tried to impose by means of gunfire its view with regard to the passage. . . . The legality of this measure taken by the Government of the United Kingdom cannot be disputed, provided that it was carried out in a manner consistent with the requirements of international law. The "mission" was designed to affirm a right which had been unjustly denied. . . .

It remains, therefore, to consider whether the *manner* in which the passage was carried out was consistent with the principle of innocent passage and to examine the various contentions of the Albanian Government in so far as they appear to be relevant. . . .

[T]he Commander-in-Chief, Mediterranean, in a telegram of October 26th to the Admiralty [said that the] guns were . . . "trained fore and aft, which is their normal position at sea in peace time, and were not loaded". . . . The main guns were in the line of the ship, and the antiaircraft guns were pointing outwards and up into the air, which is the normal position of these guns on a cruiser both in harbour and at sea. In the light of this evidence, the Court cannot accept the Albanian contention that the position of the guns was inconsistent with the rules of innocent passage.

In the above-mentioned telegram of October 26th, the Commander-in-Chief reported that the passage "was made with ships at action stations in order that they might be able to retaliate quickly if fired upon again". In view of the firing from the Albanian battery on May 15th, this measure of precaution cannot, in itself, be regarded as unreasonable. But four warships—two cruisers and two destroyers—passed in this manner, with crews at action stations, ready to retaliate quickly if fired upon. They passed one after another through this narrow channel, close to the Albanian coast, at a time of political tension in this region. The intention must have been, not only to test Albania's attitude, but at the same time to demonstrate such force that she would abstain from firing again on passing ships. Having regard, however, to all the circumstances of the case, as described above, the Court is unable to characterize these measures taken by the United Kingdom authorities as a violation of Albania's sovereignty.

In subsequent proceedings that Albania boycotted, the Court awarded Britain 843,947 pounds sterling in compensation for the damage and loss of life caused by the mines. Albania refused to pay for many years. After its hard-line communist government fell in 1989, it opened negotiations with Britain for payment in exchange for Britain's return of 1.5 tons of Albanian gold the British had seized from the Nazis during World War II. Britain agreed in 1992 to accept $2 million in compensation, one-tenth of the then current value of what the ICJ had ordered. In 1996, the UK returned the gold, but Albania claimed it lacked the funds to pay the settlement. Albania finally repaid the $2 million in 1996.

Notes and Questions

1. What sort of rights did the ICJ recognize for naval and coastal states in the *Corfu Channel* opinion?
2. Did it matter to the Court that Britain could easily have ordered its ships to avoid the Corfu Channel with minimal inconvenience to their mission? Why would the United Kingdom press the issue?
3. Later in the judgment, the ICJ found that the United Kingdom had violated international law when it conducted minesweeping operations in the Corfu Channel without the consent of Albania. It rejected the British claim that it needed to pick up evidence of mines to show Albania's responsibility for mine laying, finding that Britain's asserted "right of intervention . . . cannot, whatever be the present defects in international organization, find a place in international law." Nonetheless, the Court refused to find the manner in which the minesweeping was carried out to be illegal. The Court found the accompanying naval presence justified by the prior attacks on the ships; it further found the declaration of illegality sufficient reparation for Albania. Why was it permissible for Britain to go through the straits but not to clear the mines?

D. Toward Codification

After the *Corfu Channel* case, the United Nations convened an international conference to draft a series of treaties on the law of the sea. The 1958 Convention on the Territorial Sea and the Contiguous Zone recognized the right of innocent passage similar to that spelled out in the 1982 Convention. The states specifically accepted the rule in *Corfu Channel* by including a provision stating: "There shall be no suspension of the innocent passage of foreign ships through straits which are used for international navigation between one part of the high seas and another part of the high seas or the territorial sea of a foreign state."(Art. 16 (4).)

Yet both the major maritime states and many coastal states remained dissatisfied with this rule. The naval states—principally the USSR and United States—believed that lack of explicit rights for submarines to pass through international straits while submerged and for aircraft to fly over straits would detract from the credibility and effectiveness of both their nuclear deterrent and their ability to deploy other forces. They wanted any new convention to address this gap in the 1958 treaty. Coastal states were uncomfortable with a rule that required them to keep waters close to their territory open at all times, whether to nuclear ships and submarines or to supertankers that might spill oil.

Exacerbating these disagreements was a continued lack of consensus among states on the width of the territorial sea. Although the idea of the territorial sea goes back centuries, its width has been a subject of considerable dispute. The Dutch legal scholar Cornelius van Bynkershoek proposed in 1702 the idea of one league, or three nautical miles, which would have only a tiny impact on the principle of *mare liberum*. (Lore has it that this distance was the range of a shore-based cannon.) Many maritime states, such as the United States and the United Kingdom, adopted this limit, but it was hardly uniform. Other states adopted larger limits, such as 6 or 12 miles, arguing that such distances were necessary to protect their shores. The controversy also turned on various coastal states' interests in excluding foreign fishing vessels (an issue considered in the second Problem in this chapter). As a result, the 1958 Convention was silent on the width of the territorial sea.

The effect of such competing claims on the passage of ships through straits was highly significant. If a state's territorial sea were limited to three miles, most of the world's key straits, which are greater than six miles across, would have bands of high seas in the middle, through which ships (and aircraft above) could pass unimpeded; such passage would include the right of submarines to stay submerged. In the wake of the 1958 Convention, most coastal states, the bulk of which are located in the developing world, argued for greater widths of the territorial sea. Some states demanded a width of as much as 200 miles. If even the modest claims for a 12-mile-wide territorial sea were accepted as law, then many of the world's key straits, namely those greater than 6 miles but less than 24 miles wide, would no longer have a band of high seas within the straits but would all be within the territorial sea of the state(s) on either side of them. These included the Strait of Gibraltar (Spain-Morocco, 8 miles), the Straits of Malacca and Singapore (Indonesia-Malaysia-Singapore, two straits, 8 and 20 miles wide), the Strait of Hormuz (Iran-Oman, 21 miles), and the Bab el Mandeb Straits (Yemen-Djibouti, 14 miles). Over 135 straits worldwide exhibited this characteristic.

Despite their Cold War rivalry, both the United States and the USSR submitted proposals to the UN conference convened to draft a new law of the sea convention that provided for high seas rights of navigation and overflight in international straits. Many states bordering the straits insisted on maintaining the 1958 rule—namely, the innocent passage regime (which they believed required surfacing of submarines and banned overflight of aircraft), but without the possibility of suspension; some coastal states, however, such as Malaysia, Singapore, Japan, France, and Britain, were also major maritime or military states and endorsed the idea of special transit rights in straits.

Throughout the 1970s, participants in the UNCLOS negotiations floated various compromise positions. Some states proposed distinguishing between critical straits and less important ones in terms of the rights of ships. Other proposals focused on the need for something less than full high-seas rights in straits. In the end, both elements were incorporated in draft treaty language that the governments participating in the Conference accepted as part of a grand compromise that included recognition of the 200-mile exclusive economic zone, significant rights for coastal states over the continental shelf, and special rights for developing countries in the mining of the sea floor. (These three issues are discussed in the next two Problems in this chapter.) As a result, the Convention explicitly allows up to a 12-mile territorial sea and contains the following provisions on passage through international straits.

United Nations Convention on the Law of the Sea

1833 U.N.T.S. 3 (1982)

Article 37
Scope of this section

This section applies to straits which are used for international navigation between one part of the high seas or an exclusive economic zone and another part of the high seas or an exclusive economic zone.

Article 38
Right of transit passage

1. In straits referred to in article 37, all ships and aircraft enjoy the right of transit passage, which shall not be impeded; except that, if the strait is formed by an island of a State bordering the strait and its mainland, transit passage shall not apply if there exists seaward of the island a route through the high seas or through an exclusive economic zone of similar convenience with respect to navigational and hydrographical characteristics.

2. Transit passage means the exercise . . . of the freedom of navigation and overflight solely for the purpose of continuous and expeditious transit of the strait between one part of the high seas or an exclusive economic zone and another part of the high seas or an exclusive economic zone. However, [this] does not preclude passage through the strait for the purpose of entering, leaving or returning from a State bordering the strait. . . .

Article 39
Duties of ships and aircraft during transit passage

1. Ships and aircraft, while exercising the right of transit passage, shall:

   (a) proceed without delay through or over the strait;

   (b) refrain from any threat or use of force against the sovereignty, territorial integrity or political independence of States bordering the strait . . . ;

   (c) refrain from any activities other than those incident to their normal modes of continuous and expeditious transit unless rendered necessary by force majeure or by distress;

   (d) comply with other relevant provisions of this Part.

[Paragraphs 2 and 3 required ships and aircraft to comply with international rules on safety and pollution.]

<u>Article 42</u>
<u>Laws and regulations of States bordering</u>
<u>straits relating to transit passage</u>

1. . . . States bordering straits may adopt laws and regulations relating to transit passage through straits, in respect of all or any of the following:

    (a) the safety of navigation and the regulation of maritime traffic. . . ;

    (b) the prevention, reduction and control of pollution. . . ;

    (c) with respect to fishing vessels, the prevention of fishing. . . ;

    (d) the loading or unloading of any commodity, currency or person. . . .

<u>Article 44</u>
<u>Duties of States bordering straits</u>

States bordering straits shall not hamper transit passage and shall give appropriate publicity to any danger to navigation or overflight within or over the strait of which they have knowledge. There shall be no suspension of transit passage.

Notes and Questions

1. How does the regime of transit passage differ from the regime of innocent passage?

2. Who won the battle between the coastal states and maritime states? Was the international legal process too deferential to the wishes of a handful of maritime states?

3. How did states that are both maritime states as well as coastal states balance their competing interests? Note that the drafting of these provisions was undertaken in a committee co-chaired by the United Kingdom, which both borders the Straits of Dover and is a major maritime state.

4. The transit passage provisions do not cover all straits. For example, Article 35 of the Convention preserves the regimes on straits in long-standing conventions, such as those on the Bosporous and the Dardanelles, noted above. In such situations, innocent passage applies, although Article 45 says it may not be suspended. Article 38 makes clear that transit passage does not apply to straits between coastal states and their own islands unless there are no convenient alternatives.

5. The Convention also provides a complex regime for archipelagic states, such as Indonesia and the Philippines. Foreign ships enjoy the right of innocent

passage through archipelagic waters (see the discussion above about straight baselines that such states may draw), but states have the right to suspend passage on terms similar to their right to suspend passage through their territorial sea. Ships, as well as aircraft, also enjoy the right of so-called archipelagic lanes passage, akin to transit passage, through lanes designated by the state with the approval of the International Maritime Organization; such passage may not be suspended. Most states have not designated such lanes, in which case states may still traverse "through the routes normally used for international navigation." (Art. 53(12).)

6. In 1986, the United States accused Libya of masterminding the bombing of a German discotheque in which two American servicemen were killed. As a consequence, American F-111 bombers were dispatched from U.S. bases in Great Britain to carry out a bombing raid on various targets in Libya that the United States claimed were supporting terrorist activities. Several European countries, including France and Spain, denied the United States the right to fly over their territories to carry out the raid. As a result, the U.S. planes flew over the Strait of Gibraltar. How would the 1982 Convention have affected U.S. options during this crisis?

7. The conclusion of UNCLOS in 1982 hardly ended all disputes over nuclear-armed ships and submarines. In 1984, in response to public protests, the government of New Zealand banned the entry into its ports of all ships and aircraft carrying nuclear weapons or powered by nuclear reactors. New Zealand's decision represented an immediate challenge to U.S. policy on such ships and aircraft, which was to "neither confirm nor deny" (NCND) whether such vessels carried nuclear weapons. The United States, New Zealand, and Australia were treaty partners under the so-called ANZUS Pact of 1951, one of a series of regional treaties of mutual defense that the United States concluded early in the Cold War. In that treaty, the parties agreed "separately and jointly by means of continuous and effective self-help and mutual aid [to] maintain and develop their individual and collective capacity to resist armed attack." (Art. 2.) The United States refused to alter NCND to accommodate New Zealand's concerns; instead, on September 17, 1986, the U.S. Ambassador to New Zealand delivered a note to its foreign ministry announcing that the United States "has suspended as between the United States and New Zealand the obligations" of the ANZUS Treaty. The U.S. position was that New Zealand had committed a material breach of the treaty, justifying the suspension under the Vienna Convention on the Law of Treaties (see Chapter 2), although the decision to suspend on these grounds was apparently unprecedented in U.S. treaty practice. This situation remains in effect today.

II. EXPLOITATION AND PROTECTION OF THE WATER AND FISH: THE CANADA/SPAIN TURBOT CONFLICT

The conflicting interests of coastal states and maritime states over the territorial sea and rights of passage represent only one aspect of a process of prescription regarding the law of the sea. For however important the security interests at stake in the resolution of those claims, both coastal and maritime states have other interests, especially economic ones, that affect their approach to the law of the sea.

The oldest and most significant economic interest concerns fishing. Competition over fishing rights represents the classic tragedy of the commons problem discussed in the introduction to Part V, a problem that states have long realized had to be tackled to avoid depletion of critical stocks. As early as 1947, Chile, Peru, and Ecuador, in part to limit fishing by foreign fleets off their coasts, proclaimed full sovereignty over the waters out to 200 miles from their shores, a claim that at the time seemed outrageous to many other states. The Latin American states picked 200 miles in order to include a particular band of water off their shores that was especially rich in fish. Indeed, while fish are found in the high seas, most of the world's richest fishing areas lie within 200 miles of shore.

The allure of the 200-mile claim would become great for most coastal states, and the solution adopted in the Law of the Sea Convention would strike a balance strongly in their favor. Nonetheless, the Convention does not eliminate all sources of tension. As you read the following problem, consider why states would agree on a regime so favorable to coastal states; how the Convention protects the economic interests of states with long-distance fishing fleets; what gaps lie in the Convention and how subsequent agreements have attempted to fill them; and what aspects of the problem of fishing make enforcement of the regime especially critical.

A. The Problem

The Greenland halibut, also commonly referred to as turbot, is a species of fish primarily used to make frozen fish sticks. Turbot do not like to stay in one place. Indeed, they happily and obliviously move from areas off Newfoundland in Canada to areas well out to sea. Canadian fishermen have long relied on turbot for their livelihood. When Spain and Portugal were admitted to the European Community (EC) in 1986, they agreed to limit their fishing off the French and British coasts and shifted many of their vessels to the Northwest Atlantic (although Spanish vessels had been fishing in the area for hundreds of years). Canada, in response, sharply cut down on the amount of fish that could be caught by Canadians and foreigners within 200 miles of its shore—a right that Canada enjoys under the Law of the Sea Convention, which will be further examined below. Spanish and Portuguese vessels continued, however, to fish heavily in areas just outside of the 200-mile limit.

In the early 1990s, Canada sought to protect the turbot and Canadian fishermen by acting through the Northwest Atlantic Fisheries Organization (NAFO), an international organization of 18 parties (including the European Union (EU)) dedicated to the management and conservation of fish in the region. NAFO's Fisheries Commission, composed of representatives of member states, examines scientific evidence as to the maximum sustainable yield of a given species and serves as a forum for states to negotiate both the total catch and an allocation among member states. Based on its conclusions, NAFO sets limits on the amount of fish in the area that can be caught year-round. In late 1994, NAFO lowered the annual quota of turbot from 60,000 tons to 27,000. The following February, NAFO allocated 60 percent of that amount to Canada and 12 percent to the EU (in this case, Spain and Portugal). The EU quickly objected to the allocation, as is permitted under the NAFO Convention, and instead set its own quota of 69 percent of the 1994 limit. The Convention does not bind states to NAFO quotas if they object. When the Spanish and Portuguese fleets did not cut their fishing significantly, Canada passed legislation allowing for the interception of vessels fishing for halibut more than 200 miles from its shore. Spain, Portugal, and the EU protested vehemently that Canada had no right unilaterally to regulate fishing that far from land.

In March 1995, Canada intercepted a Spanish trawler, the *Estai,* fishing just outside the 200-mile limit in the Atlantic Ocean. After chasing it for four hours in the fog and firing warning shots across the ship's bow, Canadian officials eventually boarded the vessel, seized it, and escorted it into St. John's (Newfoundland) harbor. Canada asserted that Spain was fishing illegally in violation of NAFO quotas and was further using NAFO-prohibited fine fish nets that catch fish before they are old enough to reproduce. Accordingly, Canada stated that unilateral action was necessary to protect the depleting stocks. The move scored tremendous domestic political points for the Canadian government, turning its Minister of Fisheries, Brian Tobin, into something of a national hero. Spain countered that the NAFO quotas were voluntary and that Spain had never agreed to the turbot limits currently then in place. Moreover, Spain asserted that Canada's actions constituted piracy on the high seas. Spain threatened to send its warships off the coast of Newfoundland and to require visas from visiting Canadians.

Despite some negotiations, the situation further intensified in April, when Canadian officials, backed by two armed navy ships, threatened to board and seize two more Spanish ships, backed by two armed Spanish patrol ships, just outside Canada's 200-mile zone. In March 1995, Spain initiated a suit against Canada at the ICJ, under Article 36(2) of the ICJ Statute, alleging illegal assertion of jurisdiction on the high seas and unlawful use of force against Spanish vessels. At oral arguments, the Canadian government lawyers contended that the ICJ did not have jurisdiction because the Court had been notified in 1994 that Canada was withdrawing its consent to have the ICJ review "disputes arising out of or concerning conservation and management measures taken by Canada with respect to vessels fishing in the NAFO Regulatory Area, as defined in the Convention on Future Multilateral Co-operation in the Northwest Atlantic Fisheries, 1978, and the enforcement of such measures."

B. Earlier Fishing Disputes: The United Kingdom-Iceland "Cod Wars"

The Canada-Spain conflict was hardly the first time that two states on otherwise friendly terms (both allies in the North Atlantic Treaty Organization (NATO)) had come to blows over fish. Participants at the first UN Conference on the Law of the Sea, which convened in 1958, had hoped to prevent such incidents by addressing this question in a convention, but the Convention on Fishing and Conservation of Living Resources of the High Seas, adopted in April 1958, glossed over the most important issues. It recognized a "special interest" of a coastal state in "the living resources in any area of the high seas adjacent to its territorial sea" (art. 6(1)), and required other states to enter into agreements with coastal states on fishing (art. 6(3)), but did not provide greater rights or specify the width of this area. At the same time, the Convention on the High Seas, adopted the same day, makes clear that in the high seas all states enjoy full freedom of fishing, though it "shall be exercised by all States with reasonable regard to the interests of other States." (Art. 2.)

Frustrated by this outcome, in June 1958 Iceland extended a unilaterally established fisheries zone beyond its coast from 4 to 12 miles to protect its fish and fishermen from a large British fleet. Iceland's act followed what had by then become a pattern of states extending not only their territorial seas but also claims to the adjacent waters and the fish in them. Britain, which had supported the 1958 Conventions, protested the extension and essentially ignored it as its ships continued to fish within 12 miles of Iceland, leading to incidents where Iceland boarded British vessels, cut their fishing lines, and took fishermen into custody. In March 1961, after much negotiation, the two states concluded an exchange of notes whereby Britain recognized the 12-mile zone, and Iceland agreed periodically to allow British vessels in some areas within 12 miles for three years and to notify Britain of any further increases. Both states agreed that either could request that the ICJ settle any future disputes.

In February 1972 Iceland announced that it would extend its fisheries jurisdiction to 50 miles effective September 1, prompting Britain to file suit in the ICJ. In August the Court issued an interim order requesting Iceland not to enforce its 50-mile limit, but Iceland extended the zone to 50 miles on September 1. After more incidents at sea, including the ramming of Icelandic coast guard vessels by British warships, in November 1973 the parties reached another interim agreement further limiting British access. On July 25, 1974, the ICJ issued its judgment.

Fisheries Jurisdiction Case (United Kingdom v. Iceland)

1974 I.C.J. 3 (July 25)

51. . . . The question of the breadth of the territorial sea and that of the extent of the coastal State's fishery jurisdiction were left unsettled at the 1958 Conference [on the Law of the Sea]. These questions were referred to the Second Conference on the Law of the Sea, held in 1960. . . .

52. The 1960 Conference failed by one vote to adopt a text governing the two questions of the breadth of the territorial sea and the extent of fishery rights. However, after that Conference the law evolved through the practice of States on the basis of the debates and near-agreements at the Conference. Two concepts have crystallized as customary law in recent years arising out of the general consensus revealed at that Conference. The first is the concept of the fishery zone, the area in which a State may claim exclusive fishery jurisdiction independently of its territorial sea; the extension of that fishery zone up to a 12-mile limit from the baselines appears now to be generally accepted. The second is the concept of preferential rights of fishing in adjacent waters in favour of the coastal State in a situation of special dependence on its coastal fisheries, this preference operating in regard to other States concerned in the exploitation of the same fisheries, and to be implemented in the way indicated in paragraph 57 below. . . .

54. The concept of a 12-mile fishery zone, referred to in paragraph 52 above, as a *tertium genus* [third category] between the territorial sea and the high seas, has been accepted with regard to Iceland in the substantive provisions of the 1961 Exchange of Notes, and the United Kingdom has also applied the same fishery limit to its own coastal waters since 1964; therefore this matter is no longer in dispute between the Parties. At the same time, the concept of preferential rights, a notion that necessarily implies the existence of other legal rights in respect of which that preference operates, has been admitted by the Applicant to be relevant to the solution of the present dispute. Moreover, the Applicant has expressly recog-

nized Iceland's preferential rights in the disputed waters and at the same time has invoked its own historic fishing rights in these same waters, on the ground that reasonable regard must be had to such traditional rights by the coastal State, in accordance with the generally recognized principles embodied in Article 2 of the High Seas Convention. . . .

55. The concept of preferential rights for the coastal State in a situation of special dependence on coastal fisheries originated in proposals submitted by Iceland at the [UN's] Geneva Conference [on the law of the sea] of 1958. Its delegation drew attention to the problem which would arise when, in spite of adequate fisheries conservation measures, the yield ceased to be sufficient to satisfy the requirements of all those who were interested in fishing in a given area. Iceland contended that in such a case, when a catch-limitation becomes necessary, special consideration should be given to the coastal State whose population is overwhelmingly dependent on the fishing resources in its adjacent waters. . . .

57. [The Court noted that many states at the 1960 Conference had accepted this idea.] The contemporary practice of States leads to the conclusion that the preferential rights of the coastal State in a special situation are to be implemented by agreement between the States concerned, either bilateral or multilateral, and, in case of disagreement, through the means for the peaceful settlement of disputes provided for in Article 33 of the Charter of the United Nations. . . .

58. State practice on the subject of fisheries reveals an increasing and widespread acceptance of the concept of preferential rights for coastal States, particularly in favour of countries or territories in a situation of special dependence on coastal fisheries. . . .

59. There can be no doubt of the exceptional dependence of Iceland on its fisheries. . . .

61. The Icelandic regulations challenged before the Court have been issued and applied by the Icelandic authorities as a claim to exclusive rights thus going beyond the concept of preferential rights. . . .

62. The concept of preferential rights is not compatible with the exclusion of all fishing activities of other States. A coastal State entitled to preferential rights is not free, unilaterally and according to its own uncontrolled discretion, to determine the extent of those rights. . . . The coastal State has to take into account and pay regard to the position of such other States, particularly when they have established an economic dependence on the same fishing grounds. . . .

63. In this case, the Applicant has pointed out that its vessels have been fishing in Icelandic waters for centuries and that they have done so in a manner comparable with their present activities for upwards of 50 years. Published statistics indicate that from 1920 onwards, fishing of demersal species by United Kingdom vessels in the disputed area has taken place on a continuous basis from year to year, and that, except for the period of the Second World War, the total catch of those vessels has been remarkably steady. . . .

64. The Applicant further states that in view of the present situation of fisheries in the North Atlantic, which has demanded the establishment of agreed catch-limitations of cod and haddock in various areas, it would not be possible for the fishing effort of United Kingdom vessels displaced from the Icelandic area to be diverted at economic levels to other fishing grounds in the North Atlantic. Given the lack of alternative fishing opportunity, it is further contended, the exclusion of British fishing vessels from the Icelandic area would have very serious adverse consequences, with immediate results for the affected vessels and with damage

extending over a wide range of supporting and related industries. It is pointed out in particular that wide-spread unemployment would be caused among all sections of the British fishing industry and in ancillary industries and that certain ports—Hull, Grimsby and Fleetwood—specially reliant on fishing in the Icelandic area, would be seriously affected. . . .

67. The provisions of the Icelandic Regulations of 14 July 1972 and the manner of their implementation disregard the fishing rights of the Applicant. Iceland's unilateral action thus constitutes an infringement of the principle enshrined in Article 2 of the 1958 Geneva Convention on the High Seas which requires that all States, including coastal States, in exercising their freedom of fishing, pay reasonable regard to the interests of other States. It also disregards the rights of the Applicant as they result from the Exchange of Notes of 1961. . . .

71. . . . [I]t follows that the Government of Iceland is not in law entitled unilaterally to exclude United Kingdom fishing vessels from sea areas to seaward of the limits agreed to in the 1961 Exchange of Notes or unilaterally to impose restrictions on their activities in such areas. But the matter does not end there; as the Court has indicated, Iceland is, in view of its special situation, entitled to preferential rights in respect of the fish stocks of the waters adjacent to its coasts. Due recognition must be given to the rights of both Parties, namely the rights of the United Kingdom to fish in the waters in dispute, and the preferential rights of Iceland. . . .

72. . . . [B]oth States have an obligation to take full account of each other's rights and of any fishery conservation measures the necessity of which is shown to exist in those waters. It is one of the advances in maritime international law, resulting from the intensification of fishing, that the former *laissez-faire* treatment of the living resources of the sea in the high seas has been replaced by a recognition of a duty to have due regard to the rights of other States and the needs of conservation for the benefit of all. . . .

73. The most appropriate method for the solution of the dispute is clearly that of negotiation. Its objective should be the delimitation of the rights and interests of the Parties, the preferential rights of the coastal State on the one hand and the rights of the Applicant on the other, to balance and regulate equitably questions such as those of catch-limitation [and] share allocations. . . . This necessitates detailed scientific knowledge of the fishing grounds. It is obvious that the relevant information and expertise would be mainly in the possession of the Parties. The Court would, for this reason, meet with difficulties if it were itself to attempt to lay down a precise scheme for an equitable adjustment of the rights involved. . . .

78. In the fresh negotiations . . . [t]he task before [the parties] will be to conduct their negotiations on the basis that each must in good faith pay reasonable regard to the legal rights of the other in the waters around Iceland outside the 12-mile limit, thus bringing about an equitable apportionment of the fishing resources based on the facts of the particular situation, and having regard to the interests of other States which have established fishing rights in the area. It is not a matter of finding simply an equitable solution, but an equitable solution derived from the applicable law. . . .

79. For these reasons,

THE COURT,

by ten votes to four, . . .

[(1) and (2) hold that Iceland cannot exclude UK vessels beyond 12 miles under the 1972 regulations];

(3) holds that the Government of Iceland and the Government of the United Kingdom are under mutual obligations to undertake negotiations in good faith for the equitable solution of their differences concerning their respective fishery rights . . . ;

(4) holds that in these negotiations the Parties are to take into account [the factors noted above—namely, Iceland's right to a preferential share, the rights of the United Kingdom, the interests of other states, and the preservation of the fishery resource].

In 1975, Iceland defied the ICJ's ruling and extended its fisheries zone from 50 to 200 miles. Britain and Germany protested, and more incidents ensued. In February 1976, citing aggressive action by British warships protecting fishing vessels in Icelandic waters, Iceland severed diplomatic relations with the United Kingdom. NATO (which included both states), and the United States in particular, became concerned by public debate in Iceland calling for withdrawal from NATO and closure of a NATO intelligence-gathering facility. Mediation by NATO officials eventually led to a June 1976 agreement in which British ships were allowed within the 200-mile zone for six more months but with limited fishing rights. After that point, most foreign fishing vessels were excluded from Iceland's 200-mile zone.

Notes and Questions

1. How did the ICJ respond to the gap in the law resulting from the failure of the first and second UN Conferences on the Law of the Sea to agree on a fishing regime? Did it advance or retard the process?

2. What would have been the likely responses of states like Spain and Canada engaged in fishing disputes after the ICJ's decision above? Given Iceland's defiance of the ICJ, should such disputes be decided in international courts or other arenas of decision making?

C. Toward Codification

Negotiations during the 1970s on fishing rights proved quite contentious. Coastal states often insisted on significant rights in an area out to 200 miles, with some states suggesting that such areas constitute part of the territorial sea. States that relied upon long-distance fishing, such as Japan and the United Kingdom, favored the traditional rights of fishing in areas beyond a narrow band of territorial sea. They were willing to accept the concept of preferential rights expressed in the *Norwegian Fisheries Case*, but not more. To them, the areas near a state were still essentially part of the high seas. Maritime states wanted assurances that any fishing rights of the coastal state would not interfere with freedom of navigation. States were, moreover, negotiating in the midst of a major North-South struggle over the idea of a New International Economic Order, an agenda of developing countries at the United Nations and other fora, that called for a major rectification of the economic inequalities between developed and developing states. Many developing coastal states thus viewed the areas off their shores as natural resources subject to their permanent sovereignty, an idea the United Nations had endorsed overwhelmingly (including most developed states) in Resolution 1803 of 1962. (See Chapter 2.)

In 1977, at the sixth session of the Third Conference on the Law of the Sea, informal negotiations began under the leadership of Norwegian delegate Jens Evensen, later joined by Mexican delegate Jorge Castañeda. They crafted a careful compromise that eventually proved acceptable to the other delegations. It combined provisions granting vast rights of control—though short of those in the territorial sea—to the coastal states, while preserving some noneconomic high seas rights for the international community. The result was effectively a new zone of the seas—neither high seas nor territorial seas.

United Nations Convention on the Law of the Sea

1833 U.N.T.S. 3 (1982)

EXCLUSIVE ECONOMIC ZONE
Article 55
Specific legal regime of the exclusive economic zone

The exclusive economic zone is an area beyond and adjacent to the territorial sea . . . under which the rights and jurisdiction of the coastal State and the rights and freedoms of other States are governed by the relevant provisions of this Convention.

Article 56
Rights, jurisdiction and duties of the coastal State in the exclusive economic zone

1. In the exclusive economic zone, the coastal State has:

(a) sovereign rights for the purpose of exploring and exploiting, conserving and managing the natural resources, whether living or non-living, of the waters superjacent to the seabed and of the seabed and its subsoil, and with regard to other activities for the economic exploitation and exploration of the zone, such as the production of energy from the water, currents and winds;

(b) jurisdiction as provided for in the relevant provisions of this Convention with regard to:

(i) the establishment and use of artificial islands, installations and structures;

(ii) marine scientific research;

(iii) the protection and preservation of the marine environment. . . .

2. In exercising its rights and performing its duties under this Convention in the exclusive economic zone, the coastal State shall have due regard to the rights and duties of other

States and shall act in a manner compatible with the provisions
of this Convention. . . .

Article 57
Breadth of the exclusive economic zone

The exclusive economic zone shall not extend beyond 200 nautical miles from the baselines from which the breadth of the territorial sea is measured.

Article 58
Rights and duties of other States in the exclusive
economic zone

1. In the exclusive economic zone, all States, whether
coastal or land-locked, enjoy . . . the freedoms . . . of navigation and overflight and of the laying of submarine cables and
pipelines, and other internationally lawful uses of the sea
related to these freedoms, such as those associated with the
operation of ships, aircraft and submarine cables and pipelines. . . .

3. . . . . States shall have due regard to the rights and duties
of the coastal State and shall comply with the laws and regulations adopted by the coastal State in accordance with the provisions of this Convention. . . .

Article 61
Conservation of the living resources

1. The coastal State shall determine the allowable catch of
the living resources in its exclusive economic zone.

2. The coastal State, taking into account the best scientific
evidence available to it, shall ensure through proper conservation and management measures that the maintenance of the living
resources in the exclusive economic zone is not endangered by
over-exploitation. As appropriate, the coastal State and competent international organizations, whether subregional, regional or global, shall cooperate to this end. . . . .

Article 62
Utilization of the living resources

1. The coastal State shall promote the objective of optimum
utilization of the living resources in the exclusive economic
zone without prejudice to article 61.

2. The coastal State shall determine its capacity to harvest
the living resources of the exclusive economic zone. Where the

coastal State does not have the capacity to harvest the entire
allowable catch, it shall, through agreements or other arrangements . . . give other States access to the surplus of the allowable catch . . . especially in relation to the developing States
mentioned therein. . . .

Article 63
Stocks occurring within the exclusive economic zones of
two or more coastal States or both within the exclusive
economic zone and in an area beyond and adjacent to it

2. Where the same stock or stocks of associated species occur
both within the exclusive economic zone and in an area beyond and
adjacent to the zone, the coastal State and the States fishing
for such stocks in the adjacent area shall seek, either directly
or through appropriate subregional or regional organizations,
to agree upon the measures necessary for the conservation of
these stocks in the adjacent area.

Beyond the EEZ, the regime of the high seas prevails for fishing. Under Article
87 of the Convention, "The high seas are open to all States, whether coastal or land-
locked. Freedom of the high seas . . . comprises, _inter alia_, both for coastal and
land-locked States: . . . freedom of fishing, subject to the conditions [that t]hese
freedoms shall be exercised by all States with due regard for the interests of
other States in their exercise of the freedom of the high seas. . . ." Moreover, Article
116 grants all states "the right for their nationals to engage in fishing on the high
seas subject to: (a) their treaty obligations; [and] (b) the rights and duties as well as
the interests of coastal States provided for, _inter alia_, in article 63, paragraph 2. . . ."
Article 117 states that "[a]ll States have the duty to take, or to cooperate with other
States in taking, such measures for their respective nationals as may be necessary for
the conservation of the living resources of the high seas."

Notes and Questions

1. Does the 1982 Convention help resolve any legal issues between Spain and
Canada? Does it matter that neither Canada nor Spain was a party to UNCLOS at
the time of the dispute? Consider also Article 110's provisions on "visits" by one ship
to another on the high seas:

> 1. [A] warship which encounters on the high seas a foreign
> ship . . . is not justified in boarding it unless there is
> reasonable ground for suspecting that:
>
> > (a) the ship is engaged in piracy;
> > (b) the ship is engaged in the slave trade;
> > (c) the ship is engaged in unauthorized broad-
> >   casting . . . ;
> > (d) the ship is without nationality; or

(e) though flying a foreign flag or refusing to show
    its flag, the ship is, in reality, of the same
    nationality as the warship.

2. In the cases provided for in paragraph 1, the warship
may proceed to verify the ship's right to fly its flag. To
this end, it may send a boat under the command of an officer
to the suspected ship. If suspicion remains after the documents have been checked, it may proceed to a further examination on board the ship, which must be carried out with all
possible consideration.

3. If the suspicions prove to be unfounded, and provided
that the ship boarded has not committed any act justifying
them, it shall be compensated for any loss or damage that
may have been sustained.

2. Note the use of the term "sovereign rights" in Article 56. How does the EEZ
resemble or differ from the territorial sea? How does it resemble or differ from the
high seas?

3. Do you think the compromise reached in the UNCLOS is a fair balance
among the competing interests? What did the coastal states gain? What did they
give up?

4. How should states interpret the dictates of Article 62 requiring "optimum
utilization of the living resources" of the EEZ, a term undefined in the Convention?

5. Articles 69 and 70 grant landlocked and geographically disadvantaged states
"the right to participate, on an equitable basis, in the exploitation of an appropriate
part of the surplus of the living resources of the exclusive economic zones of coastal
States of the same subregion or region." However, the Convention does not specify
those rights, leaving it to the affected states to work out an agreement based on
criteria such as protection of the coastal state's fishing industry, the number of states
seeking access to a particular coastal state's surplus, and the extent to which any of
those states have access to another coastal state's surplus. These provisions represent somewhat poor substitutes for what these states wanted but did not achieve—a
share of the revenue from the continental shelf. (The continental shelf regime is
explored in the next section of this chapter.)

6. The compromise arrived at for defining the EEZ, like the compromises on
other issues, was the result of many meetings, most of them behind closed doors. As
one participant wrote:

It is very difficult to unravel the story of how a text came to acquire its final form,
especially, as at UNCLOS, when all substantive discussion was off the record. Instead
of the will of a majority opposed to the will of the minority, there is the interaction of
many wills within the groups and among the groups, interacting not merely in relation
to a draft text and a limited number of proposed amendments but in relation to an
infinite number of possible alternative textual formulations, as various as the ingenuity
and the patience of the negotiators will allow. A brief conversation on a social occasion
may generate a new solution or a new will to agree where more formal methods have
failed, and the promotion of a given solution may involve many kinds of interpersonal
social behavior, going far beyond the simple dialectic of debate and decision. UNCLOS
itself was dazzlingly prolific in creating ad hoc negotiating procedures, spawned by

hope out of necessity: working groups (restricted and open-ended), negotiating groups, confrontations between interest groups, "friends of the chairman" of a committee, the President's bureau, appointed and self-appointed mediators in smoke-filled rooms. . . .

Philip Allott, *Power Sharing in the Law of the Sea*, 77 Am. J. Intl. L. 1, 6-7 (1983).

What are the implications of such a negotiating process for the ability of parties to future disputes to utilize the *travaux préparatoires* of the Convention as a supplementary source of interpretation, under Article 31 of the Vienna Convention on the Law of Treaties?

D. Toward a Solution for Straddling Stocks

Turbot are an example of so-called straddling stock—fish that move in and out of a state's EEZ—addressed by Article 63 of UNCLOS. Yet the language of that article provides stark evidence of the inability of states during the Third UN Conference to agree on a regime for such fish. As a result of this failure, overfishing in areas beyond the EEZ continued, as the Spain-Canada dispute makes clear. In 1992, when the United Nations convened its Earth Summit at Rio de Janeiro, governments and non-governmental organizations (NGOs) accepted the need for a special agreement on straddling stocks. In 1993, negotiations started, wrapping up in August 1995.

Agreement for the Implementation of the Provisions of the United Nations Convention on the Law of the Sea of 10 December 1982 Relating to the Conservation and Management of Straddling Fish Stocks and Highly Migratory Fish Stocks

34 I.L.M. 1542 (1995)

Article 5
General principles

In order to conserve and manage straddling fish stocks and highly migratory fish stocks, coastal States and States fishing on the high seas shall, in giving effect to their duty to cooperate in accordance with the [1982] Convention:

(a) adopt measures to ensure long-term sustainability of straddling fish stocks and highly migratory fish stocks and promote the objective of their optimum utilization;

(b) ensure that such measures are based on the best scientific evidence available and are designed to maintain or restore stocks at levels capable of producing maximum sustainable yield . . . ;

(c) apply the precautionary approach in accordance with article 6. . . .

Article 6
Application of the precautionary approach

1. States shall apply the precautionary approach widely to conservation, management and exploitation of straddling fish stocks and highly migratory fish stocks in order to protect the living marine resources and preserve the marine environment.

2. States shall be more cautious when information is uncertain, unreliable or inadequate. The absence of adequate scientific information shall not be used as a reason for postponing or failing to take conservation and management measures. . . .

Article 8
Cooperation for conservation and management

1. Coastal States and States fishing on the high seas shall, in accordance with the Convention, pursue cooperation in relation to straddling fish stocks and highly migratory fish stocks either directly or through appropriate subregional or regional fisheries management organizations or arrangements. . . .

3. Where a subregional or regional fisheries management organization or arrangement has the competence to establish conservation and management measures . . . , States fishing for the stocks on the high seas and relevant coastal States shall give effect to their duty to cooperate by becoming members of such organization or participants in such arrangement, or by agreeing to apply the conservation and management measures established by such organization or arrangement. . . .

Article 17
Non-members of organizations and non-participants
in arrangements

1. A State which is not a member of a subregional or regional fisheries management organization or is not a participant in a subregional or regional fisheries management arrangement, and which does not otherwise agree to apply the conservation and management measures established by such organization or arrangement, is not discharged from the obligation to cooperate . . . in the conservation and management of the relevant straddling fish stocks and highly migratory fish stocks.

2. Such State shall not authorize vessels flying its flag to engage in fishing operations for the straddling fish stocks or highly migratory fish stocks which are subject to the conservation and management measures established by such organization or arrangement.

Article 19
Compliance and enforcement by the flag State

1. A State shall ensure compliance by vessels flying its flag with subregional and regional conservation and management measures for straddling fish stocks and highly migratory fish stocks. To this end, that State shall:

(a) enforce such measures irrespective of where violations occur;

(b) investigate immediately and fully any alleged violation of subregional or regional conservation and management measures. . . ;

(d) if satisfied that sufficient evidence is available in respect of an alleged violation, refer the case to its authorities with a view to instituting proceedings, without delay . . . ; and

(e) ensure that . . . the vessel does not engage in fishing operations on the high seas until such time as all outstanding sanctions imposed by the flag State in respect of the violation have been complied with. . . .

Article 20
International cooperation in enforcement

6. Where there are reasonable grounds for believing that a vessel on the high seas has been engaged in unauthorized fishing within an area under the jurisdiction of a coastal State, the flag State of that vessel, at the request of the coastal State concerned, shall immediately and fully investigate the matter. The flag State shall cooperate with the coastal State in taking appropriate enforcement action in such cases and may authorize the relevant authorities of the coastal State to board and inspect the vessel on the high seas. . . .

Article 21
Subregional and regional cooperation in enforcement

1. In any high seas area covered by a subregional or regional fisheries management organization or arrangement, a State Party which is a member of such organization or a participant in such arrangement may, through its duly authorized inspectors, board and inspect . . . fishing vessels flying the flag of another State Party to this Agreement, whether or not such State Party is also a member of the organization or a participant in the arrangement, for the purpose of ensuring compliance with conservation and management measures for straddling fish stocks and highly migratory fish stocks established by that organization or arrangement. . . .

5. Where . . . there are clear grounds for believing that a vessel has engaged in any activity contrary to the conservation and management measures referred to in paragraph 1, the inspecting State shall, where appropriate, secure evidence and shall promptly notify the flag State of the alleged violation.

6. The flag State shall respond to the notification referred to in paragraph 5 within three working days of its receipt, or such other period as may be prescribed . . . and shall either:

   (a) . . . investigate and, if evidence so warrants, take enforcement action with respect to the vessel, in which case it shall promptly inform the inspecting State of the results of the investigation and of any enforcement action taken; or

   (b) authorize the inspecting State to investigate.

8. Where . . . there are clear grounds for believing that a vessel has committed a serious violation, and the flag State has either failed to respond or failed to take action . . . the inspectors may remain on board and secure evidence and may require the master to assist in further investigation including, where appropriate, by bringing the vessel without delay to the nearest appropriate port. . . .

11. For the purposes of this article, a serious violation means [a list of nine actions, including fishing without a license and using prohibited fishing gear]. . . .

18. States shall be liable for damage or loss attributable to them arising from action taken pursuant to this article when such action is unlawful or exceeds that reasonably required in the light of available information to implement the provisions of this article.

The turbot war ended when Spain, through the EU, and Canada came to a new agreement in April 1995. Under the settlement Canada was allowed to get 10,000 tons of the 27,000 tons of annual total turbot fishing allowed by NAFO for 1995. Seven thousand tons of Canada's catch would come from its own EEZ, where only Canadian vessels could fish. The agreement allowed the EU ships to catch an additional 5,013 tons outside Canada's EEZ without stating how much turbot they had already caught that year. The EU also agreed to provide stricter monitoring mechanisms. The two sides further agreed to propose to NAFO a scheme under which they would split their share of future halibut catches outside Canada's EEZ (of the amounts not allocated to other NAFO states) in a 10:3 (EU:Canada) ratio. This was a significant concession by Spain, which in 1994 caught 44,000 tons of fish in that same area compared to Canada's 4,000 tons. NAFO endorsed this settlement in June 1995. As a result, the total halibut in the NAFO area (inside and outside Canada's EEZ) would be split roughly 41 percent for the EU, 41 percent for Canada, and 18 percent for other NAFO states, principally Japan and Russia. As part of the deal, Canada released the fishing vessel *Estai* and suspended all proceedings against the boat's crew. Spanish fishermen were angered by the agreement. They chastised their government for selling out and threatened to continue to fish illegally. Spain did not withdraw its ICJ suit after the settlement. In December 1998 the ICJ dismissed Spain's suit, agreeing with Canada's position that the ICJ did not have jurisdiction over the case.

Notes and Questions

1. What are the respective roles of the flag state, the coastal state, and the regional organization in the enforcement of the 1995 treaty?

2. How does Article 17 address the problem of fishing by states that are not parties to a particular regional fisheries arrangement and thus not bound by its catch limits?

3. Would this agreement have avoided the Spain-Canada turbot incidents?

4. How does the 1995 agreement address the possibility of violations? Consider the following:

> The chief compliance mechanism that the Straddling Stocks Agreement constructs represents a pivotal evolutionary development of the international legal order of fisheries. By allowing parties to the Straddling Stocks Agreement the right to board and inspect each others' vessels that are reasonably suspected of management/conservation violations (e.g., the use of prohibited gear, the taking of juvenile fish, as was the case in NAFO, or the taking of prohibited quantities of fish), the agreement supplies the element previously unavailable to the fisheries management order: a congruently generalized right to expect compliance from each others' fishing fleets via a legal device that reinforces that expectation. Specifically, Article 21 creates the possibility of international embarrassment and the social opprobrium that accompanies the disclosure of a state's dereliction of its obligations, without attempting to create a tool of coercion.

Jamison E. Colburn, *Turbot Wars: Straddling Stocks, Regime Theory, and a New U.N. Agreement*, 6 J. Transnatl. L. & Poly. 323, 363 (1997).

E. Note on Dispute Resolution Under UNCLOS

Part XV and several Annexes to the 1982 Convention set up a rather complex system for the resolution of disputes. Parties are free to settle their disputes by any means upon which they agree (including, of course, nonjudicial means); but if they are also party to another treaty that, by its terms, specifies particular dispute settlement provisions to the exclusion of others, that treaty's provisions shall apply if one party chooses to invoke them. If that option is not exercised, the parties can submit disputes to a new International Tribunal for the Law of the Sea (ITLOS), the ICJ, an arbitral tribunal, or a special arbitral tribunal that deals only with fisheries, pollution, research, and navigation. The 21 ITLOS members (who sit in Hamburg) are elected by the parties to UNCLOS based on geographic distribution criteria. In the arbitral tribunal, the parties each pick one arbitrator, who then must agree on three more; and in the special arbitral tribunal, each disputant picks two arbitrators, who must then agree on one more.

When signing or ratifying UNCLOS, states may indicate that they accept the jurisdiction of only some of these four means to settle disputes—except that a special chamber of the ITLOS automatically has jurisdiction over most disputes concerning the Convention's deep seabed provisions as well as disputes where a state seeks the release of a seized vessel or provisional measures (the international law term for a temporary injunction). In addition, when signing the Convention, a state may indicate that it does not accept binding dispute settlement over three issues—sea boundary delimitations and claims to historic bays, military activities, and issues under consideration by the UN Security Council. When President Clinton forwarded the Convention to the Senate in 1994 for its advice and consent to ratification, he indicated his intention to choose the arbitral and special arbitral tribunals over the ICJ and ITLOS and to exercise the right not to accept binding dispute settlement over the three issues noted above.

Since the inception of the system, some important decisions have emerged. First, in November 1997, Guinean authorities seized a vessel from St. Vincent and the Grenadines that was suspected of smuggling. Guinea detained its crew and removed its cargo of fuel oil. Two weeks later St. Vincent applied to ITLOS for the prompt release of the vessel under a dispute settlement provision of UNCLOS (Article 292) that allows states to seek release of one of their vessels if they allege that the detaining state has violated Article 73(2)'s requirement that "[a]rrested vessels and their crews shall be promptly released upon the posting of reasonable bond or other security." ITLOS examined the UNCLOS provisions that limit a state's ability to detain foreign vessels indefinitely and ordered the release if the vessel posted a bond. Guinea initially refused to accept the bond or release the vessel and crew but released them just before the ITLOS ordered it not to take any further action against the vessel. *M/V "Saiga,"* Dec. 4, 1997, 37 I.L.M. 360 (1998). In July 1999, ITLOS ordered Guinea to pay over $2 million in damages. In 2001, Guinea agreed on a payment schedule for this sum.

Second, in 1999, Australia and New Zealand instituted proceedings against Japan, claiming that Japan's experimental fishing program on the high seas violated its obligations under their trilateral Convention for the Conservation of Southern Bluefin Tuna. The applicants instituted arbitration for the merits (arbitration is the fallback provision if none of the parties has indicated a preferred method of settling the dispute), and went to ITLOS for provisional measures. As discussed more fully in Chapter 11, in August 1999, ITLOS ordered provisional measures in favor of Australia and New Zealand and required each party to refrain from experimental fishing, to limit its catch to previously agreed quotas, to avoid any other aggravation of the dispute, and to negotiate a solution. *Southern Bluefin Tuna Cases*, Aug. 27, 1999, 38 I.L.M. 1624 (1999).

In August 2000, however, the arbitral tribunal decided that it lacked jurisdiction to reach the merits. In a complex decision, the court compared the dispute resolution provisions of UNCLOS and of the tuna treaty and concluded that the parties had agreed in the latter to resolve disputes according to the tuna treaty alone. The arbitral tribunal also revoked the provisional measures awarded by ITLOS (perhaps an odd outcome given that it had determined that it lacked jurisdiction over the case). *Southern Bluefin Tuna Cases*, Award on Jurisdiction and Admissibility, Aug. 4, 2000, 39 I.L.M. 1359 (2000). The panel's decision will doubtless affect the views of future UNCLOS arbitral panels as to whether they can adjudicate disputes where other treaties—like the 1995 Straddling Stocks Convention—have dispute resolution procedures.

Third, in January 2000, three months after France had seized a Panamanian vessel for illegal fishing within the French EEZ and then had set a bond of 20 million francs for its release, Panama instituted proceedings in ITLOS under Article 292. Three weeks after the case was filed, ITLOS ordered the release of the ship upon posting of an 8 million franc bond. The bond was posted, whereupon the vessel was released. The Tribunal rejected France's argument that Panama could not apply under Article 292 until it had exhausted its appeals of the original bond order in the French courts; it further found that the original bond was unreasonable in light of the vessel's replacement value of only 3.7 million francs. *The "Camouco,"* Judgment, Feb. 7, 2000, 39 I.L.M. 666 (2000). Two commentators wrote of the outcome:

> Those who argue that the outcomes of cases often reflect the substantive predispositions of the judges' states of nationality will again be surprised by the Tribunal: the decision reveals substantially the opposite of what those so inclined might have expected in a case challenging a bond fixed by the coastal state in a fisheries arrest. The majority included most judges from countries that might be regarded as particularly sympathetic to coastal state claims to discretionary control over fisheries, whereas the dissent included judges from European (but not Asian) countries that are at times more restrained about such claims. In addition, it can be argued that regional factors were irrelevant because the dispute was in substance between France and a Spanish fishing company.

Bernard H. Oxman & Vincent P. Bantz, *International Decisions: The "Camouco,"* 94 Am. J. Intl. L. 713, 719 (2000).

As noted in the commentary, in the cases where states sought prompt release of seized vessels, the real actors seeking the release were not the petitioning states but the companies that owned the vessels, for example, the Spanish fishing company in the case of the *Camouco*. Indeed, the fishing companies did the principal legal work for the petitioning states in the ITLOS. The petitioning states (St. Vincent and the Grenadines and Panama) were flag states of convenience—that is, states chosen by the fishing or transport industry for the ease with which vessels may be registered.

Fourth, in October 2003, in a case brought by Malaysia against Singapore contesting the the latter's land reclamation plans for the Straits of Johor (which separates the two states), ITLOS made a significant decision when it ordered the two states to establish a joint panel of scientific experts to study the environmental effects of Singapore's plans and ordered Singapore not to carry out any land reclamation "in ways that might cause irreparable prejudice to the rights of Malaysia or serious harm to the marine environment." The panel eventually reached a set of unanimous recommendations in late 2004, which the parties accepted as the basis for further negotiations. On the eve of a new round of arguments before ITLOS, the parties announced a settlement under which Singapore adjusted some of its reclamation projects and compensated affected Malaysian fisherman, and the two sides agreed to cooperate on future use of the straits through binational mechanisms.

Finally, in October 2001, Ireland sued the United Kingdom over the latter's construction of a plant to make mixed oxide (MOX) fuel for nuclear reactors, alleging that radioactive wastes from the plant draining into the Irish Sea would violate UNCLOS provisions on marine pollution; it sought creation of an UNCLOS arbitral tribunal to resolve the dispute and also petitioned ITLOS for provisional measures to enjoin the operation of the plant. (Ireland had previously instituted arbitration proceedings against the United Kingdom under a treaty to protect the northeast Atlantic marine environment, though the panel created thereunder ruled against it in July 2003.) In December 2001, ITLOS rejected Ireland's request as not based on sufficient urgency but did order the parties to share information and cooperate on a plan to prevent pollution from the plant in the future. In rulings in June and November 2003, the arbitration panel refused to rule on the merits; instead, it stayed the proceedings until the European Court of Justice (the EU's highest court) decided whether only the EC (which is itself a party to UNCLOS), and not Ireland, could, under EU law, institute proceedings under UNCLOS. The panel nonetheless ordered provisional measures similar to those ordered by ITLOS, though, like ITLOS, it rejected Ireland's request for a stronger injunction. By early 2006, the ECJ had not ruled on this question, nor had the arbitral tribunal returned to the case. The involvement of two international courts, two arbitration bodies, and at least three treaties highlights the possibilities of judicial resolution of law of the sea disputes but also the risks of conflicting orders for the litigants, as well as inconsistent jurisprudence on the underlying substantive claims.

III. ECONOMIC EXPLOITATION OF THE CONTINENTAL SHELF: THE BATTLE FOR DRILLING RIGHTS IN THE CASPIAN SEA

Disputes over the extent of a coastal state's control of the waters off its shore have extended well beyond the security claims associated with the territorial sea and international straits and the economic aspects associated with the regime of the exclusive economic zone. Many states have important economic claims regarding the exploitation of lands located beneath the surface of adjacent waters. The land masses of the continents extend naturally beyond their shores to an underwater mass known as the continental shelf. (See diagram on p. 702) The shelf extends past a state's coastline before it drops into a steeper area (known as the continental slope), and then a more gradually sloping area (known as the continental rise) before eventually forming the ocean floor. The shelf averages between 42 and 47 miles in breadth, with an average depth of 210 feet and a gradient of only 0.07 degrees. That shelf represents a potential resource for the coastal state, in particular as nearly all offshore hydrocarbon deposits are located on the continental shelf and slope; it might also conceivably represent a potential security threat if an adversary were to use it to emplant weapons or intelligence-gathering capabilities (although the technical difficulties to and vulnerabilities of such uses would be significant).

Though some uses of the continental shelf are quite ancient, such as the gathering of pearls or even some mining from shore-based mineshafts, the most important claims to use of the continental shelf are fairly recent, roughly since World War II. As a result, they have not given rise to the sort of customary international law seen in the regime providing for freedom of the high seas or rights of coastal states in the territorial sea. But the newness of the claims in no way lessens their salience for the affected states. Many of these claims have been authoritatively resolved in the 1982 Law of the Sea Convention. For others, such as those between two neighboring states seeking to divide the shelf between them, the Convention provides a starting point but no definitive answer. As you read the following materials, consider how the key claimants organized themselves on this issue compared to the navigational and fishing issues discussed in the previous Problems; why states were able to agree relatively quickly on a set of norms concerning the continental shelf; and what options are open to competing claimants where the Law of the Sea Convention does not resolve their concerns.

A. The Problem

The Caspian Sea is the world's largest fully enclosed body of water. Some seven hundred miles long, for most of the twentieth century it bordered two states—the

Soviet Union (which controlled about 1,385 out of 1,704 miles of its coast) and Iran. Today, its shores touch five states—Russia, Azerbaijan, Iran, Turkmenistan, and Kazakhstan—with Kazakhstan occupying the largest single part (526 miles) of the coastline. The Caspian Sea has always had a significant economic role in the lives of the peoples living near it. Some 130 rivers flow into the Sea, including the Volga in Russia, and the Sea has long served as a major transportation route between Russia and Persia. It is also the home of some 115 species of fish, including the *osyetr* (sturgeon), which supplies eggs for the caviar industry. (See map.)

Most significantly for the states surrounding it, the Caspian contains six distinct hydrocarbon basins, with the total proven oil reserves for the sea- and land-based areas estimated at 18-35 billion barrels (compared to 17 billion for the North Sea); natural gas reserves are significantly larger. Oil exploration dates back to the nineteenth century, when many of Europe's large oil barons, including the Nobels and the Rothschilds, helped Czarist Russia develop land-based oil fields. In the late 1800s, the oil trade in the region represented 30 percent of the total global oil trade. During World War I and World War II, Germany sought without success to seize some of the Russian (later Soviet) fields in the areas around Baku (now the capital of Azerbaijan).

The Caucasus and Central Asia

SOURCE: CIA World Factbook

During the many years when only two states surrounded the Sea, Iran and Russia sought to ensure that no other state would have access to the Sea for navigation or fishing. In February 1921, Persia (Iran) and Russia (the Soviet Union had not yet formally come into existence) signed an agreement reaffirming each state's right of "free navigation" in the Caspian. In March 1940, the two sides concluded a Treaty of Commerce and Navigation, in which they agreed that each could fish exclusively up to ten miles from its shore; an exchange of notes stated that the "parties hold the Caspian to belong to Iran and to the Soviet [Union]." Neither agreement, however, provided for any division of the sea itself. In an era before significant offshore exploitation was possible, the lack of such an agreement did not have serious consequences. Technological change soon prompted states to take more decisive steps toward control of subsurface areas off their shores. As you read the following materials, you should note that the Caspian Sea is much more like a large saltwater lake vis-à-vis noncoastal states than it is like waters off the shores of a continent. Nevertheless, it has an underwater geological formation resembling the continental shelf, making the evolution of the law on the shelf pertinent to the resolution of the problem.

B. Unilateral Claims to the Continental Shelf: The Truman Proclamation and Reactions

The lack of scientific knowledge by states regarding the economic potential of the continental shelf and the technological limits on exploiting it effectively meant that no state saw any need to assert claims over the shelf. The result was that the shelf remained legally unregulated until the middle of the twentieth century. In theory the notion of high seas freedom pointed in the direction of open exploitation; yet the acceptance by states of the notion of a territorial sea suggested that coastal states did have special interests in all areas—including, potentially, the submerged land areas—near their shore.

In the early 1940s, however, the United States, the largest military and economic power, began to see the continental shelf as a valuable and exploitable part of its territory. Discussions began within the Roosevelt Administration on a national policy concerning the shelf. In a June 9, 1943, note to Secretary of State Cordell Hull, Franklin Roosevelt wrote:

> I think [Secretary of the Interior] Harold Ickes has the right slant on this [continental shelf]. For many years, I have felt that the old three-mile limit or twenty-mile limit should be superseded by a rule of common sense. For instance, the Gulf of Mexico is bounded on the south by Mexico and on the north by the United States. In parts of the Gulf, shallow water extends very many miles off shore. It seems to me that the Mexican Government should be entitled to drill for oil in the southern half of the Gulf and we in the northern half of the Gulf. That would be far more sensible than allowing some European nation, for example, to come in there and drill.

At Roosevelt's request, officials of the Departments of the Interior and State began intensive discussions on a proposal regarding the shelf. An internal Department of State memorandum noted:

> It is believed that international law does not prevent a nation acquiring by occupation or contiguity rights to lands beneath the high seas, provided the freedom of navigation is not impaired. The Legal Adviser of the Department has given his approval to the

policy. None of the governments with which the policy has been discussed indicated any opposition.

On September 28, 1945, President Harry Truman issued the following proclamation:

Policy of the United States With Respect to the Natural Resources of the Subsoil and Sea Bed of the Continental Shelf

10 Fed. Reg. 12,303 (1945)

WHEREAS the Government of the United States of America, aware of the long range world-wide need for new sources of petroleum and other minerals, holds the view that efforts to discover and make available new supplies of these resources should be encouraged; and

WHEREAS its competent experts are of the opinion that such resources underlie many parts of the continental shelf off the coasts of the United States of America, and that with modern technological progress their utilization is already practicable or will become so at any early date; and

WHEREAS recognized jurisdiction over these resources is required in the interest of their conservation and prudent utilization when and as development is undertaken; and

WHEREAS it is the view of the Government of the United States that the exercise of jurisdiction over the natural resources of the subsoil and sea bed of the continental shelf by the contiguous nation is reasonable and just, since the effectiveness of measures to utilize or conserve these resources would be contingent upon cooperation and protection from the shore, since the continental shelf may be regarded as an extension of the land-mass of the coastal nation and thus naturally appurtenant to it, since these resources frequently form a seaward extension of a pool or deposit lying within the territory, and since self-protection compels the coastal nation to keep close watch over activities off its shores which are of their nature necessary for utilization of these resources;

NOW THEREFORE I, HARRY S. TRUMAN, President of the United States of America, do hereby proclaim the following policy of the United States of America with respect to the natural resources of the subsoil and sea bed of the continental shelf.

Having concern for the urgency of conserving and prudently utilizing its natural resources, the Government of the United States regards the natural resources of the subsoil and sea bed of the continental shelf beneath the high seas but contiguous to the coasts of the United States as appertaining to the United States, subject to its jurisdiction and control. In cases where the continental shelf extends to the shores of another State, or is shared with an adjacent State, the boundary shall be determined by the United States and the State concerned in accordance with equitable principles. The character as high seas of the waters above the continental shelf and the right to their free and unimpeded navigation are in no way thus affected.

In the years after the Truman Proclamation, most coastal states issued similar statements of policy. Nonetheless, they differed on the extent of their claim, in terms of the distance from the shore, with some asserting a 200-mile limit; the areas covered, with some calling for control of the high seas over the resources of the subsoil and the seabed; and the scope of the rights, with some asserting "sovereign rights" rather than "jurisdiction and control." Indeed, the assertion of a 200-mile fishing zone by Chile, Ecuador, and Peru in 1947 discussed in the previous Problem was an attempt by states without significant continental shelves to compensate by asserting extensive fishing jurisdiction.

Notes and Questions

1. What was the legal basis for Truman's actions? Did his decision violate international law? Was it consistent with the traditional view of the high seas as free for all to use? Consider the following:

> [W]hat was the international rule concerning the continental shelf as of January 1945, just before Truman issued his proclamation? At the time there was no applicable treaty, nor was there much if any state practice relating to the continental shelf; thus, no rule of customary international law had developed. But was this issue simply outside the scope of international law? Were states free to do whatever they liked? This seems highly doubtful since, if so, this would have meant not only that a coastal state could claim its continental shelf, but that non-coastal states could do so as well—that the United States, say, could have claimed the continental shelf off the coast of France. Arguably, a more accurate way to describe the legal situation at the time of the Truman Proclamation was that there was no norm one way or the other, either supporting the right of the United States to issue the Proclamation or prohibiting it from doing so. There was a gap in the law (as the United States itself recognised at the time), which the Truman Proclamation sought to fill.

Daniel Bodansky, Non Liquet *and the Incompleteness of International Law, in* International Law, the International Court of Justice and Nuclear Weapons 153, 157 (Laurence Boisson de Chazournes & Philippe Sands eds., 2000).

2. What does the practice of other states after 1945 suggest about the effect of the Proclamation on international law? Why was it significant that the United States, as opposed to a poorer state, made the Proclamation?

3. Was the United States, as the state with the greatest potential to exploit offshore hydrocarbons around the world, losing more than it gained by creating a precedent for other states to claim their continental shelves as subject to their jurisdiction and control?

C. Prescription Through the United Nations

The uncertainties among states about the legal regime in light of the Truman Proclamation and other unilateral acts prompted a flurry of activity in the United Nations. The International Law Commission (ILC) began considering the issue as early as 1949, producing sets of draft articles on the legal regime of the continental shelf in 1951 and 1953. The UN General Assembly convened the first intergovernmental Conference on the Law of the Sea in 1958. That conference concluded a Convention on the Continental Shelf, which defined the shelf as the seabed and subsoil to a depth of 200 meters, "or, beyond that limit, to where the depth of the superjacent waters admits of the exploitation of the natural resources of the said areas." (Art. 1). Nonetheless, substantial disagreements over the definition of the shelf—how far and how deep it would extend—and the formulae for dividing it among neighboring states (see further discussion below) kept the number of states ratifying it at the rather low figure of roughly 50. Iran and the USSR both signed the treaty, but only the USSR eventually ratified it.

When governments negotiated continental shelf issues during the Third UN Conference on the Law of the Sea in the 1970s, they disagreed over whether the shelf should be regulated separately from the regime of the waters above it, a regime which, as shown in the previous Problem, would give full exploitation rights to the coastal state out to 200 miles. States with broad continental shelves favored extensive rights, even extending beyond 200 miles from shore (far beyond the 200-meter depth provided in the 1958 Convention) if the continental shelf extended that far. States without significant offshore areas—whether because they are landlocked or are so-called geographically disadvantaged states (with small shelves due to the shape of their coastline)—or those without significant resources wanted to ensure that they would benefit from the exploitation of the sea. Some argued for a regime to share the wealth from continental shelf drilling.

In 1979, the chair of the Conference offered a compromise that provided for a continental shelf of at least 200 miles in breadth but whose maximum breadth could be much larger if the shelf met certain geomorphologic criteria. In exchange, states exploiting the shelf beyond 200 miles would have to share the resources to a small extent, and the waters above remain mostly beyond coastal state control. The compromise is reflected in the following provisions of UNCLOS:

United Nations Convention on the Law of the Sea

1833 U.N.T.S. 3 (1982)

Article 76
Definition of the Continental Shelf

1. The continental shelf of a coastal State comprises the sea-bed and subsoil of the submarine areas that extend beyond its territorial sea throughout the natural prolongation of its land territory to the outer edge of the continental margin, or to a distance of 200 nautical miles from the baselines from which the breadth of the territorial sea is measured [see p. 709, note 3 concerning baselines] where the outer edge of the continental margin does not extend up to that distance. . . .

3. The continental margin comprises the submerged prolongation of the land mass of the coastal State, and consists of the sea-bed and subsoil of the shelf, the slope and the rise. It does not include the deep ocean floor. . . .

4. [This provides a complex formula for determining the outer edge of the continental margin if it is more than 200 miles from the territorial sea's baselines.]

5. The fixed points comprising the line of the outer limits of the continental shelf on the sea-bed . . . either shall not

exceed 350 nautical miles from the baselines from which the
breadth of the territorial sea is measured or shall not exceed
100 nautical miles from the 2,500 metre isobath, which is a
line connecting the depth of 2,500 metres. . . .

8. Information on the limits of the continental shelf
beyond 200 nautical miles . . . shall be submitted by the
coastal State to the Commission on the Limits of the Continental Shelf [described in detail in an Annex to the Convention].
The Commission shall make recommendations to coastal States on
matters related to the establishment of the outer limits of
their continental shelf. The limits of the shelf established
by a coastal State on the basis of these recommendations shall
be final and binding.

Article 77
Rights of the coastal State over the continental shelf

1. The coastal State exercises over the continental shelf
sovereign rights for the purpose of exploring it and exploiting its natural resources.

2. The rights referred to in paragraph 1 are exclusive in
the sense that if the coastal State does not explore the continental shelf or exploit its natural resources, no one may
undertake these activities without the express consent of
the coastal State.

3. The rights of the coastal State over the continental
shelf do not depend on occupation, effective or notional, or
on any express proclamation.

4. The natural resources referred to in this Part consist of
the mineral and other non-living resources of the seabed and
subsoil together with living organisms belonging to sedentary
species. . . .

Article 78
Legal status of the superjacent waters and air space
and the rights and freedoms of other States

1. The rights of the coastal State over the continental
shelf do not affect the legal status of the superjacent waters
or of the air space above those waters.

2. The exercise of the rights of the coastal State over the
continental shelf must not infringe or result in any unjustifiable interference with navigation and other rights and freedoms of other States as provided for in this Convention. . . .

Article 82
Payments and contributions with respect to the
exploitation of the continental shelf beyond
200 nautical miles

1. The coastal State shall make payments or contributions in kind in respect of the exploitation of the non-living resources of the continental shelf beyond 200 nautical miles from the baselines from which the breadth of the territorial sea is measured.

2. [This article specifies a gradual payment scheme from 1 percent of production until it reaches 7 percent.]

4. The payments or contributions shall be made through the [International Sea-Bed] Authority [a standing body under UNCLOS, composed of all member states, charged principally with controlling access to deep seabed mining] which shall distribute them to States Parties to this Convention, on the basis of equitable sharing criteria, taking into account the interests and needs of developing States, particularly the least developed and the land-locked among them.

Notes and Questions

1. Why is the definition of the continental shelf in the 1982 Convention more expansive than that in the 1958 Convention? How does the 1982 Convention impose limits on a coastal state's ability to define the limits of its continental shelf?

2. How do the rights of coastal states differ with respect to the continental shelf and the EEZ? How would you explain this difference? Why would they agree to the compromise?

3. The UNCLOS provisions on the continental shelf, like those for the EEZ, grant the coastal states "sovereign rights" rather than "sovereignty." What is the practical effect of this difference?

4. In late 2001, the Russian Federation became the first state to submit information to the Commission on the Limits of the Continental Shelf established under Article 76. Russia's submission contained its views on the limits of its continental shelf in those areas beyond 200 miles from its baselines and included claims to the shelves in the Bering Sea, Barents Sea, Okhotsk Sea, and Arctic Ocean. The United States and four other states responded to the Russian submission, protesting that Russia included in its delimitation parts of the deep ocean floor of the Arctic Ocean, expressly excluded from the definition of the shelf in Article 76(3). Russia insisted that the relevant areas were part of the continental margin. In June 2002, the Commission rejected Russia's claims in the Arctic Ocean areas due to lack of scientific proof, asking it to resubmit data on those claims; the claims to the other areas were generally accepted, though the Commission asked Russia to confer with its neighbors (the United States, Norway, and Japan) over the precise delimitation. In 2004 and 2005, the Commission received submissions from Brazil, Australia, and Ireland. In light of Article 76(8), what sort of decisionmaking body is the Commission?

D. Norms for Dividing the Caspian's Continental Shelf?

The evolution between 1945 and 1982 of a legal regime governing the continental shelf that was, in essence, greatly favorable to coastal states put the spotlight on another issue: the possibility that neighboring states could lay claim to the same piece of the shelf. Adjacent states on a coastline might differ as to the direction that a boundary line should follow as it went from the land border out to sea; states opposite each other across a bay, sea, or other body of water would doubtless have different senses of the best location for a continental shelf boundary. Any comprehensive convention on the law of the sea would need to address these potential disputes.

Delimitation issues are critical to the Caspian and its coastal states. Despite the importance of the underwater landmass, Iran and the USSR never agreed upon a formal division of it. The USSR conducted drilling activities beyond the ten-mile fishing limit set forth in the 1940 treaty on the theory that it could exploit seabed areas adjacent to its shores. It did not share any of the proceeds with Iran, apparently without protest.* Iran instead drilled within the areas adjacent to its coastline.

As noted earlier, the Caspian is a landlocked body of water, and the Convention and its provisions on the shelf do not per se apply to the Caspian. Although the world has numerous such bodies (mostly termed lakes rather than seas), such as the Great Lakes (Canada and the United States), Lake Victoria (Kenya, Tanzania, and Uganda), Lake Titicaca (Bolivia and Peru), and Lake Geneva (France and Switzerland), their regulation and delimitation remain a matter of treaties between the coastal states as well as some principles of customary international law formulated at a very general level. (Most of these lakes do not have oil reserves.) Nonetheless, the debates over the proper criteria for delimitation of the shelf—and their ultimate resolution in the 1982 Convention—remain quite pertinent to the Caspian.

As a theoretical matter, the continental shelf of states adjacent to each other or facing each other across a body of water could be divided along a number of different criteria:

1. *Geography*: the shelf is divided in proportion to the length of the coastline of each state (what is known as the proportionality principle); or in some way related to the shape of the coastline(s) adjacent to it;
2. *Geomorphology*: the shelf is divided according to its (underwater) shape as a natural extension of the land mass;
3. *Unity of resources*: the shelf is divided in a way that would keep certain pools of natural resources together so that only one state would exploit each one;
4. *Economics*: the shelf is divided based on the economic resources within it or based on the economic capacity of the states to exploit it;
5. *History*: the shelf is divided based on historical patterns of exploitation.
6. *Distributive justice*: the shelf is divided based on the needs of the populations of coastal or other (e.g., landlocked or poor) states.

During the first UN Conference on the Law of the Sea, states negotiated the issue intensely and eventually agreed on the following formula:

---

*Brice M. Clagett, *Ownership of Seabed and Subsoil Resources in the Caspian Sea Under the Rules of International Law,* 1 Caspian Crossroads Magazine (1995).

Convention on the Continental Shelf

516 U.N.T.S. 205 (1958)

Article 6

1. Where the same continental shelf is adjacent to the territories of two or more States whose coasts are opposite each other, the boundary of the continental shelf appertaining to such States shall be determined by agreement between them. In the absence of agreement, and unless another boundary line is justified by special circumstances, the boundary is the median line, every point of which is equidistant from the nearest points of the baselines from which the breadth of the territorial sea of each State is measured.

2. Where the same continental shelf is adjacent to the territories of two adjacent States, the boundary of the continental shelf shall be determined by agreement between them. In the absence of agreement, and unless another boundary line is justified by special circumstances, the boundary shall be determined by application of the principle of equidistance from the nearest points of the baselines from which the breadth of the territorial sea of each State is measured.

The norm in Article 6 is known as the equidistance principle, a rule based on the shape of the coastline. The line is drawn such that each point on it is equidistant from the nearest point on the coastline. One critical result of this principle is that irregularities in the coastline will inure to the benefit of one or another state. The effects of this test became clear when the states of the North Sea attempted to divide up their continental shelf, which contains rich mineral deposits.

The North Sea touches the United Kingdom, Norway, Denmark, the Federal Republic of Germany, the Netherlands, and Belgium. The United Kingdom had delimited much of the shelf in separate agreements with Norway, Denmark, and the Netherlands. Germany and Denmark partially agreed on their bilateral boundary—line A-B on the map on p. 746 (from the ICJ judgment below)—in an agreement of June 9, 1965. Germany and the Netherlands partially agreed on their boundary—line C-D in a December 1, 1964, agreement. Denmark and the Netherlands agreed on March 31, 1966, on line E-F to divide the areas based on what they believed were their full boundaries with Germany—namely, lines B-E and D-E. Denmark and the Netherlands, both parties to the 1958 Convention, had drawn the lines between their coasts as well as between them and Germany based on the equidistance principle. Germany, which had signed but never ratified the Convention, protested the 1966 agreement. Germany insisted that it had never agreed to those lines with Denmark and the Netherlands and that the equidistance principle in the 1958 Convention did not bind it. Instead, it claimed that those borders should have been based on lines B-F and D-F, which reflected more equitably the length of Germany's coastline. The three states agreed to ask the ICJ for a ruling on the "principles and rules of international law" applicable to the division of the shelf among them.

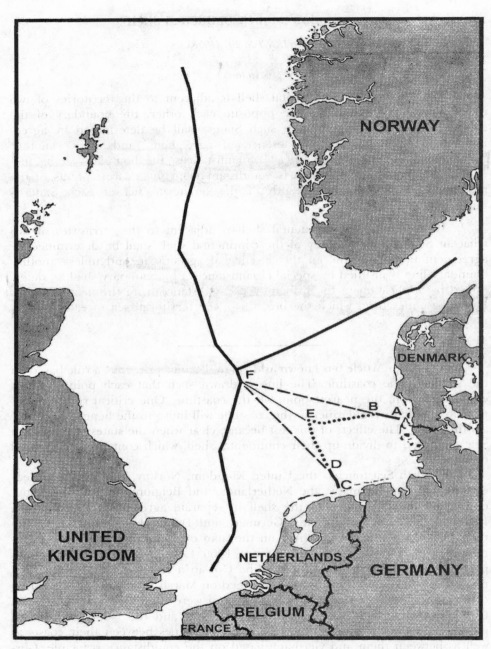

Map 3
(See paragraphs 5-9)

Carte 3
(Voir paragraphes 5-9)

The maps in the present Judgment were prepared on the basis of documents submitted to the Court by the Parties, and their sole purpose is to provide a visual illustration of the paragraphs of the Judgment which refer to them.

Les cartes jointes au présent arrêt ont été établies d'après les documents soumis à la Cour par les Parties et ont pour seul objet d'illustrer graphiquement les paragraphes de l'arrêt qui s'y réfèrent.

North Sea Continental Shelf Cases (Federal Republic of Germany/Denmark and Netherlands)

1969 I.C.J. 3 (Feb. 20)

8. [I]n the case of a concave or recessing coast such as that of the Federal Republic on the North Sea, the effect of the use of the equidistance method is to pull the line of the boundary inwards, in the direction of the concavity. Consequently, where two such lines are drawn at different points on a concave coast, they will, if the curvature is pronounced, inevitably meet at a relatively short distance from the coast, thus causing the continental shelf area they enclose, to take the form approximately of a triangle with its apex to seaward and, as it was put on behalf of the Federal Republic, "cutting off" the coastal State from the further areas of the continental shelf outside of and beyond this triangle. . . . In contrast to this, the effect of coastal projections, or of convex or outwardly curving coasts such as are, to a moderate extent, those of Denmark and the Netherlands, is to cause boundary lines drawn on an equidistance basis to leave the coast on divergent courses. . . . [See the Court's sketch below.]

37. It is maintained by Denmark and the Netherlands that the Federal Republic [of Germany], whatever its position may be in relation to the Geneva Convention, considered as such, is in any event bound to accept delimitation on an equidistance-special circumstances basis, because the use of this method is not in the nature of a merely conventional obligation, but is, or must now be regarded as involving, a rule that is part of the *corpus* of general international law;—and, like other rules of general or customary international law, is binding on the Federal Republic automatically and independently of any specific assent, direct or indirect, given by the latter. . . .

61. . . . Denmark and the Netherlands . . . stated that . . . although prior to the [1958] Conference, continental shelf law was only in the formative stage, and State practice lacked uniformity, yet "the process of the definition and consolidation of the emerging customary law took place through the work of the International Law Commission, the reaction of governments to that work and the proceedings of the Geneva Conference"; and this emerging customary law became "crystallized in the adoption of the Continental Shelf Convention by the Conference".

62. Whatever validity this contention may have in respect of at least certain parts of the Convention, the Court cannot accept it as regards the delimitation provision (Article 6), the relevant parts of which were adopted almost unchanged from the draft of the International Law Commission that formed the basis of discussion at the Conference. The status of the rule in the Convention therefore depends mainly on the processes that led the Commission to propose it . . . : [T]he principle of equidistance, as it now figures in Article 6 of the Convention, was proposed by the Commission with considerable hesitation, somewhat on an experimental basis, at most *de lege ferenda* [the law as desired], and not at all *de lege lata* [the law as it is] or as an emerging rule of customary international law. This is clearly not the sort of foundation on which Article 6 of the Convention could be said to have reflected or crystallized such a rule.

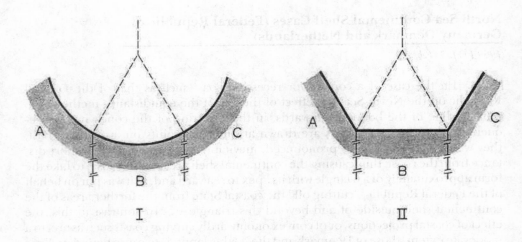

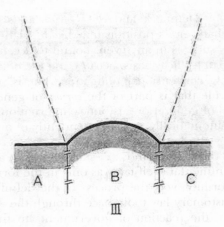

Sketches illustrating the geographical situations described in paragraph 8 of the Judgment

Croquis illustratifs des situations géographiques décrites au paragraphe 8 de l'arrêt

63. The foregoing conclusion receives significant confirmation from the fact that Article 6 is one of those in respect of which, under the reservations article of the Convention (Article 12) reservations may be made by any State on signing, ratifying or acceding,—for, speaking generally, it is a characteristic of purely conventional rules and obligations that, in regard to them, some faculty of making unilateral reservations may, within certain limits, be admitted;—whereas this cannot be so in the case of general or customary law rules and obligations which, by their very nature, must have equal force for all members of the international community, and cannot therefore be the subject of any right of unilateral exclusion exercisable at will by any one of them in its own favour. . . .

70. The Court must now proceed to the last stage in the argument put forward on behalf of Denmark and the Netherlands . . . to the effect that even if there was at

D3 Narguein alternative that it is customary law.

the date of the Geneva Convention no rule of customary international law in favour of the equidistance principle, and no such rule was crystallized in Article 6 of the Convention, nevertheless such a rule has come into being since the Convention, partly because of its own impact, partly on the basis of subsequent State practice,— and that this rule, being now a rule of customary international law binding on all States, including therefore the Federal Republic, should be declared applicable to the delimitation of the boundaries between the Parties' respective continental shelf areas in the North Sea. . . .

73. With respect to the other elements usually regarded as necessary before a conventional rule can be considered to have become a general rule of international law, it might be that, even without the passage of any considerable period of time, a very widespread and representative participation in the convention might suffice of itself, provided it included that of States whose interests were specially affected. In the present case however, the Court notes that, even if allowance is made for the existence of a number of States to whom participation in the Geneva Convention is not open, or which, by reason for instance of being land-locked States, would have no interest in becoming parties to it, the number of ratifications and accessions so far secured [this number was 37 as of the date of the judgment] is, though respectable, hardly sufficient. . . .

Not enough countries recognize it to be customary law

74. As regards the time element, the Court notes that it is over ten years since the Convention was signed, but that it is even now less than five since it came into force in June 1964, and that when the present proceedings were brought it was less than three years, while less than one had elapsed at the time when the respective negotiations between the Federal Republic and the other two Parties for a complete delimitation broke down on the question of the application of the equidistance principle. Although the passage of only a short period of time is not necessarily, or of itself, a bar to the formation of a new rule of customary international law on the basis of what was originally a purely conventional rule, an indispensable requirement would be that within the period in question, short though it might be, State practice, including that of States whose interests are specially affected, should have been both extensive and virtually uniform in the sense of the provision invoked;— and should moreover have occurred in such a way as to show a general recognition that a rule of law or legal obligation is involved.

Not customary law because it was not generally recognized as law

75. The Court must now consider whether State practice in the matter of continental shelf delimitation has, subsequent to the Geneva Convention, been of such a kind as to satisfy this requirement. . . . [S]ome fifteen cases have been cited in the course of the present proceedings, occurring mostly since the signature of the 1958 Geneva Convention, in which continental shelf boundaries have been delimited according to the equidistance principle—in the majority of the cases by agreement, in a few others unilaterally—or else the delimitation was foreshadowed but has not yet been carried out. . . .

76. To begin with, over half the States concerned, whether acting unilaterally or conjointly, were or shortly became parties to the Geneva Convention, and were therefore presumably, so far as they were concerned, acting actually or potentially in the application of the Convention. From their action no inference could legitimately be drawn as to the existence of a rule of customary international law in favour of the equidistance principle. As regards those States, on the other hand, which were not, and have not become parties to the Convention, the basis of their action can only be problematical and must remain entirely speculative. Clearly, they were not applying the Convention. But from that no inference could

ones that obeyed did so cause they were Part of Convention and

ones that didn't does not mean there is customi

justifiably be drawn that they believed themselves to be applying a mandatory rule of customary international law. There is not a shred of evidence that they did and . . . there is no lack of other reasons for using the equidistance method, so that acting, or agreeing to act in a certain way, does not of itself demonstrate anything of a juridical nature.

77. . . . [To create *opinio juris*, n]ot only must the acts concerned amount to a settled practice, but they must also be such, or be carried out in such a way, as to be evidence of a belief that this practice is rendered obligatory by the existence of a rule of law requiring it. The need for such a belief, i.e., the existence of a subjective element, is implicit in the very notion of the *opinio juris sive necessitatis*. The States concerned must therefore feel that they are conforming to what amounts to a legal obligation. The frequency, or even habitual character of the acts is not in itself enough. There are many international acts, e.g., in the field of ceremon[y] and protocol, which are performed almost invariably, but which are motivated only by considerations of courtesy, convenience or tradition, and not by any sense of legal duty. . . .

78. . . . [T]he position is simply that in certain cases—not a great number—the States concerned agreed to draw or did draw the boundaries concerned according to the principle of equidistance. There is no evidence that they so acted because they felt legally compelled to draw them in this way by reason of a rule of customary law obliging them to do so—especially considering that they might have been motivated by other obvious factors. . . .

Holding

81. The Court accordingly concludes that if the Geneva Convention was not in its origins or inception declaratory of a mandatory rule of customary international law enjoining the use of the equidistance principle for the delimitation of continental shelf areas between adjacent States, neither has its subsequent effect been constitutive of such a rule; and that State practice up-to-date has equally been insufficient for the purpose. . . .

85. [The Court then began its search for alternative governing principles:] [D]elimitation must be the object of agreement between the States concerned, and that . . . such agreement must be arrived at in accordance with equitable principles. . . . [Specifically,]

(a) the parties are under an obligation to enter into negotiations with a view to arriving at an agreement, and not merely to go through a formal process of negotiation as a sort of prior condition for the automatic application of a certain method of delimitation in the absence of agreement . . . ;

(b) the parties are under an obligation to act in such a way that, in the particular case, and taking all the circumstances into account, equitable principles are applied,—for this purpose the equidistance method can be used, but other methods exist and may be employed, alone or in combination, according to the areas involved;

(c) . . . the continental shelf of any State must be the natural prolongation of its land territory and must not encroach upon what is the natural prolongation of the territory of another State. . . .

88. The Court comes next to the rule of equity. . . . Whatever the legal reasoning of a court of justice, its decisions must by definition be just, and therefore in that sense equitable. Nevertheless, when mention is made of a court dispensing justice or declaring the law, what is meant is that the decision finds its objective justification in considerations lying not outside but within the rules, and in this field it is precisely a rule of law that calls for the application of equitable principles. . . .

89. It must next be observed that, in certain geographical circumstances which are quite frequently met with, the equidistance method, despite its known advantages, leads unquestionably to inequity, in [that the] slightest irregularity in a coastline is automatically magnified by the equidistance line. . . .

91. Equity does not necessarily imply equality. There can never be any question of completely refashioning nature, . . . [for example, by] rendering the situation of a State with an extensive coastline similar to that of a State with a restricted coastline. . . . [I]n the present case there are three States whose North Sea coastlines are in fact comparable in length and which, therefore, have been given broadly equal treatment by nature except that the configuration of one of the coastlines would, if the equidistance method is used, deny to one of these States treatment equal or comparable to that given the other two. . . . What is unacceptable in this instance is that a State should enjoy continental shelf rights considerably different from those of its neighbours merely because in the one case the coastline is roughly convex in form and in the other it is markedly concave, although those coastlines are comparable in length. . . .

93. . . . [T]here is no legal limit to the considerations which States may take account of for the purpose of making sure that they apply equitable procedures, and more often than not it is the balancing-up of all such considerations that will produce this result rather than reliance on one to the exclusion of all others. . . .

94. . . . Some [factors] are related to the geological, others to the geographical aspect of the situation. . . .

97. Another factor to be taken into consideration in the delimitation of areas of continental shelf as between adjacent States is the unity of any deposits. The natural resources of the subsoil of the sea in those parts which consist of continental shelf are the very object of the legal régime established subsequent to the Truman Proclamation. Yet it frequently occurs that the same deposit lies on both sides of the line dividing a continental shelf between two States. . . .

98. A final factor to be taken account of is the element of a reasonable degree of proportionality which a delimitation effected according to equitable principles ought to bring about between the extent of the continental shelf appertaining to the States concerned and the lengths of their respective coastlines. . . .

99. . . . [If application of these criteria leads to overlapping areas,] such a situation must be accepted as a given fact and resolved either by an agreed, or failing that by an equal division of the overlapping areas, or by agreements for joint exploitation, the latter solution appearing particularly appropriate when it is a question of preserving the unity of a deposit.

[The Court ruled, by 11-6, that in light of the inapplicability of the equidistance method, the following principles applied:]

(1) delimitation is to be effected by agreement in accordance with equitable principles, and taking account of all the relevant circumstances, in such a way as to leave as much as possible to each Party all those parts of the continental shelf that constitute a natural prolongation of its land territory into and under the sea, without encroachment on the natural prolongation of the land territory of the other;

(2) if, in the application of the preceding sub-paragraph, the delimitation leaves to the Parties areas that overlap, these are to be divided between them in agreed proportions or, failing agreement, equally, unless they decide on a régime of joint jurisdiction, use, or exploitation for the zones of overlap or any part of them;

. . . [I]n the course of the negotiations, the factors to be taken into account are to include:

(1) the general configuration of the coasts of the Parties . . . ;

(2) so far as known or readily ascertainable, the physical and geological structure, and natural resources, of the continental shelf areas involved;

(3) the element of a reasonable degree of proportionality . . . between the extent of the continental shelf areas appertaining to the coastal State and the length of its coast measured in the general direction of the coastline. . . .

In dissent, Judge Kotaro Tanaka wrote:

Reference to the equitable principle is nothing else but begging the question. . . . [T]he factors which may be taken into consideration to carry out the equitable principle are of diverse nature and susceptible of different evaluations. Consequently, it appears extremely doubtful whether the negotiations could be expected to achieve a successful result, and more likely that they would engender new complications and chaos.

It may be said that the Court's answer amounts to the suggestion to the Parties that they settle their dispute by negotiations according to *ex aequo et bono* [any right and proper factors] without any indication as to what are the "principles and rules of international law", namely juridical principles and rules vested with obligatory power rather than considerations of expediency—factors or criteria—which are not incorporated in the legal norm and about which the Parties did not request an answer. . . .

The important matter in connection with the present cases is that the Parties should have a guarantee of being able to terminate the possibly endless repetition of detailed negotiations by the final application of the equidistance principle. Another important matter should be that, the Court by according the equidistance principle the status of a world law would make a contribution to the progressive development of international law.

Philip Jessup, the U.S. national on the Court, wrote a separate opinion in which he stated:

Although . . . the Parties in this case chose to deal obliquely in their pleadings with the actuality of their basic interests in the continental shelf of the North Sea, it is of course obvious that the reason why they are particularly concerned with the delimitation of their respective portions is the known or probable existence of deposits of oil and gas in that seabed. [After citing the pleadings of the sides, he noted:] . . . [T]he problem of the exploitation of the oil and gas resources of the continental shelf of the North Sea was in the front of the minds of the Parties but that none of them was prepared to base its case squarely on consideration of this factor, preferring to argue on other legal principles which are sometimes advanced with almost academic detachment from realities.

Judge Jessup then urged the parties to consider explicitly in their negotiations the possibility of joint ownership and exploitation of parts of the continental shelf as a means of most efficiently mining the areas.

In the end, Germany concluded two separate agreements with the Netherlands and Denmark on January 28, 1971, to complete the delimitation of their boundary. Both lines were more generous to Germany than would have been the case under the equidistance principle, although Germany did agree to a line that placed some existing Danish licensees in Denmark's continental shelf.

At the negotiations for the 1982 Law of the Sea Convention, states again argued over the appropriate principles for delimitation. Not surprisingly, most states offered self-serving positions. Those benefiting from the equidistance method of the 1958 Convention called for repeating it in the new treaty; others favored the equitable principles adopted in the *North Sea Continental Shelf Cases* or even a stronger version emphasizing the special circumstances of geographically disadvantaged states. In the end, at the last working session of the Conference, its chairman, Tommy Koh of Singapore, proposed a compromise that proved acceptable to the participants. It became Article 83 of the Convention.

Article 83
Delimitation of the continental shelf between States with opposite or adjacent coasts

1. The delimitation of the continental shelf between States with opposite or adjacent coasts shall be effected by agreement on the basis of international law, as referred to in Article 38 of the Statute of the International Court of Justice, in order to achieve an equitable solution.

2. If no agreement can be reached within a reasonable period of time, the States concerned shall resort to the procedures provided for in Part XV [setting up institutions for nonbinding and binding settlement of disputes].

3. Pending agreement as provided for in paragraph 1, the States concerned, in a spirit of understanding and cooperation, shall make every effort to enter into provisional arrangements of a practical nature and, during this transitional period, not to jeopardize or hamper the reaching of the final agreement. Such arrangements shall be without prejudice to the final delimitation. . . .

The Conference participants adopted the same provision regarding the delimitation of the EEZ between states with opposite or adjacent coasts (Art. 74). As for the delimitation of the territorial sea between states with opposite or adjacent coasts, Article 15 of the Convention adopts a different rule—namely, that "neither of the two States is entitled, failing agreement between them to the contrary, to extend its territorial sea beyond the median line [except] where it is necessary by reason of historic title or other special circumstances to delimit the territorial seas of the two States in a way which is at variance therewith."

Notes and Questions

1. How could Iran, with its concave coast along the Caspian, use the *North Sea Continental Shelf Cases* for its benefit?

2. Why do you think the Court was unwilling to propose more definite criteria for the division of the continental shelf? Is Judge Tanaka correct in describing the majority's guidance as "self-evident but . . . unable to furnish any concrete criteria for delimitation"?

3. Why were the parties to the North Sea case avoiding discussion of oil exploitation and instead, in Judge Jessup's words, arguing "on other legal principles which are sometimes advanced with almost academic detachment from realities"? How important a role should economic concerns play compared to geographic realities in delimiting the shelf?

4. Does the 1982 Convention provide a norm that is more useful for governments than that offered by the ICJ? Recall the discussion in Chapter 2 regarding the ways in which international norms might vary in hardness or softness. How hard is the law in Article 83? Why do you think states could agree on a more specific norm regarding division of the territorial seas of states with adjacent or opposite coasts than they could for the division of their continental shelves or EEZs?

5. The notion of equity referred to in the *North Sea Continental Shelf Cases* and in Article 83(1) has eluded any detailed definition in international law. Scholars have regarded it as a general principle of law under Article 38 of the ICJ Statute, and it clearly implies some idea of fairness in the final outcome. In *Case Concerning the Continental Shelf* (Libya/Malta), 1985 I.C.J. 13, 39-40, the Court stated:

> 45. . . . [T]he delimitation of a continental shelf boundary must be effected by the application of equitable principles in all the relevant circumstances in order to achieve an equitable result. The Court did of course remark in its 1982 Judgment [delimiting the continental shelf between Libya and Tunisia] that this terminology . . . "is not entirely satisfactory because it employs the term equitable to characterize both the result to be achieved and the means to be applied to reach this result." . . . It is however the goal—the equitable result—and not the means used to achieve it, that must be the primary element in this duality of characterization. . . .
>
> 46. . . . That equitable principles are expressed in terms of general application, is immediately apparent from a glance at some well-known examples: the principle that there is to be no question of refashioning geography, or compensating for the inequalities of nature; the related principle of non-encroachment by one party on the natural prolongation of the other, which is no more than the negative expression of the positive rule that the coastal State enjoys sovereign rights over the continental shelf off its coasts to the full extent authorized by international law in the relevant circumstances; the principle of respect due to all such relevant circumstances; the principle that although all States are equal before the law and are entitled to equal treatment, 'equity does not necessarily imply equality' (I.C.J. Reports 1969, p. 49, para. 91), nor does it seek to make equal what nature has made unequal; and the principle that there can be no question of distributive justice.

Yet Rosalyn Higgins (now an ICJ judge) has condemned the use of equity by the ICJ, including its use in the *Libya/Malta* case: "Because judicial decision-making inevitably entails choices, and because thinness of applicable norms allows a certain freedom in that choice, it is important to make the choices to achieve justifiable and desired ends. But those ends must be articulated, and cannot be hidden behind the term 'equitable result.' . . ." Rosalyn Higgins, Problems and Process: International Law and How We Use It 227 (1994). Others, including her British predecessor on the ICJ, Robert Jennings, have expressed concern that it can become merely an excuse for decisions where the judges have made up their minds as to a fair dividing line before considering the law. Do you agree that equity's susceptibility to such abuse renders it an inappropriate factor in dividing the continental shelf (or the EEZ)? Does Article 83(1) now mean that states regard equity as a principle of *jus cogens* in the area of maritime delimitation? Could states voluntarily conclude agreements that are not equitable?

6. Many disputes over the continental shelf derive from the presence of islands off a state's shore. The Convention's provisions on islands (Article 121) state that

> the territorial sea, . . . the exclusive economic zone and the continental shelf of an island are determined in accordance with the provisions of this Convention applicable to other land territory. . . . Rocks which cannot sustain human habitation or economic life of their own shall have no exclusive economic zone or continental shelf.

E. The Caspian Today

Both Iran and the Soviet Union signed the 1982 Convention on the Law of the Sea. Iran, however, has still not ratified it. As for the Soviet Union, as noted earlier, its dissolution in 1992 created three new parties to the dispute (in addition to Russia)-Azerbaijan, Kazakhstan, and Turkmenistan. Although Russia became a party to the Convention in 1997, the other three successor states remain nonparties.

Although the Convention itself does not apply to the Caspian, the parties to the Caspian Sea dispute could choose to apply its provisions that contemplate division of overlapping shelves. In this respect the parties have offered different and at times vague positions over time. Azerbaijan has advocated division of the Sea (water and seabed) into national sectors, much like the United States and Canada have partitioned the Great Lakes. At the same time, it has called for respecting the (somewhat unclear) lines that the USSR drew in 1970 to divide up the republics' portions of the Sea, lines that give Azerbaijan the valuable Kyapaz oil field. (See Chapter 3 for a discussion of *uti possidetis*.) Russia has changed its position over time. It has at times called for equal access by the five states to the resources beyond ten miles from shore, but more recently has advocated division of the seabed along median lines adjusted for equitable and historical factors. The Russian position calls for the waters themselves to remain open to all five states. Turkmenistan's position has also changed. In 1997, its President endorsed a division along Soviet-era lines pending a final status agreement; lately, Turkmenistan has contested some of Azerbaijan's claims to the Sea.

These positions have formed the basis for some legal and political commitments that may or may not correspond to the current preferences of the states. Kazakhstan and Azerbaijan, and Kazakhstan and Turkmenistan, agreed in 1997 to respect Soviet-era lines; Russia and Kazakhstan concluded a bilateral agreement in 1998 dividing their areas of the seabed along median lines; the Russian and Azerbaijani Presidents committed themselves to the same policy in 2001; and Turkmenistan agreed in principle with Azerbaijan in 1998 to divide their areas along median lines, but they never finalized an agreement due to a difference over the Kyapaz field, which both claimed.

Iran, however, to date seems to be moving in a different direction. It has called for equal division of the water and seabed among the states (20 percent each) or, alternatively, a condominium approach whereby the Caspian would be developed jointly. It has protested exploration in parts of the Sea that it regards as reserved for Iran. Iran's insistence on its approach has been more than diplomatic. In July 2001, when the *Geofizik-3*, a research vessel leased by the Azerbaijani government to British Petroleum (BP), was exploring for oil in the Alov field, 60 miles from Iranian territorial waters but within the portion of the Caspian that Iran claims, Iranian warplanes buzzed the ship and Iranian naval vessels forced it at gunpoint to retreat. Despite protests by Azerbaijan, Turkey, and the United States over the incident, Iran reportedly dispatched jets into Azerbaijan's air space. A leading adviser to Azerbaijan's President stated that "Iran demands that the Caspian is only for the five states, not Western companies or governments. . . . [Iranian diplomats] put a finger on the map and said 'This is my part' ." Douglas Frantz, *Iran and Azerbaijan Argue Over Caspian's Riches*, N.Y. Times, Aug. 30, 2001, at A4. BP, with significant operations in Iran, agreed to suspend further exploration in the disputed area.

The condominium approach has received endorsement from the ICJ as a solution to some maritime disputes. In a conflict among Honduras, Nicaragua, and El Salvador over the Gulf of Fonseca in the Pacific Ocean, the Court decided in 1992 that all areas beyond three miles from the shore would continue to be held in common by the three states. At the same time, the ICJ put great weight on the states' historic treatment of the Gulf as a common area (including, when those three states were united in the early nineteenth century as the Federal Republic of Central America, the lack of any administrative divisions within the Gulf). The presence of some USSR-era administrative lines in the Caspian Sea might make this precedent somewhat less on point.

Two additional factors have further complicated the issue. First, the coastal states have already concluded numerous agreements with Western oil companies for exploitation of areas of the Caspian Sea at a considerable distance from their coast. In 1993, Kazakhstan reached a deal with Mobil, Shell, Total, Agip, BP, and others to create the Caspishelf Consortium to explore Kazakhstan's offshore deposits. In 1994 Azerbaijan concluded an $8 billion deal with Amoco, BP, Pennzoil, Unocal, Lukoil (Russia), Statoil (Norway), and others on the development of three large fields in the Caspian.

Second, whatever oil is produced in or around the Caspian must be transported to markets across several states. Older pipelines from the former Soviet republics all went through Russia to the Black Sea port of Novorosiisk, and additional pipelines to that port are under construction. In recent years, numerous other routes have been proposed, mostly over land. Some of these proposals face political obstacles, such as instability in Georgia and Chechnya. Others have moved forward, such as the pipeline delivering oil from Azerbaijan's fields on the Caspian to Turkey via Georgia. It avoids Russia, Iran, and the environmentally sensitive Bosphorous and Dardanelles straits in Turkey that link the Black and Mediterranean Seas.

As for routes involving the Caspian Sea, some oil is currently shipped via tanker across the Caspian from Kazakhstan and Turkmenistan to Baku, Azerbaijan. In 1998 Shell, Chevron, and Mobil agreed to conduct a feasibility study for Kazakhstan to build oil and gas pipelines under the Caspian from Kazakhstan to Baku. Iran has opposed such a pipeline (as well as the pipeline to Turkey), claiming environmental concerns, though analysts have speculated that Iran wants to delay a Caspian pipeline until the United States drops its opposition to American oil companies participating in a shorter pipeline that would transit Iran. As of 2006 the United States remained wary of approving such a pipeline.

In November 2003, the five Caspian states signed a Caspian environmental cooperation treaty that some believe may be a harbinger of a broader settlement of the shelf issue. A special working group of representatives of the five states continued meeting through 2006 to discuss the future of the sea. Despite some talk among diplomats of concluding a convention on the sea's status, the parties achieved no major breakthroughs on a comprehensive agreement.

Notes and Questions

1. Given the existing regime on the law of the sea and the situations of the parties, which policy seems most promising for the Caspian Sea—division into sectors or joint development along a condominium approach? Should it matter that a law and economics approach to this issue would generally consider the condominium approach inefficient?

2. Does the Iranian proposal for a 20 percent share of the seabed address the issue of which 20 percent each state would have? How would states negotiate this issue?

3. If the parties were to negotiate a division into sectors, should they follow any USSR-era lines according to the principle of *uti possidetis*? What if those lines differ from median lines? Consider the following two proposals for the Caspian offered by two American international lawyers:

> While states are free to agree on any boundary they wish, the overwhelming majority of treaties that delimit boundaries in lakes or inland seas have adopted the median/equidistance line between the opposite shores, occasionally modified to take account of some historic or other special circumstance. . . . [In the case of the Caspian, a] court would draw equidistance lines between all the littoral states and would regard those lines as the tentative boundaries. It would then test the tentative boundaries by conducting a proportionality study. If the study shows that the tentative boundaries result in an adequate degree of proportionality, the court would adopt the tentative boundaries as its decision, subject to considering whether there are any circumstances that require modifications. [The author showed that such lines would divide the sea in rough proportion to the length of the coastline.]
>
> The court would inquire whether the history of the area establishes any historic rights, titles or de facto boundaries that require modification of the tentative boundaries. Such a situation does exist in the Caspian, as noted above. In the former USSR, each Soviet republic was allocated an adjacent sector to administer, including the exploration and development of natural resources. Kazakstan, Azerbaijan and Turkmenistan, at least, have up to now respected these historic de facto delimitations in the conduct of their exploration and production activities. A court would conclude that de facto boundaries exist with reference to these historic and traditional administrative areas of responsibility; that the administrative internal boundaries were "transformed into international frontiers" on the dissolution of the USSR, and that those boundaries should be respected. . . .
>
> Minor adjustments of the pure equidistance line should be made, both to respect the de facto boundaries and for practical reasons, such as to avoid splitting a single oil field between two states with the resulting difficulties of administration.

Brice M. Clagett, *Ownership of Seabed and Subsoil Resources in the Caspian Sea Under the Rules of International Law*, 1 Caspian Crossroads (Fall 1995).

> [N]otwithstanding assertions by some publicists that equidistance is the rule of division particularly between opposite coasts, the practice of states with respect to the division of

lakes indicates no consistent use of equidistance. It is used most often, but not consistently, between opposite coasts, and even then is often simplified and adjusted to form long, straight lines.

Given the substantial size of the Caspian Sea, it would appear that some of the problems with strict equidistance that arise in maritime delimitation in semi-enclosed seas [like the North Sea—namely, the problem of convexity and concavity, discussed above] could arise there as well. This does not mean equidistance is not appropriate in many or even all circumstances. But it does mean that a prior insistence on equidistance without considering its effects would run counter to the vast body of learning and jurisprudence that has developed on the question of delimitation in the last quarter century. From this perspective, at least, it makes sense to apply the underlying principles in the way they might be applied in a semi-enclosed marine sea.

Perhaps more importantly, the governments concerned should consider carefully for what purposes partition is necessary or desirable at any given time. If, for example, a regime of free navigation and joint regulation of fishing are contemplated, then it could be useful to limit discussion of delimitation to other specific uses for which it is immediately relevant, such as development of hydrocarbon and mineral deposits. . . .

With respect to hydrocarbon and mineral deposits, partition would seem to be a sensible result (assuming communications and environmental concerns can be accommodated). It is supported by overwhelming state practice. This is true even in the Mediterranean Sea, where most coastal states exercise partitioned continental shelf jurisdiction over the seabed and subsoil, but have refrained from declaring or partitioning exclusive economic zones in the water column beyond the territorial sea.

Bernard H. Oxman, *Caspian Sea or Lake: What Difference Does It Make?*, 1 Caspian Crossroads (Winter 1996).

4. Several surveys of bilateral maritime boundary agreements found that geographical factors predominate over geophysical ones in delimiting maritime boundaries. As for the geographical principles used, the surveys found that equidistance remains the clearly preferred method where the opposite or adjacent coasts have comparable shape and length, but that in other cases, nonequidistance methods are more common. *See* Prosper Weil, *Geographic Considerations in Maritime Delimitation*, and Keith Highet, *The Use of Geophysical Factors in the Delimitation of Maritime Boundaries*, *in* 1 International Maritime Boundaries 126-127, 194-195 (Jonathan I. Charney & Lewis M. Alexander eds., 1993).

F. Note on the Deep Seabed Mining Regime of the 1982 Law of the Sea Convention

Most of the world's oceans lie well beyond the 200-mile EEZ or the end of the continental shelf. In these areas far from a coastal state's immediate interests, the regime of the high seas offers equal rights for all states. The deep seabed contains vast mineral wealth, though the fantastic depths at which it is located has made economic exploitation all but impossible. Over the last 50 years, governmental attention has been focused on manganese nodules, which sit at depths of 3000-6000 meters, principally in the Atlantic and Pacific. Governments saw strategic significance to the manganese; business saw a chance to make large profits; and developing states saw an opportunity to share in the income from exploiting a new resource. After several years of discussion within the UN, in 1970, the General Assembly adopted a landmark resolution that declared the deep seabed "beyond the limits of national jurisdiction" and "the common heritage of mankind"; stated that no state shall claim sovereignty over it; and called for an "international régime" to be established under which exploitation would be "carried out for the benefit of mankind as a whole," with "equitable sharing" of benefits, in particular to benefit developing states.

When the Third UN Conference on the Law of the Sea convened in 1973, developing states favored the creation of an International Seabed Authority to have exclusive rights to seabed exploration and exploitation, while industrialized nations wanted the Authority to give licenses to states and private companies. Negotiations through the late 1970s led to a narrowing of differences and general agreement on a plan under which both mining states and their nationals, as well as the Authority—through a mining arm called the Enterprise—would conduct operations. Nonetheless, the North and South differed on numerous issues, notably mandatory technology transfer from companies to the Authority, the approval process for licenses, fees to be paid to the Authority, and production quotas. When the Reagan Administration assumed power in Washington in 1981, it reviewed U.S. policy on UNCLOS and announced it would seek major changes to the seabed mining regime. In particular, the United States complained that the treaty draft gave the Authority too much monopoly power and set up decision-making structures and procedures for the Authority that did not afford enough power to the developed states—especially the United States—who would be investing in the mining. During the last round of UNCLOS talks, in part due to clumsy diplomacy by the United States, attempts at compromise failed, and the United States voted against the final text of UNCLOS in 1982. Other industrialized states, including the United Kingdom, Germany, and Japan, also opposed the mining regime, resulting in a convention regime that did not have the support of key states that would be engaging in mining. Indeed, by 1990, fewer than 40 states had ratified UNCLOS, all but two of which (Iceland and Cyprus) were developing nations.

In the years immediately after UNCLOS, the United States spoke publicly about the possibility of an alternative deep seabed mining regime to that in UNCLOS. It worked with other Western states whose companies were interested in mining the deep seabed; in 1984, it agreed with them and their companies to resolve overlapping claims to one particularly dense area of nodules between Hawaii and Baja California. Representatives of those states that were UNCLOS signatories also worked to prevent the Authority's preparatory commission (of which they were members by virtue of being UNCLOS signatories) from registering with the Authority a plan by the Soviet Union to exploit part of that site, which would have given the USSR special rights once the Convention entered into force. More negotiations inside and outside the preparatory commission followed, and by 1987, the Western governments and companies had resolved their competing claims with the Soviet Union.

Despite the flurry of activity to preserve their rights for the time when UNCLOS would come into force, neither the Authority nor any of the companies or governments were ever convinced that seabed mining was economically attractive. Indeed, during the 1980s, no mining project advanced beyond the planning stage. The low prices for metals on the world commodities market contributed to the lack of interest. The developing states sensed that the seabed mining regime would not function effectively without an infusion of capital from major industrial states, none of which had ratified the Convention. This changed perspective from the South accompanied a reduction of North-South ideological tensions in the late 1980s due to the waning of the Cold War, and the South's retreat from its agenda for a "New International Economic Order," as it became increasingly interested in investment from the North (see Chapters 2 and 11).

But Northern states were also increasingly uncomfortable with the status quo. Despite the lack of ratifications from industrialized countries, by the early 1990s, the number of states that had ratified the Convention was approaching the 60 required for the treaty to enter into force. Although the United States and others claimed that much of the treaty was customary international law, they saw a clear advantage in treaty-based rules and thus in reaching some compromise that would allow for broad adherence to UNCLOS. In 1990, the UN Secretary-General convened a series of meetings on modifying the seabed regime of the Convention. After the Clinton Administration took office in 1993, the United States assumed a leading role in the UN talks. Barely a year later, in July 1994, the parties had achieved a solution—a new "Agreement Relating to the Implementation of Part XI of the United Nations Convention on the Law of the Sea of 10 December 1982." Adopted by the General Assembly and immediately signed by the United States and other industrialized states, the agreement, despite its bland title, represents a de facto amendment of UNCLOS; it radically restructures the Authority to give the United States a veto over key decisions of the authority and a veto over other decisions if two other industrialized countries agree; it also ends production quotas and mandatory technology transfers and emphasizes free market principles.

In 1994, President Clinton submitted UNCLOS, along with the 1994 Agreement, to the Senate for advice and consent to ratification. Since that time, the treaty has languished in the Senate, though the Senate Foreign Relations Committee unanimously reported it out in 2004. The Bush Administration, with the backing of the U.S. military, urged the Senate to give its consent to ratification; the treaty also had the clear support of the American oil industry, which sought U.S. participation in the Commission on the Limits of the Continental Shelf. But some senators still believed the treaty does not sufficiently protect U.S. interests, and as of 2006, the United States was not a party to UNCLOS. As a result of its non-party status, the United States cannot invoke the compulsory dispute settlement process, and may not nominate or vote on members of the ITLOS or the Commission on the Limits of the Continental Shelf, nor serve as a member of the International Seabed Authority.

The International Seabed Authority, based in Kingston, Jamaica, is a functioning international institution. It began its work in November 1994, when UNCLOS and the 1994 Agreement both entered into force. The ISA consists of an Assembly of all parties to UNCLOS, a 36-member Council that drafts substantive rules and issues licenses, and a Secretariat. In July 2000, it adopted by consensus a set of detailed rules regarding mining for manganese nodules—effectively a sui generis international mining code. Included were standard form exploration contracts and exploitation contracts. With these regulations completed, in March 2001 the Authority concluded exploration contracts with seven pioneer investors (each of which had to pay a $250,000 application fee)—France, Japan, Russia, and India, as well as China, Korea, and an Eastern European consortium—granting them exclusive rights to explore certain designated areas for 15 years.

11

Protecting the International Environment

International environmental problems have moved to the center of the international legal and political agenda over the past four decades. Ozone depletion, species loss, deforestation, climate change, and other environmental issues have captured the attention of policy makers and the public. In response, states have negotiated hundreds of international environmental agreements and have developed a sophisticated legal regime.

International environmental efforts, however, started much earlier. Indeed, the world's earliest recorded treaty memorializes the resolution of a dispute over water resources between the Mesopotamian city states of Lagash and Umma in approximately 3100 B.C. Many early efforts to address environmental issues, like the Lagash-Umma treaty, were responses to particular events or incidents, and through the eighteenth century the creation of international environmental law was ad hoc and sporadic. In the mid-nineteenth and early twentieth centuries, states entered into environmental treaties with greater frequency, including bilateral and regional treaties to control the overexploitation of fisheries and to protect valuable land species, such as the migratory birds protected by the treaty discussed in *Missouri v. Holland* in Chapter 5.

A second stage in the development of international environmental law began in the 1930s and 1940s, as states began to enter into broader treaties that protected wildlife, plants, or habitat generally, rather than individual species. In addition, international bodies at the global and regional levels began to address environmental issues during this period. For example, in October 1948, 18 states, 7 international organizations, and 107 national organizations established the International Union for the Conservation of Nature (IUCN), to encourage the ecologically sustainable use of natural resources. Over the years, IUCN, now also called the World Conservation Union, has been extremely active in treaty preparation—it co-drafted the World Heritage Convention and contributed to the adoption of the Convention on International Trade in Endangered Species (CITES)—and treaty implementation—it prepares official reports on wildlife trade for the CITES Secretariat. IUCN illustrates the critical role that non-state actors have assumed in international efforts to protect the environment.

Finally, during this period an important international arbitral award was rendered. The *Trail Smelter* arbitration between the United States and Canada arose out of damage caused in the state of Washington by sulphur dioxide emissions from a Canadian-owned smelter plant located in Trail, British Columbia, seven miles from the border. After unsuccessful negotiations, in 1935 the parties agreed to submit the matter to an arbitral tribunal and instructed the tribunal to "apply the law and practice followed in dealing with cognate questions in the United States of America as well as International Law and Practice." The arbitral tribunal declared that:

> under the principles of international law . . . no State has the right to use or permit the use of its territory in such a manner as to cause injury by fumes in or to the territory of another or the properties or persons therein, when the case is of serious consequence and the injury is established by clear and convincing evidence.

The arbitral tribunal ordered Canada to pay compensation for past pollution damage and created a complex regime to govern the operation of the smelter to minimize damage in Washington in the future. While *Trail Smelter* is frequently cited in support of a customary duty to prevent transboundary pollution, a great amount of transboundary pollution occurs every day.

International environmental law's modern era began in 1972, when 113 states gathered in Stockholm for the United Nations Conference on the Human Environment. At Stockholm states negotiated a Declaration on the Human Environment (the Stockholm Declaration) and adopted a proposal that eventually led to the creation of a new UN body, the United Nations Environment Programme (UNEP). The conference also reaffirmed the fundamental principle that one state should not cause environmental damage to another. Principle 21 of the Stockholm Declaration provides that:

> States have, in accordance with the Charter of the United Nations and the principles of international law, the sovereign right to exploit their own resources pursuant to their own environmental policies, and the responsibility to ensure that activities within their jurisdiction or control do not cause damage to the environment of other States or of areas beyond the limits of national jurisdiction.

More broadly, the Stockholm Conference signaled recognition that international environmental problems constitute a distinct area of concern and that international environmental law is a distinct branch of international law. Thereafter, international environmental law making accelerated greatly as states entered into several hundred environmental treaties between the Stockholm Conference and the 1992 United Nations Conference on Environment and Development (the Earth Summit), which itself produced a number of important international instruments.

Thus, contemporary international environmental law consists of a dense regime of treaties, custom, and soft law covering a variety of different topics. These legal norms address a diverse range of environmental media and issues, including the atmosphere, oceans and seas, freshwater resources, wildlife and biodiversity, habitat protection, hazardous activities and wastes, industrial waste, and the polar regions. In many of these issue areas, policy makers attempt to balance the protection of human health and environmental resources with other policy goals, such as economic development. One concept that attempts to bridge these potentially conflicting goals is that of "sustainable development," understood as development that meets the needs of present generations without compromising the ability of future generations to meet their own needs. While many treaties acknowledge the goal of sustainable development, this concept remains politically controversial, because many developing states insist that sustained economic growth must precede efforts to protect the environment.

Contemporary international environmental law is also marked by innovative developments in the scope, nature, and processes of law making. For example, contemporary treaties tend to focus on the conservation of entire ecosystems rather than the preservation of enumerated species, and on the preservation of global commons areas that are outside the jurisdiction of any particular state, such as the atmosphere, rather than transboundary resources. They also increasingly include provisions that restrain activities within national borders. Modern treaties also focus on preventive or precautionary approaches to protect the global environment rather than on liability for transboundary harm. Finally, contemporary efforts frequently implicate other areas of international regulation, such as international trade, intellectual property, and human rights. Thus Chapter 10, on the law of the sea, and Chapter 12, on international economic law, both examine international environmental issues. The interplay of these issues with other international legal issues raises difficult questions about the hierarchical relationships among various bodies of international law, and about whether and how environmental issues can be addressed in an integrated manner with other international legal issues.

In the problems that follow, we shall see how many of the more challenging contemporary international environmental problems are considerably more complex than the bilateral pollution problem at issue in *Trail Smelter*, as well as a number of the innovative legislative, regulatory, and institutional mechanisms that states have developed to address these problems. In the first problem, we examine the development of the law of international watercourses through a study of conflicts arising over the use of the Nile waters. In the second problem, we explore the innovative approaches states used to address the problem of ozone depletion—and the unanticipated problems that arose when states successfully regulated ozone-depleting substances. In the third problem, we examine efforts to address climate change.

Considered together, these sections explore international efforts in two different media (air and water); the strategies used to address both transboundary and global commons problems; approaches to both pollution and the allocation of shared natural resources; and the political dynamics at play in South-South, North-North, and North-South conflicts.

I. INTERNATIONAL WATERS: RESOLVING CONFLICT OVER THE NILE

Fresh water is essential for human life as well as for economic growth and development. It is equally critical for the healthy functioning of the natural systems upon which human civilization is built. Although water covers more than 70 percent of the earth's surface, this apparent abundance is misleading. Only 2.5 percent of all water on earth is fresh water; the rest is salt water. The vast majority of fresh water is frozen in the icecaps of Antarctica and Greenland, and most of the remainder is present as soil moisture or lies inaccessible in deep underground aquifers. As a result, less than 1 percent of the world's fresh water—or about 0.007 percent of all water on earth—is readily accessible for direct human use.

These limited resources are under increasing stress. Between 1900 and 1995, humanity's use of global water resources increased by over six times, more than double the rate of population growth. At the same time, water pollution—including untreated sewage, chemical discharges, and agricultural runoff—increased significantly. In one area of the world after another, the type and amount of wastes discharged have overwhelmed nature's capacity to break them down into less harmful elements. As a result, about one-third of the world's population lives in countries that are experiencing moderate to high water scarcity. By 2025 as much as two-thirds of the world's population may face water scarcity.

Water scarcity—like scarcity of other resources—can give rise to conflict. Since nearly 300 of the world's rivers are shared by more than one nation, conflicts over freshwater resources often have an international dimension. The Problem that follows, concerning competing demands on the waters of the Nile, is designed to explore the adequacy of international legal responses to contemporary water conflicts. As you read these materials, consider whether each Nile state is free to use Nile waters in its territory in whatever way it sees fit, and whether Nile states have rights or interests in water projects in other Nile states. Consider also how international law should resolve conflicting claims to the use of freshwater resources, and whether there is—or should be—an international legal obligation on Nile states to apportion the Nile's waters equitably.

A. The Problem

The Nile is the world's longest river, stretching over 4,000 miles from its source in the mountains of Burundi to the waters of the Mediterranean Sea. The Nile is formed by three tributaries, the White Nile, the Blue Nile, and the Atbara. As shown on the map below, the White Nile starts in Burundi, passes through Lake Victoria, and flows into southern Sudan. The Blue Nile, which contains over half of the Nile's waters, has its source near Lake Tana in Ethiopia and flows into Sudan. There, near Khartoum, the White and Blue Niles meet. These waters then meet the Atbara just north of Khartoum. The river then flows through Lake Nassar and the Aswan Dam before flowing into the Mediterranean.

For millenia, Nile Valley inhabitants used traditional flood irrigation for agricultural purposes. This system, however, permits growth of only one crop per year. In the early 1900s—at a time when the British controlled much of the Nile Valley—economic pressures on Egypt and Sudan prompted the construction of waterworks to permit perennial irrigation. These pressures drove an intensive period of water development on the Nile—and gave rise to conflicts between proponents of Egyptian, Sudanese, and British interests.[*]

In 1925 a Nile Waters Commission was formed, which estimated that Egypt needed 58 billion cubic meters (bcm) of Nile waters per year and that all Sudanese needs could be met through the Blue Nile alone. These recommendations laid the groundwork for the 1929 Nile Waters Agreement between the United Kingdom (representing Sudan) and Egypt, which allocated 4 bcm per year to Sudan and 48 bcm per year to Egypt. The treaty explicitly provided that Sudan's water

[*]Great Britain had declared a Protectorate over Egypt in December 1914, terminating Turkish suzerainty. By the 1923 Treaty of Lausanne, Turkey renounced all rights over Egypt and Sudan and effectively recognized Great Britain's unilateral action. In 1922, Great Britain terminated the Protectorate and declared Egypt an independent state. Sudan achieved independence in 1956.

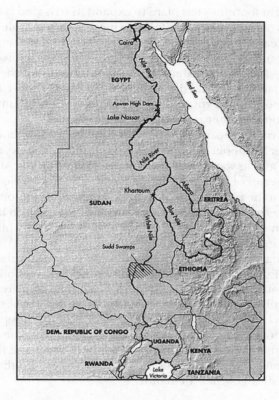

The Nile River Basin

needs would be subordinated to Egypt's water needs, and prohibited Sudanese water projects that would restrict the flow of Nile waters to Egypt.

When Sudan achieved independence, it sought to modify the 1929 treaty. Egypt argued that existing needs and historic uses should take priority, and that excess waters resulting from development projects should be apportioned on the basis of population. Egypt also sought to ensure that development projects were built in Egypt, so that it would not be dependent on projects outside its borders. Sudan argued that, in light of its population and needs, it was entitled to one-third of the Nile's waters. After extensive negotiations—and low-grade military conflict in 1958—a new treaty was signed in 1959, temporarily settling most of the outstanding water issues between the two states. As discussed below, the 1959 treaty allocates Nile waters between the states and provides for the building of dams in Sudan and Egypt.

While at present Egypt and Sudan use about 94 percent of the available Nile water, in recent years many Nile basin nations have announced ambitious plans to use more Nile waters. These efforts are driven by population pressures and by demands for economic development. In the aggregate, the Nile river basin population is expected to increase from 299 million in 1997 to 497 million in 2025, and then exceed 1 billion people by 2050. This increased population will need more water for human consumption, for livestock and agricultural uses, and for industrial and commercial activities.

For example, Egypt, which already uses at least the 14.5 trillion gallons of Nile waters allocated to it by the 1959 treaty—and whose population increases by

1 million every eight months—has plans to expand its irrigated land area by at least 1 million hectares (a hectare is 10,000 square meters, the equivalent of 2,471 acres) over the next 20 years, which could easily require an additional eight bcm of water. Sudan, which currently uses about 20 percent of the Nile's water, is expected to need 33 bcm per year—13.5 bcm greater than its allocation under the 1959 treaty—by 2025. Hence, Sudan has repeatedly demanded to modify the 1959 agreement, a move strongly opposed by Egypt. Sudan has threatened several times to redirect the Nile's flow and stop the water to Egypt.

Ethiopia contributes nearly 86 percent of the Nile's flow but uses less than 5 percent of its water. Ethiopia's population is expected to double, to 122 million, in the next 20 years, and its water needs will increase significantly. At one point Ethiopia announced a series of large-scale agricultural irrigation projects that would use about 18 bcm from the present Egyptian and Sudanese allocations. More recently, Ethiopia hired international engineering firms to begin work on hundreds of small dams. Completion of these projects could reduce the quantity and quality of Nile waters reaching Egypt.

Egypt and Sudan insist that Ethiopia undertake no works without their consent. More ominously, Egypt has declared that any significant diversion of Nile waters by upstream states would be viewed as a threat to its national security. Egypt's position is more than simply rhetorical: there have been border clashes. In 1990, Egypt reportedly blocked an African Development Bank loan to Ethiopia for new irrigation projects. In short, tensions in the area rose steadily during the 1980s and 1990s, not only because the nations that contribute the most water use the least, and vice versa, but also because Nile basin nations increasingly realized that there is insufficient water to satisfy all of their demands.

B. Allocating the Nile's Waters

States have long used treaties to assert and protect their interests in Nile waters. In an 1891 protocol, Great Britain recognized an Italian sphere of influence in the Ethiopian highlands in return for Italy's promise "not to construct [on] the Atbara, in view of irrigation, any work which might sensibly modify its flow into the Nile." At the time, the British did not realize that this treaty protected a relatively minor source (about 13 percent) of Nile waters, but left the major source (about 60 percent) to be exploited by the Italians. As a result, the 1891 treaty was augmented by a 1902 agreement in which Ethiopia agreed "not to construct or allow to be constructed, any works across the Blue Nile . . . which would arrest the flow of their waters into the Nile except in agreement with His Brittanic Majesty's Government and the Government of the Sudan."

The next major Nile treaty was concluded in 1929 between Egypt and the United Kingdom, representing Sudan. It provides that:

> 2. It is realised that the development of the Sudan requires a quantity of the Nile water greater than that which has been so far utilised by the Sudan. . . . [T]he Egyptian Government has always been anxious to encourage such development, and will therefore . . . be willing to agree . . . upon such an increase of this quantity as does not infringe Egypt's natural and historical rights in the waters of the Nile and its requirements of agricultural extension, subject to satisfactory assurances as to the safe guarding of Egyptian interests as detailed [below]. . . .

4. It is further understood that . . .

>   (b) Save with the previous agreement of the Egyptian Government, no irrigation or power works or measures are to be constructed or taken on the River Nile and its branches, or on the lakes from which it flows, so far as all these are in the Sudan or in countries under British administration, which would, in such a manner as to entail any prejudice to the interests of Egypt, either reduce the quantity of water arriving in Egypt, or modify the date of its arrival, or lower its level.

Egypt-U.K. Exchange of Notes Regarding the Use of the Waters of the Nile for Irrigation, 93 U.N.T.S. 43 (1929).

After Sudan achieved independence, it entered into the 1959 Nile Treaty with Egypt mentioned above:

Agreement for the Full Utilization of the Nile Waters

6519 U.N.T.S. 63 (1959)

First
THE PRESENT ACQUIRED RIGHTS

1. That the amount of the Nile waters used by the United Arab Republic [Egypt] until this Agreement is signed shall be her acquired right before obtaining the benefits of the Nile Control Projects and the projects which will increase its yield and which projects are referred to in this Agreement; The total of this acquired right is 48 [billion] cubic meters per year as measured at Aswan.

2. That the amount of the waters used at present by the Republic of Sudan shall be her acquired right before obtaining the benefits of the projects referred to above. The total amount of this acquired right is 4 [billion] cubic meters per year as measured at Aswan.

Second
THE NILE CONTROL PROJECTS AND THE DIVISION OF THEIR BENEFITS BETWEEN THE TWO REPUBLICS

1. In order to regulate the River waters and control their flow into the sea, the two Republics agree that the United Arab Republic constructs the [Aswan Dam] as the first link of a series of projects on the Nile for over-year storage.

2. In order to enable the Sudan to utilize its share of the water, the two Republics agree that the Republic of Sudan shall construct the Roseires Dam on the Blue Nile and any other works which the Republic of the Sudan considers essential for the utilization of its share. . . .

4. The net benefit from the [Aswan] Reservoir mentioned in the previous item shall be divided between the two Republics at the ratio of $14\frac{1}{2}$ for the Sudan and $7\frac{1}{2}$ for the United Arab Republic. . . .

6. The United Arab Republic agrees to pay to the Sudan Republic 15 Million Egyptian Pounds as full compensation for the damage resulting to the Sudanese existing properties as a result of the storage in the [Aswan] Reservoir. . . .

Fourth
TECHNICAL CO-OPERATION BETWEEN THE TWO REPUBLICS

1. In order to ensure the technical co-operation between the Governments of the two Republics . . . a Permanent joint Technical Commission shall be formed of an equal number of members from both parties; and its functions shall be: . . .

(c) The drawing up of the working arrangements for any works to be constructed on the Nile, within the boundaries of the Sudan, and also for those to be constructed outside the boundaries of the Sudan, by agreement with the authorities concerned in the countries in which such works are constructed.

(d) The supervision of the application of all the working arrangements mentioned in (c) above . . . and the supervision of the working of the upper Nile projects, as provided in the agreements concluded with the countries in which such projects are constructed. . . .

Fifth
GENERAL PROVISIONS

1. If it becomes necessary to hold any negotiations concerning the Nile waters, with any riparian state . . . the Governments of the Sudan Republic and the United Arab Republic shall agree on a unified view after the subject is studied by the said Technical Commission. The said unified view shall be the basis of any negotiations by the Commission with the said states. . . .

2. As [Nile] states, other than the two Republics, claim a share in the Nile waters, the two Republics have agreed that they shall jointly consider and reach one unified view regarding the said claims. And if the said consideration results in the acceptance of allotting an amount of the Nile water to one or the other of the said states, the accepted amount shall be deducted from the shares of the two Republics in equal parts. . . .

Notes and Questions

1. In the 1959 agreement, Sudan accepted the concept of preexisting rights, which effectively granted Egypt the right to use 12 times as much water as Sudan. At the time, Egypt's population was roughly double that of the Sudan. Why would Sudan agree to such a provision?

2. In the early 1950s, both Egypt and Sudan developed plans for large dam projects. Egypt wanted to build the Aswan High Dam, and Sudan wanted to build a dam at Roseires. But each state needed the agreement of the other to proceed. The Aswan Dam would cause flooding of Sudanese territory. More important, Egypt needed Sudan's assurance that it would not reduce the flow of the Nile into Egypt in an amount that would jeopardize operation of the High Dam. For its part, Sudan needed international financing for Roseires, which would not likely be forthcoming if Egypt objected to the project. For example, the World Bank had advised Sudan that financing for Roseires was contingent upon an agreement with Egypt. In their 1959 agreement, Egypt consented to construction of the Roseires Dam and, in exchange, Sudan consented to construction of the Aswan High Dam; Egypt also agreed to pay Sudan damages for flooding caused by the Aswan project. Thereafter,

the World Bank and West German Development Finance Bank provided financing for the Roseires project.

Many large projects of this kind require outside financing. What should the role of international financial institutions be regarding these projects? Can and should they help enforce or even create international law regarding shared watercourses? Similarly, should non-Nile basin governments assist in the planning or financing of any of these Nile River projects? Should non-Nile basin states encourage their citizens and companies to participate in these projects? Or should they discourage or prohibit participation in Nile projects that may be inconsistent with relevant international legal norms?

3. Much of the legal analysis of this problem turns on the status of colonial-era treaties. Considering the materials on treaty law in Chapter 2 and on state succession in Chapter 3, what is the legal status of these treaties? Should all treaties from this era be treated in the same way?

C. Development of Norms on International Watercourses

Over the years, there have been many international disputes involving international watercourses, and states have developed a number of procedural and substantive norms. We shall follow the widespread practice of treating procedural and substantive norms separately; but here, as in other areas of the law, there are complex interrelationships between procedure and substance.

1. Procedural Norms

An important early case involving international waters is the *Lac Lanoux* Arbitration, which arose out of France's plan to build a reservoir at Lake Lanoux, on French territory, to produce electricity. The lake feeds a river that runs into Spain. To replace the waters that Spain would otherwise lose, France proposed building an underground tunnel and drawing, from other sources, a quantity of water equal to that used in the project. Spain argued that this project would violate the 1866 Treaty of Bayonne between France and Spain and the Additional Act to this treaty. Spain also claimed that, under the Treaty, such works could not be undertaken without the previous agreement of both parties. The dispute was eventually referred to a five-person arbitral tribunal.

Lac Lanoux Arbitration (Spain v. France)

24 I.L.R. 101 (1956)

11. Before proceeding to an examination of the Spanish argument [that its consent was necessary before France could proceed with the project] . . . it will be useful to make some very general observations on the nature of the obligations invoked against the French Government. To admit that jurisdiction in a certain field can no longer be exercised except on the condition of, or by way of, an agreement between two States, is to place an essential restriction on the sovereignty of a State, and such restriction could only be admitted if there were clear and convincing evidence. Without doubt, international practice does reveal some special cases in

which this hypothesis has become reality. . . . But these cases are exceptional, and international judicial decisions are slow to recognize their existence, especially when they impair the territorial sovereignty of a State, as would be the case in the present matter.

In effect, in order to appreciate in its essence the necessity for prior agreement, one must envisage the hypothesis in which the interested States cannot reach agreement. In such case, it must be admitted that the State which is normally competent has lost its right to act alone as a result of the unconditional and arbitrary opposition of another State. This amounts to admitting a "right of assent," a "right of veto," which at the discretion of one State paralyses the exercise of the territorial jurisdiction of another.

That is why international practice prefers to resort to less extreme solutions by confining itself to obliging the State to seek, by preliminary negotiations, terms for an agreement, without subordinating the exercise of their competencies to the conclusion of such an agreement. . . . [T]he reality of the obligations thus undertaken is incontestable and sanctions can be applied in the event, for example, of an unjustified breaking off of the discussions, abnormal delays, disregard of the agreed procedures, systematic refusals to take into consideration adverse proposals or interests, and, more generally, in case of violation of the rules of good faith. . . .

13. . . . Thus, if it is admitted that there is a principle which prohibits the upstream State from altering the waters of a river in such a fashion as seriously to prejudice the downstream State, such a principle would have no application to the present case, [since the Tribunal determined that the French plan did not injure Spanish interests]. . . .

But international practice does not so far permit more than the following conclusion: the rule that States may utilize the hydraulic power of international watercourses only on condition of a *prior* agreement between the interested States cannot be established as a custom, even less a general principle of law. . . .

22. . . . The Tribunal is of the opinion that, according to the rules of good faith, the upstream State is under the obligation to take into consideration the various interests involved, to seek to give them every satisfaction compatible with the pursuit of its own interests, and to show that in this regard it is genuinely concerned to reconcile the interests of the other riparian State with its own.

23. . . . France is entitled to exercise her rights; she cannot ignore Spanish interests.

Spain is entitled to demand that her rights be respected and that her interests be taken into consideration.

As a matter of form, the upstream State has, procedurally, a right of initiative; it is not obliged to associate the downstream State in the elaboration of its schemes. If, in the course of discussions, the downstream State submits schemes to it, the upstream State must examine them, but it has the right to give preference to the solution contained in its own scheme provided that it takes into consideration in a reasonable manner the interests of the downstream State.

Notes and Questions

1. Given that France replaced the quantity of diverted waters in full, what is the basis of Spain's complaint? In addition to arguing that France could not undertake the project without prior Spanish consent, Spain also argued that the project would

enable France "to bring pressure to bear" on Spain by giving France "the physical possibility of stopping the flow of the Lanoux water" to Spain. Is this complaint one that international law should recognize?

2. What, exactly, is the nature of the duty the panel identified in this case? What is the value of this duty to a downstream state? What is an appropriate remedy if this duty is breached?

3. A more recent statement of the procedural norms applicable to the uses of international watercourses is found in the UN Convention on the Law of Non-Navigational Uses of International Watercourses, adopted by the General Assembly in 1997. The Convention, discussed in more detail below, essentially provides for "timely notification" whenever one watercourse state implements measures "which may have a significant adverse effect upon other watercourse States," as well as for consultations and negotiations concerning planned measures. A state can avoid these procedures, however, where implementation is of the "utmost urgency in order to protect public health, public safety or other equally important interests." What type of projects would this include? France's project at Lac Lanoux, which was to generate electricity? Egypt's, Sudan's, or Ethiopia's planned Nile projects?

2. Substantive Norms

The substantive norms governing international watercourses have evolved considerably over the last hundred years. An early expression of the U.S. view of the applicable norms was made in the 1890s, when Mexico complained that U.S. diversions of the Rio Grande threatened the water supply of several Mexican cities. The U.S. Secretary of State asked the Attorney General for an opinion on the applicable legal norms. Attorney General Judson Harmon responded:

> The fundamental principle of international law is the absolute sovereignty of every nation, as against all others, within its own territory. Of the nature and scope of sovereignty with respect to judicial jurisdiction, which is one of its elements, Chief Justice Marshall said (*Schooner Exchange v. McFadden,* 7 Cranch, p. 136):
>
> > The jurisdiction of the nation within its own territory is necessarily exclusive and absolute. It is susceptible of no limitation not imposed by itself. Any restriction upon it, deriving validity from an external source, would imply a diminution of its sovereignty to the extent of the restriction, and an investment of that sovereignty to the same extent in that power which could impose such restriction. "All exceptions," therefore, to the full and complete power of a nation within its own territories must be traced up to the consent of the nation itself. They can flow from no other legitimate source. . . .
>
> The immediate as well as the possible consequences of the right asserted by Mexico show that its recognition is entirely inconsistent with the sovereignty of the United States over its national domain. Apart from the sum demanded by way of indemnity for the past, the claim involves not only the arrest of further settlement and development of large regions of country, but the abandonment, in great measure at least, of what has already been accomplished. . . .
>
> It is not suggested that the injuries complained of are or have been in any measure due to wantonness or wastefulness in the use of water or to any design or intention to injure. The water is simply insufficient to supply the needs of the great stretch of arid country through which the river, never large in the dry season, flows, giving much and receiving little.
>
> The case presented is a novel one. Whether the circumstances make it possible or proper to take any action from considerations of comity is a question which does not

pertain to this Department; but that question should be decided as one of policy only, because, in my opinion, the rules, principles, and precedents of international law impose no liability or obligation upon the United States.

Attorney General Opinion, 21 U.S. Op. Atty. Gen. 274, 280-283 (1895).

During the nineteenth century, many upstream states advocated the so-called Harmon Doctrine, also known as the doctrine of absolute territorial sovereignty. Its mirror image, the doctrine of absolute territorial integrity, holds that downstream states have the right to receive the same quantity of water that they have historically received. Under this theory, upstream states have no right to interfere with the waters received by downstream states. While hints of both doctrines still exist in contemporary state practice, many experts argue that states now accept the concept known as equitable utilization. This doctrine has been endorsed, most recently, in the UN Convention on the Law of Non-Navigational Uses of International Watercourses, which provides:

Article 5
Equitable and reasonable utilization and participation

1. Watercourse States shall in their respective territories utilize an international watercourse in an equitable and reasonable manner. In particular, an international watercourse shall be used and developed by watercourse States with a view to attaining optimal and sustainable utilization thereof and benefits therefrom, taking into account the interests of the watercourse States concerned, consistent with adequate protection of the watercourse.

2. Watercourse States shall participate in the use, development and protection of an international watercourse in an equitable and reasonable manner. Such participation includes both the right to utilize the watercourse and the duty to cooperate in the protection and development thereof, as provided in the present Convention.

Article 6
Factors relevant to equitable and reasonable utilization

1. Utilization of an international watercourse in an equitable and reasonable manner within the meaning of article 5 requires taking into account all relevant factors and circumstances, including:

(a) Geographic, hydrographic, hydrological, climatic, ecological and other factors of a natural character;

(b) The social and economic needs of the watercourse States concerned;

(c) The population dependent on the watercourse in each watercourse State;

(d) The effects of the use or uses of the watercourses in one watercourse State on other watercourse States;

(e) Existing and potential uses of the watercourse;

(f) Conservation, protection, development and economy of use of the water resources of the watercourse and the costs of measures taken to that effect;

(g) The availability of alternatives, of comparable value, to a particular planned or existing use. . . .

3. The weight to be given to each factor is to be determined by its importance in comparison with that of other relevant factors. In determining what is a reasonable and equitable use, all relevant factors are to be considered together and a conclusion reached on the basis of the whole.

Article 10
Relationship between different kinds of uses

1. In the absence of agreement or custom to the contrary, no use of an international watercourse enjoys inherent priority over other uses.

2. In the event of a conflict between uses of an international watercourse, it shall be resolved with reference to articles 5 to 7, with special regard being given to the requirements of vital human needs. . . .

The Convention also contains articles on the prevention and control of water pollution. Most notably, it provides:

Article 7
Obligation not to cause significant harm

1. Watercourse States shall, in utilizing an international watercourse in their territories, take all appropriate measures to prevent the causing of significant harm to other watercourse States.

2. Where significant harm nevertheless is caused to another watercourse State, the States whose use causes such harm shall, in the absence of agreement to such use, take all appropriate measures, having due regard for the provisions of articles 5 and 6, in consultation with the affected State, to eliminate or mitigate such harm and, where appropriate, to discuss the question of compensation.

UN Convention on the Law of Non-Navigational Uses of International Watercourses, G.A. Res. 51/229 (Annex) (1997)

Notes and Questions

1. The Convention is the product of a lengthy process. In 1970, the General Assembly asked the International Law Commission (ILC), a UN body of international law experts charged with promoting the progressive development and codification of international law, to prepare a draft treaty. The ILC began work in 1974 and provisionally adopted draft articles in 1991. States were then given an opportunity to comment, and a second draft was completed in 1994. The ILC then submitted the draft articles to the General Assembly, which passed a resolution to "convene a Working Group of the Whole" to draft a convention building upon the ILC's work. The General Assembly adopted the Convention in May 1997 by a vote of 103 in favor, 3 against, 27 abstentions, and 33 members absent.

Would you have advised Ethiopia or Egypt to vote for this Convention? In fact, Ethiopia abstained from voting on it. Ethiopia's delegate stated that Article 7 was "of particular concern," that Ethiopia wanted to see the primacy of Article 5 over Articles 6 and 7 "clearly established," and that specific watercourse arrangements should be adjusted to the Convention, not the other way around. Finally, he argued that the Convention was tilted toward lower riparians. Egypt also abstained.

Reaction of the other Nile riparians was mixed. Sudan and Kenya voted for the Convention; Rwanda and Tanzania abstained; Burundi voted against; and Uganda and Zaire were absent. None of the Nile riparians have signed or ratified the Convention.

2. Do you agree with the comments of a former World Bank official who worked on international rivers issues:

> The [Convention's] approach appears to be realistic, appropriate and consistent with some state practice in the area of pollution of the marine environment. However it seems inappropriate and unattractive where the country potentially harmed is weaker than the country causing the harm. [These norms] may not be appropriately enforced in Nile River disputes for two main reasons: The approach seems to reward the countries (Egypt and Sudan) that are first in time to develop a shared river, and weaker Nile Basin nations (such as Ethiopia) that are asserting . . . the equitable utilization principle are less likely to succeed without some legal backing and pressure according primacy to the principle. In contrast with weaker countries, a relatively powerful nation is better able to apply the necessary economic and political pressure to convince other nations to cease their inequitable utilization without the support of any legal principle.

Valentina Okaru-Bisant, *Institutional and Legal Frameworks of Preventing and Resolving Disputes Concerning the Development and Management of Africa's Shared River Basins*, 9 Colo. J. Intl Envtl. L. & Poly. 331, 353-354 (1998).

3. Is there a contradiction between the principle of equitable utilization set out in Article 5 of the Convention and the obligation not to cause significant harm set out in Article 7?

4. Does the Convention affect the rights and obligations contained in the Nile treaties discussed above? The Convention provides:

Article 3
Watercourse agreements

1. . . . [N]othing in the present Convention shall affect the rights or obligations of a watercourse State arising from agreements in force for it on the date on which it became a party to the present Convention. . . .

6. Where some but not all watercourse States to a particular international watercourse are parties to an agreement, nothing in such agreement shall affect the rights or obligations under the present Convention of watercourse States that are not parties to such an agreement.

Article 4
Parties to watercourse agreements

1. Every watercourse State is entitled to participate in the negotiation of and to become a party to any watercourse agreement that applies to the entire international watercourse, as well as to participate in any relevant consultations.

2. A watercourse State whose use of an international watercourse may be affected to a significant extent by the implementation of a proposed watercourse agreement that applies only to a part of the watercourse or to a particular project, programme or use is entitled to participate in consultations on such an agreement and, where appropriate, in the negotiation thereof in good faith with a view to becoming a party thereto, to the extent that its use is thereby affected. . . .

5. In 2004, the International Law Association, a multinational NGO devoted to the development of international law, adopted the Berlin Rules on Water Resources. The Berlin Rules purport to "express international law applicable to the management of the waters of international drainage basins and applicable to all

waters." In their provisions on equitable and reasonable utilization, the Berlin Rules adopt the factors mentioned in Article 6 of the UN Convention, and add two additional factors: the sustainability of proposed or existing uses and the minimization of environmental harm. How does the addition of these factors change the analysis of whether a particular use is equitable and reasonable? Can you identify uses that would be equitable and reasonable under the UN Convention but not satisfy the Berlin Rules?

D. Guidance from the World Court?

The ICJ addressed international watercourse issues in a case arising out of a 1977 agreement between Hungary and Czechoslovakia to build a series of dams on the Danube River. The treaty provides for the construction of two series of locks at Gabcikovo, Czechoslovakia (now Slovakia), and Nagymaros, Hungary, which together were to constitute a single operational system of works financed, constructed, operated, and owned by both states.

Following the dramatic political changes of 1989, Hungary suspended construction of the Nagymoros dam and, in 1992, sought unilaterally to terminate the agreement. Czechoslovakia rejected Hungary's efforts to terminate the treaty and, after changing the original design so that the dam could be built entirely on Czechoslovakia territory, continued with the Gabcikovo project. The revised project, called the "provisional solution" and "Variant C," was completed in 1992, shortly before Slovakia became an independent state. As part of Variant C, Slovakia unilaterally diverted a substantial part of the Danube River's flow away from the Hungarian-Slovak border. After extensive negotiations, Hungary and Slovakia agreed to bring their dispute to the ICJ.

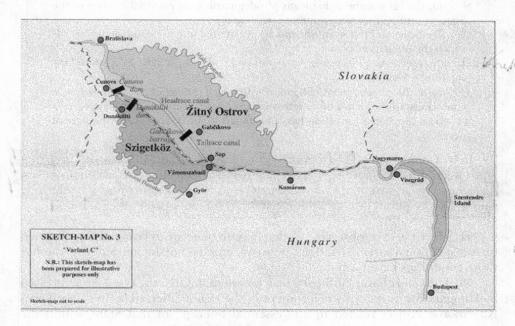

ICJ Sketch-Map of Variant C

Case Concerning the Gabcikovo-Nagymoros Project (Hungary/Slovakia)

1997 I.C.J 7

H argues

40. . . . Hungary contended that, although it did suspend or abandon certain works . . . it never suspended the application of the 1977 Treaty itself. To justify its conduct, it relied essentially on a "state of ecological necessity."

raised environmental problems

Hungary contended that the various installations in the Gabcikovo-Nagymoros System of Locks had been designed to enable the Gabcikovo power plant to operate in [a manner that] . . . carried ecological risks which it found unacceptable [including the replacement of Danube groundwater flow with stagnant upstream reservoir water, the silting of the Danube, eutrophication (the depletion of oxygen necessary for aquatic life) and serious threats to aquatic habitats]. . . .

As for Nagymoros, Hungary argued that, if that dam had been built, [the water supply to Budapest would have been significantly diminished and aquatic habitats threatened]. . . . From all these predictions, in support of which it quoted a variety of scientific studies, Hungary concluded that a "state of ecological necessity" did indeed exist in 1989. . . .

50. . . . [T]he existence of a state of necessity must be evaluated in the light of the criteria laid down by the International Law Commission in Article 33 of the Draft Articles on the International Responsibility of States [which provides:]

Article 33. State of necessity

Can't use necessity for wrongful act unless

1. A state of necessity may not be invoked by a State as a ground for precluding the wrongfulness of an act of that State not in conformity with an international obligation of the State unless:

   (a) the act was the only means of safeguarding an essential interest of the State against a grave and imminent peril; and

   (b) the act did not seriously impair an essential interest of the State towards which the obligation existed.

no necessity defense when

2. In any case, a state of necessity may not be invoked by a State as a ground for precluding wrongfulness:

   (a) if the international obligation with which the act of the State is not in conformity arises out of a peremptory norm of general international law; or . . .

   (c) if the State in question has contributed to the occurrence of the state of necessity.

In its Commentary, the Commission defined the "state of necessity" as being "the situation of a State whose sole means of safeguarding an essential interest threatened by a grave and imminent peril is to adopt conduct not in conformity with what is required of it by an international obligation to another State." . . .

Court devises

51. The Court . . . observes . . . that [a state of necessity] can only be accepted on an exceptional basis . . . and the State concerned is not the sole judge of whether those conditions have been met. . . .

53. The Court has no difficulty in acknowledging that the concerns expressed by Hungary for its natural environment in the region affected by the Gabcikovo-Nagymoros Project related to an "essential interest" of that State, within the

meaning given to that expression in Article 33 of the Draft of the International Law Commission.

The Commission, in its Commentary, indicated that . . . it included among the situations that could occasion a state of necessity, "a grave danger to . . . the ecological preservation of all or some of [the] territory [of a State]"; and specified, with reference to State practice, that "It is primarily in the last two decades that safeguarding the ecological balance has come to be considered an 'essential interest' of all States."

The Court recalls that it has recently had occasion to stress, in the following terms, the great significance that it attaches to respect for the environment, not only for States but also for the whole of mankind:

> the environment is not an abstraction but represents the living space, the quality of life and the very health of human beings, including generations unborn. The existence of the general obligation of States to ensure that activities within their jurisdiction and control respect the environment of other States or of areas beyond national control is now part of the corpus of international law relating to the environment. (*Legality of the Threat or Use of Nuclear Weapons, Advisory Opinion, I.C.J. Reports 1996*, pp. 241-242, para. 29.)

54. . . . [Regarding the alleged state of necessity, b]oth Parties have placed on record an impressive amount of scientific material aimed at reinforcing their respective arguments. The Court has given most careful attention to this material. . . . [But] it is not necessary . . . to determine which of those points of view is scientifically better founded.

55. The Court will begin by considering the situation at Nagymoros. . . . The Court notes that the dangers ascribed to the upstream reservoir were mostly of a long-term nature and, above all, that they remained uncertain. . . . It follows that, even if it could have been established . . . that the reservoir would ultimately have constituted a "grave peril" for the environment in the area, one would be bound to conclude that the peril was not "imminent" at the time at which Hungary suspended and then abandoned the works relating to the dam. . . .

56. [With respect to Gabcikovo,] the Court finds here again, that the peril claimed by Hungary was to be considered in the long term, and, more importantly, remained uncertain. As Hungary itself acknowledges, the damage that it apprehended had primarily to be the result of some relatively slow natural processes, the effects of which could not easily be assessed. . . .

The Court moreover considers that Hungary could . . . have resorted to other means in order to respond to the dangers that it apprehended. In particular . . . Hungary seemed to be in a position to control at least partially the distribution of the water between the bypass canal, the old bed of the Danube and the side-arms. It should not be overlooked that the Dunakiliti dam was located in Hungarian territory and that Hungary could construct the works needed to regulate flows along the old bed of the Danube and the side-arms. . . .

57. The Court concludes from the foregoing that . . . the perils invoked by Hungary, without prejudging their possible gravity, were not sufficiently established in 1989, nor were they "imminent"; and that Hungary had available to it at that time means of responding to these perceived perils other than the suspension and abandonment of works with which it had been entrusted. . . .

What is more, the Court cannot fail to note [that in] 1983, Hungary asked that the works under the Treaty should go forward more slowly, for reasons that were essentially economic but also, subsidiarily, related to ecological concerns. In 1989, when, according to Hungary itself, the state of scientific knowledge had undergone a significant development, it asked for the works to be speeded up, and then decided, three months later, to suspend them and subsequently to abandon them. The Court is not however unaware that profound changes were taking place in Hungary in 1989, and that, during that transitory phase, it might have been more than usually difficult to co-ordinate the different points of view prevailing from time to time.

The Court infers from all these elements that, in the present case, even if it had been established that there was, in 1989, a state of necessity linked to the performance of the 1977 Treaty, Hungary would not have been permitted to rely upon that state of necessity in order to justify its failure to comply with its treaty obligations, as it had helped, by act or omission to bring it about. . . .

[The Court then addressed whether Czechoslovakia was entitled to construct Variant C and unilaterally divert the Danube on the grounds that Hungary's actions made it impossible to carry out the original project.]

78. . . . [T]he operation of Variant C led Czechoslovakia to appropriate, essentially for its use and benefit, between 80 and 90 per cent of the waters of the Danube before returning them to the main bed of the river, despite the fact that the Danube is not only a shared international watercourse but also an international boundary river.

Czechoslovakia submitted that Variant C was essentially no more than what Hungary had already agreed to and that the only modifications made were those which had become necessary by virtue of Hungary's decision not to implement its treaty obligations. It is true that Hungary . . . had agreed to the damming of the Danube and the diversion of its waters into the bypass canal. But it was only in the context of a joint operation and a sharing of its benefits that Hungary had given its consent. The suspension and withdrawal of that consent constituted a violation of Hungary's legal obligations, demonstrating, as it did, the refusal by Hungary of joint operation; but that cannot mean that Hungary forfeited its basic right to an equitable and reasonable sharing of the resources of an international watercourse.

The Court accordingly concludes that Czechoslovakia, in putting Variant C into operation, was not applying the 1977 Treaty but, on the contrary, violated certain of its express provisions, and, in so doing, committed an internationally wrongful act. . . .

85. [Czechoslovakia argued that Variant C was a justified countermeasure in response to Hungary's breach of the 1977 Treaty.] In the view of the Court . . . the effects of a countermeasure must be commensurate with the injury suffered, taking account of the rights in question.

In 1929, the Permanent Court of International Justice . . . stated as follows:

> [the] community of interest in a navigable river becomes the basis of a common legal right, the essential features of which are the perfect equality of all riparian States in the user of the whole course of the river and the exclusion of any preferential privilege of any one riparian State in relation to the others (*Territorial Jurisdiction of the International Commission of the River Oder, Judgment No. 16, 1929, P.C.I.J., Series A, No. 23*, p. 27).

Modern development of international law has strengthened this principle for non-navigational uses of international watercourses as well, as evidenced by the adoption of the Convention . . . on the Law of the Non-Navigational Uses of International Watercourses by the United Nations General Assembly.

The Court considers that Czechoslovakia, by unilaterally assuming control of a shared resource, and thereby depriving Hungary of its right to an equitable and reasonable share of the natural resources of the Danube . . . failed to respect the proportionality which is required by international law. . . .

[The Court next considered whether new norms of international environmental law justified Hungary's 1992 termination of the treaty.]

112. Neither of the Parties contended that new peremptory norms of environmental law had emerged since the conclusion of the 1977 Treaty. . . . On the other hand, the Court wishes to point out that newly developed norms of environmental law are relevant for the implementation of the Treaty and that the parties could, by agreement, incorporate them through the application of specific treaty articles. These articles do not contain specific obligations of performance but require the parties, in carrying out their obligations . . . to take new environmental norms into consideration when agreeing upon the means to be specified in the Joint Contractual Plan.

By inserting these evolving provisions in the Treaty, the parties recognized the potential necessity to adapt the Project. Consequently, the Treaty is not static, and is open to adapt to emerging norms of international law. By means of Articles 15 and 19, new environmental norms can be incorporated in the Joint Contractual Plan.

The responsibility to do this was a joint responsibility. The obligations contained in Articles 15, 19 and 20 are, by definition, general and have to be transformed into specific obligations of performance through a process of consultation and negotiation. Their implementation thus requires a mutual willingness to discuss in good faith actual and potential environmental risks. . . .

140. It is clear that the Project's impact upon, and its implications for, the environment are of necessity a key issue. The numerous scientific reports which have been presented to the Court by the Parties—even if their conclusions are often contradictory—provide abundant evidence that this impact and these implications are considerable.

In order to evaluate the environmental risks, current standards must be taken into consideration. This is not only allowed by the wording of Articles 15 and 19, but even prescribed, to the extent that these articles impose a continuing—and thus necessarily evolving—obligation on the parties to maintain the quality of the water of the Danube and to protect nature.

The Court is mindful that, in the field of environmental protection, vigilance and prevention are required on account of the often irreversible character of damage to the environment and of the limitations inherent in the very mechanism of reparation of this type of damage.

Throughout the ages, mankind has, for economic and other reasons, constantly interfered with nature. In the past, this was often done without consideration of the effects upon the environment. Owing to new scientific insights and to a growing awareness of the risks for mankind—for present and future generations—of pursuit of such interventions at an unconsidered and unabated pace, new norms and standards have been developed, set forth in a great number of instruments during the last two decades. Such new norms have to be taken into consideration, and such new standards given proper weight, not only when States contemplate new activities but also when continuing with activities begun in the past. This need to reconcile economic development with protection of the environment is aptly expressed in the concept of sustainable development.

For the purposes of the present case, this means that the Parties together should look afresh at the effects on the environment of the operation of the Gabikovo power plant. In particular they must find a satisfactory solution for the volume of water to be released into the old bed of the Danube and into the side-arms on both sides of the river. . . .

[The Court held that the 1977 Agreement was still in force and ordered the parties to recreate a joint regime.]

147. Re-establishment of the joint rgime will also reflect in an optimal way the concept of common utilization of shared water resources for the achievement of the several objectives mentioned in the Treaty, in concordance with Article 5, paragraph 2, of the Convention on the Law of the Non-Navigational Uses of International Watercourses, according to which:

> Watercourse States shall participate in the use, development and protection of an international watercourse in an equitable and reasonable manner. Such participation includes both the right to utilize the watercourse and the duty to cooperate in the protection and development thereof, as provided in the present Convention.

148. . . . Now the Court will turn to the legal consequences of the internationally wrongful acts committed by the Parties.

149. The Permanent Court of International Justice stated in its Judgment . . . in the case concerning the *Factory at Chorzów*:

> reparation must, as far as possible, wipe out all the consequences of the illegal act and reestablish the situation which would, in all probability, have existed if that act had not been committed (*P.C.I.J., Series A, No. 17*, p. 47).

150. . . . In this case, the consequences of the wrongful acts of both Parties will be wiped out "as far as possible" if they resume their co-operation in the utilization of the shared water resources of the Danube, and if the multi-purpose programme, in the form of a co-ordinated single unit, for the use, development and protection of the watercourse is implemented in an equitable and reasonable manner. What it is possible for the Parties to do is to re-establish co-operative administration of what remains of the Project. . . .

153. Given the fact, however, that there have been intersecting wrongs by both Parties, the Court wishes to observe that the issue of compensation could satisfactorily be resolved in the framework of an overall settlement if each of the Parties were to renounce or cancel all financial claims and counter-claims. . . .

Notes and Questions

1. How does this opinion bear on the Nile waters problem? May any of the Nile states invoke a state of necessity to justify noncompliance with any of the Nile treaties? More generally, should the Nile treaties be interpreted as the ICJ interprets the Danube treaty, as "not static, and . . . open to adapt to emerging norms of international law"? If so, which Nile states would such an interpretation favor?

2. Which party won the *Gabcikovo* case? Did international environmental law emerge a winner? In particular, what does this decision imply about the relationship between international environmental law and international treaty law?

3. At the time of the *Gabcikovo* decision, the UN Convention had no parties and no immediate prospect of entering into force. What, if anything, does this decision imply about the status of the norms articulated in the Convention?

4. The Court held that the 1977 agreement continues to govern the parties' relationship, and that the parties are required to take account of evolving principles

of international environmental law. On what basis are the parties to take account of these principles? Because the 1977 agreement requires them to? Or are they required to do so even absent an express treaty provision?

5. As the Court expressly declined to evaluate the conflicting scientific evidence presented by the parties, how can it determine whether the environmental threats were sufficiently "immediate" to support Hungary's necessity argument?

E. An Institutional Approach

Assuming that international legal norms provide insufficient guidance to government officials to resolve conflicting claims to international waters, what sort of framework or process might states use to resolve their claims in an orderly manner? In recent years, Nile nations have embarked on a promising series of cooperative efforts. For example, in 1992, the Nile Basin States formed the Technical Cooperation Committee for the Promotion of the Development and Protection of the Nile Basin (TECCONILE), a transitional mechanism for Nile cooperation. Egypt, Rwanda, Sudan, Tanzania, Uganda, and Democratic Republic of the Congo are members of TECCONILE, while Burundi, Eritrea, Ethiopia, and Kenya are observers. In 1995 TECCONILE developed a Nile River Basin Action Plan. The plan contemplated 22 projects as well as creation of a "basin-wide, multidisciplinary framework for legal and institutional arrangements." The Nile states did not have the resources to implement the Nile River Basin Action Plan and thus looked to international bodies for support. The UN Development Programme provided initial funding for a project to create a cooperative institutional and legal framework acceptable to all Nile countries for the integrated management of the Nile River.

Building upon these efforts, in February 1999 the Nile countries created the Nile Basin Initiative (NBI) to replace TECCONILE. All Nile nations are members except for Eritrea, which is an invited observer. NBI is based upon the promise that cooperation on the Nile provides opportunities to eradicate poverty and promote regional economic development. Under NBI auspices, Nile states have negotiated a number of cooperative projects in recent years. In June 2001, under World Bank auspices, a group of donor nations met for the first time and pledged initial support of at least $140 million to (1) finance a program of basin-wide projects designed to lay the groundwork for future action and (2) promote investment to spur economic growth in and environmental management of the Basin.

The NBI is supported by contributions from NBI states and a number of donors. Many donors, including Canada, Denmark, the Netherlands, Norway, Sweden, and the United Kingdom offer contributions to the Nile Basin Trust Fund, which was established in 2003 and is administered by the World Bank. The Fund supports a basin-wide Shared Vision Program, which focuses on institution building, information sharing, stakeholder training, and other forms of technical assistance.

Notes and Questions

1. Does the formation of consultative and technical bodies like those described above reflect a failure of international legal norms in this area? What are the advantages and disadvantages of using a consultative approach to conflicting demands for Nile waters?

2. How could legal norms influence decisions made under the auspices of the NBI? How could outside observers evaluate whether legal norms have in fact influenced these decisions?

3. As the readings above suggest, in the last few years Nile states have begun to move from conflictual to cooperative relationships with respect to Nile waters. How might creation of an international institution—the NBI—have advanced this process? Some commentators suggest that, although much of the technical and scientific projects conducted under NBI auspices are not "legal," these interactions help promote a cooperative framework through which law emerges. Consider the following argument:

> [T]he emergence of a basin identity and shared understandings as to basin-wide interests . . . serve to constrain Nile states from making entirely self-interested arguments. . . . In addition, concepts such as sustainable development, benefit sharing, or environmental protection provide important normative guidance by directly focusing upon positive outcomes, best achieved through cooperation, not competition. These emerging norms, all reflected in the NBI, help guide the interaction of the basin states by rendering purely competitive arguments, even in the context of water scarcity, untenable or, at least, unconvincing.
>
> A further key development was the recognition, through the NBI process, that only a shared basin-wide set of normative principles would legitimize particular project activities by ensuring a perspective that was inclusive of the identities and interests of all basin states. . . . In sum, it was not possible to promote "action on the ground" before a shared framework of principles had been elaborated and inclusive processes of discussion had been created. But to insist on basin-wide cooperation on all issues and projects was unrealistic, if not impossible. [Thus, NBI places emphasis on sub-basin projects.] So, perhaps ironically, it was a basin-wide, completely inclusive process of normative evolution [under the NBI] that . . . [allowed] Nile states to move toward concrete cooperative projects, many of which will be undertaken at the sub-basin level.
>
> The recent informal processes of discussion on the Nile cannot be appropriately characterized as either "cheap talk" or purely strategic bargaining processes. Rather, they have begun to involve genuine arguments, geared toward reaching common understandings and reasoned consensus. They are interactional processes of lawmaking, contributing simultaneously to shaping state identities [as part of a Nile Basin community] and building legitimacy [for norms of cooperation]. . . .

Jutta Brunnee & Stephen J. Toope, *The Changing Nile Basin Regime: Does Law Matter?*, 43 Harv. Intl. L.J. 105, 155-156 (2002).

4. Water issues are particularly salient in the developing world. Water-borne diseases are responsible for 80 percent of illnesses and death in developing states, killing a child every eight seconds. According to the 2003 UN World Water Development Report, 1.1 billion people in developing states lack access to improved water supply and 2.4 billion to improved sanitation. Given the scale and seriousness of water issues, why do they receive relatively limited international attention and resources?

II. PROTECTING THE EARTH'S ATMOSPHERE: SAVING THE OZONE LAYER

As the Nile problem suggests, states have long used international law to address disputes arising out of shared water resources. Although transboundary air pollution is not new, using international law to address atmospheric pollution problems is a relatively new phenomenon. The 1941 *Trail Smelter* arbitral award, discussed above, was an important step in the development of international legal norms protecting the atmosphere. However, this dispute involved a single known source of pollution causing geographically limited and easily identified environmental damage. International efforts to address more diffuse forms of atmospheric pollution began with a series of UN General Assembly resolutions concerning the effects of nuclear radiation resulting from atmospheric nuclear testing in the 1950s. For the most part, however, through the 1960s states considered air pollution essentially to be a local problem.

In the 1970s, widespread concern over acid rain and developing scientific understanding regarding the existence and impact of long-range pollutants led to important international negotiations in both Europe and North America. The 1979 Convention on Long Range Transboundary Air Pollution (LRTAP), negotiated under the auspices of the UN Economic Commission for Europe, sets forth a regional framework to control and reduce transboundary air pollution. Unlike *Trail Smelter*, LRTAP applies to air pollution

> whose physical origin is situated wholly or in part within the area under the national jurisdiction of one State and which has adverse effects in the area under the jurisdiction of another State at such a distance that it is not generally possible to distinguish the contribution of individual emission sources or groups of sources.

This framework convention did not require any reductions in emissions of air pollutants but prompted information sharing and collaborative research. These processes generated increased understanding, and led to a series of protocols to LRTAP that require reductions in emissions of specific pollutants, including nitrous oxide, sulfur dioxide, volatile organic compounds, and persistent organic pollutants. During the 1970s and 1980s, the United States and Canada also negotiated over acid rain and in 1991 entered into a treaty designed to control transboundary air pollution between them.

While states addressed bilateral and regional air pollution issues like acid rain, in the late 1970s and early 1980s public concern grew over global atmospheric problems, including depletion of the earth's ozone layer and, later, climate change caused by increased emissions of carbon dioxide and other greenhouse gases. These problems differed from the acid rain and other bilateral and regional air pollution problems in that ozone depletion and climate change present a serious threat to a global commons resource and threaten to affect every state adversely. Moreover, ozone-depleting chemicals and greenhouse gases produced or released by one state do not simply affect the atmosphere above that state; rather, many of these chemicals remain in the atmosphere for decades and, literally, circulate around the globe. In many respects, the problems of ozone depletion and climate change are structurally similar to the tragedy of the commons problem identified in the readings that introduce Part IV of the book.

In the Problem that follows, we examine the innovative international legal responses to the issues posed by ozone depletion. As you read these materials, consider how concerned states created incentives for other states to sign the ozone treaties and whether these incentives themselves caused other difficulties in protecting the ozone layer. Consider also which states were advantaged and which disadvantaged by the provisions of the ozone treaties, how states attempted to incorporate rapidly changing scientific understandings into law, and whether ozone treaty states have adequately addressed the problem of noncompliance with the treaties.

A. The Problem

Most atmospheric ozone is found in the stratosphere, a part of the atmosphere that begins between 5 and 11 miles above the earth's surface and extends up to about 30 miles. The ozone layer is exceedingly thin, as the stratosphere contains about three molecules of ozone for every 10 million air molecules. Atmospheric ozone is critical to life on earth, as it is the only gas that absorbs solar ultraviolet (UV-B) radiation, protecting animal and plant life from its toxic effects. When released into the atmosphere, certain industrial chemicals destroy stratospheric ozone.

Ozone depletion threatens a number of adverse health consequences. Most notable, perhaps, is an increased incidence of skin cancers, including the most deadly skin cancer, melanoma. Increased UV radiation also causes increased cataracts, which already account for half of the blindness in the world. Increased UV exposure also is thought to suppress the human immune system.

Moreover, UV radiation can penetrate several meters into the surface of the oceans, where phytoplankton, the beginning of the food chain for all aquatic creatures, reside. Phytoplankton are highly vulnerable to damage by UV radiation, so ozone depletion also poses a serious threat to marine life. Finally, UV radiation is toxic to most plants. It causes reduced leaf areas, plant stunting, weight reduction, and increased disease. Of all the adverse consequences of ozone depletion, food shortages are likely to be the most devastating.

In May 1985, British scientists stunned the world by reporting that ozone concentrations over the Antarctic had fallen by half from levels recorded in the 1960s. Subsequent investigations found that this trend was not confined to the sparsely populated Antarctic. By 1993 the ozone layer over the heavily populated mid-latitudes of the Northern Hemisphere was also at record low levels.

The scientific cause of ozone depletion was, at that time, the subject of substantial scientific controversy. In 1974 scientists theorized that chloroflurocarbons (CFCs), a man-made chemical, were potent destroyers of stratospheric ozone, although this theory was not confirmed until the 1980s and 1990s. CFCs were produced almost entirely in the United States and Europe. However, as atmospheric CFCs circulate around the globe, no one state can solve the problem of ozone depletion. Even if the United States, for example, immediately halted the production of CFCs, European or other states could increase their production, thereby obviating any environmental benefit that might otherwise result from unilateral U.S. reductions in CFC production. Moreover, the great majority of states threatened by the adverse consequences of ozone depletion do not even produce ozone-depleting chemicals.

B. The Ozone Regime

During the 1980s and 1990s, states entered into a series of treaties designed to reduce and, in several cases, eliminate the use of CFCs and other ozone-depleting substances. In so doing, many different interests—including those of the United States, Europe, the developing states, the CFC industry, and environmentalists—had to be accommodated. The ozone regime emerged in several steps, which we review below.

1. The Politics of Ozone Depletion: The Run-up to Vienna

As nations began the negotiations that eventually led to the ozone treaties, much of the information summarized above had not yet been developed, and there was sharp dispute over the role CFCs played in ozone depletion. In particular, most of the business community strongly rejected the initial scientific findings, published in the mid-1970s, that suggested a link between CFCs and ozone depletion. However, some companies that produced or used CFCs worried about adverse publicity and potential legal liabilities. Hence, in the midst of the ongoing scientific debate, Johnson Wax Company announced that it would voluntarily replace CFCs in several of its products. This helped spark a competitive dynamic among companies that sought to capture the market power of environmentally conscious consumers. As a result of corporate and consumer action, the U.S. market for CFC aerosol propellants fell by two-thirds between 1975 and 1977. In 1978, the U.S. Environmental Protection Agency (EPA) banned the use of CFC aerosol propellents for all but essential uses. Soon thereafter, Sweden, Canada, and Norway also banned nonessential uses of CFCs as propellents. These unilateral acts introduced a new dynamic into international debates. The U.S. government, for example, did not want its unilateral efforts to reduce the pressure on other states to act, and U.S. businesses did not want to operate under restrictions that their international competitors did not face.

Nevertheless, expectations were low as governments met in March 1985 in Vienna to negotiate an ozone treaty. The United States, having already banned use of CFC aerosol propellants at home, pushed for a similar global ban. This position was supported by U.S. industry, which had seen its share of global CFC sales drop from 46 percent to 28 percent, while their European competitors had enjoyed a significant increase in their sales. In contrast, the European Community (EC) opposed restrictions on consumption and argued for restrictions on production facilities. European industry, which was not producing at full capacity and which believed that their U.S. competitors were close to developing CFC substitutes, helped drive the EC position.

Given this alignment of political and economic interests and the underlying scientific uncertainties, what sort of treaty might you expect to result from the Vienna negotiations?

Vienna Convention for the Protection of the Ozone Layer

1513 U.N.T.S. 293 (1985)

Article 2: General obligations

1. The Parties shall take appropriate measures . . . to protect human health and the environment against adverse effects resulting or likely to result from human activities which modify or are likely to modify the ozone layer.

2. To this end the Parties shall, in accordance with the means at their disposal and their capabilities:

(a) Co-operate by means of systematic observations, research and information exchange in order to better understand and assess the effects on human health and the environment from modification of the ozone layer; . . .

(c) Co-operate in the formulation of agreed measures, procedures and standards for the implementation of this Convention, with a view to the adoption of protocols and annexes; . . .

Article 3: Research and systematic observations

1. The Parties undertake, as appropriate, to initiate and co-operate in . . . the conduct of research and scientific assessments on:
(a) The physical and chemical processes that may affect the ozone layer;
(b) The human health and other biological effects deriving from any modifications of the ozone layer . . . ;
(f) Alternative substances and technologies; . . .
2. The Parties undertake to promote or establish . . . joint or complementary programmes for systematic observation of the state of the ozone layer. . . .

Article 4: Co-operation in the legal, scientific and technical fields

1. The Parties shall facilitate and encourage the exchange of scientific, technical, socio-economic, commercial and legal information relevant to this Convention. . . .
2. The Parties shall co-operate, consistent with their national laws . . . and taking into account in particular the needs of the developing countries, in promoting . . . the development and transfer of technology and knowledge. . . .

In addition to these vague commitments, the Vienna Convention also includes a number of institutional provisions that would shape future negotiations over ozone issues:

Article 9: Amendments of the Convention or protocols

3. The Parties shall make every effort to reach agreement on any proposed amendment to this Convention by consensus. If all efforts at consensus have been exhausted, and no agreement reached, the amendment shall as a last resort be adopted by a three-fourths majority vote of the Parties present and voting . . . , and shall be submitted . . . to all Parties for ratification, approval or acceptance.
4. The procedure mentioned in paragraph 3 above shall apply to amendments to any protocol, except that a two-thirds majority of the parties to that protocol present and voting . . . shall suffice for their adoption.
5. . . . Amendments . . . shall enter into force between parties having accepted them . . . after the . . . ratification, approval or acceptance by at least three-fourths of the Parties to this Convention or by at least two-thirds of the parties to the protocol concerned. . . .

Article 10: Adoption and amendment of annexes

1. The annexes to this Convention or to any protocol shall form an integral part of this Convention or of such protocol. . . . Such annexes shall be restricted to scientific, technical and administrative matters.
2. Except as may be otherwise provided . . . the following procedure shall apply to the proposal, adoption and entry into force of additional annexes to this Convention or of annexes to a protocol:

(a) Annexes to this Convention shall be proposed and adopted according to the procedure laid down in [Article 9 (3)], while annexes to any protocol shall be proposed and adopted according to the procedure laid down in [Article 9 (4)];

(b) Any party that is unable to approve an additional annex to this Convention or annex to any protocol to which it is party shall so notify the Depositary. . . . within six months from the date of the communication of the adoption by the Depositary. The Depositary shall without delay notify all Parties of any such notification received. . . .

(c) On the expiry of six months from the date of the circulation of the communication by the Depositary, the annex shall become effective for all Parties . . . which have not submitted a notification in accordance with the provision of subparagraph (b) above.

3. The proposal, adoption and entry into force of amendments to annexes to this Convention or to any protocol shall be subject to the same procedure as for the proposal, adoption and entry into force of annexes to the Convention or annexes to a protocol. . . .

Article 11: Settlement of disputes

1. In the event of a dispute between Parties concerning the interpretation or application of this Convention, the parties concerned shall seek solution by negotiation.

2. If the parties concerned cannot reach agreement by negotiation, they may jointly seek the good offices of, or request mediation by, a third party.

3. . . . [Any party] may declare . . . that for a dispute not resolved in accordance with paragraph 1 or paragraph 2 above, it accepts one or both of the following means of dispute settlement as compulsory:

(a) Arbitration in accordance with procedures to be adopted by the Conference of the Parties at its first ordinary meeting;

(b) Submission of the dispute to the International Court of Justice.

4. If the parties have not, in accordance with paragraph 3 above, accepted the same or any procedure, the dispute shall be submitted to conciliation in accordance with paragraph 5 below unless the parties otherwise agree.

5. A conciliation commission shall be created upon the request of one of the parties to the dispute. The commission shall be composed of an equal number of members appointed by each party concerned and a chairman chosen jointly by the members appointed by each party. The commission shall render a final and recommendatory award, which the parties shall consider in good faith. . . .

Notes and Questions

1. Identify the key substantive and procedural obligations undertaken by parties to the Vienna Convention. What happens if a party fails to comply with one of its obligations? What is the purpose of this treaty?

2. Do the norms set forth in the *Trail Smelter* case or Principle 21 of the Stockholm Declaration adequately address the ozone problem?

3. Does the discussion of externalities set forth at page 696 capture the dynamic driving the problem of ozone depletion? If so, does that discussion suggest the outlines of a solution? Or is the ozone problem akin to a tragedy of the

commons, as described in the Hardin extract at pages 697-698? If so, does Hardin's analysis suggest a solution to the problem of ozone depletion? Can you identify the collective action problems associated with the issue of ozone depletion?

2. The Politics of Ozone Depletion: From Vienna to Montreal

In the summer of 1985, approximately two months after the Vienna Convention was completed, British scientists announced their startling results regarding depletion of the springtime ozone layer over Antarctica. Shortly thereafter, a study funded by the United States, Germany, UNEP, and the World Meteorological Organization showed a significant increase in atmospheric concentrations of CFCs and estimated dire health effects from increasing concentrations of ozone-depleting chemicals. In 1986, DuPont, the world's leading CFC producer, announced that it could develop CFC substitutes within five years if the proper regulatory incentives were provided. By late 1986, Canada, Finland, New Zealand, Norway, Sweden, Switzerland, and the United States had publicly endorsed the new controls on ozone-depleting chemicals; and Australia, Austria, and several developing states were moving toward support for stringent controls. Hence, the run-up to the Montreal ozone meeting, scheduled for September 1987, had a dramatically different negotiating dynamic than did the run-up to Vienna. As negotiations proceeded, a number of major outstanding issues emerged, as described in the following excerpt.

Richard Benedick, Ozone Diplomacy

77-79, 83-84 (2d ed. 1998)

CHEMICAL COVERAGE

Even though discussions before the Vienna Convention had focused only on CFCs 11 and 12 [used in aerosols and the first CFC compounds over which scientists raised concerns], Canada, Norway, the United States, and others had come to insist . . . that effective protection of the ozone layer would require *all* significant ozone depleting substances to be controlled under the protocol. . . .

Arguing more legalistically than scientifically, the EC long resisted going beyond CFCs 11 and 12. The EC delegation head . . . charged in April 1987 that the Americans were complicating the negotiations by adding new chemicals. . . .

Japan was initially insistent that CFC 113 be excluded from control; it was an essential solvent in that country's expanding electronics industry. The EC and the Soviet Union were particularly reluctant to include the halons, which were important as fire extinguishants in sensitive defense and space-related technologies and for which satisfactory substitutes were unavailable. . . .

The turning point in this debate came from the conclusions of the scientific meeting held in Wilrzburg [West Germany] in April 1987. The Wilrzburg analyses convincingly indicated that failure to regulate the rapidly growing CFC 113 and the extremely potent halons 1211 and 1301 would result in significant future ozone depletion . . . even if the other CFCs were controlled. . . . In addition, the scientists had now agreed that each individual chemical could be assigned an index number representing its ozone-depleting potential (ODP). . . . The value for a given chemical was calculated relative to CFC 11, which was arbitrarily assigned an ODP of 1.0. On the basis of this weighting system, the negotiators could craft a protocol provision that allowed substances to be treated for control purposes as a combined "basket" rather than individually. . . .

PRODUCTION VERSUS CONSUMPTION

The issue of whether restrictions should be applied to the production or the consumption of controlled substances proved extremely difficult to resolve because of its commercial implications.

The EC pushed hard for the production concept. European negotiators argued that it was administratively simpler to measure, and thereby to control, output, since there were only a small number of CFC- and halon-producing countries as opposed to thousands of consuming industries and countless points of consumption. The EC also feared that, if only consumption and not production were reduced, U.S. companies—which were currently operating at full capacity to meet domestic demand—would experience excess capacity as U.S. consumption was rolled back. With such excess capacity, American producers might be tempted to compete in the world's export markets, which were the nearly exclusive preserve of the EC.

Other governments, however, pointed out that focusing on production would convey inequitable power to existing producer countries, particularly the European Community, vis-à-vis other nations. For example, a production limit would essentially lock in the Europeans' foreign markets, which absorbed about one-third of total EC output. The only way that other producers could supply those markets would be to starve their own rising domestic consumption. Thus, EC exporters, with no viable competitors, would enjoy a monopoly reinforced by treaty obligations. Moreover, if continued growth in European demand for CFCs were at some point to tempt EC manufacturers to scale back on exports in order to satisfy their domestic consumers, CFC-importing countries, having neither recourse to other suppliers nor treaty authority to expand their own production, would have to bear a disproportionate share of reducing use of CFCs. Because of this vulnerability, CFC-importing countries might choose to remain outside the protocol and build their own CFC capacity. Controlling only production thus risked undermining the effectiveness of a protocol. . . .

STRINGENCY AND TIMING OF REDUCTIONS

. . . Not unexpectedly, this . . . turned out to be the single most contentious issue. Again, the European Community and the United States were the principal opponents.

The United States originally called for a freeze, to be followed by three phases of progressively more stringent reductions. The rationale for phased reductions was to provide milestones at which the parties could review the adequacy of the schedule on the basis of periodic scientific reassessments. In the U.S. draft text presented at the first session in December 1986, these cuts (which were bracketed to mark clearly their "illustrative" nature) were shown at 20 percent, 50 percent, and 95 percent of the base year. . . .

EC representatives entered the negotiations hinting that they might consider lowering their existing capacity cap. This apparent concession, however, still implied some growth in production. At Vienna they progressed to a freeze, with a possible 10 to 20 percent reduction coming six to eight years after the protocol's entry into force. But the EC further weakened its proposal by insisting that any reduction step require an affirmative vote by at least two-thirds of the parties. . . .

Notes and Questions

1. Given the divergent U.S. and European views, how likely is a successful outcome of the Montreal negotiations? How might a treaty be designed to satisfy both of these parties?

2. How might a treaty be designed to accommodate the interests of developing states?

_____

The combination of alarming new scientific evidence on ozone depletion, significant advances in the search for alternatives to ozone-depleting chemicals; sustained public and non-governmental organization (NGO) pressure; and effective leadership from Mostafa Tolba, then Executive Director of UNEP, and the United States resulted in the parties reaching a new agreement, the Montreal Protocol, in September 1987. The Protocol requires the phased reduction, over a number of years, of various ozone-depleting substances (ODS). Note the Protocol's approach to the U.S.-EU dispute over whether to regulate production or consumption.

Montreal Protocol on Substances that Deplete the Ozone Layer

1522 U.N.T.S. 3 (1987)

Article 1: Definitions

For the purposes of this Protocol: . . .

5. "Production" means the amount of controlled substances produced minus the amount destroyed by technologies to be approved by the Parties.

6. "Consumption" means production plus imports minus exports of controlled substances.

7. "Calculated levels" of production, imports, exports and consumption means levels determined in accordance with Article 3. . . .

Article 2: Control Measures

1. Each Party shall ensure that [for the period 1 July 1992 to 30 June 1993], its calculated level of consumption of the controlled substances in Group I of Annex A [reproduced below] does not exceed its calculated level of consumption in 1986. By the end of the same period, each Party . . . shall ensure that its calculated level of production of the substances does not exceed its calculated level of production in 1986, except that such level may have increased [only so as to satisfy the basic domestic needs of the Parties operating under Article 5] by no more than ten per cent based on the 1986 level. . . .

3. Each Party shall ensure that for the period 1 July 1993 to 30 June 1994 and in each twelve-month period thereafter, its calculated level of consumption of the controlled substances in Group I of Annex A does not exceed, annually, eighty per cent of its calculated level of consumption in 1986. Each Party . . . shall, for the same periods, ensure that its calculated level of production of the substances does not exceed, annually, eighty per cent of its calculated level of production in 1986. However, in order to satisfy the basic domestic needs of the Parties operating

under Article 5 . . . its calculated level of production may exceed that limit by up to ten per cent of its calculated level of production in 1986.

4. Each Party shall ensure that for the period 1 July 1998 to 30 June 1999, and in each twelve-month period thereafter, its calculated level of consumption of the controlled substances in Group I of Annex A does not exceed, annually, fifty per cent of its calculated level of consumption in 1986. . . .

ANNEX A
Controlled Substances

Group	Substance	Ozone Depleting Potential
Group I	CFC-11	1.0
	CFC-12	1.0
	CFC-113	0.8
	CFC-114	1.0
	CFC-115	0.6
Group II	halon-1211	3.0
	halon-1301	10.0
	halon-2402	(to be determined)

Article 3: Calculation of Control Levels

For the purposes of Articles 2 and 5, each Party shall . . . determine its calculated levels of:

(a) production by:

(i) multiplying its annual production of each controlled substance by the ozone depleting potential specified in respect of it in Annex A; and

(ii) adding together, for each such Group, the resulting figures;

(b) imports and exports, respectively, by following . . . the procedure set out in subparagraph (a); and

(c) consumption by adding together its calculated levels of production and imports and subtracting its calculated level of exports as determined in accordance with subparagraphs (a) and (b). However, beginning on 1 January 1993, any export of controlled substances to non-Parties shall not be subtracted in calculating the consumption level of the exporting Party. . . .

The Protocol provides the following incentives for developing states to join.

Article 5: Special Situation of Developing Countries

1. Any Party that is a developing country and whose annual calculated level of consumption of the controlled substances is less than 0.3 kilograms per capita . . . shall, in order to meet its basic domestic needs, be entitled to delay its compliance with the control measures set out [in Article 2] by ten years. . . .

2. The Parties undertake to facilitate access to environmentally safe alternative substances and technology for Parties that are developing countries and assist them to make expeditious use of such alternatives.

3. The Parties undertake to facilitate bilaterally or multilaterally the provision of subsidies, aid, credits, guarantees or insurance programmes to Parties that are developing countries for the use of alternative technology and for substitute products.

Article 10: Technical Assistance

1. The Parties shall . . . taking into account in particular the needs of developing countries, co-operate in promoting technical assistance to facilitate participation in and implementation of this Protocol. . . .

Notwithstanding the incentives provided by Articles 5 and 10, industrialized states feared that developing states might not sign the Protocol. In particular, developed states worried that developing states could begin producing ODS and gain export markets at precisely the time that developed states were reducing their production of ODS. Article 3(c), reproduced above, is specifically designed to encourage developing states to sign the Protocol. The Protocol also provides:

Article 4: Control of Trade with Non-Parties

1. Within one year of the entry into force of this Protocol, each Party shall ban the import of controlled substances from any [nonparty].

2. Beginning on 1 January 1993, no [developing state Party] may export any controlled substance to any [nonparty].

3. Within three years of the date of the entry into force of this Protocol, the Parties shall . . . elaborate in an annex a list of products containing controlled substances. Parties that have not objected to the annex . . . shall ban, within one year of the annex having become effective, the import of those products from any [nonparty].

4. Within five years of the entry into force of this Protocol, the Parties shall determine the feasibility of banning or restricting, from [nonparties], the import of products produced with, but not containing, controlled substances. If determined feasible, the Parties shall . . . elaborate in an annex a list of such products. Parties that have not objected to it . . . shall ban or restrict, within one year of the annex having become effective, the import of those products from any [nonparty].

5. Each Party shall discourage the export, to any [nonparty], of technology for producing and for utilizing controlled substances.

6. Each Party shall refrain from providing new subsidies, aid, credits, guarantees or insurance programmes for the export to [nonparties] of products, equipment, plants or technology that would facilitate the production of controlled substances. . . .

The negotiators intended for the interplay of Articles 3 and 4 to create strong incentives for developing states that sought access to CFCs to join the treaty. Under Article 4(5), it would be difficult for nonparties to obtain technology for producing or using CFCs. Moreover, pursuant to Article 4(2), nonparties would be unable to purchase CFCs from other developing states. And they would have to pay a premium to purchase CFCs from developed states because the definition of "exports" in Article 3(c) created a powerful incentive for developed states to export only to Montreal Protocol parties.

At Montreal the parties also addressed a number of institutional issues. For example, states disagreed about when the Protocol's controls on ODS would enter into force. If parties were bound by the Protocol's reduction provisions as soon as they ratified the treaty, then states would have an incentive not to ratify quickly and thereby enjoy short-term competitive advantages. The Protocol therefore provides:

Article 16: Entry Into Force

1. This Protocol shall enter into force on 1 January 1989, provided that at least eleven instruments of ratification, acceptance, approval of the Protocol or accession thereto have been deposited by States or regional economic integration organizations representing at least two-thirds of 1986 estimated global consumption of the controlled substances . . . .

Moreover, the parties understood that scientific knowledge regarding ozone depletion was in a state of rapid flux and sought to create a regime that could quickly adjust to changing scientific understandings. Hence, the parties drafted creative provisions to facilitate amendments and adjustments to the Protocol. Article 6 provided that, at least every four years, the Treaty parties assess the treaty's obligations considering current scientific, environmental, and technical information. On the basis of this assessment:

Article 2: Control Measures

9. (a) . . . [T]he Parties may decide whether: . . .
   (ii) further adjustments and reductions of production or consumption of the controlled substances from 1986 levels should be undertaken and, if so, what the scope, amount and timing of any such adjustments and reductions should be. . . .
   (c) In taking such decisions, the Parties shall make every effort to reach agreement by consensus. If all efforts at consensus have been exhausted, and no agreement reached, such decisions shall, as a last resort, be adopted by a two-thirds majority vote of the Parties present and voting representing at least fifty per cent of the total consumption of the controlled substances of the Parties.
   (d) The decisions . . . shall be binding on all Parties [and] shall forthwith be communicated to the Parties by the Depositary. . . .
10. (a) . . . [T]he Parties may decide:
    (i) whether any substances, and if so which, should be added to or removed from any annex to this Protocol, and
    (ii) the mechanism, scope and timing of the control measures that should apply to those substances;
    (b) Any such decision shall become effective, provided that it has been accepted by a two-thirds majority vote of the Parties present and voting. . . .

Notes and Questions

1. Does this treaty focus on the consumption or the production of ozone-depleting substances? Why? Does this fairly bridge the gap between the divergent U.S. and European economic interests at stake in this treaty?

2. Would you expect developing states to sign this treaty? What incentives does the treaty offer to developing states? What negative consequences would a non-signatory developing state face? Which do you think are more likely to be effective in encouraging developing states to sign and ratify the treaty?

3. Does this treaty use, or add to, the solutions that Hardin offers to forestall a tragedy of the commons?

4. Examine the voting rules for the adjustment of control measures in Article 2(9) and 2(10). Are they consistent with the idea that international law arises out of

the consent of nations? Why would states change the amendment procedures agreed to in the Vienna Convention?

3. The Politics of Ozone Depletion: From Montreal to London and Beyond

The Montreal Protocol put the CFC industry on notice that its markets would soon disappear, and industry redoubled its efforts to develop substitute products. In short order, AT&T announced a substitute for certain uses of CFC-113, and DuPont announced plans to build a pilot plant to produce a new generation of refrigerants. Thus, as the treaty negotiators had hoped, the treaty changed industry's incentives and unleashed a potentially profitable race to develop ODS substitutes.

Negotiations took yet another dramatic turn after completion of the Montreal Protocol. Within six months after the treaty was negotiated, several studies showed that the ozone hole was rapidly expanding, and a clear link between ozone depletion and the presence of CFCs in the stratosphere was established. One influential study found that, due to the longevity and stability of CFCs in the stratosphere, atmospheric concentrations of CFCs would substantially increase, even with nearly global participation in the Protocol. As a result of this alarming new evidence, the political pressure for more stringent regulation of ODS increased. Moreover, DuPont, citing the new studies, announced that it would accelerate its research into substitutes and would halt production of all CFCs and halons by the end of the twentieth century.

New political tensions accompanied the new science. Although the Montreal Protocol attempted to address developing state concerns, North-South issues increased in prominence following Montreal. While industrialized nations accounted for less than 25 percent of the world's population, they consumed 88 percent of world CFCs. However, CFC use in developing states was rapidly increasing. For example, China's CFC consumption had been growing at 20 percent annually, and the number of refrigerators in China reportedly increased by some 80 percent in 1988 alone. Important developing countries, such as China and India (together representing nearly 40 percent of the world's population) refused to join the Protocol. They argued that they had not caused the ozone depletion problem and were therefore unwilling either to forgo use of products, such as refrigerators, that contained CFCs, or to use more expensive substitute chemicals—and thereby enrich the very industry that had caused the problem in the first place. These states also argued that, given the need to address more pressing issues, such as poverty, hunger, and disease, they could not afford the costs of CFC abatement. Finally, they highlighted a notable asymmetry in the treaty: vagueness on issues of concern to them, such as technology transfer, but clear and specific provisions on ODS restrictions. As a result, by August 1989, virtually every industrialized state had joined the Protocol, but only 14 developing states had done so. Thus, the treaty parties faced the potential for widespread nonaccession to the Protocol.

In this complex scientific and political dynamic, the parties entered into intensive negotiations. Less than 18 months after the Protocol came into effect, the parties adopted new provisions in London. The parties agreed to accelerate the Montreal Protocol's phaseout schedules by requiring parties, by 1995-1996, to cut CFC production and use to not more than 50 percent of 1986 levels. By 1997-1998, CFC use was to be not more than 15 percent of 1986 levels, and by 2000-2001, production and use of CFCs was to be eliminated. These deadlines were largely met. The parties also added phaseout schedules for ten additional CFCs not covered by the Protocol, accelerated the phaseout schedules for halons, another group of chemicals controlled by the Montreal Protocol, and added controls for new classes of chemicals. The parties also created a new fund to help developing states meet their ozone treaty obligations.

As you review these provisions, consider whether, if you were in the foreign ministry of India or China, you would advise your government to sign the ozone treaties after the London meeting.

(London) Amendment to the Montreal Protocol on Substances that Deplete the Ozone Layer

Paragraphs 1 to 5 of Article 4 [of the Montreal Protocol] shall be replaced by the following paragraphs:

1. As of 1 January 1990, each Party shall ban the import of the controlled substances in Annex A from any [nonparty]. . . .
2. As of 1 January 1993, each Party shall ban the export of any controlled substances in Annex A to any [nonparty]. . . .
3. By 1 January 1992, the Parties shall . . . elaborate in an annex a list of products containing controlled substances in Annex A. Parties that have not objected to the annex . . . shall ban, within one year of the annex having become effective, the import of those products from any [nonparty]. . . .
4. By 1 January 1994, the Parties shall determine the feasibility of banning or restricting, from [nonparties], the import of products produced with, but not containing, controlled substances in Annex A. If determined feasible, the Parties shall . . . elaborate in an annex a list of such products. Parties that have not objected to the annex . . . shall ban, within one year of the annex having become effective, the import of those products from any [nonparty]. . . .

Article 5 of the Protocol shall be replaced by the following: . . .

5. Developing the capacity to fulfil the obligations of the [developing state parties] to comply with the control measures . . . and their implementation by those same Parties will depend upon the effective implementation of the financial co-operation as provided by Article 10. . . .
6. [A developing state party] may, at any time, notify the Secretariat in writing that, having taken all practicable steps it is unable to implement any or all of the obligations laid down in [Article 2, which sets out the targets and timetables for CFC reductions] due to the inadequate implementation of [the articles on financial cooperation and technology transfer]. The Secretariat shall forthwith transmit a copy of the notification to the Parties, which . . . shall decide upon appropriate action to be taken. . . .

Article 10 of the Protocol shall be replaced by the following:

Article 10: Financial mechanism

1. The Parties shall establish a mechanism for the purposes of providing financial and technical cooperation, including the transfer of technologies, to (developing countries) . . . to enable their compliance with the control measures. . . . The mechanism, contributions to which shall be additional to other financial transfers to

Parties operating under that paragraph, shall meet all agreed incremental costs of such Parties in order to enable their compliance with the control measures of the Protocol. . . .

2. The mechanism established under paragraph 1 shall include a Multilateral Fund. . . .

3. The Multilateral Fund shall . . . [m]eet, on a grant or concessional basis as appropriate, and according to criteria to be decided upon by the Parties, the agreed incremental costs; . . . .

5. The Parties shall establish an Executive Committee to develop and monitor the implementation of specific operational policies . . . including the disbursement of resources, for the purpose of achieving the objectives of the Multilateral Fund. The Executive Committee shall discharge its tasks and responsibilities . . . with the cooperation and assistance of the International Bank for Reconstruction and Development (World Bank), the United Nations Environment Programme, [and] the United Nations Development Programme. . . . The members of the Executive Committee, which shall be selected on the basis of a balanced representation of the Parties operating under paragraph 1 of Article 5 [that is, developing states] and of the Parties not so operating, shall be endorsed by the Parties. . . .

9. Decisions by the Parties under this Article shall be taken by consensus whenever possible. If all efforts at consensus have been exhausted and no agreement reached, decisions shall be adopted by a two-thirds majority vote of the Parties present and voting, representing a majority of the [developing state parties] present and voting and a majority of the [developed state parties] present and voting. . . .

The Fund began operations in 1991, and approximately two-thirds of the Montreal Protocol Parties are eligible to receive assistance from it. Contributions to the Fund come from industrialized nations, which are assessed according to the UN scale of assessment. As of October 2005, the contributions to the Fund from some 49 industrialized states (including states with economies in transition) totaled over $2 billion. The Fund's Executive Committee has approved the expenditure of $1.97 billion to support about 5,150 projects in 139 developing states. The implementation of these projects will result in the phase-out of the consumption of more than 223,729 ODP metric tons (one metric ton equals 1000 kilograms) of ODS and the production of about 133,219 ODP metric tons of ODS. Of this total, about 169,800 tons of consumption and 74,600 tons of production have been phased out from projects approved through December 2004. Monies from the Fund, along with monies from the World Bank, have supported projects designed, for example, to lead to a complete phaseout of CFC production in India.

Notes and Questions

1. Establishment of the Multilateral Fund helped induce developing nations, including China and India, to join the ozone regime. Given the language of Article 10(1), is there any reason for a developing state not to sign the ozone treaties? Can you see any downside to creation of the Fund?

2. Note that although the London Conference was a "meeting of the parties," two of the most important actors—China and India—were nonparties. Note also that all of the decisions were adopted by consensus, including the 42 delegations

from states not yet party to the Protocol. Why would states use a consensus procedure instead of the Protocol's elaborate voting provisions?

3. In an effort to provide additional incentives to join the treaty regime, in 1991 the parties approved a list of goods containing CFCs that, as of 1993, could only be imported from parties. The banned products included car and truck air-conditioning units, residential and commercial refrigerators, air-conditioning and heat pump equipment, nonmedical aerosol products, portable fire extinguishers, and insulation boards and panels. Not coincidentally, the number of developing states that joined the ozone regime more than doubled, to nearly 70, between mid-1990 and mid-1993. By 1996, the number had reached 120.

Many observers believe that the trade restrictions were even more important than the ozone fund in motivating developing states to join the ozone treaties. However, there is significant debate over whether the various Montreal Protocol trade restrictions are consistent with international trade law. The conflict between environmental measures that restrict trade and international trade norms is considered in detail in Chapter 12.

4. Consider the different treatment of developed and developing states in the ozone treaty regime. Principle 7 of the Rio Declaration, adopted at the 1992 Earth Summit, provides:

> In view of the different contributions to global environmental degradation, States have common but differentiated responsibilities. The developed countries acknowledge the responsibility that they bear in the international pursuit of sustainable development in view of the pressures their societies place on the global environment and of the technologies and financial resources they command.

A member of the U.S. negotiating team at the Rio Conference states that

> [t]he principle is relatively straightforward on its face. . . . [It] reflects the fact that because states contribute in different ways and by different degrees to various aspects of global degradation, they have both shared and individual responsibilities as part of their common task to address that degradation. The [final] sentence reflects the developed countries' recognition that they have taken on a special role in the common partnership in light of their higher per capita consumption and pollution levels and their greater technological and financial resources. . . .

Jeffrey D. Kovar, *A Short Guide to the Rio Declaration*, 4 Colo. J. Intl. Envtl. L. & Poly. 119, 128-130 (1993).

Is the principle of common but differentiated responsibilities incorporated into the ozone regime? If so, what does this principle mean in this context? Consider the following comments from the chief U.S. negotiator at the ozone negotiations:

> [The principle of common but differentiated responsibilities] could represent a justifiable effort to achieve equity between richer and poorer states, as reflected by the framers of the original Montreal Protocol in their article 5 provision for a grace period before developing countries had to implement controls on ozone-depleting substances. It could represent a formula for balancing performance by developing countries with the technological and financial assistance made available to them, as articulated in the London Amendments. Or it could represent an opportunity to extract the maximum possible transfer of wealth, without regard to the economics of the situation, as a precondition for accepting a share of responsibility in protecting the global environment.

Benedick, *supra*, at 241.

5. Subsequent meetings of the Parties in 1992 in Copenhagen, in 1995 in Vienna, and in 1999 in Beijing similarly accelerated the phaseouts of various chemicals and added controls on new chemicals. In addition, at Copenhagen the parties decided to make the Interim Multilateral Fund permanent and created an Implementation Committee, which is discussed in more detail below.

C. Promoting Compliance with the Ozone Treaties

Creating the ozone regime described above was a substantial diplomatic achievement. However, the parties to the ozone treaties were soon to face significant new issues. First, in 1992 Russia and other central European states voiced growing concern that the imminent phaseouts required by the ozone treaties were occurring at precisely the time that their own economic crises were deepening. As we have seen above, the treaties impose differential obligations on developed and developing states; in 1993 and 1994 Russia unsuccessfully requested creation of an additional treaty category for states "with problems similar to those of developed countries" in an effort to obtain a five-to-ten year extension on its treaty obligations. The request was opposed by the United States and the EC, and was unsuccessful. By 1995, there was little doubt that Russia and the other states of the former Soviet Union would soon be in a condition of noncompliance that would last for several years. In 1996 Russia conceded that it would be unable to meet the treaties' phaseout schedules but promised to complete the phaseout if sufficient economic and technical assistance was forthcoming.

Simultaneously, a new problem emerged: the smuggling of black market CFCs and other ozone-depleting chemicals into the United States, Europe, and elsewhere. While the size of this market is difficult to determine, CFC smuggling is said to be second in value to the smuggling of narcotics in some U.S. ports, and industry estimates that up to 20 percent of the CFCs in use in the mid-1990s were smuggled. Indeed, the unaccountably low price of some CFCs offers powerful evidence of a black market. For example, although the price of CFC-12 increased by approximately 12 times in the United States following its phaseout, prices in the EU increased only three to four times despite a phaseout. In contrast, the European price of R502, a refrigerant using a CFC not produced in Russia, had increased dramatically. The profits in the illegal CFC trade are considered to rival the profits to be made by selling cocaine.

This black market trade is in part a result of the ozone treaties' successes; as developed states phased out their production, the demand for illegal CFCs rose. Moreover, detection is difficult; the treaties generally permit the use and trade of recycled CFCs to service existing equipment, but it is often difficult to distinguish between new and recycled CFCs. In addition, the fact that developing states could produce CFCs even after developed states were to phase out production meant that the mere presence of these chemicals was not evidence of their illegality. Moreover, a thriving black market threatened to undermine the treaty. The entire treaty regime is premised upon the substitution of ODS with safer chemicals; a U.S. official estimated that a "cheating rate" of only 10 percent could keep stratospheric CFC levels from declining.

States recognized in Montreal that a monitoring and compliance mechanism was essential but were unable to agree then on how to treat noncompliance. The Protocol provides that "[t]he Parties, at their first meeting, shall consider and approve procedures and institutional mechanisms for determining non-compliance with the provisions of this Protocol and for treatment of Parties found to be in non-compliance." In 1989, the Parties established a working group of legal experts to draft a noncompliance procedure. In the following year, the Parties adopted, on an interim basis, the following noncompliance procedure (NCP).

Interim Non-Compliance Procedure

UNEP/OzL. Pro. 2/3 (Annex III) (1990)

1. If one or more Parties have reservations regarding another Party's implementation of its obligations . . . ., those concerns may be addressed in writing to the Secretariat. Such a submission shall be supported by corroborating information.

2. The Party whose implementation is at issue is to be given the submission and a reasonable opportunity to reply. Such reply . . . is to be submitted to the Secretariat and to the Parties involved. The Secretariat shall then transmit the submission, the reply and the information provided by the Parties, to the Implementation Committee . . . which shall consider the matter as soon as practicable.

3. An Implementation Committee is hereby established. It shall consist of five Parties elected by the Meeting of the Parties for two years, based on equitable geographical distribution. . . .

6. The Committee shall consider the submissions, information and observations referred to [above] with a view to securing an amicable resolution of the matter on the basis of respect for the provisions of the Protocol.

7. The Committee shall report to the Meeting of the Parties. After receiving a report by the Committee the Parties may, taking into consideration the circumstances of the case, decide upon and call for steps to bring about full compliance with the Protocol, including measures to assist the Party's compliance with the Protocol, and to further the Protocol's objectives. . . .

10. The Meeting of the Parties may request the Committee to make recommendations to assist the Meeting's consideration of cases of possible non-compliance. . . .

This system was agreed to only on an interim basis because some parties, led by Norway, thought a more rigorous noncompliance system was needed. As a result, the working group was reconvened and given a mandate to deliver a stronger procedure; simultaneously the Implementation Committee (IC) began to operate under the interim procedure. In 1992, the Parties adopted a revised NCP, which expanded the IC from five to ten members. They also adopted an "indicative list of measures that might be taken in respect of non-compliance," including not only appropriate assistance but also "[s]uspension . . . of specific rights and privileges under the Protocol."

Although the IC was relatively inactive during its first few years, in 1995 the system was used for the first time to handle a situation of potential noncompliance with the Montreal Protocol's substantive provisions. Belarus, Bulgaria, Poland, Russia, and Ukraine jointly submitted a request for a special five-year grace period on their ODS phaseout obligations. Shortly thereafter, Russian Prime Minister Viktor Chernomyrdin sent a message effectively admitting that Russia would not be able to meet the 1996 CFC phaseout deadlines. At U.S. urging, this statement was routed to the IC, which deemed the request a "submission" under the NCP. Russia and the IC entered into negotiations, in which Russia agreed to provide more data and work with the IC to develop a detailed phaseout plan. The IC, and thereafter the Meeting of the Parties, officially supported international technical and financial assistance for Russia linked to trade restrictions forbidding exports of ODS to industrialized parties other than those formerly a part of the USSR. The Parties did not, however, explicitly address Russia's request for a grace period.

Thereafter, Russia created a special interagency commission on ODS involving 27 ministries and departments. With the help of Denmark, Russia promulgated a detailed plan for ODS phaseout. In March 1996, the IC expressed its satisfaction with Russia's reports and noted that Russia had "taken important steps . . . towards achieving full compliance" with the ozone treaties. In December 1996, the Meeting of the Parties noted that Russia had made "considerable progress" and urged continued international assistance contingent upon Russia's continued submission of reports to, and consultations with, the IC.

Thereafter, a complex effort involving several bodies began. Russia was not an Article 5 nation and hence was ineligible for assistance from the Multilateral Fund. As a result, the Global Environment Facility (GEF), a collaborative funding mechanism among the World Bank, UNEP, and the United Nations Development Programme, which helps developing states meet the incremental costs of efforts to address climate change, biodiversity, international water resources, and ozone depletion, along with the Danish and U.S. governments, committed to support a $60 million program for the phaseout of ODS in several sectors of the Russian economy. The World Bank prepared a $50-$60 million project focused on the shutdown and conversion of six Russian production facilities, which together accounted for nearly half of remaining global CFC production capacity.

Although funding for Russia comes from outside the treaty regime and from bodies with no official role in the treaty system, the IC continues to play a central role in regularly reviewing progress and dealing with compliance issues as they arise. For example, the Parties' decisions pertaining to Russia state that "[i]n case of any questions related to the reporting requirements and the actions [of Russia], the disbursement of the international assistance should be contingent on the settlement of those problems with the Implementation Committee." The GEF has represented that "GEF funding [is] subject to the formal processes of the Montreal Protocol for noncompliance." Hence, in practice, the ozone regime consists of a system of integrated institutions that extends beyond the formal boundaries of the ozone treaties.

The Parties continued to address the problem of Russian noncompliance. At its November 1998 meeting, the Implementation Committee drafted the following for consideration by the Meeting of Parties:

Draft Decisions Submitted by the Implementation Committee for the Consideration of the Meeting of the Parties

UNEP/OzL.Pro./ImpCom/21/3 (Annex I) (1998)

Decision (g).—Compliance with the Montreal Protocol by the Russian Federation

1. . . . . [I]n 1996, the Russian Federation was in non-compliance with its control obligations under [Article 2, setting forth targets and timetables for ODS phaseouts]

of the Montreal Protocol. The Russian Federation also expresses a belief that this situation will continue through at least the year 2000, necessitating annual review by the Implementation Committee and the Parties until such time as the Russian Federation comes into compliance;

2. . . . [T]he Russian Federation submitted a country programme in October 1995 (revised in November 1995) that contains specific benchmarks and a phase-out schedule. . . . Further steps were taken to bring the Russian Federation into compliance with its obligations under [Article 2, setting forth targets and timetables for ODS phaseouts] when, in October 1998, the "Special Initiative for ODS Production Closure in the Russian Federation" (Special Initiative) was signed [with the World Bank]. . . .

3. [The Parties decide to] closely monitor the progress of the Russian Federation with regard to the phase-out of ozone-depleting substances, particularly towards meeting the specific commitments in the 1995 country programme and the Special Initiative noted above. In this regard, the Parties request that the Russian Federation submit a complete copy of its country programme, and subsequent updates, if any, to the Ozone Secretariat. To the degree that the Russian Federation is working towards and meeting the specific time-based commitments in the country programme and the Special Initiative and continues to report data annually demonstrating a decrease in imports and consumption, the Russian Federation should continue to be treated in the same manner as a Party in good standing. In this regard, the Russian Federation should continue to receive international assistance to enable it to meet these commitments. . . . However . . . the Parties caution the Russian Federation . . . that in the event that the country fails to meet the commitments noted in prior decisions as well as in the above documents in the times specified, the Parties shall consider measures. . . . These measures could include the possibility of actions that may be available under Article 4 [i.e., treating noncompliant parties as nonparties to the Protocol], designed to ensure that the supply of CFCs and halons that is the subject of non-compliance is ceased, and that exporting Parties are not contributing to a continuing situation of non-compliance. . . .

Over the next several years, Russia received substantial World Bank assistance in phasing out its ODS production facilities. In October 2001 the ozone treaty Secretariat informed the IC that the World Bank had confirmed that all ODS-producing enterprises in Russia "had completed closure activities in accordance with the legally binding Closure Plans, and that none would be capable of future ODS production." The same month, the Montreal Protocol parties adopted a decision noting that Russia had ended CFC production and had halted the import and export of new ODS in 2000.

Notes and Questions

1. How would you characterize the purposes of the Montreal Protocol noncompliance mechanism? Is the Implementation Committee an adjudicatory, a conciliatory, or an executive organ? Is the IC designed to vindicate the rights of individual states, or the collective rights of all parties to the treaty?

2. What is the relationship between this mechanism and the dispute settlement procedure set forth in Article 11 of the Vienna Convention? Why would parties choose the NCP over the Vienna Convention provision, which has never been invoked? Might the NCP, by offering financial aid in response to noncompliance, actually encourage noncompliance?

3. Why do you think that all of the major proceedings regarding noncompliance before the NCP were initiated by the affected parties themselves?

4. It appears that, by 1995 or 1996, the amount of black market trade in CFCs had significantly declined. Do you think that the international community would have responded differently to Russian noncompliance if Russia had not been considered to be a major contributor to the black market in CFCs?

5. States have continued efforts to combat illegal trade in ODS. In 1997, parties to the ozone treaties entered into the so-called Montreal Amendment, which requires states to establish a "system for licensing the import and export" of substances controlled by the ozone treaties. Under this system, importers and exporters must register and apply for national permits. The applications identify the type and quantity of ODS, the states involved in the transaction, and other relevant information. The system is designed to enable customs and police officials to monitor trade in ODS and to detect unlicensed trade. In addition, UNEP has sponsored a series of regional trading sessions for customs officers so they can better monitor trade in ODS.

Notwithstanding these efforts, as of 2005, significant illegal trade in CFCs continues to exist. Factors that contribute to this trade appear to include the continued demand for CFCs in developed states to maintain CFC-dependent equipment; the costs associated with retrofitting or replacing CFC-dependent equipment; the absence or lack of enforcement of import and export controls; and the difficulty in distinguishing between new and used CFCs.

D. A Model for Future Efforts?

In many respects the ozone treaties are one of international law's important success stories. In 1986, total consumption of CFCs worldwide was about 1.1 million ODP tonnes; by 2004, this had dropped to roughly 70,000 tonnes. Absent the ozone treaties, global consumption would have reached an estimated 3 million tonnes in 2010 and 8 million tonnes in 2060, resulting in a 50 percent depletion of the ozone layer by 2035. Consumption in developed states fell from nearly 1 million ODP tonnes in 1986 to about 2,000 tonnes in 2004. By 2004, developing states had reduced their CFC consumption by about 60 percent from their maximum consumption in the mid-1990s.

Absent these treaties, UV-B radiation would have doubled in the North and quadrupled in the South. This would have caused an estimated 19 million cases of non-melanoma cancer, 1.5 million cases of melanoma cancer, and 130 million cases of eye cataracts. The charts on page 803 project atmospheric concentrations of ODS under the various ozone regimes and global production of ODS.

In light of this success, many have asked whether and how the ozone regime may be used as a model for other international regimes. Consider the following comments, excerpted from the 1999 Report on Multilateral Environmental Agreements published by a British House of Commons Select Committee:

34. Designing compliance mechanisms for [environmental treaties] is made more difficult by the limited number of means available for ensuring compliance.

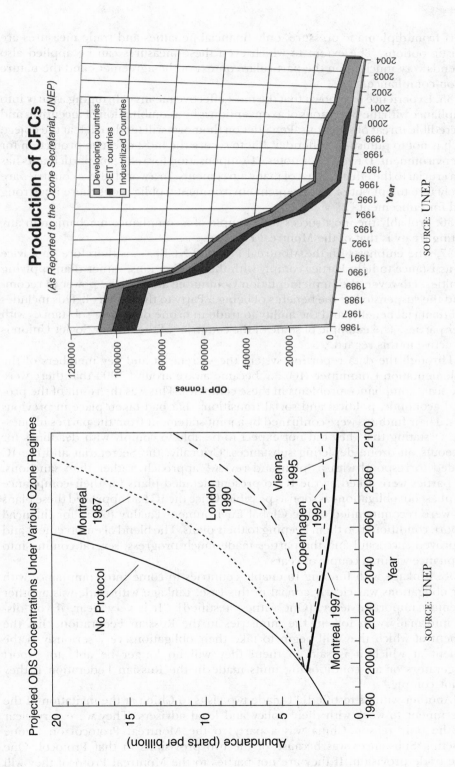

Production of CFCs
(As Reported to the Ozone Secretariat, UNEP)

- Developing countries
- CEIT countries
- Industrilized Countries

ODP Tonnes

1200000
1000000
800000
600000
400000
200000
0

1986 1987 1988 1989 1990 1991 1992 1993 1994 1995 1996 1997 1998 1999 2000 2001 2002 2003 2004

Year

SOURCE: UNEP

Projected ODS Concentrations Under Various Ozone Regimes

Abundance (parts per billion)

20

15

10

5

0

1980 2000 2020 2040 2060 2080 2100

Year

No Protocol

Montreal 1987

London 1990

Vienna 1995

Copenhagen 1992

Montreal 1997

SOURCE: UNEP

Apart from diplomatic pressure, only financial penalties and trade measures are realistic options. The extent to which even these measures can be applied also depends very much upon the particular context of the agreement and the nature of non-compliance. . . .

35. Experience has shown that the most effective means of bringing a party into compliance with the provisions of a convention is by a combination of incentives and the credible threat of sanctions. Penalties on their own will tend to defeat the object, which is not to punish the offender, but to secure the most effective protection for the environment. David Victor notes, "Compensation for reluctant participants has been crucial to the effectiveness of many agreements. In a world where countries are largely free to opt out of inconvenient environmental obligations there is a strong need for enticement."

36. Probably the most successful example of a compliance mechanism in any existing treaty is that of the Montreal Protocol. . . .

37. The emphasis [in the Montreal Protocol NCP] . . . is therefore on advice and assistance to help Parties comply with their obligations, rather than applying penalties. However, the Implementation Committee also has the power to recommend the suspension of the benefits of being a Party to the Protocol. This includes both financial benefits and the ability to trade in ozone depleting substances with other parties. The example of some of the countries of the former Soviet Union is instructive in this regard. . . .

Through the data reporting system the secretariat and key members of the Implementation Committee (IC) . . . became aware around 1994 that there were large scale compliance problems in these countries. This was the result of the profound economic, political and social transitions that had taken place in previous years. Their findings were confirmed by a joint statement from the parties in question . . . stating that they did not expect to be able to comply with deadlines for phaseouts on ozone depleting substances. Critically, the Secretariat and the IC decided to respond with a "plan and review" approach, rather than sanctions. The parties were asked by the IC to present detailed plans for their compliance with phaseout obligations as soon as possible. Once the IC had approved these plans they were recommended to the Global Environment Facility (GEF) for financial support, conditional on them keeping to their plans. The blend of enforcement and aid proved successful and the parties made much progress, several coming into compliance within a couple of years.

38. Linkage with funding to enable countries to come into compliance with their obligations was clearly crucial in this case. Linkage with trade was another extremely important lever. [One witness testified], "It is very clear, if you discuss informally with folk in the ministries in the Russian Federation, that the moment at which they will begin to take their obligations very seriously is the moment at which it is said to them they will no longer be able to export refrigerators or air conditioning units made in the Russian Federation if they do not comply." . . .

[Another witness testified] "I made two visits to China at the invitation of the Government to work with their policy and legal advisers. They were very clear that the only reason China was a party to the Montreal Protocol on Ozone Depleting Substances was because of the two provisions in that Protocol. One is the trade provision. If they are not parties to the Montreal Protocol they will not be able to trade in goods made with, containing or comprising prescribed substances. Secondly, there is the provision of financial resources to assist them into the transition to non-ozone depleting substance use. Without those two mechanisms they would not even have become [a] party [to the treaty]. Those two mechanisms will also be key to ensuring compliance by countries like China when the obligations really begin to bite."

41. We note, however, . . . that powers of enforcement must not be left only in the hands of the economically strong, not the economically weak, countries. The [IC] provides for equal representation of developed and developing countries . . . thus ensuring that it retains the confidence of all sides. It is essential that compliance mechanisms are developed and operated in a democratic manner which encourages the participation and commands the confidence of all parties. . . .

Select Committee on Environment, *Transportation and Regional Affairs, Multilateral Environmental Agreements* (16th Rep., 1999).

Notes and Questions

1. One way to interpret the ozone regime is that the parties proceeded in three sequential stages. First, the parties agreed to a substantively vague framework agreement, the Vienna Convention, which focused on research and information sharing. This was followed by agreement on a series of detailed percentage reductions in specific ODS. Finally, the parties agreed on noncompliance provisions. What is the logic behind this sequential approach? Could this strategy be successful in other contexts? What are the drawbacks to this process?

2. The Montreal Protocol imposed its most stringent obligations upon the richest states, while giving a substantial grace period and, eventually, a 100 percent subsidy to poorer nations. Several states in transition, such as Russia, have been informally given a grace period. Can or should these types of differential obligations be incorporated into more international agreements?

E. Note on the Precautionary Principle

The international response to ozone depletion involved rapidly changing scientific understandings, uncertain predictions about chemical and biological reactions decades into the future, and ongoing collaboration between scientists and policy makers. Many international environmental issues involve similar scientific complexities and uncertainties. The precautionary principle is one response to the policy dilemmas posed by scientific uncertainty. This principle has been expressed in a number of different ways in various international environmental instruments. For example, Principle 15 of the Rio Declaration provides that "[w]here there are threats of serious or irreversible damage, lack of full scientific certainty shall not be used as a reason for postponing cost-effective measures to prevent environmental degradation." A different articulation of the principle is found in the 1996 Protocol to the London Convention on the Prevention of Marine Pollution by Dumping of Wastes and Other Matter, which provides that:

Contracting Parties shall apply a precautionary approach to environmental protection from dumping of wastes or other matter whereby appropriate preventative measures are taken when there is reason to believe that wastes or other matter introduced into the marine environment are likely to cause harm even when there is no conclusive evidence to provide a causal relation between inputs and their effects.

The various articulations of the precautionary principle in international environmental instruments give rise to a number of questions. For example, what level and type of harm is necessary to trigger the principle? Does the principle require only cost-effective measures, or whatever is necessary to prevent environmental harm? What is the relationship between the magnitude of the risk and the precautionary measures taken? These and other uncertainties cause many states and scholars to question (1) whether the precautionary principle is a legal norm and (2) whether the precautionary principle can be usefully operationalized.

The status and application of the precautionary principle has been addressed in several recent international disputes. One involves an EC ban on the use of certain growth-promoting hormones in livestock production and on the importation of meat from livestock treated with these hormones. These hormones are widely used in the United States. The ban, first imposed in 1987, effectively eliminated most U.S. red meat and meat product exports to the EC, costing U.S. industry in excess of $100 million in lost sales per year. The United States and the EC disagreed over whether use of these hormones posed a health risk, and in April 1996 the United States challenged the EC ban in dispute settlement proceedings at the World Trade Organization (WTO). The legal issue presented was whether the EC's rationale for the ban had sufficient "scientific justification," as required by the WTO Agreement on the Application of Sanitary and Phytosanitary Measures (SPS Agreement). The EC argued that the SPS Agreement should be read against the background of the precautionary principle. The WTO Appellate Body stated:

121. The basic submission of the [EC] is that the precautionary principle is, or has become, "a general customary rule of international law" or at least "a general principle of law". Referring more specifically to . . . the SPS Agreement, applying the precautionary principle means, in the view of the [EC] that it is not necessary for *all* scientists around the world to agree on the "possibility and magnitude" of the risk, nor for *all* or most of the WTO Members to perceive and evaluate the risk in the same way. . . .

122. The United States does not consider that the "precautionary principle" represents customary international law and suggests it is more an "approach" than a "principle". Canada, too, takes the view that the precautionary principle has not yet been incorporated into the corpus of public international law; however, it concedes that the "precautionary approach" or "concept" is "an *emerging* principle of law" which may in the future crystallize into one of the "general principles of law recognized by civilized nations" within the meaning of Article 38(1)(c) of the [International Court of Justice Statute].

123. The status of the precautionary principle in international law continues to be the subject of debate among academics, law practitioners, regulators and judges. . . . Whether it has been widely accepted by Members as a principle of *general* or *customary international law* appears less than clear. We consider, however, that it is unnecessary, and probably imprudent, for the Appellate Body in this appeal to take a position on this important, but abstract, question. We note

that . . . the precautionary principle, at least outside the field of international environmental law, still awaits authoritative formulation.[93]

124. It appears to us important, nevertheless, to note some aspects of the relationship of the precautionary principle to the *SPS Agreement*. First, the principle has not been written into the *SPS Agreement* as a ground for justifying SPS measures that are otherwise inconsistent with the . . . particular provisions of that Agreement. . . . [A] panel charged with determining, for instance, whether "sufficient scientific evidence" exists to warrant the maintenance by a Member of a particular SPS measure may, of course, and should, bear in mind that responsible, representative governments commonly act from perspectives of prudence and precaution where risks of irreversible, e.g. life-terminating, damage to human health are concerned. Lastly, however, the precautionary principle does not, by itself, and without a clear textual directive to that effect, relieve a panel from the duty of applying the normal (i.e. customary international law) principles of treaty interpretation in reading the provisions of the *SPS Agreement*.

125. We accordingly [find] that the precautionary principle does not override the provisions . . . of the *SPS Agreement*.

EC—Measures Concerning Meat and Meat Products (Hormones), WT/DS28/AB/R (1998). The Appellate Body concluded that the EC ban was not consistent with the SPS Agreement.

More recently, the precautionary principle was at issue in a dispute between Australia and New Zealand, on the one hand, and Japan, on the other, over Japan's experimental fishing program for Southern Bluefin Tuna (SBT). During the early 1980s, these three countries entered into informal talks to cooperate in the conservation and utilization of SBT. By 1985 they concluded an informal agreement on an annual total allowable catch of SBT and an allocation among them. New totals and allocations were negotiated in subsequent years, and by 1994 the informal agreement was formalized in the Convention for the Conservation of Southern Bluefin Tuna (CSBT Convention). Under the Convention, a commission consisting of representatives from each CSBT party was charged with the establishment and allocation, by consensus, of a total allowable catch among the parties. From 1994 through 1997, the commission set total catch and allocations at 1989 levels. However, no agreement was reached in 1998 and 1999 because Japan believed that SBT stocks were recovering so that the total allowable catch could be increased; Australia and New Zealand believed that restraint was still necessary to permit the SBT stock to recover. As a result, the parties discussed creating an experimental fishing program to enhance their understanding of the SBT stock. Through the Commission, it was agreed that any experimental program would be a collaborative effort agreed to by all the parties. Thereafter, multiple proposals from Japan for an experimental fishing program were rejected.

In 1998 Japan announced plans unilaterally to begin an experimental fishing program. As a result, Japan's taking of SBT exceeded its 1997 allocation. After

---

[93]In Case Concerning the Gabcíkovo-Nagymaros Project (Hungary/Slovakia), the International Court of Justice recognized that in the field of environmental protection ". . . new norms and standards have been developed, [as] set forth in a great number of instruments during the last two decades. Such new norms have to be taken into consideration, and such new standards given proper weight . . .". However, the Court did not identify the precautionary principle as one of those recently developed norms. It also declined to declare that such principle could override the obligations of the Treaty between Czechoslovakia and Hungary of 16 September 1977 concerning the construction and operation of the Gabcíkovo/Nagymaros System of Locks.

inconclusive negotiations, in July 1999 New Zealand and Australia both notified Japan that they were instituting arbitral proceedings under Annex VII of the 1982 UN Convention on the Law of the Sea (UNCLOS) and, pending constitution of the arbitral tribunal, were seeking provisional measures from the International Tribunal for the Law of the Sea (ITLOS), as permitted under UNCLOS. This treaty, which is examined in detail in Chapter 10, authorizes provisional measures if the tribunal determines "that the urgency of the situation so requires." The applicants argued that Japan's experimental fishing program violated various provisions of UNCLOS and the precautionary principle. In August 1999, the Tribunal issued the following order:

Southern Bluefin Tuna Cases (New Zealand and Australia v. Japan)

117 I.L.R. 148 (Int'l Trib. L. Sea 1999)

29. . . . . [The applicants] alleged that Japan had failed to comply with its obligation to cooperate in the conservation of the southern bluefin tuna stock by, *inter alia*, undertaking unilateral experimental fishing for southern bluefin tuna in 1998 and 1999 and, accordingly, had requested the arbitral tribunal . . . to adjudge and declare [that Japan had breached its obligations under the UNCLOS in relation to the conservation and management of the SBT stock]. . . .

67. *Considering* that . . . the Tribunal may prescribe provisional measures to preserve the respective rights of the parties to the dispute or to prevent serious harm to the marine environment; . . .

69. *Considering* that Australia and New Zealand contend that further catches of southern bluefin tuna, pending the hearing of the matter by an arbitral tribunal, would cause immediate harm to their rights; . . .

71. *Considering* that there is no disagreement between the parties that the stock of southern bluefin tuna is severely depleted and is at its historically lowest levels and that this is a cause for serious biological concern; . . .

73. *Considering* that Japan contends that the scientific evidence available shows that the implementation of its experimental fishing programme will cause no further threat to the southern bluefin tuna stock and that the experimental fishing programme remains necessary to reach a more reliable assessment of the potential of the stock to recover;

74. *Considering* that Australia and New Zealand maintain that the scientific evidence available shows that the amount of southern bluefin tuna taken under the experimental fishing programme could endanger the existence of the stock; . . .

77. *Considering* that, in the view of the Tribunal, the parties should in the circumstances act with prudence and caution to ensure that effective conservation measures are taken to prevent serious harm to the stock of southern bluefin tuna; . . .

79. *Considering* that there is scientific uncertainty regarding measures to be taken to conserve the stock of southern bluefin tuna and that there is no agreement among the parties as to whether the conservation measures taken so far have led to the improvement in the stock of southern bluefin tuna;

80. *Considering* that, although the Tribunal cannot conclusively assess the scientific evidence presented by the parties, it finds that measures should be taken as a matter of urgency to preserve the rights of the parties and to avert further deterioration of the southern bluefin tuna stock; . . .

90. *For these reasons,*
THE TRIBUNAL,
1. *Prescribes*, pending a decision of the arbitral tribunal, the following measures: . . .
   By 18 votes to 4,
(c) Australia, Japan and New Zealand shall ensure, unless they agree otherwise, that their annual catches do not exceed the annual national allocations at the levels last agreed by the parties . . . ; in calculating the annual catches for 1999 and 2000, and without prejudice to any decision of the arbitral tribunal, account shall be taken of the catch during 1999 as part of an experimental fishing programme;
   By 20 votes to 2,
(d) Australia, Japan and New Zealand shall each refrain from conducting an experimental fishing programme involving the taking of a catch of southern bluefin tuna, except with the agreement of the other parties or unless the experimental catch is counted against its annual national allocation as prescribed in subparagraph (c); . . .

SEPARATE OPINION BY JUDGE LAING

12. . . . The Applicants based their requests for provisional measures on [UNCLOS]; the 1993 Convention . . . as well as their obligations under general international law, in particular the "precautionary principle" which, according to the [Applicants] . . .

> must be applied by States in taking decisions about actions which entail threats of serious or irreversible damage to the environment while there is scientific uncertainty about the effect of such actions. The principle requires caution and vigilance in decision-making in the face of such uncertainty.

Background on Environmental Precaution

14. The notion of environmental precaution largely stems from diplomatic practice and treaty-making in the spheres, originally, of international marine pollution and, now, of biodiversity, climate change, pollution generally and, broadly, the environment. Its main thesis is that, in the face of serious risk to or grounds (as appropriately qualified) for concern about the environment, scientific uncertainty or the absence of complete proof should not stand in the way of positive action to minimize risks or take actions of a conservatory, preventative or curative nature. In addition to scientific uncertainty, the most frequently articulated conditions or circumstances are concerns of an intergenerational nature and forensic or proof difficulties, generally in the context of rapid change and perceived high risks. The thrust of the notion is vesting a broad dispensation to policy makers, seeking to provide guidance to administrative and other decision-makers and shifting the burden of proof to the State in control of the territory from which the harm might emanate or to the responsible actor. . . .

15. Even as questioning of the acceptability of the precautionary notion diminishes, challenges increase regarding such specifics as: the wide potential ambit of its coverage; the clarity of operational criteria; the monetary costs of environmental regulation; possible public health risks associated with the very remedies improvised to avoid risk; diversity and vagueness of articulations of the notion; uncertainties about attendant obligations, and the imprecision and subjectivity of such a value-laden

notion. Nevertheless, the notion has been "broadly accepted for international action, even if the consequence of its application in a given situation remains open to interpretation."

16. Nevertheless, it is not possible, on the basis of the materials available and arguments presented on this application for provisional measures, to determine whether, as the Applicants contend, customary international law recognizes a precautionary principle.[5]

Precaution in Marine Living Resource Management

17. However, it cannot be denied that UNCLOS adopts a precautionary *approach*. . . .

18. . . . . The Tribunal also recites the apparently key importance in this case of serious harm to the marine environment as a crucial, perhaps *the* crucial criterion or condition for provisional measures and it prescribes as provisional measures a prohibition of experimental programmes in [sic] except by agreement of all three parties and annual catch limits (quotas), which include the concept of payback for catch taken over quota in 1999. . . .

19. In view of my earlier discussion, it becomes evident that the Tribunal has adopted the precautionary approach for the purposes of provisional measures in such a case as the present. In my view, adopting an *approach*, rather than a principle, appropriately imports a certain degree of flexibility and tends, though not dispositively, to underscore reticence about making premature pronouncements about desirable normative structures. . . .

Notes and Questions

1. Do either of these cases represent a victory for those who advocate use of the precautionary principle? Do the cases help resolve the controversy over whether the precautionary principle is a customary norm, or whether tribunals can meaningfully apply it?

2. Is a WTO tribunal of trade experts well-positioned to evaluate the scientific justifications offered by a government in defense of a particular health or safety regulation? Similarly, given the ITLOS's inability to evaluate the conflicting scientific evidence before it, upon what basis could the Tribunal conclude that "measures should be taken as a matter of urgency to perserve the rights of the parties and to avert further deterioration of the southern bluefin tuna stocks"?

3. UNEP's Executive Director, Mostafa Tolba, said that the Vienna Convention

> is the first global convention to address an issue that for the time being seems far in the future and is of unknown proportions. This Convention . . . is the essence of the anticipatory response so many environmental issues call for: to deal with the threat of the problem before we have to deal with the problem itself.

Would you consider the Vienna Convention and subsequent ozone treaties examples of the application—or the repudiation—of the precautionary principle?

[5]It might be noted that treaties and formal instruments use different language of obligation; the notion is stated variously (as a principle, approach, concept, measures, action); no authoritative judicial decision unequivocally supports the notion; doctrine is indecisive, and domestic juridical materials are uncertain or evolving.

III. PROTECTING THE PLANET: COMBATING CLIMATE CHANGE

Human activities produce various gases that affect the earth's atmosphere and climate. While the nature and scope of these changes is a matter of some controversy, there is little doubt that climate change threatens to alter significantly the planet's environment, human health and welfare, and the global economy. Thus, the ecological and environmental stakes associated with climate change are enormous—as are the political and legal difficulties associated with international efforts to address the issue.

The structure of the climate change problem appears at first glance to be similar to that of the ozone problem discussed in Section II of this chapter: states release emissions into the atmosphere leading to environmental changes that threaten to adversely affect human health and activities. Moreover, like the ozone problem, climate change is truly a *global* problem as greenhouse gases (GHGs) released anywhere in the world disperse rapidly in the global atmosphere.

But climate change is vastly more complex than ozone depletion. The ozone problem involved a handful of chemicals and a small number of producers located primarily in the United States and Europe. In contrast, virtually every form of human activity produces greenhouse gases, and significant reductions in GHG emissions will affect the economic competitiveness of individuals, firms and states, creating economic winners and losers. Climate policy involves cutting-edge scientific issues concerning atmospheric chemistry; the ability of forests, clouds, and oceans to absorb and store carbon; the protection of natural habitats and ecosystems; and rising sea-levels. In addition, climate policy involves major questions of economic development, the conflicting interests of developing and developed states, the interests of future generations, the diffusion of technical assistance and know-how, financial transfers, and sovereignty over natural resources.

Finally, debate over climate policy frequently focuses on the costs and benefits of various possible strategies for addressing this issue. However, given the enormous range and complexity of the potential impact, significant uncertainty surrounds almost all estimates of the costs of climate change, as well as the costs and benefits of policies designed to curb it. Some studies project high economic costs to achieve even small reductions in greenhouse gases; others show GHG reduction imposing negligible costs, while generating secondary benefits in the form of cleaner air and water—benefits that would otherwise be achieved by other means.

In the Problem that follows, we examine the evolving international legal response to the challenges posed by climate change. As we shall see, efforts to address climate change pose difficult distributional and equity issues, and have given rise to an elaborate institutional architecture for international cooperation on climate issues. As you review the materials below, consider how policymakers should address issues of scientific and economic uncertainty, and how they should balance environmental and economic goals. Consider also the various options states have in designing an institutional architecture to combat climate change, and whether any approaches can attract widespread acceptance from developed and developing states. Finally, consider which strategies the international community should pursue, given that the United States, the world's largest emitter of GHGs, has refused to ratify the central treaty mandating GHG reductions, and that rapidly industrializing developing states, such as China and India, have no obligation to control emissions.

A. The Problem

The earth's climate is driven by energy, mostly in the form of visible light, received from the sun. About 70 percent of the sun's energy passes through the atmosphere to heat the earth's surface. The earth, in turn, emits this energy in the form of infrared radiation. This energy cannot pass through the atmosphere like visible light. Instead it is carried away from the earth's surface by air currents and eventually escapes into outer space. Greenhouse gases in the earth's atmosphere, including water vapor, carbon dioxide, methane, and nitrous oxides, control this energy flow by absorbing some of the infrared radiation emitted by the earth. These gases produce a natural greenhouse effect that keeps the planet some 30 degrees (centigrade) warmer than it would be otherwise; thus, these greenhouse gases are essential for life as we know it.

However, human activities are increasing the amounts of GHGs in the atmosphere. Carbon dioxide is the most important of these, comprising nearly half of all anthropogenic GHG emissions. It is generated whenever fossil fuels—primarily coal, oil, and natural gas—are burned, and these fuels provide more than 80 percent of the world's energy. Other GHG sources include methane from agriculture and energy production and distribution; nitrous oxide from agriculture and industrial processes; and synthetic gases, such as hydrofluorocarbons, perfluorocarbons, and sulfur hexafluoride, from a variety of business and consumer uses. The loss of so-called carbon sinks, such as forests that remove and sequester carbon dioxide, is another important source of increased GHG concentrations.

For hundreds of years before the start of the Industrial Revolution, carbon dioxide concentrations in the atmosphere were about 270 parts per million. However, human activities have markedly changed the composition of the earth's atmosphere. Between 1900 and 1999, human activities added an estimated 254,845 tons of carbon dioxide into the atmosphere. As a result, atmospheric concentrations of carbon dioxide have risen from about 280 parts per million by volume (ppm) in 1815 to over 375 ppm today, and the rise seems to be accelerating. Concentrations of other GHGs have also risen sharply; methane concentrations, for example, have risen from about 700 parts per billion by volume (ppb) to over 1700 ppb.

Of course, states have not contributed equally to these changes. The United States, with approximately four percent of the world's population, emits approximately one-quarter of the planet's GHGs each year. In 1999, the United States emitted approximately 1,520 millions of tons of carbon; the EU emitted 915 million tons; China 669 million tons; and India 243 million tons. These national totals depend in part on population and levels of industrial activity. Thus, in 1999, the United States emitted approximately 5.6 tons of carbon per capita; the EU 2.4 tons; China 0.5 tons; and India 0.2 tons.

There is significant evidence that increased GHG concentrations have already started to alter the earth's climate. 2005 was the hottest year on record, and eight of the ten hottest years on record have occurred since 1980. Snow cover has declined by some 10 percent since the late 1960s in the mid- and high latitudes of the Northern Hemisphere, and rain patterns have changed over much of the globe. The global average sea level has risen by 10 to 20 centimeters over the past 100 years, some ten times faster than the rate over the previous 3,000 years. Extreme weather events have increased in frequency and intensity; the insurance industry has experienced a 15-fold increase in insured losses from catastrophic weather events in the past three decades. The Intergovernmental Panel on Climate Change (IPCC), the authoritative international scientific body that assesses the technical and socio-economic issues associated with climate change, has also identified:

> shrinkage in glaciers, thawing of permafrost, later freezing and earlier breakup of ice on rivers and lakes, lengthening of mid-to high-latitude growing seasons, poleward and altitudinal shifts of plant and animal ranges, declines of plant and animal populations, and earlier flowering of trees, emergence of insects and egg-laying in birds . . .

as consequences of increased GHG concentrations.

Using complex computer models, IPCC estimates that mean global temperatures will increase by 1.4 degrees Celsius to 5.8 degrees Celsius between 1990 and 2100. This may sound modest, but it would be a greater change in mean global temperature than that experienced over the last 10,000 years. There is significant debate over the impact such a change in the planet's climate would produce.

The IPCC estimates that global warming will produce a 9 to 88 centimeter rise in sea levels, with a "best estimate" of 50 centimeters, causing potentially catastrophic consequences in low-lying areas. Some island states, such as the Maldives and the Cook Islands, could be submerged. The expected sea level rise would inundate much of the world's lowlands, damage costal cropland, and displace millions of people from coastal and small island communities. Higher seas levels would contaminate underground fresh water supplies in China's Yangtze Delta and Vietnam's Mekong Delta and numerous atolls scattered across the Pacific and Indian Oceans.

Climate change is expected to produce more frequent and more extreme storms, droughts, floods, and heat waves. More intense rainfall will lead to greater flooding in some regions, along with more landslides, avalanches and soil erosion. Cyclones, hurricanes and tornados are expected to be larger and more intense. Changing weather patterns will affect agriculture and food security. According to the United Nations Environment Programme, drier soils may reduce yields by as much as a third in the tropics and subtropics, while the U.S. grain belt, vast sections of mid-latitude Asia, and sub-Saharan Africa are all expected to experience drier and hotter conditions. On the other hand, longer growing seasons and increased rains may increase productivity in certain regions, including the United Kingdom, Scandinavia, and parts of Russia and North America.

Climate change threatens to harm public health, particularly in developing states. Heat waves are associated with cardiovascular, respiratory, and other diseases, and illness and death from these diseases are expected to rise. Public health experts also expect increased outbreaks of some insect-borne infectious diseases, such as malaria and dengue fever, and increased cases of diarrhea and other waterborne diseases, particularly in developing states.

B. The Climate Regime

International discussions about climate change began in the 1970s, eventually leading to a series of agreements designed to avoid, or at least mitigate, the harmful impacts of climate change. The climate regime emerged in several steps.

1. The Road to Rio

The 1979 World Climate Conference recognized climate change as a serious international problem. This scientific gathering was the first of a series of technical and political conferences held over the next two decades that focused on climate change. In 1988, states created the IPCC with the mandate to assess the state of existing knowledge about the climate system and climate change; the impacts of climate change; and possible response strategies. In 1990, the IPCC released its first scientific assessment report, which had a powerful effect on both policy makers and the general public. Shortly after the report's release, in December 1990, the UN General Assembly approved the start of negotiations over a climate change treaty, with a view to drafting an agreement to be signed at the Earth Summit in Rio de Janeiro in June 1992.

At these negotiations, the EU called for binding emission reduction targets and timetables for meeting those targets. The United States opposed targets and time-tables, arguing that climate science and policy was marked by substantial uncertainty, and urged further research to resolve these uncertainties. The United States also advocated a "no regrets" policy of actions that, while reducing GHG emissions, were justified as cost-effective on other grounds. In general, developing states rejected any requirements that would slow their economic growth and argued that they were not responsible for creating the climate problem. But in other respects, developing states had divergent interests. Small island states and low-lying states like Bangladesh pushed for major cuts in developed states' GHG emissions. Oil-producing states, in contrast, opposed any mandated cuts in GHG emissions, and pressed for an international fund to compensate them for any loss due to reduced oil demand that would result from emissions reductions under a climate change regime. Brazil and other Amazon Basin states objected to treaty provisions on forest conservation and carbon sinks as a means of shifting responsibility for climate change to developing states.

After lengthy negotiations, states reached agreement in 1992 on a Framework Convention on Climate Change (FCCC).

United Nations Framework Agreement on Climate Change

1771 U.N.T.S. 107 (1992)

Article 2: Objective

The ultimate objective of this Convention . . . is to achieve . . . stabilization of greenhouse gas concentrations in the atmosphere at a level that would prevent dangerous anthropogenic interference with the climate system.

Article 3: Principles

1. The parties should protect the climate system for the benefit of present and future generations . . . on the basis of equity and in accordance with their common but differentiated responsibilities and respective capabilities. Accordingly, the developed country Parties should take the lead in controlling climate change and the adverse effects thereof. . . .

3. The Parties should take precautionary measures to anticipate, prevent or minimize the causes of climate change and mitigate its adverse effects. Where there are threats of serious or irreversible damage, lack of full scientific certainty should not be used as a reason for postponing such measures, taking into account that policies and measures to deal with climate change should be cost-effective, so as to ensure global benefits at the lowest possible cost. . . .

Article 4: Commitments

1. All Parties, taking into account their common but differentiated responsibilities . . . shall:

(a) Develop [and] publish . . . national inventories of anthropogenic emissions by sources and removals by sinks of all [GHGs]. . . .

2. The developed country Parties . . . commit themselves specifically as provided for in the following:

(a) Each of these Parties shall adopt national policies . . . limiting its anthropogenic emissions of greenhouse gases and protecting and enhancing its greenhouse gas sinks and reservoirs. These policies and measures will demonstrate that developed countries are taking the lead in modifying longer-term trends in anthropogenic emissions consistent with the objective of the Convention, recognizing that the return by the end of the present decade to earlier levels of anthropogenic emissions of carbon dioxide and other greenhouse gases . . . would contribute to such modification. . . .

(b) In order to promote progress to this end, each of these Parties shall communicate . . . detailed information on its policies and measures referred to in subparagraph (a) above, as well as on its resulting [GHG emissions] . . . with the aim of returning individually or jointly to their 1990 levels of these anthropogenic emissions of carbon dioxide and other [GHGs]. . . .

The treaty also provides for a Conference of the Parties (COP) to review implementation of the FCCC and decide on additional measures that may be necessary, a new body to provide scientific and technical advice to the COP, and a separate implementation body to assist the COP in its review of national implementation of the treaty.

The FCCC was opened for signature at the June 1992 Earth Summit in Rio. One hundred and fifty-five states signed the agreement. The treaty entered into force in March 1994, following the fiftieth ratification of the treaty. As of February 2006, 189 states had ratified the treaty.

Notes and Questions

1. Does Article 4(2) of the FCCC adopt the targets and timetables approach advocated by the EU? What, exactly, is the commitment that developed states assume under Article 4(2)? What obligation do developed states have with respect to emissions after 2000?

2. Article 3 provides that climate policy should proceed on the basis of equity. How can this term be operationalized in the climate change context? Article 3 also speaks of the parties' "common but differentiated responsibilities." Does this mean that developing states should have different obligations from developed states under the FCCC? That developed states should provide financial assistance to developing states to compensate for harms caused by climate change?

(margin note: States agreed set-up wasn't working)

2. From Rio to Kyoto

The FCCC instructed the first COP meeting, scheduled for Berlin in March 1995, to "review the adequacy" of developed states' commitments under the treaty. As parties prepared for this meeting, they generally agreed that (1) the overwhelming majority of developed states would not meet the goal of reducing their GHG emissions to 1990 levels by the year 2000 and (2) even if they did so, these reductions would not achieve the treaty's objective of stabilizing GHG concentrations at a safe level. Thus, environmentalists and many developing states urged developed states to increase their commitments to control GHG emissions. At Berlin, the parties declared that the FCCC's Article 4(2) commitments "are not adequate" and agreed "to begin a process" to "strengthen[]" these commitments through agreement on binding targets and timetables for reductions in developed states' GHG emissions. The so-called Berlin Mandate also provided that the process would "not introduce any new commitments" for developing states. Negotiations began over a new instrument with a view to its adoption at the third meeting of the COP (COP-3), scheduled for Kyoto, Japan, in December 1997.

Negotiations intensified in the months leading to the Kyoto meeting, spurred in part by a 1995 IPCC report detailing the growing scientific consensus that human activities were affecting the global climate. After this report, the United States announced, for the first time, that it would support binding targets and timetables for GHG emissions. Debate then focused on the level of targets and timetables. Developing states proposed that developed states cut GHG emissions by 35 percent below 1990 levels by 2020; the EU proposed cuts of 7.5 percent below 1990 levels by 2005; Russia and several eastern European states were urging cuts to 1990 levels by 2005 or 2010; and the United States eventually proposed cuts to 1990 levels by 2008 to 2012, with unspecified cuts thereafter. In July 1997, the U.S. Senate adopted a non-binding resolution, by a vote of 95 to 0, recommending that the United States should not enter into a treaty mandating "new commitments to limit or reduce greenhouse gas emissions" for developed states unless the treaty "also mandates new specific scheduled commitments to limit or reduce greenhouse gas emissions for Developing Country Parties," or any treaty that would "result in serious harm to the economy of the United States."

Against this backdrop, at Kyoto the parties adopted what the head of the U.S. delegation called "the most complex, broad ranging and ambitious environmental agreement ever negotiated by the international community."

Kyoto Protocol to the United Nations Framework Convention on Climate Change

Dec. 10, 1997, UN Doc. FCCC/CP/1997/7/Add.2 (1997)

Article 3

1. The Parties included in Annex I* shall, individually or jointly, ensure that their aggregate anthropogenic carbon dioxide equivalent emissions [of GHGs] . . . do not exceed their assigned amounts . . . with a view to reducing their overall emissions of [GHGs] by at least 5 per cent below 1990 levels in the commitment period 2008 to 2012. . . .

*The Annex I states consist primarily of OECD members along with some Eastern Europan states and former Soviet republics.

9. Commitments for subsequent periods . . . shall be established in amendments . . . to this Protocol. . . .

13. If the emissions of a Party . . . are less than its assigned amount . . . this
difference shall . . . be added to the assigned amount for that Party for subsequent
commitment periods.

Reaching agreement on the various reduction commitments for the Annex I
Parties was one of the most difficult issues in the negotiations. Several European
states and the United States (until the last stages of the negotiations) argued for a
uniform target for all Annex I states. Australia, Iceland, Japan, Norway and others
argued for differential targets, considering different states' natural resources, energy
use patterns and consumption profiles. After states agreed to use individual targets,
the figures themselves became the subject of heated debate. The parties agreed to
varying levels of reductions or, in some cases, reductions in emissions growth, as
summarized below. Notably, these differentiated targets did not result from a
standardized formula, but rather from complex and contentious negotiations.

Country	Target (1990** - 2008/2012)
EU-15*, Bulgaria, Czech Republic, Estonia, Latvia, Liechtenstein, Lithuania, Monaco, Romania, Slovakia, Slovenia, Switzerland	-8%
United States	-7%
Canada, Hungary, Japan, Poland	-6%
Croatia	-5%
New Zealand, Russian Federation, Ukraine	0
Norway	+1%
Australia	+8%
Iceland	+10%

*The EU's member States will redistribute their targets among themselves, taking
advantage of a provision under the Protocol known as a "bubble."
** Some states with "economies in transition" have selected a baseline year other than
1990.

The Annex I states understood that emissions reductions were potentially
costly. To reduce the costs associated with these commitments, the Protocol grants
Annex I states flexibility in meeting their emission targets through the use of several
market-based mechanisms.

Article 6

1. For the purpose of meeting its commitments under Article 3, any Party
included in Annex I may transfer to, or acquire from, any other such Party emission
reduction units resulting from projects aimed at reducing anthropogenic emissions
by sources or enhancing anthropogenic removals by sinks of greenhouse gases in
any sector of the economy, provided that: . . .

(a) Any such project provides a reduction in emissions by sources, or an
enhancement of removals by sinks, that is additional to any that would
otherwise occur; . . .

(b) The acquisition of emission reduction units shall be supplemental to
domestic actions for the purposes of meeting commitments under Article
3. . . .

Article 12

1. A clean development mechanism is hereby defined.

2. The purpose of the clean development mechanism shall be to assist Parties not included in Annex I in achieving sustainable development and in contributing to the ultimate objective of the Convention, and to assist Parties included in Annex I in achieving compliance with their quantified emission limitation and reduction commitments under Article 3. . . .

3. Under the clean development mechanism:

   (a) Parties not included in Annex I will benefit from project activities resulting in certified emission reductions; and

   (b) Parties included in Annex I may use the certified emission reductions accruing from such project activities to contribute to compliance with part of their quantified emission limitation and reduction commitments under Article 3. . . .

5. Emission reductions resulting from each project activity shall be certified by operational entities to be designated by the Conference of the Parties . . . on the basis of:

   (a) Voluntary participation approved by each Party involved; . . . [and]

   (b) Reductions in emissions that are additional to any that would occur in the absence of the certified project activity.

6. The clean development mechanism shall assist in arranging funding of certified project activities as necessary. . . .

8. The Conference of the Parties . . . shall ensure that a share of the proceeds from certified project activities is used . . . to assist developing country Parties that are particularly vulnerable to the adverse effects of climate change to meet the costs of adaptation.

9. Participation under the clean development mechanism . . . may involve private and/or public entities. . . .

10. Certified emission reductions obtained during the period from the year 2000 up to the beginning of the first commitment period can be used to assist in achieving compliance in the first commitment period.

Article 17

The Conference of Parties shall define the relevant principles, modalities, rules and guidelines, in particular for verification, reporting and accountability for emissions trading. . . . Any such trading shall be supplemental to domestic actions for the purpose of meeting [emissions reductions under Article 3].

In many respects, the market-based mechanisms contemplated by Articles 6, 12, and 17 lie at the heart of the Protocol. Article 6 provides for so-called joint implementation (JI) between Annex I states. Under this provision, Annex I states and private firms can invest in emission reduction projects in other Annex I states and then apply the emissions reductions generated by the project to their own national emission targets. The United States had proposed that the treaty authorize credit from JI with developing states. However, China and other developing states vehemently opposed this proposal on the grounds that developed states should not be able to evade their responsibility for addressing climate change through JI projects in developing states. The Protocol addresses joint projects in developing states through Article 12's provisions for a clean development mechanism (CDM). Under CDM, Annex I states or private entities can invest in emission reduction projects in developing states, and apply a portion of the emissions reduction generated by the projects to their own emissions targets. In exchange, a portion of the proceeds of these projects will be used to fund climate projects in developing states.

Article 17 contemplates emissions trading among Annex I states. The idea behind trading is that if one state does not use all of its GHG emissions, it can sell the rights to these emissions to another state. This provision creates an incentive for states to reduce emissions beyond their treaty targets and permits the treaty's emission reductions to be achieved more efficiently. However, negotiations nearly collapsed over the issue of emissions trading. The United States, other developed states, and states with economies in transition supported emissions trading as a way to allow reductions to occur in a cost-effective manner. China and other developing states viewed trading as a loophole that would permit industrialized states to avoid their duty to control emissions and strongly opposed provisions for emissions trading.

The Protocol includes other features thought to enhance the treaty's cost effectiveness and the parties' flexibility. For example, instead of addressing only carbon dioxide—the most important anthropogenic GHG—the treaty covers all of the significant GHGs, as well as all their sources. The logic of this "comprehensive" approach is that a treaty covering one gas only might encourage states to shift activities away from emissions of that gas, but increase emissions of other GHGs, causing economic dislocation but producing little environmental benefit.

Moreover, the Protocol addresses not only carbon sources but also carbon sinks. The logic behind this approach is that the sequestration of an additional ton of carbon through, for example, reforestation, is equivalent to reducing carbon emissions by one ton. But the treatment of sinks proved to be highly controversial. The ability of trees to sequester carbon decreases with age. Thus, states with large numbers of forests will not be able to maintain the same rate of carbon sequestration as their forests age; declining rates of sequestration will make it more difficult for these states to meet their emissions targets. Conversely, states that had historically engaged in deforestation can make progress toward their target by simply reducing the rate of deforestation. Thus, the treaty ran the risk of rewarding states that had been deforesters and penalizing states that historically had been afforesters. The Protocol attempts to avoid this by, in general, not including sinks in the calculation of a state's base year emissions, but including carbon removal by sinks during the commitment period that are due to human-induced activities and that began after 1990. Again, however, the parties were not able to work out all the details in Kyoto, and left this to future meetings.

Finally, as the Protocol, unlike the FCCC, contains legally binding targets, the negotiators devoted significant attention to compliance issues. The Protocol expands the reporting requirements found in the FCCC by increasing the amounts and types of information to be provided. The Protocol also provides for "expert review teams" to perform a "thorough and comprehensive technical assessment of all aspects" of a party's implementation of the Protocol and to identify "any potential problems" with a party's compliance. The Protocol Secretariat is to circulate reports identifying compliance issues to the parties, who "shall take decisions on any matter required for the implementation of this Protocol." The United States and Europe pushed for a strong enforcement mechanism. Japan, Russia and Australia resisted the effort to adopt legally binding consequences. As a result, the Protocol does not identify the consequences of failure to meet emissions targets. Instead, it directs the parties to create procedures and mechanisms to address noncompliance in the future.

Notes and Questions

1. The Berlin Mandate rejected the imposition of emission reduction targets on developing states, and the Kyoto Protocol requires only developed states to reduce emissions. However, GHG emissions from developing states are expected to surpass those from developed states early in the twenty-first century. What is the political logic behind exempting developing states from emissions reductions? What is the environmental logic? Will provisions that exempt developing states from emission reductions drive carbon-intensive industries to relocate in developing states? What arguments or actions might persuade developing states to assume binding emission reduction commitments?

2. Use of market-based mechanisms require an initial allocation of permits to emit GHGs. Many industrialized states argued that allocations to emit should track current emissions patterns. Some developing state diplomats countered that each person should be permitted to emit the same amount of GHGs, while others argued that each state should be permitted to emit the same amount of GHGs. Which states would be advantaged and which disadvantaged by each of these approaches? How can the ability to generate GHGs fairly be allocated?

3. From Kyoto to Bonn

Given the Protocol's substantial unfinished business, at a 1999 meeting in Buenos Aires, the parties agreed to a work plan designed to resolve the major open issues by the Sixth Conference of the Parties, in late 2000 at The Hague. As had been the case during earlier climate negotiations, distributional and institutional questions loomed large, and controversy erupted over a number of issues. One involved the extent to which Annex I states could meet their commitments by trading or undertaking projects in other states. The EU sought to cap emissions trading at 50 percent of a state's required reductions, relying upon Protocol language stating that "trading shall be supplemental to domestic actions. . . . " The United States, joined by Australia, Canada, Japan, Norway, and Russia, argued that the text imposed no limits on trading and that unlimited trading would permit the parties to achieve the Protocol's objective more efficiently. Other debates centered on how to ensure that the various flexibility mechanisms were leading to additional reductions—that is, reductions over and above what would have occurred absent trade or investment. For example, Russia's economic contraction during the 1990s renders it very likely that Russian emissions will be significantly less than those permitted under the Protocol. Should Protocol parties be able to meet their obligations by purchasing Russia's excess emissions credits? Related difficulties arose in considering how to credit projects in developing states, which have no quantified targets under the Protocol. Finally, the parties continued to disagree over how to treat noncompliance, with a split between states that sought to define legally binding consequences and those that wanted to employ a more political, and less legal, approach to noncompliance.

The Protocol encountered difficulties outside the negotiating sessions as well. The Clinton Administration announced that it would not submit the Protocol to the U.S. Senate for its advice and consent absent "meaningful participation" by developing states. Without the United States, other developed states were reluctant to ratify the Protocol, as they did not want to put their own industries at a competitive disadvantage vis-à-vis U.S. firms. And most developing states resisted efforts to persuade them to assume binding emission commitments, arguing that they had not caused the problem and should not be asked to pay for its solution.

Thus, the political climate heading into The Hague meeting in November 2000 was inauspicious. Intensive negotiations narrowed many of the parties' differences, but despite round-the-clock discussions, parties were unable to reach agreement. Eventually the chair "suspended" the meeting, which resumed in Bonn, Germany, in July 2001.

The failure to reach closure at The Hague assumed greater significance as incoming U.S. President George W. Bush announced in March 2001 that the United States would not ratify the Kyoto Protocol, but instead address climate change through domestic policy. The Administration claimed that the treaty would have cost the U.S. economy up to $400 billion and 4.9 million jobs, and objected to the fact that major developing states, such as China and India, were not obliged to cut their emissions. The President's decision sparked strong condemnation from political leaders around the globe. Many observers predicted that without the United States—which accounts for approximately 25 percent of the world's carbon emissions—the Kyoto process was dead.

Surprisingly, at Bonn, states reached agreement on many of the outstanding issues that could not be resolved at The Hague meeting. The meeting adopted the rules governing the CDM and created an executive board to oversee the Mechanism. Other rules addressed the international emissions trading system, and the JI regime. The Bonn agreement emphasized that all three of the above mechanisms should be supplemental to domestic action and that domestic action shall thus constitute a significant element of the effort made by each Party.

Finally, the Bonn meeting decided to create a Compliance Committee with a facilitative branch and an enforcement branch. As their names suggest, the facilitative branch will promote advice and assistance to parties to promote compliance, whereas the enforcement branch has the power to determine whether a party is in non-compliance with its emissions target and reporting requirements. The parties agreed that, for every ton of gas that a country emits over its target, it will be required to reduce an additional 1.3 tons during the Protocol's second commitment period, which starts in 2013. In addition, parties that fail to meet their targets can be suspended from the carbon emissions trading regime. Parties agreed to develop additional compliance procedures and mechanisms after the Protocol enters into force.

Daniel Bodansky, who served as the U.S. State Department's Climate Change Coordinator from 1999 through 2001, attributes the Bonn meeting's success to several factors:

> At The Hague, countries played a game of chicken, hoping that others would relent first. They waited so long to advance compromise proposals that there was insufficient time even to understand what others were suggesting, let alone engage in genuine negotiation. At Bonn, countries realized that . . . if they continued to engage in such brinksmanship . . . [they] could kill Kyoto altogether. Moreover, since The Hague failure, they had had months to analyze and digest potential compromises.

But perhaps the decisive factor contributing to Bonn's success was President Bush's own actions. Before the meeting, most observers had expected that his rejection of Kyoto would deflate the process, depriving it of the momentum necessary for its success. But Bush's decision had the opposite effect: It united countries around the Kyoto Protocol and galvanized them into action. The peremptory way in which the administration acted—repudiating years of multilateral work in response to domestic special interests, without consulting other countries or undertaking a serious policy review—combined with his failure to offer a credible alternative, stuck in other countries' craws. . . . The Bush Administration compounded its mistakes by taunting the Europeans for not having ratified Kyoto, implying that they were hypocrites. Thus, the [EU] came to Bonn determined to make whatever compromises were necessary to reach agreement and to prove Bush wrong.

American disengagement from the Bonn negotiations also made agreement easier from a substantive standpoint. In The Hague, the Clinton Administration felt it had to win on virtually every issue to have even a prayer of overcoming Senate opposition to Kyoto. By contrast, other countries had fewer walk-away issues and thus could agree more easily on a compromise package in Bonn. In particular, the U.S. absence made one of the most contentious issues easier to resolve: how much credit to give for the carbon sucked out of the atmosphere by carbon "sinks." With the United States out, the Europeans had plenty of room to accommodate the demands for sink credits by Japan and Canada, since they no longer had to satisfy the much larger demands of the United States.

Daniel Bodansky, *Bonn Voyage: Kyoto's Uncertain Revival*, The National Interest, Fall 2001, at 45, 48. A few months later, the parties met in Marrakesh, Morocco and agreed to a legal text (the Marrakesh Accords) setting our many of the key agreements reached in Bonn.

Notes and Questions

1. Even Protocol supporters concede that achieving the treaty's emissions targets will do little to stop the effects of climate change, and that there is no reason to believe that the targets set by the Protocol are the environmentally or economically optimal levels of GHG emissions, either for individual states or the planet as a whole. Given these problems with the Protocol's approach, why was there such a strong negative reaction to the United States's decision not to ratify the Protocol?

2. Kyoto's critics argue that it is unfair that rapidly industrializing states such as China and India do not have to reduce their emissions. Bodansky counters that the greater unfairness lies in the fact that these states have been full participants in the negotiations, crafting rules that do not apply to them. He suggests that developing states should have been given a choice: "acknowledge a willingness to accept new commitments or stay out of the negotiations altogether." What do you think would have happened had developing states been given this choice?

3. Given experience under the ozone regime, would you expect the facilitative branch or the enforcement branch to be more effective at inducing compliance with the Protocol's emissions targets? To the extent that the enforcement mechanism is employed, are states more likely to respond to the penalty of reduced emissions allowances in the future, or to being suspended from the emissions trading regime?

4. Next Steps?

U.S. opposition to the Protocol sparked a lively debate among states and others involved in climate policy. Some states redoubled their efforts to engage the United States on climate issues, while others argued that the Kyoto process should proceed even in the absence of the United States.

a. Kyoto Enters into Force

The Kyoto Protocol provided that it would enter into force when Annex I states accounting for 55 percent of the group's carbon dioxide emissions became parties. With the United States's announcement that it would not ratify the treaty, it became evident that the Protocol would not enter into force unless Russia—which is responsible for approximately 17 percent of world emissions—ratified the treaty. During 2003 and much of 2004, Russia sent conflicting signals regarding its intent to ratify the Protocol; many observers suggested that Russian "indecision" reflected an effort to hold out for a better deal.

In May 2004, the EU dropped its objections to Russia joining the WTO. Russia's President Vladimir Putin stated: "The fact that the European Union has met us halfway at the negotiations on membership in the WTO cannot but influence Moscow's positive attitude towards ratification of the Kyoto protocol." Putin reasoned that the agreement over the WTO "lowers the risks for our economy in the midterm and unties our hands to a certain degree to resolve the problem of joining the Kyoto protocol sooner. . . . " In late 2004, Russia ended the long period of uncertainty regarding its intentions by ratifying the Protocol.

On February 16, 2005—nearly 13 years after climate negotiations began in Rio and nearly seven years after the Protocol was negotiated—the Protocol entered into force and became legally binding upon its 136 parties. As of February 2006, 161 parties had ratified the Protocol, including 37 Annex I Parties representing 62 percent of 1990 Annex I GHG emissions. Only four developed states have not ratified the Protocol: Australia, Liechtenstein, Monaco, and the United States. However, given the U.S.'s absence, and lack of controls over emissions from developing states, the Protocol applies to less than a third of global emissions.

b. Implementing Kyoto

With the Protocol's entry into force, international efforts to combat climate change entered a new phase. In particular, following years of arduous negotiations, the Protocol's market-based mechanisms became operationalized. In October 2005, the CDM's Executive Board issued the first-ever certified emissions reductions under the Protocol. As of the end of 2005, 26 projects had been registered with the Executive Board, and approximately 300 proposed projects were awaiting validation.

In addition, many Protocol parties intensified efforts to limit GHG emissions. For example, the European Union began operations of an EU Greenhouse Gas Emission Trading Scheme (EU ETS) in January 2005. During the first trading period, from 2005 to 2007, the system will cover carbon dioxide emissions from large emitters in the power and heat generation industry and in selected energy-intensive industrial sectors. The system covers approximately 12,000 installations, which account for roughly half of the EU's total carbon emissions. Significantly, the system allows companies to use credits from JI and CDM projects, creating incentives for EU firms to invest in emission-reduction projects abroad. Following the initial two-year "warm up" phase, a second phase will run from 2008-2012, which may include additional GHGs and additional economic sectors.

c. Alternative Approaches to Addressing Climate Change

President Bush's decision to reject the Kyoto process triggered strong pressures to propose an alternative approach. In February 2002, the President announced a plan to cut "greenhouse gas intensity" by 18 percent over the next ten years. Greenhouse gas intensity is the ratio of GHG emissions to economic output. This voluntary plan would lower U.S. emissions from an estimated 183 metric tons per million dollars of GDP in 2002, to 151 metric tons per million dollars of GDP in 2012. Critics argue that the planned cuts in GHG intensity—less than 2 percent per year compounded over the next decade—are exceedingly modest and will not stop the growth in total emissions, and that the plan's voluntary nature will not give firms sufficient incentive to invest in clean technologies.

The United States has also pursued alternative international arrangements. For example, in July 2005, the United States entered into an agreement with Japan, China, India, Australia, and South Korea to create the Asia-Pacific Partnership for Clean Development and Climate. This partnership is designed to develop and deploy cleaner technologies and to focus on voluntary measures to address climate change. The parties claim that this effort is designed to "complement, but not replace, the Kyoto Protocol." The United States has also entered into 15 climate partnerships with individual states, such as Brazil, China, and Germany, and with regional organizations. These partnerships involve, inter alia, joint projects on climate research and science. Critics charge that the partnerships' voluntary plans will do little to alter emissions patterns.

In response to what they perceived as inadequate federal efforts, many states, corporations, and local communities in the United States have engaged in innovative efforts to combat climate change. For example, in June 2003, ten northeast states began negotiations over the creation of a regional market for power plants to purchase and sell carbon dioxide credits among themselves. In December 2005, Connecticut, Delaware, Maine, New Hampshire, New Jersey, New York, and Vermont agreed to create a Regional Greenhouse Gas Initiative through a mandatory emissions cap on the electricity generating sector coupled with a market-based trading program to start in 2009. Similarly, Washington, Oregon, and California are cooperating on a strategy to reduce GHG emissions, known as the West Coast Governors' Global Warming Initiative. Some of these efforts have crossed international borders. For example, in 2001, governors of New England states and premiers of Canada's Eastern provinces approved a comprehensive regional Climate Action Plan that aims to reduce GHG emissions to 1990 levels by 2010. Local governments have also become active in climate policy; in May 2005, a group of 132 mayors from 33 states pledged to have their cities meet the Kyoto Protocol's target of reducing GHG emissions to 7 percent below 1990 levels by 2012.

A growing number of businesses are undertaking significant efforts to address climate change. These efforts include setting GHG reduction targets, improving energy efficiency, increasing the use and production of clean and renewable energy technologies, increasing the use and production of renewable energy, improving waste management, investing in carbon sequestration, participating in emissions trading and developing energy saving products. Some firms state that they are undertaking these efforts because they believe that an international climate regime is inevitable and that their investments will pay off under any future treaty. Others believe that by acting now they can help government enact climate policies that work well for their business.

A number of lawsuits designed to change the United State's climate change policy have been filed. For example, 12 states, three cities, and a group of environmental organizations unsuccessfully sued the U.S. Environmental Protection Agency over the Agency's refusal to regulate carbon dioxide and other GHG emissions from new motor vehicles under the Clean Air Act. *Massachusetts v. EPA*, 415 F.3d 50 (D.C. Cir. 2005). An action by California, Connecticut, Iowa, New Jersey, New York, Rhode Island, Vermont, and Wisconsin, along with the City of New York, seeking to force five major utilities that emit about 10 percent of total U.S. emissions to reduce their emissions of carbon dioxide was dismissed as presenting a nonjusticiable political question. *Connecticut v. American Electric Power Co.*, 406 F. Supp. 2d 265 (S.D.N.Y. 2005). In international fora, in December 2005, a group of Inuits living in the Arctic regions of the United States and Canada filed a petition with the Inter-American Commission on Human Rights. The petitioners allege that retreating sea ice, caused by climate change, has exposed Inuit villages to the eroding forces of wind and waves, causing their homes to topple into the sea, and threatens polar bears and other animal resources upon which the Inuit depend for food and livelihood. The petition asks the Commission to recommend that the United States adopt mandatory limits on GHG emissions.

Notes and Questions

1. Should international efforts to address climate change focus on the development of a single, comprehensive international regime, or should efforts proceed in a decentralized manner? If a single regime is used, should it minimize the stringency of obligations and de-emphasize enforcement, so as to maximize the number of parties? Or is a stronger treaty with fewer parties more desirable? Should other regimes complement, or serve as an alternative to, the FCCC process?

2. In December 2005, Kyoto Protocol parties initiated a process to "consider further commitments" for Annex I states for the period beyond 2012, when the Kyoto emissions targets expire. The parties agreed to begin negotiations that should conclude "in time to ensure that there is no gap between the first and second commitment periods."

In a separate decision under the FCCC, parties agreed to open a nonbinding "dialogue on long-term cooperative action" on climate change. The dialogue is not intended to "open any negotiations leading to new commitments." The EU, Japan, Canada, and other states pushed for this parallel process under the FCCC as a way to engage both the United States and developing states in future efforts. How can the Kyoto framework be modified to increase the chances for constructive engagement with the United States?

3. Note that the Protocol does not have any provisions specifically aimed at non-parties, even though other environmental treaties include provisions addressing non-parties to prevent free riding and create incentives to join the regime. How could such strategies be used in the climate context?

4. In response to federal court litigation against power companies, the head of an energy trade association responded that "climate policy should be fashioned by policymakers—with due consideration to environmental, energy and economic implications—not by lawyers in the courtroom." What are the advantages, and disadvantages, of using litigation as a means to change U.S. climate policy? Would a ruling from a domestic court be more or less useful than a ruling from an international tribunal?

12

Managing the World Economy

The international economy has experienced a period of remarkable growth and integration since the end of World War II. Simultaneously, states have created a complex and rapidly expanding body of law and a set of international institutions to both guide and encourage these economic developments. Hence, in recent years international economic law—the rules and institutions that affect international business transactions and govern economic relations among states—has become one of the largest and most vibrant fields of international law. Many scholars suggest that the vast majority of international legal work today consists of the interpretation and application of international economic law. As a result, students of international law can no longer ignore this field, particularly the law of international trade—the flow of goods across national borders—and investment—the flow of capital across national borders.

International economic law is in a period of significant change. These changes both reflect and shape larger transformations in global commerce and finance. Financial flows have been liberalized throughout the world; market forces now largely determine economic outcomes in many states; and U.S. economic dominance has given way to a world where the United States, the European Union (EU), and Japan are all economic superpowers, and rapidly developing states such as China and India play increasingly important roles in the global economy. More broadly, the international economy has entered a period termed "globalization," marked by liberalized flows of goods, money, people, and ideas across national borders and heightened economic interdependence. At the same time, many issues previously regarded as purely domestic, such as environmental or labor laws, are now seen as having international economic dimensions.

In this chapter we explore three of the most important and difficult institutional and legal issues addressed by international economic law. First, we examine the interplay of law and politics in the resolution of international trade disputes and the development of the World Trade Organization's (WTO) extraordinary dispute resolution process by focusing on the so-called banana war. Next, we explore the interface of economic and other social policies and the relationship of international economic law and domestic law through an in-depth study of trade and environment issues. Finally, we focus on the emerging law of foreign investment by examining the controversial investor protection and international arbitration provisions of the North American Free Trade Agreement (NAFTA). These materials will introduce you to many of the key principles and institutions that states use to manage the world economy.

I. PROMOTING INTERNATIONAL TRADE AND RESOLVING TRADE DISPUTES: THE BANANA WAR

Many of the principles animating today's global trading system can be understood as responses to the disastrous trade policies states used during the years leading to the Great Depression and World War II. During the 1920s and 1930s, many states subsidized exports, depreciated currencies, raised tariffs, and pursued other policies designed to increase exports and decrease imports. But these mercantilist policies prompted retaliatory actions from other trading states. Thus, after the United States raised its tariffs by enacting the Smoot-Hawley Act in May 1930, Australia, Canada, Cuba, France, Italy, Mexico, New Zealand, and Spain quickly raised their tariffs, and a number of other countries imposed import quotas. In the aggregate, these actions caused a dramatic reduction in international trade, which in turn contributed to the depth and length of the Great Depression. In the post-World War II era, states decided to use international law and institutions to help them avoid a repeat of the interwar experience.

The trade system was designed to address both economic and political problems. On the economic side, political leaders believed that, in the absence of trade restrictions, each state would specialize in the production of goods that it could make more efficiently than other states. The economic theory of comparative advantage teaches that such international specialization increases the efficiency of global production and markets, thereby producing greater trade and greater aggregate wealth. From this economic perspective, the purpose of trade rules is to liberalize markets and increase global welfare.

On the political side, the dynamic driving interwar trade policy can be understood as a "prisoner's dilemma." This is a game theoretic term for situations where two or more actors have incentives to cooperate (in this context, to reduce trade barriers to increase aggregate welfare) and incentives to "defect" from cooperation, or raise trade barriers, notwithstanding any harm this might cause to other states. From any particular state's perspective, the best situation is when that state alone defects (that is, where it raises trade barriers to keep out imported goods), but other states cooperate by lowering their trade barriers (permitting the first state to expand its exports). Of course, if every state were to choose to defect, then the global economy would be marked by high trade barriers and reduced economic wealth for all—precisely the situation states faced during the interwar years. The dilemma, then, is how to avoid the counterproductive outcomes that result when each state pursues its apparent self-interest. From this perspective, the purpose of international trade law and institutions is to help states avoid the prisoner's dilemma by increasing incentives to cooperate and by raising the costs of defection.

Thus, in the immediate postwar era there were compelling economic and political rationales for the creation of an international trade regime, and one of the UN's first tasks was to sponsor a series of negotiations over a charter for a proposed International Trade Organization (ITO). The ITO was to have responsibility for international trade and other international commercial matters. At the same time, at U.S. urging, states entered into separate negotiations for a tariff reduction treaty called the General Agreement on Tariffs and Trade (GATT). By 1947 negotiators had completed the GATT, although parts of the ITO Charter were still being negotiated.

The GATT was closely tied to the prospective ITO. Many GATT provisions were taken verbatim from the ITO Charter. More important, the GATT provided that "on the day on which the [ITO Charter] enters into force," GATT's provisions "shall be suspended and superseded by the corresponding provisions of the Charter." The diplomats who negotiated the GATT were eager for it to come into force as quickly as possible. Thus, in 1947 eight GATT parties entered into the Protocol of Provisional Application, which provided that these states would apply GATT on a provisional basis from January 1, 1948.

By 1949, however, U.S. enthusiasm for the ITO had significantly diminished, due to a revival of isolationist sentiments, limited support from the business community, and a general disenchantment with international organizations. Without U.S. support, international efforts to create the ITO faltered, and the ITO Charter never entered into force. Thus, by default the GATT served for nearly 50 years as the principal mechanism governing international trade.

The GATT contains a series of rules designed to reduce government policies that distort trade and thus achieve the economic and political goals of its drafters. Most important, GATT contains two fundamental nondiscrimination rules. GATT Article I—the most-favored-nation (MFN) clause—bans discrimination among foreign country imports. Under this rule, any advantage (such as reduced tariffs) that a state extends to products imported from any of its trading partners must be extended to like products imported from all other GATT parties. An exception permits preferential tariff treatment to be extended to developing states in certain circumstances. GATT Article III contains the second nondiscrimination rule, called the national treatment obligation (NTO). This Article requires that once imported products from another GATT party have cleared customs, governments must treat them no less favorably than they do domestic products. In addition, GATT Article XI prohibits, subject to certain exceptions, the use of quotas and other nontariff trade restrictions. Finally, GATT Article II permits the use of tariffs, but not in excess of agreed-upon levels. Many states have substantially reduced their tariffs through a series of GATT negotiating "rounds."

In 1995 trading states entered into a series of agreements collectively called the Uruguay Round agreements. In addition to maintaining the basic GATT rules outlined above, these agreements created a new international organization, the WTO, and extended trade rules into several new areas, including services and intellectual property. As of December 15, 2005, 150 states, including most of the industrialized world, were members of the WTO.

Given the breadth of WTO rules and the number of WTO members, the WTO system applies to over $8 trillion, or about 90 percent, of international trade in goods and services per year. As a result, disputes frequently arise as to whether a state is complying with its WTO obligations. One of the Uruguay Round agreements—the Understanding on Rules and Procedures Governing the Settlement of Disputes (Dispute Settlement Understanding or DSU)—creates a complex system for resolving such disputes.

The WTO Director-General has called the DSU "the central pillar of the multilateral trading system and the WTO's most individual contribution to the stability of the global economy." As you read the materials that follow, consider whether the dispute settlement process is or should be primarily one of adjudication or one of negotiation; whether WTO panels do or should employ a deferential standard when reviewing national legislation; and whether the system adequately addresses the problem of noncompliance with adverse WTO rulings. More broadly, consider how to surmount the barriers to successful international cooperation in the trade area; the decision-making processes used in international trade bodies; and whether the institutional structures developed in the trade area are transferable to other areas of international law.

A. The Problem

World trade in bananas exceeds $1 billion annually. Bananas are the planet's second most traded foodstuff, behind only coffee. Bananas come primarily from three areas: the Caribbean, Central and South America (Latin bananas), and the Philippines. Latin banana plantations are typically controlled by U.S.-based transnational corporations. They frequently cover several thousand acres and often use sophisticated irrigation, drainage, and highway systems. Caribbean island plantations are generally no larger than 12 acres and cannot realistically be expanded. Given superior technology and economies of scale, Latin bananas typically sell for 20 to 25 percent of the price of Caribbean bananas.

The European Community (EC) member states consume over 4 million tons of bananas annually—nearly 40 percent of the global banana market—and are the world's largest banana importers. The Europeans likely also have the most convoluted banana import regime on the planet. Pursuant to the 1989 Lomé IV treaty between the EC and a group of former European colonies in Africa, the Caribbean, and the Pacific (the ACP states), ACP bananas enter EC nations duty-free. But, before July 1, 1993, each EC member state had its own combination of tariffs, quotas, and import licensing regulations for non-ACP bananas.

As the EC moved toward a more unified common market, it attempted to create a unified banana regime. After two years of extensive negotiations, in February 1993 the EC adopted Regulation 404/93, a complex structured tariff and quota system to replace the various national regimes. In essence, the new regulation recognized four different categories of banana suppliers and created a complicated tariff and quota scheme for bananas from each category. The regulation afforded duty-free importation of ACP bananas for up to 30 percent of all European banana consumption. Up to 2 million tons of Latin bananas could be imported per year at a 20 percent tariff, while additional Latin bananas were subject to a 170 percent tariff. An even more complex regime governed the distribution of licenses to import bananas into the EC. This regime also favored ACP nations.

Latin countries complained that the EC regime cost them millions of dollars annually in lost sales. While the United States does not export bananas, it complained that this regime discriminated against U.S.-based banana distributors, such as Chiquita and Dole Foods, which grow bananas in Central America.

B. GATT Dispute Settlement

As noted above, the ITO Charter was supposed to supersede the GATT. Hence, the GATT's provisions on institutional matters, including dispute settlement, were skeletal at best. The GATT provides a right of consultation when one party alleges that another has failed to carry out its GATT obligations. It further provides that if consultations fail to settle matters, the dispute may be referred to the Contracting Parties (that is, all the GATT parties acting jointly), who "shall promptly investigate" and are authorized to make appropriate recommendations or to "give a ruling on the matter." In appropriately serious cases, the Contracting Parties may authorize "a Contracting Party or Parties" to retaliate by restricting trade from the offending party.

During the GATT's early years, GATT parties almost always addressed trade disputes through diplomatic means. By the early 1950s, GATT parties submitted disputes to "working parties," consisting of representatives of the disputing parties and other trade diplomats. Around 1955, GATT parties developed a practice of submitting disputes to panels of three to seven experts. These experts were typically GATT delegates from neutral countries who would issue a "report" akin to a legal ruling on the merits of a complaint. Panels forwarded their reports to the GATT Council (that is, the executive committee of the full membership) for adoption. Panel reports had no official status unless and until adopted by the GATT Council.

This dispute resolution process had a number of features that, over time, proved problematic. Notably, a consensus rule governed each stage of this process. Hence, the allegedly noncomplying state had a right of veto at virtually every step of the process, from the appointment of a panel to the decision to adopt a panel report to a decision to authorize trade sanctions in response to noncompliance. Moreover, there were no set time periods for the various stages of the process, giving defending states the ability to delay—sometimes interminably—the proceedings. In addition, formal procedures for monitoring compliance with panel rulings were lacking. Finally, the consensus rule rendered remedial action to enforce compliance virtually impossible. Indeed, only once between 1948 and 1994 did the GATT Council authorize a prevailing state to retaliate or restrict trade from a noncompliant state.

Early panel reports often contained diplomatically vague language. Governments understood the implicit rulings, and losing governments nearly always complied with panel reports. This process worked in part because the GATT of the 1950s was essentially a small club of like-minded trade officials who shared a common understanding of GATT obligations.

During the 1960s, the GATT panel process fell into disuse. In part, this reflected a dramatic change in the GATT's membership, including a significant increase in the number of developing country members. In addition, developed states were frequently reluctant to litigate claims asserted by increasingly aggressive developing states, and used the consensus rules to block panel proceedings.

During the 1970s, GATT dispute settlement activity increased, reflecting in part an increased concern about the proliferation of nontariff trade barriers. While panels used the same procedures as before, in other ways it was not possible to turn back the clock:

> At first, the GATT panels appointed in the 1970s tried to follow the nuanced diplomatic style of adjudication practiced in the 1950s. But the . . . "club" of the 1950s was gone, and in its place was a much more contentious membership of over eighty nations. . . . Meanwhile, political leaders in national capitals had begun to pay greater attention to GATT legal affairs, on the one hand questioning its assertion of legal authority over their trade policies, and at the very same time demanding more aggressive prosecution of GATT legal

claims against others. The more these often contentious GATT legal proceedings fell under the political spotlight, the more difficult it became for panels of GATT diplomats to "finesse" their way to an acceptable conclusion in important legal disputes.

. . . The GATT Secretariat recognized that, in this new and more difficult setting, the dispute settlement procedure would need to rely more heavily on the authority of "law" itself. . . . And over the next decade . . . the panel procedure [produced] a string of quite sophisticated legal decisions resolving a number of very sensitive trade policy disputes. These successes stimulated governments to bring more legal conflicts to the GATT, with an ever-increasing degree of difficulty and political sensitivity. As it dealt with this growing caseload, the dispute settlement system also began to develop the substantive content of GATT law in a series of forward-looking legal precedents.

By the end of the 1980s, GATT had developed its dispute settlement procedure into a quite powerful legal instrument. In the decade as a whole the GATT procedure disposed of some 115 legal disputes, and by the end of the decade the annual volume of complaints was almost double that level. As the cases became more and more difficult, the number of failures increased, but at the end of the decade over 80 percent of the cases were still being successfully disposed of. To be sure, that rate of failure would certainly have been unacceptable for most advanced domestic legal systems. For an international legal institution, however, it was remarkably successful. Most important, it was successful in the view of the governments which participated in it. Indeed, the best measure of the success of the GATT disputes procedure by 1990 was the increasing number of complaints governments chose to bring before it and the increasing political sensitivity of the trade practices it was being asked to rule upon. . . .

Robert E. Hudec, *The New WTO Dispute Settlement Procedure: An Overview of the First Three Years*, 8 Minn. J. Global Trade 1, 7-8 (1999).

Notes and Questions

1. How could the GATT dispute resolution process resolve so many disputes over so many years given the virtual absence of legally binding enforcement powers?

2. Why would states create a dispute settlement system in which the losing party had the right to veto unfavorable decisions or the imposition of sanctions against it?

3. If you were a trade official for a GATT party, what procedural features of the GATT dispute settlement system would you seek to change? Do you think such changes would be politically viable?

C. Challenging the EC Banana Regime

Shortly before adoption of EC Regulation 404/93, five Central and South American nations requested creation of a GATT dispute resolution panel to examine the European banana regimes. The panel report (*Bananas I*), issued in June 1993, found that Europe's patchwork of preferences and different tariffs violated the GATT's ban on quantitative restrictions (quotas) and its MFN clause. However, this victory proved hollow. First, the report was never formally adopted by the GATT Council due to objections from the EC and ACP nations. Second, the various banana import regimes were terminated less than one month after the panel report was issued and were replaced by Regulation 404/93.

In 1993 the Latin American nations requested a second panel to determine the GATT consistency of the new EC banana regime. In January 1994 the second panel issued its report (*Bananas II*), finding that the new banana regime was GATT-inconsistent. In particular, the panel found that the tariff preferences granted the ACP in the new regime violated the GATT's MFN and national treatment obligations. Once again, however, the EC and ACP nations blocked adoption of the panel report. The EC argued that implementation of the panel report would cause dire political and economic consequences to ACP states and would violate the EC's obligations under the Lomé Convention.

In March 1994, the EC and four of the complaining parties negotiated the so-called Bananas Agreement. Colombia, Costa Rica, Nicaragua, and Venezuela agreed not to seek adoption of the second panel report, and the EC agreed in effect to increase the number of bananas imported from those countries. Guatemala, one of the complainants, did not participate in this agreement, which the United States and Germany (Europe's largest consumer of bananas) also opposed.

As the EC's banana regime was being challenged at the GATT, a unilateral challenge to the regime was also developing. In September 1994, Chiquita Brands International, Inc. and the Hawaii Banana Industry Association filed a petition with the U.S. Trade Representative (USTR) under section 301 of the U.S. Trade Act of 1974, alleging that the Banana Agreement unlawfully discriminated against Chiquita bananas. Section 301 authorizes the USTR, after an investigation and consultations with a foreign government, to respond to foreign government acts, practices, or policies that are "unjustifiable," "unreasonable" or "discriminatory," and that burden or restrict U.S. commerce. The statute defines as "unreasonable" any foreign government act, policy, or practice that, although "not necessarily in violation of, or inconsistent with, the international legal rights of the United States, is otherwise unfair or inequitable." Section 301 authorizes the USTR to impose duties, quotas, or other trade restrictions on nations that engage in "unreasonable" acts.

In response to the collective pressure of the adverse panel reports, splits within the EC, and the Section 301 proceedings, the EC and ACP nations sought a GATT "waiver." GATT Article XXV(5) provides that "in exceptional circumstances" the GATT parties can "waive an obligation imposed upon a contracting party." At the final GATT Council meeting in December 1994, the Contracting Parties approved a five-year waiver from Article I's MFN clause for Lomé IV's trade provisions. (Under the GATT, a waiver could be granted by a two-thirds majority vote of the Contracting Parties, while the WTO agreements, which took effect January 1, 1995, require a three-fourths majority vote to approve a waiver). The waiver reads, in part:

> Subject to the terms and conditions set out hereunder, the provisions of paragraph 1 of Article I of the General Agreement shall be waived, until 29 February 2000, to the extent necessary to permit the European Communities to provide preferential treatment for products originating in ACP states as required by the relevant provisions of the Fourth Lomé Convention, without being required to extend the same preferential treatment to like products of any other contracting party.

In the meantime, USTR was investigating the EC banana regime and on January 9, 1995, announced its preliminary determination that the EC regime was adversely affecting U.S. economic interests. USTR then entered into months of inconclusive negotiations with the Europeans. In September, the United States announced that it, along with Guatemala, Honduras, and Mexico, would challenge the EC banana regime in the new WTO. This became known as the *Bananas III* dispute.

ACP nations strongly opposed the filing of this action, arguing that the survival of thousands of small banana producers—and even the economy of several Caribbean islands—were at issue. They pointed out that in St. Vincent, for example, some 70 percent of the population depends directly or indirectly upon income from the bananas trade. More broadly, over 60 percent of export income for the Windward Islands (Dominica, Grenada, St. Lucia, and St. Vincent and the Grenadines) comes from the bananas trade. Caribbean growers argued that if they lost preferential access to European markets for legitimate goods like bananas, they would have little option but to turn to illegitimate goods, such as illegal drugs.

D. The Evolution of Dispute Settlement in the Trade Regime

When the Uruguay Round negotiations started in 1986, GATT governments sought only minor procedural changes in dispute settlement procedures. In 1988 GATT parties rejected efforts to change the consensus principle that gave the losing party a veto over adverse rulings. However, less than a year later, GATT parties agreed to a dramatically enhanced dispute resolution system in the DSU. The DSU essentially reverses the GATT consensus rule; under the DSU, requests for a panel, requests to adopt a panel report, and requests for authorization of sanctions in cases of noncompliance are all automatically granted unless there is a consensus by all WTO members sitting as the Dispute Settlement Body (DSB) *against* such a request. In addition, the DSU provides for strict deadlines at each stage of the proceedings. The DSU grants losing parties a "reasonable period" within which to comply with panel rulings, a period that can be set by WTO arbitrators. Finally, if a party refuses to comply, it is supposed to negotiate a mutually acceptable agreement with the prevailing party; if this is not possible, the winning party can receive DSB authorization for trade retaliation against the losing party by, for example, raising tariffs.

Given the considerably increased importance of panel reports, the DSU also creates a standing Appellate Body, to which parties can appeal points of law. The same WTO reverse consensus rule applies to Appellate Body reports—they automatically enter into effect unless the entire WTO membership decides by consensus not to adopt the report. This appellate procedure is unique in the history of interstate dispute resolution.

What caused this dramatic change? The immediate precipitating event was apparently the considerable strengthening of Section 301 by major trade legislation enacted in 1988. The new legislation created "Super 301," which requires USTR to identify "major [foreign government] barriers and trade distorting practices, the elimination of which are likely to have the most significant potential to increase United States exports." After identifying these practices, USTR is directed to persuade the other government to eliminate the unfair barriers or provide the United States with compensation. If the other government is unwilling to accede to U.S. demands, USTR may take retaliatory trade action.

Other governments viewed the new legislation as an unacceptable unilateral attempt by the United States to judge their trade practices and called a special GATT meeting to demand a change in U.S. policy. The United States argued that these unilateral procedures were necessary because GATT dispute settlement was too cumbersome and too weak to protect U.S. trade interests adequately. Eventually, the outlines of a global bargain emerged. In addition to compulsory jurisdiction, the reverse consensus rule, strict time limits, and provisions for sanctions in cases of noncompliance, the DSU provides:

Article 23
Strengthening of the Multilateral System

1. When Members seek the redress of a violation of obligations . . . under the [WTO] agreements. . . . they shall have recourse to, and abide by, the rules and procedures of this Understanding.

2. In such cases, Members shall:

    (a) not make a determination to the effect that a violation has occurred . . . except through recourse to dispute settlement in accordance with the rules and procedures of this Understanding. . . .

    (c) follow the procedures set forth in [this agreement] to determine the level of suspension of concessions or other obligations and obtain DSB authorization in accordance with those procedures before suspending concessions or other obligations . . . in response to the failure of the Member concerned to implement [panel or Appellate Body] recommendations and rulings. . . .

E. Testing the WTO's Dispute Settlement System

In May 1997 the *Bananas III* panel report held that the EC regime was inconsistent with a number of WTO provisions and not authorized by the WTO waiver, which covered only the EC's MFN obligations. However, obtaining a determination on the merits of the EC's banana regime proved to be the start, rather than the finish, of WTO dispute resolution proceedings. The DSU provides losing parties with a "reasonable period of time" to change their law, but the United States and the EC disagreed over how long the EC should have to change its bananas regime. The DSU provides for binding arbitration in these circumstances, and an arbitrator granted the EC until January 1, 1999, to implement the panel's report and recommendations. In July 1998 the EC adopted a new bananas regulation to take effect on January 1, 1999. However, the United States argued that the new system would also be WTO-inconsistent, that the EC would therefore not be in compliance with the *Bananas III* report, and that the United States would impose trade sanctions effective February 1. The Europeans responded that under DSU Article 23, "[n]o member has the right to unilaterally determine, without recourse to [WTO procedures], whether another member is in compliance with WTO rules," and that any U.S. sanctions would be challenged at the WTO. The United States countered that the EC position would permit a recalcitrant party to enact an endless series of

WTO-inconsistent measures, and thereby escape trade sanctions and defeat the prevailing party's automatic right to retaliate against noncompliant parties.

1. The DSU: The Death of Unilateralism?

From the U.S. perspective, the ongoing bananas dispute centered upon a discriminatory import regime and European noncompliance with multiple panel rulings. From the European perspective, the conflict was evolving into a dispute over the legality of unilateral U.S. trade actions, particularly those taken pursuant to Section 301. This law had long been a flash point in trans-Atlantic relations, and the Europeans believed that the DSU had been its death knell. Nevertheless, the United States was threatening unilateral action in this, and other, trade disputes. Hence, in a March 1999 proceeding formally unrelated to the bananas litigation, the Europeans challenged Section 301. Six months later the panel issued its report. Relevant excerpts follow:

United States—Sections 301-310 of the Trade Act of 1974
WT/DS152/R (1999)

7.2   The EC claims that by adopting, maintaining on its statute book and applying Sections 301-310 of the 1974 Trade Act after the entry into force of the Uruguay Round Agreements, the US has breached the historical deal . . . between the US and other Uruguay Round participants . . . consist[ing] of a trade-off between, on the one hand, the practical certainty of adoption by the Dispute Settlement Body ("DSB") of panel and Appellate Body reports and of authorization for Members to suspend concessions . . . and, on the other hand, the complete and definitive abandoning by the US of its long-standing policy of unilateral action. . . .

THE MEASURE IN QUESTION AND THE PANEL'S GENERAL METHODOLOGY

7.28   . . . [I]n examining the relevant provisions of Sections 301-310 we first look at the statutory language itself, severed from all other elements of the law. We then look at the other elements of Sections 301-310 which, in our view, constitute an integral part of the Measure in question and make our final evaluation based on all elements taken together. . . .

7.59   The text of [DSU] Article 23.1 is simple enough: Members are obligated generally to (a) have recourse to and (b) abide by DSU rules and procedures. These rules and procedures include most specifically in Article 23.2(a) a prohibition on making a unilateral determination of inconsistency prior to exhaustion of DSU proceedings. . . .

7.61   . . . In each and every case when a determination [of GATT inconsistency] is made [by USTR under Section 301] while DSU proceedings are not yet exhausted, Members locked in a dispute with the US will be subject to a mandatory determination by the USTR under a statute which explicitly puts them in that very danger which Article 23 was intended to remove. . . .

7.94   The more effective and quasi-automatic dispute settlement system under the WTO has often been heralded as one of the fundamental changes and major achievements of the Uruguay Round agreements. . . . If individual economic operators cannot be confident about the integrity of WTO dispute resolution and may fear unilateral measures outside the guarantees and disciplines which the DSU ensures, their confidence in each and every of the substantive disciplines of the system will be undermined as well. The overall systemic damage and the denial of benefits would be amplified accordingly. The assurances thus given under the DSU may, in our view, be of even greater importance than those provided under substantive WTO provisions. . . .

7.96   Consequently, the statutory language of Section 304[*]—by mandating a determination before the adoption of DSB findings and statutorily reserving the right for this determination to be one of inconsistency—must be considered presumptively to be inconsistent with the obligations in Article 23.2(a). . . .

7.98   In the previous analysis we have deliberately referred to the "statutory language". . . . The Measure in question includes statutory language as well as other institutional and administrative elements. To evaluate its overall WTO conformity we have to assess all of these elements together. . . .

7.110   [A Statement of Administrative Action (SAA) accompanied the US legislation implementing the results of the Uruguay Round submitted by the President to Congress. The SAA states:]

> This Statement . . . represents an authoritative expression by the Administration concerning its views regarding the interpretation and application of the Uruguay Round agreements, both for purposes of U.S. international obligations and domestic law. Furthermore, the Administration understands that it is the expectation of the Congress that future Administrations will observe and apply the interpretations and commitments set out in this Statement. . . .

7.112   [The SSA also states:] Although it will enhance the effectiveness of section 301, the DSU does not require any significant change in section 301 *for investigations that involve an alleged violation of a Uruguay Round agreement or the impairment of U.S. benefits under such an agreement.* In such cases, *the Trade Representative will:*

- invoke DSU dispute settlement procedures, as required under current law;
- base any section 301 determination that there has been a violation or denial of U.S. rights under the relevant agreement on the panel or Appellate Body findings adopted by the DSB;
- following adoption of a favorable panel or Appellate Body report, allow the defending party a reasonable period of time to implement the report's recommendations; and
- if the matter cannot be resolved during that period, seek authority from the DSB to retaliate.

This official statement in the SAA—in particular, the commitment undertaken in the second bullet point—approved by the US Congress in the expectation that it will be followed by future US Administrations, is a major element in our conclusion that the discretion created by the statutory language permitting a determination of inconsistency prior to exhaustion of DSU proceeding has effectively been curtailed. . . .

---

[*]Section 304 directs the USTR to determine whether any U.S. rights are being denied under any trade agreement, or whether a foreign government act, policy, or practice is unjustifiable or unreasonable. If so, section 304 also directs the USTR to determine what action, if any, to take. Finally, section 304 sets time limits for these determinations. These time limits are, in certain cases, shorter than the time limits used in WTO dispute resolution.—Eds.

US STATEMENTS BEFORE THIS PANEL

7.115   . . . In response to our very insistent questions, the US explicitly, officially, repeatedly and unconditionally confirmed the commitment expressed in the SAA namely that the USTR would ". . . base any section 301 determination that there has been a violation or denial of U.S. rights under the relevant agreement on the panel or Appellate Body findings adopted by the DSB". . . .

7.122   The representations and statements by the representatives of the US . . . were solemnly made, in a deliberative manner, for the record, repeated in writing and confirmed in the Panel's second hearing. . . .

7.125   Accordingly, we find that these statements . . . express the unambiguous and official position of the US representing, in a manner that can be relied upon by all Members, an undertaking that the discretion of the USTR has been limited so as to prevent a determination of inconsistency before exhaustion of DSU proceedings. . . .

7.126   The aggregate effect of the SAA and the US statements made to us is to provide the guarantees, both direct to other Members and indirect to the market place, that Article 23 is intended to secure. Through the SAA and the US statements . . . it is now clear that under Section 304 . . . the USTR is precluded from making a determination of inconsistency contrary to [DSU] Article 23.2(a). . . . It of course follows that should the US repudiate or remove in any way these undertakings, the US would incur State responsibility since its law would be rendered inconsistent with the obligations under Article 23. . . .

Notes and Questions

1. Are you persuaded by the panel's analysis? Is the Section 301 panel deciding that the U.S. statements to the panel were legally binding? If so, is this consistent with the principles governing the binding effect of unilateral statements developed in the *Eastern Greenland* and *Nuclear Tests* cases discussed in Chapter 2?

Given the panel's reliance on the Administration's representations to Congress in the SAA, is it relevant that USTR Mickey Kantor testified before Congress in 1994 that

> some countries have even tried to claim that the WTO will restrict the ability of the United States to use Section 301 because it requires a member to abide by the [dispute settlement] rules and procedures when it seeks to redress a violation of the WTO. There is however absolutely no basis for such a claim.

2. Is Section 301 consistent with the text or structure of the DSU? Is it obsolete in a post-Uruguay Round world? Or is it a legitimate form of "civil disobedience" that can achieve change in the international trading system and pressure recalcitrant foreign governments to remove barriers to trade?

One empirical study of Section 301 analyzed some 72 cases brought between 1975 and 1994 and found that about half the time the United States achieved its negotiating objectives. Another examined 77 cases between 1975 and 1990 and found that trade liberalization occurred in about one-third of the cases, and that in eight instances the United States imposed trade measures against the target country. Should Section 301's "success" rate bear on the desirability or legality of statutes like this?

3. In the course of the dispute over the WTO consistency of Section 301, the United States argued that it had always applied Section 301 in a WTO-consistent manner. The panel invited the EC to submit evidence to the contrary. The panel refused to make a "conclusive finding" on this issue but noted that "the evidence submitted to us [was insufficient] to overturn the U.S. claim" that its use of Section 301 was WTO-consistent.

2. Responding to Noncompliance

In the aftermath of the *Bananas III* ruling and adoption of the new EC banana regime, the United States and the EC bitterly contested whether the United States had a right to request immediate DSB authorization to impose sanctions under Article 22 or whether a WTO panel first had to find the new regime WTO-inconsistent under Article 21.5. Relevant provisions of the DSU provide:

Article 21
Surveillance of Implementation of Recommendations and Rulings

1. Prompt compliance with recommendations or rulings of the DSB is essential in order to ensure effective resolution of disputes to the benefit of all Members. . . .

5. Where there is disagreement as to the [GATT] consistency . . . of measures taken to comply with the [panel's] recommendations and rulings such dispute shall be decided through recourse to these dispute settlement procedures, including wherever possible resort to the original panel. . . .

Article 22
Compensation and the Suspension of Concessions

2. If the Member concerned fails to bring the measure found to be [GATT] inconsistent . . . into compliance therewith or otherwise comply with the [panel's] recommendations and rulings . . . such Member shall, if so requested . . . enter into negotiations with [the prevailing party] with a view to developing mutually acceptable compensation. If no satisfactory compensation has been agreed within [a specified time], [the prevailing party] may request authorization from the DSB to suspend the application to the Member concerned of concessions or other obligations under the covered agreements. . . .

4. The level of the suspension of concessions or other obligations authorized by the DSB shall be equivalent to the level of the nullification or impairment. . . .

6. When the situation described in paragraph 2 occurs, the DSB, upon request, shall grant authorization to suspend concessions or other obligations . . . unless the DSB decides by consensus to reject the request. However, if the Member concerned objects to the level of suspension proposed . . . the matter shall be referred to arbitration. . . . Concessions or other obligations shall not be suspended during the course of the arbitration.

7. The arbitrator . . . shall determine whether the level of such suspension is equivalent to the level of nullification or impairment. . . . The parties shall accept the arbitrator's decision as final . . . .

This dispute over whether the United States could proceed immediately to trade sanctions or had first to obtain a ruling that the new banana regulation was WTO-inconsistent unfolded in various stages. In December 1998 Ecuador, the world's largest banana exporter, requested formation of an Article 21.5 panel to examine the WTO consistency of the new EC regulation. In a highly unusual request, the EC asked for creation of an Article 21.5 panel as well. The following month the United States requested authorization under Article 22.2 to raise tariffs in the amount of $520 million on EC products ranging from Italian pecorino cheese to Scottish cashmere sweaters. The EC responded by saying that this figure was inflated and, pursuant to Article 22.6, requested arbitration on the level of concessions requested by the United States.

Meanwhile, the broader WTO membership weighed in. Many governments claimed that EC noncompliance challenged the effectiveness of the WTO dispute system. Others countered that U.S. unilateralism posed a greater threat to the system. After weeks of backroom negotiations, on February 1 the Chair of the DSB offered the following self-described "suggest[ion]":

> 1. A number of delegations have highlighted the lack of clarity in how Articles 21.5 and 22 should be interpreted and the sequence in which they should be applied. I believe that many of these concerns are legitimate, but we face the problem of how to solve our problem in this dispute today. . . . I think that the best approach is to proceed by separating the Bananas case from the more general systemic issues. The solution to the Bananas matter *would be totally without prejudice* to future cases and . . . the systemic issue of the relationship between Articles 21.5 and 22 . . . .
>
> 3. As to Bananas, the original panel is now engaged in two Article 21.5 proceedings. . . . [A]ssuming the EC makes a request for arbitration under Article 22.6, the same individuals could be given the task of arbitrating the level of suspension. . . . There remains the problem of how the panel and the arbitrators would coordinate their work, but as they will be the same individuals, the reality is that they will find a logical way forward, in consultation with the parties. . . .
>
> 4. As to the systemic issues concerning the relationship of Articles 21.5 and 22, they must be resolved expeditiously. . . . I will propose to the Chairman of the General Council that this matter be taken up by that body . . . .

Both the Article 21 and the Article 22 requests were sent to the original panelists. Under WTO rules, the Article 22 arbitration was to be completed by March 2 while the Article 21 panels were to announce their decisions by April 12. However, on March 2, the Article 22 arbitrators announced that they needed additional information before issuing a ruling. The following day, the United States announced that it was, in effect, raising tariffs on specific EC goods pending a final WTO decision on its Article 22 request.

On April 6, 1999, the Article 21.5 panels issued their reports and, simultaneously, the Article 22 arbitrators issued their award. The Article 21.5 panel requested by Ecuador concluded that various aspects of the EC's bananas regime still discriminated against Latin bananas and therefore were "inconsistent with the EC's obligations" under various WTO provisions. The Article 21.5 panel initiated by the EC rejected the EC's request for a finding that:

> . . . the new EC [banana] regime . . . adopted in order to comply with the recommendations and rulings of the [panel and Appellate Body] had to be deemed . . . to be in

conformity with the WTO covered agreements so long as those original parties had not successfully challenged the new EC regime under the relevant dispute settlement procedures of the WTO.

The EC did not appeal either panel decision.

The Article 22 arbitrators held, as the United States had argued, that they had the authority to rule on the WTO-consistency of measures taken to comply with a panel ruling.

It would be the WTO-inconsistency of the revised EC regime that would be the root cause of any nullification or impairment suffered by the United States. Since the level of the proposed suspension of concessions is to be equivalent to the level of nullification or impairment, logic dictates that our examination as Arbitrators focuses on that latter level before we will be in a position to ascertain its equivalence to the level of the suspension of concessions proposed by the United States.

The arbitrators concluded that the new EC banana regime was WTO-inconsistent and that the United States could retaliate in an amount of $191.4 million per year. On April 19 the United States requested and received DSB authorization to suspend $191.4 million worth of concessions. To do so, the United States imposed 100 percent customs duties on designated items from the EC.

In the meantime, in a formally separate proceeding, the EC challenged the U.S. decision to raise tariffs on selected imports from Europe in March, prior to the release of the arbitrators' award. A WTO panel made several relevant determinations. First, since DSU Article 23 requires WTO members to have recourse to and abide by DSU rules and procedures when they want to retaliate against alleged WTO noncompliance, sanctions imposed prior to a WTO finding of noncompliance violated Article 23. Second, the imposition of sanctions prior to the release of the Article 22 arbitrators' award violated Article 22, which states that "concessions or other obligations shall not be suspended during the course of the arbitration."

Finally, addressing the underlying doctrinal dispute of whether the United States could move immediately for authorization to impose sanctions under Article 22 or whether it first had to use the Article 21 process, the panel noted that while Article 21.5 provides that "where there is disagreement as to the existence or consistency with a covered agreement of measures taken to comply with the recommendations and rulings such dispute shall be decided through recourse to these dispute settlement procedures," it did not specify which procedures should be used. The panel agreed with the United States that an Article 22 procedure could be used and rejected the EC's argument that an Article 21.5 procedure had to be used. However, the panel held that the United States nevertheless violated Article 21.5 by imposing sanctions before any WTO body had held that the EC's implementing measures were WTO-inconsistent.

Both sides appealed this report. On the key doctrinal question of whether an Article 21.5 finding of noncompliance was a prerequisite to the imposition of sanctions, the Appellate Body found that the panel had improperly considered the U.S.'s April 19th sanctions, imposed after the Article 22 award was issued. As the April sanctions were not properly before the panel, its conclusion that an Article 22 proceeding can be used to satisfy the Article 21.5 requirements "ha[s] no legal effect." The Appellate Body continued:

> 91.   In coming to this conclusion, we are cognizant of the important systemic issue of the relationship between Articles 21.5 and 22 of the DSU . . . and [that] the relationship between these two provisions of the DSU has been the subject of intensive and extensive discussion among Members of the WTO. . . .
>
> 92.   In so noting, we observe that it is certainly not the task of either panels or the Appellate Body to amend the DSU. . . . Only WTO members have the authority to amend the DSU. . . . [T]he task of panels and the Appellate Body in the dispute settlement system of the WTO is "to preserve the rights and obligations of Members . . . and to *clarify the existing provisions* of those agreements in accordance with customary rules of interpretation of public international law." Determining what the rules and procedures of the DSU ought to be is not our responsibility nor the responsibility of the panels; it is clearly the responsibility solely of the Members of the WTO.

United States—Import Measures on Certain Products from the European Communities, WT/DS165/AB/R (2000).

On April 11, 2001, the United States and the EU reached an agreement to resolve the banana dispute. The EU agreed to eliminate its quotas and to implement a tariff-only system by 2006. On July 1, 2001, the EU instituted a new interim system for licensing banana imports that effectively increased the number of Latin bananas imported into Europe at the expense of ACP bananas. On the same date, the United States suspended the trade measures it had imposed upon the EU since 1999.

Ecuador opposed the new agreement, which it characterized as "flagrantly WTO incompatible." Ecuador threatened a WTO challenge and entered into negotiations with the Europeans. A few weeks later, the parties reached an agreement providing for an increase in Ecuador's share of exports to Europe in exchange for Ecuador's support for the U.S.-EC agreement. In December 2001, WTO members adopted a waiver covering the European quota for ACP bananas during the interim period before the Europeans moved to a tariff-only system. An annex to the waiver states that the new system "should result in at least maintaining total market access" for Latin American banana suppliers.

In October 2004, the EC announced that on January 1, 2006, it would replace the Latin American banana quota limit with a tariff of 230 euros per tonne. Nine Latin American states challenged this rate, and in August 2005, a WTO panel ruled that the proposed tariff was too high to guarantee the same market access that Latin suppliers enjoyed under the then-current system. In October 2005, the panel found that a proposed tariff of 187 euros per ton was also too high. In November 2005, the EC proposed a tariff rate of 176 euros per ton. As of December 2005, Honduras, Nicaragua and Panama had announced that they would challenge this tariff rate in WTO proceedings.

Notes and Questions

1. The chart that follows summarizes the litigation over the EC bananas regime and related issues covered in this chapter.

Complainant(s)	Respondent	Type of Proceeding	Issue	Holding
Colombia, Costa Rica, Guatemala, Nicaragua, Venezuela (*Bananas I*)	EC	GATT dispute resolution	GATT consistency of various European banana regimes	European regimes violate MFN and ban on quotas June 1993
Colombia, Costa Rica, Guatemala, Nicaragua, Venezuela (*Bananas II*)	EC	GATT dispute resolution	GATT consistency of EC Regulation 404/93	Regulation violates MFN and NTO obligations January 1994
Ecuador, Guatemala, Honduras, Mexico, U.S. (*Bananas III*)	EC	WTO dispute resolution	WTO consistency of EC Regulation 404/93	Regulation inconsistent with WTO obligations, not authorized by GATT waiver May 1997
Ecuador, Guatemala, Honduras, Mexico, U.S.	EC	WTO Article 21 arbitration	Length of time for EC to change Regulation 404/93	EC given until January 1, 1999 January 1998
EC	U.S.	WTO dispute resolution	WTO consistency of section 301	Statutory language is presumptively inconsistent, but SAA and U.S. statements before panel limiting use of statute render statute not WTO-inconsistent September 1999
EC		WTO Article 21.5 proceedings	WTO consistency of EC's January 1, 1999 banana regime	Rejects EC request to find new regime WTO-consistent. April 1999

Complainant(s)	Respondent	Type of Proceeding	Issue	Holding
Ecuador	EC	WTO Article 21.5 proceedings	WTO consistency of EC's January 1, 1999 banana regime	January 1, 1999, regime is inconsistent with EC's WTO obligations April 1999
U.S.	EC	WTO Article 22.6 arbitration	1. Can Article 22 arbitrators determine the WTO consistency of January 1, 1999 banana regime? 2. Did U.S. request excessive level of retaliatory trade sanctions?	1. Article 22 arbitrators can rule on WTO consistency of losing party's implementation measures 2. U.S. request was excessive and is reduced to $191.4 million per year April 1999
EC	U.S.	WTO dispute resolution	WTO consistency of U.S.'s unilateral trade sanctions against the EC on March 3	1. Unilateral sanctions violate Article 23 2. Unilateral sanctions violate Article 22 3. Unilateral sanctions violate Article 21.5 July 2000
U.S. (Appellant)	EC (Appellee)	WTO Appellate Body	WTO consistency of U.S.'s unilateral trade sanctions against the EC on March 3	1. Upholds panel determination that unilateral sanctions violate Article 21.5 2. Vacates panel determination that unilateral sanctions violate Article 22 as question was not properly before panel December 2000

2. Who won the banana war? The United States invested substantial legal resources and diplomatic capital over many years, yet the U.S. exports no bananas. Moreover, during the course of the bananas dispute, the EC challenged certain provisions of U.S. tax laws that distinguish between U.S. and foreign companies in the taxation of certain types of income. Many U.S. officials believe that the EC filed the tax case in retaliation for the bananas case. In October 1999, a WTO panel held that the tax breaks were WTO-inconsistent. In November 2000, the United States enacted new tax provisions in response to the panel report.

However, the EC argued that the new law was WTO-inconsistent and sought authorization to impose over $4 billion per year in punitive tariffs against U.S. goods. The United States and EC agreed that the parties would submit the WTO compliance of the new law to an Article 21.5 panel. In August 2001, a WTO panel determined that the new U.S. tax law was WTO-inconsistent. In January 2002, the Appellate Body affirmed this decision.

The United States challenged the EC request for $4 billion of trade sanctions as excessive, but in August 2002, an Article 22 arbitrator rejected the United States's arguments and approved the EC's request. In May 2003, the DSB authorized the EC to impose up to $4 billion in tariffs against U.S. goods; in March 2004, the EC began to impose additional tariffs of 5 percent on selected U.S. goods, and increased the tariffs by 1 percent each subsequent month.

In October 2004, the United States replaced the offending law with a new law and, in response, in January 2005, the EC decided to lift its punitive tariffs. However, shortly thereafter, the EC challenged provisions of the new law in WTO dispute proceedings. In September 2005, a WTO compliance panel ruled that certain "transition and grandfathering clauses" in the new law were WTO-illegal and, in February 2006, the Appellate Body affirmed. If the United States does not bring its law into compliance, the EC will be able to reimpose part of the $4 billion in annual retaliatory duties.

3. The banana dispute also illustrates the interplay of domestic and international politics in the trade area. Recall that the U.S. challenge to the EC's banana regime was triggered by a Section 301 filing by Chiquita. Chiquita was also very active in domestic trade politics. In the 2000 election cycle, Chiquita's top executive, Carl H. Linder, and American Financial Group, which owns 36 percent of Chiquita, gave $1.03 million to Republicans and $676,750 to Democrats. Chiquita also hired the brother of the White House Chief of Staff to lobby the Clinton Administration on trade issues. The U.S.-EC banana deal allocated banana import licenses based in part on how they had been allocated between 1994 and 1996, a period when Chiquita dominated the European market. A spokesperson for rival Dole Food Company complained that Dole "got sold up the river."

Is the banana dispute a dispute between the U.S. and European governments, or is it more a battle among large multinational corporations for the European banana market? Did U.S. trade policy reflect the national interest or a particular corporate interest?

4. After prevailing in April 1999 its Article 21.5 action, in November 1999 Ecuador requested authorization to suspend concessions to the EC in the amount of $450 million. The EC contested this figure, and the issue went to an Article 22 arbitration. In March 2000 the arbitrators found that Ecuador could suspend concessions in the amount of $201.6 million. Thereafter, Ecuador and the EC were unable to negotiate a mutually acceptable agreement, and in May 2000, Ecuador

requested, and received, WTO authorization to suspend concessions in the amount of $201.6 million.

In its request, Ecuador argued that the imposition of higher tariffs on imported goods from the EC would harm its domestic industries, which are dependent upon imported capital goods and raw materials. Hence, WTO parties authorized Ecuador to retaliate by suspending intellectual property protection and wholesale distribution rights for EC goods and services providers. This authority was granted pursuant to a DSU provision allowing retaliation outside the sector of the measure at issue where it is not "practicable or effective" to impose sanctions in that sector (here, the sale of goods). These actions represented the first time that the WTO had authorized a developing nation to impose sanctions on another WTO member and the first time the body had authorized "cross-retaliation" outside the goods sector. Are retaliatory trade barriers a sensible remedy for the WTO to authorize?

5. Note that the WTO dispute system does not permit the award of damages for economic losses suffered before issuance of the panel report. What is the logic behind such a system? What incentive does this provide to states considering the adoption of WTO-inconsistent measures? Given that complainants absorb the considerable cost of litigating WTO disputes and, if successful, either share the benefits of the elimination of the offending measure with other states or impose (welfare-reducing) trade restrictions, what is the incentive to file a WTO action?

6. Is the DSU a success? States submitted some 298 disputes to the GATT's dispute resolution processes over nearly 50 years. Between January 1, 1995, when the WTO came into existence, and December 12, 2005, WTO members notified some 335 complaints to the WTO. WTO parties have adopted 95 panel and Appellate Body reports, and 81 complaints have been settled or were inactive.

The compliance issues presented in the bananas dispute were, for the most part, issues of first impression. In subsequent disputes raising compliance issues, the WTO members involved have generally reached agreements affirming the need for an Article 21.5 panel to rule on whether a member has complied with a panel report before the complaining party can suspend concessions. As of December 12, 2005, WTO members had requested a panel or the Appellate Body to rule on compliance in 14 disputes. Many of the disputes that raise compliance issues, such as the bananas dispute, involve multiple complainants. As of December 2005, the WTO had authorized trade retaliation against noncompliant parties on 15 occasions.

II. BALANCING TRADE AND THE ENVIRONMENT: THE *SHRIMP-TURTLE* DISPUTE

Trade and environment issues loomed large in the public protests at the WTO's meeting in Seattle in 1999 and at subsequent international economic meetings. The trade and environment debate covers a number of issues: will the increased economic activity caused by expanded trade create pollution spillovers from one state to another, or lead to the unsustainable use of natural resources? Will governments use rules contained in trade agreements to override domestic or international environmental laws? Can states restrict trade to encourage other states to address regional or global environmental problems? Finally, beneath much of the trade and

environment debate lies the difficult question of whether states with lower environmental standards enjoy competitive advantages in international markets and, if so,
what can or should be done about this.

In this section, we explore the trajectory of WTO jurisprudence addressing
these controversial issues. As you review the materials in this section, consider
how international bodies can distinguish between environmental measures that
protect inefficient domestic industries from those that protect important environmental resources. Consider also whether the trade system should incorporate
environmental law or values, and whether environmental norms are consistent with
international trade rules. Finally, consider whether trade bodies like the WTO are
appropriate institutions for mediating the tensions between trade and environment
values.

A. The Problem

Sea turtles are air-breathing reptiles that inhabit tropical and subtropical ocean
waters throughout the world. Having traveled the seas for over 100 million years,
sea turtles have outlived virtually all the prehistoric animals, including dinosaurs,
with which they once shared the planet. However, sea turtle populations have
declined precipitously in recent decades. For example, by 1990, the number of
Kemp's ridley turtles at their only important nesting beach, on the Mexican
coast of the Gulf of Mexico, had dropped to 1 percent of their population in
1947. At present, all species of sea turtle are listed as "species threatened with
extinction which are or may be affected by trade" under the Convention on International Trade in Endangered Species; all turtle species that spend at least some
portion of their lives in U.S. coastal waters are listed as endangered or threatened
under the U.S. Endangered Species Act (ESA).

While sea turtle mortality is caused by a number of factors, including destruction and alteration of nesting and foraging habitats, predators, and diseases,
authoritative studies have found that "the most important human-associated source
of mortality is incidental capture in shrimp trawls, which accounts for more deaths
than all other human activities combined." By some estimates, during the 1980s,
commercial shrimp trawling was causing the deaths of approximately 124,000 turtles per year. As part of a program aimed at reducing turtle mortality, the U.S.
National Marine Fisheries Service (NMFS) developed Turtle Excluder Devices
(TEDs). TEDs are mechanical devices that permit turtles to escape from shrimp-
trawling nets. Properly designed and installed, TEDs can reduce turtle mortality by
approximately 97 percent.

In 1983, NMFS began to encourage U.S. shrimp vessels to use TEDs voluntarily. However, these efforts met with limited success as few shrimpers used TEDs
on a regular basis. In 1987, the United States issued regulations, pursuant to the
ESA, requiring shrimp trawlers operating in ocean waters off the southeastern
United States to use TEDs.

The shrimp fishery has the highest product value of any fishery in the United
States. But many shrimpers complained that TEDs were expensive and time-
consuming to install and clean, had to be replaced frequently, and that use of
TEDs placed them at a competitive disadvantage vis-à-vis their foreign competitors.
Environmental advocates noted that since U.S. shrimpers produce only 8 percent of
the world's shrimp catch, and since turtles migrate great distances, unilateral efforts

by U.S. shrimpers would be of limited effectiveness unless similar levels of protection were afforded throughout the turtles' migratory range.

In response to these concerns, in 1989, Congress enacted Section 609 of Public Law 101-162, which requires the federal government to initiate negotiations for agreements with nations engaged in fishing operations that might adversely affect sea turtles. Section 609 also provides that "the importation of shrimp or products from shrimp which have been harvested with commercial fishing technology which may affect adversely [sea turtles] shall be prohibited not later than May 1, 1991" unless the President certifies to Congress by May 1, 1991, and annually thereafter, that:

> (A) the government of the harvesting nation has . . . [adopted] a regulatory program governing the incidental taking of such sea turtles . . . that is comparable to that of the United States; and
> (B) the average rate of that incidental taking by the vessels of the harvesting nation is comparable to the average rate of incidental taking of sea turtles by United States vessels . . . ; or
> (C) the particular fishing environment of the harvesting nation does not pose a threat of the incidental taking of such sea turtles . . . .

The U.S. State Department issued guidelines in 1991, amended in 1993, for assessing the comparability of foreign regulatory programs with the U.S. program. To be found comparable, a foreign nation's program had to include, inter alia, a commitment to require all shrimp trawl vessels to use TEDs at all times. Foreign states were given three years to complete the phase-in of a comparable program. The guidelines also provided that Section 609 would be applied only to the following states: Mexico, Belize, Guatemala, Honduras, Nicaragua, Costa Rica, Panama, Colombia, Venezuela, Trinidad and Tobago, Guyana, Suriname, French Guyana, and Brazil. Thus, under both the 1991 and 1993 Guidelines, national certification was the only way a harvesting state could export shrimp to the United States. The import of shrimp from uncertified states was prohibited, even if those particular shrimp had been caught by a shrimper that used TEDs. In addition, at this time, the United States began efforts to negotiate a treaty to protect sea turtles with the states of the Caribbean and Western Atlantic region.*

In 1995, a coalition of environmental NGOs filed suit in the U.S. Court of International Trade, a specialized court with jurisdiction over disputes arising under U.S. trade statutes, challenging the Administration's application of the statute only to shrimp harvested in the wider Caribbean/western Atlantic region. The court found that the Administration decided to limit the geographic application of Section 609 because a worldwide ban "could affect shrimp imports from more than 80 countries totaling as much as $1.8 billion—more than 75 percent (by value) of all shrimp consumed in this country. The impact of the resulting embargoes would be unprecedented both internationally and domestically . . . , [and] create major foreign policy problems with many countries." *Earth Island Institute v. Christopher*, 913 F. Supp. 559 (Ct. Int'l Trade 1995). The court held that there was no statutory basis for limiting the geographic application of Section 609 and directed the State Department "to prohibit not later than May 1, 1996 the importation of shrimp

---

*The negotiations concluded in 1996 with the signing of the Inter-American Convention for the Protection and Conservation of Sea Turtles. The Convention entered into force in 2001 with Brazil, Costa Rica, Ecuador, Honduras, Mexico, the Netherlands, Peru, Venezuela, and the United States as parties.

or products of shrimp wherever harvested in the wild with commercial fishing technology which may affect adversely [sea turtles]."

In response, in April 1996, the State Department issued revised guidelines (1996 Guidelines) which restricted imports of shrimp harvested from all waters inhabited by sea turtles, not just those of the wider Caribbean region. However, in contrast to the 1991 and 1993 Guidelines, the 1996 Guidelines permitted imports of shrimp from waters of uncertified states if the exporter included a declaration that the shrimp were "harvested under conditions that did not adversely affect [protected species of] sea turtles." Thus, under this shipment-by-shipment approach, a state did not need to be certified to export to the United States. Instead, a nation could satisfy Section 609 simply by employing TEDs on those vessels harvesting shrimp bound for the U.S. market.

Earth Island challenged the 1996 Guidelines. In October 1996, the court determined that Section 609 applied to all "shrimp or shrimp products harvested in the wild by citizens or vessels of nations which have not been certified." The court concluded that, by permitting imports of shrimp from noncertified countries that were harvested with technology that did not adversely affect sea turtles, the 1996 Guidelines were inconsistent with Section 609. Accordingly, the court prohibited the import of shrimp from noncertified harvesting nations. *Earth Island Institute v. Christopher*, 942 F. Supp. 597 (Ct. Int'l Trade 1996). This decision was later vacated on procedural grounds.

As a result of the various regulations and court rulings, during the mid-1990s the United States banned shrimp imports from a number of states. The ban had a significant economic effect; for example, shrimp exports from Malaysia fell from $9.1 million in 1995 to $4.86 million in 1996 and $1.47 million in 1997. In 1997, India, Malaysia, Pakistan, and Thailand requested creation of WTO dispute settlement panels to determine whether the shrimp embargo violated the United States's WTO obligations.

B. The **Tuna-Dolphin** *Dispute*

The *Shrimp-Turtle* dispute was not the first time that a trade panel was asked to consider the legality of environmental measures that restrict trade under international trade law. A 1991 dispute involved a fact pattern strikingly similar to the *Shrimp-Turtle* dispute. That dispute, *United States—Restrictions on Imports of Tuna*, DS21/R-39S/155 (1991) (*Tuna-Dolphin I*) involved a challenge to certain provisions of the United State's Marine Mammal Protection Act (MMPA).* These provisions were designed to protect dolphins that were incidentally caught by the commercial tuna fleet. Under that law, the U.S. fleet had to fish in a "dolphin safe" manner in order to sell their tuna on the U.S. market. Several years later, Congress amended the MMPA to require that, to import into the United States, foreign states had to adopt a regulatory program "comparable" to that of the United States and their fleets had to achieve an incidental dolphin kill rate "comparable" to that of the U.S.

---

*Much of the account that follows is drawn from Richard W. Parker, *The Use and Abuse of Trade Leverage to Protect the Global Commons: What We Can Learn from the Tuna-Dolphin Conflict*, 12 Geo. Intl. Envtl. L. Rev. 1 (1999); James R. Joseph, *The Tuna-Dolphin Controversy in the Eastern Pacific Ocean: Biological, Economic and Political Impacts*, 25 Ocean Dev. & Intl. L. 1 (1994); Jeffrey L. Dunoff, *Reconciling International Trade with Preservation of the Global Commons: Can We Prosper and Protect?*, 49 Wash. & Lee L. Rev. 1407 (1992).

fleet. When the Administration proved reluctant to impose tuna embargoes on foreign fleets, Earth Island Institute filed a federal court action which led to an order requiring the federal government to enforce the MMPA. Thereafter, the United States enforced a tuna embargo against a number of states, including Mexico. Mexico responded by initiating dispute settlement proceedings at the GATT.

As a matter of GATT law, the dispute involved the meaning of, and relationships among, GATT articles XI, III, and XX. Article XI provides that, subject to limited exceptions, "[n]o prohibitions or restrictions other than duties, taxes or other charges, whether made effective through quotas . . . or other measures, shall be instituted or maintained" on imports from other GATT members. Article III provides that products imported from GATT parties shall "be accorded treatment no less favourable than that accorded to like products of national origin." Article XX provides, in relevant part, that:

> Subject to the requirement that such measures are not applied in a manner which would constitute a means of arbitrary or unjustifiable discrimination between countries where the same conditions prevail . . . , nothing in this Agreement shall be construed to prevent the adoption or enforcement by any contracting party of measures . . .
> (b) necessary to protect human, animal or plant life or health; . . .
> (g) relating to the conservation of exhaustible natural resources if such measures are made effective in conjunction with restrictions on domestic production or consumption; . . . .

Mexico argued that the embargo violated Article XI. The United States responded that as the MMPA applies to both domestic and imported tuna, the challenged measures were "internal regulations" and hence governed by and consistent with Article III, rather than quotas governed by Article XI. The United States argued, in the alternative, that even if the embargo violated one of these articles, it fell within the Article XX exception. In September 1991, a GATT panel issued the following report:

United States—Restrictions on Imports of Tuna

DS21/R-39S/155 (1991)

5.9   . . . While restrictions on importation are prohibited by Article XI:1, contracting parties are permitted by Article III:4 and the Note Ad Article III [an interpretative note attached to the treaty] to impose an internal regulation on products imported from other contracting parties provided that it . . . accords to imported products treatment no less favourable than that accorded to like products of national origin. . . .

5.11   The text of Article III:1 refers to the application to imported or domestic *products* of "laws, regulations and requirements affecting the internal sale . . . of *products*" . . . ; it sets forth the principle that such regulations on *products* not be applied so as to afford protection to domestic production. Article III:4 refers solely to laws, regulations and requirements affecting the internal sale, etc. of *products*. This suggests that Article III covers only measures affecting products as such. . . .

5.14   . . . The Panel noted that the MMPA regulates the domestic harvesting of yellowfin tuna to reduce the incidental taking of dolphin, but that these regulations could not be regarded as being applied to tuna products as such because they would not directly regulate the sale of tuna and could not possibly affect tuna as a product. . . .

    5.15   . . . Article III:4 calls for a comparison of the treatment of imported tuna *as a product* with that of domestic tuna as a product. Regulations governing the taking of dolphins incidental to the taking of tuna could not possibly affect tuna *as a product*. Article III:4 therefore obliges the United States to accord treatment to Mexican tuna no less favourable than that accorded to United States tuna, whether or not the incidental taking of dolphins by Mexican vessels corresponds to that of United States vessels. . . .

    [After rejecting the argument that the U.S. measure fell within the scope of Article III, the panel held that the import ban violated Article XI. The panel then considered whether the embargo fell within the scope of GATT Article XX.]

    5.24 The Panel noted that the United States considered [its embargoes] . . . to be justified by Article XX(b) because they served solely the purpose of protecting dolphin life and health and were "necessary" . . . because, in respect of the protection of dolphin life and health outside its jurisdiction, there was no alternative measure reasonably available to the United States to achieve this objective. Mexico considered that Article XX(b) was not applicable to a measure imposed to protect the life or health of animals outside the jurisdiction of the contracting party taking it. . . .

    5.25   The Panel noted that the basic question . . . whether Article XX(b) covers measures necessary to protect human, animal or plant life or health outside the jurisdiction of the contracting party taking the measure, is not clearly answered by the text of that provision. The Panel therefore decided to analyze this issue in the light of the drafting history of Article XX(b), the purpose of this provision, and the consequences that the interpretations proposed by the parties would have for the operation of the General Agreement as a whole.

    5.26   [In an earlier draft of Article XX,] exception (b) read: "For the purpose of protecting human, animal or plant life or health, if corresponding domestic safeguards under similar conditions exist in the importing country." This [final clause] reflected concerns regarding the abuse of sanitary regulations by importing countries. Later, [a drafting committee] agreed to drop this proviso as unnecessary. Thus, the record indicates that the concerns of the drafters of Article XX(b) focused on the use of sanitary measures to safeguard life or health of humans, animals or plants within the jurisdiction of the importing country.

    5.27   . . . The Panel recalled the finding of a previous panel that [Article XX (b)] was intended to allow contracting parties to impose trade restrictive measures inconsistent with the General Agreement to pursue overriding public policy goals to the extent that such inconsistencies were unavoidable. The Panel considered that if the broad interpretation of Article XX(b) suggested by the United States were accepted, each contracting party could unilaterally determine the life or health protection policies from which other contracting parties could not deviate without jeopardizing their rights under the General Agreement. The General Agreement would then no longer constitute a multilateral framework for trade among all contracting parties but would provide legal security only in respect of trade between a limited number of contracting parties with identical internal regulations.

    5.28   The Panel considered that the United States' measures, even if Article XX(b) were interpreted to permit extrajurisdictional protection of life and health, would not meet the requirement of necessity set out in that provision. The United States had not . . . exhausted all options reasonably available to it to pursue its dolphin protection objectives through measures consistent with the General Agreement, in particular through the negotiation of international cooperative arrangements. . . . Moreover . . . [t]he United States linked the maximum incidental dolphin taking rate which Mexico had to meet . . . to the taking rate actually recorded for United States fishermen during the same period. Consequently, the Mexican authorities could not know whether, at a given point of time, their policies conformed to the United States' dolphin protection standards. The Panel considered that a limitation on trade based on such unpredictable conditions could not be regarded as necessary to protect the health or life of dolphins. . . .

Notes and Questions

1. In its Article III analysis, the panel sharply distinguishes between (permissible) regulations based upon the "product as such" and (impermissible) regulations based upon the process through which a product is made. What values does this distinction further? Can you identify the economic logic, based upon a theory of comparative advantage, of this distinction? If the United States could ban tuna based on the way it is caught, could it ban products from countries where workers get paid unfair wages? On the other hand, why can the United States protect dolphins by, for example, banning the import of dead dolphins, but not do so by banning tuna caught in a way that produces dead dolphins?

2. Consider the three arguments the panel relies upon in concluding that Article XX does not reach trade measures designed to protect a resource outside a state's territory:

First, in paragraph 5.26, the panel relies on the drafters' elimination of a clause from an earlier draft of Article XX. Do you agree with the inference that the panel draws from the drafting history? Second, in paragraph 5.28, the panel argues that the U.S. measure was not "necessary" because the United States had not pursued an international agreement on dolphin protection. The panel ignored U.S. dolphin conservation efforts through the Inter-American Tropical Tuna Commission (IATTC) for many years prior to the MMPA embargoes, as well as Mexico's opposition to these efforts. Third, the panel argues that the U.S. measure is not "necessary" because it used a standard that was "unpredictable." Does the panel explain why unpredictable measures cannot be necessary measures? Does the panel suggest any alternative measures that were reasonably available to the United States?

3. The panel could have rejected the United States' article XX argument on the narrow ground that the embargo was not "necessary" as that term is used in article XX(b). Why did the panel reach the issue of whether a nation can restrict imports for the purpose of protecting environmental resources outside its own jurisdiction?

Under GATT dispute resolution procedures, panel reports could be adopted only by consensus. The United States objected to the broad language of the panel report. Mexico also did not seek adoption of the report. Many observers suggest that, given the ongoing NAFTA negotiations, Mexico sought to avoid a high-profile environmental dispute with the United States.

The panel report did not end the tuna-dolphin dispute. The United States neither lifted the embargo nor changed the MMPA. To the contrary, during 1991 and 1992, the United States banned the importation of tuna from a number of intermediary nations, including Costa Rica, Ecuador, France, Indonesia, Malaysia, Panama, Spain, Thailand, the United Kingdom, and Venezuela. In response, the EC and the Netherlands filed a challenge to the MMPA's "intermediary nation" provisions, which banned imports from "intermediary nations" unless those nations act to ban tuna imports from nations subject to direct embargos. In a lengthy report (*Tuna Dolphin II*), the panel found that the embargos violated Article XI, used the product/process distinction to reject the U.S.'s Article III argument, and found that the embargoes did not fall within the scope of Article XX. Once again, the United States blocked adoption of the panel report and maintained its tuna embargoes. The report, however, increased the international pressure on the United States to modify its tuna policy, as well as the environmental community's distrust of the GATT.

In April 1992, Colombia, Costa Rica, Ecuador, Mexico, Nicaragua, Panama, Spain, Vanuatu, Venezuela, and the United States entered into a nonbinding agreement (the La Jolla agreement), which included a schedule to reduce total dolphin takes through the imposition of annual limits to be allocated among fishing vessels that meet certain criteria, including the use of certain dolphin-safe fishing techniques. Thereafter, two bills to amend the MMPA came before the U.S. Congress. One would have implemented the La Jolla agreement, and imposed embargos on nations failing to meet their commitments under the agreement. This bill was rejected in favor of the International Dolphin Conservation Act of 1992, which lifted the U.S. embargo for nations that agreed to a five-year moratorium on fishing techniques that threatened dolphins. While Mexico and Venezuela initially expressed interest in a moratorium, no nation concluded a moratorium agreement with the United States. Thus, notwithstanding the two panel reports and the La Jolla agreement, the tuna embargoes remained in place. Nevertheless, foreign fleets followed the La Jolla agreement for several years, and dolphin mortality dropped from 15,539 in 1992 to 2,547 in 1996.

However, foreign fleets complained that they still lacked access to the U.S. market, and six of the states that had signed the La Jolla agreement threatened to withdraw from the agreement. The IATTC and the U.S. State Department argued that the embargos had outlived their usefulness. Given the two adverse GATT panel reports and significant pressure from the embargoed nations, the status quo was unsustainable. In 1995, representatives from 12 governments and five major environmental NGOs met in Panama. The resulting Panama Declaration—signed by the 12 states—formalized various components of the La Jolla agreement into a binding international agreement. Notably, it created a permanent mortality limit and provided for the lifting of the U.S. embargos on tuna caught in compliance with the La Jolla agreement. In 1997, Congress passed legislation implementing most of the Panama Declaration.

Notes and Questions

1. One commentator has observed that the Tuna-Dolphin conflict led to "the quiet emergence of one of the most innovative and effective environmental regimes in the world—a regime which has reduced dolphin mortality by over 99% while eliciting a very high level of compliance from all fishers and flag states in the fishery." Richard W. Parker, *The Use and Abuse of Trade Leverage to Protect the Global Commons: What Can We Learn From the Tuna-Dolphin Conflict*, 12 Geo. Intl Envtl.

L. Rev. 1, 6 (1999). Do the events following the *Tuna-Dolphin I* panel tend to vindicate or undermine the panel's reasoning? Was an agreement among the relevant countries rendered more or less likely by panel rulings that the U.S. embargoes were inconsistent with international trade law? What lessons does the Tuna-Dolphin dispute hold regarding the use of trade measures to achieve environmental ends?

2. Note that states used both nonbinding and binding agreements to attempt to resolve the tuna-dolphin conflict. Recalling the discussion of soft law in Chapter 2, why would states attempt to resolve this dispute through a nonbinding instrument? Why did they then employ a binding agreement?

C. The WTO Dispute Settlement Reports

In May 1998, the WTO panel issued its report in the Shrimp-Turtle dispute. It found that the U.S. embargo was inconsistent with Article XI. In rejecting the U.S. argument that the ban fell within the scope of Article XX, the panel focused on Article XX's chapeau, which provides that no trade measure shall be applied "in a manner that would constitute a means or arbitrary or unjustifiable discrimination where the same conditions prevail. . . ." The panel's key findings and supporting rationale are excerpted below.

7.40   . . . As the Appellate Body [stated], Article XX "needs to be read in its context and in such a manner as to give effect to the purposes and objects of the General Agreement" and "the purpose and object of the introductory clauses of Article XX is generally the prevention of 'abuse of the exceptions of . . . [Article XX]'." . . .

7.42   We consequently turn to the consideration of the object and purpose of the WTO Agreement. . . . While the WTO Preamble confirms that environmental considerations are important for the interpretation of the WTO Agreement, the central focus of that agreement remains the promotion of economic development through trade; and the provisions of GATT are essentially turned toward liberalization of access to markets on a nondiscriminatory basis.

7.44   Therefore, we are of the opinion that the chapeau [of] Article XX, interpreted within its context and in the light of the object and purpose of GATT and of the WTO Agreement, only allows Members to derogate from GATT provisions so long as, in doing so, they do not undermine the WTO multilateral trading system, thus also abusing the exceptions contained in Article XX. Such undermining and abuse would occur when a Member jeopardizes the operation of the WTO Agreement in such a way that guaranteed market access and nondiscriminatory treatment within a multilateral framework would no longer be possible. . . . We consequently find that when considering a measure under Article XX, we must determine not only whether the measure on its own undermines the WTO multilateral trading system, but also whether such type of measure, if it were to be adopted by other Members, would threaten the security and predictability of the multilateral trading system.

7.45   In our view, if [the chapeau of Article XX were to be interpreted to] allow a Member to adopt measures conditioning access to its market for a given product upon the adoption by the exporting Members of certain policies . . . the WTO Agreement could no longer serve as a multilateral framework for trade among Members as security and predictability of trade relations under those agreements would be threatened. This follows because, if one WTO Member were allowed to adopt such measures, then other Members would also have the right to adopt similar measures on the same subject but with differing, or even conflicting, requirements. . . . Market access for goods could become subject to an increasing number of conflicting policy requirements for the same product and this would rapidly lead to the end of the WTO multilateral trading system. . . .

7.49   Accordingly, it appears to us that, in light of the context of the term "unjustifiable" and the object and purpose of the WTO Agreement, the US measure at issue constitutes unjustifiable discrimination [and thus violates Article XX]. . . .

United States—Import Prohibition of Certain Shrimp and Shrimp Products, WT/DS58/R (1998).

———————————

The United States appealed. In a landmark report, the Appellate Body rejected much of the panel's reasoning and applied a two-part test in determining whether the U.S. measure fell within the scope of Article XX.

United States—Import Prohibition of Certain Shrimp and Shrimp Products

WT/DS58/AB/R (1998)

118.   In [a previous dispute], we enunciated the appropriate method for applying Article XX . . . :

> In order that [Article XX apply], the measure at issue must not only come under one or another of the particular exceptions—paragraphs (a) to (j)—listed under Article XX; it must also satisfy the requirements imposed by the opening clauses of Article XX. *The analysis is*, in other words, *two-tiered: first, provisional justification by reason of characterization of the measure under XX(g); second, further appraisal of the same measure under the introductory clauses of Article XX.*

127.   We begin with the threshold question of whether Section 609 is a measure concerned with the conservation of "exhaustible natural resources" within the meaning of Article XX(g). . . . India, Pakistan and Thailand contended that . . . the term refers to "finite resources such as minerals, rather than biological or renewable resources." In their view, such finite resources were exhaustible "because there was a limited supply which could and would be depleted unit for unit as the resources were consumed." Moreover, they argued, if "all" natural resources were considered to be exhaustible, the term "exhaustible" would become superfluous. . . .

129.   The words of Article XX(g), "exhaustible natural resources," were actually crafted more than 50 years ago. They must be read by a treaty interpreter in the light of contemporary concerns of the community of nations about the protection and conservation of the environment. . . .

130.   From the perspective embodied in the preamble of the *WTO Agreement* [which explicitly acknowledges "the objective of sustainable development"], we note that the generic term "natural resources" in Article XX(g) is not "static" in its content or reference but is rather "by definition, evolutionary." It is, therefore, pertinent to note that modern international conventions and declarations make frequent references to natural resources as embracing both living and non-living resources. . . . [The Appellate Body then cited several multilateral environmental agreements that referred to living natural resources.]

131.   . . . We hold that, in line with the principle of effectiveness in treaty interpretation, measures to conserve exhaustible natural resources, whether *living* or *non-living*, may fall within Article XX(g). . . .

133.   Finally, we observe that sea turtles are highly migratory animals, passing in and out of waters subject to the rights of jurisdiction of various coastal states and

the high seas. . . . We do not pass upon the question of whether there is an implied jurisdictional limitation in Article XX(g), and if so, the nature or extent of that limitation. We note only that in the specific circumstances of the case before us, there is a sufficient nexus between the migratory and endangered marine populations involved and the United States for purposes of Article XX(g). . . .

156.   Turning then to the chapeau of Article XX, we consider that it embodies the recognition on the part of WTO Members of the need to maintain a balance of rights and obligations between the right of a Member to invoke one or another of the exceptions of Article XX . . . on the one hand, and the substantive rights of the other Members under the GATT 1994, on the other hand. . . .

159. The task of interpreting and applying the chapeau is, hence, essentially the delicate one of locating and marking out a line of equilibrium between the right of a Member to invoke an exception under Article XX and the rights of the other Members under varying substantive provisions (e.g., Article XI) of the GATT 1994, so that neither of the competing rights will cancel out the other and thereby distort and nullify or impair the balance of rights and obligations constructed by the Members themselves in that Agreement. The location of the line of equilibrium, as expressed in the chapeau, is not fixed and unchanging; the line moves as the kind and the shape of the measures at stake vary and as the facts making up specific cases differ.

165.   . . . [Under Section 609,] shrimp caught using methods identical to those employed in the United States have been excluded from the United States market solely because they have been caught in waters of countries that have not been certified by the United States. The resulting situation is difficult to reconcile with the declared policy objective of protecting and conserving sea turtles. This suggests to us that this measure . . . is more concerned with effectively influencing WTO members to adopt essentially the same comprehensive regulatory regime as that applied by the United States to its domestic shrimp trawlers, even though many of those members may be differently situated. We believe that discrimination results not only when countries in which the same conditions prevail are differently treated, but also when the application of the measure at issue does not allow for any inquiry into the appropriateness of the regulatory program for the conditions prevailing in those exporting countries.

166.   Another aspect of the application of Section 609 that bears heavily in any appraisal of justifiable or unjustifiable discrimination is the failure of the United States to engage the appellees, as well as other Members exporting shrimp to the United States, in serious, across-the-board negotiations with the objective of concluding bilateral or multilateral agreements for the protection and conservation of sea turtles, before enforcing the import prohibition against the shrimp exports of those other Members. . . .

172.   Clearly, the United States negotiated seriously with some, but not with other Members (including the appellees), that export shrimp to the United States. The effect is plainly discriminatory and, in our view, unjustifiable. . . .

173. The application of Section 609, through the implementing guidelines together with administrative practice, also resulted in other differential treatment among various countries desiring certification. [Under the guidelines implementing Section 609, the 14 states in the wider Caribbean/western Atlantic region had a "phase-in" period of three years to adopt TEDs while all other states had only four months to implement the requirement of compulsory use of TEDs.] . . .

176.   When the foregoing differences in the means of application of Section 609 to various shrimp exporting countries are considered in their cumulative effect,

we find, and so hold, that those differences in treatment constitute "unjustifiable discrimination" between exporting countries desiring certification in order to gain access to the United States shrimp market within the meaning of the chapeau of Article XX. . . .

The Appellate Body report did not end the Shrimp-Turtle dispute. In July 1999, the State Department issued Revised Guidelines for the implementation of Section 609. These guidelines set forth various criteria for certification. The guidelines stated that Section 609's import ban does not apply to shrimp harvested under any circumstance "that the Department of State may determine . . . does not pose a threat of the incidental taking of sea turtles." Thus, the 1999 Guidelines continued to permit importation of TED-caught shrimp from uncertified nations under a shipment-by-shipment approach. The guidelines also attempted to provide greater flexibility to harvesting states by permitting certification "[i]f the government of a harvesting nation demonstrates that it has implemented . . . a comparably effective regulatory program to protect sea turtles in the course of shrimp trawl fishing without the use of TEDs . . . ." In addition, the United States initiated efforts to negotiate a sea turtle conservation treaty in the Indian Ocean region and offered to provide technical assistance in the installation and use of TEDs to other governments. However, the United States did not amend Section 609, and did not lift the embargo against shrimp from Malaysia.

In October 2000, Malaysia requested a WTO panel to rule on whether the United States's failure to lift the import prohibition on shrimp constituted noncompliance with the Appellate Body report. In June 2001, the panel held, inter alia, that the United States could keep its embargo so long as it demonstrated "ongoing serious good faith efforts" to reach a multilateral agreement on the protection of sea turtles in the Indian Ocean region. However, the panel emphasized that the ability to impose unilateral measures to protect sea turtles "is more to be seen, for purposes of Article XX, as the possibility to adopt a provisional measure allowed for emergency reasons than as a definitive 'right' to take a permanent measure." Malaysia appealed, and in October 2001, the Appellate Body issued the *Shrimp-Turtle II* report:

> 122.   We concluded in [*Shrimp-Turtle I*] that, to avoid "arbitrary or unjustifiable discrimination", the United States had to provide all exporting countries "similar opportunities to negotiate" an international agreement. . . . The negotiations need not be identical. . . . Yet the negotiations must be comparable in the sense that comparable efforts are made, comparable resources are invested, and comparable energies are devoted to securing an international agreement. So long as such comparable efforts are made, it is more likely that "arbitrary or unjustifiable discrimination" will be avoided between countries where an importing Member concludes an agreement with one group of countries, but fails to do so with another group of countries.
>
> 123.   . . . Requiring that a multilateral agreement be concluded by the United States in order to avoid "arbitrary or unjustifiable discrimination" in applying its measure would mean that any country party to the negotiations with the United States . . . would have, in effect, a veto over whether the United States could fulfill its WTO obligations. Such a requirement would not be reasonable. For a variety of reasons, it may be possible to conclude an agreement with one group of countries but not another. . . . In our view, the United States cannot be held to have engaged in "arbitrary or unjustifiable discrimination" under Article XX solely because one international negotiation resulted in an agreement while another did not.

134.   . . . . Therefore, we uphold the Panel's finding that, in view of the serious, good faith efforts made by the United States to negotiate an international agreement, "Section 609 is now applied in a manner that no longer constitutes a means of unjustifiable or arbitrary discrimination, as identified by the Appellate Body in its Report."

135.   We now turn to Malaysia's arguments relating to the flexibility of the Revised Guidelines. Malaysia argued before the Panel that the measure at issue results in "arbitrary or unjustifiable discrimination" because it conditions the importation of shrimp into the United States on compliance by the exporting Members with policies and standards "unilaterally" prescribed by the United States. . . .

140.   In [Shrimp-Turtle I], we concluded that the measure at issue there did not meet the requirements of the chapeau of Article XX relating to "arbitrary or unjustifiable discrimination" because, through the application of the measure, the exporting members were faced with "a single, rigid and unbending requirement" to adopt essentially the same policies and enforcement practices as those applied to, and enforced on, domestic shrimp trawlers in the United States. In contrast, in this dispute, the Panel found that this new measure is more flexible than the original measure and has been applied more flexibly than was the original measure. . . .

144.   In our view, there is an important difference between conditioning market access on the adoption of essentially the same programme, and conditioning market access on the adoption of a programme comparable in effectiveness. Authorizing an importing Member to condition market access on exporting Members putting in place regulatory programmes comparable in effectiveness to that of the importing Member gives sufficient latitude to the exporting Member . . . to adopt a regulatory programme that is suitable to the specific conditions prevailing in its territory. . . . [T]he Panel correctly reasoned and concluded that conditioning market access on the adoption of a programme comparable in effectiveness, allows for sufficient flexibility in the application of the measure so as to avoid "arbitrary or unjustifiable discrimination". . . .

152.   For all of these reasons, we uphold the finding of the Panel [that the United States is in compliance with Shrimp-Turtle I] as long as the conditions stated in the findings of this Report, in particular the ongoing serious, good faith efforts to reach a multilateral agreement, remain satisfied.

United States—Import Prohibition on Certain Shrimp and Shrimp Products, WT/DS58/AB/RW (2001).

Notes and Questions

1. The *Tuna-Dolphin I* report and the *Shrimp-Turtle* panel report suggest that unilateral measures that condition market access on the policies of exporting states are, in general, not justifiable under Article XX. In *Shrimp-Turtle I*, the Appellate Body stated:

> In the present case, the Panel found that the [U.S.] measure [was] excluded . . . because Section 609 conditions access to the domestic shrimp market of the United States on the adoption by exporting countries of certain conservation policies prescribed by the United States. It appears to us, however, that conditioning access to a member's domestic market on whether exporting Members comply with, or adopt, a policy . . . unilaterally prescribed by the importing Member may . . . be a common aspect of measures falling within the scope of one or another of the exceptions . . . of Article XX. . . . It is not necessary to assume that requiring from exporting countries compliance with, or adoption of, certain policies . . . prescribed by the importing country renders a measure a priori incapable of justification under Article XX. Such an interpretation renders most, if not all, of the specific exceptions of Article XX inutile. . . .

Shrimp-Turtle II rejected Malaysia's argument that this statement was dicta and affirmed that "this statement expresses a principle that was central to our ruling in [*Shrimp-Turtle I*]." After *Shrimp-Turtle I* and *II*, under what conditions are unilateral measures restricting trade permissible under Article XX?

2. In *Shrimp-Turtle I*, the Appellate Body stated that its "task" was to find the shifting "line of equilibrium" between conflicting trade and environmental interests, and its rationale departed sharply from that employed by previous panels. Was the Appellate Body engaged in a law-making function similar to that exercised by common law courts? Does the fact that international negotiations have failed to make significant progress on trade-environment issues justify a more activist role for panels?

3. The *Shrimp-Turtle* panel interpreted Article XX "within its context and in the light of the object and purpose of GATT." In *Shrimp-Turtle I*, the Appellate Body interpreted Article XX in an "evolutionary" manner "in the light of contemporary concerns . . . about the protection and conservation of the environment." Recalling the Vienna Convention's provisions on treaty interpretation discussed in Chapter 2, which interpretative methodology is more appropriate? Which interpretative methodology is more consistent with the DSU provision stating that "[r]ecommendations and rulings of [panels] cannot add to or diminish the rights and obligations provided in the covered agreements"? Recalling the ICJ's treaty analysis in the *Gabcikovo* case discussed in Chapter 11, are there particular reasons to adopt an "evolutionary" approach when environmental concerns are at issue?

4. Does the Appellate Body's determination in *Shrimp-Turtle II* that the United States could maintain its embargo make the negotiation of regional conservation agreements more or less likely? How does it change the strategic environment in which such negotiations take place? Consider in this regard Ronald Coase's insight that, in a world where bargaining entails significant transaction costs, negotiated agreements will be affected by background legal rules on which the parties can rely in the absence of an agreement.

5. There is significant scholarly debate over whether panels should use non-trade international law. While several GATT panels rejected attempts by parties to rely on international environmental agreements, in *Shrimp-Turtle I*, the Appellate Body explicitly invoked several such agreements. What are the advantages and disadvantages of having panels incorporate non-trade law into WTO dispute resolution processes? Are panels competent, in either a legal or technical sense, to interpret non-WTO law?

III. RESOLVING INVESTMENT DISPUTES: THE LOEWEN LITIGATION

While states created the WTO and use its dispute settlement system, today multinational corporations—and their employees—are the major creators and drivers of the world economy. They do so by producing the trillions of dollars worth of goods and services that cross international borders each year. Increasingly, these goods and services are made by local companies whose ownership and financing originates elsewhere. This section examines some of the international legal norms that apply to foreign direct investment (FDI), the process whereby an investor based in one state transfers capital to another state to create or purchase an asset in that other state, giving the investor a stake in the income the asset produces. FDI typically involves a long-term relationship reflecting the investor's ongoing interest in a foreign entity.

The amount of new global FDI has increased exponentially over the past few decades. From 1983 to 1990, for example, FDI grew at an annual rate of 26 percent. FDI inflows grew through the 1990s, then declined sharply in 2001, and moderately in 2002 and 2003. They grew by 2 percent in 2004 to $648 billion, and then jumped by 29 percent in 2005 to $897 billion. In addition to these dramatic increases, current FDI differs from that of the past in several respects. First, there has been a shift from a focus on manufacturing in the 1960s, and oil in the 1970s, to an increasing focus on services since the early 1990s. Domestic deregulation in various sectors—such as telecommunications, electricity, banking, insurance, and air-lines—along with rapid technological change, trade liberalization, and privatiza-tion have all contributed to this shift. Second, most of the growth in international production over the past decade has come from cross-border mergers and acquisi-tions (M&As); the value of cross-border M&As rose from less than $100 billion in 1987 to roughly $2.9 trillion in 2005. Cross-border M&As often represent the fastest means of establishing a strong position in new markets and allow firms to realize synergies through the pooling of proprietary resources.

While most of the debate over FDI involves North-South issues, most global FDI flows among developed states. In this sense, the Loewen case, discussed below, involving a Canadian investor in the United States, is relatively typical. In 2004, the top ten outward investor states were, in order, the United States, the United Kingdom, Luxembourg, Spain, France, Canada, Hong Kong, Japan, Belgium, and Switzerland. The top ten recipient states in 2004, in order, were the United States, the United Kingdom, China, Luxembourg, Australia, Belgium, Hong Kong, France, Spain, and Brazil.

Nevertheless, it is difficult to overstate the dramatic increase in foreign capital flows to developing states. These flows increased tenfold from 1982 to 1993 and almost twentyfold by 1996, with a 40 percent increase in FDI inflows from 1994 to 1995 alone. In 2004, FDI inflows to developing states jumped 40 percent, and increased another 13 percent in 2005 to an estimated $274 billion. However, these flows have not been evenly distributed. In 2004, for example, the top five recipients—China, Hong Kong, Brazil, Mexico, and Singapore—accounted for over 60 percent of total flows to developing states. In contrast, FDI in the least developed countries constituted only 2 percent of total FDI flows.

FDI is politically controversial. On the one hand, it promises many benefits to the host state. It brings in needed capital and provides employment and, often, increased foreign exchange earnings. It also provides a number of resources that are only imperfectly tradable on markets, such as advanced technologies and man-agement skills. But FDI can bring restrictive business practices, and international corporations can manipulate prices in interfirm transactions, which can deprive a host state of its fair share of tax revenues. Moreover, FDI can bring a perceived loss of national control or prestige through the sale to foreigners of important national assets. In addition to the political controversy over FDI, there has been significant controversy in the postwar era over the legal norms applicable to FDI, as we saw in Chapter 2.

Foreign investment—and legal efforts to protect it—long predate these con-troversies. During the eighteenth century, much foreign investment occurred in the context of colonial expansion, and the imperial system protected much of the investment that flowed to colonies. Significant international legal efforts in this area began in the nineteenth century as rapid industrialization, the spread of the corporate form of business, and creation of securities markets all combined to fuel a substantial increase in foreign investment. At the same time, the United States and other countries entered into a series of Friendship, Commerce and Navigation (FCN) treaties. While the earliest FCN treaties focused upon trade and navigation, they typically included investment provisions, such as those guaranteeing "special protection" and "full and perfect protection" of property in one state owned by the other party's nationals. By the middle of the nineteenth century, FCN treaties addressed expropriation, and by the end of the century they frequently addressed currency transfer restrictions. The United States continued to enter into FCNs in the twentieth century and, by the World War II era, the primary purpose of FCNs was the protection of foreign investment.

While the United States was negotiating FCNs into the 1960s, several European states were entering into bilateral investment protection agreements with developing states. In 1977 the United States launched its own bilateral investment treaty (BIT) program, and began to enter into BITs with developing states in the 1980s. Both the European and the U.S. investment treaties reflected a belief that guarantees in an international agreement were preferable to those provided under the host state's domestic laws, which were, of course, subject to change. Between 1980 and 2006, states from all parts of the world entered into over 2,000 BITs.

More recently, states have sought to include investment provisions in regional and global treaties. Chapter 11 of NAFTA builds upon preexisting U.S. BITs and contains some of the most comprehensive investment provisions found in a regional treaty to date. In this section, we explore the nature and scope of Chapter 11's protections and its dispute settlement mechanisms. As you review these materials, consider whether NAFTA's provisions clearly delineate the rights of investors and host states, and whether these provisions strike an appropriate balance among the interests of the investor, the host state, and other societal actors. Consider also why states have not developed a multilateral investment regime akin to the trade regime, and whether they should.

A. The Problem

The Loewen Group is a Vancouver-based funeral service provider. By 1996, it owned 856 funeral homes and 203 cemeteries and was the second largest provider of funeral services in North America. During the 1990s Loewen entered the Mississippi funeral market. Loewen first purchased the Riemann Brothers' Funeral Homes holdings in Gulfport and Biloxi and then purchased Wright & Ferguson, the largest funeral home in Jackson.

Loewen's entry into Mississippi affected Jeremiah O'Keefe, a Biloxi funeral home and insurance businessman. O'Keefe owned Gulf National Life Insurance Company (GNLIC). In 1987 Wright & Ferguson had contracted with O'Keefe to provide only GNLIC funeral insurance to its customers. However, after being purchased by Loewen, Wright & Ferguson discontinued selling GNLIC funeral insurance and instead sold Riemann Brothers' insurance.

In response, O'Keefe filed a breach of contract action against Wright & Ferguson and Loewen in Mississippi state court, seeking $500,000 in damages. Several months later, after the parties were unable to finalize a tentative settlement, O'Keefe amended his complaint to add claims of fraud, tortious interference, breach of good faith, and unfair trade practices. O'Keefe at that point sought damages of $5 million.

862 12. Managing the World Economy

In 1995, the case went to trial in Hinds County, Mississippi. Throughout the course of the seven-week trial, O'Keefe's trial counsel repeatedly referred to the nationality, race, and economic class of the litigants. During voir dire, plaintiff's counsel asked whether parties "from Canada" should be bound by "Mississippi" rules. During their opening, plaintiff's counsel encouraged the jury to exercise the "power of the people of Mississippi . . . to say to people like Loewen who would build rich fortunes upon the misery and poverty of burying loved ones of the people of the poorest state in our nation." During questioning of most of their witnesses, plaintiff's counsel once again touched on the themes of nationality, class, and race. Counsel sought, in effect, to portray the defendant as a racist foreign firm. By contrast, O'Keefe's counsel produced a series of African-American witnesses to testify that O'Keefe, who was white, was not a racist.

On November 1, 1995, the jury returned a verdict for O'Keefe for $100 million in compensatory damages and $160 million in punitive damages. However, Mississippi law prohibits juries from considering compensatory and punitive damages at the same time. The judge denied Loewen's motion for a mistrial but "reformed" the verdict to reflect only the $100 million award of compensatory damages. The following day, a brief hearing on punitive damages was held, and the jury awarded $400 million in punitive damages. This was the largest amount ever awarded in Mississippi history and was well in excess of the value of either the Loewen insurance company or the O'Keefe funeral homes that were the principal subjects of the underlying dispute.

Mississippi law requires that, before filing an appeal, appellants post a bond for 125 percent of the judgment. Loewen contacted surety bond companies, who required that Loewen post 100 percent collateral in the form of a $625 million letter of credit. Loewen lacked sufficient assets to post this amount and filed a motion to reduce the appeal bond to $125 million (125 percent of the compensatory damages). While Mississippi law permits the amount of the bond to be reduced for "good cause," the motion was denied by the trial court and ultimately by the Mississippi Supreme Court.

Given Loewen's economic resources, the $625 million bond requirement effectively foreclosed its ability to appeal, and Loewen settled the litigation, "under extreme duress," for $175 million. As a Canadian investor allegedly mistreated in the Mississippi court system, Loewen believed that the litigation implicated NAFTA Chapter 11. In October 1998, Loewen initiated the first Chapter 11 claim filed against the United States.

B. NAFTA Chapter 11

NAFTA Chapter 11 is designed to establish a secure investment environment in the NAFTA countries by providing detailed rules regarding the treatment of foreign investment and investors and establishing effective means of dispute resolution. The investor protection rules are organized around five key principles:

(1) National treatment and most-favored-nation treatment. Chapter 11 requires each NAFTA party to accord investors "treatment no less favorable than that it accords, in like circumstances, to its own investors," as well as "treatment no less favorable than that it accords, in like circumstances, to investors of any other Party or of a non-Party." These provisions are designed to ensure that parties do not favor domestic over foreign investors and do not discriminate among foreign investors. Similar obligations are found in many FCN treaties and BITs.

(2) *Minimum standard of treatment.* Each NAFTA party is to accord investments "treatment in accordance with international law, including fair and equitable treatment and full protection and security." This language incorporates customary international law norms regarding the minimum standard of treatment of foreign investment.

(3) *Prohibition on so-called performance requirements.* No NAFTA party can require that investors make certain concessions, such as promises to employ a certain number of local personnel, export a certain percentage of output, or achieve a certain percentage of domestic content in its goods. This provision eliminates the economic distortions that performance requirements create, and protects investor autonomy.

(4) *Free transfers.* NAFTA requires that all parties permit all financial transfers abroad related to an investment, including profits, dividends, interest, capital gains, and fees to be made "freely and without delay" and in a "freely usable currency at the market rate of exchange." This ensures that investors will be able to expatriate their profits.

(5) *International law standards on expropriation and compensation.* Article 1110 provides:

1. No Party may directly or indirectly nationalize or expropriate an investment of an investor of another Party in its territory or take a measure tantamount to nationalization or expropriation of such an investment ("expropriation"), except:
    (a) for a public purpose;
    (b) on a non-discriminatory basis;
    (c) in accordance with due process of law . . . ; and
    (d) on payment of compensation [as specified below].
2. Compensation shall be equivalent to the fair market value of the expropriated investment immediately before the expropriation took place ("date of expropriation"), and shall not reflect any change in value occurring because the intended expropriation had become known earlier. Valuation criteria shall include going concern value, asset value including declared tax value of tangible property, and other criteria, as appropriate, to determine fair market value.
3. Compensation shall be paid without delay and be fully realizable [and freely transferable]. . . .

Chapter 11 also contains extensive provisions regarding dispute settlement. Most notably, it grants foreign investors the ability to file direct actions against host governments to enforce their rights and the NAFTA obligations of the governments. While the investor may use domestic courts, Chapter 11 permits investors to pursue their rights against the host state in binding international arbitration. Chapter 11 arbitral panels generally consist of three individuals, one appointed by each party and the third by agreement of the parties. Panels can award monetary damages (with interest) and order restitution of property.

C. Other Chapter 11 Disputes

While Chapter 11 was designed primarily to liberalize Mexico's investment regime and calm U.S. investor fears about expropriation and other interference by the

Mexican government, investors have been quick to invoke Chapter 11 against each of the NAFTA parties. As of December 2005, at least 12 claims had been filed against Canada, at least 15 against Mexico, and at least 16 against the United States. The unexpectedly broad and aggressive use of the Chapter 11 process has sparked significant controversy. Several of the most significant Chapter 11 disputes are outlined below. As you review these materials, consider whether provisions designed to ensure security and predictability for investors have created excessive uncertainty and unpredictability for the NAFTA governments.

1. Metalclad v. Mexico

The first Chapter 11 claim against Mexico was filed by Metalclad, a U.S. corporation that sought to purchase and operate a waste facility plant near the town of Guadalcazar in the Mexican state of San Luis Potosi (SLP). Metalclad obtained the necessary federal permits, and the head of the national environmental agency assured Metalclad that the project would go forward.

However, as construction of the project neared completion, the local municipality claimed that Metalclad had to obtain a building permit, and then, 13 months after Metalclad applied for the permit, refused to issue the permit. SLP's governor then declared the area of the site to be a Natural Area for the protection of a rare cactus.

Metalclad alleged that these actions violated NAFTA's "fair and equitable treatment" obligation and constituted an expropriation. The Chapter 11 panel noted that:

> Prominent in the statement of principles and rules that introduces the Agreement is the reference to "transparency" (*NAFTA Article 102(1)*). The Tribunal understands this to include the idea that all relevant legal requirements for the purpose of initiating, completing and successfully operating investments . . . should be capable of being readily known to all affected investors of another Party. There should be no room for doubt or uncertainty on such matters. Once the authorities of the central government of any Party (whose international responsibility in such matters has been identified in the preceding section) become aware of any scope for misunderstanding or confusion in this connection, it is their duty to ensure that the correct position is promptly determined and clearly stated so that investors can proceed with all appropriate expedition in the confident belief that they are acting in accordance with all relevant laws. . . .

Metalclad Corp. v. United Mexican States, ICSID Case No. Arb(AF)/97/1 at para. 76 (2000).

The panel then determined that the confusion over the necessity of a municipal permit and the legal standards that govern the granting of such permits constituted a violation of "fair and equitable treatment."

> The absence of a clear rule as to the requirement or not of a municipal construction permit, as well as the absence of any established practice or procedure as to the manner of handling applications for a municipal construction permit, amounts to a failure on the part of Mexico to ensure the transparency required by NAFTA. . . .

Id. at para. 88.

The arbitrators then determined that, as a matter of Mexican law, the municipality had denied the permit on impermissible grounds; this act "taken together with the representations of the Mexican federal government, on which Metalclad relied [that no local permit would be necessary], and the absence of a timely, orderly or substantive basis for the denial by the Municipality of the local construction permit, amount to an indirect expropriation." Finally, the tribunal decided that the decree naming the site a Natural Area also constituted an expropriation and awarded $16,685,000 in damages.

While Chapter 11 arbitral awards are deemed final and enforceable, a party to an arbitration may petition a court at the "seat" of the arbitration for revision, setting aside, or annulment of the award under the national law of the seat of the arbitration. Thus, Chapter 11 awards are subject to limited review by national courts, primarily to deal with situations in which the tribunal allegedly was improperly constituted, there was corruption among the arbitrators or other basic violations of due process, or the arbitrators manifestly exceeded their powers. Although the *Metalclad* hearings were held in the World Bank's offices in Washington, D.C., the arbitral tribunal was technically designated as sitting in Vancouver, British Columbia. Hence, Mexico petitioned the Supreme Court of British Columbia to set aside the award. Canada filed a brief in support of Mexico. An effort by a Canadian union to intervene was denied.

The Court set aside the award in part. The Court held that the arbitral tribunal "misstated the applicable law to include transparency obligations" and hence exceeded the "scope of the transmission to arbitrate because there are not transparency obligations contained in Chapter 11." *United Mexican States v. Metalclad*, 2001 B.C.S.C. 664. The Court also concluded that to the extent the tribunal's finding of expropriation relied upon Mexico's failure to provide a transparent regulatory framework, this was also "beyond the scope of the submission to arbitrate." *Id*. The Court upheld the arbitrators' finding that the ecological decree constituted an expropriation. In October 2001, Mexico paid Metalclad just over $16 million in satisfaction of the arbitral award.

2. S.D. Myers v. Canada

S.D. Myers is a U.S. investor in the hazardous waste business. Myers wanted to transport waste contaminated with polychlorinated biphenyls (PCBs) from Canada to the United States, where it would be recycled or disposed of in a safe manner. Myers had an affiliate in Canada (Myers-Canada) that was to market Myers' services in Canada.

In 1990, Canada banned the export of PCB-contaminated waste to all countries other than the United States. Under this law, exports to the United States required the prior approval of the U.S. Environmental Protection Agency (EPA). In 1980 the United States banned the import and export of PCBs and PCB-contaminated waste for disposal but granted the EPA discretion to waive these bans if the activity would not result in an unreasonable risk to human health.

In October 1995, Myers obtained EPA permission to import PCBs into the United States. The following month, in response to significant lobbying from the Canadian disposal industry, the Canadian Environment Ministry banned the export of PCBs. Approximately 16 months later, in February 1997, Canada repealed its export ban.

Myers claimed that Canada's temporary export ban violated Chapter 11 and requested $20 million in lost profits and business opportunities. A Chapter 11 tribunal determined that the ban was motivated "to a very great extent by the desire and intent to protect and promote the market share of enterprises that would carry out the destruction of PCBs in Canada and that were owned by Canadian nationals," and that the ban violated NAFTA's requirements of "national treatment" and "fair and equitable treatment." *S.D. Myers v. Canada* (NAFTA Arb. Trib. 2000).

3. Methanex v. United States

Methanex is a Canadian petrochemical company with facilities in the United States and elsewhere; it is also the world's largest producer of methanol. Methanol is used to produce methyl tertiary butyl ether (MTBE), a gasoline component that is used, in part, to increase the oxygen content of gasoline and hence reduce certain environmentally harmful automotive exhaust emissions. However, MTBE is a known animal carcinogen and has been classified as a possible human carcinogen by the EPA. It also has a turpentine-like taste and odor. Hence, even at extremely low concentrations, it can render water unpotable.

When gasoline leaks from underground storage tanks into soil, MTBE moves very rapidly through the soil and into groundwater or surface water. MTBE contamination is a serious concern in California; a 1998 University of California study reported that MBTE had leaked into as many as 10,000 groundwater sites in the state. In response to public concern, California's governor signed an executive order requiring the phaseout of MTBE from gasoline by the end of the year 2002.

In response, Methanex filed a NAFTA Chapter 11 claim, alleging that California's executive order is "not based on credible scientific evidence" and "go[es] far beyond what is necessary to protect any legitimate public interest," and seeking damages of $970 million. More particularly, Methanex alleges that California did not afford it fair and equitable treatment, and that the MTBE ban was a measure "tantamount to an expropriation."

The United States challenged the tribunal's jurisdiction over Methanex's claims and disputed the claims on the merits. In August 2002, a NAFTA tribunal found that it lacked jurisdiction over Methanex's claims, but granted Methanex permission to submit an amended claim. Methanex's amended claim alleged that top executives from Archer-Daniels-Midland (ADM), the principle U.S. producer of ethanol, secretly met with California's Governor while he was considering whether or how to regulate MTBE. Methanex alleged that, two weeks later, "ADM made a $100,000 contribution to the [Governor's] campaign, and it made another $55,000 in contributions over the next four months." Thereafter, the Governor issued the executive order banning MTBE and indicating that ethanol would be the preferred replacement. Methanex made no allegation of bribery or criminal activity; rather it claimed that this conduct violated Chapter 11's provisions on national treatment, fair and equitable treatment, and expropriation.

In August 2005, the tribunal issued its final award on jurisdiction and the merits. The tribunal ruled, first, that there was no violation of NAFTA's national treatment provision, as the California ban on MTBE had precisely the same effect on the American investors and investments in the domestic methanol industry as it had on Methanex. The tribunal then determined that California's ban was "made for a public purpose, was non-discriminatory and was accomplished with due process" and therefore did not constitute an expropriation. In light of these findings, the tribunal turned to the United State's arguments that Methanex's claims did not meet the requirements of NAFTA Article 1101, which provides that "this Chapter [11] applies to measures adopted or maintained by a Party relating to . . . investors of another Party." The tribunal reasoned as follows:

> Having concluded on the evidential record that no illicit pretext underlay California's conduct and that Methanex has failed to establish that the US measures were intended

to harm foreign methanol producers . . . it follows on the facts of this case that there is no legally significant connection between the US measures, Methanex and its investments. As such, the US measures do not "relate to" Methanex or its investments as required by Article 1101(1). Accordingly . . . the Tribunal concludes that it lacks jurisdiction to determine Methanex's substantive claims alleged under NAFTA [Chapter 11].

Finally, the tribunal ordered Methanex to reimburse the United States over $1 million for the costs of the arbitration, as well as nearly $3 million for the "legal costs reasonably incurred" during the arbitration proceedings. *Methanex Corp. v. USA* (available at http://www.state.gov/s/l/c5858.htm).

Notes and Questions

1. Do any of these cases shed light on the likely disposition of Loewen's claims?

2. Does Chapter 11 strike an appropriate balance among competing economic and noneconomic objectives? If not, how could it be changed?

3. International arbitral proceedings are typically confidential. NAFTA does not require that governments publically disclose when they have been sued, copies of their briefs, or final arbitral awards, although NAFTA governments, at times, have made these documents public. Are there any reasons that Chapter 11 proceedings should be more transparent than other international arbitral proceedings?

4. Investors, unlike states, have only their own business interests to consider when deciding whether to initiate a claim against a NAFTA party. Does investor-state arbitration represent an inappropriate "privatization" of international economic disputes or does it properly remove what are essentially private, commercial disputes from more politically contentious interstate mechanisms?

5. NAFTA Chapter 11 provides that an interpretation by the NAFTA parties' Trade Ministers of a NAFTA provision "shall be binding" on Chapter 11 tribunals. In July 2001 the three Ministers agreed that "[t]he concepts of 'fair and equitable treatment' and 'full protection and security' do not require treatment in addition to or beyond that which is required by the customary international law minimum standard of treatment of aliens," and that "a determination that there has been a breach of another provision of the NAFTA, or of a separate international agreement, does not establish that there has been a breach of Article 1105(1) [providing for the minimum standard of treatment noted on p. 863]." These interpretations, in effect, rejected contrary determinations by Chapter 11 tribunals. Do such interpretations undermine the Chapter 11 process? Or do they provide a useful check on arbitrators? How should a panel determine whether the Ministers' statement is a binding interpretation or a treaty amendment outside the Ministers' authority?

6. As discussed in Chapter 2, efforts to create a multilateral investment regime have been unsuccessful. Why have states from all over the planet entered into hundreds of similar BITs but not into multilateral agreements? In the area of investment, do state incentives differ in the bilateral and multilateral contexts?

7. Many experts argue that the presence or absence of investment treaties is not a significant factor determining investment decisions by foreign investors. Why are treaties necessary in this area? Why not rely upon the market to discipline states that mistreat foreign investment and reward states that treat foreign investment well?

D. Loewen's NAFTA Claims

Loewen claimed that the extensive anti-Canadian and pro-American testimony introduced at trial violated Chapter 11's national treatment obligation by treating it less favorably than the treatment accorded to similarly situated U.S. investors. Loewen also alleged that the Mississippi proceedings constituted a substantive denial of justice, a procedural denial of justice (by admitting prejudicial testimony and requiring a bond that foreclosed the right of appeal), and a denial of the international legal requirement of fair and equitable treatment. Finally, Loewen argued that the "excessive verdict, denial of appeal and coerced settlement" were tantamount to an expropriation. Loewen requested $725 million in damages.

In June 2003, after years of procedural skirmishing, the Chapter 11 tribunal issued its ruling. After reviewing the trial transcript, the tribunal found "that the conduct of the trial by the trial judge was so flawed that it constituted a miscarriage of justice amounting to a manifest injustice as that expression is understood in international law." In particular, the panel noted that "[t]here was a gross failure on the part of the trial judge to afford the due process due to Loewen in protecting it from the tactics employed by O'Keefe and its counsel," and that "[b]y any standard of measurement, the trial involving O'Keefe and Loewen was a disgrace." The tribunal concluded that the trial, and resulting verdict, "cannot be squared with minimum standards of international law and fair and equitable treatment."

The tribunal nevertheless rejected Loewen's claim. It held that, under the local remedies rule, "a [domestic] court decision which can be challenged through the [domestic] judicial process does not amount to a denial of justice at the international level. . . ." Hence, the claimants had an obligation to exhaust reasonably available domestic remedies. Loewen did not pursue an appeal to the state supreme court or to the U.S. Supreme Court. Loewen argued that pursuing such appeals was not reasonable and that its financial condition forced it to settle the case. The tribunal disagreed:

> 216. Although entry into the settlement agreement may well have been a reasonable course for Loewen to take, we are simply left to speculate on the reasons which led to the decision to adopt that course rather than to pursue other options. It is not a case in which it can be said that it was the only course which Loewen could reasonably be expected to take.
> 217. Accordingly . . . Loewen failed to pursue its domestic remedies, notably the Supreme Court option and that, in consequence, Loewen has not shown a violation of customary international law and a violation of NAFTA. . . .

Loewen's claim failed for a separate and independent reason. Shortly after settling the Mississippi litigation, Loewen filed for bankruptcy and all of its business operations were reorganized as a U.S. corporation. The NAFTA claim was then assigned to a Canadian corporation owned and controlled by a U.S. corporation. Since the real party in interest was a U.S. entity, the claim failed under the "continuous nationality" rule, which provides that "there must be continuous national identity from the date of the events giving rise to the claim . . . through the date of the resolution of the claim. . . ." The tribunal reasoned that NAFTA "was not intended to and could not affect the rights of American investors in relation to practices of the United States that adversely affect such American investors." *The Loewen Group, Inc. v. United States*, ICSID Case No. ARB(AF)/98/3 (June 26, 2003).

Notes and Questions

1. Are you persuaded by the *Loewen* tribunal's rationale? Is there any reason to think that a different result might have been obtained had the judicial proceedings at issue taken place in Mexico rather than the United States?

2. Was Loewen's case, in effect, an attack on the jury system as used in the United States? Or on tort systems that permit the award of punitive damages?

3. Note that the United States, not Mississippi, was the respondent in Loewen's action. What are the incentives and disincentives that subnational units such as Mississippi face when deciding whether to have a justice system that is fair to foreigners? Considering this dispute and the one over the Massachusetts law restricting investment in Burma, discussed in Chapter 4, how should the federal government respond when a state is arguably breaching the United States's international legal obligations?

4. Do any of the decisions discussed above, let alone the sheer number and variety of disputes, suggest that states will not provide for investor-state arbitration in future investment agreements? Do they suggest the need for any changes in the language of investment treaties? Note that in November 2004, the United States released a "Model Bilateral Investment Treaty" that provides: "Except in rare circumstances, nondiscriminatory regulatory actions by a Party that are designed and applied to protect legitimate public welfare objectives, such as public health, safety, and the environment, do not constitute indirect expropriations."

E. Note on Other Methods of Resolving Investment Disputes

Traditional doctrine maintained that only states, not persons, could be subjects of international law. Therefore, individuals could not bring claims against foreign states when injured by them. Instead, under the legal fiction that whoever wronged a person indirectly harmed his state, the individual had to convince his government to adopt his private grievance and "espouse" it on the international plane against the offending state. But in practice, espousal often proved to be unsatisfactory to both claimants and states. First, states are under no legal obligation to espouse claims of their nationals. Hence, the pursuit of claims is frequently hostage to political and diplomatic expediency, and states often decline to pursue claims due to broader foreign policy concerns. Even when claims are espoused, the injured party and the espousing state often disagree over how to conduct the litigation. Finally, prevailing states are under no international legal obligation to distribute any recovered funds to the injured individual. For these and other reasons, the espousal process has proved unattractive to most investors.

Hence, pressures built for alternative mechanisms, and governments and investors have agreed upon a number of other processes for resolving disputes arising out of alleged expropriations or other mistreatment of foreign investors or investments. NAFTA and BITs represent one type of response. A few others are outlined below.

Lump-Sum Agreements. In these cases, the governments involved agree to settle outstanding claims by payment of a negotiated sum to the claimant state. The claimant state then distributes the funds according to domestic processes, including through claims commissions. While lump-sum agreements date back to the 1794 Jay Treaty and the dawn of the modern law of international claims, lump-sum agreements became the leading device for settling international claims after World War II. States have entered into approximately 200 lump-sum agreements since World War II.

In the United States, lump-sum settlements are distributed by the Foreign Claims Settlement Commission (FCSC), a quasi-judicial, independent agency within the Department of Justice. FCSC decisions are final and are not judicially reviewable. The FCSC (and its predecessor agencies) has successfully completed more than 40 claims programs, involving countries such as Iran, Yugoslavia, Bulgaria, Romania, Hungary, Czechoslovakia, the Soviet Union, Poland, Italy, Cuba, China, East Germany, Vietnam, Ethiopia, Egypt, and Panama. More than 660,000 cases have been adjudicated and billions of dollars in awards distributed.

Lump-sum agreements have a number of practical advantages. They remove large numbers of claims from the diplomatic realm and permit the prompt distribution of monies to eligible claimants. Lump-sum agreements are often a comparatively quick way to dispose of claims. On the other hand, lump-sum agreements take control away from the injured private parties and typically provide individual claimants much less than full compensation.

ICSID. The International Centre for the Settlement of Investment Disputes (ICSID) is closely associated with the World Bank. The Bank's primary purpose is to assist economic development in poorer states and, since its founding, the Bank has encouraged private foreign investment as a means to spur development. The Bank quickly realized that the prompt and effective settlement of investment disputes helped promote investment, and during its early years the Bank helped settle several disputes between governments and foreign investors.

The World Bank's role in dispute settlement suggested the absence of other mechanisms that both investors and governments were willing to use. Hence, in 1961 the Bank's President suggested the possibility of establishing a neutral international body to hear international investment disputes. Extensive preparatory work followed and, in 1964-1965, Executive Directors of the Bank, working with a committee of experts from 61 governments, drafted the Convention on the Settlement of Investment Disputes between States and Nationals of Other States (the ICSID Convention). The ICSID Convention entered into force in 1966 and, as of June 30, 2005, 142 states had ratified the Convention.

The ICSID Convention attempts to balance the interests of host states, foreign investors, and their governments. The Convention gives private parties direct access to an international arbitral forum to pursue claims against host states. In return, the Convention precludes the investor's state from exercising diplomatic protection or instituting an international claim (unless the host state fails to comply with an arbitral award). In addition, the Convention provides that, unless the parties have otherwise agreed, the arbitral tribunal "shall apply the law of the Contracting State party to the dispute (including its rules on the conflict of laws) and such rules of international law as may be applicable." Awards are binding upon the parties, and can be recognized and enforced in contracting states. The Convention provides that either party may request annulment of an award on the traditional grounds (a) that the tribunal was not properly constituted; (b) that the tribunal has manifestly exceeded its powers; (c) that there was corruption on the part of a member of the tribunal; (d) that there has been a serious departure from a fundamental rule of procedure; or (e) that the award has failed to state the reasons on which it is based.

The ICSID annulment procedure was not used during ICSID's first 17 years. The first annulment committee, formed in 1983, adopted a highly controversial reading of the Convention that expanded the grounds for annulment by, in effect, permitting a claimant to allege any violation of the Convention in the review procedure. This raised fears that many awards would be challenged and that ICSID arbitrations would become a two-stage process. However, subsequent annulment committees have retreated from the more expansive arguments made by the first committee.

Provisions for ICSID arbitration are commonly found in investment contracts between governments and investors from other member countries. Advance consent by governments to submit investment disputes to ICSID arbitration can also be found in about 20 investment laws and in over 900 bilateral and regional investment treaties, including NAFTA. Pursuant to these provisions, the number of cases submitted to the Centre has increased significantly in recent years. Between July 1, 2004, and June 30, 2005, ICSID registered 25 new cases, bringing the number of pending cases to 103.

Iran-U.S. Claims Tribunal and Other Bilateral Claims Tribunals. Investors and states can also resolve disputes through the use of bilateral claims tribunals. The outstanding example here during the postwar period is the Iran-U.S. Claims Tribunal. As discussed in Chapter 5, this tribunal was formed as part of the solution to the hostage crisis and has jurisdiction over claims by U.S. nationals against Iran and by Iranian nationals against the United States. The Tribunal also has jurisdiction over contractual claims between the two states.

The Tribunal consists of nine arbitrators: the United States selects three, Iran selects three, and then these six select three more arbitrators. After some initial delays, the Tribunal was a remarkably busy and, on balance, successful institution. The Tribunal has disposed of nearly 4,000 cases and has awarded more than $2.5 billion (including interest) to the United States and U.S. nationals and more than $900 million (including interest) to Iran and Iranian nationals. The Tribunal has also created an important body of case law that has significantly contributed to the development of international arbitral law and the international law of foreign investment.

United Nations Compensation Commission. Yet another model of claims resolution is provided by the United Nations Compensation Commission (UNCC). The UN Security Council created the Commission in 1991 to process claims and pay compensation for losses resulting from Iraq's invasion and occupation of Kuwait. Compensation is payable to successful claimants from a special fund that receives a percentage of the proceeds from sales of Iraqi oil. The Commission accepts claims of individuals, corporations, and governments, submitted by governments, as well as those submitted by international organizations for individuals who are not in a position to have their claims filed by a government.

In practice, the Commission operates more as an administrative body than as an adjudicatory tribunal. The Commission divided claims into six categories: four categories for different types of individual claims, one for corporations, and one for governments and international organizations. As Iraq accepted legal responsibility for damage arising from its invasion, detailed review of the numerous individual claims was neither necessary nor feasible. The UNCC used computerized matching of claims and verification information, sampling, individual review, and, in some instances, statistical modeling to expedite the processing of these claims. Corporate and other business claims are often more complex, limiting the ability to use expedited procedures to process these claims. Nevertheless, the UNCC has grouped together claims that present similar legal or factual issues and has developed standard valuation methods. Once precedents are set, the Commission applies them to subsequent claims, thus limiting its work to the verification and valuation of claims.

By June 2005, the UNCC had concluded its processing of claims. In over 12 years of claims processing, the UNCC considered over 2.6 million claims seeking approximately $354 billion in compensation. The Commission approved the award of approximately $52.5 billion in around 1.5 million of those claims. As of January 2006, over $20.3 billion had been made available for distribution to successful claimants. Now that it has concluded the processing of claims, the UNCC will continue its work, with a small secretariat, on the distribution of funds and a number of residual tasks.

Between 1996 and 2003, funds to pay for these awards were drawn from the UN Compensation Fund, which received a percentage of the revenue generated by exports of Iraqi petroleum and petroleum products pursuant to Security Council resolutions. In May 2005, the UN Security Council passed resolution 1483, which lifted sanctions against Iraq and provided for the establishment of a Development Fund for Iraq to receive and administer proceeds from the sale of Iraqi oil. Resolution 1483 further provided that 5 percent of the proceeds from these sales should be transferred to the UN Compensation Fund and that this requirement "shall be binding on a properly constituted, internationally recognized, representative government of Iraq. . . ."

PART VI

Challenges to International Law

For many observers, international law does not really warrant the title "law." They note, in keeping with the philosopher John Austin, that international law is not set by a single sovereign with the power to back commands by sanctions. There is no international legislature with the power to prescribe law, no international system of courts with general compulsory jurisdiction to interpret the law and authoritatively settle disputes, and no international executive to compel compliance. Moreover, according to the precepts of realism, the dominant school of thought in political science, states in their international relations act to further their own material interests. In an anarchic world system, states by necessity seek to maximize their security relative to other states. Accordingly, they will follow international law when convenient but disregard it when their interests so dictate.

Much of the skepticism surrounding international law arises in connection with decisions by states to use force to further self-interested ends. Breaches of international norms governing the use of force, though infrequent, are usually highly visible. Moreover, because decisions to use force typically involve a state's perceived vital interests, law in this context is often seen as singularly incapable of constraining state action.

At the same time, the most visible international institutions—the United Nations and the League of Nations before it—have often appeared powerless to prevent interstate conflicts or to address other pressing international issues. Powerful states may utilize international organizations for their own ends, while pressing global issues go unresolved. In this context, skeptics often question the relevance and basic fairness of international law and institutions.

The next two chapters confront these issues head-on. Chapter 13 examines the use of force in international affairs and provides a context for consideration of the extent to which international law does and can reasonably be expected to control or at least influence decisions to resort to force. The chapter begins with a historical overview of the evolution of the law governing the use of force and then moves to a Problem dealing with the role of international law in constraining aggression. Subsequent Problems focus on uses of force in the context of internal conflicts and humanitarian intervention.

The book concludes with a chapter devoted to issues of legitimacy, relevance, and justice in international law. The first Problem, UN sanctions against Libya, raises questions regarding the proper allocation of decision-making authority among international actors and institutions, and the legitimacy of outcomes generated by current decision-making processes. The next Problem, centered around the terrorist attacks of September 11, 2001, and the reaction of the United States and other actors to those attacks, raises directly the question whether international law is really law at all. The last Problem, involving the international response to the AIDS crisis in South Africa, is designed to provoke discussion of the justice of international law and institutions.

13

The Use of Force

Chapter 8 examined the law governing the conduct of armed conflict. In this chapter, we examine the law that applies to decisions to resort to force both between and within states. The circumstances that prompt the use of force in contemporary politics, and the ways in which force is applied, vary enormously. Because of the political, military, and human costs associated with any large-scale use of force, most states openly use force only rarely and only when they believe vital interests are at stake. On rare occasions, a state has invaded and sought to annex another state, as happened in 1990, when Iraq invaded Kuwait. More commonly, one or more states have offered military and other assistance to internal armed factions struggling for control of their own state. In some instances, powerful states have used military force against foreign terrorist groups or have launched preemptive strikes against foreign military installations deemed particularly threatening to the states' national interests. States have sometimes used armed force to carry out reprisals for injuries suffered at the hands of another state, to resolve disputes over a common but contested border, or to rescue nationals trapped by armed conflict abroad.

States have also used force for less self-interested reasons. With increasing frequency, coalitions of states have engaged in peacekeeping or peace enforcement missions authorized either by the UN Security Council or by the states on whose territory the missions take place. On occasion, states have also intervened militarily to avert or end serious and widespread violations of human rights or to provide relief to populations suffering from starvation or other humanitarian disaster.

States and other international actors have a long history of seeking to place limits on the use of force. But the utility of international law in this regard is subject to debate. Because decisions to use force usually implicate the vital interests of the states and substate actors involved, such actors often ignore or seek to circumvent legal constraints on their freedom to use force. In most national legal systems, the central government exercises a monopoly on the legitimate use of armed force. In the international system, no single actor exercises a similar monopoly. Under Chapter VII of the UN Charter, the Security Council may authorize states to use force in response to a threat to or breach of international peace and security. But the power to authorize and the power to implement are divided: the Council itself has no armed forces at its disposal, and it must rely on member states to carry out its decisions. Moreover, any of the permanent members of the Council can veto any resolution authorizing a use of force. For these and other reasons considered below, international law and institutions have often appeared powerless to control either interstate or internal armed conflicts.

At the same time, states using force almost invariably seek to justify their actions with reference to international law. They may invoke the right of self-defense, or claim the consent of an affected state, or offer some other legal justification. No state denies the authority of international law governing the use of force, even if many states on occasion seek to reinterpret or evade that law.

The core legal norm relating to the use of force appears in Article 2(4) of the UN Charter. That article, which prohibits the use of force against the territorial integrity or political independence of any state, was written with the experience of World War II in mind. The drafters of the Charter expressly intended to prohibit the once lawful practice of using force to assert legal rights or to obtain redress for grievances. Thus, the Charter attempts to substitute a system of collective decision making and response for unilateral decisions to engage in nondefensive uses of force. Under the Charter, the Security Council is authorized to determine the existence of any threat to or breach of the peace, and to decide on the measures to be taken in response. Individual states are allowed to use force in self-defense, but according to the Charter, must otherwise await Security Council authorization before using force and must then use force only in accordance with that authorization.

But the Charter system never functioned as its drafters intended. During the Cold War, the UN Security Council was largely paralyzed by the frequent use of the veto by one or more permanent members, especially the Soviet Union. States that were victims of a use of force by other states could seldom count on the ideologically divided Security Council to issue a condemnation, much less to take effective action in response. Moreover, the nature of warfare shifted, as internal conflicts (often fueled by outside support) largely replaced international conflicts as the dominant source of large-scale violence in international affairs. States increasingly relied on broad notions of self-defense or state consent to justify military interventions in countries around the world. As a result, the Charter framework played relatively little role in the resolution of most international conflicts. Indeed, during its first 45 years, the Security Council only once achieved the consensus necessary to authorize a collective military response to repel one state's use of force against another. On June 27, 1950, the Council adopted a resolution recommending that "the Members of the United Nations furnish such assistance to the Republic of Korea as may be necessary to repel the armed attack [launched by North Korea] and to restore international peace and security to the area." The Soviet Union did not veto the resolution, but only because its representative was not present when the resolution was adopted, due to a decision to boycott temporarily the Council's proceedings over the failure to seat the representative of the People's Republic of China in the United Nations in place of the representative of the Republic of China (Taiwan).

With the end of the Cold War, the political environment and the nature of armed conflict shifted. The Security Council could act with increasing frequency, but demands for humanitarian intervention, and more recently, demands for effective responses to terrorism, have placed new strains on the Charter's framework for evaluating uses of force.

Section I of this chapter provides a brief overview of the history of the law governing the use of force. Section II examines the history and practical application of the UN Charter template for the use of force in the context of Iraq's 1990 invasion of Kuwait and the 2003 U.S.-led intervention in Iraq. Section III examines the role of law in dealing with mixed international-civil conflicts, with a focus on the recent conflict in the Democratic Republic of the Congo. Section IV examines the international response to repression in Kosovo and the law relating to humanitarian intervention. (We consider the use of force in response to terrorism in Chapter 14, in connection with a discussion of the legitimacy and effectiveness of international law and institutions.)

I. THE EVOLUTION OF THE LAW GOVERNING THE USE OF FORCE

The UN Charter's provisions governing the use of force reflect a dramatic transformation in efforts to regulate coercion. Prior to the 1920s, states viewed war as a lawful means to redress grievances and alter legal relations between states. World War I prompted states to move toward outlawing war as an instrument of national policy, and World War II prompted states to seek to bar all nondefensive uses of force except those authorized by the Security Council. The following excerpt provides an overview of the pre-Charter era:

Peter Malanczuk, Akehurst's Modern Introduction to International Law

306-309 (7th ed. 1997)

Lawful and unlawful wars: developments before 1945

For many centuries Western European attitudes towards the legality of war were dominated by the teachings of the Roman Catholic Church. One of the first theologians to write on the subject was St. Augustine (AD 354-430), who said:

> Just wars are usually defined as those which avenge injuries, when the nation or city against which warlike action is to be directed has neglected either to punish wrongs committed by its own citizens or to restore what has been unjustly taken by it. Further, that kind of war is undoubtedly just which God Himself ordains.

These ideas continued to be accepted for over 1,000 years. War was regarded as a means of obtaining reparation for a prior illegal act committed by the other side (the reparation sought had to be proportional to the seriousness of the illegality). In addition, wars against unbelievers and heretics were sometimes (but not always) regarded as being commanded by God.

In the late sixteenth century the distinction between just and unjust wars began to break down. Theologians were particularly concerned with the state of man's conscience, and admitted that each side would be blameless if it genuinely believed that it was in the right, even though one of the sides might have been objectively in the wrong (this was known as the doctrine of probabilism). Moreover, the category of just wars (*bellum justum*) began to be dangerously extended. Although seventeenth century writers like Hugo Grotius made some attempt to re-establish traditional doctrines, the eighteenth and nineteenth centuries produced an almost complete abandonment of the distinction between legal and illegal wars. Wars were said to be justified if they were fought for the defence of certain vital interests, but each state remained the sole judge of its vital interests, which were never defined with any attempt at precision. Indeed, the whole doctrine of vital interests probably constituted, not a legal criterion of the legality of war, but a source for political justifications and excuses, to be used for propaganda purposes. The most realistic view of the customary law in the "classical" period of international law, as it came to stand towards the end of the nineteenth century, is that it placed no limits on the right of states to resort to war. . . .

[During the nineteenth century,] the balance-of-power system was fairly successful in making wars rare. The expense, destructiveness and long duration of wars, and the risks of defeat, meant that wars were not worth fighting unless a state stood to gain a large amount of territory by going to war; but a state which seized too much territory threatened the whole of Europe because it upset the balance of power, and states were usually deterred from attempting to seize large areas of territory by the knowledge that such an attempt would unite the rest of Europe against them. . . .

The unprecedented suffering of the First World War caused a revolutionary change in attitudes towards war. Nowadays people (at least in Europe) are accustomed to regard war as an appalling evil. It is hard to realize that during the eighteenth and nineteenth centuries most people (except for a few pacifists) regarded war in much the same way as they regarded a hard winter—uncomfortable, certainly, but part of the settled order of things, and providing excellent opportunities for exhilarating sport; even the wounded soldier did not regard war as wrong, any more than the skier with a broken leg regards skiing as wrong. All this changed after 1914, but the law took some time to catch up with public opinion. The Covenant of the League of Nations, signed in 1919, did not prohibit war altogether; instead, Article 12(1) provided:

> The Members of the League agree that, if there should arise between them any dispute likely to lead to a rupture, they will submit the matter either to arbitration or judicial settlement or to inquiry by the Council, and they agree in no case to resort to war until three months after the award by the arbitrators or the judicial decision, or the report by the Council.

(The three-month period of delay was intended to allow time for passions to die down; if states had observed a three-month delay after the assassination of the Archduke Franz Ferdinand in 1914, it is possible that the First World War could have been averted.) In addition, members of the League agreed not to go to war with members complying with an arbitral award or judicial decision.

During the 1920s various efforts were made to fill the "gaps in the Covenant"— that is, to transform the Covenant's partial prohibition of war into a total prohibition of war. These efforts culminated in the General Treaty for the Renunciation of War (otherwise known as the Kellogg-Briand Pact, or the Pact of Paris), signed in 1928. Almost all the states in the world became parties to this treaty, which provided:

> The High Contracting Parties solemnly declare . . . that they condemn recourse to war for the solution of international controversies, and renounce it as an instrument of national policy in their relations with one another.

The High Contracting Parties agree that the settlement or solution of all disputes or conflicts of whatever nature or of whatever origin they may be, which may arise among them, shall never be sought except by pacific means.

The UN Charter goes further than the Kellogg-Briand Pact by outlawing all uses of force against the territorial integrity or political independence of a state unless authorized by the Security Council or taken in self-defense. Prior to adoption of the Charter, a declaration of war triggered a complex set of legal rules dealing with the rights of belligerents and neutrals. To avoid the legal consequences associated with a technical state of war, states engaged in armed conflict often denied that they were actually at war. To surmount this difficulty, Article 2(4) of the UN Charter refers to all uses of force, whether they might amount to war in the technical sense or not. But as the materials that follow make clear, Article 2(4) and related Charter provisions leave abundant room for debate about whether a particular use of force is or is not lawful.

United Nations Charter

(1945)

WE THE PEOPLES OF THE UNITED NATIONS DETERMINED
    to save succeeding generations from the scourge of war, which twice in our lifetime has brought untold sorrow to mankind, . . .

HAVE RESOLVED TO COMBINE OUR EFFORTS
TO ACCOMPLISH THESE AIMS. . . .

Article 1

The Purposes of the United Nations are:

1. To maintain international peace and security, and to that end: to take effective collective measures for the prevention and removal of threats to the peace, and for the suppression of acts of aggression or other breaches of the peace, and to bring about by peaceful means, and in conformity with the principles of justice and international law, adjustment or settlement of international disputes or situations which might lead to a breach of the peace; . . . .

Article 2

The Organization and its Members, in pursuit of the Purposes stated in Article 1, shall act in accordance with the following Principles.

1. The Organization is based on the principle of the sovereign equality of all its Members.

2. All Members, in order to ensure to all of them the rights and benefits resulting from membership, shall fulfill in good faith the obligations assumed by them in accordance with the present Charter.

3. All Members shall settle their international disputes by peaceful means in such a manner that international peace and security, and justice, are not endangered.

4. All Members shall refrain in their international relations from the threat or use of force against the territorial integrity or political independence of any state, or in any other manner inconsistent with the Purposes of the United Nations.

5. All Members shall give the United Nations every assistance in any action it takes in accordance with the present Charter, and shall refrain from giving assistance to any state against which the United Nations is taking preventive or enforcement action.

6. The Organization shall ensure that states which are not Members of the United Nations act in accordance with these Principles so far as may be necessary for the maintenance of international peace and security.

7. Nothing contained in the present Charter shall authorize the United Nations to intervene in matters which are essentially within the domestic jurisdiction of any state or shall require the Members to submit such matters to settlement under the present Charter; but this principle shall not prejudice the application of enforcement measures under Chapter VII.

Article 24

1. In order to ensure prompt and effective action by the United Nations, its Members confer on the Security Council primary responsibility for the maintenance of international peace and security, and agree that in carrying out its duties under this responsibility the Security Council acts on their behalf.

2. In discharging these duties the Security Council shall act in accordance with the Purposes and Principles of the United Nations.

Article 25

The Members of the United Nations agree to accept and carry out the decisions of the Security Council in accordance with the present Charter.

CHAPTER VI
PACIFIC SETTLEMENT OF DISPUTES

Article 33

1. The parties to any dispute, the continuance of which is likely to endanger the maintenance of international peace and security, shall, first of all, seek a solution by negotiation, enquiry, mediation, conciliation, arbitration, judicial settlement, resort to regional agencies or arrangements, or other peaceful means of their own choice.

2. The Security Council shall, when it deems necessary, call upon the parties to settle their dispute by such means.

CHAPTER VII
ACTION WITH RESPECT TO THREATS TO THE PEACE, BREACHES
OF THE PEACE, AND ACTS OF AGGRESSION

Article 39

The Security Council shall determine the existence of any threat to the peace, breach of the peace, or act of aggression and shall make recommendations, or decide what measures shall be taken in accordance with Articles 41 and 42, to maintain or restore international peace and security.

Article 41

The Security Council may decide what measures not involving the use of armed force are to be employed to give effect to its decisions, and it may call upon the Members of the United Nations to apply such measures. These may include complete or partial interruption of economic relations and of rail, sea, air, postal, telegraphic, radio, and other means of communication, and the severance of diplomatic relations.

Article 42

Should the Security Council consider that measures provided for in Article 41 would be inadequate or have proved to be inadequate, it may take such action by air, sea, or land forces as may be necessary to maintain or restore international peace and security. Such action may include demonstrations, blockade, and other operations by air, sea, or land forces of Members of the United Nations.

Article 43

1. All Members of the United Nations, in order to contribute to the maintenance of international peace and security, undertake to make available to the Security Council, on its call and in accordance with a special agreement or agreements, armed forces, assistance, and facilities, including rights of passage, necessary for the purpose of maintaining international peace and security.

2. Such agreement or agreements shall govern the numbers and types of forces, their degree of readiness and general location, and the nature of the facilities and assistance to be provided.

3. The agreement or agreements shall be negotiated as soon as possible on the initiative of the Security Council. They shall be concluded between the Security Council and Members or between the Security Council and groups of Members and shall be subject to ratification by the signatory states in accordance with their respective constitutional processes.

Article 51

Nothing in the present Charter shall impair the inherent right of individual or collective self-defense if an armed attack occurs against a Member of the United Nations, until the Security Council has taken measures necessary to maintain international peace and security. Measures taken by Members in the exercise of this right of self-defense shall be immediately reported to the Security Council and shall not in any way affect the authority and responsibility of the Security Council under the present Charter to take at any time such action as it deems necessary in order to maintain or restore international peace and security.

CHAPTER VIII
REGIONAL ARRANGEMENTS

Article 53

1. The Security Council shall, where appropriate, utilize such regional arrangements or agencies for enforcement action under its authority. But no enforcement action shall be taken under regional arrangements or by regional agencies without the authorization of the Security Council. . . .

Article 43 of the Charter envisioned that UN member states would promptly conclude special agreements with the Security Council making military units available for enforcement actions undertaken under UN command. In keeping with this conception, Article 47 provided for a Military Staff Committee to "be responsible under the Security Council for the strategic direction of any armed forces placed at the disposal of the Security Council." Thus, as originally envisioned, the Security Council would have had considerable power to implement its decisions on matters involving aggression or breaches of international peace. Indeed, many of the smaller states feared that the Council had been given too much power; they floated various proposals to give the General Assembly some power to review the Council's decisions, but the major powers rejected these suggestions.

In the years immediately following adoption of the Charter, states generally assumed that completion of Article 43 agreements must necessarily precede any Security Council enforcement action. But Cold War tensions undermined the original expectations concerning the Council's operations, and although the Military Staff Committee was created, no state ever concluded an Article 43 agreement. When the Council authorized the use of force in 1950 to repel North Korea's attack on South Korea, 16 states provided military assistance to the South Korean government. The Security Council asked the United States to select the force commander, and the United States chose General Douglas MacArthur. Although the United States referred to MacArthur as the UN Commander-in-Chief, and to the forces under him as UN forces, MacArthur operated within the U.S. military chain of command. The United States provided regular reports to the United Nations concerning military operations in Korea but did not accept UN direction in the conduct of those operations. Over time, this led to considerable tension, as the United States and other UN members sometimes disagreed over the objectives of the UN force.

Because of Cold War disagreements, the Security Council after the Korean War was rarely able to muster the consensus needed to authorize any coercive measures under Chapter VII of the Charter. The one area in which the Council did manage to agree on coercive measures involved efforts to oppose apartheid and white minority rule in southern Africa. Thus, for example, the Security Council imposed economic sanctions on Rhodesia in 1966, following its declaration of independence. For most of the Cold War, however, states seeking to justify cross-border military action had to find justifications for the use of force other than Security Council authorization. The most common justifications were self-defense, invitation of the lawful authorities of the state in which force was used, authorization of regional organizations, or some combination of the above. In the following excerpt, Professor Tom Farer describes some of the ways in which scholars and governments sought to enlarge the scope for unilateral uses of force beyond that apparently permitted by Article 2(4) of the Charter:

Tom Farer, *A Paradigm of Legitimate Intervention*

Enforcing Restraint: Collective Intervention in Internal Conflicts 316, 320-321
(Lori F. Damrosch ed., 1993)

For those determined to find ambiguities, they lurked as much in what was said as in what was not. Article 2(4) prohibits force or the threat thereof against the political independence or territorial integrity of a state or for any other end incon-sistent with the purposes and principles of the Charter. In justifying Israel's 1956 thrust into Egypt's Sinai Peninsula, the Australian scholar Julius Stone denied that a temporary incursion designed to protect threatened legal rights could be deemed inconsistent with the Charter's language. Surely, he declaimed, the vindication of law is consistent with the Charter's principles.

A small covey of scholars, most of them from the United States, rather than interpreting their way through the Charter's restraints circumnavigated them. It was in contemplation of collective enforcement by the Security Council, they argued, that states had yielded their inherent right to apply force proportionally as a last resort in defense of important legal rights. Thus when the collapse of the wartime coalition paralyzed that organ, states recovered a broad right to self-help. In legal terms, either the failure of a condition or a fundamental change of circum-stances had occurred.

Imaginative exegesis and the capacity of a superpower to manufacture prece-dent also loosened the restraints on regional arrangements. That regional organi-zations could coordinate collective defense against an armed attack seemed indisputable. But could they also authorize members to use force to liquidate a still remote threat to a region's security? In other words, could they, despite the language of article 53 of the Charter, act like mini-Security Councils without benefit of Security Council authorization?

Moscow's decision at the beginning of the 1960s to emplace nuclear-armed bal-listic missiles in Cuba drew an affirmative response to this question from Washington and the great majority of its Latin American allies. Determined to force removal of the missiles, but unable plausibly to claim that Fidel Castro and Nikita Khrushchev were about to attack the United States or any other state, Washington secured OAS [Orga-nization of American States] authorization for a partial blockade of the island. In defending the "quarantine" and the 1965 occupation of the Dominican Republic, which the OAS authorized after American troops invaded that country, U.S. officials argued that authorization could be after the fact and could be induced from the silence of the Security Council. They also argued that where the OAS merely authorized, rather than ordered, military measures (under the OAS Charter and the associated Rio Treaty of Mutual Defense, the organization's political organs actually lack author-ity to order the use of force), those measures did not constitute "enforcement action" and therefore did not fall within the terms of article 53.

In the later years of the Cold War, normative dissonance intensified. To Soviet claims of right to intervene on behalf of international proletarian interests, Washington responded with the Reagan Doctrine, heralding military assistance to opponents of Marxist regimes. Meanwhile, outside the framework of bipolarity, Third World states helped to loosen restraints on intervention. They proclaimed a right to assist national liberation movements.

The end of the Cold War enabled the Security Council to reach consensus on a series of military interventions for diverse purposes, including the expulsion of Iraqi forces from Kuwait, the delivery of humanitarian assistance in Somalia and Bosnia, the restoration of the democratically elected head of state in Haiti, and the termination of genocide in Rwanda. Indeed, as discussed in Chapter 14, the Security Council used its power to order coercive measures under Chapter VII in situations well beyond those envisioned by the drafters of the Charter when they insisted on a finding of a threat to international peace and security as a pre-condition for authorizing military intervention. But as the following discussion demonstrates, the Security Council's new-found ability to reach consensus has significant limits, and leaves open important questions concerning the relationship between and the scope of the Council's coercive powers and states' inherent right of self-defense.

II. DOES INTERNATIONAL LAW CONSTRAIN AGGRESSION? THE 1991 AND 2003 GULF WARS

On its face, Iraq's 1990 invasion and annexation of Kuwait constitute a classic instance of an unlawful use of force. Iraq attacked Kuwait with overwhelming military force, occupied Kuwait's territory, installed a new government, and within a few weeks declared Kuwait a province of Iraq. In doing so, Iraq openly breached one of the core norms of the international legal system and evidently anticipated that it would benefit from doing so. In this respect, Iraq's action might be taken as a sign of the weakness of international law and institutions. International law did not deter Iraq from invading Kuwait, nor did it prevent Iraq from mistreating Kuwaiti nationals, third-country nationals, and foreign diplomats.

On the other hand, the international response may be seen as at least a partial vindication of international law and institutions. The invasion was overwhelmingly condemned by governments around the world, and the UN Security Council moved quickly to impose sanctions and, eventually, to authorize a collective military response, which succeeded in expelling Iraqi forces from Kuwait. In this respect, the international response to the Iraqi invasion illustrates how the UN collective security system is supposed to work.

However, the Gulf War was followed by a dozen years of UN sanctions and increasingly acrimonious debate within the Security Council over whether Iraq remained a threat to international peace and security. The United States, joined by some of its allies, insisted that Iraq had failed to comply with UN resolutions mandating the destruction of its weapons of mass destruction. In 2003, the United States led a coalition of like-minded states in military action against Iraq, prompting heated debate over the claimed legal basis for the coalition's use of force and renewed concerns over the Security Council's inability to reach consensus and the willingness of some states to bypass it on important matters of international peace and security. The first Gulf War raised the important question of how best to reconcile a state's right of self-defense with the Security Council's authority over the use of coercive measures taken to restore international peace and security. The second Gulf War raised even more contentious issues concerning the proper interpretation of Security Council resolutions and the legality of preemptive self-defense. As you read the following materials, consider the identity and interests of the actors involved and their relationship to one another, the role of international law in influencing decisions to use force, and the ways in which international law and institutions might be strengthened to deal with similar events in the future.

Iraq and Its Neighbors
SOURCE: CIA World Factbook, 2001

A. The Problem

Modern Iraq took shape after World War I.* With the collapse of the Ottoman Empire, Britain and France assumed control over much of the Arab world. In 1922, Britain decided the current borders of Iraq, Saudi Arabia, and Kuwait. Britain deliberately denied Iraq viable access to the Persian Gulf to limit Iraq's influence in the region and to keep it dependent on Britain.

Iraq never fully accepted this outcome and periodically laid claim to some or all of Kuwait's territory. In Iraq's view, because Kuwait was an administrative subdistrict of the Iraqi province of Basra during the Ottoman era, it should have been part of modern Iraq. In 1963, Iraq reached an agreement with Kuwait, accepting its independence and acknowledging its frontiers in a general way, but without specifying a precise border. But ten years later, Iraq briefly seized part of northeastern Kuwait before backing down at the behest of the Arab League.

In 1979, Saddam Hussein seized power in Iraq. Shortly thereafter, he launched a long and bitter war with neighboring Iran. In 1988, both sides finally agreed to a cease-fire. The war left Iraq burdened with an $80 billion debt, a large slice of which Iraq owed to Kuwait. To make matters worse, the price of oil, Iraq's only notable export and source of hard currency, was declining. The Iraqi economy was gravely

*Much of the historical account that follows is drawn from Glenn Frankel, *Lines in the Sand, in* The Gulf War Reader 16 (Micah Sifry & Christopher Cerf eds., 1991), and Whalid Khalidi, *Iraq v. Kuwait: Claims and Counterclaims, in id.* at 57.

weakened, and inflation was rampant. But Iraq did have an enormous military (some 1 million strong) and heightened prestige within the Arab world for its service in containing the perceived threat posed by Iran.

By 1990 Iraq was prepared to reassert its historical claim to Kuwait. Iraq was particularly interested in acquiring control of Warba and Bubiyan, two uninhabited islands that would give Iraq improved access to the Gulf. Perhaps to lay the ground-work for its attack on Kuwait, Iraq complained frequently that Kuwait and other Gulf states were exceeding their Organization of Petroleum Exporting Countries (OPEC) oil production quotas, costing Iraq billions of dollars. Iraq claimed that in its "present economic state this overproduction was an 'act of war.'" Iraq also complained that Kuwait had stolen $2.4 billion worth of oil in the preceding decade by slant drilling across the border into Iraq's portion of the Rumaila oil field. Iraq characterized this as "not less than an act of war."

On August 2, Iraqi tanks rumbled into the streets of Kuwait's capital. Saddam announced that the Kuwaiti government had been ousted in a coup and that the new government had requested Iraq's help. In a radio broadcast, Iraq warned against any foreign intervention and stated that "Iraq has responded to the request from the interim government of free Kuwait and decided to cooperate with it." Within a matter of hours, Iraq closed all of Kuwait's ports and airports, barred foreign travel and telecommunications, and took control of Kuwait's oil fields. Over the next several weeks, Iraq announced the annexation of Kuwait and detained hundreds of foreign nationals, including diplomats. In the process, Iraqi forces terrorized Kuwaiti civilians and committed numerous acts of murder, torture, and rape.

By invading Kuwait, Iraq accomplished, albeit only briefly, several major objectives. First, it effectively cancelled the enormous debt it incurred as a result of Kuwait's financial aid during the Iran-Iraq war. Second, it positioned itself to control Kuwait's enormous oil wealth and perhaps the many billions of dollars in Kuwaiti assets held in foreign banks. Third, it signaled neighboring Gulf states, especially Saudi Arabia, that if they did not accommodate Iraq's oil price policies, they could be next in line for attack. Finally, it eliminated Iraq's historical territorial grievance and gave it full access to the Gulf.

Notes and Questions

1. In light of Article 33 of the UN Charter, what options were open to Iraq to pursue resolution of its grievances with Kuwait? What should Iraq have done if the measures provided for in Article 33 did not yield redress?

2. Did Iraq's reliance on "the request from the interim government of free Kuwait" carry any weight under international law? Recall in this regard the Cyprus case considered in Chapter 2. Despite the absolute terms in which Article 2(4) of the UN Charter is framed, states may use force in the territory of another state if the affected state consents. Thus, states frequently seek to justify armed intervention on the basis of consent. When the Soviet Union invaded Hungary in 1956, Czechoslovakia in 1968, and Afghanistan in 1979, for example, it argued that its use of force was justified by an invitation from the lawful government. Similarly, the United States relied in part on consent of the "lawful authorities" to justify its interventions in the Dominican Republic in 1965 and Grenada in 1983. The legal issue in such cases is often whether the consent at issue is valid—that is, whether it is voluntary and issued by an official or state institution with the requisite legal authority.

3. Following Iraq's purported annexation of Kuwait, which individuals or institutions possessed legal authority to represent Kuwait's interests in international fora? In this connection, recall the discussion of the effect of changes in a state's government in Chapter 3.

B. Initial Responses: Condemnations and Sanctions

Condemnation of the invasion was widespread and swift. The United States immediately denounced the attack as a "blatant use of military aggression" and called for "the immediate and unconditional withdrawal of all Iraqi forces." The European Community (EC) and North Atlantic Treaty Organization (NATO) issued similar denunciations. The oil-rich states of the Gulf and most members of the Arab League also vigorously condemned the invasion. A few Arab states, notably Jordan and Yemen, expressed support for Iraq; they were joined by the leadership of the PLO.

On the day of the invasion, President Bush invoked his authority under the International Emergency Economic Powers Act to impose broad economic sanctions against Iraq. Among other things, he prohibited trade with Iraq, froze Iraqi government property and interests in property in the possession of U.S. persons, or U.S. companies or their overseas branches, prohibited travel between the United States and Iraq, and barred the grant of credits or loans to the government of Iraq or its instrumentalities. France and the United Kingdom soon joined the United States in freezing billions of dollars of Iraqi assets; they and other countries also froze billions of dollars in Kuwaiti assets to prevent a puppet government in Kuwait from acquiring those assets. Other countries, including European states, Japan, China, and the Soviet Union, quickly followed suit.

The UN Security Council met in emergency session the day of the invasion. By a vote of 14-0, with Yemen abstaining, the Council adopted a resolution condemning the Iraqi invasion, determining that it constituted a breach of international peace and security, and demanding "that Iraq withdraw immediately and unconditionally" from Kuwait. S.C. Res. 660 (1990). On August 6, by a vote of 13-0 (with Yemen and Cuba abstaining), the Security Council imposed broad economic sanctions on Iraq.

Security Council Resolution 661 (1990)

The Security Council, . . .

Affirming the inherent right of individual or collective self-defence, in response to the armed attack by Iraq against Kuwait, in accordance with Article 51 of the Charter,

Acting under Chapter VII of the Charter, . . .

3. *Decides* that all States shall prevent:
(a) The import into their territories of all commodities and products originating in Iraq or Kuwait exported therefrom after the date of the present resolution;
(b) Any activities by their nationals or in their territories which would promote or are calculated to promote the export or trans-shipment of any commodities or

products from Iraq or Kuwait; and any dealings by their nationals or their flag vessels or in their territories in any commodities or products originating in Iraq or Kuwait and exported therefrom after the date of the present resolution, including in particular any transfer of funds to Iraq or Kuwait for the purposes of such activities or dealings;

(c) The sale or supply by their nationals or from their territories or using their flag vessels of any commodities or products, including weapons or any other military equipment, whether or not originating in their territories but not including supplies intended strictly for medical purposes, and, in humanitarian circumstances, foodstuffs, to any person or body in Iraq or Kuwait or to any person or body for the purposes of any business carried on in or operated from Iraq or Kuwait, and any activities by their nationals or in their territories which promote or are calculated to promote such sale or supply of such commodities or products;

4. *Decides* that all States shall not make available to the Government of Iraq or to any commercial, industrial or public utility undertaking in Iraq or Kuwait, any funds or any other financial or economic resources and shall prevent their nationals and any persons within their territories from removing from their territories or otherwise making available to that Government or to any such undertaking any such funds or resources and from remitting any other funds to persons or bodies within Iraq or Kuwait, except payments exclusively for strictly medical or humanitarian purposes and, in humanitarian circumstances, foodstuffs.

On August 5, Iraq declared the establishment of a new Kuwaiti government, headed by nine military officers. Three days later, Iraq announced the formal annexation of Kuwait, and described the new "comprehensive and eternal merger" as the return of "the part and branch, Kuwait, to the whole and the Iraq of its origins." At the same time, Iraq began closing foreign embassies in Kuwait and detaining foreign diplomats and hundreds of foreign nationals. (Some 60 percent of Kuwait's population consisted of foreign nationals.) Iraq denied that those detained were "hostages."

On August 9, the Security Council promptly and unanimously denounced Iraq's purported annexation as "null and void," and called upon all states "not to recognize that annexation, and to refrain from any action or dealing that might be interpreted as an indirect recognition of the annexation." S.C. Res. 662 (1990). On August 18, the Security Council unanimously demanded that Iraq permit the departure of third-country nationals and "rescind its orders for the closure of diplomatic and consular missions and the withdrawal of the immunity of their personnel." S.C. Res. 664 (1990).

As Iraq fortified its positions in and near Kuwait, Western states increasingly expressed concern that Iraq might attack Saudi Arabia next. The combination of Iraq's own oil supplies with those of Kuwait and Saudi Arabia would give Iraq control over some 40 percent of the world's known oil reserves. Partly to forestall any such outcome, the United States began sending thousands of troops to Saudi Arabia as the vanguard of a much larger force, despite considerable Saudi reluctance to host Western troops. At the same time, the United States disclaimed any intention of immediately using force to oust Iraq from Kuwait, stating that UN sanctions should be given time to take effect. British forces joined the Americans, though other states declined to send troops.

As the U.S. military buildup progressed, the United States also worked to tighten the UN embargo on Iraq. One particularly sensitive issue was the possibility that Yemen and Jordan might help Iraq circumvent the embargo. The United States claimed that Resolution 661 and the right of self-defense enshrined in Article 51 of the UN Charter permitted the use of force to compel compliance with the embargo. The United States instructed its warships in the Persian Gulf to use "minimum force" to block Iraqi ships from loading or unloading cargo. Other states, including most other members of the Security Council, disagreed with the U.S. interpretation of Resolution 661. Similarly, the UN Secretary-General suggested at a news conference that the use of force to enforce sanctions would violate the UN Charter in the absence of Security Council authorization. Nonetheless, the embargo and the U.S. threat of force appeared sufficient to halt all trading by Iraq's fleet of 80 tankers and cargo ships and to shut off almost completely Iraqi and Kuwaiti oil exports.

On August 18 Iraqi President Saddam Hussein issued the following statement about the treatment of foreigners in Iraq.

Statement of Iraqi President Saddam Hussein*

Federal News Service, August 18, 1990

[T]he United States and its allies . . . began to blockade and use . . . military force [to impose an] economic embargo including food and medicine, which is considered an act of war [in violation of] international custom and international law. And this procedure did lead to the reduction of imported foods which includes [milk for] newborn babies . . . [I]n accordance with . . . humanitarian principles we decided to . . . treat the foreign newborn babies similarly with the Iraqi babies. And if there were to be any reduction in the necessities of babies because of the economic embargo, then . . . the same calamity affecting the Iraqi newborn will affect similarly the foreign babies.

. . . Because of the conditions of the economic embargo and blockade which were imposed by the United States and its allies . . . food cannot be secured to all [adult] persons in the manner that we wish. . . .

[Members of the Iraqi armed forces] should be provided with priority in terms of food and other necessities because they are protecting the Iraqi nation. . . . And because . . . the foreigners . . . are not going to be members of the military forces, and they are not going to be participating in the activities related to that, that means that their share of the food—the quantity and the quality will be affected by the fact that our imports of food will be reduced.

Since many states disagreed with the U.S. view that Resolution 661 authorized the use of force to prevent Iraqi ships from violating the UN embargo, the United States pressed for explicit Security Council authorization. On August 25, by a vote of 13-0 (with Yemen and Cuba abstaining), the Security Council in a compromise adopted Resolution 665, which permitted member states to use "measures commensurate to the specific circumstances as may be necessary under the authority of the Security Council to halt all inward and outward maritime shipping in order to inspect and verify their cargoes and destinations." The awkward wording emerged

---

*The statement quoted in the text reflects a somewhat rough simultaneous translation of a statement issued through an Iraqi spokesman during a television broadcast.—EDS.

after days of difficult negotiations between the United States, which wanted an explicit authorization for the use of "minimum force," and the Soviet Union, which insisted on weaker language. After the resolution was adopted, the United States declared that the wording was "sufficiently broad to use armed force . . . depending on the circumstances."

On September 25, the United Nations prohibited air traffic to and from Iraq, closing off one of the last remaining sanctions loopholes. S.C. Res. 670 (1990). A month later, the Security Council ratcheted up the pressure on Iraq by stating, in Resolution 674, that Iraq would be responsible for any mistreatment of hostages as well as for any damages arising from Iraq's invasion and occupation of Kuwait.

Notes and Questions

1. Do you agree with the United States that Resolution 661 permitted it to use force to block Iraqi vessels from loading or unloading cargo? Did Resolution 665 confer the necessary legal authority? Why would the United States push for adoption of Resolution 665 if U.S. actions under Resolution 661 sufficed to paralyze Iraqi shipping?

2. Are the measures suggested by President Hussein unlawful? Note that Resolution 674 demanded that Iraq "ensure the immediate access to food, water and basic services necessary to the protection and well-being of Kuwaiti nationals and of nationals of third states in Kuwait and Iraq." Was Iraq obligated under the circumstances to provide such necessities to foreign nationals if it lacked the means to supply them to its own nationals as a result of the UN sanctions? Recall the discussion in Chapter 7 of the right to food under the International Covenant on Economic, Social and Cultural Rights. Would Iraq violate the right to food if it failed to provide an adequate diet to detained foreign nationals? To its own nationals? Would UN sanctions relieve Iraq of responsibility for providing adequate food? Note in this regard that the sanctions exempted delivery of food to Iraq for humanitarian purposes.

3. Could the United States or other Western countries have used force to rescue their own or other foreign nationals being held by the Iraqi government? Consider the following views of Professor Oscar Schachter:

> Generally speaking, a state has no right to invade a foreign state to rescue or protect its nationals who are considered to be held unlawfully by that state or by private persons. This proposition also holds where a state fails to protect a foreign national from criminal acts or injuries by private persons in that country. A government may strongly protest a national's arbitrary detention or inhumane treatment in prison, but it must have recourse to available diplomatic and possibly judicial procedures. The government may also impose non-military sanctions on the state that shirked its obligations under international law.
>
> In some situations, however, such as the Israeli hostages held at Entebbe Airport or the American hostages held in Tehran, when lives are in imminent danger, a good case exists for an exercise of self-defense through a rescue attempt. Such attempts must be limited to the rescue and must not serve as a basis for political pressure or reprisal.

Oscar Schachter, *In Defense of International Rules on the Use of Force*, 53 U. Chi. L. Rev. 113, 138-139 (1986).

Under Article 51 of the UN Charter, only an armed attack triggers the right to self-defense. Does a state's unwillingness or inability to protect foreign nationals in its territory from a threat of imminent harm amount to an armed attack on the state of nationality? If not, how can the rescue of nationals be justified as self-defense?

C. Deciding to Use Force

As the sanctions effort intensified, so too did preparations for war. Iraq continued to build up its military forces in Kuwait and constructed massive fortifications along the Kuwait-Saudi border. At the reluctant invitation of the Saudis, the United States and other Western countries began to deploy large numbers of troops and military equipment to Saudi Arabia.

1. The UN Ultimatum

As both sides continued their military buildup, the United States, supported by the United Kingdom and others, continued to work hard to build support within the UN Security Council for a resolution authorizing the use of force. A significant number of Council members, including the Soviet Union, China, Malaysia, Colombia, Yemen, and Cuba, wanted more time to pursue a peaceful settlement. After extensive and complicated negotiations, the Security Council issued a final warning to Iraq in Resolution 678, adopted on November 29, 1990, by a vote of 12-2; Cuba and Yemen voted no, and China abstained.

Security Council Resolution 678 (1990)

The Security Council . . .

Acting under Chapter VII of the Charter,

1. *Demands* that Iraq comply fully with resolution 660 (1990) and all subsequent relevant resolutions, and decides, while maintaining all its decisions, to allow Iraq one final opportunity, as a pause of goodwill, to do so;

2. *Authorizes* Member States co-operating with the Government of Kuwait, unless Iraq on or before 15 January 1991 fully implements, as set forth in paragraph 1 above, the above-mentioned resolutions, to use all necessary means to uphold and implement resolution 660 (1990) and all subsequent relevant resolutions and to restore international peace and security in the area. . . .

The phrase "all necessary means" provided the explicit authorization to use force sought by the United States. Nonetheless, Iraq's Parliament voted unanimously to defy the Security Council and to fight to retain control of Kuwait.

Notes and Questions

1. On what basis should Security Council members rest a decision to vote in favor of a resolution authorizing the use of force? During the debates leading up to the adoption of Resolution 678, the United States lobbied heavily to generate support for military action. The Bush Administration urged Saudi Arabia to provide the Soviet Union with $1 billion in aid, and signaled China that its diplomatic isolation following the use of force to crush pro-democracy demonstrators in Tiananmen Square in 1989 would come to an end. Moreover, the U.S. Ambassador was instructed to inform the delegate from Yemen, minutes after he voted against Resolution 678, that "that was the most expensive no vote you ever cast," meaning

it would cost Yemen $70 million in U.S. aid. Were the means employed by the United States to secure a majority in favor of Resolution 678 legitimate? Did they affect the resolution's political or legal effect?

2. Does the UN Charter provide any guidance on when it is appropriate for the Security Council to move from "measures not involving the use of force" under Article 41 to "action by air, sea or land forces" under Article 42? Are such decisions entirely political, or does international law play a role?

2. The U.S. Sanctions Debate

Within the United States, opinion over how to respond to Iraq's seizure of Kuwait was sharply divided. Likening Saddam to Hitler, the Administration offered a variety of rationales to support prompt and decisive action: the escalating harm wrought by the Iraqi occupation in Kuwait, the continued danger to Saudi Arabia (and world oil supplies), Iraq's seizure of hostages, the general threat to the world economy posed by a prolonged crisis, and the danger posed by Iraqi efforts to develop weapons of mass destruction. Critics of the Administration's policy argued that the human and material costs of an invasion would be high, that the existing troop deployment would deter any attack on Saudi Arabia, that the use of force would alienate much of the Arab world, that Saudi Arabia and other oil-producing states could easily increase their own production to offset what had been lost from Kuwait and Iraq, and that the danger of Iraq acquiring weapons of mass destruction was highly exaggerated.

But the real debate centered on whether to allow more time for sanctions to work. Former President Jimmy Carter, two former chairmen of the Joint Chiefs of Staff, the commander of U.S. forces in the Gulf, and many others urged that sanctions be given more time to take effect. Proponents of sanctions argued that Iraq was vulnerable to economic coercion because of its dependence on oil revenues and the broad scope of the sanctions imposed; they urged the United States to wait at least one year for sanctions to take effect.

The Bush Administration disagreed. On January 12, 1991, a closely divided Congress voted to support the Administration's decision to use force, largely though not entirely along party lines. The Administration's rationale for using force appears in a January 15 national security directive (NSD) authorizing military action and instructing the relevant U.S. government agencies on the means to be employed to achieve U.S. policy goals. The directive, a now unclassified but formerly top secret memorandum from President Bush to the members of the National Security Council, is excerpted below.

National Security Directive 54

(1991), www.gwu.edu/~nsarchiv/NSAEBB/NSAEBB21/06-01.htm

SUBJECT: Responding to Iraqi Aggression in the Gulf

1. Access to Persian Gulf oil and the security of key friendly states in the area are vital to U.S. national security. . . . [A]s a matter of long-standing policy, the United States remains committed to defending its vital interests in the region, if necessary through the use of military force, against any power with interests inimical to our own. . . . Economic sanctions mandated by UN Security Council Resolution 661 have had a measurable impact upon Iraq's economy but have not accomplished

the intended objective of ending Iraq's occupation of Kuwait. There is no persuasive evidence that they will do so in a timely manner. Moreover, prolonging the current situation would be detrimental to the United States in that it would increase the costs of eventual military action, threaten the political cohesion of the coalition of countries arrayed against Iraq, allow for continued brutalization of the Kuwaiti people and destruction of their country, and cause added damage to the U.S. and world economies. . . .

2.   Pursuant to my responsibilities and authority under the Constitution as President and Commander in Chief . . . and in accordance with the rights and obligations of the United States under international law, . . . and consistent with the inherent right of collective self-defense affirmed in Article 51 of the United Nations Charter, I hereby authorize military actions designed to bring about Iraq's withdrawal from Kuwait. These actions are to be conducted . . . at a date and time I shall determine and communicate through National Command Authority channels. This authorization is for the following purposes:

a. to effect the immediate, complete and unconditional withdrawal of all Iraqi forces from Kuwait;

b. to restore Kuwait's legitimate government; [and]

d. to promote the security and the stability of the Persian Gulf.

3.   To achieve the above purposes, U.S. and coalition forces should seek to:

a. defend Saudi Arabia and the other GCC [Gulf Cooperation Council] states against attack;

b. preclude Iraqi launch of ballistic missiles . . . ;

c. destroy Iraq's chemical, biological, and nuclear capabilities;

d. destroy Iraq's command, control, and communications capabilities;

e. eliminate the Republican Guards as an effective fighting force; and

f. conduct operations designed to drive Iraq's forces from Kuwait, break the will of Iraqi forces, discourage Iraqi use of chemical, biological or nuclear weapons, encourage defection of Iraqi forces, and weaken Iraqi popular support for the current government. . . .

9.   The United States recognizes the territorial integrity of Iraq and will not support efforts to change current boundaries.

10.   Should Iraq resort to using chemical, biological, or nuclear weapons, be found supporting terrorist acts against U.S. or coalition partners anywhere in the world, or destroy Kuwait's oil fields, it shall become an explicit objective of the United States to replace the current leadership of Iraq. I also want to preserve the option of authorizing additional punitive actions against Iraq.

12. Military operations will come to an end only when I have determined that the objectives set forth in paragraph 2 above have been met.

George Bush

The next day, the coalition air assault commenced.

Notes and Questions

1. Was there any legal obligation to give sanctions more time? Was there an obligation to attempt sanctions at all before using force?

2. Are the reasons and goals for military action articulated in NSD 54 consistent with international law governing the use of force? Would the use of chemical, biological, or nuclear weapons by Iraq justify the use of force to replace the Iraqi leadership, as suggested in paragraph 10 of NSD 54?

3. Articles 33-42 of the UN Charter suggest a series of steps leading up to the use of force: pursuit by the parties of a solution through negotiation or other peaceful means; determination by the Security Council of the existence of a threat to or breach of the peace; recommendation or decision by the Council of the measures to be taken; decision by the Council on measures not involving armed force; decision by the Council on measures involving force. Was the process leading up to the use of force against Iraq consistent with this approach?

3. Police Action or Self-Defense?

Could the United States and its allies have used force to drive Iraqi troops out of Kuwait even in the absence of the authorization to use "all necessary means" in Security Council Resolution 678? Under the UN Charter, the Security Council is entrusted with taking the measures necessary to maintain international peace and security, which may include enforcement actions—that is, military actions to implement Council decisions on peace and security matters. At the same time, however, the Charter recognizes the "inherent right" of self-defense, which is to operate until the Security Council takes the action "it deems necessary" to secure international peace. As Professor Tom Farer explains:

> In its essential character, the model of legitimacy set out in the UN Charter corresponds structurally to the model found in national legal systems; both tolerate self-help while subjecting it to close normative discipline and authoritative review. Space for self-help exists even in efficient modern states, where courts, prosecutors, and security forces, able to concentrate power far exceeding that of any delinquent, maintain order. Take the United States: individuals can, for example, use deadly force when they reasonably believe it is necessary to protect themselves and their families from a potentially fatal assault. Since the Charter did no more than anticipate the creation of an international police force [Article 43 anticipates that states will make troops available to the Security Council], and since it made the force's use subject to veto by any one of the great powers, and since sovereign entities had perforce always assumed the principal—and often the entire—burden of protecting their interests and rights, the drafters not surprisingly left states free to defend themselves until the Security Council took action "to maintain or restore international peace and security."

Tom Farer, *A Paradigm of Legitimate Intervention, supra*, at 317-318.

But the language of the Charter does not make clear precisely when the right of self-defense must give way to collective action taken by the Security Council. During and after the Gulf War, this question provoked heated scholarly debate. Consider the three scholarly views excerpted below:

[If force is used in violation of article 2(4)], the Charter envisages two kinds of military remedies: wars of *self-defense* and *police actions*. . . .

If states use armed force under the self-defense rubric of Article 51, their individual activities are subsumed by, or incorporated into, the global police response once it is activated. That is, the old way is licensed only until the new way begins to work: "until," in the words of Article 51, "the Security Council has taken the necessary measures to maintain international peace and security." . . .

The executive hawks who champion the old order maintain that the Charter merely meant to supplement, rather than repeal, the preexisting war system. . . . They argue that [the UN] police measures [against Iraq] did not suspend the right of the United States to continue to act without Council authorization in exercise of its "inherent" unilateral power to wage wars of self-defense under Article 51.

Implicit in this argument is the erroneous assumption that the *war* power of member states was not intended to be restricted, but only augmented, by the Charter's creation of a new *police* power. This interpretation flies in the face of common sense and the literal text. A new-style, UN-authorized police action functioning alongside a traditional sovereign exercise of war powers is conceptually and operationally untenable, the more so when states seeking the freedom to act unilaterally have forces committed alongside others in a Security Council police action. As a textual matter, it is obvious on its face that the Charter, in creating the new police power, intended to establish an exclusive alternative to the old war system. The old system was retained only as a fallback, available when the new system could not be made to work; not, as some U.S. hawks argue, as an equal alternative, to be chosen at the sole discretion of the members.

. . . For U.S. hawks, this meant that they had to await the Council's consent before the United States could take offensive military action in the gulf. It also limits the purposes to which force may be directed.

Thomas M. Franck & Faiza Patel, *The Gulf Crisis in International and Foreign Relations Law: UN Police Action in Lieu of War: "The Old Order Changeth,"* 85 Am. J. Intl. L. 63, 63-64, 74 (1991).

The ultimate legal question presented by the Persian Gulf crisis of 1990-1991 is whether the Security Council can insist that no state exercise its rights of individual and collective self-defense without prior Security Council permission. Such permission could be blocked by the veto of one of the permanent members—or, indeed, by the inaction of a Council majority. . . .

The practice of subordinating the right of self-defense to a requirement of prior Security Council permission would be fatal to the right of states to defend themselves. What the Charter prescribes is precisely the opposite rule: that the aggrieved state and its friends and allies may decide for themselves when to exercise their rights of individual and collective self-defense until peace is restored or the Security Council, by its own affirmative vote, decides that self-defense has gone too far and become a threat to the peace. . . . [W]hat Franck seems to be saying is that when the Security Council accepts jurisdiction of a conflict (i.e., when the new system is activated), the injured party's right of self-defense is "suspended" until the Council affirmatively decides it cannot deal effectively with the problem. . . .

To me, what Article 51 and Resolution 661 seem to say is just the opposite—that the customary law of self-defense is not impaired in any way by the Charter but remains intact until the Council has *successfully* dealt with the controversy before it. That cautious reading of Article 51 seems to me inevitable not only because of its language but even more because of its position in the Charter as a proviso limiting the earlier parts of chapter VII, and because of its context in history. . . .

Eugene V. Rostow, *The Gulf Crisis in International and Foreign Relations Law, Continued: Until What? Enforcement Action or Collective Self-Defense?*, 85 Am. J. Intl. L. 506, 510-511 (1991).

Who is to judge whether measures authorized by the Security Council are sufficient to maintain international peace and security [within the meaning of article 51]? . . .

During the Cold War, when the Security Council was immobilized by reciprocal vetoes, the argument was perhaps available that a state acting in individual or collective self-defense could not be expected to forgo continuing action simply because the Council was debating the situation, with no likelihood of a serious substantive outcome. This also would be the case if the Council's action is plainly incommensurate with the seriousness of the situation. In those instances it would be a plausible argument that the Council was simply not exercising its functions, so that the preemption contemplated by Article 51 when the Council was truly addressing the situation does not come into operation.

From the beginning of the Iraq-Kuwait crisis, as has been widely acknowledged, the Security Council worked "as it was supposed to work" according to the design of its framers. It cannot be argued that the Council failed to address the situation with appropriate gravity or to adopt measures with real impact or to strengthen those measures as the need became apparent. If the United Nations works as intended, judgments as to the ultimate objectives of U.N. action, the sufficiency of the measures to be taken, how long to wait for the sanctions to take effect, and the like are consigned to the Council. . . . The United States can ensure by use of the veto that the Council will not act against its interests. But if the United States cannot induce the necessary number of other Security Council members to agree that additional measures involving the use of force are necessary, the Charter would clearly seem to preclude unilateral action.

Abram Chayes, *The Use of Force in the Persian Gulf, in* Law and Force in the New International Order, *supra*, at 5-6.

Notes and Questions

1. Why did the United States work so hard to obtain a majority in favor of Resolution 678?

2. What are the practical implications of the differing positions expressed above on the applicability of Articles 42 and 51 to the Gulf War? Is Rostow correct in suggesting that treating the Gulf War as an enforcement action would gravely undermine the right of self-defense? Or do you agree with Franck and Patel that the right of self-defense properly ceased to apply when the Security Council began to exercise its "police powers"?

3. Do you agree with Chayes that the Security Council should be the judge of whether it has taken the "measures necessary to maintain international peace and security"? Under this approach, would any measure taken by the Security Council to

maintain or restore peace (for example, the imposition of a trade embargo) preclude other states from taking military action in collective self-defense of a state that has been attacked? Does it matter whether the measure taken is likely to succeed in maintaining or restoring peace? If the decision on whether the "measures necessary to maintain international peace and security" is left to individual states, might not their decisions about the timing and scope of any military response to aggression interfere with the Security Council's efforts to achieve peace?

4. The Council's authorization in Resolution 678 and elsewhere to a state or group of states—a "coalition of the willing"—to use force flowed directly from the absence of any agreements under Article 43. Who should decide whether the states acting in reliance on an authorizing resolution have acted in a manner consistent with the resolution? In the case of Iraq, for example, did the coalition forces have complete discretion to decide how far into Iraq to carry the war and when to terminate hostilities?

D. The War and Its Aftermath

The coalition military campaign against Iraq proceeded in two phases. In the early morning hours of January 16, 1991 coalition forces initiated a punishing air assault on Iraqi forces that ended up lasting six weeks. The air war was followed by a brief but massive ground assault.

1. Operations Desert Storm and Desert Sabre

In the air campaign, code-named Desert Storm, hundreds of allied warplanes attacked Iraq's air defenses, SCUD missile sites, and command and control centers. Targets also included oil refineries, Baghdad's international airport, the presidential palace, and Iraqi chemical and nuclear weapons facilities. At the same time, the coalition continued to bomb targets in Baghdad, including power facilities. Civilians suffered alongside the Iraqi military, leading the Iraqi government to accuse the coalition of trying to "expel Iraq from the 20th century."

On February 21, 1991, the Soviets announced a peace proposal that would have allowed Iraq 21 days to withdraw from Kuwait and terminated sanctions immediately upon completion of the withdrawal. The following day, President Bush issued a second ultimatum to Iraq: begin withdrawal from Kuwait by noon the next day or face a ground invasion. The Deputy Chairman of Iraq's Revolutionary Council declared that the U.S. demand was "an aggressive ultimatum to which we will pay no attention."

The ground war, code-named Desert Sabre, began hours later, on the night of February 23. Some 700,000 coalition troops from 34 countries faced an Iraqi army that, at the outset of the fighting, had numbered 545,000. Backed by 2,000 warplanes and 100 warships, coalition troops rapidly outflanked (and in some areas simply rolled over) demoralized and outgunned Iraqi forces. The coalition destroyed thousands of Iraqi tanks and artillery pieces, and killed tens of thousands of Iraqi soldiers. Before long, Iraqi forces were in full retreat. One hundred hours after the ground assault began, the war was over. Coalition casualties were stunningly low; the United States lost 148 soldiers in combat. By contrast, Iraq is estimated to have suffered as many as 100,000 combat deaths (though later reports suggest the figure may have been considerably lower). The U.S. Department of

Defense estimated the cost of the war at $61 billion (though other estimates place it closer to $71 billion). Much of the cost was paid by Kuwait, Saudi Arabia, and other Gulf states ($36 billion) and by Germany and Japan ($16 billion).

On February 27, President Bush ordered a cease-fire, stopping short of the complete destruction of the Iraqi army and resisting the suggestion of some advisers that coalition forces should drive all the way to Baghdad. Bush was evidently motivated by humanitarian concerns, the desire to allow Iraq to continue to serve as a counterpoise to Iranian power in the region, and the concern expressed by some allies regarding the legal authority for continuation of the war.

2. The Cessation of Hostilities

Shortly after suspending hostilities, President Bush announced the coalition's terms for a formal cease-fire in a February 27 speech. They included immediate release of all coalition prisoners of war and Kuwaiti detainees; provision of information to Kuwaiti authorities on all land mines and sea mines; and full compliance with all relevant UN Security Council resolutions, including "a rescinding of Iraq's August decision to annex Kuwait and acceptance in principle of Iraq's responsibility to pay compensation for the loss, damage and injury its aggression has caused." On March 3, 1991, the Security Council incorporated those terms into Resolution 686.

Security Council Resolution 686 (1991)

The Security Council . . .

2. *Demands* that Iraq implement its acceptance of [12 prior resolutions] and in particular that Iraq:

(a) Rescind immediately its actions purporting to annex Kuwait; . . .

(c) Under international law immediately release . . . all Kuwaiti and third country nationals detained by Iraq . . . ; and

(d) Immediately begin to return all Kuwaiti property seized by Iraq, to be completed in the shortest possible period;

3. *Also demands* that Iraq:

(a) Cease hostile or provocative actions by its forces against all Member States including missile attacks and flights of combat aircraft; . . .

4. *Recognizes* that during the period required for Iraq to comply with paragraphs 2 and 3 above, the provisions of paragraph 2 of resolution 678 (1990) [authorizing "all necessary means" to implement prior Council resolutions] remain valid. . . .

That same day, in a letter from Deputy Prime Minister Tariq Aziz, the Iraqi government stated that it accepted Resolution 686.

3. Containing Iraq After the War

On April 13, 1991, some six weeks following the end of the Gulf War, the UN Security Council adopted Resolution 687. Resolution 687 demanded that Iraq account for detainees, accept responsibility for all harm occasioned to foreign states and nationals as a result of Iraq's invasion and occupation of Kuwait, return stolen

Kuwaiti property, renounce terrorism, and respect the inviolability of the Iraq-Kuwait border as provided in the 1963 treaty. Further, Resolution 687 established the Iraq-Kuwait Boundary Demarcation Commission to fix precisely the location of that border. Perhaps most important, Resolution 687 directed Iraq to dismantle its weapons of mass destruction (WMD), and to allow the United Nations to monitor and inspect its weapons production facilities to ensure that no further weapons of mass destruction were developed.

Security Council Resolution 687

(1991)

   The Security Council . . .

   Reaffirming the need to be assured of Iraq's peaceful intentions in the light of its unlawful invasion and occupation of Kuwait, . . .

   Conscious also of the statements by Iraq threatening to use weapons in violation of its obligations under the Protocol for the Prohibition of the Use in War of Asphyxiating, Poisonous or Other Gases, and of Bacteriological Methods of Warfare, signed at Geneva on 17 June 1925, and of its prior use of chemical weapons, and affirming that grave consequences would follow any further use by Iraq of such weapons, . . .

   Aware of the use by Iraq of ballistic missiles in unprovoked attacks and therefore of the need to take specific measures in regard to such missiles located in Iraq,

   Concerned by the reports in the hands of Member States that Iraq has attempted to acquire materials for a nuclear-weapons programme contrary to its obligations under the Treaty on the Non-Proliferation of Nuclear Weapons of 1 July 1968, . . .

   Deploring threats made by Iraq during the recent conflict to make use of terrorism against targets outside Iraq and the taking of hostages by Iraq, . . .

   Conscious of the need to take the following measures acting under Chapter VII of the Charter,

   2. *Demands* that Iraq and Kuwait respect the inviolability of the international boundary and the allocation of islands set out in the "Agreed Minutes between the State of Kuwait and the Republic of Iraq regarding the restoration of friendly relations, recognition and related matters", signed by them in the exercise of their sovereignty at Baghdad on 4 October 1963. . . ;

   8. *Decides* that Iraq shall unconditionally accept the destruction, removal, or rendering harmless, under international supervision, of:

   (a) All chemical and biological weapons and all stocks of agents and all related subsystems and components and all research, development, support and manufacturing facilities related thereto;

   (b) All ballistic missiles with a range greater than 150 kilometres, and related major parts and repair and production facilities;

   9. *Decides also*, for the implementation of paragraph 8 above, the following:

   (a) Iraq shall submit to the Secretary-General, within fifteen days of the adoption of the present resolution, a declaration of the locations, amounts and types of all items specified in paragraph 8 and agree to urgent, on-site inspection as specified below;

(b) The Secretary-General . . . with the Director-General of the World Health Organization, within forty-five days of the adoption of the present resolution shall develop and submit to the Council for approval a plan calling for the completion of the following acts within forty-five days of such approval:

(i) The forming of a special commission, which shall carry out immediate on-site inspection of Iraq's biological, chemical and missile capabilities, based on Iraq's declarations and the designation of any additional locations by the special commission itself;

(ii) The yielding by Iraq of possession to the Special Commission for destruction, removal or rendering harmless, taking into account the requirements of public safety, of all items specified under paragraph 8 (a) above, including items at the additional locations designated by the Special Commission under paragraph (i) above and the destruction by Iraq, under the supervision of the Special Commission, of all its missile capabilities, including launchers, as specified under paragraph 8 (b);
. . .

22. *Decides also* that [upon fulfillment of Iraq's disarmament and reparations obligations,] the prohibitions against the import of commodities and products originating in Iraq and the prohibitions against financial transactions related thereto contained in resolution 661 (1990) shall have no further force or effect; . . .

33. *Declares* that, upon official notification by Iraq to the Secretary-General and to the Security Council of its acceptance of the provisions above, a formal cease-fire is effective between Iraq and Kuwait and the Member States cooperating with Kuwait in accordance with resolution 678 (1990);

34. *Decides* to remain seized of the matter and to take such further steps as may be required for the implementation of the present resolution and to secure peace and security in the area.

Resolution 687 similarly requires Iraq to forgo development of nuclear weapons and to permit inspection of relevant sites and destruction of nuclear weapons materials. The International Atomic Energy Agency (IAEA) was charged with monitoring and verifying the destruction of Iraq's nuclear weapons program along lines similar to that of the Special Commission described in paragraph 9 of the resolution. Resolution 687 also continued existing sanctions against Iraq, pending its compliance with the terms of the resolution and prior resolutions.

From the outset, Iraq strongly resisted efforts to monitor its WMD programs. Iraqi officials lied to UN monitors and special commission members, concealed prohibited materials and activities, and obstructed investigations as much as possible. Nonetheless, the UN Special Commission (UNSCOM) made considerable progress in locating and overseeing the destruction of Iraqi weapons of mass destruction in the years following the Gulf War. Iraq continually threatened to end all cooperation with UNSCOM unless the Security Council agreed to set a date for the end of all inspections and sanctions. In October 1997 Iraq began to halt inspections, claiming that UNSCOM was conducting espionage activities for the United States.

The United States warned that it would use military force if needed to prevent Iraq's continued disregard for the inspections program and began to strengthen its military forces in the Persian Gulf. On December 15, 1998, after a year of further Security Council resolutions, Richard Butler, the head of UNSCOM, filed a formal report with the Security Council stating that UNSCOM "is not able to conduct the substantive disarmament work mandated to it by the Security Council." The following day, U.S. and British forces began Operation Desert Fox, a four-day air attack designed to "degrade" Iraq's military capability and limit Iraq's ability to threaten its neighbors.

Many Western countries, even some generally sympathetic to Iraq, expressed support for the strikes in light of Iraq's intransigence regarding the inspections; some of the Gulf states provided basing or other logistical support. China, Russia, and France, on the other hand, strongly criticized the action and called for an end to the oil embargo and for the retooling or abandonment of UNSCOM.

In early January 1999, a former UNSCOM official revealed that UNSCOM had closely cooperated with U.S. intelligence operations in Iraq, which reinforced the desire of many states to modify or replace UNSCOM. Some months later, a sharply divided Security Council reached a compromise: sanctions were loosened, and a new body, the UN Monitoring, Verification and Inspection Commission (UNMOVIC), was formed to replace UNSCOM. Sanctions were to continue until UNMOVIC reported that the new system was up and running. But Iraq rejected the proposal and continued to bar UN inspections.

By early 2001 it was clear that the sanctions regime could not be maintained in its then-current form. UN agencies and international human rights groups highlighted the widespread suffering in Iraq attributable to the sanctions and Iraq's failure to take full advantage of a UN program permitting Iraq to sell oil to purchase human-itarian necessities. Arab and other Muslim states increasingly opposed the restric-tions on Iraq; so did France, Russia, and many other countries. Some countries turned a blind eye to violations of the embargo on Iraq, and neighboring countries in particular permitted Iraq to smuggle oil to market to avoid the escrow system.

On May 14, 2002, the Security Council unanimously adopted Resolution 1409, which substantially revised the sanctions regime. The resolution permitted far more consumer goods to reach Iraq but continued to restrict the import of goods that might be used for military purposes, such as high-speed computers.

Notes and Questions

1. The regime established under Resolution 687 for the monitoring and destruction of Iraq's chemical, biological, and nuclear weapons capabilities was highly intrusive, open-ended, and unprecedented. Did the Security Council have the authority under the Charter to impose this inspection regime? Could the coali-tion states have legitimately established a comparable regime in the absence of Security Council authorization?

2. What means other than the use of force were open to the United States and the United Kingdom for securing compliance with the requirements of the inspec-tion regime?

3. What avenues were open to states critical of the sanctions to get them lifted? How many members of the Security Council would have had to oppose lifting the sanctions to keep them in place?

4. In addition to the Charter's requirement of an armed attack, additional conditions for the legitimate exercise of the right of self-defense may be found in

customary international law. In particular, any use of force must be both necessary and proportionate. However, governments and scholars disagree over the meaning of these two terms:

> A widely accepted test of necessity dates back to 1842 when U.S. Secretary of State Daniel Webster rejected a British claim of self-defense arising out of a raid on a small steamship that was being used in support of a Canadian insurrection against Great Britain. A British raiding party boarded the ship while it was moored on the New York side of the Niagara River, attacked those on board and set it afloat over Niagara Falls. Webster said that although a right of self-defense existed, it should be confined to cases in which the "necessity of that self-defence is instant, overwhelming, and leaving no choice of means and no moment for deliberation." The British government acquiesced in that test, and it was adopted by the International Military Tribunal at Nuremberg after World War II. It has sometimes been questioned since the Nuremberg trials, primarily in the context of defense against a threatened nuclear attack.

Frederic L. Kirgis, *Cruise Missile Strikes in Afghanistan and Sudan*, ASIL Insights, Aug. 1998, *www.asil.org/insights/insigh24.htm*. Some scholars suggest that Webster's definition of necessity, with its focus on temporality, applies only to cases of anticipatory self-defense; others argue that his definition is relevant to all uses of self-defense. A third school of thought argues that necessity simply means that force used in self-defense "must be by way of a last resort after all peaceful means have failed." Judith Gardam, Necessity, Proportionality and the Use of Force by States 5 (2004).

Proportionality in self-defense is an ill-defined concept. In general, however, it precludes a state from using force beyond that necessary to repel an attack or to restore the *status quo ante*. Professor Schachter offers the following views:

> Proportionality is closely linked to necessity as a requirement of self-defense. Acts done in self-defense must not exceed in manner or aim the necessity provoking them. . . . Governments, by and large, observe the requirement when they are faced with isolated frontier attacks or naval incidents. The "defending" state under attack generally limits itself to force proportionate to the attack; it does not bomb cities or launch an invasion. We tend to see such restraint generally as political or prudential, but that does not detract from its legal relevance. Thus, when defensive action is greatly in excess of the provocation, as measured by relative casualties or scale of weaponry, international opinion will more readily condemn such defense as illegally disproportionate. . . .
>
> Geography may also be a significant factor in determining proportionality. An isolated attack in one place—say, in a disputed territorial zone—would not normally warrant a defensive action deep into the territory of the attacking state. However, the situation may change when a series of attacks in one area leads to the conclusion that defense requires a counterattack against the "source" of the attack on a scale that would deter future attacks. . . .
>
> . . . [I]t does not seem unreasonable, as a rule, to allow a state to retaliate beyond the immediate area of attack, when that state has sufficient reason to expect a continuation of attacks (with substantial military weapons) from the same source. Such action would not be "anticipatory" because prior attacks occurred; nor would it be a "reprisal" since its prime motive would be protective, not punitive. When a government treats an isolated incident of armed attack as a ground for retaliation with force, the action can only be justified as self-defense when it can be reasonably regarded as a defense against a new attack. Thus, "defensive retaliation" may be justified when a state has good reason to expect a series of attacks from the same source and such retaliation serves as a deterrent or protective action. However, a reprisal for revenge or as a penalty (or "lesson") would not be defensive.

Oscar Schachter, *In Defense of International Rules on the Use of Force*, 53 U. Chi. L. Rev. 113, 138-139 (1986).

In light of these customary international law limitations on the use of force, were the coalition forces obligated to discontinue the attack on Iraq at the time President Bush declared a cease-fire, or could they have continued to pursue the retreating Iraqi forces? Would continued pursuit have been in defense of Kuwait? Do you agree with the following analysis?

How far could the coalition forces led by the United States have gone in carrying the war to Iraq? We should assume that the principles of reasonableness and proportionality of the customary law of self-defense apply. . . . What action against Iraq did they justify? Surely, action to liberate Kuwait, restore its legitimate government, and insist on reparations and other normal remedies within the rules of proportionality and reasonableness. Under the military circumstances, those goals required and justified whatever attacks against Iraq were deemed reasonably necessary to attain the end: i.e., bombing and other attacks on troops, installations, and military equipment in Iraq as well as Kuwait.

But the Security Council resolutions also contemplate "measures to restore international peace and security in the area." This phrase is not a rhetorical flourish. It has always been an essential ingredient of the law of self-defense. It is a recurring theme of the United Nations Charter and is reiterated in Resolution 678. It means that the lawful goal of the war, viewed as a war of self-defense, was not simply to force Iraq out of Kuwait, so that it could wait, fully armed, until the United States and other coalition forces went home and it perfected its nuclear, chemical, and biological warfare capabilities. . . .

Under accepted standards of international law—those applied in the cases of Germany and Japan after 1945—the United States and its allies could dismantle Iraq's program for building weapons of mass destruction, destroy its stocks of these weapons, and take measures to guarantee to the world that such activities on Iraq's part are effectively prevented for the future. If it had been found necessary to put Iraq under military occupation for a time in order to achieve those goals, that, too, would have been permissible under international law.

Eugene V. Rostow, *The Gulf Crisis in International and Foreign Relations Law, Continued: Until What? Enforcement Action or Collective Self-Defense?*, 85 Am. J. Intl. L. 506, 514 (1991).

5. The International Court of Justice had occasion to consider issues of necessity and proportionality in *Case Concerning Oil Platforms (Islamic Republic of Iran v. United States of America)*, 2003 I.C.J. (Nov. 6). The case arose in the context of the 1980-88 Iran-Iraq war. In that conflict, both parties launched attacks on shipping in the Persian Gulf. In 1987, a missile hit the *Sea Isle City*, a U.S.-flagged merchant vessel, and in 1988, a mine damaged the *Samuel B. Roberts*, a U.S. naval vessel. The United States attributed these and a series of other incidents to Iran, and attacked certain Iranian oil platforms in October 1987 and April 1988. The Court found the evidence of Iranian responsibility for the damage to the U.S. ships to be inconclusive; moreover, setting aside the question of responsibility, the Court concluded that the incidents did not rise to the level of an armed attack sufficient to trigger the right of self-defense. To decide whether U.S. actions violated a treaty of friendship between the United States and Iran, the Court went on to discuss whether U.S. actions were necessary and proportionate under the law of self-defense:

76.   . . . In the case both of the attack on the *Sea Isle City* and the mining of the USS *Samuel B. Roberts*, the Court is not satisfied that the attacks on the platforms were necessary to respond to these incidents. In this connection, the Court notes that there is no evidence that the United States complained to Iran of the military activities of the

platforms, in the same way as it complained repeatedly of minelaying and attacks on neutral shipping, which does not suggest that the targeting of the platforms was seen as a necessary act. The Court would also observe that in the case of the attack of 19 October 1987, the United States forces attacked the R-4 platform as a "target of opportunity", not one previously identified as an appropriate military target.

77.   As to the requirement of proportionality, the attack of 19 October 1987 might, had the Court found that it was necessary in response to the *Sea Isle City* incident as an armed attack committed by Iran, have been considered proportionate. In the case of the attacks of 18 April 1988, however, they were conceived and executed as part of a more extensive operation entitled "Operation Praying Mantis" . . . which involved, *inter alia*, the destruction of two Iranian frigates and a number of other naval vessels and aircraft. As a response to the mining, by an unidentified agency, of a single United States warship, which was severely damaged but not sunk, and without loss of life, neither "Operation Praying Mantis" as a whole, nor even that part of it that destroyed the Salman and Nasr platforms, can be regarded, in the circumstances of this case, as a proportionate use of force in self-defence.

For more on proportionality, see the discussions of that issue in connection with the *Nuclear Weapons* case in Chapter 8, the allied bombing of Kosovo in Section III of this chapter, and the U.S. response to terrorism in Chapter 14.

E. Operation Iraqi Freedom and Its Aftermath

In the aftermath of the terrorist attacks of September 11, 2001, the United States and the United Kingdom sought to induce a reluctant Security Council to take a harder line toward Iraq.

1. Increasing International Pressure on Iraq

In his January 29, 2002 State of the Union address, President George W. Bush identified Iraq as "a grave and growing danger" constituting part of an "axis of evil" that threatened international peace and security. Bush accused Iraq of developing weapons of mass destruction and supporting terrorist organizations, and warned that America "will not wait on events, while dangers gather." The U.S. government soon began talking openly of "regime change" in Iraq. President Bush promised that the United States would "work with the U.N. Security Council to meet our common challenge," yet warned that the United States was prepared to act unilaterally if necessary. As tensions between the United States and Iraq mounted, U.N. Secretary-General Kofi Annan made the following statement to the General Assembly on September 12, 2002:

> [T]he leadership of Iraq continues to defy mandatory resolutions adopted by the Security Council under Chapter VII of the Charter. . . .
> I appeal to all those who have influence with Iraq's leaders to impress on them the vital importance of accepting the weapons inspections. This is the indispensable first step towards assuring the world that all Iraq's weapons of mass destruction have indeed been eliminated. . . .
> If Iraq's defiance continues, the Security Council must face its responsibilities.

In response, Iraq insisted that it had already substantially complied with Resolution 687 and no longer possessed weapons of mass destruction. Still, on September 16, 2002, the Iraqi government agreed to the unconditional return of U.N. weapons inspectors to Iraq.

2. The UN Debate on the Use of Force Against Iraq and Resolution 1441

Iraq's announcement that it would allow U.N. Monitoring, Verification, and Inspection Commission (UNMOVIC) and International Atomic Energy Agency (IAEA) inspectors to return to Iraq sparked sharp debate within the Security Council. Given Iraq's history of non-compliance, the United States demanded a new Council resolution containing stricter verification procedures, shorter deadlines, and unconditional cooperation with inspectors, as well as a complete declaration by Iraq of all aspects of its WMD programs. The United States, supported by the United Kingdom, prepared a draft resolution providing that false statements by Iraq concerning its weapons programs or a failure to cooperate fully with inspectors would "constitute a further material breach of Iraq's obligations, and that such breach authorizes member states to use all necessary means to restore international peace and security in the area."

Other Security Council members opposed the U.S.-UK proposal. Russia, France, and China in particular opposed "automaticity"—the proposed authorization to use force in the event of a material breach without need for a further Security Council resolution. The French Foreign Minister declared that his country would not support any proposal that gave the United States a "blank check" to attack Iraq. Most other UN member states, including the 114 developing countries comprising the Non-Aligned Movement (NAM), also rejected the U.S.-UK proposal.

France, Russia, and China then attempted to forge a compromise, agreeing to back a new resolution toughening the inspection regime as long as the resolution omitted language authorizing the use of force. France insisted that the Council should meet to consider a second resolution authorizing the use of force only if, and when, Iraq defied the first resolution. The United States and the United Kingdom eventually revised their draft resolution, dropping the "all necessary means" language and adding language agreeing to consult the Security Council to determine possible consequences if inspectors reported that Iraq had failed to cooperate fully. Still, the United States emphasized that while it would discuss Iraqi violations with the Council, it would not wait for UN approval before taking military action. In addition, the United States retained a paragraph declaring that "Iraq is still, and has been for a number of years, in material breach of its obligations under relevant resolutions."

Russia initially threatened to veto any resolution declaring that Iraq was in "material breach" of past UN resolutions and warning that Iraq would face "serious consequences" if it failed to cooperate with the new weapons-inspection process. France agreed, fearing that the "material breach" language might be a "hidden trigger" for the use of force. Nonetheless, the United States and the United Kingdom pushed to a vote their revised version, which the Security Council unanimously adopted on November 8, 2002 as Resolution 1441.

Security Council Resolution 1441 (2002)

The Security Council . . .
Acting under Chapter VII of the Charter of the United Nations,
Further recalling that its resolution 687 (1991) imposed obligations on Iraq as a necessary step for achievement of its stated objective of restoring international peace and security in the area,

1. *Decides* that Iraq has been and remains in material breach of its obligations under relevant resolutions . . . in particular through Iraq's failure to cooperate with United Nations inspectors . . . ;

2. *Decides* . . . to afford Iraq, by this resolution, a final opportunity to comply with its disarmament obligations . . . ;

3. *Decides* that, in order to begin to comply with its disarmament obligations, . . . Iraq shall provide to UNMOVIC, the IAEA, and the Council, not later than 30 days from the date of this resolution, a currently accurate, full, and complete declaration of all aspects of its programmes to develop chemical, biological, and nuclear weapons . . . ;

4. *Decides* that false statements or omissions in the declarations submitted by Iraq pursuant to this resolution and failure by Iraq at any time to comply with, and cooperate fully in the implementation of, this resolution shall constitute a further material breach of Iraq's obligations . . . ;

11. *Directs* the Executive Chairman of UNMOVIC and the Director-General of the IAEA to report immediately to the Council any interference by Iraq with inspection activities, as well as any failure by Iraq to comply with its disarmament obligations, including its obligations regarding inspections under this resolution;

12. *Decides* to convene immediately upon receipt of a report in accordance with paragraphs 4 or 11 above, in order to consider the situation and the need for full compliance with all of the relevant Council resolutions in order to secure international peace and security;

13. *Recalls*, in that context, that the Council has repeatedly warned Iraq that it will face serious consequences as a result of its continued violations of its obligations.

3. U.S. Congressional Authorization for the Use of Force Against Iraq

At the same time that the United States was pushing the Security Council for a resolution authorizing military action against Iraq, the United States was preparing to act unilaterally. On October 16, 2002, President Bush signed into law a joint House and Senate resolution authorizing the use of force against Iraq:

Authorization for the Use of Military Force Against Iraq Resolution

Public Law 107-243 (2002)

Whereas Iraq both poses a continuing threat to the national Security of the United States and international peace and security . . . and remains in material and unacceptable breach of its international obligations by, among other things, continuing to possess and develop a significant chemical and biological weapons capability, actively seeking a nuclear weapons capability, and supporting and harboring terrorist organizations; . . .

The President is authorized to use the Armed Forces of the United States as he determines to be necessary and appropriate in order to—

(1) defend the national security of the United States against the continuing threat posed by Iraq; and

(2) enforce all relevant United Nations Security Council resolutions regarding Iraq.

———————————

Bush assured the Security Council that by signing the joint resolution he was not ordering the use of force, but only sending a message to the world that "the United States speaks with one determined voice." The U.S. Ambassador to the United Nations assured the Security Council that the United States would act outside the Security Council only "should diplomatic efforts fail."

4. The UN Debate on the Need for Military Action

On November 13, 2002, the Iraqi government grudgingly accepted Resolution 1441. With the new resolution in place, UNMOVIC and IAEA began formal inspections on November 27, 2002. On December 7, 2002, one day before the 30-day deadline set by Resolution 1441, Iraq delivered to UNMOVIC inspectors a 12,000 page document outlining its chemical, biological, and nuclear weapons programs. Iraq denied that it had developed weapons of mass destruction and focused primarily on civilian materials that could have military applications. The heads of UNMOVIC and the IAEA suggested that based upon previous UN disarmament records, the document was not a complete accounting of Iraq's arsenal of banned weapons. In response, U.S. Secretary of State Colin Powell declared that Iraq had "totally failed" to meet UN demands.

Inspections continued into early 2003. While inspectors discovered ballistic missiles whose range modestly exceeded UN limits, inspectors were unable to find any conclusive evidence that Iraq possessed weapons of mass destruction. Still, the U.S. government insisted that Iraq was hiding illegal weapons.

In accordance with paragraph 12 of Resolution 1441, the Security Council convened on February 5, 2003, to discuss Iraq's non-compliance. Secretary of State Powell presented to the Council intercepted telephone conversations, reports by Iraqi informants, and satellite surveillance photographs in an attempt to demonstrate that Iraq was hiding weapons, sanitizing inspection sites, and intimidating scientists in an effort to obstruct interviews. Powell urged the Council to support a military strike against Iraq. Without a "smoking gun" proving that Iraq had defied UN resolutions, however, the Council refused to authorize the use of force.

Convinced that the United Nations was not serious about disarmament, the United States put together a "coalition of the willing," including the United Kingdom, Australia, Spain, Italy, Poland, and an assortment of other countries, and began sending thousands of troops to the Persian Gulf. As the new coalition prepared to launch an assault on Iraq, the United States, the United Kingdom and Spain presented a new resolution to the Security Council on February 24, 2003, which declared that Iraq had "failed to take the final opportunity afforded to it in resolution 1441," and thereby implicitly authorized the use of force against Iraq. France, Russia, and China, insisting that force was premature and inspections should continue, threatened to veto the resolution if put to a vote.

Hoping at least to obtain majority support in the Security Council for the resolution, the United States wooed Chile, Angola, Guinea, and Cameroon with suggestions of trade benefits, loans, and economic aid. In addition, the United States warned Mexico that the U.S. Congress could hinder trade if Mexico did not support the Bush Administration. France quickly countered with a lobbying campaign of its own, making frenzied telephone calls to the swing vote countries in an effort to convince them to remain true to their anti-war positions. After much political haggling, the United States and Britain realized that they probably would not secure the nine votes required to pass a resolution even in the absence of any veto. Britain offered an amendment to the draft resolution, setting March 17, 2003, as the deadline for Iraq to disarm. Russia, France, and Germany rejected the revised draft and warned the United States not to attack Iraq. Despite this warning, on March 17, 2003, the United States, the United Kingdom, and Spain withdrew the proposed second resolution and told Saddam Hussein to leave Iraq within 48 hours in order to avoid military action. Hussein ignored the ultimatum.

5. The War in Iraq

On March 19, 2003, U.S. forces attacked a site where Saddam Hussein and his top deputies were thought to be meeting. This marked the start of Operation Iraqi Freedom. The ground offensive began on March 20, 2003, with U.S. and UK forces crossing the border from Kuwait into Iraq. The first stage of the offensive involved a massive bombing campaign intended to disable the Iraqi command and control structure. Coalition forces worked quickly, seizing oilfields and Iraqi airbases and surrounding major Iraqi cities within days. While the Republican Guard offered some resistance, many Iraqi troops surrendered to coalition forces without a fight. Coalition troops took control of central Baghdad by April 9, 2003. Tikrit, the last Iraqi stronghold, fell to coalition forces on April 14, 2003. President Bush then announced that major combat operations were over.

F. Debating the Legality of the War

Beginning in the months before the war, many governments and most academic commentators argued that an attack on Iraq would be unlawful for two reasons: first, Iraq had committed no armed attack permitting a use of force against it in self-defense; and second, Resolution 678 could not be used to justify a use of force so many years after the end of the first Gulf War. They rejected the view that the ceasefire referenced in Resolution 687 was contingent on full compliance by Iraq with all of the disarmament provisions in that resolution and argued that Resolution 1441 left it to the Security Council to decide, through adoption of a subsequent resolution, whether force should be used to coerce Iraq's compliance with its disarmament obligations.

Supporters of the war offered two principal legal arguments: (1) that Security Council resolutions 678 (1990), 687 (1991), and 1441 (2002) provided sufficient authorization for the use of force; and (2) that the war was a legitimate exercise of preemptive self-defense.

In March 2003, President Bush declared that "[u]nder Resolutions 678 and 687 . . . the United States and our allies are authorized to use force in ridding Iraq of weapons of mass destruction." The British Attorney General agreed, asserting that "[a]uthority to use force against Iraq exists from the combined effect of resolutions 678, 687 and 1441." The next day, the Australian government issued a similar statement:

Memorandum of Legal Advice on the Use of Force Against Iraq

Australian Attorney General's Dept. and the Dept. of Foreign Affairs & Trade, March 18, 2003, reprinted in 4 Melbourne J. Int'l L. 178 (2003).

Existing United Nations Security Council resolutions provide authority for the use of force directed towards disarming Iraq of weapons of mass destruction and restoring international peace and security in the area. This existing authority for the use of force would only be negated in current circumstances if the Security Council were to pass a resolution that required Member States to refrain from the use of force against Iraq. . . .

10. Between the adoption of SCR 687 and the present day, the Security Council has found that Iraq has failed to comply with its obligations under SCR 687. This culminated in the adoption by the Security Council under Chapter VII of the UN Charter of SCR 1441 (2002) on 2 November 2002. In its preamble, this resolution recalled that SCR 678 authorised Member States to use all necessary means to uphold and implement SCR 660 and all relevant resolutions subsequent to SCR 660 and to restore international peace and security to the area. It also recalled that SCR 687 "imposed obligations on Iraq as a necessary step for the achievement of its stated objective of restoring international peace and security in the area." Furthermore, the preamble provides:

> Recalling that in its resolution 687 (1991) the Council declared that a cease-fire would be based on acceptance by Iraq of the provisions of that resolution, including the obligations on Iraq contained therein. . . .

14. In our view, Iraq's past and continuing material breaches of SCR 687 have negated the basis for the "formal cease-fire." Iraq, by its conduct subsequent to the adoption of SCR 687, has demonstrated that it did not and does not 'accept' the terms of SCR 687. Consequently, the cease-fire is not effective and the authorisation for the use of force in SCR 678 is reactivated.

15. We do not believe that the authorisation contained in SCR 678 has expired or that, coupled with SCR 687, it was confined to the limited purpose of ensuring Iraq's withdrawal from Kuwait. Nor do we believe that the Security Council has either expressly or impliedly withdrawn the authority for the use of force in SCR 678 in all circumstances.

16. Operative paragraph 2 of SCR 678 set out above itself contains no limitations in terms of time. Nor is the purpose for which the authority to use force was given confined to restoration of the sovereignty and independence of Kuwait. The authority to use force also was to uphold and implement "all subsequent relevant resolutions and to restore international peace and security to the area". That purpose holds as good today as it did in 1990. There is no finite time under the Charter in which the authority given in a Security Council resolution expires. Nor is there any indication in resolutions subsequent to SCR 678 that the authority for the use of force contained in that resolution has expired. Indeed, subsequent resolutions indicate to the contrary.

17. Given the existing authority for the use of force, suggestions that there is a legal requirement for a further resolution are misplaced. Also, suggestions that the use of force in Iraq in the absence of a further Security Council Resolution would be "unilateral" are wrong.

The U.S.-UK-Australian position was not new. In 1998, after Iraq declared it would no longer cooperate with UNSCOM, the Clinton Administration advanced a similar interpretation of Resolutions 678 and 687 to justify Operation Desert Fox, a series of bombing attacks against military targets in Iraq intended to pressure Iraq to comply with its disarmament obligations. That interpretation was controversial. Consider the comments of Paul Szasz, former Deputy UN Legal Counsel, in reference to Operation Desert Fox:

Legal Authority for the Possible Use of Force Against Iraq

92 Proc. Am. Soc'y Int'l L. 136 (1998)

Resolution 678, adopted in November 1990, some weeks before the attack . . . states that the Council "*[a]uthorizes* Member States co-operating with the government of Kuwait, unless Iraq on or before 15 January 1991, fully implements . . . the above-mentioned resolutions, to use all necessary means to uphold and implement Resolution 660 and all subsequent relevant resolutions and to restore international peace and security in the area." The phrase "all subsequent resolutions" must be read in terms of the previous reference to the "above-mentioned resolutions." Thus, the word "subsequent" cannot mean resolutions subsequent to Resolution 678. It obviously refers, grammatically, to the resolutions that had already been referred to. Resolution 678 authorized the use of force if Iraq failed to comply with the requirements of the previously adopted resolutions. Those previous resolutions required that Iraq withdraw from Kuwait, release hostages, and to do a variety of other things, none of which had anything to do with the inspection systems set up some five months later in April 1991 by Resolution 687.

On March 2, 1991, immediately after General Schwarzkopf signed the cease fire agreement with the Iraqi commanders, the Security Council adopted the real cease fire resolution, 686. By that resolution, it directed that Iraq do a number of things to maintain the cease fire and it also stated that the "Security Council . . . *recognizes* that during the period required for Iraq to comply with paragraphs 2 and 3 above, the provisions of paragraph 2 of Resolution 678 (1990) remain valid." The cited paragraph is the one that authorized using "all necessary means." The Security Council deliberately kept open the authority of the allied forces to use all necessary means, but only for the purpose of implementing two particular paragraphs of Resolution 686 . . . No other resolution coming after Resolution 686 reaffirmed Resolution 678 and the authority to use force.

We then come to Resolution 687, adopted on April 3, 1991, a month and a day after Resolution 686. Resolution 687 also provided for a cease fire but in a sense, it was more of an armistice, i.e., a long-term arrangement and not merely designed to stop the shooting at a specific time. It is this Resolution that sets out . . . the inspection system that Iraq has been violating all along, and still continues to violate. . . . But that resolution itself did not reauthorize the use of force, and the primary penalty that it foresees for non-compliance with its provisions is the maintenance of economic sanctions. So, one cannot say that Resolution 678 still has a life, in terms of continuing to authorize the use of force.

Notes and Questions

1. What actions did Resolution 678 authorize? For what period of time? Under the U.S.-UK-Australian reading of the relevant resolutions, do members of the original Gulf War coalition have "in perpetuity the right to use force to restore peace" in the area?

2. Does paragraph 33 of Resolution 687 require fulfillment of the resolution's disarmament obligations or only a formal acceptance of those obligations to render the cease-fire effective? Does a breach of Iraq's disarmament obligations render the cease-fire referred to in Resolution 687 void? Does it matter whether the breach occurs immediately after passage of the resolution or years later?

3. Does the preambular paragraph of Resolution 1441 referring to Resolution 687 accurately represent the content of that resolution? Can the Security Council change the meaning of a resolution by the way it interprets that resolution in a later resolution?

4. Does Resolution 1441 indicate, explicitly or implicitly, that a further Security Council resolution is required before the "serious consequences" of which the resolution warns can include the use of force?

An additional or alternative possible justification for the war might be a claimed right of preemptive self-defense. Governments and international lawyers have long debated the legitimacy of anticipatory or preemptive self-defense. The language of Article 51 of the UN Charter, which permits self-defense "if an armed attack occurs," suggests that a use of force in anticipation of an attack is premature and thus unlawful. Some state practice suggests tolerance of a preemptive response by a state facing an imminent and potentially devastating armed attack. In 1967, for example, President Nasser of Egypt, responding to escalating tensions with Israel, demanded that the United Nations withdraw peacekeepers stationed on Egyptian territory to prevent war between Israel and Egypt, mobilized Egyptian military units in the Sinai, and closed the Straits of Tiran to Israeli shipping. Israel, anticipating an imminent full-scale armed attack, struck first. The war ended six days later, after Israel managed to seize the Golan Heights from Syria, the Gaza Strip from Egypt, and the West Bank from Jordan. The war was the subject of vigorous debate in the United Nations and elsewhere. Israel asserted that it had acted in self-defense, a position that received direct or tacit support from the United States and many western countries; the Arab states, supported by the communist bloc and many non-aligned states, characterized the Israeli attack as aggression.

On the other hand, in 1981, Israeli fighter-bombers destroyed a nuclear reactor in Osiraq, Iraq. Israel contended that its action constituted legitimate self-defense. From Israel's standpoint, Iraq was a hostile state whose possession of nuclear weapons would gravely threaten Israel's security and perhaps its very survival. At the time, international reaction was overwhelmingly critical, in part because there was little evidence that an Iraqi attack on Israel was imminent. The Security Council in Resolution 487 strongly condemned Israel's attack and determined that Iraq was "entitled to appropriate redress for the destruction it has suffered."

The Bush Administration gave a major boost to proponents of preemptive self-defense with the promulgation of a new U.S. National Security Strategy (NSS) in 2002:

The National Security Strategy of the United States of America

September 2002, http://www.whitehouse.gov/nsc/nss.html

For centuries, international law recognized that nations need not suffer an attack before they can lawfully take action to defend themselves against forces that present an imminent danger of attack. Legal scholars and international jurists often conditioned the legitimacy of preemption on the existence of an imminent threat—most often a visible mobilization of armies, navies, and air forces preparing to attack.

We must adapt the concept of imminent threat to the capabilities and objectives of today's adversaries. Rogue states and terrorists do not seek to attack us using conventional means. They know such attacks would fail. Instead, they rely on acts of terror and, potentially, the use of weapons of mass destruction—weapons that can be easily concealed, delivered covertly, and used without warning. . . .

The United States has long maintained the option of preemptive actions to counter a sufficient threat to our national security. The greater the threat, the greater is the risk of inaction—and the more compelling the case for taking anticipatory action to defend ourselves, even if uncertainty remains as to the time and place of the enemy's attack. To forestall or prevent such hostile acts by our adversaries, the United States will, if necessary, act preemptively.

The doctrine of anticipatory or preemptive self-defense remains controversial. The United States did not invoke the doctrine in support of the war in Iraq, although William Taft IV, then the legal adviser to the Department of State, noted that "the United States was prepared to deploy its forces . . . in self-defense in the face of an actual or imminent attack." In analyzing claims of anticipatory self-defense, governments and scholars have often invoked the "Caroline criteria," developed by U.S. Secretary of State Daniel Webster after an 1837 incident involving a British use of force against a vessel in the United States that had been supporting insurgents in Canada (see text at p. 900). They hold that anticipatory self-defense is lawful when there is "a necessity of self-defense, instant, overwhelming, leaving no choice of means and no moment for deliberation," and the action taken in response is not "unreasonable or excessive."

In the aftermath of the Iraq war, UN Secretary-General Kofi Annan formed a high-level panel to consider collective responses to contemporary threats. Consider the panel's view on anticipatory self-defense:

188.   [A] threatened State, according to long established international law, can take military action as long as the threatened attack is imminent, no other means would deflect it and the action is proportionate. The problem arises where the threat in question is not imminent but still claimed to be real: for example the acquisition, with allegedly hostile intent, of nuclear weapons-making capability.

189.   Can a State, without going to the Security Council, claim in these circumstances the right to act, in anticipatory self-defence, not just preemptively (against an imminent or proximate threat) but preventively (against a non-imminent or non-proximate one)? Those who say "yes" argue that the potential harm from some threats (e.g., terrorists armed with a nuclear weapon) is so great that one simply cannot risk waiting until they become imminent, and that less harm may be done (e.g., avoiding a nuclear exchange or radioactive fallout from a reactor destruction) by acting earlier.

190.   The short answer is that if there are good arguments for preventive military action, with good evidence to support them, they should be put to the Security Council, which can authorize such action if it chooses to. If it does not so choose, there will be, by definition, time to pursue other strategies, including persuasion, negotiation, deterrence and containment—and to visit again the military option.

191.   For those impatient with such a response, the answer must be that, in a world full of perceived potential threats, the risk to the global order and the norm of non-intervention on which it continues to be based is simply too great for the legality of unilateral preventive action, as distinct from collectively endorsed action, to be accepted. Allowing one to so act is to allow all.

Report of the Secretary-General's High-level Panel on Threats, Challenges and Change, *A More Secure World: Our Shared Responsibility* (2004).

Professor Michael Schmitt offers a different perspective:

[The imminency criterion for preemptive self-defense] made sense when armies had to mobilize to go to war and combat was linear, concentrated along a fairly well defined line. However, the NSS correctly points to changes in the context in which the criterion is applied. Today, attacks can be launched without warning; indeed, that is the prevailing modus operandi of terrorists. Moreover, terrorist attacks may be catastrophic in an era of WMD. To require States to wait until the blow is about to fall would often render them defenseless.

A more fruitful approach is to interpret imminency in light of its underlying purposes—permitting States to defend themselves effectively against attack while allowing the greatest opportunity possible for means short of the use of force to resolve the situation. . . . [This] allows a State to act anticipatorily (preemptively) if it must strike immediately to defend itself in a meaningful way and the potential aggressor is irrevocably committed to attack. The determinative question . . . is whether the defensive action occurred during the last possible window of opportunity in the face of an attack that was almost certainly going to occur. . . .

Should the United States have reliable evidence that a transfer [of weapons of mass destruction to terrorist groups] is looming, it may legally use force to prevent the exchange. This is justified because a State's ability to locate and destroy the weapons drops precipitously once they pass to terrorists. Similarly, if a State is developing WMD and it is reasonable to conclude that it intends to use the weapons against the United States, U.S. forces may strike anticipatorily in self-defense if they cannot reliably destroy the WMD inventory once developed. . . . Thus, the National Security Strategy's willingness to take "anticipatory action to defend ourselves, even if uncertainty remains as to time and place of the enemy's attack" is, depending on the facts at hand, lawful.

Michael N. Schmitt, *U.S. Security Strategies: A Legal Assessment*, 27 Harv. J.L. & Pub. Pol'y 737, 755-56 (2004).

Notes and Questions

1. In July 2002, British Prime Minister Tony Blair and his senior advisors discussed the possibility of military action in Iraq. Their discussion is summarized in a memorandum marked "Secret and Strictly Personal—UK Eyes Only" that was later leaked to the press:

The Foreign Secretary said he would discuss [the timing of military action] with Colin Powell this week. It seemed clear that Bush had made up his mind to take military action, even if the timing was not yet decided. But the case was thin. Saddam was not threatening his neighbours, and his WMD capability was less than that of Libya, North Korea or Iran. We should work up a plan for an ultimatum to Saddam to allow back in the UN weapons inspectors. This would also help with the legal justification for the use of force.

The Attorney-General said that the desire for regime change was not a legal base for military action. There were three possible legal bases: self-defence, humanitarian intervention, or UNSC authorisation. The first and second could not be the base in this case. Relying on UNSCR 1205 [condemning Iraq's refusal to cooperate with weapons inspectors] of three years ago would be difficult. The situation might of course change.

Memorandum from Matthew Rycroft to David Manning, Iraqi Prime Minister's Meeting, July 23, 2002. In March 2006, the New York Times reported on another memorandum by David Manning, one of Prime Minister Blair's top foreign policy advisors, describing a January 31, 2003 private meeting between President Bush and Blair. The memorandum indicates that Bush was intent on invading Iraq even in the absence of a second UN resolution, and that Bush raised several possible ways of provoking a confrontation with Iraq in the event UN inspectors could not find unconventional weapons there. According to the Times, Bush's suggestions included painting a U.S. surveillance plane in UN colors in the hope of attracting Iraqi fire, and assassinating Saddam Hussein. Do these memoranda affect your view of the legality of the use of force against Iraq in March 2003?

2. In 1962, the United States placed a naval quarantine around Cuba, in order to prevent the Soviet Union from installing missiles there capable of striking the United States. President Kennedy described the quarantine as "defensive," but the United States did not invoke anticipatory self-defense as a legal basis for the quarantine. Abram Chayes, then the State Department Legal Advisor, explains why:

> No doubt the phrase "armed attack" [in Article 51 of the UN Charter] must be construed broadly enough to permit some anticipatory response. But it is a very different matter to expand it to include threatening deployments or demonstrations that do not have imminent attack as their purpose or probable outcome. To accept that reading is to make the occasion for forceful response essentially a question for unilateral national decision that would not only be formally unreviewable, but not subject to intelligent criticism, either. . . . Whenever a nation believed that interests, which in the heat and pressure of a crisis it is prepared to characterize as vital, were threatened, its use of force in response would become permissible. . . . In this sense, I believe that an Article 51 defense would have signaled that the United States did not take the legal issues involved very seriously, that in its view the situation was to be governed by national discretion not international law.

Abram Chayes, The Cuban Missile Crisis 65-66 (1974). Does the National Security Strategy of 2002 suggest a significant change in the U.S. view of anticipatory self-defense? Why do you think the United States did not rely on anticipatory self-defense as a legal basis for the war in Iraq?

3. For many years, most scholars, and many governments, assumed anticipatory self-defense would rarely, if ever, be lawful. Yet the High-level Panel Report, prepared by a group of eminent international statesmen, suggests that preemptive self-defense is now widely accepted, and that the debate has shifted to the legality of preventive self-defense. What might account for such a shift in attitudes?

4. What sort of evidence might suffice to demonstrate that a threatened attack is imminent? Professor Schmitt suggests that "clear and convincing evidence" should be required. Is that an appropriate standard? Who should decide whether the

applicable standard has been met in a given case? What should be the consequences if one state erroneously believes itself to be subject to an imminent attack and itself initiates military action against the other state?

5. What do you think the High-level Panel meant by the suggestion in paragraph 190 of its report that a state could "visit again the military option" should the Security Council take no action in a given case?

III. INTERVENTION AND SELF-DEFENSE: TURMOIL IN THE DEMOCRATIC REPUBLIC OF CONGO

Iraq represents the paradigmatic case for application of the UN Charter's provisions relating to the use of force. But in the post-World War II era, armies seldom march openly across borders. Instead, most contemporary armed conflicts are fought largely within the territory of a single state, with consequences often as devastating as in interstate wars of the past. During the Cold War, many conflicts were fought at least in significant part over ideological differences, with the superpowers and their allies supporting pro- or anti-communist insurgent forces seeking to overthrow established governments in countries from El Salvador to Angola. In recent years, bitter and protracted conflicts in the former Yugoslavia, the former Soviet Union, and elsewhere have centered on questions of national identity and ethnic affiliations, but these conflicts have also often attracted the involvement of outside states.

In many of these conflicts, outside states attempt to conceal or understate their role in assisting one side or another in the conflict. In addition, outside states often justify their involvement as a response to the prior involvement of other states. As a result, government decision makers, international organizations, scholars, and occasionally courts are confronted with difficult questions of fact in attempting to apply international law in these various conflicts.

As you read the following materials, consider whether the UN Charter's prohibition on the use of force between states can be readily applied to internal armed conflicts that attract outside involvement; whether and when one state's intervention in an internal conflict constitutes a legitimate basis for another state to counter-intervene; and how international law and institutions could be strengthened in order to respond better to the complexities such conflicts present.

A. The Problem

The Democratic Republic of the Congo (DRC or the Congo) is a country roughly the size of Western Europe, with approximately 50 million people and enormous natural resources, including diamonds, gold, oil, timber, and ivory. (See map on p. 914.) But the Congo is also a country in collapse. For 32 years it was ruled by Mobutu Sese Seko, a legendarily corrupt autocrat supported by the United States and other Western states during much of the Cold War.

The recent crisis in the Congo began near the end of Mobutu's reign, with the outbreak of war and genocide in neighboring Rwanda. Rwanda has long been plagued by political tensions between two principal ethnic groups—the majority Hutu and the minority Tutsi. In 1994, Rwandan government officials who opposed

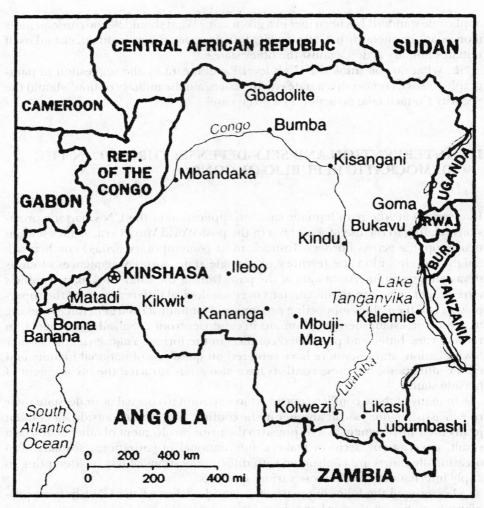

The DRC and Its Neighbors
SOURCE: CIA World Factbook, 2001

a political settlement that would have included Tutsi in the government agitated for the destruction of the Tutsi population. In the ensuing violence, majority Hutu extremists slaughtered between 500,000 and 1 million Tutsi and many moderate Hutu. (For a discussion of the international criminal law implications of these events, see Chapter 9.) But as Tutsi rebels, with support from Uganda, gained the upper hand in fighting with Rwandan government forces, hundreds of thousands of Hutu fled into the eastern provinces of neighboring Congo, many taking up residence in large, squalid refugee camps. Many of the Hutu extremists involved in the Rwandan genocide, the so-called genocidaires, allied themselves with Mobutu and used the camps as a base from which to continue attacks inside Rwanda.

Rwanda (under a new Tutsi-dominated government) and Uganda decided to support Laurent Kabila, a long-time political opponent of Mobutu, and other rebels in their campaign to depose Mobutu. Kabila promised democratic elections and national reconstruction. But soon after his forces succeeded in overthrowing Mobutu, Kabila had a falling out with his former allies, who accused him of failing to prevent Hutu genocidaires from staging cross-border attacks on Rwanda and of persecuting Congolese Tutsi. In August 1998 Rwanda, and Uganda backed a new rebel group, this one intent on ousting an increasingly repressive Kabila. But this time other regional powers intervened. Angola, Zimbabwe, and Namibia rushed troops to assist Kabila and prevented his otherwise almost certain defeat. These states were concerned about the extent of Ugandan and Rwandan involvement in the Congo. Perhaps more important, Angola and Namibia saw an opportunity to strike a blow against UNITA, the Angolan rebel force that used the Congo as a base in its long civil war against the Angolan government. Before long, thousands of foreign troops had joined Kabila's army in fighting against a proliferating number of rebel forces and their Rwandan and Ugandan allies. To make matters more complicated, Rwandan and Ugandan forces began fighting each other over territory and differences in strategy. In addition, other African states soon became involved in the fighting or threatened to do so. Burundi sent troops to battle Hutu rebels in the DRC, and Sudan, Zambia, Chad, and Libya warned that they might also dispatch forces.

B. The ICJ Opines on Intervention in Internal Conflicts

On June 23, 1999, the Congo brought suit against Uganda in the International Court of Justice (ICJ), charging Uganda with "armed aggression." (The DRC also brought, but subsequently withdrew, suits against Rwanda and Burundi; in May 2002, the DRC initiated new proceedings against Rwanda, which the ICJ dismissed in early 2006 on jurisdictional grounds.) In July 2000, the ICJ issued preliminary measures, directing both Uganda and the DRC to "prevent and refrain from any action, and in particular any armed action, which might . . . aggravate or extend the dispute before the Court." The Court did not issue its judgment on the merits until December 2005 (see Section C below). That judgment relies in part on an earlier landmark decision, *Nicaragua v. United States*, in which the Court considered at length the legality of a third state's intervention in an internal conflict.

The events leading up to that decision began in 1979, when the Sandinistas, a quasi-Marxist revolutionary front, overthrew the dictatorial regime of Anastasio Somoza, then President of the Republic of Nicaragua. The Sandinistas promptly set about the remaking of Nicaraguan society and looked to the Soviet Union and Cuba for assistance. In addition, the Sandinistas supported like-minded revolutionary movements in other countries. In particular, they provided safe haven and other assistance to Marxist rebels seeking to overthrow the government of El Salvador. When Ronald Reagan became President of the United States in 1981, relations between the United States and Nicaragua deteriorated. The United States began to support a group of Nicaraguan rebels, known as the *contras*, in their efforts to overthrow the Sandinistas. The United States supplied financial, political, and military assistance to the *contras*, who pursued their war against the Sandinistas from bases in neighboring Honduras and Costa Rica. In addition, U.S. military personnel or their agents covertly mined Nicaragua's harbors and carried out a number of attacks against Nicaraguan ports and military installations.

In 1984, Nicaragua filed suit against the United States in the ICJ. Nicaragua asserted jurisdiction on the basis of each country's declaration under Article 36(2) of the Court's Statute, which permits the Court to hear any legal disputes between countries in accordance with the terms of their declarations, as well as on a provision in the 1956 Treaty of Friendship, Commerce, and Navigation between the two countries providing for ICJ resolution of disputes relating to the treaty. The United States, getting wind of Nicaragua's intent to file the suit, attempted to modify its acceptance of the ICJ's Article 36(2) jurisdiction just a few days before the suit was filed. Relying on this attempted modification and a variety of other arguments, the United States vigorously contested jurisdiction. When the Court ruled that it did have jurisdiction, the United States refused to participate further in the case, and on October 7, 1985, terminated its acceptance of the Court's jurisdiction under Article 36(2).

Because the ICJ cannot render a default judgment, the Court proceeded to examine the merits of Nicaragua's claims. Although the United States did not participate in the merits phase of the case, its position was clear from various public statements. The United States did not deny that it had supplied the *contras* with money, training, intelligence, and other assistance, though the extent and purpose of U.S. aid was contested. The principal U.S. legal justification was collective self-defense. The United States insisted that Nicaragua was subverting or threatening the governments of neighboring countries—El Salvador, Honduras, and Costa Rica. In particular, the United States claimed that Nicaragua was assisting the Frente Farabundo Martí para la Liberación Nacional (FMLN), the Marxist rebel forces in El Salvador, in their efforts to overthrow the government of that country, by providing the FMLN with arms and other assistance. Among other things, the United States argued that its support for the *contras* was necessary to interdict arms shipments from Nicaragua (and from the Soviet Union and Cuba through Nicaragua) to the FMLN. The Nicaraguan government denied that it was supplying arms to the FMLN and argued that U.S. aid to the *contras* would in any event violate the basic principles governing the use of force.

On June 27, 1986, the Court announced its decision on the merits. This decision remains the Court's most complete pronouncement on legal issues relating to the use of force in international relations. Excerpts of the Court's lengthy judgment are presented below:

Case Concerning Military and Paramilitary Activities in and Against Nicaragua (Nicaragua v. United States)

1986 I.C.J. 14 (June 27)

[Although Nicaragua invoked various multilateral treaties in support of its claims, including the Charters of the United Nations and the Organization of American States, the Court concluded that it could not apply those treaties because of a reservation to the United States acceptance of the Court's jurisdiction that excluded "disputes arising under a multilateral treaty, unless (1) all the parties to the treaty affected by the decision are also parties to the case before the Court. . . ." Because not all the affected states were before the Court, the Court held that it had to decide the case based upon customary international law.]

188. The Court thus finds that both Parties take the view that the principles as to the use of force incorporated in the United Nations Charter correspond, in essentials, to those found in customary international law. The Parties thus both take the view that the fundamental principle in this area is expressed in the terms employed in Article 2, paragraph 4, of the United Nations Charter. They therefore accept a treaty-law obligation to refrain in their international relations from the threat or use of force against the territorial integrity or political independence of any State, or in any other manner inconsistent with the purposes of the United Nations. . . .

193. The general rule prohibiting force allows for certain exceptions [including individual and collective self-defense]. . . .

194. With regard to the characteristics governing the right of self-defence . . . [t]he Parties also agree in holding that whether the response to the attack is lawful depends on observance of the criteria of the necessity and the proportionality of the measures taken in self-defence. Since the existence of the right of collective self-defence is established in customary international law, the Court must define the specific conditions which may have to be met for its exercise, in addition to the conditions of necessity and proportionality to which the Parties have referred.

195. In the case of individual self-defence, the exercise of this right is subject to the State concerned having been the victim of an armed attack. Reliance on collective self-defence of course does not remove the need for this. There appears now to be general agreement on the nature of the acts which can be treated as constituting armed attacks. In particular . . . an armed attack must be understood as including not merely action by regular armed forces across an international border, but also "the sending by or on behalf of a State of armed bands, groups, irregulars or mercenaries, which carry out acts of armed force against another State of such gravity as to amount to" (*inter alia*) an actual armed attack conducted by regular forces, "or its substantial involvement therein." This description, contained in Article 3, paragraph (g), of the Definition of Aggression annexed to General Assembly resolution 3314 (XXIX) [1974], may be taken to reflect customary international law. . . . [I]n customary law, the prohibition of armed attacks may apply to the sending by a State of armed bands to the territory of another State, if such an operation, because of its scale and effects, would have been classified as an armed attack rather than as a mere frontier incident had it been carried out by regular armed forces. But the Court does not believe that the concept of "armed attack" includes . . . assistance to rebels in the form of the provision of weapons or logistical or other support. Such assistance may be regarded as a threat or use of force, or amount to intervention in the internal or external affairs of other States. It is also clear that it is the State which is the victim of an armed attack which must form and declare the view that it has been so attacked. There is no rule in customary international law permitting another State to exercise the right of collective self-defence on the basis of its own assessment of the situation. . . .

199. At all events, the Court finds that in customary international law . . . there is no rule permitting the exercise of collective self-defence in the absence of a request by the State which regards itself as the victim of an armed attack. The Court concludes that the requirement of a request by the State which is the victim of the alleged attack is additional to the requirement that such a State should have declared itself to have been attacked. . . .

202. The principle of non-intervention involves the right of every sovereign State to conduct its affairs without outside interference; though examples of trespass against this principle are not infrequent, the Court considers that it is part and parcel of customary international law. . . . [It is] a corollary of the principle of the sovereign equality of States. . . .

205. . . . [T]he principle [of non-intervention] forbids all States or groups of States to intervene directly or indirectly in internal or external affairs of other States. A prohibited intervention must accordingly be one bearing on matters in which each State is permitted, by the principle of State sovereignty, to decide freely. One of these is the choice of a political, economic, social and cultural system, and the formulation of foreign policy. Intervention is wrongful when it uses methods of

coercion in regard to such choices, which must remain free ones. The element of coercion, which defines, and indeed forms the very essence of, prohibited intervention, is particularly obvious in the case of an intervention which uses force, either in the direct form of military action, or in the indirect form of support for subversive or terrorist armed activities within another State. . . .

209. The Court therefore finds that no such general right of intervention, in support of an opposition within another State, exists in contemporary international law. The Court concludes that acts constituting a breach of the customary principle of non-intervention will also, if they directly or indirectly involve the use of force, constitute a breach of the principle of non-use of force in international relations.

210. [I]f one State acts towards another State in breach of the principle of non-intervention, may a third State lawfully take such action by way of counter-measures against the first State as would otherwise constitute an intervention in its internal affairs? A right to act in this way in the case of intervention would be analogous to the right of collective self-defence in the case of an armed attack, but both the act which gives rise to the reaction, and that reaction itself, would in principle be less grave. . . .

211. The Court has recalled above (paragraphs 193 to 195) that for one State to use force against another, on the ground that that State has committed a wrongful act of force against a third State, is regarded as lawful, by way of exception, only when the wrongful act provoking the response was an armed attack. . . . In the view of the Court, under international law in force today—whether customary international law or that of the United Nations system—States do not have a right of "collective" armed response to acts which do not constitute an "armed attack." . . .

227. . . . . For the most part, the complaints by Nicaragua are of the actual use of force against it by the United States. Of the acts which the Court has found imputable to the Government of the United States, the following are relevant in this respect:

—the laying of mines in Nicaraguan internal or territorial waters in early 1984 . . .

—certain attacks on Nicaraguan ports, oil installations and a naval base. . . .

228. Nicaragua has also claimed that the United States has . . . used force against Nicaragua in breach of its obligation under customary international law inasmuch as it has engaged in 'recruiting, training, arming, equipping, financing, supplying and otherwise encouraging, supporting, aiding, and directing military and paramilitary actions in and against Nicaragua' . . .

. . . [T]he Court finds that, subject to the question whether the action of the United States might be justified as an exercise of the right of self-defence, the United States has committed a prima facie violation of that principle [of non-use of force] by its assistance to the *contras* in Nicaragua, by "organizing or encouraging the organization of irregular forces or armed bands . . . for incursion into the territory of another State," and "participating in acts of civil strife . . . in another State," in the terms of General Assembly resolution 2625 (XXV). According to that resolution, participation of this kind is contrary to the principle of the prohibition of the use of force when the acts of civil strife referred to "involve a threat or use of force." In the view of the Court, while the arming and training of the *contras* can certainly be said to involve the threat or use of force against Nicaragua, this is not necessarily so in respect of all the assistance given by the United States Government. In particular, the Court considers that the mere supply of funds to the *contras*, while undoubtedly an act of intervention in the internal affairs of Nicaragua, as will be explained below, does not in itself amount to a use of force.

229. The Court must thus consider whether, as the Respondent claims, the acts in question of the United States are justified by the exercise of its right of collective self-defence against an armed attack. . . .

230. As regards El Salvador, the Court has found . . . that it is satisfied that between July 1979 and the early months of 1981, an intermittent flow of arms was routed via the territory of Nicaragua to the armed opposition in that country. The Court was not however satisfied that assistance has reached the Salvadorian armed opposition, on a scale of any significance, since the early months of 1981, or that the Government of Nicaragua was responsible for any flow of arms at either period. Even assuming that the supply of arms to the opposition in El Salvador could be treated as imputable to the Government of Nicaragua, to justify invocation of the right of collective self-defence in customary international law, it would have to be equated with an armed attack by Nicaragua on El Salvador. As stated above, the Court is unable to consider that, in customary international law, the provision of arms to the opposition in another State constitutes an armed attack on that State. Even at a time when the arms flow was at its peak, and again assuming the participation of the Nicaraguan Government, that would not constitute such armed attack.

232. [T]he Court is entitled to take account . . . of the actual conduct of El Salvador, Honduras and Costa Rica at the relevant time, as indicative of a belief by the State in question that it was the victim of an armed attack by Nicaragua. . . .

233. [W]hile El Salvador did in fact officially declare itself the victim of an armed attack, and did ask for the United States to exercise its right of collective self-defence, this occurred only on a date much later than the commencement of the United States activities which were allegedly justified by this request. . . . It was only in its Declaration of Intervention filed on 15 August 1984, that El Salvador referred to requests addressed at various dates to the United States for the latter to exercise its right of collective self-defence. . . .

234. As to Honduras and Costa Rica, they also were prompted by the institution of proceedings in this case to address communications to the Court; in neither of these is there mention of armed attack or collective self-defence. . . .

235. There is also an aspect of the conduct of the United States which the Court is entitled to take into account as indicative of the view of that State on the question of the existence of an armed attack. At no time, up to the present, has the United States Government addressed to the Security Council, in connection with the matters the subject of the present case, the report which is required by Article 51 of the United Nations Charter in respect of measures which a State believes itself bound to take when it exercises the right of individual or collective self-defence. . . . [T]his conduct of the United States hardly conforms with the latter's avowed conviction that it was acting in the context of collective self-defence as consecrated by Article 51 of the Charter. . . .

236. Similarly, while no strict legal conclusion may be drawn from the date of El Salvador's announcement that it was the victim of an armed attack, and the date of its official request addressed to the United States concerning the exercise of collective self-defence, those dates have a significance as evidence of El Salvador's view of the situation. The declaration and the request of El Salvador, made publicly for the first time in August 1984, do not support the contention that in 1981 there was an armed attack capable of serving as a legal foundation for United States activities which began in the second half of that year. The States concerned did not behave as though there were an armed attack at the time when the activities

attributed by the United States to Nicaragua, without actually constituting such an attack, were nevertheless the most accentuated. . . .

[The Court goes on to question whether U.S. actions met the requirements of necessity and proportionality, noting that "these measures were only taken . . . several months after the major offensive of the armed opposition against the Government of El Salvador had been completely repulsed," and that "the United States activities . . . relating to the mining of the Nicaraguan ports and the attacks on ports, oil installations, etc." were disproportionate to any aid provided by Nicaragua to the Salvadoran armed opposition.]

240. Nicaragua has laid much emphasis on the intentions it attributes to the Government of the United States in giving aid and support to the *contras*. It contends that the purpose of the policy of the United States and its actions against Nicaragua in pursuance of this policy was, from the beginning, to overthrow the Government of Nicaragua. . . .

241. The Court however does not consider it necessary to seek to establish whether the intention of the United States to secure a change of governmental policies in Nicaragua went so far as to be equated with an endeavour to overthrow the Nicaraguan Government. It appears to the Court to be clearly established first, that the United States intended, by its support of the *contras*, to coerce the Government of Nicaragua in respect of matters in which each State is permitted, by the principle of State sovereignty, to decide freely (see paragraph 205 above); and secondly that the intention of the *contras* themselves was to overthrow the present Government of Nicaragua. . . . The Court considers that in international law, if one State, with a view to the coercion of another State, supports and assists armed bands in that State whose purpose is to overthrow the government of that State, that amounts to an intervention by the one State in the internal affairs of the other, whether or not the political objective of the State giving such support and assistance is equally far reaching. . . .

242. The Court therefore finds that the support given by the United States, up to the end of September 1984, to the military and paramilitary activities of the *contras* in Nicaragua, by financial support, training, supply of weapons, intelligence and logistic support, constitutes a clear breach of the principle of non-intervention. . . .

244. As already noted, Nicaragua has also asserted that the United States is responsible for an 'indirect' form of intervention in its internal affairs inasmuch as it has taken, to Nicaragua's disadvantage, certain action of an economic nature. The Court's attention has been drawn in particular to the cessation of economic aid in April 1981; the 90 per cent reduction in the sugar quota for United States imports from Nicaragua in April 1981; and the trade embargo adopted on 1 May 1985. While admitting in principle that some of these actions were not unlawful in themselves, counsel for Nicaragua argued that these measures of economic constraint add up to a systematic violation of the principle of non-intervention.

245. . . . . At this point, the Court has merely to say that it is unable to regard such action on the economic plane as is here complained of as a breach of the customary-law principle of non-intervention.

246. . . . . As the Court has stated, the principle of non-intervention . . . would certainly lose its effectiveness as a principle of law if intervention were to be justified by a mere request for assistance made by an opposition group in another State. . . . Indeed, it is difficult to see what would remain of the principle of non-intervention in international law if intervention, which is already allowable at the

request of the government of a State, were also to be allowed at the request of the opposition. This would permit any State to intervene at any moment in the internal affairs of another State, whether at the request of the government or at the request of its opposition. . . .

247. The Court has already indicated . . . its conclusion that the conduct of the United States towards Nicaragua cannot be justified by the right of collective self-defence in response to an alleged armed attack on one or other of Nicaragua's neighbours. So far as regards the allegations of supply of arms by Nicaragua to the armed opposition in El Salvador, the Court has indicated that . . . the supply of arms and other support to such bands cannot be equated with armed attack. Nevertheless, such activities may well constitute a breach of the principle of the non-use of force and an intervention in the internal affairs of a State, that is, a form of conduct which is certainly wrongful, but is of lesser gravity than an armed attack. The Court must therefore enquire now whether the activities of the United States towards Nicaragua might be justified as a response to an intervention by that State in the internal affairs of another State in Central America.

249. On the legal level the Court cannot regard response to an intervention by Nicaragua as such a justification. While an armed attack would give rise to an entitlement to collective self-defence, a use of force of a lesser degree of gravity cannot, as the Court has already observed (paragraph 211 above), produce any entitlement to take collective counter-measures involving the use of force. The acts of which Nicaragua is accused, even assuming them to have been established and imputable to that State, could only have justified proportionate counter-measures on the part of the State which had been the victim of these acts, namely El Salvador, Honduras or Costa Rica. They could not justify counter-measures taken by a third State, the United States, and particularly could not justify intervention involving the use of force.

[Senior U.S. officials and members of Congress, in addition to relying on collective self-defense, sometimes justified U.S. support for the *contras*, described by the United States as "freedom fighters," as necessary to oppose what the United States described as a dictatorial, communist regime that did not respect the human rights of its citizens and that was engaged in an arms buildup threatening to its neighbors. The Court offered the following assessment of the legal significance of these claims.]

263. . . . However the regime in Nicaragua be defined, adherence by a State to any particular doctrine does not constitute a violation of customary international law; to hold otherwise would make nonsense of the fundamental principle of State sovereignty, on which the whole of international law rests, and the freedom of choice of the political, social, economic and cultural system of a State. Consequently, Nicaragua's domestic policy options, even assuming that they correspond to the description given of them by the Congress finding, cannot justify on the legal plane the various actions of the Respondent complained of. The Court cannot contemplate the creation of a new rule opening up a right of intervention by one State against another on the ground that the latter has opted for some particular ideology or political system.

268. [W]hile the United States might form its own appraisal of the situation as to respect for human rights in Nicaragua, the use of force could not be the appropriate method to monitor or ensure such respect. With regard to the steps actually taken, the protection of human rights, a strictly humanitarian objective, cannot be compatible with the mining of ports, the destruction of oil installations, or again with the

training, arming and equipping of the *contras*. The Court concludes that the argument derived from the preservation of human rights in Nicaragua cannot afford a legal justification for the conduct of the United States.

By a vote of 12-3, the Court held, among other things, that the U.S. justification of self-defense could not be sustained; that by arming, equipping, and supporting the *contras*, the United States had violated the non-intervention principle; that by its attacks on Puerto Sandino and other Nicaraguan facilities and by laying mines in Nicaraguan waters, the United States had violated the prohibition on the use of force against another State; that the United States was under an obligation to desist immediately from further violations; and that it was under a duty to make reparation to Nicaragua for the injuries caused by its unlawful acts.

Despite the Court's decision, the United States continued to support the *contras*. The Court scheduled further proceedings to determine the amount of reparations to be paid by the United States to Nicaragua. In the late 1980s, at the urging of other Central American states, the Nicaraguan government entered into negotiations with the *contras* and others over a political settlement to the conflict. These negotiations resulted in the Sapoa peace accord, pursuant to which Nicaragua agreed to hold internationally monitored elections. All parties to the conflict, including the United States, tacitly agreed to respect the outcome of the elections. In February 1990, Violeta Barrios de Chamorro defeated Daniel Ortega, the Sandinista incumbent, for the presidency. The United States, which had strongly supported Chamorro's candidacy, was dismayed when Chamorro did not immediately agree to terminate Nicaragua's suit against the United States in the ICJ. The United States indicated its reluctance to provide economic aid to the new government while the suit was still pending. In September 1991, Nicaragua withdrew its suit, prior to a decision on damages.

Notes and Questions

1. Note the asymmetry between the law governing the use of force and the law of self-defense under the Court's decision. Article 2(4) of the UN Charter prohibits all uses of force except those taken in self-defense or with the authorization of the Security Council. But according to the ICJ, Article 51 permits self-defense only in response to an armed attack. Why might the framers of the UN Charter have built that asymmetry into the Charter's design? From the standpoint of the ICJ, what effect did this asymmetry have on the U.S. claim of collective self-defense?

2. In light of the ICJ's decision in the *Nicaragua* case, what could the United States have done lawfully to oppose efforts by Nicaragua to supply the FMLN with arms? Does the Court's decision mean, in essence, that the United States cannot do to Nicaragua what Nicaragua was accused of doing to El Salvador? Note that under the Court's decision, one state may not use forcible countermeasures in the territory of another state for a wrong committed by that state against a third state. Such a use of force would only be permissible as an exercise of collective self-defense in response to an armed attack on that third state.

3. Under the Court's decision, what could El Salvador have done lawfully to block Nicaragua or other states from supplying arms to the FMLN?

4. Does the Court recognize any exceptions to Article 2(4)'s prohibition on the use of force other than self-defense in the event of an armed attack?

5. Can one country's assistance to rebels ever amount to an illegal use of force against that country? To an armed attack? What level of force is required to cross the armed attack threshold? In a recent arbitration decision, the Eritrea-Ethiopia Claims Commission concluded that "geographically limited clashes between small Eritrean and Ethiopian patrols along a remote, unmarked, and disputed border . . . were not of a magnitude to constitute an armed attack." Partial Award, Eritrea Ethiopia Claims Commission, December 19, 2005.

6. Paul S. Reichler, a U.S. lawyer who played a leading role in representing Nicaragua in the ICJ, provides the following account of Nicaragua's aims in suing the United States. Reichler notes that U.S. aid to the *contras* was highly controversial within the United States, in particular within the U.S. Congress. He goes on to explain:

> It was clear that to win the debate in Congress we had to change the question. That was the reason for proposing that Nicaragua sue the United States in the World Court: to change the focus of the debate in Congress in order to win forthcoming votes on Contra aid. The question would no longer be the simplistic one asked (and answered) by the Reagan Administration: whether the Sandinistas were Communists whose very existence threatened U.S. interests. With the United States in the defendant's dock in The Hague, members of Congress would have to ask themselves whether U.S. national interests were truly served when America wantonly disregarded, and thereby undermined, the most fundamental principles of international law. As Abe Chayes [a member of Nicaragua's legal team] put it during our meeting in Cambridge, the suit would force a change in the debate by holding up a mirror to America's face and challenging its image of itself as a law-abiding nation proud of its role in creating, supporting and defending the international legal order.

Paul S. Reichler, *Holding America to Its Own Best Standards: Abe Chayes and Nicaragua in the World Court*, 42 Harv. Intl. L.J. 15, 22-23 (2001). Is this an appropriate use of the ICJ's contentious jurisdiction?

C. The Congo Revisited

Facing a rapidly widening regional conflict involving the DRC and other African states, the United Nations struggled to broker a cease-fire and to formulate a viable peace plan. Early peacekeeping proposals ran aground for a variety of reasons, including U.S. concerns about attempting peacekeeping in a dangerous and unstable environment. On July 7, 1999, representatives of the DRC, Angola, Namibia, Uganda, and Zimbabwe, as well as three of the principal Congolese rebel groups, signed the Lusaka Agreement, calling for a cease-fire, withdrawal of foreign forces, an inter-Congolese political dialogue, and an international peacekeeping force to monitor implementation of the agreement. The Annex to the Agreement provides a timetable for the completion of tasks set out in the text of the Agreement, and provides, among other things, for the orderly withdrawal of foreign forces within 180 days. Excerpts of the Agreement follow:

Lusaka Cease-Fire Agreement

U.N. Doc. S/1999/815 (1999)

Article I

<u>THE CEASE-FIRE</u>

1. The Parties agree to a cease-fire among all their forces in the DRC. . . .

Article II

<u>SECURITY CONCERNS</u>

4. On the coming into force of this Agreement the Parties commit themselves to immediately address the security concerns of the DRC and her neighbouring countries.

Article III

<u>PRINCIPLES OF THE AGREEMENT</u>

11. a. The United Nations Security Council, acting under Chapter VII of the UN Charter and in collaboration with the OAU [Organization of African Unity], shall be requested to constitute, facilitate and deploy an appropriate peacekeeping force in the DRC to ensure implementation of this Agreement; and taking into account the peculiar situation of the DRC, mandate the peacekeeping force to track down all armed groups in the DRC. In this respect, the UN Security Council shall provide the requisite mandate for the peacekeeping force.

    b. The Parties shall constitute a Joint Military Commission (JMC) which shall, together with the UN/OAU Observer group be responsible for executing, immediately after the coming into force of this Agreement, peacekeeping operations until the deployment of the UN peace-keeping force. . . .

12. The final withdrawal of all foreign forces from the national territory of the DRC shall be carried out in accordance with . . . a withdrawal schedule to be prepared by the UN, the OAU and the JMC. . . .

15. Nothing in the Agreement shall in any way undermine the sovereignty and territorial integrity of the Democratic Republic of Congo.

16. The Parties re-affirm that all ethnic groups and nationalities whose people and territory constituted what became Congo (now DRC) at independence must enjoy equal rights and protection under the law as citizens.

17. The Parties to this Agreement shall take all necessary measures aimed at securing the normalisation of the situation along the international borders of the Democratic Republic of Congo, including the control of illicit trafficking of arms and the infiltration of armed groups. . . .

19. On the coming into force of this Agreement, the Government of the DRC, the armed opposition . . . as well as the unarmed opposition shall enter into an open national dialogue. These inter-Congolese political negotiations involving

les forces vives shall lead to a new political dispensation and national reconciliation in the DRC. The inter-Congolese political negotiations shall be under the aegis of a neutral facilitator to be agreed upon by the Congolese parties. . . .

22.   There shall be a mechanism for disarming militias and armed groups, including the genocidal forces. In this context, all Parties commit themselves to the process of locating, identifying, disarming and assembling all members of armed groups in the DRC. Countries of origin of members of the armed groups commit themselves to taking all the necessary measures to facilitate their repatriation. Such measures may include granting of amnesty in countries where such a measure has been deemed beneficial. It shall, however, not apply in the case of suspects of the crime of genocide. The Parties assume full responsibility of ensuring that armed groups operating alongside their troops or on the territory under their control, comply with the processes leading to dismantling of those groups in particular.

In the months following the Lusaka Agreement, various summit meetings were held among heads of state in the region, with the support of both the United Nations and the OAU, to discuss ways to facilitate implementation of the agreement. But progress was slow, and fighting within the DRC continued to flare up periodically. On June 16, 2000, the UN Security Council adopted Resolution 1304.

Security Council Resolution 1304 (2000)

The Security Council . . .

1. *Calls on* all parties to cease hostilities throughout the territory of the Democratic Republic of the Congo and to fulfil their obligations under the Ceasefire Agreement and the relevant provisions of the 8 April 2000 Kampala disengagement plan [a follow-on agreement supplementing the Lusaka cease-fire agreement];

2. *Reiterates* its unreserved condemnation of the fighting between Ugandan and Rwandan forces in Kisangani in violation of the sovereignty and territorial integrity of the Democratic Republic of the Congo, and *demands* that these forces and those allied to them desist from further fighting;

3. *Demands* that Ugandan and Rwandan forces as well as forces of the Congolese armed opposition and other armed groups immediately and completely withdraw from Kisangani, and calls on all parties to the Ceasefire Agreement to respect the demilitarization of the city and its environs;

4. *Further demands:*

(a) that Uganda and Rwanda, which have violated the sovereignty and territorial integrity of the Democratic Republic of the Congo, withdraw all their forces from the territory of the Democratic Republic of the Congo without further delay, in conformity with the timetable of the Ceasefire Agreement and the 8 April 2000 Kampala disengagement plan;

(b) that each phase of withdrawal completed by Ugandan and Rwandan forces be reciprocated by the other parties in conformity with the same timetable;

927

28 13. The Use of Force

(c) that all other foreign military presence and activity, direct and indirect, in the territory of the Democratic Republic of the Congo be brought to an end in conformity with the provisions of the Ceasefire Agreement.

Notwithstanding Resolution 1304, the Lusaka Agreement, and the partial withdrawal of foreign troops, fighting continued in the Congo, albeit at a lower level. On January 18, 2001, President Laurent Kabila was assassinated by a member of his own security forces. His son, Joseph Kabila, assumed the presidency and began to moderate some of the policies pursued by his father. In particular, Joseph Kabila showed himself more open to peace talks. In the following months, international pressure built on Uganda and Rwanda to withdraw their troops from the DRC, and both countries began to reduce their presence in the DRC.

In July 2002, the DRC and Rwanda reached an agreement on the withdrawal of Rwandan forces from the territory of the DRC. Several months later, Uganda and the DRC signed the Luanda Agreement, which provided for the withdrawal of Ugandan troops and the creation of a joint border security commission. By the end of 2002, most foreign forces had withdrawn from the DRC. Nonetheless, fighting among the various internal factions intensified in 2003, and incidents of ethnic cleansing took place throughout the region, even next to the UN compound. As the violence spiraled out of control, the UN Security Council authorized the deployment of a French-led International Emergency Multinational Force (IEMF) to restore security in Bunia, the administrative center of Ituri province. Given its small size and limited mandate, however, IEMF has had only a modest impact on the continuing violence in the region.

In 2003, several of the principal internal warring factions joined a Government of National Unity and Transition, and substituted political infighting for armed conflict. Critics charged that government ministers were interested principally in enriching themselves. Moreover, several warring factions did not join the new government, and fighting continued in the more remote parts of the country. In addition, some of the warring groups continued to engage in occasional massacres of civilians and attacks on UN peacekeepers. After almost four million deaths over the course of the last ten years, the political situation in the DRC remains fragile at best.

In its 1999 application to the ICJ, the DRC accused Uganda of "acts of armed aggression . . . in flagrant violation of the United Nations Charter and of the Charter of the Organization of African Unity," of providing "unlimited aid to rebels in the form of arms and armed troops, in return for the right to exploit the wealth of the Congo," and of gross violations of international humanitarian and human rights law. Uganda in its counterclaims accused the DRC of acts of aggression and attacks on Ugandan diplomatic premises and nationals in Kinshasa. Excerpts of the Court's December 2005 judgment follow:

Case Concerning Armed Activities on the Territory of the Congo (Democratic Republic of the Congo v. Uganda)

2005 I.C.J. (Dec. 19)

43. In response to the DRC's allegations of military and paramilitary activities amounting to aggression, Uganda states that from May 1997 (when President Laur-

ent-Désiré Kabila assumed power in Kinshasa) until 11 September 1998 (the date on which Uganda states that it decided to respond on the basis of self-defence) it was present in the DRC with the latter's consent. It asserts that the DRC's consent to the presence of Ugandan forces was renewed in July 1999 by virtue of the terms of the Lusaka Agreement and extended thereafter. Uganda defends its military actions in the intervening period of 11 September 1998 to 10 July 1999 as lawful self-defence. . . .

45. Relations between Laurent-Désiré Kabila and the Ugandan Government had been close, and with the coming to power of the former there was a common interest in controlling anti-government rebels who were active along the Congo-Uganda border, carrying out in particular cross-border attacks against Uganda. It seems certain that from mid-1997 and during the first part of 1998 Uganda was being allowed to engage in military action against anti-Ugandan rebels in the eastern part of Congolese territory. . . . The DRC has acknowledged that "Ugandan troops were present on the territory of the Democratic Republic of the Congo with the consent of the country's lawful government". . . .

46. A series of bilateral meetings between the two governments . . . culminated in a Protocol on Security along the Common Border being signed on 27 April 1998. . . . The two parties agreed that their respective armies would "co-operate in order to insure security and peace along the common border". The DRC contends that these words do not constitute an "invitation or acceptance by either of the contracting parties to send its army into the other's territory". The Court believes that both the absence of any objection to the presence of Ugandan troops in the DRC in the preceding months, and the practice subsequent to the signing of the Protocol, support the view that the continued presence as before of Ugandan troops would be permitted by the DRC by virtue of the Protocol. . . .

52. [T]he Court draws attention to the fact that the consent that had been given to Uganda to place its forces in the DRC, and to engage in military operations, was not an open-ended consent. The DRC accepted that Uganda could act, or assist in acting, against rebels on the eastern border and in particular to stop them operating across the common border. Even had consent to the Ugandan military presence extended much beyond the end of July 1998, the parameters of that consent, in terms of geographic location and objectives, would have remained thus restricted. [The Court later finds the capture of certain border towns in August 1998 to be "quite outside any mutual understanding between the Parties as to Uganda's presence on Congolese territory. . . ."]

53. [A]t the Victoria Falls Summit [a multilateral peace conference] the DRC accused Rwanda and Uganda of invading its territory. Thus, it appears evident to the Court that . . . any earlier consent by the DRC to the presence of Ugandan troops on its territory had at the latest been withdrawn by 8 August 1998, i.e., the closing date of the Victoria Falls Summit.

[The Court then considers whether the Lusaka agreement constituted consent to the presence of Ugandan troops in the DRC for the post-August 1998 period.]

95. The Lusaka Agreement does not refer to "consent". It confines itself to providing that "[t]he final withdrawal of all foreign forces from the national territory of the DRC shall be carried out in accordance with the Calendar in Annex 'B' of this Agreement and a withdrawal schedule to be prepared by the UN, the OAU and the JMC [Joint Military Commission]". Under the terms of Annex "B", the Calendar for the Implementation of the Ceasefire Agreement was dependent upon a series of designated "Major Events" which were to follow upon the official signature of the

Agreement ("D-Day"). This "Orderly Withdrawal of all Foreign Forces" was to occur on "D-Day plus 180 days." It was provided that, pending that withdrawal, "[a]ll forces shall remain in the declared and recorded locations" in which they were present at the date of signature of the Agreement. . . .

97. The Lusaka Agreement is, as Uganda argues, more than a mere ceasefire agreement, in that it lays down various "principles" (Art. III) which cover both the internal situation within the DRC and its relations with its neighbours. . . . However, the Court cannot accept the argument . . . that the Lusaka Agreement constituted "an acceptance by all parties of Uganda's justification for sending additional troops into the DRC between mid-September 1998 and mid-July 1999."

98. A more complex question . . . was whether the calendar for withdrawal and its relationship to the series of "Major Events," taken together with the reference to the "D-Day plus 180 days", constituted consent by the DRC to the presence of Ugandan forces for at least 180 days from 10 July 1999—and indeed beyond that time if the envisaged necessary "Major Events" did not occur.

99. The Court is of the view that, notwithstanding the special features of the Lusaka Agreement just described, this conclusion cannot be drawn. The Agreement took as its starting point the realities on the ground. Among those realities were the major Ugandan military deployment across vast areas of the DRC and the massive loss of life over the preceding months. The arrangements made at Lusaka, to progress towards withdrawal of foreign forces and an eventual peace, with security for all concerned, were directed at these factors on the ground and at the realities of the unstable political and security situation. The provisions of the Lusaka Agreement thus represented an agreed *modus operandi* for the parties. . . . In accepting this *modus operandi* the DRC did not "consent" to the presence of Ugandan troops. It simply concurred that there should be a process to end that reality in an orderly fashion. [The DRC] did not thereby recognize the situation on the ground as legal, either before the Lusaka Agreement or in the period that would pass until the fulfilment of its terms.

[After concluding that subsequent agreements modifying the Lusaka withdrawal timetable also did not constitute consent to the presence of Ugandan troops in the DRC, the Court turns to Uganda's claims of self-defense, focusing on the period after September 11, 1998, the date of a change in Uganda's policy toward the DRC.]

108. . . . 11 September was the date of issue of the "Position of the [Ugandan] High Command on the Presence of the UPDF [Ugandan Peoples' Defence Forces] in the DRC" (hereinafter "the Ugandan High Command document"). . . . Uganda now greatly increased the number of its troops from that date on. Uganda acknowledges that its military operations thereafter can only be justified by reference to an entitlement to act in self-defence.

109. . . . The High Command document . . . provides the basis for the operation known as operation "Safe Haven." The document reads as follows:

> WHEREAS for a long time the DRC has been used by the enemies of Uganda as a base and launching pad for attacks against Uganda;
> AND
> WHEREAS the successive governments of the DRC have not been in effective control of all the territory of the Congo; . . .
> NOW THEREFORE the High Command sitting in Kampala this 11th day of September, 1998, resolves to maintain forces of the UPDF in order to secure Uganda's legitimate security interests which are the following: . . .

2. To enable UPDF neutralize [sic] Uganda dissident groups which have been receiving assistance from the Government of the DRC and the Sudan.

3. To ensure that the political and administrative vacuum, and instability caused by the fighting between the rebels and the Congolese Army and its allies do not adversely affect the security of Uganda.

4. To prevent the genocidal elements . . . which have been launching attacks on the people of Uganda from the DRC, from continuing to do so.

5. To be in position to safeguard the territory [sic] integrity of Uganda against irresponsible threats of invasion from certain forces.

119. The Court first observes that the objectives of operation "Safe Haven," as stated in the Ugandan High Command document (see paragraph 109 above), were not consonant with the concept of self-defence as understood in international law.

120. Uganda in its response to the question put to it by Judge Kooijmans confirms that the changed policies of President Kabila had meant that co-operation in controlling insurgency in the border areas had been replaced by "stepped-up cross-border attacks against Uganda by the ADF [the Allied Democratic Forces, a rebel group opposed to the Ugandan government with bases in the DRC], which was being re-supplied and re-equipped by the Sudan and the DRC Government." [After reviewing the evidence adduced in support of Uganda's claim of DRC support for ADF attacks on Uganda, the Court continues:]

143. The Court recalls that Uganda has insisted in this case that operation "Safe Haven" was not a use of force against an anticipated attack. [After noting it would not express a view on the legality of anticipatory self-defense, the Court continues:] The Court feels constrained, however, to observe that the wording of the Ugandan High Command document on the position regarding the presence of the UPDF in the DRC makes no reference whatever to armed attacks that have already occurred against Uganda at the hands of the DRC (or indeed by persons for whose action the DRC is claimed to be responsible). Rather, the position of the High Command is that it is necessary "to secure Uganda's legitimate security interests." The specified security needs are essentially preventative—to ensure that the political vacuum does not adversely affect Uganda, to prevent attacks from "genocidal elements," to be in a position to safeguard Uganda from irresponsible threats of invasion, to "deny the Sudan the opportunity to use the territory of the DRC to destabilize Uganda." Only one of the five listed objectives refers to a response to acts that had already taken place—the neutralization of "Uganda dissident groups which have been receiving assistance from the Government of the DRC and the Sudan."

144. While relying heavily on this document, Uganda nonetheless insisted to the Court that after 11 September 1998 the UPDF was acting in self-defence in response to attacks that had occurred. . . .

145. The Court would first observe that in August and early September 1998 Uganda did not report to the Security Council events that it had regarded as requiring it to act in self-defence.

146. It is further to be noted that, while Uganda claimed to have acted in self-defence, it did not ever claim that it had been subjected to an armed attack by the armed forces of the DRC. The "armed attacks" to which reference was made came rather from the ADF. The Court has found above that there is no satisfactory proof of the involvement in these attacks, direct or indirect, of the Government of the DRC. The attacks did not emanate from armed bands or irregulars sent by the DRC or on behalf of the DRC, within the sense of Article 3(g) of General Assembly

resolution 3314 (XXIX) on the definition of aggression, adopted on 14 December 1974. The Court is of the view that, on the evidence before it, even if this series of deplorable attacks could be regarded as cumulative in character, they still remained non-attributable to the DRC. . . .

153. The evidence has shown that the UPDF traversed vast areas of the DRC, violating the sovereignty of that country. It engaged in military operations in a multitude of locations. . . . These were grave violations of Article 2, paragraph 4, of the Charter.

The Court goes on to observe that Uganda helped "launch an offensive together with various factions which sought to overthrow the Government of the DRC," and that by providing training and military support to rebel forces Uganda had violated the principles of non-use of force and non-intervention. The Court further found Uganda responsible for grave violations of humanitarian and human rights law, and ordered Uganda to pay reparations to the DRC. Finally, while the Court dismissed most of Uganda's counterclaims, it did find the DRC responsible for attacks on the Ugandan embassy and diplomatic personnel in Kinshasa, and ordered the DRC to pay reparations to Uganda for those assaults.

Notes and Questions

1. Do you agree with the Court's interpretation of the Lusaka agreement? Once a state withdraws its consent to the presence of foreign troops, how quickly must those troops be removed?

2. Do you agree with the Court that the objectives of Operation Safe Haven, as expressed in the High Command document, are inconsistent with a claim of self-defense? What steps were lawfully open to Uganda to oppose attacks launched against it by rebel forces based in the DRC? How might the analysis change if it could be shown that the rebel forces were sent across the border by the DRC?

3. Given that the Court's decision came after most foreign forces had been withdrawn from the DRC, what impact is the decision likely to have? Would you anticipate that the DRC will comply with the order to pay reparations?

D. Note on Peacekeeping

The Lusaka Cease-Fire Agreement of July 1999 called for the creation of "an appropriate" force to be constituted and deployed by the United Nations in collaboration with the OAU. In November 1999, the Security Council, acting on the recommendation of the Secretary-General, authorized the establishment of the United Nations Mission in the Democratic Republic of the Congo (MONUC), consisting at the outset of a 90-member team. MONUC's mandate included the following tasks: monitor implementation of the cease-fire and investigate violations; develop an action plan for the disengagement, disarmament, demobilization, and resettlement of the warring factions and the withdrawal of foreign forces; work with the parties to obtain release of prisoners; and facilitate the provision of humanitarian assistance and human rights monitoring, especially for members of vulnerable groups. As of October 24, 2005, MONUC had 16,199 uniformed personnel from 45 countries and approximately 2,600 international and local civilian staff.

Notwithstanding MONUC's deployment, the situation remains precarious. Progress on disarmament and demobilization of combatants remains elusive and may require the deployment of additional peacekeepers. MONUC can claim to have contributed to a lessening of tensions in the region, but a final resolution of the conflict there is not yet in sight.

MONUC is only one in a long line of UN peacekeeping operations. Some experts trace the history of UN peacekeeping back to 1948, when the Security Council stationed 36 unarmed military observers in the Middle East to monitor a tenuous truce in the first Arab-Israeli war. A year later the UN sent military personnel to monitor a cease-fire between India and Pakistan. For many UN historians, however, UN peacekeeping was launched in 1956, when the General Assembly created the UN Emergency Force (UNEF) to secure a cease-fire by deploying between the Egyptian and Israeli armies following the 1956 Sinai war. The force remained in place until Egypt demanded its withdrawal in 1967. Since these early operations, hundreds of thousands of peacekeepers have served in over 60 separate UN peacekeeping operations. More than 1,700 peacekeepers have died while part of UN peacekeeping missions.

For most of the Cold War, peacekeeping constituted the principal UN contribution to the maintenance of international peace. Yet the UN Charter never mentions peacekeeping. Secretary-General Dag Hammarskjold, who was instrumental in the deployment of UNEF, suggested authority for peacekeeping could be found in "Chapter Six and a Half" of the Charter, since peacekeeping falls somewhere between the peaceful measures referred to in Chapter VI and the coercive measures outlined in Chapter VII.

Early peacekeeping operations, sometimes referred to as first-generation peacekeeping, followed a fairly standard pattern. Military personnel, mostly from developing countries, deployed under UN command between warring armies to monitor a previously agreed upon cease-fire and to report any violations. The Security Council authorized peacekeeping operations only with the consent of the warring parties. Consent served two important functions. First, it provided the legal basis for the deployment of armed forces to the territory of a foreign state. Consent distinguished peacekeeping from peace enforcement; the latter involves the use of military force under Chapter VII of the Charter to create peace when one or more parties are unwilling to agree to a cease-fire or to the Security Council's terms for ending a conflict. Second, consent reduced the physical risk to the usually lightly armed peacekeepers, who might otherwise expect a hostile reception from one or more parties. Consent remains a fundamental characteristic of peacekeeping, which continues to operate under a different set of operational and conceptual premises than UN-authorized military operations such as those in the Gulf War.

The presence of peacekeepers, often called "Blue Helmets," has helped stabilize tense situations in many countries. Parties to a conflict are often reluctant to incur the international opprobrium that would follow breach of a UN-supervised ceasefire. But traditional peacekeeping forces are not asked or expected to deal with the issues underlying the conflicts in which they are deployed. Instead, their mere presence is supposed to provide the political space for others to find diplomatic solutions. In some cases, however, the presence of UN peacekeepers may hinder the final resolution of conflicts. Parties to the conflicts sometimes refuse to compromise, preferring the status quo to any available negotiated settlement, and knowing that a military resolution to the underlying dispute is unlikely with peacekeepers in place. As a result, some peacekeeping operations have dragged on for many years. The peacekeeping mission in Cyprus, for example, described in Chapter 2, has been in place continuously since 1964, at considerable expense to UN members.

The United Nations still engages in traditional, first-generation peacekeeping. But in the late 1980s, as the Cold War and various conflicts fueled by it wound down, UN peacekeeping underwent a dramatic metamorphosis. The Security Council and other actors sought to adapt UN peacekeeping to the long-term settlement of various regional conflicts in which peacekeepers actively seek to assist in the implementation of these political settlements. This vastly more complicated and challenging form of peacekeeping is sometimes referred to as second-generation peacekeeping. (The term "generation" refers to the different nature of the two kinds of peacekeeping rather than the period in which an operation began; both types of operations are in place today.) The following excerpt highlights some of the differences between the two "generations" of peacekeeping:

• *Second-generation operations aim primarily at assisting a state or group of states in executing an agreed political solution to a conflict.* During the Cold War, the UN and its member states seized upon peacekeeping as a way to preserve a truce, while assuming that other mechanisms would be employed to settle the underlying issues. . . . [P]eacekeeping . . . aimed to prevent conflicts in the Third World outside the immediate spheres of interest of the United States and Soviet Union from escalating into superpower confrontations. . . . The new peacekeeping rejects this limitation. By working from the starting point of a political settlement, it seeks to end the underlying dispute, not simply avoid its aggravation. It is thus directed more at the long-term than the immediate goal of termination of armed hostilities. . . .

• *Second-generation peacekeeping has complex agendas.* . . . The new peacekeeping includes the broad notion of peace-building, namely creation of conditions for the long-term preservation of the peace brought about by the settlement. This peace-building entails promotion of reconciliation among the former combatants and assisting them in identifying and responding to the longer-term needs of the nation. Fulfilling these agendas has thus far meant that the new peacekeeping undertakes the following nonmilitary functions: verification, supervision, and conduct of elections; supervision of civil administration; promotion and protection of human rights; supervision of law and order and police activities; economic rehabilitation; repatriation of refugees; humanitarian relief; de-mining assistance; public information activities; and training and advice to governmental officials. . . .

• *The new peacekeeping is as likely to respond to an ostensibly internal conflict as to an interstate conflict.* First-generation peacekeeping operations were and are primarily deployed in situations of international conflict. . . . The new peacekeeping responds to both domestic conflicts and international ones. It reflects the realization that separation of and distinction between the two is anachronistic, as most civil wars are both fueled by foreign supporters and have ramifications beyond a state's borders. The UN's horizon of attention has thus fundamentally expanded. Operations can take place in the context of termination of colonial situations, such as Namibia or the Western Sahara, disputes between factions in one state, such as Haiti or Liberia, and wars with a significant interstate dimension, such as Cambodia or Central America. The competing parties will seek out the United Nations to provide international legitimacy to their peace settlement and assistance in implementing it. . . .

• *Second-generation peacekeeping operations involve numerous types of actors.* First-generation operations engaged primarily two sets of participants: military personnel under UN auspices—the Blue Helmets—and states, principally the combatants and a handful of others, such as troop donors and members of the Security Council. The new peacekeeping includes those two groups, but also the following: guerrilla movements; domestic political parties; regional organizations; nongovernmental organizations (for example, in the fields of economic development, human rights, and humanitarian relief); civilian participants in the mission, whether from within the Organization or seconded from governments; international financial institutions; specialized and technical agencies of the United Nations; private foundations; foreign investors; academic institutions; and even domestic criminal organizations. Each has demands and expectations regarding the operations, and can thereby aid or aggravate the UN's work. . . .

• *The new peacekeeping is a fluid phenomenon.* The paradigmatic first-generation operations tended to have one mandate that scarcely changed over time. The new peacekeeping is, however, inherently mercurial and versatile. The UN may adjust the mandate of an operation to respond to the political situation on the ground, adding or eliminating tasks at the behest of the parties and the international community.

Steven R. Ratner, The New UN Peacekeeping: Building Peace in Lands of Conflict After the Cold War 22-24 (1995).

In the late 1980s and 1990s, the United Nations achieved some important, if partial, successes in second-generation peacekeeping. In particular, UN peacekeepers helped countries such as Namibia, El Salvador, and Mozambique make difficult political transitions after periods of protracted conflict. One notable example was the UN Transitional Administration in Cambodia (UNTAC), which was established in 1992 to oversee the 1991 Cambodian peace accords, which provided for the disarmament of Cambodia's four warring factions and the establishment of a new government through the conduct of national elections. UNTAC, with some 20,000 personnel, was given direct control over government ministries dealing with foreign affairs, national defense, finance, public security, and information, and substantial influence over other government agencies that might influence the outcome of the elections. The UN Special Representative to Cambodia was given the authority to assign UN personnel to positions within government agencies, and to reassign or remove Cambodian personnel. Though UNTAC encountered numerous obstacles, it did conduct free and fair elections in 1993. Although the results were problematic in some respects, the peace accord held sufficiently to permit UNTAC to withdraw as planned at the end of 1993.

Encouraged by UNTAC's apparent success, UN peacekeeping operations expanded rapidly in the early 1990s, with many new and complex missions. But along with some limited successes came some highly visible problems. Peacekeepers were deployed with increasing frequency in conflicts where there was no peace to keep, and casualties and criticism mounted. UN peacekeepers in Bosnia and in Somalia from 1992 to 1995, and in Rwanda in 1994, lacked the resources or mandate to compel warring factions to cease fighting. The factions often saw UN forces as partial to one or another side to the conflict, particularly when the peacekeepers used force in self-defense or in furtherance of their mandate. Even the delivery of humanitarian assistance was sometimes seen as assisting one party at the expense of another. As a result, peacekeepers increasingly came under fire or were forced to stand by while civilians were killed by warring factions. The United Nations was humiliated when peacekeepers in Bosnia were chained to artillery pieces in 1995 by Bosnian Serbs seeking to ward off NATO air strikes; the United States was humiliated when its forces suffered casualties in a 1993 firefight in Mogadishu, Somalia, while trying to apprehend a local war lord whose activities had obstructed efforts to achieve a lasting peace. Critics accused the United Nations of trying to combine peacekeeping with peace enforcement, with disastrous results.

In response, individual states and the UN Secretariat began to express doubts about the deployment of new peacekeeping operations absent a clear commitment from member states of the necessary resources and mandate. In 1994, following the debacle in Somalia, the United States promulgated a new policy governing U.S. support for peace operations (including both peacekeeping and peace enforcement), known as Presidential Decision Directive 25. The document itself is classified, but a published executive summary articulated U.S. policy as follows:

> The U.S. will support well-defined peace operations, generally, as a tool to provide finite windows of opportunity to allow combatants to resolve their differences and failed societies to begin to reconstitute themselves. Peace operations should not be open-ended commitments but instead linked to concrete political solutions; otherwise, they normally should not be undertaken.

The Clinton Administration's Policy on Reforming Multilateral Peace Operations, 33 I.L.M. 798, 802-803 (1994).

The Bush Administration entered office reluctant to support broad "nation-building" missions, though it was prepared to support limited peacekeeping efforts it viewed as in U.S. interests. But the aftermath of the wars in Afghanistan and Iraq convinced many U.S. government officials of the need for greater U.S. and international post-conflict peacekeeping and reconstruction capabilities. Thus, in 2004, the Bush Administration proposed a five-year, multilateral Global Peace Operations Initiative (GPOI) to train and equip up to 75,000 peacekeeping troops by the year 2010, most expected to come from various African states. Congress appropriated some $100 million for 2005. Moreover, in November 2005, the Department of Defense issued a new directive intended to enhance U.S. capabilities to conduct "stability operations" and to make such operations "a core U.S. military mission . . . with priority comparable to combat operations." Department of Defense Directive 3000.05 (November 28, 2005).

The earlier reluctance of the United States to support new peacekeeping operations played a role in the debate over whether to expand a small UN peacekeeping mission in Rwanda in 1994, prior to the outbreak of genocide there. A majority of the Security Council, reluctant to put peacekeepers in the middle of an ongoing conflict and unwilling to authorize a Chapter VII mission, decided to reduce the size of the force. The genocide that followed forced yet another reassessment of UN peacekeeping operations. This led to more muscular mandates and more "robust" peacekeeping operations, with peacekeepers more heavily armed and prepared to use force in exceptional cases. In Sierra Leone, for example, UN peacekeepers conducted a military operation in July 2000 to free more than 200 peacekeeping forces that had been held for over two months by anti-government factions.

UN peacekeeping missions remain deployed in many countries, often working in close collaboration with regional organizations. As of January 2006, the United Nations had 15 peacekeeping missions in place, with almost 70,000 uniformed personnel from 108 countries, at an annual cost of over $5 billion.

Efforts to improve the UN's capacity for peacekeeping continue. In August 2000, a special Panel on Peacekeeping Operations released a report containing detailed recommendations on improving UN peace operations. In December 2005, the Security Council and General Assembly jointly created a new Peacebuilding Commission and an associated Peacebuilding Fund. The new body is intended to improve existing efforts to set priorities, mobilize resources, and coordinate post-conflict planning and implementation. It is also supposed to provide strategic-level planning and to ensure that resources are matched to needs in a timely and adequate fashion. The Commission was established as an intergovernmental advisory body, with a core membership of 31 states, including key Security Council members, donors, troop contributors, and others.

Increasingly, UN peacekeeping efforts are being supplemented by regional organization peacekeeping missions. For example, when civil war decimated Liberia in 1990, the Economic Community of West African States (ECOWAS), a subregional organization, took the lead in peace enforcement and peacekeeping operations intended to end the fighting there. But ECOWAS forces (composed principally of Nigerian troops) were accused of bias by one of the principal warring factions and were sometimes heavy-handed in their methods. In Bosnia, UN peace-keepers worked closely with NATO troops and Organization on Security and Cooperation in Europe (OSCE) monitors. In Georgia, a UN mission works together with OSCE monitors and a Commonwealth of Independent States peacekeeping force. In Kosovo, a major effort at the political and economic reconstruction of the province is under way: the United Nations takes the lead on civil administration; the UN High Commissioner on Refugees is responsible for coordinating humanitarian assistance; the OSCE heads democratization and institution-building efforts; and the EU is working on economic development.

IV. HUMANITARIAN INTERVENTION: STOPPING REPRESSION IN KOSOVO

In the vast majority of cases, states that use force internationally do so to further strategic or economic self-interest. Iraq invaded Kuwait to acquire territory and oil; Rwanda intervened in the DRC to secure its border and install what it hoped would be a friendly government. Other states involved in both conflicts had their own economic and strategic interests in mind.

On occasion, however, states use force for what they claim to be disinterested and humanitarian reasons. In the past, such uses of force typically involved efforts by one state to protect a religious minority (sharing the same creed as the intervenors) in another state. In the 1820s, for example, Great Britain, France, and Russia intervened in Greece (then under Ottoman control) following massacres of Greek Christians; similarly, France intervened in Syria in 1860 following massacres of Christians there. More recently, states have used force against governments responsible for widespread atrocities, though usually for self-interested reasons. India invaded East Pakistan (which later became Bangladesh) in 1971 and stopped indiscriminate killings committed by the West Pakistani army; Vietnam invaded Cambodia in 1978 and ousted the murderous Khmer Rouge; Tanzania invaded Uganda in 1979 and ousted the brutal Idi Amin. Significantly, the intervenors in these later cases did not rely on any claimed legal right to intervene for humanitarian reasons. Instead, they sought to justify their actions as self-defense, pointing in each case to acts of alleged aggression by the state in which they intervened.

The legal, political, and moral issues raised by such interventions have provoked long and sometimes passionate debate. Scholars and human rights activists have advanced a variety of legal theories to justify humanitarian intervention—that is, the use of force by one or more states to protect another state's citizens from serious and widespread abuse of human rights. Some contend that humanitarian intervention is not directed against a state's territorial integrity or political independence and thus should not be deemed contrary to the UN Charter's Article 2(4). Others suggest that states exist to further the rights of their citizens and conclude that states that attack their own people, or fail to protect them, should forfeit the legal protections associated with statehood. Some contend that when the Security Council is deadlocked, a claimed preexisting customary international law right of humanitarian intervention should revive. Still others argue that a theory of necessity permits the use of force to avert a humanitarian disaster as the lesser of two evils.

During the Cold War, few governments manifested much interest in any formal acceptance of a doctrine of humanitarian intervention. Most feared that a right to intervene for humanitarian ends would be too vulnerable to abuse, since too many states might invoke it as a pretext for self-interested interventions. Moreover, as the Cold War came to an end, the need for unilateral interventions appeared initially to diminish. The UN Security Council seemed finally to be in a position to reach consensus on interventions with humanitarian aims. In 1991 the Council commended a group of West African states for their intervention to end the civil war then raging in Liberia. Also in 1991, the United States and others interpreted various Gulf War resolutions as providing the "legal space" necessary for military intervention in support of Iraqi Kurds. In December 1992, the Security Council authorized a U.S.-led force to enter Somalia to secure a safe environment for the distribution of humanitarian relief to a starving population. Thereafter, the Council authorized military intervention to provide humanitarian relief in Bosnia, to protect non-combatants threatened by genocide and internal conflict in Rwanda, the DRC, Liberia and Sudan, and to restore democratically elected governments in Haiti and Sierra Leone.

To justify the exercise of its coercive powers under Chapter VII, the Security Council determined that events in each of these cases posed a threat to international peace and security. At times these determinations appeared rather strained. In its December 1992 Somalia resolution, for example, the Council determined "that the magnitude of the human tragedy caused by the conflict in Somalia . . . constitutes a threat to international peace and security," even though the conflict between warring factions was almost exclusively internal. Recall also the Security Council's determination, discussed in Section I of this chapter, that refugee flows rendered Iraq's mistreatment of its nationals a threat to international peace. The Council's finding of a threat to the peace in these and other cases initially generated considerable debate about whether the Council had exceeded its authority in situations of internal turmoil. Currently, however, most states accept that the Council has broad authority to respond to a humanitarian disaster, including through the use of force.

But the Security Council's early post-Cold War harmony did not last long. The brutal disintegration of the Socialist Federal Republic of Yugoslavia placed considerable strain on the relationship between the United States and its allies and the Russian Federation. Those strains came to a head over Kosovo.

A. The Problem

For many years, Kosovo was an autonomous province within the Republic of Serbia, itself part of the Socialist Federal Republic of Yugoslavia. Kosovo was once predominantly Serb. At the end of World War II, its population was approximately half Serb and half Albanian. By 1980, however, Kosovar Albanians constituted approximately 80 percent of the local population, and ethnic Serbs in Kosovo were often the victims of discrimination. Slobodan Milosevic, a rising politician, seized on the situation of Serbs in Kosovo as the basis for a nationalist political platform that ultimately carried him to the presidency of Serbia and later of the Federal Republic of Yugoslavia (FRY), even as nationalism helped break former Yugoslavia apart. In 1989 Milosevic (as President of Serbia) revoked Kosovo's long-standing autonomy. Ethnic Albanians, facing discrimination in employment, education, and public life generally, created a set of parallel institutions to govern their daily life. At the same time, many Kosovars employed insurrectionist tactics in pursuit of independence. Most western governments viewed those tactics as often reprehensible. Indeed, the United States and others characterized the Kosovo Liberation Army (KLA), the primary ethnic Albanian rebel force, as a terrorist organization. As the KLA escalated its attacks on Yugoslav police and other targets, Belgrade intensified its repression of the Kosovar Albanians, leading tens of thousands to flee their villages and seek refuge in the hills.

Western states feared a reprise of the bloody conflicts in Croatia and Bosnia and were determined to act before events escalated into a possible regional conflict involving neighboring Albania and Macedonia, a country with its own large Albanian minority. In 1998 Belgrade agreed under international pressure to accept unarmed international observers in Kosovo to monitor the conduct of Serb police. But human rights abuses by Serb security forces continued. On January 15, 1999, teams of Serb police, apparently retaliating for a recent KLA ambush in which three Serb policemen were killed, entered the town of Racak, where they tortured and brutally murdered some 45 inhabitants. The FRY government announced that those killed in Racak were terrorists who had "opened fire at the police from automatic weapons, bazookas and mortars," but the FRY's actions were widely condemned and prompted Western states to press hard for a political resolution to the conflict.

In February 1999, the Contact Group—the United States, the United Kingdom, France, Germany, Russia, and Italy—pushed both sides into negotiations in Rambouillet, France, over enhanced autonomy for Kosovo. At Rambouillet, the United States and others insisted that Belgrade accept broad but interim autonomy arrangements and permit NATO full access to Kosovo to ensure that the arrangements were carried out. Both sides in the conflict balked. The Kosovar Albanians wanted full independence; Belgrade did not want armed NATO troops roaming part of its territory. Eventually, Western states prevailed on the Kosovars to accept the Rambouillet agreement, but Belgrade refused, despite explicit warnings that NATO might use force if the talks did not succeed. When it became apparent that no agreement would be reached, on March 18, 1999, the talks were suspended. Two days later, Belgrade launched a spring offensive directed in large part against the KLA, but that also encompassed areas in which the KLA was not active. Serb forces expelled or killed many civilians and looted and burned numerous homes in ethnic Albanian villages.

On March 24, 1999, NATO began bombing selected targets in Kosovo and in Serbia proper. Instead of accepting NATO's proposals on Kosovo, Milosevic rapidly escalated his offensive against the Kosovar Albanians. Serb troops and para-military forces wearing black ski masks deported over 800,000 Kosovars in a matter of weeks. In the process, many were physically abused; as many as 10,000 may have been killed. Although NATO initially hoped that its bombing campaign would yield results in a matter of days, the campaign lasted several months. It ended in early June 1999 with a peace agreement and a related Security Council resolution that compelled Milosevic to adhere to terms similar to (though not quite as onerous as) those offered in Rambouillet. By August some 90 percent of the Kosovars who had been forced to flee the province to Albania, Macedonia, and other countries had returned under the protection of NATO peacekeepers.

As Kosovar Albanians returned, many Kosovar Serbs left. Within a matter of months, perhaps half of the Serb population of Kosovo had relocated to Serbia proper. Tensions between the two communities persist. NATO peacekeepers continue to protect the small remaining Serb population from revenge attacks while debate over Kosovo's future status continues.

B. Debating the Legality of NATO Intervention

Government officials, human rights groups, philosophers, and legal scholars alike have vigorously debated the compatibility of NATO's military intervention with Article 2(4) of the UN Charter. Supporters of the intervention emphasize the need to respond to a humanitarian emergency and the multilateral character of NATO decisionmaking. Further, they point to numerous Security Council resolutions in advance of the bombing determining that Belgrade's attacks on Kosovar Albanians threatened international peace and security and demanding an end to violations of the Kosovars' human rights. In Resolution 1160, for example, the Council demanded on March 31, 1998, that Belgrade withdraw its "special police units and cease[] action by the security forces affecting the civilian population." Similarly, in Resolution 1199, adopted on September 23, 1998, the Security Council demanded that Belgrade cease hostilities and negotiate a political settlement. The Council warned that "should the concrete measures demanded in this resolution . . . not be taken . . . [it would] consider further action and additional measures to maintain or restore peace and stability in the region."

But as critics of the intervention point out, the Security Council never expressly authorized NATO's military campaign. NATO's members would have liked, but did not seek, such authorization because it was clear that Russia, with its long historical ties to Serbia, and perhaps also China, which has long opposed what it sees as attempts at asserting Western hegemony, would veto any authorizing resolution. At the same time, by a vote of 12-3, the Security Council on March 26 (two days into the war) rejected a draft resolution introduced by Russia, China, and Namibia condemning the bombing campaign as a violation of international law. Moreover, in Resolution 1244, adopted on June 10, 1999, the Security Council welcomed the political settlement reached at the conclusion of the bombing campaign and the "international presence" that followed the FRY's June agreement with NATO.

For some observers, NATO's action without prior and explicit Security Council authorization amounted to a clear violation of Article 2(4) of the Charter. In their view, humanitarian concerns of the sort that precipitated NATO action do not and should not suffice to override the Charter's norms on the use of force. They argue that the Charter's design reflects a simple but crucial utilitarian calculus: the risk of escalating interstate conflict inherent in any weakening of the constraints on the use of force outweighs the possible benefits of carving out exceptions for cases of grave humanitarian need that, for one reason or another, cannot generate the Security Council consensus needed to authorize military intervention.

Others resist this conclusion as insufficiently responsive to humanitarian concerns and as incompatible with recent state practice. In their view, it is impossible to dismiss an action carried out by the world's richest and most powerful states, all democracies committed to the rule of law, as a simple breach of international law. They argue that the intervention was morally and politically justified and that international law must be flexible enough to accommodate such interventions. Some of these divergent views are reflected in the materials that follow.

1. International Views on NATO's Decision to Use Force

On March 23, 1999, just prior to the commencement of the NATO bombing, NATO Secretary-General Javier Solana made the following statement:

Press Statement of Javier Solana

NATO Press Release 040 (1999)

Good evening, ladies and gentlemen,

I have just directed SACEUR [Supreme Commander Europe] General Clark, to initiate air operations in the Federal Republic of Yugoslavia.

I have taken this decision after extensive consultations in recent days with all the Allies, and after it became clear that the final diplomatic effort of [U.S.] Ambassador [Richard] Holbrooke in Belgrade has not met with success.

All efforts to achieve a negotiated, political solution to the Kosovo crisis having failed, no alternative is open but to take military action. . . .

This military action is intended to support the political aims of the international community.

It will be directed towards disrupting the violent attacks being committed by the Serb Army and Special Police Forces and weakening their ability to cause further humanitarian catastrophe.

We wish thereby to support international efforts to secure Yugoslav agreement to an interim political settlement. . . .

Let me be clear: NATO is not waging war against Yugoslavia.

We have no quarrel with the people of Yugoslavia who for too long have been isolated in Europe because of the policies of their government.

Our objective is to prevent more human suffering and more repression and violence against the civilian population of Kosovo.

We must also act to prevent instability spreading in the region. . . .

We must halt the violence and bring an end to the humanitarian catastrophe now unfolding in Kosovo. . . .

We must stop an authoritarian regime from repressing its people in Europe at the end of the 20th century.

We have a moral duty to do so.

The responsibility is on our shoulders and we will fulfil it.

On March 24, 1999, the day NATO commenced bombing, UN Secretary-General Kofi Annan issued the following statement:

Secretary-General's Statement on NATO Military Action Against Yugoslavia

UN Doc. SG/SM/6938 (1999)

I speak to you at a grave moment for the international community.

Throughout the last year, I have appealed on many occasions to the Yugoslav authorities and the Kosovo Albanians to seek peace over war, compromise over conflict. I deeply regret that, in spite of all the efforts made by the international community, the Yugoslav authorities have persisted in their rejection of a political settlement, which would have halted the bloodshed in Kosovo and secured an equitable peace for the population there. It is indeed tragic that diplomacy has failed, but there are times when the use of force may be legitimate in the pursuit of peace.

In helping maintain international peace and security, Chapter VIII of the United Nations Charter assigns an important role to regional organizations. But as Secretary-General I have many times pointed out, not just in relation to Kosovo, that under the Charter the Security Council has primary responsibility for maintaining international peace and security—and this is explicitly acknowledged in the North Atlantic Treaty. Therefore the Council should be involved in any decision to resort to the use of force.

Shortly before the NATO military campaign began, State Department spokesman James Rubin explained the U.S. position regarding the legality of military action:

There has been extensive consideration of the international legal issue with our NATO allies. We and our NATO allies have looked to numerous factors in concluding that such action, if necessary, would be justified—including the fact that Yugoslav military and police forces have committed serious and widespread violations of international law, and have used excessive and indiscriminate force in violation of international law. The Serbs have failed to comply with the Organization of Security and Cooperation in Europe and NATO verification agreements. They've violated UN Security Council agreements. They're in violation of the requirements of the International Criminal Tribunal and its own unilateral commitments.

Therefore, the Serbs are way out of line and far out of compliance with any reasonable standard of international law. With Belgrade giving every indication that it will prepare a new offensive against Kosovar Albanians, we face the prospect of a new explosion of violence if the international community doesn't take preventative action. Humanitarian suffering and destruction could well exceed that of the 1998 offensive. Serb actions also constitute a threat to the region, particularly Albania and Macedonia and potentially NATO allies, including Greece and Turkey. In addition, these actions constitute a threat to the safety of international observers in Kosovo.

On the basis of such considerations, we and our NATO allies believe there are legitimate grounds to threaten and, if necessary, use military force. These issues have been considered repeatedly in the international bodies—the Organization of Security and Cooperation in Europe, in the North Atlantic Treaty Organization, and in the United Nations and in other international bodies. So we believe, for all these reasons, the Serb side is so far out of line with accepted norms of international behavior, and the dangers of not taking preventative action are so great in terms of humanitarian suffering and further violations of international law that we believe we have legitimate grounds to act.

James P. Rubin, U.S. Department of State, Daily Press Briefing, Mar. 16, 1999.

Asked whether international law permits the use of force against states that "misbehave," Rubin replied:

No, I said that there are principles of international law and specific provisions of international law that they have violated repeatedly. In addition, there is a danger to NATO allies in the region, which thereby brings in the NATO charter. In addition, there is the prospect of a further humanitarian catastrophe. These three reasons, in our view, are legitimate grounds . . . to threaten and, if necessary, use force. That is our view.

Id.

In Senate testimony on April 21, 1999, Assistant Secretary of State Franklin Kramer discussed the Strategic Statement that NATO members intended to issue that year in connection with NATO's fiftieth anniversary summit. Kramer noted that "[w]hile collective defense continues to be the core function of the Alliance, future missions should include 'out-of-area' contingencies such as Bosnia and Kosovo, which threaten the overall strategic stability of Europe." He then added:

As you know, in taking any such NATO action, it is our strong belief that UN Security Council resolutions mandating or authorizing NATO efforts are not required as a matter of international law—and, as the Kosovo situation has shown, that view is widely shared in the Alliance. NATO's actions have been and will remain consistent with the purposes and principles of the United Nations—a proposition reflected in the Washington Treaty [which established NATO] itself. The United States will not accept any statement in the new Strategic Concept that would require a UN Security Council resolution for NATO to act.

NATO's 50th Anniversary Summit: Hearing Before the Senate Committee on Foreign Relations, S. Hrg. 106-144 (1999), at 53.

Other states had varying reactions to NATO's military action in Kosovo:

Reactions to the air strikes outside of the NATO member states were largely supportive, with some notable exceptions. Austria closed its airspace to NATO strike aircraft, stating that there was no UN mandate for the strikes. Russia withdrew its ambassador to NATO and condemned the NATO attacks, arguing that regional alliances may act to restore peace and security only upon specific authorization by the Security Council. For the same reason, Belarus, China, Cuba, India, and Ukraine joined in Russia's condemnation of the attacks.

Many states, however, supported the action. For instance, states from the Organization of the Islamic Conference asserted that "in view of the failure of all diplomatic efforts, due to the intransigence of the Belgrade authorities, a decisive international action was necessary to prevent humanitarian catastrophe and further violations of human rights" in Kosovo. Most significantly, at a meeting on March 26, the Security Council voted down a Russian proposed resolution condemning the attack as a "threat to international peace" and a "flagrant violation" of the UN Charter by a margin of 12 (Argentina, Bahrain, Brazil, Canada, France, Gabon, Gambia, Malaysia, Netherlands, Slovenia, United Kingdom, United States) to 3 (Russia, China, Namibia).

In comments to the press after the vote, Argentina's representative stated that a "large majority of nations have acted together to say that no longer will you be able to violate human rights massively over a long period of time without evoking a reaction." The representative also stated that, while not a UN endorsement of the NATO attacks, the vote bolstered the "legitimacy of what NATO is doing." . . . In the meantime, public demonstrations against the air strikes occurred in various European countries, Australia, and the United States.

Contemporary Practice of the United States Relating to International Law, 93 Am. J. Int'l L. 628, 633-634 (Sean D. Murphy ed., 1999).

Notes and Questions

1. Does Dr. Solana's statement offer a legal justification for NATO's decision to use force? Why might he have avoided articulation of a specific legal rationale?

2. Is Secretary-General Kofi Annan's statement supportive or critical of NATO's use of force?

3. Is the U.S. State Department position persuasive as a legal basis for the use of force? Is the U.S. position on the new NATO Strategic Concept consistent with the UN Charter? Why might the United States have taken such a position?

4. What is the legal significance, if any, of the fact that the Russian draft resolution condemning the bombing failed by a vote of 12-3? Would it have mattered if the resolution failed only because of a U.S. veto? Why would states such as Russia, which voted to condemn the bombing while it was ongoing, later vote in favor of Resolution 1244, which approved the settlement reached as a result of the bombing?

2. Yugoslavia Sues NATO in the ICJ

The FRY condemned NATO's action as blatant aggression. On April 28, 1999, Yugoslavia initiated a complex litigation strategy. In the course of one day, Yugoslavia accepted the compulsory jurisdiction of the Court under Article 36(2) of its Statute, filed applications against the United States, the United Kingdom, France, Germany, Italy, Netherlands, Belgium, Canada, Portugal, and Spain "for the violation of the obligation not to use force," and requested the Court to issue a provisional measures order directing NATO members to refrain from any further use of force. Excerpts from Yugoslavia's Application against Belgium, which is representative of the other applications, follow:

Legality of Use of Force
Application of the Federal Republic of Yugoslavia

(Yugoslavia v. Belgium) 1999 I.C.J. 105 (Apr. 29)

The Government of The Kingdom of Belgium, together with the Governments of other Member States of NATO, took part in the acts of use of force against the Federal Republic of Yugoslavia by taking part in bombing targets in the Federal

Republic of Yugoslavia. In bombing the Federal Republic of Yugoslavia military and civilian targets were attacked. Great numbers of people were killed, including a great many civilians. Residential houses came under attack. Numerous dwellings were destroyed. Enormous damage was caused to schools, hospitals, radio and television stations, cultural and health institutions and to places of worship. A large number of bridges, roads and railway lines were destroyed. Attacks on oil refineries and chemical plants have had serious environmental effects on cities, towns and villages in the Federal Republic of Yugoslavia. The use of weapons containing depleted uranium is having far-reaching consequences for human life. The above-mentioned acts are deliberately creating conditions calculated at the physical destruction of an ethnic group, in whole or in part. . . .

The above acts of the Government of Belgium represent a gross violation of the obligation not to use force against another State. By financing, arming, training and equipping the so-called "Kosovo Liberation Army", support is given to terrorist groups and the secessionist movement in the territory of the Federal Republic of Yugoslavia in breach of the obligation not to intervene in the internal affairs of another State. . . . Furthermore, the obligation contained in the Convention on the Prevention and Punishment of the Crime of Genocide not to impose deliberately on a national group conditions of life calculated to bring about the physical destruction of the group has been breached.

During oral argument, held on May 10, 1999, Professor Ian Brownlie, an Oxford University professor of international law serving as a member of the FRY legal team, urged the Court to reject humanitarian intervention as a legal justification for NATO's bombing campaign. After reviewing various legal authorities in support of his position, Professor Brownlie quoted from a 1986 British Foreign Office Memorandum:

> In fact, the best case that can be made in support of humanitarian intervention is that it cannot be said to be unambiguously illegal. To make that case, it is necessary to demonstrate, in particular by reference to Article 1(3) of the UN Charter, which includes the promotion and encouragement of respect for human rights as one of the Purposes of the United Nations, that paragraphs 7 and 4 of Article 2 do not apply in cases of flagrant violations of human rights. But the overwhelming majority of contemporary legal opinion comes down against the existence of a right of humanitarian intervention, for three main reasons: first, the UN Charter and the corpus of modern international law do not seem specifically to incorporate such a right; secondly, state practice in the past two centuries, and especially since 1945, at best provides only a handful of genuine cases of humanitarian intervention, and, on most assessments, none at all; and finally, on prudential grounds, that the scope for abusing such a right argues strongly against its creation. As Akehurst argues, 'claims by some states that they are entitled to use force to prevent violations of human rights may make other states reluctant to accept legal obligations concerning human rights'. In essence, therefore, the case against making humanitarian intervention an exception to the principle of non-intervention is that its doubtful benefits would be heavily outweighed by its costs in terms of respect for international law.

Oral Pleadings, 10 May 1999, *Legality of Use of Force* (Yugo. v. Belg.) CR/99/14.

After reviewing further legal authorities, Professor Brownlie argued that NATO's motive for intervention was geopolitical rather than humanitarian, and that its tactics (including high-altitude bombing), choice of weapons, and choice of targets were inconsistent with a humanitarian effort. He concluded:

> If the views of the few exponents of humanitarian intervention are studied, it becomes clear that they did not envisage anything like the NATO bombing of the populated areas of Yugoslavia, the damage to the system of health care, the destruction of the civilian infrastructure, the use of prohibited weapons, and the destruction of cultural property on a large scale.

Id.

a. Belgium's Defense

Most of the respondent States confined their arguments principally to the question of the Court's jurisdiction, arguing (among other things) that Yugoslavia's acceptance of jurisdiction should not apply retroactively. Professor Rusen Ergec, speaking for Belgium, went on to address the legality of humanitarian intervention.

Legality of the Use of Force (Yugoslavia v. Belgium)

Oral Pleadings, CR/99/15 (1999)

As regards the intervention, the Kingdom of Belgium takes the view that the Security Council's resolutions . . . provide an unchallengeable basis for the armed intervention. They are clear, and they are based on Chapter VII of the Charter, under which the Security Council may determine the existence of any threat to international peace and security. But we need to go further and develop the idea of armed humanitarian intervention. NATO, and the Kingdom of Belgium in particular, felt obliged to intervene to forestall an ongoing humanitarian catastrophe, acknowledged in Security Council resolutions. To safeguard what? To safeguard, Mr. President, essential values which also rank as *jus cogens*. Are the right to life, physical integrity, the prohibition of torture, are these not norms with the status of *jus cogens*? They undeniably have this status, so much so that international instruments on human rights (the European Human Rights Convention, the agreements mentioned above) protect them in a waiver clause (the power of suspension in case of war of all human rights except right to life and integrity of the individual): thus they are absolute rights, from which we may conclude that they belong to the *jus cogens*. Thus, NATO intervened to protect fundamental values enshrined in the *jus cogens* and to prevent an impending catastrophe recognized as such by the Security Council. There is another important feature of NATO's action: NATO has never questioned the political independence and the territorial integrity of the Federal Republic of Yugoslavia—the Security Council's resolutions, the NATO decisions, and the press releases have, moreover, consistently stressed this. Thus this is not an intervention against the territorial integrity or independence of the former Republic of Yugoslavia. The purpose of NATO's intervention is to rescue a people in peril, in deep distress. For this reason the Kingdom of Belgium takes the view that this is an armed humanitarian intervention, compatible with Article 2, paragraph 4, of the Charter, which covers only intervention against the territorial integrity or political independence of a State.

There is no shortage of precedents. India's intervention in Eastern Pakistan; Tanzania's intervention in Uganda; Vietnam in Cambodia, the West African countries' interventions first in Liberia and then in Sierra Leone. While there may have been certain doubts expressed in the doctrine, and among some members of the international community, these interventions have not been expressly condemned by the relevant United Nations bodies. These precedents, combined with Security Council resolutions and the rejection of the draft Russian resolution on 26 March, which I have already referred to, undoubtedly support and substantiate our contention that the NATO intervention is entirely legal. . . .

The intervention is of a quite exceptional character, prompted by entirely objective criteria. In the circumstances do we need to add another consideration, the tendency in contemporary international law towards a steadily greater protection of minorities? We are accused of encroaching on sovereignty, but the Government of the Kingdom of Belgium would like to quote a passage from a speech given by Mr. Kofi Annan, United Nations Secretary-General, on 30 April last, at the University of Michigan. Mr. Annan said "no Government has the right to hide behind national sovereignty in order to violate the human rights or fundamental freedoms of its peoples", and heralded a very important point, "Emerging slowly, but I believe surely is an international norm against the violent repression of minorities that will and must take precedence over concerns of State sovereignty."

NATO's action has had and still has a further dimension. The aim is to protect a distressed population in the throes of a humanitarian catastrophe, but there is also a need to safeguard the stability of an entire region, for the Security Council resolutions have also noted that the behaviour of the Federal Republic of Yugoslavia in Kosovo was generating a threat to international peace and security by impairing the stability of the whole area. . . . [T]he Government of the Kingdom of Belgium will also plead, in the alternative, that there is a state of necessity.

The state of necessity

The notion of a state of necessity, which is enshrined in all branches of the law, is unquestionably acknowledged in international law. . . .

Allow me to suggest a definition to the Court: what is a state of necessity? A state of necessity is the cause which justifies the violation of a binding rule in order to safeguard, in face of grave and imminent peril, values which are higher than those protected by the rule which has been breached. Let me review the elements of this definition one at a time and set them against the case we are dealing with today.

First, what rule has been breached? We do not accept that any rule has been breached. However, for the sake of argument, let us say that it is the rule prohibiting the use of force. Where is the imminent peril, the grave and imminent peril? There it was— . . . there it is still—the humanitarian catastrophe recorded in the resolutions of the Security Council—an impending peril. What are the higher values which this intervention attempts to safeguard? They are rights of *jus cogens*. It is the collective security of an entire region. And the final element of a state of necessity, I almost forgot, is that the acts must be proportionate; the intervention must be proportional to the threat. The intervention is wholly in proportion to the gravity of the peril; it is limited to aerial bombardments directed solely and exclusively against the war machine of the aggressor and against its military-industrial complex.

b. Yugoslavia's Position on Necessity

In anticipation of Belgium's necessity argument, Professor Paul de Waart argued for the FRY that NATO's action did not satisfy the criteria for necessity:

NATO Member States have no right under the Washington Treaty [establishing NATO] to humanitarian intervention in Kosovo under the pretext of acting in a state of necessity. . . . [According to the International Law Commission, a] state of necessity may not be invoked by a State to defend the wrongfulness of an act unless

(a) the act was the only means of safeguarding an essential interest of the State against a grave and imminent peril; and

(b) the act did not seriously impair an essential interest of the State towards which the obligation existed.

Moreover a state of necessity may not be invoked by a State as a ground for precluding wrongfulness, if, amongst other things, the international obligation with which the act of the State is not in conformity arises out of a peremptory norm of international law or if the State in question has contributed to the occurrence of the state of necessity. . . .

The NATO Members contributed to the state of necessity themselves by their illegal and premature threat of the aerial bombardments. . . .

The NATO aerial bombardments do not meet the [above] criteria. . . . The bombardments were certainly not the only means. Some NATO States have had at their disposal a number of peaceful means for the settlement of disputes. The bombardments impair an essential interest of the Federal Republic of Yugoslavia. Finally but not lastly, the international prohibition of the use of force arises out of a peremptory norm of international law. Moreover, the threat or use of force is a prohibited countermeasure.

Oral Pleadings, 10 May 1999, *Legality of Use of Force* (Yugo. v. Belg.), CR/99/14.

c. The Court's Decision on Jurisdiction

On June 2, 1999, the ICJ rejected Yugoslavia's request for provisional measures. It found that the dispute arose prior to the date of Yugoslavia's acceptance of the jurisdiction of the court, precluding jurisdiction under Article 36(2) of the Court's Statute. The Court also concluded that NATO's acts did not appear to have been "carried out with the intent to destroy a national, ethnical, racial, or religious group," as would be necessary to find jurisdiction under the Genocide Convention.

On December 15, 2004, the Court concluded unanimously that it lacked jurisdiction to decide the FRY's claims. The Court focused on whether the FRY was a party to the Statute of the Court at the time it instituted the proceedings. Under Article 35 of the Statute, the Court is open to "states parties to the present Statute." The FRY's claim to be a party to the Statute rested on its membership in the United Nations. After reviewing the circumstances surrounding the FRY's relationship to the United Nations and the FRY's claim that it continued the legal personality of the Socialist Federal Republic of Yugoslavia following that state's dissolution (see the discussion in Chapter 3), the Court stated that the status of the FRY's UN membership from 1992-2000 was "ambiguous and open to different assessments." The Court concluded that this confusing situation ended when the FRY's newly elected president requested UN membership in 2000 and the Security Council and General Assembly approved the request. In view of these developments, the Court held that the FRY's ambiguous status prior to 2000 did not constitute membership, and thus the FRY was not a party to the ICJ's Statute when it initiated the proceedings. The Court also rejected several alternative grounds on which the Court might have been deemed open to the FRY. *Legality of Use of Force* (Serb. and Mont. v. Belg.), Preliminary Objections, 2004 I.C.J. (Dec. 15).

Seven judges issued a Joint Declaration stating that, although they agreed with the outcome, they disagreed with the Court's reasoning. They noted that at the provisional measures phase of the case, the Court had questioned its jurisdiction to rule on Yugoslavia's application on different grounds, focusing then on the fact that the cause of action arose prior to the filing of Yugoslavia's declaration accepting the jurisdiction of the Court. The Declaration noted further that the Court's opinion "could call into question" the Court's prior rulings on jurisdiction "in the case brought by Bosnia-Herzegovina against Serbia and Montenegro for the application of the Genocide Convention," since those rulings seem to assume that Yugoslavia was a party to the Court's statute at the relevant time.

Notes and Questions

1. Do you agree with Professor Brownlie that NATO's motivation for intervention was geopolitical rather than humanitarian? Does NATO's motivation affect the legality of the intervention?

2. How should the Court have ruled on Yugoslavia's claims if the Court had reached the merits? Do you agree with Belgium that Security Council resolutions provide "an unchallengeable basis for the armed intervention?" Do you find Belgium's necessity defense persuasive? What would be the implications for the UN Charter use-of-force framework if the Court accepted Belgium's necessity defense?

3. Some U.S. allies, most notably the United Kingdom, declared, in the words of Foreign Secretary Robin Cook, that "states do have the right to use force in the case of overwhelming humanitarian necessity." The United States, however, refused to embrace humanitarian intervention as a legal justification. In discussing the U.S. position, State Department Legal Adviser William Taft later posed the following question:

> Is it better to have a very strict rule prohibiting the use of force that is in some rare cases simply not complied with, or should we adopt a broader rule that attempts to anticipate those rare cases and approve them in advance generically? Advocates of a strict rule argue that states will inevitably interpret a broader rule too liberally; it is better, they say, to maintain a tight rule and accept that in limited contexts the rule might have to be broken. Others argue that even though it is difficult to formulate a rule that covers all cases wisely, an admittedly imperfect rule that states are not expected to follow in every situation undermines the credibility of the law.

William Taft, IV, *International Law and the Use of Force*, 36 Geo. J. Int'l L. 659, 662 (2004). Which do you think is preferable, a strict rule or a broad one?

3. Scholarly Reactions to Kosovo

Legal academics were sharply divided in their response to NATO's intervention in Kosovo. Some condemned it as an open breach of the UN Charter and customary international law. Others praised it as ushering in a new era in which the protection of human rights would take precedence over outmoded notions of state sovereignty. But many scholars offered a more nuanced evaluation, as reflected in the following excerpts.

Ruth Wedgwood, *NATO's Campaign in Yugoslavia*

93 Am. J. Intl. L. 828, 828-833 (1999)

The lack of any simple precedent for the air campaign is only a starting place in deciding upon legality, for the formal system of international law cannot claim a monopoly on generative power. The lack of any single source of rules or ultimate arbiter of disputes in international affairs means that state practice remains key to the shaping of legal norms. When an action is deemed morally urgent by a majority of states—even an action involving the use of force—it is likely to shape a legal justification to match.

The war over Kosovo may mark the end of Security Council classicism—the common belief that all necessary and legitimate uses of force outside the Council's decision can necessarily be accommodated within the paradigm of interstate self-defense. It may also mark the emergence of a limited and conditional right of humanitarian intervention, permitting the use of force to protect the lives of a threatened population when the decision is taken by what most of the world would recognize as a responsible multilateral organization and the Security Council does not oppose the action. . . .

In its explanation of the Kosovo military intervention, the United States has emphasized the goals of the NATO action, rather than the basis in international law for authorization of the use of force. President Clinton stated that the action was designed to avert a humanitarian catastrophe, preserve stability in a key part of Europe, and maintain the credibility of NATO. U.S. government lawyers, perhaps more mindful of precedent, have rested on a so-called elements approach—also styled as "fact-based factors." Elegant or not, this is in part a practical prudence, mixing circumstances and principle to qualify any universalist theory or wide-ranging rule that might prove less attractive in other hands. There is, in fact, no shortage of theories to legitimate the Kosovo campaign. But the legal scholar faces a paradox reminiscent of Justice Cardozo's famously maddening opinions—no single argument quite carries the day, even while the ensemble seems sufficient. . . .

Within the ken of treatise writers, humanitarian intervention has inconstant support. Some note its infrequent use and the danger of pretextual disguise of national ambitions. Others argue that a more direct assignment of the task of humanitarian protection to the United Nations might increase its legitimacy, and hence the willingness to discharge the duty through collective means. But many have argued against procedural perfectionism in times of emergency, when key normative principles are at stake, and United Nations security machinery fails to work. The aims of the UN Charter are to guarantee human rights and international security, and while the danger of increasing the scale of a conflict is always to be considered, the use of military action to protect a beleaguered population may advance humane values without significant danger to stability.

Richard A. Falk, *Kosovo, World Order, and the Future of International Law*

93 Am. J. Intl. L. 847, 848, 852 (1999)

It is jurisprudentially problematic *both* to regard "ethnic cleansing" as intolerable to the international community and to condemn the form and substance of the NATO interventionary response designed to prevent it. And yet just such a doctrinal tension seems to follow from the perspectives of international law and world order. My attempt here is to defend such a double condemnation as posing the essential normative challenge for the future: *genocidal behavior cannot be shielded by claims of sovereignty, but neither can these claims be overridden by unauthorized uses of force delivered in an excessive and inappropriate manner.*

[Professor Falk then reviews the Kosovo policy dilemma. He notes that in the view of proponents of the intervention, the Kosovar Albanian population was in "severe jeopardy," the UN appeared incapable of effectively addressing the problem, and diplomatic remedies had been exhausted. On the other hand, he notes that critics respond that the Security Council did not authorize the intervention, that a less rigid and confrontational diplomacy might have produced a satisfactory resolution, and that "the massive Serb resort to ethnic cleansing by the most brutal means [may be regarded] as largely an effect of the bombing rather than as an urgent stimulus for a plan that would otherwise have been carried out more gradually."]

Putting these two major lines of interpretation together leaves one with the disturbing impression that humanitarian intervention on behalf of Albanian Kosovars was *necessary* but, under the circumstances, *impossible.* It was necessary to prevent a humanitarian catastrophe in the form of ethnic cleansing. It was impossible because of the political unavailability of an appropriate means. The selection of such a means was blocked by deep divisions between leading European states, and by the resolve to insist on a NATO solution. It also reflected the disinclination of the citizenry of the NATO countries, especially Germany and the United States, to bear the considerable human costs that might have followed from the adoption of a legally and morally more acceptable form of intervention. As this phrasing suggests, the most helpful form of legal appraisal is one of *degree*, conceiving of legality and illegality by reference to a spectrum. The more "reasonable" a response, the closer to the legality end of the spectrum. In relation to Kosovo, the contention here is that plausible options were available to give the action taken a higher degree of legality (without compromising the humanitarian mission), and thus to improve its status as a precedent for the future.

III. REJECTING LEGALISM

[R]eliance on legalistic analysis is particularly unfortunate for the future of international law. It puts international lawyers in the uncomfortable role that Immanuel Kant accused them of in *Perpetual Peace*, namely, that of being "miserable consolers". . . . The basic undertaking of the Charter was to assign exclusive control over nondefensive uses of force to the Security Council, and to accept the limits on response that this entailed as a result of vesting the five permanent members with a right of veto. In the setting of the Persian Gulf war, this Charter framework was reaffirmed in the form of China's agreeing to "abstain,". . . .

Similarly, the legalistic contentions of those that point to domestic jurisdiction and veto powers as precluding humanitarian intervention occupy untenable ground. It is correct that normal textual readings are on their side, and that the Charter system cannot be legally bypassed in the manner attempted by NATO. Yet it is equally true that to regard the textual barriers to humanitarian intervention as decisive in the face of genocidal behavior is politically and morally unacceptable, especially in view of the qualifications imposed on unconditional claims of sovereignty by the expanded conception of international human rights. . . .

In essence, the textual level of analysis, upon which legalists rely, cannot give a satisfactory basis for NATO intervention; nor can it provide a suitable rationale for rejecting the humanitarian imperative to rescue the potential victims of genocidal policies in Kosovo. Moreover, textualism does not help focus attention on whether the means chosen were legally acceptable in light of the goals being pursued. More nuanced attention to context is required so that the debate can be reformulated in a manner corresponding with the broad injunction to seek a global security system that contributes to the achievement of "humane governance" on a global scale. Otherwise, the self-marginalization of international law and international lawyers is assured in contemporary situations involving claims to use force, consigning their vocational fate to the demeaning roles of "apologist" or "utopian."

IV. THE GEOPOLITICAL PREROGATIVE

The main problem with presupposing the validity of NATO's response is that it focuses exclusively on the injustice of Milosevic's policies in Kosovo, and does not consider the injustice of the NATO response. My contention is that, unless this double injustice is placed in focus, no jurisprudential appraisal will be generally convincing, nor should it be. . . .

Against this background, my argument centers on the need to ground a legal appraisal, and an appeal to justice, on the contextual reality of Kosovo, which includes the inability and unwillingness of NATO to fashion a response that was commensurate to the challenge. Because of this fundamental circumstance, no clear line of legal inference can be persuasively drawn: in effect, it was justifiable to act, but not in the manner undertaken.

[Professor Falk then goes on to identify options NATO could have pursued, including more flexible diplomacy and tactics of warfare more sensitive to the risks to civilians.]

Notes and Questions

1. Do you agree with Professor Wedgwood that the "ensemble" of arguments supporting NATO intervention in Kosovo adds up to an adequate legal justification? Does NATO's status as a "responsible multilateral organization" influence your evaluation of the legality of the intervention in Kosovo? Of the legitimacy of that intervention? If so, what other organizations, if any, might be entitled to similar deference?

2. Do you agree with Professor Falk that humanitarian intervention in NATO was both "necessary" and "impossible"? What factors rendered it "impossible"? What should NATO have done differently?

3. What are the implications of NATO's action for the UN Charter legal framework for dealing with interstate uses of force? Consider the views of Professors Simma and Cassese excerpted below:

[A] potential boomerang effect of such breaches can never be excluded, but this danger can at least be reduced by indicating the concrete circumstances that led to a decision *ad hoc* being destined to remain singular. In this regard, NATO has done rather a convincing job. . . . But should the Alliance now set out to include breaches of the UN Charter as a regular part of its strategic programme for the future, this would have an immeasurably more destructive impact on the universal system of collective security embodied in the Charter. To resort to illegality as an explicit *ultima ratio* for reasons as convincing as those put forward in the Kosovo case is one thing. To turn such an exception into a general policy is quite another.

Bruno Simma, *NATO, the UN and the Use of Force: Legal Aspects*, 10 Eur. J. Intl. L. 1, 22 (1999).

The breach of the United Nations Charter occurring in this instance cannot be termed minor. The action of NATO countries radically departs from the Charter system for collective security. . . . It would not be appropriate to object that the United Nations Charter has been violated on many occasions by states resorting to force in breach of Article 2 para. 4: on those occasions states have always tried to justify their action by relying upon (and abusing) Article 51. In the present instance, the member states of NATO have not put forward any legal justification based on the United Nations Charter. . . .

Nor can one confine oneself to hoping that this dramatic departure from UN standards will remain an exception. Once a group of powerful states has realized it can freely escape the strictures of the UN Charter and resort to force without any censure, except for that of public opinion, a Pandora's box may be opened. What will restrain those states or other groups of states from behaving likewise when faced with a similar situation or, at any event, with a situation that in their opinion warrants resort to armed violence? [Cassese goes on to argue that NATO's action was ethical but not legal, and that a limited international law exception for forcible humanitarian countermeasures might be in the process of emerging.]

Antonio Cassese, Ex iniuria ius oritur: *Are We Moving towards International Legitimation of Forcible Humanitarian Countermeasures in the World Community?*, 10 Eur. J. Intl. L. 23, 24-25 (1999).

4. Critics of NATO's intervention note that Western states have refused to intervene in many other countries in which the human rights situation was far worse than that in Kosovo. Does such selectivity undermine the legitimacy of NATO's action? Consider the following comments by Professor Christine Chinkin:

Finally, the Kosovo intervention shows that the West continues to script international law, even while it ignores the constitutional safeguards of the international legal order. The instances since 1990 that are most frequently cited as evidence that humanitarian intervention is evolving as a doctrine of post-Charter international law were initiated by the West and involved action in non-Western states (Iraq, Somalia and Haiti). . . . The alleged doctrine seems to exemplify international lawmaking by the West for its own application, in the name of its "civilizing" mission. Internal disorder and human rights violations are explained in terms of local nationalisms and power struggles without reference to other causes of violence such as economic intervention. The West assumes that its wealth, power and assurance bestow a normative authority that discounts alternative views. Accordingly, it is hard to envisage that other states would be able to undertake such a campaign, either unilaterally or together, against the wishes of permanent members of the Security Council and without being challenged by them.

At the same time, the commitment to human rights that humanitarian intervention supposedly entails does not mean equality of rights worldwide. The human rights of some people are more worth protecting than those of others. Military intervention on behalf of the victims of human rights abuses has not occurred in, inter alia, Sudan, Afghanistan or Ethiopia. It was woefully inadequate and delayed in Rwanda. . . . . It is better to be a refugee in Europe (where "they look like us") than in Africa, although greater efforts are also made to ensure that there is no expectation of long-term shelter from us. "Money for peace" is more likely to be found for some areas than for others. Such selectivity undermines moral authority. It is also reflected in legal scholarship, where, for example, interstate conflict in Central Africa has remained largely unremarked.

Christine M. Chinkin, *Kosovo: A "Good" or "Bad" War?*, 93 Am. J. Intl. L. 841, 846-847 (1999).

C. Evolving Norms: Approaches to Humanitarian Intervention After Kosovo

In the aftermath of Kosovo, UN officials, governments, scholars, and non-governmental organizations (NGOs) have urged the development of clearer norms and procedures to guide decision makers confronted with future cases of widespread and grave human rights abuses. UN Secretary-General Kofi Annan eloquently summarized the need for new approaches:

Secretary-General's Address to the General Assembly

Press Release SG/SM/7136, GA 9596 (1999)

State sovereignty, in its most basic sense, is being redefined by the forces of globalization and international cooperation.

The State is now widely understood to be the servant of its people, and not vice versa. At the same time, individual sovereignty—and by this I mean the human rights and fundamental freedoms of each and every individual as enshrined in our Charter—has been enhanced by a renewed consciousness of the right of every individual to control his or her own destiny. . . .

While the genocide in Rwanda will define for our generation the consequences of inaction in the face of mass murder, the more recent conflict in Kosovo has prompted important questions about the consequences of action in the absence of complete unity on the part of the international community.

It has cast in stark relief the dilemma of what has been called humanitarian intervention: on one side, the question of the legitimacy of an action taken by a regional organization without a United Nations mandate; on the other, the universally recognized imperative of effectively halting gross and systematic violations of human rights with grave humanitarian consequences.

The inability of the international community in the case of Kosovo to reconcile these two equally compelling interests—universal legitimacy and effectiveness in defence of human rights—can only be viewed as a tragedy.

It has revealed the core challenge to the Security Council and to the United Nations as a whole in the next century: to forge unity behind the principle that massive and systematic violations of human rights—wherever they may take place—should not be allowed to stand. . . .

To those for whom the greatest threat to the future of international order is the use of force in the absence of a Security Council mandate, one might ask—not in the context of Kosovo—but in the context of Rwanda: If, in those dark days and hours leading up to the genocide, a coalition of States had been prepared to act in defence of the Tutsi population, but did not receive prompt Council authorization, should such a coalition have stood aside and allowed the horror to unfold?

To those for whom the Kosovo action heralded a new era when States and groups of States can take military action outside the established mechanisms for enforcing international law, one might ask: Is there not a danger of such interventions undermining the imperfect, yet resilient, security system created after the Second World War, and of setting dangerous precedents for future interventions without a clear criterion to decide who might invoke these precedents, and in what circumstances?

———

In September 2000, the Government of Canada responded to Kofi Annan's challenge by establishing the independent International Commission on Intervention and State Sovereignty (ICISS), with 12 prominent individuals from around the world as members. In December 2001, the Commission released a report arguing "that sovereign states have a responsibility to protect their own citizens from avoidable catastrophe—from mass murder and rape, from starvation—but that when they are unwilling or unable to do so, that responsibility must be borne by the broader community of states."

The Commission identified a set of criteria that in its view justified military intervention to protect human rights, including ongoing or imminent "serious and irreparable harm" involving "large scale loss of life," or "large scale 'ethnic cleansing';" the use of force as a last resort; and the use of "proportional means" meaning that "[t]he scale, duration and intensity of the planned military intervention should be the minimum necessary to secure the defined human protection objective." The Responsibility to Protect: Report of the International Commission on Intervention and State Sovereignty (2001). Other organizations and, in some cases, individual governments also proposed similar criteria.

The Secretary-General's High-level panel on Threats, Challenges and Change echoed the ICISS by stating in its December 2004 report that "[w]e endorse the emerging norm that there is a collective international responsibility to protect, exercisable by the Security Council authorizing military intervention as a last resort, in the event of genocide and other large scale killing, ethnic cleansing or serious violations of international humanitarian law which sovereign Governments have proved powerless or unwilling to prevent." The Panel urged the Security Council to adopt an agreed set of guidelines "to maximize the possibility of achieving Security Council consensus around when it is appropriate or not to use coercive action, including armed force . . . and to minimize the possibility of individual Member States bypassing the Security Council." The Panel's proposed guidelines provide:

207. In considering whether to authorize or endorse the use of military force, the Security Council should always address—whatever other considerations it may take into account—at least the following five basic criteria of legitimacy:

(a) *Seriousness of threat.* Is the threatened harm to State or human security of a kind, and sufficiently clear and serious, to justify *prima facie* the use of military force? In the case of internal threats, does it involve genocide and other large-scale killing, ethnic

cleansing or serious violations of international humanitarian law, actual or imminently apprehended?

(b) *Proper purpose.* Is it clear that the primary purpose of the proposed military action is
to halt or avert the threat in question, whatever other purposes or motives may be
involved?

(c) *Last resort.* Has every non-military option for meeting the threat in question been
explored, with reasonable grounds for believing that other measures will not succeed?

(d) *Proportional means.* Are the scale, duration and intensity of the proposed military
action the minimum necessary to meet the threat in question?

(e) *Balance of consequences.* Is there a reasonable chance of the military action being
successful in meeting the threat in question, with the consequences of action not
likely to be worse than the consequences of inaction?

———————————

The Security Council has not adopted the Panel's proposed criteria. However,
the Secretary-General has endorsed the responsibility to protect idea. Similarly, the
heads of state who gathered at the United Nations for the Millenium + 5 Summit
also endorsed the idea, stating "we are prepared to take collective action, in a timely
and decisive manner, through the Security Council, in accordance with the UN
Charter, including Chapter VII, on a case-by-case basis and in cooperation with
relevant regional organizations as appropriate, should peaceful means be inadequate and national authorities are manifestly failing to protect their populations
from genocide, war crimes, ethnic cleansing and crimes against humanity."

Notes and Questions

1. What is Kofi Annan's solution for situations in which a government fails to
curb massive human rights abuses? Is that solution adequate?

2. Do you agree with the High-level Panel that the United Nations should
develop guidelines for intervention in cases involving massive human rights
abuses? Are the guidelines the Panel proposes good ones?

3. Do the proposed guidelines contemplate bypassing the UN Security Council
in some instances? Under what circumstances would that be appropriate?

4. Do you agree with the view that states have a responsibility to protect
nationals of other countries from avoidable catastrophe? What is the basis for
such an obligation? Is the proposal to judge a state's motives realistic or helpful?

5. In the following excerpt, Professor Jane Stromseth argues that it is premature
to set criteria for lawful humanitarian intervention. Do you agree with her analysis?

Any decision to intervene with force for humanitarian purposes inevitably will
involve a delicate and context-specific balancing of principles—the principle of
non-use of force, the central role accorded the Security Council and the reasons behind
it, the importance of protecting fundamental human rights. The goal of resolving
conflicts between such principles abstractly in advance in a doctrinal formulation,
and thus delineating a legal right of intervention, is in tension with the usually
messy, complicated and uncertain way in which conflicts actually present themselves.
Indeed, the historical record of humanitarian intervention is sufficiently ambiguous
that it argues for humility regarding efforts to specify in advance the circumstances in

which states can use force, without Security Council authorization, against other states to protect human rights.

Rather than attempt prematurely to codify legal criteria for humanitarian intervention, it is better to continue the gradual process of normative evolution under the UN Charter framework. Over time, as the cases of the Kurds and Kosovo suggest, the elements of a normative consensus regarding intervention for humanitarian purposes gradually may develop. In this process, any conflicts between the non-intervention norm and the human rights principles at the heart of the UN Charter can be addressed and resolved in concrete situations. Indeed, an international consensus on when humanitarian intervention should be deemed both legitimate and lawful is more likely to emerge over time from the international community's assessment of concrete interventions such as these than from an exercise in codification. Perhaps some day, if sufficient consensus develops, it might be possible to achieve codification on some aspects of humanitarian intervention, but any such effort would be more promising if it were built on a solid foundation of consensus developed through a process of incremental change.

Jane Stromseth, *Rethinking Humanitarian Intervention: The Case for Incremental Change, in* Humanitarian Intervention: Ethical, Legal, and Political Dilemmas 256-57 (J. L. Holzgrefe & Robert O. Keohane eds., 2003).

14

Conceptual Challenges to International Law: Legitimacy, Relevance, and Justice

The second half of the twentieth century witnessed an explosive growth in international law and institutions. The congerie of processes collectively labeled "globalization"—increased trade, the interpenetration of financial markets, the exponential growth of telecommunications and information technologies, and the burgeoning movement of people and ideas across borders—has driven a corresponding boom in international law making. An increasingly dense network of treaties and other law-making instruments purports to govern important aspects of virtually all areas of international life, from trade to the environment, from international criminal law to the law of the sea. Institutions such as the UN Security Council, the World Bank, and the World Trade Organization exercise new or newly expanded authority to address problems between or within states; others, such as the European Court of Human Rights, render decisions on claims raised by individuals against states; still others, such as the International Criminal Court, adjudicate claims that individuals have violated international norms. Some of this vast and growing body of law represents an elaboration of past law in areas previously only thinly regulated; but much of it involves the regulation of areas of life not previously addressed by international law or in ways that intrude on national decision-making authority to an extent that would have seemed inconceivable only a few decades ago.

The trend toward expanded international governance accelerated greatly after 1990. The disintegration of the Soviet Union worked a dramatic and fundamental change in the structure of world politics. Among other things, it revitalized the UN Security Council, allowing it to overcome, at least temporarily, the paralysis engendered by the Cold War. More broadly, it has facilitated increased international cooperation in areas as diverse as the regulation of antipersonnel landmines, arms control, and foreign investment.

As positive as these developments have been in many respects, they have also raised, or at least rendered more pressing, a set of fundamental questions about the legitimacy, relevance, and justice of contemporary international law and institutions. Although these issues overlap to a significant degree, for the sake of analytical clarity we explore each of them in turn.

Legitimacy refers, among other things, to the capacity of legal institutions and norms to engender respect and confidence in those who are subject to them. Legitimacy has procedural as well as substantive components. A particular decision, action, or law may be procedurally legitimate—that is, formulated in accordance with agreed-upon rules, or substantively legitimate—that is, consistent with some theory of justice or morality, or both.

As Professor Daniel Bodansky notes, questions concerning the legitimacy of international law and institutions command considerably more attention now than they have in the past.

> [T]he legitimacy of international governance has, until recently, received little attention. What accounts for this discrepancy? . . .
>
> The answer has two parts. First, until recently international institutions have generally been so weak—they have exercised so little authority—that the issue of their legitimacy has barely arisen. Indeed, many political scientists have questioned whether international institutions have any significant influence at all. Hence, international relations scholars have traditionally focused on the causal role—if any—of international institutions, rather than on their legitimacy.
>
> Second, to the extent that international institutions do influence the behavior of states—to the extent that we can speak of "international governance"—this authority has generally been self-imposed, it rests on the consent of the very states to which it applies. Theories of legitimacy focus on the problem of domination, the imposition of one's will on another. By contrast, the legitimacy of consensual obligations such as contracts or treaties is generally regarded as unproblematic. . . .
>
> As international institutions gain greater authority, however, and their consensual underpinnings erode, questions about their legitimacy are beginning to be voiced. The reinvigoration of the Security Council following the end of the Cold War, for example, has raised concerns about the Council's authority under the UN Charter to make decisions that bind all UN member states, even those that disagree. Although the Security Council's decision-making authority has a consensual origin—the acceptance by the member states of the UN Charter—the relationship between consent and authority has become too attenuated to provide an unproblematic basis of legitimacy, particularly given the domination of the Security Council by its five permanent members. So the question arises: Can the Council's authority be legitimated on some other basis? Is it justified, for example, by the Council's composition and voting rules? Similarly, the strengthened system of dispute resolution under the GATT Uruguay Round Agreements, which created the World Trade Organization (WTO), has raised questions about the de facto authority of the WTO to override domestic environmental and health laws.

Daniel Bodansky, *The Legitimacy of International Governance: A Coming Challenge for International Environmental Law?*, 93 Am. J. Int'l L. 596, 596-597 (1999).

"Relevance" as we use the term in this chapter relates to the efficacy of international law and institutions. For many years, most political scientists and many lawyers have largely relegated international law to the realm of "positive morality." In their view, states acted on the basis of fixed interests dictated by the anarchic nature of the international system. In the absence of any centralized authority capable of making and enforcing international law, states were forced to compete for power and relative status. In this environment, international law could provide only a mask for states pursuing their interests. Powerful states would invoke international law when convenient, and otherwise ignore it. In a nutshell, many political scientists and lawyers denied that international law was really "law" at all.

By contrast, most international lawyers have long maintained that international law, even if it differs from national law in many respects, nonetheless does influence and constrain states and other actors in important ways. They argue that the enforcement model of national legal systems is incomplete, and that states and other actors comply with international law for a variety of reasons, including the law's perceived legitimacy. Increasingly, this position has commanded support from within political science itself. Some political scientists see international law as instrumental to achieving cooperation among states for mutual gains that could not be as efficiently realized in the absence of international law and institutions; others view international law as helping to shape states' identities and therefore their interests.

Finally, in the last Problem in this casebook, we explore the extent to which international law and institutions may be deemed fair or just in their effect on the ability of states, and individuals and groups within states, to achieve desired ends. Justice in this sense has many facets. It involves the equitable distribution of political power and material resources both among and within states. It also relates to the ability of states and individuals to meet pressing social needs, to satisfy different conceptions of the good life, and to share equitably in the burdens and responsibilities of members of an international community.

As a formal matter, of course, all states are juridically equal. But this juridical equality does little to obscure the vast difference in bargaining power among states and other actors. These differences in bargaining power are in turn reflected in the structure, institutions, and norms of international law. To what extent, then, is it possible for international actors to arrive at just outcomes when negotiating treaties and other arrangements dealing with the divergent social, economic, and cultural interests of different political communities? What theories and standards should be employed in attempting to determine what constitutes a just outcome? As international institutions and law proliferate and penetrate more deeply into the life of local communities, these questions have become ever more pressing.

Section I of this chapter considers the legitimacy of UN Security Council decision making in the context of the economic sanctions imposed on Libya following its refusal to surrender two nationals accused of participation in the destruction of Pan Am Flight 103. Section II examines the effectiveness of international law and institutions in responding to the events of September 11, 2001, and their aftermath. Section III examines the justice and allocational fairness of international law in the context of the international response to the AIDS crisis in South Africa.

I. LEGITIMACY AND AUTHORITY IN THE INTERNATIONAL SYSTEM: SECURITY COUNCIL SANCTIONS AGAINST LIBYA

Issues of legitimacy pose difficulties for many international organizations, particularly those with broad mandates and substantial decision-making authority. The European Union (EU), for example, is struggling to address the "democracy deficit," the perception that its executive institutions are overly bureaucratic and excessively remote from the citizens of the member states. Similarly, WTO dispute resolution panels are accused of making decisions in closed proceedings that override decisions made by democratically elected national leaders. But the UN Security Council's authority to impose decisions binding on all states and the formalized inequality of its membership (which includes five veto-wielding members) have rendered the Security Council the principal focus of the legitimacy debate.

Professor W. Michael Reisman describes some of the factors giving rise to concerns about Security Council activism in the early 1990s:

[T]he Cold War has ended and, suddenly, the Council, by national or international governmental standards, seems remarkably effective, as was most recently demonstrated by the expulsion of an aggressor and the liberation of Kuwait. That was a campaign all could applaud because it responded to the sort of international delinquency that, writ large, may threaten every small state. But the expulsion was followed by deployment of the military, economic and diplomatic means at the Council's disposal, with the manifest objective of forcing a leader from power and changing a government. Using the powers of the United Nations to change a national government that two or three of the permanent members dislike is quite different from expelling an aggressor. The UN branch of Saddam Hussein's fan club may be small and shrinking, but actions like these may have precedential dimensions. The permanent members also, in effect, ordered the demarcation of a boundary, a dramatic new policy that makes many political elites elsewhere uneasy. Moreover, the permanent members undertook to sequester the natural resource wealth of a state without its agreement and to require it to pay a potentially large amount of damages, whose quantum and beneficiaries will be determined, in the ultimate instance, by the Council. Thus, with the end of the Cold War, the Council not only has revived atrophied functions, but also has undertaken activities that, arguably, may not have been contemplated at its inception.

Magnifying the disquiet is the fact that, as the Council has become more effective and powerful, it has become more secretive. . . . Before the plenary Council meets in "consultation," in a special room assigned to it near the Security Council, the P-5 have met in "consultation" in a special room now assigned to them outside the Security Council; and before they meet, the P-3, composed of the United States, the United Kingdom and France, have met in "consultation" in one of their missions in New York. . . . After the fifteen members of the Council have consulted and reached their decision, they adjourn to the Council's chamber, where they go through the formal motions of voting and announcing their decision. Decisions that appear to go further than at any time in the history of the United Nations are now ultimately being taken, it seems, by a small group of states separately meeting in secret.

As long as the target was Iraq and the context the continuing UN response to its aggression against Kuwait, the Council's activities, if innovative, were undertaken within a framework clearly contemplated by the Charter. . . . But in its Resolution 731, on January 21, 1992, the Council shifted its attention to Libya and its alleged export of state terrorism. . . . Were the P-3 of the Security Council proclaiming, in fact, a "new world order" in which they constituted, in the vivid expression of Professor Rene-Jean Dupuy, "a world directorate" for anything they determined to be a "threat to the peace"?

W. Michael Reisman, *The Constitutional Crisis in the United Nations*, 87 Am. J. Int'l L. 83, 85 (1993).

Concerns over Security Council activism accelerated as the Council increasingly began to identify threats to international peace and security and to authorize coercive measures in internal conflicts, such as those in Somalia, the former Yugoslavia, Rwanda, and elsewhere, and even in cases involving the overthrow of an elected head of state (in Haiti and Sierra Leone). The Council's imposition of sanctions to compel Libya's surrender of two of its nationals for aircraft sabotage was paralleled by an October 1999 resolution imposing sanctions on Afghanistan to force it to surrender Osama bin Laden. Moreover, the Council has increasingly taken to establishing judicial or quasi-judicial bodies, such as the UN Compensation Commission and the ad hoc international criminal tribunals for the former Yugoslavia and Rwanda, a quasi-legislative endeavor that some doubt is within the Council's powers under the UN Charter. All of this heightened activity, much of it extending well beyond the traditional sphere of the Council's work, has generated demands for greater Security Council accountability.

The limits of Security Council activism were starkly illustrated by the willingness of NATO members to take military action against Yugoslavia over Kosovo in 1999, and by the willingness of the United States and its coalition partners to take military action against Iraq in 2003, in each case without express Security Council authorization. Nonetheless, the Council remains activist in many spheres. In 2001, for example, the Security Council adopted a sweeping anti-terrorism resolution mandating all states to criminalize terrorist acts, freeze funds that might be used to support terrorism, cooperate in law enforcement efforts aimed at terrorism, and report to a new Security Council committee the steps they have taken to implement the resolution. Thus, many states, NGOs, and others continue to urge that the Security Council be reformed to make it more representative, transparent, and accountable.

Such demands tend to take one of two forms. First, some scholars, non-governmental organizations (NGOs), judges, and governmental officials have suggested that the Security Council's decisions should be subject to some form of judicial review by the International Court of Justice (ICJ) to ensure their compatibility with the principles and purposes of the Charter and perhaps with general international law. Second, many states, as well as NGOs and academics, have called for reform of the Security Council's membership and procedures, with the goal of making it more democratic, more transparent, and ultimately, more legitimate. The *Lockerbie* case, discussed below, deals with the issue of judicial review; it is followed by materials dealing with Security Council reform.

A. The Problem

On December 21, 1988, a bomb exploded in the forward cargo hold of Pan Am Flight 103 en route from London to New York. The explosion shattered the plane, which was flying at 31,000 feet. Witnesses on the ground saw "a great ball of flame" and heard what sounded like thunder. All 259 persons on board, including 189 U.S. nationals, were killed. Fiery debris rained down on the small Scottish town of Lockerbie, killing 11 residents and destroying homes and automobiles. (See photo.)

Scotland Yard, assisted by U.S. and other states' law enforcement and intelligence agencies, launched an immediate and massive criminal investigation. Ultimately, over 15,000 people were questioned in more than 30 states. The plane itself was reconstructed from hundreds of thousands of pieces scattered over 845 square miles of Scottish countryside.

Over the course of several years, investigators focused their attention on two Libyan nationals, Abdel Basset Ali al-Megrahi and Lamen Khalifa Fhimah, who worked in Malta for the Libyan national airline. Forensic evidence suggested that close to a pound of plastic explosives had been concealed inside a cassette recorder and packed in a brown Samsonite suitcase. A fragment from the timing device used to detonate the bomb appeared to match one of 20 timers previously sold to a Libyan official. A charred piece of shirt matched one sold to al-Megrahi in Malta, where the bomb was placed on an Air Malta flight for eventual transfer to Pan

Nose Section of Pan Am Flight 103
SOURCE: AP/Wide World Photos

Am 103. An entry found in Fhimah's diary referred cryptically to obtaining Air Malta baggage tags. U.S. and British intelligence agencies concluded that both men were Libyan intelligence officials. But both suspects have steadfastly maintained their innocence and have denied working for Libyan intelligence.

In November 1991, a U.S. grand jury indicted the two Libyan nationals for destruction of a civil aircraft and the killing of U.S. nationals. Similar charges were brought by the Lord High Advocate of Scotland. Lacking an extradition treaty with Libya, the United States and the United Kingdom asked Belgium, which represents U.S. interests in Libya in the absence of a U.S. embassy there, to explore the possibility of an informal arrangement for the surrender of the two suspects for trial in either the United States or Scotland. Libya rejected these overtures. On November 27, 1991, the United States and the United Kingdom issued a joint declaration:

> The British and American Governments today declare that the Government of Libya must:
>   —surrender for trial all those charged with the crime; and accept responsibility for the actions of Libyan officials;
>   —disclose all it knows of this crime, including the names of all those responsible, and allow full access to all witnesses, documents and other material evidence, including all the remaining timers;
>   —pay appropriate compensation.
> We expect Libya to comply promptly and in full.

Statement Announcing Joint Declarations on the Libyan Indictments, http://bush-library.tamu.edu/papers/1991/9142702.html.

Libya rejected these demands and announced its intention to conduct its own judicial investigation. Libya claimed it was entitled to do so under the 1971 Montreal Convention for the Suppression of Unlawful Acts Against the Safety of Civil Aviation (the Montreal Convention). That Convention, excerpted below, requires states either to prosecute or to extradite individuals accused of aircraft sabotage if present on their territory:

Convention for the Suppression of Unlawful Acts Against the Safety of Civil Aviation

974 U.N.T.S. 177 (1971)

Article 1.   1. Any person commits an offence if he unlawfully and intentionally:

(a) performs an act of violence against a person on board an aircraft in flight if that act is likely to endanger the safety of that aircraft; or
(b) destroys an aircraft in service or causes damage to such an aircraft which renders it incapable of flight or which is likely to endanger its safety in flight; or
(c) places or causes to be placed on an aircraft in service, by any means whatsoever, a device or substance which is likely to destroy that aircraft, or to cause damage to it which renders it incapable of flight, or to cause damage to it which is likely to endanger its safety in flight; . . .

Article 3.   Each Contracting State undertakes to make the offences mentioned in Article 1 punishable by severe penalties.

Article 5.   1. Each Contracting State shall take such measures as may be necessary to establish its jurisdiction over the offences in the following cases:

(a) when the offence is committed in the territory of that State;
(b) when the offence is committed against or on board an aircraft registered in that State;
(c) when the aircraft on board which the offence is committed lands in its territory with the alleged offender still on board; . . .

2. Each Contracting State shall likewise take such measures as may be necessary to establish its jurisdiction over the offences mentioned in Article 1 . . . in the case where the alleged offender is present in its territory and it does not extradite him pursuant to Article 8 to any of the States mentioned in paragraph 1 of this Article.

Article 7.   The Contracting State in the territory of which the alleged offender is found shall, if it does not extradite him, be obliged, without exception whatsoever and whether or not the offence was committed in its territory, to submit the case to its competent authorities for the purpose of prosecution. . . .

Article 8.   2. If a Contracting State which makes extradition conditional on the existence of a treaty receives a request for extradition from another Contracting State with which it has no extradition treaty, it may at its option consider this Convention as the legal basis for extradition in respect of the offences. . . .

Article 11.   1. Contracting States shall afford one another the greatest measure of assistance in connection with criminal proceedings brought in respect of the offences. The law of the State requested shall apply in all cases. . . .

Article 14.   1. Any dispute between two or more Contracting States concerning the interpretation or application of this Convention which cannot be settled through negotiation, shall, at the request of one of them, be submitted to arbitration. If within six months from the date of the request for arbitration the Parties are unable to agree on the organization of the arbitration, any one of those Parties may refer the dispute to the International Court of Justice. . . .

B. Forum Shopping: The Security Council and the ICJ

In January 1992, the United States and the United Kingdom, with support from France, which considered Libya responsible for the September 1989 destruction of UTA Flight 772 over Niger, took the issue to the UN Security Council. On January 21, the Council unanimously adopted the following resolution:

Security Council Resolution 731 (1992)

Deeply concerned over results of investigations which implicate officials of the Libyan Government . . . ,

Determined to eliminate international terrorism,

1. *Condemns* the destruction of Pan Am flight 103 and Union de transports aériens (UTA) flight 772 and the resultant loss of hundreds of lives;

2. *Strongly deplores* the fact that the Libyan Government has not yet responded effectively to . . . requests to cooperate fully in establishing responsibility for the terrorist acts referred to above against Pan Am flight 103 and Union de transports aériens (UTA) flight 772;

3. *Urges* the Libyan Government immediately to provide a full and effective response to those requests so as to contribute to the elimination of international terrorism;

4. *Requests* the Secretary-General to seek the cooperation of the Libyan Government to provide a full and effective response to those requests; . . .

6. *Decides* to remain seized of the matter.

In keeping with paragraph 4 of the Resolution, a special envoy of the UN Secretary-General met with Libyan leader Colonel Muammar Qaddafi to seek his cooperation. Qaddafi stated that he could not act inconsistently with Libyan law, which precluded the extradition of Libyan nationals in the absence of an extradition treaty. He further stated that judicial proceedings had already commenced in Libya and that countries with relevant information should provide it to the Libyan authorities. In subsequent discussions, Qaddafi suggested that trial in Malta or any Arab country might be acceptable. Qaddafi also claimed that Libya would sever all ties to terrorist organizations and punish anyone found to be involved in terrorist acts. The United States and the United Kingdom found these proposals unacceptable and returned to the UN Security Council to seek sanctions against Libya to force it to surrender the two suspects for trial.

In response, Libya filed essentially identical Applications in the International Court of Justice (ICJ) against the United States and the United Kingdom, basing jurisdiction on Article 36(1) of the Statute of the Court and Article 14(1) of the Montreal Convention. Libya claimed that the Montreal Convention was the only relevant treaty in force between the parties; that the United States and the United Kingdom were improperly acting to prevent Libya from exercising its jurisdiction over an alleged offender present in Libyan territory in violation of Articles 5 and 7 of the Convention; and that the United States and the United Kingdom were failing to provide Libya with the greatest measure of assistance in its criminal proceedings against the accused offenders, in violation of Article 11 of the Convention.

Three days after oral arguments on Libya's request for provisional measures but prior to the issuance of the Court's decision, the United States and the United Kingdom prevailed on the Security Council to adopt Resolution 748, by a vote of 10-0; Cape Verde, China, India, Morocco, and Zimbabwe abstained.

Security Council Resolution 748 (1992)

Determining . . . that the failure by the Libyan Government to demonstrate, by concrete actions its renunciation of terrorism and in particular its continued failure to respond fully and effectively to the requests in resolution 731 (1992), constitute a threat to international peace and security . . .

Acting under Chapter VII of the Charter of the United Nations,

1. *Decides* that the Libyan Government must now comply without any further delay with paragraph 3 of resolution 731 (1992) . . . .;

2. *Decides also* that the Libyan Government must commit itself definitively to cease all forms of terrorist action and all assistance to terrorist groups and that it must promptly, by concrete actions, demonstrate its renunciation of terrorism;

3. *Decides* that on 15 April 1992 all States shall adopt the measures set out below, which shall apply until the Security Council decides that the Libyan Government has complied with paragraphs 1 and 2 above;

4. *Decides also* that all States shall:

(a) Deny permission to any aircraft to take off from, land in or overfly their territory if it is destined to land in or has taken off from the territory of Libya, unless the particular flight has been approved on grounds of significant humanitarian need . . . ;

(b) Prohibit, by their nationals or from their territory, the supply of any aircraft or aircraft components to Libya. . . .

In addition, Resolution 748 prohibited the export of arms to Libya and required all states to "[s]ignificantly reduce the number and the level of the staff at Libyan diplomatic missions and consular posts," and to close "all Libyan Arab Airlines offices" on their territory. Resolution 748 marked the first time the Council used its coercive powers under Chapter VII to respond to terrorism.

In its April 14, 1992 decisions on Libya's request for provisional measures, the ICJ considered the effect of Resolution 748 on Libya's rights under the Montreal Convention. The decision in the suit against the United States is excerpted below:

Case Concerning Questions of Interpretation and Application of the 1971 Montreal Convention Arising from the Aerial Incident at Lockerbie (Libya v. United States)

1992 I.C.J. Rep. 114 (April 14)

38. Whereas in its observations on Security Council resolution 748 (1992) . . . Libya contends as follows: first, that that resolution does not prejudice the rights of Libya to request the Court to indicate provisional measures, inasmuch as by deciding, in effect, that Libya must surrender its nationals to the United States and the United Kingdom, the Security Council infringes, or threatens to infringe, the enjoyment and the exercise of the rights conferred on Libya by the Montreal Convention and its economic, commercial and diplomatic rights; whereas Libya therefore claims that the United States and the United Kingdom should so act as not to infringe Libya's rights, for example by seeking a suspension of the relevant part of resolution 748 (1992);

39. Whereas Libya in its observations contends, secondly, that the risk of contradiction between the resolution and the provisional measures requested of the Court by Libya does not render the Libyan request inadmissible, since there is in law no competition or hierarchy between the Court and the Security Council, each exercising its own competence; whereas Libya recalls in this connection that it regards the decision of the Security Council as contrary to international law, and considers that the Council has employed its power to characterize the situation for purposes of Chapter VII simply as a pretext to avoid applying the Montreal Convention;

40. Whereas in its observations on Security Council resolution 748 (1992) . . . the United States observes that that resolution was adopted under Chapter VII rather than Chapter VI of the Charter and was framed as a "decision" and contended that, given that binding decision, no object would be served by provisional measures; that, irrespective of the right claimed by Libya under the Montreal Convention, Libya has a Charter-based duty to accept and carry out the decisions in

the resolution, and other States have a Charter-based duty to seek Libya's compliance; that any indication of provisional measures would run a serious risk of conflicting with the work of the Security Council; that the Council had rejected (inter alia) Libya's contention that the matter should be addressed on the basis of the right claimed by Libya under the Montreal Convention, which Libya asks the Court to protect through provisional measures; and that the Court should therefore decline the request;

41. Whereas the Court, in the context of the present proceedings on a request for provisional measures . . . cannot make definitive findings either of fact or of law on the issues relating to the merits, and the right of the Parties to contest such issues at the stage of the merits must remain unaffected by the Court's decision;

42. Whereas both Libya and the United States, as Members of the United Nations, are obliged to accept and carry out the decisions of the Security Council in accordance with Article 25 of the Charter; whereas the Court, which is at the stage of proceedings on provisional measures, considers that prima facie this obligation extends to the decision contained in resolution 748 (1992); and whereas, in accordance with Article 103 of the Charter, the obligations of the Parties in that respect prevail over their obligations under any other international agreement, including the Montreal Convention;

43. Whereas the Court, while thus not at this stage called upon to determine definitively the legal effect of Security Council resolution 748 (1992), considers that, whatever the situation previous to the adoption of that resolution, the rights claimed by Libya under the Montreal Convention cannot now be regarded as appropriate for protection by the indication of provisional measures; . . .

46. For these reasons,

THE COURT,

By eleven votes to five,

Finds that the circumstances of the case are not such as to require the exercise of its power under Article 41 of the Statute to indicate provisional measures.

IN FAVOUR: Vice-President Oda [Japan], Acting President; President Sir Robert Jennings [United Kingdom]; Judges Lachs [Poland], Ago [Italy], Schwebel [United States], Ni [China], Evensen [Norway], Tarassov [Russian Federation], Guillaume [France], Shahabuddeen [Guyana], Aguilar Mawdsley [Venezuela];

AGAINST: Judges Bedjaoui [Algeria], Weeramantry [Sri Lanka], Ranjeva [Madagascar], Ajibola [Nigeria]; Judge ad hoc El-Kosheri [Egypt].

In separate opinions, several of the judges discussed the respective roles of the Court and the Security Council when their functions overlap. Judge Christopher Weeramantry offered the following observations in a dissenting opinion:

An important difference must also be noted between the division of powers in municipal systems and the distribution of powers between the principal organs of the United Nations, for there is not among the United Nations organizations the same strict principle of separation of powers one sometimes finds in municipal systems. . . .

As a judicial organ, it will be the Court's duty from time to time to examine and determine from a strictly legal point of view matters which may at the same time be the subject of determination from an executive or political point of view by another principal organ of the United Nations. The Court by virtue of its nature and constitution applies to the matter before it the concepts, the criteria and the methodology of the judicial process which other organs of the United Nations are naturally not obliged to do. The concepts it uses are juridical concepts, its criteria are standards of legality, it [sic] method is that of legal proof. Its tests of validity and the bases of its decisions are naturally not the same as they would be before a political or executive organ of the United Nations.

Yet this much they have in common—that all organs alike exercise their authority under and in terms of the Charter. There can never truly be a question of opposition of one organ to another but rather a common subjection of all organs to the Charter. The interpretation of Charter provisions is primarily a matter of law, and such questions of law may in appropriate circumstances come before the Court for judicial determination. When this does occur, the Court acts as guardian of the Charter and of international law for, in the international arena, there is no higher body charged with judicial functions and with the determination of questions of interpretation and application of international law. . . . [T]he fact that its judicial decision based upon the law may have political consequences is not a factor that would deflect it from discharging its duties under the Charter of the United Nations and the Statute of the Court.

[Judge Weeramantry goes on to describe the Court as an organ of the United Nations with responsibility as appropriate to support the Security Council in its efforts to maintain international peace and security. He concludes, however, that:]

Since the Court and the Security Council may properly exercise their respective functions with regard to an international dispute or situation, each must in the exercise of the undoubted authority conferred on it exercise its independent judgment in accordance with the Charter. It follows that their assessment of a given situation will not always be in complete coincidence. Especially where matters of legal interpretation are involved, the Court will naturally zealously preserve its independence of judgment, for to do any less would not be a proper compliance with the requirements of the Charter.

1992 I.C.J. Rep. at 160, 165-166, 169.

After reviewing the legislative history of the UN Charter, Judge Weeramantry concludes that the Security Council in discharging its functions must act consistently with the purposes and principles of the UN Charter and in accordance with international law, pursuant to Article 24 of the Charter. Nonetheless, he finds that "the determination under Article 39 of the existence of any threat to the peace, breach of the peace or act of aggression, is one entirely within the discretion of the Council." Judge Weeramantry concludes that the Security Council did not take any binding decisions in Resolution 731; by contrast, he finds that Resolution 748 "must be treated as binding on Libya as on all countries in terms of Article 25 of the United Nations Charter and that, in terms of Article 103, the obligations it lays down prevail over the obligations flowing from any other international agreement. In specific terms, this means that Libya is, *prima facie*, bound by the provisions of that resolution even if they should conflict with the rights Libya claims under the Montreal Convention." Nonetheless, Judge Weeramantry disagrees with the majority's decision on provisional measures, because he believes that the Court could have fashioned a provisional measures order directing the parties to prevent "such aggravation or extension of the dispute as might result in the use of force by either or both Parties" without running counter to Resolution 748.

Judge Mohamed Shahabudeen agreed that by virtue of Article 103, the Council's decision took precedence over Libya's rights under the Montreal Convention. But, he noted, the majority opinion left key questions unresolved:

. . . In this case, it happens that the decision which the Court is asked to give is one which would directly conflict with a decision of the Security Council. That is not an aspect which can be overlooked. Yet, it is not the juridical ground of today's Order. This results not from any collision between the competence of the Security Council and that of the Court, but from a collision between the obligations of Libya under the decision of the Security Council and any obligations which it may have under the Montreal Convention. The Charter says that the former prevail. . . .

The question now raised by Libya's challenge to the validity of resolution 748 (1992) is whether a decision of the Security Council may override the legal rights of States, and, if so, whether there are any limitations on the power of the Council to characterize a situation as one justifying the making of a decision entailing such consequences. Are there any limits to the Council's powers of appreciation? In the equilibrium of forces underpinning the structure of the United Nations within the evolving international order, is there any conceivable point beyond which a legal issue may properly arise as to the competence of the Security Council to produce such overriding results? If there are any limits, what are those limits and what body, if other than the Security Council, is competent to say what those limits are?

If the answers to these delicate and complex questions are all in the negative, the position is potentially curious. It would not, on that account, be necessarily unsustainable in law; and how far the Court can enter the field is another matter. The issues are however important, even though they cannot be examined now.

1992 I.C.J. Rep. at 140, 141-142.

The following year, as the impasse among the three states persisted, the Security Council adopted Resolution 883. The resolution tightened the sanctions on Libya by, among other things, directing all states to freeze any funds owned or controlled by the Libyan government, to preclude the provision to Libya of equipment used to export oil and gas, and to close all Libyan Arab Airlines offices within their territories. Eleven states voted in favor of the resolution; four states—China, Djibouti, Morocco, and Pakistan—abstained.

In 1994, Libya responded to the heightened sanctions regime by suggesting that it might accept a trial before a Scottish court, provided that it sit in a neutral country. The United States and the United Kingdom were initially skeptical of this proposal, viewing it as a Libyan propaganda effort. But Libya's offer, and its rejection of UN sanctions as illegitimate, were beginning to generate significant support from many developing states, including members of the Arab League, the Islamic Conference, and the Organization of African Unity (OAU). In June 1994, for example, the OAU adopted the following resolution.

Resolution on the Crisis Between the Great Jamahiriya and the USA, UK, and France

OAU Res. 1525 (1994)

[The OAU] . . .

1. EXPRESSES ITS APPRECIATION for the declaration by the Great Jamahiriya [Libya] of its repeated condemnation of terrorism and its full readiness to

cooperate, in the context of international efforts, with any party fighting terrorism and working to eradicate it, and commends its self-restraint and the sense of responsibility with which it has adressed the crisis; . . .

3. EXPRESSES ITS GRAVE CONCERN at the escalation of the crisis and the threats of additional sanctions and the use of force as a pattern of relations among states, in violation of the Charters of the Organization of African Unity and the United Nations as well as international laws and norms;

4. CALLS ON all the parties concerned to commit themselves to the initiatives advocating dialogue and negotiations, with a view to arriving at a peaceful solution to the crisis in conformity with Article 33 of Chapter VI of the United Nations Charter which calls for the resolution of conflicts through negotiations, mediation, and legal settlement. It also calls for a just and fair trial of all the suspects in a neutral country agreed upon by all parties concerned;

5. URGES the Security Council to reconsider its resolutions 731/92, 748/92 and 883/93 and lift the embargo imposed on Libya in appreciation of the positive initiatives taken by the Great Jamahiriya in addressing the crisis, and CALLS ON the Security Council to adopt a new resolution securing a fair trial for the suspects in a location agreed upon, and leading to the uncovering of the truth and doing justice to the victims and their families.

As the dispute persisted, and as the sanctions took an increasing toll on Libya, states sympathetic to Libya increased their criticism of the sanctions regime and on occasion openly defied it. In 1996, for example, Saudi Arabia permitted a Libyan-registered aircraft to fly from Tripoli to Saudi Arabia, carrying passengers participating in the Hajj, the annual pilgrimage to Mecca. In response, the Security Council issued a Presidential Statement condemning Libya for a "clear" and "totally unacceptable" violation of Resolution 748. As instances of "sanctions-busting" increased, both in frequency and in terms of the number of countries involved, some Security Council members became concerned at what they saw as a threat to the Security Council's authority.

In February 1998, the ICJ rendered its judgment on jurisdiction. The Court first determined that a dispute between the parties existed concerning the interpretation and application of the Montreal Convention and was properly before the Court. The Court rejected the U.S. objection that the relevant Security Council resolutions rendered the application moot. In deciding that issue, the Court noted that the U.S. objection had to possess an exclusively preliminary character to be decided during the proceedings on jurisdiction. The Court concluded that to decide the objection, which in effect asked the Court to determine that the Security Council resolutions barred consideration of Libya's claims under the Montreal Convention, would amount to a ruling on the merits.

However, on September 9, 2003, following the settlement described below at page 976, the United States and the United Kingdom notified the ICJ that they had agreed "to discontinue with prejudice the proceedings." The Court removed the *Lockerbie* case from the list of pending cases the following day.

Notes and Questions

1. What was Libya obligated to do under Resolution 731? Under Resolution 748? Is it significant that Resolution 748 was adopted after Libya filed its Application?

2. In the absence of an applicable treaty, states ordinarily have no obligation to extradite a national to another state. Article 5 of the Montreal Convention gives the custodial state the option of extraditing an accused or submitting the case to its authorities for prosecution. What then was the legal basis for the U.S. and UK extradition demands? Did Libya's failure to surrender the Lockerbie suspects constitute a threat to international peace and security? Do you agree with Judge Weeramantry that such determinations are entirely within the discretion of the Security Council?

3. Is it legitimate for the Security Council to impose sanctions on Libya when it is not represented on the Council and the two states seeking sanctions are influential permanent members? Does Libya's ratification of the UN Charter provide a satisfactory basis for the Council's exercise of authority in this case?

C. Should the ICJ Engage in Judicial Review?

The ICJ has been called on to consider the legality of acts by the political organs of the United Nations on several occasions. In its 1962 Advisory Opinion in the *Certain Expenses of the United Nations* case, the Court determined that member states were required to pay expenses incurred in peacekeeping operations in the Congo and the Middle East undertaken pursuant to General Assembly and Security Council resolutions. Similarly, in the 1971 *Legal Consequences for States of the Continued Presence of South Africa in Namibia* case, the Court (although expressly disclaiming a power of judicial review) issued an advisory opinion upholding, among other things, the legality of a General Assembly resolution finding South Africa's presence in Namibia illegal. Still, the *Lockerbie* case seems to pose the issue of judicial review more starkly than any prior case. The Court majority concluded that it was unnecessary to reach that issue prior to a decision on the merits. But Judge Schwebel, the U.S. national on the court, addressed it in the following dissent to the court's 1998 judgment on preliminary objections:

The texts of the Charter of the United Nations and of the Statute of the Court furnish no shred of support for a conclusion that the Court possesses a power of judicial review in general, or a power to supervene the decisions of the Security Council in particular. On the contrary, by the absence of any such provision, and by according the Security Council "primary responsibility for the maintenance of international peace and security", the Charter and the Statute import the contrary. So extraordinary a power as that of judicial review is not ordinarily to be implied and never has been on the international plane. If the Court were to generate such a power, the Security Council would no longer be primary in its assigned responsibilities, because if the Court could overrule, negate, modify—or, as in this case, hold as proposed that decisions of the Security Council are not "opposable" to the principal object State of those decisions and to the object of its sanctions—it would be the Court and not the Council that would exercise, or purport to exercise, the dispositive and hence primary authority. . . .

. . . [T]he Security Council is subject to the rule of law; it shall act in accordance with the Purposes and Principles of the United Nations and its decisions must be adopted in accordance with the Charter. At the same time, as Article 103 imports, it may lawfully decide upon measures which may in the interests of the maintenance or restoration of international peace and security derogate from the rights of a State under international law. . . .

Judicial review could have been provided for at San Francisco, in full or lesser measure, directly or indirectly, but both directly and indirectly it was not in any measure contemplated or enacted. . . . Proposals which in restricted measure would have accorded the Court a degree of authority, by way of advisory proceedings, to pass upon the legality of proposed resolutions of the Security Council in the sphere of peaceful settlement—what came to be Chapter VI of the Charter—were not accepted. What was never proposed, considered, or, so far as the records reveal, even imagined, was that the International Court of Justice would be entrusted with, or would develop, a power of judicial review at large, or a power to supervene, modify, negate or confine the applicability of resolutions of the Security Council whether directly or in the guise of interpretation. . . .

. . . Judicial review, in varying forms, is found in a number of democratic polities. . . . But it is by no means a universal or even general principle of government or law. It is hardly found outside the democratic world and is not uniformly found in it. Where it exists internationally, as in the European Union, it is expressly provided for by treaty in specific terms. The United Nations is far from being a government, or an international organization comparable in its integration to the European Union, and it is not democratic.

1992 I.C.J. Rep. 64.

Professor Thomas Franck offers a contrasting view in an article written shortly after the 1992 provisional measures decision, in which he compares the *Lockerbie* case to *Marbury v. Madison*.

Thomas M. Franck, *The "Powers of Appreciation": Who Is the Ultimate Guardian of UN Legality?*

86 Am. J. Intl. L. 519, 519-523 (1992)

The similarities of the *Libyan* case to *Marbury* extend beyond judicial tactics. Both raise the specter of political actors exercising powers *mala fide* and *ultra vires* and what courts are to do about them. . . .

As in *Marbury*, the Court superficially appears to accede to the broad discretionary power of the system's political "branch." But, as in *Marbury*, it accedes not by refusing to decide, but by exercising its power of decision. The Security Council's action in imposing sanctions is adjudged *intra vires* precisely because the majority of judges seems to agree that, for purposes of interim measures, Article 103 of the Charter "trumps" any rights Libya might have under the Montreal Convention, and thus frees the Security Council to apply sanctions as a suitable remedy in exercise of its powers under chapter VII. On the other hand, had Libya been able to allege a more general ground of *ultra vires*—that a coercive demand for extradition of a state's own national "could be deemed contrary . . . to protection of sovereign rights under general international law"—then, in the words of Acting President

Oda, that "would have instituted a totally different litigation, and whether or not the Court has jurisdiction to deal with that issue is certainly a different matter." . . .

The majority and dissenting opinions seem to be in agreement that there are such limits and that they cannot be left exclusively to the Security Council to interpret. The legality of actions by any UN organ must be judged by reference to the Charter as a "constitution" of *delegated* powers. In extreme cases, the Court may have to be the last-resort defender of the system's legitimacy if the United Nations is to continue to enjoy the adherence of its members. . . .

What distinguishes the Court's majority from its minority is the degree of caution exhibited by the former in staking any *Marbury*-like claim to umpire the system. The majority, implicitly, reserves that function to itself by finding that the Security Council's action was valid by operation of Charter Article 103.

The opposing views expressed by Judge Schwebel and Professor Franck represent two commonly held positions in the judicial review debate. In the following excerpt, Professor Jose Alvarez describes these two viewpoints as the "realist" and "legalist" positions, respectively, and suggests that both may miss a more complex reality of "variegated forms" of ICJ review of decisions by the political organs of the United Nations.

Jose E. Alvarez, *Judging the Security Council*

90 Am. J. Intl. L. 1, 3-4 (1996)

Despite their differing conclusions, many realists and those they would call "judicial romantics" make many of the same assumptions. Both sides suggest that the ICJ now faces a decision like the one the U.S. Supreme Court confronted in 1803 in *Marbury v. Madison;* that is, ICJ judges need to decide whether to "cross the 'Rubicon'" and assume the power, without express constitutional warrant, to render the decision of a coordinate political organ null and void. They tend to ask the question as it seems to be posed in the *Lockerbie* . . . case[] now before the Court: that is, as either praiseworthy or wrongheaded attempts by states to "judicialize" determinations under chapter VII, especially Article 39. . . .

They assume that the Court's answer will be apparent when it comes and that the Court's ability to engage in "review" turns on textual determinacy: that is, legalists posit that there are textually determinate rules judges can apply or discover, while realists tend to disagree. Many, on both sides of the issue, also propose that the Court find "the answer" in the text of the Charter and its negotiating history. Finally, both sides tend to see proposals for change in the Council's membership or procedures and proposals for judicial review as rival alternatives, political or juridical, intended to foster institutional legitimacy.

Professor Alvarez argues that the relevant texts will not yield definitive answers and that the "all-or-nothing alternatives sometimes suggested are deceptive." He points out that the ICJ "cannot make the Council a party to a binding judgment," since only states may be parties in cases heard under the Court's contentious jurisdiction. The real issue, he suggests, concerns the possible "delegitimating consequences" of judgments contrary to Security Council decisions, "not the threat of a binding finding of nullity." Such consequences will vary depending on the issue, the parties to the case, and the nature of the Court's decision. Further, challenges to the Council's authority may arise in other fora, including other UN bodies and other judicial bodies, such as the International Criminal Tribunal for the former Yugoslavia.

Alvarez argues that as Security Council determinations on issues involving international law proliferate, the Court will find it increasingly "difficult to avoid reexamining some of that Council-generated law," even though it will probably avoid any finding that a Council decision is void. Alvarez concludes:

> No one model of judicial review for Council/Court interaction has yet been articulated by the Court and perhaps no *one* model is appropriate. In the meantime, reality cannot be denied. Aspects of "review" by the Court are already here and, especially through the Court's advisory jurisdiction, have been here for some time. . . .
>
> Given the many modes of Council action with potential legal effect and the many possible modes of World Court "review," the issue need not be seen as a choice between hegemonic (or systemic) needs and the "rule of law." Even more activist forms of judicial review than have appeared to date may prove to be neither utopian nor calamitous—especially if the permanent members of the Security Council come to appreciate that they have long-term interests in pursuing peace through law.

Id. at 39.

Notes and Questions

1. Did the Court's decision on provisional measures in the *Lockerbie* case enhance or undermine the Council's authority and legitimacy? Professor Franck suggests that the Court in *Lockerbie* implicitly asserted the right to judicially review the Council's decision to impose sanctions on Libya. Do you agree with that characterization of the Court's holding?

2. Should the ICJ have the authority to determine that Council actions on peace and security matters are *ultra vires* and therefore void? If so, does the UN Charter provide manageable standards for determining when the Council acts *ultra vires*? What would be the practical effect of such a determination?

3. Do the justifications for judicial review in national legal systems apply with equal force to the international system?

4. Judge Schwebel states that the Council has the authority to derogate from the rights of individual states under international law. Does his position imply that the Council operates outside or above the law? What would be an example of an unlawful Security Council decision?

5. Proponents of judicial review often argue that it will enhance the legitimacy of the Security Council, which is an unrepresentative and otherwise largely unaccountable actor. On the other hand, international tribunals established under the WTO and NAFTA are themselves said to lack legitimacy. But what does "legitimacy" mean in this context? Professor Alvarez argues that the legalists have failed to articulate this concept adequately.

> Without a clearer description of the Court's mission and how it is supposed to accomplish it, one is hard put to discern which of several theoretical justifications for judicial review legalists have in mind. . . . The possibilities include (1) a consent-based

model, grounded in the proposition that whatever the Court does is ultimately subject to correction via amendment of the Charter; (2) a minority protection model, under which the Court's role is to protect a particular state or minority group of states whenever the majoritarian or hegemonic processes of the Council threaten their rights; (3) a participation-based model, under which the Charter scheme is premised, more narrowly, on sovereign equality as to participation in UN governance, so that the Court is authorized to step in only when a state's participation rights are denied (but is not authorized to alter the substantive outcomes produced by those processes); (4) a teleological model, grounded in achieving international peace and security at all costs; and, most broadly of all, (5) a rights-based model, according to which the Charter is ultimately grounded in protecting the human rights of people, not states, and which authorizes the Court to review all legislative outcomes, including those produced by the Council, for consistency with these norms. Each of these presents a very different conception of the Court's (de)legitimation role.

Id. at 18-19. Which of these models would support judicial review in the *Lockerbie* case? Which is the strongest argument for judicial review?

D. The Trial of the Lockerbie Defendants

Shortly after the ICJ concluded that it had jurisdiction in the *Lockerbie* case, the United Kingdom persuaded the United States to accept Libya's proposal for a trial in a neutral country. As described by Professor Michael Scharf, the final deal contained the following elements:

(1) The Security Council sanctions would be suspended when Libya surrendered Al-Megrahi and Fhimah to the Netherlands for trial before a Scottish panel of judges at Camp Zeist, part of the decommissioned U.S. Soesterberg air base outside of Utrecht; (2) Al-Megrahi and Fhimah would be permitted to fly on a non-stop flight from Libya to the Netherlands so that they would not be susceptible to arrest in a third country; (3) While in the Netherlands, Al-Megrahi and Fhimah would stand trial only for the Pan Am 103 case, and if acquitted, would be returned directly to Libya; (4) If Al-Megrahi and Fhima are convicted, U.N. monitors would be permanently stationed inside "Barlinnie Prison" in Scotland where the two would serve sentence; and (5) The United Kingdom would permit Libya to establish a consulate in Edinburgh to watch over Al-Megrahi and Fhima's interests, despite the absence of diplomatic relations between the United Kingdom and Libya. In addition to these five conditions, press reports indicated that the United Kingdom had agreed that no senior Libyan intelligence officers would be required to testify at the trial and that the prosecution would not try to trace the orders for the bombing to Libyan leader Muammar Khaddafi himself. Scottish prosecutors have insisted that no such deal concerning senior Libyan intelligence officials has been made.

Michael P. Scharf, *A Preview of the Lockerbie Case*, ASIL Insights, May 2000, *asil.org/ insights/insigh44.htm*.

Al-Megrahi and Fhimah arrived in the Netherlands on April 6, 1999. Later that day, the Security Council suspended the sanctions imposed on Libya by prior resolutions. The trial lasted eight months and involved more than 200 witnesses. On January 31, 2001, the three-judge Court found Fhima not guilty. The Court found al-Megrahi guilty of murder and sentenced him to life imprisonment in Scotland, with a possibility of parole after 20 years. The Court did not express a view on the possible involvement of higher-ranking Libyan officials in the bombing. As

Professor Scharf observes, although the judgment was unanimous, it was "a close call, with the three judges acknowledging that the prosecution's case had 'uncertainties and qualifications' and that key witnesses had repeatedly lied. Indeed, portions of the judgment read as though the text had been drafted for a 'not proven' verdict, which is used under Scottish law when the court is convinced of guilt but the evidence does not rise to the level of 'beyond reasonable doubt.'" Michael P. Scharf, *The Lockerbie Trial Verdict*, ASIL Insights, Feb. 2001, *asil.org/insights/insigh61.htm*.

On August 15, 2003, as part of an agreement with the United States, the United Kingdom, and the families of those killed in the Lockerbie bombing, Libya formally accepted responsibility for the actions of Libyan officials in the destruction of Flight 103. Libya also deposited $2.7 billion in an escrow account in a Swiss bank, an amount sufficient to provide $10 million in compensation to each of the victims' families. Libya agreed to pay $4 million to each family on the lifting of UN sanctions, and the remainder when all sanctions are lifted.

On September 13, 2003, the Security Council voted 13-0 (with France and the United States abstaining) to lift UN sanctions on Libya. The vote had little immediate practical effect, since the UN had suspended its sanctions on Libya following Libya's decision four years earlier to surrender for trial the two suspects in the Lockerbie bombing. Nonetheless, for Libya, the vote was another step toward ending its long international isolation. On September 20, 2004, the United States revoked its trade embargo on Libya, clearing the way for further payments to the families of the victims of the Flight 103 bombing. In mid-2006, the United States removed Libya from a list of countries that sponsor terrorism, and resumed full diplomatic relations.

E. Security Council Reform

While judicial review is one possible means to enhance the legitimacy of the Security Council's decisions, the "democratization" of the Council through reform of its membership and procedures is an alternative often suggested by the many states that feel underrepresented on the Council. Not surprisingly, however, there is little agreement on what a reformed Council should look like.

Changes in political and economic realities, and in the UN's membership, did prompt Security Council reform once before. By 1965 the UN's membership had grown from 51 to 112, as many states emerging from decolonization joined the organization. In response to pressure from new UN members for increased representation in the Security Council, the Charter was amended to add four new nonpermanent seats, giving the Council a total of five permanent members and ten nonpermanent members. This reform effectively permitted the nonaligned states, by voting as a bloc, to bar Council action and thus created a check on the power of the permanent five (the so-called nonaligned veto).

So long as the Security Council remained largely paralyzed by Cold War tensions and the frequent use of the veto, the Council's current structure did not particularly offend most states. But the decline of the U.S.-Soviet rivalry inaugurated a newly active Security Council. Council meetings increased exponentially— so much so that the Council is now effectively in continuous session. The use of the veto declined correspondingly, as indicated on the chart below.

Changing Patterns in the Use of the Veto in the Security Council*

Table shows number of times veto was cast, by country[1]

Period	China*	France	Britain	US	USSR/Russia	Total
Total	4-5	18	32	80	122	257
2005	-	-	-	-	-	-
2004	-	-	-	2	1	3
2003	-	-	-	2	-	2
2002	-	-	-	2	-	2
2001	-	-	-	2	-	2
2000	-	-	-	-	-	0
1999	1	-	-	-	-	1
1998	-	-	-	-	-	0
1997	1	-	-	2	-	3
1996	-	-	-	-	-	0
1986-95	-	3	8	24	2	37
1976-85	-	9	11	34	6	60
1966-75	2	2	10	12	7	33
1956-65	-	2	3	-	26	31
1946-55	(1)*	2	-	-	80	83

Table compiled by Global Policy Forum from UN information

Between 1946 and 1971, the Chinese seat on the Security Council was occupied by the Republic of China (Taiwan), which used the veto only once (to block Mongolia's application for membership in 1955). The first veto exercised by the present occupant, the People's Republic of China, was therefore not until 25 August 1972.

[1]Only a minority of vetoes have been cast in cases where vital international security issues were at stake. 59 vetoes have been cast to block admission of member states. Additionally, 43 vetoes have been used to block nominees for Secretary General, although these vetoes were cast during closed sessions of the Council and are not included in the table above. Limitation of veto use to Chapter VII (threats to international peace and security), as many members propose, would be a long step towards total veto abolition.

The new political climate in the Security Council not only enabled it to become the activist body described above, but also contributed to sharply increased pressure for Security Council reform. In 1992, the General Assembly asked the Secretary-General to invite states to submit comments on reform, and 80 states did so. The following year, the General Assembly set up an Open-Ended Working Group to consider proposals for restructuring the Security Council and increasing the transparency of its operations. This working group has met repeatedly since then and has considered dozens of proposals. But so little progress has been made that critics of the reform process refer to the group as the "Never-Ending Working Group."

Pressures for restructuring come principally from developing countries. Indonesia's views, as reflected in the following statement by its UN representative, are illustrative:

[D]eveloping countries continue to be disenfranchised as four out of five permanent members are from the developed nations, an anomaly which can not be perpetuated. It is also pertinent to note that two thirds of the world's population in the developing countries is without representation in the permanent membership. . . .

Likewise . . . only 8% of the general [UN] membership is now represented in the Council. Further compounding the situation is the fact that although the membership of the Organization has grown by nearly 60% since its last increase in 1965, there has not been a corresponding increase in the membership of the Security Council for over three decades. Consequently, any review of the Council's composition must . . . ensure a balanced configuration in the composition of the Council which would inevitably lead to the widening of its decision-making basis.

[A]pproximately 280 vetoes [have been] cast, most of them during the Cold War era. To contend that these were cast in the interests of the international community in accordance with Article 24 of the Charter would be a travesty of facts; on the contrary, it would be more closer to truth to contend that these were used to promote the national interests of the countries concerned. It gave rise to a widely shared perception that the Security Council was being used as an institution for the imposition of the will of the strong over the weak or world affairs being run by a small group of powerful nations. And this is the raison d'etre for the near universal denunciation of the exercise of veto which violates the wishes of the majority—one of the cardinal principles of democracy. The insistence on this presumed right may buttress the disturbing trends witnessed in recent times of the marginalization of the Council's role and the erosion of its authority in the maintenance of international peace and security. It is in the interest of all nations to reverse these trends through flexibility and compromise, realism and pragmatism, . . . and this in turn will enable the Council to cope with the challenges that it will surely face in the millennium.

Statement by Ambassador Makarim Wibisono, U.N. Doc. A/54/PV. 82 at 12 (1999).

Pressures for reform also come from developed countries, such as Japan and Germany, which feel their UN contributions and geopolitical clout entitle them to Security Council permanent membership. But sharp disagreements remain between individual states, and between different regional groups, over such questions as the number of states that should be added to the Council, the criteria for choosing those states, which if any of those states should become permanent members, and whether any new permanent members should be entitled to exercise the veto.

In December 2004, the Secretary-General's High-level Panel on Threats, Challenges and Change offered the following analysis of efforts at Security Council reform:

> 246. Since the end of the cold war, the effectiveness of the Council has improved, as has its willingness to act; but it has not always been equitable in its actions, nor has it acted consistently or effectively in the face of genocide or other atrocities. This has gravely damaged its credibility. The financial and military contributions to the United Nations of some of the five permanent members are modest compared to their special status, and often the Council's non-permanent members have been unable to make the necessary contribution to the work of the Organization envisaged by the Charter. Even outside the use of a formal veto, the ability of the five permanent members to keep critical issues of peace and security off the Security Council's agenda has further undermined confidence in the body's work.

> 248. Thus, the challenge for any reform is to increase both the effectiveness and the credibility of the Security Council and, most importantly, to enhance its capacity and willingness to act in the face of threats. . . .

249. We believe that reforms of the Security Council should meet the following principles:

(a) They should, in honouring Article 23 of the Charter of the United Nations, increase the involvement in decision-making of those who contribute most to the United Nations financially, militarily and diplomatically—specifically in terms of contributions to United Nations assessed budgets, participation in mandated peace operations, contributions to voluntary activities of the United Nations in the areas of security and development, and diplomatic activities in support of United Nations objectives and mandates. Among developed countries, achieving or making substantial progress towards the internationally agreed level of 0.7 per cent of GNP for ODA [official development assistance] should be considered an important criterion of contribution;

(b) They should bring into the decision-making process countries more representative of the broader membership, especially of the developing world;

(c) They should not impair the effectiveness of the Security Council;

(d) They should increase the democratic and accountable nature of the body.

In 2005, three different groups of countries submitted rival proposals for reforming the Council. The first came from a group of 27 states led by the G4 — Brazil, Germany, India, and Japan, the second from the African Union, and the third from a group of middle-sized states calling itself the Uniting for Consensus (UfC) group, led in part by Italy and Pakistan. Each proposal provoked fierce opposition from members of the other two camps, enough to block any of the proposals from coming to a vote.

The G4 proposal called for adding ten states to the Council's membership, six permanent (but without the veto power) and four non-permanent members. The plan was roundly attacked by African Union states, which wanted two or more of their number to join the Council with the veto power, by regional rivals of the G4 (Argentina and Mexico oppose Brazil, Italy opposes Germany, Pakistan opposes India, and China and Korea oppose Japan), and by mid-size states that oppose any new permanent seats for fear it would reduce their chances to obtain a non-permanent seat on a rotating basis.

Consider the comments of the Pakistani ambassador:

7. The views of Pakistan, and other UfC members . . . are no secret. We oppose this resolution strongly, for several reasons.

First, the proposal is contrary to the principle of sovereign equality of states enshrined in the UN Charter. Most of us, when we entered the United Nations, were given no choice regarding the existing permanent members. But, today, we do have a choice. And, we will not choose to anoint six States with special privileges and stamp ourselves as second class members in this Organization. . . .

Second, it is unequal. It will give permanent membership to 11 states, consigning 180 others to compete for 14 seats.

Third, it will erode—not enhance—democracy and accountability in the Security Council. The ratio of permanent (unelected) to non-permanent (elected) members would increase from 1:2 to almost 1:1. Half of the Council's membership will be unaccountable (the word "accountability" does not appear in the G-4's resolution).

Fourth, it will enlarge the "club of the privileged" who will have a vested interest in addressing most issues in the Security Council, further draining the oxygen out of the General Assembly, and enhancing the domination of the Security Council.

Fifth, it will reduce, not improve, the effectiveness and efficiency of the Security Council by requiring the constant reconciliation of the interests of 11 instead of 5 permanent members.

Statement by Ambassador Munir Akran, Permanent Representative of Pakistan to the United Nations, July 11, 2005.

The African Union introduced its own proposal by noting "the undeniable fact that in the year 1945, when the United Nations was being formed, most of Africa was not represented and that, as a result, Africa remains to this day the only continent without a permanent seat in the Council." The African proposal called for 11 new members, including two permanent and two non-permanent seats for both Africa and Asia, one permanent and one non-permanent seat for Latin America and the Caribbean, one permanent seat for Western Europe, and one non-permanent seat for Eastern Europe. Under the African proposal, the new permanent members would receive "the same prerogatives and privileges as those of the current permanent members, including the right of veto." The African proposal attracted little support, however; the G4 and others considered it unrealistic, since the existing permanent members would not accept such a stark dilution of their own power, and because it would likely foster Security Council gridlock. The UfC group also opposed it, since none of their members was a likely candidate for one of the proposed new permanent seats.

The UfC called instead for ten new elected, non-permanent members to be added to the Council with "due regard being specially paid, in the first instance to the contribution of Members of the United Nations to the maintenance of international peace and security and to the other purposes of the Organization, and also to equitable geographical distribution." UfC Draft Resolution, July 21, 2005. The Canadian ambassador extolled the proposal in the following terms:

[The UfC] proposal—instead of adding additional permanent members—would add seats that would be permanently allocated to regions, while leaving the member states in those regions to decide, from time to time, which of their number is best suited to serve and for how long. The Uniting for Consensus proposal is flexible in leaving it to the regions to determine the duration of each regional mandate. Its approach is democratic and accountable in providing for periodic elections and re-elections at intervals that each region would determine. In that way, there would always be an opportunity to adjust to changing circumstances and to evolving needs. It would also, Mr. President, spare us the damaging and divisive decision which the pending resolution would force on us now, of choosing among candidates—each of them worthy in its own right—who seek special status in a permanent seat that they will hold into the future, no matter what the future may hold.

Statement by Ambassador Alan Rock, July 12, 2005.

The United States did not support any of the three proposals tabled in 2005. At a press conference, Under Secretary for Political Affairs Nicholas Burns explained why:

We think it's very important as we look at Security Council enlargement, not just to look at it as a debate of what parts of the world should be represented, which geographic region should have the greatest number of seats or the least number of seats. We think it's more important to look at the criteria for which countries are now eligible and which countries are supremely well qualified to become members of the Council. . . .

Certainly, the size of a country's economy is important; the size of its population; its military capacity, its potential to contribute militarily to United Nations peacekeeping missions; its contributions to peacekeeping; its commitment to democracy and human rights; its financial contributions to the United Nations system; its record and commitment on counterterrorism; its record and commitment on nonproliferation; and we have to look, of course, at the geographic balance, overall, of how the Security Council is constituted. . . .

    [W]e would likely support adding two or so new permanent members to the Council, based on the set of criteria that I've just read out to you. And of course you know that we have longstanding support for Japan. . . .

    In addition to our likely support for two or so new permanent members, we will also support two or three additional non-permanent seats. And that would expand the Council from its current size of 15 members to 19 or 20. . . .

    We have to be concerned, as one of the custodians of the Security Council, as a member of the Permanent Five . . . about the effectiveness of [the] Security Council. And so we believe that an intake of nine or ten countries is not easily digestible. . . . We wouldn't be able to be assured that the Council's effectiveness could be continued. . . .

Nicholas Burns, On-the-Record Briefing on UN Reform, June 16, 2005. As of early 2006, discussions on Security Council reform continued, but with little prospect of near-term success.

Notes and Questions

1. What criteria should be considered in determining the size and composition of the Council? As David Malone, former President of the International Peace Academy, a think-tank, has observed, "[t]he obvious truth is that every country looks to its own advantage when it comes to reform of the composition of the Council, and countries want to be on the Council as often as possible and will assess any proposal for change relative to their own prospects of getting on more often . . .".

2. Most of the states urging Security Council reform claim that they wish to see a more representative, democratic, accountable, transparent, and effective Council. Would any of the reform proposals described above be likely to achieve these goals?

3. Should new permanent members be entitled to exercise a veto on Council decisions? Should the veto be eliminated or, more plausibly, restricted even for existing Council members? Would existing members of the Council, who can veto the Charter amendments necessary to restrict the exercise of the veto, have any incentive to accept such restrictions?

4. As a practical matter, is there a way to address concerns that the Security Council acts inconsistently in carrying out its mandate? Could the General Assembly or a Citizen Assembly act as a check on Security Council actions such as those at issue in the *Lockerbie* case?

II. THE ONTOLOGICAL CHALLENGE: THE "WAR ON TERRORISM"

The problem of the Security Council's sanctions against Libya demonstrates the challenges to creating a legitimate system of law in a world where the UN's key enforcement body reflects a highly selective—and anachronistic—distribution of states. But the Libya situation, and others, highlight a more profound challenge to international law, one made by skeptics for hundreds of years—namely, is international law really law in the sense generally understood in national legal systems?

How can there be binding rules and acceptable rates of compliance when, in the end, there is no guarantee of enforcement by some supranational authority?

This ontological challenge has been leveled at international law by scholars and practitioners in both fields that it straddles—namely, domestic law and international relations. The skeptics offer two fundamental critiques. First, they say that only domestic systems have the characteristics of true legal systems—a legislature, executive, and judiciary, each with real authority. In the absence of such institutions to make, implement, and interpret rules, international law may be morally persuasive but cannot be law. Second, critics, particularly international relations scholars in the realist school, argue that the lack of a centralized authority able to guarantee compliance means that international law does not really control or even affect very much the behavior of states. They note correctly that the ICJ has never been a major player in international affairs and point to key instances where states have violated important treaties, such as the many neutrality and nonaggression treaties ignored at the start of World War II. The shape of the international system in the Cold War reinforced this skeptical attitude, as the United Nations was hobbled by both East-West and North-South tensions. While the end of the Cold War has loosened many of the blockages to international law making and implementation, the skepticism remains.

Not surprisingly, international lawyers have heard both these critiques and have developed their own responses, often with support from political scientists who believe norms are important in international affairs. This book has attempted to highlight both the critiques and the responses to them in a variety of situations. In this section, we consider these ontological challenges more directly. The Problem that follows considers the role of international law in a crisis facing a major world power. The Problem appraises the responses of states and international organizations to the September 11, 2001, terrorist attack on the United States. It focuses principally, but not exclusively, on the second ontological critique—namely, that international law does not influence state decision making. Following the Problem are a series of readings addressing both critiques. As you read the Problem, consider whether and how each actor took into account existing legal norms in formulating its response to the terrorist attacks; whether some norms influenced the key actors more than others, and why; how the political, economic, and military power of the United States influenced those responses; whether such crises can change international law and, if so, the legitimacy of such rapid change; and the extent to which international law can or should constrain state behavior during crises of this sort.

A. The Problem

On the morning of September 11, 2001, four U.S. commercial aircraft en route from the eastern United States to California were hijacked within an hour of takeoff by a total of 19 men. The assailants threatened the passengers and crews with box cutters and other sharp objects they had brought with them and took control of the aircraft. The results of the assailants' efforts became clear by mid-morning. At 8:48 A.M. local time, the first set of hijackers crashed American Airlines flight 11, a Boeing 767 jet en route from Boston to Los Angeles, into the north tower of New York City's World Trade Center. The second set of hijackers flew United Airlines flight 175, a 767 also flying from Boston to Los Angeles, into the south tower of the World Trade Center at 9:03 A.M. The third set steered American Airlines flight 77, a 757 jet, which took off that morning from Dulles Airport outside Washington, D.C., into the Pentagon, the headquarters of the U.S. Department of Defense, at 9:40 A.M. At 10:03 A.M., United Airlines flight 93, a 757 en route from Newark Airport to San Francisco,

Attack on the World Trade Center
SOURCE: AP/Wide World Photos

crashed in a field in south central Pennsylvania. It appears that the passengers and crew of the last flight, alerted by cellular telephone conversations to the events in New York and Washington, were able to overcome the fourth team of hijackers, though not in time to regain control of the aircraft.

The damage from the attack on the World Trade Center towers—at 110 stories each, the tallest buildings in New York City—was catastrophic. The impact ignited thousands of gallons of jet fuel on the two aircraft, setting the upper floors of each tower on fire. The intense heat melted the steel and concrete supporting structures in the towers. At 10:05 A.M., the entire south tower collapsed in a matter of seconds; at 10:29 A.M., the north tower collapsed. Later in the day, other lower buildings in the complex also collapsed. After the impact, the vast majority of workers and visitors inside the Trade Center managed to escape the burning buildings. But nearly all those on and above the floors where the aircraft crashed had no chance of survival. Approximately 2,700 people in the towers were killed in the crash, fire, and subsequent collapse, including over 350 fire, police, and rescue workers. At the Pentagon, 125 people were killed, and a large portion of one of the building's sides was destroyed. The total number of deaths, including all the passengers and crew on the four doomed planes, was over 3,000. Over 80 nations counted one or more of their citizens among the victims.

Within hours of the attacks, senior officials of the U.S. government concluded that they were planned and initiated jointly and from outside the United States. Based on the passenger manifests of the four hijacked planes, the U.S. Attorney General announced the names of the 19 persons suspected of participating in the hijackings. All were foreign nationals of Middle East origin: identification papers showed them to be citizens of Egypt, Saudi Arabia, Lebanon, and the United Arab Emirates, though investigators were not certain of all their nationalities. On the evening of September 11, President George W. Bush, in an address to the nation, stated:

> The search is underway for those who are behind these evil acts. I've directed the full resources of our intelligence and law enforcement communities to find those responsible and to bring them to justice. We will make no distinction between the terrorists who committed these acts and those who harbor them.

On September 20, in a speech to a joint session of Congress, President Bush announced that the United States had concluded that the hijackers were part of a network of anti-American radical Muslim saboteurs known as Al Qaeda. Al Qaeda's leader was said to be a Saudi-born millionaire named Osama bin Laden. The United States accused bin Laden of setting up training camps in Afghanistan and arranging for the financing of terror cells around the world, which would recruit and train new members and then deploy them against American interests. The United States asserted that Al Qaeda had organized the 1999 bombings of the American embassies in Nairobi, Kenya, and Dar es Salaam, Tanzania, that had killed hundreds, principally local residents, as well as the 2000 bombing of an American naval ship docked in Yemen. President Bush declared that these "enemies of freedom committed an act of war against our country," adding, "[w]hether we bring our enemies to justice, or bring justice to our enemies, justice will be done."

President Bush also accused the government of Afghanistan, controlled by an ultra-orthodox group of Muslims known as the Taliban, of "threatening people everywhere by sponsoring and sheltering and supplying terrorists. By aiding and abetting murder, the Taliban regime is committing murder." He then made the following "demands" to the Taliban government:

> Deliver to United States authorities all the leaders of al Qaeda who hide in your land. Release all foreign nationals, including American citizens, you have unjustly imprisoned. Protect foreign journalists, diplomats and aid workers in your country. Close immediately and permanently every terrorist training camp in Afghanistan, and hand over every terrorist, and every person in their support structure, to appropriate authorities. Give the United States full access to terrorist training camps, so we can make sure they are no longer operating. These demands are not open to negotiation or discussion. The Taliban must act, and act immediately. They will hand over the terrorists, or they will share in their fate.

Address Before a Joint Session of Congress on the United States Response to the Terrorist Attacks of September 11, 37 Weekly Comp. Pres. Doc. 1347 (2001).

President Bush also announced the beginning of a "war" on terrorism, whose confines he characterized as follows:

We will direct every resource at our command—every means of diplomacy, every tool of intelligence, every instrument of law enforcement, every financial influence, and every necessary weapon of war—to the disruption and to the defeat of the global terror network. . . .

. . . We will starve terrorists of funding, turn them one against another, drive them from place to place, until there is no refuge or no rest. And we will pursue nations that provide aid or safe haven to terrorism. Every nation, in every region, now has a decision to make. Either you are with us, or you are with the terrorists. From this day forward, any nation that continues to harbor or support terrorism will be regarded by the United States as a hostile regime.

Id.

In the days and weeks after the speech, American foreign policy became almost exclusively focused on the new war on terrorism. The U.S. government froze the American bank accounts of numerous organizations that it asserted had served to funnel funds to and from Al Qaeda; threatened sanctions against foreign banks that failed to do the same; and began a series of intense consultations with European and other states on law enforcement cooperation. At President Bush's urging, Congress passed legislation in the fall of 2001 providing for the payment to the United Nations by the end of 2001 of $1.4 billion in current dues and arrearages, funding that had been held up in Congress by House Republicans opposed to a variety of UN initiatives.

B. International Reactions

Condemnation of the attacks by world leaders was swift. On September 12, the Security Council adopted the following resolution unanimously.

Security Council Resolution 1368 (2001)

The Security Council . . .

Recognizing the inherent right of individual or collective self-defence in accordance with the Charter,

1. *Unequivocally condemns* in the strongest terms the horrifying terrorist attacks which took place on 11 September 2001 in New York, Washington, D.C. and Pennsylvania and *regards* such acts, like any act of international terrorism, as a threat to international peace and security . . .

3. *Calls* on all States to work together urgently to bring to justice the perpetrators, organizers and sponsors of these terrorist attacks and *stresses* that those responsible for aiding, supporting or harbouring the perpetrators, organizers and sponsors of these acts will be held accountable . . .

5. *Expresses* its readiness to take all necessary steps to respond to the terrorist attacks of 11 September 2001, and to combat all forms of terrorism, in accordance with its responsibilities under the Charter of the United Nations. . . .

The same day, the General Assembly adopted the following resolution by consensus:

General Assembly Resolution 56/1 (2001)

The General Assembly . . .

1. *Strongly condemns* the heinous acts of terrorism, which have caused enormous loss of human life, destruction and damage in the cities of New York, host city of the United Nations, and Washington, D.C., and in Pennsylvania . . .

3. *Urgently calls* for international cooperation to bring to justice the perpetrators, organizers and sponsors of the outrages of 11 September 2001;

4. *Also urgently calls* for international cooperation to prevent and eradicate acts of terrorism, and stresses that those responsible for aiding, supporting or harbouring the perpetrators, organizers and sponsors of such acts will be held accountable.

On September 28, the Security Council passed a broad sanctions resolution:

Security Council Resolution 1373 (2001)

The Security Council . . .

Reaffirming further that such acts, like any act of international terrorism, constitute a threat to international peace and security,

Reaffirming the inherent right of individual or collective self-defence as recognized by the Charter of the United Nations as reiterated in resolution 1368 (2001) . . .

Acting under Chapter VII of the Charter of the United Nations,

1. *Decides* that all States shall:

(a) Prevent and suppress the financing of terrorist acts;

(b) Criminalize the wilful provision or collection, by any means, directly or indirectly, of funds by their nationals or in their territories with the intention that the funds should be used, or in the knowledge that they are to be used, in order to carry out terrorist acts;

(c) Freeze without delay funds and other financial assets or economic resources of persons who commit, or attempt to commit, terrorist acts or participate in or facilitate the commission of terrorist acts; of entities owned or controlled . . . by such persons; and of persons and entities acting on behalf of, or at the direction of such persons and entities . . . ;

(d) Prohibit their nationals or any persons and entities within their territories from making any funds . . . available, directly or indirectly, for the benefit of persons who commit or attempt to commit or facilitate or participate in the commission of terrorist acts, of entities owned or controlled . . . by such persons and of persons and entities acting on behalf of or at the direction of such persons;

2. *Decides also* that all States shall:

(a) Refrain from providing any form of support, active or passive, to entities or persons involved in terrorist acts, including by suppressing recruitment of members of terrorist groups and eliminating the supply of weapons to terrorists; . . .

(c) Deny safe haven to those who finance, plan, support, or commit terrorist acts, or provide safe havens; . . .

(e) Ensure that any person who participates in the financing, planning, preparation or perpetration of terrorist acts or in supporting terrorist acts is brought to justice . . . ;

3. *Calls* upon all States to . . .

(d) Become parties as soon as possible to the relevant international conventions and protocols relating to terrorism, including the International Convention for the Suppression of the Financing of Terrorism of 9 December 1999; . . .

In addition, the members of NATO, the 19-member security alliance among the United States, Canada, and 17 European states, made key decisions in the wake of September 11. The North Atlantic Council, NATO's policy-making organ under the 1949 Treaty of Washington, and consisting of representatives of all NATO's members, issued the following statement on September 12:

Statement by the North Atlantic Council

Press Release (2001) 124, www.nato.int/docu/pr/2001/p01-124e.htm.

The Council agreed that if it is determined that this attack was directed from abroad against the United States, it shall be regarded as an action covered by Article 5 of the Washington Treaty, which states that an armed attack against one or more of the Allies in Europe or North America shall be considered an attack against them all.

The commitment to collective self-defence embodied in the Washington Treaty was first entered into in circumstances very different from those that exist now, but it remains no less valid and no less essential today, in a world subject to the scourge of international terrorism. . . .

Article 5 of the Washington Treaty stipulates that in the event of attacks falling within its purview, each Ally will assist the Party that has been attacked by taking such action as it deems necessary. Accordingly, the United States' NATO Allies stand ready to provide the assistance that may be required as a consequence of these acts of barbarism.

The September 12 statement was NATO's first formal invocation of Article 5 of the Washington Treaty. Article 5 states:

> The Parties agree that an armed attack against one or more of them in Europe or North America shall be considered an attack against them all and consequently they agree that, if such an armed attack occurs, each of them, in exercise of the right of individual or collective self-defence recognised by Article 51 of the Charter of the United Nations, will assist the Party or Parties so attacked by taking forthwith,

individually and in concert with the other Parties, such action as it deems necessary, including the use of armed force, to restore and maintain the security of the North Atlantic area.

Any such armed attack and all measures taken as a result thereof shall immediately be reported to the Security Council. Such measures shall be terminated when the Security Council has taken the measures necessary to restore and maintain international peace and security.

During the next few weeks, American officials conducted a series of secret briefings of NATO leaders regarding the evidence linking the September 11 events to overseas organizations and states. On October 2, 2001, the NATO Secretary-General, Lord George Robertson, issued the following statement:

This morning, the United States briefed the North Atlantic Council on the results of the investigation into who was responsible for the horrific terrorist attacks which took place on 11 September. . . .

Today's was a classified briefing and so I cannot give you all the details. . . .

The facts are clear and compelling. The information presented points conclusively to an Al-Qaida role in the 11 September attacks.

We know that the individuals who carried out these attacks were part of the world-wide terrorist network of Al-Qaida, headed by Osama bin Laden and his key lieutenants and protected by the Taleban.

On the basis of this briefing, it has now been determined that the attack against the United States on 11 September was directed from abroad and shall therefore be regarded as an action covered by Article 5 of the Washington Treaty, which states that an armed attack on one or more of the Allies in Europe or North America shall be considered an attack against them all. . . .

Statement by NATO Secretary General Lord Roberton, *www.nato.int/docu/speech/2001/s011002a.htm.*

In addition, the members of the Organization of American States (OAS), which are also party to a mutual defense treaty for the Americas (the Rio Treaty), met in Washington and adopted a resolution on September 21. It "recogniz[ed] the inherent right of individual and collective self-defense in accordance with the Charters of the Organization of American States and the United Nations," "condemn[ed] vigorously the terrorist attacks perpetrated within the territory of the United States of America on September 11, 2001," and "call[ed] upon all member states and the entire international community to take effective measures to deny terrorist groups the ability to operate within their territories, noting that those responsible for aiding, supporting, or harboring the perpetrators, organizers, and sponsors of these acts are equally complicit in these acts."

The reactions from Afghanistan to the attacks were inconsistent. At first, the Taliban government condemned the attacks but insisted bin Laden was not responsible; then it refused to hand over bin Laden, but within a few days suggested he might be handed over. On September 20, the day before President Bush's speech, Afghanistan's senior Muslim leaders—not the government itself—issued a decree, which stated: "To avoid the current tumult, and also to allay future suspicions, the Supreme Council of the Islamic clergy recommends [that the government] persuade Osama bin Laden to leave Afghanistan whenever possible. . . . The [clergy] voice their sadness over American deaths and hope America does not attack Afghanistan." After the Bush speech, the Taliban reaffirmed through various emissaries that it had no intention either to hand bin Laden over to American authorities or to eject him from the country.

As for the Taliban's handful of allies, on September 22 the United Arab Emirates, one of only three states to recognize the Taliban as the government of Afghanistan (despite its control of some 90 percent of Afghan territory, the regime did not hold Afghanistan's UN seat), broke off relations with the regime. Saudi Arabia severed diplomatic relations on September 25. Pakistan, which had supported the Taliban because of ethnic ties to the group and its support for Pakistani paramilitaries engaging in attacks against India in the disputed province of Kashmir, came under intense pressure to break ties with the regime. Yet despite an early October briefing by the American ambassador to Pakistani officials, a foreign ministry spokesman said: "We have yet to receive any detailed evidence about the persons responsible for the horrendous act of terrorism or other links with bin Laden or Al Queda." Pakistan never formally severed diplomatic relations, though its military leader, General Pervez Musharraf—whom the United States had previously ostracized for coming to power via a coup against the democratically elected government—announced that Pakistan stood behind the United States.

C. A War in Afghanistan

On the evening of October 7, the United States and Great Britain initiated a massive set of air strikes against Afghanistan. President Bush stated:

> On my orders, the United States military has begun strikes against al Qaeda terrorist training camps and military installations of the Taliban regime in Afghanistan. These carefully targeted actions are designed to disrupt the use of Afghanistan as a terrorist base of operations, and to attack the military capability of the Taliban regime.
>
> We are joined in this operation by our staunch friend, Great Britain. Other close friends, including Canada, Australia, Germany and France, have pledged forces as the operation unfolds. More than 40 countries in the Middle East, Africa, Europe and across Asia have granted air transit or landing rights. Many more have shared intelligence. We are supported by the collective will of the world.

That same day, the U.S. Representative to the United Nations circulated a letter to the Security Council, reprinted below.

Neither the Security Council nor the General Assembly adopted any resolutions in the immediate aftermath of the U.S. actions, although the Council did meet to discuss the humanitarian crisis in Afghanistan. On October 15, Secretary-General Kofi Annan issued a statement in which he "regret[ted] the tragic loss of life caused by the intensified conflict in Afghanistan" and expressed concern about the safety of UN and humanitarian aid workers. Annan's statements in the ensuing weeks focused on the plight of Afghan refugees and the need for a broad-based government to assume power in the country.

Governmental reactions to the operation varied from strong support from U.S. allies to silence to a few condemnations. Among U.S. allies, for instance, on October 16, an OAS committee of senior officials adopted a resolution stating that "the measures being applied by the United States of America and other states in the exercise of their inherent right of individual and collective self-defense have the full support of the states parties to the Rio Treaty." In addition, some NATO allies offered logistical support for the operations in Afghanistan. Beyond NATO and the OAS, the United States secured the permission of key central Asian states

UNITED
NATIONS

S

Security Council

Distr.: General

S/2001/946
7 October 2001

Original: English

**Letter dated 7 October 2001 from the Permanent Representative
of the United States of America to the United Nations addressed
to the President of the Security Council**

In accordance with Article 51 of the Charter of the United Nations, I wish, on behalf of my Government, to report that the United States of America, together with other States, has initiated actions in the exercise of its inherent right of individual and collective self-defence following the armed attacks that were carried out against the United States on 11 September 2001.

On 11 September 2001, the United States was the victim of massive and brutal attacks in the states of New York, Pennsylvania and Virginia. These attacks were specifically designed to maximize the loss of life; they resulted in the death of more than 5,000 persons, including nationals of 81 countries, as well as the destruction of four civilian aircraft, the World Trade Center towers and a section of the Pentagon. Since 11 September, my Government has obtained clear and compelling information that the Al-Qaeda organization, which is supported by the Taliban regime in Afghanistan, had a central role in the attacks. There is still much we do not know. Our inquiry is in its early stages. We may find that our self-defence requires further actions with respect to other organizations and other States.

The attacks on 11 September 2001 and the ongoing threat to the United States and its nationals posed by the Al-Qaeda organization have been made possible by the decision of the Taliban regime to allow the parts of Afghanistan that it controls to be used by this organization as a base of operation. Despite every effort by the United States and the international community, the Taliban regime has refused to change its policy. From the territory of Afghanistan, the Al-Qaeda organization continues to train and support agents of terror who attack innocent people throughout the world and target United States nationals and interests in the United States and abroad.

In response to these attacks, and in accordance with the inherent right of individual and collective self-defence, United States armed forces have initiated actions designed to prevent and deter further attacks on the United States. These actions include measures against Al-Qaeda terrorist training camps and military installations of the Taliban regime in Afghanistan. In carrying out these actions, the United States is committed to minimizing civilian casualties and damage to civilian property. In addition, the United States will continue its humanitarian efforts to alleviate the suffering of the people of Afghanistan. We are providing them with food, medicine and supplies.

I ask that you circulate the text of the present letter as a document of the Security Council.

(Signed) John D. Negroponte

near Afghanistan to allow U.S. troops to operate there. These included not only long-time allies like Pakistan, but the former Soviet republics of Uzbekistan and Kyrgyzstan, where the United States improved airports and built other facilities.

Iran was among the handful of states vocally critical of the U.S. response. Iran's foreign ministry spokesman stated: "The attacks which have been launched in defiance of the public opinion in the world and in Muslim countries in particular, and will hurt the innocent and oppressed people of Afghanistan are unacceptable." In an October 18 interview with an Italian newspaper, Iran's foreign minister, Kamal Kharrazi, stated:

> Under the UN law [the United States has] the right to defend itself, but first those behind the attack should be identified and then punished. What we are presently witnessing is that the Afghan people are compensating for the September 11 terrorist attack. . . . People in the Muslim countries do not believe that bin Laden is implicated in the attack on the US. No evidence has been offered to show his implication in the attack. If there is such evidence it should be offered to the people.

Other Islamic states stated in more nuanced rhetoric that military action was not the way to end international terrorism, but that its roots had to be understood and removed. Yet, on the same day as the issuance of the above statement, Iran also secretly offered to the United States to rescue any American air crew that had to conduct an emergency landing in Iranian territory.

The U.S.-British action in Afghanistan expanded over the next month to include aerial bombardments of suspected Al Qaeda training camps as well as installations and forces of the Afghan government. The United States coordinated much of its actions with the Northern Alliance, a loose affiliation of groups that had ruled Afghanistan from 1996-1998 before their ouster by the Taliban. Aided by American and British bombing, the Northern Alliance quickly swept across much of the country, killing many Taliban soldiers. Many other Taliban soldiers surrendered en masse. By December 2001, the Northern Alliance and its allies were in control of most of the country. Most Al Qaeda camps had been destroyed, but, despite heavy bombing of caves in eastern Afghanistan said to house bin Laden and his supporters, many Al Qaeda fighters evaded capture through mid-2002.

To plan for the future of Afghanistan after the Taliban, UN officials initiated a series of consultations during the fall of 2001 among various Afghan groups inside and outside of Afghanistan. On November 14, 2001, the Security Council adopted Resolution 1378. It called for

> a new and transitional administration leading to the formation of a government, both of which should be broad-based, multi-ethnic and fully representative of all the Afghan people and committed to peace with Afghanistan's neighbours, [and which] should respect the human rights of all Afghan people, regardless of gender, ethnicity or religion.

After intense negotiations at a luxury hotel outside Bonn, the leaders of the various Afghan groups announced in early December the formation of a temporary government to assume power. That new government took office on December 22, 2001. British troops soon led a small peacekeeping force to preserve order in Kabul, while a massive relief effort began to avert a humanitarian crisis and to start the rebuilding of Afghanistan's infrastructure. A June 2002 assembly of tribal representatives elected an interim administration to serve for two years. Meanwhile, large numbers of U.S. forces remained in Afghanistan, hunting for Taliban and Al Qaeda fighters and, at times, using military force against elements opposed to the new government.

A second assembly in 2004 adopted a new constitution. Internal conflict continued throughout Afghanistan, as Taliban remnants continued to fight against forces from the United States and its coalition partners, which numbered some 20,000 troops. NATO deployed a 9000-person International Security Assistance Force to help the government maintain order and aid in reconstruction. Many observers claimed that central government control remained limited.

D. International Law: Relevant or Rhetorical?

The events and aftermath of September 11 concern many areas of international law discussed earlier in this book: the use of force; international humanitarian law; the status of Afghanistan's government; the reach of jurisdiction of American and European regulations aimed at entities cooperating with Al Qaeda; the limits on states' ability to capture suspected criminals in other states; and the best arenas for bringing international criminals to justice. Each of these issues raises exceedingly complex legal issues, some of which the earlier chapters of this book help clarify.

Here we address two main issues: (1) the lawfulness of the United States military campaign in Afghanistan and (2) the treatment and potential prosecution of those persons apprehended and suspected of involvement in the September 11 events or other unlawful acts against the United States or other countries. We treat these issues here because they raise significant questions about whether and why states pay attention to international law; the role of disparities in power in the way states treat international law; and, ultimately, whether international law is simply a mask for power or reflects some notions of legitimacy and justice.

1. The Legality of Force Against Afghanistan

The U.S. government has repeatedly asserted that its military response to the events of September 11 is justified as self-defense under Article 51 of the UN Charter. Yet the U.S. response—a wait of approximately four weeks and then a massive deployment of force against Afghanistan—caused some observers in the United States and elsewhere to question whether the U.S. action was indeed a lawful act of self-defense. Critics—most of them academics—made at least five distinct arguments:

1. the self-defense rationale does not apply because the United States was the victim of a criminal act by non-state actors, rather than an armed attack by another state;
2. the link between the attackers and the state of Afghanistan was not sufficiently close to impute to Afghanistan responsibility for the events of September 11;
3. the United States failed to exhaust nonmilitary alternatives;
4. the delay in the use of force turned it into an illegal act of reprisal (essentially, unlawful revenge) rather than a legitimate act of self-defense; and
5. the use of force against the entire Taliban regime, rather than Al Qaeda, was not proportional to the threat.

These critiques may be grouped and examined as follows:

Armed Attack or Criminal Act?   Article 51 of the UN Charter begins by stating that "[n]othing in the present Charter shall impair the inherent right of individual or collective self-defense if an armed attack occurs against a Member of the United Nations, until the Security Council has taken measures necessary to maintain international peace and security." The first of these criticisms essentially challenged whether the self-defense paradigm even applied to the September 11 events. Some critics suggested that the only legal option for the United States was to wait for Afghanistan to turn any attackers over for trial. Consider the following appraisal:

> The attacks can be looked at through two lenses. First they might be viewed as an armed attack on the United States. . . . The problem with calling it an armed attack is that traditionally that term has been defined as an act committed by a state or by state agents. Nonetheless, the Security Council's recent resolution condemning the incidents [S.C. Res. 1368, reprinted above] refers to a state's right of inherent self-defense against armed attack. Looked at through the second lens, these were criminal acts against persons on U.S. soil. They are clearly violations of U.S. law and also international crimes—aircraft hijacking, aircraft sabotage, and probably crimes against humanity.
>
> The United States has acted in accordance with both views in previous cases of terrorist attacks on U.S. targets. After suspecting that Libya had organized the 1985 bombing of a Berlin night club in which one U.S. armed service member was killed, the U.S. engaged in air strikes against Libya in 1986, justifying its actions as self-defense in response to an attack. In addition, the United States used air strikes against Iraq in 1993 after suspecting it was behind a conspiracy to kill former President Bush during a visit to Kuwait. On the other hand, after the bombing of Pan Am Flight 103 in 1988, the United States did not respond militarily, but instead demanded the extradition of those whom it suspected were responsible. Other terrorist attacks on American targets, including the 1993 World Trade Center bombing, were also handled through law enforcement, rather than military, channels.

Steven R. Ratner, *Terrorism and the Laws of War—September 11 and its Aftermath: Expert Analysis*, Crimes of War Project Web site, *www.crimesofwar.org*.

The Link to Afghanistan. An essential part of the U.S. legal justification of the campaign in Afghanistan was that by "harboring" terrorists, a state commits an armed attack and can become a legitimate target of force used in self-defense. Indeed, the Clinton Administration had made a similar argument in August 1998, when the United States conducted air strikes against Al Qaeda bases in Afghanistan and a suspected chemical weapons facility in Sudan following the Al Qaeda-organized attacks on U.S. embassies in Kenya and Tanzania. In a message to the Congress, President Clinton invoked Article 51 of the Charter, noting that the "strikes were intended to prevent and deter additional attacks by a clearly identified terrorist threat"; in his address to the nation, Clinton stated:

> Our forces targeted one of the most active terrorist bases in the world. It contained key elements of the bin Laden network's infrastructure and has served as a training camp for literally thousands of terrorists from around the globe. . . . The United States does not take this action lightly. Afghanistan and Sudan have been warned for years to stop harboring and supporting these terrorist groups. But countries that persistently host terrorists have no right to be safe havens.

States, international organizations, and international courts have frequently made decisions as to whether a government was responsible for the action of non-state actors on its territory. The *Nicaragua* and *Tadic* cases, discussed in Chapters 13 and 8, respectively, are two examples. In *Nicaragua*, the ICJ held that the acts of the Nicaraguan *contras* could be imputed to the United States only if the latter had issued specific instructions to them; in *Tadic*, the International Criminal Tribunal for the Former Yugoslavia held that the acts of the Bosnian Serb army could be imputed to Serbia as long as Serbia exercised "overall control" over the former. The UN's International Law Commission, after extensively examining the issue for years, put forth its view of extant law in a 2001 set of principles (for possible later codification into a treaty)—the Draft Articles on Responsibility of States for Internationally Wrongful Acts. With respect to imputing to states the acts of non-state actors, it described the existing law as follows:

Article 8
Conduct directed or controlled by a State

The conduct of a person or group of persons shall be considered an act of a State under international law if the person or group of persons is in fact acting on the instructions of, or under the direction or control of, that State in carrying out the conduct.

Article 9
Conduct carried out in the absence or default of the
official authorities

The conduct of a person or group of persons shall be considered an act of a State under international law if the person or group of persons is in fact exercising elements of the governmental authority in the absence or default of the official authorities and in circumstances such as to call for the exercise of those elements of authority.

Article 11
Conduct acknowledged and adopted by a State as its own

Conduct which is not attributable to a State under the preceding articles shall nevertheless be considered an act of that State under international law if and to the extent that the State acknowledges and adopts the conduct in question as its own.

Report of the International Law Commission on the work of its fifty-third session, U.N. Doc. A/56/10, at 45 (2001).

Academic critics asserted that the government and state of Afghanistan had neither instructed nor directed Al Qaeda; that Al Qaeda was not exercising governmental authority when it carried out the acts; and that Afghanistan had not endorsed the attacks on the World Trade Center and the Pentagon. Thus, they asserted, Afghanistan could not be held responsible for the September 11 attacks. Professor Gregory Fox observes that there is some precedent for this view.

On October 1, 1985 Israeli planes bombed the headquarters of the Palestine Liberation Organization at Hammam-Plage, near Tunis, Tunisia. In explaining its action to
the Security Council, Israel argued that the bombing was justified by Tunisia having
knowingly harbored terrorists who had targeted Israel. . . . The Security Council evidently rejected this claim and voted in Resolution 573 to condemn the Israeli action by
a margin of 14-0, with the United States abstaining. The resolution condemned "vigorously the act of armed aggression perpetrated by Israel against Tunisian territory in
flagrant violation of the Charter of the United Nations, international law and norms of
conduct." It described the air raid as a "threat to peace and security in the Mediterranean region." The resolution further requested UN member states "to take measures
to dissuade Israel from resorting to such acts against the sovereignty and territorial
integrity of all States." Finally, it stated "Tunisia has the right to appropriate reparations as a result of the loss of human life and material damage."

Gregory H. Fox, *Addendum to ASIL Insight on Terrorist Attacks*, *www.asil.org/insights/
insigh77.htm#addendum*.

International law does recognize that states may have some affirmative duties
regarding the conduct of non-state actors on their territory. Thus, for example, the
Convention for the Suppression of Unlawful Acts Against the Safety of Civil Aviation, to which both the United States and Afghanistan are party (the treaty at issue in
the Lockerbie episode above), states that all parties "shall, in accordance with international and national law, endeavour to take all practicable measures for the purpose of preventing" sabotage, and requires all states to either extradite or prosecute
offenders. But critics pointed out that any violation of that treaty by Afghanistan
would not mean that the United States can attack Afghanistan, because, under the
UN Charter, states may not use force to remedy treaty violations, but only to
respond to armed attacks.

With respect to evidence linking Afghanistan to Al Qaeda, one U.S. scholar,
Jonathan Charney wrote:

> The United States should have disclosed the factual bases for its claim of self-defense
> against the terrorist attacks before engaging in military action. It had time to do so, as it
> waited nearly a month before initiating the use of force. . . . Its failure to do so in this
> situation makes it easier for others to take unjustifiable military actions based on
> unsupported assertions of self-defense.

Jonathan I. Charney, *The Use of Force Against Terrorism and International Law*, 95 Am.
J. Intl. L. 835, 836 (2001). But another scholar, Thomas Franck, replied:

> [T]he right of a state to defend itself against attack is not subordinated in law to a *prior*
> requirement to demonstrate to the satisfaction of the Security Council that it is acting
> against the party guilty of the attack. . . . [I]f a state claiming to be implementing its
> inherent right of self-defense were to attack an innocent party, the remedy would be the
> same as for any other aggression in violation of Article 2(4). The innocent party would
> have the right of self-defense under Article 51, which is exercisable at its sole voli-
> tion. . . . Any other reading of Article 51 would base the right of self-defense not on a
> victim state's "inherent" powers of self-preservation, but upon its ability, in the days
> following an attack, to convince the fifteen members of the Security Council that it has
> indeed correctly identified its attacker. . . .

Thomas M. Franck, *Terrorism and the Right of Self-Defense*, 95 Am. J. Intl. L. 839, 842-
843 (2001).

Timing and Necessity. The last three critiques above concern the manner of the
U.S. response. With respect to timing, some critics asserted that the United States

failed to exhaust nonmilitary alternatives. Indeed, the arguments from the Gulf War regarding whether the imposition of economic sanctions by the Security Council constitutes Security Council "action" under the terms of Article 51 such as to cut off a state's right of self-defense were made again here. When the United States did use force, some critics asserted that the use violated a fundamental norm of the customary international law of self-defense—namely, that self-defense is only legal when an attack is ongoing. They cited the 1837 incident between the United States and England when the British army set fire to and towed into Niagara Falls a U.S. private vessel, the *Caroline*, that had been assisting Canadians during a rebellion against British colonial control (discussed in Chapter 13). After the episode, both governments accepted that self-defense must be based on real necessity—that is, when the danger is "instant, overwhelming, and leaving no choice of means, and no moment for deliberation." (They differed on whether the British had met the test.) Thus, because the September 11 attack on the United States was over, self-defense was not permitted. Moreover, they asserted that, even if the attack against the United States were ongoing, the United States was using force to topple the Taliban as a whole, not merely to eliminate the threat of Al Qaeda. Professor Antonio Cassese, for instance, asserted:

> [T]he use of military force must be *proportionate* . . . to the purpose of such use, which is (i) to detain the persons allegedly responsible for the crimes, and (ii) to destroy military objectives, such as infrastructures, training bases and similar facilities used by the terrorists. Force *may not* be used to wipe out the Afghan leadership or destroy Afghan military installations and other military objectives that have nothing to do with the terrorist organizations, unless the Afghan central authorities show by words or deeds that they approve and endorse the action of terrorist organizations. . . .

Antonio Cassese, *Terrorism Is Also Disrupting Some Crucial Legal Categories of International Law*, 12 Eur. J. Intl. L. 993, 999 (2001). In response, other scholars noted that the *Caroline* case concerned only *anticipatory self-defense*—namely, the right of a state to use force *before* it had been attacked, and that the attacks on Afghanistan were proportionate to the threat to the United States.

Notes and Questions

1. Compare the legal determinations made by the Security Council, General Assembly, and North Atlantic Council. Did these bodies endorse the United States view that it was entitled to use force against Afghanistan in self-defense? What did the United States achieve from these resolutions?

2. What are the contours of the U.S. notion of "harboring"? Were they accepted by the Security Council, General Assembly, OAS, and NATO in their resolutions? by Iran? Is Switzerland harboring terrorists if its bank secrecy laws allow them to deposit and withdraw money with difficulty of detection?

3. What happened to the norms of state responsibility for illegal activities after September 11 and the norms of self-defense? Did they change? Were they too outdated to respond to modern threats by non-state actors? Did the United States violate those norms?

4. The U.S. government initially promised to provide a detailed public statement of the evidence linking the attacks to Al Qaeda but later refrained from doing so, asserting that public revelations might compromise U.S. intelligence

capabilities, such as electronic eavesdropping targets or spies within Al Qaeda, and limit the government's ability to prevent further attacks. Do you think that the United States had a duty to provide greater public evidence before using force against Afghanistan?

5. What does the endorsement by the United Nations of an interim government to replace the Taliban suggest about international attitudes toward the U.S. action?

6. Why did the U.S. claim of self-defense meet with such apparent acceptance by other states? Does it reflect a change in the law? A response to a compelling human tragedy? The power of the United States? One scholar has commented:

> It was the good fortune of the Bush Administration that Osama bin Laden had been operating from Afghanistan under Taliban rule in recent years. . . . Afghanistan had practically no diplomatic friends in the world since the Taliban came to power. . . . Indeed, Afghanistan itself was treated as an outlaw state, a status confirmed by a Special Rapporteur appointed by the UN Human Rights Commission, who reported annually on the severe human rights abuses and crimes against humanity that were routinely taking place in the country. As well, Afghanistan was the recipient of universal censure, including from Islamic governments, for its insistence on removing any taint of non-Islamic religious devotion by the deliberate destruction of the huge world renowned statues of The Buddha at Budiman just months earlier.

Richard Falk, *Appraising the War in Afghanistan*, Social Science Research Council Web site on After Sept. 11, *www.ssrc.org*.

7. United States forces have worked closely with a variety of Afghan armed elements, in particular those of the anti-Taliban Northern Alliance. In a November 30, 2001, briefing, Secretary of Defense Rumsfeld noted that the United States has provided food, ammunition, clothing, and air support to various anti-Taliban groups. He added, "We've worked with them closely. We have troops embedded in their forces and have been assisting with overhead targeting and resupply of ammunition. It's a relationship." In light of the discussion above of state responsibility, do these links make the United States responsible if those groups were found to have committed war crimes against civilians or others during the conflict in Afghanistan?

2. U.S. Detention of Suspected Taliban and Al Qaeda Personnel

As the U.S. campaign in Afghanistan intensified, U.S. military personnel and their new allies in the anti-Taliban alliance began occupying large areas of the country and, in the process, capturing thousands of persons, both Afghan and foreign in nationality. In addition, in the wake of the September 11 attacks, the U.S. government engaged in intensive law enforcement cooperation with governments in Europe, Asia, and elsewhere to locate other members of Al Qaeda who might be planning future operations against the United States.

Beginning in the fall of 2002, hundreds of those captured in Afghanistan and other countries were transferred to U.S. detention facilities, in particular at Bagram air base outside Kabul and at a new camp built at the U.S. naval base at Guantanamo Bay, Cuba. The United States reportedly operated smaller facilities in Afghanistan, on board naval vessels, and in other states. The United States asserted several different purposes for detaining persons it caught in the Afghan war and elsewhere and whom it claimed were members of the Taliban or Al Qaeda. These included removal of elements destabilizing to the new Afghan regime, prevention of future attacks on U.S. interests, interrogation regarding past and possible future attacks, and possible trial of those implicated in such attacks. As the numbers of detainees increased, the U.S. government considered whether those captured should be treated as prisoners of war (POWs) under international humanitarian law. Such status applies to certain persons captured in armed conflicts and confers on them special protections.

a. What Kind of Armed Conflict?

The critical threshold question for those inside and outside the U.S. government in determining the treatment to be afforded detainees was whether the United States was engaged in an armed conflict, as defined by international humanitarian law, and if so, whether it was an international or non-international armed conflict. This question proved complex because of the multifaceted aspects of U.S. military action. On the one hand, the war in Afghanistan represented an interstate conflict insofar as the forces of the United States and its allies were fighting the forces of the Taliban government. On the other hand, that war included actions against nonstate actors, namely Al Qaeda elements. More significantly, the Bush Administration's declaration of a "global war on terror" meant that the United States viewed the armed conflict as extending far beyond Afghanistan, both in terms of the zone of conflict and its endpoint. Indeed, the United States asserted that the war against Al Qaeda was open-ended, with victory difficult to measure. The extent to which international humanitarian law addresses such a vision of armed conflict became quite controversial.

Consider the following provisions, common to all four Geneva Conventions, which describe their general scope of application:

ARTICLE 2

[T]he present Convention shall apply to all cases of declared war or of any other armed conflict which may arise between two or more of the High Contracting Parties, even if the state of war is not recognized by one of them. . . .

Although one of the Powers in conflict may not be a party to the present Convention, the Powers who are parties thereto shall remain bound by it in their mutual relations. They shall furthermore be bound by the Convention in relation to the said Power, if the latter accepts and applies the provisions thereof.

ARTICLE 3

In the case of armed conflict not of an international character occurring in the territory of one of the High Contracting Parties, each Party to the conflict shall be bound to apply, as a minimum, the following provisions:

(1) Persons taking no active part in the hostilities, including members of armed forces who have laid down their arms and those placed hors de combat by sickness, wounds, detention, or any other cause, shall in all circumstances be treated humanely, without any adverse distinction founded on race, colour, religion or faith. . . . To this end, the following acts are and shall remain prohibited at any time and in any place whatsoever with respect to the above-mentioned persons:

(a) violence to life and person, in particular murder of all kinds, mutilation, cruel treatment and torture;

(b) taking of hostages;

    (c) outrages upon personal dignity, in particular, humiliating and degrading treatment;

    (d) the passing of sentences and the carrying out of executions without previous judgment pronounced by a regularly constituted court, affording all the judicial guarantees which are recognized as indispensable by civilized peoples.

(2) The wounded and sick shall be collected and cared for.

Under these provisions, the conflict against the Taliban government in Afghanistan (which was a party to the Geneva Conventions) would seem to fall within Article 2. As for armed action against Al Qaeda in Afghanistan and elsewhere, the question arises as to whether Article 2 covers all transnational military action. If it does not, would Article 3 apply on the theory that it encompasses all conflicts not covered by Article 2? Or would neither apply? If the Geneva Conventions do not apply to military actions against Al Qaeda, then what law would apply? One possibility would be customary international humanitarian law, which many scholars have asserted incorporates most of the core elements of the Geneva Conventions. Another is international human rights law, with its extensive set of norms constraining governmental conduct, on the view that actions against Al Qaeda should not be characterized as an armed conflict at all, but instead as a law enforcement action during peacetime.

b. Treaty Law on Detainees

Both international humanitarian law and international human rights law include specific rules on the treatment of detainees. The key treaty regarding POW status is the 1949 Geneva Convention Relative to the Treatment of Prisoners of War, known as the Third Geneva Convention. Consider the following provisions:

Geneva Convention Relative to the Treatment of Prisoners of War

75 U.N.T.S. 135 (1949)

ARTICLE 4

A. Prisoners of war, in the sense of the present Convention, are persons belonging to one of the following categories, who have fallen into the power of the enemy:

(1) Members of the armed forces of a Party to the conflict, as well as members of militias or volunteer corps forming part of such armed forces.

(2) Members of other militias and members of other volunteer corps, including those of organized resistance movements, belonging to a Party to the conflict and operating in or outside their own territory, even if this territory is occupied, provided that such militias or volunteer corps, including such organized resistance movements, fulfil the following conditions:

    (a) that of being commanded by a person responsible for his subordinates;

    (b) that of having a fixed distinctive sign recognizable at a distance;

    (c) that of carrying arms openly;

    (d) that of conducting their operations in accordance with the laws and customs of war.

(3) Members of regular armed forces who profess allegiance to a government or an authority not recognized by the Detaining Power.

(4) Persons who accompany the armed forces without actually being members thereof, such as civilian members of military aircraft crews, war correspondents, supply contractors, members of labour units or of services responsible for the welfare of the armed forces, provided that they have received authorization from the armed forces which they accompany. . . .

ARTICLE 5

The present Convention shall apply to the persons referred to in Article 4 from the time they fall into the power of the enemy and until their final release and repatriation.

    Should any doubt arise as to whether persons, having committed a belligerent act and having fallen into the hands of the enemy, belong to any of the categories enumerated in Article 4, such persons shall enjoy the protection of the present Convention until such time as their status has been determined by a competent tribunal.

In addition, the 1977 Additional Protocol I elaborates on the Third Geneva Convention. The United States is not a party to Protocol I.

Protocol Additional to the Geneva Conventions of 12 August 1949, and Relating to the Protection of Victims of International Armed Conflicts

1125 U.N.T.S. 3 (1977)

    Article 43. ARMED FORCES 1. The armed forces of a Party to a conflict consist of all organized armed forces, groups and units which are under a command responsible to that Party for the conduct of its subordinates, even if that Party is represented by a government or an authority not recognized by an adverse Party. Such armed forces shall be subject to an internal disciplinary system which, inter alia, shall enforce compliance with the rules of international law applicable in armed conflict.

    2. Members of the armed forces of a Party to a conflict . . . are combatants, that is to say, they have the right to participate directly in hostilities.

    3. Whenever a Party to a conflict incorporates a paramilitary or armed law enforcement agency into its armed forces it shall so notify the other Parties to the conflict.

    Article 44. COMBATANTS AND PRISONERS OF WAR 1. Any combatant, as defined in Article 43, who falls into the power of an adverse Party shall be a prisoner of war.

    2. While all combatants are obliged to comply with the rules of international law applicable in armed conflict, violations of these rules shall not deprive a combatant of his right to be a combatant or, if he falls into the power of an adverse Party, of his right to be a prisoner of war, except as provided in paragraphs 3 and 4.

3. In order to promote the protection of the civilian population from the effects of hostilities, combatants are obliged to distinguish themselves from the civilian population while they are engaged in an attack or in a military operation preparatory to an attack. Recognizing, however, that there are situations in armed conflicts where, owing to the nature of the hostilities an armed combatant cannot so distinguish himself, he shall retain his status as a combatant, provided that, in such situations, he carries his arms openly:
(a) during each military engagement, and
(b) during such time as he is visible to the adversary while he is engaged in a military deployment preceding the launching of an attack in which he is to participate. . . .

4. A combatant who falls into the power of an adverse Party while failing to meet the requirements set forth in the second sentence of paragraph 3 shall forfeit his right to be a prisoner of war, but he shall, nevertheless, be given protections equivalent in all respects to those accorded to prisoners of war by the Third Convention and by this Protocol. This protection includes protections equivalent to those accorded to prisoners of war by the Third Convention in the case where such a person is tried and punished for any offences he has committed.

5. Any combatant who falls into the power of an adverse Party while not engaged in an attack or in a military operation preparatory to an attack shall not forfeit his rights to be a combatant and a prisoner of war by virtue of his prior activities. . . .

Protocol I also includes a number of basic protections for all persons in the power of a party to a conflict who are not otherwise protected by other parts of the Conventions (such as the provisions on POWs). Article 75 prohibits "violence to the life, health, or physical or mental well-being of persons," including murder, torture, and humiliating treatment; and requires that detainees be "informed promptly" of the reasons for their detention.

POW status, if granted, has significant advantages for those captured. The Third Geneva Convention grants POWs detailed rights and provides specific standards concerning housing, food, hygiene, medical attention, religious observance, discipline, labor, and delivery and receipt of mail. Consider one small example: Article 25 grants POWs the right to "be quartered under conditions as favourable as those for the forces of the Detaining Power who are billeted in the same area." Moreover, as discussed below, the Convention provides detailed rights if POWs are put on trial. And it requires states to release and repatriate POWs "without delay after the cessation of active hostilities."

International human rights law represents an alternative or supplementary framework for examining the legality of detentions. Consider the following provisions of the International Covenant on Civil and Political Rights, to which the United States is a party:

International Covenant on Civil and Political Rights

999 U.N.T.S. 171 (1966)

Article 9

1. Everyone has the right to liberty and security of person. No one shall be subjected to arbitrary arrest or detention. No one shall be deprived of his liberty

except on such grounds and in accordance with such procedure as are established by law.

2. Anyone who is arrested shall be informed, at the time of arrest, of the reasons for his arrest and shall be promptly informed of any charges against him.

3. Anyone arrested or detained on a criminal charge shall be brought promptly before a judge or other officer authorized by law to exercise judicial power and shall be entitled to trial within a reasonable time or to release. It shall not be the general rule that persons awaiting trial shall be detained in custody, but release may be subject to guarantees to appear for trial, at any other stage of the judicial proceedings, and, should occasion arise, for execution of the judgement.

4. Anyone who is deprived of his liberty by arrest or detention shall be entitled to take proceedings before a court, in order that court may decide without delay on the lawfulness of his detention and order his release if the detention is not lawful.

5. Anyone who has been the victim of unlawful arrest or detention shall have an enforceable right to compensation.

Article 10

1. All persons deprived of their liberty shall be treated with humanity and with respect for the inherent dignity of the human person.

2. (a) Accused persons shall, save in exceptional circumstances, be segregated from convicted persons and shall be subject to separate treatment appropriate to their status as unconvicted persons;

(b) Accused juvenile persons shall be separated from adults and brought as speedily as possible for adjudication.

---

c. The Unfolding U.S. Policy

In assessing whether detainees would be granted POW status, some lawyers, particularly the White House Counsel, questioned whether the Geneva Conventions, to which both the United States and Afghanistan are party, even applied to such a conflict. They argued that the entire conflict was essentially against Al Qaeda forces in Afghanistan rather than against Afghanistan itself, and thus not covered by the Conventions.

In mid-January 2002, U.S. newspapers reported that President Bush had secretly determined that the Geneva Conventions did not apply to the conflict in Afghanistan and that, consequently, none of those captured would be entitled to POW status. In a January 28 press briefing, the White House Press Spokesman, Ari Fleischer, stated:

MR. FLEISCHER: . . . [A]s for the people who are the detainees who are being held in Cuba, the determination has been made that they are not and will not be considered POWs. That, in the tradition of this country, and it should go without saying, that anybody in the custody of our military will, at all times, be treated humanely. That is the American way.

As for some of the legal issues involving the applicability of the Geneva Convention, the President received the advice of his counsel and the President has made no determinations, having received that advice. . . .

. . . They will be allowed, for example, to receive and to send correspondence. They will be allowed to receive and send—receive food and clothing, subject to proper security clearance screenings.

But one of the things, for example, if they were POWs, that they'd be entitled to, which they are not going to get, is going to be a stipend for tobacco. Those are things they would be entitled to. They'd be entitled to advances on their pay, if they were declared POWs. And the United States is not going to pay them stipends. I think that's widely supported.

Question: It's not just the question of whether or not they are POWs. The Geneva Conventions provide for a review of each individual case, to determine whether that captive is [a] POW or not. And it seems that the United States position is that the Geneva Conventions don't even apply as far as that. Why not? What is the administration's position why the Geneva Convention shouldn't apply at all?

MR. FLEISCHER: . . . [W]hat you have to recognize that is so different—and the President has always said this is a different kind of war, a new kind of war—is the situation surrounding the detainees in Cuba is unlike any conditions before, in previous wars, where there were simple, black and white cases of troops, typically who were drafted, who had been captured in accord with fighting for a recognized country.

That's not at all the case here. What you have here are typically non-uniformed people who moved to Afghanistan—from more than 30 nations in the case of the detainees in Cuba—for the purpose of engaging in terror, not for the purpose of engaging in military combat, which is typically what you think of when you think of the Geneva Convention. . . .

Question: So out of that, just to nail it down, the United States is not going to provide an individual, case-by-case determination of whether or not these captives count as prisoners of war or not? We're just saying, blanket—they aren't even covered by the Geneva Convention.

MR. FLEISCHER: That issue is resolved. The issue is resolved. They are not POWs.

Press Briefing by Ari Fleischer, *www.whitehouse.gov/news/releases/2002/01/20020128-11.html.*

Yet the determination not to apply the Geneva Conventions would not last long. On February 7, 2002, the White House issued the following "Fact Sheet" on the status of the detainees at Guantanamo Bay:

United States Policy.

—The United States is treating and will continue to treat all of the individuals detained at Guantanamo humanely and, to the extent appropriate and consistent with military necessity, in a manner consistent with the principles of the Third Geneva Convention of 1949.

—The President has determined that the Geneva Convention applies to the Taliban detainees, but not to the al-Qaida detainees.

—Al-Qaida is not a state party to the Geneva Convention; it is a foreign terrorist group. As such, its members are not entitled to POW status.

—Although we never recognized the Taliban as the legitimate Afghan government, Afghanistan is a party to the Convention, and the President has determined that the Taliban are covered by the Convention. Under the terms of the Geneva Convention, however, the Taliban detainees do not qualify as POWs.

—Therefore, neither the Taliban nor al-Qaida detainees are entitled to POW status. Even though the detainees are not entitled to POW privileges, they will be provided many POW privileges as a matter of policy. . . .

Fact Sheet: Status of Detainees at Guantanamo Bay, *www.whitehouse.gov/news/releases/2002/02/20020207-13.html*

The White House press secretary stated that Taliban detainees did not enjoy POW status because they "have not effectively distinguished themselves from the civilian population of Afghanistan" and "have not conducted their operations in accordance with the laws and customs of war." The Fact Sheet noted that detainees were provided "three meals a day that meet Muslim dietary laws," medical care, adequate shelter, basic amenities, the opportunity to worship, and the ability to send and receive mail. It promised that the detainees would not be subject to "physical or mental abuse or cruel treatment" and that the International Committee of the Red Cross would be allowed to meet with detainees privately. It concluded:

> The detainees will receive much of the treatment normally afforded to POWs by the Third Geneva Convention. However, the detainees will not receive some of the specific privileges afforded to POWs, including: access to a canteen to purchase food, soap, and tobacco; a monthly advance of pay; the ability to have and consult personal financial accounts; [and] the ability to receive scientific equipment, musical instruments, or sports outfits. . . .

The President's change of course in deciding that Geneva Convention III "applies to the Taliban detainees," as well as the Administration's continued position that the Taliban detainees did not qualify as POWs, were the result of an extraordinary debate among top officials of the Departments of State, Justice, and Defense, as well as White House officials, over the applicability of the Conventions.

Thom Shanker & Katharine A. Seelye, *Behind-the-Scenes Clash Led Bush to Reverse Himself on Applying Geneva Conventions*

N.Y. Times, Feb. 22, 2002, at A12

President Bush's decision this month to reverse himself and apply the Geneva Conventions to the Afghan war came after the Pentagon and State Department lined up against the administration's top lawyers, senior administration officials now say.

Senior officials also disclosed for the first time that NATO allies were so concerned with Mr. Bush's initial decision to reject the conventions that Britain and France warned they might not turn over Taliban and Al Qaeda fighters captured by their troops in Afghanistan unless Mr. Bush pledged to honor the treaties. "What we heard from the French and the British was that if we didn't determine that the Geneva Conventions applied, then they would find it difficult to transfer to our custody people that they might take into custody that we'd want," a senior administration official said. These complaints were voiced informally, the official said.

Further pressure on Mr. Bush to shift his stance came when the Defense Department agreed with warnings from the State Department that ignoring the treaties could put American troops at risk if they were captured. The State Department and the Pentagon have not always seen eye to eye on how to carry out antiterror policy; in other debates since Sept. 11, defense officials have sometimes adopted a harder line and more hawkish stance than State.

Mr. Bush's first decision to reject the conventions, reached in secret on Jan. 18 and never announced, was based on advice from the Justice Department and from the White House counsel, Alberto Gonzales.

Their views reflected the administration's basic reluctance to be bound automatically by international treaties. In this particular case, the president feared that giving adversaries like Taliban and Al Qaeda the status—and protections—of formal enemies would limit his flexibility in the long-term, global campaign against terrorism, officials said.

By denying captives full Geneva protections, the administration said, it could more thoroughly interrogate them to uncover future terrorist plots, bring a wide array of charges against them, try them before military tribunals and administer the death penalty.

The treatment of detainees complicated relations with European allies, many of whom oppose the death penalty. This was particularly acute with Britain and France, which have a handful of citizens among the detainees, officials said.

Secretary of State Colin L. Powell was particularly influential in getting the president to change his mind, officials said.

On Feb. 7, 20 days after his original decision, the president dispatched the White House press secretary to announce at a hastily arranged news conference that the Geneva Conventions would apply to the conflict and to the Taliban detainees, but not to Al Qaeda—and that neither Taliban nor Al Qaeda would be granted prisoner-of-war status.

Several international legal scholars were outraged at what they saw as a picking and choosing of which parts of the treaty to apply. The decision drew a rare statement of disapproval from the International Committee of the Red Cross, which said its views were "divergent" with those of the United States. . . .

At a Pentagon news conference, [Secretary of Defense Donald Rumsfeld] blasted critics of America's treatment of the prisoners as "isolated pockets of international hyperventilation."

But when asked to explain the legal underpinnings of the new policy, he distanced himself from the whole process. "I do not have the power to deliver White House lawyers or the president of the United States, who made the decision," he said. . . .

Mr. Rumsfeld eventually agreed with Secretary Powell in asking the president to review the question of whether the Geneva Conventions applied to these captives. Senior Pentagon officials also said Mr. Rumsfeld came to reflect the concerns of the Joint Chiefs of Staff, who rely on the Geneva Conventions to protect captured Americans, and was displeased by what he saw as the clumsy public release of the administration's decisions.

"We are the country that has most to gain from the universal application of these principles," a senior Rumsfeld adviser noted.

International legal scholars point out that many of the administration's goals in denying prisoner-of-war status to the detainees could be accomplished even under the Geneva Conventions. Interrogations are not prohibited. And while prisoners not charged with war crimes are to be released at the end of a conflict, the administration could argue that the broader war on terror simply opened with a front in Afghanistan, and was still continuing elsewhere in the world and that these fighters cannot be released.

Many of the key internal U.S. governmental memoranda surrounding these determinations were leaked to the press in 2003 and 2004. Consider the following memoranda from the White House and the State Department:

January 25, 2002, Draft Memorandum from the White House Counsel to President Bush

http://msnbc.msn.com/id/4999148/site/newsweek

MEMORANDUM FOR THE PRESIDENT

FROM: ALBERTO R. GONZALES

SUBJECT: DECISION RE APPLICATION OF THE GENEVA CONVENTION ON PRISONERS OF WAR TO THE CONFLICT WITH AL QAEDA AND THE TALIBAN

Purpose

On January 18, I advised you that Department of Justice had issued a formal legal opinion concluding that the Geneva Convention III on the Treatment of Prisoners of War (GPW) does not apply to the conflict with al Qaeda [and] that there are reasonable grounds for you to conclude that GPW does not apply with respect to the conflict with the Taliban. I understand that you decided that GPW does not apply and, accordingly, that al Qaeda and Taliban detainees are not prisoners of war under the GPW.

The Secretary of State has requested that you reconsider that decision. Specifically, he has asked that you conclude that GPW does apply to both al Qaeda and the Taliban. . . .

Ramifications of Determination that GPW Does Not Apply

The consequences of a decision to adhere to what I understood to be your earlier determination that the GPW does not apply to the Taliban include the following:

Positive:

- Preserve flexibility:
  - ☐ As you have said, the war against terrorism is a new kind of war. It is not the traditional clash between nations adhering to the laws of war that formed the backdrop for GPW. The nature of the new war places a high premium on other factors, such as the ability to quickly obtain information from captured terrorists and their sponsors in order to avoid further atrocities against American civilians, and the need to try terrorists for war crimes such as wantonly killing civilians. [T]his new paradigm renders obsolete Geneva's strict limitations on questioning of enemy prisoners and renders quaint some of its provisions requiring that captured enemy be afforded such things as commissary privileges, scrip (i.e., advances of monthly pay), athletic uniforms, and scientific instruments.

☐   Although some of these provisions do not apply to detainees who are not POWs, a determination that GPW does not apply to al Qaeda and the Taliban eliminates any argument regarding the need for case-by-case determinations of POW status. It also hold open options for the future conflicts in which it may be more difficult to determine whether an enemy force as a whole meets the standard for POW status. . . .

Negative:

[T]he following arguments would support reconsideration and reversal of your decision that the GPW does not apply to either al Qaeda or the Taliban:

- Since the Geneva Conventions were concluded in 1949, the United States has never denied their applicability to either U.S. or opposing forces engaged in armed conflict, despite several opportunities to do so. . . .
- The United States could not invoke the GPW if enemy forces threatened to mistreat or mistreated U.S. or coalition forces captured during operations in Afghanistan, or if they denied Red Cross access or other POW privileges. . . .
- Our position would likely provoke widespread condemnation among our allies and in some domestic quarters, even if we make clear that we will comply with the core humanitarian principles of the treaty as a matter of policy. . . .

Response to Arguments for Applying GPW to the al Qaeda and the Taliban

- In response to the argument that we should decide to apply GPW to the Taliban in order to encourage other countries to treat captured U.S. military personnel in accordance with the GPW, it should be noted that your policy of providing humane treatment to enemy detainees gives us the credibility to insist on like treatment for our soldiers. . . . I note that our adversaries in several recent conflicts have not been deterred by GPW rules in any event.
- The statement that other nations would criticize the U.S. because we have determined that GPW does not apply is undoubtedly true. . . . On the other hand, some international and domestic criticism is already likely to flow from your previous decision not to treat the detainees as POWs. And as we can facilitate cooperation with other nations by reassuring them that we fully support GPW where it is applicable. . . .

January 26, 2002 from Secretary of State Powell to the White House Counsel

http://msnbc.msn.com/id/4999363/site/newsweek

United States Department of State
Washington, D.C. 20520

TO: Counsel to the President
             Assistant to the President for National Security Affairs

FROM: Colin L. Powell

SUBJECT: Draft Decision Memorandum for the President on the Applicability
             of theGeneva Convention to the Conflict in Afghanistan

I am concerned that the draft does not squarely present to the President the options that are available to him. Nor does it identify the significant pros and cons of each option.

Option 1 - Geneva Convention does not apply to the conflict

Pros:

- This is an across-the-board approach that on its face provides maximum flexibility, removing any question of case-by-case determination for individuals.

Cons:

- It will reverse over a century of U.S. policy and practice in supporting the Geneva Conventions and undermine the protections of the law of war for our troops.
- It has a high cost in terms of negative international reaction, with immediate adverse consequences for our conduct of foreign policy.
- It will undermine public support among critical allies, making military cooperation more difficult to sustain.
- Europeans and others will likely have legal problems with extradition or other forms or cooperation in law enforcement.
- It may provoke some individual foreign prosecutors to investigate and prosecute our officials and troops.
- It will make us more vulnerable to domestic and international legal challenge and deprive us of important legal options:

  - We will be challenged in international fora (UN Commission on Human Rights; World Court; etc.).
  - The Geneva Conventions are a more flexible and suitable legal framework than other laws that would arguably apply, [e.g.,] human rights conventions. [Geneva Convention III] permits long-term detention without criminal charges.
  - Determining GPW does not apply deprives us of a winning argument to oppose habeas corpus actions in U.S. courts.

Option 2 - Geneva Convention applies to the conflict

Pros:

- By providing a more defensible legal framework, it preserves our flexibility under both domestic and international law.
- It provides the strongest legal foundation for what we actually intend to do.
- It presents a positive international posture, preserves U.S. credibility and moral authority by taking the high ground, and puts us in a better position to demand and receive international support.
- It maintains POW status for U.S. forces, reinforces the importance of the Geneva Conventions, and generally supports the U.S. objective of ensuring its forces are accorded protection under the Convention.
- It reduces the incentives for international criminal investigations directed against U.S. officials and troops.

Cons:

- If, for some reason, a case-by-case review is used for Taliban, some may be determined to be entitled to POW status. This would not, however, affect their treatment as a practical matter.

In a memorandum to Gonzales on February 2, 2002, the State Department Legal Adviser stated, "The Conventions call for a decision whether they apply to the conflict in Afghanistan. If they do, their provisions are applicable to all persons involved in that conflict—al Qaeda, Taliban, Northern Alliance, U.S. troops, civilians, etc." At the same time, he noted that all the U.S. government lawyers involved agreed that "al Qaeda or Taliban soldiers are presumptively not POWs, consistent with the President's determination of January 18," suggesting that the President's mid-January determination of the status of the detainees was not up for reconsideration during the debate over the application of the Conventions. He added that lawyers from the Defense and State Departments and the Joint Chiefs of Staff (but not the White House Counsel, Office of the Vice-President, or Justice Department) believed that should doubt arise as to the detainees' status, the United States would need to do further screening either under Article 5 or at least consistent with its procedures.

On March 12, 2002, in response to a petition by the New York-based Center for Constitutional Rights alleging U.S. violations of international human rights and humanitarian law regarding the Guantanamo Bay detainees, the OAS's Inter-American Commission on Human Rights issued "precautionary measures" to the United States—a type of interim relief that the Commission views as binding on all OAS member states. It stated:

[W]here persons find themselves within the authority and control of a state and where a circumstance of armed conflict may be involved, their fundamental rights may be determined in part by reference to international humanitarian law as well as international human rights law. Where it may be considered that the protections of international humanitarian law do not apply, however, such persons remain the beneficiaries at least of the non-derogable protections under international human rights law. In short, no person under the authority and control of a state, regardless of his or her circumstances, is devoid of legal protection for his or her fundamental and non-derogable human rights. . . .

. . . [D]oubts exists as to the legal status of the detainees. This includes the question of whether and to what extent the Third Geneva Convention and/or other provisions of international humanitarian laws apply to some or all of the detainees and what implications this may have for their international human rights protections. [The U.S.] Executive Branch has most recently declined to extend prisoner of war status under the Third Geneva Convention to the detainees, without submitting the issue for determination by a competent tribunal or otherwise ascertaining the rights and protections to which the detainees are entitled under US domestic or international law . . . [T]he detainees remain entirely at the unfettered discretion of the United States government. . . .

On this basis, the Commission hereby requests that the Untied States take the urgent measures necessary to have the legal status of the detainees at Guantanamo Bay determined by a competent tribunal.

Inter-American Commission on Human Rights, Detainees in Guantanamo Bay, Cuba, Request for Precautionary Measures, 41 I.L.M. 532 (2002).

In April 2002, within the 30 day-limit set by the Commission for a response, the United States government sent a lengthy reply to the Commission. Its primary assertion was that, under the jurisprudence of the Inter-American Court of Human Rights, the Commission had the competence to address only violations of international human rights law and not those of international humanitarian law.

Second, the United States reiterated its position of February 7, 2002, that the Taliban and Al Qaeda detainees' legal status was clear, and it was one of unlawful combatants, rather than prisoners of war; thus no competent tribunal needed to be convened under Article 5 of the Third Geneva Convention.

Third, the United States argued that precautionary measures were unnecessary because the detainees were being treated humanely and faced no prospect of irreparable harm. With respect to petitioners' allegations of mistreatment, the United States stated:

> [D]etainees have communicated with each other, their families, representatives of the ICRC, and government officials from the country of nationality. Representatives of the ICRC have met the detainees individually and privately. . . .
>
> . . . [T]he detainees are being held lawfully as unlawful enemy combatants in connection with an ongoing armed conflict. They are not POWs, but even if they were, the United States would not have any obligation to release and repatriate them until at least the close of hostilities [citing article 118 of the Third Geneva Convention]. Petitioners have mistakenly applied the peacetime human rights law concept of "prolonged detention" to the wartime humanitarian law concept of capture and detention of enemy combatants, lawful and unlawful.

Id. at 35-36.

Notes and Questions

1. Was the conflict against Al Qaeda an armed conflict for purposes of international humanitarian law? Should international human rights law apply to the treatment of detainees? Why does the U.S. government call its policy a "war on terrorism?"

2. What would you need to know about Taliban and Al Qaeda personnel captured in Afghanistan to decide whether any are entitled to POW status under the Third Geneva Convention?

3. Is the U.S. position that none of the Taliban fighters qualify as POWs consistent with Articles 4 and 5 of the Third Geneva Convention? Does the United States have a duty under Article 5 to convene a "competent tribunal" to determine their status?

4. Why was the Bush Administration willing to state that the Conventions apply but was unwilling to recognize POW status for any of the Taliban? What are the implications for the possibility of their eventual release?

5. Do the internal United States government debates—and the eventual U.S. decision to apply the Conventions to the conflict with Afghanistan but deny POW status to all detainees—deny or confirm the relevance of international law to decisionmakers? What do the process and outcome suggest about the reasons that states comply or do not comply with international law?

d. Judicial Review and Reaction

Detainees in Guantanamo and elsewhere soon began to seek judicial review of their detention, claiming violations of U.S. statutory law, constitutional law, and international law. By 2004, the U.S. Supreme Court had issued two major decisions on the status of detainees. In *Rasul v. Bush*, 542 U.S. 466 (2004), the Court ruled that the U.S. federal habeas corpus statute applied to detainees (all non-U.S. nationals) at Guantanamo. Although the Court did examine briefly the legal status of Guantanamo, the decision was principally a broad construction of the habeas statute that made scant reference to international law.

In *Hamdi v. Rumsfeld*, 542 U.S. 507 (2004), the plaintiff seeking habeas relief was a U.S. citizen captured in Afghanistan and held, without any charges, at the prison at Norfolk Naval Station. The Administration claimed that a declaration by a Department of Defense official explaining the government's views concerning the circumstances of his capture was a sufficient basis to hold a U.S. citizen caught in a zone of combat. More broadly, it asserted that the constitutional separation of powers required deference to the Executive Branch on military matters such as this determination, and that the Constitution did not require any further review, even in the case of a U.S. citizen. In the Administration's view, the Third Geneva Convention remained inapplicable pursuant to the President's determination, and, in any case, did not confer private rights of action on Hamdi. The U.S. Court of Appeals for the Fourth Circuit ruled for the Administration, but the Supreme Court overturned the ruling. In a number of different opinions, eight of the nine justices agreed that the United States could not hold Hamdi based on the information provided thus far. The Court's central holding was that a "citizen-detainee seeking to challenge his classification as an enemy combatant must receive notice of the factual basis for his classification, and a fair opportunity to rebut the Government's factual assertions before a neutral decisionmaker." The Court did not decide whether these protections would apply to a non-citizen.

The opinions were generally confined to a discussion of U.S. constitutional law. Nonetheless, the plurality opinion of Justice O'Connor included the following discussion:

Hamdi v. Rumsfeld

542 U.S. 507 (2004)

The threshold question before us is whether the Executive has the authority to detain citizens who qualify as "enemy combatants." . . . [F]or purposes of this case, the "enemy combatant" that it is seeking to detain is an individual who, it alleges, was "'part of or supporting forces hostile to the United States or coalition partners'" in Afghanistan and who "'engaged in an armed conflict against the United States'" there. We therefore answer only the narrow question before us: whether the detention of citizens falling within that definition is authorized. . . .

The AUMF [Congress's Authorization for the Use of Military Force] authorizes the President to use "all necessary and appropriate force" against "nations, organizations, or persons" associated with the September 11, 2001, terrorist attacks. There can be no doubt that individuals who fought against the United States in Afghanistan as part of the Taliban, an organization known to have supported the al

Qaeda terrorist network responsible for those attacks, are individuals Congress sought to target in passing the AUMF. We conclude that detention of individuals falling into the limited category we are considering, for the duration of the particular conflict in which they were captured, is so fundamental and accepted an incident to war as to be an exercise of the "necessary and appropriate force" Congress has authorized the President to use.

The capture and detention of lawful combatants and the capture, detention, and trial of unlawful combatants, by "universal agreement and practice," are "important incident[s] of war." *Ex parte Quirin*, 317 U.S., at 28. The purpose of detention is to prevent captured individuals from returning to the field of battle and taking up arms once again. . . .

It is a clearly established principle of the law of war that detention may last no longer than active hostilities. See Article 118 of the Geneva Convention (III) Relative to the Treatment of Prisoners of War. . . . See also Article 20 of the Hague Convention (II) on Laws and Customs of War on Land, July 29, 1899 ([release] as soon as possible after "conclusion of peace"); Hague Convention (IV), supra, Oct. 18, 1907 ("conclusion of peace" (Art. 20)); Geneva Convention, supra, July 27, 1929 (repatriation should be accomplished with the least possible delay after conclusion of peace (Art. 75)). . . .

Hamdi contends that the AUMF does not authorize indefinite or perpetual detention. Certainly, we agree that indefinite detention for the purpose of interrogation is not authorized. Further, we understand Congress' grant of authority for the use of "necessary and appropriate force" to include the authority to detain for the duration of the relevant conflict, and our understanding is based on longstanding law-of-war principles. If the practical circumstances of a given conflict are entirely unlike those of the conflicts that informed the development of the law of war, that understanding may unravel. But that is not the situation we face as of this date. Active combat operations against Taliban fighters apparently are ongoing in Afghanistan. . . .

[With respect to the type of court proceedings required by its holding, the plurality stated:]

There remains the possibility that the standards we have articulated could be met by an appropriately authorized and properly constituted military tribunal. Indeed, it is notable that military regulations already provide for such process in related instances, dictating that tribunals be made available to determine the status of enemy detainees who assert prisoner-of-war status under the Geneva Convention. See Enemy Prisoners of War, Retained Personnel, Civilian Internees and Other Detainees, Army Regulation 190-8, §1-6 (1997). In the absence of such process, however, a court that receives a petition for a writ of habeas corpus from an alleged enemy combatant must itself ensure that the minimum requirements of due process are achieved.

The most extensive discussion of international law was by Justices Souter and Ginsburg:

[T]he Government's stated legal position in its campaign against the Taliban (among whom Hamdi was allegedly captured) is apparently at odds with its claim here to be acting in accordance with customary law of war and hence to be within the terms of the Force Resolution in its detention of Hamdi. In a statement of its legal position cited in its brief, the Government says that "the Geneva Convention applies to the Taliban detainees." Hamdi presumably is such a detainee, since according to the Government's own account, he was taken bearing arms on the Taliban side of a field of battle in Afghanistan. He would therefore seem to qualify for treatment as a prisoner of war under the Third Geneva Convention. . . .

By holding him incommunicado, however, the Government obviously has not been treating him as a prisoner of war, and in fact the Government claims that no Taliban detainee is entitled to prisoner of war status. This treatment appears to be a violation of the Geneva Convention provision that even in cases of doubt, captives are entitled to be treated as prisoners of war "until such time as their status has been determined by a competent tribunal." The Government answers that the President's determination that Taliban detainees do not qualify as prisoners of war is conclusive as to Hamdi's status and removes any doubt that would trigger application of the Convention's tribunal requirement. But reliance on this categorical pronouncement to settle doubt is apparently at odds with the military regulation, . . . Army Reg. 190-8 . . . , adopted to implement the Geneva Convention, and setting out a detailed procedure for a military tribunal to determine an individual's status. See, e.g., id., §1-6 ("A competent tribunal shall be composed of three commissioned officers"; . . . "[p]roceedings shall be open" with certain exceptions; "[p]ersons whose status is to be determined shall be . . . allowed to call witnesses if reasonably available, and to question those witnesses called by the Tribunal," and to "have a right to testify"; and a tribunal shall determine status by a "[p]reponderance of evidence"). One of the types of doubt these tribunals are meant to settle is whether a given individual may be, as Hamdi says he is, an "[i]nnocent civilian who should be immediately returned to his home or released." Id., §1-6e(10)(c). . . . The regulation also incorporates the Geneva Convention's presumption that in cases of doubt, "persons shall enjoy the protection of the . . . Convention until such time as their status has been determined by a competent tribunal." Id., §1-6a. Thus, there is reason to question whether the United States is acting in accordance with the laws of war it claims as authority.

Whether, or to what degree, the Government is in fact violating the Geneva Convention and is thus acting outside the customary usages of war are not matters I can resolve at this point. What I can say, though, is that the Government has not made out its claim that in detaining Hamdi in the manner described, it is acting in accord with the laws of war authorized to be applied against citizens by the Force Resolution. . . .

One month after the Supreme Court's decisions above, the Defense Department announced the creation of a Combatant Status Review Tribunal (CSRT), composed of three military officers, one of them a lawyer, to allow those at Guantanamo to challenge their status. The order grants each detainee a "personal representative" military officer, and the right to testify, call witnesses, and present evidence. Human rights NGOs objected to the proceedings as not providing a truly impartial forum. Between July 2004 and March 2005, the CSRT held proceedings for 558 detainees; it determined that 520 were enemy combatants and 38 were not; those in the latter group were released. The Defense Department stated that it had also notified all Guantanamo detainees of their right to petition for habeas corpus relief in a U.S. federal court under the ruling in *Rasul*, and dozens of detainees filed habeas petitions, though as of May 2006, none had been successful. As for Hamdi, the U.S. released him in September 2004 to his family in Saudi Arabia in return for his surrender of his U.S. citizenship and a promise not to engage in terrorist activity or sue the United States over his detention. By May 2006, Guantanamo held just over 500 detainees; the United States had released another 180 and transferred approximately 70 to the governments of Pakistan, Morocco, France, Russia, Saudi Arabia, Spain, Sweden, Kuwait, Australia, Great Britain, and Belgium, in some cases following intense lobbying by the detainees' state of nationality for their release. The U.S. military asserted that release decisions were based upon an assessment of the individual's threat to the United States and any intelligence value from his continued detention and interrogation.

International attention on detainees at Guantanamo did not diminish despite the possibility of judicial recourse. ICRC officials continued to monitor their treatment at the detention facility. In a 2005 Operational Update, the ICRC stated:

> For many detainees at Guantanamo Bay nearly four years have passed since their arrest. The ICRC has always maintained that those detainees remaining at Guantanamo Bay should either be charged and tried, released, or be placed within a legal framework that governs their continued detention. . . .
>
> The ICRC believes that the uncertainty about their fate has added to the mental and emotional strain experienced by many detainees at Guantanamo Bay.
>
> The ICRC has had regular access to the persons detained at Bagram, but not immediately after their arrest. Initially detainees were only held for limited periods of time before being transferred to Guantanamo Bay or released. However, since mid-2003 many persons have been detained for longer periods at Bagram, in some cases for more than a year. Therefore, the ICRC remains concerned by the fact that the US authorities have not resolved the questions of their legal status and of the applicable legal framework. . . .
>
> Beyond Bagram and Guantanamo Bay, the ICRC is concerned about the fate of an unknown number of people detained at undisclosed locations. For the ICRC, obtaining information on these detainees and access to them is a priority and a logical continuation of its current detention work in Afghanistan and Guantanamo Bay. Although no agreement has as yet been reached on the notification of these detainees to the ICRC and ICRC access to them dialogue continues with the US authorities on this issue.

In February 2006, a panel of UN experts under the auspices of the UN Human Rights Commission found that the detentions at Guantanamo amounted to unlawful arbitrary detention; it called on the United States to close the facility and either transfer its inmates to regular judicial processes or release them.

In London, the mother of a British national detained at Guantanamo sued to compel the British Foreign Office (FCO) to inquire of U.S. officials the reasons for his detention, asserting that the FCO's stance denied him his human right against arbitrary detention. In *Abbasi v. Secretary of State*, decided in November 2002, the Court of Appeal rejected Abassi's claims. After canvassing the opinions of leading British international lawyers, the court found that human rights law, whether British or under the European Convention on Human Rights, does not impose any duty on a state to protect (including by diplomatic intervention) its citizens overseas when they are in distress. While not ruling out the possibility that some decisions of the FCO concerning diplomatic protection of British nationals might be reviewable (if the government somehow acted irrationally or contrary to clearly stated policy), it found the determination generally one within the discretion of the government and thus nonjusticiable. The Court of Appeal nonetheless went out of its way in dicta to criticize the U.S. detention policy, stating, "We do not find it possible to approach this claim for judicial review other than on the basis that, in apparent contravention of fundamental principles recognised by both jurisdictions and by international law, Mr. Abbasi is at present arbitrarily detained in a 'legal black-hole.' . . . What appears to us to be objectionable is that Mr. Abbasi should be subject to indefinite detention in territory over which the United States has exclusive control with no opportunity to challenge the legitimacy of his detention before any court or tribunal."

Meanwhile, Bagram continued to hold some 500 detainees as of early 2006. The *New York Times* reported in February 2006 that, following *Rasul*'s holding that Guantanamo detainees could file habeas petitions, the military sharply reduced the number of detainees transferred from Bagram to Guantanamo and enlarged Bagram's capacity. The Defense Department did not extend the coverage of the CSRTs to Bagram, instead relying on more summary review proceedings in which neither the detainee nor any representative are involved. Although much of the reasoning in *Rasul* suggested that it could apply to the Bagram detainees as well, lawyers were reluctant to take on Bagram detainees as clients, in part because U.S. courts had not yet determined whether the Guantanamo detainees filing habeas petitions were entitled to any relief.

Notes and Questions

1. To what extent do the various Supreme Court justices take international law seriously in *Hamdi*? Why do you suppose that most justices chose not to address the claim that Hamdi was entitled to a competent tribunal under Article 5 of the Third Geneva Convention?

2. In the Vietnam and first Persian Gulf War, the United States convened thousands of Article 5 tribunals — each staffed by a handful of officers — to determine whether captured Vietnamese or Iraqis should receive POW status or be released as civilians. Do the CSRTs satisfy the demands of Article 5?

3. To what extent should the diplomatic overtures of the state of nationality of detainees affect the prospect for their release? What does this suggest about the role of law in the detention process?

4. The United States has been subject to significant international criticism for mistreatment of detainees. Protests focused on conditions at Guantanamo and abuses at Abu Ghraib prison in Baghdad. For further discussion of these issues, see Chapter 7, Section I, and Chapter 9, Section II. In addition, in 2005 and 2006, news media reported on the secret arrest of suspected terrorists in Europe and elsewhere by U.S. intelligence services and their transfer to states where the detainees were allegedly tortured. This irregular rendition process created particular alarm among governments and the public in Europe, because those rendered included European citizens, because the United States was said to be operating so-called "black camps" in Europe where interrogations took place, and because the transfer of suspects through Europe to states engaging in torture would likely violate the European Convention on Human Rights. In response to these reports, both the European Union and the Council of Europe began investigations into the practice in 2005, with promises of repercussions against states violating their human rights commitments. The United States engaged in intense diplomacy with governments in Europe, emphasizing the need for cooperation against terrorism and the benefits

to Europe of U.S. intelligence-gathering. Much of the practice remained shrouded in secrecy, in particular the extent to which particular European leaders or intelligence services may have provided their consent to these operations without informing other players in the government or parliament.

5. The question of indefinite detention has arisen not only for the United States, but also for the United Kingdom. In 2001, Parliament passed legislation allowing the Home Secretary to order the indefinite detention of suspected foreign (but not British) terrorists without access to legal counsel, although such persons could leave the UK voluntarily for a country willing to take them; in so doing, Parliament formally derogated from the European Convention on Human Rights with respect to the right to liberty. In a landmark decision in December 2004, the House of Lords ruled 8-1 that the law was not narrowly tailored as required by the derogation clause of the European Convention. In the words of Lord Bingham, "the choice of an immigration measure to address a security problem had the inevitable result of failing adequately to address that problem (by allowing non-UK suspected terrorists to leave the country with impunity and leaving British suspected terrorists at large) while imposing the severe penalty of indefinite detention on persons who, even if reasonably suspected of having links with Al-Qaeda, may harbour no hostile intentions towards the United Kingdom." *A and Others v. Secretary of State for the Home Department*, [2004] UKHL 56. It also found that the law unlawfully discriminated based on nationality. In response, Parliament passed new legislation in 2005 that requires the Home Secretary to make more stringent, individuated determinations and to tailor any limitation on liberty to the potential danger; it also provides for greater judicial and parliamentary review.

3. Options for Prosecuting Captured Suspected Terrorists

The U.S. government repeatedly stated in the wake of September 11 that its strategy against Al Qaeda included bringing its members to justice. In most previous cases of terrorist attacks by non-American citizens against the United States, the United States prosecuted such individuals in federal courts under federal criminal laws. These statutes are broad enough to cover attacks on Americans overseas-for instance, the terrorist attacks on the U.S. embassies in Kenya and Tanzania in 1999. Yet on November 13, 2001, the President issued the following Military Order:

Detention, Treatment, and Trial of Certain Non-Citizens in the War Against Terrorism

66 Fed. Reg. 57,833 (2001)

Section 1. *Findings*

(b) In light of grave acts of terrorism and threats of terrorism, including the terrorist attacks on September 11, 2001, on the headquarters of the United States Department of Defense in the national capital region, on the World Trade Center in New York, and on civilian aircraft such as in Pennsylvania, I proclaimed a national emergency on September 14, 2001. . . .

(c) Individuals acting alone and in concert involved in international terrorism possess both the capability and the intention to undertake further terrorist attacks against the United States that, if not detected and prevented, will cause mass deaths,

II. The Ontological Challenge: The War on Terrorism

mass injuries, and massive destruction of property, and may place at risk the continuity of the operations of the United States Government. . . .

(e) To protect the United States and its citizens, and for the effective conduct of military operations and prevention of terrorist attacks, it is necessary for individuals subject to this order pursuant to section 2 hereof to be detained, and, when tried, to be tried for violations of the laws of war and other applicable laws by military tribunals.

(f) Given the danger to the safety of the United States and the nature of international terrorism, and to the extent provided by and under this order, I find . . . that it is not practicable to apply in military commissions under this order the principles of law and the rules of evidence generally recognized in the trial of criminal cases in the United States district courts.

(g) Having fully considered the magnitude of the potential deaths, injuries, and property destruction that would result from potential acts of terrorism against the United States, and the probability that such acts will occur, I have determined that an extraordinary emergency exists for national defense purposes, that this emergency constitutes an urgent and compelling government interest, and that issuance of this order is necessary to meet the emergency.

Sec. 2. *Definition and Policy.*

(a) The term "individual subject to this order" shall mean any individual who is not a United States citizen with respect to whom I determine from time to time in writing that:

(1) there is reason to believe that such individual, at the relevant times,

(i) is or was a member of the organization known as al Qaida;

(ii) has engaged in, aided or abetted, or conspired to commit, acts of international terrorism, or acts in preparation therefor, that have caused, threaten to cause, or have as their aim to cause, injury to or adverse effects on the United States, its citizens, national security, foreign policy, or economy; or

(iii) has knowingly harbored one or more individuals described in sub paragraphs (i) or (ii) of subsection 2(a)(1) of this order; and

(2) it is in the interest of the United States that such individual be subject to this order.

(b) It is the policy of the United States that the Secretary of Defense shall take all necessary measures to ensure that any individual subject to this order is detained in accordance with section 3, and, if the individual is to be tried, that such individual is tried only in accordance with section 4. . . .

Sec. 3. *Detention Authority of the Secretary of Defense.*

Any individual subject to this order shall be—

(a) detained at an appropriate location designated by the Secretary of Defense outside or within the United States;

(b) treated humanely, without any adverse distinction based on race, color, religion, gender, birth, wealth, or any similar criteria;

(c) afforded adequate food, drinking water, shelter, clothing, and medical treatment;

(d) allowed the free exercise of religion consistent with the requirements of such detention. . . .

Sec. 4. *Authority of the Secretary of Defense Regarding Trials of Individuals Subject to this Order.*

(a) Any individual subject to this order . . . may be punished in accordance with the penalties provided under applicable law, including life imprisonment or death.

(b) . . . [T]he Secretary of Defense shall issue such orders and regulations . . . as may be necessary to carry out subsection (a) of this section.

(c) [These will include] rules for the conduct of the proceedings of military commissions, including pretrial, trial, and post-trial procedures, modes of proof . . . and qualifications of attorneys, which shall at a minimum provide for . . .

(2) a full and fair trial, with the military commission sitting as the triers of both fact and law;

(3) admission of such evidence as would, in the opinion of the presiding officer . . . have probative value to a reasonable person; . . .

(6) conviction only upon the concurrence of two-thirds of the members of the commission present at the time of the vote, a majority being present;

(7) sentencing only upon the concurrence of two-thirds of the members of the commission present at the time of the vote, a majority being present; and

(8) submission of the record of the trial, including any conviction or sentence, for review and final decision by me or by the Secretary of Defense. . . .

Sec. 7. *Relationship to Other Law and Forums* . . .

(b) With respect to any individual subject to this order—

(1) military tribunals shall have exclusive jurisdiction with respect to offenses by the individual; and

(2) the individual shall not be privileged to seek any remedy or maintain any proceeding, directly or indirectly, or to have any such remedy or proceeding sought on the individual's behalf, in (i) any court of the United States, or any State thereof, (ii) any court of any foreign nation, or (iii) any international tribunal. . . .

Criticism of the proposal for military tribunals was swift. Leading American constitutional scholars and civil rights organizations attacked the plan as unconstitutional. Some asserted that the President lacked the authority to create such tribunals without congressional approval, while others asserted that even a federal statute would violate defendants' rights to a fair trial. Many of these constitutional arguments hinged on differing interpretations of *Ex Parte Quirin*, 317 U.S. 1 (1942), in which the Supreme Court upheld the conviction before a secret military commission of German saboteurs caught in New York during World War II.

But the idea of such commissions also raised important questions under international law. The International Covenant on Civil and Political Rights (ICCPR), to which the United States is a party, contains detailed provisions on the right to a fair trial, including the following.

International Covenant on Civil and Political Rights

999 U.N.T.S. 171 (1966)

Article 14. 1. All persons shall be equal before the courts and tribunals. In the determination of any criminal charge against him, or of his rights and obligations in a suit at law, everyone shall be entitled to a fair and public hearing by a competent, independent and impartial tribunal established by law. The press and the public may be excluded from all or part of a trial for reasons of morals, public order (*ordre public*) or national security in a democratic society, or when the interest of the private lives of the parties so requires, or to the extent strictly necessary in the opinion of the court in special circumstances where publicity would prejudice the interests of justice; but any judgement rendered in criminal case or in a suit at law shall be made public. . . .

2. Everyone charged with a criminal offence shall have the right to be presumed innocent until proved guilty according to law.

3. In the determination of any criminal charge against him, everyone shall be entitled to the following minimum guarantees, in full equality:

(a) To be informed promptly and in detail in a language which he understands of the nature and cause of the charge against him;

(b) To have adequate time and facilities for the preparation of his defence and to communicate with counsel of his own choosing;

(c) To be tried without undue delay;

(d) To be tried in his presence, and to defend himself in person or through legal assistance of his own choosing; to be informed, if he does not have legal assistance, of this right; and to have legal assistance assigned to him, in any case where the interests of justice so require, and without payment by him in any such case if he does not have sufficient means to pay for it;

(e) To examine, or have examined, the witnesses against him and to obtain the attendance and examination of witnesses on his behalf . . . ;

(f) To have the free assistance of an interpreter if he cannot understand or speak the language used in court;

(g) Not to be compelled to testify against himself or to confess guilt. . . .

5. Everyone convicted of a crime shall have the right to his conviction and sentence being reviewed by a higher tribunal according to law. . . .

The European Court of Human Rights has interpreted a similar provision in the European Convention on Human Rights—requiring "an independent and impartial tribunal"—to prohibit the presence of military officers on special national security courts. In the 1998 case of *Incal v. Turkey*, 1998-IV Eur. Ct. H.R. 1547, the Court found that because the accused, tried for circulating pro-Kurdish information, "ha[d] legitimate cause to doubt the independence and impartiality" of the special court, Turkey had breached the Convention. In response, Turkey removed military officials from these courts. In addition, the United States has condemned the use of military courts by other states; for example, it issued a protest to Peru for its military trial of an American citizen accused of participation in terrorist activities.

Nevertheless, as discussed in Chapter 7 of this book, Article 4 of the ICCPR provides the following exception to Article 14 and most (but not all) of the other articles in the Covenant:

In time of public emergency which threatens the life of the nation and the existence of which is officially proclaimed, the States Parties to the present Covenant may take measures derogating from their obligations under the present Covenant to the extent strictly required by the exigencies of the situation, provided that such measures are not inconsistent with their other obligations under international law and do not involve discrimination solely on the ground of race, colour, sex, language, religion or social origin.

Article 4 further requires any state declaring a national emergency to "immediately inform the other States Parties to the [ICCPR] through the intermediary of the Secretary-General of the United Nations, of the provisions from which it has derogated and of the reasons by which it was actuated." The United States has not issued any notice invoking Article 4.

Also at issue is whether military commissions satisfy international humanitarian law's detailed rules on trials of prisoners of war. Consider the following provisions from Geneva Convention III:

Geneva Convention Relative to the Treatment of Prisoners of War

75 U.N.T.S. 135 (1949)

ARTICLE 84

. . . . In no circumstances whatever shall a prisoner of war be tried by a court of any kind which does not offer the essential guarantees of independence and impartiality as generally recognized, and, in particular, the procedure of which does not afford the accused the rights and means of defence provided for in Article 105. . . .

ARTICLE 87

Prisoners of war may not be sentenced by the military authorities and courts of the Detaining Power to any penalties except those provided for in respect of members of the armed forces of the said Power who have committed the same acts. . . .

ARTICLE 99

No prisoner of war may be tried or sentenced for an act which is not forbidden by the law of the Detaining Power or by international law, in force at the time the said act was committed.

No moral or physical coercion may be exerted on a prisoner of war in order to induce him to admit himself guilty of the act of which he is accused. . . .

ARTICLE 102

A prisoner of war can be validly sentenced only if the sentence has been pronounced by the same courts according to the same procedure as in the case of members of the armed forces of the Detaining Power, and if, furthermore, the provisions of the present Chapter have been observed.

ARTICLE 103

Judicial investigations relating to a prisoner of war shall be conducted as rapidly as circumstances permit and so that his trial shall take place as soon as possible. A prisoner of war shall not be confined while awaiting trial unless a member of the armed forces of the Detaining Power would be so confined if he were accused of a similar offence, or if it is essential to do so in the interests of national security. In no circumstances shall this confinement exceed three months. . . .

ARTICLE 105

The prisoner of war shall be entitled to assistance by one of his prisoner comrades, to defence by a qualified advocate or counsel of his own choice, to the calling of witnesses and, if he deems necessary, to the services of a competent interpreter. [Other rights include the right of counsel to conduct a full defense and the right to know the charges against him.]

ARTICLE 106

Every prisoner of war shall have, in the same manner as the members of the armed forces of the Detaining Power, the right of appeal or petition from any sentence pronounced upon him, with a view to the quashing or revising of the sentence or the re-opening of the trial. . . .

Last, Article 75 of Protocol I provides a variety of minimal protections for persons not protected by the other Geneva Conventions, such as detainees not given POW status. It requires that any trials of such detainees be undertaken by "an impartial and regularly constituted court respecting the generally recognized principles of regular judicial procedure." It lists ten such principles, including "all necessary rights and means of defence," *nullum crimen sine lege*, the presumption of innocence, a ban on self-incrimination, the right to cross-examine witnesses, and the right to have a judgment pronounced publicly.

On December 14, 2001, Human Rights Watch wrote a lengthy letter to the U.S. Secretary of Defense criticizing the proposed commissions and urging him to ensure that the regulations drafted to implement the President's Order complied with international human rights and humanitarian law. It noted that the Order provided fewer protections than either those provided for American service members under the Uniform Code of Military Justice (which governs court-martial proceedings) or the Statutes and Rules of the UN's International Criminal Tribunals for the former Yugoslavia and for Rwanda.

In January 2002, the Parliamentary Assembly of the Council of Europe, composed of elected delegates from the 43 member states of the Council of Europe, adopted Resolution 1271, titled Combating Terrorism and Respect for Human Rights. Among its provisions were the following:

> 5. The combat against terrorism must be carried out in compliance with national and international law and respecting human rights. . . .
>
> 7. The Assembly, which has declared itself to be strongly opposed to capital punishment and which has succeeded in ridding Europe of the death penalty, tolerates no exceptions to this principle. Therefore, prior to the extradition of suspected terrorists to countries that still apply the death penalty, assurances must be obtained that this penalty will not be sought.
>
> 8. The Assembly also insists on the fact that member states should under no circumstances extradite persons who risk being subjected to ill-treatment in violation of Article 3 of the European Convention on Human Rights [which prohibits torture and other inhuman or degrading treatment or punishment] or being subjected to a trial which does not respect the fundamental principles of a fair trial, or, in a period of conflict, to standards which fall below those enshrined in the Geneva Convention.

Resolution 1271 (2002), *http://assembly.coe.int.*

On March 21, 2002, Secretary of Defense Rumsfeld issued procedures to govern the trials by military commissions. The Order provides that the commissions have from three to seven members. Each panel's presiding officer, and each case's prosecutor and lead defense counsel are judge advocates of the armed forces. (The accused may retain a civilian lawyer as well.) The Order includes the following rights for the accused:

Department of Defense Military Commission Order No. 1

(2002), http://defenselink.mil/news/Mar2002/d20020321ord.pdf

5. PROCEDURES ACCORDED THE ACCUSED

The following procedures shall apply with respect to the Accused:

A. The Prosecution shall furnish to the Accused, sufficiently in advance of trial to prepare a defense, a copy of the charges in English and, if appropriate, in another language that the Accused understands.

B. The Accused shall be presumed innocent until proven guilty.

C. A Commission member shall vote for a finding of Guilty as to an offense if and only if that member is convinced beyond a reasonable doubt, based on the evidence admitted at trial, that the Accused is guilty of the offense.

D. At least one Detailed Defense Counsel shall be made available to the Accused sufficiently in advance of trial to prepare a defense. . . .

E. The Prosecution shall provide the Defense with access to evidence the Prosecution intends to introduce at trial and with access to evidence known to the Prosecution that tends to exculpate the Accused. Such access shall be consistent with Section 6(D)(5). . . .

F. The Accused shall not be required to testify during trial. A Commission shall draw no adverse inference from an Accused's decision not to testify. This subsection shall not preclude admission of evidence of prior statements or conduct of the Accused. . . .

H. The Accused may obtain witnesses and documents for the Accused's defense, to the extent necessary and reasonably available as determined by the Presiding Officer. Such access shall be consistent with the requirements of Section 6(D)(5). . . .

6. CONDUCT OF THE TRIAL

B. Duties of the Commission During Trial

The Commission shall:

(1) Provide a full and fair trial. . . .

(3) Hold open proceedings except where otherwise decided by the Appointing Authority [the Secretary of Defense or his designee] or the Presiding Officer. . . . Grounds for closure include the protection of [classified] information . . . ; information protected by law or rule from unauthorized disclosure; the physical safety of participants in Commission proceedings, including prospective witnesses; intelligence and law enforcement sources, methods, or activities; and other national security interests. The Presiding Officer may decide to close all or part of a proceeding on the Presiding Officer's own initiative or based upon a presentation, including an *ex parte, in camera* presentation by either the Prosecution or the Defense. . . .

D. Evidence

(1) Admissibility

Evidence shall be admitted if, in the opinion of the Presiding Officer . . . the evidence would have probative value to a reasonable person. . . .

(2) Witnesses

The Prosecution or the Defense may request that the Commission hear the testimony of any person, and such testimony shall be received if found to be admissible and not cumulative. . . . The Commission may permit the testimony of witnesses by telephone, audiovisual means, or other means; however, the Commission shall consider the ability to test the veracity of that testimony in evaluating the weight to be given to the testimony of the witness. . . .

(5) Protection of Information

(a) Protective Order

The Presiding Officer may issue protective orders as necessary to carry out the Military Order and this Order, including to safeguard "Protected Information," which includes: (i) [classified] information . . . ; (ii) information protected by law or rule from unauthorized disclosure; (iii) information the disclosure of which may endanger the physical safety of participants in Commission proceedings, including prospective witnesses; (iv) information concerning intelligence and law enforcement sources, methods, or activities; or (v) information concerning other national security interests. . . .

F. Voting

. . . A Commission member shall vote for a finding of Guilty as to an offense if and only if that member is convinced beyond a reasonable doubt, based on the evidence admitted at trial, that the Accused is guilty of the offense. An affirmative vote of two-thirds of the members is required for a finding of Guilty. . . . An affirmative vote of two-thirds of the members is required to determine a sentence, except that a sentence of death requires a unanimous, affirmative vote of all of the members. . . .

G. Sentence

. . . [T]he Commission shall impose a sentence that is appropriate to the offense or offenses for which there was a finding of Guilty, which sentence may include death, imprisonment for life or for any lesser term, payment of a fine or restitution, or such other lawful punishment or condition of punishment as the Commission shall determine to be proper. Only a Commission of seven members may sentence an Accused to death. . . .

The Order also provides for a review panel of three military officers, and possibly civilians as well, to review the trial. It can order new proceedings if "a majority of the Review Panel has formed a definite and firm conviction that a material error of law occurred." The President retains the authority of final review over convictions and sentences.

The same day, Human Rights Watch issued a statement noting that "[t]he Administration went a long way towards meeting human rights concerns and preserving the reputation of U.S. military justice," but criticizing the rules as "fail[ing] to meet the core human rights requirement of appellate review by an independent and impartial court, or to meet the requirements of the Geneva Conventions. They also leave intact the sweeping military jurisdiction over non-citizens contained in President Bush's November 13 order authorizing military trial of suspected terrorists."

In 2003 and 2004, President Bush determined that 15 detainees fell under the terms of his 2001 military order; during that time the Defense Department also issued orders regarding the mechanics of the trials and appointed judges, prosecutors, and defense counsel. An April 2003 instruction from the Department of Defense to military prosecutors specified the crimes to be tried by the commissions, noting that the crimes "constitute violations of the law of armed conflict or offenses that, consistent with that body of law, are triable by military commissions." The crimes included 18 offenses generally accepted as war crimes under the Geneva Conventions, customary law, and the Statute of the International Criminal Court— killing protected persons, attacking civilians and civilian objects, pillage, denying quarter, taking hostages, use of poison weapons, use of human shields, torture, rape, causing serious injury, and others. They also included 8 other crimes—hijacking, terrorism, murder by unprivileged combatants, destruction of property by unprivileged combatants, aiding the enemy, spying, and obstruction of justice— some of which the United States apparently viewed as implicit in the law of armed conflict (such as the acts by unprivileged combatants and spying). Military prosecutors prepared indictments against ten detainees.

Meanwhile, despite the Court of Appeals' ruling in *Abbasi*, the United Kingdom and Australia did put diplomatic pressure on the United States regarding at least one issue concerning British and Australian detainees—the possibility that, if tried by a commission, they would receive the death penalty, allowed under the U.S. military order but deeply opposed in Britain and Australia. After a series of intense meetings, both among legal officials and between President Bush and Prime Minister Blair, the Department of Defense announced in 2003 that it would not seek the death penalty against Abbasi, another British detainee, and an Australian detainee, nor would the United States eavesdrop on conversations between them and their counsel.

The first U.S. military commission since World War II convened on August 24, 2004, against Salim Hamdan, who was captured in Afghanistan in late 2001 and said by the United States government to be a driver and bodyguard for Osama Bin Laden. Proceedings against Australian citizen David Hicks began the next day. The Department of Defense invited representatives from the media as well as Human Rights Watch, Amnesty International, Human Rights First, and the American Civil Liberties Union to attend. After the first week of hearings, Human Rights Watch expressed a number of concerns over possible bias. In November 2004, a federal district judge in Washington, D.C. ordered a halt to the commission proceedings against Hamdan. The judge concluded that the President lacked the legal authority to create the commissions without prior passage of a statute by Congress; that Hamdan was presumptively a POW unless a competent tribunal established under Article 5 of the Third Geneva Convention found otherwise and thus, under the Third Convention, he could be tried only by a civilian court or a court-martial; and that if a competent tribunal found him not to be a POW, his rights under common Article 3 of the Conventions could not be met by the military commissions as established. In July 2005, the U.S. Court of Appeals for the District of Columbia Circuit overturned the district court.

Salim Ahmed Hamdan v. Donald H. Rumsfeld

415 F.3d 33 (D. C. Cir. 2005)

[The court began by rejecting the government's argument that it should abstain from ruling on the merits and by rejecting Hamdan's argument that the creation of the military commissions violated the separation of powers between Congress and the President, holding that Congress had authorized such commissions.]

III.

This brings us to Hamdan's argument, accepted by the district court, that the Geneva Convention Relative to the Treatment of Prisoners of War . . . may be enforced in federal court.

[T]his country has traditionally negotiated treaties with the understanding that they do not create judicially enforceable individual rights. As a general matter, a "treaty is primarily a compact between independent nations," and "depends for the enforcement of its provisions on the interest and honor of the governments which are parties to it." *Head Money Cases, Edye and Another v. Robertson*, 112 U.S. 580 (1884). If a treaty is violated, this "becomes the subject of international negotiations and reclamation," not the subject of a lawsuit. *Id.* . . .

In *[Johnston v.] Eisentrager*, [339 U.S. 763 (1950),] German nationals, convicted by a military commission in China of violating the laws of war and imprisoned in Germany, sought writs of habeas corpus in federal district court on the ground that the military commission violated their rights under the Constitution and their rights under the 1929 Geneva Convention. The Supreme Court [wrote] that the Convention was not judicially enforceable: the Convention specifies rights of prisoners of war, but "responsibility for observance and enforcement of these rights is upon political and military authorities." *Id.* at 789 n.14. . . . This aspect of

Eisentrager is still good law and demands our adherence. . . . [W]e have compared the 1949 Convention to the 1929 Convention. There are differences, but none of them renders *Eisentrager*'s conclusion about the 1929 Convention inapplicable to the 1949 Convention. [The court found that both treaties contemplated enforcement through interstate channels, not by courts addressing claims by individuals.] . . . The Supreme Court's *Rasul* decision did give district courts jurisdiction over habeas corpus petitions filed on behalf of Guantanamo detainees such as Hamdan. But *Rasul* did not render the Geneva Convention judicially enforceable. That a court has jurisdiction over a claim does not mean the claim is valid. The availability of habeas may obviate a petitioner's need to rely on a private right of action, but it does not render a treaty judicially enforceable. . . .

IV.

Even if the 1949 Geneva Convention could be enforced in court, this would not assist Hamdan. He contends that a military commission trial would violate his rights under Article 102, which provides that a "prisoner of war can be validly sentenced only if the sentence has been pronounced by the same courts according to the same procedure as in the case of members of the armed forces of the Detaining Power." One problem for Hamdan is that he does not fit the Article 4 definition of a "prisoner of war" entitled to the protection of the Convention. He does not purport to be a member of a group who displayed "a fixed distinctive sign recognizable at a distance" and who conducted "their operations in accordance with the laws and customs of war." See 1949 Convention, arts. 4A(2)(b), (c) & (d). If Hamdan were to claim prisoner of war status under Article 4A(4) as a person who accompanied "the armed forces without actually being [a] member[] thereof," he might raise that claim before the military commission under Army Regulation 190-8. . . .

Another problem for Hamdan is that the 1949 Convention does not apply to al Qaeda and its members. The Convention appears to contemplate only two types of armed conflicts. The first is an international conflict. Under Common Article 2, the provisions of the Convention apply to "all cases of declared war or of any other armed conflict which may arise between two or more of the High Contracting Parties, even if the state of war is not recognized by one of them." Needless to say, al Qaeda is not a state and it was not a "High Contracting Party." . . .

The second type of conflict, covered by Common Article 3, is a civil war—that is, an "armed conflict not of an international character occurring in the territory of one of the High Contracting Parties. . . . " In that situation, Common Article 3 prohibits "the passing of sentences and the carrying out of executions without previous judgment pronounced by a regularly constituted court affording all the judicial guarantees which are recognized as indispensable by a civilized people." Hamdan assumes that if Common Article 3 applies, a military commission could not try him. We will make the same assumption arguendo, which leaves the question whether Common Article 3 applies. Afghanistan is a "High Contracting Party." Hamdan was captured during hostilities there. But is the war against terrorism in general and the war against al Qaeda in particular, an "armed conflict not of an international character"? See INT'L COMM. RED CROSS, COMMENTARY: III GENEVA CONVENTION RELATIVE TO THE TREATMENT OF PRISONERS OF WAR 37 (1960) (Common Article 3 applies only to armed conflicts confined to "a single country"). President Bush determined . . . on February 7, 2002, that it did not fit that description because the conflict was "international in scope." . . . Hamdan was captured in Afghanistan in November 2001, but the conflict with al Qaeda arose before then, in other regions, including this country on September 11, 2001. Under the Constitution, the President "has a degree of independent authority to act" in foreign affairs, *Am. Ins. Ass'n v. Garamendi*, 539 U.S. 396, 414 (2003), and, for this reason and others, his construction and application of treaty provisions is entitled to "great weight." *United States v. Stuart*, 489 U.S. 353, 369 (1989). [T]he President's decision to treat our conflict with the Taliban separately from our conflict with al Qaeda is the sort of political-military decision constitutionally committed to him. . . . .

V.

Suppose . . . Common Article 3 . . . does cover Hamdan. Even then we would abstain from testing the military commission against the requirement in Common Article 3(1)(d) that sentences must be pronounced "by a regularly constituted court affording all the judicial guarantees which are recognized as indispensable by civilized peoples." Unlike his arguments that the military commission lacked jurisdiction, his argument here is that the commission's procedures—particularly its alleged failure to require his presence at all stages of the proceedings—fall short of what Common Article 3 requires. The issue thus raised is not whether the commission may try him, but rather how the commission may try him. That is by no stretch a jurisdictional argument. No one would say that a criminal defendant's contention that a district court will not allow him to confront the witnesses against him raises a jurisdictional objection. Hamdan's claim therefore falls [under precedents that require] that we defer to the ongoing military proceedings. If Hamdan were convicted, and if Common Article 3 covered him, he could contest his conviction in federal court after he exhausted his military remedies.

VI.

After determining that the 1949 Geneva Convention provided Hamdan a basis for judicial relief, the district court went on to consider the legitimacy of a military commission in the event Hamdan should eventually appear before one. In the district court's view, the principal constraint on the President's power to utilize such commissions is found in Article 36 of the Uniform Code of Military Justice, 10 U.S.C. §836, which provides:

> Pretrial, trial, and post-trial procedures, including modes of proof, for cases arising under this chapter triable in courts-martial, military commissions and other military tribunals . . . may be prescribed by the President by regulations which shall, so far as he considers practicable, apply the principles of law and the rules of evidence generally recognized in the trial of criminal cases in the United States district courts, *but which may not be contrary to or inconsistent with this chapter.*

(Emphasis added.) The district court interpreted the final qualifying clause to mean that military commissions must comply in all respects with the requirements of the Uniform Code of Military Justice (UCMJ). This was an error.

Throughout its Articles, the UCMJ takes care to distinguish between "courts-martial" and "military commissions." *See, e.g.*, 10 U.S.C. §821 (noting that "provisions of this chapter conferring jurisdiction upon courts-martial do not deprive military commissions . . . of concurrent jurisdiction"). The . . . majority of the UCMJ's procedural requirements refer only to courts-martial. The district court's approach would obliterate this distinction. A far more sensible reading is that in establishing military commissions, the President may not adopt procedures that are "contrary to or inconsistent with" the UCMJ's provisions governing military commissions. In particular, Article 39 requires that sessions of a "trial by court-martial . . . shall be conducted in the presence of the accused." Hamdan's trial before a military commission does not violate Article 36 if it omits this procedural guarantee. . . .

VII.

Although we have considered all of Hamdan's remaining contentions, the only one requiring further discussion is his claim that even if the Geneva Convention is not judicially enforceable, Army Regulation 190-8 provides a basis for relief. This regulation, which contains many subsections, "implements international law, both customary and codified, relating to [enemy prisoners of war], [retained personnel], [civilian internees], and [other detainees] which includes those persons held during military operations other than war." The regulation lists the Geneva Convention among the "principal treaties relevant to this regulation." . . . One subsection, §1-5(a)(2), requires that prisoners receive the protections of the Convention "until some other legal status is determined by *competent authority.*" (Emphasis added.) The President found that Hamdan was not a prisoner of war under the Convention. Nothing in the regulations, and nothing Hamdan argues, suggests that the President is not a "competent authority" for these purposes.

Hamdan claims that AR 190-8 entitles him to have a "competent tribunal" determine his status. But we believe the military commission is such a tribunal. The regulations specify that such a "competent tribunal" shall be composed of three commissioned officers, one of whom must be field-grade. A field-grade officer is an officer above the rank of captain and below the rank of brigadier general—a major, a lieutenant colonel, or a colonel. The President's order requires military commissions to be composed of between three and seven commissioned officers. The commission before which Hamdan is to be tried consists of three colonels. We therefore see no reason why Hamdan could not assert his claim to prisoner of war status before the military commission at the time of his trial and thereby receive the judgment of a "competent tribunal" within the meaning of Army Regulation 190-8. . . .

[A concurring judge agreed with all of the opinion except the view that Common Article 3 did not apply to U.S. conduct, noting:]

Common Article 3 fills [a] gap, providing some minimal protection for such non-eligibles in an "armed conflict not of an international character occurring in the territory of one of the High Contracting Parties." The gap being filled is the non-eligible party's failure to be a nation. Thus the words "not of an international character" are sensibly understood to refer to a conflict between a signatory nation and a non-state actor. The most obvious form of such a conflict is a civil war. But given the Convention's structure, the logical reading of "international character" is one that matches the basic derivation of the word "international," i.e., between nations. Thus, I think the context compels the view that a conflict between a signatory and a non-state actor is a conflict "not of an international character." In such a conflict, the signatory is bound to Common Article 3's modest requirements of "humane[]" treatment and "the judicial guarantees which are recognized as indispensable by civilized peoples."

Notes and Questions

1. Compare the President's Military Order to the ICCPR, the Third Geneva Convention, and Protocol I. Do any provisions of the Order facially violate those

treaties? Did the Department of Defense order provide for commissions consistent with the President's Order as well as those three treaties?

2. Why would the Executive Branch include many procedural protections in the Department of Defense order? What actors and norms were influencing them?

3. How do the options for prosecuting suspected terrorists in a manner consistent with international law turn on their status as prisoners of war or mere "detainees"?

4. Should the President's Executive Order constitute a notice of an emergency under Article 4 of the ICCPR? Why might the United States not wish to make a formal notification?

5. Does the court of appeals' approach to the Geneva Conventions in *Hamdan* give ample consideration to international law in determining the legality of military commissions? If the United States had declared Hamdan a POW, would the case have come out differently?

E. Ontological Doubts and Their Origins

However interesting and important the questions regarding the substantive law on the use of force and international humanitarian law to the U.S. response to September 11, the attacks and their aftermath raise more fundamental questions about the nature, legitimacy, and efficacy of international law. Viewed rather starkly, the episode was an attack on a great power, an inevitable response from it, support from its friends, and an unwillingness of nearly all states to challenge most of the U.S. action publicly. Would any nation allow international law to stand in its way in the face of such an attack? Can powerful states simply change the law unilaterally? Was the acquiescence by other states a reflection of their shock at the attacks, their distaste for the Taliban regime, or their fear of antagonizing the United States? Does their response suggest they were more influenced by political factors than legal ones?

Consider the following traditional (though well argued) attack on international law.

Charles Krauthammer, *The curse of legalism: International law? It's purely advisory*

The New Republic, Nov. 6, 1989, at 44-46, 50

. . . Americans have a propensity to see the international arena as a court of law, an ordered world regulated by word and contract. The resulting American foreign policy [is] informed less by national interest than by the dictates of a particularly disabling diplomatic disease: legalism.

Legalism starts with a naive belief in the efficacy of law as a regulator of international conduct. But it does not stop there. Legalism means operating abroad by an international rule book, acting on the basis of written and verbal promises, trusting to paper international institutions . . . to put things right. Legalism is a kind of diplomatic literalness, and, like all forms of literalness, it lacks imagination. Because it cannot imagine the infinite capacity of nation-states for duplicity, mendacity, and malice—in short, for lawlessness—it is not only naive but dangerous.

America tends to see the international arena as domestic life writ large. The fundamental difference between domestic and international life, of course, is that in the international arena the legal structure is not agreed upon and there is no enforcement mechanism. States are free to ignore the law. If the leader of Iran decides, say, to contract for the killing of a British writer [as was done to Salman Rushdie] (payment: a ticket to heaven and change), what is to stop him?

Legalism is international relations for lawyers. But the international arena is not a court. It is more a state of nature. That is how the world looks from Kurdistan, Afghanistan, and the other convulsed-stans of this world. That is not how it looks from Washington.

Consider, for example, the [1989] attempted coup in Panama. In the midst of the fighting, the U.S. Embassy in Panama City cabled Washington that the rebels were holding Gen. Manuel Noriega [Panama's dictator] and wanted to turn him over to the United States. . . . The New York Times describes what happened next: "That fact was reported to the State Department and Central Intelligence Agency simultaneously, prompting the State Department to call a hurried meeting with government lawyers to consider such a step. Minutes later, the coup collapsed."

The bullets are flying. A score of lives hang in the balance. Panama's future is about to be decided. And the State Department calls together its lawyers. Only in America. . . .

Nor was it only the State Department that in the fog of war kept a clear eye on the law. The United States had been asked by the coup's plotters to block two roads to prevent Noriega's reinforcements from reaching army headquarters. Noriega then flew his men to an airport on the other side of town and brought them in by a third route. These reinforcements turned the tide and saved him. What did the United States do? It did comply with the first request to block the two roads, because, American officials subsequently explained, these roadblocks could be justified as permitted under existing treaty arrangements with Panama. Blocking the third approach would take American forces off their bases and would clearly be "illegal." What could be disguised as a legal maneuver was undertaken. What could not was not, despite the fact that it would probably have tipped the balance of forces and toppled Noriega.

What should President Bush have done? . . . Go in, do what you have to do, and then call in the lawyers to find some retroactive legal justification for what you've done. . . .

Allowing policy to be driven by legal formulas rather than by national purpose is the heart of legalism. This is not, however, to say that treaties are meaningless. Reciprocal agreements . . . between countries that mutually agree to abide by agreements and can be trusted to do so are in the interests of both parties. If the United States and Canada draw up a fishing agreement, they have every reason to be legalistic in carrying it out, since if both countries are scrupulous in carrying it out, both profit. But this situation simply does not obtain when dealing with countries for which law of any kind is a mere instrument, infinitely adaptable to the requirements of power.

[I]nternational relations is not contract law. And treaties are not retained simply because their provisions are fully observed or renounced simply because they are breached. One has to make a larger judgment. . . . That is a policy judgment to which a reading of treaty text, no matter how close, contributes nothing. . . .

In this case, as in many of the tough ones, the law—international law—is an ass. It has nothing to offer. Foreign policy is best made without it.

   Much of Krauthammer's argument reflects the views of English jurist John Austin (1790-1859), whose ideas of law in turn were primarily influenced by Jeremy Bentham (1748-1832). Bentham had argued in favor of a positivist conception of law that sought to describe the existing rules with reference to formal, rather than moral, criteria. Law was a signal—a command—from the sovereign to those subject to his power concerning conduct; compliance was assured because the target knew with certainty of the repercussions for violating it. *See* Jeremy Bentham, Of Laws in General, ch. 1 (H.L.A. Hart ed., 1970). Bentham's positivism led Austin to conclude with respect to international law:

> [The] writers on the so-called law of nations, have fallen into a . . . confusion of ideas: they have confounded positive international morality, or the rules which actually obtain among civilised nations in their mutual intercourse, with their own vague conception of international morality as it *ought to be*. . . . [T]he law obtaining between nations is not positive law: for every positive law is set by a given sovereign to a person or persons in a state of subjection to its author. . . . The duties which [the law of nations] imposes are enforced by moral sanctions: by fear on the part of nations, or by fear on the part of sovereigns, of provoking general hostility, and incurring its probable evils, in case they shall violate maxims generally received and respected.

John Austin, The Province of Jurisprudence Determined 187, 201 (Berlin, Hampshire & Wollheim eds., 1954) (1832).

   The pure positivism of Bentham and Austin has faded in popularity as an understanding of law. The most significant rejection of Bentham and Austin came from within positivism itself, in particular from the work of the English scholar H.L.A. Hart. Hart rejected coercion as the basis for law and pointed out that people comply with law for a variety of reasons and that law itself emerges from custom as much as from sovereign commands. In response to Austin's views of international law, Hart wrote:

H.L.A. Hart, The Concept of Law

212-215, 222-226 (1961)

   We shall take it that . . . Chapter VII of the United Nations Charter [did not] introduce[] into international law anything which can be equated with the sanctions of municipal law. . . . [W]e shall suppose that . . . the law enforcement provisions of the Charter are likely to be paralysed by the veto and must be said to exist only on paper.
   To argue that international law is not binding because of its lack of organized sanctions is tacitly to accept the analysis of obligation contained in the theory that law is essentially a matter of orders backed by threats. . . . Yet, as we have argued, this identification distorts the role played in all legal thought and discourse of the ideas of obligation and duty. . . .
   [Hart assumes the law's inability to prohibit aggression but says states are most often at peace with each other. He continues:] These years of peace are only rationally to be expected, given the risks and stakes of war and the mutual needs of states; but they are worth regulating by rules which differ from those of municipal law in . . . not providing for their enforcement by any central organ. Yet what these rules require is thought and spoken of as obligatory; there is general pressure for conformity to the rules; claims and admissions are based on them and their breach is

held to justify not only insistent demands for compensation, but reprisals and countermeasures. When the rules are disregarded, it is not on the footing that they are not binding; instead efforts are made to conceal the facts. . . . [N]o simple deduction can be made from the necessity of organized sanctions to municipal law . . . to the conclusion that without them international law . . . imposes no obligations, is not "binding", and so not worth the title of "law". . . .

Sometimes insistence that the rules governing the relations between states are only moral rules, is inspired by the old dogmatism, that any form of social structure that is not reducible to orders backed by threats can only be a form of 'morality'. . . .

. . . [But the] appraisal of states' conduct in terms of morality is recognizably different from the formulation of claims, demands, and the acknowledgments of rights and obligations under the rules of international law. . . .

. . . What predominate in the arguments, often technical, which states address to each other over disputed matters of international law, are references to precedents, treaties and juristic writings; often no mention is made of moral right or wrong. . . .

. . . [In addition, t]he rules of international law, like those of municipal law, are often morally quite indifferent. . . . Hence legal rules, municipal and international, commonly contain much specific detail, and draw arbitrary distinctions, which would be unintelligible as elements in moral rules or principles. . . .

. . . [S]o we expect international law, but not morality, to tell us such things as the number of days a belligerent vessel may stay for refuelling or repairs in a neutral port; the width of territorial waters; the methods to be used in their measurement. . . .

. . . [As to whether law only exists when there is a moral obligation to comply,] it is difficult to see why . . . it *must* exist as a condition of the existence of international law. . . . [C]ertain rules are regularly respected even at the cost of certain sacrifices; claims are formulated by reference to them; breaches of the rules expose the offender to serious criticism and are held to justify claims for compensation or retaliation. These, surely, are all the elements required to support the statement that there exist among states rules imposing obligations on them. The proof that "binding" rules in any society exist, is simply that they are thought of, spoken of, and function as such. . . . It is, of course, true that rules could not exist . . . unless a preponderant majority accepted [them] and voluntarily cooperated in maintaining them. It is true also that the pressure exercised on those who break or threaten to break the rules is often relatively weak, and has usually been decentralized or unorganized. But as in the case of individuals, who voluntarily accept the far more strongly coercive system of municipal law, the motives for voluntarily supporting such a system may be extremely diverse. It may well be that any form of legal order is at its healthiest when there is a generally diffused sense that it is morally obligatory to conform to it. Nonetheless, adherence to law may not be motivated by it, but by calculations of long-term interest, or by the wish to continue a tradition or by disinterested concern for others. There seems no good reason for identifying any of these as a necessary condition of the existence of law either among individuals or states.

Notes and Questions

1. How would Krauthammer react to the interagency debate on POW status for those detained by U.S. forces in the war in Afghanistan? Does the debate support or undermine his position?

2. How effective a response does Hart offer to Austin? How meaningful can law be without some mechanisms to ensure compliance?

F. Two Affirmations of International Law's Utility

International lawyers have taken up Hart's ideas and expanded upon them to defend the reality of international law. Consider the following excerpt from a January 1994 speech by Boutros Boutros-Ghali, the UN's Secretary-General from 1992-1996 and an Egyptian professor of international law.

> Today, even those who do not respect international law adopt its language and its terms of reference. Today, even the most flagrant violators of international law feel compelled to assert the compatibility of their actions with its principles. International law has helped both to create our vision of progress, and to give that vision substance. Through international law we proclaim the universal aspirations and values that are common to all societies. . . . International law is, I am proud to say, humanity's common language of communication.
>
> By means of this common language of communication, we are able, in a practical way, to address the challenges that constitute our most fundamental societal concerns. . . .
>
> As we face the challenges that lie ahead our goal must be to transform human relations so that international law becomes a true code of conduct, as well as a means of human communication. In international law itself we have both a strategy for pursuing this goal and a very practical means of taking action.

U.N. Doc. SG/SM/5202 (1994).

Professor Louis Henkin has offered one of the most enduring defenses of international law.

Louis Henkin, How Nations Behave

42-44, 88-90, 93 (2d ed. 1979)

Violations of law attract attention and the occasional important violation is dramatic; the daily, sober loyalty of nations to the law and their obligations is hardly noted. It is probably the case that almost all nations observe almost all principles of international law and almost all of their obligations almost all of the time. Every day nations respect the borders of other nations, treat foreign diplomats and citizens and property as required by law, observe thousands of treaties with a hundred countries. . . .

. . . [I]nternational law achieves—and reflects—a measure of order in the life of nations. . . .

Much is made of the fact that, in international society, there is no one to compel nations to obey the law. But physical coercion is not the sole or even principal force ensuring compliance with law. Important law is observed by the most powerful, even in domestic societies, although there is no one to compel them. In the United States, the President, Congress, and the mighty armed forces obey orders of a Supreme Court whose single marshal is unarmed.

Too much is made of the fact that nations act not out of "respect for law" but from fear of the consequences of breaking it. And too much is made of the fact that the consequences are not "punishment" by "superior," legally constituted authority, but are the response of the victim and his friends and the unhappy results for friendly relations, prestige, credit, international stability, and other interests which in domestic society would be considered "extra-legal." The fact is that, in domestic society, individuals observe law principally from fear of consequences, and there are "extra-legal" consequences that are often enough to deter violation, even were official punishment lacking. . . . In international society, law observance must depend more heavily on these extra-legal sanctions, which means that law observance will depend more closely on the law's current acceptability and on the community's—especially the victim's—current interest in vindicating it. It does not mean that law is not law, or that its observance is less law observance.

There are several mistakes in the related impression that nations do pursuant to law only what they would do anyhow. In part, the criticism misconceives the purpose of law. Law is generally not designed to keep individuals from doing what they are eager to do. Much of law, and the most successful part, is a codification of existing mores, of how people behave and feel they ought to behave. . . . If there were no law against homicide, most individuals in contemporary societies would still refrain from murder. Were that not so, the law could hardly survive and be effective. . . .

At the same time much law (particularly tort law and "white collar crimes") is observed because it is law and because its violation would have undesirable consequences. The effective legal system, it should be clear, is not the one which punishes the most violators, but rather that which has few violations to punish because the law deters potential violators. . . . This suggests that the law does not concern itself principally to "criminal elements" on the one hand or to "saints" on the other. . . . The law is aimed principally at the mass in between—at those who, while generally law-abiding, may yet be tempted to some violations by immediate self-interest. In international society, too, law is not effective against the Hitlers, and is not needed for that nation which is content with its lot and has few temptations. International law aims at nations which are in principle law-abiding but which might be tempted to commit a violation if there were no threat of undesirable consequences. . . .

In large part . . . the argument that nations do pursuant to law only what they would do anyhow is plain error. The fact that particular behavior is required by law brings into play those ultimate advantages in law observance that suppress temptations and override the apparent immediate advantages from acting otherwise. In many areas, the law at least achieves a common standard or rule and clarity as to what is agreed. . . .

The most common deprecation of international law, finally, insists that no government will observe international law "in the crunch, when it really hurts." If the implication is that nations observe law only when it does not matter, it is grossly mistaken. Indeed, one might as well urge the very opposite: violations in "small matters" sometimes occur because the actor knows that the victim's response will be slight; serious violations are avoided because they might bring serious reactions. The most serious violation—the resort to war—generally does not occur, although it is only when major interests are at stake that nations would even be tempted to this violation. On the other hand, if the suggestion is that when it costs too much to observe international law nations will violate it, the charge is no doubt true. But the implications are less devastating than might appear, since a nation's perception of "when it really hurts" to observe law must take into account its interests in law and in its observance, and the costs of violation. The criticism might as well be leveled at domestic law where persons generally law-abiding will violate laws, commit even crimes of violence, when it "really hurts" not to do so. Neither the domestic violations nor the international ones challenge the basic validity of the law or the basic effectiveness of the system.

Notes and Questions

1. How would Boutros-Ghali and Henkin explain the behavior of the United States and other states in the "war on terrorism?"

2. Is Boutros-Ghali's conception of international law sufficient for it to make a difference in the behavior of states? How important is a language of communication?

3. Is the picture of international law Professor Henkin portrays too optimistic? Does his view that states act in accordance with international law mean that international law actually influences their decision making? How would Krauthammer respond to Henkin? Who has the better argument?

4. What do the Problems in this book suggest about Henkin's analysis of the reasons states comply or do not comply with international law?

G. Two Perspectives on Law and Power

Many defenders of international law, such as Boutros-Ghali and Henkin, focus on the role of international law in serving as the language of claims in the international system and on actual compliance with it. Yet the relationship of power to law, evidenced by the "war on terrorism," is not central to their analysis. Other scholars have explored the law-power relationship more explicitly.

W. Michael Reisman, *Law From the Policy Perspective*

International Law Essays 1, 6-9 (Myres S. McDougal &
W. Michael Reisman eds., 1981)

. . . For a variety of reasons, deriving from culture, inertia, professional self-interest or ignorance, we tend to think of the law as a thing found in a book, a sort of autonomous control system which is preprogrammed and which can be predicted by logic or professional hunch. But it is not. It is a process of making decisions in conformity with the expectations of appropriateness of those who are politically relevant: more concisely, a process of authoritative decision. Who is politically relevant in a particular setting, whose norms "apply" is never self-evident; complex assessments are involved and they themselves become factors in the outcome. [T]he norms of a contemporary industrial-based system . . . are in a constant flux with pressures for stasis and change from the many features of the process. . . .

Decisions are effective social choices about dividing up the good and bad things of life. Politics are the processes by which decisions are made and law, in common parlance, refers to certain unique political processes, distinctive because of their techniques for recruitment of personnel, their manifest and latent criteria of choice their situations, the special symbols deployed and so on. The conventional wisdom . . . holds that there is a sharp distinction between law and politics, a mutual exclusiveness, even an antithesis. Law is decision according to principles, we are told: reasoned decision. Politics is decision according to power. If you are a lawyer, the word "politics" or "political decision" often has a pejorative tone. . . .

A moment's reflection will show that this distinction between law and politics is artificial, even preposterous. Notions of authority, expectations of what is right with regard to social choices, play a major role in politics; conversely power is a very critical and indispensable factor in law. . . . This does not mean that every exercise of power is lawful or that every putative act by someone in a manifest law role is effective. But it does mean that lawful acts, to be such, will require a minimum degree of effectiveness and that, over time, effective acts are likely to be deemed lawful. Power and authority are always co-present in varying degrees. This notion of the co-presence of authority and power or control is fundamental to legal theory and absolutely necessary for the performance of legal functions. . . .

There are dramatic instances in which the authority process and the power process of a group seem sharply separated. . . . If you go to an American town, as a journalist or perhaps a lawyer sent by a client considering moving his plant there, your first question will be, "Who's the mayor?" Your second question will be, "Who's the boss?" Your questions bespeak a keen recognition of the fact that the process of law and the process of power, as popularly conceptualized, need not and often do not overlap. Because you are interested in really understanding what is going on or in getting things done, you wish to identify those social sectors in which decisions are made by authority and those made with little reference to authority.

. . . [I]t is plain that power and authority are in a sort of symbiotic relationship. Now it is probable that discrepancies between power and authority over an extended period of time will lead to readjustments in peoples' minds as to what is authoritative. Power can "legitimize" or "authorize" itself. . . . Some members who resent the change may, of course, leave the group or disrupt the group and it is quite possible that the group will be terminated. . . .

At any particular moment, it may be hard to determine accurately where authority ends and power begins in the expected handling of certain matters. . . .

From the most inclusive international arena to a tiny social circle like the friendship group, there is always a power elite: individuals who draw on resources—military, economic, charismatic and so on—which give them in a particular social situation predominant power. Anyone who wishes to operate effectively, within a group, and *a fortiori* the lawyer, must develop a keen sense of where the power elite is and the structure of the processes through which it operates. The lawyer cannot afford to become hyper-realistic and overlook the authority component, for just as it is influenced by power, it too influences power. . . . Nor can the lawyer afford to become excessively "proper" and refuse to take account of the power realities. What is called for is a balanced focus on both authority and control.

I am describing a phenomenon and not appraising its moral dimension. That, international law notwithstanding, a large state will intervene in the affairs of a smaller state if it deems its own security threatened does not mean that it is right for it to do so. . . . It does mean that people in the smaller and larger state who are trying to develop a realistic set of matter-of-fact expectations of future probabilities and possibilities in order to maintain wealth, security and life itself, will be wise to put this possibility into their reckoning.

Martti Koskenniemi, *The Politics of International Law*

1 Eur. J. Intl. L. 4, 9, 28-29, 31-32 (1990)

Two criticisms are often advanced against international law. One group of critics has accused international law of being too political in the sense of being too dependent on states' political power. Another group has argued that the law is too political because [it is] founded on speculative utopias. The standard point about the non-existence of legislative machineries, compulsory adjudication and enforcement procedures captures both criticisms. From one perspective, this criticism highlights the infinite flexibility of international law, its character as a manipulable facade for power politics. From another perspective, the criticism stresses the moralistic character of international law, its distance from the realities of power politics. According to the former criticism, international law is too *apologetic* to be taken seriously in the construction of international order. According to the latter, it is too *utopian* to the identical effect.

International lawyers have had difficulty answering these criticisms. The more reconstructive doctrines have attempted to prove the normativity of the law, its autonomy from politics, the more they have become vulnerable to the charge of utopianism. The more they have insisted on the close connexion between international law and state behaviour, the less normative their doctrines have appeared. [Koskenniemi reviews and criticizes the responses of four different schools of international law to this dilemma.]

The Rule of Law constitutes an attempt to provide communal life without giving up individual autonomy. Communal life is, of course, needed to check individualism from leading either into anarchy or tyranny. Individualism is needed because otherwise it would remain objectionable for those who feel that the kind of community provided by it does not meet their political criteria. From their perspective, the law's communitarian pretensions would turn out as totalitarian apologies.

The law aims to fulfil its double task by becoming formal: by endorsing neither particular communitarian ideals nor particular sovereign policies. Or, conversely, an acceptable legal rule, argument or doctrine is one which can explain itself both from the perspective of enhancing community (because it would otherwise seem apologist) as well as safeguarding sovereignty (because its implications would otherwise remain totalitarian). The problem is that as soon as any of these justifications are advanced to support *some particular kind of communal existence or some determined limit for sovereign autonomy*, they are vulnerable from an opposing substantive perspective. So, while an advocate justifies his preferred substantive outcome by its capacity to support community, it becomes simultaneously possible for his counterpart-not sharing the same communal ideal—to challenge the very justification as totalitarian. Correspondingly, a rule, principle or solution justified by recourse to the way it protects sovereignty may—for someone drawing the limits of "sovereignty" differently—be objected as furthering egoism and anarchy. . . .

Kind of Paradox

. . . Because the world—including lawyers' views about it—is conflictual, any grand design for a "world order" will always remain suspect. Any legal rule, principle or world order project will only seem acceptable when stated in an abstract and formal fashion. When it is applied, it will have overruled some interpretation, some collective experience and appear apologist.

Social theorists have documented a recent modern turn in national societies away from the *Rechtstaat* [state based on law] into a society in which social conflict is increasingly met with flexible, contextually determined standards and compromises. The turn away from general principles and formal rules into contextually determined equity may reflect a similar turn in the development of international legal thought and practice. . . . Their solution requires venturing into fields such as politics, . . . [which has been] formally delimited beyond the point at which legal argument was supposed to stop in order to remain "legal." To be sure, we shall remain uncertain. Resolutions based on political acceptability cannot be made with the kind of certainty post-Enlightenment lawyers once hoped to attain. And yet, it is only . . . their remaining so which will prevent their use as apologies for tyranny.

Notes and Questions

1. How would Reisman and Koskenniemi explain the actions of the United States and other international actors in response to September 11? Would they see American power as leading to a violation of international law or a change in the law? Do their perspectives suggest that law was relevant to the decision makers in that episode?

2. Does Reisman's attempt to understand the relationship of law and power make the former a slave to the latter? How central is the "control" element of law? What does this suggest about the validity of treaties that are routinely violated?

3. Do you agree with Koskenniemi that international lawyers are trapped between apology and utopia? Is there a way out of the conundrum?

H. Two Views from International Relations

International relations theorists have adopted a vast range of attitudes toward international law. At one end, the realist approach believes that state behavior is determined by structural factors in the international system alone, in particular the relative political, economic, and military power of states. The extent to which a state's behavior in fact conforms to international norms concerning a particular issue depends upon these factors and not norms at all; norms merely reflect the interests of states exogenously determined. Realists may thus accept that international law exists, but they argue that it has no independent effect on state behavior.

Other schools of international relations are more open to the possibility that norms can indeed influence behavior. Those under the label "institutionalism" believe that states can combine to create institutions that can make rules affecting state behavior. At the same time, however, institutionalists argue that these norms influence states not because of any internal characteristics as law, but because they form part of an entire regime—that is, a "set[] of implicit or explicit principles, norms, rules, and decision-making procedures around which actors' expectations converge in a given area of international relations." Stephen D. Krasner, *Structural Causes and Regime Consequences: Regimes as Intervening Variables, in* International Regimes 1, 2 (Stephen D. Krasner ed., 1983). Institutionalists posit that regimes change state behavior by creating incentives for compliance—such as linking compliance on one issue with rewards or penalties on other issues or highlighting a state's reputation as one that complies or violates regime policy. Some institutionalists have specifically focused on international law.

Robert O. Keohane, *International Relations and International Law: Two Optics*

38 Harv. Intl. L.J. 487, 487-488, 489-494, 501-502 (1997)

. . . Traditionally, political scientists have styled themselves as "realistic" rather than "idealistic." They are utilitarians of one form or another. According to this view, elite states seek to maintain position, wealth, and power in an uncertain world by acquiring, retaining, and wielding power—resources that enable them to achieve multiple purposes. States use the rules of international law as instruments to attain their interests. International law can thus be interpreted through such an "instrumentalist optic." . . .

The "instrumentalist optic" focuses on interests and argues that rules and norms will matter only if they affect the calculations of interests by agents. International institutions exist because they perform valuable functions for states. They can make a difference, but only when their rules create specific opportunities and impose constraints which affect state interests. A crude version of instrumentalism discounts the observation that states often conform to rules. In this view, states only accede to rules that they favor, and comply because such conformity is convenient. . . .

Subtler instrumentalist arguments recognize that rules, as part of the environment faced by a state, exert an impact on state behavior. They do so, in this view, not because the norms they reflect persuade people that they should behave differently. Rather, they alter incentives, not merely for states conceived of as units, but for interest groups, organizations, members of professional associations, and individual policymakers within governments. . . .

[Keohane contrasts the "instrumentalist optic" with the "normative optic" held by some international lawyers.] International lawyers often argue that the legitimacy of norms and rules has causal effect. . . . Legitimacy, says Thomas M. Franck, exerts a "compliance pull," which competes with the pull exerted by interests in reneging. Rules that are determinate and coherent—important components of legitimacy—are associated with greater compliance than those that are not, at least in part because their clarity makes it possible "to dismiss bogus, self-serving interpretations." Officials may routinely keep many commitments because they have respect for law. . . .

According to this "normative optic," norms have causal impact. . . . They exert a profound impact on how people think about state roles and obligations, and therefore on state behavior. This "normative optic" shows respect for the discourse that takes place when commitments are contested. It is also consistent with the attention that policymakers pay to norms and ideas about what makes norms legitimate. How else can one account for the enormous amount of argument over rule interpretation? . . .

Empirically, it is hard to validate causal arguments about the impact of norms or discourse. . . . "Legitimacy" is difficult to measure independent from the compliance that it is supposed to explain. For instance, Franck describes a rule's compliance "pull power" as "its index of legitimacy." Yet legitimacy is said to explain "compliance pull," making the argument circular. . . .

Both of these optics seem necessary, yet neither is sufficient. . . . It can hardly be disputed that some states follow the instrumentalist optic some of the time. Most of the time, however, the policies of all states are affected by their material interests, as perceived by their elites; and the relative power capabilities of states are relevant to the degree to which they can achieve their purposes. The literature on international institutions has demonstrated, over the last twenty years, that states do modify their behavior in light of rules, although the extent to which they do so is contested.

What is at issue, however, is not the relevance of the instrumentalist optic, but its sufficiency. . . . Do discourse and persuasion matter, or are calculations of interest and power all that really count?

To answer this question, we need somehow to trace out the causal pathways on which these two optics rely and to generate testable propositions from them. . . . [R]esearchers should eventually test these hypotheses against evidence chosen to minimize bias, rather than merely to illustrate arguments. . . .

[After reviewing the role of reputation, state interests, and institutions on the effect of norms on state behavior, Keohane concludes:] Interests are changeable, responding to changes in descriptive information, causal beliefs, and principled beliefs. Hence norms matter for interests. So do beliefs about others' beliefs; that is, reputation. Concern for reputation can be a means of reconciling instrumentalist prescriptions with normative ones. However, this reconciliation only takes place reliably within the context of highly valued institutions, which align material and extra-material incentives. Institutions are especially important for the way in which they can alter beliefs, can sometimes influence what we want or do, and can always affect how others will behave if they have any impact at all.

A more recent school of international relations has proved even more receptive to the role of law in international affairs. The constructivist ontology starts from a completely different point compared to other international relations schools by seeing the interests and identities of states as, in the words of John Ruggie, "socially constructed." As part of their focus on ideas as constituting the makeup and interests of international actors, constructivists embrace norms. For them, legal rules and other norms do not only respond to or merely influence the fixed interests of actors or the structure of the international system. Rather, they help define identity, interests, and structure. Leading scholars have sought to describe how international norms effect these changes. The following excerpt offers one such explanation.

Martha Finnemore & Kathryn Sikkink, *International Norm Dynamics and Political Change*

52 Intl. Org. 887, 895-896, 901-902, 904 (1998)

Norm influence may be understood as a three-stage process. . . . [T]he first stage is "norm emergence"; the second stage involves broad norm acceptance, which we term . . . a "norm cascade"; and the third stage involves internalization. The first two stages are divided by a threshold or "tipping" point, at which a critical mass of relevant state actors adopt the norm. . . .

The characteristic mechanism of the first stage, norm emergence, is persuasion by norm entrepreneurs. Norm entrepreneurs attempt to convince a critical mass of states (norm leaders) to embrace new norms. The second stage is characterized more by a dynamic of imitation as the norm leaders attempt to socialize other states to become norm followers. . . . At the far end of the norm cascade, norm internalization occurs; norms acquire a taken-for-granted quality and are no longer a matter of broad public debate. . . . Completion of the "life cycle" is not an inevitable process. Many emergent norms fail to reach a tipping point. . . .

Research on women's suffrage globally provides support for the idea of the life cycle of norms and the notion of a "tipping point" or threshold of normative change. Although many domestic suffrage organizations were active in the nineteenth century, it was not until 1904, when women's rights advocates founded the International Women's Suffrage Association (IWSA), that an international campaign for suffrage was launched. In fact, rather than a single international campaign for women's suffrage, there were three or four overlapping campaigns with different degrees of coordination. A quantitative analysis of the cross-national acquisition of suffrage rights reveals a different dynamic at work for early and late adopters of women's suffrage. Prior to a threshold point in 1930, no country had adopted women's suffrage without strong pressure from domestic suffrage organizations. Between 1890 and 1930, Western countries with strong national women's movements were most likely to grant female suffrage. Although some original norm entrepreneurs came from the United States and the United Kingdom, this was not a case of "hegemonic socialization," since the first states to grant women the right to vote (New Zealand, Australia, Finland) were not hegemons, and the United States and the United Kingdom lagged ten to twenty years behind. After 1930, international and transnational influences become far more important than domestic pressures for norm adoption, and countries adopted women's suffrage even though they faced no domestic pressures to do so. For women's suffrage, the first stage of norm emergence lasted over eighty years: it took from the Seneca Falls Conference in 1848 until 1930 for twenty states to adopt women's suffrage. In the twenty years that followed the tipping point, however, some forty-eight countries adopted women's suffrage norms. . . .

[In the first stage, it] matters which states adopt the norm. Some states are critical to a norm's adoption; others are less so. What constitutes a "critical state" will vary from issue to issue, but one criterion is that critical states are those without which the achievement of the substantive norm goal is compromised. Thus, in the case of land mines, a state that did not produce or use land mines would not have been a critical state. By contrast, the decision in mid-1997 by France and Great Britain, both land mines producers, to support the treaty [banning land mines] could well have contributed to the norm cascade that happened in late 1997. . . .

[In the second stage, m]ore countries begin to adopt new norms more rapidly even without domestic pressure for such change. . . . [T]he primary mechanism for promoting norm cascades is an active process of international socialization intended to induce norm breakers to become norm followers . . . : emulation (of heroes), praise (for behavior that conforms to group norms), and ridicule (for deviation). In the context of international politics, socialization involves diplomatic praise or censure, either bilateral or multilateral, which is reinforced by material sanctions and incentives. States, however, are not the only agents of socialization. Networks of norm entrepreneurs and international organizations also act as agents of socialization by pressuring targeted actors to adopt new policies and laws and to ratify treaties and by monitoring compliance with international standards. . . .

Socialization is thus the dominant mechanism of a norm cascade—the mechanism through which norm leaders persuade others to adhere—but what makes socialization work? . . . We argue that states comply with norms in stage 2 for reasons that relate to their identities as members of an international society. Recognition that state identity fundamentally shapes state behavior, and that state identity is, in turn, shaped by the cultural-institutional context within which states act, has been an important contribution of recent norms research. . . . What happens at the tipping point is that enough states and enough critical states endorse the new norm to redefine appropriate behavior for the identity called "state" or some relevant subset of states (such as a "liberal" state or a European state).

[In stage 3], norms may become so widely accepted that they are internalized by actors and achieve a "taken-for-granted" quality that makes conformance with the norm almost automatic. For this reason, internalized norms can be both extremely powerful (because behavior according to the norm is not questioned) and hard to discern (because actors do not seriously consider or discuss whether to conform). . . .

Notes and Questions

1. How would Keohane explain the actions of the United States in response to September 11? What international regimes, if any, are enabling or constraining U.S. actions, and by what causal pathways?

2. Do the constructivist scholars help explain the actions of the United States in response to September 11? Is the U.S. identity as a global actor shaped by international norms concerning *jus ad bellum* and *jus in bello*?

3. Would these international relations scholars argue that international law affected the United States more or less than, for example, Henkin would assert?

4. To what extent do these international relations scholars care about norms themselves—their internal properties, as it were—in explaining why states observe them? What do their views suggest about the differences between hard and soft law?

5. What does international relations theory offer compared to approaches from within international law in helping us understand whether law matters in international affairs?

III. JUSTICE, INEQUALITY, AND INTERNATIONAL LAW: THE AIDS PANDEMIC AND ACCESS TO AFFORDABLE MEDICINES

Having considered international law's legitimacy and efficacy, we now turn to issues of inequality, fairness, and justice. Although international law treats states as equal in a formal and juridical sense, the world states inhabit is marked by dramatic inequalities in wealth, power, and security. If more powerful states can disproportionately shape international rules and influence international bodies, as suggested by the materials above, then the growth in international legal norms and institutions threatens to further entrench these inequalities.

Moreover, many contemporary economic processes may be widening the gaps between rich and poor both within and among states; critics charge that globalization not only increases inequalities of political power and influence but also highlights new dimensions of inequality. And, by increasing the inequalities in resources and capabilities among states, globalization may also be exacerbating the differences in states' abilities to make and to break rules of international law. Whether international law directly or indirectly contributes to growing inequality is thus a pressing question.

Finally, some international legal norms may erode the ability of states, particularly weak states, to address effectively a growing number of social, economic, and political issues on the domestic plane. So another important question is whether international law, which reaches increasingly deeply into the domestic realm, helps or hinders states in their efforts to address pressing social and economic issues. More broadly, the critical inquiry is whether international law helps produce justice at either the international or the domestic level.

Our focus in this section will be on international responses to the AIDS pandemic, but these questions are germane to many of the problems discussed throughout this book. We focus on the AIDS crisis in part because it involves one of the most devastating epidemics in human history and is therefore an urgent humanitarian crisis. Moreover, the AIDS crisis has given rise to a highly visible conflict between developing state governments and AIDS activists on the one hand, both of whom insist on affordable access to safe medicines, and developed state governments and pharmaceutical firms on the other, which advocate the commercial interests of patent rights holders. Finally, it presents a complex mix of economic, scientific, social, and public health issues. For these reasons, the conflict over access to AIDS drugs not only implicates issues of inequality, distributional fairness, and justice; it also illustrates many of the profound structural transformations in the issues and actors that constitute the contemporary international legal arena.

As you read the materials that follow, consider which interests are served by the international legal norms relevant to developing states' access to affordable medicines, the legitimacy of the processes used to make new norms in this area, how the different levels of political power of different actors affected the content of these norms, and whether the relevant legal norms represent a fair balance among the competing interests. More broadly, consider whether international law advances or impedes the quest for a more just world and how international legal norms and processes could be changed to promote justice more effectively.

A. The Problem

The numbers are staggering: HIV/AIDS has killed more than 25 million people worldwide since it was first recognized in 1981, making it one of the most destructive pandemics in recorded history. In 2005, the total number of people living with HIV reached an estimated 40.3 million, the highest level ever. 2005 also witnessed some five million new HIV infections and around three million deaths due to AIDS-related diseases. In short, despite advances in medical technologies and access to treatment, the AIDS epidemic continues to outstrip global efforts to contain it.

Sub-Saharan Africa has been the region hardest hit by this pandemic. This area contains just over 10 percent of the world's population, but is home to more than 60 percent of all people living with HIV. In 2005, an estimated 3.2 million people in the region became newly infected, and 2.4 million adults and children died of AIDS. These bleak figures led the Joint UN Programme on HIV/AIDS (UNAIDS) to conclude that "Southern Africa remains the epicentre of the global AIDS epidemic."

Moreover, for all the devastation that it has already caused, the AIDS epidemic may still be in its early stages. Between 2003 and 2005, the number of people living with AIDS increased in all but one region of the world; in the Caribbean, the second-most affected region in the world, HIV prevalence remained constant. Growing epidemics are underway in Central Asia and Eastern Europe, where the number of people infected with HIV increased by one quarter (to 1.6 million) since 2003, and the number of AIDS deaths almost doubled. In East Asia, the number of people living with HIV in 2005 increased by one fifth, to 870,000, compared with two years earlier. Finally, there are alarming signs that other populous states, including Indonesia and Pakistan, could be on the verge of serious epidemics.

Unlike many diseases, AIDS robs societies of their most productive adults during the prime of their life. In many developing states AIDS is literally eliminating the products of decades of investment in education and human capital; Zimbabwe, Botswana, and Namibia could each lose up to one-third of their labor force by 2020. As a result, AIDS has a devastating economic impact in addition to its emotional and social costs.

While there is no cure or vaccine for AIDS, powerful medications can transform AIDS from a deadly into a manageable disease by delaying the onset of AIDS symptoms and prolonging the lives of those infected. However, these drug therapies often cost more than $15,000 per year per person in Western countries, which place them economically out of reach of most HIV-infected individuals. Indeed, in 2005, no more than one in ten Africans and one in seven Asians in need of anti-retroviral treatment were receiving it. Some developing states have responded to the high cost of patented drugs by either producing or importing generic drugs, which sometimes cost a tenth of the price of patented drugs. Drug companies argue that these actions violate international legal norms and discourage the development of new drugs, as high prices permit companies to recover their considerable research and development costs and to fund new projects. The firms also argue that reduced drug prices will not guarantee that medicines will reach the poorest and neediest populations in the developing world. They contend that accessibility to drugs is hampered by many factors other than price, including a lack of trained medical personnel, health facilities located great distances from rural populations, inadequate infrastructure (roads, electricity, water), and illiteracy that inhibits health awareness and treatment compliance.

B. The International Legal Framework: TRIPs and Public Health

Much of the debate over access to affordable medicines in developing states has focused on the relationship of domestic intellectual property (IP) law and international economic law, particularly the multilateral Agreement on Trade-Related Intellectual Property Rights (TRIPs agreement). Intellectual property rights are granted under domestic law and confer exclusive rights within the territory of a particular state. Historically, the levels of protection and enforcement of intellectual property rights have varied considerably among states. In the 1980s and 1990s, trade in the products of knowledge-based industries (including chemical, pharmaceutical, and software companies) grew significantly, and the differences in national IP regimes increasingly gave rise to international tensions. Many high technology companies in developed states argued that lax IP laws and enforcement in developing states permitted widespread counterfeiting that distorted international markets.

The TRIPs agreement, negotiated as part of the 1994 Uruguay Round agreements, was an attempt to narrow the gaps in various domestic systems and ensure that adequate minimum levels of IP protection existed in the domestic laws of all WTO member states. With respect to patents, TRIPs provides that domestic patent laws "shall confer on [the patent owner] the following exclusive rights . . . to prevent third parties not having the owner's consent from the acts of: making, using, offering for sale, selling, or importing" the patented product. TRIPs further requires that states must provide patent protection to medicines and pharmaceutical processes. Prior to TRIPs, approximately 50 states excluded pharmaceutical products from patent protection.

However, patent rights are not absolute. TRIPS permits governments to issue so-called compulsory licenses, or authorization to third parties to produce a patented product or use a patented process without the patent holder's consent, under certain conditions. TRIPs Article 31 permits compulsory licensing

> (b) . . . only . . . if, prior to such use, the proposed user has made efforts to obtain authorization from the right holder on reasonable commercial terms and conditions and that such efforts have not been successful within a reasonable period of time. This requirement may be waived by a Member in the case of a national emergency or other circumstances of extreme urgency or in cases of public non-commercial use. . . .
> (f) such use shall be authorized predominantly for the supply of the domestic market of the Member authorizing such use. . . .

As patent holders enjoy monopoly rights, they often charge different prices in different jurisdictions. Differential pricing and currency fluctuations create the opportunity for parties to purchase a patented good in one state and then resell it in a second state without the patent holder's consent. The TRIPs provision quoted above appears to require states to grant patent holders the right to prohibit these so-called parallel, or grey market, imports. However, different states have different rules about parallel imports; many adopt the legal principle known as "exhaustion," which means that once a patent holder has sold its good in one state, its patent is "exhausted," and the patent holder no longer can control what happens to the product. The TRIPs agreement states that "nothing in this Agreement shall be used to address the issue of the exhaustion of intellectual property rights" in WTO dispute resolution. In other words, even if a state allows parallel imports in a way that might violate the TRIPS agreement, this cannot be challenged in WTO dispute resolution proceedings.

Many developing states opposed the TRIPs agreement, in part out of a fear that the agreement would lead to higher pharmaceutical prices, particularly in states that historically had not patented medicines. However, developing states accepted TRIPs as part of the entire package of Uruguay Round agreements, including agreements that promised greater access to developed state markets in textiles and agricultural goods. Developed states had to ensure that their IP laws complied with TRIPs by January 1, 1995; developing states were given until January 1, 2000; and least developed states until January 1, 2006.

C. Two Domestic Responses

The tensions between the interest in protecting IP rights and providing affordable AIDS medications have risen most sharply in South Africa and Brazil. The South African case involves the issue of parallel imports, while the Brazilian case primarily revolves around the issue of compulsory licensing. Both fact patterns were driven in large part by non-state actors, involved conflict between developing and developed states, and entailed complex relationships between international and domestic legal processes.

1. South Africa

The devastation wrought by the AIDS pandemic is perhaps felt most dramatically in South Africa, which has more HIV-positive people than any other state in the world. With over 5.6 million people infected, South Africa has more people living with HIV than North and South America and Europe combined. Having lagged behind most other epidemics in the region, AIDS in South Africa is now taking a devastating toll in human lives. A 15-year-old in South Africa has a better than 50 percent chance of dying of AIDS and the U.S. government estimates that, at current infection rates, AIDS could kill as many as one-quarter of South Africa's approximately 40 million citizens.

In an effort to reduce drug prices, the South African government amended the Medicines and Medical Devices Regulatory Act (Medicines Act) in 1997 to permit compulsory licensing and parallel imports. As South Africa lacked a highly developed domestic pharmaceutical industry, the parallel import provisions were of greater practical import. The United States denounced the amendments as "clearly inconsistent with South Africa's obligations under TRIPs," and, in the words of a State Department report, launched "a full court press" to persuade the South African government to withdraw or modify the amendments. The Pharmaceutical Research and Manufacturers of America (PhRMA), an industry trade group, was also active, declaring South Africa a "test case" for states that oppose U.S. efforts to strengthen IP protections around the world and urging the U.S. government to impose trade sanctions on South Africa. Shortly thereafter, the United States placed South Africa on a special "watch list," with the explicit threat of trade sanctions, largely because of the Medicines Act. In June 1998 the White House announced that it would postpone consideration of South Africa's request for preferential tariff treatment for various goods pending progress on the dispute over IP protections. In October 1998 the U.S. House of Representatives passed a bill that would temporarily cut off aid to South Africa.

While the United States was pressing South Africa to change its law, 39 drug companies from the United States, Europe, and South Africa challenged the Medicines Act in the South African courts, alleging that it unconstitutionally granted the Health Minister too much discretionary power and violated the TRIPs agreement. Given the various pressures at both international and domestic levels, in September 1999, South Africa agreed to review the Medicines Act in return for the drug firms' agreement to suspend the lawsuit. At the same time, the U.S. and South African governments reached an understanding that South Africa had an "urgent need to provide better, more affordable health care while ensuring that intellectual property rights are protected," and agreed to "set aside this issue from our bilateral trade agenda."

However, the South African government made no significant changes to the law, and industry revived its lawsuit in late 2000. This sparked a political firestorm; AIDS activists launched a media campaign attacking the industry's insensitivity to Africa's AIDS crisis, and Germany, France, the Netherlands, and the European Parliament—as well as a petition signed by a quarter million people worldwide—urged the companies to drop the suit. In light of mounting public pressure and after

UN Secretary-General Kofi Annan's personal intervention, the companies agreed to drop the suit in April 2001 in exchange for the government's promise that it would implement the law in accordance with TRIPs.

As noted above, TRIPs appears to prohibit parallel imports, but it also provides that disputes over a state's policy in regard to the exhaustion of IP rights cannot be brought to WTO dispute resolution. Thus, AIDS activists hailed the settlement, which in effect preserved the ability to engage in parallel imports, as a dramatic victory over the pharmaceutical companies and predicted that the industry would not challenge other developing states' efforts to obtain cheaper AIDS drugs. In December 2001, the South African NGO Treatment Action Campaign, acting with Oxfam and Médecins Sans Frontières, began to import into South Africa generic AIDS drugs produced in Brazil.

During the years when South Africa's AIDS crisis was taking root, many government officials, including President Thabo Mbeki, openly questioned the link between HIV and AIDS, and suggested that anti-retroviral drugs (ARVs) were part of a genocidal campaign to poison blacks. South Africa's Health Minister suggested that a diet of sweet potatoes and garlic can be as important as ARVs in treating AIDS. These and similar statements sparked strong criticism from both within and outside the country and, by 2002, the government's policy began to shift. In April 2002, the government announced that it would no longer oppose the use of ARVs to treat rape victims. In November 2003, the Cabinet approved a plan for a national HIV/AIDS treatment program, including the distribution of free ARVs and, in April 2004, the government began the rollout of its national ARV distribution program at five hospitals. The program aims to treat 1.2 million people, about one-fourth of the country's HIV-positive population, by 2008.

This dramatic shift in policy was driven by the spread of the pandemic, sustained public pressure, and falling drug prices. For example, in 2001, GlaxoSmithKline (GSK) granted a voluntary license to Aspen PharmaCare, the largest generic producer in South Africa, for three different ARVs. The license enabled Aspen to manufacture and sell the drugs to the South African government and others in the nonprofit sector. Thereafter, a number of similar agreements were concluded, permitting Aspen and other producers to manufacture a variety of ARVs.

The AIDS epidemic has imposed a heavy economic toll on South African businesses. In response, many South African firms initiated AIDS programs, including some that provide HIV medications. For example, in 2001, BMW began providing free AIDS drugs to its workers at an assembly plant outside of Pretoria; in 2002, South Africa's largest mining company began to distribute HIV medicines to infected employees. However, despite these and other programs, as of 2005 only about 4 percent of employees at South Africa's largest companies were participating in HIV/AIDS disease-management plans, and less than 1 percent of employees at these companies were receiving ARV drugs.

2. Brazil

Prior to TRIPs, Brazil did not patent pharmaceuticals. As a result, Brazil developed a large and sophisticated generic drug industry, including FarManguinhos, a state-owned laboratory and production facility. Since 1996, Brazil has guaranteed free distribution of generic anti-retroviral drugs to Brazilians infected with AIDS. As a result, between 1996 and 2001, the number of HIV-infected Brazilians taking these powerful drugs increased fourfold, and Brazil's HIV infection and death rates fell by about half.

In 1996, Brazil passed a new IP law providing for patents on medicines. However, as permitted under TRIPs, the new law did not permit the patenting in Brazil of medicines patented in other states prior to 1997 (including many of the most popular AIDS drugs). The new law also provided that patent holders must "work" their patent in Brazil—for example, by producing the patented good in the country. If the patent holder fails to do so, the government can issue a compulsory license allowing others to utilize the patent.

Pharmaceutical firms and several states objected to the provisions that patents be worked in Brazil. The pharmaceutical industry argued that the law protected local manufacturing capacity, rather than access to medicines. Several international drug firms threatened to stop investing in Brazil unless the government changed the law, and the United States argued that the law violated a TRIPs provision stating that patents may be used regardless of "whether the products are imported or locally produced."

Efforts by the United States to persuade Brazil to change its law proved unsuccessful, and in January 2001 the United States initiated WTO dispute resolution proceedings against Brazil. This action sparked strong opposition from AIDS activists, who claimed that the United States was attacking Brazil's anti-AIDS efforts. The United States countered that it was only challenging the section of the law that required that a patent be worked in Brazil, not the separate section of the law that authorizes compulsory licensing to address medical emergencies.

As the WTO dispute proceeded, the United States and Brazil sparred over IP rights in other arenas. For example, Brazil led efforts at the World Health Organization (WHO) to obtain resolutions, over U.S. objections, emphasizing the importance of generic drugs and the local production of pharmaceuticals. In April 2001, Brazil successfully introduced a nonbinding resolution at the UN Commission on Human Rights calling upon states to promote "the accessibility . . . and affordability to all" of AIDS medicines. The resolution was approved by 52 of the Commission's 53 voting members; the United States abstained.

Non-state actors also stepped up their activities in opposition to U.S. policy. Two weeks after the United States initiated the WTO proceedings against Brazil, Oxfam launched a campaign to cut the costs of drugs for developing states because of "a concern that international trade rules, dictated by Northern governments and pharmaceutical companies . . . will further diminish the access of poor people to vital medicines." Shortly thereafter, the Indian pharmaceutical company Cipla announced that it would make available a generic version of the combination of AIDS drugs known as a "triple therapy" to Médecins Sans Frontières for around $350 per person per year for use in Africa and around $600 per year to governments and UN agencies. GlaxoSmithKline—which had dropped its price for these drugs to around $700 per year for governments and NGOs in Africa—threatened Cipla with legal action as the pharmaceutical firm claimed the exclusive rights over one of the drugs in the triple therapy.

In the midst of all this activity, on June 25, 2001—the opening day of a special General Assembly session on the AIDS crisis—the United States unexpectedly agreed to drop its WTO complaint against Brazil and instead pursue the issue through a newly formed bilateral consultative mechanism. In return, Brazil agreed to provide advance notice to the U.S. government in the event Brazil decided to use generic copies of drugs that U.S. companies had patented. AIDS activists hailed the agreement as "an important precedent for other nations desperate for ways to make treatment more affordable to their populations against the strong patent protections and pricing policies of companies in rich nations." The activists argued that the U.S. decision signaled that pharmaceutical companies can no longer expect governments to protect them against the rising public concern over the price of AIDS medicines in developing states.

In addition to its efforts in international fora, the Brazilian government was also active on the domestic front. In 2000 Brazil's Health Minister openly threatened to override patents on AIDS drugs produced by Merck unless the company lowered its prices. After months of negotiations, in March 2001 the Health Ministry announced that Merck had agreed to lower prices by 65 percent and 59 percent on two AIDS drugs. Brazil then announced plans to issue a compulsory license authorizing a Brazilian drug manufacturer to produce a generic version of an AIDS drug made by Roche, a Swiss firm. Two weeks later Brazil and Roche reached an agreement providing that Roche would produce the drug in Brazil and sell the drug in Brazil at a 40 percent discount. Brazil pursued similar strategies over the next several years. In November 2003, Brazil negotiated a 25 percent discount on an ARV produced by Merck. In January 2004, it reached agreements with several pharmaceutical firms, including Roche, Gilead, and Abbott, to reduce prices on the five most expensive ARV medications by between 10 and 76 percent. In October 2005, Brazil entered into an agreement with Abbott Laboratories to lower the price of an AIDS treatment from $1.17 to 63 cents; in addition, Abbott agreed to donate $3 million worth of other pharmaceuticals and to transfer its technology to the government so that a state-owned laboratory can produce a generic version of the drug when the firm's patent expires in 2015. In each case, the Brazilian government had threatened to issue compulsory licenses if prices were not lowered. In the aggregate, these agreements saved the Brazilian government hundreds of millions of dollars per year, and enabled the government to expand the number of citizens that received ARV treatments.

Finally, Brazil has assumed a highly visible role in working with other developing states, including several efforts to help them improve access to medicines. For example, in July 2004, Brazil entered into an alliance with seven other developing states to promote local capacity for producing generic drugs and to jointly negotiate prices with pharmaceutical companies. The following year, Brazil and ten other Latin American states concluded an agreement with 26 pharmaceutical firms to secure discounts of up to 66 percent on ARVs. In January 2006, Brazil agreed to purchase second-line AIDS drugs, taken by patients who have developed resistance to first-line drugs, from Indian generic producers.

Notes and Questions

1. The United States was a driving force behind negotiation of the TRIPs agreement and an aggressive critic of developing states who used compulsory licensing or parallel imports of pharmaceutical products. Yet in May 2000 President Clinton issued an Executive Order prohibiting "the United States Government from taking action . . . with respect to any law or policy in beneficiary sub-Saharan African countries that promotes access to HIV/AIDS pharmaceuticals or medical technologies and that provides adequate and effective intellectual property protection consistent with the TRIPs Agreement." The next day, the world's five largest

pharmaceutical companies signed an agreement with the United Nations to cut the price of AIDS drugs up to 80 percent for impoverished states. Do you think there is a connection between the U.S. action and the UN agreement? Why would the United States shift its position on these issues? Why would the companies agree to reduce their prices so dramatically?

2. The readings above suggest that the issue of access to affordable AIDS medicines can be considered as a trade, intellectual property, development, or national security issue. Recalling the materials covered in Chapter 7, should access to HIV medications be treated as a human rights issue?

Article 3 of the European Convention on Human Rights provides that "No one shall be subjected to torture or to inhuman or degrading treatment or punishment." The European Court of Human Rights held that the United Kingdom's plan to deport an individual in the final stages of AIDS-related illnesses to St. Kitts, where the individual would receive neither medical care nor family support, would violate Article 3. *D. v. United Kingdom*, 1997-III Eur. Ct. H.R. 777. In later cases involving individuals who were not near death, the court held that deportation of HIV-infected individuals would not violate Article 3. See, e.g., *Ndangoya v. Sweden*, App. No. 17868/03 (2004); *Amegnigan v. The Netherlands*, App. No. 25629/04 (2004).

The British House of Lords recently had the opportunity to consider this line of cases. *N v. Sec. of State*, 2005 UKHL 31 (2005), involved an HIV-infected Ugandan who was receiving advanced medical treatment in the United Kingdom. The government sought to deport her, and the House of Lords considered whether deportation would violate Article 3. Lord Nichols of Birkenhead wrote:

> 12. In the case of D the court . . . applied article 3 in what it described as the 'very exceptional circumstances' of that case.
> 13. The difficulty . . . is that, with variations in degree, the humanitarian considerations existing in the case of D are not 'very exceptional' in the case of AIDS sufferers. . . . If unavailability of appropriate medical care or family support was regarded as an exceptional circumstance for the purpose of article 3 in the case of D, why is this not equally so in the case of other AIDS sufferers? In D's case there was the additional feature that D was dying. But . . . why is it unacceptable to expel a person whose illness is irreversible and whose death is near, but acceptable to expel a person whose illness is under control but whose death will occur once treatment ceases (as may well happen on deportation)?
> 14. As I see it, these questions are not capable of satisfactory humanitarian answers. . . . A supposed difference of degree in humanitarian appeal, with emphasis on a claimant's current state of health, is not a satisfactory basis for distinguishing between D's case and other AIDS cases. . . .
> 15. Is there, then, some other rationale underlying the decisions in the many immigration cases where the Strasbourg court has distinguished D's case? . . . The essential distinction is not to be found in humanitarian differences. Rather it lies in recognising that article 3 does not require contracting states to undertake the obligation of providing aliens indefinitely with medical treatment lacking in their home countries. . . . [T]he Strasbourg court has constantly reiterated that in principle aliens subject to expulsion cannot claim any entitlement to remain in the territory of a contracting state in order to continue to benefit from medical, social and other forms of assistance provided by the expelling state. Article 3 imposes no such 'medical care' obligation on contracting states. This is so even where, in the absence of medical treatment, the life of the would-be immigrant will be significantly shortened. But in the case of D, unlike the later cases, there was no question of imposing any such obligation on the United Kingdom. D was dying, and beyond the reach of medical treatment then available.

16. I express the obligation in terms of provision of medical care because that is what cases of this type are all about. The appellant, and others in her position, seek admission to this country for the purpose of obtaining the advantages of the medical care readily available to all who are here. . . .

18. No one could fail to be moved by the appellant's situation. But those acting on her behalf are seeking to press the obligations arising under the European Convention too far. The problem derives from the disparity of medical facilities in different countries of the world. Despite this disparity, an AIDS sufferer's need for medical treatment does not, as a matter of Convention right, entitle him to enter a contracting state and remain there in order to obtain the treatment he or she so desperately needs.

D. The Evolving International Response

The international community was slow to respond to the developing AIDS crisis. The WHO was the primary international body addressing AIDS issues during the 1980s. In subsequent years, a number of other international organizations, including the United Nations Development Programme (UNDP), the United Nations Children's Fund, and the World Bank, developed their own AIDS programs. By the mid-1990s, however, it was clear that the emerging pandemic required a greatly expanded multilateral effort, and, in 1996, the United Nations drew six international organizations together to form the Joint United Nations Programme on HIV/AIDS (UNAIDS). UNAIDS has been a key advocate for the expansion of international efforts to prevent the spread of HIV and provides developing states with technical and institutional support to respond to AIDS. UNAIDS also sponsors a program designed to provide enhanced access to affordable medications by working with states and the largest pharmaceutical firms. This program has cut the prices of some AIDS medications in some sub-Saharan states by nearly 85 percent, but the program reaches only a small fraction of those in need.

More recently, other parts of the UN system have also become involved. In January 2000 the UN Security Council met to discuss the AIDS pandemic, the first time in its history that the Council met to discuss action on a health issue. In July 2000 the Council adopted its first resolution ever on a health issue, recognizing AIDS as a significant security concern and calling for member states and peacekeeping missions to develop prevention and treatment programs. The Security Council has discussed AIDS several other times, and the issue remains on the Council's agenda.

Activity at the United Nations accelerated in June 2001, when the General Assembly held a special session on AIDS. The session produced a Declaration of Commitment on HIV/AIDS calling for specific funding levels and national strategies to address the pandemic. The Declaration also called for annual General Assembly reviews of progress made on meeting the Declaration's goals. Secretary-General Annan proposed creation of a Global Fund to raise the level of spending on AIDS prevention and care in low- and middle-income countries to between $7 and $10 billion annually, five times the amount that states and international donors were spending. As of January 2006, the Global Fund had received donations or pledges of approximately $8.5 billion from industrialized and developing state governments, corporations, foundations, and individuals. The Fund has approved grants of nearly $5 billion to over 350 projects in 131 states. As of January 2006, the

Fund had disbursed approximately $2 billion to recipients in 127 countries. Approximately 55 percent of the grants were awarded to projects in Africa. Despite the Fund's impressive fund raising efforts, the Fund accounts for only a fraction of the estimated immediate program needs for AIDS in developing states.

Notes and Questions

1. AIDS cases were first diagnosed in 1980. Why did it take two decades and millions of deaths for states to mobilize on this issue? Should improved public health in Africa, like the earth's atmosphere, be considered an international public good that international law ought to protect? Or is public health in African states an issue for African governments? Did international legal norms help accelerate or retard efforts to address the AIDs pandemic?

2. If poor people in developing states should get access to AIDS drugs at reduced prices, should they also get access to treatments for cancers and other deadly diseases at reduced prices? Should poor people in developed states get access to AIDS and other life-saving drugs at reduced prices?

E. The Doha Declaration

In 2001 the debate over access to affordable medicines moved to the center of the WTO's agenda. In the months preceding the November 2001 Ministerial meeting in Doha, Qatar—which was supposed to announce the start of new trade negotiations—developing states forcefully pressed for a WTO declaration that TRIPs allows governments freedom to pursue their public health objectives. The United States and Switzerland objected on the grounds that patent protection for pharmaceuticals serves public health policies because it provides incentives for companies to develop new medicines. They also argued that the lack of access to affordable medicines in developing states results in part from underfunded health budgets and poor distribution networks. Several trade ministers characterized the TRIPs issue as a potential "deal-breaker." However, in the run-up to the meeting, the United States unexpectedly proposed that least-developed states be granted a ten-year extension to comply with all pharmaceutical-related provisions of TRIPs, with a moratorium on WTO challenges to possible TRIPs violations by sub-Saharan states. Critics charged that these proposals were designed to split the African states (which can engage in parallel imports but lack the capacity to produce generics) from supporting a proposal by India and Brazil (which have companies that can produce generic drugs and are not least-developed states), declaring that "nothing" in the TRIPs agreement prevents WTO members "from taking measures to protect public health."

Nevertheless, the U.S. proposals, along with the withdrawal of the WTO action against Brazil, signaled a dramatic change in the U.S. position. This, along with significant pressure from AIDS activists and developing-state flexibility, produced the conditions for a compromise. At Doha, the world's trade ministers adopted the following declaration, which was drafted by Mexico, in cooperation with the United States, the EU, Brazil, India, Zimbabwe, Kenya, Peru, Nigeria, and New Zealand.

WORLD TRADE

WT/MIN(01)/DEC/2
20 November 2001

ORGANIZATION

(01-5860)

MINISTERIAL CONFERENCE
Fourth Session
Doha, 9-14 November 2001

DECLARATION ON THE TRIPS AGREEMENT AND PUBLIC HEALTH

3. We recognize that intellectual property protection is important for the development of new medicines. We also recognize the concerns about its effects on prices.

4. We agree that the TRIPS Agreement does not and should not prevent Members from taking measures to protect public health. Accordingly, while reiterating our commitment to the TRIPS Agreement, we affirm that the Agreement can and should be interpreted and implemented in a manner supportive of WTO Members' right to protect public health and, in particular, to promote access to medicines for all.

In this connection, we reaffirm the right of WTO Members to use, to the full, the provisions in the TRIPS Agreement, which provide flexibility for this purpose.

5. Accordingly and in the light of paragraph 4 above, while maintaining our commitments in the TRIPS Agreement, we recognize that these flexibilities include . . .

    b.   Each Member has the right to grant compulsory licences and the freedom to determine the grounds upon which such licences are granted.

    c.   Each Member has the right to determine what constitutes a national emergency or other circumstances of extreme urgency, it being understood that public health crises, including those relating to HIV/AIDS, tuberculosis, malaria and other epidemics, can represent a national emergency or other circumstances of extreme urgency.

    d.   The effect of the provisions in the TRIPS Agreement that are relevant to the exhaustion of intellectual property rights is to leave each Member free to establish its own regime for such exhaustion without challenge, subject to [MFN and national treatment obligations].

6. We recognize that WTO Members with insufficient or no manufacturing capacities in the pharmaceutical sector could face difficulties in making effective use of compulsory licensing under the TRIPS Agreement. We instruct the Council for TRIPS to find an expeditious solution to this problem and to report to [WTO Members] before the end of 2002. . . .

AIDS activists hailed the Declaration as "the strongest and most important international statement yet on the need to refashion national patent laws to protect human health interests." Yet the Declaration did not resolve all issues regarding access to medicines. In particular, the Declaration was of primary interest to the handful of developing states, such as China, India, Brazil, and Argentina, that had sufficient manufacturing capacity to produce generic drugs. For the great majority of developing states, which lack such manufacturing capacity, the only realistic method for obtaining essential medicines is through importation. However, these states cannot import drugs from other developing states who produce them under compulsory license because TRIPS Article 31(f) limits compulsory licensing to situations "predominantly for supply of the domestic market." Paragraph 6 of the Doha Declaration recognized this concern, and instructed WTO members to "find an expeditious solution to this problem."

However, efforts to address the difficulties faced by states that lack the ability to produce medicines quickly turned contentious. Developed and developing states sparred over several issues, including the "scope of diseases" for which compulsory licensing could be used. Paragraph 1 of the Doha Declaration recognized "the gravity of the public health problems afflicting many developing and least-developed countries, especially those resulting from HIV/AIDS, tuberculosis, malaria and other epidemics." The United States argued that any solution to the problem of developing states that lack manufacturing capacity should be limited to these three diseases. Developing states flatly rejected the U.S. approach; a South African submission argued:

> *Scope of diseases*: Paragraph 1 of the Declaration does not in any manner . . . limit the scope of diseases that may be addressed when finding an expeditious solution to the problem referred to in paragraph 6. There must therefore be no a priori exclusions regarding diseases that may be addressed. . . . It is neither practicable nor desirable to predict the pharmaceutical product needs of Members desiring to protect the public health by promoting access to medicines for all.

A draft Ministerial Decision circulated by the Chair of the WTO's TRIPs Council attempted to resolve the impasse by proposing a definition of "pharmaceutical products" that included the phrase "public health problems referred to in paragraph 1" of the Doha Declaration. Developing states rejected this language on the grounds that it might be read to imply that they could import medicines, produced under compulsory licence in other states, only for the diseases specifically referenced in paragraph 1. The language was eventually changed to read "'pharmaceutical product' means any patented product . . . needed to address the public health problems as recognized in paragraph 1 of the Declaration." All WTO members except for the United States agreed to this language. As a result of the U.S. objection, the paragraph 6 problem remained unresolved.

At the same time that it was blocking consensus at the WTO, the United States pledged "not to challenge any WTO Member that breaks WTO rules to export drugs produced under compulsory licence to a country in need," and called on other states to join this moratorium. The USTR announced that this "interim solution" was designed to help those countries combat HIV/AIDS, malaria, tuberculosis, and other infectious epidemics of comparable gravity and scale, such as, for example "ebola, . . . cholera, dengue, typhoid, and typhus fevers." The European Union and Switzerland followed with their own moratoriums.

In early 2003, several proposals were offered to bridge the disagreement over the scope of diseases. Eventually, the United States signaled that it was willing to abandon its insistence that a paragraph 6 solution address only specific diseases, and shifted its focus to limiting the eligible states and creating safeguards against the diversion of low-cost medicines into other markets. This shift in the U.S. position led to an August 2003 meeting that included the United States, Kenya, Brazil,

South Africa, and India, and that produced a draft text acceptable to all WTO members.

On August 30, 2003, WTO members adopted the Decision on Implementation of Paragraph 6 of the Doha Declaration. The Decision provides for a temporary waiver of Members' obligations under TRIPs Article 31(f), which permits compulsory licenses "predominantly for the supply of the domestic market," until such time as Article 31(f) is amended. The Decision thus authorizes developing states to issue compulsory licenses to produce generic drugs for the purpose of exporting those drugs to other developing states. The Decision defines "pharmaceutical product" with reference to the "public health problems as recognized in paragraph 1 of the Declaration"; hence, the scope of diseases provision is identical to that rejected by the United States in December 2002.

The Decision sets out a number of safeguards designed to ensure that low-cost drugs manufactured under compulsory licenses and intended for developing states are not diverted to developed states. For example, exporting states are to provide detailed notifications to the WTO of the type and quantity of products licensed and a certification that the importing state lacks domestic manufacturing capability. In addition, anti-diversion strategies, such as distinctive labeling and packaging of generic products, are to be used.

The 2003 Decision was accompanied by a "Chairperson's Statement," which purports to describe WTO members' "shared understanding" on how the Decision is to be interpreted and implemented. The statement provides that members will take all reasonable steps to prevent and discourage medicines produced under compulsory licenses from being diverted to developed state markets, and that they will allow for expeditious review of any complaints regarding the new system.

In November 2004, the African Group proposed an amendment to TRIPs Article 31 that would incorporate the basic elements of the waiver, but not mention the safeguard provisions. The United States argued that any amendment should reference the Chairperson's Statement, thus making it part of the legally binding amendment. Brazil, Argentina, India, and the Philippines, among other developing states, rejected the claim that the elements in the Chairperson's Statement should be treated as legally binding obligations. Finally, in December 2005, WTO members reached agreement on an amendment. The agreed language incorporates the terms of the August 2003 decision into a legally binding, permanent TRIPS amendment. The August 2003 Chairperson's Statement was reread when the Members adopted the amendment. The amendment will become effective when two-thirds of the WTO's members have ratified the change. The August 2003 Decision will remain in effect until then.

Notes and Questions

1. Does the TRIPS amendment adequately account for the concerns of developing states? Does it appropriately balance developing and developed state interests? If not, what changes to TRIPS would you recommend?

2. Is it relevant that, as of December 2005, no developing state had yet utilized the compulsory licensing system to import essential medicines? Does this suggest that the procedural and administrative burdens associated with the licensing system are too onerous?

3. As intellectual property issues have moved toward the center of the international legal and policy agenda, states and NGOs have raised IP issues in an increasing number of international fora, including human rights bodies, the World Health Organization, the Food and Agriculture Organization, and various treaty bodies. Professor Laurence Helfer suggests that this activity reflects dissatisfaction with TRIPS provisions and that the strategy of "regime shifting" is a way to destabilize TRIPS norms. What are the advantages and disadvantages of considering IP issues before a number of international bodies? Should the WTO be the lead international institution addressing the issue of developing states' access to essential medicines?

F. Non-State Actors in the Battle Against HIV/AIDS

Non-state actors were important participants in many of the domestic and international struggles over access to medicines outlined above. For example, in response to significant public pressure, some large pharmaceutical companies took steps to increase access to medications in developing states. As noted above, several pharmaceutical firms entered into agreements with developing states or with large employers to lower the price of essential medications. Some firms, such as Roche, announced that they would not file or enforce patents on medicines in least developed states, would not take actions against generic manufacturers in those states, and would not file patents on new ARVs in sub-Saharan Africa. In 2006, pharmaceutical companies began to enter into agreements concerning second line treatments. For example, in February 2006, Bristol-Myers Squibb announced an agreement to license one of its newest and most powerful AIDS drugs to generic drug producers in South Africa and India. The agreement permits the generic manufacturers to set the pricing for the drug in sub-Saharan Africa and India.

Large foundations also assumed significant roles in the effort to combat HIV/AIDS. For example, between 1994 and 2006, the Bill and Melinda Gates Foundation awarded over $5.8 billion to global health projects. Other foundations launched efforts specifically targeted at increasing access to medicines in developing states. For example, in 2003, the Clinton HIV/AIDS Initiative reached agreement with five suppliers of generic ARV medications to cut the price of the most commonly used triple drug therapies to less than $140 per person per year in some developing states. In 2004, the Initiative entered into a similar agreement with five health care companies to reduce pricing for two key diagnostic tests.

Other NGOs assumed important operational responsibilities. The French-based NGO, Médecins Sans Frontières (MSF), began caring for people living with HIV/AIDS in developing states in the 1990s, and began offering ARV drugs in Cameroon, Thailand, and South Africa in 2000. By December 2005, MSF was providing ARVs to over 57,000 individuals in nearly 30 developing states. By early 2006, MSF had started the process of transferring its health care work to local health authorities in several states, including Honduras, Indonesia, and Thailand.

Finally, various individuals and groups launched efforts to harness the power of the global marketplace to raise funds for fighting AIDS. In one high-visibility effort, in 2006, rock star Bono and others organized a global business initiative to support the Global Fund. Under this initiative, a number of multinational corporations, including American Express, Converse, Gap, and Armani, agreed to create products for a new brand called Product RED. Firms that participate in the program pledge to contribute a portion of their profits from the sale of RED products to Global Fund-financed programs in Africa.

These various efforts increased the number of people in developing states who had access to essential AIDS medicines. Nevertheless, as of early 2006, approximately nine out of ten individuals, the majority of whom live in sub-Saharan Africa, remain in need of treatment.

Notes and Questions

1. As outlined above, a number of European and U.S.-based pharmaceutical firms have offered medicines to developing state free of charge or at greatly reduced rates. However, developing states have, at times, been reluctant to accept these offers. Why would developing states not eagerly accept these offers? What risks do pharmaceutical companies face when they offer low-cost drugs to developing states?

2. Why would non-state actors play a more prominent role in the access to medicines issue than in many of the other issues discussed in this book? In light of the concerns over NGO legitimacy and accountability discussed in Chapter 4, what are the drawbacks or limitations of private party initiatives in this area?

3. Should efforts to increase developing states' access to medicines be driven by international agencies, national governments, or non-state actors?

G. International Law and Inequality

While the problem of access to affordable medicines is in part a story about the TRIPs agreement, it is also a story about poverty and economic inequality, about various ways that weaker states can respond to international rules that disadvantage them, and about how international law affects the ability of states to address social problems. Thus, the AIDS crisis raises larger questions about international law and inequality.

Equality has many dimensions. The readings that follow address sovereign equality, economic equality, and gender equality. As you read them, consider which form of equality is most relevant to the problem of access to AIDS drugs and, more broadly, whether international law does or should promote greater equality.

Benedict Kingsbury, *Sovereignty and Inequality*

9 Eur. J. Intl. L. 599, 600-602 (1998)

. . . Inequality . . . has received minimal consideration as a theoretical topic in the recent literature of international law. While the reluctance formally to confront inequality has many causes, it has been made possible—and encouraged—by the centrality of sovereignty as a normative foundation of international law. . . .

First, the concept of sovereignty underpins a principle of sovereign equality that has attained almost an ontological position in the structure of the international legal system. This ontological status makes enough difference in the processes of international law and politics to modestly vindicate the significance and effectiveness of the system of sovereign equality: thus very small states are procedurally on an equal footing with the largest or most powerful states in the International Court of Justice, and groups of small states have made some difference in the dynamics of multilateral bargaining on issues such as climate change. In the same spirit, legal doctrines of the special status of great powers have been in the descendant since 1945, and such matters as the structure of the UN Security Council are dealt with by most legal writers as anomalies, however necessary or enduring, in the scheme of sovereign equality. This conceptual scheme serves, if very unevenly, as a counter to the vast inequalities that might otherwise be expected to feature in the formal structure of the legal system.

Second, the concept of state sovereignty allows questions of social and economic inequality among people to be treated in international law as a responsibility of territorial states. International law and legal institutions are able to promote market activity, for example through the [WTO] or the [IMF], while in theory leaving largely to states the responsibility of mitigating social and economic inequalities associated with markets. Episodic attempts to address economic and social inequality directly through substantial non-market changes in the international legal order have met with little success outside the established human rights and environmental programmes. . . . International institutions continue to play important roles in economic development, and political leaders in prosperous countries confronted with concerns about poverty or dislocation or maldistribution abroad increasingly hope for solutions from the World Bank and other intergovernmental agencies along with bilateral assistance and the much-vaunted voluntary sector. There is however a growing incongruence between the increasing market orientation of international law and the inability of international governance institutions or of many sovereign states to cope with problems of inequality that markets alone do not resolve. Intra-societal inequality in some countries, and unevenness in the global distribution of human flourishing whether defined in terms of well-being, capabilities, wealth, or a human development index, appears to have been intensifying rather than diminishing. . . .

There is thus a relationship of mutual containment between sovereignty and inequality. The system of sovereignty at least notionally precludes some forms of inequality, while helping to exclude other forms of inequality from real consideration.

Sovereign equality does not, of course, guarantee substantive equality, and, from the 1960s onward, developing states have attempted to move international law beyond a commitment to formal equality and toward rules producing greater distributional equality. During the early 1970s, developing states called for a New International Economic Order (NIEO) based upon a more equal distribution of economic wealth. Many developing states justified this redistribution of wealth as an appropriate response to colonialism and other historic injustices. However, developed states, including the United States, resisted various efforts to establish a NIEO, and developing states were unable to secure many significant economic concessions from the North.

During the 1980s, much of the debate over economic inequality focused on an asserted right to development. Proponents of this controversial right argued that it would address the economic imbalance between developed and developing states, and integrate human rights and development issues. Critics argued that it was an ill-defined concept that would do little to improve the living standards of the world's poor. In December 1986, the General Assembly adopted the Declaration on the Right to Development, which provides that "every human person and all peoples are entitled to participate in, contribute to, and enjoy economic, social, cultural and political development, in which all human rights and fundamental freedoms can be fully realized." The United Nations has since devoted considerable attention to promoting the implementation of this right. For example, several UN World Conferences have reaffirmed the right to development as a "universal and inalienable right and an integral part of fundamental human rights," and the right to development features prominently in the mandate of the UN High Commissioner for Human Rights. Although significant uncertainty remains over the scope and status of this right, it has potentially profound implications for development assistance, debt policies, foreign investment, and international trade law.

More recently, increased globalization, the creation of new international regimes such as the WTO, and the emergence of problems like the AIDS pandemic have sparked renewed debates over the complex relationships among international law, poverty, development, and equality. Hence, in recent years many developing states and NGOs have questioned whether the international norms, organizations, and processes that helped produce and further globalization increase or decrease economic inequality. Many developing state officials agree with a 2004 International Labour Organization report, which argued that "[t]he current process of globalization is generating unbalanced outcomes, both between and within countries. Wealth is being created, but too many countries and people are not sharing in its benefits. They also have little or no voice in shaping the process. . . . These global imbalances are morally unacceptable and politically unsustainable."

However, even assuming that globalization exacerbates wealth inequalities among and within states, it is not clear whether growing inequality reflects too much globalization, or not enough. Consider the following argument from two World Bank economists:

. . . a strong correlation links increased participation in international trade and investment on the one hand and faster growth on the other. The developing world can be divided into a "globalizing" group of countries that have seen rapid increases in trade and foreign investment over the last two decades — well above the rates for rich countries — and a "nonglobalizing" group that trades even less of its income today than it did 20 years ago. The aggregate annual per capita growth rate of the globalizing group accelerated steadily from one percent in the 1960s to five percent in the 1990s. During that latter decade, in contrast, rich countries grew at two percent and nonglobalizers at only one percent. Economists are cautious about drawing conclusions concerning causality, but they largely agree that openness to foreign trade and investment (along with complementary reforms) explains the faster growth of the globalizers.

. . . [G]lobalization has not resulted in higher inequality within economies. Inequality has indeed gone up in some countries (such as China) and down in others (such as the Philippines). But those changes are not systematically linked to globalization measures such as trade and investment flows, tariff rates, and the presence of capital controls. Instead, shifts in inequality stem more from domestic education, taxes, and social policies. In general, higher growth rates in globalizing developing countries have translated into higher incomes for the poor. Even with its increased inequality, for example, China has seen the most spectacular reduction of poverty in world history — which was supported by opening its economy to foreign trade and investment.

Although globalization can be a powerful force for poverty reduction, its beneficial results are not inevitable. . . .

David Dollar & Aart Kraay, *Spreading the Wealth*, 81 For. Aff. 120, 121 (Jan./Feb. 2002).

International human rights norms prohibiting certain forms of unequal treatment are another dimension of the relationship between international law and equality. In Chapter 7 we explored international norms pertaining to gender discrimination. Despite these norms, significant gender gaps remain regarding access to education and health care and women's participation in political and economic activities. In 1995 women constituted 70 percent of the 1.3 billion people living in poverty; women worked two-thirds of the world's working hours but earned only one-tenth of the world's income and owned less than one-tenth of the world's property.

Gender issues have special relevance in the context of the AIDS pandemic. In many African states, adolescent girls are eight times more likely than boys to contract HIV. Moreover, many married, monogamous women in Africa (and elsewhere) are infected with HIV:

> Although these women know about HIV, and condoms are accessible in the marketplace, their risk factor is their inability to control their husbands' sexual behavior, or to refuse unprotected and unwanted sexual intercourse. Refusal may result in physical harm, or in divorce, the equivalent of social and economic death for the woman. Therefore, women's vulnerability to HIV is now recognized to be integrally connected with discrimination and unequal rights, involving property, marriage, divorce and inheritance.

Jonathan Mann, et al., *Health and Human Rights*, 1 Health & Hum. Rts 7, 20 (1994).

The excerpt that follows offers a feminist analysis of the challenges globalization poses to the achievement of gender equality.

Shelley Wright, *Women and the Global Economic Order: A Feminist Perspective*

10 Am. U. J. Intl. L. & Poly. 861, 861-862, 867, 886-887 (1995)

Numerous studies provide unassailable evidence that the stereotypical gender division of labor is a reality throughout the world. . . . Women almost universally work longer hours than men. The addition of remunerated activities to women's workload [made possible by globalization] leads to little or no reduction in their domestic tasks. . . .

[The shift of jobs from developed to developing states that globalization accelerates] also has a major impact on women. Women who have relied on the traditional role of housewife and mother within a monogamous marriage are vulnerable to poverty, marital violence and disruption as the shutting down of traditional male jobs increases. Such women are forced to look for work which is often low-paid. The alternative is social assistance. Women's responsibilities for feeding, clothing and providing shelter and education for their children again remains the same. Western women who engage in paid work generally spend around thirty to forty hours per week on housework. This expenditure occurs regardless of whether or not they have remained in a relationship with a man. Their paid work tends to earn considerably less than men's work so that women are underpaid for one job and unpaid for their second. . . .

A feminist analysis might question the aim of unlimited economic growth and replace it with a more balanced and rational approach to the distribution of wealth and resources. "Economic rights" would cease to be either marginalized into the ghetto of social and cultural concerns or operate as a corporate power base hidden from international regulation. The connections between the right to work and the mobility of labor and capital under free trade might be more clearly (and less emotively) addressed. There is already evidence that policies of the World Bank are becoming more sensitive to formerly irrelevant "externalities" such as the role of women as productive workers both at the subsistence and cash economy level. The fever for corporate downsizing and labor reductions may already be subsiding as corporate decision makers recognize that making a large sector of the labor market redundant has a profound impact on consumer driven economic spending. Finally, the huge and growing disparity between rich and poor both within national boundaries and internationally could be seen, not as a natural product of economic development, but as the result of politically motivated and economically short-sighted policies instituted by mainly male leaders. A feminist analysis can, at the very least, open up for question what has hitherto been treated as "natural," inevitable or even desirable in the global disparity of work, resources and value.

Notes and Questions

1. Which type(s) of inequality underlie the problem of access to affordable medicines? Which form(s) of inequality should states address through international law?

2. Do the readings above suggest that globalization exacerbates or diminishes inequality among and within states?

3. Does the debate over TRIPs and public health suggest that globalization and contemporary international law enhance or diminish weaker states' ability to address social and economic issues, such as the AIDS pandemic?

H. International Law and Justice

Many of the arguments over developing states' access to affordable AIDS medications—and much international legal argument in general—invoke justice claims, at least implicitly. Moreover, the debates over international law and equality and international law's legitimacy, reviewed above, are often closely related to arguments about international law and justice. Hence, we turn to an examination of three different perspectives on the relationships between international law and justice.

The first reading adopts a fairly traditional approach to international law and justice by exploring whether international legal norms represent a fair balance between the competing interests within the international community. The second reading looks at the structural features of the international legal system and asks whether international law will be better at achieving retributive justice, corrective justice, or distributive justice. The third reading questions whether, given power differentials and realpolitik, international law can ever achieve justice. As you review these materials, consider whether the international response to the AIDS pandemic tends to support one or another of the arguments presented and, more broadly, how to enhance international law's ability to promote justice.

A former Principal Legal Adviser to the British Foreign and Commonwealth Office presents a traditional approach to the relationships between international law and justice.

Sir Arthur Watts, *The Importance of International Law*

The Role of International Law in International Politics 5, 15-16
(Michael Byers ed., 2000)

The existence of competing interests is a normal feature of any society: international society is no different. But not all States are at the forefront of such competition: most just want order. However, some States seek to impose their own kind of order. Over the past fifty years there have been great conflicts of this kind. For example, the order of the old, imperial world was ranged against that of the newer, post-colonial world. The order of the economically developed world confronted that of the economically developing world. There was also the order of the communist world, pitted against that of the Western democratic world. . . .

None of this is inimical to the existence or effectiveness of an international legal order. It is natural for social groups to struggle for what they see as their own best interests. Out of that struggle emerges a balance, which reflects the new order. The process is dynamic, not static: interests fade, existing interests change their emphasis, and new interests emerge. Moreover, the balance changes not just because of the changing interest of international society's component groupings, but also because of changing technologies which open up new areas in which balances have to be struck, and because of changes in the focus of States as they respond to world events.

As all these changes occur, the balances within the international community change too. International law, which can only be important to the international community if it reflects the balances within that community, must therefore change as well. An out-of-date law is an irrelevant law and an irrelevant law cannot be an important law.

The processes of change in international law are, however, imperfect. Much of the law is customary international law, based on the general practice of States—a phenomenon which is as imprecise a source of law as it is a slow vehicle for change. . . . Judicial involvement with the law is . . . essentially haphazard, since it depends entirely on what particular matters States may choose to bring forward for judicial settlement. . . . Treaties can generate general changes in the law, but only slowly, as part of a process involving the growth of new customary international law. For the most part treaties only bind the parties and do not, even when participation in them is widespread, approach the status of true law of general application. The reality is that the international legal system has no legislative process capable of producing instant and general change in the law.

An equal reality, however, is that international law does change. The processes of change may not be rapid, or reliable, or straightforward, but somehow the necessary changes occur. "Muddling through" can be as effective in practice as it is unsatisfactory in principle. At least it shows that the international legal system does not suffer from so substantial an inability to change that the system itself is undermined. The problems lie more in the timeliness of change, and in securing the right direction for change.

Professor Lea Brilmayer distinguishes among different types of justice that international law might produce. Retributive justice requires that norm breakers receive penalties commensurate with their violations. It can be analogized to domestic criminal law. Corrective justice requires that a wrongdoer compensate the victim for the harm that it has caused. It can be analogized to domestic tort law. Distributive justice calls for a redistribution of unjust allocations of economic (and other) resources. The closest domestic analogue is entitlements supported by tax revenues. Brilmayer argues that, given the structure of the international legal system, we should expect it to be better at retribution than corrective or distributive justice, and that the system would be better at maintaining peace and facilitating cooperation than at achieving justice.

Lea Brilmayer, *International Justice and International Law*

98 W. Va. L. Rev. 611, 627-628, 632-633 (1996)

. . . The logic behind this claim rests on the simple truisms that the ability to achieve a goal depends on the extent to which that goal is in the mutual interests of the parties, and, when the goal imposes costs on one of the parties, this is more of an impediment when that party is a strong state than a weak state. Because promotion of cooperation and maintenance of peace involve, essentially, the identification of mutual interests and the deterrence of violation of norms, they are easier to achieve with the tools available to international law than the forms of justice which require transferring assets from one state to another. . . .

It is clear that if international law is to be able to redistribute wealth systematically, as opposed to simply doing so when rich nations happen to feel like making voluntary contributions, or steering a greater share to poor nations when the pie itself is increasing, then it has to have some kind of sanctioning power at hand. . . . [T]he tool typically used for wealth distribution in the domestic context—the taxing authority's power to seize assets—is virtually completely lacking in the international context. This means that the sole device for ensuring compliance with norms of redistribution is application of pressure. But not only would distributive justice require large amounts of pressure (because massive transfers of resources would be involved) but also the pressure must be directed against precisely those actors that are best situated to resist that pressure: the wealthy and powerful. . . .

The basic difficulty with the pursuit of international justice is that it does not privilege the status quo the way that international law does. . . . [I]nternational law is at its best when the object is either to maintain the status quo or to move the status quo in some direction that is preferable from the point of view of all parties. This makes a certain amount of sense; for when there are limited tools available, it is easiest to start at the point where one currently finds oneself rather than insisting first on a radical rearrangement. But international justice searches for ideals, not practical solutions. . . .

Just as there is no reason to think that the ideal state of affairs is identical to the status quo, there is no particular reason to think that the ideal state of affairs . . . will make all states better off. There are likely to be losers. Indeed, it is virtually built in with at least two of the forms of justice that there be losers. The whole point of retributive justice is that something be taken away from the state that violated international norms. And part of the point of corrective justice is that the compensation given to the victim comes from the violator. International justice, therefore, is swimming against the tide. It requires international legal mechanisms that are not generally available. It requires the ability to redistribute when what we primarily have is the ability either to maintain the status quo or to move it in a Pareto superior direction. . . .

Finally, a prominent international relations scholar links the themes explored in this chapter by highlighting the ways in which power and inequality can undermine international law's normative aspirations.

Andrew Hurrell, *International Law and the Changing Constitution of International Society*

The Role of Law in International Politics 327, 334-336 (Michael Byers ed., 2000)

International order is made up of far more than simply law. There remains in much legal writing the implication that the progressive development of international law would in and of itself lead to a more stable and perhaps equitable world. And yet much of what makes for international order stands outside the domain of law and would not be helped by legal regulation. Some disputes are unsuited either to framing or to resolution in legal terms. . . . Equally, and far more commonly, the management of many aspects of international life depends quite directly on hierarchy and unequal power in ways that sit uneasily with the norms and proclaimed standards of international legal order. . . .

The[] weaknesses [in the UN system] do not mean that the normative aspirations of international law do not matter. It is impossible to think seriously about international relations today without reference to norms prohibiting the aggressive use of force or proscribing genocide, or upholding self-determination and human rights. Such norms have a powerful political as well as moral reality. Even on purely pragmatic grounds, States need to justify their actions in terms of these norms and to seek legal endorsement and legitimacy from those international bodies that are the repositories of those norms—which is one way to deal with the United Nations. But it is to say, first, that the aspirations of this normatively ambitious international society remain deeply contaminated by the interests and values of powerful States and of the private actors that they may represent; and, second, that international law can only ignore the persistence of this structural contamination at the cost of empty formalization. The character of international law will always be influenced by the broader distribution of power both within the international political system and the global economy.

. . . Inequality is partly a matter of the distribution of State power, both material and ideational. But it also flows from the close links between globalization and inequality: in terms of the distribution of the costs and benefits of economic globalization; in terms of the dominant position of powerful States in setting the ground rules of the global economy and in choosing when, how, and if markets are to be regulated; and in terms of the ever-widening differential capacity of States to adapt to the demands of a global economy.

Notes and Questions

1. How would Watts, Brilmayer, and Hurrell explain the developments in the debate over developing states' access to affordable medicines, particularly changes in the U.S. position?

2. What criteria does Watts provide for determining whether any particular international rule represents a fair balance among competing state interests? Does Watts's argument suggest that existing rules tend to reflect a fair resolution of competing interests, or that existing rules are likely to reflect an obsolete balance of them? How could states and other international actors improve international law's ability to strike a fair balance among different interests in a timely manner?

3. Is Brilmayer correct in saying that international law is better at addressing claims of retributive justice than distributive justice? What fact patterns from the book tend to prove or undermine this claim? What are the implications of Brilmayer's claim that international law is relatively poor at addressing claims of distributive justice for those groups with valid claims to distributive justice? Does this justify these parties taking matters into their own hands through whatever means are available?

4. Hurrell argues that some international disputes are outside the domain of law. What types of disputes? For Hurrell, can international law ever produce justice? If not, what is the value of international law?

5. A December 2001 report commissioned by the WHO calls upon rich states to spend an extra one-tenth of 1 percent of their wealth on the health of developing world citizens. This money, along with higher health spending by developing states, would save at least eight million lives a year, according to the report. The report estimates that increased health spending of $62 billion per year would produce economic gains of at least $360 billion per year. This plan would cost each rich-country citizen approximately $25 per year.

As a normative matter, should there be a duty on developed states to participate in projects such as this? If so, on what grounds? Human rights? Equity? Justice? Considering the arguments presented by Watts, Brilmayer, and Hurrell, is it likely that international law will recognize a duty to participate in projects such as those outlined in the WHO report?

I. International Law: Change and Continuity

This case book has emphasized the changes that mark contemporary international law, including the rise of non-state actors, the growth of international institutions, the birth of new substantive areas and norms and, more broadly, the general increasing legalization of international relations. But, like all disciplines, international law is marked by continuity as well as change. In this final set of readings, we examine divergent views that challenge, at least in certain respects, the claim that international law has radically changed. The first reading argues that international law's colonialist legacy, introduced in Chapter 1 and discussed in Chapters 3 and 4, continues to define the field. It suggests that change is unlikely, if not impossible. The second extract suggests that while international law was changing for some period of time, since the end of the Cold War the field is now returning, like a pendulum, to an earlier form. It suggests that the scope and direction of change are historically contingent. The third reading suggests that international law projects and arguments tend to recur over time, that what appears to be change is instead a cyclical movement. As you read these excerpts, consider how the Problems in the book tend to support, or to undermine, the arguments presented.

First, consider the argument that contemporary international law reinscribes international law's colonial legacy.

Makau Mutua, *What Is TWAIL* [Third World Approaches to International Law]?

94 Proc. Am. Socy. Intl. L. 31, 34-35 (2000)

Immediately after World War II, many colonies overthrew the yoke of direct colonial rule. But they quickly realized that political independence was largely illusory. Although now formally free, Third World states were still bonded—politically, legally, and economically—to the West. . . .

Ostensibly, the United Nations was the neutral, universal and fair guardian of the new order. But in reality, European hegemony over global affairs was simply transferred to the big powers . . . which allotted themselves permanent seats at the Security Council, the most powerful UN organ. The primacy of the Security Council over the UN General Assembly . . . made a mockery of the notion of sovereign equality among states. . . . As noted by others, the use of the United Nations as a front by the big powers "simply changed the form of European hegemony, not its substance."

In the economic arena, Third World states found themselves vised by the Bretton Woods institutions—the World Bank, International Monetary Fund (IMF), and General Agreement on Tariffs and Trade (GATT)—multinational corporations and the Western states. In the eyes of all of these institutions, the newly emergent states remained marginal, and at the mercy of Western capital. . . . Crushing debt, which the West advanced to corrupt, undemocratic regimes, now ensures that many countries in Africa, Asia, and Latin America cannot create meaningful development programs. Yet the international financial institutions refuse to do the right thing and either write off or forgive the debt. . . .

. . . Today, globalization and the ubiquity of free markets, and the push for a single global market, simply underscore these evil imbalances which characterize the international order. The World Trade Organization, which is an opaque undemocratic bureaucracy, is the latest in a series of international institutions perpetuating Western hegemony over the rest of the world.

The Third World consists of the victims and the powerless in the international economy. . . . Together we constitute a majority of the world's population, and possess the largest part of certain important raw materials, but we have no control and hardly any influence over the manner in which the nations of the world arrange their economic affairs. In international rule-making, we are recipients not participants.

In the next reading, Professor Georges Abi-Saab reflects upon Wolfgang Friedmann's argument, made in 1964, that international law was moving from a "law of coexistence" designed to manage relations among independent (if not antagonistic) states, to a "law of cooperation," which recognizes common interests that can only be pursued through collective efforts. Abi-Saab discusses whether this trajectory has continued in the post-Cold War era, particularly with respect to the right of development.

Georges Abi-Saab, *Whither the International Community?*

9 Eur. J. Intl. L. 248, 263-265 (1998)

. . . As regards the *sphere of expansion* of the law of cooperation in non-political fields, the end of the Cold War has had very variable effects according to the matter in question. . . .

The main problem remains, however, that of North-South cooperation in development. In this area, change has been radical. It is true, as we have shown, that a large part of the impressive normative body of the international law of development had not yet crossed the threshold of [ripening into customary international law], yet it was either part of *soft law* or at least a legal prophecy in the process of realization. The end of the Cold War opened the era of triumphant neo-liberalism, which is poles apart from the protective and 'affirmative action' strategy of the international law of development. . . .

Such a return to the wild liberalism of the nineteenth century, trusting entirely in the 'invisible hand' and the supreme law of the market . . . in reality leaving it to crude power relations in society . . . cannot but aggravate potential . . . disorders, just as it did at the time of the Industrial Revolution and the rise of the international economy before the First World War. . . .

Thus, the international law of development . . . is stopped dead in its evolution; a progressive deconstruction of this law's normative structure can now be seen, together with a total about-turn in the opposite direction, towards policies of privatization and the dismantlement of all protections. These new strategies, in the 'spirit of the times', to favour globalization, with the World Trade Organization as their flagship, place themselves squarely in the pure tradition of the law of coexistence. . . .

. . . [W]e must conclude that the end of the Cold War, far from pushing international society towards a global international community, has introduced new dangers together with new bones of contention among the members of this society, which run the risk of making it evolve in the opposite direction.

A final perspective understands international law less as a collection of norms and institutions, or even a process, than a disciplinary consciousness or vocabulary that international lawyers share. This perspective stresses the continuity in the projects that international lawyers pursue, and the strategies they employ.

David Kennedy, *When Renewal Repeats: Thinking Against the Box*

22 N.Y.U. J. Intl. L. & Pol. 335, 348-349, 351-353, 372-373 (2000)

Whether in practice or the academy, whether working on particular legal issues or generating broad new proposals for the field as a whole, the work international lawyers do is in large part the generation of arguments for reforms. . . . [Hence] the institutional setting for international law is less that of a court than a permanent standing constitutional convention, working to inaugurate a new legal and political order. Specific problems and disputes are debated as opportunities to develop the system. International lawyers do appear as advocates before courts disposing of stakes . . . [but more often,] international lawyers appear as advisors from a higher plane, offering advice about systemic interests. The instances for generation of work by international lawyers are less often disputes than reform projects. The call for and promise of new thinking is, in this sense, the central activity of the profession. . . .

As international lawyers elaborate a legal system to function outside of and between states, they also differ about the emphasis that should be placed on [international legislation, administration, and adjudication]. . . . Across the last century, the discipline's overall emphasis has repeatedly shifted among these areas. During the inter-war period, the most innovative work was done in the domain of legislation—both establishing the League of Nations' plenary and working on normative codification. After the Second World War, we find far more innovative energy building the administrative empire of the United Nations and specialized agencies. The last twenty or thirty years have seen the emphasis shift back to dispute resolution and adjudication—precisely where it was in the period before the First World War. . . .

Within each domain, some choices reappear across the period. Are international norms best built by custom or treaty? International lawyers have worried about this for at least a century, one or the other mode coming in and out of fashion at various points. Should only the most firmly followed norms be thought law, or should the field be open to one or another type of "soft" law? Are international organizations more or less than the sum of their members? . . . Should international law rely on courts or other, less formal, modes of dispute resolution? The field develops by changing the emphasis it places on one or another side in these debates.

Although such choices are often presented as intensely pragmatic matters . . . looking back, it is striking how one or another solution comes in and out of fashion for the field as a whole, irrespective of the issue involved. For a time, everyone is making norms with multilateral treaties; then, no one is. For a time, the field struggles to codify rights; then, international lawyers in one domain after another prefer working with principles. For a time, international institutions are emphasizing their autonomy, personality, and discretion; then, across dozens of different issue areas, they adopt a more clerk-like posture. . . .

The terms employed to debate these issues are surprisingly consistent across the last century. . . . Repeatedly, a focus on norms rather than on institutions, on rules rather than principles, on treaties rather than custom, on the authority of member states rather than institutions, and on adjudication rather than other dispute resolution techniques, have all been defended in similar terms. To defend [the first of the terms in these pairings] international lawyers stress the importance of sovereignty . . . as well as the need to root international law firmly in the consent of sovereigns and the importance of establishing an international law distinct from political calculation. In defending [the second terms] international lawyers stress the desirability of indirectly sneaking up on sovereignty. An international law more embedded in its political context, in this view, will both be more likely to dislodge sovereignty, and more adequately express the will of the current and future "international community."

. . . If we look back at a century of proposals to renew international law . . . two things remain striking. First, doctrinal and institutional reforms are overwhelmingly evaluated in terms of these broad arguments about their significance for the system as a whole. It is surprising how rarely international lawyers argue for particular projects in terms of the specific distributional or strategic consequences for particular groups that will result. Second, the field's general terms . . . are understood by most everyone not to be entirely persuasive, nor nearly as dispositive, as the arguments made using them would suggest. . . .

Notes and Questions

1. How would Mutua, Abi-Saab, and Kennedy account for the developments in the debate over developing states' access to affordable medicines, particularly the change in the U.S. position?

2. What do the Problems in this book suggest about Mutua's argument that the United Nations and other international bodies purport to be neutral guardians of a new order but simply provide cover for continued Western hegemony over international affairs?

3. Considering the Problems discussed in this chapter, do you think that international law is more a law of coexistence or a law of cooperation? Or are these not helpful categories in understanding contemporary international law?

4. Considering the three Problems and the scholars surveyed in this chapter, is Kennedy correct that international lawyers typically evaluate doctrinal and institutional arguments from a systemic perspective, rather than by how they impact upon particular states or groups? For Kennedy, what is the value of international law?

Table of Authorities

References are to page numbers. Principal entries are in italics.

I. TREATIES, DECLARATIONS, AND OTHER INTERNATIONAL INSTRUMENTS

II.   Judicial, Arbitral, and Other Decisions and Opinions

III. DOMESTIC STATUTES AND CONSTITUTIONS

Index

By subject matter. References are to page numbers. Please consult the Table of Authorities for individual treaties, international instruments, cases, and domestic codes.